A Handbook for the Study o
Second Edition
Social Contexts, Theories, and Systems

The second edition of *A Handbook for the Study of Mental Health: Social Contexts, Theories, and Systems* provides a comprehensive review of the sociology of mental health, with chapters written by leading scholars and researchers. The volume presents an overview of historical, social, and institutional frameworks for understanding mental health and illness. Part I examines social factors that shape psychiatric diagnosis and the measurement of mental health and illness, the theories that explain the definition and treatment of mental disorders, and cultural variability in mental health. Part II investigates effects of social context on mental health and illness. Individual chapters consider the role of social statuses, including class, gender, race, and age. Several chapters focus on the critical role played by stress, marriage, work, and social support, with a concluding chapter focusing on terrorism. Part III focuses on the organization, delivery, and evaluation of mental health services, including a discussion of the criminalization of mental illness, the mental health challenges posed by HIV, and the importance of stigma in meeting the mental health needs of individuals. *A Handbook for the Study of Mental Health* is a key resource that will be useful to both undergraduates and graduate students studying mental health and illness from any number of disciplines.

Teresa L. Scheid is Professor of Sociology and serves on the faculty for doctoral programs in public policy, organization science, and health services research at the University of North Carolina at Charlotte. She has published widely on the organization and delivery of mental health care services with a focus on the work of mental health care providers. This work is reflected in her book, *Tie a Knot and Hang On: Providing Mental Health Care in a Turbulent Environment* (2004). Professor Scheid's current work has expanded to examine the mental health consequences of HIV.

Tony N. Brown is Associate Professor of Sociology and holds secondary appointments in Psychology and Human Development, and Human and Organizational Development at Vanderbilt University. He also serves on the faculty of the Program in African American and Diaspora Studies; the Developmental Psychopathology Research Training Program; the Center for Medicine, Health, and Society; and the Center for Evaluation and Program Improvement. His research interests include the mental health impact of race-related stressors, racial identity, ethnic/race socialization, the conceptualization of mental health, and psychiatric epidemiology. In recent work, he examines the psychological costs of racism for Blacks as well as the mental health benefits that some Whites receive because of racism.

A Handbook for the Study of Mental Health
Second Edition

Social Contexts, Theories, and Systems

Edited by

TERESA L. SCHEID
*University of North Carolina
at Charlotte*

TONY N. BROWN
Vanderbilt University

CAMBRIDGE UNIVERSITY PRESS
Cambridge, New York, Melbourne, Madrid, Cape Town, Singapore,
São Paulo, Delhi, Dubai, Tokyo

Cambridge University Press
32 Avenue of the Americas, New York, NY 10013-2473, USA

www.cambridge.org
Information on this title: www.cambridge.org/9780521728911

First published 2010

Printed in the United States of America

A catalog record for this publication is available from the British Library.

Library of Congress Cataloging in Publication data

A handbook for the study of mental health : social contexts, theories, and systems /
edited by Teresa L. Scheid, Tony N. Brown. – 2nd ed.
    p.   cm.
Includes bibliographical references and index.
ISBN 978-0-521-49194-5 (hardback) – ISBN 978-0-521-72891-1 (pbk.)
1. Social psychiatry.   I. Scheid, Teresa L.   II. Brown, Tony N.   III. Title.
RC455.H285   2010
362.196'89 – dc22   2009014768

ISBN   978-0-521-49194-5 Hardback
ISBN   978-0-521-72891-1 Paperback

We dedicate this volume to James R. Greenley,
who devoted his personal and professional
life to the improvement of mental health services.

Contents

Contributors

Kateri Berasi, EdM
Graduate Student
Teachers College
Columbia University

Carol A. Boyer, PhD
Associate Director, Institute for Health,
    Health Care Policy, and Aging Research
Rutgers, The State University of
    New Jersey

Diane R. Brown, PhD
Professor
Health Education and Behavioral
    Science
Institute for the Elimination of Health
    Disparities
UMDNJ-School of Public Health

Robyn Lewis Brown, MS
Doctoral Candidate, Department of
    Sociology
Florida State University

Tony N. Brown, PhD
Associate Professor of Sociology
Faculty Head of Hank Ingram House,
    The Commons
Research Fellow, Vanderbilt Center for
    Nashville Studies
Vanderbilt University

Padraic J. Burns, MA
Doctoral Candidate, Department of
    Sociology
North Carolina State University

Cleopatra Howard Caldwell, PhD
Associate Professor
Department of Health Behavior and
    Health Education
School of Public Health
University of Michigan, Ann Arbor

Daniel L. Carlson, MA
Doctoral Candidate, Department of
    Sociology
The Ohio State University

Cheryl Corcoran, MD
Florence Irving Assistant Professor of
    Clinical Psychiatry
Columbia University and Director
    Center of Prevention and
    Evaluation
New York Psychiatric Institute

Manuela Costa, MPH
Doctoral Candidate, Department of
    Society, Human Development, and
    Health
Harvard School of Public Health

Stephen Crystal, PhD
Director, Center for Pharmacotherapy,
    Chronic Disease Management and
    Outcomes and Center for Education
    and Research on Mental Health
    Therapeutics
Research Professor and Chair, Division
    on Aging

Associate Institute Director for
  Health Services Research, Institute
  on Health, Health Care Policy, and
  Aging Research
Rutgers, The State University of
  New Jersey

Gary S. Cuddeback, PhD
Assistant Professor of Social Work
Research Fellow, Cecil G. Sheps Center
  for Health Services Research
University of North Carolina at
  Chapel Hill

William W. Eaton, PhD
Sylvia and Harold Halpert Professor
  and Chair, Department of Mental
  Health
Johns Hopkins Bloomberg School of
  Public Health

Adrianne Frech, PhD
Postdoctoral Fellow
Rice University

Virginia Aldigé Hiday, PhD
Professor, Department of Sociology and
  Anthropology
North Carolina State University

Stevan E. Hobfoll, PhD
The Judd and Marjorie Weinberg
  Presidential Professor and
  Chair
Rush University Medical Center

Allan V. Horwitz, PhD
Professor of Sociology and Dean of Social
  and Behavioral Sciences
School of Arts and Sciences
Rutgers, The State University of
  New Jersey

Robert J. Johnson, PhD
Professor and Chairperson
Department of Sociology
University of Miami

Verna M. Keith, PhD
Professor
Department of Sociology
Center for Demography and Population
  Health
Florida State University

Ronald C. Kessler, PhD
Professor, Department of Health Care
  Policy
Harvard Medical School

Corey L. M. Keyes, PhD
Associate Professor, Department of
  Sociology
Emory University

Jacinta P. Leavell, PhD
Associate Professor, School of
  Dentistry
Meharry Medical College

Harriet P. Lefley, PhD
Professor, Department of Psychiatry and
  Behavioral Sciences
University of Miami Miller School of
  Medicine

Mary Clare Lennon, PhD
Professor
PhD Program in Sociology
The Graduate Center
City University of New York

Laura Limonic, MA
The Graduate Center
City University of New York

Bruce G. Link, PhD
Professor, Epidemiology and
  Sociomedical Sciences
School of Public Health
Columbia University

Athena McLean, PhD
Professor of Anthropology, Department
  of Sociology, Anthropology and
  Social Work
Central Michigan University

David Mechanic, PhD
Director and Rene Dubos University
  Professor
Institute for Health, Health Care Policy,
  and Aging Research
Rutgers, The State University of
  New Jersey

Elizabeth G. Menaghan, PhD
Professor, Department of Sociology
The Ohio State University

Barret Michalec, PhD
Assistant Professor, Department of
  Sociology
University of Delaware

John Mirowsky, PhD
Professor, Department of Sociology and
  Population Research Center
University of Texas

Shirin Montazer
Doctoral Candidate
Department of Sociology
University of Toronto

Joseph P. Morrissey, PhD
Professor of Health Policy, Management,
  and Psychiatry
Deputy Director, Cecil G. Sheps Center
  for Health Services
University of North Carolina at Chapel
  Hill

Carles Muntaner, PhD
Psychiatry and Addictions Nursing
  Research Chair
Social Equity and Health Section,
  Social Policy and Prevention
  Department
Center for Addictions and Mental Health
  and
Professor of Nursing, Public Health and
  Psychiatry
University of Toronto

Bernice A. Pescosolido, PhD
Professor, Department of Sociology and
  Consortium for Mental Health Services
  Research and
Director, Indiana Consortium for Mental
  Health Services Research
Indiana University-Bloomington

Christopher Peterson, PhD
Professor, Department of Psychiatry
University of Michigan

Jo C. Phelan, PhD
Associate Professor of Sociomedical
  Sciences

School of Public Health
Columbia University

Michael Polgar, PhD
Department of Sociology
Penn State University

Sarah Rosenfield, PhD
Department of Sociology
Institute for Health, Health Care Policy,
  and Aging Research
Rutgers, The State University of
  New Jersey

Catherine E. Ross
Professor, Department of Sociology and
  Population Research Center
University of Texas, Austin

Ebony Sandusky, MPH
Doctoral Student, Department of Health
  Behavior and Health Education
School of Public Health
University of Michigan, Ann Arbor

Jaime C. Sapag, MD, MPH
Special Advisor, Office of International
  Health
Centre for Addiction and Mental
  Health
Ontario, Canada

Teresa L. Scheid, PhD
Professor, Department of Sociology
University of North Carolina at
  Charlotte

Mark F. Schmitz, PhD
Associate Professor, School of Social
  Administration
Temple University

Sharon Schwartz, PhD
Professor of Clinical Epidemiology
Mailman School of Public Health
Columbia University

Dena Smith, MA
Doctoral Student, Department of
  Sociology

Rutgers, The State University of
    New Jersey

David T. Takeuchi, PhD
Professor, Department of Sociology and
    Social Work
University of Washington

Peggy A. Thoits, PhD
Professor
Department of Sociology
Indiana University

R. Jay Turner, PhD
Marie E. Coward Professor of Sociology
    and Epidemiology
Professor of Psychology
Florida State University

Edwina S. Uehara, PhD
Professor
Department of Sociology
University of Washington

Jerome C. Wakefield, PhD, DSW
University Professor, Silver School
    of Social Work and Department
    of Psychiatry, School of
    Medicine
New York University

James Walkup, PhD
Graduate School of Applied and
    Professional Psychology and
Institute for Health, Health Care Policy,
    and Aging Research
Rutgers, The State University of
    New Jersey

Emily Walton
Department of Sociology
University of Washington

Blair Wheaton, PhD
Professor and Chair, Department of
    Sociology
University of Toronto

David R. Williams, PhD
Florence and Laura Norman Professor of
    Public Health
Professor of African and African
    American Studies and of
    Sociology
Staff Director, RWJF Commission to
    Build a Healthier America
Harvard School of Public Health

Kristi Williams, PhD
Associate Professor, Department of
    Sociology
The Ohio State University

Foreword

The National Institute of Mental Health (NIMH), established at the end of World War II, had an important influence on the growth of medical sociology and especially on social research in mental health. Its first director, Robert Felix, sought to include the social sciences as basic sciences for the study of mental health issues and problems. He strongly supported PhD training and extramural research and contributed to the growth of sociology, anthropology, and psychology as disciplinary areas. The fact that initially public support for sociology largely came through NIMH rather than other disease-oriented institutes explains the dominance of mental health concerns within the development of medical sociology. With increasing numbers of sociologists trained in NIMH programs, medical sociology became one of the largest and most active sections of the American Sociological Association (ASA). Felix was committed to bringing a public health perspective to the study and treatment of persons with mental illness, a viewpoint that began to erode during the Reagan administration when politics forced NIMH into a more insular disease perspective. The public health view has now again gained some traction on the nation's health agenda, with a renewed interest in social determinants of health and socioeconomic and ethnic/racial disparities.

In earlier decades, training programs encompassed broad areas of social psychology, social organization, and social methodology; this breadth encouraged the wide range of substantive interests and theoretical and methodological approaches exhibited in this *Handbook*. NIMH predoctoral and postdoctoral awards supported my training in the 1950s, and probably many, if not most, of the contributors to this *Handbook* had similar support during their disciplinary training. I have been involved for almost 50 years in running such training programs at the University of Wisconsin and Rutgers University; in the earlier decades these programs had a strong focus on promoting and expanding knowledge and methods in the basic areas of the discipline. Many of those who participated in these and related programs have contributed importantly not only to mental health but also to their disciplines. Programs funded today are much more focused on problem areas and interdisciplinary efforts, but it remains essential for researchers to be strongly involved with the conceptual, theoretical, and methodological advances in their disciplines if they are to be effective partners in interdisciplinary collaborations.

This *Handbook* nicely informs readers on conceptual, substantive, and policy aspects of mental health. A core issue that engages every aspect of mental health research and practice is the conceptualization of mental health itself: Is it seen most usefully in terms of discrete disorders or in terms of continua of affect and function? There is some resurgence of interest in conceptualizing positive mental health as well, although determining the role of culture and values in framing what is seen as positive remains a difficult challenge. As the mental health field prepares to introduce version V of the *Diagnostic and Statistical Manual of Mental Disorders* (DSM-V), many groups have intense interest in its structure and content. Whatever one might think of DSM, it will continue to have an important role in reimbursement arrangements, disability determinations, legal contests, and the promotion and marketing of drugs and other therapies. We clearly need a reliable classificatory basis for research, for treatment assessment, and for communication, but absence of a theoretical basis for DSM entities and disagreements about its inclusiveness leave much room for controversy and debate. It remains uncertain whether social understanding is enhanced more by a focus on discrete disorders as defined by DSM or whether we might benefit more by attention to dimensional conceptualizations and inquiries. Both are important and respond to different purposes and needs, but it is clear that the balance among approaches requires reexamination.

The excesses of pharmaceutical marketing, its role in expanding concepts of disorder, and its influence on drug research and professional education have done a great deal to undermine trust in psychiatric research results and psychiatric expertise. Selective publication of drug trials in research funded and controlled by pharmaceutical companies has cast suspicion on the validity of psychiatric knowledge and effectiveness claims. There is now a considerable backlash against many of the marketing and funding practices of these large companies and much greater skepticism among educators, editors of major journals, and the media. Social research has been an important antidote to this negative pattern and has contributed importantly to revealing and understanding these patterns of professional and commercial self-interest and how they have helped shape trends in the mental health sector.

The substance of mental health inquiry is very much focused on the study of developmental processes across the life course and the influence on those processes of social stratification and important social institutions such as the family, the labor market, and work. Social and epidemiological surveys have become the core tools for many of these studies that seek to understand human development and social behavior across age cohorts and historical periods while being sensitive to the crucial way in which biological predispositions interact with social context and the environment. Surveys have become larger, technically more sophisticated and longitudinal in scope, and the ability to link varying sources of data makes it increasingly possible to examine causal ideas with more credibility. Randomized studies remain the "gold standard" because social selection is so powerful and pervasive and difficult to discount, but increasingly, natural experiments, longitudinal databases, and the use of instrumental variables and sophisticated multivariate approaches make causal interpretations more convincing in the typical instance in which randomization is not feasible or ethical.

We value knowledge and understanding for their own sake, but most of us study mental health issues and are supported by research agencies because of the expectation that enhanced knowledge will improve people's lives. The American health system, even more its mental health system, is dysfunctional and in shambles. Dealing effectively with serious mental illness involves many sectors from general medicine to the criminal justice system, but there is little effective coordination or integration. Some of what we already know has been implemented in a constructive way, but far too much of what we have learned remains to be applied. Whether we are concerned with broad social determinants such as extreme poverty, child abuse and neglect, inferior schooling, and stigmatization on the one hand or the lack of access to mental health services and a lack of appropriate balance in treatment among medication, supportive care, and rehabilitative services on the other, there remains a great gap between what we know and what gets done. Some positive changes have occurred, such as the growing acceptance of mental health as an important aspect of health, the move to greater health insurance parity, more coverage for serious mental illness in public programs such as Medicaid, and more accessibility to treatment and trained mental health professionals. But as this *Handbook* makes clear, the social determinants of mental health problems and their management will continue to remain challenging for scientists, professionals, and policy makers.

David Mechanic
Rutgers University

Preface

We are pleased to edit the second edition of *A Handbook for the Study of Mental Health*. We worked hard to bring it out on roughly the 10-year anniversary of the first edition, which is still widely used in many classrooms and by many researchers. Allan V. Horwitz was the senior editor on the first edition, and he suggested Tony N. Brown as someone who would be most instrumental in rethinking the second edition. As a consequence, we have included a number of new chapters that target emerging areas of research. We are especially pleased to have a chapter on subjective well-being to augment the theories presented in Part I. In Part II we have added several chapters that focus on mental health among minority groups: one chapter on Black adolescents and a second on the intersection of race, socioeconomic status, and gender. Part II also includes a new chapter on marriage and another on mental health and terrorism. Part III includes two new chapters on organizations and mental health care providers.

We want to thank everyone who worked so hard to update and extend their chapters, as well as those who wrote new material for the volume. We owe much to the students who handled many of the more tedious details in putting the *Handbook* together: Radhi Gosai at University of North Carolina-Charlotte, who merged the references, and Whitney Laster and Nakia Collins at Vanderbilt University, who took on the indexing. Ed Parsons at Cambridge University Press was patient and always available for any question and has been a pleasure to work with. As with the first edition, proceeds from this volume benefit the American Sociological Association Section on Mental Health.

Part I

Approaches to Mental Health and Illness: Conflicting Definitions and Emphases

Teresa L. Scheid and Tony N. Brown

Mental health and mental disorder represent two different areas of theory, research, and policy implications, reflecting our tendency to dichotomize healthy and sick, normal and abnormal, and sane and insane. David Mechanic (2006) has argued that the term "mental health" has no clear or consistent meaning, and in the sociological literature, this argument is generally true. Mental health is not merely the absence of disease or disorder; it involves self-esteem, mastery, and the ability to maintain meaningful relationships with others. The concept of mental health is better developed in the psychology literature, and Carol Ryff has provided an exceptional account of "happiness" that draws on the theories of Maslow, Rogers, Jung, and Allport to develop a multidimensional construct of psychological well-being (Ryff, 1989). Although most of us fall short of achieving optimal well-being or happiness, those who experience mental health problems or psychological distress have been the focus of most sociological research.

However, definitions of mental health problems, or illnesses, or disorders are also not so straightforward. According to Horwitz (2002), "mental diseases" reflect underlying internal dysfunctions that have universal features (e.g., schizophrenia and to a lesser degree bipolar disorder). A valid "mental disorder" reflects some internal psychological system that is unable to function as it should, and this dysfunction is socially inappropriate. For most disorders, symptoms are not specific indicators of discrete underlying diseases (such as schizophrenia); instead many conditions (such as depression, anxiety, and eating disorders) arise from stressful social conditions. Thus symptoms associated with mental disorders are shaped by cultural processes, and it is important to distinguish mental disorders from normal reactions to social stressors. Horwitz (2002) used the terminology of "mental illness" to refer to those conditions that a particular group has defined as a mental illness and that often includes behaviors that are deemed deviant; for example, homosexuality in previous psychiatric classifications. In Chapter 1, Horwitz argues that sociological approaches regard mental health and mental health problems as aspects of social circumstances. He provides a very thorough overview of how various social conditions affect degrees of mental health and mental health problems and, consequently, how social context shapes the definition as well as the response to mental health problems.

It is also important to understand that there have been two different approaches to differentiating between mental health and illness. One approach views mental health and illness in terms of a continuum, with health and illness at opposite ends of the poles and most of us falling somewhere in between. In other words, there are varying degrees of healthy and sick, normal and abnormal. In the second approach are theories that view health and illness as opposites, as forming a dichotomy such that one is either sick or well and that, furthermore, one will fit into a specific disease category once specific symptoms are identified. Of course, these two approaches to the definition of mental health and illness may be reconcilable if you can find the point on the continuum that differentiates health from illness. A special issue of the *Journal of Health and Social Behavior* (2002, volume 43) focused on whether sociologists should privilege diagnoses or continuum measures. Medically oriented thinking emphasizes diagnoses – that is, dichotomous categories that determine whether one is sick or not. Such an approach is the basis of the *Diagnostic and Statistical Manual of Mental Disorders* (DSM), which is used in clinical practice as well as in a great deal of epidemiological studies that seek to determine levels of mental disorder in the general population. Currently in the version IV-TR (version V is due to be published in 2011 or 2012), the DSM identifies more than 400 distinct mental disorders. These disorders are assumed to be discrete (i.e., they do not overlap with one another). Other researchers prefer to use continuum assessments of mental health and mental health problems such as scales to assess psychological well-being or distress. Indices assess not only the problem but also its severity and frequency along a continuum (Mirowsky & Ross, 2002).

In Chapter 2, Jerome Wakefield and Mark Schmitz provide an overview of how researchers have measured and assessed mental disorder and illness. In assessing mental illness there are a variety of terms with which the student needs to be familiar. *Epidemiology* refers to the study of the distribution of illness in a population. *Morbidity* is the prevalence of diseases in a population, whereas *comorbidity* is the co-occurrence of disease and associated risk factors. Hence epidemiological research not only assesses rates of disease but also, by identifying who is susceptible to particular conditions, can lead us to an understanding of the specific causes of a disorder or disease. *Point prevalence* refers to the percentage of the population affected with an illness at a given point in time; *lifetime prevalence* refers to the percentage of the population *ever* affected with an illness. *Incidence rate* is the rate at which new cases of an illness or disorder form in the population; for example, many are now concerned with the prevalence rate at which depression is found among all age groups and the fact that incidence rates seem to be increasing for young women. Ronald Kessler in Chapter 3 describes the most recent estimates of community incidence, age of onset, and prevalence of mental disorders.

People with mental health problems fall into three groups (Mechanic, 2006). First are those with acute mental health problems such as normal depression following a loss or some other stressful event. In the second group are those with acute mental health problems that are more severe or those who have chronic conditions but who can maintain normal role functioning. The third group is made up of those with serious, chronic mental diseases that involve significant functional disability. Although only a small percentage of the population is affected by serious mental illness, the majority of public mental health monies are directed toward members of that third group, most of whom need a wide array of services and long-term supports. The shortage of such services in the past decade has resulted in the criminal justice system becoming the de facto system of care for many with chronic and serious mental diseases. Reflecting the medicalization of mental health care described by Horwitz in Chapter 1, most people with mental health problems receive medication, which is the primary expenditure for mental health care under Medicaid (Mechanic, 2006).

Reliance on psychiatric medication is in keeping with a medical model, rather than a social or psychological model, of the etiology of mental health problems. *Etiology* refers to theories about the causes of illness, yet the etiology of mental illness (or disorder, as mental illness has only recently been considered a disease) is influenced by specific historical and social frameworks, as illustrated by Michel Foucault in *Madness and Civilization* (1965/1988). The DSM-III, which was hotly contested during the 1980s, was a significant factor in the re-medicalization of American psychiatry (M. Wilson, 1993) and served as a catalyst for debate among sociological, psychological, psychiatric, and biological understandings of mental disorder. In essence, "clinicians were replaced by biomedical investigators as the most influential voices in the field" (M. Wilson, 1993, p. 400).

Included in a more organic or biological approach to mental illness are theories that postulate that mental illnesses have genetic, biological, biochemical, or neurological causes (Michels & Marzuk, 1993). This approach conceptualizes mental illness as a disease and places increasing reliance on medication to provide treatment while deemphasizing psychotherapy. There has been much recent work in neuroscience, which combines the findings from several scientific disciplines, that seeks to understand the relationships between brain structure and human behavior. The biological approach to mental illness, as well as sociology's relationship to the biolological approach, is described in Chapter 4 by Sharon Schwartz and Cheryl Corcoran.

The psychosocial model of mental illness, dominant until the 1970s, was based on a continuum definition of mental health and illness in which the boundary between health and illness was fluid and subject to social and environmental influences. That is, it was widely accepted that anyone could become "sick" if subject to the right conditions or environmental stressors. Since the 1980s, there has been an increased emphasis on biological or organic views of mental illness and a corresponding narrowing of the psychiatric gaze, which has deemphasized the idea of the unconscious, historical development, family dynamics, and social factors (M. Wilson, 1993). Christopher Peterson provides a thorough overview of the various psychological approaches to mental health and illness in Chapter 5. He describes the overlap between the psychological and sociological in a comprehensible way.

And where does sociology fit into this debate between psychologists and psychiatrists? Cooperation between sociology and psychiatry faces fundamental obstacles because of their diverging theoretical perspectives and research agendas (Coopers, 1991). Most critical is the issue posed posed by Mirowsky and Ross (1989a): Do mental disorders represent disease entities or are mental disorders related to social context, which affects the rates of generalized distress, abnormal behavior, and social deviance? Traditionally, sociologists have viewed mental disorder as deviance from institutional expectations – often referred to as *social reaction theory* (Horwitz, 1982; Perrucci, 1974; Scheff, 1984; Turner, 1987). Rather than focusing on the individual, sociologists focus on the social context of illness and treatment and also tend to take a critical or oppositional stance to the biomedical model of mental disorders as diseases (Turner, 1987). Consequently, mental disorder is generally referred to as abnormal behavior or simply disorder as opposed to mental illness. Peggy Thoits in Chapter 6 provides a thorough analysis of the various sociological approaches to stress and to mental health and illness.

Despite the widespread use of the DSM to classify mental disorders, sociologists have been sharply critical of the underlying assumption that DSM categories reflect underlying pathophysiological entities or disease states. Mirowsky and Ross (1989a) charged that such diagnoses are reified measurement: what is assessed are psychiatry's *views* of mental illnesses based on clinical observations of those with psychiatric problems. They assert that "the absence of gold standards, the paucity and uncertain relevance of latent biological classes, and the symptom factors that bear little resemblance to diagnostic 'syndromes' lead us to believe that psychiatric diagnoses, whether simulated or clinical, are mythical entities" (Mirowsky & Ross, 1989a, p. 17).

Others have also researched the politics of the DSM (Caplan, 1995) and have raised serious questions about the validity and reliability of the diagnostic categories (Kirk & Kutchins, 1992). Debates continue over the use of the DSM classification system as more and more behaviors come to be defined as "abnormal"; see for example an *American Journal of Psychiatry* article that addressed the question of whether or not caffeine abuse should be added to the DSM-IV (Hughes et al., 1992). Students are directed to a 2007 book by Allan Horwitz and Jerome Wakefield (*The Loss of Sadness*), which is sharply critical of the classification of "normal sadness" as a DSM depressive disorder. The problem is that the DSM does not take into account contextual factors that may account for the existence of various symptoms.

An important addition to the sociological literature since the first edition of the *Handbook* is Corey Keyes' distinction between languishing and flourishing, a conceptualization that includes continuum measures of both mental health and mental disorder. This is a model that moves sociologists well beyond debates over the validity of diagnostic criteria and to a useful approach to understanding the mental health profile of a given community or population. In Chapter 7, Corey Keyes and Barret Michalec provide a philosophical and theoretical justification for a "dual continua" model, as well as a description of research contributing to the ongoing dichotomy versus continuum debate.

If mental health and illness are indeed in some part produced by social context, one would expect some degree of cultural variability in the prevalence and symptomatology of behaviors and disorders characterized as mental illness or insanity. Although some forms of mental illness are universal (i.e., all cultures characterize some forms of behavior as mental illness or disorder), there is much disagreement over whether specific categories of mental illness are indeed universal (Patel & Winston, 1994). Recent research has challenged the widely held belief that rates of schizophrenia are culturally invariant (Morgan, McKenzie, & Fearon, 2008). The question of the universality or culturally specific nature of mental illness presents a test of the medical etiology model that asserts that the source of mental illness is biological, neurological, biochemical, or genetic. If the cause of mental illness is organic in nature, then such behaviors should be invariant across different cultures. However, evidence demonstrates that the social environment influences both the course and the outcome of psychosis (Morgan et al., 2008). Harriet Lefley in Chapter 8 examines the role of cultural context in defining mental health and mental illness and provides an overview of cross-cultural research. She describes the relationship between culture and the experience of stress, as well as a variety of culture-bound syndromes. Services and interventions to treat mental health problems follow from beliefs about the etiology of these problems, and Chapter 8 introduces students to diverse mental health systems.

As this overview should indicate, much more research needs to be done to extend our understanding of mental health and illness before we will be able to resolve the ongoing debates on the existence and causes of mental illnesses, much less that on suitable treatments. We do know that social conditions and environments are critical in understanding not only what constitutes a mental health problem but also the course and outcome of mental health problems. However, the mechanisms by which the social environment influences mental health have not been thoroughly studied (Morgan et al., 2008). Part II will direct more focused attention to the social context of stress, coping, and mental health and illness.

1

An Overview of Sociological Perspectives on the Definitions, Causes, and Responses to Mental Health and Illness

Allan V. Horwitz

Sociological approaches regard mental health and illness as aspects of social circumstances. One type of sociological study examines the sorts of social conditions, such as negative life events, ongoing stressful circumstances, demanding social roles, levels of social support, and the strength of cultural systems of meaning, that affect levels of mental health and illness. Another type of study focuses on how social and cultural influences shape the definitions of and responses to mental health problems. These kinds of studies show how key recent trends – including the medicalization of a growing number of conditions, the increased use of prescription drugs to deal with mental health problems, and a greater willingness to identify emotional suffering as mental illnesses that require professional help – are transforming how modern societies deal with psychological problems. The sociological study of mental health and illness is both distinct from and complementary to more individualistic psychological and biological approaches to these topics. What would be an example of the difference between how a sociologist and a psychiatrist might view someone's mental health problems? What are the advantages and disadvantages of each approach? Some people think that using prescription drugs for mental health problems is a helpful way of responding to suffering, whereas others emphasize the dangers involved in growing rates of prescription drug use. Which view do you think is best supported?

Introduction

Why do some people seem to be always cheerful, whereas others are often sad? Most of us believe that our moods have to do with aspects of our personalities that make us more or less depressed, anxious, or exuberant. Others think that temperament results from biological factors such as our genes and neurochemicals. People usually also assume that engaging in therapies that change their states of mind is the natural response to mental problems. These treatments might involve psychotherapies that modify the way people view the world or drugs that alter their brain chemistry. Thus, typical approaches to the nature, causes, and cures of various states of mind emphasize individual traits, temperaments, and behaviors.

Sociological approaches to psychological well-being are fundamentally different. Unlike psychological and biological perspectives that look at personal qualities and brain characteristics, sociologists focus on the impact of social circumstances on mental health and illness. The distinctive emphasis of sociological approaches is on how processes such as life events, social conditions, social roles, social structures, and cultural systems of meaning affect states of mind. Social perspectives assume that different individuals who are in the same circumstances will have similar levels of mental health and illness. That is, what determines how good or bad people feel does not just depend on their own personalities or brains but also on the sorts of social conditions they face. These conditions vary tremendously across different social groups, societies, and historical eras.

Some important social influences involve how many stressful life events people confront (Holmes & Rahe, 1967). These events include such circumstances as getting divorced, losing a valued job, having a serious automobile accident, receiving a diagnosis of a serious physical illness, or having a close relative die. Especially serious stressors such as being a victim of a violent crime, natural disaster, military combat, or physical or sexual abuse during childhood are particularly powerful causes of adverse mental health outcomes (Dohrenwend, 2000). The more frequently such events occur and the more serious they are, the worse any person's mental health is likely to be.

Other social causes of poor mental health lie in persistent living conditions that do not appear at a particular time and then go away but are instead rooted in ongoing circumstances (Turner, Wheaton, & Lloyd, 1995). For example, people who live in social environments that feature high rates of poverty, neighborhood instability, crime rates, dilapidated housing, and broken families are likely to have high rates of psychological distress (Ross, 2000). Other enduring stressful circumstances are troubled marriages, oppressive working conditions, or unreasonable parents. Sociological perspectives predict that especially taxing living conditions, roles, and relationships are related to low levels of psychological well-being, over and above the qualities of the particular individuals who must deal with these situations.

Many sociologists study how social conditions affect levels of mental health. Others look at the social reactions to mental health problems. Some factors that lead people to respond to emotional difficulties in different ways involve social characteristics such as gender, ethnicity, age, and education. These traits make people more or less likely to define themselves as having some kind of psychological problem and to seek help once they have made these definitions. Other aspects involved in the reaction to mental troubles concern varying cultural values toward mental health and illness. *Culture* refers to socially shared systems of beliefs, values, and meanings. It encompasses, among many other factors, people's ethnic heritage, religious beliefs, and political principles and the tastes of their age peers. For example, responses to emotional problems in cultures that stigmatize the mentally ill will be very different from those in cultures that highly value professional treatment for these problems. Additional factors that shape the social response to psychological problems involve the accessibility, quality, type, and amount of health care that is available to people.

Sociological approaches share the idea that mental health and illness are not just qualities of individuals but also stem from various aspects of social circumstances. What social groups people belong to, what historical periods and societies they live in, and what cultural values they hold profoundly shape how people feel about themselves, how likely they are to become mentally ill, the kinds of problems they are likely to develop, what they do if they develop mental difficulties, and the kinds of help that are available to them.

What Outcomes Do Sociologists Study?

Most sociologists examine levels of mental health and illness in the natural settings where people live. Sociological research is more likely to take place in schools, family settings, neighborhoods, and communities than in clinical settings where people seek professional mental health care. Therefore, the kinds of mental health conditions that sociologists study are usually different from those examined by other disciplines such as psychiatry or clinical psychology.

Most research that takes place in clinical settings examines particular types of mental illnesses, such as schizophrenia, bipolar disorder, major depression, and obsessive-compulsive disorder. These conditions have symptoms that are believed to indicate the presence of some underlying disease entity and that are different from the symptoms of other diseases. Diagnoses of particular mental disorders are usually dichotomous; that is, someone either has or does not have an anxiety, depressive, substance abuse, attention-deficit, or eating disorder.

In contrast, most sociologists use outcomes that reflect more generalized conditions of distress, not particular types of mental illnesses. For example, the Center for Epidemiologic Studies–Depression scale (CES-D) is the most common instrument that sociologists use to measure mental health (Radloff, 1977). It consists of 20 questions that ask people how they have felt over the past week; for example, "I enjoyed life," "My sleep was restless," or "I felt lonely." The scale is not comparable to any specific mental illness, but instead contains items relating to more global states of well-being. Many of its items (e.g., "I felt hopeful about the future," "I felt I was just as good as other people") tap general attitudes about life or personal qualities such as self-esteem. The CES-D and other scales that sociologists typically use measure global qualities of well-being rather than discrete psychiatric conditions.

The broad nature of these outcomes means that they provide good measures of general states of psychological well-being or ill health, but are not comparable to psychiatric diagnoses and do not measure mental illness. In addition, scales such as the CES-D are limited because they only measure qualities of mental health that reflect internal types of suffering. They do not contain items that ask about other possible indicators of mental health such as heavy drinking or drug taking, violent and aggressive behavior, or severe symptoms such as delusions and hallucinations.

To adequately capture the full range of psychological symptoms, these scales need to be supplemented by a broader range of mental health outcomes.

Sociologists who examine the social response to emotional problems must use different sorts of outcomes from those used in studies that examine the social determinants of well-being and distress. They do not try to explain how symptoms develop in the first place; rather, they ask how, once symptoms emerge, sufferers themselves and others around them define, classify, and respond to experiences of mental distress. Some of these studies ask people about their attitudes toward mental illness and see how their answers reflect who does or does not enter mental health treatment. Others use official statistics that are collected about how many people with psychological problems enter different kinds of facilities such as general medical practices, outpatient psychiatric care, or inpatient mental hospitals. They then view how rates of various kinds of treatment vary across groups with divergent social characteristics such as race, socioeconomic circumstances, and immigrant status. Another type of study compares treatment rates across large geographic areas such as different states, regions of the country, or different countries to see how general aspects of the mental health system influence patterns of seeking professional help. For example, far more people with mild psychological problems are likely to enter professional mental health treatment in the United States than in other countries (Katz et al., 1997).

Sociological studies, then, are less likely than clinical studies to use small groups of people who are found in mental health treatment. Instead, they use general scales that measure mental health in samples of community members. They also rely on statistics about rates of mental health care across a wide range of facilities and regions. These studies are good at showing broad social variations in the development of and response to psychological problems, although they are unable to say much about individual experiences of mental health and illness.

What Social Factors Relate to Mental Health and Illness?

Sociological studies reveal that psychological well-being and distress are related to several general aspects of social life: the degree of social integration, inequality, and meaningful collective belief systems. In addition, the periods of time when individuals were born and the countries they live in are associated with their states of mental health. The influence of these factors means that levels of mental health diverge considerably among people in different social locations.

Social Integration

Emile Durkheim's study, *Suicide*, is generally regarded as the first explicitly sociological study of mental health (Durkheim 1897/1951). Durkheim compared the rates of suicide in different European countries at the end of the 19th century and correlated them with various social characteristics of the populations of these countries. His central theme was that the nature of the connections people have with each other and with social institutions shapes the likelihood that they will commit suicide. He found that people with strong social ties were least likely to commit suicide. Conversely, people who were socially isolated were more likely to commit what Durkheim called "egoistic" suicides. For example, married people had lower suicide rates than the unmarried, and married people with children were especially unlikely to commit suicide. Likewise, members of religions such as Catholicism that shared common practices and beliefs committed a smaller number of suicides than members of Protestant groups that permitted more free inquiry among individuals. In addition, Durkheim discovered that few people commit suicide during wars and revolutions because of the intensity of shared collective experiences in such periods.

Durkheim also found that a second aspect of social integration, which he termed "social regulation," affected levels of what he named "anomic" suicide. Groups that could successfully control individual expectations for constant happiness and great achievement had lower suicide rates than groups in which most people think that limitless possibilities for success exist. This was because people who always expect to be happy and believe that there are no limits on what they can achieve are bound to suffer serious disappointments. Periods of sudden economic prosperity, for example, can lead people to think they can satisfy all of their desires. Such unrealistic beliefs lead some people to become frustrated and consequently to commit suicide. Durkheim concluded that optimal mental health was found in societies that had strong systems of social integration that connected people to each other and of social regulation that moderated their desires.

Contemporary studies in the sociology of mental health confirm the importance of social integration as a fundamental cause of well-being. For example, people with more frequent contacts with family, friends, and neighbors and who are involved with voluntary organizations such as churches, civic organizations, and clubs report better mental health than those who are more isolated (Thoits & Hewitt, 2001). Married people have less distress than unmarried people because they have more supportive relationships and more ties to community institutions (Umberson & Williams, 1999). Marriage also serves the regulative functions of promoting conformity to social norms, more conventional lifestyles, and lower levels of all kinds of deviance (Umberson, 1987). Conversely, the loss of social attachments that may be caused by the death of intimates, divorce, and the breakup of romantic attachments is associated with growing levels of distress. Socially integrated people not only are less likely to develop mental health problems but they are also better able to cope with stressful experiences that they face (e.g., House, Landis, & Umberson, 1988; Turner, 1999). This is because they receive more social support, help, and sympathy from the members of their social networks.

Residents of communities that feature more social integration also have better mental health. After taking into account the characteristics of individuals who live in them, localities that are clean and safe, feature strong and respectful relationships among residents, and have well-maintained housing foster mental health (Aneshensel & Sucoff, 1996; Ross, 2000). In contrast, areas with little cohesion and connectedness among their residents promote psychological distress. Social integration is associated with positive mental health – humans derive satisfaction from valued intimate relationships and suffer when their circumstances deprive them of these relationships.

Social Stratification

Whereas social integration involves relationships characterized by closeness, support, and friendship, social stratification involves interactions featuring differences in power, status, and resources. A considerable body of research indicates that people who are more powerful, of higher status, and wealthier also have better mental health compared with those who possess fewer resources. In addition, relationships that are relatively egalitarian promote more overall positive mental health than those that feature sharp distinctions in the amount of power and control that each member has (Mirowsky & Ross, 2003).

Inequality

Inequalities in wealth, power, knowledge, influence, and prestige, which define social class status, have powerful impacts on mental health (Link & Phelan, 1995). Poverty, which involves not only economic deprivation but also undesirable working conditions, physically hazardous environments, marital instability, and unhealthy lifestyles, is especially associated with poor mental health (McLeod & Nonnemaker, 1999). High socioeconomic status (SES) also enhances well-being, although the negative effects of impoverished circumstances on poor mental health are stronger than the positive impact of economic abundance on psychological welfare. Likewise, people who suffer declines in their economic status see their mental health deteriorate, whereas those who gain resources also achieve better mental health.

One unresolved issue is whether well-being depends on the absolute or the relative amount of resources people have. If the absolute amount of assets predicts happiness, then the wealthy will have good and the poor will have inferior states of mental health. If, however, mental health depends on how one's own resources compare to those of other people, then even the very wealthy can be unhappy when they have fewer goods than others to whom they compare themselves. For example, a professional basketball player who is a millionaire might be unhappy because he is the lowest paid member of his team. Conversely, people who don't make much money might be quite happy if those that they evaluate themselves with are also poor.

Work conditions also have important impacts on psychological well-being (Lennon, 1994). Jobs that are autonomous, creative, and complex and in which a person has control over others enhance mental health. Conversely, those that are tedious, routine, oppressive, and lack autonomy lead to much distress. Worst of all is having no job: unemployed people have the poorest mental health of any economic group.

Social inequality relates not only to economic and work conditions but is also an aspect of all social institutions. For example, the dominant party in a marriage reports better mental health than the less powerful spouse. Because husbands are usually more powerful than wives, they generally also report better mental health. However, this is not always the case. In the relatively few cases in which married men have fewer resources than their wives, they also have higher rates of distress than their spouses (Rosenfield, 1980). Egalitarian marriages lead to the best mental health (Mirowsky, 1985). Spouses who share child rearing and chores report better mental health than do those for whom one partner (almost always the wife) does much more of the household labor than the other.

Different social groups and societies are also marked by more or less economic inequality. Overall, societies that have low levels of inequality have high levels of mental health, whereas those that feature sharp differences in resources have worse overall well-being (Marmot & Wilkinson, 1999). In general, subordinate social positions and inequality are associated with poor mental health, dominant ones with well-being, and egalitarian relationships with the best mutual states of happiness.

Cultural Values

A third source of psychological well-being involves possessing meaningful systems of cultural values. Social groups that provide their members clear and attainable goals foster mental health. Those that create expectations that many people cannot fulfill are marked by widespread frustration and unhappiness. For example, American values traditionally have stressed that all people, regardless of their backgrounds, can achieve material success (Merton, 1938/1968). In fact, only a relatively small proportion of people will attain high-paying, prestigious, and fulfilling positions. Those who fail to realize their goals will tend to blame themselves, rather than the cultural values that emphasize success or the structural conditions that place limits on how many people can actually reach such high levels of accomplishment. High levels of distress result from the inability of people to attain the values their cultures encourage them to achieve.

Religion provides another example of the importance of cultural values. In general, religious people report less distress, especially when they undergo highly stressful life experiences, than those who are not religious (Idler, 1995). Members of ethnic groups that promote values emphasizing the importance of cohesion and support for fellow group members also have better mental health than members of groups with more individualistic value systems (Vega & Rumbaut, 1991). Overall, cultural values that provide group cohesion, meaning, and purpose to life are conducive to mental health. These values are not psychological characteristics of individuals, but they are socially generated and shared group properties.

Cohort Membership

Birth cohorts are another social influence that shapes mental health. A *birth cohort* is a group of people born in a particular time and place; for example, all Americans who were born in the decade of the 1980s. Each cohort shares common historical and social experiences that are different from the experiences of other cohorts. People born at different times have witnessed different historical events, different trends in marriage and divorce rates, different occupational and educational opportunities, and changes in fashion, technology, world views, and cultural patterns. To the extent that such factors are related to mental health, members of different generations have divergent rates of psychological well-being and distress because of the time period when they were born.

Differing levels of abuse of alcohol and drugs indicate the importance of cohort membership. One large study compared such abuse among 15- to 24-year-olds born between 1966 and 1975, 25- to 34-year-olds born between 1956 and 1965, 35- to 44-year-olds born between 1946 and 1955, and 45- to 54-year-olds born between 1936 and 1945 (Warner et al., 1995). Although only 2.1% of the oldest birth cohort reported a history of substance dependence by age 24, 17.3% of the youngest cohort did so. This means that there was an 800% difference in the chances of a 24-year-old having had a substance dependence disorder, depending on whether he or she was born between 1966 and 1975 or between 1936 and 1945.

Rates of many mental disorders reflect the importance of the time period when someone is born. For example, younger generations in the first decade of the 21st century report far higher levels of attention-deficit hyperactivity disorder (ADHD), eating disorders, autism, and bipolar conditions than earlier birth cohorts. Although it is not clear what factors account for the growing levels of reported mental disorders of these kinds, it is apparent that any given individual's chances of being diagnosed with many types of psychiatric conditions are related not only to individual characteristics but also to when he or she happened to be born.

Generational factors also affect general levels of well-being and distress (Yang, 2008). A sociological perspective indicates that frustration and distress from failed ambitions stem from the social structural conditions that are present in any particular time period. For example, many young people now face a growing gap between their aspirations for material achievements and the opportunities that are available to them. Cultural values still promote the possibility of high levels of financial success for everyone, but declining economic conditions allow fewer people to reach their goals. The result of waning opportunities for material accomplishments might be worse levels of mental health overall among current generations of young adults.

Cross-Cultural Differences

The importance of social factors such as social integration, stratification, and culture becomes especially apparent when levels of mental health and illness across different countries are examined. Rates of depression provide an example. These rates vary enormously across different societies. One set of studies showed that the amount of depression varied from a low of 3% of women in a rural area of Spain to a high of more than 30% of women in an urban township in Zimbabwe (G. W. Brown, 2002). Another summary of community surveys in 10 countries found amounts of depression that ranged from a low of 1.5% in Taiwan and 2.9% in Korea to a high of 16% in Paris and 19% in Beirut, Lebanon (Weissman et al., 1996). A third study found that rates of depression varied by a factor of 15 among primary medical care patients in 14 different countries (Simon et al., 2002).

Other mental disorders show equally steep divergences across cultures. For instance, social phobias ranged from a low of 1.7% in Puerto Rico to a high of 16% in Basel, Switzerland (Merikangas et al., 1996). Rates of alcohol and drug dependence show even larger variations across national contexts. One cross-national study of alcoholism found that the highest lifetime prevalence rate of 23% among a Native American population exceeded the lowest rate of 0.45% in Shanghai, China, by more than 46 times (Helzer & Canino, 1992)! The importance of social and cultural factors is also shown by the fact that the United States has far higher rates of many kinds of mental illnesses than the rest of the world. For example, nearly 20% of Americans reported having an anxiety disorder and almost 10% reported a depressive condition compared to only about 2% of Chinese who said they have each of these conditions (World Health Organization World Mental Health Survey Consortium, 2004).

These diverse rates could stem from differences in the rates of social stressors across cultures; disparities in social integration, stratification, and cultural systems of meaning; varied expressions of distress in each culture; or measures of mental illness that are not sensitive to cultural contexts. Although it is not clear what exact factors account for the huge differences in prevalence across cultures, these differences suggest that societal impacts on the development of emotional problems cannot be ignored in explanations of well-being and distress.

Social Responses to Mental Disorder

Another type of sociological research examines how people themselves, those around them, and their societies define and respond to psychological problems.

Social influences profoundly affect how people and groups react to mental health troubles.

Images of mental illness have undergone radical changes in recent decades. For most of history, people associated mental illness with crazy, mad, and bizarre behaviors (Grob, 1995). These conceptions also carried a great deal of stigma so that people would resist defining themselves as mentally ill and seeking mental health treatment. Because only the most severe and disruptive conditions would come to the attention of mental health professionals, treatment often occurred in locked wards of inpatient mental hospitals.

An enormous change has occurred in recent decades in how Americans define, seek help for, and treat psychological and behavioral problems. In particular, a dramatic upsurge in the medicalization of social life occurred in the 1990s and 2000s. *Medicalization* means that conditions that previously had been defined as nonmedical difficulties are now seen as medical problems that ought to be treated through medical techniques (Conrad, 2007). Troubles that in the past were considered as spiritual, moral, or behavioral harms that were handled through prayer, counseling, or punishment or were simply tolerated are now defined as diseases and addressed through biomedical treatments. In the field of mental health, medicalization has had these effects: people are more willing to seek professional help for their emotional problems, social definitions emphasize how mental troubles are signs of diseases, and treatments primarily involve biomedical interventions, especially drugs.

The fundamental categories of mental illness themselves have undergone notable changes in recent years. For example, distressing and disruptive but not necessarily disordered childhood behaviors are increasingly being labeled as mental illnesses. Children have always behaved in ways that annoy and frustrate their parents and disturb their teachers. Only recently, however, have these behaviors been considered to be mental disorders that must be treated with medications. Just 20 years ago less than 1% of children were diagnosed and treated for ADHD (Olfson, Gameroff, Marcus, & Jensen, 2003). By 2003, ADHD had become a widely prevalent psychiatric condition among children and adolescents, with 7.8% of youth aged 4 to 17 years reporting a diagnosis of ADHD and 4.3% taking medication for the condition (Visser, Lesesne, & Perou, 2007).

The spectacular rise in rates of bipolar (or manic-depressive) disorder in youth provides another dramatic instance of a new childhood mental disorder. This disorder was traditionally thought to arise in mid-life and until recently was virtually unknown among youth. Then, in 2007 a national survey discovered an astonishing *40-fold* increase in the number of children and adolescents treated for bipolar disorder from 1994 to 2003 (Moreno et al., 2007). The common denominator among children treated for this condition seems to be that their behavior is extremely disturbing to adults, usually their parents or teachers. The rising rates of the pediatric bipolar diagnosis and resulting prescriptions for powerful drugs seem more due to their usefulness for pacifying disruptive behavior than to the discovery of a previously unknown disease.

Among adults, major depressive disorder (MDD) is the most common diagnosis in psychiatric treatment and one of the most common conditions reported in community surveys. Its typical symptoms are states of low mood, diminished pleasure, sleep and appetite difficulties, fatigue, and lack of concentration that persist for a 2-week period. Studies estimate that about 17% of people suffer from MDD over their lifetime (Kessler, Berglund, et al., 2005). In the past, the symptoms of MDD would often have been viewed as natural responses to some serious loss such as the breakup of a marriage or a long-term romantic relationship, the unexpected loss of a valued job, or the discovery that an intimate has a life-threatening illness. The expansion of medicalization has led American culture to define sadness as a depressive mental disorder and to treat it with medications (Horwitz & Wakefield, 2007).

Social phobia provides another example of medicalization. Social phobias are conditions that feature extreme anxiety over situations in which people are exposed to the scrutiny of others, such as when they must speak in public, have their performance evaluated, or attend social events that involve interacting with strangers. When this condition first appeared in the official psychiatric manual in 1980, it was noted that "the disorder is apparently relatively rare" (American Psychiatric Association, 1980, p. 228). Initial studies of the disorder in the early 1980s indicated that about 1% to 2% of the population reported this condition. Yet, more recent studies indicate that about 13%, or one of eight people, has had a social phobia at some point in their lives (Magee et al., 1996). Indeed, by the early 2000s, social phobias were one of the two most common mental disorders. Rising rates of conditions such as social phobia largely result from growing cultural tendencies to treat personality traits such as shyness as if they were diseases and from widespread drug advertisements that urge people to seek medical help for their distressing conditions (Lane, 2007).

It is not just conceptions of what mental disorders are that have changed in recent years. People are now far more willing to seek mental health treatment than they were just 20 years ago. The treatment of depression illustrates this change. The percentage of the population in therapy for depression in a given year increased by 76% between the early 1980s to the early 2000s (Wang et al., 2006). Although the willingness to seek professional help for mental health problems such as depression has increased among all social groups in recent years, a number of social characteristics are associated with defining oneself as in need of mental health treatment. Women, younger and middle-aged people, Whites, and highly educated individuals are considerably more likely to seek professional treatment than men, the elderly, racial and ethnic minorities, and the less educated (Pescosolido & Boyer, 1999).

The places where people receive mental health treatment have also dramatically changed in recent years. Since the 1950s rates of inpatient treatment in mental hospitals have plunged, and few mentally ill people now enter these institutions (Grob, 1995). When people do receive inpatient treatment it is likely to be given in general hospitals or private clinics. The vast majority of people treated in the mental health system now go to outpatient facilities in the community or see general physicians for their emotional problems.

Several factors account for the dramatically rising rates of professional treatment during the recent past. The earlier emphasis of cultural conceptions of mental illness on the most serious and stigmatizing conditions has shifted toward a focus on a broad range of emotional and psychosocial problems. Younger birth cohorts, in particular, have been socialized to a therapeutic culture that emphasizes using mental health services and, especially, taking psychotropic medications to ease suffering. Various mental illnesses are common topics in television shows, movies, and popular magazines. Direct-to-consumer (DTC) advertisements of medications that treat psychological problems are another prominent reason for rising rates of treatment. These ads, which have only been allowed since the late 1990s, are now widely featured in the media.

The drug industry has had an especially important influence on the growth and evolution of mental health treatment (Barber, 2008). The most striking change in treatment is the vast increase in prescriptions for antidepressant medications. The use of antidepressants, including fluoxetine (Prozac), paroxetine (Paxil), sertraline (Zoloft), venlafaxine (Effexor), and fluvoxamine (Luvox), nearly tripled between 1988 and 2000; in any given month, 10% of women and 4% of men use these drugs (*Health United States*, 2004). The increasing use of antidepressants is especially apparent among young adults. The period from 1994 to 2001 witnessed a 250% increase in the number of visits to physicians that resulted in a prescription for some medication that treats psychological problems among adolescents (Thomas, Conrad, Casler, & Goodman, 2006). Recent years have also seen rising rates of stimulant drugs such as Ritalin that treat ADHD. More than two million children now receive these drugs each year (Zuvekas, Vitiello, & Norquist, 2006). The numbers of persons 20 years old and younger who received a prescription for the strongest kind of medications, the antipsychotics, jumped from about 200,000 in 1993–1995 to about 1,225,000 in 2002, a more than sixfold increase in less than a decade (Olfson et al., 2006). A sharp drop in the use of psychotherapies – treatments of emotional disorders that rely on talk therapies – has accompanied the growing reliance on drugs (Olfson et al., 2002).

On the one hand, changes in the social response to mental health conditions have meant that far more people are getting professional help for their psychological problems. The stigma associated with seeking help for emotional problems and mental illness has also declined as a broader range of conditions have become associated with this label. However, people who suffer from more serious types of mental disorders such as schizophrenia remain highly stigmatized. The availability of effective medications is also partly responsible for why far fewer people enter mental hospitals and far more live in the community than in past decades. Psychotropic drugs allow many people to lead brighter lives and accomplish more than they would if they were not taking medications for their problems.

On the other hand, critics have emphasized how a number of problems are due to the rising use of drug therapies (Conrad, 2007; Elliott, 2003; Healy, 2004). Growing medicalization has led to the assumption that drugs are the treatment of choice for numerous psychosocial problems. Prescribing a pill can communicate the message that issues such as unfulfilling marriages, poor parenting, and inadequate finances are easily remedied through pharmaceuticals. Current health policy might be overly reliant on using medical remedies for concerns that often can be addressed through alternative social policies. For example, enhancing parenting skills, investing in childhood development programs and child care, and creating more stimulating classroom experiences might be more effective responses to childhood behavioral problems than pharmaceutical treatments. It is possible that promoting healthy lifestyles and reducing socioeconomic inequality, workplace pressures, and family demands could enhance mental health to a greater extent than telling people they have a disease and prescribing pills to remedy their conditions.

Another problem is that the benefits of medicalization are often overstated. Although these drugs do help control the worst symptoms of serious mental illnesses, their effectiveness for less severe conditions does not greatly exceed that of placebo treatments (Kirsch et al., 2008). If the benefits of drugs have been exaggerated, their risks including negative side effects such as diminished sexual desire, increased somatic symptoms, and sleep problems, withdrawal problems from ceasing use, and heightened suicidal potential might be underestimated (Healy, 2004). An additional issue is that little is known about the impact of long-term use of psychotropic medications, an especially important concern for young adults who begin using them during early stages of their life cycle. Whatever the exact balance is between the benefits and risks of the medicalized response to emotional problems, it is undoubtedly one of the most important recent trends in the field of the sociology of mental health and illness.

Conclusion

Sociological research about mental health and illness shows how the emergence of psychological well-being and distress are consequences of basic aspects of social organization (Pearlin, 1989). Dimensions of social life including integration, stratification, and cultural systems of meanings shape resulting rates of emotional problems. Even such extreme behaviors as suicide can often result from the way people are attached to social institutions rather than from the irrational behavior of abnormal individuals. From a sociological point of view, regular features of social life rather than abnormal processes within individuals explain how much distress will emerge among people living in any given time and place.

The response to mental problems is also rooted in essential dimensions of social life. Social processes influence how people classify what kinds of problems they have, what sort of remedies they seek, and what kind of resources are available to treat them. Cultural conceptions of what it means to be emotionally healthy or disturbed have radically altered in recent decades. A number of particular social groups including pharmaceutical companies, the mental health professions, the media, and governmental bodies encourage people to medicalize their emotional suffering. The result is that notions of mental illness are far broader than in the past, allowing many more people to view themselves as having emotional problems that require professional treatment.

Rooting the emergence and response to psychological problems in social practices rather than within individuals might seem to be counterintuitive. Most people think that their emotions are profoundly individual processes that are uniquely their own. Yet, as the various chapters in this volume will demonstrate, the kinds of societies we live in and the sorts of cultural beliefs that we share shape the seemingly most innermost aspects of our thoughts, feelings, and behaviors. They will also suggest some answers to what is possibly the most important sociological question: What sorts of social arrangements can optimize happiness and minimize distress?

2

The Measurement of Mental Disorder

Jerome C. Wakefield and Mark F. Schmitz

This chapter examines the assessment and measurement of mental disorders. Researchers must distinguish between clinical prevalence (i.e., people who are currently being treated for mental disorder) and true prevalence (i.e., the actual rate of disorder in a community, including those not in treatment). The measurement of mental illness must be conceptually valid; that is, there must be criteria that successfully distinguish cases of disorder from cases of nondisordered distress. In the past, researchers relied on general symptom checklists, which identify a threshold above which an individual is considered disordered but without specifying a particular disorder. An alternative to checklists is provided by the American Psychiatric Association's *Diagnostic and Statistical Manual of Mental Disorders* (DSM), which provides sets of diagnostic criteria for specific disorders. The assumption underlying the DSM is that mental disorders result from internal psychological dysfunctions (i.e., failures of proper functioning of mental processes), a presumption that we accept but demonstrate is often violated by the DSM's own criteria for mental disorder. We illustrate this critique of the DSM's approach to measurement with several DSM diagnoses. In addition to discussing the conceptual basis of the DSM, this chapter provides examples of attempts to use DSM-derived criteria to measure the prevalence of mental disorder in the community. These examples demonstrate the recurrent problems with creating conceptually valid measures for use in psychiatric epidemiology. It is unclear whether these problems can be overcome or circumvented with methodological innovations. Why is it so difficult to determine who is mentally disordered and to distinguish mental disorder from intense normal distress? Is a conceptually valid resolution of these problems possible?

Introduction

How many people in the United States suffer from mental disorder in general and from each specific mental disorder, and what characteristics are correlated with each disorder? The answers to such questions are important in formulating mental health policy, in evaluating theories of the causes of disorder, in planning the efficient distribution of mental health care, and in justifying funding for mental health services and research. Thus, there have long been efforts to measure the rate, or *prevalence*, of mental disorder both in the population as a whole and in various segments of the population. *Psychiatric epidemiology*, the discipline that pursues such studies, is logically part of medical epidemiology, the study of the occurrence and correlates of medical disorders in various populations. However, psychiatric epidemiology has remained as much within the province of sociologists as of physicians and psychiatrists because many of the questions that psychiatric epidemiologists attempt to answer, such as those concerning the effects of social stress on mental health or the prevalence of mental disorder in various socioeconomic, gender, racial, and ethnic groups, as well as the survey methodology often used in this field, traditionally fall within the domain of sociology.

Good clinicians, with the help of an adequately detailed history and diagnostic interview, can generally recognize a case of mental disorder when they see one. It is a very different matter to measure how many people in the general population, most of whom have never seen a clinician, suffer from mental disorder. Epidemiological surveys in which nonclinicians interview members of the community about symptoms they have experienced lack many of the safeguards and corrective mechanisms available in a clinical evaluation and may be more prone to diagnostic error. Thus, the creation of valid measures that identify mental disorders is a crucial challenge for psychiatric epidemiology. This chapter explores the special problems that have arisen in epidemiologists' attempts to transfer diagnostic criteria from the domain of clinical evaluation to the much different epidemiological arena in which disorder is measured in the general population by survey.

The Current Crisis in Psychiatric Epidemiology

It is generally too costly to have clinicians do full diagnostic interviews with large samples of the general population, so psychiatric epidemiologists have come to rely on structured interviews administered by lay interviewers to distinguish disordered from nondisordered individuals. Three particularly comprehensive studies using such instruments and for which the data have been released at this writing, all well funded and using the best methodological resources available, have been mounted in recent years in the United States in an attempt to obtain valid, definitive answers to psychiatric epidemiologists' questions. The first is the Epidemiological Catchment Area Study (ECA; Robins & Regier, 1991), which surveyed samples of the general population at five sites (or "catchment areas" as they were called in community mental health legislation) across the United States, from New Haven, Connecticut, to Los Angeles. The second is the National Comorbidity Survey (NCS; Kessler et al., 1994), so named because it focused on establishing the degree to which different disorders occur in the same individuals (or are "comorbid"). The third is the National Comorbidity Survey Replication (NCS-R; Kessler, Berglund, et al., 2005), which was an attempt to replicate and extend findings from the NCS.

However, rather than resolving the challenges of psychiatric epidemiology, the ECA, NCS, and NCS-R may be considered to have instead thrown the field into something of a crisis. These studies ran into two basic difficulties. First, the estimated prevalence rates of mental disorder seemed to many observers to be too high; for example, the ECA found that about one-third of all Americans suffer from a mental disorder at some point in their lives, and the NCS and NCS-R indicated that the figure is closer to one-half. The prevalence rates for many specific disorders also seemed high; for example, the ECA claims that about 14% of Americans suffer from alcohol abuse disorder or alcohol dependence disorder at some point in their lives; the NCS found that 13% of the U.S. population has at some point in life experienced social phobia; and the NCS-R reports that about 17% have had major depressive disorder (MDD). Second, the studies, although using very similar instruments and other research technology, yielded surprisingly different results in many instances. For example, the ECA found that about 6% of Americans suffer at some time in their lives from a major depressive disorder, whereas the comparable NCS and NCS-R figures were about 17%; the prevalence of alcohol dependence was about 14% in the NCS and about 5% in the NCS-R, and that of agoraphobia (without panic) was about 5% in the NCS and about 1% in the NCS-R. As indicated earlier, the studies' overall lifetime prevalence rates for all psychiatric disorders differed quite substantially as well (i.e., one-third versus one-half of the population). It is implausible that real changes in the rates of disorders over a few decades could explain such divergent estimates. Changing diagnostic criteria across the DSM editions no doubt account for some of these disparities, but not all, and generally these studies offered no systematic argument as to why one result based on one criteria set was more valid than another.

Many possible reasons have been proposed for these problematic results, but no clear agreement on the explanation has yet emerged. In addition to somewhat changed diagnostic criteria, many other factors may have played a role, such as the failure of subjects to remember painful symptoms, the varying effectiveness of techniques for prompting subjects' memories used by interviewers in different studies, and the subjects' interpretations or misinterpretations of what the questions were intended to elicit, their desire to avoid answering lengthy lists of questions (e.g., subjects' perception that if they answer "yes" to a question, that will mean extensive follow-up and a lengthier interview), and their resistance to reporting mental problems because of potential feelings of shame or stigma – a resistance that may have lessened over time as some mental disorders became less stigmatized.

However, it seems likely that the way in which mental disorder was measured in these studies had something to do both with the high absolute magnitudes of the rates and the differences in the rates. When such well-funded, state-of-the-art studies in a field yield such potentially troubling and divergent results with no clear, agreed-on explanation, one might consider the field to be in a scientific crisis that demands reexamination of the fundamentals. This situation with respect to current measures led us to take a rather different approach in this chapter than we otherwise might. Rather than surveying the measurement of mental disorder in psychiatric epidemiological studies as if such measures are an accomplished fact, we approach the measurement of mental disorder as an ongoing challenge that has yet to be satisfactorily resolved. This chapter provides glimpses of aspects of this problem using specific examples that represent broader issues.

True Prevalence versus Clinical Prevalence

One obvious way to try to measure the rate of mental disorder in the community is to take a census of how many mental patients are being treated in hospitals, psychiatric clinics, mental health professionals' offices, and general medical practices or are being dealt with by other community authorities. Such surveys of patients yield what might be called the *clinical prevalence* of mental disorder. For purposes of scientific theory and social policy, however, epidemiologists are mainly interested not in the apparent, clinical prevalence of disorder but rather in the *true prevalence* of disorder; that is, the actual rate of disorder in the community, whether treated or not.

Some early psychiatric epidemiological studies were based on the assumption that clinical prevalence could be used to validly infer the community population's true prevalence. Unfortunately, using clinical prevalence to measure true prevalence begs one of the central questions of psychiatric epidemiology; namely, to what degree do mental disorders in the general population go untreated? It is the rate of *untreated* mental disorder that most forcefully argues for the need for greater funding of mental health services, and it has long been an article of faith – and more recently an empirically demonstrated fact – that large numbers of people who are classified as disordered do not have access to or do not make use of mental health services. Thus, clinical surveys cannot be used to measure true prevalence rates.

Moreover, the characteristics of the community's patient population may not be a valid guide to the characteristics of the community's overall disordered population. There are many possible reasons, such as the availability or mix of community services, why the makeup of the clinical population might diverge from that of the overall disordered population. For example, Ruesch (1949) studied clinic populations in New Haven and concluded, "We can state that the lower class culture favors conduct disorders and rebellion, the middle class culture physical symptom formations and psychosomatic reactions" (cited in Srole et al., 1978, p. 294). But when Srole et al. (1978) did their community population study of midtown Manhattan (the "Midtown Study"), they did not find this to be the case:

> The data ... do not support that generalization. A more plausible interpretation of Ruesch's observation is that (1) rebellious lower class individuals with 'acting out' character disorders tend to be shunted to psychiatric facilities by action of community authorities or agencies; (2) their status peers with psychosomatic reactions get strictly medical or no attention; (3) middle-class individuals with psychosomatic disorders tend to be referred to psychiatric outpatient services, generally on the advice of their own physician. (p. 294)

Thus, social factors that determine how a problem is dealt with in the community can dramatically affect how frequently patients in different subpopulations with a given problem show up in mental health clinics.

Consequently, a patient census cannot tell us the true prevalence of mental disorder in a population or the relative rates of disorder across socioeconomic status (SES) or other subgroups of the population, the critical variables that psychiatric epidemiology attempts to study. So psychiatric epidemiologists have largely rejected patient surveys for these purposes and focused instead on establishing true prevalence by direct surveys of community populations. In comparison to patient surveys, this strategy entails considerable methodological demands and costs. Mental health professionals have already screened clinical populations, and patients have often been observed over a period of time so that the validity of their diagnoses can be confirmed. Thus the patients who are counted in clinical surveys are to a large extent already "validated" as patients with specific disorders. Clinical prevalence can thus be ascertained simply by obtaining summary statistics from each community setting.

However, the population at large has not been prescreened, so each individual must be surveyed directly. Moreover, the rates of some mental disorders are quite low, so one must interview a very large number of individuals to get a sufficient sample to establish the population prevalence. Many other problems arise in such surveys; for example, in the space of a short interview, individuals may not accurately remember symptoms that may have occurred some time before, they may be reluctant to reveal such symptoms to a lay interviewer, or they may misinterpret the meaning of symptom questions that ask about unusual and subtle matters of subjective experience. Each of these possible sources of error poses a challenge to the methodologist. But the most difficult and fundamental challenge in community surveys – and the one on which we focus here – is to construct an instrument that validly distinguishes disordered from nondisordered individuals once the subject does provide the information ascertained by the interview instrument. That is, by what sort of algorithm can one most validly infer disorder or nondisorder from the reports of experiences of the subject?

Conceptual Validity and Symptom Checklists

It has often been observed that there is no "gold standard" by which the presence of a mental disorder can be conclusively inferred, as there is in the case of certain physical disorders that can be conclusively identified through laboratory tests. In the absence of such markers, we must judge as best we can from apparent symptoms and other available information whether a condition is or is not a disorder.

Criteria for a specific disorder that successfully distinguish cases of disorder from cases of nondisorder are *conceptually valid* criteria (Wakefield, 1992a, 1992b, 1993). Because the cost of using professionals to diagnose or even to administer survey instruments to large samples is so high, epidemiologists have turned to structured questionnaires that can be administered by a lay person and analyzed by computer and that contain all the questions necessary to make a diagnosis. At no point does clinical or professional expertise enter into the process of administration and analysis of such structured survey instruments. Thus, the entire diagnostic process must be based on explicit, rigid rules about how the answers to a fixed set of questions determine whether a diagnosis is appropriate. The challenge of community studies, then, is to construct conceptually valid rules for diagnosing specific mental disorders.

The important role that diagnostic criteria play in an epidemiological study cannot be overemphasized. The logical structure of an epidemiological study is like an upside-down pyramid: the wide base of the pyramid consists of a vast array of activities, from sample selection and data collection to instrument development and data analysis, the usefulness of all of which rests on the narrow point of the pyramid, which consists of a handful of diagnostic criteria for the disorders that are being studied. The entire enterprise has its foundation in, and its potential for success depends on, these few definitions of disorder. No matter how sophisticated and flawless are instrument development, sampling procedures, data collection techniques, and methods of data analysis, if the diagnostic criteria used to identify disorders are invalid. then all the other efforts will be to no avail in achieving the goal of accurately estimating true prevalence. Conceptual validity, then, is critical to the epidemiological enterprise.

Before creation of the new wave of DSM-based instruments used in most recent epidemiological studies, which we consider shortly, most studies used instruments consisting of general symptom checklists and simply defined some threshold of number of symptoms as the point above which an individual is considered psychiatrically disordered. These instruments generally yielded an overall, unidimensional score of degree of disordered status rather than specific diagnoses, although sometimes specific disorders were inferred from the nature of the specific symptoms. For example, the Langner (1962) scale, used in the landmark Midtown Manhattan Study (Srole et al., 1978), contained 20 questions about symptomatic experiences. In general, a score of four or more positive answers to questions on the Langner scale was considered to indicate disorder. Yet many of the listed symptoms could be normal reactions to misfortunes in life (e.g., "Are you ever bothered by nervousness . . .", "Do you ever have any trouble in getting to sleep . . ."), or could represent a general state of demoralization (e.g., feeling alone, feeling that one's wishes are not fulfilled, feelings of worry, nervousness, or low spirits; (Dohrenwend, Shrout, Egri, & Mendelsohn, 1980), or even could be symptoms of physical disorder (e.g., "Have you ever had any fainting spells?"; "Every so often I suddenly feel hot all over"). The challenge of the problem of false positives (that is, the misclassification of nondisordered individuals in distress as disordered) is brought out by the fact that, in Srole et al.'s (1978) study, fully 82% of the surveyed population reported some psychiatric symptomatology.

More recently devised instruments deal with the problems of symptom checklists in a variety of ways. First, they present separate sets of symptoms for each

the use of *disorder* in the broader medical sciences. DSM's definition according to the American Psychiatric Association (2000) is as follows:

> In *DSM-IV*, each of the mental disorders is conceptualized as a clinically significant behavioral or psychological syndrome or pattern that occurs in an individual and that typically is associated with present distress (e.g., a painful symptom) or disability (i.e., impairment in one or more important areas of functioning) or with a significantly increased risk of suffering death, pain, disability, or an important loss of freedom. In addition, this syndrome or pattern must not be merely an expectable and culturally sanctioned response to a particular event, for example, the death of a loved one. Whatever its original cause, it must currently be considered a manifestation of a behavioral, psychological, or biological dysfunction in the individual. Neither deviant behavior (e.g., political, religious, or sexual) nor conflicts that are primarily between the individual and society are mental disorders unless the deviance or conflict is a symptom of a dysfunction in the individual, as described above. (APA, 2000, pp. xxx–xxxi).

The definition makes four useful points. First, disorder is something in the individual; it is not an unfortunate environmental stress to which a person responds with proportionate emotional pain, but a condition in which something has gone wrong inside the person. Second, the internal condition, which must be inferred from manifest symptoms, is a dysfunction; that is, something must have gone wrong with the way that the internal mechanism normally functions. Not all problematic internal states are disorders; for example, ignorance and appropriate sadness over a loss are problematic internal states, but they are not disorders. Only those problematic internal states that are also dysfunctions are disorders in the medical sense. In the case of mental disorders, the dysfunctional mechanism must be a cognitive, motivational, behavioral, emotional, or other psychological mechanism. Of course, "dysfunction" itself is an obscure concept and requires its own analysis. A series of articles (Wakefield, 1992a, 1992b, 1993, 1999a, 1999b; Wakefield & First, 2003) provide such an analysis, according to which a dysfunction, in the sense relevant to both physical and mental medical disorder, is a failure of some internal mental or physical mechanism to perform a natural function for which it was designed by natural selection.

Third, a dysfunction of some internal mechanism is not enough to imply disorder. Many things go wrong with various mental and physical mechanisms – these breakdowns in the functioning of specific mechanisms constitute what Donald Klein (1978) has called "part dysfunctions" – that do not deserve to be called disorders because they do not have sufficiently negative implications for the individual's overall well-being. The difference between dysfunctions that can be classified as disorders and dysfunctions that cannot be classified as disorders thus lies in whether the dysfunction causes real harm to the person. In DSM's definition, the main harms that occur as a result of dysfunctions and are useful in diagnosis are divided into two kinds, distresses and disabilities.

Finally, the distress, disability, or other harm must come about as a direct result of a dysfunction and not just because society disapproves of the person's condition or for other reasons originating in interpersonal conflicts or in conflict between the individual and society. Such conflicts may at times be so stressful that they bring about an internal dysfunction and disorder that go beyond the normal response to stress, but the painful reaction to such a conflict is not in and of itself a disorder. This last condition is meant to preclude the misuse of psychiatry for sheer social control purposes, as occurred in Soviet psychiatry when dissidents who opposed the oppressive Soviet political system were labelled as disordered. But it also reflects the critical insight in DSM's definition that mental disorders, like all medical disorders, are distresses or disabilities resulting from internal dysfunctions: "Whatever its original cause, it must currently be considered a manifestation of a . . . dysfunction in the individual" (American Psychiatric Association, 2000, p. xxxi). A disorder is more than just appropriate unhappiness or distress or reduced functioning because of unfortunate circumstances.

In sum, the concept of disorder, as it applies to both physical and mental conditions, is that of a "harmful dysfunction" (Wakefield, 1992a, 1992b, 1993, 1997, 1998, 1999a, 1999b; Wakefield & First, 2003). The harm can be any negatively evaluated, undesirable outcome; the dysfunction must involve something going wrong with the functioning of some internal mechanism, so that the mechanism is not performing one of the functions for which it is "designed" by natural selection.

Specificity and the Problem of False Positives

Conceptual validity is not easy to attain for one basic reason: the symptoms of many mental disorders can also be normal reactions when they occur in response to certain kinds of stressful environments. For example, deep sadness can indicate major depressive disorder, or it can indicate a normal reaction to loss; intense anxiety can be a symptom of generalized anxiety disorder, or it can be a normal response to an unusually stressful set of circumstances; antisocial behavior can represent a breakdown in the ability to function according to social rules and thus a conduct disorder, or it can represent a decision to join a gang and go along with gang activities in a dangerous neighborhood where one's life is otherwise in danger; and excessive alcohol intake can be a manifestation of an addiction that is a disorder, or it can be a youthful attempt to be exuberantly excessive, having no long-lasting negative implications and involving no addiction. In these and many other instances, criteria that use symptoms to pick out disorders might also pick out large numbers of normal conditions that have the same "symptoms" as the disorders. This is the problem of *false positives*, and it is a serious challenge to the conceptual validity of epidemiological surveys.

Mental disorders are relatively rare, whereas normal misery in response to problems in the environment is relatively common. Consequently, if an instrument does not successfully distinguish problems in living from true disorders, the estimate of the prevalence of disorder in the population could easily be greatly inflated by a large number of false-positive diagnoses.

In epidemiology, sensitivity and specificity of criteria are two important aspects of conceptual validity. Criteria are *sensitive* if they are satisfied by all disorders in the domain of interest, so that if the criteria are applied correctly there are no false negatives (i.e., no genuine disorders are mistakenly classified as nondisorders). Criteria are *specific* if they are only satisfied by disorders, so that if the criteria are applied correctly, there are no false positives (i.e., no nondisorders are mistakenly classified as disorders). If criteria lack specificity, then nondisordered individuals may be falsely classified as disordered, and the criteria are said to be overinclusive. Therefore, criteria are sensitive to the degree that they identify as disorders *all* the true disorders and do not miss any disorders; criteria are specific to the extent that they identify as disorders *only* the true disorders and do not classify any nondisorders as disorders.

We are concerned in this chapter only with the conceptual specificity of criteria for mental disorder. Although we could address many important problems with the sensitivity of diagnostic criteria, such as problems with potential underdiagnosis, or false negatives, in our view, specificity – and the problem of overdiagnosis – is by far the more difficult and important measurement issue of the two. Underdiagnosis is a serious problem with some disorders, but this is generally not because of inherent problems with the validity of the diagnostic criteria themselves so that they fail to correctly classify disordered conditions as disorders; rather, underdiagnosis occurs because disordered individuals may fail to seek treatment, may not accurately report their symptoms, or may fail to be recognized by a professional as having a disorder for a variety of other reasons. It should also be noted that even those disordered conditions that do not fall under standard diagnostic criteria for a given disorder may still be diagnosed as a disorder under DSM's "wastebasket" category of diagnosis: "not otherwise specified" (NOS; e.g., "mood disorder not otherwise specified"). For example, even "subthreshold" conditions that do not have enough symptoms to satisfy diagnostic criteria can be classified as disorders via the corresponding NOS category. In contrast, there is no mechanism within the DSM allowing the classification of a condition that does satisfy the diagnostic criteria to be classified as a normal reaction rather than a disorder, even if the clinician judges it to be not a disorder.

Specificity is generally more difficult to achieve than sensitivity. Although there are atypical instances of every disorder, most disorders are accompanied by certain predictable kinds of behaviors, so reasonably high levels of sensitivity are not hard to attain. For example, all phobias involve intense and irrational fears, all alcoholic disorders involve heavy drinking, and all depressions and anxiety disorders involve inordinate sadness and anxiety, respectively. So it is generally not hard to find criteria that apply to most or all instances of a disorder. The harder problem is to make the criteria specific enough to pick out only disorders from among the broader realm of problems in living. In some disorders, such as schizophrenia, the typical symptoms are far enough from the normal that there is relatively little problem with specificity, though even here the variations in the normal, including the presence of dissociative and even hallucinatory experiences that are not pathological (e.g., hallucinations of seeing a deceased spouse during some normal grief reactions), can lead to false positives. But with many disorders, such as depression, anxiety, phobias, and alcohol and drug abuse and dependence, the same or very similar kinds of behaviors that are typically manifested by disordered people are also manifested by nondisordered people, so specificity becomes a very challenging problem.

Within psychiatric epidemiology, specificity is of particular importance because of the well-known fact that even small problems with specificity can be devastating to the validity of epidemiological prevalence estimates. The reason for the disproportionate power of specificity is that, with respect to any given disorder, the samples in epidemiological studies of the general population generally contain many more people who do not have the disorder than who do have the disorder. Indeed, it is common to have 10 to 100 times as many nondisordered as disordered individuals with respect to a given disorder in such samples. Consequently, failures of specificity that yield only small percentages of errors can still lead to many incorrect diagnoses.

This point can be illustrated with the following example. Suppose a disorder has an actual prevalence of 1% of the general population. Suppose further that a set of diagnostic criteria for identifying the disorder has identical 10% rates of error for false positives and false negatives. That is, of all those who actually have the disorder, the criteria correctly identify 90% of them as disordered and incorrectly classify 10% as nondisordered. And of all those who actually do not have the disorder, the criteria correctly identify 90% of them as nondisordered and incorrectly classify 10% of them as disordered. Although the error rates for false negatives and false positives are the same, the two error rates have very different impacts on the resulting prevalence estimates because the populations involved – the normal and the disordered – are of such different sizes. The rate of false negatives means that 10% of the disordered 1% of the population, or 0.1%, are misdiagnosed as nondisordered. In contrast, the rate of false positives means that 10% of the nondisordered 99% of the population, or 9.9% of the population, are misdiagnosed as having the disorder. In this example, the 10% false-positive rate has an effect on the prevalence estimate that is 99 times as large as the effect of the 10% false-negative rate. Together, both 10% error rates change the prevalence estimate from the true prevalence of 1% to an estimated prevalence of 10.8%, for about a 1,000% increase over true prevalence. The power of small errors in specificity to yield such large prevalence errors is the central challenge of measurement in psychiatric epidemiology aimed at establishing true prevalence in community samples.

The implication is simple: to accurately measure the prevalence of disorder in community samples, diagnostic criteria must, if anything, err on the side of specificity. Unfortunately, as we shall see, specificity has not been the highest priority in formulating such criteria.

DSM-IV and the Problem of False Positives

As noted earlier, contemporary psychiatric epidemiological studies take their diagnostic criteria from DSM, generally without substantial change. When diagnostic instruments for community epidemiological studies were designed, much effort was expended on translating DSM criteria into questions appropriate to an epidemiological interview and to validating such instruments against other DSM-based standards. There was little attempt, however, to independently assess whether DSM criteria worked appropriately in the community context. The assumption was that such an instrument would identify those in the community who have conditions comparable to those who are diagnosed within clinical situations. However, the extreme importance of specificity to epidemiology raises the question of whether DSM, a manual designed to be used primarily with a clinical population, adequately addressed specificity in the construction of its diagnostic criteria. Although in principle the goal of diagnosis in DSM and epidemiological instruments is the same – namely, valid diagnoses using operationalized criteria for specific mental disorders – divergent features of clinical and epidemiological contexts express themselves in different implicit emphases when constructing diagnostic criteria. For several reasons, these different emphases lead DSM criteria to be weaker with respect to specificity than would be desirable for epidemiological criteria.

First, clinical interviewing and treatment extend over time and allow the clinician the luxury of correcting a mistaken initial diagnosis based on later findings. As new information emerges, the clinician might even conclude that there were extenuating circumstances and that the individual does not genuinely suffer from a disorder after all. The clinician can even "disagree" with the official DSM criteria when the context of symptoms warrants such an exception. For these and other reasons, the cost of an initial false-positive diagnosis in a clinical setting is not as great as the cost of a false negative, where an individual may not get the treatment that is needed. And, even if there is a false-positive diagnosis, some purpose may be served because treatment may still be useful with subclinical conditions.

In contrast, epidemiological diagnoses are almost always based on one contact, and there are no feedback loops or corrective mechanisms by which diagnostic evaluations can be reconsidered in light of emerging information. Nor is there second-guessing the criteria; epidemiological surveys rely exclusively on the diagnostic criteria in the epidemiological instrument in an algorithmic all-or-none fashion. Thus false positives remain false positives – and false positives defeat the essential point of an epidemiological study, which is to identify and count disorders to shape policy and discover the causes of disorder.

Second, clinical populations are highly self-selected and contain individuals who have been willing to undergo considerable inconvenience to obtain help with their problems. The psychological and institutional obstacles that help-seekers must overcome mean that members of the clinical population are likely to be suffering from very high levels of distress, disability, or other harm, which may be indicative of a genuine disorder. This tends to make the issue of conceptual specificity superfluous. Diagnosis then becomes a matter of choosing the category of disorder that best applies to the patient. This is a very different kind of problem from the one that faces epidemiologists. Epidemiological surveys encompass many people who report problems similar to those of clinical populations, but who have never sought out a mental health professional. In such cases, the seriousness of the condition and thus its disorder status are questionable. Consequently, there is a much greater danger that the epidemiological survey will incorrectly diagnose nondisordered people as disordered. These divergent features of clinical and epidemiological contexts should make one wary about uncritically transposing clinically derived criteria into the epidemiological domain.

It turns out (Wakefield, 1993, 1996, 1997) that many DSM criteria are inconsistent with DSM's own definition of disorder and consequently give rise to false positives. In particular, two of DSM's definitional requirements for disorder are frequently violated by its own criteria. The first is that the condition must be due to a psychological or biological dysfunction; many of the criteria describe human harms (e.g., intense anxiety, excessive use of alcohol) that need not originate in dysfunctions. The second requirement that is often violated is the stipulation that the harm cannot be the result of social conflict or the attempt by society to control disapproved behavior; in fact, many of the criteria involve "symptoms" that are clearly manifestations of social conflict (e.g., arrest for the use of illegal drugs, disapproval of one's alcohol use by one's family) and are not harms directly caused by dysfunctions.

In this section we present a few examples to illustrate how DSM's rules for the diagnosis of specific disorders diverge from the concept of disorder and are likely to encompass nondisordered problems of living. We thank the American Psychological Association for permission to use here some material previously published in Wakefield (1996).

Conduct Disorder

DSM-IV diagnostic criteria for conduct disorder (CD), an adolescent disorder involving antisocial behavior, require the presence of at least three of the following behaviors in the past year (and one in the past 6 months): intimidating others, initiating fights, using a weapon, being cruel to people or animals, stealing while confronting a victim, forcing someone into sexual activity, setting fires, destroying others' property, breaking into a house or building, lying to obtain goods, stealing, staying out late despite parental prohibitions, running away from home, and being truant from school. DSM-IV criteria for CD additionally include a clinical significance requirement (see the later discussion of such DSM clinical significance requirements): that "the disturbance in behavior causes clinically significant impairment in social, academic, or occupational functioning" (American Psychiatric Association, 2000, p. 91). This addition seems unlikely to have a great impact on diagnosis simply because it is likely that any adolescent satisfying three of the symptom criteria would thereby tautologically be classifiable as displaying impaired social functioning and thus would satisfy the clinical significance requirement; in addition, some of the criteria (e.g., truancy, running away) strongly imply impaired school functioning as well.

It is manifest that these DSM diagnostic criteria for CD allow the diagnosis of adolescents as disordered who are responding with antisocial behavior to peer pressure, to the dangers of a deprived or threatening environment, or to abuses at home. For example, a girl who, in an attempt to avoid escalating sexual abuse by her stepfather, lies to her parents about her whereabouts, often stays out late at night despite their prohibitions, and then, tired during the day, often skips school, and her academic functioning is consequently impaired, can be diagnosed as having a CD. Rebellious kids or those who fall in with the wrong crowd and who skip school and do a bit of shoplifting and vandalism also qualify for diagnosis. However, in an acknowledgment of such problems of diagnosis, there is a unique paragraph added to DSM-IV's textual discussion of CD that states that "consistent with the DSM-IV definition of mental disorder, the Conduct Disorder diagnosis should be applied only when the behavior in question is symptomatic of an underlying dysfunction within the individual and not simply a reaction to the immediate social context." It further notes that "it may be helpful for the clinician to consider the social and economic context in which the undesirable behaviors have occurred" (American Psychiatric Association, 2000, p. 96). If this paragraph's substance had been incorporated into the diagnostic criteria, many potential false positives could have been eliminated. Unfortunately, in epidemiological studies and research contexts, as well as in some clinical contexts, such nuances of the text are ignored.

Substance Abuse

Diagnosis of substance abuse requires any one of four criteria: poor role performance at work or home due to substance use; substance use in hazardous circumstances, such as driving under the influence of alcohol; recurrent substance-related legal problems; or social or interpersonal problems due to substance use, such as arguments with family members about substance use. Contrary to DSM's definition of mental disorder, these criteria allow diagnosis on the basis of conflict between the individual and social institutions such as police or family. Arguments with one's spouse about alcohol or drug use or between a child and his or her parent are sufficient for diagnosis, as is being arrested more than once for driving while under the influence of alcohol or for possession of marijuana. These social problems and interpersonal conflicts need not be caused by mental disorders.

Clinical Significance

The most notable attempt in DSM-IV to make general progress on the false-positives problem has been the development of a clinical significance (CS) criterion for use in evaluating mental disorder. The CS criterion proposed in DSM-IV addresses the basic concern that the symptoms cause clinically significant distress or impairment in social, occupational, or other important areas of functioning. It aims to set an impairment/distress threshold for diagnosis so as to eliminate false positives where there is minimal harm to the individual, and in a few instances it does improve validity. However, requiring "clinically significant" distress or role impairment as a criterion for distinguishing disorder from nondisorder involves circular reasoning because the amount of distress or impairment varies greatly with both normal and disordered negative conditions. Thus, to say that distress or impairment is "clinically significant" in this context can only mean that the distress or impairment is significant enough to imply the existence of a disorder, a tautologous criterion. The phrase offers no real guidance in deciding whether the level of impairment is or is not sufficient to imply disorder.

Furthermore, the CS criterion does not deal with a large number of potential false positives, specifically those where there may be harm but no dysfunction. For example, the normal child in a threatening environment whose aggressive behavior meets the criteria for CD or the normal girl threatened by a school bully, who meets the selective mutism criteria by virtue of her not speaking at school because of her fear, do experience distress and significant impairment in functioning as part of their normal reactions and so are not excluded from diagnosis by the CS criterion. Although there is obviously a thorny issue lurking here about the point at which motivations become so intense and rigid as to be pathological, it seems clear that in some cases such motivations (e.g., not to talk to avoid being beaten up by a bully) can be perfectly normal, even though they impair performance and are distressful. Thus, clinical significance by itself does not imply disorder.

Another problem with the CS criterion is the potential for yielding false-negative misdiagnoses when it is indiscriminately added to criteria sets, because it requires such specific forms of harm. For example, DSM-IV's requirement that a pattern of substance use cause clinically significant impairment or distress before dependence can be diagnosed could yield large numbers of false negatives. It is not uncommon to encounter addicted individuals whose health is threatened by drug use and who surely have a disorder, but who are not distressed and who can carry on successful role functioning. The proverbial cocaine-addicted successful stockbroker may be an example, as may be many tobacco users. The problem in many of these cases is that distress and role impairment are not the only kinds of harms that can be caused by dysfunctions. Disorder simply requires "significant harm."

Use of clinical significance criteria played a prominent role in an attempt to resolve the significant discrepancies in prevalence estimates in the ECA and NCS studies (Narrow et al., 2002). Unfortunately, the ECA and NCS datasets did not include operationalizations of the DSM-IV CS criterion, because they were based on the earlier DSM-III and DSM-III-R criteria, respectively, which included no CS criterion. In their attempt to reconcile the differences in prevalence estimates between the ECA and NCS, Narrow et al. (2002) operationalized the CS requirement using retroactively imposed criteria, but they based it on questions regarding service use and interference with life activities, rather than distress and role impairment, because the latter DSM criteria were not available within the ECA and NCS datasets. Their attempt is consequently hard to interpret and in any event showed limited success in accomplishing the goal of reconciling the prevalence estimate differences in the two studies (Wakefield & Spitzer, 2002a).

A few studies have empirically tested the impact of the CS criterion on community (Beals et al., 2004; Slade & Andrews, 2002) or clinical (Zimmerman et al., 2006) samples. These studies overall suggest that applying the CS criterion may increase the likelihood of false negatives in community samples and does little in reducing the likelihood of false positives in either community or clinical samples (Beals et al., 2004; Zimmerman et al., 2006). The Beals et al. (2004) study validated the CS against a standardized interview (the Structured Clinical Interview for DSM Disorders [SCID]) that is itself based on DSM criteria and thus may have a substantial false-positives problem in its own right, making the interpretation of the results difficult. Some authors have suggested that the CS criterion may obscure racial health disparities, particularly when it is operationalized with service use indicators (Coyne & Marcus, 2006).

Perhaps the most problematic aspect of the CS criterion is that it reflects a misunderstanding of the main problem underlying false positives and thus a misdirection of effort. The CS criterion is based on the assumption that the way to ensure that a condition is pathological is to establish that it causes sufficient distress or impairment in social or role functioning, an assumption at odds with broader diagnostic practice in medicine and that fails to recognize that there are mild disorders (Kessler, Merikangas, et al., 2003). Moreover, DSM false positives are most often due not to a failure of symptoms to reach a threshold of harmfulness but to a failure of symptomatic criteria to indicate the presence of an underlying dysfunction. Thus, ratcheting up the level of harms such as distress or impairment is not sufficient for distinguishing disorder from nondisorder. There are two good indicators of this failure in DSM itself. The first is that the most obvious potential false positive in the manual, uncomplicated bereavement as distinguished from major depressive disorder, must be dealt with by an additional special exclusion clause and is not eliminated by the CS criterion that is added to the criteria set, because normal grief can be just as distressful and role impairing as pathological depression, even though it is not caused by a dysfunction. The second indicator is that, although the CS is added to the criteria for conduct disorder (see earlier text), the DSM still adds a textual note that adolescents may satisfy the criteria and still not be disordered because their antisocial behavior may not be due to a dysfunction but to a normal reaction to a problematic environment. Clearly, the CS criterion does not address the dysfunction problem. Both distress and role impairment can be the result of normal or disordered emotions and behaviors.

With all of the conceptual and empirical difficulties of the CS criterion, particularly its tautological nature (Frances, 1998) and its apparently poor conceptual validity in restricting diagnosis to genuine mental dysfunctions (Spitzer & Wakefield, 1999; Wakefield & Spitzer, 2002a, 2002b), another approach is necessary. Wakefield and Spitzer (2002b) suggested that the issue of false positives in diagnosis is better approached by examining the context of the particular symptoms and adjusting the details of the diagnostic criteria.

Extended Example: Major Depressive Disorder

In this section, we present an extended example of a recent attempt to use DSM-derived criteria in an epidemiological study to measure the prevalence of a particular mental disorder, namely, major depressive disorder (MDD). We selected this example because MDD is among the disorders with the highest prevalence rates and its defining criteria warrant special attention to specificity.

The DSM defines MDD based on three criteria: (1) presence of a major depressive episode; (2) the major depressive episode is not better accounted for by a schizoaffective disorder, schizophrenia, or similar types of disorders; and (3) there has never been a manic episode, mixed episode, or hypomanic episode. The key criterion for our discussion is the first one – presence of a major depressive episode.

Five criteria need to be met to diagnose a major depressive episode: (1) at least five out of nine symptoms present nearly every day for 2 weeks or longer; (2) the symptoms do not meet criteria for a mixed episode; (3) the symptoms cause clinically significant distress or impairment in social, occupational, or other important areas of functioning; (4) the symptoms are not due to the physiological effects of a substance or general medical condition; and (5) the symptoms are not better accounted for by bereavement.

Two issues are of interest in the above criteria. First, the only place in which the context of symptoms is considered is in the last criterion, where bereavement is allowed as a potential exclusion for the diagnosis. Second, the clinical significance criterion is quite broad, and, as noted in the previous, more general discussion about the CS criterion in DSM, anyone meeting the symptom criteria will also very likely meet the CS criterion for major depressive episode. This is a good example of how the CS criterion does no real work in the diagnosis.

The strength of carefully delineated, operationalized criteria with respect to reliability is obvious, and such criteria generally lead to excellent sensitivity. We focus our comments in this section on the kinds of problems that can occur with false positives and a lack of specificity when such DSM-style criteria are used. The example is drawn from the NCS-R (Kessler & Merikangas, 2004), and the criteria are part of the World Mental Health Initiative version of the Composite

International Diagnostic Interview (WMH-CIDI; Kessler & Üstun, 2004), developed specially for and used in that study. The WMH-CIDI is essentially a translation of DSM-IV criteria into the format of an epidemiological instrument.

The NCS-R, like many epidemiological studies, presented estimates for both lifetime and active (i.e., current) prevalence of disorders. Lifetime prevalence refers to the percentage of people who have ever had a given disorder in their lives. Active prevalence, in the context of the NCS-R, refers to the percentage of people who have had a given disorder at any time in the past year. We are concerned here only with lifetime prevalence. Note that lifetime prevalence includes "active" people who currently have the disorder.

According to Kessler, Berglund, et al. (2005), the lifetime prevalence of MDD in the general population is 16.6%. At the heart of the WMH-CIDI criteria for MDD is the notion of a major depressive episode, which is defined essentially as a 2-week period during which five or more of the following symptoms occurred: depressed mood, loss of interest in daily activities, significant weight loss or gain, sleep disturbance, changes in psychomotor activity, feelings of worthlessness or guilt, difficulty in concentrating, and preoccupation with death or a wish to die. At least one of the symptoms has to be either depressed mood or loss of interest.

An individual is classified as having a major depressive episode if the individual answers "yes" to each of the following categories:

A. Symptom criteria, requiring both Part 1 and Part 2.

Part 1: Symptoms have been present during the same 2-week period and at least one symptom is either depressed mood or loss of interest, assessed by a yes response to at least one of the following:

"Did you feel sad, empty, or depressed most of the day nearly every day during that period of two weeks?"

"Did you feel so sad that nothing could cheer you up nearly every day?"

"During that period of two weeks, did you feel discouraged about how things were going in your life most of the day nearly every day?"

"Did you feel hopeless about the future nearly every day?"

"During that period of two weeks, did you lose interest in almost all things like work and hobbies and things you like to do for fun?"

"Did you feel like nothing was fun even when good things were happening?"

Part 2: At least five of the following symptoms must be present and represent change from previous functioning:

Depressed mood, assessed by yes to one of the first four questions in Part 1 above.

Loss of interest, assessed by yes to one of the last two questions in Part 1 above.

Significant weight loss or gain, assessed by asking "Did you have a much larger [smaller] appetite than usual nearly every day?"

Sleep trouble, assessed by asking "Did you have a lot more trouble than usual either falling asleep, staying asleep, or waking too early nearly every night during that period of two weeks," and "Did you sleep a lot more than usual nearly every night during that period of two weeks?"

Changes in psychomotor activity, assessed by asking "Do you talk or move more slowly than is normal for you nearly every day and did anyone else notice you were talking or moving slowly," and "Were you so restless or jittery nearly every day that you pace up and down or couldn't sit still and did anyone else notice you were restless?"

Fatigue, assessed by asking "Did you feel tired or low in energy nearly every day during that period of two weeks even when you had not been working very hard?"

Feelings of worthlessness, assessed by asking "Did you feel totally worthless nearly every day?"

Trouble concentrating, assessed by asking "Did your thoughts come much more slowly than usual or seem mixed up nearly every day during that period of two weeks" and "Did you have a lot more trouble concentrating than is normal for you nearly every day" and "Were you unable to make up your mind about things you ordinarily have no trouble deciding about?"

Recurrent thoughts of death, suicide ideation, or suicide attempt, assessed by asking "Did you often think a lot about death, either your own, someone else's, or death in general" and "During that period, did you ever think that it would be better if you were dead," and "Did you think about committing suicide," and "Did you make a suicide plan," and "Did you make a suicide attempt?"

B. Symptoms do not meet criteria for a mixed episode – not operationalized in the NCS-R dataset.

C. Symptoms cause clinically significant distress or impairment in social, occupational, or other important areas of functioning.

Assessed by several questions about symptom impact on activities.

D. Symptoms are not due to the direct physiological effects of a substance or are not due to a general medical condition.

E. Symptoms not better accounted for by bereavement – not operationalized in NCS-R dataset.

The central validity problem for any definition of depressive disorder is to distinguish pathological depression from the common and normal depressive reactions that occur in response to significant losses or failures of all kinds. Unfortunately, the DSM criteria that are the basis for the WMH-CIDI criteria do not themselves validly distinguish normal sadness responses from disorders, and these invalidities are inherited by the WMH-CIDI. The basic problem is that having several symptoms of intense sadness could represent intense normal sadness rather than a depressive disorder. Unfortunately, the WMH-CIDI did not consider symptom context at all and thus was unable to distinguish disorder from normal sadness responses.

The DSM-IV criteria for MDD, as we saw, correctly contain an exclusion for uncomplicated bereavement (i.e., one is not diagnosed as disordered if the symptoms are due to a normal-range response to having recently lost a loved one, with up to 2 months of symptoms allowed as normal). However, they contain no exclusions for equally normal reactions to other losses, such as a terminal medical diagnosis in oneself or a loved one, separation from one's spouse, or losing one's job. If in grappling with such a loss, one's reaction includes just 2 weeks of depressed mood, diminished pleasure in usual activities, insomnia, fatigue, and a diminished ability to concentrate on work tasks, then one satisfies DSM criteria for MDD, even though such a reaction need not imply pathology any more than it does in bereavement (Horwitz & Wakefield, 2007; Wakefield, Schmitz, First, & Horwitz, 2007). This problem is exacerbated in the WMH-CIDI in that it does not even operationalize the DSM bereavement exclusion, which would have offered at least a minimal consideration of environmental context. Clearly, the prevalence estimates from the NCS-R for MDD are too high, given the complete lack of consideration of the depressive symptom context in the structured interview.

To appreciate the validity problem with respect to DSM-IV criteria for MDD, it is useful to start by reflecting on why grief reactions are justifiably excluded from the category of disorder in the first place, even though such reactions can contain all the symptoms characteristic of a pathological depression. The exclusion is justified because such grief reactions appear to be normal-range responses that play an adaptive role in coming to terms with loss, and so they are presumed to be part of how human beings are designed to react to such losses. The occurrence of such loss responses, however painful they may be, does not represent a dysfunction in which some psychological mechanism fails to perform its function; rather, it represents the proper workings of emotional mechanisms. In fact, the lack of such a response may be indicative of dysfunction. Therefore, the exclusion of grief reactions from the category of disorder is essential to validity. Obviously only those grief reactions that are "uncomplicated," meaning that they do not involve excessive persistence or severity of symptoms given the nature of the loss, are excluded from disorder status; grief reactions can be pathological when unduly persistent or severe.

From the viewpoint of validity, it is entirely arbitrary to exclude grief reactions to loss of a loved one from the category of disorder but not to exclude all the other uncomplicated, normal sadness reactions to life's losses and failures that are comparable to grief in the nature of the experienced symptoms (Horwitz & Wakefield, 2007). There are an endless number of circumstances of loss or failure under which people normally and appropriately experience sadness that meets the criteria for a depressive episode. Consider, for example, the following vignettes, taken from Wakefield (1998). We thank the American Psychological Association for permission to use this material here:

Vignette 1 Reaction to a life-threatening medical diagnosis

The patient, a 35-year-old physician, had been diagnosed 3 weeks before with a malignant brain tumor and was told by his physician that there is no effective treatment. He came to a research medical center for a second opinion and was given some hope that an experimental treatment might give him 5 to 10 years of life. Referred by the neurosurgical staff for a psychiatric assessment, he reports that since his diagnosis he has experienced chronic feelings of sadness over the loss of his health and the implications for his wife and child, markedly diminished interest or pleasure in his usual activities as he focused on possible treatments, insomnia due to thinking about his illness and his prospects, lack of energy due to sadness and insomnia, diminished ability to concentrate on everyday tasks due to his attempting to come to terms with the possibility that he might soon die, and some suicidal ideation when he earlier thought the course of his illness would be more rapid and hopeless and he considered whether it would be better for him and his family to end his life before the occurrence of deterioration due to the disease.

This patient's response qualifies him for a DSM-IV diagnosis of major depressive disorder. However, once one takes into account the subjective meanings that are causing the loss response – namely, his discovery that he is suffering from an imminently life-threatening illness – his reaction appears to be consistent with a normal-range, nondisordered response. This is perhaps especially so because he is a physician and fully understands the implications of his diagnosis. Note that although he has stopped functioning in his normal routines – which is entirely understandable given his prognosis – he has continued to assertively seek out the best available medical care. The failure to distinguish normal from pathological sadness responses to threatening medical diagnoses could be seriously iatrogenic in this case; if the clinician had followed DSM and offered a diagnosis of MDD, this could have placed this normal individual outside the parameters of the research protocol governing the experimental treatment he is seeking.

Not only the patient but also the patient's family and other loved ones may experience severe sadness reactions to news of a life-threatening medical diagnosis, as seen in Vignette 2.

Vignette 2 Reaction to a life-threatening medical diagnosis in a loved one

A woman who is visiting a medical center distant from her home consults a psychiatrist at the center asking for medication to help her sleep. In the diagnostic interview, it emerges that the woman's son, a physician, to whom she is very close and who is the pride of her life, has just 3 weeks before been diagnosed with a malignant brain tumor. The woman has traveled to the medical center to be with her son for an evaluation and possible immediate operation. After the news of her son's diagnosis, the patient was devastated by feelings of sadness and despair and was unable to function at work or socially. She did, however, devote herself to helping her son arrange for a visit to the medical research center for further evaluation and possible treatment and offered him and his wife emotional support. Although she kept up a brave front for her son, the patient has been in a state of great distress since the diagnosis, crying intermittently, unable to sleep, lacking the ability to concentrate, and feeling fatigued and uninterested in her usual activities, as she attempted to come to terms with the news of her son's diagnosis.

This woman satisfies the WMH-CIDI and DSM-IV criteria for diagnosis with a major depressive disorder, yet her reaction appears to be within normal range for a loving parent in such a situation. The horror of such an illness in a beloved child who is still young, who carries one's hopes for the future and thus one's sense of life's meaningfulness, and to whom one has devoted much of one's life, appropriately causes an extreme and enduring emotional reaction. Once the subjective meaning to the mother of her son's diagnosis is taken into account, her reaction is consistent with a nondisordered response.

Vignette 3 Ending of a passionate romantic relationship

The patient, a male professor in the social sciences, comes to the consultation seeking antidepressant medication and medicine for insomnia. He must present a paper in another city as part of a job interview and is afraid he cannot function adequately to do so. He reports that for the past month he has experienced depressed mood and extreme feelings of sadness and emptiness, as well as a lack of interest in his usual activities (in fact, when not with friends, he has largely lain in bed or watched television). His appetite has diminished, and he lies awake long into the night unable to fall asleep due to the pain of his sadness. He is fatigued and lacking in energy during the day and does not have the ability to concentrate on his work. There is no suicidal ideation or feelings of guilt or worthlessness. However, there is functional impairment: the patient is barely managing to meet minimal occupational obligations (e.g., he has shown up at class relatively unprepared and has not attended the monthly faculty meeting or worked on his research). He has also avoided social obligations, except to be with close friends to lessen his pain.

When asked what event might have precipitated these distressing feelings, the patient reports, holding back tears as he speaks, that about a month before, an extremely intense and passionate 5-year love affair with a married woman (the patient is single) to whom he had been completely devoted had been ended by the woman after she made a final decision that she could not leave her husband. Both lovers had perceived this relationship as a unique, once-in-a-lifetime romance in which they had met their "soulmate" and experienced an extraordinary combination of emotional and intellectual intimacy. If one is left by a lover whom one believes (perhaps with good reason) is a once-in-a-lifetime "soulmate," it is not abnormal or inappropriate to feel extreme sadness and even despair, with all the associated depressive symptoms. The meaning to the patient of this relationship reveals that the reaction is not necessarily disordered, despite its intensity. Similarly, loss of a partner due to separation or divorce may also cause a normal loss response of great and enduring intensity. In general, the end of a serious relationship can cause a feeling that the world is drained of meaning as the person struggles to no longer see the world partly through the eyes of the other, and the associated feelings may satisfy DSM criteria without actually being a MDD.

All the patients described in these vignettes satisfy DSM criteria for MDD, and if they had been subjects in the NCS-R study, they would have correctly answered the questions in a way that qualified them for diagnosis under WMH-CIDI criteria as well. Yet, none of them need be disordered. Of course, the experiences suffered by these patients could trigger a genuine depressive disorder, but there is no evidence in these cases of such a pathological reaction. The distinction between nonpathological depression and pathological depression is not adequately drawn by DSM-IV or the WMH-CIDI, and without that distinction there is no way to tell how many of the depressive episodes reported by the NCS-R are actually disorders. Indeed, recent reanalyses of the NCS data showed that lifetime prevalence estimates of MDD are likely 25% too high, given even a limited ability to incorporate into the diagnostic algorithm other types of losses in triggering a depressive episode (Wakefield et al., 2007).

Recent Issues: Dimensionality and Subthreshold Disorder

In preparations for the fifth edition of the DSM, a vigorous debate has arisen regarding the basic categorical approach used in the manual. Because epidemiological studies, such as the NCS and NCS-R, found very high comorbidity among disorders, extensive variability within disorders regarding types of symptoms exhibited and disorder prognosis, and a lack of discrete cutoffs in symptom distribution (Krueger, Watson, & Barlow, 2005), several authors have proposed using a dimensional typology in assessing disorder in the DSM (Clark, 2005; Krueger, Watson, et al., 2005; Watson, 2005; Widiger & Samuel, 2005). Dimensional approaches have been shown to give higher levels of diagnostic reliability and validity

(Widiger & Samuel, 2005). However, other authors have argued that the most important issue is the clinical utility of diagnosis and that a dimensional approach to diagnosis, although perhaps more effective for researchers, may not be so helpful for clinicians (First, 2005). Proposals for including dimensional components in clinical diagnosis are being explored, with the possible addition of indicators of symptom severity and patient functioning (First & Westen, 2007).

However, given that almost everyone will fall somewhere along various emotional and symptom dimensions, a basic question is how dimensional approaches will address the question of who is disordered and who is not disordered. Establishing thresholds on various dimensions for considering a patient to have a disorder seems to recreate all the problems of the categorical approach. Yet, some such system is essential for the clinical utility of a dimensional system and for avoiding invalidly pathologizing those who are experiencing normal-range distress. The dimensional approach, for all its appeal, faces challenging issues of validity (Wakefield, 2008).

In a related issue, numerous authors have advocated the inclusion as disorders of those cases that do not meet the minimum symptom count for a given diagnosis (Angst et al., 2003; Kendler & Gardner, 1998). For example, cases of depression exhibiting four symptoms or fewer would be identified as mild depression (Judd et al., 1997; Kramer, 2005; Sullivan, Kessler, & Kendler, 1998). Subthreshold cases of depression have been found to exhibit similar correlates as major depression, as well as significant levels of impairment (Kessler, Zhao, et al., 1997). These authors have concluded that minor depression cannot be dismissed as nondisorder and that prevalence estimates of depressive disorder, based on the five-symptom cutoff, are actually much too low.

Granted, the symptom cutoffs in diagnoses are rather arbitrary, and there are people exhibiting only a few symptoms who are experiencing conditions that should be diagnosed as disorder. However, the key is to distinguish normal responses to circumstances from dysfunctional responses to those circumstances, and emphasizing the counting of symptoms simply misses this fundamental point regarding the assessment of dysfunction and disorder. Any number of symptoms may or may not indicate disorder, depending on their environmental context.

Conclusion

When the United States some years ago launched the Hubble Space Telescope at a cost of more than 1 billion dollars, it was discovered after the launch that the mirror suffered from a degree of distortion, yielding fuzzy images that could not provide the new view of the universe that was the goal of the project. As a result, the many other aspects of the program – the rest of the telescope, the computers and motors that aimed the telescope with extreme precision, the solar panels providing power, the telemetry that allowed the telescope's readings to be transmitted to earth, and even the successful launch itself – all became relatively worthless. The value of every other aspect of the enterprise depended on the expectation that the mirror could yield clear pictures. Fortunately, a later repair mission was able to fix the mirrors and allow the entire project to go forward and fulfill its mission of providing sharp images of our universe.

We find ourselves today in a somewhat similar position with respect to psychiatric epidemiology and its measuring instruments. The entire, extremely expensive apparatus of such studies – from instrument development, sample selection, and data collection to the statistical analysis of data – depends for its meaningfulness on the validity of a few definitions of mental disorders, generally taken from DSM. Yet if the argument presented in this chapter is correct, there is reason to believe that these definitions do not give a clear and valid picture of the domain of disorder. Instead, they seem to fuzzily encompass a broad range of abnormal and normal situations in which human beings feel distress or are impaired in their usual functioning. For all their innovation and sophistication, DSM-derived criteria do not overcome some of the problems in distinguishing disorder from nondisorder that beset the earlier symptom checklists. The question that faces psychiatric epidemiology is whether some kind of "repair mission" can succeed in fixing these criteria or, alternatively, whether some methodological innovation can circumvent these validity problems.

There is reason to hope that refined criteria and tailored methodologies can finally overcome the problem of false positives. For example, future epidemiological studies may use a two-stage process in which subjects are first screened using DSM or comparable criteria and then those meeting DSM criteria for disorder are interviewed by a professional to distinguish genuine cases from false positives. Criteria may be refined to take the situational context of the symptoms into account and thus reduce the magnitude of the problem of specificity (Wakefield, 1996). In any event, current studies, though flawed, do provide large amounts of valuable data on the prevalence of disorder, distress, and impairment. However, for now, the question remains open as to whether or when psychiatric epidemiology will reach its ultimate goal of accurately measuring the true prevalence of mental disorder in community populations.

3

The Prevalence of Mental Illness

Ronald C. Kessler

A very important question is, How many people suffer from mental health problems? In this chapter Ronald C. Kessler provides a thorough answer to this question, relying primarily on the most recent data source available, the National Comorbidity Survey Replication (see the Acknowledgments). Kessler begins by addressing issues raised by both David Mechanic in the foreword and Allan Horwitz in Chapter 1: should measures of mental health and illness be discrete or continuous? He then reviews sources of data and describes prevalence rates in great detail. An advantage of the recent data is that researchers also ascertained whether people who did experience mental health problems received treatment for these problems and whether this treatment was adequate. The chapter concludes with an extended discussion of the implications of this research. In considering the overall prevalence rates, are you surprised by the widespread prevalence of mental illnesses in the population? What is the meaning of comorbidity, and why is it important?

The NCS-R is carried out in conjunction with the World Health Organization World Mental Health (WMH) Survey Initiative. We thank the staff of the WMH Data Collection and Data Analysis Coordination Centres for assistance with instrumentation, fieldwork, and consultation on data analysis. These activities were supported by the NIMH (R01 MH070884), the John D. and Catherine T. MacArthur Foundation, the Pfizer Foundation, the U.S. Public Health Service (U13-MH066849, R01-MH069864, and R01 DA016558), the Fogarty International Center (FIRCA R03-TW006481), the Pan American Health Organization, Eli Lilly and Company, Ortho-McNeil Pharmaceutical, Inc., GlaxoSmithKline, Bristol-Myers Squibb, and

---

The National Comorbidity Survey Replication (NCS-R) is supported by the National Institute of Mental Health (NIMH; U01-MH60220) with supplemental support from the National Institute on Drug Abuse (NIDA), the Substance Abuse and Mental Health Services Administration (SAMHSA), the Robert Wood Johnson Foundation (RWJF; Grant 044780), and the John W. Alden Trust. Collaborating NCS-R investigators include Ronald C. Kessler (Principal Investigator, Harvard Medical School), Kathleen Merikangas (Co-Principal Investigator, NIMH), James Anthony (Michigan State University), William Eaton (Johns Hopkins University), Meyer Glantz (NIDA), Doreen Koretz (Harvard University), Jane McLeod (Indiana University), Mark Olfson (New York State Psychiatric Institute, College of Physicians and Surgeons of Columbia University), Harold Pincus (University of Pittsburgh), Greg Simon (Group Health Cooperative), Michael Von Korff (Group Health Cooperative), Philip Wang (Harvard Medical School), Kenneth Wells (UCLA), Elaine Wethington (Cornell University), and Hans-Ulrich Wittchen (Max Planck Institute of Psychiatry; Technical University of Dresden). The views and opinions expressed in this report are those of the authors and should not be construed to represent the views of any of the sponsoring organizations, agencies, or the U.S. government. A complete list of NCS publications and the full text of all NCS-R instruments can be found at http://www.hcp.med.harvard.edu/ncs. Send correspondence to ncs@hcp.med.harvard.edu.

Shire. A complete list of WMH publications can be found at http://www.hcp.med. harvard.edu/wmh/.

Background

The answer to the question, How many people have a mental illness?, depends on how one conceptualizes and measures mental illness. This chapter focuses on measures of mental disorder as assessed in the *Diagnostic and Statistical Manual* (DSM) of the American Psychiatric Association (APA) or the World Health Organization's (WHO) International Classification of Diseases (ICD) and as operationalized in lay-administered fully structured diagnostic interviews like the Diagnostic Interview Schedule (DIS; Robins et al., 1981) or the Composite International Diagnostic Interview (CIDI; Robins et al., 1988). Although a number of versions of the DSM and ICD classification schemes exist, the results reported here are based on the DSM-IV (American Psychiatric Association, 1994) because this system has been the basis for most recent general population research on the prevalence of mental disorders.

It is worth noting at the onset that most of the research on the prevalence of mental illness by sociologists over the years has not focused on DSM or ICD disorders. Measures of nonspecific psychological distress have been used much more commonly as outcomes (for a review, see Link & Dohrenwend, 1980). Research based on these continuous measures of distress have an advantage over research based on the assessment of dichotomous measures of mental disorder in that the former deal much more directly with the actual constellations of signs and symptoms that exist in the population than with the classification schemes imposed on these constellations by the committees that created the DSM and ICD diagnoses. However, there is also a disadvantage of working with distress measures: There is nothing in these measures themselves that allows us to discriminate between people who do and do not have clinically significant emotional problems. This discrimination is important for purposes of making social policy decisions based on such issues as the number of people in need of mental health services. Researchers who work with measures of nonspecific psychological distress often deal with this lack of discrimination by developing rules for classifying people with scores above a certain threshold as "cases" (e.g., Radloff, 1977). The cut-points are usually based on statistical analyses that attempt to discriminate optimally between the scores of patients in mental health treatment and those of people in a community sample. In contrast, dichotomous diagnostic measures allow this sort of discrimination to be made directly based on an evaluation of diagnostic criteria, which is why we prefer using them in analyses that require some case distinction.

It is important to recognize that there is an inherent ambiguity in making the dichotomous decision that is required to define some people as cases and others as not cases. This ambiguity is recognized by the clinicians who are involved in work to establish diagnostic criteria (Frances, Widiger, & Fyer, 1990). However, there are some ways in which this ambiguity is not terribly different from the situation in areas of physical medicine where yes–no treatment decisions have to be made based on continuous data, such as the decision of where to draw the line in blood pressure readings to define hypertension. Decisions of this sort are usually made on the basis of actuarial evidence regarding the subsequent risk of some fairly well-defined outcome (e.g., stroke) associated with the continuous measure, but there is certainly no expectation that 100% of the people on one side of the line and 0% on the other side of the line will experience that outcome.

However, the situation is more difficult in the area of psychiatric assessment because there are no relatively unequivocal dichotomous outcomes like having a heart attack or stroke or developing cancer that can be used as a gold standard against which to calibrate the dichotomous case decisions. This ambiguity is also more pronounced in the study of mental illness because of the absence of medical tests to make diagnoses and the inherent political nature of some distinctions regarding the types of behaviors that are socially normative. As a result, caution is needed not to read too much into results regarding prevalence estimates. Nonetheless, it is necessary for treatment purposes as well as for social policy purposes to make dichotomous diagnostic distinctions of this sort.

Data Sources

The need for general population data on the prevalence of mental illness was noted three decades ago in the report of President Carter's Commission on Mental Health and Illness (1978). It was impossible to undertake such a survey at that time because of the absence of a structured research diagnostic interview capable of generating reliable psychiatric diagnoses in general population samples. Recognizing this need, the National Institute of Mental Health (NIMH) funded the development of the Diagnostic Interview Schedule (DIS; Robins et al., 1981), a research diagnostic interview that can be administered by trained interviewers who are not clinicians. The DIS was first used in the Epidemiologic Catchment Area (ECA) Study, a landmark study that interviewed more than 20,000 respondents in a series of five community epidemiological surveys (Robins & Regier, 1991). The ECA was the main source of data in the United States on the prevalence of mental disorders and utilization of services for these disorders over the next decade (Bourdon et al., 1992; Regier et al., 1993; Robins, Locke, & Regier, 1991).

Development of a lay-administered diagnostic interview was critical to the implementation of the ECA study because it would have been prohibitively expensive to carry out a large national survey that used clinician-administered diagnostic interviews. A few community surveys using clinician-administered diagnostic interviews have been carried out, but these have either been quite small local surveys (e.g., Weissman & Myers, 1978) or surveys based on samples that are not representative of the general population (e.g., the sample of twins interviewed by Kendler, Neale, Kessler, Heath, & Eaves, 1992) or that were carried out outside the United States (e.g., Dohrenwend et al., 1992). At the same time, it is important to establish comparability between diagnoses based on lay-administered interviews and those based on clinician-administered interviews. This sort of comparison was made in the ECA study by having small subsamples of respondents interviewed a second time by clinical interviewers and comparing the diagnoses obtained in the main survey with the diagnoses based on these clinical follow-up interviews (Anthony et al., 1985; Helzer et al., 1985). These methodological studies showed generally low agreement between DIS classifications and the classifications independently made by clinical interviewers, thereby raising questions about the accuracy of the ECA results (e.g., Parker, 1987; Rogler, Malgady, & Tryon, 1992). However, others noted that the validity problems in the DIS are concentrated among respondents who either fall just short of meeting criteria or just barely meet criteria and that the errors due to false positives and false negatives tend to balance each other out to produce fairly accurate total population prevalence estimates (Robins, 1985). Although this observation provides no assurance that the different errors are counterbalanced in all important segments of the population (Dohrenwend, 1995), the documentation that this is true in the population as a whole suggests that the ECA results yielded useful overall prevalence data.

Critics raised other concerns about the ECA as well, perhaps the most important being that the ECA was carried out in only five local areas around the country rather than in a nationally representative sample. This problem was subsequently addressed in a second survey carried out a decade after the ECA. This survey, known as the National Comorbidity Survey (NCS; Kessler et al., 1994), was based on a national sample and used a modified version of the DIS known as the Composite International Diagnostic Interview (CIDI; Robins et al., 1988). The CIDI expanded the DIS to include diagnoses based on DSM-III-R (American Psychiatric Association, 1987) criteria, as well as the ICD-10 (World Health Organization, 1991). WHO field trials of the CIDI documented adequate reliability and validity for all diagnoses (Wittchen, 1994). A clinical reappraisal study in the NCS documented generally good concordance between diagnoses based on the CIDI and diagnoses based on subsequent clinician-administered reappraisal interviews (Kessler, Wittchen, et al., 1998).

An NCS replication survey (NCS-R; Kessler & Merikangas, 2004) was carried out a decade after the NCS to monitor trends in the prevalence and treatment of mental disorders in the United States. The NCS-R also expanded the diagnostic coverage of the earlier ECA and NCS surveys, though none of the surveys covered all Axis I disorders. The ECA focused on mood disorders (major depression, dysthymia, mania), anxiety disorders (generalized anxiety disorder, panic disorder, phobia, obsessive-compulsive disorder, posttraumatic stress disorder), addictive disorders (alcohol abuse and dependence, drug abuse and dependence), nonaffective psychoses (schizophrenia, schizophreniform disorder, schizoaffective disorder, delusional disorder, brief psychotic reaction), and somataform disorder.

Neither did the surveys cover Axis II disorders, which include the personality disorders and mental retardation, although antisocial personality disorder (ASPD) and some measures of cognitive impairment were assessed. The absence of information on personality disorders other than ASPD was a major omission, but was necessitated by the fact that valid structured diagnostic interview methods to assess personality disorders did not exist at the time these surveys were carried out.

Another major gap is the absence of assessments of disruptive behavior disorders, most notably attention-deficit/hyperactivity disorder (ADHD) and intermittent explosive disorder (IED). Although ADHD has traditionally been thought of as a disorder that affects only children, recent follow-up studies of clinical samples have shown clearly that many cases persist into adulthood (Wilens, Faraone, & Biederman, 2004), making it important to include an assessment of ADHD in epidemiological surveys of adult mental illness. IED is important because it is the only disorder in the DSM in which the core symptoms are anger and violence. Based on these considerations, both adult ADHD (Kessler, Adler, et al., 2006) and IED (Kessler, Coccaro, et al., 2006) were included for the first time in the NCS-R. The NCS-R also included screening measures of personality disorders (Lenzenweger et al., 2007). Results from the NCS-R are the focus of the current chapter.

Plan of the Chapter

The chapter begins with a broad overview of results concerning the estimated lifetime prevalence, age-of-onset distributions, projected lifetime risk, cohort effects, and sociodemographic correlates of the DSM-IV disorders assessed in the NCS-R. It then turns to a discussion of the prevalence of these same disorders in the year before the NCS-R interview. This is followed by a brief review of data regarding trends in disorder prevalence and treatment in the NCS-R compared to a decade earlier in the baseline NCS. The chapter closes with a discussion of interpretations and implications of these results along with anticipated future directions in the investigation of the prevalence of mental disorders.

Lifetime Prevalence and Age-of-Onset of DSM-IV Disorders

Lifetime Prevalence

The ECA (Robins & Regier, 1991) and the NCS (Kessler et al., 1994) both reported high lifetime prevalence and generally early age-of-onset (AOO) distributions of most DSM-III (NCS) and DSM-III-R (NCS-R) disorders. As shown in Table 3.1, similar results were found in the NCS-R (Kessler, Berglund, et al., 2005). The most prevalent lifetime disorders were major depression (16.6%), alcohol abuse (13.2%), specific phobia (12.5%), and social phobia (12.1%). Anxiety disorders were the most prevalent class of disorders (28.8%), followed by disruptive behavior disorders (24.8%), mood disorders (20.8%), and substance use disorders (14.6%). The lifetime prevalence of any disorder was 46.4%, whereas 27.7% of respondents had two or more lifetime disorders and 17.3% had three or more. A discussion of the symptom requirements for being classified as having each of these disorders is beyond the scope of this chapter, but can be found by referring to the DSM-IV manual (American Psychiatric Association, 1994).

Lifetime prevalence estimates varied significantly with age for all but a handful of disorders. A monotonic increase in prevalence was generally found from the youngest (18–29) to a higher (for the most part, 30–44) age group, and then there was a decline in the older age group(s). Prevalence was always lowest, and sometimes substantially so, in the oldest age group (60+). The most dramatic differences of this sort were for drug abuse and dependence, posttraumatic stress disorder (PTSD), and bipolar disorder. Prevalence differences were much less marked among the other three age groups.

Age-of-Onset Distributions

The NCS-R asked respondents with lifetime disorders retrospectively to report their AOO. The two-part actuarial method (Halli & Rao, 1992) was used to generate AOO curves and estimates of projected lifetime risk as of age 75. The distributions of cumulative lifetime risk estimates were standardized and examined for fixed percentiles. As shown in Table 3.2, two clear patterns emerged from these data. First, median AOO (i.e., 50th percentile on the AOO distribution) was found to be much earlier for anxiety disorders (age 11) and disruptive behavior disorders (age 11) than for substance use disorders (age 20) and mood disorders (age 30). Second, AOO was found to be concentrated in a very narrow age range for most disorders, with interquartile ranges (IQR; the 25th–75th percentiles of the AOO distributions) of only 8 years (ages 7–15) for disruptive behavior disorders, 9 years (ages 18–27) for substance use disorders, and 15 years (ages 6–21) for anxiety disorders compared to 25 years (ages 18–43) for mood disorders.

Table 3.2 shows that most disorder-specific AOO distributions share important features with other disorders in their class. In particular, median AOO was earlier for each disruptive behavior disorder (ages 7–15) than for any substance (ages 19–23) or mood (ages 25–32) disorder, whereas the IQR was consistently narrower for each of the disruptive-behavior control (1–6 years) and substance (6–12 years) disorders than for any mood disorder (25–26 years). The AOO distributions of anxiety disorders were more diverse, with specific phobia and separation

Table 3.1. *Estimates of the lifetime prevalence of DSM-IV disorders in the NCS-R (n = 9,282)*

	Total		18–29		30–44		45–59		60+		$c^{2,3}$
	%	(SE)	%	(SE)	%	(SE)	%	(SE)	%	(SE)	
I. Anxiety disorders											
Panic disorder	4.7	(0.2)	4.4	(0.4)	5.7	(0.5)	5.9	(0.4)	2.0	(0.4)	52.6*
Agoraphobia without panic	1.4	(0.1)	1.1	(0.2)	1.7	(0.3)	1.6	(0.3)	1.0	(0.3)	4.5
Specific phobia	12.5	(0.4)	13.3	(0.8)	13.9	(0.8)	14.1	(1.0)	7.5	(0.7)	54.3*
Social phobia	12.1	(0.4)	13.6	(0.7)	14.3	(0.8)	12.4	(0.8)	6.6	(0.5)	109.0*
Generalized anxiety disorder	5.7	(0.3)	4.1	(0.4)	6.8	(0.5)	7.7	(0.7)	3.6	(0.5)	39.9*
Posttraumatic stress disorder[1]	6.8	(0.4)	6.3	(0.5)	8.2	(0.8)	9.2	(0.9)	2.5	(0.5)	37.9*
Obsessive-compulsive disorder[2]	1.6	(0.3)	2.0	(0.5)	2.3	(0.9)	1.3	(0.6)	0.7	(0.4)	6.8
Separation anxiety disorder[3]	5.2	(0.4)	5.2	(0.6)	5.1	(0.6)	—[3]	—[3]	—[3]	—[3]	0.0[5]
Any anxiety disorder[4]	28.8	(0.9)	30.2	(1.1)	35.1	(1.4)	30.8	(1.7)	15.3	(1.5)	89.9*
II. Mood disorders											
Major depressive disorder	16.6	(0.5)	15.4	(0.7)	19.8	(0.9)	18.8	(1.1)	10.6	(0.8)	49.9*
Dysthymia	2.5	(0.2)	1.7	(0.3)	2.9	(0.4)	3.7	(0.7)	1.3	(0.3)	10.6*
Bipolar I–II disorders	3.9	(0.2)	5.9	(0.6)	4.5	(0.3)	3.5	(0.4)	1.0	(0.3)	62.0*
Any mood disorder	20.8	(0.6)	21.4	(0.9)	24.6	(0.9)	22.9	(1.2)	11.9	(1.0)	58.0*
III. Disruptive behavior disorders											
Oppositional-defiant disorder	8.5	(0.7)	9.5	(0.9)	7.5	(0.8)	—	—[3]	—	—[3]	3.0[5]
Conduct disorder	9.5	(0.8)	10.9	(1.0)	8.2	(0.8)	—	—[3]	—	—[3]	7.6*[5]
Attention-deficit/hyperactivity disorder	8.1	(0.6)	7.8	(0.8)	8.3	(0.9)	—	—[3]	—	—[3]	0.2[5]
Intermittent explosive disorder	5.2	(0.3)	7.4	(0.7)	5.7	(0.6)	4.9	(0.4)	1.9	(0.5)	74.7*
Any disruptive disorder	24.8	(1.1)	26.8	(1.7)	23.0	(1.3)	—	—[3]	—	—[3]	4.0*[5]

IV. Substance disorders

	%	(SE)	%	(SE)	%	(SE)	%	(SE)	%	(SE)	χ^2
Alcohol abuse	13.2	(0.6)	14.3	(1.0)	16.3	(1.1)	14.0	(1.1)	6.2	(0.7)	60.2*
Alcohol dependence	5.4	(0.3)	6.3	(0.7)	6.4	(0.6)	6.0	(0.7)	2.2	(0.4)	45.2*
Drug abuse	7.9	(0.4)	10.9	(0.9)	11.9	(1.0)	6.5	(0.6)	0.3	(0.2)	168.7*
Drug dependence	3.0	(0.2)	3.9	(0.5)	4.9	(0.6)	2.3	(0.4)	0.2	(0.1)	90.0*
Any substance disorder	14.6	(0.6)	16.7	(1.1)	18.0	(1.1)	15.3	(1.0)	6.3	(0.7)	71.4*
V. Any disorder											
Any[4]	46.4	(1.1)	52.4	(1.7)	55.0	(1.6)	46.5	(1.8)	26.1	(1.7)	115.4*
Two or more disorders[4]	27.7	(0.9)	33.9	(1.3)	34.0	(1.5)	27.0	(1.6)	11.6	(1.0)	148.3*
Three or more disorders[4]	17.3	(0.7)	22.3	(1.2)	22.5	(1.1)	15.9	(1.3)	5.3	(0.7)	140.7*

*Significant age difference at the .05 level.

[1] PTSD was assessed only in the Part II sample ($n = 5,692$).

[2] Obsessive-compulsive disorder was assessed only in a random one-third of the Part II sample ($n = 1,808$).

[3] Separation anxiety disorder, oppositional-defiant disorder, conduct disorder, ADHD, and any disruptive behavior disorder were assessed only among Part II respondents in the age range 18–44 ($n = 3,199$).

[4] These summary measures were analyzed in the full Part II sample ($n = 5,692$). Separation anxiety disorder, oppositional-defiant disorder, conduct disorder, and ADHD were coded as absent among respondents who were not assessed for these disorders.

[5] The c^2 test evaluates statistical significance of age-related differences in estimated prevalence; c^2 is evaluated with one degree of freedom for SAD, ODD, CD, ADHD, and any disruptive behavior disorder.

Table 3.2. *Ages at selected percentiles on the standardized age-of-onset (AOO) distributions of DSM-IV disorders with projected lifetime (LT) risk at age 75 in the NCS-R* (n = 9,282)

	Projected LT risk at age 75		Ages at selected AOO percentiles							
	%	(SE)	5	10	25	50	75	90	95	99
I. Anxiety disorders										
Panic disorder	6.0	(0.3)	6	10	16	24	40	51	56	63
Agoraphobia without panic	1.6	(0.2)	6	7	13	20	33	48	51	54
Specific phobia	13.2	(0.4)	4	5	5	7	12	23	41	64
Social phobia	12.6	(0.4)	5	6	8	13	15	23	34	52
Generalized anxiety disorder	8.3	(0.4)	8	13	20	31	47	58	66	75
Posttraumatic stress disorder[1]	8.7	(0.6)	6	9	15	23	39	53	61	71
Obsessive-compulsive disorder[2]	1.9	(0.3)	10	11	14	19	30	48	54	54
Separation anxiety disorder[3]	5.2	(0.4)	5	5	6	7	10	13	14	17
Any anxiety disorder[4]	31.5	(1.1)	5	5	6	11	21	41	51	65
II. Mood disorders										
Major depressive disorder	23.2	(0.6)	12	14	19	32	44	56	64	73
Dysthymia	3.4	(0.3)	7	11	17	31	43	51	57	73
Bipolar I–II disorders	5.1	(0.3)	11	13	17	25	42	50	57	65
Any mood disorder	28.0	(0.8)	11	13	18	30	43	54	63	73
III. Disruptive behavior disorders										
Oppositional-defiant disorder[3]	8.5	(0.7)	5	6	8	13	14	16	17	18
Conduct disorder[3]	9.5	(0.8)	6	7	10	13	15	17	17	18
Attention-deficit/hyperactivity disorder[3]	8.1	(0.6)	5	6	7	7	8	11	11	16
Intermittent explosive disorder	5.4	(0.3)	6	8	11	15	20	26	37	46
Any disruptive behavior disorder[3]	25.4	(1.1)	5	6	7	11	15	18	23	36
IV. Substance disorders										
Alcohol abuse[1]	15.1	(0.7)	15	16	18	21	29	39	44	54
Alcohol dependence[1]	6.5	(0.4)	16	17	19	23	31	41	50	56
Drug abuse[1]	8.5	(0.4)	15	16	17	19	23	29	36	46
Drug dependence[1]	3.4	(0.3)	15	16	18	21	28	36	41	49
Any substance use disorder[4]	16.3	(0.6)	15	16	18	20	27	37	41	54
V. Any disorder										
Any[4]	50.8	(1.2)	5	5	7	14	24	42	51	64

[1]PTSD and substance disorders were assessed only in the Part II sample ($n = 5,692$).

[2]Obsessive-compulsive disorder was assessed only in a random one-third of the Part II sample ($n = 1,808$).

[3]Separation anxiety disorder, oppositional-defiant disorder, conduct disorder, ADHD, and any disruptive behavior disorder were assessed only among Part II respondents in the age range 18–44 ($n = 3,199$).

[4]These summary measures were analyzed in the full Part II sample ($n = 5,692$). Separation anxiety disorder, oppositional-defiant disorder, conduct disorder, and ADHD were coded as absent among respondents who were not assessed for these disorders.

anxiety disorder having a very early median AOO (age 7) and very narrow IQRs (4–7 years), social phobia having a later median AOO (age 13) and a narrow IQR (7 years), and other anxiety disorders having much later median AOOs (ages 19–31) and much wider IQRs (16–27 years).

Projected Lifetime Risk

Projected lifetime risk as of age 75 based on the AOO distributions (Table 3.2) was 9% higher than lifetime prevalence estimates reported in Table 3.1 for anxiety disorders, 34% higher for mood disorders, 2% higher for disruptive behavior disorders, 12% higher for substance use disorders, and 9% higher for any disorder. Disorders with the highest increases between prevalence and projected risk were, predictably, those with late AOO distributions: major depression, generalized anxiety disorder, and PTSD. Consistent with the prevalence data, projected risk was highest for anxiety disorders (31.5%), but the order was reversed for disruptive behavior and mood disorders – with the former having a higher prevalence (24.8% vs. 20.8%) and the latter a higher projected risk (28.0% vs. 25.4%). Substance use disorders had the lowest projected risk (16.3%). Individual disorders with the highest projected risk were identical to those with the highest prevalence. More than 80% of projected new onsets are estimated to occur to people who already had earlier disorders. This can be seen by noting that the overall projected risk in the total sample was only 4.4% higher than the lifetime prevalence reported in Table 3.1 (50.8% vs. 46.4%), whereas disorder-specific risk vs. prevalence differences summed to 20.4%.

Cohort Effects

Dummy variables defining age groups 18–29, 30–44, 45–59, and 60+ (corresponding roughly to cohorts born in the years 1970+, 1955–1969, 1940–1954, and earlier than 1940) were used to predict lifetime disorders using discrete-time survival analysis. The odds ratios (ORs) were statistically significant in the vast majority of comparisons, with a consistently positive association between recency of cohorts and OR of onset. The largest cohort effects were associated with drug use disorders and the smallest with phobias and childhood-onset disruptive behavior disorders. The cohort model was elaborated to evaluate whether inter-cohort differences decrease significantly with increasing age, a pattern that might be expected either (1) if lifetime risk was actually constant across cohorts but appeared to vary with cohort due to onsets occurring earlier in more recent than in later cohorts (either caused by secular changes in environmental triggers or age-related differences in AOO recall accuracy) or (2) if differential mortality had an increasingly severe effect on sample selection bias with increasing age. Differences were examined separately for first onsets in the age ranges 1–12,

13–19, 20–29, 30–39, 40–49, and 50–59; because the last of these age intervals was the upper end of the age distribution of the second oldest cohort quartile, it was not possible to study intercohort differences beyond this age. No evidence of decreasing cohort effects with increasing age was found for anxiety or mood disorders. In contrast, dramatic differences emerged for substance use disorders, with much higher cohort effects in the teens and 20s than in either childhood or in the 30s through the 50s.

Sociodemographic Predictors

Several sociodemographic variables were significantly related to lifetime risk of the NCS-R disorders in survival analyses that controlled for cohort. Most notably, women had significantly higher risk of anxiety and mood disorders than men. Men had significantly higher risk of disruptive behavior and substance use disorders than women. Non-Hispanic Blacks and Hispanics had significantly lower risk of anxiety, mood, and substance use disorders (the last only among non-Hispanic Blacks) than non-Hispanic Whites. Low education was associated with high risk of substance disorders. Marital disruption was associated with three out of four classes of disorder, the exception being disruptive behavior disorder.

The possibility was also considered that sociodemographic correlates might vary by cohort so that increasing prevalence in recent cohorts would be concentrated in certain population segments. Although at least one significant interaction was found for each sociodemographic predictor, the pattern was not consistent. The most notable results were that gender differences in anxiety, mood, and disruptive behavior disorders did not differ across cohort, but women were more similar to men in substance disorders in recent cohorts. In addition, the significant inverse associations of education and being married with substance disorders were found to exist only in recent cohorts.

Past Year Prevalence, Severity, and Comorbidity of DSM-IV Disorders

Twelve-Month Prevalence

As shown in Table 3.3, the disorders found in the NCS-R to be most prevalent in the year before the interview (12-month disorders) were specific phobia (8.7%), social phobia (6.8%), and major depression (6.7%; Kessler, Chiu, et al., 2005). Anxiety disorders were the most prevalent class (18.1%), followed by mood disorders (9.5%), disruptive behavior disorders (8.9%), and substance disorders (3.8%). Twelve-month prevalence of any disorder was estimated to be 26.2%, with more than half of cases (14.4% of the total sample) meeting criteria for only one disorder and smaller proportions meeting criteria for two (5.8%) or more (6.0%) disorders.

Table 3.3. *Estimates of 12-month prevalence and severity of DSM-IV disorders in the NCS-R* (n = 9,282)

| | Total | | Severity[1] | | | | | |
| | | | Serious | | Moderate | | Mild | |
	%	(SE)	%	(SE)	%	(SE)	%	(SE)
I. Anxiety disorders								
Panic disorder	2.7	(0.2)	44.8	(3.2)	29.5	(2.7)	25.7	(2.5)
Agoraphobia without panic	0.8	(0.1)	40.6	(7.2)	30.7	(6.4)	28.7	(8.4)
Specific phobia	8.7	(0.4)	21.9	(2.0)	30.0	(2.0)	48.1	(2.1)
Social phobia	6.8	(0.3)	29.9	(2.0)	38.8	(2.5)	31.3	(2.4)
Generalized anxiety disorder	3.1	(0.2)	32.3	(2.9)	44.6	(4.0)	23.1	(2.9)
Posttraumatic stress disorder[2]	3.5	(0.3)	36.6	(3.5)	33.1	(2.2)	30.2	(3.4)
Obsessive-compulsive disorder[3]	1.0	(0.3)	50.6	(12.4)	34.8	(14.1)	14.6	(5.7)
Separation anxiety disorder[4]	0.9	(0.2)	43.3	(9.2)	24.8	(7.5)	31.9	(12.2)
Any anxiety disorder[5]	18.1	(0.7)	22.8	(1.5)	33.7	(1.4)	43.5	(2.1)
II. Mood disorders								
Major depressive disorder	6.7	(0.3)	30.4	(1.7)	50.1	(2.1)	19.5	(2.1)
Dysthymia	1.5	(0.1)	49.7	(3.9)	32.1	(4.0)	18.2	(3.4)
Bipolar I–II disorders	2.6	(0.2)	82.9	(3.2)	17.1	(3.2)	0.0	(0.0)
Any mood disorder	9.5	(0.4)	45.0	(1.9)	40.0	(1.7)	15.0	(1.6)
III. Disruptive behavior disorders								
Oppositional-defiant disorder[4]	1.0	(0.2)	49.6	(8.0)	40.3	(8.7)	10.1	(4.8)
Conduct disorder[4]	1.0	(0.2)	40.5	(11.1)	31.6	(7.5)	28.0	(9.1)
Attention-deficit/hyperactivity disorder[4]	4.1	(0.3)	41.3	(4.3)	35.2	(3.5)	23.5	(4.5)
Intermittent explosive disorder	2.6	(0.2)	23.8	(3.3)	74.4	(3.5)	1.7	(0.9)
Any disruptive behavior disorder[4,6]	8.9	(0.5)	32.9	(2.9)	52.4	(3.0)	14.7	(2.3)
IV. Substance disorders								
Alcohol abuse[2]	3.1	(0.3)	28.9	(2.6)	39.7	(3.7)	31.5	(3.3)
Alcohol dependence[2]	1.3	(0.2)	34.3	(4.5)	65.7	(4.5)	0.0	(0.0)
Drug abuse[2]	1.4	(0.1)	36.6	(5.0)	30.4	(5.8)	33.0	(6.8)
Drug dependence[2]	0.4	(0.1)	56.5	(8.2)	43.5	(8.2)	0.0	(0.0)
Any substance disorder[2]	3.8	(0.3)	29.6	(2.8)	37.1	(3.5)	33.4	(3.2)
V. Any disorder								
Any[5]	26.2	(0.8)	22.3	(1.3)	37.3	(1.3)	40.4	(1.6)
One disorder[5]	14.4	(0.6)	9.6	(1.3)	31.2	(1.9)	59.2	(2.3)
Two disorders[5]	5.8	(0.3)	25.5	(2.1)	46.4	(2.6)	28.2	(2.0)
Three or more disorders[5]	6.0	(0.3)	49.9	(2.3)	43.1	(2.1)	7.0	(1.3)

[1] Percentages in the three severity columns are repeated as proportions of all cases and sum to 100% across each row.
[2] PTSD and substance disorders were assessed only in the Part II sample (*n* = 5,692).
[3] Obsessive-compulsive disorder was assessed only in a random one-third of the Part II sample (*n* = 1,808).
[4] Separation anxiety disorder, oppositional-defiant disorder, conduct disorder, ADHD, and any disruptive behavior disorder were assessed only among Part II respondents in the age range 18–44 (*n* = 3,199).
[5] These summary measures were analyzed in the full Part II sample (*n* = 5,692). Separation anxiety disorder, oppositional-defiant disorder, conduct disorder, and ADHD were coded as absent among respondents who were not assessed for these disorders.
[6] The estimated prevalence of any disruptive behavior disorder is larger than the sum of the individual disorders because the prevalence of intermittent explosive disorder, the only disruptive behavior disorder that was assessed in the total sample, is reported here for the total sample rather than for the subsample of respondents among whom the other disruptive behavior disorders were assessed (Part II respondents in the age range 18–44). The estimated prevalence of any disruptive behavior disorder, in comparison, is estimated in the latter subsample. Intermittent explosive disorder has a considerably higher estimated prevalence in this subsample than in the total sample.

Severity of 12-Month Disorders

Among respondents with a 12-month disorder, 22.3% were classified as serious, 37.3% moderate, and 40.4% mild based on a standard clinical severity rating scheme (Kessler, Chiu, et al., 2005). Severity was strongly related to comorbidity: 9.6% of respondents with one diagnosis, 25.5% with two, and 49.9% with three or more diagnoses were classified as serious. Nearly 80% of all serious cases were concentrated in the 9.6% of the population with comorbidity. The distribution of severity was quite different from the distribution of prevalence across classes of disorder, with mood disorders having the highest percentage of serious cases (45.0%) and anxiety disorders the lowest (22.8%). The anxiety disorder with the highest percentage of serious cases was obsessive-compulsive disorder (50.6%), whereas bipolar disorder had the highest percent serious (82.9%) among mood disorders, oppositional-defiant disorder (ODD; 49.6%) among the disruptive behavior disorders, and drug dependence (56.5%) among substance disorders.

Comorbidity

The severity data showed clearly that comorbidity is important, as the vast majority of serious cases were concentrated in the small proportion of the population with comorbid disorders. Correlations among disorders were calculated to study the dominant patterns of comorbidity. Tetrachoric correlations between hierarchy-free 12-month disorders were almost all positive (98%) and statistically significant (72%). After excluding the small number of disorders associated with negative correlations, exploratory factor analysis of the correlation matrix showed there to be two strong factors, one representing internalizing disorders (anxiety disorders, major depressive episode) and the other externalizing disorders (conduct disorder, substance disorders). Five disorders had factor loadings of .30 or higher on both factors (dysthymia, mania-hypomania, ODD, ADHD, and IED), although all five had higher loadings on the internalizing than externalizing factors.

Trends in Prevalence and Treatment

Although enormous changes in the mental health care system took place in the 1990s in the United States, little was known about changes in patterns of treatment of mental disorders prior to the NCS-R. Comparisons of data about treatment patterns in the year of interview of the baseline NCS (1990–1992) and the NCS-R (2001–2003) provided unique information about these changes (Kessler, Demler, et al., 2005). The treatment rate increased dramatically over this decade, from 20.3% of respondents with a 12-month disorder receiving treatment in the baseline survey to 32.9% a decade later. This increase in treatment was limited, though, to three sectors: general medical (where the number of people receiving treatment for a mental disorder increased by 159% over the decade), psychiatry (a 117% increase), and other specialty mental health (e.g., primarily psychologists and psychiatric social workers, a 59% increase). There were no significant increases, in comparison, in treatment for mental disorders either in the human services sector (e.g., spiritual advisors, marital counselors) or in the complementary-alternative medical sector (e.g., most notably self-help groups). Importantly, these increases in treatment occurred despite there being no change in the 12-month prevalence of mental disorders over the decade. Furthermore, the increases in treatment were independent of severity of the disorder; that is, the proportion increase in treatment over the decade was roughly the same among people with mild, moderate, and severe disorders.

When we look at the proportion of treatment given in each sector, we see that the importance of the general medical sector increased dramatically over the decade, to the point where the majority of treatment occurred in the general medical sector by the time of the second survey. In contrast, the majority of treatment was provided by psychiatrists and other mental health specialists at the time of the baseline survey. A companion trend was that the main type of treatment was medication in the absence of psychotherapy at the time of the second survey. In contrast, psychotherapy in combination with medication was the main type of treatment in the baseline survey. Because of these shifts in sector and mode of treatment, the adequacy of treatment declined over time as the proportion of people receiving treatment increased.

Overview

The NCS-R results suggest that mental disorders are highly prevalent in the general population. These estimates are broadly consistent with those of other community surveys in the United States (Kessler et al., 1994; Regier et al., 1998) and elsewhere in the world (Demyttenaere et al., 2004; WHO International Consortium in Psychiatric Epidemiology, 2000). Although no truly comprehensive assessment of all mental disorders has ever been carried out in a general population sample, it is almost certainly the case that such a study would find that an even higher proportion of the population met criteria for at least one of these disorders at some time in their life than estimated in the NCS-R. This result – that a majority of the population have a mental disorder at some time in their life – might initially seem remarkable, but it is actually quite easy to understand. The DSM and ICD classification systems are very broad. Both include a number of disorders that are usually self-limiting and not severely impairing. It should be no more surprising to find that half the population have met criteria for one or more of these disorders in their lifetime than to find that the vast majority of the population have had the flu or measles or some other common physical malady at some time in their life.

High prevalence estimates in previous psychiatric epidemiological surveys have been a source of two concerns to mental health policy analysts. The first is that the estimates are so high as to be scientifically implausible (Brugha, Bebbington, &, Jenkins, 1999). The NCS-R addressed this issue by showing that concordance was generally good between diagnoses generated in the survey and independent diagnoses made in clinical reappraisal interviews. A critic might conclude from this finding that the DSM-IV system itself is overly inclusive. However, it is noteworthy that analyses of the 12-month NCS-R data showed that even those 12-month CIDI disorders classified as mild are associated with levels of impairment equivalent to those caused by clinically significant chronic physical disorders (Merikangas et al., 2007). Based on this evidence, it would be difficult to make a principled argument for narrowing diagnostic criteria in future editions of the DSM to increase the threshold for clinical significance.

The second concern about high prevalence estimates is that, even if accurate, they correspond to many more people than can be helped by currently available treatment resources (Narrow et al., 2002) and consequently have no practical short-term implications other than perhaps reducing support for parity of treatment with physical disorders (Peck & Scheffler, 2002). In considering these issues it is important to note that mental disorders, like physical disorders, differ widely both in severity and in need for treatment (Kendell, 2002; Spitzer, 1998). The fact that nearly half the population meet criteria for a mental disorder in their life does not mean that they all need treatment. In addition, treatments with demonstrated cost effectiveness are not available for all mental disorders. If cost-effective treatments were to become available, it is likely that anticipated resource deficits would be at least partly counterbalanced by increased demand and willingness to pay, consistent, for example, with reactions to recently published research on the cost effectiveness of treating subthreshold hypercholesterolemia (Cannon et al., 2004; Nissen et al., 2004; Sacks, 2004; Topol, 2004).

The NCS-R results are also consistent with those of other studies in finding that depression, phobias, and alcohol abuse are the most common individual disorders and that anxiety disorders are the most common class of disorders. Although we know of no previous attempt to estimate the lifetime prevalence of DSM-IV disruptive behavior disorders in a nationally representative sample of adults, the NCS-R estimates are in the range reported in epidemiological surveys of adolescents (Loeber et al., 2000; Scahill & Schwab-Stone, 2000). The NCS-R prevalence estimate for IED is also consistent with the scant data on the prevalence of that disorder (Olvera, 2002). Given that previous epidemiological surveys excluded these impulse-control disorders, it is striking that their combined lifetime prevalence is higher than for either mood disorders or substance disorders.

Perhaps the more surprising NCS-R prevalence result is that, although many people have been touched by mental illness at some time in their life, the major burden of mental disorder in the population is concentrated in the relatively small proportion of people who are comorbid. This means that a pile-up of multiple disorders is the most important defining characteristic of serious mental illness, a result that points to the previously underappreciated importance of research on the primary prevention of secondary disorders (Kessler & Price, 1993). It also means that epidemiological information about the prevalence of individual disorders is much less important than information about the prevalence of functional impairment, comorbidity, and chronicity. This realization has led to a recent interest in functional impairment in revising diagnostic code-x DSM-IV criteria (American Psychiatric Association, 1994). This same emphasis can also be seen in the focus of the National Advisory Mental Health Council (1993) on what it defined as "severe and persistent mental illness" (SPMI) and the Substance Abuse and Mental Health Service Administration (1993) on what it defined as "serious mental illness" (SMI). The 1-year prevalences of SPMI and SMI are approximately 3% and 6%, respectively (Kessler, Berglund, et al., 1995), compared to 1-year prevalences of any DSM-IV disorder of about 26%.

The NCS-R AOO distributions, again consistent with those reported in previous epidemiological surveys (Christie et al., 1988; WHO International Consortium in Psychiatric Epidemiology, 2000), are striking in demonstrating that most mental disorders start at an early age and are concentrated in a relatively narrow time span. These patterns are opposite to those found for most chronic physical disorders, where conditional risk increases with age and the upper bound of the IQR is in late middle age or old age (Murray & Lopez, 1996). Whatever else we can say about mental disorders, they are distinct from chronic physical disorders because they gain their strongest foothold by attacking youth, with risk substantially lower among people who have matured out of the high-risk age range.

An important issue in assessing the societal burden of mental disorders is whether the evidence of increasing prevalence in recent cohorts is real or a methodological artifact. The fact that NCS-R cohort effects vary in plausible ways (e.g., the largest ORs are associated with drug use disorders, which are known independently to have increased among cohorts that went through adolescence beginning in the 1970s) and the fact that sociodemographic correlates of cohort effects are substantively plausible (e.g., the increasing similarity of women and men in substance use disorders in recent cohorts) argue for the observed cohort effect being at least partly caused by substantive rather than methodological factors. In addition, no evidence was found for the convergence among cohorts with increasing age that would be expected if methodological factors were responsible for intercohort variation in prevalence estimates. Nonetheless, residual effects of methodological factors are likely, based on the fact that longitudinal studies show mental disorders to be associated with early mortality (Bruce & Leaf, 1989) and that resolved mental disorders reported in baseline interviews often are not reported in follow-up interviews (Badawi et al., 1999). To the extent that these biases are at work, the high prevalence found in the younger NCS-R cohorts might also apply to older cohorts.

Based on the considerations in the last paragraph, we suspect that NCS-R intercohort differences in AOO are caused by a combination of substantive and methodological factors. A more definitive evaluation will require longitudinal trend comparisons. Even before such data become available, though, the NCS-R results clearly document that mental disorders are highly prevalent, that lifetime prevalence is, if anything, underestimated, that AOO distributions for most of the disorders considered here are concentrated in a relatively narrow age range during the first two decades of life, and that later onset disorders largely occur as temporally secondary comorbid conditions. To the extent that the evidence of cohort effects in the data is due to methodological factors, similar patterns might have occurred in earlier cohorts. Given the enormous personal and societal burdens of mental disorders, these observations should lead us to direct a greater part of our thinking about public health interventions to the child and adolescent years and, with appropriately balanced considerations of potential risks and benefits, to focus on early interventions aimed at preventing the progression of primary disorders and the onset of comorbid disorders.

The results reviewed here regarding trends in prevalence in the NCS-R compared to the earlier NCS survey are surprising in finding that 12-month prevalence of mental disorders stayed fairly constant over time. This is surprising if for no other reason than because the percentage of Americans receiving treatment for mental disorders rose by roughly 50% overall during that period. Does this imply that prevalence would have increased had it not been for the increase in treatment? That is certainly a possibility, although the fact that the ratio of current prevalence to 12-month prevalence did not decrease in the NCS-R compared to the NCS suggests that this is not the case in that episode duration has remained fairly similar. As treatment of mental disorders is largely treatment of episodes after they occur rather than prophylactic treatment to prevent episode recurrence, the finding that episode length has not decreased argues against the suggestion that the increase in treatment has led to a substantial reduction in disorder prevalence. What, then, has been the benefit of the enormous rise in treatment of mental disorders?

One possibility is that there has been no benefit, that this treatment was largely ineffective. This possibility is consistent with the NCS-R finding that a substantial proportion of treatment of mental disorders fails to meet even the minimum requirements in published treatment guidelines (Wang, Lane et al., 2005). Another possibility is that positive effects of treatment exist that are undetected by the nonexperimental NCS-R design. The only rigorous way to adjudicate between these possibilities is to carry out a long-term ongoing tracking study that includes an intervention component rather than once-a-decade naturalistic snapshot studies like the ECA, NCS, and NCS-R. Discussions are underway for the implementation of a major tracking study of this sort, although it is as yet unclear if it will be implemented.

Regardless of whether a major tracking study is implemented, it is likely that epidemiological research on adult mental disorders over the next decade will focus more than in the past on serious and severe disorders rather than on overall prevalence. To the extent that the prevalence of particular disorders is emphasized, it will likely be to study the underlying pathologies associated with ongoing impairment in functioning. There is also likely to be a considerable expansion of research on the epidemiology of child and adolescent disorders, a topic that has not been covered in this chapter, based on the realization that most mental disorders have early ages of onset and because of new initiatives to study child and adolescent mental disorders (Merikangas et al., 2009).

4

Biological Theories of Psychiatric Disorders: A Sociological Approach

Sharon Schwartz and Cheryl Corcoran

The biological understanding of mental illness views it as a disease of the brain. The biological revolution in psychiatry was sparked by evidence for a genetic component to psychiatric disorders and by pharmaceutical advances in drug therapies that added to our understanding of the chemistry of the brain and neuronal communication (i.e., neurochemistry). Furthermore, advances in neuroscience and neuroanatomy, fields that combine the findings from several scientific disciplines, have furthered our understanding of the relationship between the structure of the brain and human behavior. Schwartz and Corcoran provide an overview of what biological psychiatrists know about the brain and its function and dysfunction (i.e., neuroanatomy), neurochemistry, and genetics. They also provide an excellent analysis of the role of neurotransmitters. Psychiatric medications affect the level of neurotransmitters and hence correct dysfunctions in the neuronal communication systems. Schizophrenia has been hypothesized to result from an excess of dopamine, and the symptoms of schizophrenia are often reduced with the administration of medications that block specific dopamine receptors. Yet this evidence does not demonstrate that the cause of schizophrenia is a chemical imbalance, as not all people respond to medications, the medications only affect some of the symptoms of schizophrenia, and studies report inconsistent responses. Contradictory findings and gaps also exist in knowledge of the role played by neurotransmitter dysfunctions in depression. Although the evidence for a genetic link to schizophrenia and depression is compelling, Schwartz and Corcoran describe a variety of methodological problems that make heritability estimates questionable. Furthermore, the specific mode of transmission and interactions among genetic and environmental factors need further examination. The biological revolution has highlighted the complexity of understanding mental illness. Schwartz and Corcoran conclude by outlining what role sociologists can play in researching the factors that affect the etiology and course of mental disorder and in using the information gained by biological psychiatrists to further our understanding of the relationship between social and biological factors. Read this chapter carefully and identify what information you previously thought was incontrovertible (i.e., schizophrenia is caused by a particular gene) that has in fact not yet been verified.

Introduction

That a biological revolution in psychiatry has occurred in recent decades is undeniable. The presidential proclamation branding the 1990s "The Decade of the Brain," frequent newspaper headlines announcing the location of yet another gene for some psychiatric or behavioral condition, an advertising campaign pronouncing

"Depression: A Flaw in Chemistry, Not Character," and T-shirts and greeting cards with one-liners about medication for a psychiatric disorder (e.g., "Don't Worry, Take Prozac") all suggest that the biological revolution has become entrenched.

This revolution was sparked by two achievements in biological psychiatry – the compelling evidence from twin and adoption studies for a genetic component to psychiatric disorders and pharmaceutical advancements in the development of drugs that target specific symptom constellations (Chua & McKenna, 1995). It has gained momentum from technological advances in molecular genetics and neuroscience and the increased ability to visualize the structure and functioning of the brain (Pilowsky, 2001). Stunning victories in understanding the biological mechanisms of some disorders such as Huntington's and Alzheimer's dementias have fanned hopes for the future of this revolution in psychiatry (Heninger, 1999).

However, as Andreasen (1984), a prominent biological psychiatrist, noted a quarter-century ago, the onset of this revolution was not based on breakthroughs in knowledge about the etiology of psychiatric disorders but rather on new conceptualizations of where to look for etiologic factors:

> It is a revolution not so much in terms of what we know as in how we perceive what we know. This shift in perception suggests that we need not look to theoretical constructs of the "mind" or to influences from the external environment in order to understand how people feel, why they behave as they do, or what becomes disturbed when people develop mental illnesses. Instead, we can look directly to the brain and try to understand both normal behavior and mental illness in terms of how the brain works and how the brain breaks down. The new mode of perception has created the exciting feeling that we can understand the causes of mental illness in terms of basic biological mechanisms. (p. 138)

But what is this revolutionary shift in perception all about? How do biologically oriented researchers approach the search for the causes of psychiatric disorders? What constructs, tools, and paradigms do they employ, and what have they concluded about the development of mental illness? And indeed, why should sociologists care? Is there a place for sociologists in a revolution that seems to dismiss the need to consider "impacts from the external environment," or is our only recourse to become counterrevolutionaries?

Given the huge and complex literature in biological psychiatry, addressing these questions, even in a very preliminary way, is a daunting task. Nonetheless, in this chapter we attempt to (1) provide a general overview of some of the main biological approaches in psychiatry, (2) illustrate some of the main findings regarding two psychiatric disorders – schizophrenia (the disorder most frequently studied from a biological perspective) and depression (the disorder most frequently studied in sociology), and (3) discuss some of the implications of this approach for sociologists interested in mental health.

Biological Approaches to Psychiatric Disorders

From a biological perspective, psychiatric disorders are illnesses like any other; they are diseases of the body, specifically the brain. Therefore, the goal is to understand how disruptions in brain functioning lead to the development of psychiatric disorders (Andreasen, 1984; Andreasen & Black, 1995; Cowan, Harter, & Kandel, 2000; Joffe, 2001).

The constructs of interest are "disease entities," with the ultimate goal being to define diseases by their particular biological mechanisms (i.e., pathophysiology) and, if possible, distinct causes (i.e., pathogenesis). Currently, however, there are no neurobiological markers that define psychiatric disorders (First & Zimmerman, 2006; Heninger, 1999); diagnoses are still defined by clinical symptoms that seem to cluster and form similar patterns that may help predict course and treatment response (Robins & Guze, 1970; Sadock & Sadock, 2003). The relationship between diagnosis and etiology is therefore recursive: current diagnostic categories are used to search for pathophysiology, and knowledge of pathophysiology will be used to refine diagnostic categories. For example, many biological psychiatrists speak of "schizophrenias" rather than schizophrenia, suggesting that the category as currently defined is heterogeneous; that is, the symptoms may have different etiologies and biological pathways. There may be more than one genetic form of schizophrenia, or there may be genetic and environmental forms (Karayiorgou & Gogos, 2006). Schizophrenia may be the result of injury to different brain systems that causes somewhat different symptom patterns (Widiger & Clark, 2000). The definitions of the outcomes of interest, specific psychiatric diseases, are therefore dynamic. As knowledge about causes and mechanisms increases, so too will diagnostic precision (Abou-Saleh, 2006; Eaton & Merikangas, 2000). The current imprecision in diagnosis is a great challenge to biological psychiatry and is frequently invoked as an impediment to advancement and the reason for inconsistent and unreplicated research findings.

Biological psychiatry is rooted in neuroscience, an integrated field that uses the tools and paradigms of many different disciplines to understand how neurons communicate, form connections, and give rise to thoughts and behaviors (Cowan et al., 2000). In this chapter we focus on three areas: brain structure and function (neuroanatomy), brain activity (functional brain imaging), and gene effects (genetics). Information from each area is beginning to be integrated, with the goal of understanding biological disease processes. To understand how this interrelationship works, we need to have some crude, if extremely oversimplified, understanding of what biological psychiatrists mean by the brain and its function and dysfunction.

A common metaphor used to understand the brain and its functioning is that of the neural network. The brain is conceptualized as an integrated system of command centers composed of bodies of nerve cells (*gray matter*) connected to each other by branches (*white matter*) that communicate through electrical impulses and chemical and molecular exchanges. Instructions for the synthesis and metabolism of these chemical and molecular messengers (i.e., neurotransmitters) and complex proteins that form other components of this communication system are coded in DNA. Further, whether genes are expressed or not depends on whether they are turned on or off (i.e., blocked by proteins, tagged with "methyl" groups, or tightly wound; Szyf, McGowan, & Meaney, 2008). These chemical exchanges are conceptualized as the biological substrate of thought, emotion, memory, judgments, and feelings – the components of what we think of as our inner life and the processes that are affected in psychiatric disorders (Andreasen & Black, 1995, Joffe, 2001; Lickey & Gordon, 1991).

The "brain can be broken" (Andreasen, 1984) at many points in this system – the neural command centers malfunction, the connections are disrupted, the chemical balances and feedback loops are not working, the proteins are not synthesized in appropriate quantities, the implicated genes are mutated, or their expression is abnormally regulated (i.e., epigenetics). Biologically oriented researchers look for brain dysfunction in all of these areas. We discuss the approaches to this search from the most macro level (anatomy and function) to the most micro level ([epi]genetics). The goals of such research are to provide a coherent picture of the pathophysiology of disorders; for example, the genetic defects are related to the synthesis of proteins that are involved with particular types of chemical communication, which occur in the areas of the brain that are working abnormally and produce the symptoms of the disorder (Deakin, 1996).

Such a picture has yet to fully materialize, but the field seems excited about the prospects (e.g., Andreasen, 1984; Lieberman, 2006). Alzheimer's dementia comes closest to fulfilling this model: it has a characteristic neuropathological marker – deposits of the β-amyloid peptide that form plaques and tangles in the brain associated with neuronal loss and distinct genetic mutations – and mutations in the amyloid precursor protein gene, presenilin 1 and 2 genes, and apolipoprotein E gene alleles that all lead to changes in β-amyloid metabolism. Although these genetic mutations are absent in many people with Alzheimer's disease and present in many without the disease, the convergence of their functions on a particular pathogenic pathway provides an impressive example for the aspirations of biological psychiatry.

Brain Structure and Function: Neuroanatomy

Szasz (1961) had long argued that psychiatric disorders do not deserve the appellation "disease" unless they are associated with brain lesions – actual pathological alterations in body tissue. Research on anomalous brain structure and function is the most direct way to search for such "lesions." Central to this search is the premise that the brain is composed of highly specialized and differentiated areas. Although there are redundancy and plasticity in the system, different parts of the brain perform different functions. Here we just give a brief overview of the brain structures thought to be important in psychiatric disorders.

The brain's surface appearance is composed of ridges (*gyri*) and fissures (*sulci*). It is divided by a furrow into right and left hemispheres that are connected by a large number of fibers called the corpus callosum. As you look "through" the brain, from the top of the head downward, the forebrain, the midbrain, and the hindbrain come into view sequentially. The complexity of the functions performed by these brain components declines from the top to the bottom of the brain. The higher, more uniquely human functions (e.g., thought, speech, emotions) are performed in the forebrain. The midbrain controls sleep, alertness, and pain, whereas the hindbrain takes care of vegetative functions such as respiration and heart rate. The spinal cord is connected to the bottom of the brain; it receives sensory information from the rest of the body, gives commands to the muscles, and controls balance and our sense of ourselves in physical space (U.S. Congress, 1992).

The forebrain is the brain area most implicated in psychiatric symptoms so we discuss it here in somewhat more detail. The part closest to the skull is the cerebral cortex, which has a grayish hue because it is densely packed with neuronal cell bodies. Each half of the cerebral cortex is divided into four lobes: the frontal, parietal, occipital, and temporal lobes. The frontal lobe is thought to perform functions related to various aspects of thinking, feeling, imagining, and decision making. The parietal lobe controls information about bodily sensations, movement, and spatial orientation; the occipital lobe controls visual information; and the temporal lobe controls auditory information, memory, and language. Underneath the cerebral cortex, deeper within the forebrain, is a group of control centers that form the limbic system (see Fig. 4.1). These structures – the thalamus, striatum, hippocampus, and amygdala – are of great interest to psychiatry because they relate to cognition, emotion, learning, memory, and motivation. The limbic system also includes some regions of the cortex, including the orbitofrontal cortex and medial frontal cortex, which are involved in social cognition, theory of mind, and empathy. In the inferior frontal gyrus are located the famous "mirror neurons," which fire both when an individual performs an action and when an individual perceives another performing the same action (Rizzolatti & Craighero, 2004).

The ventricular system is also of interest because it can index brain abnormalities. This system is composed of four cavities filled with cerebral spinal fluid that project into the cerebral cortex. When cells of the brain or their connections are damaged or reduced, the ventricles may enlarge to fill the space. Ventricular enlargement may therefore be an indicator of brain atrophy.

The functional mapping of the brain is an ongoing process. What is known about normal brain functioning provides hypotheses about where to look for abnormalities that would be likely to produce the specific symptoms of the disorders of interest. For example, in schizophrenia, in which integrative problems seem central,

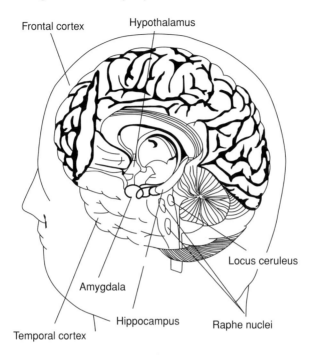

Figure 4.1. Brain structures involved in mental disorders. *Source*: Adapted from Lewis E. Calver, University of Texas, Southwestern Medical Center, Dallas, Texas; reproduced in U.S. Congress (1992).

frontal lobe involvement is a reasonable hypothesis. In turn, knowledge from brain lesions informs brain mapping.

Because the brain should not normally be biopsied, early knowledge about brain function was based on autopsies and serendipitous situations, such as the correlation between obvious brain damage and symptom patterns (Heninger, 1999). A famous example in psychiatry is that of Phineas Gage, an efficient and capable railroad worker who had a stake go through his frontal lobe in an explosion. Although he survived the accident, he experienced a dramatic change in personality, becoming impatient, irresponsible, and socially inappropriate (Plotnik, 1993). The changes in his behavior led to deductions about the tasks performed by the frontal lobe. However, serendipity, being serendipitous, is of limited usefulness as the basis for brain mapping. In addition, the usual long time lag between disorder onset and death makes it difficult to determine if the brain damage was the cause of the symptoms or if the symptoms (or treatment for the symptoms) caused the brain damage.

The search for anatomical and functional brain deficits has gained new impetus from remarkable technological advances in brain imaging that allow for the examination of brain structure and function in living people (Abou-Saleh, 2006). The main structural brain imaging techniques are CT (*computerized tomographic*) and MRI (*magnetic resonance imaging*) scans. In CT scans, low-level radiation is emitted, and its absorption in different parts of the brain is measured. The denser the brain area through which the radiation passes, the more radiation is absorbed. This absorption is mapped onto a grid. A computer assigns numbers to these differences in absorption and translates them into a visual picture, with levels of absorption indicated by different shades of gray. In MRI scans, the head is placed in a magnetic field that disturbs the spins of atoms – typically either hydrogen or phosphorus. Their relaxation time is determined by their local environment (i.e., whether the hydrogen atoms are part of water or part of a large organic molecule), which is again translated by computer into pictures of brain structures. Although MRI scans give clearer and more detailed images than CT scans, both can visualize the size and shape of various brain structures and therefore provide evidence of atrophy, damage, and tumors (Andreasen & Swayze, 1989). MRI can also provide information about brain activity, neurochemistry, and the integrity of white matter tracts.

Methods have also been developed to visualize brain functioning, most notably PET (*positron emission tomography*) and fMRI (*functional magnetic resonance imaging*). In PET, radioactive tracers are injected that differentially localize in the brain based on brain activity (e.g., radioactive glucose), affinity for receptors (e.g., radioactive analogues of neurotransmitters), or affinity for abnormal proteins (e.g., β-amyloid in Alzheimer's dementia). With fMRI, which does not involve radioactivity, brain functioning is detected by changes in blood flow and oxygen concentration (Bullmore & Suckling, 2001); the amount and location of brain activity among people with and without the disorder of interest can then be compared while the subjects are participating in a variety of cognitive tasks. With both PET and fMRI, information is again translated into images.

Since the first CT scan in psychiatric research in 1976 and the first MRI study in 1983, there have been thousands of brain imaging studies of schizophrenia. This work has identified small and subtle structural brain anomalies associated with this disorder (Brambilla & Tansella, 2008; Steen et al., 2006). The most replicated finding has been evidence of enlargement of the lateral and third ventricles, which are surrounded by the thalamus, basal ganglia, and hippocampus (Brambrilla & Tansella, 2008; Lewis & Lieberman, 2000; Pfefferbaum et al., 1990; Raz & Raz, 1990; Sawa & Snyder, 2002; Shenton et al., 2001). There is also moderately consistent evidence for abnormalities in the frontal, temporal, and parietal lobes (Abou-Saleh, 2006; Shenton et al., 2001).

There have also been a substantial number of functional brain imaging studies of schizophrenia using PET and fMRI scans (Lewis, 1990). PET studies have been very powerful in schizophrenia – showing us that people diagnosed with schizophrenia have changes in the number of dopamine receptors in the striatum and increased dopamine release there in response to amphetamine challenge (Guillin, Abi-Dargham, & Laruelle, 2007; Miyamoto et al., 2003). In addition, fMRI scans have indicated hypofrontality – less activation of the frontal lobe – among people with schizophrenia, particularly during cognitive tasks (Lieberman, Brown, & Gorman, 1994; Weinberger et al., 2001; Yoon et al., 2008).

The timing of these abnormalities has not yet been determined; many are evident when the individual is first symptomatic, but a subset does change over course of illness (Lieberman et al., 2001). Ventricular enlargement, for example, may occur early in the development of the disorder and be nonprogressive and independent of medication history (Deakin, 1996; Dwork, 1996). If ventricular enlargement indexes an etiological component, then these factors suggest that schizophrenia may be a neurodevelopmental disorder (Lewis & Levitt, 2002), lending credence to the potential etiological significance of early developmental assaults such as maternal viral infections, nutritional deficits, and obstetrical complications (Bradbury & Miller, 1985; Crow, 1994; Susser & Lin, 1992). It should be noted, however, that these changes reflect average differences between people with and without schizophrenia – they cannot provide the basis for a diagnosis. That is, in general one cannot look at the brain scan of a particular individual and determine whether the person has the constellation of signs and symptoms that we call schizophrenia.

It is also possible to conclude that schizophrenia and other neuropsychiatric disorders (except for dementias) may be related to subtle brain anomalies for which there is no unique anatomical lesion (Bogerts & Lieberman, 1989). Indeed, the early models that explained brain dysfunction in terms of single lesions have been abandoned in favor of more dynamic models (Heinrichs, 1993). For example, brain pathology in schizophrenia may be qualitative rather than quantitative, making it difficult to assess given the large variation in normal samples (Chua & McKenna, 1995; Drevets, 1998). It seems in some ways that the most startling finding of brain imaging studies is that a disease such as schizophrenia can so severely compromise presumed brain functions without evidence of gross anatomical abnormalities (Malaspina, Kegeles, & Van Heertum, 1996). Schizophrenia may be better conceptualized as a problem of neural connectivity rather than the result of a specific lesion or as a disruption in developmental processes rather than a structural deficit (Andreasen, 1999). The current challenge is to understand the functioning of neural networks and the interconnections among brain regions. Newer technologies, particularly functional brain imaging, open the door to this possibility (Shenton et al., 2001).

Neuronal Communication – Neurochemistry

When we turn a microscope on the brain structures that we have been discussing, we see that the brain is composed of millions of nerve cells of different sizes and

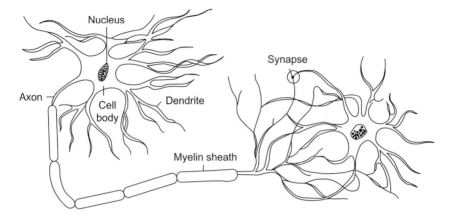

Figure 4.2. Two neurons in synaptic contact. *Source: The Brain* by Richard
Restak, M.D. [© 1984 by Educational Broadcasting Corporation and Richard
M. Restak, M.D. Used by permission of Bantam Books, a division of Bantam Doubleday Dell Publishing Group, Inc.; reproduced in U.S. Congress
(1992).]

shapes. Nerve cells come in two main types: glial cells (the most numerous) and
neurons. The *glial cells* serve as supporting, connecting, and nourishing structures
for the neurons. In this chapter, we focus attention on the neurons because it
is their functioning that is largely the basis of theories of psychiatric disorders
at this level of analysis, with the recognition that the glial cells that support the
neurons may also be relevant. To understand these theories, we need some basic
outline of the neuronal communication system.

Neurons have four basic components: (1) the cell body that directs the communication process and provides the DNA instructions for the production of the
chemicals involved in neuronal communication; (2) dendrites – branch-like structures that protrude from the cell body and receive information from other neurons;
(3) axons – longer extensions from the cell body that are insulated by a covering called the myelin sheath through which electrical messages are sent, and
(4) axon terminals, from which chemical messages (i.e., neurotransmitters) are
released when the electrical message arrives (see Fig. 4.2). Neurons that are in
close proximity send messages to each other. They are separated by a tiny space
called the synapse (or the synaptic cleft), through which they communicate by
neurotransmitters (U.S. Congress, 1992).

Overall, when a neuron is activated, an electrical impulse (or an action potential)
flows down to the end of the axon to bulb-like swellings called axon terminals. In
these axon terminals are numerous sac-like structures (i.e., synaptic vesicles) that
contain chemical substances called neurotransmitters. When the electric charge

reaches these synaptic vesicles in the axon terminal – in this instance called the presynaptic terminal because it is sending the message – the sacs fuse with the cell membrane and release neurotransmitters into the synapse.

These neurotransmitters react with receptors on adjacent neurons – the post-synaptic neuron in this case because it is receiving a message. These receptors are highly specialized and respond only to specific types of neurotransmitters. Indeed, specific subtypes of receptors for the same neurotransmitters have been discovered. When a neurotransmitter is of the type to which the particular receptor can respond, it binds to the receptor. This binding either encourages an action potential in the postsynaptic neuron (if the message is excitatory) or it discourages an action potential (if the message is inhibitory). The sensitivity of the postsynaptic neuron to this message can be influenced by its proximity to the cell body, the other messages the neuron is receiving, the number of receptors for a particular neurotransmitter, the affinity of the receptor for the neurotransmitter, and the efficiency with which the binding is translated into a message to the receiving neuron (second messenger system; Sadock & Sadock, 2003).

Each neuron receives messages from dozens of other neurons (Andreasen, 1984). The postsynaptic neuron, however, will only send a message if the excitatory messages exceed the inhibitory ones. Some inhibition and excitation messages work directly through the receptors and are therefore instantaneous. Other neurotransmitters, including many that are important in psychiatry, work indirectly by activating enzymes that cause biochemical changes in the postsynaptic cell that can influence the action potential after a delay of minutes or hours (Lickey & Gordon, 1991). This communication decision, to fire or not, is therefore extremely complicated and involves the integration of many different messages.

The neurotransmitter is removed from the synapse either through enzyme action in the synapse that decomposes the neurotransmitter (through metabolism) or through reentry into the presynaptic neuron, a process called reuptake, which is mediated also by receptors and "transporters." It then either reenters the vesicle, to be released again at a later date, or is destroyed by enzymes in the presynaptic terminal (Lickey & Gordon, 1991).

Several regulatory mechanisms maintain an adequate supply of neurotransmitters in synaptic vesicles (see Fig. 4.3). In the short term, enzymes may slow down synthesis from neurotransmitter precursors (i.e., the substances from which neurotransmitters are synthesized) if there is a sufficient supply of neurotransmitters. In contrast, if the neuron has been very active and there is neurotransmitter depletion, the production of these precursors can be increased. If there is long-term hyperactivity and synaptic depletion, the DNA of the neuron can be transcribed to code for the increased production of neurotransmitter precursors. In addition, some neurons have receptors in the presynaptic membrane (called autoreceptors) that, when bound by released neurotransmitters, can decrease the amount of neurotransmitters released (Andreasen & Black, 1995).

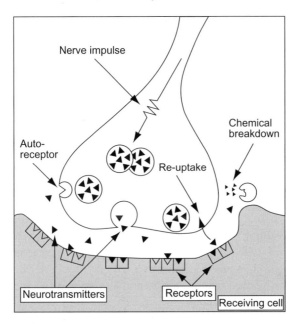

Figure 4.3. The synapse and associated structures. *Source*: U.S. Congress (1992).

There are two main groupings of classic neurotransmitters: biogenic amines (e.g., dopamine, norepinephrine, and serotonin) and peptides (e.g., GABA and glutamate). It was originally thought that different parts of the brain use different neurotransmitters. Now it is understood that individual neurons can have receptors for different neurotransmitters and that many neurotransmitters can be released in any region of the brain. For example, dopaminergic neurons are concentrated in the midbrain and hypothalamus, but project to the limbic system and the cerebral cortex. Neurons that release norepinephrine (also called noradrenaline) and serotonin are located in the brainstem (norepinephrine in the locus coeruleus and serotonin in the raphe nuclei) and project throughout the cerebral cortex. These neurotransmitter systems appear to play a role in producing the symptoms of schizophrenia (primarily dopamine) and depression (primarily serotonin and norepinephrine; Sadock & Sadock, 2003), although the peptides GABA and glutamate are increasingly recognized as important in schizophrenia as well.

Researchers have used several methods to test the hypothesis that psychiatric disorders reflect dysfunctions in neuronal communication systems. One way is to examine the mechanisms of psychiatric medications and their effects on levels of neurotransmitters and their receptors in both humans and in animal models of illness through PET imaging. Researchers have also examined postmortem brain tissue to see changes in the shapes of neurons and their connections.

Currently, the hypothesis that schizophrenia is related to an excess of dopamine in the striatum is probably the most widely supported and viable theory in the neurochemistry of this disorder. Evidence for this hypothesis comes from the mechanism of antipsychotic medications that block the transmission of dopamine between neurons (Andreasen & Black, 1995), as well as from PET studies (Guillin et al., 2007). The involvement of numerous neurotransmitters is consistent with the anatomical findings that various parts of the brain are involved in the disorder, supporting the concept of connectivity as a major issue in the pathogenesis of schizophrenia.

In depression, norepinephrine and serotonin are the neurotransmitters most widely implicated and studied (Belmaker & Agam, 2008). The original hypothesis derived from a serendipitous finding that 15% of people treated for hypertension with reserpine, which depletes norepinephrine, became depressed (Kaplan, Sadock, & Grebb, 1994). Here too, the best evidence for the role of a deficit in these neurotransmitters in depression comes from the known effects of antidepressant medications and from PET imaging studies (Parsey et al., 2006). The serotonin hypothesis has gained strength from the success of serotonin-specific reuptake inhibitors (SSRIs) in treating depression, which, as the name suggests, specifically inhibit serotonin reuptake, leaving more serotonin in the synapse for a longer time.

A role for norepinephrine in depression is indirectly supported by evidence suggesting a relationship between depression and dysfunction in the endocrine system (i.e., dysregulation of the hypothalamic-pituitary-adrenal axis). A role for this system is suggested by symptom similarity between adrenal gland disorders and depression (i.e., fatigue and disturbances in appetite and sleep). The most compelling evidence for such a connection comes from drug challenges with dexamethasone. When the brain perceives a stressful situation, the hypothalamus releases corticotrophin-releasing factor (CRT), which stimulates the pituitary to release adrenocorticotropic hormone (ACTH), which in turn stimulates the adrenal glands to release cortisol, a substance released in response to stress. To test the hypothesis that this system is dysfunctional in people with depression, patients with depression and control subjects are given dexamethasone, a synthetic substance that resembles cortisol. When dexamethasone levels increase in the blood the hypothalamus stops producing CRT, just as it would when the levels of cortisol increase. It was originally hoped the dexamethasone suppression test could be used to diagnose depression. Only a minority of people with depression test positive, however, and dexamethasone "nonsuppression" seems instead to be a hallmark specifically of major depression with psychotic features (Gold, Goodwin, & Chrousos, 1988b; Sadock & Sadock, 2003).

Other endocrine problems have also been found with other drug challenges. The pattern of endocrine results suggests that the problem may lie with the regulation of the hypothalamus, which uses norepinephrine as its main neurotransmitter

(Andreasen, 1984). However, what is problematic for all these etiological theories is that most positive findings support a state effect of neurotransmitter excess or deficit, rather than a trait effect; that is, there is little evidence for neurotransmitter deficits occurring before active symptom formation (Nathan & Schatzberg, 1994). This leaves unresolved whether the symptoms cause the neurotransmitter abnormalities or they are the neurotransmitter expression of the symptoms. Improved techniques allowing for expanded use of PET and fMRI scans in neurotransmitter functioning should provide better evidence regarding these hypotheses (Belmaker & Agam, 2008; Sharif, 1996).

Our vastly increased understanding of neuronal communication suggests another reason for inconsistent findings: etiological hypotheses based on an excess or deficit in a specific neurotransmitter are too simplistic. The number of neurotransmitters and neurotransmitter-like substances discovered in the brain has multiplied. Complex interactions among neurotransmitters, the specification of multiple receptors for the same neurotransmitters, and complexities in second messenger systems call for more sophisticated explanations (Gold, Goodwin, & Chrousos, 1988a; Kaplan et al., 1994). Progress may come not in the specification of the neurochemical processes underlying schizophrenia and depression, but rather in a fuller understanding of the systems of neuronal communication in general.

Genetics

The genetic component of the biological revolution in psychiatry has had perhaps the greatest influence on the popular imagination. Rapid advances in genetic methodology and the sequencing of the human genome have expanded greatly the potential for progress in this area (Cowan et al., 2000; Karayiorgou & Gogos, 2006). Three central tasks, each with its associated methodology, guide genetic research in psychiatric disorders: (1) identifying those disorders that have a genetic basis, (2) identifying the specific genetic mutations involved in the disorder, and (3) identifying what the genetic mutation does (Kendler, 2005). In what follows we discuss the basic methodological approaches and some basic findings for each task.

Identification of Disorders with a Genetic Basis. Disorders with a genetic basis often, but not always, aggregate in families; that is, the disorder rates for the biological relatives of probands (i.e., persons with the disorder) are higher than for the biological relatives of controls (i.e., people without the disorder). In addition, the disorder rates should correlate with the degree of biological relationship (Faraone & Tsuang, 1995).

Early studies of familial aggregation of schizophrenia found rates averaging 6% for parents, 10% for siblings, and 13% for children compared with general population rates of around 1%. However, these early studies were fraught with methodological difficulties. Often, there was no specific control group (e.g., rates in relatives were compared with general population rates), diagnostic criteria were often not explicit, and researchers were not blind to proband disorder status when examining relatives, leading to the potential for interviewer bias (Kendler, 1983). More recent studies, using more rigorous methods, generally find increased risk for family members but the risks are lower than those found in earlier studies (Lyons et al., 1991).

There have been fewer studies of familial aggregation in depression, and some of these do not differentiate bipolar depression (i.e., depression alternating with mania) from unipolar depression (i.e., depression without manic episodes). However, a number of studies have demonstrated an increased risk of depression for offspring of depressed women (e.g., Beardslee et al., 1983; Downey & Coyne, 1990; Sullivan, Neale, & Kendler, 2000). The strongest evidence comes from a number of well-controlled studies (Gershon et al., 1982; Tsuang, Winokur, & Crowe, 1980; Weissman, Gershon, G Kidd, 1984; Weissman et al., 2006, 2008) that found elevated rates of unipolar depression in the biological relatives of depressed probands, providing evidence of familial aggregation (Tsuang, Faraone, & Lyons, 1989). The amount of familial aggregation varied with phenotypic variation (e.g., early vs. late onset, single vs. repeat episode; Shih, Belmonte, & Zandi, 2004).

It should be noted, however, that familial aggregation is not consistently specific; that is, probands with one type of disorder may have biological relatives with an excess of many different types of disorders. For example, there seems to be overlap in the heritability of bipolar depression, unipolar depression, schizoaffective disorder, anorexia, bulimia, anxiety disorders, substance use disorders, and alcoholism (Gershon & Nurnberger, 1995; Weissman et al., 2006). Similarly, the heritability of schizophrenia overlaps with that for schizotypy, suggesting these disorders are related. Although it is reasonably clear from these studies that both schizophrenia and depression aggregate in families, the source of the familial aggregation is left unaddressed because families share many potential risk factors for disorder in addition to genes (e.g., socioeconomic status, exposure to viruses, coping mechanisms; Von Knorring et al., 1983). To test and attempt to quantify the genetic contribution to familial aggregation, twin and adoption studies are often used.

Twin and adoption studies capitalize on special circumstances that allow for the separation of genetic and social inheritance. The basic assumption underlying these designs is that variance in any disorder can be divided into three general categories: genetic factors, shared environmental factors (i.e., aspects of the environment that family members, in this case, siblings, have in common such as childhood socioeconomic status, exposure to household toxins, and parenting style), and unique environmental factors (i.e., risk factors that siblings do not share like peers and exposure to accidents). Shared risk factors for disease (whether environmental

Table 4.1. *Heritability estimates from twin studies*

Disorder variance = GENES + SHARED ENVIRONMENT + UNIQUE ENVIRONMENT
MZ concordance = (100% GENETIC + 100% SHARED ENVIRONMENT)/TOTAL
DZ concordance = (50% GENETIC + 100% SHARED ENVIRONMENT)/TOTAL
MZ discordance = (100% UNIQUE ENVIRONMENT)/TOTAL
DZ discordance = (50% GENETIC + 100% UNIQUE ENVIRONMENT)/TOTAL

Therefore: MZ CONCORDANCE − DZ CONCORDANCE = 50% OF THE GENETIC EFFECT

E.G., MZ CONCORDANCE = 90%, DZ CONCORDANCE = 50%

    90% − 50% = 40% = HALF OF THE GENETIC PORTION OF THE TOTAL VARIANCE
    40% × 2 = 80% = GENETIC PORTION OF THE TOTAL VARIANCE
    90% − 80% = 10% = SHARED ENVIRONMENT PORTION OF THE TOTAL VARIANCE
    100% − 90% = 10% = UNIQUE ENVIRONMENT PORTION OF THE TOTAL VARIANCE

VARIANCE IN THIS EXAMPLE: 90% GENETIC, 10% SHARED ENVIRONMENT,
  10% UNIQUE ENVIRONMENT

Source: Adapted from Plomin (1990).

or genetic) increase concordance – similarity in disease status – for twin pairs. Unique risk factors, risk factors to which only one twin is exposed (whether environmental or genetic), increase discordance; that is, dissimilarity in disease status for twin pairs.

In this section, we go into some detail about how twin studies assess the relative magnitudes of these genetic and environmental contributions because they are the source of considerable confusion. In addition, the results of twin studies often contradict the results of sociological studies, mainly because of methodological considerations. Twins studies capitalize on the fact that whereas monozygotic (MZ) – identical – twins share 100% of their genes, dizygotic (DZ) – fraternal – twins share only 50% of their genes, on average, like any other sibling pair. For this reason, the factors that lead to concordance and discordance differ for MZ and DZ twins. For MZ twins, the concordance rate reflects 100% of the genetic component of the variance in the disorder plus 100% of the shared environmental component. For DZ twins, the concordance rate reflects 50% of the genetic component (the proportion of genes that, on average, DZ twins share) and 100% of the shared environment. As seen in Table 4.1, these differences can be mathematically modeled to estimate the proportion of the variance in an outcome that is due to genetic factors, shared familial environment, and unique environmental factors (Plomin, 1990; Plomin et al., 2000).

In adoption studies, social and genetic inheritance are separated in a different way. Because adopted children are reared by parents with whom they do not share genes, any correlation between their disorder and that of their adopted parents is due to shared environmental factors. Conversely, because adoptees are not reared by their biological parents, any concordance with their biological parents is likely due mainly to genetic components rather than a shared environment; a possible exception is the influence of a shared in utero environment (Cadoret, 1991).

Twin and adoption studies of schizophrenia provide strong evidence for a genetic component to this disorder. Based on data from eight twin studies of schizophrenia reviewed by Torrey (1992), the concordance rates for MZ twins is between 30% and 40%, depending on the specific method used to estimate concordance, and the concordance for DZ twins is between 6% and 15%. More recent estimates suggest that heritability for schizophrenia is in the 60% to 90% range (Rutter, 2004). Results of adoption studies, using several different designs, are fairly consistent as well. Some studies compare rates of disorder for the biological and adoptive relatives of adoptees with schizophrenia with the rates in relatives of control adoptees. Others compare disorder rates in adoptees whose birth mother had schizophrenia with adoptees whose mothers did not have schizophrenia. Most of these studies show a higher concordance for biological than adoptive relatives (Shih et al., 2004). However, the extremely low rate of schizophrenia in the adoptive relatives of the probands in these studies – below general population estimates – suggests that these results should be interpreted with caution.

Although fewer in number than studies of schizophrenia, twin studies support a genetic component to depressive disorders, with concordance rates for MZ twins in the 20% to 40% range (Belmaker & Agam, 2008; Sullivan et al., 2000; Tsuang & Faraone, 1990). Adoption studies are less consistent: Some support a genetic component (Medelwicz & Rainer, 1977; Wender et al., 1986), whereas others do not (Cadoret, 1978; Cadoret, O'Gorman, & Heywood, 1985; von Knorring et al., 1983). However, all these studies suffer from diagnostic or power problems (Sullivan et al., 2000).

Although twin and adoption designs and heritability estimation are appealing methods for separating genetic and environmental effects, they are based on assumptions that warrant discussion. One basic assumption is that twinship and adoption per se are not correlated with risk factors (or protective factors) for the disorder of interest. In schizophrenia research at least, this problem has been recognized, and the rate of schizophrenia among twins has been estimated; it appears to approximate general population rates (Rose, 1991).

One of the most contested assumptions of twin studies is the "equality of environmental co-variance" for MZ and DZ twins (e.g., Lewontin, Rose, & Kamin, 1984). Monozygotic twins clearly experience greater environmental similarity than DZ twins. For example, they are more likely to dress alike, play together, share a room, and have frequent contact. However, it is less clear if MZ twins experience greater environmental similarity on factors that relate to psychiatric disorders (Rose, 1991). This assumption can also be contested from the other direction – certain aspects of the environment of MZ twins may not be as similar as was once thought (e.g., in utero environment and genetic differences; see Bruder et al., 2008; Rutter, 2006a, 2006b; Torrey et al., 1994).

Additivity is another problematic assumption. Heritability estimates assume an additive relationship among genetic, and shared and unique environmental risk factors. This assumption is almost certainly unjustified. Indeed, most theories of depression and schizophrenia assume gene–environment interactions, with certain genes sensitizing people to environmental risk factors or certain environmental risk factors activating dormant genes (Kendler, Lyons, & Tsuang, 1991). In addition, gene–environment correlations, in which certain genotypes influence the types of environments to which individuals are exposed, are ubiquitous (Rutter, 2006a, 2006b; Rutter, Moffitt, & Caspi, 2006; Scarr & McCartney, 1983). Gene–gene interactions have been hypothesized that would also violate the assumption of additivity. It is almost certain that these assumptions are violated in the study of schizophrenia and depression because the DZ concordance rate is frequently less than half the MZ concordance rate, a situation that should not happen if the assumptions of additivity hold.

Although twin and adoption studies provide compelling evidence for a genetic component to depression and schizophrenia, their methodological problems make heritability estimates questionable, an issue to which we return later (Schwartz & Susser, 2006). Nonetheless, these studies do provide strong grounds for rejecting an extreme environmental position that either disorder is of purely environmental origins (Kendler, 2005). They tell us that there is a genetic component to the disorder, but not what the genetic component is; other methods are required for this task.

Gene Identification. For psychiatric disorders, which are assumed to be complex disorders for which single genes are neither necessary nor sufficient, gene identification is extraordinarily difficult (Karayiorgou & Gogos, 2006). Two main methods are used to identify genes: linkage studies and association studies. Animal studies are also used in which the effects of gene "knockouts" or "knockdowns" are examined.

Linkage studies have produced numerous headlines in recent years with the discovery of the location of the genes associated with Huntington's disease, Alzheimer's, and breast cancer, to name just a few. Once located the genes can be isolated, their functions identified, and the pathophysiology of the disorder specified (Risch, 1991).

Linkage analyses are based on estimations of the probability that within a family a genetic propensity for a particular disease is inherited along with a genetic marker (i.e., a gene with a known location on a particular chromosome). If the probability is high, it is assumed that a gene making a major contribution to the appearance of the disease under study is in close physical proximity to the genetic marker. Advances in molecular genetics have led to the discovery of new types of genetic markers, including restriction fragment length polymorphisms (RFLPs). This discovery has greatly enhanced the utility of linkage studies because these markers cover the entire human genome, allowing for a full search for a gene's location. Other approaches to gene location such as association studies (i.e., looking for genes that are linked in the population), the use of candidate genes (i.e., genes with known pathogenic effects), and mutation screening (i.e., searching for genetic mutations that differentiate people with and without the disorder of interest) are also being employed.

Linkage analyses and association studies have met with tremendous success in the location of genes associated with many medical disorders, but have been a disappointment in psychiatry (Risch, 1991). Numerous studies suggesting linkage have failed replication attempts or have been disconfirmed after longer observation of the pedigrees (e.g., Bassett et al., 1988; Gershon et al., 1979; Hallmayer et al., 1992; Kennedy et al., 1988; Sherrington et al., 1988). Disorder complexity, in which individual genes are neither necessary nor sufficient, and genetic hetero-geneity – the probability that currently defined disorder categories can be caused by different genes in different people – are likely reasons for the slow progress (Rutter, 2004). However, recent advances that allow saturation of the human genome with markers make it easier to find relevant loci (Cowan et al., 2000). Indeed, some linkage results have been replicated, suggesting that the neuregulin-1 and dys-bindin genes (both implicated in neuronal communication) are involved in the pathophysiology of schizophrenia (Karayiorgou & Gogos, 2006). Yet, caution is still warranted because of many extant methodological issues (e.g., confounding occurs especially through population stratification, selection biases, multiple com-parisons, and publication bias; Karayiorgou & Gogos, 2006; Kelsoe, 2004). For depression, there are currently no accepted genetic association findings although there are some promising candidate genes (Detera-Wadleigh & McMahon, 2004; Levinson, 2006; Lopez-Leon et al., 2008).

Function. Yet, even a successful linkage or association finding only identifies the location of the gene; it does not identify the allelic variant that causes the disease nor does it tell us what the gene does. Once a likely gene is identified, the next stage is to identify a functional mutation and to understand how it leads to the disease phenotype (Detera-Wadleigh & McMahon, 2004). Many different biological approaches are being developed for this crucial step (Kelsoe, 2004). One method that has gained traction in psychiatry is the use of gene knockout models, in which mouse models of the genotype are developed and then the gene is rendered nonfunctional ("knocked out") and the effect is observed. This method has been used to examine the effect of neutralizing the neuregulin 1 gene – a gene that has been implicated in schizophrenia – on receptor expression (Kendler, 2005).

Status of the Revolution

So what have biologically oriented researchers concluded about the search for the biological causes of psychiatric disorders, particularly for schizophrenia? Optimism prevails (Bilder, 2008; Brambilla & Tansella, 2008; Iritani, 2007). For example, Joffe (2001, p. 102) concludes, "The progress in psychiatric research over the last 100 years has been remarkable, and although there is still very little known about the illnesses we confront and treat, there is reason for optimism." In reading the literature one gets the feeling that we are on the edge of a new way of thinking – one that fully embraces the complexity of psychiatric disorders and will finally lead to fundamental advances.

Indeed, in each of the areas we have discussed – (1) brain structure and function, (2) neuronal communication, and (3) genetic effects – it would appear that instead of answering existing questions, methodological breakthroughs have given rise to new questions of greater complexity. The pathophysiology and etiology of psychiatric disorders are not likely to be as straightforward as early hypotheses suggested. In the biological revolution, as in most revolutions, maturity brings complexity. It is unlikely that a single lesion will be found for most psychiatric disorders; rather the presence of subtle, diffuse, qualitative brain representations is more probable. Deficits or excesses of single neurotransmitters are not likely to yield compelling explanations for psychiatric disorders. Rather, symptoms are probably explained by interactions over development among neurotransmitters, specific receptors, and complex second messenger systems and among neurons and brain regions. Although evidence for a genetic component to many disorders is substantial, single genes are not responsible. The specific mode of transmission and interactions among genetic and environmental factors remain to be explicated. Thus although clinical practice has been dramatically altered, with advances in psychopharmacology offering new hope to many people with severe psychiatric disorders, the shift from mind to brain in the search for etiology is likely to advance slowly, with frequent setbacks that increase the sophistication of the paradigm.

Implications of this Revolution for Sociology

Do participants in the biological revolution see a place for sociologists? Some clearly do. As they eagerly point out, a concordance rate of less than 100% for MZ twins indicates an environmental component to psychiatric disorders. Indeed, some see genetic research in particular as providing the best evidence that environmental factors play a role (Lyons et al., 1991; Reiss, Plomin, & Hetherington, 1991). Others demur (Heston, 1992; Klein & Wender, 1993). They argue that a concordance rate of less than 100% could still imply only biological causes because MZ twins may not be as alike as we once assumed: DNA to RNA transcription errors, effects of placental differences, or phenotyping errors could account for these genetic differences (see McGuffin et al., 1994; Torrey, et al., 1994). In addition, "environmental" does not imply psychological or sociological; it just means not genetic. Such influences could still be biological (e.g., viral infection, brain damage) and, in fact, must ultimately be so. Sociology may have a place in understanding "normal depression," for example, but depressive disorder is a biological phenomenon for which psychological and surely sociological explanations are not sufficient in and of themselves.

And how have sociologists responded? Some have argued, much like their biological counterparts, for a separatist position. Sociologists should not concern themselves with psychiatric phenomena such as schizophrenia that have a powerful genetic etiology and fit well within the medical paradigm. Rather, sociologists should concern themselves exclusively with mental phenomena that are likely to have a powerful social etiology, such as anxiety and subclinical depression (e.g., Mirowsky & Ross, 2002; Pearlin, 1989).

The separatist position seems to be based on a distinction between mental health problems that are largely genetic and those that are largely environmental. This distinction itself is problematic on several grounds. It seems to imply an acceptance of heritability estimates as providing limits on the importance of social etiological factors. That is, if schizophrenia is 70% heritable, then, barring methodological errors, the environment is of minimal importance in its etiology. This assumption treats the heritability estimate as if it were inherent in the disorder. However, this interpretation is problematic. The parcelling out of nature–nurture influences is environmentally specific. If you change the environment, the heritability estimate may change as well. The more environmentally homogeneous the study population, the larger the heritability estimate, all other things being equal (Kendler, 2005; Tucker, 1994). Furthermore, there is a disjuncture between apparent causal importance and appropriate intervention. Despite the fact that the heritability estimate is huge, a successful intervention may be entirely environmental (Jencks, 1980). A commonly cited example is phenylketonuria, a genetic disorder that leads to an inability to metabolize phenylalanine: its heritability estimate is virtually 100%, but the successful intervention in the disorder is completely environmental (i.e., a diet without phenylalanine). A high heritability estimate tells you nothing about either the importance of environmental causal factors or the potential efficacy of environmental interventions.

In addition, when we try to identify the cause of a condition, we usually begin by examining how the factor varies in a population. If you want to know the causes of depression you look at how depression is distributed in the population. However, as Lieberson (1985) has pointed out, what we learn from this research is the cause of the variation of this factor in a population, but not necessarily the cause of the factor itself or its magnitude. What causes the distribution of a factor within a population will not be what causes the rate of the factor. For example, depression seems to be a disorder with a genetic component. However, there is also evidence for a cohort effect in depression, with rates increasing and age of onset decreasing in recent cohorts. The cause of any increase in the rate of depression is likely to be entirely environmental. But even if the etiology of the increased rate is environmental the proportion of the variance explained by genetic factors in any population may be unaffected. Sociological explanations could account entirely for the rate of disorder, whereas genetic influences explain who within a population is more likely to get the disorder.

Furthermore, as discussed in the section on genetic approaches, heritability estimates do not take interactions into account. Twin studies are modeled in such a way that any genetic interaction with a shared familial environment, which includes the most powerful sociological variables, is included in the genetic effect (Schwartz & Susser, 2006). Advances in molecular genetics itself point to the futility in trying to parcel out gene–environment interactions into their contributory components. Gene–environment interactions are dynamic, with the brain responding in a development-specific way to environmental phenomena (Sharif, 1996). Although genes are inherited at conception and are basically unchangeable, what are inherited are genes and not disease outcomes. Genes do not cause disease or behavior; they only code for proteins that interact in minute and ongoing ways with the environment, which provides feedback to the body to change the proteins and their products. Genes can be turned on and off (Rutter, Moffitt, et al., 2006). Although a separatist position has appeal, the parcelling off of mental phenomena, with large genetic components as "off limits" to sociologists, renders too much to biology.

But if we reject a separatist position, how can sociologists relate to this revolution? There are many possible options, depending on the particular questions that sociologists wish to address. We briefly outline three options: active participation in the revolution, cooptation, and counterrevolution.

Active Participation

Sociologists can participate in and advance research that is conducted from within the biological paradigm, an approach congruent with what Aneshensel, Rutter, and Lachenbruch (1991) referred to as the "sociomedical" paradigm. In this paradigm the problematic is the disorder; factors influencing the etiology and course of the disorder are of primary interest. Sociologists can delineate the types of environmental factors that are implicated in the cause and course of these disorders. The interactions between biological vulnerability and sociological factors are central to such work. This approach is exemplified by the collaboration of Kendler and Kessler (e.g., Kendler, et al., 1993, 2002; Kendler, Kessler, et al., 1991; Kendler, Neale, Prescott, & Kessler, 1996) in which sociological phenomena are explicitly measured and included in twin studies. One exciting advance in this direction is the examination of the interaction of specific susceptibility genes with environmentally relevant risk factors. For example, Caspi and colleagues (2003) have examined the interaction of stressful life events and a polymorphism in the 5-HTT gene, a gene related to serotonin reuptake, in causing depression.

In such analyses, sociology plays a supporting role. Diagnostic categories, the focus of interest, are defined and refined by criteria that are unique to the disorder. This specificity increases the importance of individual-level variables over social-level variables. As knowledge about the pathophysiology of psychiatric disorders increases, and with it diagnostic precision, biological factors will, by definition, become the necessary if not sufficient causes of the disorder. Within this paradigm, sociology can identify factors that trigger these biological dysfunctions and social factors that influence the course of these disorders. In this way sociology can play an important but secondary role in advancing the biological revolution.

Co-optation

Another possibility is to use biological explanations to advance the cause of sociology. Several review articles have identified the examination of multiple outcomes as a promising direction for stress research, a prominent paradigm within the sociology of mental health (Aneshensel et al., 1991; Horwitz, 2002; McLean & Link, 1994; Thoits, 1995). They argue that because sociological factors influence a broad range of both physical and psychiatric disorders, we underestimate the effects of such factors if we examine only a limited number of outcomes. Research deriving from the biological perspective can help advance this agenda by encouraging the search for unifying theories that encompass both physical and psychiatric disorders. There has been a tendency in sociological research to create an artificial separation between mental and physical disorders, emphasizing different social risk factors in each area (Thoits, 1995). In part we think this is because mental disorders are considered basically as psychological phenomena, ending in the mind rather than in the body. Our theories of how social factors influence mental health have therefore been derived from, and, one can argue often been reduced to, psychological factors such as self-esteem, locus of control, learned helplessness, and mastery. In physical disorders the pathway ends in the body – implying different sets of causal variables. Biological explanations of psychiatric disorders suggest there may be more unifying sociological theories, because psychiatric disorders also have biological representations.

However, as Mclean and Link (1994) point out, although multiple outcomes need to be examined, it is not fruitful to simply clump all socially relevant risk factors with all health outcomes to which they may be linked. We need to develop theories that would suggest boundaries for both risk factors and outcomes. Ideas deriving from biological psychiatry can serve as a useful supplement to our repertoire of theoretical ideas. Biological theory may suggest novel approaches to deciding which outcomes to examine in the same study. Currently, when multiple outcomes are examined, this usually means merely the combination of several psychiatric disorders in one study (e.g., Dohrenwend et al., 1992; Kessler, Turner, & House, 1989; Thoits, 1995). The implied commonality between disorders such as antisocial personality and schizophrenia is that they are conceptualized as psychological phenomena. But once we see psychiatric disorders also as biological phenomena, new combinations are suggested. For example, coronary artery disease and depression are not only comorbid, but at least one set of social factors has been suggested as etiologically significant for both: jobs lacking direction, control, and planning (Karasek et al., 1988; Link, Lennon, & Dohrenwend, 1993). Is this occupational phenomenon related to bodily changes that are common to both disorders? Can these changes help explain their comorbidity? In more general terms, the physiology of stress may suggest the types of social risk factors that may be most fruitfully explored for specific constellations of disorders. For example, chronic strain and life events have very different effects on the body. Understanding the biological substrate of physical and psychiatric disorders may suggest which types of stress may be more important for which types of outcomes (Sapolsky, 1994). Biological theories may also suggest the stage of development when sociological phenomena of different types may exert their effects. For example, if schizophrenia is a progressive neurodevelopmental disorder, then social factors influencing early development may have greatest salience.

Examining the biological substrate of psychiatric disorders may also broaden the types of linkages between social factors and psychiatric disorders that we examine. Instead of limiting ourselves to linkages through psychological phenomena, we can also examine nonpsychological phenomena. For example, social class may be related to psychiatric disorder not only through its effect on stressful life events, coping, and the like but also through increased exposure to viral infections, head injuries, birth trauma, and other physical phenomena. The influence of social structure is no less important if it works through the disparate and unequal distribution of physical risk factors than through psychological ones.

Biological linkages may also strengthen the need for investigations of psychiatric disorders outside the framework of survey research. Sociological phenomena may influence disorder through direct effects on the body that are not consciously recognized by the individual. For example, the effects of unrecognized and unnamed racial discrimination have been implicated in high blood pressure (Krieger, 1990). It may be that such factors also have connections with depression, where bodily responses to stress are intimately tied to the neurotransmitters identified in biological theories as implicated in the etiology of depression. Such theories may suggest linkages between social phenomena and biological expressions of stress that can be exploited.

Anomalous findings from a biological perspective may also suggest fruitful avenues for sociological examination. At the anatomical, neurochemical, and genetic levels, there are often biological deficits that are common for disparate disorders. For example, there is some evidence for a shared biological vulnerability to depression and alcoholism. Yet these disorders have very different distributions. Indeed, whereas depression and alcoholism are comorbid on the individual level, there are social groupings that have high rates of one and low rates of the other (i.e., gender groupings and some ethnic groupings). This may suggest a venue for examining the relationship between biological substrate and disease expression. These are just a few ideas of how the biological approach can be used to inform sociological understandings of the relationship between the social world and mental health.

Counterrevolution

Although an understanding of the biological perspective of psychiatric disorders is important for sociology as the basis to advance both the social component in biological theories of psychiatric disorders and to use such theories to advance the sociology of mental health, it is also important to provide the basis of a sociological critique of the biological approach. The biological revolution in psychiatry carries along with its promise the dangers of biological reductionism, biological determinism, and the hegemony of biological explanations for psychiatric disorders and other social problems. There are many fronts from which this counterrevolution must be fought. We just outline a few here.

The dominance of the biological perspective in psychiatry was enhanced by the scientific successes of genetic and pharmaceutical research, but that is clearly only a part of the story. Sociologists do and should examine the interrelationships between social and political phenomena and the rise of the biological revolution. Why does this paradigm have such appeal in the current social context? Who are the beneficiaries of this revolution and who the losers? Proponents of a biological perspective suggest that this revolution would decrease the stigma associated with psychiatric disorders. Has it decreased stigma? For whom? (See Conrad, 2005; Conrad & Leiter, 2004.)

Sociological analyses of the social construction of psychiatric disorders are also important, particularly at this juncture when the number of disorders officially recognized in psychiatry is growing at an unprecedented rate. All behaviors have biological, psychological, and sociological components. The question is, On which level of analysis is the phenomenon defined and why? Defining a phenomenon in terms of its biological component and naming it a disease is a political decision, one that demands sociological analysis. The medicalization of social phenomena and the labeling of biological differences as biological defects need to be discussed (Horwitz, 2007). What phenomena should be defined on the basis of their biological representations and which should not? How are these decisions being made and by whom? What are the consequences of these decisions? Should phenomena with similar biological representations be considered the same thing, regardless of contextual differences? Advances in biological psychiatry itself point to the problems of diagnosis. What may be a unitary phenomenon from a genetic perspective may be diverse phenomena from a neurochemical perspective. What definitions will be most useful depends on the discipline involved.

Sociologists also need to examine the types of questions that a biological perspective can and cannot address. For example, questions about the causes of an increase in the rate of a disorder or differences between disorder rates in different areas are generally not answerable from a biological perspective. In addition, studies designed to examine biological phenomena, which benefit from socially and psychologically homogeneous samples, are ill suited to examining the causes of disease rates. Yet biological studies are often used to address such questions. Sociology needs to critique such analyses and to delineate the types of questions for which biological approaches are unsuitable. This counterrevolution cannot be waged without understanding the basis for biological explanations of psychiatric disorders.

5

Psychological Approaches to Mental Illness

Christopher Peterson

Psychologists focus attention on individual factors that produce abnormal thoughts, feelings, and behaviors. Psychologists also provide therapies that try to alleviate the distress caused by mental illness. In this chapter, Peterson provides an overview of the views of human nature, abnormality, and treatment found in four psychological models of mental illness. The psychoanalytic model, which originated with Freud, assumes that people are closed energy systems motivated by a variety of drives. Abnormality can be understood developmentally, so early childhood events affect adult functioning. Psychoanalytic treatment generally involves helping the individual achieve insight and free energy from unhealthy purposes through catharsis. A second model is the cognitive-behavioral one, which emphasizes cognition and learning. It views people as information-processing systems, who attempt to maximize pleasure and minimize pain. All types of learning (i.e., classic conditioning, operant conditioning, and modeling) must be placed in a cognitive context because learning takes place within a thinking context. Abnormalities arise when individuals are placed in highly unusual situations or have unusual ways of thinking. Interventions encourage adaptive habits and teach individuals to perceive the world more accurately and to solve problems more efficiently. The third psychological model of mental illness is the humanistic-existential-phenomenological approach, represented by such psychologists as Abraham Maslow and Karl Rogers. It emphasizes the need for self-actualization rather than the diagnosis of mental illness. The focus lies in the individual's experience of the world and the creation of a supportive atmosphere characterized by genuineness, empathy, and unconditional positive reward. A final model is the family systems approach, which sees most problems as originating in the family. Accordingly, couples or family therapy, in which the therapist intervenes to develop healthy ways of relating to one another, is undertaken. Each model works well with some types of problems and falls short with others. An integrated approach may be best, in which one identifies the purposes best suited for a particular model.

Here are questions to consider while reading this chapter. What assumptions are embodied in each psychological model of abnormality? How do these shape the recognition and treatment of psychological problems? What are strengths and weaknesses of each model?

Introduction

Psychology is but one of several disciplines concerned with abnormality. Although psychologists throughout much of the 20th century pursued theoretically focused strategies, recent years have demonstrated that the topic demands a broader approach (Castonguay & Goldfried, 1994; Omer, 1993). The biochemical underpinnings of particular types of abnormality need to specified, along with the possible contribution of genetic influences (see Chapter 4). At the same time, abnormality must be placed in its larger social context – that provided by history, society, and culture (see Chapters 8 and 20, for example).

Today many psychologists endorse Engel's (1980) biopsychosocial model, which calls for theorists to consider biological mechanisms, psychological processes, and social influences on abnormality. This model remains just a slogan, however, until one can fill in the details of specific instances of abnormality – for example, anxiety, depression, substance abuse, and schizophrenia – and much work remains to be done before this vision is achieved.

The purpose of this chapter is to discuss major psychological perspectives on mental illness. In terms of the biopsychosocial model, the unique contribution of psychology lies in its attention to the intraindividual mechanisms that produce abnormal thoughts, feelings, and behaviors (Persons, 1986). Although psychologists today take diagnosis seriously, most are not satisifed with simply showing that individuals whose problems fall into different diagnostic categories are different. Their goal is to explain why these differences exist. Often, psychological theorists assume that abnormality and normality are continuous; because the same psychological mechanisms presumably produce both abnormal and normal behavior, there is no discrete break between the two.

Another contribution of psychology to the field of mental illness has been the development of individual therapies that try to undo or neutralize psychological mechanisms specified by various theories of abnormality, thereby alleviating distress. Research testifies to the effectiveness of a variety of psychological therapies (Nathan & Gorman, 2002).

Psychological Models of Abnormality

All useful psychological models of abnormality share a common form. At the core of each is a set of assumptions about human nature. Each model takes a stance on the nature of behavior (general psychology), on how behavior can go awry (psychopathology), and on how abnormality can be prevented or corrected or both (intervention). Although there are a number of popular psychological models of abnormality, this chapter focuses on four: the psychoanalytic, cognitive-behavioral, humanistic-existential-phenomenological, and the family systems approaches (see Table 5.1).

Psychoanalytic Model

The psychoanalytic model on abnormality originated in Sigmund Freud's influential theorizing. At its core, this model implies that people are closed energy

Table 5.1. *Psychological models of abnormality*

Model	Assumptions
Psychoanalytic	People are energy systems Problems result from the investment of energy in symptoms Treatment releases energy by encouraging insight
Cognitive-behavioral	People are information-processing systems Problems result from inappropriate learning or thinking or both Treatment changes the environment or thoughts or both
Humanistic-existential- phenomenological	People choose and define their own existence Problems result from the failure of self-actualization Treatment encourages authentic living
Family systems	People are products of their family Problems result from family dynamics and the creation of an unhealthy homeostasis Treatment changes the family status quo

systems. Freud (1895/1950) seemed to regard psychological energy (or libido, to use his term) as an actual thing, which neurologists would eventually discover. Subsequent versions of psychoanalytic theory used the notion of energy in a more metaphorical way, but common to all these theories are assumptions stemming from the view of people as engaged in the transformation and redirection of psychological energy.

Key Concepts. One of the overarching ideas of psychoanalytic theorizing is that behavior is overdetermined, meaning that even the most simple of our actions has numerous causes. The assumption of overdetermined behavior helps explain why the psychoanalytic model has been controversial. On the one hand, psychoanalytic theorizing about abnormality does justice to the complexity of the subject. On the other hand, because so many theoretical notions must be brought to bear in a single psychoanalytic explanation, the process may become unwieldy and appear arbitrary (Rapaport, 1959).

Another important aspect of the psychoanalytic model is that it takes a developmental approach to abnormality, stressing events and occurrences early in life that affect adult functioning. This emphasis stems from Freud's original medical training in neurology, where it is a truism that early structures form the foundation that underlie later structures. Put another way, the behavioral styles that children develop early in life become the ingredients of their adult personalities.

Freud believed that children develop by passing through a fixed sequence of psychosexual stages – discrete periods defined by the part of the body that provides gratification of the sexual drive. The child who passes through these stages – oral, anal, phallic, latency, and genital – in satisfactory fashion becomes a normal adult. But frustration or indulgence at any stage may leave the child with a fixation at that stage that influences adult character. An orally fixated person, for example, might drink too much or eat too much as an adult, creating such problems as alcoholism or obesity.

Yet another noteworthy psychoanalytic idea is that of the dynamic unconscious. According to Freud and subsequent psychoanalytic theorists, there exists important mental activity of which we are not aware. The unconscious is not just a deficit in knowledge but is also an active process that motivates us to keep threatening material from our conscious minds. Chief among these threatening contents are the sexual and aggressive motives that underlie our every action.

Where does psychological energy originate? Freud's answer is that we have certain innate drives, in particular sexuality and aggression, that demand discharge. The term for the sexual drive is *Eros* (after the Greek god of love). Eros is manifest not just in the narrow sense of genital activity culminating in orgasm but also, more broadly, in any and all activities that involve bodily pleasure. The aggressive drive is sometimes called *Thanatos* (after the Greek god of death). This drive is presumably behind the destructive acts we direct against ourselves and others: suicide, drug abuse, murder, and war.

Another important concern is the struggle between individuals and their drives and the restrictions placed by the larger social groups to which they belong. According to Freud (1930/1961), civilization would not be possible if people directly satisfied all their sexual and aggressive drives as they arose. Who would raise children, harvest crops, or pay taxes? For society to exist, people's drives must be curbed.

Freud held that drives could not be eliminated. But people could be induced to compromise, either to delay their gratification or to find indirect or symbolic means of satisfying them. In the course of socialization, children are transformed from bundles of drives – literally wild animals – into creatures capable of modifying their impulses or holding them in check. Socialization is never fully achieved, and it produces casualties: both people who never learn to control their drives and those who control them too well.

When infants are born, their only mental structure is what Freud termed the *id*, which is responsible for our irrational and emotional aspects. The id operates according to the pleasure principle: gratification without delay. In the course of socialization, the infant develops an *ego*: this mental structure operates according to the reality principle: adaptation to external constraints. The internalization of parental dictates – mainly "thou shalt nots" – is accomplished by the development of yet a third structure, the *superego*. In the adult, these three systems – the id, ego, and superego – interact continually. Their dynamic balance determines an individual's personality in general and his or her problems in particular.

How does the mind defend itself? One of Freud's most important contributions to psychological thought is the notion of *defense mechanisms*. These are mostly unconscious strategies that the ego uses to protect itself from anxiety. All people presumably use defense mechanisms, but they may show considerable variation in those they habitually favor (Vaillant, 1977). Some people rely mainly on primitive defenses that distort or deny reality, such as denial or repression. Other people use more subtle ones, such as humor or sublimation. People with severe problems tend to use particularly immature or exaggerated defenses. Indeed, the psychoanalytic model gives us a rich vocabulary for describing various disorders in terms of the defense mechanisms that people typically use. For example, paranoid individuals use projection, and phobic individuals use displacement.

Psychopathology. Psychoanalytic theorists see problems as resulting from defects in the transformation and use of psychological energy. These ideas explain both circumscribed and pervasive problems. So, in dysphoria – that is, general anxiety or depression – a person invests too much energy in defenses, thus having less available energy for more gratifying activities. In severe forms of abnormality such as schizophrenia, a person may not invest enough energy in defenses and as a result becomes overwhelmed by drives.

Defenses can end up being problems in their own right. Consider multiple personality disorder, the existence within the same individual of discrete personalities with little awareness of one another. Research implicates sexual or physical abuse in the childhood of most people with this disorder (Putnam, Guroff, Silberman, Barban & Post, 1986). One interpretation is that individuals who later develop multiple personality disorder create in childhood an alternative personality as a defense against abuse. It is a way to escape an intolerable situation, psychologically if not physically. This strategy, although useful at the time, creates obvious problems for those who continue to use it.

Intervention. The first modern "talking cure" was Freud's psychoanalysis, and subsequent psychological therapies have often used it as a model (Luborsky, 1984). Even psychotherapists who take issue with psychoanalysis have been influenced by it. Many believe that talking about problems in a special way is curative, that insight into the source of one's own problems is a critical ingredient in improvement, and that a nonjudgmental relationship between client and therapist is crucial.

Psychoanalytic treatment usually involves releasing energy and freeing it from investments in unhealthy purposes so that it is available for use elsewhere. The process by which energy is freed is termed *catharsis*, which is accompanied by sudden emotional relief.

As noted, attaining insight, thus bringing conflicts and motives into conscious awareness, is a major strategy in this kind of intervention. If people become conscious of ideas and impulses heretofore repressed, they have taken a major step toward helping themselves because it makes psychological energy available for pursuits more gratifying than the maintenance of defenses.

Psychoanalysts have developed a host of strategies for revealing unconscious conflicts. The technique of *free association* is one example. Here the person is instructed and encouraged to say anything that comes to mind, one idea leading to another and then another. The hope is that the train of emotional associations will lead eventually back to unconscious memories.

Dream interpretation is another strategy for accomplishing the same purpose. According to Freud (1900/1953), dreams are "the royal road to the unconscious," and he theorized extensively about how dreams may represent disguises of our unconscious wishes and fears. We can gain insight once these disguises are stripped away. Just like defense mechanisms, dreams disguise conflicts, but at the same time hint of them via symbolism.

Another strategy emerging from psychoanalytic theory is the analysis of the *transference relationship* between therapist and client. According to this view, clients in therapy inevitably react to therapists as they reacted earlier to those people with whom their conflicts originated. If the therapist and client can re-create these conflicts, then they have clues about how conflicts operated in the past. Again, insight is the goal. To help this process along, the therapist deliberately cultivates a pose of neutrality, a so-called blank screen.

It is quite difficult to say, fully one century after Freud first began to treat hysterical patients by asking them to free associate, whether this type of treatment is effective (Henry et al., 1994). Its terms are ambiguous, the duration of psychoanalytic therapy is typically years, the clients are highly select, and some psychoanalytic therapists are reluctant to subject their efforts to scientific investigation. Few if any methodologically sound investigations of psychoanalysis have been conducted.

Psychodynamic Approaches. Throughout his long career, Freud attracted a number of followers. Many of these individuals proposed their own versions of psychoanalysis, and what we have today are many such approaches, each with somewhat different emphases. It is customary to refer to Freud's original theory as psychoanalysis and to the family of related approaches as psychodynamic theories, because they are concerned with the dynamic workings of the mind. These theories in general assume that people's problems result from inner conflicts that overwhelm their defenses.

Contemporary psychodynamic theorists often follow the lead of Alfred Adler (1927), Carl Jung (1924), and the neo-Freudians – such as Erich Fromm (1947), Karen Horney (1937), Harry Stack Sullivan (1947), and Erik Erikson (1963), among others – by placing less emphasis on the purely biological or sexual aspects of personality. They are more likely to be interested in social determinants. Along these lines, they tend to downplay or even eliminate references to psychological energy and drives.

Contemporary psychodynamic theorists have also followed the lead of the ego psychologists – such as Anna Freud (1937), Heinz Hartmann (1939), and Robert White (1959) – by placing less emphasis on the conflict between id and superego and more stress on the ego as an active – not reactive – agent. Sometimes these theorists refer to defense mechanisms as coping mechanisms to emphasize their active nature.

Many psychodynamic theorists today are particularly interested in the mental representations that people have of themselves and others. These representations are called *object relations* (Greenberg & Mitchell, 1983). "Object" was Freud's term for people or things, and the term "relations" refers to the perceived link between these objects and the individual. In one sense, this emphasis on object relations reflects the trend for psychology to be more interested in cognition (Gardner, 1985). But object relations theories maintain the traditional psychoanalytic emphases on unconscious, irrational, and emotional processes.

Cognitive-Behavioral Model

A second psychological perspective on abnormality combines approaches that emphasize cognition on the one hand and processes of learning on the other. Early theories of learning stemmed from behaviorism and thus made no use of cognitive explanations. Indeed, throughout most of the 20th century, learning theories and cognitive theories were clearly distinct and often antagonistic (Sweet & Loizeaux, 1991). Although some contemporary therapists regard themselves as strictly behavioral or strictly cognitive, in recent years many other therapists have successfully combined these approaches (Peterson, 1992, 1996). The resulting cognitive-behavioral model of abnormality views people as information-processing systems, attempting to predict and understand events in the world with the goal of maximizing pleasure and minimizing pain. Said another way, the cognitive-behavioral model regards people as thinking hedonists.

Explicit in the cognitive-behavioral view of human nature is the assumption that people constantly interact with the world. Bandura (1986) termed this give-and-take between a person and the world *reciprocal determinism*. Each of us is influenced by prevailing patterns of rewards and punishments in the environment, and our actions in turn influence these patterns. Furthermore, this transaction is mediated cognitively. We react to the world in terms of how we interpret events. The "reality" in which our behavior takes place is a perceived reality.

Forms of Learning. Cognitive-behavioral theorists emphasize several psychological processes, especially several basic forms of learning. Classical conditioning – remember Pavlov's salivating dogs? – is the process by which people come to associate particular emotional reactions with previously neutral stimuli.

Imagine people who have had a series of traumatic experiences with dogs, or airplane travel, or sexual relations. They may well develop fears or aversions to them.

Operant conditioning is the process by which we come to associate responses with their consequences. If the consequences are reinforcing, we are more likely to repeat the actions that preceded them. Children might throw tantrums when doing so is the only way they can get attention from their parents or teachers. If the consequences of responses are painful, then we tend to refrain from repeating those actions.

Modeling – or vicarious conditioning – is the process by which we learn new behaviors by watching others perform them. If the person we watch, called a model, meets with reward, then we are more likely to follow his or her example, even in problematic directions. Any of a number of problems can be produced by modeling.

Cognitive Contents and Processes. Cognitive-behavioral theorists believe that all of these types of learning (i.e., classical conditioning, operant conditioning, and modeling) must be placed in a cognitive context. Learning does not automatically occur just because certain environmental events take place. It occurs most readily for a thinking organism. Even the simplest examples of learning may reflect the influence of expectations (Schwartz, 1984). Theorists have accordingly introduced a host of cognitive constructs.

One way to bring some order to cognitive theorizing is by distinguishing the content of thought from its process. Cognitive contents are mental representations: particular thoughts and beliefs. We transform and utilize these representations by using cognitive processes: judging, decision making, and problem solving.

Our cognitive contents are organized. A *schema* refers to an organized set of beliefs about some subject; for example, your sense of who you are: your strengths, weaknesses, hopes, dreams, and fears. The key characteristic of a schema is that it has a structure.

Various principles have been suggested as a way of describing the organization of our different schemas (Taylor, 1981). One guiding principle is consistency (Festinger, 1957). People often seek out balance and harmony among their thoughts (Heider, 1958). They want their ideas to be consistent with one another. Consistency can take an insidious turn, however, if individuals happen to have a negative view of themselves. Consistency may lead them to notice only events that confirm their negative views and to ignore disconfirming ones (Mischel, Ebbesen, & Zeiss, 1973). Another guiding principle is accuracy. People try to understand the facts of the world. In particular, they notice very quickly what makes them feel good or bad. A third guiding principle is self-aggrandizement. Many individuals put a positive spin on their experiences whenever possible (Taylor, 1989). Depression is a notable exception.

The needs for consistency, accuracy, and self-aggrandizement influence our thoughts, and they may push us in different directions. What we think is always a compromise among them. Sometimes consistency or self-aggrandizement wins out, in which cases we change our perceptions of reality to fit how we think. Other times accuracy wins out, and we change how we think to fit the available evidence.

Psychopathology. According to the cognitive-behavioral model, people's problems are not intrinsically different from their normal behavior; rather, all actions are produced by the same processes of learning and thinking. People encounter difficulties either when they are placed in situations that encourage problems or when they happen to be ignorant, confused, or mistaken.

General dysphoria is often explained by the cognitive-behavioral model in terms of exposure to unpredictable and uncontrollable events coupled with exaggerated beliefs about vulnerability and loss. Severe mental illness is seen in similar terms, presumably brought out by highly unusual experiences or ways of thinking. For example, schizophrenic individuals have difficulties in the psychological mechanisms responsible for selective attention. Too much information is available to them, and they think in overly inclusive terms. The hallucinations and delusions that characterize schizophrenia are derived from these attentional problems.

Intervention. To treat problems from the cognitive-behavioral view, the therapist encourages adaptive habits: behavioral or cognitive or both. Clients are helped to see the world more accurately and to solve problems more efficiently. Therapists equate their treatment with education, because they conceive it as learning or relearning.

In the past few decades, a host of cognitive-behavior therapies have been developed. First was behavior therapy, which applied ideas of classical conditioning and operant conditioning to people's problems. Joseph Wolpe's (1958) *systematic desensitization* was one of the first such therapies to be widely used. A person is asked to imagine a series of increasingly disturbing images while deeply relaxed. This process is repeated until the images no longer elicit fear. Systematic desensitization continues to this day to be one of the most effective treatments for specific phobias.

Next was the development of strategies based on modeling (Bandura, 1969). Behavior change need not occur through trial and error. Sometimes people can shed old habits and acquire new ones by watching other individuals behave in adaptive ways. A person who is afraid of spiders or snakes is helped by watching someone else approach them without fear.

At the same time, therapies appeared assuming that people's problems are brought about by the thoughts and beliefs that they entertain. An effective way to treat problems would thus involve changing these thoughts and beliefs. These cognitive interventions were foreshadowed by the approaches of George Kelly (1955), whose fixed-role therapy encouraged people to try out specific roles in order to experience the perspectives that went along with them, and of Albert Ellis (1962), whose rational-emotive therapy identified and challenged people's irrational beliefs, chiefly those that were rigid and absolutist (i.e., "I must make $125,000 per year in order to be happy").

Today, one of the best-known cognitive interventions is *cognitive therapy*, which targets for change the negative thoughts that depressed people hold about themselves (Beck et al., 1979). They are encouraged to evaluate their ideas against relevant evidence, testing the "reality" of their beliefs. Cognitive therapy has also been used to treat anxiety disorders characterized by exaggerated beliefs about vulnerability.

In cognitive therapy, a client may be told to carry out experiments that allow the gathering of pertinent evidence. Clients who regard themselves as social losers might be instructed to invite 10 people to share a cup of coffee during a break at work. What is the anticipated versus actual result? Of course, if a therapist suggests such experiments, they should not be overly stringent. Then the client will fail, thereby confirming his or her negative views. If there is reason to suspect that all 10 people will refuse to have coffee with the client, this experiment is best left on the drawing board. Maybe the person should be instructed on *how* to ask somebody to have a cup of coffee.

In this example, you see how cognitive treatment slides into behavioral treatment; hence, the growing trend to combine these approaches to abnormality and its remediation. This combination is called cognitive-behavior therapy. Indeed, one of the good ways to change how people think is to change how they behave, and vice versa (Bandura, 1986).

Today it makes sense to speak of a cognitive-behavioral model of abnormality, to subsume the various techniques of behavior therapy and cognitive therapy under this umbrella, and to call them cognitive-behavior therapy (Mahoney, 1974; Meichenbaum, 1977). Many "behavioral" techniques pay attention to mental occurrences; even the epitome of behavior therapy – systematic desensitization – employs mental images to bring about behavioral change. And many cognitive therapies take into account rewards and punishments.

Cognitive-behavioral techniques have been used with a variety of problems, often with very good success (Emmelkamp, 1994; Engels, Garnefski, & Diekstra, 1993; Hollon & Beck, 1994). In some cases, like infantile autism or organic brain disorder, the problem is not eradicated so much as the individual is helped to compensate or cope. In other cases, such as specific phobias or sexual dysfunction, the problem indeed goes away. These techniques are presumably effective in eliminating problems when they can undo basic causes. They may also be effective in helping an individual cope by providing an alternative way of reaching some goal.

Cognitive-behavioral approaches also have their share of difficulties. They seem to work best when problems fit their formula; that is, when they are circumscribed, behavioral, or associated with immediately accessible thoughts. When problems do not readily fit this framework, cognitive-behavior therapy is apt to be misdirected.

Some advocates regard cognitive-behavioral approaches as superior to drug-based therapies because they effect long-lasting changes in behavior or cognition or both, as opposed to temporary changes in biochemistry (Rush et al., 1977). But the facts do not support the conclusion that cognitive-behavioral changes are always permanent. In many cases, they are not, nor are they as general across situations as we might want.

This failure represents not only a practical problem but also a theoretical one. Part of the rationale for cognitive-behavioral approaches is the assumption that people have problems because they have not learned appropriate ways of being happy and winning rewards. Therapy facilitates this new learning. The person without social skills should find a whole new world opened up once these skills have been acquired. Depression or anxiety stemming from this lack of knowledge about social skills should be permanently precluded. But this is not always so. Short-term benefits are sometimes simply that. Why do the new skills not lead to a dramatically different life?

One possible answer is that the environment did not change, and thus it cannot sustain the changes in behavior. If a person lives in an objectively distressing world, any therapy, no matter how successful, is likely to seem ineffective when he or she returns home. Treatment cannot make someone oblivious to the world.

Another possible answer is that the changes brought about by cognitive-behavior therapy are not always sufficiently deep. If these changes take place only on a superficial level, they can be dislodged. This criticism points, perhaps, to the need for these approaches to address the physiological, emotional, or unconscious levels of problems.

Humanistic-Existential-Phenomenological Model

The psychodynamic and cognitive-behavioral models try to specify the causes of problems. Their approach to behavior very much characterizes 20th-century psychology, especially in the United States. But voices of dissent have given rise to several important strands of thought. These dissenting traditions regard human behavior as freely chosen and therefore inappropriately explained in cause–effect terms. These traditions also have something to say about the nature of abnormality and its treatment.

Key Concepts. Humanism is the doctrine that the needs and values of human beings take precedence over material things and, further, that people cannot be studied simply as part of the material world. Humanists argue that psychologists may miss what is most important about people by focusing on the supposed causes of behavior, as if people were simply billiard balls, doing poorly or well depending on whatever happens to ricochet into them. Many psychologists are in turn impatient with humanistic theories because they seem vague and impossible to test.

Well-known psychologists within this tradition include Abraham Maslow (1970) and Carl Rogers (1961). Both emphasized that people strive to make the most of their potential in a process called *self-actualization*. Self-actualization can be thwarted by various conditions, but if these conditions are changed, then the potential within each individual will necessarily unfold.

This approach is a very different way of thinking about human nature: it emphasizes the goals for which people strive, their conscious awareness of this striving, the importance of their own choices, and their rationality. Its focus is thereby directed away from mechanical causes and toward fundamental questions about existence and meaning.

The humanistic models often overlap with another viewpoint that is termed *existentialism*. The critical idea of existentialism is that a person's experience is primary. To understand any individual is to understand him or her subjectively, from the inside out.

Existentialists see people as products of their own choices, which are freely undertaken. To use their phrase, existence precedes essence, with essence understood to mean a person's particular characteristics. They also stress that there is no fixed human nature, only the sort of person that each unique individual becomes by the self-definition he or she chooses.

As applied specifically to psychology, these humanistic and existential viewpoints have several emphases (Urban, 1983):

- the significance of the individual
- the complex organization of the individual
- the capacity for change inherent in the individual
- the significance of conscious experience
- the self-regulatory nature of human activity

Implicit here is a criticism of scientific psychology as typically conducted, because it does not deal with what is most important about people (Maslow, 1966).

Humanists and existential theorists believe that psychologists must pay more attention to an individual's way of seeing the world, and here they join ranks with yet another intellectual movement, phenomenology, which attempts to describe a person's conscious experience in terms meaningful for that individual. Phenomenology has a superficial resemblance to cognitive approaches, in that both are concerned with thoughts and thinking, but this similarity is misleading. Cognitive approaches start by specifying the terms with which to describe "cognition" and then use this theoretical language to describe the thoughts of all people. In contrast, phenomenologists start with the experience of a specific individual and then attempt to describe it.

Many models of abnormality are antithetical to the phenomenological goal of describing experience, because the theoretical terms introduced by these models turn people into objects, denying them – by implication – any experience. Scottish psychiatrist Ronald D. Laing (1959) eloquently phrased this critique. He pointed out that psychologists and psychiatrists describe schizophrenic symptoms with colorful terms like *word salad, loose associations,* and *poverty of speech,* which make schizophrenic individuals seem like broken machines. Laing (1959) advised us to listen to what "abnormal" people communicate, because their experience – even when at odds with our own – is still their defining characteristic, just as our own experience defines us.

Psychopathology. Humanistic, existential, and phenomenological psychologists are not much concerned with traditional diagnosis. Although they recognize that people have problems, their view of them is quite different than the one inherent in traditional diagnosis. Problems ensue when people experience a discrepancy between their sense of who they are and the way the world treats them. Sometimes the world is to blame, in the sense of creating circumstances that lead them to doubt their own choices (Rogers, 1942). And sometimes people make poor choices by not declaring to themselves their true intentions. Simply put, problems are seen as derailments along the way to self-actualization.

People have a central fear, according to many theorists in this tradition, and this fear is one of nonexistence – death. Needless to say, all of us will die, but many of us fail to confront this eventuality. In denying death, we fail to live in an authentic way, and we fall short of actualizing our potential. Fear of death and our failure to deal with this fear may figure in cases of general dysphoria characterized by anxiety and depression.

Severe mental illness must similarly be examined from the inside out. In a well-known case study, Laing (1959) recounted the story of Peter, a young man diagnosed as schizophrenic. Among his symptoms was smelling something rotten that no one else could detect. We could simply call this an olfactory hallucination and be done with it, but Laing delved into Peter's experience. He discovered that Peter had been raised in a family where he was not exactly abused but rather was ignored – in a profound way. His parents fed him and clothed him, but otherwise paid him absolutely no heed. They went about their business in their small apartment as if their son did not exist.

Peter came to experience the world in a highly idiosyncratic way. He never developed a sense of intersubjective reality, the convention that certain experiences are "public" because other people treat them as real, whereas other experiences are "private" because other people do not acknowledge them. Peter never regarded his experiences as public versus private because his parents never validated or invalidated any of them. So what if other people did not experience smells in the way that Peter did? None of his experiences had intersubjective reality. To call his experience a hallucination is to disregard its significance. Simply diagnosing Peter as a schizophrenic is inadequate if our goal is to understand and eventually help another human being.

Forms of Learning. Most humanistic-existential-phenomenological approaches to treatment were proposed by therapists originally trained in the psychoanalytic tradition. Disenchanted, these therapists articulated their own views of human nature, problems, and treatments. They described people's problems with terms like *angst, despair, crisis,* and *failure to take responsibility.* These terms refer to aspects of the human experience, and they can only be changed by encouraging the person to confront them and choose to act more forthrightly (Greenberg, Elliott, & Lietar, 1994).

Viktor Frankl (1975), a well-known existential theorist and therapist, devised strategies that illustrate this point. For example, in dereflection, people are encouraged to turn from their own problems to those of others. An insecure and depressed individual might be told to do volunteer work in a hospice. An aggressive and hostile person might be asked to undertake relief work for victims of famine. The intent of dereflection is not to distract, but rather to cultivate self-understanding and to provide meaning to one's own life.

Among the best-known humanistic therapies is client-centered therapy as developed by Carl Rogers (1951). Although he was originally trained in psychoanalytic therapy, he found it less than useful for many of the problems he encountered among his clients. He proposed his own view of human nature, one in which people know their own problems and how to solve them, if they could be placed in a setting that encouraged their natural wisdom. And thus his therapy emphasized the creation of a supportive atmosphere, one characterized by genuineness, empathy, and unconditional positive regard. As in psychoanalysis, there is an emphasis on the characteristics of the therapist, but in contrast to a carefully cultivated neutrality, we see warmth and concern stressed.

Therapists try not to judge or evaluate what clients say. Rather, they repeat disclosures back to them to convey understanding and positive regard. When clients can speak openly and without hesitation about their problems, then solutions may follow.

Unlike many therapists in this tradition, Rogers believed that the effectiveness of therapy was an open question that could be investigated scientifically. He conducted pioneering investigations of psychotherapy effectiveness. Several conclusions emerged from his studies (Beutler, Crago, & Arizmendi, 1986). First, personal qualities of the therapist such as warmth, genuineness, and empathy are important ingredients in effective therapy, but in themselves they are not enough. Second, therapy works to the extent that people's perceptions of themselves become more congruent. Third, client-centered therapy is effective with milder forms of anxiety and depressive disorders, in which problems with self-esteem and self-perception predominate, but it is of more limited use when problems are more severe. Rogers conducted a well-known investigation of client-centered therapy with schizophrenia but found little evidence for its effectiveness (Rogler et al., 1967).

Family Systems Model

Some problems can be described as existing between and among people. This perspective is embodied in the family systems model, which takes the position that most problems – depression, anxiety, and substance abuse – are manifestations of disturbances in the family (Jacobson & Addis, 1993). Family systems theories usually agree on main points (Haley, 1976; Minuchin, 1974; Stanton, 1981).

Key Concepts. Most basically, individuals must be located in their immediate social context, and usually this means their family. Each family has a unique style or character that shows itself in repetitive patterns of interactions among family members. In addition, each family is regarded as a complex system, with every person's behavior simultaneously a cause and an effect of everyone else's behavior. It is therefore difficult, if not impossible, to specify simple cause–effect relationships within the family. This model instead focuses on the factors existing among family members that maintain the behavioral status quo. The status quo is called *homeostasis*: balance among the behaviors of the family members. Conflicts in one aspect of the system are counteracted by changes elsewhere in an attempt to restore homeostasis.

Psychopathology. In a healthy family, the status quo is one in which the individuals can thrive both as individuals and as family members. But in other families, the status quo is achieved at a cost. An individual might develop "symptoms" as a way of compensating for problems elsewhere in the family. Family systems theorists call the family member with symptoms the identified patient, making the point that this person is merely the one who shows family problems most blatantly.

Stanton (1981, p. 364) provided the following example of how a disturbed family takes its obvious toll on one family member:

> Spouse A is driving and Spouse B is in a hurry to get to their destination. . . . A accelerates through a yellow light, B . . . criticizes A, who retorts and steps on the gas. B protests more loudly, A shouts back, and the child, C, starts to cry. At this point the argument stops, while B attends to C and A slows down. If this pattern repeats itself over and over, then the child, C, runs the risk of being seen as having an emotional problem, although the child's "problem" obviously serves a purpose. It reduces the tension between the parents and restores homeostasis.

The family systems approach often places great emphasis on triangles like the one just described, regarding them as the basic unit of family interaction. When there is tension between two people in the family, a third person will often diffuse or eliminate it. Appreciate the complexity involved here, because all sorts of possible triangles exist even within a small family.

The general problem with the family systems approach is that it may be circular. Given a family member with a problem, it is often assumed without independent verification that family dynamics must be responsible. Other family members may be blamed for enabling the difficulty rather than seen simply as bystanders or indeed as victims themselves.

Different psychological problems are explained in terms of the particular ways in which a family achieves homeostasis. A family member may develop a circumscribed symptom – such as a phobia about traveling – as a way to distract the family as a whole from fighting about how to spend summer vacations. More severe problems reflect gross difficulties in family styles of communication.

Several theories of schizophrenia, for example, propose that the disorder is most likely to occur in families in which messages are consistently disguised, contradictory, or accompanied by strong criticism (Bateson et al., 1956; Lidz, 1975). Although research does not support the hypothesis that such family styles cause schizophrenia, there is good evidence that the family environment plays a role in maintaining or exacerbating schizophrenia once it is present (Leff & Vaughn, 1985).

Intervention. Family systems theorists, not surprisingly, feel that problems are best dealt with by treating the family as a whole. Couples therapy or family therapy accordingly is undertaken. The goal of the therapist is to intervene so that a new equilibrium can be established in the couple or the family, one without victims.

The idea of homeostasis leads the family systems therapist to expect resistance by the family to change. The family's style of relating, however unhealthy, is the status quo, and it maintains itself. Therefore, the therapist must be a strategist, planning treatments that create change (Haley, 1973). One way of conducting this strategic form of therapy is with reframing interventions: techniques that encourage a more benign interpretation of what is going on. Also part of the repertoire of family systems therapists are paradoxical interventions, suggestions that subtly communicate the message "don't change." In resisting these sorts of interventions, the family ends up changing (Haley, 1973, 1987).

On the average, couples who go through couples therapy fare better than those who do not; they tend to resolve conflicts more satisfactorily and stay together longer (Alexander, Holtzworth-Monroe, & Jameson, 1994; Dunn & Schwebel, 1995). It seems to work better for younger couples and for those who have not begun divorce proceedings. In any event, this kind of therapy proves more effective in solving marital problems than individual therapy undertaken with only one spouse.

Couples therapy can also be of help as a treatment for ostensibly "individual" problems, including depression, substance abuse, and obesity (Black, Gleser, & Kooyers, 1990; Jacobson, Holtzworth-Munroe, & Schmaling, 1989; O'Farrell, 1989). Although each of these problems has numerous determinants, among the important influences may be interpersonal processes that couples therapy can address.

In family therapy, the therapist attempts to establish a healthy equilibrium within the family. Studies show that this kind of therapy is often effective for reducing conflicts and resolving specific problems such as bulimia (Cox & Merkel, 1989). It sometimes exceeds individual therapy in effectiveness (DeWitt, 1978). As an adjunct to individual treatment of problems like substance abuse, bipolar disorder, and schizophrenia, family therapy also has proven to be of value (Lebow & Gurman, 1995). This kind of therapy can also help individuals and their families adjust to life-threatening and chronic physical illnesses, such as cancer, AIDS, or Alzheimer's disease.

Conclusions

Psychologists have long hoped that a given approach would answer all of the questions we might pose about each and every disorder. This hope has not been realized for any of the existing models. Rather, each model has what Kelly (1955) termed a focus of convenience, a domain of the world (in this case abnormality) where it works particularly well. And each model certainly encounters abnormality. Indeed, it may be impossible to evaluate any of these models as a whole, much less to compare them across the board. The task of the theorist and the practitioner is to identify those purposes for which a given model is best suited. For a given disorder, which model best accounts for its risk factors and mechanisms? And again for a given disorder, which model generates the most effective treatments?

As noted in the introduction to this chapter, many psychologists today try to integrate the insights of the different models of abnormality, along with the contributions of biological and sociocultural perspectives (Peterson, 1996). All problems, circumscribed or severe, are profitably viewed as having a biological basis and as residing in a social context. The psychological mechanisms specified by the theories described in this chapter play critical roles as well. Adding to the complexity of a fully integrated perspective on abnormality is the mutual influence between and among all of these factors.

6

Sociological Approaches to Mental Illness

Peggy A. Thoits

The sociological approach focuses on the factors external to the individual – the environmental or social context – and views mental illness as a breakdown in the face of overwhelming environmental stress. Thoits provides an overview of three dominant theories, or models, and describes their basic assumptions, advantages and limitations, and implications for treating or preventing mental illness. Stress theory is based on evidence that accumulations of social stressors can precipitate mental health problems. The relationship between stress exposure and psychiatric symptoms, however, is not strong because individuals have extensive coping resources to help them handle stress. Researchers focus on the relationship between stress and coping mechanisms and also on the unequal distribution of stressful experiences and a variety of coping resources in the population. One reason why higher rates of mental disorder and psychological distress are found in lower status, disadvantaged groups is that these groups are more likely to be exposed to stressors and less likely to have important coping resources. To treat mental illness, one needs to eliminate or reduce stressors, teach individuals different coping strategies, and bolster their personal resources. Structural strain theory locates the origins of disorder and distress in the broader organization of society. Mental illness may be an adaptive response to structural strain or to one's degree of integration into society. For example, during periods of high unemployment, admissions to treatment for psychosis increase, whereas periods of economic upturns are associated with lower rates of hospitalization. A structural condition, hard economic times, causes people to experience major stressors and provokes mental illness. Society's organization places some groups at a social or economic disadvantage. To prevent or reduce mental illness, society must be restructured in a fairly major way, for example, by creating a guaranteed minimum income to eliminate the strains of unemployment. A third approach to mental illness is labeling or social reaction theory. The logic behind labeling theory is that people who are labeled as mentally ill, and who are treated as mentally ill, become mentally ill. Symptoms of mental illness are viewed as violations of the normative order whereby individuals violate taken-for-granted rules about how one should think, feel, and behave. The way to reduce or prevent mental illness is to change those norms that distinguish what is normal behavior from that considered abnormal. Although this approach may seem idealistic, labeling theory has been very important in alerting us to the consequences of labeling and institutionalization. Students should think about the various ways the three sociological approaches to mental illness complement each other and contribute to the biological and psychological understandings of mental disorder.

Introduction

The three general approaches to mental illness that are discussed in this volume can be broadly characterized by their underlying metaphors. The biological or medical approach views mental illness as if it were a disease or physical defect in the brain or body. The psychological approach treats it as if it were a sickness or abnormality in the mind or psyche (i.e., the soul). And the sociological approach views mental illness as if it were a breakdown in the face of overwhelming environmental demands. The key distinction between the biological and psychological perspectives on the one hand and the sociological perspective on the other is the location of the primary cause of mental illness. From the biological and psychological approaches, the determinants of mental illness are internal – "in" the person (in the physical body or in the person's mind). From a sociological approach, the cause is external – in the environment or in the person's social situation. Although obviously oversimplifying the differences among the three approaches, this characterization helps clarify the focus of this chapter – on the social, rather than biological and psychological, origins of mental illness.

Within the social approach, there are three dominant theories of mental illness etiology (where etiology means the study of the origins or causes of a disease): (1) stress theory, (2) structural strain theory, and (3) labeling theory. This chapter describes each theory's basic concepts and assumptions, theoretical limitations and advantages, and implications for treating or preventing mental illness.

Stress Theory

Hans Selye, a medical researcher, introduced the term *stress* into scientific discourse in the mid-1930s. By stress or stressors he meant anything that puts wear and tear on the body, usually noxious environmental stimuli. Because he experimented with laboratory animals, stressors meant such conditions as extreme heat or cold, overcrowded cages, and repeated electric shocks. Selye (1956) argued and showed that prolonged or repeated exposure to noxious stressors eventually depleted the body's physical defenses and that laboratory animals almost inevitably succumbed to disease or infection when that happened.

Because laboratory studies convincingly established a relationship between prolonged or repeated stress exposure and disease in animals, speculation turned to the effects of stress on human beings. Researchers began to focus on social stressors, in particular, on major life events (Holmes & Rahe, 1967). Thomas Holmes and Richard Rahe defined life events as major changes in people's lives that require extensive behavioral readjustments. They hypothesized that having to readjust one's behavior repeatedly or substantially could overtax a person's ability to cope or adapt, thus leaving him or her more vulnerable to physical illness, injury, or even death. To test this hypothesis, Holmes and Rahe first went through the medical records of Navy personnel, recording the most common life events that preceded Navy men's doctor visits and hospitalizations and abstracting a list of 43 major life events. Next they asked groups of people to judge (independently of one another) how much behavioral readjustment each event on their list required. Table 6.1 shows the resulting Social Readjustment Rating Scale, with the 43 events ordered by their average "life change unit" scores, that is, by the amounts of behavioral readjustment (from 0 to 100 units) that people believed they require.

This life events checklist gave social researchers an easy way to assess whether exposure to social stressors would have health consequences for human beings. The answer was clear: The more life events that individuals experienced in a given period of time (say, during 6 months or a year) and the higher their readjustment scores, the more likely they would have an injury, an illness, or even die (Cooper, 2005; Cohen, Janicki-Deverts, & Miller, 2007; Tennant, 1999). Literally hundreds of studies showed a significant relationship between the amount of life change that one experienced and illness, including heart attacks, strokes, tuberculosis, ulcers, asthma attacks, flu, and even the common cold (S. Cohen, 1996). More exciting to mental health researchers, studies found that major life changes were significantly associated with the onset of anxiety, depression, schizophrenia, and generalized states of psychological distress (Thoits, 1983, 1995). An accumulation of social stressors, then, could precipitate mental health problems.[1]

Soon after the discovery of these basic relationships, investigators' attention turned to the types of stressors that were most likely to precede the onset of mental illness.[2] Notice that Holmes and Rahe's Social Readjustment Rating Scale implicitly assumes that all life events, both positive and negative, can require behavioral readjustment and thus overtax individuals' coping resources and leave them physically or emotionally vulnerable. However, researchers next found that

---

[1]   You may have noticed that there are several problems with Homes and Rahe's SSRS. For example, many important life events are missing from the list (e.g., losing custody of one's children, "coming out of the closet," a parent remarries); in fact subsequent life events checklists have been expanded to include anywhere from 100 to 200 events (Dohrenwend et al., 1978). Another problem is that the events on the SRRS tend to be ones that happen primarily to males and Whites; events that are experienced more by women or minority group members are underpresented. Also, many items on the SRRS are possible symptoms of psychological problems rather than events in themselves, for example, changes in eating habits, changes in sleeping habits, sexual difficulties). Researchers have since gone to extensive lengths to eliminate these and other problems (Wethington, Brown, & Kessler, 1995). However, even with improved life events measurement, the same basic relationships reported in your text are still found.

[2]   It is important to understand that laypersons often use the term *stress* ambiguously and that this ambiguity must be avoided for clarity. *Stress* can refer to the cause of the psychological problems (e.g., negative events), or it can describe one's subjective emotional experience (e.g., "I feel so stressed). To avoid this ambiguity, researchers usually restrict the term *stress* or *stressor* to refer to major life events and chronic strains – the environmental causes of emotional problems. The phrases "stress reaction" or "stress response" are used to distinguish emotional consequences from their environmental causes. In this book, psychological distress and mental disorder are the stress reactions of primary concern, and major life events and chronic strains are the causal factors.

Table 6.1. *Social readjustment rating scale*

Rank	Event	Life change units
1	Death of spouse	100
2	Divorce	73
3	Marital separation	65
4	Jail term	63
5	Death of close family member	63
6	Personal injury or illness	53
7	Marriage	50
8	Fired at work	47
9	Marital reconciliation	45
10	Retirement	45
11	Change in health of family member	44
12	Pregnancy	39
13	Sex difficulties	39
14	Gain of new family member	39
15	Business readjustment	39
16	Change in financial state	38
17	Death of close friend	37
18	Change to different line of work	36
19	Change of number of arguments with spouse	35
20	Mortgage or loan over $10,000	31
21	Foreclosure of mortgage or loan	30
22	Change in responsibilities at work	29
23	Son or daughter leaving home	29
24	Trouble with in-laws	29
25	Outstanding personal achievement	28
26	Wife begins or stops work	26
27	Begin or end school	26
28	Change in living conditions	25
29	Revision of personal habits	24
30	Trouble with boss	23
31	Change in work hours or conditions	20
32	Change in residence	20
33	Change in schools	20
34	Change in recreation	19
35	Change in church	19
36	Change in social activities	18
37	Mortgage or loan less than $10,000	17
38	Change in sleeping habits	16
39	Change in number of family get-togethers	15
40	Change in eating habits	15
41	Vacation	13
42	Christmas	12
43	Minor violations of the law	11

Source: Thomas A. Holmes and Richard H. Rahe (1967), "The Social Readjustment Rating Scale," *Journal of Psychosomatic Research, 11,* 213–218.

when events were subdivided into culturally desirable (positive) and culturally undesirable (negative) types, undesirable events were more strongly associated with psychological problems than desirable events were (Ross & Mirowsky, 1979; Brown & Harris, 1978). George Brown and Tirril Harris's path-breaking socio-logical study of life events and depression offered compelling evidence for this relationship.

Brown and Harris randomly selected about 460 women in the city of Camber-well, outside London, for in-depth interviews. Through the interviews they estab-lished whether any of the women met the clinical criteria for major depression and, if so, the month when the depression had begun. About 15% of the women in the Camberwell community sample were found to be clinically depressed at the time of the study. A central part of the interview canvassed all of the major life changes and chronic difficulties the women had experienced over the past year or up to the point of depression onset. Importantly, this was not a simple checklist type of assessment, but instead an in-depth, probing discussion of the various changes and difficulties the women had been through in the past year.

Brown and Harris defined "severe" life events as negative events that most people would agree are serious long-term threats to personal well-being. They found that severe events predicted the onset of major depression much better than "non-severe" events, which referred to minor negative events and positive events. These researchers discovered, too, that ongoing difficulties (sometimes called chronic strains) were almost as important as severe negative events in predicting depression. Examples of ongoing difficulties are living in overcrowded conditions, having persistent family arguments, and having too little money to buy necessary food, clothes, or medicine. When severe events and long-term major difficulties were considered together, Brown and Harris found that 89% of the depressed women had experienced one or both types of stressors in the past 9 months whereas only 30% of the nondepressed women had experienced those conditions during the same time period. So Brown and Harris concluded that acute negative events and chronic strains put individuals at much higher risk of developing major depression. Note that it is not all changes, positive and negative, but only negative changes in people's lives that are causes of psychological problems.

Subsequent research showed that negative events and chronic strains also pre-dicted the onset of schizophrenia, anxiety attacks, and milder states of depression and generalized distress (Thoits, 1983, 1995; Turner, 1995; Turner & Lloyd, 1999). In other words, acute events and chronic strains (the latter defined as environmen-tal demands that require repeated or daily readjustments in behavior over long periods of time) are causally implicated in a variety of forms of mental illness, from mild to severe.[3] Research has also pinpointed the types of events that more

---

[3] Researchers have also studied "hassles" as types of stressors that may cause psychological problems (Kanner et al., 1981). Hassles are mini-events, small changes requiring immediate readjustment in one's behavior. Examples include getting stuck in traffic, having unexpected company arrive, and losing one's wallet. Although there is evidence supporting a relationship between mounting hassles

often precede psychological disorder, such as events that are unexpected, uncontrollable, and clustered in time; traumatic experiences; and unresolved problems. You will learn more about these various types of stressors and their effects in Part II of this volume.

As findings on the psychological effects of stress mounted, researchers began to turn their attention to a related problem: Although there clearly is a relationship between exposure to stressors and the subsequent development of psychological problems, this relationship is not strong. The strength of a relationship is measured as a *correlation*. A correlation between two variables ranges in value from .00 (no relationship at all) to 1.0 (a perfect positive relationship – that is, for each negative event experienced, there is an accompanying unit increase in psychological symptoms). Most studies report correlations around .30, which is a very modest correlation between stressors and symptoms of psychological distress or disorder. In other words, many people who experience severe stressors do not become disturbed, whereas others who experience few or minor stressors do. Why is this?

According to elaborations of stress theory (Lazarus & Folkman, 1984; Pearlin, 1989; Pearlin, Lieberman, Menaghan, & Mullan, 1981), the modest correlation between stress exposure and symptoms occurs because many individuals have extensive coping resources and use effective coping strategies when handling stressful demands, thus buffering the negative psychological impacts of those demands. *Coping resources* refer to social and personal reserves from which people draw when dealing with stressors (Pearlin & Schooler, 1978). Social support is a key social coping resource; it consists of emotional, informational, or practical assistance with stressors from significant others such as family or friends. Two important personal coping resources are self-esteem and a sense of control or mastery over life. People who have high self-esteem and those who strongly believe that they are in control of their lives are more likely to engage in active problem-solving efforts to overcome problems (Folkman, 1984; Pearlin et al., 1981; Taylor, 2007; Taylor & Aspinwall, 1996) or to use a variety of coping strategies flexibly to meet stressful demands (Folkman & Moskowitz, 2004; Mattlin, Wethington, & Kessler, 1990; Pearlin & Schooler, 1978).

Coping strategies are usually defined as behavioral or cognitive attempts to manage situational demands that one perceives as taxing or exceeding one's ability to adapt (Lazarus & Folkman, 1984). They are typically subdivided into two types: problem-focused and emotion-focused coping strategies. Problem-focused coping efforts are directed at changing or eliminating the stressful demands themselves. Emotion-focused strategies are attempts to alter one's emotional reactions to stressful demands, for example, through distraction, avoidance, or tension release. Pearlin and Schooler (1978) distinguished what might be called

---

and emotional upset, hassles scales are problematic because they mix in major events, chronic strains, and possible psychological symptoms with true mini-events (Dohrenwend et al., 1984). Hence, the findings of hassles scales are not emphasized here.

meaning-focused coping, or cognitive coping, from other emotion-focused strate-gies. Meaning-focused coping consists of mental efforts to alter one's perceptions of stressful demands so that they seem less threatening or overwhelming (e.g., reinterpreting the situation, looking on the bright side of things). Lazarus and Folkman (1984) classified such cognitive strategies as emotion focused in nature because they can reduce emotional reactions to demands, but do not change the demands themselves.

Research shows that, in most stressful episodes, people use both problem-focused and emotion-focused strategies, including meaning-focused ones (Folkman & Lazarus, 1980; Taylor & Aspinwall, 1996). For example, when facing a major exam, students may attack the problem by studying an hour or two each day and practicing answers to possible test questions. They may control their anxiety by telling themselves that they understand more of the material than other students do, reminding themselves that they have done well before on these kinds of tests, and perhaps, engaging in some strenuous exercise to ease physical tension. Despite the fact that most people use a variety of coping strategies when facing stressors, difficulties that can be changed or controlled tend to elicit more problem-focused efforts, whereas intractable problems tend to generate more strategies that are emotion focused (Taylor & Aspinwall, 1996). Escapist or avoidant strategies are consistently associated with poor mental health (Folkman & Moskowitz, 2004).

As Chapter 10 shows in more detail, coping resources (e.g., social support, self-esteem, sense of control) and certain types of coping strategies buffer or reduce the negative psychological impacts of stressors. This is why the relationship between stress exposure and psychological problems is far from perfect – in essence, people are able to protect themselves from being overwhelmed by stressful demands. However, some people are poorly equipped to protect themselves because they lack social support or a sense of control over their lives or have not acquired efficacious coping strategies. Of crucial importance to sociologists of mental health is the finding that life events and chronic strains, as well as social support, self-esteem, and a sense of mastery, are unequally distributed in the population, leaving some groups of people (e.g., women, the elderly, the very young, the unmarried, those of low socioeconomic status) both more likely to experience certain stressors and more vulnerable to the effects of stressors in general (Turner, 1995; Turner & Marino, 1994; Turner & Roszell, 1994). These key findings point very clearly to the important role that social factors can play in the etiology of mental illness and psychological distress. Moreover, they suggest an explanation for the higher rates of mental disorder and psychological distress found in lower status, disadvantaged groups (see Chapter 12) – these are the groups that are more likely to be exposed to stressors and less likely to have important coping resources.

The advantages of stress theory are several. First, the theory focuses on aspects of the individual's current social situation that the biological and psychological approaches tend to deemphasize or ignore as etiologically important. Second, it helps explain why psychological distress and disorder occur more frequently in lower status groups than in higher status groups, patterns that the biological and psychological perspectives have difficulty explaining parsimoniously. Third, stress theory allows for more direct empirical testing than the biological and psychological approaches do. Conventional survey and interview methods allow researchers to measure key concepts (e.g., stressors, coping resources, social support) and to test relationships among them explicitly, unlike biological studies in which researchers must infer from the effects of specific drugs an association between, for example, serotonin uptake and major depression. Similarly, psychological researchers must assume a relationship between childhood traumatic experiences and mental illness from the effects of psychotherapy, which often unearths such past experiences. Finally, as you will see in later chapters, considerable empirical evidence supports the stress explanation of psychological disturbance. Despite these advantages, however, the limitations of the theory should not be ignored.

One key limitation is that stress theory cannot explain why this person and not that one became mentally ill; in other words, it cannot explain individual cases of psychological disorder. Stress theory is better suited to explaining group differences in psychological problems – for example, why lower class persons are more likely to have a mental disorder in their lifetimes than are middle and upper class people or why individuals without social support are more vulnerable to stressors than people who have it. Second, stress theory is nonspecific with respect to outcomes; it does not explain why some groups are more prone to certain disorders, whereas other groups develop different disorders (for example, why women become depressed and anxious and why men develop antisocial personality disorder and more often abuse drugs and alcohol). Finally, the theory does not apply equally well to all types of mental disorders. Stress theory is most relevant to affective and anxiety disorders (i.e., mood-related disorders) and to adjustment disorders; people clearly become depressed or anxious in response to stressors or have trouble adjusting to them. It is more difficult to explain the etiology of psychoses with stress theory; psychoses by their very seriousness and complexity seem to require additional explanatory factors, such as genetic predisposition, imbalances of certain chemicals in the brain, and faulty childhood socialization. In short, to explain psychoses, and perhaps to explain most clinical disorders adequately, one might better employ diathesis-stress theory (Rosenthal, 1970), which posits that disorder is the result of a diathesis (technically, a constitutional or genetic weakness, but more generally used to mean "vulnerability") combined with exposure to stress. Diathesis-stress theory suggests that the experience of stress alone is not sufficient to cause mental disorder; instead, stressors may cause disorder when they occur along with other vulnerability factors in a person's body, psyche, or circumstances.

The treatment implications of stress theory are straightforward and quite different from biological and psychological approaches. To treat or prevent mental illness one needs to change the person's situation (i.e., eliminate or reduce stressors), teach the person different coping responses (i.e., encourage better management of stressors), or bolster his or her personal and social resources (i.e., increase available social support, raise self-esteem, or empower a stronger sense of control). Because directly changing people's life situations can be intrusive or expensive, interventions aimed at people's actual sources of stress are less frequently attempted than efforts aimed at enhancing their coping strategies or their personal and social resources. Some well-crafted experiments (see Caplan, Vinokur, & Price, 1997, for examples) have shown quite clearly that interventions to change people's coping strategies and to bolster their social support do, in fact, reduce their emotional reactions in response to major life events (e.g., a diagnosis of cancer, major surgery, divorce, unemployment). Thus, stress theory offers real promise for devising preventive mental health interventions.

Structural Strain Theory

Structural strain theory is an umbrella term that covers several more specific sociological hypotheses about mental illness etiology. In contrast to stress theory, which focuses on specific events and strains in people's social lives as causal, structural strain theory locates the origins of distress and disorder in the broader organization of society, in which some social groups are disadvantaged compared to others. Merton's (1938/1968) *anomie theory of deviance* provides a useful example of a structural strain theory.

Merton's anomie theory attempts to explain the occurrence of deviant behavior in general (including criminal, addictive, and rebellious behaviors), not just mental illness. Merton argued that American culture emphasizes success and wealth as important values; Americans are taught to desire and strive for economic success above almost all other goals. American society also views educational attainment as one key means, if not the key means, to economic success. Merton assumed that most people view the educational system as a legitimate route to the widely shared goal of financial success. Unfortunately, large segments of society also perceive (correctly) that their avenues to success are systematically blocked. The poor and minority group members live in neighborhoods with inadequate school facilities and poorly trained teachers; they lack the preparation, encouragement, and financial assistance to pursue higher education; and they experience class-based and race-based discrimination in schools and in the labor force, which defeats efforts to succeed while following legitimate paths.

Merton used the term *anomie* to describe the gap between cultural goals (e.g., desires for financial success) and the structural means to those goals (e.g., access to adequate education and employment). He argued that people who experience anomie adapt to that dilemma in one of several possible ways: by changing their

Table 6.2. *Merton's anomie theory of deviance:*
Responses to anomie

	Adherence to cultural goal of economic success	Seek legitimate means to success
Conformity	+	+
Ritualism	−	+
Innovation	+	−
Retreatism	−	−
Rebellion	+/−	+/−

Notes: +, acceptance; −, rejection; +/−, rejection and substitution of new goals and means.

goals, pursuing alternative means, or both. Merton described five adaptive responses, which are displayed in Table 6.2.

"Conformists" are people who continue to adhere to culturally shared goals and to pursue conventional means to those goals, despite the awareness that these efforts are unlikely to pay off. "Ritualists" are those who reduce their aspirations (give up the possibility of ever achieving success), yet continue to behave in socially acceptable ways (they perhaps finish high school and work steadily at some low-pay, low-prestige job). Neither conformist nor ritualist responses create major social problems. However, the remaining three adaptive responses are generally viewed as behaviorally deviant and hence socially problematic. "Innovators" are people who continue to desire and seek wealth, but resort to illegitimate means to reach that goal, rejecting legitimate means; innovators are essentially society's criminals, from simple thieves to executives engaged in fraud and tax evasion. "Retreatists" are those who give up the goal of success and who stop attempting to follow legitimate avenues. Instead, they retreat from the world into substance abuse or mental disorder. Finally, "rebels" are people who reject both the goals and the socially acceptable means to those goals and substitute both new goals and new avenues; these are people who lead or participate in social movements or, more threateningly, riots and rebellions. Although it is clear that Merton could have generated additional adaptive responses (a person could substitute new goals while following legitimate avenues, for example), the central point to be extracted from his analysis is this: Mental illness is an adaptive response to structural strain. Specifically, it is a response to finding one's legitimate roads to valued rewards irrevocably blocked. Importantly, that blockage is not due to one's own inadequacies but to the structure (hierarchical organization) of society, which unfairly privileges the desires and efforts of some social groups over others.

Like Merton's more general theory of deviance, most structural strain explanations of mental illness suggest that strains in macro (i.e., large-scale) social and economic systems cause higher rates of mental disorder or mental hospitalization for certain groups. Before Merton, Emile Durkheim, a French sociologist, analyzed the social causes of suicide, a behavior that on the surface seems highly psychological and individual in nature (1897/1951). Durkheim found unequal distributions of suicide within and across societies. For example, Protestants had higher rates of suicide than either Catholics or Jews; unmarried people, especially those without children, had higher rates than married people or parents; military men committed suicide at higher rates than civilians; and suicide rates were higher during times of rapid economic expansion and depression than during more stable economic periods, among many other patterns. Searching for an underlying explanatory factor, Durkheim eventually argued that groups and societies differ in their social integration, which he defined as the degree to which people are bound together and regulated by shared norms. He maintained that norms (i.e., rules that guide appropriate behavior in specific situations) serve to moderate our passions and sustain our ties to others, preventing our desires and emotional impulses from spiraling out of control. Members of groups that are weakly integrated, then, suffer from disappointment and misery because their escalating passions, unregulated by norms or relations with others, inevitably go unfulfilled. Durkheim called this kind of suicide "egoistic suicide," because individuals in poorly integrated groups are more likely to succumb to despair caused by unchecked and unfulfilled personal desires. On the other hand, Durkheim recognized that social integration can be too strong, leading some to commit what he called "altruistic suicide." In overly integrated groups, individuals subordinate their passions and impulses for the good of the group, adhering to strong rules that guide almost all aspects of daily experience (military life is a good example). When the group or society is threatened, its members are therefore more likely to sacrifice themselves for the community. Finally, Durkheim described "anomic suicide," a condition induced by rapid changes in social structure and breakdowns in norms. Durkheim's concept of anomie refers to a state of normlessness or normative confusion (notice that Merton's term "anomie" means something different, although related). Societies or groups undergoing rapid social or economic change (e.g., sudden increases in the divorce rate, sudden changes in the unemployment rate) frequently find that traditional rules for behavior no longer apply. The resulting sense of confusion or normlessness causes individuals' passions once again to become unregulated, often plunging them into disappointment and despair. In short, according to Durkheim, the cause of suicide resides in the degree to which a society's members are tied tightly or loosely together through shared normative expectations for behavior. A too weakly or too strongly integrated society and a society undergoing rapid change are conditions of structural (in this case, system-level) strain, manifested in noticeably higher rates of suicide in its members, relative to groups with moderate degrees of integration.

Evidence for Durkheim's structural theory of suicide has accumulated over the years. In a classic study, Faris and Dunham (1939) plotted the previous residences of all patients admitted to hospitals for schizophrenia and other psychoses in Chicago during the mid-1930s. They found clear patterns: Schizophrenic patients had lived in poor areas of the city, concentrated in the inner urban core, with high population turnover, a high percentage of rental apartments and boarding houses, and a high percentage of foreign-born (probably immigrant) residents. Thus, they lived in neighborhoods in which few people knew one other or formed lasting ties. Faris and Dunham concluded that schizophrenia was caused, in part, by social disorganization and the prolonged or excessive social isolation that it produced.[4] A dramatic example of the consequences of social disorganization can be found in Kai Erikson's study (1976a, 1976b) of the survivors of the 1972 Buffalo Creek flood in the Appalachian hills of West Virginia. Early on a Saturday morning after heavy rainfall, a dam constructed poorly by the Buffalo Mining Company crumbled and released tons of floodwater, which washed out 13 small coal mining communities in the valley below. Most people, still asleep, were caught by surprise. Many were injured, 125 people were killed, and literally everything in the floodwater's path was destroyed or swept away. Federal authorities trucked in hundreds of trailers to house surviving residents, freezing people in the scattered locations of their displacement for the next few years (the parallels to the aftermath of Hurricane Katrina in New Orleans in 2005 should be obvious). Through in-depth interviews with survivors, Erikson and other researchers found that the shocks of destruction and damage caused by the flood were compounded by the sudden and permanent loss of community. Connections with kin and long-term neighbors and friends were cut by the survivors' placements in haphazard emergency housing. Almost all of the survivors suffered from at least some symptoms of posttraumatic stress disorder, which took years to dissipate (Green, Grace, Vary, & Kramer, 1994; Green, Lindy, Grace, & Gleser, 1990). The Buffalo Creek flood is an example of Durkheim's concept of anomie – a sudden, massive structural change that produced a sense of normlessness in survivors, causing psychological harm over and above the stressful events of bereavement, injury, and property loss.

Erikson's study reminds us that structural strains need not be at the macro or system level to have consequences; they can be more proximate or local. In recent years, there has been a surge of interest in the impacts of local social structures,

---

[4] It should be noted that Dunham later repudiated the original study's conclusions. Dunham argued that schizophrenic patients' residences were likely a result of their mental disorder, rather than a cause of it (Dunham, 1965). In other words, he contended that disorganized neighborhoods do not produce mental health problems in residents; instead, disturbed persons selectively migrate into such neighborhoods because their poor mental health prevents them from having the jobs or money needed to live elsewhere. Although this is a plausible argument, the bulk of the evidence favors the causal influence of disorganized neighborhoods on mental health.

especially the effects of poor neighborhoods on residents' mental health. Poor neighborhoods are characterized by high rates of racial segregation, unemployment, single-headed families, residential instability, crime, and physical decay, among an array of other disadvantages. These features of neighborhood organization have distressing and depressing influences in themselves while also generating concrete difficulties in residents' lives and exacerbating the negative psychological consequences of their sparse social support, weak sense of control, and alienation (Aneshensel, 1996; Silver, Mulvey, & Swanson, 2002; Stockdale et al., 2007). Neighborhoods, in short, are contexts or structures that generate chronic strain as well as magnify community members' personal difficulties.

The theme of harmful consequences of social isolation or the lack of social integration recurs in these examples of structural strain. Up to this point, measures of social isolation have been at the group or aggregate, level (e.g., high rates of residential turnover, disruption in a community's organization). But social isolation can also be conceptualized and measured at the individual level, in terms of holding few social roles. *Roles* are sets of reciprocal rights and obligations attached to specific positions in the social structure, such as husband–wife, parent–child, teacher–student, and physician–patient. These rights and obligations tell incumbents how to act in relationships with other people and why they should do so. Thus, roles provide behavioral guidance and supply individuals with purpose and meaning in life (Thoits, 2003). Given this, people who have few or no social roles are at greater risk of engaging in deviant behavior (e.g., drug or alcohol abuse, aggressive or impulsive acts) and experiencing anxiety or despair. Considerable research to date confirms that holding multiple roles promotes psychological well-being; conversely, a lack of roles or social isolation is psychologically damaging (Thoits, 2003). Hence, even at the individual level, social isolation has mental health implications, consistent with Durkheim's original thesis developed long ago.

Note that stress theory implicitly underlies these examples of structural strain approaches. Structural theorists usually do not spell out the stress implications explicitly because their thinking and empirical research usually stay at the aggregate or group level (i.e., their studies examine percentages of female-headed families or rates of unemployment, for example, rather than examining individual people as cases). But it is fairly easy to see the implications of, say, high unemployment rates in a community for individuals who are living there. They may be increasingly anxious about losing their jobs; if they are laid off, they may have more trouble finding new jobs with steady pay; and persistent financial difficulties in turn may lead to marital conflict or lack of access to needed medical care, all of which are stressors that may overwhelm individuals' abilities to cope.

That stress theory is necessary to make the link between structural strains and mental health sensible is one of the weaknesses of structural approaches. Structural theorists generally do not elaborate the ways in which broad social structures and broad socioeconomic trends become actualized in the lives of specific individuals, and thus they do not clarify how or why macro social trends can produce psychological distress or disorder. Structural approaches, especially studies that focus on neighborhoods, also tend to emphasize class-related or socioeconomic disadvantages as etiologically crucial while neglecting the effects of other large-scale societal changes on mental health. For example, changing trends in the organization and quality of family relationships (e.g., high rates of divorce, more absentee fathers, and increasing numbers of parents or grandparents who are frail and elderly) may be particularly important structural sources of stress in people's lives.

On the other hand, structural strain theories have advantages. The most important is the unique contribution they make to theories of mental illness etiology. As mentioned earlier, mental illness is not randomly distributed in society; it is concentrated in several demographic groups that are socially and economically disadvantaged or low in power and influence. The theory suggests that the very structure or organization of society itself may play a role in the epidemiology and etiology of mental illness, which is an idea that stress theory, for example, does not capture well and psychological and biological theories miss altogether. (Stress theorists certainly recognize but usually do not capitalize on the idea that stressors may themselves be a product of the very way our society is organized.) If our goal is to understand thoroughly the complex and multiple causes of mental illness, then the strains induced by social systems, social institutions, and community contexts surely must be taken into account.

Structural strain theory suggests that to prevent or reduce mental illness in society one must intervene in fairly large-scale ways, for example, by combating racial segregation, bolstering access to college education, buffering spikes in the unemployment rate, and expanding services for the elderly. Such system-level solutions to prevent mental illness require massive (and thus usually expensive) social programs that are difficult for legislators to pass and fund; therefore, the preventive implications of structural strain theory usually go untested and untried (although there have been social experiments that provide guaranteed incomes to poor and working-class families; see Robins, Spiegelman, Weiner, & Bell, 1980, for an example). However, given recent evidence of the importance of local neighborhood contexts for the mental health of their residents, more delimited community-focused interventions might be economically and politically feasible, which target problematic aspects of neighborhood life to better promote members' social integration and well-being.

Labeling Theory

Like structural strain theory, *labeling theory* (sometimes called societal reaction theory) offers a uniquely sociological explanation of the causes of mental illness;

some have described it as a radical sociological explanation. The theory has had enormous intellectual impact and has played an important role in the movement to deinstitutionalize the mentally ill.

Labeling theory is based on one key idea: People who are labeled as deviant and treated as deviant become deviant. *Deviance* refers to violation of norms or rule-breaking. In the case of mental illness, symptoms of psychiatric disorder are themselves viewed as normative violations. Symptoms essentially break taken-for-granted rules (Scheff, 1984) about how people should think, feel, and behave (for example, it is not appropriate to believe that the Central Intelligence Agency is tapping your phones; you should not constantly feel anxious or depressed; you should not run naked and screaming through the streets).

Labeling theorists (Becker, 1973; Lemert, 1951; Scheff, 1984) assume that everyone violates norms at some time in his or her life for any of a multitude of reasons. Reasons for rule-breaking can include biological causes (e.g., fatigue, undernourishment, genetic abnormalities, illness), psychological causes (e.g., unhappy childhood, a need for attention, internal conflicts, low self-esteem), sociological causes (e.g., role conflict, peer pressure, exposure to stressors), cultural causes (e.g., following subcultural norms that differ from those of the dominant society), economic causes (e.g., a need for money, buying prestige in the eyes of others), and even miscellaneous reasons (e.g., carelessness, accidents, sheer ignorance of the rules). Labeling theorists regard these various causes of primary deviance (initial rule-breaking acts, in this case, psychological symptoms) as relatively unimportant. What matters is how the social group reacts to an individual's primary deviance. This is why the theory is often called "societal reaction theory."

Most often, rule-breaking acts are ignored, denied, or rationalized away by family, friends, and the rule-breakers themselves, and (according to the theory) those primary acts are then rarely repeated. However, when individuals' norm violations are frequent, severe, or highly visible, or when rule-breakers are low in power and status relative to "agents of social control" (i.e., police, social workers, judges, psychiatrists), rule-breakers are much more likely to be publicly and formally labeled as deviant (in this case, mentally ill) and forced into treatment.

Why is public, official labeling so important? That is because, once labeled and in psychiatric care, rule-breakers begin to experience differential treatment on the basis of their label (Rosenhan, 1973). People labeled as mentally ill or disturbed are stereotypically viewed as unpredictable, dangerous to themselves or others, unable to engage in self-care, and likely to behave in bizarre ways (Scheff, 1984). These still-common stereotypes cause others, even mental hospital staff, to treat patients as though they were irresponsible children (Goffman, 1961; Rosenhan, 1973). Mental patients hear jokes about crazy people, are reminded of their past failures or inadequacies, and are prevented from resuming conventional adult activities (e.g., leaving the hospital grounds without permission, using the showers or a razor without staff present, making private phone calls, driving a car, returning to work, voting, or seeing family or friends at will). One consequence of differential treatment, then, is blocked access to normal activities. Differential treatment also leads to association with similar deviants. In hospitals or treatment centers, patients spend more time in the company of other mental patients than with nonpatients. This increased contact in turn allows socialization into the subculture of mental patients; one learns a deviant world view, or a deviant set of values, which reinforces adopting a simple life within the safe, protective walls of the hospital or outpatient day program (Braginsky, Braginsky, & Ring, 1969; Estroff, 1981; Goffman, 1961).

The unfortunate outcome of differential treatment, according to labeling theory, is identification with the mental patient role: one takes on the identity of a mentally ill person. And because this identity becomes "who I am," mental patients continue to expect psychiatric symptoms from themselves and to exhibit symptoms. In labeling theory terms, the patient displays secondary deviance or continued rule-breaking (i.e., continued abnormal behavior or symptoms) because he or she has internalized and identified with the patient role. This process is an example of a "self-fulfilling prophecy" (Merton, 1938/1968). In short, people who are labeled as deviant and treated as deviant become deviant. Mental illness becomes the issue around which one's identity and life become organized – it becomes a "deviant career."

Why the theory has sometimes been described as radically sociological may now be clear: it turns our usual causal thinking about mental illness on its head. Deviance or mental illness is not "in" the person's biology or psyche, nor even is it primarily caused by the individual's life situation. Instead, mental illness is created and sustained by society itself. In his book *Outsiders*, Becker (1973, p. 9) sums it up this way:

> Social groups create deviance by making rules whose infraction constitutes deviance, and by applying those rules to particular people and labeling them as outsiders. From this point of view, deviance is not a quality of the act the person commits, but rather a consequence of the application by others of rules and sanctions to an "offender." The deviant is one to whom that label has been successfully applied; deviant behavior is behavior that people so label.

Essentially, then, chronic mental patients are victims of labeling and differential treatment by others and would not be chronic patients otherwise.

There is a more subtle process by which mental illness labels can have deleterious consequences. In his "modified labeling theory," Bruce Link (1987; Link, Cullen, Frank, & Wozniak, 1987) has argued that outright rejection and discrimination by other people are not necessary for a self-fulfilling prophecy to occur. Instead, persons who have been diagnosed and hospitalized are well aware that negative stereotypes of mental patients are generally held by the public (Link et al., 1999). These stereotypes take on acute personal significance once the patient has been discharged back into the community. Because the former mental patient expects rejection and discrimination from other people, he or she engages in at least one of three coping strategies: (1) avoiding contact with other people, (2) concealing information about his or her psychiatric past, and (3) attempting to educate others about mental illness to combat their stereotypes. Link shows that these strategies tend to backfire, leaving former patients isolated, demoralized, and distressed and with fewer employment opportunities. Thus, expectations of rejection are sufficient to start a negative self-fulfilling process, regardless of the actual reactive behaviors of other people.

Link and Phelan's Chapter 29 elaborates on labeling theory, presenting the evidence both for and against various tenets of the theory. For now it is sufficient simply to point out that there are several limitations to and problems with the theory in its original formulation. Clearly, classic labeling theory best applies to patients who have been involuntarily committed to treatment and to those who have become chronically ill. Because a majority of patients seek treatment voluntarily (Pescosolido, Gardner, & Lubell, 1998) and most episodes of disorder are short-lived, the theory has limited explanatory power. The theory does not explain how or why individuals voluntarily self-label and seek treatment (although see Thoits, 1985). It tends to ignore the crucial role of informal labeling by family members and neighbors; mental patients are usually brought to psychiatric attention through the tentative preliminary labeling of these "unofficial" agents of social control. Also problematic are two implicit assumptions of the theory. One is that a behavior or symptom will usually stop if it is not labeled. This is an assumption that flies in the face of casual observation as well as considerable evidence. The other problematic assumption is that labeling and differential treatment are the key causes of continued psychiatric symptoms (Scheff, 1984); this implies that the initial causes of psychological symptoms (biological, psychological, sociological, and so on) cease to have major influences on the individual's thoughts, feelings, or behaviors after labeling has occurred – which of course is not a sensible implication. In short, the theory in its original form probably overestimated considerably the importance of labeling as a cause of sustained mental disorder. Link's modification of the theory supplies a more realistic account of how fears of rejection and discrimination can start a harmful self-fulfilling process.

Although flawed, labeling theory still has major advantages. Perhaps most important, it has sensitized psychiatric social workers, psychiatrists, and judges to the potential for bias or error in diagnostic judgments when patients are poor, female, elderly, or minority group members (i.e., low in power and status). Relatedly, state laws have been revised to make involuntary commitments more difficult, giving the accused access to legal representation and ensuring that involuntary hospitalization lasts no longer than so many days without a formal review (Gove, 1982). Labeling theory has also made policymakers and hospital administrators more aware of the problem of "institutional syndrome," in which long-term patients become overly dependent on hospital staff, unable to care for themselves, and passive and compliant as a result of their hospital experience. One of the goals of the deinstitutionalization movement was to prevent institutional syndrome by moving patients back into the community before they became overly dependent on the hospital. Labeling theory is especially valuable because it reminds us that mental illness is, to some extent, socially created and sustained and that there are risks to accepting psychiatrists' judgments as invariably valid assessments of mental disorder. Wrongful commitments can occur and societal reactions based on stereotypes can make the experience of disturbance more severe and potentially more long-lasting. Finally, strong evidence for the existence and negative effects of stigma has accumulated.

The treatment implications of labeling theory are quite different from those of stress and structural strain approaches. Potential ways to reduce or prevent mental illness include changing social norms that define "normal" thoughts, feelings, and behaviors; attacking widely held misperceptions of the mentally ill; avoiding the formal diagnosis and hospitalization of individuals for aberrant behavior; and reducing the length of stay of hospitalized individuals to prevent them from acquiring a deviant identity. Although many of the treatment and preventive implications of labeling theory seem overly idealistic – you will learn more about the (mostly negative) consequences of deinstitutionalization in Part III of this volume – the theory remains important for its sensitizing, critical perspective on psychiatric diagnosis, mental hospital life, and the stigma attached to mental illness, which is as strong today, if not stronger, than 50 years ago (Pescosolido et al., 2008b; Phelan, Link, Stueve, & Pescosolido, 2000).

Integrating the Three Sociological Theories

By this point, the careful reader might see how the three dominant sociological explanations of mental illness could be integrated. Structural strain theories suggest that the ways in which societies, institutions, and neighborhoods are organized create general patterns of advantage or risk for particular social groups. Stress theory bridges the gap between macro structures and micro (i.e., individual-level) experiences by explaining how structured risks become actualized in the lives of individuals as stressful experiences. According to stress theory, when events and strains accumulate in people's lives, they can overwhelm people's psychosocial resources and abilities to cope and then generate symptoms of psychological disorder (primary deviance, in labeling theory's terms). Labeling theory picks up at this point and suggests that frequent, severe, or highly visible symptoms, or symptoms exhibited by those with little social prestige or power, can launch a victimizing process. Societal reactions to symptoms may result in the person's receiving a formal psychiatric diagnosis, becoming hospitalized, and, ultimately, accepting a mental patient identity. Alternatively, fears of rejection may lead former psychiatric patients to adopt dysfunctional coping strategies that perpetuate their isolation and disturbance. As mentioned earlier, however, evidence shows that chronic patienthood is not an inevitable consequence of labeling processes, despite the assertions of labeling theorists to the contrary (e.g., Scheff, 1984). Explaining how and why the majority of people who have been diagnosed and hospitalized do not become chronically mentally ill is the next theoretical task for sociologists to tackle.

Concluding Commentary

It is important to remember that sociological theories of etiology do not claim to explain fully the causes of mental illness. No single approach to mental illness – biological, psychological, or sociological – can completely explain its origins. For example, even if deficits of certain neurotransmitters in the brain were shown to be directly responsible for major depression (a biological explanation), the onset of a depressive episode is probably due to multiple factors operating simultaneously: a person's gender, age, social class, current stressful experiences, past unresolved psychological conflicts, and a strain-producing structural context. Each broad theoretical approach to mental illness tends to focus on only certain kinds of causes (biological, psychological, or sociological ones), and thus each approach inadvertently deemphasizes the importance of other causes. Although we focus on sociological approaches in this volume, the intention is not to downplay the importance of other causal factors. Instead, the goal is to deepen and elaborate your appreciation of the sociological factors involved in the causes, consequences, treatment, and prevention of mental illness because these sociological factors are the most likely to be ignored or neglected in the field of mental health in general. Mental illness is not randomly distributed in the population, but is socially patterned. Patients in treatment are not a random set of individuals, but once again are socially patterned. Effective treatments, excellent hospitals, and beneficial community services are not equally available, but yet again are socially patterned. Grasping the impact of these social inequalities in the experience of mental disorder, in the quest for treatment, and in the availability of mental health services is crucial for a well-rounded understanding of the causes and consequences of mental disorder.

7

Viewing Mental Health from the Complete State Paradigm

Corey L. M. Keyes and Barret Michalec

Is illness more serious than health? Is it enough to seek cures, treatment, and protection from disease and illness as the way toward achieving better mental health in the U.S. population? If your answers to both questions are yes, then the complete state model and research should lead you to reconsider your position. Everyone who studies health is familiar with the World Health Organization's 1948 definition of health as "not merely the absence of disease and infirmity" but also the presence of various forms of well-being. Clearly, health has been viewed as a complete state for a long time. However, until recently there was no body of empirical research that tested hypotheses that flow from the complete state model. Why? Public health policy aspires to create health in the population and therefore to direct all resources toward reducing illness. We operate "as if " health were the absence of illness, suggesting that health and illness belong to a single latent measurement continuum. In contrast, the complete state model predicts that measures of positive mental health reflect a separate latent measurement continuum (the "salutogenic" factor, where *salus* means the presence of health) from measures of mental illness, which belong to a second latent measurement continuum (the "pathogenic" factor, where *pathos* means the presence of illness). The problem, we are led to believe, is that we know little about mental illness, and what we know either does not get translated into practical solutions soon enough or those solutions are not accessible. Perhaps another problem is with our starting assumptions about health, particularly whether research supports the "dual continua" model of mental health and mental illness. What this research has shown thus far is that (1) the absence of mental illness does not translate into the presence of mental health and (2) that any condition less than "flourishing" (which is the absence of mental illness and the presence of sufficiently high levels of subjective well-being) results in elevated "burden" to self and society (e.g., missed workdays and more disability). Moreover, the dual continua model suggests that causes of true mental health may be distinct processes from those now understood as causes of mental illness. Rather than intensifying the exclusive focus on mental illness, nations must adopt two complementary approaches to tackle the problem of mental illness and achieve the goal of increasing their populations' mental health: (1) protecting and promoting flourishing mental health while (2) improving the prevention and treatment of mental illness.

Introduction

There have been at least three conceptions of health throughout human history. The *pathogenic* approach is the first, most historically dominant vision, derived from the Greek word *pathos*, meaning suffering or an emotion evoking sympathy. The pathogenic approach views health as the absence of disability, disease, and premature death. The second approach is the *salutogenic* approach, which can be found in early Greek and Roman writings and was popularized by Antonovsky (1979) and humanistic scholars (e.g., Abraham Maslow). Derived from the word *salus*, the Latin word for health, the salutogenic approach views health as the presence of positive states of human capacities and functioning in thinking, feeling, and behavior (Strümpfer, 1995). The third approach is the complete state model, which derives from the ancient word for health as being *hale*, meaning whole. This approach is exemplified in the World Health Organization's (1948) definition of overall health as a complete state, consisting of the presence of the positive state of human capacities and functioning as well as the absence of disease or infirmity.

By combining the pathogenic and salutogenic paradigms, the complete state approach is the only paradigm that can achieve true population mental health. This chapter illustrates the model of health as a complete state through a review of research on mental health as a complete state. Borrowing from the World Health Organization's (1948) definition of health, here we define mental health as not merely the absence of psychopathology but also the presence of sufficient levels of emotional, psychological, and social well-being (Keyes, 2002, 2005a, 2005b).

Mental Health as "Something Positive"

Until recently, mental health as something more than the absence of psychopathology remained undefined, unmeasured, and therefore unrecognized at the level of governments and nongovernmental organizations. In 1999, the Surgeon General, then Dr. David Satcher, conceived of mental health as "a state of successful performance of mental function, resulting in productive activities, fulfilling relationships with people, and the ability to adapt to change and to cope with adversity" (Surgeon General, 1999, p. 4). In 2004, the WHO published a historic first report on mental health promotion, conceptualizing mental health as not merely the absence of mental illness but also as the presence of "a state of well-being in which the individual realizes his or her own abilities, can cope with the normal stresses of life, can work productively and fruitfully, and is able to make a contribution to his or her community" (World Health Organization, 2004, p. 12).

These definitions affirmed the existing behavioral and social scientific vision of mental health as not merely the absence of mental illness but also as the presence of something positive (e.g., Gurin, Veroff, & Feld, 1960; Jahoda, 1958). Social and psychological scientists have been studying "something positive" in the domain of subjective well-being – individuals' evaluations and judgment of their own lives – for roughly 50 years (Keyes, 2006). This research has yielded as many as 13 specific dimensions of well-being in the U.S. population. Using factor analysis, studies have shown that the manifold scales measuring subjective well-being represent the latent structure of hedonic well-being (i.e., positive emotions

Table 7.1. *Factors and dimensions reflecting mental health as flourishing*

Hedonia
Emotional well-being
  1) *Positive affect*: is cheerful, interested in life, in good spirits, happy, calm and peaceful, full of life
  2) *Avowed quality of life:* is mostly or highly satisfied with life overall or in domains of life positive functioning
  3) *Self-acceptance:* holds positive attitudes toward self, acknowledges and likes most parts of self, personality
  4) *Personal growth:* seeks challenge, has insight into own potential, feels a sense of continued development
  5) *Purpose in life:* finds own life has a direction and meaning
  6) *Environmental mastery:* exercises ability to select, manage, and mold personal environs to suit needs
  7) *autonomy:* is guided by own, socially accepted, internal standards and values
  8) *Positive relations with others:* has, or can form, warm, trusting personal relationships
  9) *Social acceptance:* holds positive attitudes toward, acknowledges, and is accepting of human differences
 10) *Social actualization:* believes people, groups, and society have potential and can evolve or grow positively
 11) *Social contribution:* sees own daily activities as useful to and valued by society and others
 12) *Social coherence:* has interest in society and social life and finds them meaningful and somewhat intelligible
 13) *Social integration:* has a sense of belonging to, and comfort and support from, a community

toward one's life) and eudaimonic well-being (i.e., psychological well-being and social well-being) in adults (Keyes, Shmotkin, & Ryff, 2002; McGregor & Little, 1998; Ryan & Deci, 2001) and adolescents (Keyes, 2005c).

Subjective well-being research yielded clusters of mental health symptoms that mirror the cluster of symptoms used in the DSM-IV-TR (American Psychiatric Association, 2000) to diagnose a major depressive episode (MDE; see Table 7.1). In the same way that depression requires symptoms of *an*-hedonia, mental health consists of symptoms of hedonia such as emotional vitality and positive feelings toward one's life. In the same way that major depression consists of symptoms of *mal*-functioning, mental health consists of symptoms of positive functioning.

The diagnosis of states of mental health was modeled after the DSM-III-R approach to diagnosing MDE (Keyes, 2002). Each measure of subjective well-being is considered a symptom insofar as it represents an outward sign of an unobservable state. In the absence of specific diagnostic tests, underlying conditions must be inferred from symptoms. Lacking specific diagnostic tests, mental health and mental illnesses remain identifiable only as collections of signs and symptoms that, as a syndrome, reflect an underlying state of health or illness.

To be diagnosed as flourishing in life, individuals must exhibit high levels on at least one measure of hedonic well-being and high levels on at least six measures of positive functioning. Individuals who exhibit low levels on at least one measure of hedonic well-being and low levels on at least six measures of positive functioning are diagnosed as languishing in life. Adults who are moderately mentally healthy do not fit the criteria for either flourishing or languishing in life. A continuous assessment sums all measures of mental health that are then coded into 10-point ranges after the Global Assessment of Functioning (GAF) approach in the DSM-III-R. For reasons reviewed by Kessler (2002) in the domain of psychopathology, we have used – and would recommend that others use – both the categorical and continuous assessments for mental health for two reasons: Each approach provides valuable information, and using both enables one to see whether results and conclusions vary by approach.

The following sections consist of reviews of several published papers using data from the MacArthur Foundation's 1995 Midlife in the United States survey (MIDUS). This survey was a random-digit-dialing sample of noninstitutionalized English-speaking adults between the ages of 25 to 74 living in the 48 contiguous states. The MIDUS used DSM-III-R (American Psychiatric Association, 1987) criteria to diagnose four mental disorders – MDE, panic, generalized anxiety, and alcohol dependence – that were operationalized by the Composite International Diagnostic Interview Short Form (CIDI-SF) scales (Kessler, Andrews, et al., 1998).

Mental Health Is More Than the Absence of Mental Illness

Confirmatory factor analysis was used to test the theory that the MIDUS measures of mental health and mental illness belong to two latent continua. Three scales served as indicators of mental health: the summed scale of emotional well-being (i.e., single item of satisfaction + scale of positive affect; items 1–2 in Table 7.1), the summed scale of psychological well-being (i.e., six scales summed together; items 3–8 in Table 7.1), and the summed scale of social well-being (i.e., five scales summed together; items 9–13 in Table 7.1). Four summary measures served as indicators of mental illness as operationalized as the number of symptoms of MDE, generalized anxiety, panic disorder, and alcohol dependence.

Two competing theories – the single-factor and the two-factor model – were tested. The single-factor model hypothesizes that the measures of mental health and mental illness reflect a single latent factor, support for which would indicate that the absence of mental illness implies the presence of mental health. The two-factor model hypothesizes that the measures of subjective well-being represent the latent factor of mental health that is distinct from, but correlated with, the latent factor of mental illness that is represented by the measures of mental illness. The two-factor – or *dual continua*– model supports the complete state approach to mental health, because it implies that mental health is more than the absence of mental illness. The data strongly supported the two-factor model, which fitted nearly perfectly to the MIDUS data (Keyes, 2005a).

DSM 12-Month Mental Illness Diagnosis	Mental Health Assessment		
	Languishing	Moderate	Flourishing
No	*Mentally Unhealthy*	*Moderately Mentally Healthy*	*Complete Mental Health*
Yes	*Mental Illness and Languishing*	*Mental Illness with Moderate Mental Health*	*Mental Illness but Flourishing*

Figure 7.1. Diagnostic categories of the complete mental health model.

The latent factor of mental illness correlated −.53 with the latent factor of mental health. Although there is a tendency for mental health to improve as mental illness symptoms decrease, this connection is relatively modest. Languishing adults had the highest prevalence of any of the four mental disorders as well as the highest prevalence of reporting two or more mental disorders during the past year. In contrast, flourishing individuals had the lowest prevalence of any of the four 12-month mental disorders or their comorbidity. Compared with languishing or flourishing individuals, moderately mentally healthy adults were at intermediate risk of having any of the mental disorders or of having two or more mental disorders during the past year. The modest correlation between the latent continua reflects the tendency for the risk of mental illness to increase as mental health decreases. For example, the 12-month risk of MDE is more than five times greater for languishing than for flourishing adults.

Support for the two-factor model provides the strongest scientific evidence to date in support of the complete health approach to mental health. That is, the evidence indicates that the absence of mental illness does not imply the presence of mental health and the absence of mental health does not imply the presence of mental illness (see Greenspoon & Saklofske, 2001; Headey, Kelley, & Wearing, 1993; and Suldo & Shaffer, 2008, for additional support of the dual continua model). Thus, neither the pathogenic (i.e., focus on the negative) nor salutogenic (i.e., focus on the positive) approaches alone accurately describe the mental health of a population. Rather, mental health is a complete state that is best studied though the combined assessments of mental health with mental illness. Complete mental health, as shown in Figure 7.1, is a state in which individuals are free of mental illness and are flourishing. Of course, flourishing may sometimes occur with an episode of mental illness, and moderate mental health and languishing can both occur with and without a mental illness. In papers published to date, individuals with a mental illness who were moderately mentally healthy or flourishing were collapsed into one group, because few flourishing individuals report an episode of mental illness and pooling these groups did not affect the results.

Mental Health as Flourishing Is Good for Society

Research has supported the hypothesis that anything less than complete mental health results in increased impairment and disability (Keyes, 2002, 2004, 2005a, 2005b). Adults who were diagnosed as completely mentally healthy functioned in a superior manner to all others in terms of the fewest workdays missed, fewest half-days or fewer cutbacks of work, lowest level of health limitations of activities of daily living, fewest chronic physical diseases and conditions, lowest health care utilization, and highest levels of psychosocial functioning. In terms of psychosocial functioning, completely mentally healthy adults reported the lowest level of perceived helplessness (e.g., low perceived control in life) and the highest levels of functional goals (e.g., knowing what they want from life), self-reported resilience (e.g., learning from adversities), and intimacy (e.g., feeling very close with family and friends). In terms of all of these measures, completely mentally healthy adults functioned better than adults with moderate mental health, who in turn functioned better than adults who were languishing.

Adults with a mental illness who were also classified as moderately mentally healthy or flourishing reported more workdays missed or more work cutbacks than languishing adults. However, languishing adults reported the same level of health limitations of daily living and worse levels of psychosocial functioning than adults with a mental illness who also had moderate mental health or were flourishing. Individuals who were completely mentally ill (i.e., languishing and with one or more of the mental disorders) functioned worse than all others on every criterion. In general, adults with a mental illness who also had either moderate mental health or were flourishing functioned no worse than adults who were languishing and did not have a mental disorder. Thus, mental illness, when combined with languishing, is more crippling than when it occurs in the context of moderate mental health or flourishing.

The complete mental health diagnostic states have been shown to be independent risk factors for cardiovascular disease (CVD; Keyes, 2004). This study focused on the combination of the categorical diagnosis of mental health with major depressive episode, because the latter has been shown to be a risk factor for heart and arterial diseases. The unadjusted prevalence of any CVD was 8% among completely mentally healthy adults, compared with 12% of adults with moderate mental health, 12% of adults who were languishing, and 13% of adults with "pure" depression (i.e., those who had MDE but also fit the criteria for moderate mental health or flourishing). Among adults who were languishing and had an episode of major depression, the prevalence of any CVD was 19%. In multivariate analyses, completely mentally healthy adults had the lowest risk of CVD. In fact, adults who fit the criteria for anything less than complete mental health had levels of relative risk for CVD that were comparable to the relative risk associated with diabetes, smoking cigarettes, and lack of physical exercise.

A recent paper (Keyes, 2005b) investigated the association of the complete mental health diagnoses with chronic physical conditions and with age. The MIDUS study included self-reported assessments of 27 chronic physical health conditions adapted from the Medical Outcomes Study. The complete mental health diagnosis was associated with 85% of the chronic physical conditions measured in the MIDUS study; note that this paper focused only on major depressive disorder as the form of mental illness. The prevalence of chronic physical conditions was highest among adults who were languishing and had an episode of major depression, and lowest among completely mentally healthy adults. The prevalence of chronic physical conditions was slightly higher among moderately mentally healthy adults than completely mentally healthy adults, whereas languishing adults reported even more chronic conditions than adults with moderate mental health.

Overall, adults with major depression and languishing had an average of 4.5 chronic conditions. Adults with depression but who also had moderate mental health or were flourishing had an average of 3.1 chronic conditions, which was the same as adults who were languishing but without any mental illness. Moderately mentally healthy adults without any mental illness had an average of 2.1 chronic conditions, compared with adults with complete mental health who had on average 1.5 chronic conditions. Multivariate regression analyses confirmed that, when compared against completely mental healthy adults, chronic physical conditions increased as the level of mental health decreased. It is noteworthy that mental health status was a significant predictor of chronic physical conditions even after adjustment for the usual sociodemographic variables as well as body mass index, diabetes status, smoking status, and level of physical exercise.

Multivariate analyses also revealed statistically significant interactions of age with two of the complete mental health diagnostic states. Although chronic physical conditions increased with age, there were two interaction effects: pure languishing by age and languishing with an episode of major depression by age. Young languishing adults had an average of 1 more chronic condition than young flourishing adults; languishing adults in midlife reported an average of about 1.7 more conditions than flourishing midlife adults; and languishing older adults had an average of 2.6 more chronic conditions than flourishing older adults. Similarly, young languishing adults with MDE reported an average of 2.6 more chronic conditions than flourishing young adults, midlife languishing adults with MDE had an average of 3.5 more conditions than flourishing midlife adults, and languishing older adults who also had MDE had an average of 4.2 more chronic conditions than flourishing older adults.

In short, adults who were completely mentally healthy had the lowest number of chronic physical conditions at all ages. Moreover, the youngest adults who were languishing had the same number of chronic physical conditions as older flourishing adults. Younger languishing adults who also had MDE had 1.5 more chronic conditions than older flourishing adults. In other words, the absence of mental health – whether it is pure languishing or languishing combined with a mental illness – seems to compound the risk of chronic physical disease with age.

In turn, we (Keyes & Grzywacz, 2005) have found health care utilization to be lowest among adults who are flourishing. Rates of overnight hospitalizations over the past year, outpatient medical visits over the past year, and number of prescription drugs were lowest among adults who were flourishing and physically healthy, followed by adults who were either flourishing but had physical illness conditions or adults who were not flourishing but were physically healthy. In short, complete mental health (i.e., flourishing and the absence of mental illness) should be central to any national debate about health care coverage and costs. Rather than focusing all discussions around health care delivery and insurance, our nation must also increase and protect the number of individuals who are healthy, thereby driving down the need for health care.

Complete Mental Health: Abundant or Scarce?

Evidence to date suggests that flourishing, a central component of complete mental health, is a desirable condition that any community, corporation, or government would want to protect or promote in its citizens. Yet, how much of the adult population is actually mentally healthy?

Figure 7.2 presents the point prevalence estimates previously reported in Keyes (2005a) with two exceptions. First, it reports the prevalence of the relatively rare but important group of adults who, despite flourishing, reported at least one or more mental disorders. Second, it also contains the ideal distribution of the various categories of mental health and illness in the population. Although arbitrary, this ideal distribution suggests that any country purporting to value and promote health should create a skewed distribution in which flourishing is the most abundant category of people in a population.

If close is good enough, the current approach to national mental health is succeeding, as approximately one-half of the adult population is moderately mentally healthy. However, because true mental health should be our goal, the current approach to national mental health is a failure, because only 17% of adults are completely mentally healthy. Worse yet, 10% of adults are mentally *un*healthy, as they are languishing and did not fit the criteria for any of the four mental disorders

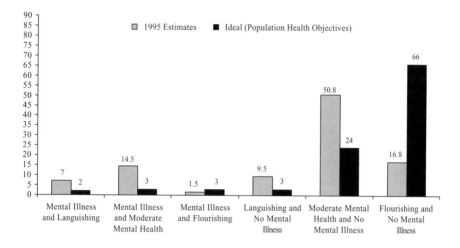

Figure 7.2. Point prevalence of complete mental health in the U.S. adult population, ages 25–74 in 1995 (data from Keyes, 2005a) compared with the ideal distribution.

(and they averaged about one symptom of mental illness, suggesting that languishers may not be subsyndromal). In addition, 23% of adults fit the criteria for one or more of the four mental disorders measured in the MIDUS. Of that 23%, 7% had a mental illness and fit the criteria for languishing, 14.5% had moderate mental health, and 1.5% were flourishing.

The disparities in Figure 7.2 between the actual and ideal point prevalence provide strong justification for continued national investment in the reduction of mental illness. However, they also suggest the need for new investments in the promotion of mental health as flourishing. The cluster of the adult population with moderate mental health and its proximity to being completely mentally healthy suggest one of the most potentially cost-effective leverage points for increasing national mental health. Evidence reviewed earlier suggests that reducing the size of the moderate mental health group by increasing its mental health could substantially reduce direct (e.g., health care usage) and indirect (e.g., workdays missed) costs.

Conclusions

There is mounting evidence that the paradigm of mental health research and services in the United States must shift toward the complete state approach in the 21st century. First, measures of mental illness and measures of mental health form two distinct continua in the U.S. population. Second, measures of disability, chronic physical illness, psychosocial functioning, and health care utilization reveal that anything less than flourishing is associated with increased impairment and burden to the self and society. Third, only a small proportion of those otherwise free of a common mental disorder are mentally healthy (i.e., flourishing).

Put simply, the absence of mental illness is not the presence of mental health; flourishing individuals function markedly better than all others. Yet, barely one-fifth of the U.S. adult population is actually flourishing. The U.S. strategy for mental health must continue to seek to prevent and treat cases of mental illness, but it must simultaneously seek to understand how to promote flourishing in individuals who are not mentally healthy but are otherwise free of mental illness.

8

Mental Health Systems in a Cross-Cultural Context

Harriet P. Lefley

Concepts of mental health, distinctions between mental health and mental illness, and distinctions between mental and physical illness are highly variable across cultures. Lefley examines the cultural context of defining mental health and mental illness. The first part of the chapter explores the relationship between culture and the experience of stress and describes a variety of culture-bound syndromes. The second part of the chapter turns to international research and provides an integration of its empirical findings. The third part focuses on cultural diversity in mental health service systems and describes the important role played by social stressors, ethnicity, and minority and refugee status. It contrasts the traditional and biomedical healing systems and describes the Italian experiment to improve the quality of life of persons with mental illness. Self-help groups and the consumer movement have also emerged internationally, and the chapter examines some of these movements. The chapter concludes by considering the future of mental health services and the merging of Western concepts with that of the developing world. Is there a universal or optimal way to describe mental health and illness? Students should consider variability among meanings attached to mental health and illness.

Introduction

In this chapter I deal with culture as a major variable in the conceptualization, development, and administration of mental health systems. The study of culture has typically focused on the beliefs, values, symbolic meanings, and normative behavioral practices of a specific human group. But in social science research today, cultural groups are usually categorized and compared along axes such as Western versus non-Western or modern versus traditional. In recent years there has been increasing attention to differentiating individualistic cultures, which give primacy to individual rights, from collectivist or sociocentric cultures that focus on group loyalties and social role obligations (Triandis, 1995). These respective modes of categorization in many ways tend to distinguish the wealthier, industrialized nations from the developing world. Thus they represent not only differences in world view and norms but also in resources available for the provision and structure of health care. Within nation-states, modal cultural attitudes as well as intergroup differences may shape the accessibility, appropriateness, and effectiveness of services for population subgroups such as racial or ethnic minorities (Takeuchi, Uehara, & Maramba, 1999).

Cultural belief systems determine whether specific behaviors are identified as deviant and the types of deviance that are classified as illness. These beliefs inform concepts of etiology and cure, as well as the designation of appropriate healers. In any cultural system, modal concepts of mental illness, help-seeking paths, and utilization patterns are intermeshed with the organization and structure of service delivery systems. Belief systems, value orientations, religious and medical practices, social organization, and family structure are related to the modes of developing and delivering services to persons identified as needing interventions. Additionally, a culture's assessed needs for social control and order, its prevailing political philosophies and legal protections, and its economic organization and resources have a significant impact on the structure of mental health service delivery systems (Lefley, 1994).

Concepts of mental health, distinctions between mental health and mental illness, and distinctions between mental and physical illness are highly variable across cultures. These conceptualizations generally determine the nature of the resources devoted to their service. Almost all cultures in the world, from tribal units to nation-states, recognize an officially sanctioned Western medical and mental health system. The people in these nations, and often the governments themselves, also support a variety of traditional healing systems. Most of these systems focus on the curing of illness or disability rather than on the diffuse concept of promoting mental health.

Cultural Context of Defining Mental Health

Psychiatrists associated with the Division of Mental Health of the World Health Organization (WHO) remind us that the WHO Constitution merges the definitions of health and mental health as "a state of complete physical, mental and social well-being, not merely the absence of disease" (Kuyken & Orley, 1994, p. 3). Throughout the world, personal well-being is largely contingent on economic survival and on family and societal stability. Given these essentials, the source and expression of well-being are affected by the interactions of an individual's personal characteristics with at least three interrelated variables: cultural norms and expectations, the status of the population subgroup of which an individual is a member, and the social stability of that subgroup within the dominant culture.

As noted, cultures vary in having an individualistic versus a sociocentric or collectivist orientation. These orientations affect the extent to which individuals value personal autonomy and devalue dependency. Anthropologist Francis Hsu (1972) has characterized the American core value as fear of dependency. Cultural norms and social structures that promote values of independence versus interdependence and that denigrate the status of dependency have particular relevance to concepts of mental health and the treatment of both mental and physical disability.

In a culture that values individualism, a person's need for support from others can be ego-threatening, generating a diminished self-concept and often a defensive denial of illness.

In defining mental health, cultures have ideal role types, as well as normative expectations that may generate a sense of well-being in very different individuals under very different conditions. Other things being equal, cultural norms determine whether the traits of submissiveness or assertiveness are likely to be linked with a sense of well-being in women. Men who are highly competitive may be revered in one setting and despised in another. There may be very different thresholds for physical well-being in agrarian and industrial economies, for persons engaged in manual and cognitive labor, or for cultures where somatization of emotional states is a normative pattern of behavior (Kleinman & Good, 1985). Research indicates that cultural norms and values affect the development of social competence in children, particularly with respect to the meaning and evaluation of behaviors such as sociability, shyness-inhibition, cooperation-compliance, and aggression-defiance (Chen & French, 2008).

The Basic Behavioral Science Task Force of the National Advisory Mental Health Council (NAMHC; 1996) focused on these interactions of individual characteristics and cultural context. It noted the important role of culture in grounding and identifying one's sense of self; in subjective interpretations of emotional states (including the experience and communication of symptoms of depression); in motivations for success (on behalf of the self or for others); and in fundamental attributions; that is, ways of explaining the behavior of others. "Cross-cultural research has shown that in cultures that stress interdependence, people tend to explain others' actions in terms of situational factors rather than internal or personal factors" (NAMHC, 1996, p. 724). This is a mode of externalizing the causes of unfortunate events or behaviors, rather than perceiving deficits in individuals. Cultural differences in attribution may have great power in explaining differential responses to mental illness and different prognoses in various parts of the world.

Individual characteristics also interact with social roles in specific cultural contexts. In the United States, a large literature suggests that the mental health of members of at least two subpopulations – minority groups and women – is affected by racism and sexism in the dominant culture (Willie et al., 1995). Throughout the world, characteristics such as socioeconomic status, gender, age, color, ethnicity, religion, sexual orientation, minority status, or, in some places, tribal/caste status or immigration status affect not only role definitions but also self-evaluations, employment opportunities, and quality of life. These social perceptions clearly interact with the preexisting strains and stigmas of mental illness. In any culture and with most disorders, whether medical or psychiatric, insults to one's mental health may adversely affect an existing vulnerability or dysfunction.

Cultural Context of Defining Mental Illness

There is now ample empirical evidence that enables us to go beyond earlier debates about the transcultural validity of mental illness as a construct (Gorenstein, 1984). As Horwitz (1982) has noted, every culture recognizes forms of negatively valued deviant behaviors that are differentiated from antisocial behaviors by their incomprehensibility within that cultural idiom. The major issues are whether certain classes of deviant behaviors are manifested uniformly, with similar etiologies and comparable distributions across cultures, and whether they can be treated with the same technologies. To answer some of these questions, increasing attention is being devoted to epidemiology, to biological and genetic parameters, and to analysis of cultural factors in diagnosis and treatment (Mezzich, Lewis-Fernandez, & Ruiperez, 2008). There is also attention to differential use of services by those with needs for psychiatric interventions (Commander, Odell, Surtees, & Sashidharan, 2003; Neighbors et al., 2007).

Anthropological research has disproved earlier speculations that psychotic conditions derive from the pressures of civilization and therefore are unlikely to be found among non-Western or more "primitive" populations:

> Acute psychotic breakdowns, as well as conditions characterized by chronic, often progressively deteriorating, nonorganic psychotic and asocial behavioral patterns, have not only been identified in all contemporary Western and non-Western urban societies, but also in tribal villages . . . and among hunter-gatherer groups . . . living in remote mountainous areas . . . or on isolated Pacific islands (Lin, 1996, p. 50).

The universal prevalence of syndromes does not mean universal modes of recognition and labeling. The major mental illnesses are characterized by recognizable impairments of cognition and affect. Although they may not differ in biological substrates, symptoms may be manifested differently and evoke different social reactions. The syndromes may be recognized as disordered states beyond personal volition or control, yet evoke different interpretations of their meaning, source, temporal nature, and curability. Because schizophrenia is the most highly studied psychiatric disorder, the literature is filled with proliferating research findings from epidemiology, neuroradiology, neuropathology, neurochemistry, hematology, pharmacology, and genetics, indicating biological parameters of what was once considered a psychogenic or sociogenic disorder (Hirsch & Weinberger, 1996; Mueser & Jeste, 2008). Similar evidence is accumulating with respect to bipolar disorder, major endogenous depression, obsessive-compulsive disorders, and some other DSM-IV Axis I disorders as well (Tasman et al., 2008). These Axis I diagnoses may ultimately turn out to be heterogeneous syndromes rather than single disease entities, and their symptoms may vary in patterning and virulence as a function of environmental and cultural influences (Mezzich et al., 2008).

Despite the burgeoning biogenetic and epidemiological research findings, it is important to acknowledge the scope and variability of disorders found in our diagnostic and statistical manuals. Some social scientists still dispute the extent to which behavioral disorders are true disease entities or simply deviations from a cultural norm (Gaines, 1992). They are concerned about the relationship of mental health to mental illness and whether these constructs refer to continuous or dichotomous variables; that is, whether given sufficient stress anyone may decompensate, or whether a prior vulnerability for a specific mental disorder is required.

Culture and Stress

Many experts today tend to accept the diathesis-stress hypothesis in the case of major psychiatric diagnoses with known biological and genetic parameters, such as schizophrenia, bipolar disorder, or obsessive-compulsive disorder. That is, stressful environmental events are presumed to trigger a biological vulnerability to a specific condition. Nevertheless, some major researchers claim that biological vulnerability alone is the first and only necessary cause for a neurodevelopmental disorder to emerge (Hirsch & Weinberger, 1996). If stress is involved in etiology, moreover, the stressful environment may be in utero or in physical conditions that affect uterine development, rather than in the psychosocial or rearing environment. There is ample presumptive evidence that war, famine, and flu virus may affect the fetal development of the person who in later years develops schizophrenia (Castle & Morgan, 2008; Hirsch & Weinberger, 1996). Two major questions today involve the interactions of the social and cultural environment with the expression of a biological vulnerability and the contributions of these interactions to relapse (Warner, 1994). To what extent do social pressures affect decompensation and hospitalization rates?

Leff's (1988) overview of studies of Asian and West Indian immigrants to the United Kingdom (UK) concluded that both groups showed above-average levels of admissions for schizophrenia to psychiatric hospitals. These admission rates were not reflected in higher prevalence data in the community nor in the home countries. "Hence, we have solid evidence that the high level of schizophrenia in Asian immigrants to the UK is not due to a constitutional liability to develop that condition. The alternative explanations, as with any immigrant group, are selective migration and the stress of living in an alien country" (Leff, 1988, p. 205). Numerous other studies have confirmed higher rates of psychiatric hospitalization for immigrants, both in England (Cochrane & Bal, 1989) and other European countries (Selten & Sijben, 1994).

In the United States, on the other hand, the highest rates of psychiatric hospital admissions have been found among groups that have been in the country the longest – African Americans and American Indians (National Institute of Mental Health [NIMH], 1987). These groups have been subjected not to the strains of migration, but to the stresses of long-term discrimination and forced culture loss imposed by the mainstream society. To determine the variables involved in the emergence of schizophrenia spectrum disorders, a major study in the United States followed for 16 years the course of more than 12,000 live births of women, who were enrolled in the study during their pregnancy. African Americans were three times more likely than Whites to be diagnosed with schizophrenia. After adjusting for indicators of family socioeconomic status (SES) at birth, the ratio was still about 2:1 (Bresnahan et al., 2007). Among the explanations offered for this disparity was the use of discriminatory police and diagnostic practices that promote psychiatric labels for African Americans and American Indians, thereby generating more admissions to crisis and hospital units. Therefore, more than SES may be involved in the development of schizophrenia – living in a racist society may in itself be sufficiently stressful to trigger decompensation in vulnerable individuals.

In contrast, there are relatively low rates of hospital admissions but longer durations of hospital stays for the two major immigrant groups – Hispanics and Asians (NIMH, 1987). A recent study that sampled a decade of psychiatric hospital admissions in Illinois confirmed that the proportion of foreign-born patients, including Asian and Mexican immigrants, was below their percentage in the overall population (Appleby et al., 2008). It has been suggested that Asians and Hispanics may keep ill family members at home until they reach advanced stages of disability; hence, their longer lengths of stay (Lefley, 1990).

The immigration–stress issue is further compounded by what has been termed the "immigrant paradox, i.e., that foreign nativity protects against psychiatric disorders" (Alegria et al., 2008, p. 359). In examining the combined data from the National Latino and Asian American Study and the National Comorbidity Survey Replication, two of the largest nationally representative samples of psychiatric information, these researchers found that the risk of most psychiatric disorders was lower for Latino than for non-Latino White subjects and that U.S.-born Latino subjects had higher rates for most psychiatric disorders than did Latino immigrants. However, under the rubric of "Latino" there was considerable within-group variance: "The immigrant paradox consistently held for Mexican subjects across mood, anxiety, and substance disorders, while it was only evident among Cuban and other Latino subjects for substance disorders. No differences were found in lifetime prevalence rates between immigrant and U.S. born Puerto Rican subjects" (Alegria et al., 2008, p. 359).

For individuals with long-term mental illness, the role of stressful life events in relapse is still unclear. There is some international research suggesting that stressful life events are likely to precede acute episodes of schizophrenia (Day et al., 1987). However, the potential for the prevention of stress in anyone's life is clearly problematic. For persons with mental illness, some interpersonal stressors may be avoided or minimized with appropriate education of caregivers or others in the person's social network, but existential stressors, such as accidents, loss of a job, economic problems, or death of a loved one, are usually not preventable for anyone. Other research has failed to confirm that life events triggered relapse in persons with long-term schizophrenia, whereas withdrawal from medication clearly did (Hirsch et al., 1996). Similarly, one prospective study indicated that stressful life events had no effect on the recurrence of primary affective disorder (Pardoen et al. 1996), whereas a study of recurrent clinical depression showed that relapse occurred an average of 7 months after the stressful life event (Monroe et al., 1996).

Culture-Bound Syndromes

In any discussion of epidemiology and culture, it is important to distinguish between the universality of certain diagnostic syndromes as demonstrated by cross-national studies and the meanings attached to these syndromes by different populations (Mezzich et al., 2008). The cross-cultural literature has also reported seemingly unique syndromes; that is, patterned clusters of disordered or psychotic behaviors that seem to be found only in specific cultural settings (Hughes, 1996). The following are examples of some of the better known culture-bound syndromes, the population affected, and some of the hypotheses advanced regarding nosological characteristics and possible antecedents.

- *Koro*: Southern China, Southeast Asia, India. This is a mental disturbance characterized by a man's belief that his penis is shrinking into his abdomen. It is now considered an acute anxiety state associated with sexual dysfunction.
- *Windigo psychosis*: Cree Eskimos and Ojibwa of Canada. This disturbance is characterized by cannibalistic delusions. The victim believes he has been transformed into a giant monster that eats human flesh. This delusion is possibly derived from tribal mythology and reflects the survival struggle in the Arctic.
- *Arctic hysteria*: Polar Eskimos. The person may scream for hours, imitating animal cries, while thrashing about on the snow in the nude or partially undresssed. Some attribute the condition to diet, to hypocalcemia, or hypervitaminosis A.
- *Latah*: Southeast Asia. This syndrome appears most commonly among women who break into obscenities and echolalia after an event that startles them. They may also follow commands automatically or repetitively imitate another person. It has been suggested that latah is an arousal state (possibly located in the amygdala) that may have developed as an adaptive response to snakes. Seeing a snake is a common precipitant of the startle response in Malayan and Filipino cultures, where snake bite is a major cause of morbidity.

- *Susto or espanto*: Latin American Indians. It is a fear state or sudden fright attributed to loss of soul by the action of spirits, the evil eye, or sorcery. Symptoms include weakness, loss of appetite, sleeplessness, nightmares, and trembling, and their frequency in this population has sometimes been attributed to hypoglycemia. Susto may be diagnosed as a brief reactive dissociative disorder, but it is unlikely to be healed by modern psychiatry. Its cure requires a traditional healer whose ministrations will influence the spirits to release the soul and return it to the host body.

Culture-bound syndromes may either form a distinctive class of disordered behaviors or ultimately turn out to be local variants of known psychiatric diagnoses (Hughes, 1996). As indicated, some may have biologically based parameters related to the local diet, climate, or unique features of the physical environment.

Epidemiology, Diagnosis, and Treatment: Biological and Cultural Aspects

Modern mental health systems throughout the world, despite their numerous local distinctions, all tend to honor the diagnostic categories found in the *Diagnostic and Statistical Manual* (DSM-IV) of the American Psychiatric Association (American Psychiatric Association, 1994), which is now the psychiatric component of the World Health Organization (1992) International Classification of Diseases (ICD-10). Although psychiatric nomenclature and some Western nosological categories continue to be questioned (Gaines, 1992), numerous international studies show agreement on core symptom clusters and comparable incidence rates of major psychiatric disorders such as schizophrenia (Sartorius et al., 1993).

International research also informs us, however, that cultural variables may have a significant impact on the manifestations of psychopathology and the developmental course of illness. The same studies that informed us of panhuman incidence also informed us that the course of mental illness may vary greatly in different parts of the world (Harrison et al., 2001; Jablensky et al., 1991).

Most of our knowledge of genetic factors in schizophrenia has come from the Scandinavian countries, where national registers permit researchers to find and interview the biological relatives of adopted-away children whose parents were schizophrenic. "High-risk" studies (i.e., comparisons of these offspring with adopted counterparts of nonschizophrenic parents), twin studies comparing monozygotic (MZ) and dizygotic (DZ) twins with concordant or discordant mental illness, and similar research have provided compelling evidence of a genetic factor in schizophrenia and major affective disorders, leading the way to further research on the still unknown modes of genetic transmission.

The research also indicates, however, an interplay of epidemiology, genetics, and culture. Despite comparable distributions across nation-states, some isolated populations with cultural barriers to intermarriage tend to show elevated levels of particular subtypes of schizophrenia (Goodman, 1996) or major affective disorders (Egeland & Hostetter, 1983). Cultural factors may also mask symptoms that affect the epidemiological picture. Egeland, Hostetter, and Eshleman (1983), for example, noted that, although most epidemiological studies indicated a ratio of 4:1 for unipolar depression over manic depression, in cultures that prohibit alcohol and severely sanction acting-out behaviors, the ratio is closer to 1:1. This is because in such cultures manic episodes are easier to identify and less likely to be confused with antisocial or substance-induced behaviors.

World Health Organization International Studies: Schizophrenia

The International Pilot Study of Schizophrenia (IPSS) was a WHO-sponsored transcultural investigation to determine whether the same symptom clusters would be similarly diagnosed in widely dispersed areas of the world. The initial research sites were in Colombia, Czechoslovakia, Denmark, India, Nigeria, Taiwan, the United Kingdom, the former Soviet Union, and the United States. Using the same interview tool with 1,202 first-contact patients, psychiatrists in different cultures generally agreed on the diagnostic screening criteria for schizophrenia, apparently confirming a universally recognized disease entity. The epidemiological picture has been similarly comparable. In a 1990s report to the World Health Assembly, the WHO Director-General stated that there were no demonstrable differences in the incidence and prevalence of schizophrenia between developing and developed countries. A uniform annual incidence rate of 0.1 per thousand and prevalence rates of 2 to 4 per thousand for schizophrenia were reported (Sartorius et al., 1993).

Cultural differences, however, were found in follow-up studies 2 and 5 years later. The course of illness was significantly better in the developing world than in the more technologically advanced countries. Good outcome figures ranged from 58% in Nigeria and 51% in India to 7% in Moscow and 6% in Denmark (Sartorius et al., 1986). Follow-up studies of first-episode patients in 10 countries found a continuing difference in outcome that favored the developing nations (Jablensky et al., 1991). Nearly two-thirds (63%) of the patients in the developing world experienced a benign course and full remission, and only 16% suffered impaired social functioning, compared to 37% experiencing remission and 42% having functional impairment in the industrialized countries (Warner, 1994). At 15- and 25-year follow-ups, about 75% of the subjects had been traced. About 50% of the surviving cases had favorable outcomes, but there was marked heterogeneity across geographic centers. Sociocultural factors seemed to modify the long-term course, with the number of deaths due to suicide significantly higher in industrialized countries. However, the most robust variables were acute onset and whether the person experienced psychotic symptoms in the 2 years following onset, suggesting biological parameters for outcome prediction (Harrison et al., 2001).

Interpreters of the data have previously raised the issue of different vulnerabilities within the schizophrenia syndrome, specifically with respect to acute versus gradual onset. For example, Warner (1992) has suggested that in the IPSS the incidence of cases with acute types of schizophrenia (i.e., no gradual onset, good premorbid adjustment) was four times as common in the developing world samples (40% of cases) as in the developed countries (11%). Because acute cases are known to show better rates of recovery than those with slow insidious onset, this difference indeed may have accounted for the better prognosis. However, as the same author noted elsewhere, the outcome in the developing world subjects was better regardless of whether their onset was acute or insidious: "The general conclusion is unavoidable. ... The majority of Third World schizophrenic people achieve a favorable outcome. The more urbanized and industrialized the setting, the more malignant becomes the illness" (Warner, 1994, p. 157).

The literature interpreting the findings of more benign outcome in developing countries postulates a hypothesis of relatively lower stress and higher social support. Common themes are that traditional cultures offer the following: (1) cultural belief systems that externalize causality, freeing the patient and family of blame, (2) greater opportunities for social reintegration and normalized work roles in agrarian economies, and (3) extended kinship networks to buffer the effects of illness on the patients and their caregivers (Leff, 1988; Lefley, 1990; Lin & Kleinman, 1988).

Different concepts of selfhood, of dependency and autonomy, and of obligations to kin are subsumed under some of these explanatory categories. In Western individualistic cultures even the first episode of mental illness connotes a depreciated personal identity, particularly if it involves psychiatric hospitalization (Estroff, 1989). Patients in Western cultures are more likely to deny illness, reject medications, and fight the intrinsic dependency status of mental illness. Paternalistic control and loss of individual autonomy are less of a threat in traditional, family-oriented cultures. Lin and Kleinman (1988) suggest also that traditional collectivist cultures are characterized by less social isolation, a more tolerant family milieu, and extended human resources to buffer family burden, in contrast to the burdened nuclear family in Western societies.

World Health Organization Studies: Epidemiology, Resources, and Service Utilization

In any country, mental health systems are driven by epidemiological need, available resources, and the interest and commitment of ruling bodies. They are also driven by service utilization patterns and their responsiveness to consumer expectations. In this section we review some major current epidemiological findings, available resources, and patterns of utilization by different ethnic groups.

Epidemiological Need

The WHO Mental Health (WMH) survey assessed epidemiological patterns through face-to-face household interviews with 84,850 adult respondents in 17 countries in Africa, Asia, the Americas, Europe, and the Middle East. Countries were assessed as low or middle income (Colombia, Lebanon, Mexico, Nigeria, China, South Africa, Ukraine) and high income (Belgium, France, Germany, Israel, Italy, Japan, Netherlands, New Zealand, Spain, United States). Lifetime prevalence, projected lifetime risk, and age of onset of DSM-IV disorders were assessed with the WHO Composite International Diagnostic Interview (CIDI) in a fully structured lay-administered diagnostic interview. It assessed the prevalence and severity of mental disorders and use of mental health services over 12 months, together with an estimate of lifetime risk. Although mental disorders occur throughout the world, the highest rates of projected lifetime risk were found in countries exposed to sectarian violence – Israel, Nigeria, and South Africa (Kessler, Angemeyer, et al., 2007).

Resource Availability

In 2000 and again in 2005, the World Health Organization (WHO) conducted the Mental Health Atlas project to provide information on mental health resources and services in 203 countries and territories representing approximately 99% of the world's population (WHO, 2005). Information related to policy, programs, financing, and mental health resource indicators (e.g., beds, personnel, medication availability, special population services, etc.) was solicited from the Ministry of Health of each country. These data were verified by an exhaustive literature search on mental health resources in low- and middle-income countries from numerous other data sources. Specific policies on mental health were present in 63% of all countries and 70% of high-income countries, although the majority of policies and legislation were relatively recent. Expenditures for mental health represented from 1% to 5% of the total country's health budget. About 30% of the countries did not have a specific budget for mental health care. Globally, 68% reported having at least some community care facilities; 52% of low-income versus 93% of high-income countries had such facilities.

The number of psychiatric beds varied greatly. In 39% of the countries there was less than one psychiatric bed per 10,000 in the population. The median number of beds per 10,000 in the population in countries with low, lower middle, upper middle, and high income was 0.2, 1.6, 7.5, and 7, respectively. The number of mental health providers was also much lower in low-income than in high-income countries: The median number of psychiatrists per 100,000 varied from 0.1 to 9.2, psychiatric nurses from 0.2 to 31.8, psychologists from 0.04 to 11, and social workers from 0 to 18.

Although programs for elderly persons and children were reported in 51% and 65% of the countries, respectively, special programs for indigenous people and minority groups were largely absent. Between 2001 and 2004, there was a worrisome trend in financing of mental health care. A decrease in social insurance (−8.9%) and an increase in private insurance (+8%) were observed in lower middle-income countries and decreased social insurance (−8.3%) in high-income countries. An analysis concluded that in addition to the clear disparities across nations, "The results of the Mental Health Atlas 2005 demonstrate that the resources that the world spends on mental health are grossly inadequate in comparison to the needs" (Saxena Sharan, Garrido, & Saraceno, 2006, p. 184).

Service Utilization

Research has long shown that cultural groups vary in their acceptance and utilization of standard mental health services versus indigenous healers. WHO's WMH survey found substantial delay and failure in treatment seeking after the first onset of a mental disorder. Although these delays were generally longer in developing countries, older cohorts, men, and patients with earlier ages of onset, there were pervasive problems worldwide (Wang et al., 2007). To evaluate utilization patterns, WHO has used a responsiveness concept to assess mental health care performance vis-à-vis the expectations of service users (WHO, 2000). One European study assessed responsiveness of mental health providers in the following domains: attention, dignity, clear communication, autonomy, confidentiality, basic amenities, choice of health care provider, continuity, and access to social support. It found that providers' responsiveness in outpatient care was rated worse by lower SES patients and may be related to social class (Bramesfeld, Wedegartner, Elgeti, & Bisson, 2007).

European Studies: Quality of Life, Services, and Treatment Efficacy

Together with the WHO international data we have findings from a number of studies from European conglomerates. The 2000 European Study of the Epidemiology of Mental Disorders (ESEMed/MHEDEA) was a cross-sectional study investigating the prevalence and associated factors of mental disorders, their effects on quality of life, and use of services in Belgium, France, Germany, Italy, the Netherlands, and Spain. With a sample size of 21,425 people, initial data indicated that, among participants with a 12-month mental disorder, fewer than 26% had consulted a formal mental health service, with proportions higher for those with mood disorder than those with anxiety disorders (Alonso et al., 2004). The European Schizophrenia Cohort study (EuroSC) was a naturalistic investigation of the quality of life (QOL) of people with schizophrenia living in France, Germany, and the UK. German participants had the highest subjective QOL. The authors felt that more daytime and structured activities in mental health service provision in Germany, as well as social welfare policy, may in part explain the differences (Marwaha et al., 2008). Another study indicated that, in Germany, persons with schizophrenia, bipolar disorder, and major depression who required hospitalization remained in the hospital significantly longer than their counterparts in the United States. The researchers suggested that, in the United States, "shorter length of stay is probably caused by cultural differences and discharging patients to aftercare facilities sooner. However, the main difference originated in the diversity of health system and pressure on doctors to discharge patients much earlier" (Auffarth, Busse, Dietrich, & Emrich, 2008, p. 40).

Perhaps the most advanced program for schizophrenia was developed by the Optimal Treatment Project (OTP) of Ian Falloon and his associates and was located in various psychiatric centers in Germany, Hungary, Italy, Japan, New Zealand, Norway, Sweden, and Turkey. OTP was set up as an international collaborative group to promote the routine use of evidence-based strategies for schizophrenic disorders in typical clinical care. These strategies were as follows: giving antipsychotic drugs at the lowest levels for effectiveness; providing education about medications, early warning signs of illness exacerbation, stress management strategies for both patients and caregivers, and psychotic disorders and their treatments; training in medication adherence; using effective interpersonal communication and problem-solving skills; providing assertive case management and outreach; gaining effective social support (including housing, finances, health, safety); providing early detection and care to resolve clinical and social crises; offering goal-oriented social skills training for patients and caregivers; using specific pharmacological and psychological strategies for recurring symptoms; and using strategies for managing negative symptoms and coping with persistent psychosis, anxiety and panic, mood swings, dysphoria, and suicidal thoughts (Falloon et al., 2004).

As a demonstration project, the OTP evaluated the benefits of applying evidence-based treatment for schizophrenia and other nonaffective psychotic disorders over a 5-year period. Fifty-three geographic sites in 21 countries were included when the study began in 1994, and 35 sites continued to participate. More than 80 mental health centers in over 20 countries began the project since 1994. Forming the basis of the review were 14 centers with patients who received optimal treatment for at least 24 months according to the project protocol.

At each program site, a multidisciplinary team was trained to administer the optimal treatment strategies, with continuous audits of fidelity to the model, annual independent reviews of services, and further training as needed. A core battery of global measures was used to assess outcomes, including symptom impairment, psychosocial functioning, disability scales, and global caregiver stress. At the end of 2002, 1,012 patients had participated in the project, with 603 having completed at least 2 years of optimal treatment. Complete data were available on 594 cases,

99% of the sample. On clinical, social, and caregiver indices significant improvements were found after 24 months. The average percentages of improvement were 41% on the impairment index, 39% on disability, and 48% on reduced stress for caregivers. Direct comparison of patients randomly assigned to OTP (n = 146) or routine case management (n = 114) at four sites (Ankara, Turkey; Trondehim, Norway; Benvento, Italy; and Gothenburg, Sweden) showed even greater contrast, with OTP cases showing more than twice the benefits of routine case management.

Recovery was assessed at two levels: full (no significant impairment or disability) and partial (substantial improvement in impairment and disability). Thirty-five percent of the OTP patients met the criteria for full recovery at 24 months versus 10% of those in routine case management. When a recent-onset (i.e., onset within 10 years) group was considered separately, 43% had made a full recovery. The researchers concluded, "On all measures, the evidence-based OTP approach achieved more than double the benefits associated with current best practices. One half of recent cases had achieved full recovery from clinical and social morbidity. These advantages were even more striking in centres where a random-control design was used" (Falloon et al., 2004, p. 104).

Family Psychoeducation in Service Systems

With progressive deinstitutionalization of the mentally ill, families are now the major caregivers and support systems of people with schizophrenia and other major psychiatric disorders throughout the world. In Italy, for example, a 2000 study found that 70% to 84% of discharged patients lived with their families (Warner, 2000). In the United States, many patients are discharged to their families: A recent study found that about 40% of White patients continued to share the same household with their families, and co-residence figures and caregiving responsibilities were considerably higher among African American, Hispanic, and Asian families (Lefley, 2004).

Theories that families play a causal role in major psychiatric disorders such as schizophrenia have now been discredited by prominent family therapists. Specifically rejecting older family therapy models that focused on presumed dysfunction of the family system (Leff, 2005), these therapists developed family psychoeducation (FPE), a family intervention that addresses the multiple issues involved in living with or being the support system for someone with a serious mental illness. There is now a substantial international research literature indicating that FPE is a powerful tool for alleviating family burden and deterring patients' relapse (Dixon & Lehman, 1996; Magliano & Fiorillo, 2007). In contrast to traditional family therapies, psychoeducational approaches are responsive to families' expressed needs for information and coping techniques. FPE education presents a diathesis-stress model of schizophrenia and other major disorders. Its core elements are state-of-the-art information about the illness, empathic support for families, illness management techniques, and problem-solving strategies. Families learn that schizophrenia and other disorders are no-fault biologically based disorders that result in thought disturbances, erratic behaviors, and problems in living. They are taught communication, behavioral, and problem-solving skills and how best to help the patient manage the illness (Dixon & Lehman, 1996; McFarlane, 2002).

Numerous models for involving families in the treatment process have been developed in diverse sites throughout the world (Lefley & Johnson, 2002). Reports on psychoeducational interventions for ethnically diverse families in the United States suggest possible adaptations. These might include involving extended family networks or community support persons, reducing the length of sessions, focusing on economic survival issues, eschewing egalitarian approaches and confirming the authority of group leaders, and other special cultural considerations (Jordan, Lewellen, & Vandiver, 1995).

Many studies of the efficacy of FPE have been conducted in a variety of settings worldwide, with continuing long-term results showing significant reductions in relapse and rehospitalization rates of patients and a lessening of family burden and distress (Magliano & Fiorillo, 2007). In a review of research, Johnson (2007) found that outcomes were much the same in these countries: Australia, China, Denmark, Germany, India, Ireland, Italy, Japan, Norway, Spain, Sweden, the UK, and the United States.

From 2000 to 2004, the European Commission promoted research on the impact of training programs for staff professionals on the implementation and effectiveness of FPE for schizophrenia in mental health centers in six countries: Germany, Greece, Italy, Portugal, Spain, and the United Kingdom. Each national center selected four mental health centers in which two professionals were randomly assigned to two different modes of training, regular practice and FPE. A total of 55 patients and 118 relatives received FPE for 1 year. At follow-up, there were significant improvements in patients' clinical status and social functioning. For families, there was a significant reduction in caregiver burden and in their use of coercion and resignation as coping strategies and an increase in relatives' positive communication with the patient; in addition they reported a higher level of professional support at follow-up than at baseline (Magliano et al., 2006).

A psychoeducational program for families of patients with schizophrenia in five cities in China reduced relapse rates from 35% to 20% per year and also demonstrated reductions in patients' disability levels and in family burden (Zhang & Yan, 1993). A unique, culturally appropriate FPE model in China not only educated families about the illness but also in one case focused on helping parents arrange a marriage for their child, as a means of providing caregiving when the parents were gone. In a randomized controlled trial with three follow-ups, this family intervention in China had these highly significant effects: reduced number and shorter duration of rehospitalizations, longer duration of employment, and reduction of family burden (Xiong et al., 1994).

A recent study in Hong Kong merged cultural content (Confucian precepts) with educational content developed in the West (Chien & Wong, 2007). These researchers conducted a randomized controlled trial of 18 sessions of psychoeducation for families of patients with schizophrenia based on the multifamily model of McFarlane (2002). There were four stages in the psychoeducational program: orientation and engagement (three sessions), educational workshops (six sessions), therapeutic family role and strength building (seven sessions), and termination (two sessions). The program content was designed based on the results of a needs assessment of 180 family members: "The program used a culturally sensitive family intervention model, which considered many of the cultural tenets that were taught by Confucius (for example, valuing collectivism over individualism and giving great importance during the needs assessment to family and kinship ties) in respect to family relationships and value orientation" (Chien & Wong, 2007, p. 1004).

The Chinese studies were particularly rigorous methodologically, with fairly large sample sizes. But as indicated, family interventions in China were quite variable. Most were modeled on basic Western content, some added Confucian precepts, and others were based on content quite at variance with the Western model. Yet all were well designed, and all yielded positive outcomes, in rural as well as urban settings. These findings seem to largely confirm the transcultural appropriateness of basic FPE.

Unfortunately, family psychoeducation is still largely offered only in research projects. Despite the need and the powerful findings of FPE's effectiveness, most service delivery systems in the United States make little effort to offer family education and training for the caregiving role. Regardless of their ethnicity and expectations of the system, most families continue to complain about a lack of communication and information from mental health professionals (Drapalski et al., 2008).

Cultural Diversity in Mental Health Service Systems

In 1963, federal legislation, with accompanying funding, mandated the development of networks of community mental health centers. Today, public mental health services are threatened by greatly reduced federal and state funding and by the constraints of managed care. In contrast, in other industrialized countries, many programs in both the public and private sectors are still oriented toward serving the mental health needs of the general population. In countries with few resources, mental health systems inevitably are geared toward the most needy population – persons with overt symptomatology who suffer from major psychiatric disorders. Most of the developing world is still dependent on a few large isolated mental hospitals, with short-term clinical care limited to major cities and few community-based resources such as halfway houses or psychosocial rehabilitation programs.

Paradoxically, the scarcity of resources in the developing world has necessitated creative approaches to service delivery that are sometimes superior to those in the West, such as the integration of mental health services with primary health care at the village level in India (Nagaswami, 1990), China (Yucun et al., 1990), and Africa. The model rehabilitation program found primarily in African countries is referred to as the ARO village system (Asuni, 1990). In the ARO village system, after treatment in a Western-style mental hospital or clinic, psychiatric patients live with a relative in a traditional village close to the mental health facility for several months to a year or longer. Patients are involved in household chores and other village community activities as their mental state improves. The relative is involved in treatment and trained as a lifetime caregiver and support system and may be paid to compensate for income lost during this period.

Although developing nations may make creative attempts to deal with mental illness, most have to deal with massive social stressors. The sequelae of colonialism, intertribal warfare, destabilization of once peaceful agrarian economies, and ravages of famine are some of the problems in the developing world that profoundly affect mental health. Industrial nations have to deal with fluctuating economies and numerous stressors linked to rapid culture change. Most Western nations are experiencing increasing racial and ethnic diversity, and there are numerous mental health problems related to the status of minority populations.

Service Delivery Issues

Research on culture and mental health in the United States has largely focused on two domains. One domain has involved differences in population characteristics that affect service utilization. These include cultural concepts of mental disorder, help-seeking patterns, modes of using services, and the use of alternative healing systems. The other, interrelated domain has targeted service system deficits such as accessibility barriers, diagnostic and treatment errors, and lack of culturally competent personnel. In addition, there is now a large clinical literature devoted to case studies and guidelines for working with different ethnic groups (e.g., Fernando & Keating, 2008).

Over time, around each service innovation has developed a discussion of cultural applications, such as ethnicity and family therapy (McGoldrick, Pearce, & Giordano, 1995) or the cross-cultural practice of clinical case managment (Manoleas, 1996). There are also models for restructuring the delivery system itself to respond to the cultural needs of specific ethnic groups, including community interventions to alleviate social stressors (Lefley & Bestman, 1991). In most of these applications, the focus is on how best to help clients with existential problems in living. Typical problem areas include generational and marital conflict, substance-abusing youth, the oppression and rage of minority status, the translocations and loss of refugee status, and adaptation to a foreign culture.

In modern industrial nations, members of ethnic minority groups are particularly vulnerable to the stresses of poverty, economically or politically forced migration, family disintegration, and the outrages of diminished status in the mainstream society. The malaise engendered by feelings of oppression and loss and the interpersonal conflicts generated by poverty, crowding, and family disruption are often attributed to external malevolence. As in more traditional countries, these problems are frequently brought first to a religious practitioner or alternative healer rather than to a mental health professional.

Traditional and Biomedical Healing Systems

Distinctions between physical and mental illness and the resources required to heal them are based on a Cartesian mind/body dichotomy that is alien to most non-Western or traditional cultures (Gaines, 1992). Symptoms of mental illness such as apathy and withdrawal, culturally atypical delusions or hallucinations, fluctuating mood states, or bizarre verbalizations are found throughout the world, but they may be viewed variably as either spiritual, psychological, or somatic in origin. Treatment of these symptoms that are characteristic of any experience of human malaise may be split among different healing systems or incorporated in a holistic approach to treatment.

In many countries parallel healing systems coexist, with reciprocal referrals. In hospitals in the People's Republic of China, a pharmacopoeia of herbal remedies coexists with the latest in psychotropic medications. A building devoted to Ayurvedic Medicine is found at the National Institute of Mental Health and Neuorsciences in Banagalore, India, a major center of psychiatric training and research. In many African countries, indigenous healing is integrated with modern psychiatry. In the ARO village system mentioned earlier, treatment typically combines native healing rituals with psychotropic medication and a type of milieu therapy in a traditional setting. Relatives live with their ill member in a compound of traditional healers both to provide for the needs of the patient and to participate in the healing rituals. The treatment consists of the administration of herbs, performance of rituals, and recitation of incantations (Asuni, 1990).

Anthropologists generally agree that, in most non-Western societies, traditional healers are the first resort in mental health problems, and they continue to be used even after psychiatric services are enlisted. According to Jilek (1993), prohibitive restrictions on nonprofessional health care were largely imposed by European authorities in their former colonial possessions. With the demise of colonialism, however, many developing nations have legalized the practice of traditional medicine. The officially sanctioned coexistence of traditional and modern medical systems is found in most African countries, Bangladesh, China, Korea, India, Nepal, Myanmar, Sri Lanka, and Thailand, to name a few. Countries that do not officially recognize but do not legally prohibit "nonscientific" medicine are Australia, Canada, Germany, most Latin American countries, the Netherlands, the Scandinavian countries, the United Kingdom, and the United States. Although some European countries have legal prohibitions, they are unlikely to proceed against non-European traditional healers practicing with their immigrant compatriots (Jilek, 1993).

In most traditional or folk healing systems, human behavior is mediated by multiple forces, both natural and supernatural. Diagnostic and treatment models are based on etiological concepts that typically involve some imbalance in life forces. The imbalance can be corrected only by invoking appropriate counterforces through the ritualistic fulfillment of religious obligations. Most rituals require the intercession of supernatural powers either directly or through the mediums of a healer (Lefley, Sandoval, & Charles, 1997).

Although cultures tend to distinguish between religious practitioners and herb doctors, in many traditional cultures the priest and healer are one. Both Western and traditional healers use medications and somatic therapies as needed. Some medications used by traditional healers have tranquilizing or antipsychotic properties (e.g., extracts of the *Rauwolfia serpentina* plant have been used to control psychotic symptoms in the ARO village programs and elsewhere in Africa and Asia).

When comparing Western psychiatry and traditional healing, it is evident that different etiological paradigms have generated different treatment modalities. Western healers look to psychodynamic issues or maladaptive behavioral patterns in fashioning cures, whereas ritual healers look to supernatural causality or external malevolence. Traditional healing rituals may exorcise a curse, propitiate gods, redress a wrong, or otherwise balance unequal forces. Through trance possession, believers may become imbued with the power of a personal god to control their malaise and improve their fortunes.

There are no adequately controlled studies comparing the effectiveness of traditional and Western psychiatric healing interventions. An admittedly limited study was reported by Koss (1987), in which 56 patients receiving either mental health care or spiritist healing in Puerto Rico rated their therapist for symptom alleviation or problem resolution. Patients' outcome ratings were significantly better for spiritists than for mental health professionals. Koss felt the difference could be accounted for by the higher expectations of the spiritists' competency in controlling fate. She also reported that spritists' patients who had first encountered and then expressed dissatisfaction with medical or psychiatric personnel were the most hopeful, because they viewed the traditional healer as a last resort. In most ethnographic reports, however, many patients and families continue to use dual systems to serve different needs (Bilu & Witztum, 1993; Lefley et al., 1997; Weiss, 1992).

Rehabilitation and the Self-Help Experience

Desinstitutionalization, the emptying of mental hospitals, is proceeding at an uneven pace throughout the world. Nevertheless, with the increasing availability of antipsychotic medications, almost every culture has seen an increased emphasis on community tenure and the need for rehabilitative services. In the international mental health literature, there is an increasing emphasis on improving quality of life (Kuyken & Orley, 1994). One of the most important attempts to deinstitutionalize, rehabilitate, and improve the quality of life of persons with mental illness has taken place in Italy.

Mental Health Systems and Changes in Italy

In 1978, Italy passed Law 180, which banned all new admissions to public mental hospitals, setting the stage for an allegedly more humane policy of deinstitution-alization and community tenure. Community mental health services have subse-quently developed very unevenly, with great disparities in the resources available in southern and northern Italy. An overview of studies of the Italian reform move-ment found that, in the south of Italy, community support services were virtually nonexistent compared with other areas of the country (Bollini & Mollica, 1989). Other studies reported that families are greatly burdened with a major caregiv-ing role and with totally inadequate clinical supports to deal with even floridly psychotic behavior (Jones & Poletti, 1985).

A 15-year follow-up study looked at the long-term psychosocial outcome of schizophrenic patients in southern Italy (Sardinia) who were discharged after the 1978 reform. The investigators found that 70% of the patients showed poor or very poor adjustment or severe maladjustment. Most were single and 85% were unemployed. Their treatment histories were marked by a large number of hospi-talizations and rare or irregular outpatient contacts (Fariante et al., 1996).

In stark contrast to Sardinia, northern Italy, particularly Trieste, has resources on the cutting edge of psychiatric rehabilitation. Numerous cooperatives employ people with psychiatric disabilities. Marianne Farkas, an international trainer in psychiatric rehabilitation for Boston University's Center for Psychiatric Rehabili-tation (Farkas & Anthony, 1989), visited these businesses many times and reported that their products were of excellent quality, with enthusiastic, often elite patron-age. Examples were a fine costume jewelry shop, a leather handbag factory and boutique, a moving company, and a radio station. The specialized industries were developed by experts and run jointly by patients and staff proficient in that indus-try. The radio station recruits top-flight people to donate 1 hour a month to these enterprises. From this outreach, they have developed a pool of expert consultants who help with product design, advertising, training, and marketing.

Several factors are readily apparent in this northern Italian experiment. First, patients work in first-class businesses of which they can be proud. There are no artificial work situations or demeaning entry-level jobs to erode an already diminished self-concept. Second, they work under conditions that are probably optimal for persons with a major mental illness. All businesses are small, with no more than 15 to 20 staff. Psychiatric patients have difficulty tolerating overstimulating, high-demand environments, and in these cooperatives they can work without excessive interpersonal stimulation and at their own pace. Cohen and Saraceno (2002) attribute the Trieste success to the establishment of an array of community services and the reorientation of care toward the social reintegration of patients. The data on northern and southern Italy tell us much about the structure of good and bad mental health systems and the interaction of these systems with psychosocial outcomes and prognosis.

Mental Health Systems and Changes in Europe

Service disparities are also found in many other countries. A study of nine European countries, from 2002 to 2006, found an ongoing but inconsistent trend toward increasing institutionalized care across Europe. Although most countries showed a slight decrease in the number of conventional inpatient beds from 1990 to 2006, in Italy, which began with the fewest beds, there was almost a fourfold increase. All the countries – Austria, Denmark, England, Germany, Ireland, Italy, Netherlands, Spain, and Switzerland – showed an increase in prison populations. In addition, the move toward reinstitutionalization coincided with a lack of adequate residential resources in the community: "Quality standards for supervised and supported housing services are often low and poorly defined, with limited incentives for provider organizations to help patients move to more independent form of living" (Priebe et al., 2008, p. 573).

Muijen (2008) has noted that "mental health systems across Europe are diverse in governance, human resources, funding systems, and service delivery" (p. 479). Although in every country treatment and medications are free for people with mental disorders, there are differences between the western European Union countries and the formerly sovietized Eastern European countries, which are developing mental health policies based on market reforms and attempts to cut public spending. "Many of the more developed countries are moving toward community-based mental health services. In poor countries, however, hospitals still dominate services, absorbing up to 90% of mental health resources" (Muijen, 2008, p. 480).

The European Study of the Epidemiology of Mental Disorders (ESEMed) studied epidemiology, comorbidity, service use, and prescribing patterns in six relatively wealthy European countries and found considerable diversity in patterns of service and drug prescribing (Alonso et al., 2004). Most service research has focused on the effectiveness of local service models and national policies, but "it is uncertain whether conclusions drawn from sophisticated service models in rich parts of the world can be applied to scenarios in middle- and low-income countries" (Muijen, 2008, p. 481).

Transforming Mental Health Systems

In the United States, the President's New Freedom Commission on Mental Health (2003) report focused on transforming the mental health system. It had the following goals and recommendations: (1) Americans understand that mental health is essential to overall health; (2) mental health care is consumer and family driven; (3) disparities in mental health services are eliminated; (4) early mental health screening, assessment, and referral services are common practice; (5) excellent mental health care is delivered and research is accelerated; (6) technology is used to enable increased access to mental health care and information.

Unfortunately these goals have not been accompanied by funding to accomplish them. Disparities in services to different ethnic groups still prevail, and although early screening and referrals are slowly increasing, these increases have been largely in the domain of prevention research rather than standard practice. Despite the increased use of technology, excellent mental health care is largely an unrealized dream in an increasingly fragmented mental health system.

During the past decades, however, there has been a substantial transformation of the types of services available for persons with serious mental illness. Reductions in institutional beds have been accompanied by the addition of paraprofessional case managers in community services. There is some increasing acceptance of the need for assistance to family caregivers. There is increasing emphasis on implementing evidence-based practices (EBPs) for persons with major disorders such as schizophrenia. In addition to medication, these EBPs include empirically validated psychosocial services such as assertive community treatment – delivered by teams that provide psychiatric services and case management in the home, integrated mental health and substance abuse treatment, supported housing, supported employment, and family psychoeducation. Despite their demonstrated efficacy and cost benefit, EBPs also remain largely absent from most clinical facilities (Torrey et al., 2001).

Worldwide, the World Health Organization has promoted both research and services for underserved populations. WHO established Nations for Mental Health in 1996, a program that supported demonstration projects for countries such as Mongolia, Sri Lanka, Argentina, Zanzibar, and the Marshall Islands. Subsequently the World Bank created a position for a specialist to stimulate and review proposals for mental health projects that it would then fund. WHO has formulated a Global Action Program, a 5-year plan aimed at reducing the stigma and burden of mental disorders through advocacy, research, and the improvement of policies and services in underdeveloped areas of the world. *The World Mental Health Casebook* presents a description of such social and mental health programs in low-income countries (Cohen, Kleinman, & Saraceno, 2002).

Advocacy and Consumer Self-Help Movements

Concurrent but not consonant with the growing emphasis on empirically supported professional services is the burgeoning of consumer movements throughout the world. When the President's Commission emphasized that mental health systems must be consumer and family driven, it was largely in acknowledgment of the political influence of service recipients in defining their own needs and appropriate remedies.

Probably the most notable development in mental health systems is the world-wide growth of advocacy and self-help organizations. Some movements are largely composed of family members and concerned citizens, but also include many consumers. Others are self-help groups for consumers alone. In the United States, a scientific national survey in 2002 found 7,467 groups and organizations run by and for mental health consumers or family members or both. Among these groups were 3,315 mutual support groups, 3,019 self-help organizations, and 1,133 consumer-operated services. Most consumer organizations enable people to access services such as disability benefits, housing, Medicaid, and health insurance and provide help with the legal or justice system (Goldstrom et al., 2006). The World Federation for Schizophrenia and Allied Disorders (WFSAD), with headquarters in Toronto, is an international umbrella organization for family groups, with representatives from all major continents. It recently published a guidebook for implementing family work (Froggatt et al., 2007).

Major supportive resources have been developed by citizen organizations, such as Mental Health America (formerly the National Mental Health Association), but service recipients themselves – consumers and their families – have become exceptionally active in recent years. Since its inception in 1979, the U.S. organization, the National Alliance on Mental Illness (NAMI), formerly the National Alliance for the Mentally Ill, has become a powerful political force at both national and state levels. With a primary focus on public education, legislative initiatives to increase funding for research and services, and mutual support, NAMI has helped develop private foundations for basic scientific research. The organization has been influential in extending the Americans with Disability Act to mentally ill individuals and attaining insurance parity for persons with mental illness and is currently engaging the media in a massive antistigma campaign. State affiliates have also developed a range of rehabilitative facilities, including housing, employment opportunities, psychosocial rehabilitation programs, and clubhouses as adjuncts to the professional service delivery system.

Consumer organizations range from strictly nonpolitical self-help models to social action movements invested in political and legal change. In the United States, there are numerous self-help organizations for persons with psychiatric diagnoses ranging from agoraphobia and anxiety disorders to schizophrenia (White & Madara, 2002). The Depressive and Bipolar Support Alliance (DBSA), formerly the National Depressive and Manic-Depressive Association, is an active self-help organization promoting research and services for the major affective disorders. There are also general groups for persons recovering from mental illness, such as Recovery Inc. or Grow, which was born in Australia. Their support groups are typically used in tandem with medication management, but they often replace the need for ancillary psychotherapy.

In the United States, most state mental health administrations today have a Mental Health Consumer Affairs office, organized and staffed by one or more former psychiatric patients. Members of state consumer organizations meet at annual national Alternatives Conferences that bring together consumers from all over the country for organizational skill building and knowledge sharing. However, consumers felt that a national presence was needed, and in October, 2006, the National Coalition of Mental Health Consumer/Survivor Organizations was organized, with representatives from 28 states and the District of Columbia and a national office in Washington, D.C.

In the United States, the dual functions of self-help and political advocacy have been merged not only in state consumer organizations but also in national centers like the National Empowerment Center in Lawrence, Massachusetts, and the National Self-Help Clearinghouse in Philadelphia. Today numerous consumer-operated enterprises serve persons with severe and persistent mental illness. These organizations offer housing and residential placement services, case management, peer counseling programs, social centers, employment services, crisis respite houses, and special programs for the homeless. Most of these enterprises were initiated with funding from the Community Support Program of the Substance Abuse and Mental Health Administration (SAMHSA). This support has demonstrated that the promotion of independence, empowerment, and skill development in people with mental illness provides valuable tools for productivity and an improved quality of life.

In Europe, the oldest national organization with substantial numbers of consumers is the Association for Social and Mental Health, founded in Sweden in 1966. In 2000, this movement reportedly had 10,000 members in 26 regional divisions (Brody, 2000). In the Netherlands, the European Network of Users and Ex-Users of Mental Health was formed between 1991 and 1993. In Central Europe, some consumer groups have developed the types of consumer-run rehabilitative facilities that were already implemented in other countries. In Slovenia, they are operating two halfway houses and a drop-in center and are working on developing sheltered employment. In Hungary, consumers have a radio program and are training people in the skill of bookbinding. Consumer groups are also found in Japan, Australia, New Zealand, and Latin America.

Continental and world conferences facilitate cross-fertilization of ideas among these groups. International consumer organizations with a focus on social change include the World Network of Users and Survivors of Psychiatry (http://www .wnusp.net/) with offices in Aukland, New Zealand, and the Mental Disability Rights International, based in Washington D.C. International organizations such as the World Federation of Mental Health (WFMH) and the World Association for Psychiatric Rehabilitation (WAPR), both largely professional organizations, frequently bring consumer leaders together at their conferences. According to Brody (2000), the WFMH assisted in forming the World Federation of Mental Health Users and in 1993 elected that group's president as the first consumer member of the WFMH board.

With a major focus on the human rights of persons with mental illness, these self-help movements offer a forum for persons with psychiatric disabilities to utilize and refine their intelligence and skills in pursuit of a social agenda and a more meaningful life. Almost all the consumer movements offer knowledge dissemination and training for advocacy roles. They offer an understanding of shared experiences, mutual support, peer counseling, and role modeling. They have the capability for providing a new identity and revived strengths to persons whose mental health has been profoundly diminished by the social devaluation of their mental illness.

Today, consonant with and perhaps as a result of the consumer movement, there is a definite emphasis on recovery from mental illness, particularly in the United States and most European countries. Recovery does not mean return to a premorbid state, but rather functional and emotional improvements that enable one to live a satisfying life despite the limitations of the illness. The recovery movement has led to greater equality in the relationships between persons with mental illness and the professionals who treat them, an advance that may have therapeutic implications. As of this writing, a new issue of *Current Psychiatry*, for example, contains an optimistic article on recovery from schizophrenia that is co-authored by two psychiatrists and two persons with mental illness (Manschreck et al., 2008).

Conclusions

The mental health/mental illness distinction has particular relevance to the changing structure of services and training in the Western world. With the worldwide emergence of managed care systems, whether publicly or privately operated, mental health service providers are under increasing attack unless they can demonstrate a medical, illness-based rationale for their interventions. Insurers are increasingly unwilling to pay for psychotherapy addressed to psychological problem-solving, personal growth, or self-actualization.

We are seeing a reorientation of disciplinary training and a restructuring of systems in advanced nations that paradoxically move those systems closer to those of the developing world. Consider the anticipated future for psychiatry in the United States. The predictions are that psychiatrists will (1) place increasingly greater emphasis on the major mental illnesses and neurobehavioral disorders than on psychological problems in living, (2) focus on psychosocial rehabilitation efforts for the disabled rather than on psychotherapy for the general population, and (3) deal more with the psychopathological aspects of general medical conditions, a move toward non-Cartesian concepts of health and illness (Lieberman & Rush, 1996). Psychoanalysis, no longer reimbursed by insurance and increasingly viewed as a personal growth enhancer rather than a treatment modality, will continue to be utilized primarily by the educated few who comprehend its premises and can invest the time and money. Developments that focus on biologically based disorders, develop a seamless view of psyche and soma, and retreat from prolonged psychotherapies indeed move us more toward the treatment systems of the developing world.

In many ways, Western concepts of mental illness are beginning to merge with those in the developing world. Western scientific thought and its correlative healing systems were traditionally based on Descartes' mind/body dichotomy, which tended to separate medicine from psychological practice. For many years the conceptual basis and the behaviors of both mental health and mental illness were ascribed to psychogenic factors, or to psychogenic nested within sociogenic factors. The proliferation of research findings pointing to the biogenesis of the major disorders has led to a more holistic view in which somatic vulnerabilities interact with psychosocial stressors, which affect the course if not the etiology of the disorders. Mental illnesses generate a fragmented sense of self; they are intrinsically frightening, and the mode of social response determines the extent to which the individual will feel diminished and stigmatized or able to cope with a disability of cognition or affect.

Social scientists have turned their attention to the social meaning of illness and illness behaviors and their interactive effects. Cultural constructivists and symbolic interactionists remind us that all human behavior must be viewed in fluid interaction with ever moving cultural currents. They note correctly that mental illness can be studied only as an interactive, constantly changing process within and among patients, families, healers, and other figures in the social environment (Gaines, 1992). These interactive variables determine how a biologically based psychopathology is defined and experienced by individuals and their significant others. They also determine the societal architecture for diagnosis, treatment, and rehabilitation.

The cross-cultural literature tells us much about the architecture of healing. The findings from WHO research suggest that culture can profoundly affect the experience of mental illness as well as its course – through cultural acceptance, social support, balanced expectations of persons with core cognitive and perceptual impairments, and cultural mechanisms for meeting the needs of individuals at variable levels of functioning.

The consumer movement has demonstrated that many people who were psychiatrically hospitalized are able to offer services, counseling, and role modeling to their peers. As an embodiment of realized hope, recovered peers also offer a dimension of self-esteem that cannot be provided by loving families or by mental health professionals alone. For many persons with mental illness, negative cultural attitudes have led to self-devaluation, abandonment of hope, and behavioral regression. Research in the years ahead may tell us whether members of the consumer movement, many of whom have triumphed over profound adversity, are able to counteract and change that social reflection.

Part II
The Social Context of Mental Health and Illness

Tony N. Brown and Teresa L. Scheid

Stress and Social Support

Social context defines not only appropriate responses to stress but also the nature of distress and emotional deviance itself. Social context in Part II of this volume situates stress that accompanies role occupancy (e.g., caregiver, spouse, and worker) and status assignment (e.g., female, Black, and middle-aged). Further, social context here helps explain within-group (or subgroup) variation in mental health and illness, thus "unpacking the average." We hope to convey that, without a sense of the context-specific norms and expectations plus attention to the intersection of roles and statuses, scholars studying mental health and illness are prone to mischaracterize its etiology and subjective experience (Moodley, 2000; Rogler, 1999). Further, scholars are likely to mischaracterize dysfunctional coping responses. These types of mischaracterizations have serious implications for the measurement of mental health and illness, affecting our ability to address overarching questions regarding the stress process, inequality, and mental health and illness. Such questions, for example, include whether stress exposure or vulnerability has been properly specified (Turner, Wheaton, & Lloyd, 1995), whether social context changes the measurement of mental health and illness (Brown, 2003; Lopez & Guarnaccia, 2000; Takeuchi, Chun, Gong, & Shen, 2002), and whether low status causes stress and distress (Dohrenwend et al., 1992).

The sociological study of stress has dominated mental health research since the 1960s; 40 years of research have demonstrated a consistently positive relationship between stress and distress. In the 1970s, researchers modified the stress model to take into account the important role played by social support and other resources that allow individuals to cope with stressful events in their lives. Intervening models, or coping theories, focus on how coping resources are mobilized after the stressful event, whereas distress-deterring models argue that coping resources such as a supportive family may actually reduce the likelihood of stress occurring in the first place or else can help alter the meaning of stress in salubrious ways.

Because stress does not affect everyone the same way, researchers must also take into account vulnerability to stress. Vulnerability was originally conceived as a purely psychological concept; sociologists now view it as a group concept as well. For example, membership in some social categories (e.g., racial minority status or gender) provides an individual with differential access to resources and a different socialization experience that may structure his or her reaction to both stress and illness. In addition, exposure and vulnerability to status-based experiences of institutional and individual discrimination have recently become interesting to stress scholars; they argue that one's position in society and access to resources result in divergent mental health experiences. Link and Phelan (1995) identified lack of access to resources as a fundamental cause of disease because it influences exposure to various risk factors including stress and one's ability to either avoid or cope with psychological distress.

Increasingly researchers are concerned with the measurability of stress and major life events, yet there is also the recognition that the meaning of an event exhibits great social variability (Aneshensel, Rutter, & Lachenbruch, 1991; Thoits, 1995). For example, one person may experience a divorce as devastating, resulting in multiple losses – a significant other, social position, family, and friends. Severe depression may thus be a likely outcome as that individual experiences grief and guilt, as well as the painful necessity of reconstructing a shattered sense of self. However, if the marriage was especially burdensome or if one was subject to emotional or physical abuse, divorce may be a welcome release and may produce a sense of freedom, autonomy, and mastery. Simple life event scales, commonly used in the 1970s and the 1980s, that sum the number of stressful life events an individual experiences fail to capture how the same event is experienced in different ways by different individuals and groups. The status quo prior to such common life transitions as job loss and divorce is far more consequential than either the transition itself or the coping strategies used (Wheaton, 1990). Furthermore, chronic stress arising from continuous and persistent social environmental conditions plays a critical role and is more important in understanding mental health than acute stressors (Wheaton, 1990). In Chapter 9 Wheaton and Montazer provide an extended discussion of stressors and stress, encouraging their more specific conceptualization and operationalization.

In addition to stress, sociologists have focused a great deal of attention on social support networks; that is, the role played by family and friends and others in helping an individual cope with stress or in exposing an individual to additional stressors. We may receive primarily emotional support (i.e., love, empathy, and understanding), structural forms of support such as money or a place to live, or some combination of the two. Structural forms of support may also be referred to as tangible or instrumental support. Although much theoretical attention has been given to how social support can reduce mental disturbance, Thoits (1995) has argued that researchers have not examined the intervening mechanisms by which social support influences one's ability to cope, or the selection of coping mechanisms, or how social support affects feelings of self-esteem and mastery, which are so crucial to mental health. Furthermore, Thoits (1995) has noted that we do not understand how an individual's existing social network and perceived social support influence support-seeking or help-seeking behavior. Often a family's shame or ignorance of the reality of mental illness can prohibit its members from seeking out professional help or therapy. Alternatively, a family with a good bit of positive experience with professional care providers may routinely access mental health services, hence forestalling problems that can lead to stress down the road. The most common example would be the benefits of couples therapy in facilitating communication and ensuring that problems do not build to the point where they become insurmountable. Issues needing further research are how stress affects social support (Taylor & Turner, 2004) and how social capital affects health (Carpiano, 2006). Many events that are considered stressful (i.e., divorce or unemployment) may also have negative impacts on social support and social capital by altering the social networks in which individuals are embedded. Turner and Lewis-Brown in Chapter 10 more fully address the complex relationship between social support and mental health, as they examine how social networks can be activated or damaged by stress.

Unemployment and underemployment are major sources of stress, especially when the economy retracts and there are few job options. In an extensive review of the literature, Perrucci and Perrucci (1990) concluded that there is strong aggregate support for the positive relationship between unemployment and poor mental health. At the individual level, Reynolds and Gilbert (1991) found that unemployment contributed to psychological distress, and Warner (1985) has argued that the effects of extended unemployment – isolation, withdrawal, anxiety, and depression – are similar to the symptoms commonly associated with schizophrenia. At the same time, work can also be a major source of stress, especially when it decreases individual opportunities for autonomy and self-control or is a source of anxiety. Job stress has been rising in the United States, and the recent trends of downsizing, downward mobility, and declining wages all compound the experience of job-related distress. Karasek and Theorell (1990) found that high-strain jobs (i.e., those with high levels of psychological demands and low degrees of autonomy, or decision latitude) resulted in moderately severe rates of depression and exhaustion as well as higher levels of pill consumption. Workers in jobs with little discretion over their work (i.e., low in autonomy and control or decision latitude) experienced higher rates of physical illness and depression, as well as a loss of self-esteem. Such job experiences are more common among the lower and working classes. Furthermore, job control and decision latitude are also important to a sense of mastery, which we have seen is important to one's mental health. Mary Clare Lennon and Laura Limonic focus on qualities of work and transitions to unemployment as stressors in Chapter 11.

Socioeconomic Status and Gender

One of the most consistent research findings has been the inverse relationship between social class and various types of mental disorder (Dohrenwend, 1990). The Epidemiological Catchment Area (ECA) studies conducted in the 1980s found that those in the lower social classes had higher levels of schizophrenia, depression, alcohol abuse, and general mental impairment (Dohrenwend, 1990).

Social class is generally referred to by sociologists as one's socioeconomic status (SES) and is determined by three factors. First is economic position, reflecting one's income and wealth including inheritance, property, and savings. Second is status or prestige, reflecting the type of occupation and education one possesses. Although economic position is a fairly objective measure, prestige is subjective and is determined by society's ranking of the prestige of various occupations. A third determinant of one's SES is the amount of power one possesses. This may be political power (i.e., the ability to influence the political process) or having power over other people. C. W. Mills (1956, p. 5) in *The Power Elite* defined the powerful as those "whose positions enable to transcend the ordinary environments of ordinary men and women; they are in positions to make decisions having major consequences."

Those in lower SES groups are subject to higher levels of chronic stress; that is, their social environments subject them to more stressful conditions and also limit their coping resources available to deal with chronic stresses such as unemployment or poverty. Social class can also affect people's sense of control over the conditions in their lives and therefore self-esteem and mastery. Lifelong exposure to chronic stress can erode one's sense of self-efficacy; furthermore, if stressors cannot be controlled then a belief in personal control (or self-efficacy) may even be detrimental and may have a negative impact on mental health (Aneshensel, 1992).

There are two explanations offered for the inverse relationship between SES and mental disorder: social causation or social selection. Social causation models postulate that those in lower status groups are subject to higher levels of stress such as poverty, unemployment, discrimination, and dangerous neighborhoods, and it is the higher levels of stress that account for higher levels of mental disorder. Social selection models focus on the individual and postulate that those with mental disorders will end up in the lower stratum of society. Such individuals would not be able to hold a job or sustain meaningful relationships with others and are likely to "drift" down the SES ladder (social selection is also referred to as social drift). William Eaton, Carles Muntaner, and Jaime Sapag in Chapter 12 provide a more in-depth explanation of the relationship between SES and mental health and illness.

Men and women exhibit different types of mental illness and disorder: Women have higher levels of mood disorder, anxiety, and depression, and men have higher rates of personality disorder and substance abuse, although rates of schizophrenia are similar in both genders. From the late 1800s until very recently, women's higher levels of mood disorder were felt to be a result of either their hormones, their more expressive, emotional personalities, or their greater propensity to seek out medical and psychiatric help. We now know that, in fact, women do experience higher levels of distress. Sharon Schwartz (1991) has argued that men and women respond to the stress in their lives in different ways. Drawing on the theories of Emile Durkheim, Schwartz focused on the social context of depression and differentiated between levels of integration and regulation. Altruism, or other-oriented valuative preferences, is associated with high levels of group integration, whereas fatalism, a belief that one has little control, is associated with high degrees of regulation whereby others in fact do control an individual's choices and actions. Girls are socialized to be both other-oriented and to accept strong normative controls over their behavior. The most obvious example is found in rules governing sexual behavior. These dual conditions of high integration and high regulation produce both altruism and fatalism, which result in lowered self-esteem in response to stress. Girls are more dependent on others for self-worth and valuation and thus more likely to feel helpless and powerless and to have lower self-esteem. Anger may also be turned inward. All of these conditions are consistent with the etiology of depression (Schwartz, 1991).

Boys, on the other hand, are socialized in a context with less emphasis on group membership (i.e., low integration or egoism in Durkheim's terminology) as well as lower levels of normative regulation on behavior (i.e., anomie). Consequently, boys and men are more likely to display antisocial behaviors in response to stress. That is, they are more likely to act out, to display aggressive or hostile behavior, or to resist normative authority and seek to actively break rule systems. This could account for the recent finding that men have higher rates of alcoholism in response to stress, whereas women have higher rates of depression. Schwartz (1991) referred to her theory as the norm hypothesis and contrasted it with the more traditional role stress hypothesis. According to that latter hypothesis, women experience higher levels of mental distress because their traditional roles, as well as their changing roles, produced higher levels of stress for which they were inadequately prepared. Role stress theory explains the higher rates of depression among housewives by arguing that the single occupational role of housewife provides few sources of gratification and reward, is relatively low skilled, and lacks social prestige. Working wives experience higher levels of depression and stress because they are, by and large, working in jobs that are lower in status and pay and also have to face the conflicting role pressures of working the "second shift," caring for home as well as maintaining a job (Hochschild & Machung, 1989). Child rearing compounds these sources of stress. Depression among professional women is attributed to role strain and tension between professional obligations and aspirations and family commitments. Finally, the higher levels of depression among older women are explained by their role loss; specifically the loss of family (both children and eventually spouse) that effectively removes a woman's reason for being, her purpose in life. Sara Rosenfield and Dena Smith provide an extended discussion of gender and mental health in Chapter 13 by invoking gendered distinctions in power, responsibilities, and selfhood.

Race and Racism

Chronic stressors (i.e., poverty, unemployment, marital and family disruption, discrimination, and poor physical health) fall disproportionately on minority groups. Members of minority groups must also face higher levels of stigma (T. Brown, Sellers, & Gomez, 2002) as well as conflicting cultural messages as they are expected to conform to the values and standards of the dominant "White" culture (Jackson & Stewart, 2003). Racism and discrimination are significant sources of stress (T. Brown et al., 2000; Williams, Yu, Jackson, & Anderson, 1997; Williams & Williams-Morris, 2000). The ECA studies found that lower SES Blacks were more likely to experience stress, particularly unemployment, poverty, and marital disruption, and would subsequently be more vulnerable to mental distress (Williams, Takeuchi, & Adair, 1992b). However, because Blacks are also disproportionately concentrated in the lower SES ranks, it is difficult to untangle the separate effects of social class and race on mental health.

McLeod and Shanahan (1993) examined the effects of persistent poverty in the underclass – the mostly minority urban population with the highest rates of unemployment, female-headed households, and crime as identified by William Julius Wilson (1993). Although Blacks and Hispanics had higher rates of current and persistent poverty than Whites, McLeod and Shanahan (1993) found little evidence of race or ethnic differences in the relationship between poverty and children's mental health. Data on the mental health status of other minority groups are lacking, despite the 2001 Supplement to the Surgeon General's Report on Mental Health, which analyzed the effects of race and culture on mental health (Sue & Chu, 2003). As noted by Vega and Rumbaut (1991, p. 357) in their review of the research and literature on minority mental health, this area has "been seriously understudied because there have been few minority researchers, and people of color often have not been presented in the clinical patient populations used to develop the epidemiologic data based over the decades of research." More than a decade later, Sue and Chu (2003, p. 447) still found that a "paucity of research exists on the mental health of ethnic minority populations." In 2003 the *Journal of Health and Social Behavior* published a special issue, "Race, Ethnicity, and Mental Health," that presented an excellent selection of research and theoretical models. The articles in this volume focused on understanding racial disparities in prevalence, diagnosis, and treatment of mental health problems in minority communities. This evidence is discussed by David Williams, Manuela Costa, and

Jacinta Leavell in Chapter 14. Deeper theorization regarding race-related stress is required and will be facilitated by new, large epidemiological studies of Blacks, Asians, and Hispanics (Alegria, Mulvaney-Day, Woo et al., 2007; Jackson et al., 2004), which include more information on social context and larger samples than any prior studies.

An important extension of research on gender differences in mental health is explaining the differential experiences of minority and White women. SES, gender, and race are interrelated in a complex manner with multiple feedback loops. Female and Black are two statuses that are socially devalued, and African American women are more likely to live in poverty than are White women. African American women also face demanding social networks, which may be a unique source of stress, rather than a coping resource. In Chapter 15 Verna Keith and Diane Brown provide a conceptual framework for understanding the intersection of race, gender, and SES, and the connection between physical and mental well-being among African American women. This framework may challenge perspectives in Chapters 12–14 that focus on a single status one at a time, rather than systematically considering intersectionality. Future research focusing on race and racism must seriously consider how incarceration, migration, residential segregation, inequality-related fatalism, and immigration (among other factors) shape experiences of mental health and illness among ethnic/racial minority groups.

Life Course

In addition to social class, gender, race and ethnicity, our social position is also structured by our age and social roles, which change as we age. An individual's social involvement and investment in meaningful role relationships clearly play an important role in mental health. The key to the positive role played by multiple role identities is that they provide multiple sources of satisfaction and different opportunities to develop a sense of efficacy and mastery. Likewise, multiple roles provide multiple opportunities for social support. For example, married people report consistently better mental health outcomes, due primarily to their higher levels of social and emotional support, than unmarried people. Yet relationship quality and the division of labor, both housework and paid work, are important conditions that cannot be ignored. In Chapter 16, Kristi Williams, Adrianne Frech, and Daniel Carlson summarize extant research on the impact on mental health of marriage, remarriage, cohabitation, and divorce for men and women.

Children and adolescents experience unique forms of stress, and Elizabeth Menaghan describes the experiences of this population in Chapter 17. Increasing attention is now being being placed on the mental health experiences of minority youth because they make up a population that many believe is highly vulnerable to stress. Vega and Rumbaut (1991) reported that American Indian children (aged between 10 and 19) are three times more likely to commit suicide than

White children, and between 18% and 23% have had a family member attempt or commit suicide. Aneshensel and Sucoff (1996) found that youth growing up in lower SES neighborhoods in Los Angeles perceived greater hazards such as crime, violence, and drug use than youth in high-SES neighborhoods and that the perception of a neighborhood as dangerous influenced mental health. The more dangerous and threatening the perception of the neighborhood, the more common the symptoms of internalizing disorders, such as anxiety and depression, and of externalizing disorders such as conduct disorder and oppositional defiant disorder. The fact that approximately three of five Black children grow up in poverty and in neighborhoods considered less than desirable obviously has serious mental health implications. Cleo Caldwell and Ebony Sandusky examine the relationship among social environment, depression, and risky sexual behaviors for Black adolescents in Chapter 18. Adolescence is a component of the life course full of change and increased risk.

Moving forward in the life course and focusing on another component of it (i.e., middle age), John Mirowsky and Catherine Ross in Chapter 19 provide a comprehensive model to understand how age (in its multiple forms) influences mental health. Their chapter demonstrates the normativity of certain transitions as we move through adulthood, and in so doing, it shows how middle age is often a period of high levels of well-being.

We conclude Part II with a chapter on terrorism and mental health. Obviously in the decade since the first edition of this volume, fear of terrorism has been stimulated by the traumatic events of 9/11, and local mental health issues have been overshadowed by efforts to ensure preparedness for terrorist attacks as well as for natural disasters such as Hurricanes Katrina and Rita that devastated (mostly disadvantaged) communities. In Chapter 20, Robert Johnson and Stevan Hobfoll provide a nuanced discussion on terrorism and mental health that demonstrates the need for far more extensive research in this area. This chapter incorporates theories of stress and social support described in Chapters 9 and 10 and does an excellent job of demonstrating how social context influences mental health.

As this overview should indicate, there is much we do not know about how social context shapes experiences of mental health and illness. No doubt social context has the capacity to define mental health through shared experiences, to produce mental illness through stress, and to determine the resources available in a crisis. Given that we are unlikely to be able to reduce stress in the lives of low-status individuals and groups, better and more comprehensive treatment options must be made available. As such, the final section of the volume, Part III, turns to treatment and management in mental health and illness from an organizational perspective. The care of and treatment provided to individuals with mental health problems reflect wider social values and priorities, and sometimes that care is uneven and unequal.

9

Stressors, Stress, and Distress

Blair Wheaton and Shirin Montazer

In this chapter, Wheaton and Montazer distinguish among commonly used terms for stress, stressors, and distress. They then examine models that have shaped our understanding of the stress concept, differentiating between the two original models of stress: the biological stress model and the engineering stress model. The authors go on to define and distinguish among different types of stress lying along a "stress continuum," from discrete events to continuous chronic stressors. Beyond these conceptual distinctions is the empirical issue of whether we need to measure diverse sources of stress. Wheaton and Montazer argue that we do – and that we need to assess the "unique" effects of diverse sources of stress (controlling for other stressors) as well as the "total" effect of stressors on mental health. This point is illustrated with data from the Toronto Mental Health and Stress Study and the National Population Health Survey of Canada. The authors then address a number of misconceptions about what stress is and is not, and conclude the chapter with a thorough review of past research and recent trends in stress research.

Introduction

Stress is a term used regularly in popular books, in the media, and in daily life. From the perspective of someone who studies stress, it is difficult not to notice the differences in meaning and understandings of stress in daily use. There is substantial confusion about what stress is and is not, and yet the overuse of this term – as a vague catch-all explanation of all that ails us – continues without any sign of letting up. When people say, "I feel stressed," they are in fact referring to distress because they are implicitly referring to the behavioral response to stressful conditions, manifest in the form of a mixture of depression and anxiety. When people say, "I have a lot of stress in my life," they typically are referring to stressors, the forces acting on us that constitute either threats to or demands on our current life and that are located in our social environments. Ironically, people rarely use the term *stress* to refer to the "stress" in the sequence of stressors, stress, and distress, primarily because that term is reserved in the dominant stress model in the social sciences to refer to the organism's physiological response to stressors, as in a state of activation, alarm, and defense. In that approach, stress is the thing that turns stressors into distress.

It is difficult to write about something that everyone feels is already well understood. Explain to someone that you study stress, and you are likely to hear a few prototypical responses, such as "I have so much stress, you should study my life,"

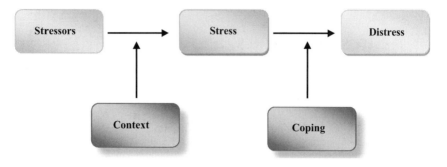

Figure 9.1. Stressors, stress, and distress.

or "but stress is everywhere and in everything we do," or "stress is just an excuse when people have problems," or "isn't it related to everything?" or the ubiquitous "life is stressful." These responses reveal a strange mixture of overgeneralized skepticism and the unconditional belief that stress is a fundamental explanation for life problems.

In this chapter, we clarify current misconceptions in these responses and, in so doing, discuss a series of distinctions that must be in place to understand the current literature on stress. We consider the following issues:

- distinguishing among commonly used terms – *stressors*, *stress*, and *distress*
- distinguishing the two original stress models from each other
- defining and distinguishing different types of stress in the "stress universe" (Wheaton, 1994)
- investigating the empirical distinctiveness of different types of stress to assess the need for these distinctions
- clarifying misconceptions or confusion about what stress is and is not
- reviewing the growth of and recent trends in stress research

Stressors, Stress, and Distress

Figure 9.1 presents some of the fundamental distinctions we need to make, showing a sequence of stressors that may precipitate *stress* depending on the context, or social circumstances, of the occurrence of the stressor and therefore its meaning, which in turn may precipitate *distress*, depending on the state of coping resources when the stressor occurs. The multiple contingencies in this process suggest that many things we think of as stressful turn out not to be, and even when they are stressful, they may not translate into increased distress. A stressor may not be as threatening to one person as to another because he or she has experienced it before; stress may not turn into distress because that person has high levels of social support or engages in active attempts to resolve the situation.

To provide focus in the psychosocial approach to stress, we argue that it is more important to define stressors than even to define stress. Given that stress itself is usually defined in terms of a biological state of the body – a generalized physiological alert – in response to threatening agents, stressors have sometimes been defined as "that which produces stress" (Selye, 1956, p. 64). The problem with this definition is that a biological response is required to define something as stressful. It is not at all clear that stressors turn into distress only because and through the stage of a bodily stress response. Some specific problems that people face may not be defined as a problem for them, but this does not mean that those problems will have no impact on their mental health over time – only that the person has habituated to them.

As a reference point, we define *stressors* as conditions of threat, challenge, demands, or structural constraints that, by the very fact of their occurrence or existence, call into question the operating integrity of the organism. This definition implies that stressors can occur in different ways, with each still representing a type of environmental pressure. Threats involve the possibility or expectation of potential harm. Challenges question the current fundamental assumptions within which a person operates – they imply that more is necessary and the usual response won't do. Demands involve the load component of stressors, also commonly referred to as "burden" or "overload." Finally, structural constraints stand for reduced opportunities, choices, or rewards resulting from severe or non-self-limiting social disadvantage. The structural constraints referred to here are features of social structure and thus are a function of social location. Living with the constant fear of victimization may be threatening, overcoming a serious stroke may be a challenge, work overload and work–family strain reflect undue demands, and the absence of job opportunities or the presence of persistent discrimination may result from the structural constraints accompanying disadvantage.

Two Stress Models

There are actually two related versions of the stress concept, one anchored in the biological stress model of Selye (1956) and the other the standard engineering stress model (Smith, 1987). These two approaches do not exactly say the same thing about stress, so it is important to understand how they are different, as well as the ways in which they converge.

The Biological Stress Model

Selye's biological stress model (1956) includes four stages: (1) stressors: in Selye's approach, a wide variety of events and conditions that represent threat or insult to the organism; (2) conditioning factors that alter the impact of the stressor on the organism, as in coping resources in the psychosocial model; (3) the general adaptation syndrome (GAS), an intervening state of stress in the organism; and (4) responses, adaptive or maladaptive (i.e., distress). This conceptual model still informs the study of stress to this day, because it incorporates essential distinctions in an overall process from stimulus problem to response. For example, we still see coping resources such as social support as a conditioning factor that alters the impact of stress. The separation of stressors from coping capacity is an important contribution to the study of stress, because it allows us to discover how the two combine to produce adaptive or maladaptive outcomes. Further, the biological model makes the point, albeit implicitly, that the occurrence of stress is separate from more general behavioral responses, such as distress or depression, which form and stabilize over time.

For Selye, the heart of the matter of stress was the general adaptation syndrome itself. He defined this syndrome in terms of physiological indications of a three-stage response sequence to "noxious agents": the alarm reaction, the stage of resistance, and the stage of exhaustion (Selye, 1956). Thus, Selye's primary interest was in identifying and describing a biologically based response syndrome to threatening agents. To help with the metaphor, he added that stress could be defined as the "state of wear and tear of the body" (p. 55). When Selye defined a stressor as "that which produces stress" (p. 64), he linked the fact of occurrence of a stressor to the observation of a biological stress response. There are at least three fundamental problems with this approach. First, a stressor is simply a putative problem, whose actual threat value is still to be defined by contextual circumstances (as in Fig. 9.1). A stressor cannot be defined purely (and retrospectively) by its consequences, because in so doing we seriously impair the identification of classes or types of social environments that are problematic to mental health in the population. Second, exposure to stressors over time may undermine mental health without the occurrence of a biological stress response as a necessary condition. The biological stress model would exclude such stressors. Importantly, these are exactly the types of stressors that may bypass consciousness because they grow insidiously, are not defined as threatening, seem to call for only routine responses, and yet eat away at the coping capacity of the person. Third, stressors may have other consequences beyond health outcomes per se that are important to understanding the broader sociological consequences of their occurrence (Aneshensel, Rutter, & Lachenbruch, 1991). Stressors may undermine educational performance, lead to marrying earlier, or cause interruptions in labor force activity.

The biological model gives minimal guidance on bounding or delimiting what social stressors are or, for that matter, what they are not. We believe that this lack of guidance implies that one cannot use the biological stress model as a basis for defining a universe of stressors or deriving particular measures of stressors.

And yet, as the concept of stress evolved from research conducted in the 1960s, that is precisely what was done.

Life Change Events: The Model Stressor

When the word *stress* is used in research circles, the most common operational link that gives expression to this word is the life change event, a discrete, observable, and "objectively" reportable event that requires some social or psychological adjustment on the part of the individual – the operant word here being *event*. Although the early research on important life changes included positive events, the usual approach over the past three decades has been to focus on negative events, because those events have been found to be much more harmful to mental health than positive events have been found to be harmful or helpful (Ross & Mirowsky, 1979). To give some flesh to the kinds of events studied, here are some examples: getting fired from a job, getting a divorce, experiencing the death of a spouse or loved one, having an abortion or miscarriage, being assaulted or robbed, and ending a romantic relationship. The lists used in research include from about 30 to well over 100 such events, with each list attempting to capture the essential set of stressful life changes (Dohrenwend et al., 1978; Holmes & Rahe, 1967). In the development of these inventories we see the opportunity to study stress using a set of objectively verifiable occurrences.

If we look to Selye's actual examples for clues as to what stressors are, we find examples that are quite instructive. The noxious agents cited include things such as toxic substances, noise, extreme heat or cold, injury, and weight (Selye, 1956). Although there are some agents here that qualify as "events," it is also clear that some qualify as conditions or continuous states. In fact, it has never been the case that biological stressors were restricted to the notion of an event (Hinkle, 1987). Thus, it is something of a mystery as to why the concept of life change events was assumed to be closer to the core of what is stressful than other life problems, other than their relative measurement expediency. Of course, the idea was that change is a challenge, but so is dealing with unremitting sameness. The problem in defining more continuous life conditions as stressors seemed to be that it was difficult to designate at what point, at what level, they become stressful. But the problems in measuring more continuous, ongoing problems as stressors should not distract attention from these sources of stress, if in fact they are important in terms of risk to mental health.

Probably because life events could be self-reported and therefore measured more straightforwardly, the measurement of other forms of stress waited while the life events tradition flourished. But our intuitions and our experience tell us that a stressor can also exist as a *state*, a continuous and persistent problem. Another stress model explicitly distinguishes between types of stressors and includes as well a flexible metaphor for how stress works in humans. Ironically, this model is derived from the stress model of physical mechanics.

The Engineering Stress Model

The "original" stress model was formulated to understand the effects of external forces on the integrity of metals. This model helps us explain, for example, dramatic metallurgical failures, as in the case of the shocking collapse of the I-35W bridge in the summer of 2007 in St. Paul, Minnesota, and in the equally unexpected collapse of a bridge over a river on Interstate 95 in Connecticut in 1984. In both cases, the main span of the bridge collapsed without the provocation of an "event" – there were no high winds, no unusual rate of traffic that day. In both cases, the cited problem referred to more long-term processes, such as metal fatigue, excessive loads, and rust. Breakdowns regularly occur in both the physical and social world without an observable precipitating event and thus require explanation using concepts beyond the very notion of an event. It may be the continual stress to the bridge of unobserved rusting (captured in the metaphor "rust never sleeps"), or the inadequacy of a design that leaves bent gusset plates in the bridge under recurrent high loads. In every case the collapse results from a slow process of decline in structural integrity that one day reaches a threshold, resulting in collapse. There may be a precipitating event (e.g., bridge repairs causing unusual weight distributions on the bridge), but this event only helps push the situation over the edge sooner rather than later.

In the engineering model, stress is essentially an external force acting against a resisting body (Smith, 1987). One could say that stress becomes a stressor when the level of force exceeds limits defining structural integrity, known in the engineering model as the "elastic limit" of the material. It appears that stressors and stress are not distinct phases in the engineering model – they both refer to the external force or threat. As a metaphor, this makes the engineering model both a more straightforward and a more general model for the study of social stressors.

Figure 9.2 reproduces from Smith (1987) the curve showing the relationship between stress and strain according to the engineering model. In the engineering model, strain is the response state of the material (distress); technically, the state of the elongation and compression of the material. The level of stress is shown on the Y axis, the level of strain on the X axis. The material, in a pristine healthy state, starts at zero. As long as the stress applied does not exceed point A on the stress scale, the material will not exceed its elastic limit, and it will return to its original shape after the stress is removed. The model does allow for changes in the elastic limit of the material, however. When stress exceeds A, say to level B, the material is able to adjust by elongation or compression (coping) and, in the process, achieve a new, greater elastic limit. In other words, it is stronger. This feature of the engineering model offers flexibility via the explicit allowance for

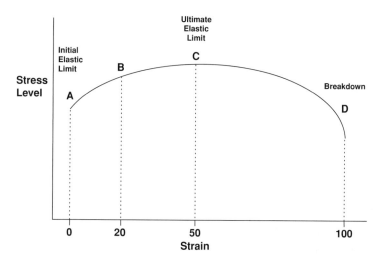

Figure 9.2. The stress versus strain curve in the engineering stress model.

enhancement of coping capacity as a result of facing stressful situations, rather than just the minimization of damage to existing capacity.

The model also allows for deterioration of the capacity to resist, because the material has an ultimate elastic limit. The implication is that at some point the individual's ability to respond with adjustments that enhance strength will no longer be possible. The size and force of the stressor will overwhelm the human capacity to withstand. Point C in Figure 9.2 represents the ultimate elastic limit of the material: the point of maximum strength. If stress is applied beyond point C, the stress the material can resist actually decreases, heading toward point D, known in the engineering model as fracture or breakdown. The curve in Figure 9.2 can be considered a representative curve, although materials and persons will differ in the amount of rise and fall of the curve and in the left-to-right distance for enhancements versus deteriorations in strength.

A fundamental point of the engineering model is that stress occurs in more than one form, sometimes as a catastrophic event and sometimes as a continuous force. This distinction was articulated in the psychosocial stress model in the work of Pearlin and his colleagues (Pearlin, 1983; Pearlin & Schooler, 1978; Pearlin, Lieberman, Menaghan, & Mullan, 1981), Brown and his colleagues (e.g., Brown & Harris, 1978), and around the same time by Wheaton (1980, 1983). Different terms were used at the time, but the most general accounts emphasized the importance of what have come to be known as chronic stressors, rather than event stressors. The distinction between catastrophic and continuous forces maps directly in the psychosocial approach to event versus chronic stressors.

Why is this distinction important in the engineering model? In effect, the types of adjustments possible on the part of the material are defined by whether the force is a trauma or a continuous force. Thus, we expect that the model showing how chronic stress affects mental health will be quite distinct from the model showing how life events affect mental health. For example, one can imagine that dealing with life event stress may involve a stronger role for coping resources that can be easily mobilized but only exist over short periods (e.g., unusually high levels of social support after a spouse dies), whereas chronic stress may demand more stable resources that are automatically rather than conditionally activated (e.g., beliefs about self-efficacy).

Allostatic Load

Recent updates of the biological stress model include the notion of *allostatic load*, which is close in purpose to the notion of a continual long-term load or force in the engineering model. First introduced by McEwen and Stellar (1993), the concept of allostatic load refers to the long-term wear and tear across multiple physiological systems resulting from stable or cumulative stress exposure (Vanitallie, 2002). According to Carlson and Chamberlain (2005, p. 309), "an underlying assumption is that the allostatic load of any biological organism will increase over time," and only a resilient organism that is able to improve with environmental challenges – that is, displays adaptive plasticity – will be able to minimize this physiological wear and tear and thus its allostatic load. Note that the concept of adaptive plasticity is the same as a dynamic elastic limit for materials.

The contribution of stress (e.g., chronic economic strain) to allostatic load is likely to accumulate over considerable amounts of time. This accumulation will in turn eventually lead to a decreased resistance to illness and disease with age (Hayward, Crimmins, Miles, & Yang, 2000). These parallels with the engineering model suggest that the historical evolution of social stress from its origins in the biological stress model focused more on certain features than others. In fact, the notions of discrete and continuous stress, short-term and long-term processes, adaptive versus maladaptive responses, and contextual circumstances that help define the level of threat are available in both approaches.

Varieties of Stress

Whether or not the engineering model is invoked, the importance of more contin-uous and ongoing sources of stress can be argued from a psychosocial perspective per se (Pearlin, 1989). This argument includes the notion that more stable forms of stress are likely to result from stable features of differences in position in a social structure. Pearlin has also made consistently clear in his work the impor-tance of distinguishing among stressors because they are involved in a dynamic interplay of causation over time, leading to either the spread or containment of stress experience over people's lives, depending on the sequence and the types of stressors involved. Earlier stressors may change the level of threat resulting from later stressors, as when exposure to an earlier stressor, such as parental divorce, changes not only the likelihood of a personal divorce occurring but also the mental health consequences, or when the chronic stress in a marriage actually reduces the threat to mental health of a divorce (Wheaton, 1990). In this approach, earlier stress in the life course can be part of the context of the meaning of later stress. Thus, distinguishing types of stressors is a necessary condition of understanding the complex interrelationships among distinct stress experiences over the life course, as well as the collective and cumulative impacts of stress on mental health.

Events versus Chronic Stressors

Life change events, known here as event stressors, have the following characteristics: They are discrete, observable events standing for significant life changes, with a relatively clear onset and offset, made up of – once in motion – a relatively well-defined sequence of subevents describing the "normal" progress of the event. Some life events, of course, have little internal structure, such as the death of a pet, but most others actually involve a process, often a partially ritualized process. Divorce, job loss, and death of a spouse are classic examples. The defining issue in a life event is its discreteness, both in its typical time course and its onset and offset. In most cases, life events do not slowly emerge as an issue; instead, they begin with the announcement of the unfortunate news that begins the event. As stressors, they typically have a clear offset, a point at which the stressor ends; for example, the court settlement of the divorce or the actual death of the spouse. Note that the actual divorce is just the end point of the stressor, not the stress that may follow, which can continue due to related sequences of stressors that follow after the initial life event.

Taking events as a point of departure, then, we can define a very different class of stressors, referred to as *chronic stressors*, that (1) do not necessarily start as an event, but develop slowly and insidiously as continuing and problematic conditions in our social environments or roles; (2) typically have a longer time course than life events, from onset to resolution; and (3) are usually less self-limiting than life events.[1] The crux of the distinction between event stressors and chronic stressors is the time course of the stressor, but there is more involved, including differences in the ways in which the stressor develops, exists, and ends.

---

[1] Chronic stressors are, in fact, "continuous" only in an approximate sense, standing for problems and issues that are either so regular in the enactment of daily roles and activities or so defined by the nature of daily role enactments or activities that they behave as if they are continuous for the individual.

There is, of course, the inevitable fact that some life events will be more chronic than others and some chronic stressors will act more like discrete problems. These examples at the border of two classes should be expected, because some specific stressors will have mixed or blended characteristics, and our categorical distinctions are only intended to describe ideal-typical examples of each class. The distinction between event stressors and chronic stressors is meant to contrast qualitatively distinct phenomenologies of stress that in fact present very different types of problems as a result. A stressor may begin as an event, with sudden news or a clear change, but then become open ended and protracted. In many such cases, it is likely that two stressors, and not one, have occurred and they have been "spliced" together. The distinction between event and chronic stressors allows us to distinguish, for example, the effects of *getting* divorced from *being* divorced. Keeping the stressors separate allows us to distinguish between the problems of identity threat and identity adjustment, on the one hand, and the problems of continual vigilance and pressure, on the other. When analyzing the stress of loss, we can correspondingly distinguish between the loss of another and the absence of another as two stressors.

Forms of Chronic Stress

Chronic stress can occur in a number of ways. Wheaton (1997) distinguished seven kinds of problems that suggest chronic stress: (1) threats, as in the threat of regular physical abuse or the threat of living in a high-crime area, where it is the threat itself that is the chronic stressor; (2) demands, as in facing levels of expectation or duty that cannot be met with current resources, including overload caused by cross-role and within-role expectations; (3) structural constraints, including the lack of access to opportunity or the necessary means to achieve ends or the structured reduction in available alternatives or choices; (4) underreward, literally, reduced outputs from a relationship relative to inputs, as in being paid less for a job than others with the same qualifications, as a result of discrimination; (5) complexity, as in the number of sources of demands, or direct conflict of responsibilities across roles, or constant contingency and instability in life arrangements, or complex content in role responsibilities; (6) uncertainty, a problem only when one desires or needs resolution of an ongoing issue, in effect, unwanted waiting for an outcome; and (7) conflict, when regularly reenacted and thus institutionalized in relationships without apparent resolution, as embodied by fundamental differences over goals or values.

It should be clear that the concept of chronic stress is not coextensive with the concept of role strain. Pearlin (1989) explicitly used the phrase "chronic stress" to include not only role-based or role-defined stressors but also what he called "ambient stressors" that cannot be attached to any one role situation. The importance of this point cannot be overstated. If chronic stress is tied exclusively

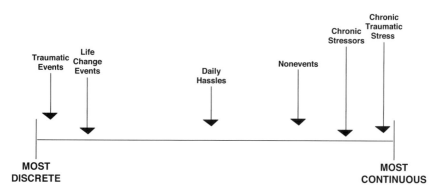

Figure 9.3. The stress continuum.

to occupancy in major social roles – spouse, worker, parent – then role occupancy becomes conceptually confounded with the experience of chronic stress because it becomes a necessary condition for reporting that type of stress. This is especially unfortunate when one realizes that selection into these roles is based partly on whatever is taken for social competence, and this component could suppress relationships between chronic stress and mental health outcomes. Thus, we need to be mindful, in measuring stressors of this kind, that we need to measure stressors that not only accompany role occupancy (e.g., work overload, marital conflict) but that also accompany role inoccupancy (e.g., not having children when you want to, not having a partner when you do want to be in a relationship), as well as a range of ambient stressors that are not role bound (e.g., time pressure, financial problems, or living in a place that is too noisy).

The Stress Continuum

In Figure 9.3, we portray the stress universe, including a range of different types of stressors, as arrayed along a continuum from discrete to continuous. This continuum is one way to compare the types of stressors discussed predominantly in the stress literature over the past 40 years. Life events are near the discrete end of the continuum, based on a typical profile of the clear onset of an event and a defined course until resolution. At the other end of the continuum is chronic stress, characterized by its slow, sometimes imperceptible onset and its open-ended recurring character as a problem. The fact that some stressors are indeed chronic is suggested by findings using a 90-item measure of different and diverse chronic stressors (Wheaton, 1991), in which each person was asked how long each problem had been present in his or her life. The problems cited included time pressures, economic hardship, fear of crime, ongoing health problems of family members, problems with children, wanting but not finding a relationship, and inability to conceive. The average time of the problems cited was 5 years, suggesting that some stressors do have a typically chronic course.

Daily Hassles

A concept that is often mistaken for chronic stress is that of daily hassles (Kanner, Coyne, Schaefer, & Lazarus, 1981). *Daily hassles* are defined as "the irritating, frustrating, distressing demands that to some degree characterize everyday trans-actions with the environment" (p. 3). In fact, there is considerable variability in the degree to which the daily hassles used in measures are regular features of daily life. Interestingly, the examples of daily hassles given by Kanner and colleagues – work overload, status incongruity between spouses, noise – are chronic stressors, but significantly, they are not at all typical of what is measured in the Daily Hassles Scale.

The Daily Hassles Scale itself has been the subject of some controversy. Complaints that a significant number of items are really measures of other concepts in the stress process model, including outcomes such as distress, seem all too valid (Dohrenwend, Dohrenwend, Dodson, & Shrout, 1984). For example, items such as "thoughts about death," "use of alcohol," "trouble making decisions," "being lonely," and "not getting enough sleep" are very clearly measures of distress (responses to stress) and not stressors. Other items sound very much like life events and should not be included as daily hassles per se – "laid off or out of work," "problems with divorce or separation" – whereas a large number indeed reflect standard chronic stress items but have little to do with the stated definition of daily hassles as daily minor stresses: for example, "not enough money for basic necessities," "overloaded with family responsibilities," and "prejudice and discrimination from others."

At their core, daily hassles do stand for a unique area of stress that is not tapped by the more general conceptualization of chronic and event stressors.[2] What is unique about this concept is its focus on insidious aspects of the mundane, its specification of a level of social reality at which other stressors are not usually distinguished. The concerns expressed in these types of items on the Daily Hassles Scale – grocery shopping, traffic jams, caring for a pet, misplacing things, repairing things around the house, the weather – nicely express the mundane realities of daily life that, when experienced cumulatively, may be annoying and stressful. But

---

[2] In the findings reported later, we include a highly edited version of the Daily Hassles Scale, focusing on 25 of the original 117 hassles that seemed to operationalize the thinking behind daily hassles most straightforwardly. These items refer to such issues as "troublesome neighbors," "misplacing or losing things," "caring for a pet," "planning meals," "repairing things around the house," "having to wait," "too many interruptions," "preparing meals," "filling out forms," "the weather," and "traffic problems."

note that they do not consistently refer only to regular features of daily life. Some items clearly refer to the almost automatic or ritualized concerns of daily life and thus may be more chronic in their manifestations (e.g., troublesome neighbors, preparing meals, and grocery shopping). Such issues are defined as chronic by the unavoidability of their enactment. At the same time, a number of these items refer to more contingent, irregular, micro-events that cannot be anticipated daily and only occur episodically (e.g., "misplacing or losing things," "having to wait," or "the weather"). In the case of each of these items, the usual scenario would be that the problem occurs sometimes, and not others, and usually unpredictably.

Thus, daily hassles span the realm of both events and more chronic problems. In general, daily hassles tap something that would be better termed micro-events; they are at the border between more occasional events that are larger in scope and more continuous life "conditions" that suggest chronic stress per se. Therefore, Figure 9.3 shows daily hassles as occupying a middle point on the stress continuum. Daily hassles are the true borderline stressor in this classificatory scheme.

Nonevents

Gersten, Langner, Eisenberg, and Orzeck (1974) used arousal theory to point out that lack of change can be as stressful as change. They used this point, however, not to suggest the importance of chronic stressors, but rather to call attention to a closely related kind of stressor that they termed "nonevents." They defined a nonevent as an "event that is desired or anticipated and does not occur. . . . Alternatively, a nonevent could be seen as something desirable which does not occur when its occurrence is normative for people of a certain group" (1974, p. 169). Thus, an anticipated promotion that does not occur or not being married by a certain age can be considered nonevents. These examples raise the clear possibility that nonevents are a form of chronic stressor. But nonevents also have the additional ironic quality of seeming like events at the same time. This quality is even clearly stated in Gersten et al.'s definition. It is clearest in the case of nonevents that reflect the absence of specific expected events – like a scheduled promotion or not having a child by a given age.

Nonevents that derive from nontransitions to desired roles and are not tied to normative timing, in contrast, seem more clearly like classic chronic stressors. Even the absence of a promotion can be seen as role captivity, the inability to leave or alter a given role situation. In these situations it is the unwanted waiting for an outcome or the very lack of change that becomes the problem. Seen from this perspective, nonevents look very much like a type of chronic stressor. In the stress measurement study reported in Wheaton (1991), respondents were asked to report any expected things that didn't happen in the last year that they wanted to happen. They gave a wide array of answers, many of which qualified as classic nonevents: hoped for a loan for low-income housing but didn't get one, wanted a relationship with a parent to improve but it didn't, planned a trip that didn't happen, or expected higher marks in school. Many of these issues also reflect chronic ongoing problems in which the person takes issue with the current state of affairs and wants change; thus, the lack of change is stressful.

Figure 9.3 appropriately shows nonevents as close to the continuous end of the stress continuum, with a qualifier. Even if we basically understand nonevents as the conjunction of ongoing chronic conditions and passing markers in time, they do have one characteristic of events: Because they refer to expected or desired events, the nonevent is itself like an event – and thus nonevents are placed closer to the discrete end of the continuum than chronic stressors.

Traumatic Stress

Some stressors are thought to be so serious and so overwhelming in their impact that we must give them a separate status to distinguish them from the usual class of events that we designate as stressful. The most applicable term for these stressors is *traumas*.

It is necessary to clarify what is meant by this term as opposed to, for instance, the usual stressful life event. The DSM-III-R defined a traumatic event as one "that is outside the range of usual human experience and . . . would be markedly distressing to almost anyone" (American Psychiatric Association, 1987, p. 250). This definition emphasizes one of the essential characteristics distinguishing traumas from the kinds of life events commonly seen in life event inventories: the magnitude of the stressor. Norris (1992, p. 409) defined traumas in terms of a population of events marked by a sudden or extreme force and denoting "violent encounters with nature, technology, or humankind." Both this and the definition by the American Psychiatric Association point to important classes of traumas, but they are incomplete. First, not all traumas occur only as events. For example, a single sexual assault would be considered a traumatic event, but repeated, regular, and therefore expected sexual abuse is best thought of as a chronic traumatic situation. Including chronic situations allows us to broaden the definition to include Terr's (1991, p. 11) consideration both of events and of situations marked by "prolonged and sickening anticipation." Second, obviously, not all traumas need be violent; some, like having a life-threatening illness or a partner ending an important and valued romantic relationship, need not involve violence at all.

Thus, several elements of traumas are important: (1) they must be more severe in level of threat than the usual life change event; (2) they may occur either as isolated events or long-term chronic problems and thus can be placed, in different forms, at both ends of the stress continuum; and (3) because of their severity, they are thought to have greater potential for long-term impacts than most other types of stressors.

Traumas include a potentially wide range of severe situations and events, such as war stress (Laufer, Gallops, & Frey-Wouters, 1984), natural disasters (Erikson,

1976a, 1976b; Kessler et al., 2008), mass violence and terrorism (Knudsen, Roman, Johnson, & Ducharme, 2005; North et al., 1999; Silver et al., 2002), sexual abuse or assault during childhood or adulthood (Burnam et al., 1988; Kendall-Tackett, Williams, & Finkelhor, 1993), physical violence and abuse (Bryer, Nelson, Miller, & Krol, 1987; Gelles & Conte, 1990; Kessler & Magee, 1994; Turner, Finkelhor, & Ormrod, 2006), parental death (Brown, Harris, & Bifulco, 1986; McLeod, 1991; Saler, 1992), and parental divorce (Amato & Keith, 1991).

The most distinguishing feature of traumas is the level of imputed seriousness of the stressor – which is an order of magnitude beyond what is included on life event or chronic stress scales. Some events on life event inventories, such as the death of a child, could also be considered traumatic stressors. There is no clear-cut division between traumas and life events, only the obvious fact that many traumatic experiences are not measured in life event approaches, presumably because they are too rare. Using an inventory of 20 lifetime traumas, Wheaton, Roszell, and Hall (1997) reported that the prevalence rates of these experiences in a general population ranged from a low of 3.5% for being sent away from home in childhood to nearly 50% for experiencing the death of a spouse, child, or other loved one. In general, these stressors are not that rare: the average prevalence was close to 20%.

One prevalent and typical form of trauma – the sudden traumatic event, as in a sexual assault involving a stranger or the sudden death of a loved one – is re-presented at the most discrete end of the stress continuum in Figure 9.3. At the other end, we have chronic traumatic life conditions, reflecting recurring and deeply embedded features of the social roles or statuses one occupies, such as persistent parental sexual abuse, long-term partner substance abuse, and growing up in a war zone. Thus, traumatic stress is distinguished by the level of threat posed by the stressor and less by its inherent natural discreteness or chronicity.

A Two-Way Classification: Adding Contextual Stressors

Many terms have been used to describe stressors that occur at levels of social reality above the individual – in the neighborhood, the workplace, the family, or the community or nation as a whole. These terms include *macro-stressors*, *systemic stressors*, and *ecological stressors* (Wheaton 1994, 1999). The problem with these terms is that they tend to focus on system-level macro-stressors that affect a whole nation or lower level meso-stressors, but not both. As a result, we now prefer the more general term *contextual stressors*, referring to all forms of stress occurring at both meso and macro levels of social reality in which the individual is embedded.

Figure 9.4 adds a vertical dimension to the horizontal dimension of the stress continuum, standing for levels of social reality, broadly distinguished by meso and macro levels. "Meso" refers to all levels of social reality from the most proximal in which we are immediately embedded, like family, neighborhood, and workplace, to the most distal that are circumscribed at least by community or social boundaries,

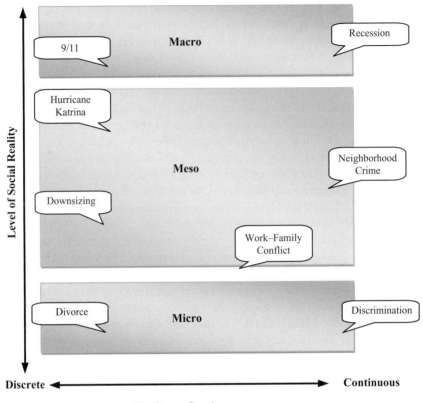

Figure 9.4. A two-way classification of stressors.

such as networks. "Macro" refers to levels described by political units like states, regions, and nations.

The early study of contextual stress focused on economic recessions, as reflected by studies of the unemployment rate (Brenner, 1974; Dooley & Catalano, 1984). There is no reason to see the macro level as embodied only by economic issues. Figure 9.4 shows that the types of stressors that can occur at this level can be widely varying in character: recessions are a type of chronic macro-stressor, but 9/11 was an event, with various other more chronic macro-stressors following as sequelae.

The micro level contains the usual individual-level stressors we study as life change events, chronic stress, traumatic stress, daily hassles, and nonevents. Beyond the individual level, the issue of classifying the stressor is the level of reality at which it occurs naturally – whether in the workplace, neighborhood, school, community, or region. The meso level of stress covers a wide range between the micro and the macro level, and all of these levels stand for different versions of contextual stress.

At the more proximal meso levels, we see stressors that occur at the family level because they result from family-level structure, demands, and expectations, such as work–family conflict (see Fig. 9.4). Beyond the family, neighborhoods, schools, and workplaces occupy a middle-range set of social contexts. In Figure 9.4, we show "neighborhood crime" as an example of a chronic neighborhood stressor and "downsizing" as a discrete workplace stressor. Disasters often occur at the community or regional level, and thus we show "Hurricane Katrina" as a discrete meso-level stressor, albeit at the more distal levels of meso-stress. Note that the classification in Figure 9.4 locates the stressor only by the level at which it occurs and not necessarily by the number of people affected. Community-level stressors can have national repercussions.

The Empirical Distinctiveness of Stressors

The discussion to this point suggests that stressors come in a variety of manifestations while sharing the qualities of a significant threat, demand, or constraint. Beyond the conceptual distinctions, a basic issue is whether there is empirical support for the idea that different types of stressors have independent effects on mental health or are part of a larger "stress package" that does not require these distinctions. This section makes two simple but essential points. First, there are no "fundamental" stressors that absorb and express the impacts of all other sources of stress. Second, the types of stress distinguished here have independent effects on mental health, so that proper assessment of the total impact of stress requires consideration of multiple sources of stress. This is especially the case when we consider the issue of estimating the impacts of combinations of stressors over time or across levels of social reality.

In considering the impact of stressors, we must remember that stressors are also related to each other (i.e., they occur in some sequence, so that some act as the foundation for others). This point is important because the true overall impact of a source of stress will be manifest not only as its unique, independent effect on mental health, taking into account other stress experiences, but also as its indirect effects on mental health via its consequences for the risk of experiencing later stressors, which then in turn also affect mental health. These indirect effects are part of the overall impact of the original stressor; thus, in what follows, we distinguish the "unique" effects of each stressor (i.e., its net effect on mental health after controlling for other stressors) from its "total" effect on mental health (i.e., the unique effect plus all indirect effects through other stressors).

To operationalize this distinction when studying an array of stressors, we must make some assumptions about the probable causal sequence in which different

Table 9.1. *Standardized effects of stressors on distress in three studies:*
Unique and total effects

	Stress Measurement Study		Toronto Mental Health and Stress Study		National Population Health Survey	
	Unique	Total	Unique	Total	Unique	Total
Childhood traumas	.145**	.387**			.105**	.273**
Earlier adult life events	.128*	.191**				
Lifetime traumas			−.002	.209**		
Recent life events	.215**	.289**	.184**	.270**	.122**	.242**
Chronic stressors	.396**	.425**	.406**	.406**	.374**	.374**
Nonevents	−.062	−.054				
Daily hassles	.133*	.128*				
R^2	.43		.25		.23	

* $p < .01.$ ** $p < .001.$

types of stressors typically occur. The causal sequence among types of stressors is likely to be complex, but guidelines are available. Using assumptions or findings reported in the literature (Pearlin et al., 1981; Wheaton, 1994), we assume that life events are more likely to set in motion chronic stressors than vice versa, although both are clearly possible; that both nonevents and daily hassles are basically epiphenomenal outcomes of current chronic stress and recent life events; and that childhood traumas (or early adult life traumas in some samples) temporally precede all other forms of current or recent stress experience. All of these assumptions are made more difficult by the fact that we are talking about overall classes of stressors, rather than individual stressors. Some nonevents may lead to chronic stress, and some chronic stressors may increase the risk of life events. The assumptions used here reflect only the modal reality for the causal sequences involved.

Table 9.1 presents results from three different studies: a stress measurement study based on randomly selected households in three Canadian cities with a sample size of 530; the Toronto Mental Health and Stress Study, a longitudinal study of 1,393 randomly selected adults in Toronto between the ages of 18 and 55 (Turner, Wheaton, & Lloyd, 1995); and the National Population Health Survey (NPHS) of Canada conducted in 1994–1995, with a sample of 16,291 adults. This last study is among the few to attempt to measure a range of stressors systematically in a national population. Each of these studies included measures of multiple sources of stress, and the measures of stress used in these studies had much in common.

In Table 9.1, we show standardized regression coefficients, meaning that the size of effect can be compared relatively within each study. Results in the first column from the stress measurement study show five basic and important findings. First, five out of six stressors measured in this study had significant independent effects on distress. In fact, the level of explained variance in distress was 43%, indicating that the overall impact of stressors is strong. The obvious implication is that unless we measure a variety of stressors, we will underestimate their impacts on mental health. Second, looking at the unique impacts, chronic stressors seemed to have the greatest importance as predictors of distress ($\beta = .396$). However, even childhood traumas that may have occurred 20 to 50 years earlier had a distinct impact. Third, among current stressors, daily hassles did have some influence, but nonevents had little, at least when controlling for other chronic stressors. Fourth, the effects of other stressors did not replace the role of life events; rather, they supplanted this role. In fact, the size of the effects for life events in these findings was very close to what is reported in the life events literature when other stressors are not measured. Thus, we cannot conclude that life events are less important than they have seemed, but simply that other stressors also matter. Finally, focusing on the total effects of each stressor, we see that childhood traumas indeed had a considerable influence on later mental health as measured by distress, second only to current chronic stressors.

Only three types of stress were measured in the Toronto study and the NPHS. Looking at the total effects in particular in the Toronto study, we see again that three sources of stress had independent influences and thus a distinct role to play, with chronic stress again having the largest impact. It should be noted here that the total impact of lifetime traumas is much larger than the unique influence because most of trauma's impact is in fact indirect (i.e., because traumas increase the risk of both stressful events and chronic stressors later in life). In the NPHS, we see a similar pattern for these three stressors, although only childhood-stage traumas were measured. Further, the chronic stress index used was much shorter than in the other studies, and so its slightly smaller impact may simply reflect the fact that not all the most important chronic stressors were included in this survey. Again, as in the stress measurement study, childhood traumas had the second largest total effect on distress.

We present these results both to demonstrate the stability of findings across studies and to underline a fundamental point: stress comes in a number of forms, and we cannot understand its role without measuring a number of sources of stress over the entire life course.

Misconceptions about Stress

We began this chapter with some examples of "typical" misconceptions about stress. With a conceptual framework in place, we can consider these misconceptions more fully.

The Illusion of Personal Stress

It is difficult to avoid the assumption that the stress in one's own life is worse than others: one feels that stress, but not the stress that others experience. The fact is, however, that some people, in fact a majority of people, must experience only average amounts of stress or less. When we measure stress by asking people specific questions about problems or events that have occurred to them, we find clear variability in lives in terms of stress. An important point is that some lives are indeed characterized by low stress, and this fact must be remembered when considering the specific problems posed by high amounts of stress. We should also remember that it is not enough to ask people how stressful their lives are, because the compression in these reports hides real and important differences in the exposure to stressors across lives.

The Illusion of Constant Stress

A related illusion reported by many is that they are always stressed, as if life never ebbs and flows in terms of demands, threats, and constraints. Obviously, this cannot be so, but it does suggest that, as observers, people are forgetting about or not noticing when things improve, as in "good news is no news at all." The bias toward perception of problems, but not their relief, leaves the impression that stress acts as a constant over time and thus cannot really be involved causally in the development of mental health problems. To understand the role of stress properly, it is necessary to see that the periods of greater stress could only have an impact because of a contrast with periods of lesser stress.

The Illusion of Useful Vagueness

Stress is indeed cited all too easily as a cause of all sorts of ills in life, especially when it is not clear exactly what the cause is. This kind of substitution of stress for uncertainty leaves the impression that stress is a vague concept that is best suited to a residual role in the explanation of mental health problems: "When in doubt, it must be stress." The standard response of both medical experts and the lay public to an unexplained or a sudden illness is to imagine stress as an invisible amorphous but powerful force that somehow accounts for the problem. Retrospectively, once a maladaptive response has occurred, anything that preceded the illness can be seen as "stressful." Thus, even relatively benign experiences for many can be transformed into stressors with the knowledge of what resulted. In this chapter, we have argued that experiences must qualify as stressors on one of four grounds: as an excessive threat, demand, challenge, or constraint. If one gets shingles, everyone will certainly feel that stress is somehow involved. But it may be that it is coping capacity – bodily defenses – that is particularly compromised, not excessive levels of stress. In this case, we should conceptualize the problem as the effect of low resources in coping more than a high amount of stress.

The Illusion of Ubiquitous Stress

If there is one most prevalent illusion about stress, it is that it is everywhere, inherent in every life experience. This illusion is not essentially an illusion of the self, but rather the illusion that stress is a built-in quality of all striving. When we measure stress in surveys, asking about the occurrence or presence of hundreds of stressors of various types, the fact is that not one stressor occurs in even a majority of the population. Even the most common of assumed stressors, "taking on too many things at once," was only reported by 44% of the sample in the stress measurement study. Some traumas are, of course, prevalent because they measure built-in life course events, such as the death of a loved one. Yet, this kind of stressor is still reported by just under 50% of an adult general population (Wheaton et al., 1997), because age is a major factor explaining exposure to this event. Most chronic stressors and traumas are actually much less prevalent, affecting only 10% to 20% of the population. Life events, measured within the past year, are by necessity much rarer than that.

It is necessary to understand that stress is not as omnipresent as is commonly assumed. If it was, its influence on most life outcomes would surely be trivial, because prevalent experiences are assumed to be by definition less dangerous or threatening. If we asked people whether their life was stressful, they may report a much higher rate than what we would usually measure as effective stress. It is true that personal reports about what is stressful will echo some differences in stress input, but they commit two other errors: (1) they imagine important stressors that demonstrably have little impact, and (2) more important, they are circumscribed by consciousness, so that whatever is beyond awareness is not stressful. This latter problem suggests that things can be stressful in consequence even though a person is not aware there is a problem. Habituation gets in the way of valid self-reports.

Past and Future: The Historical Trajectory of Stress Research

Some years ago, Kaplan concluded that "in the last analysis, the term stress may be unnecessary to accomplish analyses that are executed under the rubric of stress research" (1996, p. 374). In fact, much research on stress goes on without specific reference to the term *stress*. When we study disasters such as Hurricane Katrina (Kessler et al., 2008) or the impact of 9/11 (Knudsen et al., 2005), or the mental health consequences of sexual abuse or violence (Turner et al., 2006), or the impact of perceived discrimination (Brown et al., 2000), we are studying the impact of various kinds of stressors – whether the word is used or not.

Is there a point to calling these diverse situations and events "stressors"? There is, because there is an enfranchisement that comes with the use of that term. Connecting these specific issues to stress immediately raises a series of questions and draws on a history of concepts that follow from posing stress as a problem to be addressed – such concepts include context, coping, counteracting influences, outcomes, and social origins. By using the term *stress* for these experiences, we gain access to the stress process model (Pearlin, 1989; Pearlin et al., 1981). This famous model posed an entire process around the occurrence of stress, anchoring it in social origins rather than treating it as free-floating; distinguishing events from chronic stressors and thus beginning to consider chains of stressors, primary to secondary; elaborating the notions of coping resources to include both social (social support) and personal (sense of control) resources; distinguishing resources from actual coping behavior in the face of stress; and posing multiple outcomes of stress, rather than considering each health outcome in turn. The center of the model was the inputs to and outputs of stress – the entire process surrounding the production of and life consequences of stress.

Some believe that the golden era of stress research is essentially a late-20th-century phenomenon. In fact, we can demonstrate that the basic frameworks and concepts in stress research are not only surviving but also flourishing – while using the term *stress* explicitly. Figure 9.5 shows the counts of articles with an explicit reference to the "stress process" in abstracts from 1981–2007, using the Scholar's Portal database. Rather than seeing the rise and fall of an era of stress research, we see here the continued upward trajectory of use of the stress process paradigm. The rise between 1995 and 2002 was especially noteworthy, and since 2003, this paradigm has been holding its own and is not in decline.

When Holmes and Rahe published their now famous inventory of stressful life events in 1967, including death of a spouse, divorce, job loss, deaths of parents and loved ones, financial loss, marriage, personal injury, sexual difficulties, and foreclosure of a mortgage – clearly a diverse group of challenging events – this measure became the *sine qua non* of stress research. Over the following decade, it became commonplace to invoke some version of the life events inventory as the embodiment of the concept of social stress. When the accumulated findings indicated that the relationship of these life events to mental health outcomes appeared to be modest, if not disappointing, a number of hypotheses and research traditions were spawned. Hypotheses growing out of the early research on life events assumed that the observed modest correlations mask differential effects of stress of some sort, so that some people are subject to very large impacts, whereas others experience no effects at all. These differential impacts were either caused by differences in vulnerability to stress (e.g., varying levels of coping resources), differences in the inherently stressful characteristics of different life events (e.g., more undesirable, more uncontrollable), or differences in the context in which stressors occur that confer different meanings and therefore different levels of threat (Wheaton, 1999).

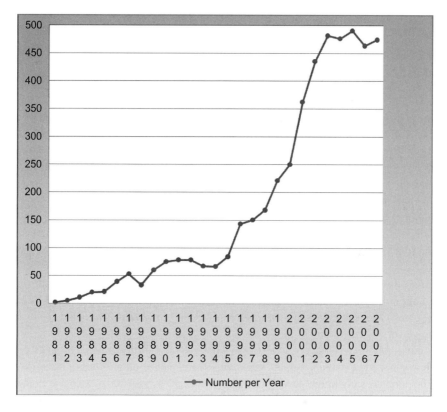

Figure 9.5. Published articles citing the stress process, 1981–2007.

Wheaton (1999) posed the *stress domain hypothesis* to help explain the earlier modest findings about the impact of stress using only life events. The stress domain hypothesis focuses on distinguishing the full array of varieties of stress in the stress universe – as in this chapter, and it argues that life events are only one component of what we can designate as stressful. And because no one source of stress will capture the full impact of the stress domain, we can readily see why events alone may produce modest findings. This hypothesis encourages consideration of sequences of stressors, termed *stress proliferation* by Pearlin, Schieman, Fazio, and Meersman (2005), where the occurrence of some types of stress, such as traumatic stressors, may set in motion the spin-off of other stressors and adversity. The findings reported in Table 9.1 support the stress domain hypothesis – one cannot specify stress entirely by referring to just one type of or one specific stressor. Instead, we need to consider both stress histories and adjunct stressful situations in people's lives when a stressor occurs; we need to surround even the study of specific stressors with the reality of stressors occurring in life history and the multiple layers of stress embedded in their social contexts.

Recent Trends

A number of reviews during the 1990s helped establish various ways of distinguishing stressors (see Aneshensel, 1992; Thoits, 1995; Wheaton, 1994, 1999). A basic question is whether the distinctions used in this chapter have taken root in the literature on stress – that is, whether there is evidence of diffusion of the stress domain hypothesis. In Figure 9.6, we show article counts from 1981–2007 that explicitly address life events, chronic stress, traumatic stress, and contextual stressors as separate entities and as a type of stress (using a variety of synonymous search terms, but all including *stress*). Because of the differences in scale of the growth of research on these different types of stressors, we include life events and chronic stress in Figure 9.6A and contextual stress and traumatic stressors in Figure 9.6B.

Trends in these article counts clearly show a rise in the explicit use of all of the four types of stressors. If it were the case that life events still dominated the discussion, we would not see these results. And if researchers had not found the distinctions among types of stressors in the stress domain necessary or useful, we would not expect such a growth over time in the use of all of these stressors in research. The result is that today, we have a much more clearly differentiated stress universe.

Research on different types of stressors has grown at different rates. Figure 9.6a shows that life events, naturally, began in 1981 ahead of other types of stressors. This emphasis continued through 1995, when there was a sudden increase in the study of life events. However, after that point, the steady linear increase in the study of chronic stress continued, whereas the study of life events fluctuated, so that by 2004, chronic stress caught up with life events as a focus of stress research.

The situation for the other two types is quite different. In 1990, all four types of stress were addressed about equally in the literature. The situation changed by 1995, when research on traumatic stress and life events increased suddenly and then stayed at these higher levels over time. Research on contextual stress increased more slowly, until 2003, after 9/11 and after the Iraq War had begun; then it increased rapidly over the 4 following years. We believe that part of this increase is in fact due to the diffusion of interest in neighborhood stress over this same period (Ross & Mirowsky, 2001; Schieman, Pearlin, & Meersman, 2006; Wheaton & Clarke, 2003; Wight et al., 2008).

By 2007, research on contextual stress was reported in at least twice the number of articles than were both life events and chronic stress, and research on traumatic stress is now occurring at six times the rate of research on life events and chronic stress. These changes reflect important trends overall in stress research that started decades ago but have come to fruition recently. We highlight three of these changes. First, the life course perspective (Elder, George, & Shanahan, 1996; George, 1999) provided a clear rationale for the study of the long-term impacts of stress

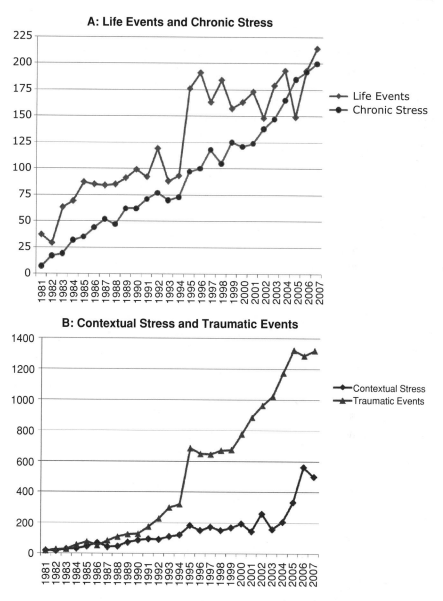

Figure 9.6. Counts of articles citing specific types of stressors, 1981–2007. A: Life events and chronic stress. B: Contextual stress and traumatic events.

across stages of life, from early childhood to later adulthood. This perspective argues for the importance of processes set in motion by stressors, which lead to reproduction of adversities, cumulative disadvantage, or redirection of lives via "turning points." The interest in the longer term impacts of stress led naturally to increased attention to childhood traumatic experiences and connections among stressors over time, and apparently to an increased emphasis on major stressors that were capable of long-term impacts. Second, the multilayered approach to stress shown in Figure 9.4 was encouraged by the co-occurrence of a number of events – crucial methodological advances in the form of the hierarchical linear model (Raudenbush & Bryk, 2002), the natural affinity of sociology for studying stress emanating from and defined by social contexts and not just in individual lives, the importance of studying combinations of stressors across social levels, and the unfortunate increased visibility of major macro events that brought national attention to stress at the system level, including the Oklahoma City bombing, 9/11, Hurricane Katrina, the I-35W bridge collapse in Minnesota, and the Columbine shootings in 1999 through to the recent shootings at Virginia Tech, to name some of the more prominent examples.

Third, and most important, even though Figure 9.6 shows that the study of distinct classes of stress is increasing, the basic impact of increased attention to how stressors combine, layers of stress accumulate, and stress sequences proceed; to contextual stress; and to long-term impacts of stress has led to a disaggregation of stressors, especially in studies since 2000. Disaggregation here refers to the study of individual stressors, such as sexual abuse, or job loss, or an act of terrorism, or work–family conflict, rather than the entire class of stressors to which they belong. It is helpful to locate these specific stressors in the classification scheme for stress, because it makes clear what kinds of stressors may or may not have similar origins and consequences. More and more, however, to understand the level of threat posed by a specific stressor, research focuses on it and then surrounds that stressor with the history of stress leading to the present, as well as the stressful circumstances in other roles, in social contexts, or in others' lives in a network.

Studying Individual Stressors

To determine trends in the use of individual stressors, we searched articles in the *Journal of Health and Social Behavior* – a central journal in the sociology of health and mental health – from 1999 through early 2008. During this period, there were 116 articles published in this journal alone on stress. We found that a large number of the articles over that period looked at individual stressors as cases.

In addition to the popular examination of the effect of such specific chronic stressors as economic or financial stress (e.g., Avison, Ali, & Walters, 2007; Kahn & Pearlin, 2006; Lantz, House, Mero, & Williams, 2005; Pearlin, Nguyen, Schieman, & Milkie, 2007) on mental health outcomes, newer research examines the role of such specific chronic stressors as crowding stress (i.e., living in crowded homes; Regoeczi 2008), including the multilayered effects of crowding in the neighborhood; nonnormative parenting stress, which refers to the stress of having children with developmental or mental health problems (Ha, Hong, Seltzer, & Greenberg, 2008); goal-striving stress – the stress resulting from the discrepancies between socially derived aspiration and achievement (Sellers & Neighbors, 2008); work-to-home conflict (Avison et al., 2007; Schieman, Whitestone, & Van Gundy, 2006); parental stress (Lantz et al., 2005); stress caused by racial/ethnic discrimination (Martin, Tuch, & Roman, 2003; Mossakowski, 2003); specific work stressors such as token stress, which occurs "when black middle class (workers) are discounted and negatively evaluated by whites and other blacks because they are often viewed as tokens who are occupying positions of authority" (Jackson & Stewart, 2003, p. 445); social rejection stress both in the area of work stress (Jackson & Stewart, 2003), as well as in the everyday lives of former psychiatric patients (Wright, Gronfein, & Owens, 2000); stress regarding debt (Drentea, 2000); acculturative stress among immigrants (Finch, Kolody, & Vega, 2000); and stressors in the form of role captivity and role overload (Aneshensel, Botticello, & Yamamoto-Mitani, 2004).

According to our search, specific contextual stressors under study are often those pertaining to neighborhood-level stressors, such as neighborhood structural disadvantage (Boardman et al., 2001; Hill, Ross, & Angel, 2005; Latkin & Curry, 2003; Ross & Mirowsky, 2001; Schieman et al., 2006). However, another contextual stressor under study is communal bereavement (Catalano & Hartig, 2001), which is the widespread experience of distress among individuals who have collectively experienced the loss of a person or persons they have never met. A perfect example of this type of stressor is that of the terrorist destruction of the World Trade Center and the attack on the Pentagon that "clearly induced communal bereavement in the United States" (Catalano & Hartig, 2001, p. 338).

Finally, apart from the usual inclusion of lifetime exposure to major and potentially traumatic events (Turner, Russell, Glover, & Hutto, 2007), the disaggregation of traumatic stressors is also evident in studies that examine the effects that childhood victimization and maltreatment have on mental health later in life (Finkelhor, Ormrod, Turner, & Hamby, 2005; Horwitz, Widom, McLaughlin, & White, 2001; Turner et al., 2006). Furthermore, studies of the effect of catastrophic events such as Hurricane Katrina (Kessler et al., 2008) and 9/11 (Knudsen et al., 2005) on mental health outcomes exemplify not only the effect of macro-stressors but also the effect of disaggregated traumatic events on a number of health-related outcomes.

These examples make clear that, as we consider both the longer view of stressors occurring over lives and the more inclusive approach that combines stress at the individual level with stressors in embedded social contexts, we naturally evolve to a focus on individual stressors as cases of more general types.

Conclusions

It may be useful at this point to review some fundamental points in this chapter: (1) we distinguished *stressors*, *stress*, and *distress* in the interest of bringing the use of these terms more into line with the way they are used in the stress literature and to reduce the problems of inconsistent usage prevalent in the discussion of stress in everyday life; (2) we distinguished the two original stress models – biological and engineering – from each other, while also pointing out areas of convergence, including the need to distinguish among types of stressors; (3) we distinguished varieties of stress, from life events to chronic to traumas to nonevents to daily hassles, at the individual level, before (4) adding layers of social reality to distinguish these stressors from contextual stressors, defined by the fact that they occur at a level of social reality above the individual; (5) we demonstrated that these distinctions are empirically supported by findings that different sources of stress have distinct impacts on mental health outcomes; (6) we returned to the issue of misconceptions about stress to argue that stress, although a general concept, is a concept with theoretical and operational borders; and (7) we reviewed trends in stress research, which reveal an upward trajectory in the study of all of the kinds of stress discussed in this chapter and an increasing focus on individual stressors, rather than classes of stressors.

This is the time to remind everyone to avoid the mistake of assuming that the term *stressor* means stressful to everybody in every circumstance. This issue has unnecessarily plagued stress research. The fact is that a stressor only needs to have the *potential* to be a stressor in most instances – that is why we measure it. It is necessary to distinguish between a realm of potential stressors, the starting point in what we measure, and stressful stressors, defined in addition by features of context, life history, and individual vulnerability that make that stressor threatening to that person. We do not need to specify context to designate a class of potential stressors, only to define the stressfulness of stressors as a subset of the total.

In defining a class of potential stressors, what are we trying to do? Basically, we have to refer to the vague referent of what is challenging for "most people." This is unfortunately imprecise, but it does imply the point of measuring stressors in the first place: We are trying to capture the most important threats to mental health in the population in the broadest terms, so that the largest sources of mental health risk are identified. We cannot make the goal of research to capture every stress story at the individual level; we already know that there will always be someone, somewhere, who will find a particular situation stressful. But such specificity does not deny the fact that there are stressors that are difficult in a broad range of situations in too many lives.

Finally, we do not need to specify a priori what level a stressor has to attain to exceed elastic limits in general – this is not what is done in the engineering model or the biological or the psychosocial model. All we need to do is measure the current level of coping capacity that applies to an individual so that we can detect when the combination of a certain level of stress and weak resources exceeds their elastic limit at that point in time.

Perhaps the most general theme of this chapter is the safety and wisdom and clarity afforded by the differentiation and disaggregation of stress concepts and of other concepts in the stress process, even if we must reaggregate concepts to understand the full power of stress. In the case of specifying social context and in extricating coping from its dependence on stress, disaggregation is the key to understanding. In a differentiated and disaggregated stress process model, no one form of stress is close to sufficient to capture all that is stressful. If we are ultimately interested in a full representation and a fair evaluation of the relevance of stress to mental and physical health or to a range of life outcomes, we must consider a range of types of stressors that vary in their typical time course and that occur at different stages in the life course and at different levels of social reality; we must specify the social and biographical context of each stressor; we must investigate the buffering effects of coping resources for stressors defined as contextually threatening; we must specify the foundations of stress; and we must be sensitive to the full range of outcomes possible and the level at which these outcomes are specified. This may seem to be an impossible task, but at least at this point in history, the task is much better defined than it was a quarter-century ago.

10

Social Support and Mental Health

R. Jay Turner and Robyn Lewis Brown

Social support refers to one's social bonds, social integration, and primary group relations – all concepts central to sociological theory and research. Social bonds and supportive relationships with others are essential to mental health; furthermore, social support can protect one from the effects of stress. Turner and Lewis Brown overview the various conceptual understandings of social support that guide the research literature, demonstrating how social support is a multidimensional concept involving perceived, structural, and received support. The major hypothesis behind a large body of research is that low levels of social support increase the risk for depressive symptomatology. Although studies consistently find support for this hypothesis, the models that explain how social support affects mental health (as a main effect or as a mediating variable) differ. The degree to which social support affects one's mental health (main effect) and the degree to which it buffers the effects of stress (mediating effect) also vary across different social status groups of the population. Social status (e.g., gender, socioeconomic status, marital status) affects the availability of social support, as well as one's exposure to stress. It is also probable that one's mental health status and personality influence the availability and perception of social support. Whom do you have available for support in your networks, and whom would you actually approach for support in a variety of stressful situations (i.e., getting sick, doing poorly in school, an unwanted pregnancy)?

Introduction

The *Oxford Illustrated Dictionary* defines support, in part, as to "keep from failing or giving way, give courage, confidence, or power of endurance to . . . supply with necessities . . . lend assistance or countenance to" (1975, p. 850). What distinguishes social support from this broader definition is that it always involves either the presence or implication of stable human relationships. The domain of social support has been addressed under a variety of labels, including "social bonds" (Henderson, 1977), "social networks" (Wellman & Wortley, 1989), "meaningful social contact" (Cassel, 1976), "availability of confidants" (Brown, Bhrolchain, & Harris, 1975), and "human companionship" (Lynch, 1977), in addition to social support. Although these concepts are not identical, they are similar and share a focus on the relevance and significance of human relationships.

This focus has been the subject of considerable attention and research effort, particularly during the 1980s but continuing to the present. As Veil and Baumann (1992, p. 1) remarked, "Measured by both its impact on current thinking concerning the social etiology of mental and physical disorders, and by the sheer volume of publications, social support has joined stress and coping as one of the

200

three most important constructs in current mental health research." However, this intense recent interest hardly signals the discovery of a new idea. In Genesis 2:18, the Lord judges that "it is not good that [one] be alone," and philosophers from Aristotle to Martin Buber have emphasized that the essence of human existence is expressed in our relationships with others.

Social bonds, social integration, and primary group relations, in general, are central constructs in sociological theory and have long been prime considerations within sociological analyses. As Hammer, Makiesky-Barrow, and Gutwirth (1978, p. 523) observed, social linkages "may be thought of as the basic building blocks of social structure; and their formation, maintenance, and severance are universal and fundamental social processes." A central hypothesis of primary group theory "holds that our morale, our sense of well-being is sustained by membership in primary groups, and that without any primary group affiliations we would become despairing. ... Withdrawing from primary contacts would be seen as dangerous to an individual's cognitive and emotional states" (Weiss, 1974, p. 18). Focusing on heart disease rather than mental health, Lynch (1977, p. xv) concluded from wide-ranging evidence that "there is a biological basis for our need to form loving human relationships. If we fail to fulfill that need, our health is in peril."

Perhaps nowhere has the significance of human associations been more dramatically demonstrated than with respect to child development. For example, Spitz (1946) long ago observed that, in institutionalized infants who are deprived of contact with their mothers, the nervous system is profoundly affected, influencing nearly all aspects of social, emotional, and psychological development and functioning among these infants. Harlow's (1959) research with baby monkeys and Bowlby's (1969, 1973) dissertations on the significance of parental attachment for healthy human development are other prominent examples of the numerous investigations that illustrate the similar implications of unresponsive mothering. As Pierce and associates (1996) noted, developmentalists and family researchers have long viewed social support, particularly that provided by parents, as a crucial contributor to personality and social development (e.g., Rollins & Thomas, 1979; Symonds, 1939).

From evidence of the significance of social support as a developmental contingency, it was only a minor leap of faith to the now pervasive assumption that this important developmental factor must also be significant for personal functioning and psychological well-being throughout the life course. This view – that social bonds and supportive interactions are important for maintaining mental health – seems to have a long history. For example, Durkheim long ago documented that suicide was more often committed by individuals who were not sufficiently socially integrated and, as a consequence, were believed to lack social support (Durkheim 1897/1951). However, specific research evidence on the connection between social support and mental health has accumulated mostly over the past 30 years. The immense growth in research on the significance of social support was stimulated by the publication of seminal review articles by John Cassel (1976) and Sidney Cobb (1976). These papers set forth preliminary evidence for a hypothesis that remains dominant within current theory and research – that social support may represent an important buffer against the impact of life stress and thereby protect one's mental health.

In the remainder of this chapter, we discuss the development of this field of research and our current understandings of the relationship between social support and mental health. We begin with a description of prominent conceptualizations of social support. Next, we discuss current knowledge of this topic, paying particular attention to the challenges of assessing both (1) the mechanisms underlying the association between social support and mental health and (2) the causal direction of this association. Finally, we consider how the relationship between social support and well-being is importantly influenced by one's social location.

Concepts of Social Support

Diversity of opinion with respect to how social support should be conceptualized and measured has been widely commented on in the literature for more than 20 years (see, e.g., Gottlieb, 1983; Kawachi & Berkman, 2001; Turner, Frankel, & Levin, 1983), and this diversity remains apparent today. Social support has been used to refer to an ever-widening domain of content that seems almost coextensive with the structural and social aspects of human relationships and interactions. In seeking to delimit the meaning of social support, several researchers have concluded that social support is a multifactorial construct. They have described different types or categories of social support that should be considered and that may have differing consequences (Dean & Lin, 1977; Funch & Mettlin, 1982; Hirsch, 1980; House, 1981b).

Cobb (1976) provided perhaps the best-known and most influential conceptualization of social support known today. He viewed social support as "information belonging to one or more of the following three classes: (1) information leading the subject to believe that he is cared for and loved; (2) information leading the subject to believe that he is esteemed and valued; and (3) information leading the subject to believe that he belongs to a network of communication and mutual obligation" (1976, p. 300). In other words, social support refers to the clarity or certainty with which an individual experiences being loved, valued, and able to count on others should the need arise.

Cobb (1979) also emphasized the importance of distinguishing social support from support that is instrumental (e.g., counseling, assisting), active (e.g., mothering), or material (e.g., providing goods or services). However, he did not suggest that these other forms of support were not important or that they lacked relevance for health and well-being. His point was simply that we should distinguish between the perception of social support and the actual receipt of supportive resources or engagement in supportive activities.

More recently, Vaux (1988, p. 28) argued that social support is best viewed as a metaconstruct, "comprised of several legitimate and distinguishable theoretical constructs." He specified three such constructs: support network resources, supportive behavior, and subjective appraisals of support. These dimensions or constructs correspond closely with Cobb's definition noted earlier.

These influential perspectives are also evident in the dominant view of social support among sociologists and psychologists today: that social support is best understood as a multidimensional construct. Descriptions of relevant elements vary somewhat, but most include the dimensions of perceived support, structural support, and received support. *Perceived support*, which is also sometimes referred to as "emotional support," is the subjective belief or appraisal that one belongs to a communicative and caring social network (Cobb, 1976; Lakey & Scoboria, 2005). *Structural support* refers to the organization of individuals' ties to one another, involving the frequency of contact with social network members and the structural characteristics of social ties (Pearlin, 1989; Umberson et al., 1996). Relevant structural characteristics include the degree of reciprocity of exchanges between provider and receiver, the strength of the bonds involved, the degree of similarity among network members, and the density of relationships among network members (Wellman, 1981, 1990). As Thoits (1995) noted, network measures often reflect the individual's level of social isolation or social involvement. *Received support* refers to the actual help that one's loved ones extend in providing either instrumental or informational assistance (House, Umberson, & Landis, 1988).

There seems ample basis for concluding that social support phenomena involve objective elements (such as the frequency of our contact with others or helping behaviors) and subjective ones. Indeed, as Pearlin (1989) argued, an understanding of the significance of social institutions and contexts will ultimately require the consideration of social networks and resources along with perceived support. However, the great bulk of evidence pointing to the significance of social support for psychological health and well-being comes from studies focused on perceived or emotional support (Berkman & Glass, 2000; House, 1981b; House et al., 1988; Lin, Ye, & Ensel, 1999; Thoits, 1995). As an illustration, House's (1981b) review of this literature found that emotional support was the common element across most conceptualizations, that it was what most people meant when they spoke of being supportive, and that, indeed, it seemed to be the most important dimension of social support.

Since that time, studies have repeatedly demonstrated that the strongest correlations between measures that purport to assess social support and indices of psychological distress or well-being are found with measures of perceived social support. For example, Wethington and Kessler (1986, p. 85) presented specific evidence for the primacy of perceived over received support. They documented "not only that perceptions of support availability are more important than actual support transactions but that the latter promotes psychological adjustment through the former, as much as by practical resolutions of situational demands." This finding further supports House's (1981b, p. 27) suggestion that "social support is likely to be effective only to the extent perceived."

Given the observations that (1) perceived social support is most persistently and powerfully associated with mental health and (2) that other elements of social support apparently exert their effects by influencing this perception, perceived support may represent the most direct criterion for assessing the broader role and significance of social support. The importance of this concept is that perceived social support may provide a basis for identifying behaviors and circumstances as promising targets for intervention efforts to prevent or ameliorate mental health problems. Thus, we now further discuss the current understanding of the nature of perceived social support.

The Nature of Perceived Social Support

Two general views have been offered to explain the protective benefits of perceived social support. The first is a situation-specific model that asserts that perceived support performs as a coping resource in relation to particular stressful events or circumstances. The second is a developmental perspective that sees social support as a crucial factor in social and personality development (Cohen, 1992; Pierce et al., 1996). These views are not contradictory, but reflect the likelihood that our perceptions of social support are influenced by both current and long-ago experiences (Pierce et al., 1996). Although both of these perspectives view the social environment as the primary source of supportive experiences, the first focuses largely on the contemporary social environment, whereas the second emphasizes the effects of the social environmental context on personality over time, attaching special significance to the developmental years.

This second view also acknowledges the role of individual personality, in addition to social influences, in the formation of support perceptions. That the tendency to believe or perceive others to be supportive may partially reflect stable personality characteristics makes intuitive sense in the context of Cobb's (1976) definition of social support described earlier. Recall that this definition describes social support as information that one is loved and wanted, valued and esteemed, and able to count on others should the need arise. Thus, reflected appraisal, which is a central component of self-esteem (Rosenberg, 1965, 1979, 1985), also represents an element of perceived social support, and experiences that foster or challenge one of these constructs must also be relevant to the others. Moreover, there is a basis for assuming a degree of reciprocal causation. Surely, the experience of being supported by others contributes to more stable and positive self-esteem, and one's level of self-esteem must set at least broad limits on the perceived level of social support. It is clear that individuals vary in their tendency or capacity to derive meaning and emotional sustenance from a given amount of evidence of positive regard and affection. Everyone has encountered individuals who cannot seem to incorporate messages of social and emotional support, no matter how frequently or clearly they are delivered. Self-esteem presumably contributes to such differences in receptiveness, because one's capacity to experience the esteem of others must require some minimum level of esteem of self.

Other grounds for assuming that personality factors are implicated in perceptions of support include evidence that such perceptions tend (1) to be consistent over time and reasonably consistent across situations (Sarason, Pierce, & Sarason, 1990) and (2) to be related to various personality characteristics such as social competence and personal control (Lakey & Cassady, 1990). It has been hypothesized that appraisals of the supportiveness of the social environment reflect, at least in part, "support schemata" – referring to "knowledge structures whose content include information about the likelihood that others, in general, will be able or willing to meet one's needs for support. Support schemata encompass one's expectations about the forthcomingness of the social environment in providing aid should one need it" (Pierce et al., 1996, p. 5). The schemata are seen as substantially rooted in early experience with attachments, especially attachments to parents (Sarason, Pierce, et al., 1990).

From this perspective, an important part of the linkage between perceived social support and the objective supportiveness of the environment derives from the tendency for those high in perceived support to be more effective at developing and maintaining supportive relationships, on the one hand, and to interpret ambiguous actions and statements as supportive in nature, on the other (Cohen et al., 2000; Lakey & Dickinson, 1994). As Pierce et al. (1996, p. 6) noted, those with the firm expectation that others will be supportive "create supportive relationships in new social settings, thereby further confirming their expectation that others are likely to be supportive."

However, the evidence seems compelling that these expectations, beliefs, or confidence about the availability of social support cannot be independent of one's history (including recent history) of real-world experiences of being supported by others (Berkman & Glass, 2000; Cutrona, 1986; Gracia & Herrero, 2004; Lakey & Scoboria, 2005; Sarason, Pierce, et al., 1990; Vinokur, Schul, & Caplan, 1987). Thus, expressions of support and supportive actions may be seen as important in the short term for the coping assistance provided and, in the long term, for the contribution made to the receiver's expectation or confidence that such support will be available in the future. Although early attachment experiences may well influence the individual's tendency to foster and perceive environmental supportiveness, there seems to be a good basis for concluding that later experiences can profoundly shape and modify these tendencies. The perception of being loved and wanted, valued and esteemed, and able to count on others must be a function of one's history of supportive and unsupportive experiences, with both early life and recent experiences representing major influences.

Social Support and Mental Health

An ever-growing number of volumes and reviews document the apparent significance of perceived social support for emotional health and well-being (Berkman & Glass, 2000; Cohen & Syme, 1985; Cohen et al., 2000; Cohen & Wills, 1985; Dean & Lin, 1977; Gottlieb, 1981a; Kawachi & Berkman, 2001; Kessler, McLeod, & Wethington, 1985; Sarason & Sarason, 1985; Sarason, Sarason, & Pierce, 1990; Turner, 1983; Turner et al., 1983; Vaux, 1988; Veil & Baumann, 1992). Perhaps the largest portion of this very substantial research effort has been focused on the hypothesis that low levels of social support increase risk for depression. Taking note of this hypothesis, Henderson (1992) identified and evaluated 35 separate studies that addressed the relationship between social support and depression. These studies used measures of depression that varied from very brief self-report inventories to standardized interviews based on accepted diagnostic criteria. Similarly, procedures for indexing social support differed widely, varying from the use of a single item on the presence or absence of a confidant to sophisticated multi-item interviews or interviewer-based methods. Despite such variable assessments of both social support and depression, Henderson observed remarkable consistency across studies. Virtually all reported a clear inverse association between social support and depression, with studies employing more brief measures of one or both variables demonstrating just as strong relationships as studies employing more elaborate methods. The connection between perceived social support and mental health status, generally, and depression in particular, seems to be highly robust.

Main versus Buffering Effects

Much of the strong interest in social support effects on mental health has been associated with the hypothesis, strongly articulated in the influential papers by Cassel (1976) and Cobb (1976), that social support may act to buffer or moderate the effects of life stress. From this perspective, social support tends to be viewed as having mental health significance only within stressful circumstances. As Cobb (1976, p. 502) argued, "Social support facilitates coping with crises and adaptation to change. Therefore, one should not expect dramatic main effects from social support. There are, of course, some main effects simply because life is full of changes and crises. The theory says that it is in moderating the effects of the major transitions in life and of the unexpected crises that the effects should be found." Here the concept of "main effects" refers to the idea that social support is of relevance in all circumstances, whether or not significant stress is present.

In influential studies, Brown and his colleagues (1975; Brown & Harris, 1978) considered factors that might influence vulnerability to depression in the face of adversity. Specifically, they examined the influence of a close, confiding relationship in reducing the risk of depression following a major life event or long-term difficulty. Among those women who lacked a confiding relationship with a husband or boyfriend, 38% developed depression following life stress or major difficulties, compared with only 4% of women who did have such a confiding relationship. Consistent with this result, Henderson's (1992) review of 35 studies assessing the relationship between social support and depression revealed only 4 that did not report such a buffering or protective effect.

However, it is also clear from Henderson's review and from the wider literature that a number of studies have found that a low level of support increases the risk for depression or for mental health problems generally, whether or not exposure to unusual stressors had also taken place. Whether these findings allow the conclusion that social support can be of importance in the absence of social stress – which is to say that there is a main effect of social support – cannot be easily answered. Antonovsky (1979, p. 77) forcefully argued that "all of us . . . even in the most benign and sheltered environments, are fairly continuously exposed to what we define as stressors. . . . We are able to get low scores on stress experience [only] because we do not ask the right questions or do not ask patiently enough and not because there really are any low scorers." He insisted that "even the most fortunate of people . . . know life as stressful to a considerable extent" (1979, p. 79). If this constancy-of-stress argument is accepted, then both the main and interactive effects that have been observed would be theoretically interpretable in terms of the buffering hypothesis.

From this perspective, it might seem to follow that the debate over buffering versus main effects is not worth worrying about. However, even if what looks like main effects are really buffering effects, it would remain important to determine whether social support is of greater significance when stress is relatively high than when it is relatively low. Given the inevitability of limited resources, it would be useful to identify those who most need and who might most benefit from a social support intervention. In other words, although everyone might benefit from enhanced social support, the issues of relative need and relative benefit with respect to psychological distress and disorder remain salient.

Evidence from a study of young mothers has shed some additional light on the inconsistency of findings relating to the buffering hypothesis (Turner, 1981; Turner & Noh, 1983). Turner and colleagues found in initial analyses that social support was related to psychological distress, independent of stress level. In addition, these analyses did not find evidence of buffering effects. These findings are consistent with the hypothesis of "main" or direct social support effects and with the significant minority of other studies that have reported no evidence for a stress-buffering role.

Further analyses of these same data, however, indicated that the question – whether social support is an influence in its own right or is important wholly (or largely) as a buffer against unusual stress – may not be so simply answered. With young mothers of lower socioeconomic status distinguished from middle-class study participants, Turner and Noh (1983) assessed the relationship between psychological distress and perceived social support within each of three stress-level categories. Within the lower class grouping, the significance of social support varied substantially by level of stress. No significant relationship was observed among the lower class group in either the low- or medium-stress circumstance; however, perceived support was of dramatic significance in the high-stress circumstance. Results for the middle-class group contrasted sharply with these findings. Clear and quite consistent social support effects were observed regardless of stress level. Thus, the answer to the question of whether social support has main or buffering effects is both conditional and complex. The significant associations observed among the middle class at all three stress levels demonstrated a main effect. In sharp contrast, no main effects were observed among the lower class, as evidenced by small and nonsignificant associations observed within the low- and medium-stress conditions. Social support was found to matter, and matter importantly, only among those lower class individuals experiencing a high level of stress. This finding provides clear support for the buffering hypothesis while also suggesting that the significance of social support varies with both social class position and stress level.

More recently, researchers including Berkman and Glass (2000) have suggested that the main effects and buffering hypotheses are not necessarily mutually exclusive. That is, it is possible that different social support processes may exert different influences on mental health. Specifically, it is suggested that the structural and objective aspects of social relationships, such as the number of friends an individual has or the frequency of contact with these friends, may exert main effects. This stands to reason, if we consider that having sufficient social contact is likely to matter for our well-being regardless of the level of life stress we experience (Berkman & Glass, 2000). In contrast, perceived support is hypothesized to operate primarily through a stress-buffering mechanism (Berkman & Glass, 2000). This perspective is consistent with the view that one's perception of being loved and valued in the face of hardship is a coping resource that may combat the distressing effects of such hardship. However, further research is needed to determine whether different aspects of social support do, indeed, uniquely influence mental health outcomes.

At this point, available evidence suggests the appropriateness of three working hypotheses with respect to the main effects–buffering debate: (1) social support tends to matter for psychological well-being in general, and for depression in particular, independent of stressor level; (2) social support seems to matter more where level of stress exposure is relatively high; and (3) the extent to which these two hypotheses hold varies across population subgroups and, perhaps, according to other variables, including the form of social support assessed.

Causal Interpretation

A fundamental assumption among those who investigate the social correlates of psychological distress and depression is that there is an etiological message to be found within these well-documented linkages. However, in the case of social support, as with other social variables, there has been difficulty in reaching a clear conclusion about the nature of this message. Most of the studies reporting this relationship have been cross-sectional or epidemiological in character, and they consequently confront the classic dilemma of whether the finding should be interpreted from the perspective of social causation or social selection. Does perceived support operate (directly or indirectly) to make psychological distress and depression less likely? Do high levels of distress or depression limit the likelihood that the individual will secure and maintain social relationships or experience the social support that is, in fact, available? The first of these questions is a social causation hypothesis, whereas the second points to social selection processes.

A second form of the selection interpretation proposes that the observed connection between social support and mental health may simply be an artifact deriving from the personal inadequacies of those who later become distressed or depressed – inadequacies that also limit the ability to secure and maintain supportive relationships. One version of this latter form of social selection hypothesis proposes that dispositional characteristics, as opposed to the nature of the social environment, largely account for differences in perceived social support (Heller, 1979; Sarason, Sarason, & Shearin, 1986) – characteristics that may also be associated with an increased risk for distress and depression.

As noted earlier, it is clear that supportive experiences in the family context represent crucial early developmental contingencies that importantly influence personality. Thus, social support is causally relevant to personality processes and, by extension, to psychological well-being. However, the question remains whether social support represents a promising intervention target throughout the life course or only during early developmental phases. To answer this question in the affirmative requires that some part of the causal flow involved in the social support–mental health connection go from social support to distress and depression, and that the level of perceived support be at least partially a function of contemporary processes and circumstances.

At this point it seems clear that no single study provides persuasive evidence on these matters. However, more than 25 years ago, House (1981b, p. 51) reached the conclusion that much of the causal flow is from social relationships to health, rather than vice versa. Although much of the evidence supporting this conclusion involved physical rather than mental health outcomes, its applicability to phenomena such as psychological distress and depression seems apparent. John Cassel's (1974, 1976) early argument on the health significance of social support was substantially based on evidence derived from animal studies on the effects of laboratory-induced stress. Examples included Liddell's (1950) finding that suggested the presence of the mother protects young goats from experimental neurosis; the Conger, Sawrey, and Turrell (1958) observation of the relevance of isolation for the occurrence of ulceration in rats; and the Henry and Cassel (1969) report on the significance of littermate presence for the prevention of persistent hypertension in mice. Other kinds of studies reviewed by House (1981b, 1987) and others (e.g., Turner, 1983) – including laboratory analog studies with humans, intervention studies, and longitudinal and panel studies – strongly suggest that some important portion of the causation involved in the well-established link between perceived social support and mental health status goes from social support to mental health.

In considering the issue of causation, it is useful to acknowledge that neither human development nor functioning is likely to proceed in terms of linear or clear-cut causes and effects. Rather, most causes and effects in human affairs are likely to be reciprocal in nature. As Smith (1968, p. 277) argued long ago, development is a matter of benign circles or vicious ones, and causation in personal and social development is "inherently circular or spiral, rather than linear, in terms of neatly isolable causes and effects." In the present case, evidence suggests that the perceived availability of social support has important consequences for distress and depression. At the same time, it is probable that one's mental health status and personality characteristics affect the availability of social support and the ability or tendency to experience the support that is available. Accumulated evidence from diverse sources seems to constitute a compelling case for the causal impact of social support. It thus also follows that social support represents a promising target for intervention efforts aimed at reducing rates of psychological distress and depression in high-risk populations or subgroups.

Social Status and Social Support

The starting point for a great deal of research on the sociology of mental health has been evidence connecting certain social statuses with mental health problems. The most persistently observed and provocative of these linked low socioeconomic status (SES; Gurin, Veroff, & Feld, 1960; Hollingshead & Redlich, 1958; Srole et al., 1961), being unmarried (Gurin et al., 1960), and being female (Al-Issa, 1982; Nolen-Hoeksema, 1987) to increased risk for psychological distress and depression. As noted previously and argued elsewhere (Pearlin, 1989; Turner & Marino, 1994), variations in the perceived availability of social support arise out of developmental (and contemporary) life conditions to which individuals have been (and are being) exposed. To the extent that significant differences in such life conditions are importantly influenced or defined by one's ascribed and achieved social statuses, it may be that the observed relationships between these statuses and mental health arise, at least in part, from associated differences in the level of social support.

For this hypothesis to be plausible, variations in support across social statuses must show a pattern that is the inverse of the known distributions of mental health problems across these statuses. That is, low levels of social support should be found where rates of psychological distress or depression are highest, and vice versa. This is precisely what has been found with respect to associations among perceived social support, SES, and marital status, respectively, by studies that have examined this issue. Married individuals quite consistently report higher levels of perceived social support than do the unmarried, and social support appears to increase with levels of SES (Mickelson & Kubzansky, 2003; Ross & Mirowsky, 1989; Thoits, 1995; Turner & Marino, 1994).

In contrast, observed gender differences in perceived support do not turn out to be the inverse of differences in distress and depression. Although some studies have reported no gender difference in perceived support, most have found substantially higher levels of such support among women (Belle, 1982; Flaherty & Richman, 1986; Leavy, 1983; Ross & Mirowsky, 1989; Turner & Marino, 1994). Because women tend to experience higher levels of perceived support than do men, it may seem that social support can provide little assistance in understanding the tendency for women to experience higher levels of psychological distress and depression. However, it should be borne in mind that, among women (as among men), a higher level of perceived support is clearly associated with lower levels of distress and depression (Thoits, 1995). It thus follows that, without the advantage of higher perceived support, distress levels among women would be even more elevated relative to men.

That the level of perceived social support varies systematically with one's gender, SES, and marital status supports the argument that social support is importantly conditioned by differences in social experience and contemporaneous life circumstances. These findings thus illuminate ways in which social structures affect the processes relevant to social support. Specifically, they suggest the appropriateness of two assumptions: (1) that variations in the availability of social support arise, as do differences in exposure to social stress, substantially out of developmental and contemporaneous conditions of life (Aneshensel, 1992; Pearlin, 1989); and (2) that one's gender, SES, and marital status effectively define significant differences in such conditions of life. House, Umberson, and Landis (1988) suggested that these status differences are associated with variations in exposure to structural barriers and opportunities in society, which tend to shape social relationship structures and processes and, hence, the availability of social support.

Conclusions

Despite the huge volume of research and publications on social support, much remains to be learned about how and why social support matters for health and well-being and about the circumstances and processes that promote and enhance its availability. As outlined in this chapter, however, several conclusions are warranted from available evidence. These conclusions may be summarized as follows.

1. The ever-growing number of studies and reviews on the subject leave little doubt that social support is importantly associated with mental health status generally and depression in particular.

2. Although social support phenomena clearly involve objective elements (such as network size, structure, and density and actual events and activities), it is one's perception or belief about the availability of support that is found to be most protective against distress and depression. This means that the love or esteem of others – or the availability of emotional, material, or instrumental assistance – is likely to be of little protective utility if kept a secret.

3. Social support tends to matter for psychological distress and depression independent of stress level. However, it tends to matter more where stress exposure is relatively high.

4. Combined evidence from laboratory animal studies, experimental human studies, and longitudinal field studies provides clear support for the contention that some part of the causality involved in the persistently observed relationship between social support and mental health flows from support to mental health status.

5. That perceived levels of social support vary reliably with location in the social system (as observed with respect to SES, marital status, and gender), in combination with an array of other evidence, makes it clear that the experience of being supported by others arises substantially out of the ongoing social context within which the individual is located.

11

Work and Unemployment as Stressors

Mary Clare Lennon and Laura Limonic

Lennon and Limonic examine the mental health consequences of work and unemployment. Changes in the nature of work and the entry of women into the workforce have had important consequences for psychological well-being. Jobs that are stressful and that provide few opportunities for control have negative consequences for mental health. The authors discuss different theoretical models for understanding the relationship between control and psychological well-being. Lennon and Limonic also consider the effect of unpaid work, specifically housework, on mental health and well-being. Similar to paid work, housework involves varying levels of control and stressful demands. Unemployment has a negative effect on well-being because it may reduce self-esteem and economic security and thus produce anxiety and depression. Yet it is also important to examine the economic context within which individuals experience unemployment. This chapter describes several recent approaches that integrate community-level conditions and individual characteristics. The authors conclude by describing a promising area of research on the effects of relational justice within the workplace. Relational justice is part of a larger framework of organizational justice and encompasses the employees' perceptions of fairness of the decision-making process within the workplace, the fairness of decisions themselves, as well as the perceived fairness of treatment received from supervisors. Considering your own job experiences, can you describe the relationship between relational justice and the stress you have experienced at work?

Introduction

This chapter considers some of the mental health consequences of work and unemployment. In examining the effects of work, it focuses on specific work conditions that both theory and empirical studies indicate are important for psychological well-being. Rather than restricting its attention to paid work, this chapter also examines research on unpaid work. In examining unemployment, it gives attention to both the effects of individual job loss and of community-level unemployment.

Background

Americans spend large portions of their adult life working. Considering waged work, the average workweek is about 34 hours (U.S. Department of Labor, 2008a). Given that approximately 90% of men and 75% of women aged 25 to 54 are in the paid labor force (Cotter, Hermsen, & Vanneman, 2004), jobs hold a central place in the daily lives of most of the adult population.

Recently, various social and economic changes have affected the availability and quality of jobs for a substantial number of workers. The latter half of the 20th century saw dramatic changes in the labor market experiences of a large share of the population. Two major changes involved the nature of work and participation of women in the labor force. This section briefly describes each of these changes, providing a context for the consideration of the relation of work and unemployment to mental health.

First, there have been a number of changes in the types of work available in the United States. Looking at changes by industrial sector (e.g., mining, manufacturing, retail trade, services), the percentage of workers who held jobs in manufacturing declined from 32% (of nonfarm, private workers) in 1972 to 14% in 2008, whereas the proportion of service workers increased from 20% to 32% during the same period (U.S. Department of Labor, 2008b; see also Bell, 1973; Gittleman & Howell, 1995; Wetzel, 1995).

This shift in the economy has transformed the work experiences of many workers. Analyses of changes in the occupational structure indicate that job quality has declined within the low-skilled occupational sector (Gittleman & Howell, 1995; Rex, 2005) whereas rates of joblessness have increased (Swinnerton & Wial, 1995). Although these declines have disproportionately affected young inner-city minority men (Kasarda, 1995; Wilson, 1985, 2003), their effects have been felt as well by a broader range of the population (Swinnerton & Wial, 1995). Moreover, research (reviewed later) has suggested that the experience of poor quality jobs and unstable employment undermines the individual's sense of competency, psychological well-being, and health.

Second, women have entered the labor force in increasing numbers, partly in response to changes in the occupational structure. The most dramatic increase has been seen for married women with young children. In 1960, one in five married women with children under age 6 was in the labor force; by 2005, this rate had tripled (U.S. Department of Labor, 2007). Participation of mothers of older children has been even greater: about three-quarters are now in the labor force (U.S. Department of Labor, 2007). A large body of literature has considered the consequences of maternal employment for women, their spouses, and their children. Even with the decline in the quality of men's jobs (Gittleman & Howell, 1995; Rex, 2005), the average woman's job continues to be of lower quality, more insecure, and less well paid than the average man's job (Cotter et al., 2004; Gittleman & Howell 1995; Kilbourne et al., 1994). Moreover, when married women are employed, they remain responsible for the bulk of household chores (Bartley, Blanton, & Gilliard, 2005). This situation means that the work that women do in the home is likely to be an important contributor to reductions in their psychological well-being.

These broad social changes – in the nature of work and woman's participation in the labor force – have wide-ranging effects on individuals, not the least of which involve their sense of psychological well-being. Both the type of work available and the unavailability of work affect mental health in many ways, some of which are outlined in this chapter. Starting with paid work, we review studies linking job conditions to psychological well-being. We then examine extensions of this framework to the study of the unpaid work done at home. Finally, we consider the consequences of job loss.

Paid Work and Psychological Well-Being

Paid work can have a range of mental health consequences, both positive and negative. Jobs provide economic rewards and may be a source of identity, competence, and self-esteem (Jahoda, 1982, 1997; Morse & Weiss, 1955). Jobs may also involve excessive pressures and demands and exposure to dangerous or toxic conditions, and they may be unchallenging and routine, all of which can undermine physical and mental health (Frankenhaeuser, Lundberg, & Chesney, 1991; Kahn, 1981; Karasek & Theorell, 1990). The focus of this section is on the stressful aspects of work; the benefits of work are examined indirectly when we consider the effects of unemployment.

Studies examining the relation of work to health and mental health have generally posited a central role for control over one's work (e.g., Ganster, 1989; Mausner-Dorsch & Eaton, 2000; Spector, 1986). Control over one's life has generally been shown to contribute to satisfaction and well-being (Costello, 1982; Pearlin et al., 1981; Rosenfield, 1989; Ross & Mirowsky, 1992; Rotter, 1966). In the workplace, control may be experienced by the worker who can set the pace of the work, as well as by the worker who can determine whom to hire or fire. Various dimensions of "control" have been examined in the literature (see Kasl, 1989, and Frese & Zapf, 1989, for reviews), and central domains of work control are discussed briefly in this section.

In evaluating the distinctive contribution of different dimensions of control, it is especially important to distinguish between autonomy and other aspects of control. Although the terms "autonomy" and "control" often have been used interchangeably in the literature (see Halaby & Weakliem,1989), control tends to have a broader meaning, ranging from a lack of close supervision, to control over others, to control over general organizational policies and procedures. Autonomy is a major component of control. It involves the exercise of discretion in one's own work activities. This concept is similar to what Karasek et al. (1988) called "decision authority" and what Blauner (1964) called "control." Autonomy may entail several components: freedom of physical movement, freedom to establish plans for one's own task accomplishment, or freedom from close supervisory attention (Schwalbe, 1985).

Another form of control is what Kohn, Schooler, and colleagues (Kohn & Schooler, 1982, 1983; Schooler et al., 2004) have called "occupational self-direction," which they define as the use of initiative and personal judgment by the worker. Occupations that permit self-direction involve substantive and complex work with data, people, or things; work that is not closely supervised; and work that is not routine. This configuration, which occurs more frequently in highly skilled occupations, promotes intellectual flexibility in job incumbents and enhances the perception of the self as competent and in control of one's own fate (Kohn & Schooler, 1983).

Yet another important dimension of control is control over others' work activities. This dimension differs from self-direction in that it involves control not only over one's own work but also over the work of others. Existing literature on the psychological consequences of control typically has not distinguished control over others' work from control over one's own work. Although, as described later, several studies have implicated self-direction or control over one's own work as consequential for well-being (Kohn & Schooler, 1982, 1983; Kohn et al., 1990; Schooler et al., 2004), some investigations have demonstrated positive psychological consequences of the direction, control, and planning of others' activities (Lennon & Rosenfield, 1994; Link et al., 1993; Semmer, 1982). At this time it is unclear whether these latter findings are due to the high levels of self-direction that accompany controlling others' work rather than to control over others' work per se.

Another dimension of control is organizational control (i.e., the ability to direct and plan organizational procedures and policies). This feature has not been investigated adequately relative to other dimensions of control in terms of its impact on psychological functioning. However, it is an important aspect of control and thus is expected to contribute to feelings of mastery and well-being.

Two theoretical frameworks are prominent in the sociological literature that assesses the relationship between control at work and psychological well-being. The first, by Kohn, Schooler, and colleagues (Kohn & Schooler, 1982, 1983; Kohn et al., 1990), has attempted to explain social class differences in psychological functioning by positing the importance of occupational self-direction. They have argued that certain aspects of work permit the exercise of self-direction: work that entails complex tasks related to data, people, and things, work that is not routine, and work that is not closely supervised. In terms of its mental health consequences, work that is substantively complex is expected to reduce anxiety and improve self-esteem. Kohn, Schooler, and colleagues have conducted a number of studies that support their arguments empirically. These studies included cross-sectional and longitudinal designs, samples of men and women, and a range of cultural settings (Kohn & Schooler, 1982, 1983; Kohn et al., 1990; Miller et al., 1979; Schooler et al., 1983, 2004). They generalized their results to nonoccupational activities, including housework (Schooler et al., 1983).

A second framework frequently used in sociological studies of work stress was proposed by Karasek and colleagues (1988; Karasek & Theorell, 1990). Their theoretical model has posited that control over work is related to health outcomes primarily among individuals who experience high levels of psychological demands on the job. In their early work, Karasek and colleagues (1988) defined control as consisting of two dimensions: (1) skill discretion, which involves nonrepetitive work, high skill requirements, and new learning on the job; and (2) decision authority or freedom to decide about aspects of work tasks or about nonwork elements, such as breaks and telephone calls. It is important to note that there is considerable overlap between these elements and the components of self-directed work. High skill requirements and new learning are involved in substantively complex work. Nonrepetitive work and nonroutine work overlap considerably, and decision authority includes freedom from close supervision.

However, Karasek's model differs from Kohn, Schooler, and colleagues' model on several dimensions. One important difference is that, for Karasek and colleagues, low control is problematic for health primarily when demands are high. They define "high strain" jobs as those in which the worker experiences excessive demands but little control. Although the strongest evidence that high job strain affects health is found in studies associating job stressors to physical health detriments such as increases in cardiovascular disease (Belkic et al., 2004; Karasek, 1979; Karasek, Gardell, & Windell, 1987; J. Schwartz, Pickering, & Landsbergis, 2001; Theorell & Karasek, 1996), recent studies have presented empirical evidence in support of the interaction of job control and demands in predicting psychological distress (Bourbonnais et al., 1996; Cropley, Steptoe, & Joekes, 1999; Karasek & Theorell, 1990; Mausner-Dorsch & Eaton, 2000; Niedhammer et al., 1998; Paterniti et al., 2002; Stansfeld et al., 1999). Karasek's framework has been expanded to incorporate the role of social support in the workplace (Johnson & Hall, 1988; Johnson, Hall, & Theorell, 1989). Jobs with high demands, low support, and low control have been associated with earlier onset of cardiovascular disease (Johnson et al., 1989).

As Kohn and Schooler (1983) recognized, one mechanism by which lack of job control can come to increase psychological distress is by contributing to a more general sense of not being in control of one's life (see also Theorell et al., 1984). Link and colleagues (1993) investigated this mechanism in relation to depression and depressive symptomatology. They defined job control somewhat differently than did either Kohn and Schooler or Karasek, arguing that jobs that permit direction, control, and planning (DCP) of others' work activities may protect against the development of depression and psychological distress by contributing to a sense of mastery over the environment. They argued further that mastery protects against depression. To investigate this issue empirically, these authors used data from a case control study and a community cross-sectional design. They showed (1) that individuals of lower socioeconomic status (SES) are less likely to be involved in DCP occupations than individuals of higher SES, (2) that exposure to occupations involving DCP accounts for the associations of SES with depressive disorder and psychological distress, and (3) that the association between DCP and depressive disorders is mediated by mastery. Furthermore, these relationships cannot fully be accounted for by social selection processes, which could cause depressed persons to gravitate toward the type of work that does not require exerting control over the work of others. In conclusion, Link and colleagues suggested that DCP operates as a protective factor that reduces the risk for the development of depression and psychological distress.

Moreover, lack of self-direction or control in one's current work situation may be compensated for by the anticipation of future control. Thus, jobs that offer opportunities for advancement may mitigate the negative consequences of low levels of job control. In this regard, advantage will accrue to individuals employed in the core industrial sector, which is characterized by well-defined internal labor markets that present opportunities for advancement (Edwards, 1979; Ward & Mueller, 1985). There is some evidence that "motivators" at work such as recognition of achievement and possibilities of future advancement mediate the effects of high job strain and stress (Wallgrena & Hanse, 2006). Thus, low-level jobs in the core sector may not be as stressful as low-level jobs in the peripheral industrial sector, for which chances for advancement and job security are limited.

Taking a broad view of occupational control as encompassing self-direction, decision latitude, control over the work of others, and autonomy, it is clear that control over work is central to psychological well-being. The role of demands, such as time pressure and excessive hours, is less clear. According to Karasek and colleagues, the effect of demands occurs in interaction with control: only at low levels of control are demands hypothesized to be relevant. However, evidence to support this view is mixed as many studies have found independent effects of demands and control, rather than interactive effects (see Bromet et al., 1988; Demerouti et al., 2001; Lennon, 1995).

An alternative way of conceptualizing the role of workplace demands is suggested by Rosenfield (1989) in her studies of power and demands in family life. Rosenfield hypothesized that excessive household demands (such as having a number of young children at home or having sole responsibility for housework) undermine an individual's sense of control, leading to higher levels of depressive symptoms. Thus, she argued that excessive demands have a similar psychological effect as low levels of control: they undermine personal sense of control or mastery. Rosenfield (1989) found support for this perspective in the conditions of family life. If her reasoning generalizes to other spheres of life, then it is plausible that excessive work demands may also limit the exercise of control. Jobs that entail heavy workloads and frequent deadlines can make it difficult for the worker to control the pacing or scheduling of tasks. Thus, job demands may reduce the possibilities for exerting control. Following Rosenfield then, we would expect to find that demands of the job, like demands at home, operate through the same mechanism as lack of control or power: diminishing both opportunities for control and feelings of mastery.

An additional theoretical framework is the effort/reward imbalance (ERI) model proposed by Siegrist (1996). The ERI model differs from the two models discussed earlier in that control over work or the lack thereof is not a factor in the development of psychological distress. The ERI model posits that the lack of reciprocity between effort and present or anticipated reward leads to adverse health outcomes and emotional distress. Effort is defined as the demands and obligations imposed by the employer, and the rewards consist of money, esteem, prestige, job security, and career opportunities. Recent empirical studies have found that an imbalance between effort and reward is associated with higher depression, anxiety, and psychological distress (see Rafferty, Friend, & Landsbergis, 2001; Stansfeld et al., 1999; Tsutsumi et al., 2001; van Vegchel, et al. 2005).

Unpaid Work and Psychological Distress

The study of work stress has generally focused on paid work. However, many women, at some point in their lives, devote substantial effort to unpaid work in the home. The study of housework as work attempts to extend the study of work conditions from the job into the home. Many researchers seeking to understand gender differences in mental health have often compared homemakers to employed wives, generally assuming that full-time housework will increase levels of distress. More symptoms among housewives, found in several studies (e.g., Gove & Geerkin, 1977; Rosenfield, 1980), have been assumed to derive from the burdensome and tedious nature of housework or from the positive features of employment. These investigations have not examined directly the characteristics of housework and paid work. However, this research has made clear that conditions of housework, like job conditions, vary among women and may include positive, as well as negative, dimensions (Berk & Berk, 1979; Bird & Ross, 1993; Oakley, 1974; Schooler et al., 1983). Housework, like paid work, involves varying levels of control and demands. For example, in households with low levels of income and many young children, housework may be quite demanding. In dual-career households, housework may be highly routinized and scheduled, and once a routine becomes established, opportunities for control become restricted, which may lead to higher levels of distress (see Oakley, 1974).

Several investigators have systematically examined housework as work (Berk, 1985; Berk & Berk, 1979; Oakley, 1974). A number of these studies used comparable measures of dimensions of paid work and housework (Bird & Ross, 1993; Kibria et al., 1990; Lennon, 1995; Schooler et al., 1983), and a few compared the conditions of work for full-time homemakers and employed women (e.g., Bird & Ross, 1993; Lennon, 1995; Matthews et al., 1998). Bird and Ross (1993) reported that housework is more routine and less intrinsically gratifying and provides fewer extrinsic rewards than waged work. These authors also found that the routine, ungratifying, and unrewarding nature of the work accounts for home-makers' lower sense of personal control relative to employed women. Lennon found similar results in a study comparing conditions of housework for home-makers with conditions of jobs for employed wives. Homemakers experienced more advantageous work conditions in terms of greater autonomy, fewer time pressures, and less responsibility for matters outside their control, whereas they experienced less advantageous conditions in terms of more routine, more phys-ical demands, and more interruptions (Lennon, 1995). The study undertaken by Matthews et al. (1998) concluded that women who are full-time homemakers have fewer opportunities for learning and experience greater monotony than women employed outside the home. However, homemakers have more flexibility and can better control their work pace.

Even though the job conditions of employed wives differ from the housework conditions of homemakers, both employed wives and full-time homemakers expe-rience surprisingly similar housework conditions, according to a study by Lennon (1998). Employed wives and full-time homemakers alike considered housework as permitting a high degree of autonomy, being highly routine, involving extensive physical effort, being subject to frequent interruptions, and entailing a moderate degree of responsibility for things outside their control. There were, however, two interesting differences between these groups: homemakers saw housework as more complex and less time pressured than did employed wives. Employed wives and homemakers differed as well on the number of hours that they spent on housework each week, with employed wives averaging fewer hours than full-time homemakers. However, when hours on the job are were added to the time spent on housework, employed wives exceeded homemakers in total hours per week (Lennon, 1998).

These differences – in specific work conditions and hours – have implications for the levels of depressive symptoms among employed wives and homemakers. Before work conditions and hours were taken into account, employed wives and homemakers did not differ in levels of depressive symptoms. However, when the impact of housework conditions was statistically controlled, employed wives averaged significantly fewer depressive symptoms than nonemployed wives. In other words, the relationship between work status and symptoms appears to have been suppressed by the characteristics of housework that distinguish employed wives from homemakers.

Although employed women experience more time pressure in their housework than do full-time homemakers, they appear to be no more disadvantaged than homemakers with respect to depressive symptoms and may in fact have lower rates of depression (Johnson & Hall, 1988). Benefits of employment, such as earnings and access to networks of social support, may compensate for the disadvantages of housework. This suggests that employed wives experience rewards from paid work that offset the difficulties they encounter with housework. Some studies have suggested, however, that this may be true only up to a certain threshold, and in fact, women who have the burden of being both employed and primarily responsible for housework and child care have similar or higher rates of anxiety than homemakers (Haavio-Mannila, 1986). Thus, future research on these issues should consider aspects of jobs as well as aspects of housework in understanding symptoms among employed wives.

Unemployment and Psychological Well-Being

A large number of investigators have documented the detrimental effects of unemployment on psychological well-being (for reviews see Dew, Penkower, & Bromet, 1991; Horwitz, 1984; Perrucci & Perrucci, 1990; Theodossiou, 1998; Warr, Jackson, & Banks, 1988; see also Brenner, 1974; Catalano, Dooley, & Jackson, 1981, for ecological studies). Research on this topic ranges from Durkheim's classic study of suicide (1897/1951), to studies of the impact of the Depression of the 1930s (e.g., Eisenberg & Lazarsfeld, 1938; Elder, 1977; Jahoda, 1982), to more recent investigations of the effects of the economic changes of the 1970s and 1980s (e.g., Conger & Elder, 1994; Dooley et al., 1988; Kessler, Turner, & House, 1989). Cross-sectional, longitudinal, and prospective studies of individuals and time-series aggregate studies of communities have shown that unemployment increases symptoms of anxiety and depression and reduces self-esteem and security (for a review of studies see Murphy & Athanasou, 1999). Evidence suggests that this effect is not entirely due to selection processes through which individuals in poor mental health are more apt to become unemployed. In fact, when unemployed persons obtain new jobs, their distress levels decline (Jackson et al., 1983), suggesting that the episode of unemployment had contributed to their initial poor mental health.

Although most research on the consequences of unemployment is descriptive, some investigators have provided conceptual frameworks for understanding the mechanisms through which unemployment comes to have negative psychological effects. Jahoda (1981, 1982, 1997) put forward a latent deprivation model whereby employment serves both manifest and latent functions: The manifest or intended function is earning a living, whereas the latent or unintended functions include definition of identity and connection to important social institutions and associations. Unemployment is stressful because it involves the loss of all of these types of benefits. Using the latent deprivation model as a theoretical framework, recent studies have demonstrated a negative effect of unemployment on psychological well-being resulting from the loss of latent employment benefits (see Creed & Macintyre, 2001; Haworth, 1997; Waters & Moore, 2002).

Whereas Jahoda's model concentrates on the latent benefits of employment, Fryer's (1986) agency restriction model is focused on employment's manifest benefits (i.e., financial income). Fryer has posited that the effects of unemployment on mental health are primarily due to financial strain. Research has shown that lowered levels of income are associated with higher psychological distress (Feather, 1989; Rowley & Feather, 1987). Pearlin and colleagues (1981), on the basis of their stress process model, considered unemployment to be a primary stressor that may set into motion disruptive secondary stressors, such as economic deprivation (see also Conger et al., 1994). Thus, unemployment may bring in its wake a range of losses, including of social ties and economic stability, and these losses may be stressful in themselves.

Many studies have found that the effect of unemployment is more negative among persons of low socioeconomic status (Dooley & Catalano, 1979; Pearlin & Lieberman, 1979). Because the pre-unemployment economic circumstances of women (especially single mothers) are likely to be more insecure than those of men (Bianchi, 1995; Dew et al., 1991) and because women are more likely to experience discrimination in the labor market, which diminishes their opportunities for reemployment (Perrucci, Perrucci, & Targ, 1997), it is likely that the economic effects of unemployment will be more problematic for women, especially those who are single parents. The poverty rate for single-parent families headed by women is 30.5% (U.S. Census Bureau, 2007). Unemployment for the breadwinner in these circumstances can exacerbate an already unstable financial situation.

In addition to examining mediators and moderators of unemployment on an individual level, research on unemployment has been extended into two promising areas: specifying further the effect of the broader economic context in which unemployment occurs and assessing the effects of unemployment on family members. Each of these areas is described briefly in this section.

Several investigators have shown the importance of examining the economic context in which individuals experience unemployment. The meaning and consequences of job loss will vary depending on the state of the economy at a given point in time and at a given place. A number of ecological studies have examined changes in broad economic indicators, such as the presence of manufacturing jobs, in relation to indicators of mental health problems, such as rates of psychiatric hospitalizations (Brenner, 1974). Problems with ecological-level studies have been well documented (Catalano, 1981; Kasl & Cobb, 1979; Perrucci & Perrucci, 1990). Even though much of this criticism is justified, the studies have the advantage of emphasizing the broader economic forces that may underlie individual episodes of unemployment.

One promising line of research has examined the mental health effects of macroeconomic conditions, including community-level unemployment rates, in addition to individual unemployment. Several investigators have reported results from such cross-level analyses. Prominent among these is the research program of Dooley, Catalano, and colleagues (Catalano & Dooley, 1977, 1983; Catalano et al., 1981; Dooley, Catalano, & Rook, 1988) that has found independent effects of community-level unemployment rates as well as of individual unemployment. Aggregate unemployment is associated with subsequent increases in depressive mood and stressful life events in metropolitan areas (Catalano & Dooley, 1977). However, these investigators did not find evidence for an interaction between these broad economic changes and unemployment on an individual level.

Another cross-level study conducted by Turner (1995) did find such an interaction effect. In areas where unemployment was high, the currently unemployed had higher rates of depressive symptoms. Moreover, this association was stronger among those with lower levels of education. The author noted that low education is a risk factor for unemployment. Thus, those with low education are more likely to become unemployed and when unemployed would have less chance of being reemployed. Considering the greater mental health cost to this group caused by their being unemployed in an adverse economy, individuals with low educational attainment appear to be highly vulnerable to macroeconomic downturns.

Conclusion

Research on the relation of work and unemployment to mental health has demonstrated both the rewards and stressors associated with working and the difficulties that are likely to ensue when jobs are lost. For the most part, however, studies of job conditions and unemployment have not been integrated. More recent research has examined the effects of macroeconomic changes, such as high levels of unemployment, on the conditions of work for those who retain their jobs. One such study, conducted by Fenwick and Tausig (1994), examined the relationship between community-level unemployment and levels of job stress. The authors hypothesized that widespread unemployment would be detrimental not only to those directly affected (i.e., the unemployed) but also to those workers who remain employed. If these workers can be easily replaced, then employers may reduce beneficial aspects of their jobs, for example by increasing workloads. Additionally, the authors observed that, in times of economic downturns, firms that survive hard times are likely to do so at the expense of the quality of jobs they offer workers. Fenwick and Tausig found support for their hypotheses in the association between higher occupational unemployment rates and decreased life satisfaction and increased stress. This effect was mediated by lower decision latitude and increased job demands associated with higher occupational unemployment. Thus, broad economic downturns have implications for mental health not only by increasing unemployment risk for individuals but also by reducing job quality. Tausig and Fenwick (1999) furthered explored their theory in their study of the 1974–1975 recession and its effect on the aggregate well-being of the population. Similar to the findings of their earlier study, they concluded that the recession experienced by the U.S. population in the 1970s contributed significantly to the distress and dissatisfaction levels of full-time workers because of labor market experiences and changes in job characteristics. The recession of the 1970s was plagued by high oil prices, high inflation, and high unemployment. Although the current economic downturn is not characterized by high oil prices or high inflation, the rate of unemployment is similar to that of the 1970s. Future research in this area, through a closer examination of the current economic downturn, will expand our knowledge on the effects of macroeconomic changes on mental health.

In addition to investigating the interaction between community economic changes and individual work experiences, more remains to be learned about the effects of unemployment on families (for a review of the literature see Ström, 2003). Investigations of families in the Depression of the 1930s noted the consequences of husbands' unemployment for their spouse and their children (Elder, 1977). Research conducted in the 1980s by Conger and Elder (1994) extended the scope of study to examine the consequences of unemployment for either spouse. They found that when mothers experience economic deprivation, their distress influences their children's well-being. In a similar vein, McLoyd et al. (1994) found that current unemployment is associated with adolescent depression primarily through the effect of unemployment and maternal depression on the quality of interactions between mothers and their children. Parental unemployment has also been found to have long-term effects on children, through the children's lowered self-esteem (Christoffersen, 1994).

The reform of the U.S. welfare system in the 1990s provided an opportunity to study the psychological effects of movement into employment among low-income women. Although additional research in this area will provide more clarity, recent studies have found that welfare reform has produced mixed results in terms of the mental health of former welfare recipient and their families. Research has indicated that both mothers and their children are likely to benefit from efforts directed at improving employment and providing higher quality jobs, because good jobs can compensate for other difficulties that single families generally face (Menaghan, 1991. However, although some studies have found that mothers who enter the workforce benefit from increased social ties, higher self-esteem, and psychological well-being (Anderson, Halter, & Gryzlak, 2004; London et al., 2004), the likelihood that women leaving welfare will enter into low-skill, low-paying service-sector jobs suggests that employment may have negative effects on mental health (Acs, Loprest, & Roberts, 2001; Cancian & Meyer, 2000; Corcoran, et al., 2000; Lichter & Jayakody, 2002). Welfare leavers are also more likely than welfare recipients to face barriers in accessing health and dental care, because their income often disqualifies them from receiving Medicaid and other government-sponsored health programs, yet is not sufficient to enable them to participate in private health plans (Danziger et al., 2002). These studies point to the importance of including the type, condition, and benefits of work in analyzing the consequences of welfare reform. Because the current economic contraction will have a direct impact on the types of jobs available to former welfare recipients, this should be a consideration in future research.

Another promising area of research that has emerged in recent years concentrates on the effects of relational justice within the workplace. Relational justice is part of the larger framework of organizational justice and encompasses the employees' perception of the fairness of the decision-making process within the workplace, the fairness of decisions themselves, as well as the perceived fairness of treatment received from supervisors. Research on organizational justice seeks to add to the existing theoretical frameworks used in studying the psychosocial aspects of the work environment and their effects on mental health (Kawachi, 2006). A study by Ferrie and colleagues (2006) suggested that this framework is useful in examining workplace stressors and mental health. Their study on British civil servants found that unfair treatment of employees by their supervisors is linked to higher risk of poor mental health in employees. Future investigation of relational justice at work is called for to more fully specify the processes through which work may affect mental health.

12

Socioeconomic Stratification and Mental Disorder

William W. Eaton, Carles Muntaner, and Jaime C. Sapag

This chapter reviews sociological theories and measurements of stratification and social class in the process of relating inequality to mental disorder. The authors argue that processes of stratification and periods of high vulnerability to mental disorder are related to different stages in the life course. Consequently, stratification and one's place in the socioeconomic system have a complex relationship to the occurrence of mental disorder. Both individual and environmental factors must be taken into account. This chapter reviews the major research studies, noting differences in indicators of social class and methodological variations. In general, researchers have found that socioeconomic status (SES) is inversely related to mental disorder; that is, those in the lower classes experience higher rates of disorder. Two contrasting frameworks for understanding the relation of SES to mental disorder are selection and drift on the one hand and social causation on the other hand. Selection refers to the idea that individuals who are predisposed to mental disorder have lower than expected educational and occupational attainment. Drift refers to the idea that those with mental disorders are likely to drift down the SES ladder, as they will have more trouble with employment and other means of attaining higher SES positions. In contrast, social causation explanations emphasize how the social experiences of members of different social classes influence their likelihood of becoming mentally ill or distressed. The authors conclude by reviewing two studies that illustrate the complexity of the relationship between social class and mental disorder. We need more research on the specific ways in which social class affects mental disorder and on how mental disorder affects the attainment of social status. Students should compare the selection and drift frameworks. Is it likely that an individual born of a wealthy family will drift down the socioeconomic ladder if they experience a mental health problem? Consider the role of social support and stress in understanding the relationship between SES and mental health.

Introduction

Inequality is the simplest concept that applies to the group but not the individual. As such, the study of inequality has always been central to sociology. Inequality in social resources seems to be present in every current society (Flanagan, 1989) and brings with it a wide range of associated differences that might be related to mental disorder. The inequity is systematic, produced by social norms, policies, and practices that tolerate or actually promote unfair distribution of and access to power, wealth, and other necessary social resources (Commission on the Social

Determinants of Health, 2008). Although the study of mental disorders formed part of the earliest empirical work in sociology, as in Durkheim's (1897/1951) *Suicide*, the initial work on the relationship of social inequality to mental disorder was done by individuals in other fields (e.g., Commission on Lunacy, 1855; Nolan, 1917). A review of the literature on social status and specific mental disorders in 1969 included 25 studies of social class and mental disorder, of which 20 revealed the inverse relationship between social class and prevalence of disorder; that is, the highest rate of disorder was found in members of the lowest social class (Dohrenwend & Dohrenwend, 1969). A review in 1990 referred to 60 studies published between 1972 and 1989 (Ortega & Corzine, 1990). Of these, 46 revealed an inverse relationship between social class and mental disorder. New studies bring more evidence supporting this association worldwide (Egan et al., 2008; Kuruvilla & Jacob, 2007).

The literature reflects the slow progress made in specifying useful details and implications of the overall research. Gradually, however, a picture is emerging that reflects both the complexity of mental disorders and the complexity of social class and SES. One of the questions that research has been trying to address is how to explain this relationship among SES and mental health and illness. This chapter reviews the existing evidence in this regard from a critical and historical perspective.

Definition of Mental Disorder

Mental disorders are defined here as disturbances in the mental life of the individual that have deleterious consequences for the individual's relationship to others. The concept of "mental disturbance" focuses both on (1) time-limited perturbations from the individual's usual pattern of thinking and feeling, such as a sudden panic attack or a month-long episode of depression, and (b) long-term deviations – in this case, from the statistical norm of mental functioning of most individuals – that have no apparent cause, like schizophrenia and antisocial personality disorder. This definition places less emphasis on behavioral deviations that have little cognitive or emotional component, such as those that can occur with addictions or homicides. Use of alcohol or other psychoactive substances does not, in itself, meet the criteria for mental disorder unless there is other evidence of mental disturbance.

Most mental disorders involve deviations in cognition or emotion that are part and parcel of everyday human existence, necessitating an arbitrary threshold of measurement. The requirement that mental disturbances lead to interference with social relationships excludes trivial disturbances such as daydreaming, brief confusion, temporary irritation, or trivial anxiety. Thus, the individual's relationship to others operationally defines the threshold for the presence of disorder. Deterioration in social functioning can have a variety of causes, such as physical illnesses or injuries, and is not in itself a mental disturbance. Mental disturbances – even nontrivial ones such as the trance of a shaman (Ellenberger, 1970) – do not qualify as mental disorders unless they bring about a disruption of the individual's social relationships. Thus, the social network is a defining concept in the operational definition of mental disorder.

This definition focuses on the nature of the disturbance (mental) and its implication for functioning (social); it thus requires psychological *and* sociological conceptualization and measurement. However, this definition does not specify the nature of the cause. Mental disorders can have infectious, toxicologic, genetic, neurodevelopmental, psychological, and social causes. Comprehensive theoretical explanatory models for mental illness are required to understand their multiple causes in a cultural context as well as to make progress in creating and evaluating appropriate treatments and recovery processes (Kendler, 2008; Kiesler, 2001).

Socioeconomic Stratification

Socioeconomic stratification is defined as the process by which individuals are accorded unequal access to rewards and resources in society. Individuals in social structures characterized by socioeconomic stratification are hierarchically ordered along a continuum as to wealth, power, and prestige – that is, economic, political, and cultural rewards and resources (as discussed in the 19th century by Weber). These rankings are sometimes referred to as "simple gradational measures" (Wright, 2000).

An important form of socioeconomic stratification is the social class structure. *Social classes* are defined here as groups of individuals who are similar in their wealth, power, and prestige and who either (1) interact with one another more often than randomly or (2) are aware of some common interest. According to the Marxian tradition, social classes are groups of individuals defined by their relationship to the ownership and control of the means of production, or by the process of appropriation, production, and distribution of surplus value in the economy. This definition leads to at least two basic classes: those who own and control the means of production and receive the benefits of others' labor (i.e., the capitalist class) and those whose labor is exploited in that the surplus value produced is taken from them (i.e., the working class). Although Marx emphasized the process of exploitation as the major determinant of class, later evolutions of this concept have emphasized the importance of power and the capacity of the individual to influence decisions about the structure of the economy. Individuals in similar socioeconomic strata form into social classes, in part, to retain control over the economic and political process (Mills, 1956). Some recent theorists have emphasized the importance of the relational concept of exploitation based on control of productive assets beyond the material means of production to organizational power and the influence of credentials such as educational degrees, as opposed to simple measures of domination or power (Western & Wright, 1994; Wright, 1985). For the purposes of our discussion, the glue holding together these notions of social class is the concept of the social group: Social classes, according to this view of the Marxian tradition and its heirs, are social groups with differential control over productive assets. In itself, socioeconomic stratification indicates only an ordering of individuals who may or may not be formed into groups.

The study of social class and socioeconomic stratification includes many diverse traditions (Collins, 1994; Farley, 1994; Matras, 1984), and views on measurement (Oakes & Rossi, 2003). These various perspectives on socioeconomic stratification and social class have formed a central part of the discipline of sociology, and it is reasonable to consider different mental health outcomes associated with various definitions. Usually SES is measured/represented by one or more of the following indicators/concepts: education, occupational status or prestige, and economic resources, which is typically measured by annual income. Although there are substantial correlations among these concepts, it is well established that each also has unique antecedents and consequences.

Education, measured either as years of education or as credentials such as certifications and degrees, is the most common index of social class in psychiatric epidemiology and public health research (Liberatos, Link, & Kelsey, 1988). Its stability over adult life – as well as it reliability, efficiency of measurement, and good validity – are presumably the main reasons for its popularity (Kaplan & McNeil, 1993). Education represents knowledge, skills, and training, which might have an influence over health behaviors (Sorlie, Backlund, & Keller, 1995). According to neoclassical economists, education might also increase the value of an individual's contribution to the productive process, which translates into greater social rewards. In contrast, some neo-Marxists maintain that the social rewards associated with greater education stem from its association with skills that are in short supply (Wright, 1985). Another view is that the credential provided by educational attainment may be more a sign of lifestyle, class of origin, or "attitude" than of actual ability; these latent features may be what actually generates the higher salary.

Occupation, measured according to the Bureau of Census Classification of Occupations or as occupational prestige, is a major social class indicator in psychiatric epidemiology (Muntaner & Eaton, 1996). Occupation strata identify technical aspects of work (Muntaner et al., 1991) and are also associated with prestige, wealth, skills, and specific working conditions (Sorlie et al., 1995). Some authors in the functionalist tradition of medical sociology emphasize that occupational prestige and SES are consequences of educational achievement (Ross & Wu, 1995). Other models of occupational stratification emphasize that the rewards associated with positions in society derive from their location in the hierarchical structure of the workplace and not from the workers' education (Krieger et al., 1993). For example, managerial and professional occupations obtain higher wages partly as compensation for the self-monitoring required by such positions.

A third way of measuring social stratification has been the assessment of a person's economic resources by using personal and household income (Kessler et al., 1994), but occasionally measures of poverty (Bruce, Takeuchi, & Leaf, 1991), wealth (Muchtler & Burr, 1991) or financial dependency (Eaton et al., 2004) have also been used. In a money economy, income and wealth are the most straightforward measures of the ability to acquire resources and influence a wide range of outcomes. However, these measures present their own set of limitations. Questions about income typically show a higher nonresponse rate than those about education and occupation, presumably because respondents are unwilling to disclose their financial situation (Kaplan & McNeil, 1993; Liberatos et al., 1988). Furthermore, although income can be conceptualized as a measure of social class, several research programs consider income as a dependent variable to be explained by social class theories (Halaby & Weakliem, 1993; Robinson & Kelley, 1990; Smith, 1990; Wright, 1979). Positions in the social structure are associated with various kinds of income (e.g., rents derived from renting land versus wages derived from being an employee) and differentials in wealth (e.g., value of assets owned; Callinicos & Harman, 1989; Wright, 1993). Finally, because wealth is more unequally distributed than income (Matras, 1984; Wolff, 1995), it is likely that reliance on income as the preferred indicator of economic resources may overlook larger differentials in mental health.

There are other ways to measure SES or social class, including area of residence, level of deprivation, and combinations of the indicators described earlier. All of them have their own limitations and strengths. It is important to recognize the limitations of these measurements, which may be related to their inherent conceptual clarity or to psychometric problems (Oakes & Rossi, 2003).

Marxian *class analysis* represents an alternative approach to measurement (Wright, 1993). Class analysis maintains that several societal relations (e.g., owner versus worker, manager versus nonmanager) generate inequalities in social resources such as income. For example, in traditional Marxian analysis, owners of the means of production generate excess wealth for themselves from the surplus value they appropriate from laborers. In some modern versions of Marxian class analysis, managers are thought to receive higher incomes to reward their additional loyalty exercised in supervising others in line with the desires of owners (Wright, 1985). Other complexities in the measurement of SES are discussed later with respect to specific research studies.

The Causes of Inequality

There are two main contending paradigms for explaining the existence of social classes and socioeconomic differences (e.g., as in Matras, 1984). One explanation arises from the sociological theory of functionalism, a major sociological paradigm (Davis & Moore, 1974; Merton, 1956). Functionalists argue that in a complex modern society there are differences in the individual qualities required for different occupations. Some occupations require extremely persistent, skillful, and intelligent individuals, whereas other jobs can be performed by almost anybody. In addition, some jobs are more important than others for the welfare of the society as a whole. Rewards are distributed unequally in society in order to attract individuals with specific and rare skills and abilities into important jobs. Thus, the social class system serves the function of sifting and sorting people into appropriate occupations for the greatest good of society.

The second main explanation for the existence of socioeconomic stratification and social classes comes out of the conflict paradigm, which finds its most developed expression in the Marxian tradition. According to this tradition, classes are thought to exist because individuals higher up in the hierarchy are more powerful, preserving the class structure to hold on to privileged and advantageous positions for themselves and their heirs (Mills, 1956). Such control is exercised in a variety of ways. For instance, the upper classes may attempt to manipulate the political process to favor those already in power (Ferguson, 1995; Navarro, 1994). High-status individuals will attempt to ensure that their sons and daughters are provided with educational credentials for entering high-status positions in the occupational structure. The upper classes, consciously or unconsciously, may manipulate the mass culture so that explanations for the class system are expressed in terms of individual differences in ability instead of differences in power or inequalities of institutions (Chomsky, 1989). The functional explanation of the class system just described may here be thought of as an ideology that elites maintain to draw attention away from their privileges and power (Laurin-Frenette, 1976).

Socioeconomic stratification is a process generating a structure that tends to persist through time, even though the individuals holding positions within the structure are constantly being replaced over the generations (Erikson & Goldthorpe, 1993). Each generation of individuals joins the current structure of socioeconomic stratification via both intergenerational mobility (i.e., from one generation to the next) and intragenerational mobility (i.e., within one generation, over the lifetime of an individual). If individuals – regardless of their personal characteristics – inherit class position from parents, then the class system is said to be "rigid" or "closed," and the data are thought to support the conflict interpretation for the existence of classes. If individuals can enter the upper class no matter what their background, then the system is thought of as "open" and the functional theory is supported.

In the past few decades, there have been considerable advances in the quantitative study of the dynamics of this replacement process (sometimes referred to as "status attainment" – a phrase and an approach with a slightly functionalist orientation). The quantification of the process of stratification has the potential to illuminate the relative adequacy of the functionalist versus conflict explanations for the existence of socioeconomic inequality. For example, useful empirical studies of the stratification process have taken the form of path models of intergenerational mobility – that is, the relationship of the acquisition of the socioeconomic position of the child to the position of the parents (Blau & Duncan, 1967). In Western societies during the first three-quarters of the 20th century, there was considerable intergenerational movement from the lower class into the middle and upper middle classes. The movement was due partly to the expansion of the middle class. But along with the movement out of the lower class, there was a strong tendency for those born into the upper class to remain there throughout their lifetimes. In other words, some evidence is consistent with the functionalist approach and some with the conflict approach. Another study found that the effect of health selection on the social gradient, even when individuals with poor health were more likely to move down and less likely to move up the social scale, especially at the intergenerational transition, is variable and of modest size and cannot be considered as a main explanation for health inequalities in early adulthood (Manor, Matthews & Power, 2003). Finally, it is important to make the distinction between social inequalities and social inequities. Although the first concept is more descriptive in terms of the social differences, the second one assumes that those differences are avoidable and unfair (Whitehead, 1990).

Causation, Selection, and the Life Course

At any given point in time, the individual brings to the social environment a biological organism with a history of learning and experience. These all affect the numerous capabilities and inclinations that make the individual unique and contribute to his or her sense of identity and life plan, as well as to the probability of successes in various endeavors – the so-called life chances described by Weber. The organism begins at conception with genetic material, and the history of learning and experience start at that moment. The organism is sometimes obdurate in the face of environmental experience (e.g., sustaining personal identity in an oppressive prison or concentration camp) and sometimes exquisitely sensitive (e.g., exhibiting neurological changes as a result of experience; Eisenberg, 1995). It is still hard to predict the realms, and the times, of obduracy and sensitivity. As the life course progresses, the capabilities and inclinations that make the individual unique are constantly evolving as experience is acquired. Age-related periods of relatively rapid or relatively stable evolution are called "developmental periods"; these are demarcated by more or less regular age-related patterns – in the way the environment changes and in the way the organism matures – called "life transitions" (Baltes, Reese, & Lipsitt, 1980).

The process of stratification, and the periods of highest vulnerability to mental disorder, are developmentally staged. During some stages of life, the effects of the environment, the choices individuals make, and the successes and failures in tasks (related to the social environment in particular) are more important for the future evolution of the life course than they are at other stages. It is also true that each stage of life influences the next stage. Advantages and disadvantages for the life chances of the individual – in terms of socioeconomic position and also in terms of mental disorders – accumulate over the life span. Combined focus on the importance of critical developmental stages, as well as the more continuous and languid accumulation of advantage and disadvantage, are the central tenets of the emerging field of life course epidemiology, and are applicable to the issue of socioeconomic position and mental disorder (Kuh & Ben-Shlomo, 1997).

Adolescence and young adulthood appear to be important developmental periods, both for the process of socioeconomic stratification and for the onset of mental disorders. For example, elaborations of status attainment models show that the periods of high school and young adulthood are very important in determining ultimate socioeconomic position. In high school, educational and occupational aspirations (as well as other factors such as the socioeconomic position of the family) are influential in determining whether the individual attends college; college attendance, in turn, is important in determining the first job (Sewell, Haller, & Ohlendorf, 1970). Still other models of the process show that the first job has a strong influence on the entire later career (Blau & Duncan, 1967). Likewise the age of risk of first onset for many mental disorders is in adolescence and young adulthood. For males, schizophrenia arises just after adolescence; for females it arises about a decade later, during young adulthood (Eaton, 1985). Depression arises in the early 20s to early 30s (Fava & Kendler, 2000; Giaconia et al., 1994; Lewinsohn et al., 1993). Simple phobic disorder, extreme shyness, and general nervousness usually start as early as when the infant learns to talk (Eaton, Dryman, & Weissman, 1991; Giaconia et al., 1994), but social phobia arises in puberty (Giaconia et al., 1994) and panic attacks start in adolescence (Hayward, Killen, & Taylor, 1989). Conduct disorder arises in males in the middle of their childhood, followed by mental disturbances connected to use of alcohol and drugs after puberty and to antisocial personality disorder in the late teenage years (Mrazek & Haggerty, 1994).

It is abundantly clear that socioeconomic position is strongly associated with the occurrence of mental disorder (as noted in reviews just cited and in work subsequently described). Two alternative explanations for the association are the causation explanation and the selection/drift explanation. The causation explanation posits that conditions associated with lower socioeconomic position raise risk for the occurrence of mental disorders. The selection/drift explanation posits that the occurrence of mental disorder affects the attainment of socioeconomic position. The selection interpretation focuses on intergenerational socioeconomic mobility, that is, changes from the socioeconomic position of the parents to the position of the offspring. The drift interpretation focuses on intragenerational socioeconomic mobility, that is, changes in the socioeconomic position of the individual after the onset of mental disorder. The processes of selection occur during the early stages of the socioeconomic career, in adolescence and young adulthood, when education is being completed, the choice of career is being made, and the first job is sought. Because many mental disorders do not have overt onset until young adulthood, the

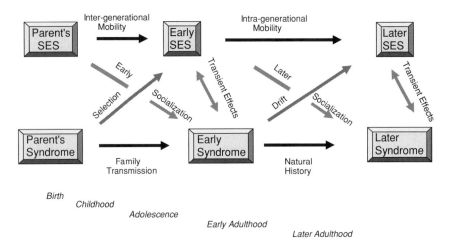

Figure 12.1. Socioeconomic status and psychopathology intergenerational and intragenerational models.

effects of selection must necessarily be influenced by premorbid characteristics of individuals who are destined to later acquire a mental disorder. The processes of drift occur somewhat later, after onset. Thus, the status attainment process and the natural history of mental disorders operate simultaneously, sometimes independently, and sometimes in synergy, as shown in Figure 12.1.

The general focus of this developmental approach is the ongoing reciprocal relationship between the age-graded expectations of the social system, the adequacy of the individual's performance in the context of those expectations, and the consequent mental life of the individual. The rating of performance by others affects aspirations for future performance; the school system and the occupational system both regularly provide such ratings (Kellam et al., 1983). How does the attainment of a given letter grade in elementary school affect risk for conduct disorder in the following year, and vice versa? How does the onset of depression or other disorder affect educational, occupational, and income aspirations (Crespo, 1977; Kessler, Foster, et al., 1995; Link, 1982), and vice versa? How does significant others' influence regarding occupational aspirations affect risk for schizophrenia, and vice versa (Parker & Kleiner, 1966)? How does the first job affect risk for schizophrenia (Link, Dohrenwend, & Skodol, 1986), and vice versa? How does the occupational career affect panic disorder, and vice versa (Keyl & Eaton, 1990)? How does an episode of schizophrenia affect occupational mobility after the first job, and vice versa (Goldberg & Morrison, 1963)? The point of listing these questions, and repeating the obverse, is to show the reader that the process of socioeconomic stratification is related to the occurrence of mental disorder in a subtle and complex manner. The effects of many variables that mediate the relationship ebb and flow over the life course, interacting in a constantly evolving codependent manner. It is necessary also to remark that the health effects of socioeconomic disadvantage may accumulate over the life course (Singh-Manoux et al., 2004). Both the selection/drift interpretation and the causation interpretation are equally important as empirical sociological research.

Mental disorders with significant chronic impairment are likely to affect attainment of occupational roles. Consider the contrast in the manner of hiring that might occur in lower- versus upper-class occupations. Application for a job as construction worker or fruit picker is sometimes as simple as showing up at the construction trailer or street corner when workers are needed. Verbal or social skills, judgment, independence, persistence, and other traits may not be assessed prior to being hired. Application for an executive or professional position is more likely to require the possession of professional certifications, assessment by professional placement firms, and interviews – sometimes over several days – with prospective supervisors and co-workers. Paper-and-pencil tests, including intelligence tests, may be included in the requirements for obtaining positions, or for the educational background of degrees and certifications required even to apply. Social impairment is one of the defining criteria for mental disorders, and the more severe disorders like schizophrenia involve lower cognitive ability in some persons (Bilder et al., 1992). Individuals with chronic social and cognitive impairments, as is likely to be the case for schizophrenia and antisocial personality disorders, are likely to suffer in the more rigorous selection procedure and so gravitate down the social scale to positions with less demanding entrance requirements.

The causation interpretation focuses on the myriad factors associated with low socioeconomic position that might raise risk for mental disorders. These are subsequently considered in some detail. Lower-class life is posited to be more stressful. When stressful conditions arise, resources to cope with the stress are less available to individuals in lower socioecononomic positions. The culture of those in low socioeconomic position may be different in some way that predisposes persons in that position to mental disorders. Physical risk factors for mental disorders such as toxins are more common in areas in which persons in low socioeconomic positions reside.

Socioeconomic Status as Outcome

Lunacy and Poverty in 19th-Century America

A classic early study of social class and mental disorder concluded that selection and drift, rather than social causation, were the dominant explanation for the relationship between socioeconomic status and mental disorder. In 1854 Edward Jarvis led a legislative commission "to ascertain the number and condition of the insane in the State, distinguishing as accurately as may be between the insane, properly so considered, and the idiotic or *non compos*; between the furious and the harmless, curable and incurable, and between the native and the foreigner, and the number of each who are State paupers" (Commission on Lunacy, 1855, p. 9). Letters of inquiry were sent to hospitals, to physicians in each town, and to clergy and other responsible persons in towns without physicians. It was apparently assumed that the physicians could make a reliable diagnosis, as they were presumed to "understand the nature of defective or diseased minds, and [were] competent to testify" (Commission on Lunacy, 1855, p. 17). The study gives the appearance of extreme effort to be comprehensive and of exacting efforts in the presentation of data. At the tenth meeting of the Association of Medical Superintendents of American Institutions for the Insane (the forerunner organization of the American Psychiatric Association), a motion was unanimously adopted praising the Jarvis commission work "as the first successful attempt, in America, to secure entirely reliable statistics on this subject" (Grob, 1971, p. 65).

A principal finding of the Jarvis report was that poverty was associated with lunacy (Table 12.1). There were 2,622 lunatics in a population of more than 1 million, for a prevalence proportion of 2.33 per thousand. This proportion is slightly lower than (but of the same order of magnitude as) the prevalence of psychosis today, which might be estimated as about one half of 1%, or 5 per thousand. The prevalence of lunacy among paupers, who formed about 2% of the population, was 65 per thousand (over 6%) but only 1 per thousand among persons of independent means. The resulting odds ratio, estimated and presented by Jarvis in the report (pp. 52–53) is nearly 70 – a size any modern-day epidemiologist would pay attention to.

What did Jarvis conclude from these data? One conclusion was that insanity caused individuals to become paupers – this is the "drift" interpretation: "It needs no philosophy to show that some, perhaps many, lunatics, by their disease lose their power of self-sustenance, and are thereby removed from the independent to the pauper class" (Commission on Lunacy, 1855, p. 53). But he also concluded (p. 55) that "much of poverty has a common origin with insanity" – this is the "selection" interpretation:

> It is worthwhile to look somewhat at the nature of poverty, its origin, and its relation to man and to society. It is usually considered as a single outward circumstance – the absence of worldly goods; but this want is . . . only one of its manifestations. Poverty is . . . enrooted deeply within the man . . . ; it reaches his body, his health, his intellect, and his moral powers, as well as his estate. In one or other of these elements it may predominate, and in that alone he may seem to be poor; but it usually involves more than one of the elements. Hence we find that, among those whom the world calls poor, there is less vital force, a lower tone of life, more ill health, more weakness, more early death, . . . less self-respect, ambition and hope, more idiocy and insanity, and more crime, than among the independent. (p. 52)

The Jarvis report raises several issues that form themes for later work on the subject. The comprehensive definition of the target population and the comprehensive

Table 12.1. *Report of the Jarvis commission*

	Lunatics	Idiots	Total
Paupers			
Number	1,522	418	23,125
Prevalence	65.82	18.08	
Independents			
Number	1,110	671	1,102,551
Prevalence	1.01	0.61	
Total			
Number	2,622	1,089	1,124,676
Prevalence	2.33	0.97	

Source: Commission on Lunacy (1855), Tables IV, VIII, XIX, XXI, and frequencies in text on page 52.

quality of case finding is important, and it would appear that the Jarvis commission was more inclusive in this respect than other work until the Epidemiologic Catchment Area study, more than 120 years later. The use of specific categories of mental disturbance ("lunatic" and "idiot"), and the presentation of data that allows distinctive relationships to social variables between the categories, contrasts favorably with some later work. However, the categories studied – both the focus variables of lunacy and idiocy and the social definition of "pauperism" – are on the rare end of the continuum.

The idea that mental illness produces a downward shift in the individual's financial status (drift), or that some trait or group of traits of the personality structures of affected individuals predisposes them simultaneously to pauperism and insanity (selection), is not proven in the cross-sectional work of Jarvis but is consistent with the functionalist view of the formation and maintenance of the social classes. This point of view suggests that individuals in poverty acquire that status because of their own lack of ability or ambition.

Longitudinal Studies

Because they sort out temporal order, longitudinal data are preferred for assessing the selection/drift theory. This assessment requires a longitudinal follow-up of the social class attainment of a population of individuals after the occurrence of mental disorder in some proportion of them. About a dozen studies address the issue of mobility of individuals with severe mental disorders; most indicate some support for either the selection or drift hypothesis (e.g., Eaton & Lasry, 1978). A methodologically rigorous study of intragenerational mobility in England gave strong evidence of downward mobility following an episode of schizophrenia (Goldberg & Morrison, 1963). Two convincing studies compared intergenerational mobility

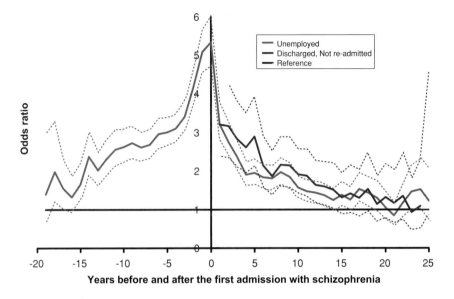

Figure 12.2. Odds ratio of being unemployed more than 1% of the year, versus employed, for schizoprenics and controls; adjusted for age, sex, calendar year, and marital status, with 95% confidence bands. *Source:* Agerbo et al. (2004).

of schizophrenics and control individuals born in the same cohort and showed that the trajectory for individuals who would later be diagnosed as schizophrenic was not as high as that in the general population (U.K. cohort – Goldberg & Morrison, 1963; U.S. cohort – Turner & Wagenfeld, 1967). These studies of intergenerational mobility suggest that the incidence findings are artifactual, because many schizophrenics have insidious onset of disorder and this type of onset is presumed to hinder upward mobility. The intergenerational and intragenerational mobility of persons with schizophrenia and of the general population have been used to parameterize a multigenerational Markov model, which can then be extrapolated to estimate a distribution of schizophrenia by socioeconomic position in a state of equilibrium. When this has been done (Eaton, 1980), the equilibrium distribution looks very similar to the distribution of the prevalence of schizophrenia by socioeconomic position – supporting the selection and drift interpretations for this disorder.

An elegant study by Agerbo et al. (2004) provides evidence of selection and drift (Figure 12.2). This study applied the case control approach to estimate the relative odds of schizophrenia for those who were employed versus unemployed. The use of comprehensive population-based registers in Denmark allowed study of these relative odds at the time of first admission to psychiatric treatment for schizophrenia, as well as at each year for 19 years prior to the admission and 25 years following the admission. The relative odds were highest at the time of admission, but also well above 1.0 even 19 years prior to admission, suggesting that impairments in finding and keeping a job were present for persons later diagnosed, well before the observed onset.

There are few follow-up studies of the effects on attainment of socioeconomic position of such milder mental disorders as depression, anxiety, and alcohol dependence, but retrospective cross-sectional data presented by Kessler et al. (2005) support the idea that insidious onset of depressive and anxiety disorders hinders the process of educational attainment (Kessler et al., 2005).

Socioeconomic Position as Cause

Prevalence and Incidence: The New Haven Study

The monograph *Social Class and Mental Illness* (Hollingshead & Redlich, 1958) is one of the most important early studies of the relationship of class to mental disorder that assumes the direction of causation from class to mental disorder. It represents one of the strongest collaborations between sociology and psychiatry. Hollingshead, the sociologist, had done earlier work on the structure of social class in America. This work included the creation of the Hollingshead Index of Social Position, which produced five categories of social class by combining information about education, occupation, and area of residence for each respondent. This index presumes that social class can be represented and measured via a single dimension. Although the Index of Social Position was ordinal in nature and is named with reference to the individual, the presentation in *Social Class and Mental Illness* indicates that the concept is consistent with the foregoing definition of social classes, that is, groups of individuals that are not only similar (in terms of wealth, power, and prestige) but that also exhibit structured patterns of interaction and discontinuous culture and lifestyles. This conception of social class is no longer dominant in sociological research, even if the Index of Social Position still appears in psychiatric journals, five decades later. The monograph – often referred to as "the New Haven study" – presents no theory as to how social class might cause mental illness. Instead, the focus was on presenting the details of the relationship, by type of disorder and by treatment facility. The impact of this study on the popular culture was dramatic, powerfully linking social class with mental illness in the public mind.

Social Class and Mental Illness had the advantage of presenting data on specific categories of disorder, but it also had the disadvantage of using data only from facilities that treat mental illness. Table 12.2 presents the central findings. Psychosis is strongly associated with class, showing more than eight times the prevalence in the lower class as in the upper two classes (1,505 versus 188 per 100,000). Some of this association must be due to higher chronicity among the lower classes, because the relationship of class to incidence is weaker (73 versus 28

Table 12.2. *The New Haven study social class and mental disorder*

	Level of social class Rates per 1,000			
	I–II	III	IV	V
Neurosis				
Point prevalence	3.49	2.50	1.14	0.97
Annual incidence	0.69	0.78	0.52	0.66
Psychosis				
Point prevalence	1.88	2.91	5.18	15.05
Annual incidence	0.28	0.36	0.37	0.73

Source: Hollingshead and Redlich (1958), Table 16.

per 100,000). Chronicity of neurosis, on the other hand, is associated with higher class status, even though the relationship of neurosis to incidence is flat. Treatment for psychosis was available in 1950 through publicly financed mental hospitals, but long-term treatment for neurosis had to be paid for by the patient. The higher prevalence rate of neurosis for the upper classes thus presumably reflects data gathered solely from treatment facilities and not the general population.

    The New Haven study was the first among many later examples of studies of socioeconomic stratification and mental disorder. Most of the studies are cross-sectional in nature, yielding only *prevalence* rates; thus, the observed association between class position and mental disorder could have resulted either because lower class position causes mental disorder ("causation") or because those with mental disorder end up in lower class positions ("selection"). Prospective studies of *incidence* – new cases – of mental disorder show that the class position actually precedes the disorder and thereby establish class as a more credible potential cause. The incidence results from the New Haven study regarding schizophrenia (Table 12.2) have been replicated in dozens of studies, with all but a handful showing the inverse relationship of incidence with social class (Eaton 1985) and thus providing consistent support for the causation explanation. Studies in the past decade do not confirm the finding, suggesting that the relationship may be evolving in some way (Byrne et al., 2004). Because schizophrenia is so rare, data on its incidence are uniformly from treatment agencies. Yet because schizophrenia is a severely impairing disorder, most schizophrenics are treated by psychiatrists, and data from the treatment sector are more credible than for other disorders (Eaton, 1985).

    There are more limited incidence data for other disorders. Data from the Epidemiologic Catchment Area (ECA) program show that indicators of poverty (Bruce et al., 1991) and of occupational status and education (Anthony &

Petronis, 1991) are risk factors for depression in a 1-year follow-up supporting the causation model for that disorder. A later study of incidence of depressive disorder in the Baltimore ECA cohort was able to control for family history of depressive disorder, and the occurrence of life events, and this analysis showed little or no effect of occupational prestige, income, or educational attainment on incidence of depressive disorder. This finding was consistent with the meta-analysis of Lorant et al. (2003), which summarized four additional studies of incidence of depressive disorder and socioeconomic position, finding a mean relative risk across the five studies of only 1.2, in spite of a mean relative odds for low socioeconmomic position and prevalence of depressive disorder of about 2.0. These results suggest that low socioeconomic position is associated with the persistence of depression but not with its start (Miech et al., 2005). Another recent longitudinal study in the United Kingdom suggests that subjective financial difficulties are independently associated with depression at follow-up (Skapinakis et al., 2006). Depressive symptoms and perceived stress are more frequent among those with fewer resources (Hamad et al., 2008). These findings on prevalence and depression contrast with several analyses on panic disorder (Keyl & Eaton, 1990), agoraphobia (Eaton & Keyl, 1990), and social phobia (Wells et al., 1994), which all showed statistically significant relationships between indicators of low social class and incidence, supporting the causation explanation for anxiety disorders generally.

Stress: The Midtown Manhattan Study

Some explanations for the effects of lower class status on mental disorder concentrate on the social environment of the individual, especially its stressful qualities. Other studies focus on individual differences in coping with the social environment. Increased stress is the most widely accepted causal explanation for higher rates of mental disorder among the lowest class. Stress evolves from the "discrepancy between the demands of the environment and the potential responses of the individual" (Mechanic, 1978). This is closely allied with "distress," which may be defined as the individual's perception of the discrepancy between the environment and the individual's potential to respond (i.e., a subjective assessment of stress). The idea that lower-class life produces mental disorder through increased stress fits naturally within the conflict theory of formation and maintenance of the social classes. Conflict theorists would contend that lower-class life is certainly less pleasant than life in the upper class, in part because of additional stresses. Many of these stresses are described in vivid detail in Marx's depiction of lower-class life in 19th-century England (Engels, 1958; Marx, 1967).

A variety of stresses that are relatively normal can contribute to one's mental disorder if they cluster together in a short period of time. These "life event" stresses are more frequent in the developmental periods of adolescence and young adulthood (Goldberg & Comstock, 1980). Many of these relatively normal stresses

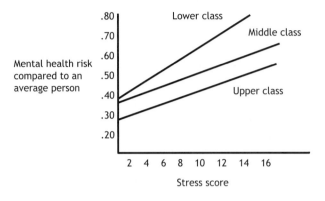

Figure 12.3. The Midtown Manhattan Study. *Source:* Redrawn from Langner and Michael (1963), Figure 14.2. Adapted with permission of the publisher.

involve the economic system, where the lower-class person is at a distinct disadvantage compared with the upper-class person. Individuals in the lower class are more likely to have financial difficulties, for instance (Wright, 1979), or to lose their jobs (Granovetter, 1995). Stresses resulting from illness in oneself or one's friends and from death of friends or relatives are important causes of mental disturbance, and these illness-related stresses have repeatedly been shown to be more common in lower classes than in the upper classes (Marmot & Koveginas, 1987; Susser, Watson, & Harper, 1985). Contemporary reviews of a variety of causes of morbidity and mortality confirm the finding (Krieger et al., 1993). Another major type of stress is related to divorce and separation, and these events may occur more frequently in the lower classes as well (Cherlin, 1992). Stress indices, which collect these types of stressful life events into a score, are related to lower social class position (Turner et al., 1995).

The Midtown Manhattan Study was conceived by sociologists and psychiatrists working together, but the major psychiatrist (Thomas Rennie) died before the collection of data began (Langner & Michael, 1963). The methodology shifted considerably: data were collected via household surveys, and the emphasis was on a global concept of mental illness rather than specific diagnostic categories. The substantive focus shifted from social class to social stress, but the issue of social class remained important. The concept of social stress provided an etiological explanation for the association of social class and mental disorder, as shown in Figure 12.3. This example is one of many ways in which lower socioeconomic position could raise the risk for mental disorder. The figure shows that higher levels of stress are related to higher risk for mental illness, all along a continuum of stress from very low to very high. It also shows that individuals in the lower class have a higher risk of mental illness for any given level of stress. Finally, the figure suggests that stress is a more potent activator of mental illness in the lower class than in the middle and upper classes: the slope of the line for the lower class is steeper. This difference in slope picks up the issue of the linearity of the relationship of social class to mental illness, which is a continuing theme in the literature (Kessler, 1979; Kohn, 1968).

Coping and Fatalism

Variation in the population regarding many individual characteristics tends to expand over the life course, as the combination of genetic endowment and environmental experiences produces individuals with more and more unique qualities (Baltes et al., 1980). A natural research focus for the functional perspective is the study of individual differences in ability – whether they are presumed to be inherited or the result of socialization processes. The question for the functionalist is this: How does an individual with a given set of characteristics end up in a given social position? For the conflict theorist the parallel question is, How does position in the socioeconomic structure affect the wide range of abilities associated with raised risk for mental disorder? In the field of socioeconomic stratification, any abilities that are broadly advantageous in a range of occupational positions are important.

Many cognitive abilities are relevant to performance of occupational duties. Some scholars feel that intelligence – the ability to perform in modern school systems and to survive and advance in a given culture – is a broad, stable, and general dimension along which individuals differ (Anastasi, 1988). There is considerable controversy over how broad and general the trait of intelligence is (Sternberg, 1995). This concept of general intelligence, if correct, has consequences for the functionalist theories of class because more intelligent individuals will be suited to a wider range of jobs than less intelligent individuals. There is evidence (reviewed by Jensen, 1969) that intelligence as measured by standard psychometric tests is correlated with socioeconomic position. The continual calibration and recalibration of intelligence tests, with validation by a range of indicators, naturally tends to produce a measure that predicts broadly for the majority of the population and is longitudinally stable. But the degree to which intelligence tests actually are predictive, whether it is fair to use them in judging individuals' abilities, and the degree of changeability over the life span are issues of intense debate. Ambition is also important to consider. In a true functionalist "meritocracy," the only determinants of reward should be an individual's ambition and intelligence (Young, 1994). At any given level of ability, ambitious people who set high aspirations for themselves are likely to have higher educational and occupational attainments.

Some status attainment models have incorporated measures of mental ability and ambition (Sewell et al., 1970). The occupational status of the parents, as well as the mental ability of the offspring, have strong influences on ultimate attainment. Mental ability has a strong influence on grades, which in turn affect educational ambition and educational attainment. Thus, early variables like mental ability and parental occupational status also pass effects on status attainment through sociopsychological variables (e.g., ambition and peer effects) measured in high school. But social class background also affects aspirations because individuals may become aware that upward mobility is closed to them, or because they are taught that it is inappropriate for them to aspire to upper-class status. Stress is a situation requiring intensive problem solving, to which the general trait of intelligence is relevant. The power of early measures of intelligence in predicting later performance in the occupational system – as shown, for example, in the Wisconsin model of status attainment (Sewell et al., 1970) – is strong enough to consider in any comprehensive model of social stratification and mental disorders.

Other types of coping abilities are important to consider. Kohn (1977) feels that lower-class children are brought up in an atmosphere that encourages a "conformist orientation," without the flexibility necessary to deal with a stressful situation. Lower-class adults, perhaps because of the type of occupations in which they find themselves (Kohn & Schooler, 1983), value conformity to authority more than upper-class people and socialize their children to their own value systems. Upper-class individuals and their children value self-direction more than conformity to authority. Conformity to authority contributes to inflexibility in coping with stress; this inflexibility, interacting with genetic factors, could explain some or all of the social class differences in rates of mental disorder. Kohn (1977) provides abundant data, from several industrialized nations, showing that social classes do differ in their conformity orientations in this way; as yet, however, there is no evidence that the differences are connected to mental disorder.

The relationships of social class, stress, coping, and psychological disorder have been examined in detail by Wheaton (1980) in what he terms an "attributional" theory. As a result of reinforcement contingencies associated with social class position, individuals develop biases in their attribution of the causes of changes in their situations. The general notion from attribution theory is that success is more likely to be attributed to the individual's efforts, whereas failure is more likely to be attributed to the external environment. Because of their disadvantaged position in the social structure, lower-class individuals are less successful in the everyday challenges of life and so acquire the habit of attributing causes to the external environment. Upper-class individuals are more successful, in general, and attribute causes to their own efforts. The external attribution, termed "fatalism," increases vulnerability to psychological disorder because active attempts at coping are viewed by the individual as unlikely to be successful. In this case, the individual's characteristics interact with the stressful environment to precipitate disorder. Individuals may not emerge successfully from stressful situations when they do not attempt to deal with them actively but instead let events overtake them (Seligman, 1975). Upper-class individuals are more optimistic because their backgrounds

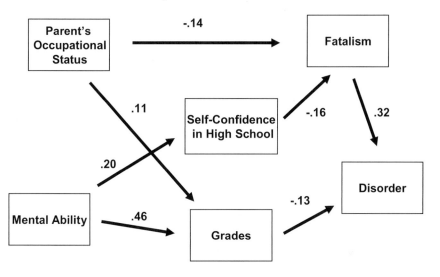

Figure 12.4. Fatalism model of SES and psychological disorder. *Note:* Residual and unanalyzed correlations are omitted. *Source:* Adapted from Wheaton (1980), Table 5 and Figure 5.

have led them to think of themselves as successful, and this optimism leads to greater persistence in the face of stress.

Wheaton (1980) provides analyses from three separate longitudinal data sets that are consistent with the fatalism theory. Figure 12.4 shows the simplified model of one of them. The data derive from a study of all 17-year-old male high school students in the Lenawee County (Michigan) school system in 1957. In 1972, 291 of these were reinterviewed. The father's occupational status is weakly related to the school ability of the respondent (correlation of 0.16). School ability affects self-confidence in high school, and school ability and father's occupational status are both related to the grades received in school. The fatalistic orientation is affected both by the father's status (−0.14) and the level of self-confidence (−0.16). Poor grades affect vulnerability to disorder (−0.13). There is a relatively strong effect of fatalism on disorder (coefficient of 0.32).

The advantage of this analysis is that it provides an empirical test of an explicit model of the effects of low social class on mental disorder. The model has the advantage of its foundation in social psychological theory and of linkage to laboratory studies of attribution for success and failure. It builds elegantly on advances in stratification theory and research.

Curiously, results for the fatalism model of Wheaton (1980) are consistent with Jarvis's contention that "among those whom the world calls poor, there is less vital force, a lower tone of life, more ill health, more weakness, . . . less self-respect, ambition, and hope"; for "less self-respect, ambition, and hope" substitute "fatalism." Data from the Jarvis commission, and from the Lenawee

County study one century later, provide strong evidence that mental disorder is related to social class position. Jarvis's notion that a wide range of personal dispositions is associated with mental disorder and with social class position receives empirical support from the work of Wheaton and others. The direction of causation is presumed by each author, but differently: from disorder to class for Jarvis; from class to disorder for Wheaton. The presumption of direction may have been affected by Jarvis's focus on relatively severe disorders as opposed to the relatively milder distress studied by Wheaton.

The Physical Environment

Many mediators of the effects of low social class have been overlooked or under-valued, perhaps because they require multidisciplinary work. The physical and biological environment can affect the individual's risk for mental disorder at any time from the moment of conception to death. Because there are enormous differences in lifestyles between the various social classes, and because the causes of mental disorders are not yet well understood, there are numerous other specific possibilities (e.g., fetal damage or toxic environments) for explaining why lower-class life may cause an increased risk for mental disorder.

A variety of disturbances during pregnancy and birth can increase the risk of disease, injury, or death of a newborn child (Bracken, 1984). These pregnancy and obstetric complications can also lead to relatively subtle disturbances in mental functioning in later life (Pasamanick & Knobloch, 1961). The link to social class exists because many aspects of fetal damage are more common among the lower classes (e.g., mortality – Bakketeig, Hoffman, & Titmuss-Oakley, 1984; low birth weight – Strobino et al., 1995; prematurity – Alberman, 1984). This suggests the possibility that lower-class infants are more likely to be born with some slight fetal damage, which may contribute later to a mental disorder. The pregnancy and obstetric complications also may interact with social class in that fetal damage may be potentiated only among lower classes (Drillien, 1964).

Mental disorders can be produced by toxins and physical deprivation. Many aspects of lower-class residential environments are potentially toxic. Lead and other heavy metals, which can cause mental deficiencies (Needleman & Bellinger, 1991), are more common in lower-class urban neighborhoods. Toxic waste sites are more likely to be situated in lower-class than in upper-class residential neighborhoods (Bullard, 1993). Dangerous occupational environments contribute to risk for mental disorder and are found more frequently in jobs held by lower-class individuals. The dangers include toxins (such as heavy metals) found in battery plants as well as organophosphate herbicides and pesticides used by migrant workers (Needleman, 1995). Other dangers include the psychological characteristics of the occupational environment. For example, Link and others have suggested that jobs with certain noisome characteristics (e.g., steam, heat or cold, odors, confined spaces) contribute to risk for schizophrenia (Link et al., 1986; replicated by Muntaner et al., 1991), and that jobs in which individuals have little influence over the pace of work may contribute to risk for depression (Link et al., 1993).

Access to Health Care

Socioeconomic class matters also in terms of health care access (Krieger et al., 2005). Many studies show that SES influences mental health services utilization. The factors linking SES and mental health services utilization still remain unclear (Amaddeo & Jones, 2007). In one side, there is an unequal distribution of funding, community and human resources for mental health services between countries, between regions, and within communities; the lack of mental health services, their unequal distribution, as well as the ineffective use of them are specially affecting people from low socioeconomic position (Saxena et al., 2007). There is also a large disparity among countries and regions in terms of resources invested in mental health (Saxena, Sharan, & Saraceno 2003).

The odds of not seeking treatment for mental health disorders tend to be higher among people in low socioeconomic position (Gadalla, 2008). Another study found a mismatch in the treatment of depression relative to apparent clinical need, with the lowest levels of treatment concentrated in the lower socioeconomic groups, despite evidence of their increased prevalence of depression and suicide (Kivimäki et al., 2007).

There are other factors associated with poverty that affect use of mental health services. For example, mothers attributed their distress to external causes (e.g., poverty, negative life stressors), which they believed individually focused mental health services could not affect; having negative consequences for seeking care, including being labeled unfit mothers, and thus potentially losing custody of their children (Anderson et al., 2006). These inequities might be even more complex among people with other conditions associated with discrimination. For example, a study in United States indicated that poor Latinos have lower access to specialty care than poor non-Latino whites (Alegría et al., 2002).

Complexities in the Study of Social Disadvantage and Mental Disorder

The Importance of Life Stage

This chapter has focused on socioeconomic position of adults and mental disorder. But there are many concomitant aspects of social position that may be related to mental disorders. These are considered below.

One important aspect of socioeconomic position is the life stage at which it is measured. For children, the impact of low socioeconomic position of their family may raise their risk for mental disorders, which have onset years or decades later, and not for the same reasons or due to the same mediators as occurs among adults. For example, social adversity during the early childhood stage might be related to mental illness (Stansfeld et al., 2008) and lower psychosocial functioning during the adult stage (Harper et al., 2002). Material and emotional adversity might influence the development of attachment through parental style, notably parental warmth. On the other hand, some authors argue that attachment style, associated with the style of parenting encountered during early childhood, may act as a source of resilience for children facing adversity. There are some emerging findings providing neurophysiological evidence that social inequalities might be associated with alterations in the prefrontal cortex in low-SES children; this damage might be explained, for example, by greater levels of stress and lack of access to cognitively stimulating environments and experiences among this group of children (Kishiyama et al., 2009). Another recent meta-analysis suggested that lower SES is associated with higher rates of depressed mood and anxiety in youth (Lemstra et al., 2008).

The most convincing demonstration of social factors in the etiology of any mental disorder is *Social Origins of Depression*, by George Brown and Tirril Harris (1978). That work demonstrates the importance of life event stresses and chronic difficulties in depression for females. The methodology involved in-depth diagnostic and etiologic interviews with a sample of 114 patients, as well as a sample of 220 community residents of a lower middle-class area of London. Of particular interest was the relationship of social class to onset of depression (Brown et al., 1975). Social class was defined by combining measures of occupation, educational attainment, and assets. Women living alone who were professionals, managers, or small business owners – or whose husbands (or fathers, if not living with their husbands) were professionals, managers, or small business owners – were defined as belonging to the middle class. Those in skilled manual or routine nonmanual occupations were included in the middle class if they or their husbands had completed school through age 16 or if they had both a car and a telephone. The lower class included semiskilled or unskilled workers or, for those with intermediate occupations, those who did not own both a car and a phone.

There was strong evidence of a relationship between life event stressors and depression. For example, 86% of the recent cases from the community, and 75% of patients, had a severe event or major difficulty, but only 31% of the women without depression had such events or difficulties (Brown et al., 1975). There also was strong evidence of a relationship between social class and depression. For example, 25% of the lower class in the community residents – versus 5% of the middle-class community residents – were recent or chronic cases (Brown et al., 1975). Likewise, there was strong evidence that stresses were related to social class (e.g., 54% of the lower class, versus 30% of the middle class, had a severe

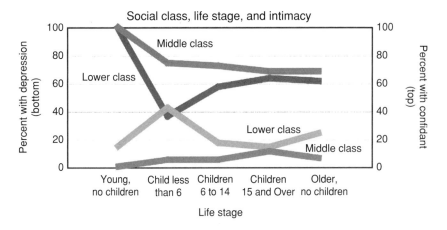

Figure 12.5. Depression among women in London. *Source:* Brown et al. (1975).

event or major life difficulty). Of interest here is the elaboration of this relationship when the data are analyzed in terms of (a) life stage and (b) the availability of an individual with whom the respondent could talk about personal problems or intimate relationships. Figure 12.5 shows the complexity of the relationships by combining two separate analyses from Brown and colleagues (1975). The bottom two lines in the figure show that social class interacts with life stage in affecting depression; there are no statistically significant differences between the classes, except for women who have one or more children younger than 6 years old living with them. But for women at this life stage, more than 40% are recent or chronic cases of depression in the lower class, versus only 5% in the middle class. That three-way relationship stretches the data about as thinly as is possible, but there is evidence of a separate interaction of class with the availability of a confidant in the top two lines in Figure 12.5. Here again, the classes differ most in the life stage of women who have children younger than 6 living with them. Less than 40% of lower-class women report having someone they can talk to about personal problems, whereas more than 75% of middle-class women have this kind of relationship available to them. Because most of these women are married, this suggests that lower-class marital life does not support or include a psychologically intimate component during this life stage. Other data in the London study, as well as data reviewed elsewhere in this volume, strongly suggest that social supports of this type are an important buffer of social stress, protecting the individual from onset of depression and other types of psychopathology. It could be that social supports are more important for women than for men in influencing risk for mental disorders (Kessler & McCleod, 1984). Regardless of this possibility, the London study reinforces the importance of life stage in understanding the relationship of class and mental disorder; it also reveals (again) the importance of young adulthood as a critical developmental period.

Additional Indicators of Socioeconomic Position

In spite of the central importance of social class to sociology – and despite the importance of the issue of mental disorders and social class – there has been only limited comparison of the effects of different measures of social class on the rate of mental disorder (Eaton, 1974; Eaton & Kessler, 1981; Kessler & Cleary, 1980). Therefore, the Baltimore ECA follow-up included several measures whose effects could be compared. The goal of including the different measures is to gain insight into the nature of the relationship between social class position and mental disorder.

The ECA program (Eaton et al., 1981; Eaton & Kessler, 1985; Regier et al., 1984) was designed to estimate prevalence and incidence of specific mental disorders, to study risk factors, and to study patterns of use of facilities. It consisted of panel surveys of populations of community mental health catchment areas in five metropolitan areas of the United States, with one year between panels. About 20,000 individuals were interviewed with a structured survey questionnaire called the Diagnostic Interview Schedule (DIS). From 1993 to 1996, the Baltimore ECA site followed up its cohort of 3,481 individuals, again using the DIS. Of the 2,635 individuals known to be alive and with an address, 73% participated in re-interviews (Eaton et al., 1997).

Results from the Baltimore ECA follow-up regarding social class are shown in Table 12.3. The DIS produces specific diagnoses according to criteria used by psychiatrists. Table 12.3 includes the diagnosis of major depression and a group of anxiety disorders, including panic disorder, phobic disorders, and obsessive-compulsive disorder. The table explores differences between the two types of mental disorders, as well as differences that may exist between measures of social class. The numbers shown are odds ratios from a multivariate logistic regression, with all variables included together in the same model. Each variable includes a category that is designated as the "reference," with an odds ratio of 1.0. Odds ratios for other categories in that variable are estimated relative to the reference category. When odds ratios are close to 1.0 there is no association, when they are greater than 1.0 there is positive association, and when they are less than 1.0 there is inverse association. The association is statistically significant when the confidence interval for the odds ratio does not include the value of 1.0, in which case the odds ratio (OR) is followed by an asterisk.

Education is not significantly related to major depression or to anxiety disorder, but low household income is related to both disorders. Respondents whose household income is less than $17,500 are 16 times as likely to meet the criteria for major depressive disorder as those whose household income is over $35,000;

Table 12.3. *Alternative measures of socioeconomic position*

| | Baltimore ECA follow-up | | | |
| | Major depression | | Anxiety disorder | |
Measure of socioeconomic position	Percent	Odds ratio	Percent	Odds ratio
Education of respondent				
Less than high school	1.2	1.0	16.0	1.0
High school graduate	2.5	1.9	14.8	1.3
Some college	2.7	3.5	7.6	0.3
College graduate	2.7	6.5	13.3	0.8
Graduate school	0.7	1.9	13.9	0.8
Household income				
Less than $17,500	1.2	16.2*	19.1	2.9*
$17,500–$34,999	3.8	11.5*	16.3	1.6
$35,000 or more	2.0	1.0	10.8	1.0
Household physical assets				
Does not own car	1.8	0.6	19.3	1.6
Owns car	2.1	1.0	13.0	1.0
Does not own home	2.2	1.3	19.3	1.1
Owns home	1.8	1.0	12.1	1.0
Household financial assets				
No dividend income	2.0	1.0	16.3	1.0
Dividend income	2.1	2.9	11.6	1.2
No savings income	2.9	1.5	18.3	1.2
Savings income	1.5	1.0	13.3	1.0
No property income	2.0	1.0	15.7	1.0
Property income	1.9	1.8	4.7	0.1*
Respondent occupation				
Labor	2.9	*	14.8	0.5
Craft	1.9	1.1	8.5	0.3
Service	0.9	0.6	14.1	0.6
Technical	2.7	0.6	19.0	0.8
Professional	2.6	1.0	14.7	1.0
Respondent organizational assets				
Not management	1.4	0.5	15.7	2.1
Supervisor	3.6	2.0	15.7	2.6*
Manager	1.0	1.0	8.1	1.0

Notes: Table includes 877 respondents in the labor force at the time of the interview.
Odds ratios adjusted for age, gender, race/ethnicity, and other variables in the table.
*Statistically significant difference at $p < 0.05$.
**No respondents with depression in this occupational category.

those with household incomes in the middle range are 11 times as likely to meet the criteria for major depressive disorder. For anxiety disorders, the relationship is significant but smaller (nearly three times the rate of anxiety disorder in the low-income group as in the reference group).

Measures of assets – such as owning one's home, having a car, owning stock, or having a savings account – are not related to rate of depression or anxiety disorder, with income and education controlled. But receiving income from property royalties, estates, or trusts is strongly associated with low rate of anxiety disorder (OR = 0.1). This type of income protects individuals from year-to-year fluctuations in salary and possibly inoculates them, to some degree, from day-to-day difficulties in achieving success at work.

The occupational setting is related to depression and anxiety disorder, but not in the predicted direction. After adjustment for education, income, and assets, the respondent's occupation does not have a strong effect. But the organizational assets of the individual do have effects in that supervisors have higher rates of depressive disorder (OR = 2.9, not significant) and anxiety disorder (OR = 2.6, significant) than both management and workers. The concept of organizational asset derives from a reconceptualization of Marxian class theory in the modern context (Wright, 1985). Supervisors are in the lower tier of management, with authority over other workers. But they have little influence over the decisions made by management and are accountable to them for the performance of workers. This class location is often filled by former workers, who may experience role conflict and divided loyalties. They have the trappings of authority but may experience little freedom in controlling their own day-to-day work. This finding is consistent with studies of the role of direction, control, and planning in the workplace as it relates to depression.

Ethnic Disadvantage

Social determinants of health interact among themselves and usually are unequally distributed, affecting the same population groups, which might be implying a higher impact on mental health among them. For example, there is an association between gender, race/ethnicity, and social class and prevalence of depressive disorders in many places (Almeida-Filho et al. 2004). These inequities might be even more complex among people with other conditions associated with discrimination. For example, a study in United States indicated that poor Latinos have lower access to specialty care than poor non-Latino Whites (Alegría et al., 2002). Social determinants of health interact among themselves and usually they are unequally distributed affecting the same population groups affecting mental health. For example, there is an association between gender, race/ethnicity, and social class and prevalence of depressive disorders in many places (Almeida-Filho et al., 2004).

There are other studies showing how socioeconomic position might negatively affect mental health even more among people who are discriminated against for other reasons, such as racial and ethnic inequities (Oliver & Muntaner, 2005). Nevertheless, it is important to note that in many contexts, processes of ethnic stratification place disproportionate numbers of persons from some ethnic groups at a substantial social disadvantage, so ethnic disadvantage might overlap with low socioeconomic position (Eaton & Harrison, 2000). For example, there are many studies (Castle, Wessely, Der, & Murray, 1991; Harrison et al., 1997; Louden 1995; Selten & Sijben, 1994) showing that Afro-Caribbeans have higher rates of schizophrenia than Whites in the United Kingdom and the Netherlands, establishing a possibility of psychological causation, because Afro-Caribbean persons remaining in the Caribbean and Africa do not have this elevated risk. One of the most likely explanations appears to be connected to social deprivation in some manner, and not just especially to the stresses of immigration per se, because the second generation also appears to be at high risk.

In reviewing the evidence on social class and mental disorder, Dohrenwend and Dohrenwend (1969) helped to inaugurate the so-called third generation of research, in part because they showed that results for social class differed for specific disorders, thus challenging the point of view that mental disorder was a global concept. They decided upon a strategy of research that would support either the stress or selection interpretation of the social class–mental disorder relationship. They argued that individuals in certain ethnic groups, such as African Americans in the United States, have less opportunity for upward mobility in societies that discriminate against them. These persons in disadvantaged ethnic groups also suffer a greater amount of stress than those in advantaged ethnic groups. The finding that social class is related to mental disorder is hard to interpret because social class status is constantly changing over the lifetime of the individual. But ethnic status does not change over the lifetime. This situation is an experiment of nature, or quasi-experiment, that provides the leverage to decide between stress and selection as an explanation for the social class–mental disorder relationship (Dohrenwend & Dohrenwend, 1974).

In analyzing data on social class, ethnic group, and mental disorder, it is important to compare rates in ethnic groups at the same level of social class. At any given level of social class, if *stress* is the explanation then the more highly stressed individuals (i.e., those in the disadvantaged ethnic groups) will have *higher* rates of disorder. If selection is the explanation, then (a) upwardly mobile individuals (in the advantaged groups) will leave behind a residue of impaired individuals in lower levels of the class structure, whereas (b) healthy individuals in disadvantaged ethnic groups, who would otherwise be upwardly mobile, will be held to lower-class positions. Hence the quasi-experimental design predicts that, if selection obtains, disadvantaged ethnic groups will have a *lower* rate of mental disorder.

The quasi-experimental design was executed in Israel, which was in many ways an ideal setting. Israel possessed excellent record-keeping systems that facilitated drawing samples, and is sufficiently small so that high completion rates could be achieved. Israeli society fit the design requirements of an open society with substantial upward mobility yet with large differences in social advantage between

Table 12.4. *Social class and ethnic disadvantage in Israel*

	European origin (*N* = 1,197)		North African origin (*N* = 1,544)	
Educational attainment	Men (*n* = 602)	Women (*n* = 595)	Men (*n* = 852)	Women (*n* = 692)
Schizophrenia				
Less than high school	4.18	0.84	1.19	0.00
High school graduate	0.29	0.39	0.17	0.00
College graduate	0.00	0.39	0.00	0.00
Major depression				
Less than high school	3.01	4.81	3.47	6.60
High school graduate	2.06	2.93	4.61	12.11
College graduate	0.66	1.68	2.94	10.70
Antisocial personality				
Less than high school	0.73	0.82	6.97	0.73
High school graduate	0.15	0.00	0.79	0.30
College graduate	0.00	0.00	0.00	0.00

Source: Dohrenwend, B. P., Levav, I., Shrout, P. E., Schwartz, S., Naveh, G., Link, B. G., et al. (1992). Socioeconomic status and psychiatric disorders: The causation-selection issue. *Science*, 255, 946–952. Table 2. Reprinted with permission from the authors.

certain ethnic groups. The Dohrenwends focused on the comparison between Jews born in Israel from European heritage versus those born in Israel of North African (mostly Moroccan) heritage, using educational attainment as the indicator of social class. Table 12.4 shows the results for three disorders: schizophrenia, major depression, and antisocial personality disorder. The selection interpretation is supported for schizophrenia, because the Jews of European heritage have higher rates at each level of education, for both sexes (e.g., 4.18 per thousand for European heritage males with low education versus 1.91 for North African heritage males; 0.84 versus 0.0 for females with low education). The results for antisocial personality disorder, on the other hand, support the stress interpretation for males, because the North African heritage group has higher rates than the European heritage group at all levels of educational attainment (e.g., 6.97 per thousand versus 0.73 at the lower level of education; 0.79 versus 0.15 at the middle level of education). For depression the results are equivocal: Even though the North African group has the higher rate at all levels of education and for both sexes, the table does not display the expected inverse relationship between social class and disorder.

The quasi- experimental strategy is bold in conception, and its execution in Israel was methodologically rigorous. However, it requires assumptions that vitiate its power. It must be assumed that the stresses (and psychological consequences of stresses) associated with low social class status are similar or identical to those associated with membership in a disadvantaged ethnic group. The perceived cause of the stress will render different psychological consequences: Lower-class individuals in the dominant ethnic group may be more willing to blame themselves for the stresses they suffer, in part because of the functionalist ideology (Hochschild, 1995; Matza, 1967), whereas individuals in disadvantaged ethnic groups may be more likely to blame the structure of society for the stresses they suffer. The quasi-experiment requires the assumption that ethnic groups do not differ in their genetic propensity for mental disorders. Although there is wide variation within any given ethnic group (often greater than variation across ethnic groups, as shown by Cavalli-Sforza, Menozi, & Piazza, 1994), it is nevertheless true that a large number of diseases differ greatly in their prevalence between groups (McKusick, 1967); often the differences are larger than the differences shown in Table 12.4. The quasi-experiment requires the assumption that mental disorders are equivalent across cultures and can be measured equivalently. The quasi-experimental data cannot determine whether or not both the causation and selection processes are operating simultaneously – the results reflect only the relative preponderance of one or the other process. Finally, the quasi-experiment fails to provide evidence as to how lower social class position affects risk for mental disorder.

Conclusion

As long as inequalities exist, they are likely to be associated to some degree with the extent of mental disorder in society. Changes in socioeconomic structure will lead to consequent changes in the mental structure of society, including rates of mental disorders. Thus, research describing the relationship will always be central to sociology's interest in the causes and consequences of inequality. As society evolves, there is a continuing role for descriptive studies of social class and mental disorder because the possibilities for both causation and selection to operate will continue to exist. There are different theoretical subjects and assumptions in their conceptualizations (Muntaner, Eaton, & Chamberlain, 2000).

   In the half-century since the New Haven study there have been many descriptive studies of the prevalence of mental disorders that document the evolving relationship. There has been slow but measurable progress in understanding the mediators: how social class affects mental disorder; and how mental disorder, or the predisposition to it, affects attainment of social status. Research on the mediating variables may eventually prove more helpful in improving the lives of individual human beings. Eliminating social inequality may be difficult, but identification of causal mechanisms may lead to (less global) societal programs for preventing the onset of mental disorder. Identification of factors mediating the process of selection may lead also to programs that lessen the impact of mental disorder once it has occurred.

13

Gender and Mental Health: Do Men and Women Have Different Amounts or Types of Problems?

Sarah Rosenfield and Dena Smith

Are there differences between men and women in mental health and why? These are the questions taken up by Rosenfield and Smith. They begin by providing an overview of classical psychoanalytical theory (Freud's conceptualization) and more recent approaches (such as by Nancy Chodorow) that represent the major positions on gender differences: Women have more mental health problems than men, men have more than women, or both have equal amounts. Evidence reveals that there are no differences in their overall rates of psychopathology, but men and women do differ in the type of psychopathology experienced. Women suffer from higher rates of depression and anxiety (referred to as internalizing disorders), and men have higher rates of substance abuse and antisocial disorders (referred to as externalizing disorders). Rosenfield and Smith consider various explanations for these differences. They concentrate on dominant gender conceptions – those held by groups in positions of power, which in this society, are primarily White, middle-class conceptions. Divisions between men and women in power, responsibilities (i.e., different role positions), and personal characteristics are relevant for mental health. For example, women earn less money, have jobs with less power and autonomy, and experience an overload of job and family demands more often than men. They have closer social ties, which bring more support but also more negative interactions. Women have personal characteristics of low self-esteem and mastery compared to men, as well as high emotional reliance as opposed to men's greater independence. Finally, men and women differ in self-salience, which constitutes beliefs about the importance of the self versus others in social relations: Women put others' interests first more often, which promotes internalizing problems, while men tend to privilege the self more strongly, facilitating externalizing problems. As African Americans exemplify, the authors suggest that socializing practices encouraging high self-regard along with high regard for others benefit mental health. This is an interesting idea, and students may want to discuss their own socialization into "appropriate" feminine and masculine behaviors.

Introduction

Among the most profound social divisions in our culture is the one we make by gender. Whether we are male or female shapes our access to resources and our life choices and options. It colors the ways we relate to others, what people expect of us, and what we expect of ourselves. Clearly, then, this division should affect our internal states and compasses: the way we feel about ourselves, how we experience the world, and our emotional reactions. Because our social practices are fundamentally gendered, mental health and emotional troubles should also differ for men and women.

For some time, however, there have been heated debates over the differences between the mental health of men and women. Some argue that women have more psychopathology than men, and some claim men have more. Others think that both genders suffer equally, but from different maladies. In this chapter, we present examples of these conflicting positions, examine the evidence for them, and discuss social explanations for disparities by gender. This discussion ultimately points us to situations that are best for the mental health of men and women.

Examples of the Positions on Gender Differences in Mental Health

Freud was probably the first to design a systematic theory comparing men's and women's mental health. Classical Freudian theory holds that men are superior to women psychically – a view that persists among many today. For these reasons, we start the debate with Freud's approach.

Generally, Freud posited that humans acquire a separate sense of self – including an ego and a superego – in the course of several stages of development. In the phallic stage of development (around ages 3–5), an event occurs that marks the beginning of a radical distinction between the genders in the nature of the self. This event is children's recognition of the genital differences between males and females. At this point, boys are indifferent to or deny the sight of the female genitals (Freud, 1959a). For girls, however, this discovery is a major crisis in their development. In Freud's words, girls "notice the penis of a brother or playmate, strikingly visible and of large proportions, at once recognize it as a superior counterpart to their own small and inconspicuous organ, and from that time forward fall victim to envy for the penis" (Freud, 1959a, p. 190). The "normal" outcome of this crisis for girls is hostility and resentment toward their mother for bringing them into the world "so ill-equipped." As a result, the girl turns from her mother to her father as her primary love object, thereby forming the female Oedipus complex (Freud, 1949, 1959a, 1959b, 1966a).

For boys, the dynamics of development are less complicated. A boy's crisis in the phallic stage comes when his attachment to the mother intensifies and becomes more sexual in tone (Freud, 1949). This desire for the mother and the resulting rivalry with the father constitute the Oedipal situation for boys. In trying to deflect this situation, the parents threaten the boy with castration, which is taken seriously only when he recalls the earlier sight of female genitals (Freud, 1949, 1959a). This results in the castration complex, in which the boy perceives that the girl has been castrated and therefore believes that the threat to himself is real. The boy renounces his desire for possession of the mother and represses the Oedipus complex (Freud, 1949). As the replacement for this loss, the child identifies with the authority of the father and with the position that he will some day inherit. This identification with the morals and standards of the father forms the basis for the superego or conscience (Freud, 1959a, 1959c).

There are several ways that girls or boys can veer off these normal paths of development. But only for girls is the normal path itself flawed. According to Freud, women are stunted in both ego and superego development. In turning toward the father, girls repress active sexual impulses, which results in passivity as a personality characteristic (Freud, 1959b). Similarly, the shift from mother to father attachment involves turning aggression toward the self, resulting in masochistic tendencies (Freud, 1966b). The wound to girls' self-image in discovering they have no penis predisposes them to more vanity and jealousy than boys (Freud, 1959a). Finally, there is no force comparable to the castration complex in boys to motivate girls to give up the Oedipus complex; they may remain in this situation indefinitely (Freud, 1959a). Because the superego depends on resolving the oedipal situation, girls have a less developed superego than boys do.

Some of Freud's own followers (for example, Horney, 1926/1967; and Thompson, 1942) criticized his positions on women, and critiques have also increased in the past decade. Research on early childhood finds that girls make positive attributions to others of their own gender and to femininity in general, questioning the validity of the idea that girls see themselves as physically and therefore psychologically lacking (De Marneffe, 1997). Rigid adherence to a predetermined, biological unfolding of developmental stages has become more tempered in recent literature, although some retain the assumption that girls and boys differ in thought, behavior, and emotion because of endowment (Friedman & Downey, 2008; Gilmore, 1998).

More recent approaches have turned these general views upside down. For example, Daniel Stern (1985) questions the basic assumptions of Freudian theory as well as most current theories of development (e.g., Erikson, 1950/1963; Kohlberg, 1969). All of these theories assume that humans start out totally connected to the world around them, especially their mothers, unable to make a distinction between themselves and the external world. Mature, successful development involves becoming an independent, self-sufficient, autonomous adult. This version of development links what we think of as masculine (autonomous, separate) with mature, developed selves and links what we think of as feminine (connected, attached to others) with immature, undeveloped selves. Therefore, these assumptions about how people develop favor males and produce the view that male psychology is superior. Stern (1985) proposes instead that humans start out as separate, unconnected creatures and become more and more attached to those around them over time. The self-in-relation theory from the Stone Center at Wellesley posits that females' sense of self is strongly based in their connections to others. The hallmark of maturity is the development of greater and greater complexity in relationships over time (Jordan et al., 1991). Thus, these approaches reverse previous models of development: Connections with others are the mark of maturity, and the model of male as superior is replaced with a model of female as superior.

Some argue that models of female superiority are just as problematic and insidious as models of male superiority. Either way, they piece apart the world and set up destructive hierarchies (Tavris, 1992). A few theories, in contrast, emphasize the problems and strengths in both male and female development. Nancy Chodorow's object relations theory (1978) is probably the best known. Chodorow claims that certain positive and negative characteristics of women and men come from the fact that women are mostly responsible for parenting. Out of their presumed similarity, mothers tend to identify more strongly with their daughters than with their sons. Because of this overidentification, mothers often hold daughters back from experiences of independence. In contrast, sons are pushed away into a position of independence too early. These different ways of treating daughters and sons underlie the development of the self, which is reinforced later by more obvious forms of socialization. Girls are more preoccupied with their relationships with others. This focus gives them a lifetime capacity for rich social connections, more flexible boundaries between themselves and others, and a large capacity for empathy. Boys' greater separateness and distance set them up to adapt effectively to the work world. However, each gender also suffers from tendencies toward problematic extremes. The overembeddedness and lack of separation for girls lead to dependency on others for a sense of self. Low self-esteem also results from identification with a mother whose own self-regard is often low and whose social position is undervalued (Chodorow, 1974). Boys, on the other hand, experience problems with and fears of emotional connection. In sum, Chodorow writes that the results of present family structures for girls and boys, respectively, are "either ego-boundary confusion, low self-esteem, and overwhelming relatedness to others, or compulsive denial of any connection to others or dependence upon them" (Chodorow, 1974, p. 66).

The theories above are examples of the three general views on gender and mental health. Although there are disputes within these approaches, they illustrate the positions that women exceed men in psychopathology, that men exceed women in psychopathology, and that both men and women experience problems but of different types. Given these views, we turn to the evidence on gender differences and mental health.

What Is the Evidence on Gender Differences in Mental Health?

Recent large-scale epidemiological studies have assessed the rates of mental disorders in the United States (Kessler, 1993; Kessler et al., 1993, 1994; Kessler, Demler, et al., 2005). Taking all psychological disorders together, these studies show that there are no differences overall in men and women's rates of psychopathology. It is therefore clear that neither gender is worse off than the other in mental health overall.

However, there are gender differences in particular types of psychiatric disorders. Women exceed men in internalizing problems of anxiety and depression, in which problematic feelings are turned inward against the self. This includes both milder and more severe forms of depression, as well as most types of anxiety, including generalized anxiety disorder and phobias. Greater depression means that more women than men live with feelings of profound sadness and loss, serious problems with negative self-concept, and feelings of guilt, self-reproach, and self-blame. Women experience a great loss of energy, motivation, and interest in life more often than men. They more frequently feel that life is hopeless, coupled with a deep sense of helplessness to improve their circumstances. They more often have trouble concentrating as well as with sleeping and appetite, which can be too much or too little. Greater anxiety means that women suffer more often from fears of specific objects or situations (i.e., phobias), panic attacks, and free-floating anxiety states that attach themselves to seemingly random thoughts and situations (American Psychiatric Association, 2000).

In contrast, men more frequently exhibit externalizing problems of substance abuse and antisocial behavior, which are more destructive and problematic to others. Greater substance abuse means that men more often consume excessive amounts of alcohol and other drugs – in both quantity and frequency – than women. They more often experience extreme physical consequences from substances, such as blackouts or hallucinations. Drugs or alcohol interfere with their lives more often, causing problems at work or school or in the family. Men are more likely to be dependent on a substance, needing to use more and more to get the same effect, and to have serious psychological or physical consequences from attempts to stop. Greater antisocial behavior includes disruptive disorders in childhood and adolescence – such as attention deficit/hyperactivity disorder, conduct disorder, and oppositional defiant disorder – as well as antisocial personality disorder in adulthood. This means that, beginning at an early age, males are more often aggressive or antisocial in a wide range of areas, including violence toward people and animals, the destruction of property, lying, and stealing. Partly as a result, males more often have problems forming close, enduring relationships (American Psychiatric Association, 2000).

In sum, neither men nor women exceed the other in mental health problems, but rather experience very different kinds of problems. Given these findings, we discuss the social explanations for these differences.

What Explains the Gender Differences in Mental Health?

We first give a brief historical perspective on our current dominant definitions of gender. Dominant gender conceptions are those held by groups in positions of power, which, in this society, are primarily White, middle-class conceptions (Connell, 1995). Explanations for gender differences in mental health problems focus on aspects of these dominant gender conceptions and practices.

The rise of industrial capitalism in the 1800s heralded a shift of major consequence in the social situations of men and women. In the agricultural societies
before this, both men and women produced goods within the home. In addition
to raising children, women had central productive responsibilities such as making
clothing and working in the fields along with men. With industrialization, the
workplace became divided from the home. Middle-class men began to leave home
to work, and women stayed to care for the children in the household. This seemingly simple split in the realms of men and women had ramifications throughout
all levels of social and personal life. The productive work of the public sphere
became primarily associated with men and masculinity. The socioemotional work
and domestic labor of the private sector became primarily linked with women
and femininity. A so-called cult of domesticity arose to validate the assignment
of women to the private sphere. This middle-class ideology dictated that women
were fragile and emotional beings and that children required their mothers' (not
fathers') special care for moral and psychic development. Thus it was that public
and private realms became divided and gendered: Men belonged in the realm
of economic productivity, and women belonged in the realm of emotions, social
relations, and caretaking. Consistent with these splits, dominant conceptions of
femininity came to associate women with personal characteristics of nurturance,
sensitivity, and emotional expressiveness. In contrast, dominant conceptions of
masculinity associated men with characteristics of assertiveness, competitiveness,
and independence (Connell, 1995; Flax, 1993; Rosenfield, Lennon, & White,
2005). *gender*
    This division of public and private has had strong implications for power differ- *roles*
ences between men and women. The economic resources of the public sphere are
more transferable than the socioemotional resources of the private sphere (Lennon
& Rosenfield, 1994). Money is a resource that can be used or transferred in any
context, exchanged for the same rewards, and accumulated without limit. In contrast, caretaking skills and emotional sensitivity are resources that are tailored to
particular individuals – one's specific husband, children, or friends – and cannot
easily be transferred to other individuals or extended indefinitely. In this sense, the
economic resources of the public sphere bring greater power and are hence more
socially valued than the socioemotional resources of the private sphere. Because
men and women are split along public–private lines, they hold different amounts
of power and esteem in the social eye (Rosenfield, 1995).
    With this background in mind, we examine the ways these gender conceptions
and practices – including the division of labor, power relations, and dimensions
of the self – shape the divergent psychological troubles of men and women. The
differences in power and responsibilities translate into lower earnings for women
than men, even in the same jobs that require the same training and experience – a
wage gap caused in part by the devaluation of women's skills (Cohen & Huffman,
2003); Kilbourne et al., 1994). In addition, average incomes are lower in professions where women make up a significant percentage (Cohen & Huffman, 2003).

Often, income is also divided unequally within the family, with husbands receiving more than wives, who spend larger proportions of their share on their children (Becker, 1976). Scores of studies attest to the negative effects of low income on mental health (see Chapter 12 in this volume).

The division of public and private spheres results in women's greater responsibility for domestic labor, regardless of their employment status. Most women are employed currently, including those with small children. Women do the bulk of child care and housework even if they work hours comparable to their husbands outside the home and bring in the same income (Greenstein, 2000; Hochschild & Machung, 1989; Lennon & Rosenfield, 1994; Pleck, 1985). These responsibilities for the household work often result in an overload of demands that raises women's levels of depressive and anxious symptoms (Bird, 1999; Krause & Markides, 1985; Lennon & Rosenfield, 1992; Mirowsky, 1995; Rosenfield, 1989, 1992a). When household tasks are split, women tend to do the kinds of tasks over which there is less discretion and that must be repeated often, such as preparing meals, shopping, cleaning, and laundry. These kinds of tasks produce a strong sense of time pressure, which also engenders depressive symptoms (Roxburgh, 2004). In addition, the stress of managing often unpredictable child care arrangements also takes a psychological toll, and women who have trouble with such arrangements suffer high levels of distress (Mirowsky & Ross, 1988, 1989b; Ross & Mirowsky, 1992). In contrast, when child care is secure and when husbands share the work at home, women's symptoms of depression and anxiety resemble the low levels among men. Thus, women's excess in internalizing problems is partly caused by the greater time pressure of their household tasks and the overload of job and family demands that they experience more often.

The separation of spheres by gender also has consequences for the social relationships of men and women and, in turn, their mental health. Consistent with their identification with the private sphere, women maintain more social ties that are emotionally intimate (Belle, 1987; Turner, 1981). For example, women enjoy higher levels of mattering in relationships; that is, the feeling that others care deeply about them (J. Taylor & Turner, 2004). However, the close ties that bring women support can also be sources of negative interactions, such as conflicts, demands, and guilt (Cohen & Wills, 1985; J. Taylor & Turner, 2004; Turner, 1981, 1994). These negative interactions can offset the benefits of supportive interactions, leaving women with higher levels of distress than men overall (Roxburgh, 2004; Turner, 1994). In addition, women experience more distress over the problems of those they care about than do men (Kessler, McLoed, & Wethington, 1985). For this reason also, women can suffer greater anxiety and depression – what some call the "costs of caring" – from their closer social connections (Kessler et al., 1985; Turner, 1994).

The dimensions of the self that differentiate men and women also have implications for mental health. Gender differences in internalizing and externalizing problems emerge in childhood and adolescence, which indicates the importance of socialized dimensions of selfhood (Avison & McAlpine, 1992; Compas, Orosan, & Grant, 1993; Gore, Aseltine, & Colten, 1993; Kessler 2000, 2003; Kessler, et al., 1994; Rosenfield, Vertefuille, & McAlpine, 2000; Turner & Lloyd, 1995). Consistent with the divisions in spheres and in power, women have more negative self-evaluations than men, a difference that also arises in adolescence. For example, women have less self-esteem and a lower sense of mastery or personal control than men (Avison & McAlpine, 1992; Barnett & Gotlib, 1988; Craighead & Green, 1989; Nolen-Hoeksema, 1994; Pearlin et al., 1981; Rosenberg, 1989; Rosenfield, 1989). These negative self-evaluations increase the risk of mental health problems, especially internalizing problems. In contrast, high self-esteem and sense of mastery are positive for mental health, operating as personal resources that protect the self in the face of stress (Pearlin et al., 1981; Rosenfield, 1992a; Rotter, 1966; Thoits, 1995). These differences in aspects of the self contribute to women's higher rates of anxious and depressive symptoms (Avison & McAlpine, 1992; Nolen-Hoeksema, 1987; Pearlin et al., 1981).

Consistent with the division into public and private spheres, women possess higher levels of emotional reliance and empathy, whereas men are more independent in relationships (Hirschfeld et al., 1976; Rosenfield et al., 2000; Turner & Turner, 1999). Extreme degrees of connectedness or dependency raise the risk of internalizing symptoms. In contrast, extreme independence and low empathy increase externalizing problems such as antisocial behavior (Guisinger & Blatt, 1994; Hagan, 1991; Hagan & Gillis, & Simpson, 1985; Heimer, 1995; Heimer & De Coster, 1999; Miedzian, 1991; Ohbuchi, Ohno, & Mukai, 1992; Rosenfield et al., 2000; Turner & Turner, 1999). There is some evidence that the gender differences in connectedness and autonomy contribute to the disparities in internalizing and externalizing problems (Rosenfield et al., 2000; Turner & Turner, 1999).

Corresponding to the differences in economic resources, men and women differ in perceptions about the amount of power they possess in relationships. Low perceptions of power raise the risk of internalizing symptoms in particular (Lennon & Rosenfield, 1994; Mirowsky, 1985). For instance, individuals who think they have few alternatives to a relationship endure higher levels of depressive symptoms than those who perceive that they have more options (Lennon & Rosenfield, 1994). Gender differences in perceived power also contribute to the disparities in internalizing symptoms between men and women.

Consistent with these differences, men and women vary in self-salience, which are schemas about the importance of the self versus others in social relations. Basically, self-salience involves who we put first, ourselves or other people. At the extremes, self-salience shapes individuals' tendencies toward internalizing or externalizing problems (Rosenfield, Lennon, & White, 2005). Schemas that elevate others at the expense of the self raise the risk of internalizing symptoms, whereas those that promote the self at the expense of others predispose individuals to externalizing behavior. Dominant conceptions of femininity privilege the needs of others above the self, whereas conceptions of masculinity privilege the self more strongly. These differences in self-salience help explain why women predominate in internalizing problems and men exceed in externalizing problems (Rosenfield et al., 2005; Rosenfield, Phillips, & White, 2006). Studies showing that internalizing symptoms are associated with lower levels of "masculine" traits are consistent with these findings (Barrett & White, 2002; Bassoff & Glass, 1982; Horwitz & White, 1987; Huselid & Cooper, 1992; Whitley & Gridley, 1993).

All of these gender differences – in power, responsibilities, and dimensions of the self – shape men's and women's experiences and reactions under stress, which have implications for mental health. Stressors that challenge valued roles or cherished goals and ideals are especially destructive to well-being (Brown & Harris, 1978; Thoits, 1992). Thus, for example, women's greater responsibility for caretaking and domestic life can make problems with their children particularly stressful. For the same reason, women feel more distress than men when spending time away from young children (Milkie & Peltola, 1999). There are also different meanings for men and women in combining work and parent roles (Simon, 1995). Men's conceptions of themselves as paid workers are consistent with their conceptions of being a good parent. They see breadwinning as part of their parental role. For women, paid work and being a parent overlap less – income is not as central to their notion of parenting. Because of these different social conceptions, women with children more often experience intense internal conflicts and challenges to identity when they are employed. These reactions in turn contribute to their higher distress in combining these roles compared with their husbands (Simon, 1995). The costs and benefits of role meanings are different for men and women, particularly for the work role (Simon, 1997). Although most meanings associated with work outside the home are positive for men and women, there is a central cost for women: Work outside the home detracts from time spent with family. Thus, the meaning of work has a cost to women that it does not for men, which helps explain why married mothers have greater internalizing problems than married fathers (Simon, 1997).

Given the differences above, men and women vary in their specific strategies for coping with stressful events and circumstances. Men are more stoic and less expressive in their responses to stressors than women. They more often try to control the problem, accept the problem, not think about the situation, and engage in problem-solving efforts. Women more often pray, solicit social support, express their feelings, and try to distract themselves (Thoits, 1995). Overall, problem-focused coping strategies, which attempt to control the stressful situation and reflect a high sense of mastery, are associated with lower depression and help explain men's lower rates (Folkman & Lazarus, 1980; Kessler et al., 1985). However, different strategies are effective for particular kinds of problems (Mattlin, Wethington, & Kessler, 1990; Pearlin & Schooler, 1978). Generally, strategies that keep partners engaged are more effective for interpersonal problems. For impersonal problems like those on the job, coping mechanisms that allow distancing or devaluation of the problem are most helpful. In this sense, women's typical coping techniques stand them in good stead for dealing with problems in relationships; men's techniques benefit them for dealing with problems at work. We see the division of spheres again reflected in this distribution. We also see that flexibility in coping may be the most effective strategy of all, allowing one to use the best technique for the specific problem at hand.

The explanations presented so far hold that gender differences in mental health result from different underlying experiences of women and men, which divisions in power, responsibilities, and aspects of selfhood produce. In contrast, another approach claims that different norms for expressing emotion rather than different underlying experiences explain the mental health disparities. Norms for the expression of emotion, or what are called "feeling rules," vary dramatically for men and women and prompt different responses to similar situations. There are "proper" or "appropriate" ways for men and women to emote, the genesis of which can be explained by differential socialization for boys and girls (Simon, 2002). As suggested earlier, children internalize messages that equate masculinity with assertiveness, dominance, aggressiveness, independence, and risk-taking, but girls are raised to be the opposite, most notably nurturing and caring (Hagan, 1991; Hagan et al., 1985; Heimer, 1995; Heimer & De Coster, 1999; Miedzian, 1991; Steffensmeier & Allan, 1991). Males are expected to suppress emotions defined as feminine and weak, such as feelings like helplessness, worry, and insecurity – all of which are associated with anxiety and depression. Anger is somewhat more tolerated even though not welcomed. In contrast, emotions such as fear and helplessness – consistent with anxiety and depression – are more normative for women (Simon, 2007; Simon & Nath, 2004).[1]

Some argue that these feeling rules leave men and women little choice in expressing their troubles. For example, because open displays of anxiety and depression are relatively forbidden, men may attempt to hide, remove, shorten, or deflect any such feelings. Drinking accomplishes this goal, under the cover of relative acceptability. For these reasons, some see substance abuse as a male version of depression; that is, a gender-equivalent expression of depression (Horwitz et al., 1996b; Rosenfield et al., 2005). Both come from the same underlying feelings, one allowing direct expression and the other indirect. As some evidence of this,

---

[1] Cross-gender emotions such as anger and antisocial behavior are discouraged. We can witness the operation of these norms clearly when men and women display the "wrong" emotional problems for their gender. For example, men who come into psychiatric emergency rooms with depressive symptoms are hospitalized at much higher rates than women with the same symptomatology. Likewise, women who come in with antisocial disorders or substance abuse are more likely to be hospitalized than men with the same problems. These cases of double deviance are treated much more severely, showing us there are norms even in deviating (Rosenfield, 1984).

low-level jobs increase psychological distress for women and increase drinking for men. Thus the same problematic circumstances can result in divergent disorders in men and women (Lennon, 1987).

What Are the Best Situations for Men's and Women's Mental Health?

Based on the evidence presented, we can point out some conditions that are positive for women and for men. The same principles hold for both genders: Greater power and reasonable levels of demands are beneficial for mental health. Thus, for women or men, one positive situation is full-time employment when there are no children in the home. Women who are employed part time with kids at home also seem to be in good shape (Rosenfield, 1989). Those women who work full time with kids at home benefit only if they have secure child care arrangements or if their husbands share in the domestic labor, especially in the highly time-pressured tasks. Because men and women gain and lose from the same conditions, a danger is trading off benefits for one gender at the expense of the other. For instance, there is evidence that, when married women's income increases, so does their happiness, both in terms of mood as well as feelings about their marriage (Rogers & DeBoer, 2001). However, wives' greater income can result in lower well-being among husbands (Rogers & DeBoer, 2001; Rosenfield, 1992b).

Within the workplace, high job autonomy and complexity – as well as low time pressure – are the most positive conditions for mental health for both men and women. Other research shows that positive job conditions can even offset negative family arrangements. Specifically, high autonomy and low time pressure on the job reduce the stress women experience in combining jobs and families and the negative effect of child care demands (Lennon & Rosenfield, 1992).

It is also clear that certain kinds of social relations and dimensions of the self are quite beneficial for men and women. High self-esteem and mastery are necessary for optimal mental health. Balanced self-salience – that is, equal esteem for the self and others, equal amounts of autonomy and connectedness, and equal regard for one's own and others' interests – reduces the chances of veering toward externalizing or internalizing disorders.

In concluding, we have reviewed some of the evidence for differences between men and women in mental health and the social underpinnings of those differences. Looking at numerous levels, from macro-level broad sociohistorical forces to micro-level aspects of the self, we see how social differentiation by gender shapes the psychological problems of men and women. One side of the division involves a constellation of low power and caretaking responsibilities; low levels of self-evaluations, autonomy, and self-salience; and feeling rules dictating expressivity of less potent and active emotions – all of which are consistent with internalizing disorders. The other side consists of a constellation of greater power and productive responsibilities; high levels of self-evaluation, independence, and self-salience; and feeling rules of emotional stoicism with the exception of more potent and active emotions – which are consonant with externalizing disorders

This is not to underestimate the variation that exists between groups in this society. Most research on gender and mental health compares all groups of men to all groups of women, rather than comparing within different subgroups. Gender differences do vary by race and ethnicity; for example, African Americans differ in gender conceptions and gender differences in mental health problems (Rosenfield, et al., 2006). Although these interactions are beyond the scope of this chapter, we recommend their further investigation.

In addition, there is substantial variation that exists among men and among women. As many observe, there is great diversity among particular men and women. We also do not want to go to the other extreme and imply that there is something necessary about these differences. Ultimately, gender differences are largely caused by things other than gender. They are a result of certain social practices such as economic inequality, that have become associated with gender but whose associations can be altered. Going full circle back to Freud, we can trace the advances in understanding the differences between the genders, showing us that anatomy is not necessarily destiny. Instead, a complexity of social forces converges to push men and women toward different psychological troubles. The more we understand these forces and their sources and consequences, the more reasons and power we gather to change them.

14

Race and Mental Health: Patterns and Challenges

David R. Williams, Manuela Costa, and Jacinta P. Leavell

Williams and colleagues provide an overview of the mental health status for members of five U.S. minorities, evaluating the available scientific evidence of racial variations in mental health. Because of different research methodologies and varying criteria for the identification of both mental disorder and minority status, it is difficult to make many generalizations about mental health differences. The intersection of race, socioeconomic status, and gender within and between populations varies, thereby contributing to additional difficulties in assessing group differences. Consequently, despite decades of research, we lack a clear picture of the mental health status of the major minority populations. Research must overcome problems with inadequate coverage of the population and find ways to capture the considerable heterogeneity of minority groups. A second group of problems concerns limitations on the measurement of mental health status. Finally, culture affects the manifestation of mental health problems because cultures vary in their emphasis on particular emotions and standards for acceptable expression and emotion. That is, culture affects the interpretation of symptoms of disorder. Research must identify the ways in which social, economic, political, and cultural factors affect the health status of minority groups. Racism and migration experiences are also critical to mental health and need further investigation. What is this multifaceted phenomenon called race and how can it lead to variations in mental health?

Introduction

In the United States, federal statistical agencies are required to report statistics for five racial groups (White, Black, Asian, Native Hawaiian or other Pacific Islander, and American Indian or Alaskan Native) and one ethnic category: Hispanic (Office of Management & Budget [OMB], 1997). These categories are socially constructed; in one study, almost 70% of Hispanics preferred to have Hispanic included as a racial category (Tucker et al., 1996). Therefore, this chapter treats all the categories as "races" and examines the extent to which these categories predict variations in mental health status. It also uses the most preferred terms for each group interchangeably (Black or African American, Hispanic or Latino, American Indian or Native American). Racial groups are more alike than

---

Preparation of this chapter was supported in part by Grant R01 MH 59575 from the National Institute of Mental Health.

different in terms of genetic characteristics, with humans being identical for about 75% of known genetic factors and with 95% of human genetic variation existing within racial groups (Lewontin, 1972; Lewontin, Rose, & Kamin, 1984). Since the first U.S. Census in 1790, no two censuses have used the same racial categories (Nobles, 2000), with historical events and political factors playing an important role in determining which racial categories are officially recognized at any given time (Williams, 1997a). The current racial categories reflect the convergence of geographic origins, exposure to prejudice and discrimination, and socioeconomic disadvantage (Williams, 1997b). Consensus does not exist within the official racial groups on a preferred racial label. Accordingly, in an effort to respect individual dignity, this chapter uses the most preferred terms for each group (Tucker et al., 1996) interchangeably (i.e., Black or African American, Hispanic or Latino, White or Caucasian, and American Indian or Native American).

This chapter provides an overview of the mental health status for each minority population and evaluates the available scientific evidence of racial variations in mental health. The term *minority* is used here not in reference to numerical size, but in the sociological sense of a nondominant group that lacks social status and political power relative to the dominant group. In considering directions for future research to enhance our understanding of race and mental health, we emphasize the need to identify the ways in which the mental health problems of each group emerge from the larger social context in which the group is embedded.

Early Studies of African-American Mental Health

Until recently, Blacks were the largest minority racial group in the United States, and early studies of racial differences in mental health focused largely on this population. Reflecting the prevailing social ideology of their time, racial categories were used in research to classify human variation and also to provide a scientific justification for the exploitation of groups that were regarded as inferior (Montagu, 1965). The very first Article of the U.S. Constitution required the enumeration of three races: Whites, Black slaves as three-fifths of a person, and Indians who paid taxes (Anderson & Fienberg, 1995). The discounting of Blacks and the exclusion of "noncivilized" Indians reflected the social and political standing of these groups. Early studies of racial variations in mental health status further reflected this racist ideology. Krieger (1987) showed that, regardless of their findings, these studies were used to demonstrate Black inferiority and provide a scientific rationale for policies of inequality and exploitation. A report based on rates of mental illness from the 1840 Census falsified Black insanity rates to show that the further north Blacks lived, the higher their rates of mental illness. This was interpreted as evidence that freedom made Blacks crazy. In fact, Blacks were regarded as so constitutionally suited for slavery that the very desire to escape slavery was defined as a mental illness called "drapetomania." Another disease, "dysesthesia

Ethiopia," readily identifiable by slave masters, was the attempt to avoid work. One of its symptoms was sleeping during the day.

Consistently, racial ideology and the social position of Blacks formed the interpretive context for all data on the mental health of Blacks. For example, Babcock (1895) argued that the newly freed slaves would be less prone to mental illness than Whites because of the excellent care and supervision received during slavery. In contrast, Lind (1914) indicated that rates of mental illness would be high for Blacks because of their inherent biological inferiority. The best available evidence on Black mental health in the early 20th century came from rates of insanity from the U.S. Census based on counts of the institutionalized and noninstitutionalized mentally ill. These data indicated that the rates of mental illness were lower for Blacks than for Caucasians (Malzberg, 1944). In 1930, the Census based its prevalence rates of mental illness only on the number of patients in state mental health facilities. After this change, census data revealed that Blacks had higher rates of mental illness than Whites (Malzberg, 1944). Other early studies that estimated prevalence using first admission rates of patients in mental hospitals, both nationally and in selected states, also found elevated rates of psychiatric illness for the African American population (Fischer, 1969).

From a methodological viewpoint, studies based on treatment rates are flawed. These rates do not capture the psychiatric problems of persons who have not entered treatment. Accordingly, they are affected by health care access and financing options, distance to health care facilities, available transportation, racial discrimination, the client's economic status, and other structural and cultural barriers that affect the likelihood of seeking and receiving medical care and of being appropriately diagnosed. For example, a national study of population-based rates of treated and untreated cases of mental illness found that only 40% of persons who have had a psychiatric illness have ever received treatment (Kessler, McGonagle, Zhao, et al., 1994). Moreover, almost half of all persons in treatment did not meet the criteria for any of the psychiatric disorders assessed. State hospitals continue to be an important source of mental health care for African Americans, and studies have indicated that rates of mental illness for persons in these health facilities are higher for Blacks than for Whites (Snowden & Cheung, 1990; U.S. Department of Health and Human Services [USDHHS], 2001).

As studies expanded their population to include outpatients, private patients, and community residents, the biases inherent in some of the earlier treatment studies were reduced, and findings of racial differences became more inconsistent (Jaco, 1960). For example, one Baltimore study found that Blacks had higher rates of mental illness than Whites only when the analyses were restricted to patients in state hospitals. Rates for Whites exceeded those at for Blacks when the state hospital data were combined with data from private mental hospitals, veterans administration hospitals, and a community survey of Baltimore residents (Pasamanick, 1963).

After World War II, community surveys emerged as a new source of information on the distribution of mental health problems. By using statistical methods to select a sample of individuals representative of an entire community, these surveys avoided major selection biases associated with treatment samples. However, psychiatry had not yet reached consensus on the criteria for the formal diagnosis of discrete psychiatric disorders, and the technology to obtain standardized information based on structured or semistructured interviews did not yet exist. Accordingly, these studies measured nonspecific emotional symptoms or psychological distress, but did not assess specific psychiatric disorders. These scales of psychological distress were brief, easy to administer, and provided the distribution of mental health status on a continuum. Typically, these symptom checklist scales included items that assessed depressed mood and anxiety and served as indicators of dysfunction (Link & Dohrenwend, 1980; Vega & Rumbaut, 1991).

In an early review of community-based studies, Dohrenwend and Dohrenwend (1969) indicated that half of the eight studies they reviewed showed higher rates of mental health problems for Blacks and half showed higher rates for Caucasians. Subsequent studies have frequently found higher rates of psychological distress for Blacks than for Whites, with the racial difference reduced to nonsignificance when adjusted for socioeconomic status (SES); however, the pattern is not uniform (Vega & Rumbaut, 1991, Wilson & Williams, 2004). The reasons for these inconsistencies are not well understood. Future research should assess the extent to which variation in racial differences on nonspecific measures of distress is linked to the differences on the specific symptoms that constitute the composite measures.

Many of the early classic community studies in psychiatric epidemiology (Weissman, Myers, & Ross, 1986) did not make special efforts to include African Americans in sufficient numbers to make reliable racial comparisons. The landmark study of social class and mental illness in New Haven, Connecticut had only 96 Blacks; the Sterling County Study, an important ongoing prospective study of mental illness, included 47 Blacks; and the Midtown Manhattan Mental Health Study, an important early study of mental health status in an urban population, was drawn from a population that was 99% White.

An important methodological innovation in the 1970s was the development of semistructured and structured interviews to obtain standardized information that could be used to generate the diagnosis of psychiatric illness. One of the first studies of this kind was a community survey in New Haven, Connecticut that found no significant racial difference for anxiety disorders, but higher rates of major depression, minor depression, and depressive personality for non-Whites (mainly Blacks), compared to Whites (Weissman & Myers, 1978). One limitation of this study was that non-Whites were only 12% of the 511 respondents. This study was a precursor to the National Institute of Mental Health Epidemiologic Catchment Area Study (ECA), with Weissman and Myers serving as investigators

Table 14.1. *Rates of psychiatric disorder for Blacks, Whites, and Hispanics in the epidemiologic catchment area study*

Disorders	Current			Lifetime		
	Black	White	Hispanic	Black	White	Hispanic
1. Affective	3.5	3.7	4.1	6.3	8.0	7.8
2. Alcohol abuse	6.6	6.7	9.1	13.8	13.6	16.7
3. Drug history	—	—	—	29.9	30.7	25.1
4. Drug abuse	2.7	2.7	1.9	5.4	6.4	4.3
5. Schizophrenia	1.6	0.9	0.4	2.1	1.4	0.8
6. Generalized anxiety	6.1	3.5	3.7	—	—	—
7. Phobic	16.2	9.1	8.1	23.4	9.7	12.2
8. Any disorder	26.0	19.0	20.0	38.0	32.0	33.0

Source: Robins & Reiger (1991).

at the first ECA site, Greater New Haven. The ECA was the first large mental health study in the United States to use a structured diagnostic interview (Robins & Regier, 1991). Between 1980 and 1983, 20,000 adults in five communities were interviewed as part of the ECA. This study used the Diagnostic Interview Schedule (DIS), a research diagnostic interview that uses operational criteria and algorithms based on the *Diagnostic and Statistical Manual of Mental Disorder* to assign persons to specific diagnostic categories (Robins et al., 1981). It is a fully structured, lay-administered interview that generates diagnoses based on the presence, severity, and duration of symptoms. Its structured nature allows for the reliable assessment of psychiatric illness without clinical judgment. The ECA thus provided estimates of the prevalence and incidence of specific psychiatric disorders in samples of institutionalized and noninstitutionalized persons.

Table 14.1 presents current and lifetime rates of disorder by race in the ECA. These data come from a summary of ECA findings that weighted the data from five regional sites of the ECA to the national demographic distribution to produce prevalence rates for the entire United States (Robins & Regier, 1991). The first two columns under the current and lifetime categories of Table 14.1 show very few differences between Blacks and Whites in rates of psychiatric disorders. Especially striking is the absence of a racial difference in drug use history and the prevalence of alcohol and drug abuse/dependence. More detailed analyses revealed that the age trajectory of lifetime rates of alcoholism varied by race. The rate of alcohol abuse for Whites was twice that of Blacks in the youngest age group (18–29), but the Black lifetime rate exceeded that of Whites in all remaining age groups, with the gap being largest in the 45–64 age category. Rates of depression among African Americans and White were generally similar, and though Blacks had higher rates

Table 14.2. *Rates of psychiatric disorders and Black/White, Hispanic/White ratios in the National Comorbidity Study*

	%	B/W Ratio	H/W Ratio
Any affective disorder	11.3	0.78	1.38
Any anxiety disorder	17.1	0.90	1.17
Any substance abuse/dependence	11.3	0.47	1.04
Any disorder	29.5	0.70	1.11

Source: Kessler et al. (1994).

of schizophrenia than Caucasians, this difference disappeared when adjusted for age, gender, marital status, and SES.

Anxiety disorders stand out as the one area in which Blacks had considerably higher rates than Whites, and this disparity is responsible for the elevated rates for Blacks in the "any disorder" category. African Americans had higher lifetime rates of simple phobia, social phobia, and agoraphobia than Whites (D. R. Brown, Eaton, & Sussman, 1990). The findings were less consistent for other anxiety disorders. Whites tended to have lower rates of generalized anxiety disorder than Blacks, but there were no consistent racial differences for panic disorder. However, comparisons of current and lifetime rates suggested that, compared to Whites, Blacks have longer durations of panic disorder, but briefer durations of phobic disorders (D. R. Brown et al., 1990).

Findings from the National Comorbidity Study (NCS) are even more striking (Kessler, McGonagle, Zhao, et al., 1994). The NCS interviewed more than 8,000 adults and was the first study to use a national probability survey to assess psychiatric disorders in the United States. Table 14.2 presents findings from this study. The first column shows the overall rate for each major class of disorders, and the second column shows the Black/White ratio. A ratio greater than 1 means that Blacks have a higher rate of disorder than Whites. The pattern in Table 14.2 is impressive. Blacks do not have higher rates of disorder than Whites for any of the major classes of disorders. Instead, lower rates for Blacks than Whites are particularly pronounced for the affective disorders (depression) and the substance abuse disorders (alcohol and drug abuse). Instructively, the NCS reported no racial differences in panic disorder, simple phobia, or agoraphobia (Kessler et al., 1994). However, detailed analyses suggested that the associations between phobia and race may be importantly patterned by gender. Using data from the NCS, Magee (1993) showed that White men tend to have higher current and lifetime rates of agoraphobia, simple phobia, and social phobia than their Black counterparts, but Black women have higher rates of agoraphobia and simple phobia than White women.

Early Studies of Hispanic Mental Health

Hispanics are the largest minority group in the United States, and the number of Hispanics continues to grow rapidly. Although most Hispanics have a common language, religion, and various traditions, the timing of immigration and incorporation experiences in the United States have varied for the more than 25 national origin groups that make up the Hispanic category, such that each group is distinctive. The largest Hispanic groups are Mexican Americans (59%), Puerto Ricans (10%), Central Americans (5%), South Americans (4%), and Cubans (4%). For multiple indicators of SES such as education, income, occupational status, and home ownership, Hispanics have lower levels than Whites (Williams, 2005). However, there is considerable variation within the Hispanic category, with immigrants from Venezuela, Brazil, and Argentina having markedly higher levels of SES than those from Mexico, the Dominican Republic, and El Salvador (Williams, 2005).

Early studies of the mental health of Hispanics did not provide a clear picture of the distribution of mental health problems for the Hispanic population, compared to other major racial groups or for subgroups within the Latino category (Rogler, 1989; Vega & Rumbaut, 1991). For example, using two Alameda County samples, Roberts (1980) found that Mexican Americans did not differ from Whites and Blacks on psychological distress. At the same time, two other California studies using the Center for Epidemiologic Studies–Depression scale (CES-D) found that Mexican Americans have higher rates of distress than either Blacks or non-Hispanic Whites (Frerichs, Aneshensel, & Clark, 1981; Vernon & Roberts, 1982). Inpatient and outpatient treatment data from the Los Angeles County Mental Health System revealed that Hispanics tend to have lower levels of psychotic disorders than Whites (Flaskerud & Hu, 1992). Some studies suggested that Puerto Ricans may be especially vulnerable to mental health problems. In a study of 1,000 New York City residents, Dohrenwend and Dohrenwend (1969) found that Puerto Ricans reported more psychiatric symptoms than Whites or Blacks, even after SES was controlled. Immigrants from Cuba and Mexico seem to enjoy better mental health than non-Hispanic Whites, but the opposite seems to be true about immigrants from Puerto Rico to the mainland (Vega & Rumbaut, 1991).

One of the best early sources of comparative data on Hispanic populations is the Hispanic Health and Nutrition Examination Survey (HHANES). The HHANES, conducted between 1982 and 1984, was a major federal effort to obtain comparable data on the populations in the continental United States with Mexican, Cuban, and Puerto Rican origins. It used a stratified cluster sample drawn from specific geographic areas where large proportions of Latinos were living. The sample size was more than 8,000. Mental health status was assessed by both CES-D depression symptoms and DIS-defined major depressive disorder. The HHANES data revealed that Puerto Ricans had the highest levels of psychological distress and the highest rates of depression (Narrow et al., 1991). In addition, Cuban

Americans had lower levels of psychological distress and lower rates of major depression than either the Mexican American or Puerto Rican population. At the same time, scores for Mexican Americans on the CES-D were lower than those found in previous studies of non-Hispanic Whites, as well as in previous community samples of Hispanics (Moscicki et al., 1989).

The ECA study provided some information on the distribution of psychiatric disorders for Latinos. However, the Hispanic sample in the ECA came from only one geographic area (the Los Angeles ECA site). Table 14.1 shows that, compared to Blacks and Whites, Hispanics had the lowest current and lifetime rates for schizophrenia and drug abuse. They also had the lowest rates of drug use history. At the same time, the current rates of alcohol abuse and affective disorder were higher than those of both Blacks and Whites. Current rates of anxiety disorder were intermediate between those of Blacks and Whites. The NCS also provided data on the prevalence of psychiatric disorders for the Hispanic population. These data, shown in Table 14.2, should be interpreted with caution because of the relatively small sample ($n = 737$) of Hispanics (Kessler et al., 1994). In contrast to the pattern for African Americans, Hispanics' rates of the major psychiatric disorders tended to be higher than those of Whites. Thus, given the quantity and quality of the available evidence from early studies, it was difficult to arrive at firm conclusions about the distribution of mental health problems for the Hispanics and major subgroups within that population.

Early Studies of Asian-American Mental Health

In the 2000 Census, Asians comprised 3.6% of the American population and included an ethnically and nationally diverse group of peoples who originated from China, Japan, Korea, the Philippines, the continent of India, and the countries of Southeast Asia. Asian countries have been major contributors to the immigration stream to the United States over the past few decades, and the population composition of the Asian American community has changed significantly over that time. Japanese Americans represented the majority of Asian Americans up to the 1960s, but the 2000 Census revealed that Chinese and Filipinos took over that position. In addition, in contrast to the 1960s when most Asian Americans had been born in the United States, as of the 2000 Census, almost 70% of Asians are foreign born.

Because Asian Americans constitute only a small portion of the U.S. population, traditional surveys do not include adequate numbers of this diverse racial group to yield reliable estimates of the distribution of health problems. Accordingly, early research on Asian American health attempted to estimate the level of mental health problems based on the utilization of mental health services. These early studies found that Asian Americans were consistently underrepresented in clinical populations, and it was assumed that they experienced lower levels of mental health problems (Sue et al., 1995). However, several small community studies suggested that at least some Asian populations in the United States were experiencing more mental health problems than previously thought. A small community sample of Chinese Americans found that between 20% and 40% reported that they experienced high levels of psychological distress (Loo, Tong, & True, 1989). Similarly, a study of Asian Americans in Seattle found that Chinese, Japanese, Filipinos, and Korean Americans reported higher levels of depressive symptoms than did White Americans (Kuo, 1984). The sampling strategies used in this last study reflect some of the challenges in attempting to sample a relatively rare population. The Seattle sample was compiled from lists provided by ethnic organizations, pooling Asian last names from the telephone directory, and lists generated from snowball techniques. Other evidence has suggested that the Chinese and Japanese American elderly have higher rates of suicide than their non-Asian peers (Lui & Yu, 1985). Refugees, especially those from Southeast Asia, have been a part of recent waves of immigration. Several studies have found high rates of mental health problems for this group (Buchwald et al., 1993; Kinzie et al., 1990; Lum, 1995).

Large epidemiological surveys like the ECA and NCS provided no comparative data on the mental health status of Asian Americans. The Chinese American Psychiatric Epidemiological Study (CAPES) was the first large study of mental disorders in any Asian group in the United States (Sue et al., 1995). It collected data from a probability sample of 1,700 native-born and immigrant Chinese living in the Los Angeles area. Overall, the rates of mental health problems for Chinese Americans were low compared to the overall rates reported in the ECA and NCS. Rates of generalized anxiety disorder, simple phobia, and panic disorder were considerably lower in the CAPES than those reported in the other studies. However, the rate of major depression (6.9%) was higher than that in the ECA (4.9%), but considerably lower than the 17.1% reported in the NCS (Sue et al., 1995).

With the revision of the Office of Management and Budget (OMB) racial categories prior to the 2000 Census, Native Hawaiians and other Pacific Islanders were separated from the Asian category as a new distinct group (OMB, 1997). This group consisted of 874,000 persons or 0.3% of the U.S. population in the 2000 Census. Much remains to be learned about the extent of psychopathology for the diverse populations that make up the Pacific Islander category.

Early Studies of American-Indian Mental Health

In the 2000 Census, 1.5% of the U.S. population or just more than 4 million persons reported that they were American Indian and Alaskan Native alone or in combination with one or more races. About 2.5 million or 0.9% of the population indicated that they are American Indian and Alaska Native alone. Despite the small size of this racial group, the diversity within its ranks is extensive, with more than

500 federally recognized tribes and entities. Though some original languages have been lost over time, many tribes have their own language and distinct customs. Almost one-quarter of the populace lives below the poverty level, and American Indians have a rate of college graduation that is comparable to that of Hispanics but lower than that of Whites, Blacks, and Asians (Williams, 2005).

There has been a dearth of information from early epidemiological studies regarding the mental health of American Indians (Manson, Walker, & Kivlahan, 1987). Two issues that have received some research attention are substance abuse and depression. Some research suggested that Indian adolescents abuse alcohol at two to three times the rate of their non-Indian peers (Mail, 1989; Mail & Johnson, 1993). Drug and alcohol abuse may exacerbate some of the health and social problems that American Indians experience, and there has been interest in the high rates of alcohol problems within some American Indian communities (Johnson, 1994). Closely related to the problem of alcohol abuse is the high rate of suicide among American Indians. It is estimated that they commit suicide at two times the national average (DeBruyn, Hymbaugh, & Valdez, 1988). Alcohol plays a role in a majority of Indian suicides (Johnson, 1994).

Studies of clinic populations or convenience samples have suggested that there might be high rates of depression among American Indians (Napholz, 1994). For example, Wilson, Civic, and Glass (1994), in a study of 102 clinic patients, found that 21% met DSM-III-R criteria for depressive disorder. Other data suggested that, as in the general population, comorbid psychopathology may also be prevalent for Native Americans (Walker & Kivlahan, 1993). For example, in a study of 104 adult Indians from three reservation-based mental health clinics, Shore (1987) found that 83% of the adults had more than one psychiatric disorder. Of the 86 individuals diagnosed as depressed, half had a secondary diagnosis of alcohol abuse.

Minority Mental Health: Current Status

In recent years, there has been a substantial increase in our knowledge of the distribution of mental disorders in minority populations in the United States. Much of this increase can be credited to three large population-based studies funded by the NIMH known as the Collaborative Psychiatric Epidemiology Surveys (CPES) initiative. These studies used common core questions and field procedures (Heeringa et al., 2004). The first study is the National Comorbidity Survey Replication, a national sample of 9,282 adults with no oversampling of any minority groups (Kessler, Berglund, et al., 2005). Second, there is the National Survey of American Life (NSAL) – the largest study of Black mental health ever conducted, including 1,621 Blacks of Caribbean ancestry, 3,570 African Americans, and 891 Whites (Jackson et al., 2004). The third study is the National Latino and Asian American Study (NLAAS). It consisted of a nationally representative sample of 868

Table 14.3. *Prevalence of lifetime and past-year psychiatric disorders according to race and ethnicity*

Race/country of origin	Lifetime disorders[a] %	Past-year disorders[a] %
White American	37.37	19.00
Latino American		
Puerto Rican	38.98	22.88
Cuban	28.38	15.91
Mexican	28.42	14.48
Other Latino	27.29	14.42
Asian American		
Chinese	18.00	10.00
Filipino	16.74	8.99
Vietnamese	13.95	6.69
Other Asian	18.29	9.55
Black American		
African American	30.54	14.79
Black Caribbean	27.87	16.38
American Indian		
Northern Midwest*	74.60	25.30
Southwest	41.90	21.00
Northern Plains	44.50	24.30

[a]Psychiatric disorders include major depressive disorder, dysthmia, social phobia, generalized anxiety disorder, posttraumatic stress disorder, drug abuse, drug dependence, alcohol abuse, and alcohol dependence.
Source: White American, Kessler, Berglund, et al. (2005); Latino American, Alegría et al. (2007); Asian American, Takeuchi et al. (2007); Black American, Williams, Haile, et al. (2007); American Indian, Northern Midwest, Whitbeck et al. (2006); American Indian, Southwest and Northern Plains, Beals et al. (2005).

Mexican Americans, 577 Cubans, 495 Puerto Ricans, and 614 other Latinos and a nationally representative sample of 600 Chinese, 508 Filipinos, 520 Vietnamese, and 467 other Asians (Alegria, Mulvaney-Day, Torres et al., 2007; Takeuchi et al., 2007). This study provides the first and most comprehensive national picture of psychiatric disorders for Hispanics and Asians in the United States.

Table 14.3 presents data from the CPES. It shows that Hispanics (with the exception of Puerto Ricans), Blacks, and Asians have lower rates of lifetime and 12-month disorders than Whites. The prevalence of disorders in Asians, in particular, is markedly lower than for Whites. These data also illustrate the heterogeneity of racial/ethnic populations. Puerto Ricans have disorder rates that are elevated compared to all other Latino groups. We are uncertain of the reasons for these differences, although Puerto Ricans differ from the other Latino groups in terms of their closer relationship to the United States and their elevated levels of residential racial segregation. Among Asians, Vietnamese have lower rates than their counterparts. This pattern is unexpected because Vietnamese immigrants have lower levels of SES than their Chinese or Filipino peers (Williams, 2005).

African Americans and Caribbean Blacks have similar rates of mental disorder. However, other analyses reveal that these overall comparisons mask intriguing patterns of variations by gender. Although Black Caribbean women have lower rates of disorder than African American women, the opposite pattern is evident among men (Williams, Haile, et al., 2007). Regarding our ethnic terminology for Blacks, we use the term *Caribbean Blacks* to refer to immigrants from Caribbean basin countries and persons of Caribbean ancestry in the United States. We use the term *African Americans* to refer to all other persons of African ancestry in the United States who do not identify with Caribbean origins. We acknowledge the limitations of this terminology given that, in our sample, (1) *Black* is preferred over *African American* as the desired term for racial designation among all persons of African ancestry; (2) our African American category includes a small number of recent immigrants from Africa to the United States, and (3) some in our Caribbean sample indicate that *African American* is their preferred racial designation.

American Indians were not included in the CPES study, but Table 14.3 includes prevalence data from three recent studies that assess the prevalence of mental health problems using diagnostic criteria. Rates of lifetime and past-year disorders for American Indians were slightly higher than those of Whites in both a probability sample of 1,446 members of a Southwest tribe and a similar sample of 1,638 members of Northern Plains Indian tribes (Beals et al., 2005). The third study used a sample of 861 parents and caretakers of early adolescents who were enrolled in American Indian and Canadian First Nations tribes. It found that lifetime rates of disorder were very high, reflecting high rates of substance abuse in this group (Whitbeck et al., 2006). These studies and the dramatic variation in disorder rates emphasize how much we yet need to learn about the mental health of American Indians. Importantly, they also highlight the need to situate the mental health of American Indians in the historical context and contemporary realities of the adversities and protective factors faced by both reservation-based and urban Indians (Alcantara & Gone, 2007).

Cross-Cutting Issues in Minority Mental Health

Our review of the available evidence clearly indicates that, although we have learned much in recent years, there is still much that we need to learn regarding the mental health status of the major minority populations in the United States. There are several issues that must be resolved before we can obtain an accurate picture of the distribution of mental health problems for minority populations. In addition, some important issues must be addressed to enhance our understanding of the determinants of variations in mental health status. These issues are considered in this section. They include data quality issues, as well as the need to pay greater attention to the specific social conditions faced by minority populations.

Data quality issues crucial to the assessment and interpretation of minority mental health status include (1) coverage of the population, (2) limitations of the measurement of mental health status, and (3) the role of culture.

Coverage of the Population

Despite large epidemiological studies like the CPES, we still lack basic information on mental disorders for Pacific Islanders, American Indians, several subgroups of both Asian and Hispanic populations, and even for some demographic and ethnic subgroups of the Black population. For example, noncoverage of African American men is a serious problem in most epidemiological surveys. Black men tend to have low response rates in survey research studies, and they are overrepresented in marginal and institutional populations that are likely to have higher rates of morbidity. High rates of nonresponse in a particular group may bias estimates of the distribution of disease for that group. This problem is typically addressed in epidemiological studies by using poststratification weights to make samples correspond to that of the census estimates of the population. This strategy does not solve the problem because it is likely that nonrespondents differ systematically from respondents and because census estimates of the population are importantly affected by the degree of census undercount. The U.S. Census estimates that it fails to count more than 10% of all Black men between the ages of 25 and 64 (Williams, 1996a). These national estimates are likely to vary by specific geographic areas and can seriously distort estimates of the population in particular areas. Although the Census has historically devoted more attention to the undercount problem for the Black and White population, the undercount problem may also be acute for Hispanics and American Indians (Williams, 1996a). Low response rates for racial minorities can be eliminated by a commitment of adequate financial resources and the use of appropriate field methods (McGraw et al., 1992).

Another issue related to data coverage is the considerable heterogeneity of minority populations. There is considerable ethnic heterogeneity within each of the OMB categories, and an understanding of mental status requires that health status variations within these categories be disaggregated whenever possible. Subgroups of the Asian, American Indian, Hispanic, and even the Black and White population vary across a broad range of sociodemographic characteristics. For example, Arab Americans are a subgroup within the White population and recent African immigrants are a subgroup within the Black population that we currently know little about in terms of their mental health risk. There is also considerable heterogeneity within even an ethnic subgroup of a global racial category. For example, the Chinese American population, one of the largest subgroups of the Asian and Pacific Islander category, is in itself diverse (Sue et al., 1995). It consists of individuals born in the United States, as well as immigrants born in different regions of China who speak a variety of dialects and languages. Some of these individuals are highly educated, whereas others may be barely literate.

The problem of noncoverage in psychiatric epidemiology studies is also evident in the absence of small groups that are relatively rare and widely dispersed in the population. The small sample size of subgroups of the Asian, Hispanic, American Indian, and Pacific Islander population in most mental health studies is a particularly serious problem. The lack of adequate data renders these groups invisible or yields unreliable estimates of the distribution of disease. It also precludes assessment of heterogeneity within a given racial group. The small sizes and geographic concentrations of these populations suggest the importance of geographically focused surveys, as opposed to national ones, as the optimal cost-effective strategy to obtain data for these groups. However, if racial identifiers exist for these populations that capture the heterogeneity of these populations in national databases, combining multiple years of data can be a useful strategy for obtaining mental health data for rare populations.

Measuring Mental Health

Historically, mental disorder and normal functioning have been conceived as polar ends of a scale, with self-reported symptoms of psychological distress or depression being on a continuum with defined psychiatric disorders. Thus, some researchers viewed scales of psychological distress as a substitute for studies of psychiatric disorders (Downey & Coyne, 1991). There is a growing recognition that scales of psychological distress capture qualitatively different phenomena than measures of psychiatric disorder. Research has shown that although most clinically depressed persons have scores in the depressed range on self-report questionnaires, relatively few persons from community samples who have high scores on self-report scales of depression meet diagnostic criteria for clinical depression (Downey & Coyne, 1991). In addition, the social correlates of self-reported symptoms differ from those of interview-generated diagnoses of clinical depression (Downey & Coyne, 1991).

Importantly, conclusions about the distribution of mental health problems for at least some minority populations seem to be linked to the measurement of mental health status. As noted earlier, compared to Whites, African Americans tend to have higher levels of symptoms but equivalent or lower rates of disorder. Some limited evidence has suggested that Puerto Ricans (Canino et al., 1987) and Chinese Americans (Sue et al., 1995) may also have high levels of symptoms but low rates of disorder. This pattern is consistent with the notion that psychological distress scales capture not clinical diagnosis but aspects of demoralization that are likely to be more common at the low end of the SES spectrum (Link & Dohrenwend, 1980).

Other data reveal even more complexity in the association between race and mental health. For example, compared to Whites, Blacks tend to report lower levels of psychological well-being on cognitively focused measures such as life satisfaction and happiness (Hughes & Thomas, 1998). At the same time, African Americans report higher levels of flourishing than Whites (Keyes, 2007). Flourishing refers to the absence of mental disorders *and* the presence of high levels of psychological well-being. We do not currently have a clear sense of either the determinants of the levels of various indicators of mental health for Blacks and Whites or of the patterning of these other dimensions of mental health for all of the other minority populations. Future research on minority mental health should assess mental health status comprehensively and seek to understand how these multiple dimensions relate to each other and are embedded in larger contextual factors.

Another problem affecting the quality of measures of psychiatric status is language proficiency. Challenges associated with mental health assessment among racial and ethnic minorities are often exacerbated by language barriers. This problem is especially acute for subgroups of the Asian American and Hispanic populations that have a high percentage of foreign-born persons. A lack of language proficiency in the client or clinician can create bias when individuals are being diagnosed. In many instances, a diagnosis of psychiatric disorder is determined by the use of a formal assessment tool. Fluency is particularly important in the determination of psychotic thought processes. If a clinician were to have difficulty comprehending the speech pattern of an individual with limited mastery of the English language, he or she could erroneously diagnose a patient as having a thought disorder (Cervantes & Arroyo, 1994).

The assessment of psychiatric disorders requires recall of specific symptoms. There are validity problems with lifetime measures of psychiatric illness that may be especially acute for members of minority populations. The available evidence indicates that respondents have difficulty in accurately recalling and dating psychiatric episodes that occurred over their lifetime (Rogler et al., 1992). These recall problems are likely to differ by racial group status as education level and level of language proficiency are probably associated with the accuracy of recall.

Culture

Inattention to the role of culture in shaping the manifestation of mental health problems could also contribute to systematic patterns of misdiagnosis across racial groups. Races belonging to different cultures may have distinct belief systems and standards for acceptable behavior. It is thus possible that the specific symptoms related to a psychiatric disorder would vary across different cultural groups.

Depression, for example, may have a stronger somatic component for individuals raised in cultures that frowned at the expression of emotion. Manson (1995) emphasized the importance of the cultural context in the presentation of symptoms among Native Americans. He indicated that cultures may differentially emphasize particular emotions, intensity of emotional expression, and the ways in which emotions is expressed. For example, some evidence has suggested that Eskimos seldom display anger (Briggs, 1970).

Rogler, Cortes, and Malgady (1991) have called attention to another methodological issue that can affect the diagnosis of mental health. Researchers, in deciding what measures to use to determine mental health, tend to use "etic" classifications. These are broad taxonomies of mental health that tend to ignore unique domains of the patient's culture, which can influence how symptoms are interpreted and treated. "Emic" classifications, on the other hand, would reflect forms of psychological distress specific to a cultural group – for example, expressions of anger if one were an Eskimo. When researchers privilege the etic over the emic, they may fall prey to the tendency of categorically applying a classification of malady that is developed for one culture to another culture.

Several studies have found that there are differences between Blacks and Whites in the type and quantity of symptoms displayed for both depression and schizophrenia (Williams & Fenton, 1994). At the present time, we do not know how generalizable this problem is, but it is likely that the standard measures of mental health may not appropriately fit all of the racial and ethnic subgroups that make up America's multiracial diversity (Rogler et al., 1991). The literature also describes several examples of how culture affects the assessment of mental health status for Hispanics. Studies have revealed that the assessment of mental health status of Puerto Ricans often confounds beliefs in spiritualism with psychotic symptoms (Guarnaccia, 1992). Similarly, cultural adaptations were made to the DIS for the assessment of several disorders (i.e., obsessive-compulsive disorder, psychosexual dysfunction, dysthymia, and cognitive impairment) in Puerto Rico (Canino et al., 1987).

An effective research strategy is the use of in-depth cognitive interviewing to assess the extent to which there might be subgroup differences in the understanding and interpretation of questions. Cognitive interviewing techniques are designed to identify the extent of variation in comprehension and other cognitive processes, such as the response editing of sensitive questions, that survey respondents use when answering standardized questions (Forsyth & Lessler, 1991). If racial groups belong to different subcultures, a single approach to eliciting symptoms could be insensitive to cultural nuances and lead to significant response errors. Cognitive interviewing has not yet been systematically applied to the examination of potential racial differences in answering questions in standardized psychiatric diagnostic interviews.

The problem of misdiagnosis may be exacerbated when sociocultural distance between clients and patients is combined with racial bias (Adebimpe, 2004). The misdiagnosis of major psychotic illnesses and psychological distress in racial and ethnic minorities has been addressed by a number of researchers (Lum, 1995; Neighbors et al., 2003). In a review of the literature pertaining to the diagnosis and treatment of African American patients in the mental health system, Worthington (1992) reported that the misdiagnosis of Black patients is common. Loring and Powell (1988) investigated the objectivity of psychiatric diagnosis using the formal diagnostic criteria of the DSM-III. They presented two case studies of undifferentiated schizophrenia to a random sample of psychiatrists. This study found that, even in the face of unambiguous diagnostic criteria, diagnosis was related to the race and sex of the client and the race and sex of the clinician. For example, both Black male and female psychiatrists tended to give the least severe diagnosis to White male patients. The most severe labels of psychopathology tended to be given to Black patients, for whom ascriptions of violence, suspiciousness, and dangerousness were often made, even though the case studies of the Black men were identical to those for the White men. Instructively, Black and Hispanic psychiatrists also misdiagnosed or failed to correct the misdiagnosis of minority patients (Loring & Powell, 1988; Mukherjee et al., 1983). Thus, skin color match per se between the client and the clinician may not overcome deeply entrenched stereotypes and norms of medical practice.

The Social Context of Minority Mental Health

Greater attention to understanding what racial categories measure can lead to the development of research agendas that shed light on the distribution of diseases across social groups. Williams (1997a) emphasized that research that will enhance our understanding of racial differences in mental health must seek to identify the ways in which social, economic, political, and cultural factors, as well as racism and the migration experience, shape the experiences of minority populations in ways that can adversely affect their mental health status.

Socioeconomic Status

SES is one of the strongest known determinants of variations in health status, both in developed countries and in the developing world (Williams & Collins, 1995). There is also a well-established pattern of variations in mental health status by SES (Kessler et al., 1994). For example, in the ECA data, low-SES persons tended to have rates of psychiatric illness that were twice as high as those of high-SES persons (Holzer et al., 1986). Race is strongly associated with SES, with American Indians, Hispanics, Blacks, and certain subgroups of the Asian and Pacific Islander population having lower levels of multiple indicators of SES than the White population (Williams, 2005). Accordingly, adjusting racial differences in mental health status for SES sometimes eliminates but always substantially reduces these differences. This pattern has been consistently found for Black/White differences in psychological distress (Neighbors, 1984) and for the higher rates of schizophrenia for Blacks, compared to Whites, in the ECA data (Robins & Regier, 1991). Lower levels of SES can lead to greater exposures to stress (Kessler, 1979), as well as higher levels of alienation and powerlessness (Mirowsky & Ross, 1989b). Moreover, SES also predicted variations in mental health status within racial groups (Williams et al., 1992b).

There is growing recognition that the relationship between race and SES is neither simple nor straightforward. Kessler and Neighbors (1986) reanalyzed data from eight epidemiological surveys and showed that there was a robust interaction between race and SES. That is, although adjustment for SES tends to reduce elevated Black levels of psychological distress to nonsignificance, low-SES Blacks had higher rates of psychological distress than low-SES Whites. A similar pattern has been found in other studies, but the findings are not uniform (Nuru-Jeter, Williams, & LaVeist, 2008). Analyses of the ECA data suggested that the association between race and SES also importantly varied by gender (Williams et al., 1992b). Among women, low-SES Black females had higher rates of alcohol and drug abuse disorders than their White counterparts. However, surprisingly, low-SES White males had *higher* rates of psychiatric disorder than their low-SES Black counterparts.

The health literature has also been giving increasing attention to the nonequivalence of SES measures across racial groups. There are racial differences in the quality of education, income returns for a given level of education, wealth or assets associated with a given level of income, the purchasing power of income, the stability of employment, and the health risks associated with occupational status (Williams & Collins, 1995). The literature has also emphasized that SES is not just a confounder of the relationship between race and mental health, but is part of the causal pathway by which race affects health status (Cooper & David, 1986). That is, race is antecedent to SES, and SES differences between the races reflect, in part, the impact of economic discrimination produced by large-scale societal structures. Measurements of SES also have considerable error, and continuing efforts are needed to identify all of the relevant aspects of position in social structure that might be linked to health status (Krieger, Williams, & Moss, 1997).

Racism

Understanding the social contexts of minority populations will require increased attention to the ways in which racism affects health (Ahmed, Mohammed, & Williams, 2007; Jones, 2000; Williams & Whitfield, 2004). We use the term *racism* to include ideologies of superiority, negative attitudes and beliefs about outgroups, and differential treatment of members of those groups by both individuals and societal institutions. There is growing attention to the pervasiveness and persistence of racial discrimination in the United States (Blank & Dabady, 2004; Fix & Struyk, 1993). Descriptions of these experiences have suggested that they incorporate important elements of stressful situations that are known to adversely affect mental health status (Essed, 1991; Feagin, 1991). The literature on the health of the Black population has long indicated that prejudice and discrimination can adversely affect Black health (McCarthy & Yancey, 1971). It has been argued that racial discrimination is an important part of the stressful life experiences of minority group members that are not captured by the traditional scales used to assess stress (Williams, Neighbors, & Jackson, 2003).

In recent years there has been an explosion of research on the relationship between experiences of discrimination and health (Krieger, 1999; Paradies, 2006; Williams et al., 2003). For example, a recent review found that between 2005 and 2007, there were 115 published studies in the PubMed database that examined the association between discrimination and health (Williams & Mohammed, 2009). Instructively, mental health status was the most frequently used health outcome, and virtually every study found an inverse relationship between discrimination and mental health. Several patterns are noteworthy in the research in discrimination and health (Williams & Mohammed, 2009). First, most early studies were U.S.-based and disproportionately focused on the African American experience. Recent studies have focused on every major racial group in the United States, immigrant groups in most European countries, and racial minority groups in Canada, New Zealand, South Africa and Australia. Second, a broad range of mental health outcomes have been considered, ranging from common psychiatric disorders and schizophrenia to cognitive impairment, daily moods, and burnout. Third, there is a small but slowly increasing number of prospective studies that link perceptions of discrimination to changes in mental health status. Fourth, a growing number of studies indicate that discrimination remains related to health even after adjustment for potentially confounding psychological characteristics such as social desirability bias and negative affect. Finally, several studies reveal that discrimination can adversely affect physical and mental health by increasing the likelihood of risk-taking behaviors such as legal and illegal substance use and by altering health-care-seeking and adherence behaviors. Future research in minority mental health status must give more serious and sustained research attention to categorizing exposure to discrimination and patterns of response and systematically assessing their implications for mental health status.

The literature also suggests that the internalization of racist beliefs within the larger culture can lead to negative self-evaluations that can adversely affect psychological well-being. Research by Taylor and colleagues (Taylor & Jackson, 1990, 1991) found a positive association between internalized racism (belief in the innate inferiority of Blacks and feeling uncomfortable around other Blacks) and alcohol consumption and psychological distress among African Americans. Williams-Morris (1996) has outlined a number of ways in which racism in the larger culture can adversely affect the psychological development of minority children. She indicated that a potential role of racism is implicit in most of the major theoretical models in developmental psychology and outlined a research agenda in that area.

Coping Processes and Resources

Minority racial status can capture not only differential exposure to stress but also variations in coping processes and in resources to cope with stress. A range of social and psychological factors have emerged as risk factors for health status or can reduce levels of stress or the adverse consequences of stress on mental health. These psychosocial variables include self-esteem, social support, perceptions of mastery or control, anger or hostility, feelings of helplessness or hopelessness, and the repression or denial of emotions (Kessler, House, Anspach, & Williams, et al., 1995). The literature clearly documents that the distribution of most of these risk factors varies by SES and race (Mirowsky & Ross, 1989; Williams, 1990), but few attempts have been made to systematically explore how psychosocial risks and resources relate to race and combine with environmental constraints to affect mental health. The literature also indicates that there is a need to pay greater attention to the health-enhancing cultural resources that minority group members have that may shield them from some of the adverse consequences of stress (Rogler, Malgady, & Rodriguez, 1989; Williams & Fenton, 1994). It has been suggested that a broad range of cultural resources, including family support and religious involvement, may play an important role in buffering minority populations from the negative effects of stress. However, the processes and mechanisms through which these resources operate to affect mental health status are not well understood.

Analyses of the Detroit Area Study data highlight the importance of understanding coping processes and testing for interactions among the predictors of mental health status. In this study, for both measures of mental health status (psychological distress and psychological well-being), the mental health of Blacks was better than that of Whites once adjustment was made for discrimination and stress (Williams et al., 1997). This pattern is consistent with the notion that these stressful experiences may more adversely affect the health of Whites than of Blacks. A review noted that for a number of child and infant health outcomes, although Blacks were more exposed to adverse risk factors, these factors had a larger impact on the health status of Whites than of Blacks (Williams & Collins, 1995). Kessler (1979) documented a similar pattern for the relationship between stressful life events and psychological distress for non-Whites (mainly Blacks) and low-SES persons. Both of these economically disadvantaged groups were more exposed to stress. However, compared to non-Whites and low-SES individuals, comparable stressful events more adversely affected the mental health of Whites and high-SES persons, respectively. Kessler (1979) suggested some possible reasons for this relative advantage. First, because of earlier or more frequent exposure to adversity, African Americans could become more accustomed to dealing with stress, such that a new stressful experience has less of an impact. Second, compared to Whites, African Americans may respond to stress with greater emotional flexibility (that is, emotional expression), which may facilitate recovery. In addition, African Americans may have greater access than Caucasians to other coping resources, such as religious involvement, that some have argued may importantly reduce the negative effects of stress (Williams & Fenton, 1994).

Migration/Acculturation

The migration experience is a salient characteristic of the lives of many minority populations and may be an important influence on the level of mental health problems within these groups. However, despite numerous studies on this topic, our understanding of the ways in which acculturation/migration affects mental health status is still modest (Rogler et al., 1991). Several studies of Asian American students have found an inverse relationship between length of time in the United States and levels of psychological distress (Sue et al., 1995). Similar findings also came from probability samples of Asian populations (Sue et al., 1995). Other studies of nonrefugee immigrants showed that the most significant risk factors for mental health are the stressors associated with migration (Furnham & Shiekh, 1993; Lum, 1995). These stresses include feelings of isolation from peers and the challenges of economic survival in an unfamiliar socioeconomic system and acquiring a new language. The new immigrant must also learn new behavioral norms and values of the host country.

In the Los Angeles site of the ECA, rates of depression were lower for immigrant Mexicans than U.S.-born Mexican Americans (Burnam et al., 1987). In contrast, Puerto Ricans in New York seemed to have higher levels of depressive symptoms than island Puerto Ricans (Vega & Rumbaut, 1991). In an analysis of the literature on acculturation and mental health among Hispanics, Rogler et al. (1991) reviewed the results of 30 studies (published since 1960) on the subject. The authors found that of the studies that were examined, 12 showed a negative relationship – that is, individuals who were low in acculturation (i.e., not fully integrated into the host society) were more prone to suffer from low self-esteem and lack of psychological well-being. Thirteen studies reported a positive relationship between acculturation and mental health. Individuals who became more and more integrated into the new society experienced greater psychological strain in the forms of self-depreciation or self-hatred and isolation from traditional support systems. In three studies, a curvilinear relationship was found. Good mental health was a product of the ability to obtain a balance between traditional cultural norms and the host country's norms and values. As one moved away from this place of equilibrium toward either acculturation extremes, psychological distress increased (Rogler et al., 1991).

Table 14.4. *Lifetime and past-year rates of psychiatric disorders for U.S. immigrants*

	Caribbean Blacks[a]		Latinos[b]		Asians[c]	
	Lifetime (%)	Past-year (%)	Lifetime (%)	Past-year (%)	Lifetime (%)	Past-year (%)
Gender						
Male	31.10	19.97	28.14	13.47	17.18	8.44
Female	24.56	12.70	30.23	17.40	17.43	9.87
Nativity						
U.S. born	43.11	25.60	36.77	18.57	24.62	13.22
Foreign born	19.37	11.05	23.76	13.12	15.16	8.00
Generation						
First	19.36	11.05	23.76	13.12	15.16	8.00
Second	35.27	22.31	30.12	15.11	23.97	13.92
Third or later	54.64	30.45	43.39	21.80	25.58	12.19

Source: Caribbean Blacks, Williams et al. (2007); Latinos, Alegría et al. (2007); Asians, Takeuchi et al. (2007).

When migration is coupled with refugee status, further implications exist for mental health. Using the Vietnamese Depression Scale, a prospective study of 467 adult refugees who sought health care in 10 public health clinics in four states revealed a 20% prevalence rate for depression (Buchwald et al., 1993). Another study of 322 refugees at a psychiatric clinic reported that 70% of their Southeast Asian refugee patient sample met the criteria for current posttraumatic stress disorder (PTSD) and that 82% of these individuals experienced the most common symptom of PTSD – depression (Kinzie et al., 1990). What is striking about this study is that most of the individuals who were assessed had experienced the trauma more than a decade prior to the assessment. High rates of refugee trauma were also found in Southeast Asian refugee populations outside of the United States. The Harvard Program in Refugee Trauma assessed the mental status of displaced Cambodians living on the Thailand-Cambodia border. Using a household survey of 993 randomly selected adults, they found a prevalence rate of 55% depression and 15% PTSD (Mollica et al., 1993).

Data from the recent CPES studies also provide a previously unavailable glimpse of the association between migration history and status variables with mental health for Black, Hispanic, and Asian immigrant populations. Three patterns are noteworthy in Table 14.4. First, among Black Caribbean immigrants, men have higher rates of lifetime and past-year disorders than women. A similar pattern is not evident for Asians or Latinos. It may be that migration and its consequences may be gendered for Caribbean immigrants in ways that have mental health consequences (Williams, Gonzalez, et al., 2007; Williams, Haile, et al., 2007). Specifically, Black

Caribbean men who were socialized in societies that were more patriarchal than the United States may confront the unique stressors of thwarted aspirations linked to coping with the personal challenges of socioeconomic mobility in the United States, as well as with the stress generated by coping with the new social and economic freedoms that Black Caribbean women enjoy in the new society, which spill over into the domestic sphere.

Second, for all groups, there are striking variations in mental health risk by nativity status, with immigrants reporting lower rates of disorder than their native-born peers. Third, for all groups, increasing exposure to American society as captured by generational status is associated with increasing mental health risk. The differences between the second and third generation in the prevalence of mental disorders are small for Asians but substantial for Hispanics and especially for Caribbean Blacks. Hispanic and Caribbean Black immigrants arrive in the United States with lower levels of SES than many Asian immigrant groups and may face greater challenges with socioeconomic mobility (Williams, 2005). Future research needs to carefully delineate the factors that are responsible for this downward trajectory in mental health status that is associated with increasing exposure to U.S. society.

Conclusion

One of the most critical issues in the study of the mental health of minority populations in the United States is the identification of the extent to which minority status itself is a predictor of increased risk for mental health problems (Vega & Rumbaut, 1991; Williams & Fenton, 1994). Such research is contingent on the delineation of the specific factors linked to race that influence health status. Challenges deriving from the adaptation to mainstream American culture and socioeconomic disadvantage can lead minority group members to experience high levels of stressful experiences that could adversely affect health. Recent research reveals that comprehensive measures of stress account for substantially more variability in mental health status than previous studies of life events and chronic stressors (Turner et al., 1995). Future research must characterize this full range of stress variables for minority populations and identify how they combine with stressors (such as residence in deprived geographic areas and racial discrimination) that may be unique to, or more prevalent among, racial minority populations to affect their mental health. An enhanced understanding of the role of the larger social environment in mental health requires integrative models that examine how stress in the larger environment develops over the life course and combines with appraisal processes, emotional states, and behavioral, psychological, and physiological responses and vulnerabilities, in additive and interactive ways, to affect mental health.

15

African American Women and Mental Well-Being: The Triangulation of Race, Gender, and Socioeconomic Status

Verna M. Keith and Diane R. Brown

Keith and Brown present a conceptual model for understanding the way in which the interrelationships among race, gender, and socioeconomic status (SES) influence mental well-being for African American women. Mental well-being is affected by social, cultural, and psychological factors as well as by physical health and health behavior; in turn these factors are influenced by one's social status (i.e., race, gender, SES). African American women are subject to both racism and sexism, which diminish their educational attainment, personal and household incomes, occupational status, wealth accumulation, and opportunities for socioeconomic advancement. Consequently, African American women have fewer resources than their White counterparts and are far more limited in their capacity to cope with crises and adversities. Stressors such as poverty and economic hardship also challenge the adaptive abilities of many African American women. They are less likely to be married and, if they are married, more likely to be employed and responsible for more household chores than White married women. Parenthood often is another source of stress as many African American women are single parents. The particular set of roles that African American women must fulfill may also expose them to more stressful life circumstances. Combining employment and parenthood roles increases the likelihood that they will experience role overload and role conflict, especially when coping resources are limited. A key argument made by Keith and Brown is that there is a strong connection between mental and physical health. African American women have poorer physical health with higher rates of diabetes, hypertension, HIV infection, and lupus, which lead to higher mortality rates than White women. Additionally, African American women are less likely to use health care, which may be due to a lack of access. However, the extended social networks of African American women may provide important sources of social support. What other types of social support would help African American women cope with the many sources of stress in their lives?

Introduction

African American women are disproportionately challenged by a host of social conditions that are linked to higher risk for poor mental health, including low incomes, high levels of poverty and unemployment, single motherhood, poor physical health, and residence in economically disadvantaged neighborhoods where these problems are compounded (Murry et al., 2008; Schulz et al., 2000). Yet, even in the face of such overwhelming threats to their emotional well-being, African American women are remarkably resilient, with research revealing a complex portrait of mental health advantages and disadvantages relative to other race and gender groups. These complexities are illustrated by a few examples drawn from our analysis of data from the National Comorbidity Study Replication (NCS-R), a survey designed to evaluate the prevalence and correlates of mental disorders in the United States (see Kessler & Merikangas, 2004). On the one hand, the percentage of African American women who have experienced a major mental disorder at some point in their lives is similar to that of African American men, but lower than the percentages for White men and women. An examination of specific disorders also shows that African American women report lower lifetime prevalence of major depressive disorder and drug and alcohol disorders than White women. On the other hand, data from the NCS-R indicate that African American women are more likely to have experienced a mental disorder in the past year than either Black men or Whites, and they have higher rates of posttraumatic stress disorder (PTSD) than White women. Further, most studies have found that, compared to men of both races and White women, African American women have lower life satisfaction and are more likely to exhibit general psychological distress and depressive symptoms that do not meet the criteria for a diagnosis of mental disorder (Brown & Keith, 2003; Bratter & Eschbach, 2005). These patterns of similarities and differences point to an amalgamation of strengths and vulnerabilities that culminate in a differential risk profile for African American women's mental well-being that requires explanatory models specific to them.

This chapter presents a discussion of societal factors that affect mental health and illness among African American women, which we contend are more salient than biological or genetic factors. The discussion is guided by the diagram depicted in Figure 15.1, which illustrates that structural location as defined by the triangulation of race, gender, and class can influence mental well-being directly or indirectly by impinging on other more proximate processes. As used here, the term *mental well-being* refers to the full array of mental states, ranging from indicators of mental health such as life satisfaction to mental illnesses/disorders such as major depression (see Chapter 7 in this volume).

The Primacy of Race, Gender, and Class

Race, gender, and class converge in the lives of African American women to create a unique set of circumstances that shape their emotional well-being. In American society, being Black and female is less valued than being White and male. Simultaneously occupying two devalued statuses influences how African American women see themselves, how they are perceived by others, and how others respond to them. African American women are often viewed by the larger

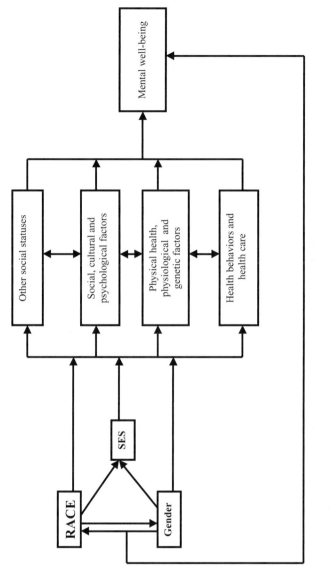

Figure 15.1. Conceptual framework of African American women's mental well-being. *Source*: Brown & Keith (2003).

American women fell below the poverty line, compared to only 20.4% of families headed by White women (U.S. Census Bureau, 2004d). For many African American women, daily life is a continuous struggle to supply such basic necessities as food and shelter. Poverty and low income increase the likelihood that African American women will also be exposed to *classism*, or prejudice and discrimination against the poor. Work by Russell (1996) indicated that the devaluation and stigmatization associated with classism can potentially affect the mental well-being of African American women by further undermining their self-concept and their relationship with others. Moreover, social class hierarchies within the Black community leave many poor African American women, especially mothers, isolated from cross-class interactions and communal support. Classism, along with racism and sexism, can have a devastating impact on the lives of African American women.

As shown in Figure 15.1, the triangulation of race, gender, and SES is a primary factor that is critical to African American women's well-being. Each system of inequality may operate independently to affect well-being, but their combined effects are more powerful. Further, these intersecting social forces may affect African American women's mental well-being indirectly though several pathways: (1) other social statuses; (2) social, cultural, and psychological factors; (3) physical health and biological and genetic factors; and (4) health behaviors and health care.

Other Social Statuses: Age, Marriage, Parenthood, and Employment

The mental well-being of African American women varies by age, marital status, household headship, parenthood, and employment. Although some studies have shown that depressive symptoms are more prevalent among younger adults than midlife adults and those just entering old age, depression increases at ages 70 and older (George, 1999). These findings may reflect the differing challenges faced across the life course, along with changes in sociocultural context and SES that occur over time. Younger women are heavily involved in balancing the demands of intimate relationships, childbearing and child rearing, and establishing careers or stable employment. Many midlife women and the "young elderly" may be at a point where children have left the home, they are in reasonably good health, have reached a point of economic stability, and have developed effective strategies for coping with a host of problematic life circumstances. As African American women age, however, they must confront declining physical health, loss of independence, and another form of discrimination – ageism.

Marriage, a highly valued status in American society, generally brings emotional, instrumental, and economic forms of support, which are beneficial to the mental health of African American women (Brown, 1996; Tucker, 2003). African

American women are less likely to marry than White women, and if ever married, they are more likely to be divorced or widowed. In 2004, 30.3% of African American women aged 15 and older were married, compared to 55.3% of White women (U.S. Census Bureau, 2004e). Further, 42.5% of African American women were never married, 9.2% were widowed, and 18% were separated or divorced. Among White women, 21.5% were never married, 10.4% were widowed, and 12.8% were separated or divorced. Major factors contributing to lower marriage rates among African American women are Black male joblessness, incarceration, and economic marginality (Harknett & McLanahan, 2004; Tucker, 2003), circumstances that in large part derive from the racial discrimination experienced by Black men. More than other ethnic groups, African American men and women believe that economic stability is critical for marital success (Haynes, 2000; Tucker & Mitchell-Kernan, 1995), and many opt for alternative domestic arrangements that result in fewer resources with which to deal with life problems (Miller & Browning, 2000). In particular, Black men's lack of adequate finances may strain relationship quality and lead to separation and divorce. Even among married women, the benefits of marriage may not be the same as they are for White women. More likely to be employed than married White women, Black women still perform most of the traditional chores of cooking and cleaning and are more likely to feel overworked than men (Broman, 1988). Most important, African American women must cope with the effects of racism on their husbands' earning ability and mental well-being, sometimes at the cost of their own (Beauboeuf-Lafontant, 2007).

Parenthood can be psychologically challenging for African American women in large part because they are more likely than White women to be mothers, to be raising children without men, and to be doing so under financially stressful conditions (Page & Steven, 2005). In 2003, the birth rate for African American women aged 15 to 44 was 15.7 per 1,000, but only 13.6 per 1,000 for White women (Martin, Hamilton, et al., 2005). Among unmarried women, the birth rates were 67.8 per 1,000 African American women and 30.1 per 1,000 for White women. Some non-marital births occur in cohabiting unions, but such births are less likely among young Black women (Schoen, Landale, & Daniels, 2007). Single mothers who head households must assume primary responsibility for meeting all household needs, including housing, food, clothing, and transportation, as well as ministering to the emotional and nurturing needs of household members. According to the U.S. Census Bureau (2004f), in 2004 African American women householders constituted approximately 44.7% of the total number of Black family households. In contrast, White women householders with no spouse present constituted approximately 13.2% of the total White family households. On average, the households headed by Black women are larger and often multigenerational, so that they may include minor children, sometimes adult children as well as older adults, and often nonrelatives or pseudo-kin. Among female householders with no spouse present, 59.7% of households headed by African American women had three or more members in comparison to 45.2% of those headed by Whites (U.S. Bureau of the Census, 2004g).

Being employed outside the home is essential to maintaining African American women's mental well-being as well as their family's quality of life, particularly because Black women are often the major breadwinners in their households, whether or not there are spouses or partners living with them. Historically, African American women have been more likely to engage in paid work than White women, but as the economy has shifted from manufacturing to services, Black–White differences have narrowed. Among women in the labor force in 2004, 55.5% of African American women were employed compared to 56.1% of White women (U.S. Department of Labor, Bureau of Labor Statistics, 2005). In contrast to these employment figures, unemployment was higher among African American women (9.8%) than for White women (4.7%). These unemployment figures reflect racial and gender dynamics in the labor force that make maintaining gainful employment more difficult for African American women. In her longitudinal analysis of labor force dynamics among women, Reid (2002) found that African American women left full-time employment at a higher rate than White women because they were more likely to be laid off, to work in seasonal or temporary jobs, and to specify other reasons for leaving work, including low wages, poor work conditions, and to obtain better jobs. Kennelly's (1999) analysis of data from employers surveyed in the Atlanta area documented that stereotyping of all Black working-class women as single mothers had negative effects on hiring practices and evaluations of job performance. Given that younger cohorts of working-class African American women have less labor market experience relative to younger White and Hispanic women, attaining stable employment and wages may become even more problematic in the future (Alon & Haberfeld, 2007).

Social, Cultural, and Psychological Influences: Life Stressors and Coping Resources

Any number of social, cultural, and psychological factors may enhance or diminish mental well-being. Among the social factors that diminish well-being among African American women are stressors resulting from the triangulation of racism, sexism, and low SES (Allen & Britt, 1983; Schulz, Gravlee, et al., 2006). Stressors such as poverty and economic hardship challenge the adaptive abilities of many African American women. The particular set of roles that African American women must fulfill may also expose them to more stressful life circumstances. Combining employment and parenthood roles increases the likelihood that they will experience role overload and role conflict, especially when coping resources are limited. A nontrivial number of African American women hold demanding jobs, are raising children without the support of the father, and are engaged in multiple caregiving roles for grandchildren, aging relatives, adult children, and other kin who may be unemployed, ill, or disabled. Consequently, these women are at high risk for role overload. Discrimination or unfair treatment at the interpersonal level is another stressor that is heavily implicated in African American women's well-being (Ryff, Keyes, & Hughes, 2003). Whether these encounters constitute major events such as being denied a bank loan or chronic, everyday events like being treated with less courtesy or respect, personal discrimination undermines mental well-being (Schulz, Gravlee, et al., 2006; Schulz, Israel, et al., 2006).

It is important to note that upwardly mobile and middle-class African American women are not exempted from exposure to stressors and strains, although certainly possessing greater economic resources provides them with some protection. Professional African Americans, both female and male, experience a myriad of strains and frustrations, including underemployment in which their skills are underutilized and concentration in jobs that are expendable because they primarily provide services to Blacks and other minority clients (Collins, 1997). Tokenism, the stress associated with being the only or one of a few African Americans in a work setting, can result in heightened pressure to perform and the expenditure of energy to combat negative stereotypes (Jackson & Stewart, 2003). As noted previously, African American women in the corporate sector are especially likely to experience the isolation that comes from tokenism, given their small numbers and the absence of collegial support. Notable also is that professional and middle-class African American women are strained from the marginality that results from being split between African American and Euro-American culture. Many African American women experience a profound schism between their professional lives and their personal lives and may be treated with suspicion and be rejected by less affluent African Americans (Chisholm, 1996; Jackson & Stewart, 2003).

Residential and physical environments are additional social influences on the mental well-being of African American women. The combination of race, gender, and low SES tends to circumscribe the choice of residential settings available to them, increasing the likelihood that they will reside in economically deprived rural areas or in equally deprived inner-city, segregated neighborhoods characterized by substandard housing, inadequate services, poor quality schools, and threats to personal safety. Residents in such locales are exposed to acute and chronic stressors that diminish optimal mental well-being as well as physical health (Cutrona et al., 2000; Hill, Ross, & Angel, 2005). Living in substandard housing is associated with exposure to environmental hazards such as asbestos insulation, lead poisoning, pest infestation, and adverse health effects from housing decay, inadequate ventilation, air and noise pollution, and faulty heating, wiring, and plumbing systems (Zsembik, 1995). These socially and economically deprived physical environments offer African American women limited access to jobs, transportation, grocery stores, health care, and other goods and services. Poor inner-city neighborhoods offer few if any recreational and cultural amenities such as the parks, playgrounds, fountains, jogging and bicycle paths, libraries, museums, and arboretums that are available in more affluent neighborhoods (Zsembik, 1995). Even when such amenities exist, they are often not well maintained or safe, given higher rates of crime in inner-city neighborhoods. Moreover, even African American middle-class women are more likely to live in highly segregated, poor neighborhoods than White or other women (Pattillo-McCoy, 1999).

Racism, sexism, and classism also contribute to increasing African American women's vulnerability to sexual harassment (Hine, 1995; Wyatt & Riederle, 1995), domestic violence, sexual assault, and physical injuries (Marsh, 1993; Leigh & Lindquist, 1999). They are more likely than White women to find themselves in life-threatening situations where they are the victims of homicide (Stevens et al., 1999). African American women are often the victims of the internalized rage of Black men against their own mistreatment. This violence has resulted in the highest reported spousal homicide rates to be those against Black women. According to Leigh and Lindquist (1999), African American women often are unwilling to call the police for fear that the police will brutalize the men who have battered them. Keeping silent about the violence perpetrated on them undermines African American women's emotional well-being, perhaps as much as the violence itself (Barbee, 2003).

The cultural values, beliefs, and practices that undergird the Black community can have a positive or negative impact on the mental well-being of African American women. Culture influences one's perceptions of the world, shapes interpretations of life experiences, and affects responses to stressors. It also provides a sense of identity, along with norms and customs pertaining to social interaction. Given the historical background of African Americans in the United States, African American culture is an amalgamation of an African heritage and Euro-American culture, among other influences. However, there is also great cultural diversity among African Americans (V. Green, 1978; Williams, Lavizzo-Mourey, & Warren, 1994). The cultural background of contemporary African Americans represents nearly every region of the globe from Africa, Europe, the Caribbean, to South America, as well as varying degrees of urbanicity (urban, small city, rural) and regional locations within the United States (north, south, east, and west). Although aspects of culture at times may be a powerful source for promoting mental well-being, at other times and under other circumstances aspects of culture can be detrimental. A few examples make this differential impact clear.

Involvement in extended family and friendship networks is among the characteristics of African American culture that can enhance the mental well-being of African American women (Akbar, 1991). Sharing close personal relationships with kin, friends, and co-workers provides opportunities to receive social support and to derive satisfaction from giving support to others (Brown & Monye, 1995; Lawton et al., 1992). Extended family and friends have traditionally provided African American women with the emotional and material resources needed to cope with family, job, and other demands. These networks of kin and pseudo-kin play especially critical roles in relieving the work and family role strain of young or poor women (Billingsley, 1992) and in caring for older women when they become ill and are no longer able to manage day-to-day activities (Dilworth-Anderson, Williams, & Gibson, 2002). Changing demographics and economic opportunities in African American communities are raising questions whether the extended family will continue to fulfill its traditional support functions (Benin & Keith, 1995). Especially notable is the declining extended family child care, even among families headed by single African American women (Brewster & Padavic, 2002).

African American women's spirituality and involvement in religious and community organizations are additional positive cultural influences on their mental well-being. African American women have high levels of church attendance (Fitchett et al., 2007), and involvement in church activities has traditionally been linked to their participation in civil rights, neighborhood, community action, political, and economic organizations (Gilkes, 2000). Participation in voluntary organizations has been a source of empowerment that has helped them combat the oppression associated with race, gender, and poverty (Collins, 2000). Like the extended family, church membership is an important source of emotional support and facilitates the exchange of goods and services (R. J. Taylor, Chatters, & Levin, 2004). Further, both church and nonchurched African American women use prayer and bible reading to effectively cope with a variety of stressors, including chronic poverty, illness, caregiving, and neighborhood problems (R. J. Taylor et al., 2004). Praying and reading religious material are thought to have positive effects on mental health by fostering emotions such as hope and forgiveness.

However, some features of African American culture can be sources of distress for African American women. On the one hand, family and friend relationships can be positive and supportive, making one feel loved and cared for. On the other hand, they can be demanding and a source of strain that is detrimental to mental well-being (Lincoln, Chatters, & Taylor, 2003; Okun & Keith, 1998). Involvement with family members can be particularly stressful if they have chronic, financial, physical, or emotional problems. Problematic relationships with family members may take a particularly heavy emotional toll on African American women, who appear to be much more deeply embedded in social networks than are African American men.

African American cultural stereotypes and socialization practices may also affect African American women's perceptions and expectations of themselves. Socialized differently than White women (Ladner, 1972), they are expected to be mothers, to be independent, to be caregivers, and to assume all manner of extended-family obligations. Although the enactment of multiple roles may serve as positive influences on the mental well-being of many African American women, it may have deleterious effects for others. Beauboeuf-Lafontant (2007) has argued that the cultural image of the "strong Black woman" has served to establish a highly valued ideal that poses an alternative to the denigrating stereotypes generated by the larger society and a feminine norm that stands in direct contrast to that of White women as weak and delicate. Many African American women, however, cannot live up to the ideal, or they do so at the expense of their mental well-being. Her interviews with African American women revealed that, in trying to live up to the strength mandate, they engage in a form of self-silencing whereby depression and distress go unrecognized or unvoiced or are not deemed legitimate by others.

An additional source of distress for African American women is the continuing social preferences in their communities and in the larger society for lighter skin color, long straight hair, and Eurocentric facial features (Hunter, 2005). Arguably the social value given to the beauty of "Blackness" is greater now than in the past, but African American women are still confronted with Euro-American standards of beauty (St. Jean & Feagin, 1998). Greene, White, and Whitten (2000) noted that excessive concern with length and texture of hair, especially among young African American girls, may have negative consequences for social adjustment. For African American women of all ages, hair and skin color are linked to complex social, political, and economic issues that impinge on their self-esteem, perceived attractiveness, life satisfaction, and overall quality of life (Hunter, 2005; M. S. Thompson & Keith, 2001).

Physical Health and Mental Well-Being

The conceptual framework presented in Figure 15.1 also contends that there are substantial interactions between physical health and mental well-being. Poor health can be emotionally upsetting, especially if the condition is disabling or life threatening or requires a drastic change in lifestyle. Some research has shown that physical illness is accompanied by anxiety (C. L. Cohen et al., 2006) as well as by depressive symptoms (Furner et al., 2006). African American women have poorer health than White women (D. R. Williams, 2002), and it is also likely that their mental health is more affected by their poorer health status. For example, chronic diseases such as hypertension, diabetes, HIV/AIDS, and lupus are more prevalent among African American than White women (Leigh & Lindquist, 1999; National Center for Health Statistics [NCHS], 2007). With higher death rates from heart disease, cancer, stroke, AIDS, and diabetes, African Americans women have an overall mortality rate that is 30% higher than the rate for White women, and they live 4.3 fewer years on average (NCHS, 2007).

Geronimus coined the term "weathering" to suggest that African American women's excessive disease rates reflect a faster aging process that stems from the cumulative burden of social and economic adversities (Geronimus et al., 2006). She and her colleagues tested the weathering hypothesis by calculating allostatic load, a health measure that includes physiological risk factors for chronic disease such as blood pressure, cholesterol, and various other biological markers obtained from blood samples. Allostatic load is thought to capture the body's reaction to stressors. Their research revealed that, compared to Whites and African American men, poor African American women had the highest allostatic load scores followed by nonpoor African American women. This study and others that noted higher disability among women suggested that African American women seem to carry a heavy disease burden despite their longer life expectancy relative to men.

In the face of physical illness and disability, African American women are much more likely than White women to continue working and fulfilling household responsibilities (D. R. Brown, 1988). An illustration of the multiple demands that many African American women face even when confronted with a life-threatening illness came from a focus group of women recently diagnosed with breast cancer. One participant said the following:

> Could not even think about it (breast cancer) because of taking care of my mother . . . there was just too much happening. It was a shock when I found out. . . . I was in denial. I can't believe this is happening. I'm taking care of too many people, you know . . . the grandkids . . . my mother, and I don't really even have the time.

Lipscomb and colleagues (2006) observed that African American women and other minority workers continue to work when ill or injured because they are overrepresented in jobs that have no or limited paid sick and vacation time. In addition, minority workers are more likely to have worker's compensation claims denied and to fear job loss after illness or injury.

The conceptual model presented in Figure 15.1 assumes that biological and genetic factors may potentially affect African American women's mental well-being. The relationship between biological or genetic factors and mental well-being is the subject of intense investigation. For example, researchers have identified genetic factors that predispose individuals to major depressive disorder (Malhi, Moore, & McGuffin, 2000). Studies have also linked genetic factors to antisocial behavior among women (Goldstein, Prescott, & Kendler, 2001), and the genetic epidemiology of Alzheimer's disease was shown to differ between African Americans and Whites (Froehlich, Bogardus, & Inouye, 2001). To date, however, there is no evidence that any biological or genetic factor is uniquely associated with the mental well-being of African American women. Further research is needed to determine the extent to which the interplay among race, gender, biology, and genetics affects mental well-being, with careful attention given to social and environmental effects on biology.

Health Behaviors and Access to Health Care

Figure 15.1 posits that health behaviors have implications for the mental well-being of African American women. Health-promoting behaviors such as getting enough regular exercise and eating a balanced, nutritious diet are generally assumed to have positive effects on mental health (Fox, 1999). Current research is documenting a negative association between obesity and mental health (Carpenter et al., 2000;

Roberts et al., 2003), although the causal sequence remains unclear. Findings from these investigations are particularly important for African American women, given their greater prevalence of obesity. According to the National Center for Health Statistics (2007), 51.6% of African American women aged 20 and older are obese, compared to 30.7% of White women. Baltrus and colleagues (2005) found that, in association with their lower childhood SES, African American women had greater body weight initially and gained more weight than men or White women over the 34-year time period of their study. Thompson (1996) contended that eating problems begin as survival strategies to cope with traumas stemming from sexual abuse, racism, classism, sexism, and poverty. Some writers have suggested that body size norms are more flexible and large body size is less stigmatized in African American culture (see Lovejoy, 2001), but others have found that concerns about weight and body image are distressing especially to African American girls (see Grandberg et al., 2008). Other lifestyle behaviors such as cigarette smoking, use of alcohol and illicit drugs, and engaging in risky sexual behavior may also impinge on the mental well-being of African American women. Although African American women are less likely to use alcohol and cigarettes and have a lower lifetime use of illicit drugs than White women (Wiemann, Berenson, & San Miguel, 1994), their use of these substances may help alleviate the distress associated with race, gender, and class oppression (Hummer, 1996; Leigh & Lindquist, 1999; Thompson, 1996). Health behaviors are not just a matter of individual preferences and choices but are also influenced by racism, sexism, socioeconomic instability, targeted marketing, education, and cultural values (F. Ahmed et al., 1994; Cooper & Simmons, 1985; Hummer, 1996).

Access to health care is critical for mental well-being because it contributes to healthier, longer lives (Hummer, 1996). Quality health care for African American women requires access and utilization of mental health services that are culturally appropriate and sensitive to the social context of their lives (Chisholm, 1996), as well as access and use of primary care. Indeed, primary care physicians often serve as the gatekeepers to mental health services, particularly in managed care organizations. Access to both primary care and mental health services may be restricted by lack of health insurance coverage. Even the insured may incur out-of-pocket expenses because of restrictions on services, especially mental health services. Additional barriers to mental health care for African American women include factors such as cultural beliefs, stigma, and lack of understanding of the nature and treatability of mental illness (U.S. Department of Health and Human Services, 2001).

Summary

The conceptual framework presented in this chapter provides a basis for linking what we know about the lives of African American women and research on mental well-being. The model emphasizes the primacy of race, gender, and SES and how these forces converge to transform more proximate influences on mental health. It recognizes that the various components combine in different ways for different African American women, encompassing their diversity. Some African American women are poor and some are middle class; some are mothers, but others are not. Despite this heterogeneity, the reality of race, gender, and SES means that they share many common experiences.

16

Marital Status and Mental Health

Kristi Williams, Adrianne Frech,
and Daniel L. Carlson

Williams, Frech, and Carlson examine the evidence for an effect of marital status on mental health, with a particular focus on the factors that identify who
benefits from marriage, who suffers from marital dissolution, and under what
circumstances. They evaluate three possible explanations for observed associations of marital status with mental health: (1) the marital resource model, (2) the
marital crisis model, and (3) selection bias. They conclude that the best recent
evidence suggests that, on average, entering marriage improves mental health and
exiting marriage undermines mental health, at least in the short run. However,
their central argument is that these average associations obscure a great deal of
heterogeneity in the experience of marriage and in its consequences for mental
health. The authors consider a range of individual, demographic, and relationship
characteristics that likely moderate the effect of marriage and marital dissolution on mental health. These include gender, marital quality, age/life course,
race/ethnicity, values and beliefs, and prior mental health. What other factors
likely influence whether marriage and divorce are beneficial, neutral, or harmful
for mental health? How might the impact of marriage and divorce on mental
health change with the times, particularly as alternative family forms become
more prevalent?

Introduction

A general consensus exists among social scientists and the public at large that marriage provides substantial benefits to mental health. For many years, this conclusion
was based on cross-sectional studies comparing the average mental health of the
married to that of the unmarried at a single point in time. This research clearly
showed that married individuals report lower average levels of depression, psychological distress, and psychiatric disorder and higher levels of life satisfaction and subjective well-being (see Umberson & Williams, 1999, and Waite &
Gallagher, 2000, for reviews) than the unmarried. The consistency and relatively
large magnitude of observed differences, as well as their persistence across time
and in numerous countries (Mastekaasa, 1994; Stack & Eshleman, 1998), led to
the conclusion that marriage improves mental health for most people.

Research findings about marital status differences in mental health strongly res-
onate with cultural views about the individual and societal importance of marriage.
Perhaps as a result, they are frequently heralded by the news media with headlines

This chapter was prepared with support from Grant R01 HD054866–01A1 from the National Institute
of Child Health and Human Development, National Institutes of Health.

like "Stressed Out? Say 'I Do'" (2005), "Lonely? Feeling Low? Try a walk . . . Down the Aisle" (2006), and "Feel Blue? Say 'I Do'" (2006). Such generalizations – both in the popular press and, to some extent, in the scientific literature – suggest that marriage is a panacea for a range of individual and societal ills. They also have real consequences for the lives of individuals. For example, social science research on average marital status differences in mental health is commonly cited in support of government policies that encourage disadvantaged single mothers to wed (Maher, 2005; Nock, 2005; Rector, Pardue, & Noyes, 2003). Further, some argue that the universality of marriage's mental health benefits is overstated, which contributes to the stigmatization of unmarried adults in the United States (DePaulo, 2006).

Despite these deeply ingrained beliefs about the importance of marriage for mental health, recent evidence suggests a more nuanced perspective. The emerging view among social scientists, based primarily on longitudinal research that follows a group of individuals over time, is that the often-cited benefits of marriage and the costs of marital dissolution are highly dependent on a range of individual and contextual factors. These associations also appear to vary depending on which group (divorced, widowed, never married) is compared to the married, how marital status and living arrangements are defined (first married, remarried, cohabiting), and the duration of time spent in particular statuses. This chapter examines the evidence for an effect of marital status on mental health, with a particular focus on the factors that identify who benefits from marriage, who suffers from marital dissolution, and under what circumstances. Because several excellent reviews of earlier literature exist (Avison, 1999; Ross, Mirowsky, & Goldsteen, 1990; Umberson & Williams, 1999; Waite & Gallagher, 2000), we highlight research published since 1999.

Measures of Mental Health

Studies of marital status differences in mental health commonly employ outcome measures of psychological distress and depressive symptoms. Most have used the Center for Epidemiologic Studies–Depression scale (CES-D), which measures both emotional and physiological symptoms of depression. A substantial body of research also has considered the importance of marital status for positive indicators of subjective well-being, including happiness and life satisfaction, thereby recognizing that mental health is more than the absence of distress (Diener, Lucas, & Oishi, 2002; Keyes, 1998; Ryff, 1989). Although more limited in number, a few studies have tested the association of marital status with specific diagnosable psychiatric disorders such as schizophrenia, anxiety disorder, and major depression (e.g., Afifi, Cox, & Enns, 2006; Overbeek et al., 2006; Williams, Takeuchi, & Adair, 1992a).

An additional outcome that has received increasing attention in recent years is alcohol use or abuse. This reflects the recognition that men and women may express distress in different ways. A growing body of evidence suggests that depressive symptoms and other internalizing or emotional reactions to stress are more common among women, whereas externalizing or behavioral expressions of distress such as alcohol abuse or even violence (Umberson, Williams, & Anderson, 2002) are more common among men (Horwitz & Davies, 1994). Thus, studies that focus only on depressive symptoms may overstate the effects of marital status on women's mental health and underestimate its effects on men's health.

Why Is Marriage Associated with Better Mental Health?

For more than a century (Durkheim 1897/1951), sociologists have argued that social relationships, in general, and marriage, in particular, connect individuals to society and to each other in ways that enhance mental health. Marriage is thought to confer a sense of obligation, belonging, meaning, and purpose – aspects of social integration that facilitate trust and the provision and receipt of emotional support (Umberson & Williams, 1999; Waite, 2009). The economies of scale associated with co-residence and the specialization that occurs in marriage provide economic resources that are protective of mental health (Oppenheimer, 2000; Ross & Huber, 1985). The special legal status of marriage also confers a number of rights including access to Social Security and public pensions, spousal health insurance benefits, and the ability to make health care decisions for one another. The sense of security provided by these spousal safety nets may have some positive consequences for mental health.

The dominant explanation for the mental health benefits of marriage focuses on these economic and psychosocial resources. At its most basic level, this *marital resource model* predicts that all unmarried individuals, including the never married, divorced, and widowed, will have poorer mental health than the married because they lack the health-enhancing resources provided by marriage. Similarly, entering marriage should improve mental health, and exiting marriage should have enduring negative consequences.

In contrast, the *marital crisis model* suggests that the strains of marital dissolution undermine mental health more than the resources of marriage protect it. If this is true, there should be few differences in the mental health of the married compared to the never married, who have never experienced marital dissolution. Further, entering marriage should not substantially improve mental health. The crisis model also generally predicts that exits from marriage should be associated with transient declines in mental health from which individuals eventually recover, although it remains possible that some strains associated with marital dissolution and their effects on mental health persist.

Selection bias is an alternative explanation for marital status differences in mental health. Selection bias attributes mental health differences between married and unmarried persons to two sources. First, married individuals may have better mental health to begin with: Rather than marriage causing improvements in well-being, mentally healthier people may simply be more likely to enter into and remain in marriage. This is essentially a problem of reverse causal order. Second, there may be numerous other preexisting differences between married people and unmarried people that cannot be completely measured by researchers. If those who choose to marry (or divorce) differ from those who do not in characteristics that affect mental health, associations of marital status with health may be biased or spurious (Ribar, 2003). Because most sociological research relies on observational data, selection bias is usually addressed through statistical correction or the inclusion of control variables, with the goal of isolating the effect of marital status on mental health. Researchers who study marital status differences in mental health cannot use experimental research designs because this would mean that, based on random assignment by the researcher, some people in the study would be required to get married, whereas others would be required to stay single, divorce, or even become widowed. Clearly people are not willing to change their marital statuses for the sake of research, and asking them to do so would be highly unethical. The result, though, is that married people differ from unmarried people in many different ways, and this makes it difficult to determine if marriage causes mental health.

The majority of the historical evidence for a beneficial effect of marriage on mental health is based on cross-sectional data collected at one point in time, which is severely limited in its ability to differentiate among these competing explanations. Certainly, cross-sectional studies that compare the married to an aggregate group of all unmarried individuals cannot provide compelling evidence for one explanation over another. Research that disaggregates the unmarried typically indicates that marital status differences in mental health are greatest when the comparison group is the divorced or widowed and smaller or nonsignificant when the comparison group is the never married (Cairney & Krause, 2005; Williams et al., 1992a), suggesting partial support for the crisis model. Most studies conducted in the past 10 years used longitudinal data that followed the same individuals over time to more directly address these questions. The strengths of this research are that it assesses how mental health changes in response to entrances into and exits from marriage, considers whether changes in mental health associated with marital transitions persist over time, and examines whether earlier mental health predicts entry into or exit from marriage.

Marital Status and Mental Health: Recent Evidence

Marriage

Several recent longitudinal studies have demonstrated that entering marriage is associated with increases in psychological well-being and declines in psychological distress (Evans & Kelley, 2004; Frech & Williams, 2007; Horwitz, White, &

Howell-White, 1996a; Kim & McHenry, 2002; Lamb, Lee, & DeMaris, 2003; Marks & Lambert, 1998; R. Simon, 2002; Strohschein et al., 2005; K. Williams, 2003; Wu & Hart, 2002). These patterns appear to provide strong support for the marital resource model. However, some scholars have raised the possibility that improvements in well-being associated with entering marriage may be temporary (i.e., a honeymoon effect). This could explain why longitudinal studies that span a relatively short time period find evidence of increased well-being with entry into marriage, but cross-sectional studies (which include those in longer term marriages) find smaller differences between the never married and married.

Surprisingly little research directly tests this honeymoon effect for mental health. Research on German adults indicates that life satisfaction increases in the time surrounding marriage, but then declines again within about 5 years (Lucas, et al., 2003; Zimmerman & Easterlin, 2006). After this point, scholars disagree about whether life satisfaction completely returns to levels that existed prior to marriage. Studies of changes in the quality of the marital relationship over the life course have indirectly suggested that the mental health benefits of marriage may dissipate with time. Marital quality appears to decline the longer people are married (D. Johnson, Amoloza, & Booth, 1992; Umberson, Williams, Powers, Chen, & Campbell, 2005; Van Laningham, Johnson, & Amato, 2001). This could mean that the mental health benefits of marriage, which are dependent on marital quality (Hawkins & Booth, 2005; K. Williams, 2003), also diminish over time.

Further, the evidence for even short-term improvements in mental health associated with entry into marriage remains mixed. A few studies indicate no improvement in mental health with entry into marriage (Hope, Power, & Rodgers, 1999; Horwitz & White, 1991; Wu & Hart, 2002), and others suggest that "losing a marital partner has a greater impact on psychological distress than gaining one" (Strohschein et al., 2005, p. 2299), suggesting some support for the crisis model.

Several issues complicate comparisons across studies and are likely to be at least somewhat responsible for discrepant findings. First, not all research distinguishes entry into first marriage from remarriage. Studies focused specifically on remarriage suggest that it improves well-being relative to remaining divorced or widowed (Barrett, 2000; Evans & Kelley, 2004; Kim & McHenry, 2002; Strohschein et al., 2005; K. Williams, 2003), but conveys fewer mental health benefits than first marriage (Barrett, 2000; Marks & Lambert, 1998). Combining the remarried and the first married may, therefore, produce weaker associations of marriage with mental health.

Second, variation exists across studies in the comparison group employed. Arguably the most logical approach in determining whether marriage improves mental health is to compare never-married individuals who transition into marriage to those who remain continually never married. This is the design employed in most studies, but others use a comparison group of the continually married or a combined group of those in all marital statuses who experience no change. Fewer differences can be expected when the newly married are compared to the stably married, and greater differences may be seen when they are compared to an aggregate group that includes the continually divorced and widowed.

Third, the choice of control variables and the timing of their measurement are of great importance. Some studies ambitiously control for contemporaneous changes or later values on a range of variables that are associated with mental health, including income, social integration, and social support (e.g., Wu & Hart, 2002). Such an approach can obscure a true effect of marital status if the control variables are, in fact, mechanisms through which the mental health effects of marital transitions are conferred (Lieberson, 1985). In other words, marriage may improve mental health in part because it increases financial resources and gives people greater access to sources of social support. If these factors are held constant (essentially made equal for those who marry and those who do not), the association of marriage with mental health is minimized. Variables such as income, financial strain, emotional support, and others thought to mediate the marital status–mental health association are generally best measured before the union transition of interest or considered separately to test a possible mediating effect. As longitudinal data create opportunities for increasingly sophisticated analyses, we must think even more carefully about the implications of modeling strategies and study design.

The extent to which prior mental health selects individuals into marriage (i.e., reverse causality) remains unclear. Several studies suggest that neither depressive symptoms nor alcohol abuse is associated with subsequent entry into marriage (vs. remaining single; Kim & McHenry, 2002; Lamb, Lee, & DeMaris, 2003). However, others indicate that, before marriage, those who eventually marry already show lower psychological distress (Hope et al., 1999) and greater life satisfaction (Lucas et al., 2003; Stutzer & Frey, 2006) than those who remain single. Most scholars generally agree that selection explains some but not all of the association between marital status and mental health. An advantage of longitudinal studies is that, because they follow individuals over time, they can use statistical methods to hold constant levels of mental health prior to marriage. Doing so allows researchers to estimate the effect of entering marriage on mental health, assuming that those who marry had the same prior levels of prior mental health as those who do not. This reduces the role of selection in explaining observed associations of marital status with mental health. However, other preexisting differences between the married and the unmarried may still not be accounted for in this approach (see Ribar, 2003).

Ultimately, determining whether marriage has a causal effect on mental health requires a much more complete understanding of the processes through which any effects are produced. Empirical evidence lags far behind theory in this respect. The marital resource model suggests that marriage benefits mental health because it provides economic and psychosocial resources, including social support and social integration, but few studies directly test this hypothesis. In many cases, the existence of social integration or receipt of social support is simply equated with occupying a particular marital status. Recent research seriously challenges this approach. In contrast to long-held assumptions about the integrative functions of marriage, Gerstel and Sarkisian (2006) reported that married people have less contact and fewer support exchanges with parents, siblings, friends, and neighbors than the unmarried (also see Sarkisian & Gerstel, 2008). This finding is consistent with research on single mothers that finds they have more frequent contact with family and friends and receive more support from them than do married mothers (Marks & McLanahan, 1993). Future studies should continue to examine whether entrances into and exits from marriage precipitate change in a range of personal and social circumstances associated with mental health and identify the extent to which these changes contribute to (or perhaps detract from) any mental health benefits of marriage.

Divorce and Widowhood

Compared to the somewhat mixed findings for mental health benefits of entering marriage, research is much more conclusive regarding the costs of marital dissolution. Numerous longitudinal studies have provided convincing evidence that the transition to divorce is associated with increases in depressive symptoms and declines in well-being (Hope et al., 1999; Kalmijn & Monden, 2006; Kim & McHenry, 2002; Marks & Lambert, 1998; Mastekaasa, 1995; Simon, 2002; Strohschein et al., 2005; K. Williams, 2003; Wu & Hart, 2002). Widowhood, too, is clearly accompanied by declines in mental health (Carr et al., 2000; Lee & DeMaris, 2007; Lucas et al., 2003; Strohschein et al., 2005; Wade & Pevalin, 2004; Wilcox et al., 2003; K. Williams, 2003).

An unresolved issue is whether dissolution represents a temporary crisis from which individuals recover or whether its negative consequences persist. One of the earliest longitudinal studies to examine this question for divorce suggested that individuals recover from the stress of marital dissolution after about 2 years (Booth & Amato, 1991). More recent evidence, however, suggests that negative effects persist despite some initial recovery (Hetherington & Kelly, 2003; Johnson & Wu, 2002; Lucas, 2005). In contrast, research on widowhood generally supports a crisis model, indicating that mental health rebounds within a few years after the spouse's death (Harlow, Goldberg, & Comstock, 1991; Lee & DeMaris, 2007; Lund, Caserta, & Dimond, 1993; McCrae & Costa, 1993; Mendes de Leon, Rapp, & Kast, 1994; Stroebe & Stroebe, 1993; Wilcox et al., 2003, but see Lucas et al., 2003).

Marital dissolution is best viewed as a process because its effects on mental health unfold over time, even before the exit from marriage occurs. For example, Lucas (2005) found that life satisfaction drops sharply in the 4 years preceding divorce and reaches its lowest point about a year before the divorce occurs.

Therefore, support for the crisis model, which indicates that individuals return to baseline mental health a few years after divorce, may be misleading if that baseline is measured after the anticipatory increase in distress has already occurred (Lee & DeMaris, 2007). In other words, divorced or widowed individuals may return to their already elevated prior levels of distress, but still have worse mental health than they did before their marital problems began. Although much progress has been made in understanding the longitudinal course of marital dissolution, greater attention to measurement timing combined with the increasing availability of data spanning longer periods will help more fully address these questions.

Declines in well-being before marital dissolution also complicate tests of differential selection out of marriage. Several studies show that, before their marriage ends, those who will subsequently divorce already have elevated distress levels compared to those who do not divorce (Aseltine & Kessler, 1993; Hope et al., 1999; D. R. Johnson & Wu, 2002; Lucas, 2005; Simon, 2002; Stutzer & Frey, 2006; Wade & Pevalin, 2004). This lower well-being of those who later divorce compared to those who remain married may simply reflect the anticipation of marital dissolution (Hope et al., 1999), rather than an effect of poor mental health on the probability of divorce. Stronger support for selection is provided by a recent study that demonstrates that those who later divorce are already less happy with life before they even enter marriage than those who will not divorce (Stutzer & Frey, 2006), but it is unclear whether this pattern exists for measures of psychological distress. Selection is generally thought to play less of a role in widowhood as individuals have little control over this form of marital loss. Direct empirical tests generally have found no evidence of lower well-being or elevated distress several years prior to widowhood (Lucas et al., 2003; Wade & Pevalin, 2004, but see Lee & DeMaris, 2007, and Wilcox et al., 2003).

Cohabitation

As cohabitation has outpaced marriage as the first union entry experienced by young adults in the United States, its importance to mental health has received growing attention. Compared to marriage, cohabiting unions are less stable (Bumpass & Lu, 2000; Raley & Bumpass, 2003), offer fewer economic resources (Brines & Joyner, 1999; Lerman, 2002), and have lower levels of relationship quality and commitment (S. L. Brown & Booth, 1996; Marcussen, 2005; Thomson & Colella, 1992). Because of these differences, scholars have theorized that cohabitation should provide some but not all of the mental health benefits of marriage (Ross, 1995). Cross-sectional research has generally supported this conclusion with evidence that cohabitors are more depressed than their married counterparts (Brown, 2000; Kim & McHenry, 2002; Marcussen, 2005; Wu, Penning, Pollard, & Hart, 2003; but see Horwitz & White, 1998) but less depressed than unmarried noncohabitors (Kurdek, 1991; Ross, 1995; but see Horwitz & White, 1998).

Recent longitudinal evidence, however, calls into question the conclusion that cohabiting unions offer any benefits for mental health. In several studies, entering cohabitation is not associated with improved mental health over time (Kim & McHenry, 2002; Lamb, Lee, & DeMaris, 2003; Musick & Bumpass, 2006; Williams, Sassler, & Nicholson, 2008; Wu & Hart, 2002). However, the average associations that are examined may obscure important variation in the nature and duration of cohabiting unions. Cohabitation is a precursor to marriage for many adults: Half of cohabitors marry their partners (Bumpass & Lu, 2000). For others, cohabiting unions function more as alternatives to singlehood than as trial marriages (Manning & Smock, 2005) and appear to be motivated in part by economic concerns and convenience (Sassler, 2004). A promising avenue for future research is to consider whether long-term cohabiting unions that more closely resemble or lead to marriage have different effects on well-being than those that are short lived or are characterized by lower levels of commitment. Understanding how different types of cohabiting unions affect mental health may also offer insight into the more general mechanisms through which any protective benefits of marriage are conferred.

Is Everyone Affected Equally by Marriage and Marital Dissolution?

In sum, the best recent research suggests that, on average, entering marriage (but not cohabitation) is associated with improvements in mental health and exiting marriage is associated with declines in mental health, at least in the short run. One of the most important – yet most frequently ignored – components of the preceding statement is the phrase "on average." Social science findings about the benefits of marriage for mental health are based on average associations. Although it can be tempting to conclude that averages apply to all or even most people, this is not always the case. Averages are highly influenced by extreme cases (i.e., outliers) so that what appear to be substantial differences in mental health between the married and the unmarried may in fact only apply to a small group of relatively anomalous individuals. A growing body of research provides convincing evidence that the mental health benefits of marriage and the costs of marital dissolution vary greatly, depending on a range of individual, demographic, and relationship characteristics. These are commonly referred to as moderators of the relationship between marriage and mental health. We explore some of the most important moderators in this section.

Gender

Of all of the moderators of the effect of marriage on mental health, gender has received the greatest attention. In the early 1970s, sociologists argued that marriage is less beneficial to women's mental health than to men's in part because women's marital roles are more demanding and require greater self-sacrifice (Bernard, 1972; Gove & Tudor, 1973). In fact, in describing what she called "his" and "her" marriage, Jessie Bernard (1972, p. 37) wrote that "marriage introduced such profound discontinuities into the lives of women as to constitute genuine emotional health hazards." Early studies generally supported the hypothesis that women benefit less than men from marriage, but more recent research has challenged this conclusion. Across a range of studies, the average mental health benefits associated with entering marriage are similar for men and women (Evans & Kelley, 2004; Kim & McKenry, 2002; Marks & Lambert, 1998; Simon, 2002; Strohschein et al., 2005; K. Williams, 2003). Some studies indicated that men benefit more than women from entering marriage in terms of reduced alcohol use (Marcussen, 2005; Simon, 2002), but this benefit is balanced against women's reductions in depressive symptoms.

Interestingly, contemporary evidence for Jessie Bernard's notion of "his" and "her" marriage appears to be limited to remarriage following divorce or widowhood. The best evidence suggests that, compared to men, women receive fewer mental health benefits from remarriage (Marks & Lambert, 1998; K. Williams, 2003). As K. Williams (2003) notes, these lower benefits may reflect the persistence of gender roles that assign women primary responsibility for negotiating complex interpersonal relationships between two families, a stressful process, especially when children are involved (Whitsett & Land, 1992). Overall, though, very little is known about men's and women's experiences in remarriage, and some studies have found no gender differences in its mental health consequences (Evans & Kelley, 2004; Strohschein et al., 2005).

Evidence for gender differences in the effects of marital dissolution on mental health is mixed. With respect to divorce, several longitudinal studies suggest that there is no significant gender variation in the effect of divorce on psychological well-being (Kim & McKenry, 2002; Strohschein, et al., 2005; K. Williams, 2003) or alcohol use (Simon, 2002). Others, however, indicate that women experience greater increases in symptoms of depression and feelings of hostility, and greater decreases in self-esteem, environmental mastery, and self-acceptance than men after a divorce (Kalmijn & Monden, 2006; Marks & Lambert, 1998; Simon, 2002). Gender differences in the impact of widowhood on mental health also depend in part on the outcome examined. Relative to the continually married, men who become widowed report larger increases in depressive symptoms than women, but women appear to experience greater losses to life satisfaction (Lee & DeMaris, 2007; K. Williams, 2003). Even if the effects of marital dissolution are similar for men and women, the explanations for these patterns likely differ at least somewhat by gender. For example, marital dissolution appears to exact a greater financial cost for women than for men, but men may face greater challenges in managing a household on their own or maintaining relationships with children (Peterson, 1996; Smock, 1994; Umberson & Williams, 1993; Umberson, Wortman, & Kessler, 1992).

Marital Quality

Among the most important findings to emerge from the literature on marital status and mental health in recent years is the observation that any psychological benefits of marriage are highly dependent on the quality of the marital union. In fact, several studies suggest that being in a strained, unhappy, or inequitable marriage is worse for mental health than being single (Gove, Hughes, & Style, 1983; Hagedoorn, Van Yperen, Coyne, & van Jaarsveld, 2006; Hawkins & Booth, 2005; K. Williams, 2003). Poor marital quality directly undermines mental health (Evans & Kelley, 2004; Frech & Williams, 2007; Hagedoorn et al., 2006; Hawkins & Booth, 2005; K. Williams, 2003) and increases the risk of experiencing a range of mood, anxiety, and substance disorders (Overbeek et al., 2006). Further, strained marriages do not provide the same levels of emotional support and closeness as happy marriages, and these are likely key resources through which any mental health benefits of marriage are conferred. In sum, recent evidence strongly suggests that statements about the mental health benefits of marriage should refer more specifically to the mental health benefits of *high-quality* marital unions.

Because poor marital quality and divorce go hand in hand, it is important to distinguish between their effects on mental health. Some evidence, for example, has suggested that what appear to be negative effects of marital dissolution on psychopathology are explained by the much stronger impact of the poor marital quality that precedes divorce (Overbeek et al., 2006). Similarly, the extent to which marital dissolution undermines mental health depends on predissolution marital quality. The negative mental health consequences of divorce are notably weaker for those exiting an inequitable or unsatisfying marriage (Hawkins & Booth, 2005; Kalmijn & Monden, 2006; Wheaton, 1990; K. Williams, 2003). In fact, in some cases a transition to divorce may be better for mental health – or, at least, appears to be no worse – than remaining in a long-term unhappy marriage (Hawkins & Booth, 2005; K. Williams, 2003). Hawkins and Booth (2005, p. 445) sum up the evidence as follows: "Unhappily married people may have greater odds of improving their well-being by dissolving their low-quality unions as there is no evidence that they are better off in any aspect of overall well-being than those who divorce."

Age and Life Course

The life course perspective emphasizes that life course stage shapes the social context and normative status of roles such as widowhood, divorce, or singlehood (Bengtson & Allen, 1993; Elder, 1985) in ways likely to influence their effects on mental health. Social stress theory has much in common with the life course perspective in this regard as both emphasize the importance of the timing and sequencing of transitions into and out of social roles (Pearlin & Skaff, 1996). Taken together, these theoretical orientations suggest that several features of the life course should be important to the effect of marital status on mental health, including age, marital history, and the existence and age of children.

With respect to age, Marks and Lambert (1998) report that being unmarried and exiting marriage more strongly undermine the well-being of younger compared to midlife adults. Although being single is more normative at younger ages, this pattern may reflect an accumulation of psychosocial resources by midlife that facilitate coping with any strains of singlehood (Marks & Lambert, 1998). The extent to which this is true, however, may also depend on prior marital history. Barrett (2000) finds that second and, especially, third marriages offer fewer benefits to mental health than first marriage. She also observes that the negative consequences of divorce and widowhood are amplified among those who have experienced these events previously. This latter finding is consistent with a life course stress perspective that suggests that, over time, the accumulation of stress, like the strains associated with marital dissolution, can make individuals more vulnerable to additional stressors (Ulbrich, Warheit, & Zimmerman, 1989). It is likely that multiple dimensions of the life course interact in complex ways to impinge on the association of marital status with well-being. For example, experiencing a second divorce or entering a second marriage by age 30 is probably a qualitatively different experience than doing so at age 50. Future research should consider how multiple dimensions of the individual and marital life course work together to influence well-being over time.

The sequencing and timing of key family roles like marriage and parenthood are also important. For example, Williams and Dunne-Bryant (2006) find that the negative mental health consequences of divorce are greatest for those with preschool-aged children and smaller or negligible for others. Greater parenting strains and more frequent contact with the former spouse experienced by parents (especially mothers) of young children appear partly responsible for this finding. These results are noteworthy because only 20% of divorces in the United States involve preschool-aged children (Fields & Casper, 2001; U.S. Bureau of the Census, 1998). For those divorcing later in the life course, divorce may have only a minor impact on well-being. Similarly, Williams and colleagues (2008) find that entering and exiting marriage has more negative effects for single mothers than for childless women but that both groups of women experience similar mental health benefits from marriages that endure. For single mothers, who tend to have a high risk of divorce, entering marriage may pose some risks to mental health as entering and exiting marriage are marginally worse for well-being than remaining single for this group (Williams et al., 2008).

Race/Ethnicity

To date, little research has considered whether the relationship between marital status and mental health differs by race/ethnicity. This is an important and timely question, especially given striking race/ethnic variations in patterns of family formation. Although 90% of Americans will marry at least once, only two-thirds of African Americans can expect to marry during their lifetime (Teachman, Tedrow, & Crowder, 2000). The intersection of marriage and childbearing, too, varies substantially by race. In 2000, 27.1% of births to White women occurred outside of marriage, compared to 42.7% of Hispanic births, and 68.5% of African American births (Dye, 2005). That race/ethnicity is associated with such large variations in patterns of marriage and family formation provides sufficient motivation to consider how it might shape the consequences of marriage (and divorce) for mental health and well-being. African Americans are also disproportionately affected by government efforts to promote marriage among low-income single mothers, so understanding the effects of marriage on the mental health of African American women has substantial policy relevance.

The limited evidence available suggests that Whites benefit more from marriage than other groups. Williams, Takeuchi, and Adair (1992) find that the cross-sectional association of marital status with psychiatric disorder is much stronger for Whites than for Blacks. In ongoing work, Kroeger and Williams (2007) observe that a mental health advantage of marriage is largely limited to Whites and Black men, with few marital status differences in mental health observed for Hispanics or Black women. Other evidence indicates that Black mothers show better adjustment to marital dissolution than their White counterparts (McKelvey & McKenry, 2000) and that the stress associated with being single is significantly lower for Black compared to White older adults (Pudrovska, Schieman, & Carr, 2006).

At this point we can only speculate about the why marital status may be more important to the mental health of White compared to Black or Hispanic adults. Nonmarital childbearing, long-term cohabitation, and permanent singlehood have become increasingly normative experiences among African Americans (Edin & Kefalas, 2005; Lichter, Qian, & Mellot, 2006; Sigle-Rushton & McLanahan, 2002). This likely shapes the meaning of being single for African Americans in ways that are beneficial or, at least, less detrimental to mental health. Further, some evidence has suggested that African Americans who marry experience lower levels of marital quality than Whites (Broman, 1993; Goodwin, 2003), which may attenuate any benefits of marriage or costs of dissolution. Race/ethnicity may also influence the resources and strategies that individuals employ to manage stressful marital experiences (Williams & Harris-Reid, 1999). As McKelvey and McKenry (2000) illustrate, the better psychosocial adjustment to marital dissolution of Black mothers as compared to White mothers results in part because of Black women's higher levels of personal mastery and utilization of formal instrumental support after divorce. Family scholars have also made much of the role that extended kin plays in African American and Hispanic families (Cherlin, 1998; Sarkisian & Gerstel, 2004), and these sources of social support may serve some of the same functions as marriage in protecting mental health.

Values, Beliefs, and Prior Mental Health

People enter marriage with a set of beliefs about the nature of the marital union and their own level of commitment to its permanence. They also bring preexisting mental health problems with them into marriage. Current research shows that these factors strongly moderate the association of marriage and, in some cases, marital dissolution, with mental health. For example, Simon and Marcussen (1999) find that the negative effects of marital dissolution and the positive effects of entering marriage are substantially greater for those with strong beliefs in the permanency, desirability, and importance of marriage. Similarly, Booth and Amato (1991) show that exiting marriage is most stressful for those who have high levels of commitment to marriage.

Prior mental health history also plays a role in the benefits of entering a union. Those who are depressed or least satisfied with life prior to marriage benefit most from a transition into marriage (Frech & Williams, 2007; Lucas, 2005). In fact, Frech and Williams (2007) find that entering marriage is associated with only modest mental health benefits for those do not have symptoms of depression prior to marriage – a group that makes up about 70% of their sample. The apparent mental health advantage of entering marriage is approximately four times greater for those who are highly depressed prior to marriage despite their lower levels of marital quality (Frech & Williams, 2007). Although explanations for these patterns await further investigation, highly depressed individuals likely have more to gain than others from the companionship, emotional support, and stability of marriage. It remains unclear, though, whether the spouses of previously depressed persons benefit similarly to their partners or whether the average benefits experienced by the depressed persist over time.

Conclusion

So, does marital status affect mental health? Although causality is difficult to determine, social science research on marriage and mental health suggests three general conclusions. First, marriage does appear to offer some benefits to mental health, at least in the short run. On average, those who enter marriage experience greater improvements in well-being than those who remain single, providing support for the marital resource model. Although prior mental health may play some role in selecting individuals into marriage, it likely does not completely explain improvements in psychological well-being associated with entering marriage. However, the duration of any mental health benefits of marriage and the specific mechanisms through which such benefits are conferred remain somewhat unclear. It is also possible that the specific aspects of marriage that are most important to well-being change over the life course.

Second, on average, exiting marriage appears to undermine mental health, but at least some of these negative effects dissipate with time. It is likely that both the marital resource model and marital crisis model are applicable to understanding the impact of marital dissolution on psychological well-being. Clearly divorce and widowhood involve numerous stressors, but the strong initial impact of many of these stressors may be relatively short lived. Even after the dust settles and individuals adjust to these stressful life events, the absence of several key resources provided by marriage, such as emotional and financial support, may have some enduring, albeit weaker, negative consequences for mental health.

Third, the average effects of marriage and marital dissolution on mental health are far from universal. Although it can be tempting to conclude that the benefits of marriage apply equally to all individuals, the best evidence suggests a great deal of variation. Clearly, those with poor marital quality receive fewer if any mental health benefits of marriage. Other factors that shape the meaning and experience of marriage, including race/ethnicity, the presence and age of children, prior mental health, and life course experiences, are also highly relevant. The result is that social science research findings about the average mental health benefits of marriage should never be used to guide decisions about whether an individual or specific group of people should be encouraged to marry or remain married. And headlines such as "New Treatment for Depression – Marriage" (MSNBC, 2007) should obviously be viewed with a healthy dose of skepticism.

Finally, it is important to remember that marriage and marital dissolution both involve a combination of rewards and strains. Most theorizing and research on marriage focus on its rewards, whereas work on marital dissolution highlights its strains. However, the extent to which either affects mental health likely depends on the way in which the benefits stack up against the costs. We need to know much more about the aspects of marriage that detract from its mental health benefits and the positive changes that may follow from marital dissolution. The ability to uncover these factors depends in part on the indicators of mental health that we choose to examine. For example, research that examines other outcomes in addition to depressive symptoms finds that the unmarried report greater levels of personal growth and more personal autonomy than the married (Marks & Lambert, 1998). As Marks and Lambert (1998, p. 676) conclude, "Marriage is not a universal beneficial determinant of well-being. It appears wise, therefore, to continue evaluating the effects of marriage on well-being with a multidimensional lens whenever possible, so that we can obtain a more precise understanding of how and when marriage is important for mental health."

17

Stress and Distress in Childhood and Adolescence

Elizabeth G. Menaghan

Menaghan emphasizes that family composition and parental employment contribute to family economic resources, which in turn shape the overall emotional climate of the family as well as strategies for child socialization and support. She identifies a number of family-linked factors, including parental conflict, unstable family composition, difficult parental working conditions, and inadequate incomes, which are likely to influence behavior problems observed in childhood and adolescence. These family-linked factors also affect the quality of the children's environment outside the home, including child care arrangements, schools, and neighborhoods. Consequently, to reduce behavior problems in early life, the social stressors that have an impact on parents must be considered. If the well-being of children is influenced by family circumstances, what type of interventions could have important impacts on children's mental health?

Introduction

An enduring interest for social scientists and everyday observers alike is the question of continuity and change in individual well-being over the life course. Although some accounts focus on genetic and biological factors that may foster continuity over time, most social scientists emphasize the broad range of social factors that may be implicated in both continuity and change. Persistent social circumstances will tend to be echoed in persistent behavior patterns, whereas changes in social context should be linked to changes – for better or worse – in well-being. In this chapter I focus primarily on one subset of the social stressors that impinge on children and adolescents: stressors that are linked to their social memberships in particular families. I examine how family composition and parental employment patterns, which together shape family economic position, are linked to patterns of parent–child interaction as well as to the development and persistence of behavior problems. I also explore how experiences outside the family in child care settings and neighborhoods may also affect childhood and adolescent emotional and social development.

National data suggest that increasing numbers of children and adolescents in the United States are exhibiting severe manifestations of aggressive and depressed behavior. Successive birth cohorts have shown increased rates and earlier onset of depression and suicide (National Institute of Mental Health [NIMH], 2001; National Research Council, 1993). These trends raise questions about how stability and change in everyday life circumstances may be linked to stability and change in children's and adolescents' emotional well-being and behavior. A better understanding of these processes promises scientific and social benefits. It can contribute to social scientific theories regarding the development of social competence and mental health over the life course. It also can help identify children and adolescents who are at risk of reaching adulthood without having developed the behavioral skills needed to sustain satisfying interpersonal relationships, enjoy a satisfying level of emotional well-being, and be effective parents to their own children. Finally, it may suggest strategies for intervention that can improve the life chances of those at high risk for adverse outcomes.

Behavior Problems: Explanations for Persistence over Time

What do we know about behavior problems in childhood and adolescence? Two dimensions of behavior problems have consistently emerged in the literature (see Achenbach, 1984; Rutter, 1970). *Externalizing behavior*, also referred to as under-controlled or troublesome behavior, refers to behavior that is troubling to others, especially aggressive and antisocial behavior. *Internalizing behavior*, sometimes labeled overcontrolled or troubled behavior, is marked by withdrawal from interaction, anxiety, and depressed mood. Because both have implications for later life chances, I focus here on what the current literature suggests about their development and change over time.

Researchers are concerned with the origins of these problems early in the life course precisely because they believe that, once established, they tend to persist. In a recent review of longitudinal studies on externalizing problems (NICHD Early Child Care Research Network, 2004), the authors concluded that, although aggressive problems tend to diminish over time for most children, about 5% show high levels of problems very early on that do not improve. Stability increases after early childhood (Burt, Obradovic, Long, & Masten, 2008; Caspi, Roberts, & Shriner, 2005; see also Rutter, Kim-Cohen, & Maughan, 2006), with externalizing problems tending to be more stable than internalizing ones.

At any particular point in time, behavior problems may be painful but self-limiting expressions of temporary emotional distress, or they may become an established pattern of learned behavior that tends to be self-reinforcing. What seems to make the difference? Elder and Caspi (1988) discussed two major social processes that sustain maladaptive behavior over time: interactional and cumulative continuity. *Interactional continuity* refers to the repeated give-and-take between individuals who interact with one another over long time periods. People tend to fall into recurrent patterns, each playing the same role or repeating the same behavior and in turn evoking the same response from the other. These reciprocal patterns of interaction, particularly in families, may repeatedly provide short-term reinforcements or rewards for problematic behavior, making its recurrence more likely (see also Patterson, 2002). *Cumulative continuity* emphasizes more long-range consequences of early problems. Over time, the consequences of such behavior accumulate, systematically selecting children into social environments that reinforce and sustain established behaviors.

Children's internal explanations and beliefs about themselves and others also play a role in maintaining established patterns. Dodge (1993, 2006) has discussed how children develop attributions about the motivations and intents of others that shape their own behavior. For example, children who perceive hostile intent are more apt to exhibit "preemptive aggression" or to take harsh retaliatory action after perceived slights. This type of behavior is self-fulfilling: The child who strikes out first, anticipating the worst, is likely to elicit an angry or punitive response – just what he or she expected. Hence, the child's own actions tend to elicit behavior that confirms the initial reading of the situation. This dynamic suggests that, once problematic attributions have become established, they will tend to persist and contribute to the persistence of problematic behavior. Consistent with this argument, Dodge and colleagues (2003) found that more negative social attributions contribute to the growth in antisocial behavior over time.

Do these attributions and their sources differ for children with externalizing versus internalizing difficulties? Dodge (see also Burgess, Wojslawowicz, Rubin, Rose-Krasnor, & Booth-LaForce, 2006) suggested that early exposure to aggressive models, insecure attachment relationships, and early experiences of abuse lead children to see the world as a hostile place, to be hypervigilant and hyperreactive to possible hostility, and to be prone to aggressive behavior. In contrast to these children with externalizing problems who selectively attend to hostile acts that may be directed toward them, depressed children selectively attend to failure and loss and tend to blame problems they may encounter on their own shortcomings. The social sources of these depressogenic attributions are likely to include prior experience with interpersonal instability and loss of relationships. These experiences incline the child to develop a negative self-schema; to attribute negative events to internal, stable, and global factors; and so to be prone to depressive behavior.

Peer Interaction and Social Distress

Friendship ties may help children modify their attributions and behaviors in more adaptive ways over time, but early behavior problems may limit children's interaction with peers. Some research has found that more disruptive behavior and, to a lesser extent, also anxiety and social withdrawal, measured around age 6, are linked to more peer rejection and fewer friendships several years later, which in turn predict greater depressive symptoms and loneliness in early adolescence (Pedersen, Vitaro, Barker, & Borge, 2007). Ladd and Troop-Gordon (2003) also found that more aggressive behaviors observed in kindergarten have significant effects on later peer experiences, including peer rejection, friendlessness, and victimization by peers. These negative peer experiences affect both externalizing and internalizing outcomes, with friendlessness particularly important in predicting internalizing symptoms.

However, other studies have suggested that peer relationships affect behavior problems more than behavior problems predict poorer peer relationships. Studying children from year to year from ages 5 through 12, Ladd (2006) concluded that peer rejection is more likely to lead to later externalizing and internalizing behavior problems, rather than the reverse. Following children from around age 10 to 17, Burt, Obradovic, Long, and Masten (2008) similarly found that poorer earlier social competence is linked to increasing later internalizing problems, but that the presence of earlier internalizing symptoms does not undermine later social competence.

Thus, further study of how other social factors shape child and adolescent peer relationships may help us better understand behavior problems. One recent study found that boys and girls whose behavior is less conforming to stereotypically feminine and masculine ideals experience more rejection from peers (Rieger, Linsenmeier, Gygax, & Bailey, 2008). Crosnoe, Frank, and Mueller (2008) found that among adolescents, higher body mass index is associated with fewer peer friendship nominations, especially for girls.

Although friendships and peer acceptance may have positive impacts, early romantic relationships may not (Davila, 2008). Joyner and Udry (2000) found that heterosexual romantic involvements in early adolescence, rather than benefiting well-being, are linked to increasing depressive symptoms for both boys and girls, especially if they have a succession of short-term involvements or have recently experienced a relationship breakup. In their study, girls seemed especially adversely affected by these early heterosexual relationships. In more qualitative analyses of early adolescent romantic relationships, however, Giordano, Longmore, and Manning (2006) found that boys also express considerable vulnerability as they enter into intimate romantic relationships; they express similar levels of emotional engagement as girls, but feel less confident than girls about navigating heterosexual relationships and less powerful in these relationships.

Social Stressors, Parent–Child Interaction, and Children's Distress

The story thus far emphasizes forces for continuity once behavioral difficulties are established, as well as internal attributions and peer interactions as potential factors. Clearly, family environments also matter, and research has focused on both parental warmth and stimulation as important dimensions (Bradley, 1985). Other important aspects of childhood socialization include the form and consistency of discipline and the extent of parental monitoring and supervision (Crouter, MacDermid, McHale, & Perry-Jenkins, 1990), explicit parental socialization/control efforts, and appropriate autonomy opportunities. Both theory and research have suggested that parental control must gradually yield to co-regulation of behavior and eventual self-regulation (Lamborn, Mounts, & Steinberg, 1991). Finally, as children spend more and more time away from the direct supervision of parents, parents must increasingly turn to more long-range monitoring and more distal supervision strategies (Crouter et al., 1990).

Particularly for initial levels of behavior problems, the characteristics that parents and children bring to their interaction also have important effects on outcomes. Maternal educational attainment and maternal cognitive skills are associated with more parental warmth and stimulation (Bradley, 1985). Mothers' psychological resources such as self-esteem and sense of mastery over life events also matter (Menaghan & Parcel, 1991, 1995). When fathers are present in the household, parallel paternal characteristics also shape interaction and well-being. Children's own attributes may also be correlated both with home environments and with other explanatory variables. For example, serious child health problems may simultaneously strain family economic resources, constrain maternal employment, and prompt parents to try to compensate for the child's limitations by providing an especially stimulating and supportive environment. Serious health problems may also hinder children's social development by limiting normal educational and social opportunities. It is clear that research linking social stressors and child and adolescent outcomes needs to take such parent and child factors into account. The effects of stressful change in family work and family circumstances may be particularly negative for children who are already having emotional or behavior difficulties before that stressful change. More generally, it is important to take explicitly into account the level of prior behavior problems when assessing the effects of subsequent events.

What social factors affect parents' abilities to provide more effective and nurturant supports for their children? We argue that family composition, parental employment, and family economic status play critical and interwoven roles. Family composition and parental employment patterns operate in part by shaping family economic resources, and these economic resources shape relations among adults in the household as well as relations between adults and children, including the strategies of child socialization, support, and control that are used, the overall emotional climate of the family, and the consistency and contingency of parental action. Changes in family composition or in parental employment are likely to affect economic resources and may each alter children's behavior patterns.

Stability and Change in Family Composition

A wide range of studies have suggested that two-biological-parent families tend to be advantaged in many ways relative to single-parent and stepparent families, even after adjusting for prior characteristics including education, and that these advantages are reflected in better child outcomes across a range of dimensions (for review, see Parcel & Menaghan, 1994, as well as McLanahan, 2004). Part of the effects of family structure on children is due to the significantly poorer economic circumstances of single relative to married mothers (McLanahan & Percheski, 2008). Much may depend, however, on the quality of the relationship between the parents, which itself may be affected by occupational difficulties or economic problems. Whatever the social sources of parental conflict, research has suggested that when parents are more hostile or withdrawn in interactions with each other, they also tend to be less emotionally available to their children, and this lower emotional availability, especially of fathers, is linked to heightened levels of internalizing and externalizing symptoms in children (Sturge-Apple, Davies, & Cummings, 2006). Their awareness of parents' conflict also increases adolescents' sense of threat, emotional insecurity, and reactivity; these in turn are linked to more internalizing and externalizing problems (Buehler, Lange, & Franck, 2007).

Several studies have suggested that parental disagreements about their children have an impact that is distinct from the effect of more general or global marital unhappiness. When parents disagree about how to rear their children, their children tend to have higher levels of externalizing problems (Feinberg, Kan, & Hetherington, 2007; Jenkins, Simpson, Dunn, Rasbash, & O'Connor, 2005). Over time, these higher levels of externalizing problems also contribute to increasing parental conflicts and negativity between spouses (Jenkins et al., 2005), particularly in remarriages (Hetherington, Henderson, & Reiss, 1999).

Adult family membership is not a stable property of all families, and changes in family composition have implications for changes in child behavior outcomes as well. Breakups of marital or quasi-marital relationships may have a particularly negative impact, as the surrounding emotional difficulties and attendant economic losses tend to compromise parents' abilities to provide appropriate stimulation and support, at least in the short run (for a recent review, see Formby & Cherlin, 2007). However, the impact of marital disruptions is less when marital conflict has been high, suggesting that for some children and adolescents, marital disruption may reduce behavior problems (Jekelek, 1998; Strohschein, 2002).

Conversely, the addition of a male spouse or partner should increase family economic resources, provide more emotional and instrumental support for mothers, and improve the overall quality of home environments. However, the establishment of these new ties may be difficult. Some evidence has suggested that stepfathers are typically less involved in interaction with children than are fathers, and children and adolescents are both more negative and noncompliant and express less warmth and affection toward their stepparents than toward their biological parents (Hetherington et al., 1999). S. J. Rogers, Parcel, and Menaghan (1991) found that both recent marital disruption and recent remarriage are associated with elevated behavior problems for young children.

However, not all stepfamilies are alike. A recent study of stepfamilies who have been married at least 5 years suggested that adolescents in simple stepfamilies (where all of the children are full biological siblings from a mother's earlier marriage) differ little from children in married two-biological-parent families. Those in more complex stepfamilies, with a mixture of step- and half-siblings as well as full siblings, however, have more parent–child conflict and higher levels of externalizing problems (Hetherington et al., 1999).

Whereas earlier studies have focused on legal marriages and remarriage, more recent studies have explicitly considered informal unions – young children living with both their biological parents who have not married and older children living with one biological parent and his or her new partner. These couples differ in numerous ways that complicate such comparisons. For example, Artis (2007) found that, for young children living with both of their biological parents, parents who are in informal unions on average have less education and earn less total income than parents who have married, and it is these differences, not cohabitation status per se, that are linked to greater problems with self-control for the children in cohabiting families. However, for adolescents, cohabiting family structures are associated with poorer child outcomes than marital households even after extensive controls for such factors (S. L. Brown, 2004). In both studies, maternal depressive symptoms tend to be higher in cohabiting arrangements than in marriages, and this factor is a strong predictor of child outcomes.

Informal unions are more likely to break up than married-parent families, although again this partly reflects preexisting differences. Using the Fragile Families data of couples with a recent shared birth, Osborne, Manning, and Smock (2007) found that cohabiting parents have lower education, are younger, and have more prior marriages than do married parents. They are also more likely to have prior births from other relationships, so that these families resemble the complex stepfamilies that Hetherington et al. (1999) found to be more problematic. As more recent studies expand their measures of compositional change to include arrivals and departures of cohabiting partners and changes in visiting romantic partners, they are documenting that multiple changes seem to have a cumulative impact on children. Given the greater fragility of cohabiting unions than marriages, children living in these arrangements are more likely to experience a series of family changes. Osborne and McLanahan (2007) found that each additional transition is associated with higher levels of aggressive behavior and anxious-depressed behaviors among children at age 3. These impacts are mediated by poorer observed mother–child interactions and mothers' reports of greater stress in their lives.

Parents' Employment, Occupational Conditions, and Economic Hardships

The number of adults in the family, depending on the quality and stability of their employment, also affects the family's economic resources. Across all father-present families, fathers' lower earnings and more limited work hours are associated with higher levels of behavior problems (Hofferth, 2006). Foster and Kalil (2007) found that when fathers are present but total family income remains very low, presumably because of the men's unemployment or intermittent employment, then being in a two-parent family offers no greater protection from internalizing or externalizing problems than other family forms. These findings are consistent with classic and more recent studies finding that unemployment and underemployment of fathers are associated with more troubled couple relationships and more hostile and withdrawn family interaction patterns (Elder, 1974; McLoyd, 1998). Clearly, the employment status and earned income of fathers, not simply their presence, matter for father–child interaction as well as for family economic well-being and in turn child outcomes.

Fathers' unemployment or underemployment has long been recognized as a risk factor for children (McLoyd, 1998). In contrast, mothers who do not work outside the home, especially when their children are young, have been viewed as beneficial. However, maternal employment has become economically essential for many families even when a second adult is present, and it is especially critical for single-mother families, for which low or intermittent employment and earnings may be common. Studying unmarried mothers with adolescent children, Kalil and Ziol-Guest (2005) found that over a 2-year period only 22% of these mothers are continuously employed in a job that provided sufficient hours and wages to rise above poverty-level incomes. Many mothers experience a sequence of low-wage jobs interspersed with lengthy unemployment spells, and such maternal employment instability is linked with worsening adolescent self-concepts and higher likelihood of school dropout.

Whether because of intermittent employment, low-wage jobs, limited work hours, or reliance on a single wage earner, a large literature supports the negative effects of economic pressures on child outcomes (see Bradley & Corwyn, 2002, and McLoyd, 1998, for reviews of the theoretical and empirical underpinnings for this link). Both the persistence of low overall economic levels and the experience of economic losses (which may reflect job loss or a partner exit) can lead to parental demoralization and depression and disrupt skillful parenting, with negative effects on children's emotions and behavior; these overall processes appear fairly similar across European American, Mexican American, and African American families (Conger, Conger, et al., 1992; Conger, Wallace, et al., 2002; Parke et al., 2004). Studies of economic factors have typically focused on household income (but see Yeung & Conley, 2008, who discussed the volatility of income, especially for families with young children, and who proposed a range of measures of family wealth that may better capture family economic resources). Strohschein (2005) found that low household income in early childhood is associated with more depressive symptoms and more antisocial behavior as early as age 4 and that these initial levels are associated with increases in problems over time. Several studies have suggested that the timing and duration of economic hardship matter, with persistent low income associated with the worst levels of both externalizing and internalizing symptoms (NICHD Early Child Care Research Network, 2005; see also Macmillan, McMorris, & Kruttschnitt, 2004).

In addition to the adverse impact of economic hardship on parental well-being and in turn on their parenting, economic hardship can have an impact on children in other ways. As we discuss further, family economic resources are also linked to the quality of nonparental child care early in life and to the quality of the children's neighborhood. And by the time children reach adolescence, their own awareness of family economic hardship is associated with a reduced sense of mastery and control over their own lives, leading to greater distress (Conger, Conger, et al., 1999).

The effects of both parents' employment depend in part on both the quality and quantity of their work. Social-psychological theory and empirical research both have suggested that the conditions adults experience at work affect their own cognitive functioning and emotional well-being and shape values they hold for their children (Kohn & Schooler, 1983; Menaghan, 1991). When parents' work is more substantively complex and offers greater opportunities for self-direction, parents place greater value on their children's developing self-direction, and they are less concerned with behavioral conformity per se. Such parents display more warmth and involvement, restrict their children's actions less frequently, and report less frequent physical punishment (Luster, Rhoades, & Haas, 1989). Studies of employed mothers have shown that more complex maternal occupations exert significant positive effects on a child's family environment (Menaghan & Parcel, 1991). Although many studies of employment quality focus in particular on mothers, it is clear that fathers' employment quality, particularly supportive work environments, also matters for children, and these effects are apparent even when children are infants (Goodman, Crouter, Lanza, & Cox, 2008).

The effects of work quality are not limited to shaping parental values. Work stress research has shown that the conditions of work that are more common in less desirable jobs – routinization, low autonomy, heavy supervision, and little opportunity for substantively complex work – exacerbate psychological distress and reduce self-esteem and personal control. When work experiences leave parents feeling uncertain of their own worth and emotionally distressed, they are less able to be emotionally available to their children or to provide them with responsive, stimulating environments (Belsky & Eggebean, 1991; McLoyd, 1998; Menaghan, 1991). Such effects may be exacerbated by other difficult family conditions, such as absence of a spouse or large family size.

Work schedules also affect children. Increasing numbers of parents work evening or nights and on Saturdays or Sundays as well, instead of the Monday-through-Friday "standard" workweek (see Presser, 2005, for a review of these patterns and their effects). Recent studies of low-income mothers with children aged 2 to 4 years old found that, even with extensive controls for education and other household characteristics, children whose mothers work nonstandard schedules have more externalizing and more internalizing problems (Joshi & Bogen, 2007). These effects are partially explained by mothers' greater stress and lower parenting satisfaction when work schedules are nonstandard. Similarly, Strazdins, Clements, Korda, Broom, and D'Souza (2006), studying dual-earner couples with children aged 2 through 11, found that when either or both parents work nonstandard work schedules, children have more behavior problems, in part because these parents more commonly report angry and ineffective parent–child interactions and mothers report greater depressive symptoms.

Finally, very long work hours of either parent may negatively affect home environments and children's behavior outcomes (Parcel & Menaghan, 1994). When parents' long work hours leave little time to transmit values, norms, and skills from parents to children, higher family economic well-being may not translate into better environments for children.

To what extent have parental employment trends put more children at risk for negative outcomes? Perhaps surprisingly, studies of time usage in families have shown that mothers' increased labor force participation in the past several decades has reduced their time with children less than expected. Bianchi, Robinson, and Milkie (2006) suggested that employed mothers have made strategic time choices, reducing time spent doing household work and on their own leisure-time activities to maximize time with children. And over the past few decades, married fathers' time with children has been increasing (although as fewer fathers are married and living with their children, this does not mean that all children have benefited from this increase).

Nonparental Child Care

As more children live with two working parents or a single parent, increasing numbers of young children now spend substantial time in care settings outside their own homes, with caregivers other than their own parents and with playmates other than their own siblings. The impact of such care on children's peer relationships and on their social adjustment is likely to vary depending on the quality of that care (for a recent review, see Vandell, 2004). In preschool programs, higher observer ratings of teachers' emotional support (i.e., establishing a positive climate; preventing and redirecting misbehavior; providing comfort, support, and encouragement; and inhibiting the expression of anger, aggression, and harshness) have predicted higher social competence and fewer problem behaviors (Mashburn et al., 2008). For nonparental care as for parent–child interaction, large numbers of children and poor ratios of children to caregivers are likely to reduce the quality of care.

Although excellent nonparental child care is likely to be especially important in compensating for strained family resources, studies have suggested that poorer families are typically limited to poorer care. The NICHD Study of Early Child Care found that the quality of home environments and the quality of nonmaternal care settings tend to be similar, especially for infants and toddlers, and low family incomes predict both poorer home environments and lower quality child care (NICHD Early Care Research Network, 1997). Although home environments have stronger effects on children than do child care settings, spending longer hours in poorer quality care also seems to carry some risks (NICHD Early Care Research Network, 2002). Early reports from this study suggested that higher proportions of children who had experienced extensive care in child care centers (many of which had poor child–caregiver ratios) were prone to more aggressive and noncompliant behavior problems in kindergarten. This small but statistically significant effect appeared to fade by Grade 3, but reemerged in sixth grade, and it also seemed to depend on the quality of attachment between mother and child (for a summary, see Belsky et al., 2007).

Multiple changes in caregiving arrangements may also take a toll. In a recent meta-analysis of young toddlers (average age 30 months) in child care, Ahnert, Pinquart, and Lamb (2006) found that children's attachment to caregivers is more secure after more time in the setting and when care arrangements have been stable rather than changing over time.

Some studies have suggested that the number of hours in care has differing effects, depending on the quality of care: Votruba-Drzal, Coley, and Chase-Landsdale (2004) found that among low-income families longer hours in high-quality care are associated with lower levels of externalizing problems; Loeb, Fuller, Kagan, and Carrol (2004) reported similar results. Intervention studies also have suggested the importance of high-quality, stable care arrangements for children already at risk for adverse outcomes. One long-term study randomly assigned some children in low-income families to attend a stable, full-time, university-affiliated day care center beginning in infancy through age 5, whereas others in similar economic circumstances were cared for at home or in a range of local child care arrangements. The researchers found that both groups had relatively poor home environments, but participation in the intervention appeared to buffer that group from later depressive symptoms (McLaughlin, Campbell, Pungello, & Skinner, 2007). But such compensating experiences for children in poorer home environments are rare.

Neighborhood Effects

Family composition and parental employment quality also affect where families can afford to live, and many studies have demonstrated associations between poorer neighborhoods and poorer child outcomes (for a review, see Leventhal & Brooks-Gunn, 2000). More economically disadvantaged neighborhoods have been linked to greater maternal depression; less consistent, less stimulating, and more punitive parenting; and poorer outcomes for young children (Kohen, Leventhal, Dahinten, & McIntosh, 2008). Lower family economic resources also constrain the quality of the neighborhood and schools that children attend, and these social contexts are increasingly powerful as children grow older. Following children over time, Hart, Atkins, and Matsuba (2008) found that living in neighborhoods with a high percentage of residents below federal poverty thresholds is associated with worsening behavior problems, even after controlling for family-level variables including maternal education and the level of cognitive and emotional supports in the home environment.

Although studies of neighborhood effects tend to link current neighborhood conditions with current child and adolescent outcomes, Wheaton and Clarke (2003) suggested that the impact of adverse neighborhood contexts may take some time to become visible. In fact, they found that neighborhood socioeconomic disadvantage experienced at ages 6 to 11 is linked to both adolescent and early adult externalizing problems, overshadowing the effects of current neighborhood conditions. They suggested that these effects operate in part by compromising parental mental health, which in turn increases risk for children and exposes them to more stressful life events over time.

Poorer neighborhoods may also experience less residential stability. Kowaleski-Jones (2000; see also Aneshensel & Sucoff, 1996) found that living in a neighborhood with more residential turnover is associated with more aggressive behavior in adolescence, net of a wide range of individual and family characteristics. Beyond effects of individual neighborhoods, the overall state of the economy and its reflection in unemployment, underemployment, and low wages can create a powerful but insufficiently studied climate of hope or pessimism that affects both parents and children (National Research Council, 1993).

How parents interact with their children and how effective their socialization efforts are may both vary depending on the supportiveness or constraints present in the surrounding community. This in turn may explain observed ethnic differences in outcomes. On average, ethnic minorities face greater economic hardships and, at any given level of economic resources, tend to live in poorer areas with greater crime and fewer community resources. On the one hand, we may expect that levels of parental support and supervision will be particularly important when family economic well-being is low and community contexts are more negative. More pessimistically, parental efforts to nurture and support their children may be overwhelmed by very low levels of economic and community support. Adjudicating between these two possibilities is an important task for future research.

Conclusion

In summary, we argue that a range of social factors may combine to shape the development of children's behavior problems during childhood and adolescence.

Stable maternal characteristics, including such resources as intellectual skills, educational attainments, and self-concept, shape children's socialization experiences and thus influence their trajectory of behavior problems. Where fathers are present, their resources also influence children's socialization environments. Because these parental characteristics are relatively stable over time, such influences arc likely to have their strongest effects on initial levels of children's behavior problems and on their stability over time. Children's own attributions about threat and loss, and the quality of their experiences with peers, also contribute to sustaining these behavior styles.

Social stressors – particularly parental conflict and unstable adult family composition, difficult parental working conditions, and inadequate incomes – undermine the quality of parental child rearing and so make the development of behavior problems more likely. When such stressors increase, children will exhibit more behavior problems. Conversely, decreases in social stressors should diminish children's behavior problems over time.

These social stressors also constrain the quality of child care that working parents can arrange, as well as the neighborhood conditions in which they raise their children, and these two social contexts have direct effects on children's levels of aggressive and depressed behavior and thus their life chances. These interdependent explanatory variables – parent and child characteristics, social stressors, and experiences beyond the family – contribute to a social explanation of children and adolescents' behavior problems. By investigating their interwoven effects, social scientific research may suggest the most promising pathways for social intervention to reduce the proportions of children who emerge with behavior styles that are associated with poor outcomes when they become adults.

18
Psychopathology and Risky Sexual Behaviors among Black Adolescents

Cleopatra Howard Caldwell and Ebony Sandusky

Caldwell and Sandusky focus on Black adolescents and the most common adolescent mental health concern: depression. They discuss prevalence estimates and identify environmental and cultural risk and protective factors associated with depression. Specifically, they consider the role of racial discrimination and neighborhood influences as structural factors that have implications for psychopathology. The authors also examine what is known about the relationship between depression and risky sexual behaviors as a way to better understand the complexity of adolescent mental health and a prevalent problem behavior among Black youth. By highlighting structural conditions that can impinge on the mental health of Black youth, Caldwell and Sandusky avoid the tendency to attribute poor outcomes solely to inherent predispositions of adolescents, thus providing a more comprehensive approach for conceptualizing adolescent depression. Why do racial discrimination and neighborhood characteristics influence the association between adolescent depression and risky sexual behaviors?

Introduction

Previous estimates indicated that 1 in 5 children and adolescents had a mental disorder (U.S. Department of Health and Human Services [USDHHS], 1999). More recent evidence, however, has suggested that childhood psychiatric disorders may have been underestimated. Costello, Mustillo, Erkanli, Keeler, and Angold's (2003) longitudinal study found prevalence rates for child and adolescent mental disorders to be closer to 1 in 3 by age 16. A review of prevalence research on childhood mental disorders by Roberts, Attkisson, and Rosenblatt (1998) reported estimates ranging from 1% to 51%, depending on a number of factors, including age of study participants, method of data collection, and case definition (i.e., method of diagnosis). Across the 12 adolescent studies included in the Roberts et al. review article, the average prevalence rate of mental disorders among adolescents was 16.5%, with a range from 6.2% to 41.3%. The authors concluded that inconsistencies in prevalence estimates exist because many studies have small sample sizes, poor case definitions, inadequate instrumentation, inconsistencies in data sources (i.e., one vs. multiple informants), and discrepant approaches to data analysis. Costello, Egger, and Angold's (2005) recent update review of research showed progress in some of these areas. In any event, the prevalence of psychiatric disorders raises questions about the influence of psychopathology in the lives of adolescents.

The lack of diverse samples in many studies of adolescent psychopathology has resulted in a predominance of information about White adolescents, with limited information about psychopathology in youth of color (Roberts et al., 1998; USDHHS, 1999). This limitation ignores the potential distinctiveness that stressful environments and culture may have on the mental health of this adolescent subgroup. Further, the 1999 Surgeon General's Report on Mental Health (USDHHS, 1999) highlighted national concerns regarding racial disparities in access to and use of mental health services for ethnic minority adolescents with psychiatric disorders. More recent studies have continued to find disparities in mental health services utilization among youth of color (Angold et al., 2002; Elster, Jarosik, VanGeest, & Fleming, 2003). More information about the social context and correlates of psychopathology for youth of color would better inform mental health services and preventive interventions provided to address their needs.

In this chapter we focus on Black adolescents and the most common adolescent mental health concern: depression. We discuss prevalence estimates and identify environmental and cultural risk and protective factors associated with depression. Specifically, we consider the role of racial discrimination and neighborhood influences as structural factors that have implications for psychopathology. We also examine what is known about the relationship between depression and risky sexual behaviors as a way to better understand the complexity of adolescent mental health and a prevalent problem behavior among Black youth. By highlighting structural conditions that can impinge on the mental health of Black youth, we hope to avoid the tendency to attribute poor outcomes solely to inherent predispositions of adolescents. Our goal is to provide a more comprehensive approach for conceptualizing adolescent depression.

Throughout this chapter we use the term *Black adolescents* to refer to the numerous distinct cultures that characterize people of African ancestry who have settled in the United States. Most research does not distinguish between various Black cultures or ethnicities (e.g., African American, Caribbean Black, African), instead labeling all Black youth as African American. Such an approach obscures the social and historical backgrounds of different groups of Black adolescents that could provide perspective into their lived experiences. Research on adolescent mental health is rich with racial and ethnic group comparisons that focus on decontextualized outcomes (Cole & Stewart, 2001), suggesting similarities or differences across groups with few explanations that consider social context beyond low socioeconomic status (SES). Paying attention to additional sociocultural features of Black adolescents' environments could offer more insights into the meaning of the racial and ethnic group differences observed in mental health research. Therefore, when possible, we highlight the role that poverty or sociocultural factors play in depression.

Prevalence of Depression among Black Adolescents

Kaslow, Croft, and Hatcher (1999) noted that depression among youth was first mentioned in the 17th century, but it received little attention until 1970 when it was recognized as a mental disorder at the Fourth Congress of the Union of European Pedopsychiatrists. Discussions about depression among racially and ethnically diverse adolescents are more recent phenomena that are continuing to evolve as scholars seek to understand adolescent depression in a diversifying society. Several literature reviews emerged during the latter part of the 1980s and throughout the 1990s that acknowledged the exclusion of or limited focus on youth of color in studies of depression. In their comprehensive review of depressive disorders, Fleming and Offord (1990) identified five of nine community studies that included Black adolescents, whereas Petersen and colleagues (1993) concluded that too few studies consider subgroup variation, except for gender, even though they identified more than 2,000 studies of depressive symptoms and depression in their initial search from 1987 to 1991.

Earlier investigations examined racial differences in prevalence estimates between Black and White adolescents (for reviews, see Fleming & Offord, 1990; Petersen et al., 1993). In the late 1990s, however, multiethnic samples of adolescents began to be included in more research. Determining race and ethnic differences in depression remained the focus of this research. However, a number of studies began offering cultural explanations for observed ethnic differences, especially for Hispanic youth. These explanations now include language barriers, acculturative stress, neighborhood stress, and ethnic identity (Allen & Mitchell, 1998; Roberts & Roberts, 2007; Van Voorhees et al., 2008).

The onset of depression is influenced by a complex set of biological, psychological, social, and environmental conditions that result in serious impairment and a lack of adaptive functioning (Kaslow et al., 1999). A desire to understand how the development of such disorders interacts with the added challenge of the developmental tasks of adolescence, such as puberty and separation and individuation from family, has led to the emergence of the field of developmental psychopathology (Cicchetti & Rogosch, 2002). Advances in the conceptualizations and measurement of adolescent psychopathology have sparked a proliferation of research on the prevalence, correlates, and comorbidity of depression during adolescence over the past two decades. Yet, depression in adolescents continues to be diagnosed using the same criteria as those used for adults (Bhatia & Bhatia, 2007; Poznanski & Mokros, 1994). Most of what is known about depression in Black adolescents is based on studies using self-report depressive symptomatology scales. Reliance on depressive symptoms scales in multiethnic research requires careful attention to measurement issues. Therefore, we provide an overview of depressive symptom and depression instruments before presenting what is known based on these measures.

Depressive Symptoms

The most extensive body of research on Black youth has examined depressive symptomatology rather than depressive disorders. From a theoretical perspective, depressive symptomatology represents a complex syndrome involving feelings of helplessness and hopelessness, guilt and worthlessness, loss of appetite, sleep disturbances, and psychomotor retardation (Radloff, 1977). Self-report symptomatology scales with adequate reliability and validity, such as the Center for Epidemiologic Studies–Depression scale (CES-D; Radloff, 1977, 1991), the Beck Depression Inventory (BDI; Beck, Rush, Shaw, & Emery, 1979), and the Children's Depression Inventory (CDI; Kovacs, 1992), are often used to measure depressive symptoms in adolescents (see Reynolds, 1994, for review). These scales do not measure clinical depression; rather, they assess who may be at risk for depression or who may be experiencing psychological distress. Higher scale scores than those prescribed for assessing symptomatology have been established to better approximate clinical depression; however, these scales can overestimate symptoms when compared with results from clinical interviews.

Measurement equivalence is an important concern when depressive symptomatology scales are used with multiple racial and ethnic groups because most have been validated with White adolescents (McLaughlin, Hilt, & Nolen-Hoeksema, 2007; Perreira, Deeb-Sossa, Harris, & Bollen, 2005). Few studies of multiethnic groups have assessed cultural biases or reporting differences across groups despite available validity information (Reynolds, 1994). It is unclear what is actually being measured when a scale has not been validated with specific race/ethnic groups. Observed differences in depressive symptoms may result from measurement error rather than group differences for a number of reasons, including variations in meaning across items, a lack of cultural sensitivity in items, or differences in expressions of psychopathology.

Perreira et al. (2005) tested the quality of the CES-D for measurement structural invariance and equivalence among Black, White, Asian, and Hispanic adolescents using data from the National Longitudinal Study of Adolescent Health (Add Health). They made assessments by race/ethnicity and immigrant generation. They determined that changes had been made to the original 20-item CES-D to create a 19-item CES-D measure for the Add Health dataset. Using this measure, Perreira et al. (2005) conducted a series of analyses showing that models of the underlying structure of the CES-D19 for non-Whites did not fit as well as models for Whites. That is, when compared to third- or higher generation Whites, the model fits were worse for second- and third- or higher generation Blacks, third- or higher generation Asians, and all Hispanic generations. They noted that the CES-D19 mixes cause, effect, and outcome indicators of depression when all indicators should be effects. Mixed indicators can bias parameter estimates of depression across racial/ethnic groups. Only 5 of the original 19 items were effects indicators for depression, and those items were comparable across the 12 racial/ethnic/immigrant status groups assessed in this study. These items are "blues," "depressed," "happy," "sad," and "life was not worthwhile"; the last item was added to the Add Health measure from the child CES-D scale (Perreira et al., 2005).

The reliability of the five-item CES-D was lower across the 12 race/ethnic/ immigrant groups (alpha = .73 −.78) than reliabilities for the CES-D19. The patterns of mean differences in scores, however, were similar for the two measures. Perreira et al. (2005) argued that the general pattern of responses across ethnic/immigrant groups with the CES-D19 taps constructs other than depression because of measurement structural invariance and a lack of item equivalence across groups. Testing the CES-D12, Roberts (1992) also found that a reduced 12-item measure was appropriate to use in a multiethnic national study of psychopathology with Black, White, Mexican American, and other Hispanic adolescents. Others have found that Black adolescents respond differently than White adolescents to some of the original CES-D20 items (McDowell & Newell, 2006; Schoenbach, Kaplan, Wagner, Grimson, & Miller, 1983). Thus, racial/ethnic similarities or variations in estimates of depressive symptoms may be a function of symptom expression elicited by measures rather than differences in depressive symptomatology. Before conclusive statements can be made, more methodological research is needed to determine the validity of different depressive symptomatology scales for youth of color. Such research is critical because of the increasing volume of multiethnic studies that use these measures for assessing risk for depression during adolescence and adulthood.

Another issue is that studies of depressive symptoms involving Black adolescents often are based on specialty samples, such as teenage mothers (Shanok & Miller, 2007), college students (Banks & Kohn-Wood, 2007), juvenile offenders (Kuo, Vander Stoep, & Stewart, 2005) or treatment populations (Crum et al., 2008), which limits the generalizability of findings. The number of large-scale community or national studies that include Black adolescents has increased over the past 25 years. Prevalence estimates of depressive symptoms based on these studies have been equivocal. Some studies have reported lower levels of depressive symptoms in Black adolescents than White adolescents (Franko et al., 2005), whereas others have reported higher (Brooks, Harris, Thrall, & Woods, 2002) or equivalent levels in Blacks when compared to Whites (McLaughlin, Hilt, & Nolen-Hoeksema, 2007). Inconsistencies in racial/ethnic differences in depressive symptomatology may be attributable to differences in instrumentation, settings, and samples across studies; however, ruling out measurement inequivalence within studies as an explanation for differences should be a high priority for future research with multiethnic youth.

Gender differences in depression typically occur between the ages of 13 and 15. There is little gender variation before puberty, although some research has found that prepubertal boys exhibit more depressive symptoms than girls (Twenge &

Nolen-Hoeksema, 2002). By age 15, girls are twice as likely as boys to be depressed, and this pattern of gender differences persists throughout the life-span (Nolen-Hoeksema & Girgus, 1994). Reports of gender differences in depression among Black youth have not been as consistent (girls higher: Carlson & Grant, 2008; McKeown et al., 1997; Roberts & Sobhan, 1992; boys higher: Nebbitt & Lombe, 2007; no difference: Hawkins, Hawkins, Sabatino, & Ley, 1998). These varying results have prompted some to suggest that gender differences may occur at a later developmental stage for Black adolescents (Nolen-Hoeksema, 2002).

A recent longitudinal study of depressive symptoms in 777 Black early adolescents from rural and suburban neighborhoods found no gender differences at age 11. At age 13, gender differences emerged, with girls having more depressive symptoms than boys, lending support to findings for a gender difference in depressive symptoms among Black youth at early adolescence (Natsuaki et al., 2007). In addition to the longitudinal design, Natsuaki et al.'s (2007) study is significant for highlighting the need to consider social context when determining the role of gender in depression for Black youth. The youth in this study were not from urban inner-city areas, and the researchers examined the role of stress and other factors to account for their findings. The role of chronic stressors in depression during early adolescents has emerged as an active research area because of the social disadvantage that many Black youth are exposed to at an early age. Natsuaki et al. (2007) found that stressful life events experienced at age 11 predict depressive symptoms at ages 11 and 13 for both boys and girls. The severity of stressful life events did not differ by gender at age 11, which is when no gender differences in depressive symptoms were evident. By age 13, gender differences in depressive symptoms may then have emerged as a function of differential responses to early stressful life events among boys and girls.

A consistent and compelling finding with adults is the association between severe life stress and depression (Monroe & Hadjiyannakis, 2002). Research on gender differences in depression in adults has indicated that men and women respond to stress in different ways, with women often vulnerable to psychological distress (Twenge & Nolen-Hoeksema, 2002). For example, women are more likely than men to report stressful events involving significant others and to engage in ruminative coping strategies that amplify depressive symptoms (Nolen-Hoeksema & Girgus, 1994; Petersen, Sarigiani, & Kennedy, 1991). Women are likely to assume their own burdens as well as the burdens of others while turning inward to cope with cumulative stressors. Black youth are often part of complicated extended family systems that value interconnectedness as part of their culture. Consequently, exposure to interpersonal family stress can occur for them at a young age, with girls learning to assume the burdens of others. Focusing on the negative aspects of stressors, self, or mood is reflective of a ruminative coping style versus coping styles that involve distractions. Few studies have tested the ruminative coping hypothesis with adolescents, although available evidence has suggested that the same pattern of gender differences found with adults may exist for White youth (see Grant et al., 2004, for a summary).

Studies of rumination and Black adolescents are almost nonexistent. In one of the only studies involving Black adolescents, Grant et al. (2004) tested hypotheses regarding interpersonal stressors and rumination as mediators of gender differences in depression with 622 low-income, urban Black youth (mean age = 12.73). Incorporating a sociocultural perspective into their work, they speculated that cultural values may result in increased involvement of boys in the lives of others, effectively diminishing the expected gender effect of interpersonal stressors on depression. Their hypothesis was supported as they found similar patterns of interpersonal involvement for boys and girls, so that interpersonal involvement was not a mediator of gender and depressive symptoms. Their study supported the cognitive vulnerability explanation for gender differences in depression in that more rumination was associated with higher levels of depressive symptoms and girls ruminated more than boys.

More long-term longitudinal research is needed to determine if a clear pattern of gender differences in depressive symptoms emerges between the ages of 13 and 15 or if later developmental stages are better reflective of the experiences of Black youth. Clarifying the role of stressful life events during early adolescence and identifying mediating factors in the link between gender and depressive symptomatology will be necessary to better understand when and why gender matters in the course of depression for Black youth.

The intersection of race and gender further illustrates the complexity of adolescent depression as questions about persistence and developmental course are examined. Franko et al. (2005), for example, found that White girls had higher depressive symptomatology than Black girls at age 16, but their symptoms diminished over time and by age 22, they no longer exhibited higher symptomatology. Depressive symptoms in Black girls remained stable from mid-adolescence until early adulthood. The within-gender race difference initially observed at midadolescence was no longer present at early adulthood. One explanation for race differences in depressive symptoms among girls during adolescence is differential adaptation skills. That is, Black girls often learn to survive and cope with adversity at an earlier age, which is due, in part, to living in harsh environmental conditions. Studies of racial socialization practices within Black families, such as the transmission of messages to promote positive ethnic identity and to prepare youth to succeed in the face of racial discrimination (D. Hughes, 2003), have shown that protective racial socialization messages are associated with less depressive symptoms in Black youth (Davis & Stevenson, 2006). Future research into the deliberate preparation of Black adolescents for adversity should identify additional cultural practices and values within families that may protect youth from depression such as egalitarian gender roles and religious beliefs.

The inconsistent findings for depressive symptoms in Black adolescents underscore the need for better measures and a broadening of the focus of inquiry beyond seeking patterns of racial/ethnic differences in depression to more explanatory models. As Roberts, Roberts, and Chen (1997) similarly asked, "What is it about race or ethnicity that increases or decreases the risk for psychiatric disorder?" (p. 107). Embedded in this question is a call to identify underlying mechanisms and social contexts that influence adolescent psychopathology that are typically represented as race/ethnicity in studies of youth of color. Families have been identified as critical risk factors in the etiology and maintenance of depression during adolescence (Lewinsohn & Essau, 2002). Substantial research supports the position that adolescents with depressed parents are at greater risk for depression than those with nondepressed parents. Genetics as well as dysfunctional family processes, including poor parent–child interactions, parental emotional unavailability, and high family conflict, account for the association between parental and adolescent depression (Lewinsohn & Essau, 2002; McLoyd, 1990). Additional family stressors exacerbate these conditions.

Some Black families face enormous stressors such as chronic poverty, un- or underemployment, financial difficulties, living in disadvantaged neighborhoods, and cumulative negative and stressful life events. Adolescents who are part of such family systems are expected to be at increased risk for depression because of the associated social disadvantages in their lives. Characterizing Black adolescents as being "at risk" simply because of their race and low socioeconomic backgrounds, however, is misleading. Farmer et al. (2004) assessed the validity of the "at risk" argument by examining the effects of single versus multiple risk profiles of Black early adolescents in two separate studies to determine who was at risk for later problem behaviors. One study focused on Black and White youth from a low-income, inner-city neighborhood, whereas the other involved Black youth from a rural environment. The majority of Black adolescents from both environments did not evidence risk for later problem behavior, regardless of their risk profiles. Determining which adolescents may be at risk for depression will be more complicated than assuming that inner-city low-income Black youth will have the worst outcomes.

Cultural strengths exist that that can protect against psychopathology. Strengths of Black families include a commitment to religious beliefs, egalitarian gender roles, a collectivist orientation, and connections to extended family systems (Hill, 1972; R. J. Taylor, Chatters, & Levin, 2004). Few studies with Black adolescents have examined these strengths as a way to better understand which adolescents may be at greater risk than others. R. D. Taylor, Casten, and Flickinger (1993) considered the protective effects of kinship support on the depressive symptoms of Black adolescents by examining the moderating effects of family structure. They found that kinship support promoted lower levels of depressive symptoms, but only among Black adolescents living in single-parent households. The availability of extended family members to provide support to adolescents living with one parent highlights a cultural strength that can be used in assessing risk assumptions to better target services and intervention. More research is needed that offers potential underlying mechanisms for relationships and sociocultural explanations for findings, thereby advancing knowledge about depression in Black adolescents.

Depression

Clinical or major depression represents a more severe and chronic form of depression than depressive symptomatology (Petersen et al., 1993; Roberts, 1992). It is defined as a clinical syndrome of at least five symptoms that cluster together, last for at least 2 weeks, and cause impairment in functioning. The syndrome includes mood symptoms (e.g., being depressed or sad or loss of interest in usual activities), cognitive symptoms (e.g., inability to concentrate, difficulty making decisions), and physical symptoms (e.g., lack of energy, or change in sleep, appetite, and activity levels; American Psychiatric Association, 2000; Pratt & Brody, 2008). Diagnostic criteria are essentially the same for adolescents and adults, although symptom expression may vary at different developmental stages (Bhatia & Bhatia, 2007; Poznanski & Mokros, 1994). Treatment populations are often the source for studies of depressive disorders in Black adolescents (Fabrega, Ulrich, & Mezzich, 1993; Jainchill, De Leon, & Yagelka, 1997). Consequently, less is known about depressive disorders in the general population of Black adolescents.

We identified 10 studies of adolescent depression with large community or national samples that included substantial numbers of Black youth. Table 18.1 provides a summary of these studies, including sample size and diagnostic measures used to assess depression and prevalence rates. Studies included in Table 18.1 are intended to be representative rather than exhaustive of the available studies that included Black adolescents in sizable numbers. We reviewed studies that used a structured diagnostic interview schedule or standardized clinical interview based on a recent version of the *Diagnostic and Statistical Manual of Mental Disorders* (DSM-III or later; American Psychiatric Association, 2000). In this section, we limit our focus to studies of adolescents with depressive disorders rather than depressive symptomatology. Although research on psychiatric disorders in Black adolescents is appallingly lacking, extant studies are instructive for understanding prevalence, correlates, and directions for future research.

Prevalence estimates for depression in Black adolescents have ranged from 0.5% to 6.8% in community samples (Angold et al., 2002; Cuffe et al., 1995; Roberts, Roberts, & Xing, 2006; Simons, Murry, McLoyd, Lin, Cutrona, & Conger, 2002) to 2.9% to 14.6% in national studies (Saluja et al., 2004; USDHHS, 1999). Structured diagnostic interview schedules or standardized clinical interviews that are used to assess depressive disorders in adolescents can assess multiple disorders, which

Table 18.1. *Community and national studies of depression including Black adolescents*

Study	Purpose	Study design	Sample/setting	Measure	Depression findings
Cuffe et al. (1995)	Examines race and gender differences in treatment of adolescent psychiatric disorders	Longitudinal Two-stage assessment process Four public middle and two high schools from a Southeast school district	Wave 1: Total N = 3,283 screened n = 478 diagnosed School-based 17.0% Black 83.0% White 50.0% Female *Age: 10–20*	CES-D K-SADS Global Assessment Scale (GAS) - impairment 12 months Validity: Not discussed	Prevalence: *Wave 1* 6.8% Blacks 6.8% Whites No difference
Doi et al. (2001)	Compares prevalence rates of major depression for multiethnic samples of U.S. and Japanese adolescents	Cross-section Cross-cultural U.S. and Japan	Total N = 2,046 n = 636 Black n = 539 Whites n = 409 Mexican Americans n = 462 Japanese *Age: 12–15*	DSM Scale/Depression (Roberts et al., 1997) Based on the DISC 2.3 MDD Validity: Construct – loneliness, self-esteem, and social support	Prevalence: Without impairment: 13.4% Blacks 9.6% Whites 16.9% Mexican 5.6% Japanese With impairment: 6.1% Blacks 4.3% Whites 9.0% Mexican 1.3% Japanese
Angold et al. (2002)	Examines race and gender differences in psychiatric disorders and correlates of service use	Cross-section Two-stage assessment process Rural state	N = 4,500 screen n = 1,302 screen n = 920 – Final School-based 4 NC counties 53.8% Black 44.4% White 50.0% Female *Age: 9–17* Parents by phone	Child and Adolescent Psychiatric Assessment (CAPA) (DSM-IV only) Impairment 3 months Validity: Original	Prevalence: 1.4% Blacks* 4.6% Whites *Blacks lower than Whites Blacks less likely to use specialty mental health services than Whites

(continued)

Table 18.1 (continued)

Study	Purpose	Study design	Sample/setting	Measure	Depression findings
Simons et al. (2002)	Examines correlates of childhood depressive symptoms	Cross-section Rural sample in two states	Total N = 867 Iowa = 462 Georgia = 405 Community 100% Black 54.0% Female Age: 10–12 Caretaker IW	DISC-IV Symptoms count used – low disorders 12 months 22-item scale, alpha = .86 Validity: Original	Prevalence: 1.3% Blacks
Saluja et al. (2004)	Examines prevalence, risk factors, and risk behaviors associated with depression	Cross-section National	Total N = 9,863 Nationally representative School-based 13.6% Black 48.0% White 28.2% Latino 08.7% Asian 01.5% AI/PI 52.2% Female Age: 11–15	Dichotomous variable created based on 12 questions from the DSM-III-R Macro International; SAMSHSA, NICHD Fund 12 months Self admin. Validity: Not discussed	Prevalence: 14.6% Blacks* 18.4% Whites 21.7% Latinos 16.6% Asians 29.0% AI/PIs *Blacks lower than Whites, Latinos and American Indian/Pacific Islanders
Roberts, Roberts, & Xing (2006)	Examines prevalence data and functional impairment and demographics as correlates of disorders	Cross-section One urban city	Total N = 4,175 Households in Houston, TX 35.35% Black 35.43% White 20.53% Mexican Age: 11–17	DISC-IV [a]CGAS – impairment 12 months Lay interviewers Validity: Original	Prevalence: Without impairment 2.0% Blacks* 3.2% Whites 3.4% Mexicans [a]With impairment 0.5% Blacks* 1.3% Whites 1.2% Mexicans
Natsuaki et al. (2007)	Examines the prospective effects of neighborhood disorder, stressful life events, and parenting on depression	Longitudinal 2-year follow-up Rural sample in two states	Total N = 777 Parent-child Neighborhood Iowa/Georgia 100% Black 54.0% Female Age: 9–12 at Wave 1	DISC-IV Symptoms count used 20 questions 12 months Lay interviewers Validity: original	Symptom scores: (Low prevalence estimates) Age: 11 Mean = 6.04 Age: 13 Mean = 6.52 Girls have more symptoms than boys

Author (year)	Purpose	Design	Sample	Measure / Validity	Results
Vega, Chen, & Williams (2007)	Estimates smoking prevalence and its relation to psychiatric disorders	Cross-section National	Total N = 19,430 Nationally representative 2000 National Household Survey on Drug Abuse (NHSDA) % Black, not reported % Female, not reported Age: 12–17	Adapted the DISC for a national household survey 12 months Validity: Not discussed	Adjusted odds ratios: (Demographics & substance use adj.) 1.72 Blacks* (1.54–1.91) 1.20 U.S. Latinos (1.07–1.35) 1.20 Immigrants (0.97–1.48) *Blacks higher than White comparison group
Williams, Gonzalez, et al. (2007)	Estimates prevalence, persistence, treatment, and disability of depression in African Americans, Caribbean Blacks, and Whites	Cross-section National	Total N = 6,082, age ≥18 n = 806 African Americans Age: 18–29 n = 436 Caribbean Blacks Age: 18–29 n = 150 Whites Age: 18–29	WHO Composite International Diagnostic Interview (CIDI) DSM-IV MDD Sheehan Disability Scale and WHO's Disability Assessment Schedule II Validity: CIDI higher rates of MDD than SCID for Caribbean Blacks	Prevalence rates: Lifetime MDD 12.8% African American 18- to 29-year-olds 19.9% Caribbean Black 18- to 29-year-olds 14.7% White 18- to 29-year-olds [Author's Note: Pattern similar for 12-month MDD but figures not reported.]
Van Voorhees et al. (2008)	Identifies factors predicting new onset of depressive episodes	Longitudinal Cohort study 1-year follow-up National	Total N = 4,791 National Longitudinal Study of Adolescent Health (Add Health) % Black not reported % Gender not reported Grades: 7–12	CES-D using DSM-III criteria (depressed mood or anhedonia most or all of the time, 5–7 days, for the last week and three other DSM-III symptoms) 1 week Interviews Validity: Original as reported by Radloff (1991) for adolescents	Adjusted odds ratios for Wave II: (CES-D Wave I, income, age, and gender adjusted) 1.62 Blacks (0.95–2.77) 1.56 Hispanics (0.82–2.98) 0.80 Asians (0.28–2.63) 0.86 Other (1.10–1.16) Blacks higher than White comparison group unadjusted, but not adjusted

Note: Although advances have been made in the use of structured or clinical interviews with adolescents, methodological approaches continue to vary across studies. What sounds like the same diagnostic measure is sometimes not the same. As indicated earlier, two studies adapted a version of the DISC using DSM criteria, one study enhanced the CES-D following DSM criteria, and one study followed DSM criteria and described a procedure as compatible with structured diagnostic interviews. Other variations occur in the "reporting of results. Prevalence estimates versus odds ratios or the use of symptom scores when prevalence estimates are too low for data analysis are examples. These issues contribute to the inconsistencies in prevalence estimates found in the literature.

CGAS = Children's Global Assessment Scale; measures impairment in functioning at home, at school and with peers.

is a useful strategy for determining comorbidities in psychopathology. The major limitations of these measures are that they can be labor intensive and costly to administer. Some require clinicians as interviewers for data collection, whereas others can be administered by well-trained lay interviewers with no clinical training (Hodges, 1994).

Based on the availability of psychometric data, Hodges (1994) critiqued five measures frequently used with adolescents to assess major depressive disorder and dysthymia : (1) the Child Assessment Schedule (CAS), (2) the Interview Schedule for Children (ISC), (3) the Schedule for Affective Disorders and Schizophrenia in School Age Children (K-SADS), (4) the Diagnostic Interview for Children and Adolescents (DICA), and (5) the Diagnostic Interview Schedule for Children (DISC-R). In their recent comprehensive review, Renou, Hergueta, Flament, Mouren-Simeoni, and Lecrubier (2004) assessed these and two additional measures: the Child and Adolescent Psychiatric Assessment (CAPA) and the Children's Interview for Psychiatric Syndromes (ChIPS). Each measure has a complementary parent version that gathers information about the adolescent's symptom from his or her parent because multiple informants are important.

The CAS, ISC, and K-SADS require clinical interviewers, whereas lay interviewers can collect disorder data using the DICA, DISC-R, CAPA, and ChIPS. Clinical interviews provide some flexibility in interpretation, so that the judgment of the clinician can be taken into account as part of the assessment process. The structured diagnostic interview schedule does not have this flexibility; classifications for disorders are made on the basis of a series of standardized questions. Structured diagnostic interview schedules are more likely to be used in large, population-based surveys. These measures have been revised to be consistent with revisions in the DSM from versions DSM-III to DSM-IV-TR. In addition, self-administration of the structured diagnostic interview has been applied in survey research, especially with computer-assisted methodologies (Costello, Egger, & Angold, 2005). Strengths and weaknesses are evident with each measure; most telling, however, is the limited reported details of systematic validity assessments with different racial/ethnic subgroups of adolescents.

Measurement validity for ethnically diverse youth has been extensively addressed for the DISC-Version 2.3 based on the Methodology for Epidemiology in Children and Adolescents study (MECA; Shaffer et al., 1996). It has been tested with Puerto Rican adolescents in the United States and Puerto Rico (Bird et al., 2001) and with American Indian adolescents (Beals et al., 1997). Roberts, Solovitz, Chen, and Casat (1996) assessed the validity of the DISC-2.1C with Black, White, and Hispanic adolescents; however. the small number of cases and the small sample size did not allow the reporting of results by race/ethnic group. Other measures have been used with multiethnic groups of adolescents, but often reliability reports are more extensive than validity reports. This either highlights the need for validity studies with multiethnic samples or more balanced reporting of validity findings with commonly used classification measures of psychiatric disorders.

Prevalence estimates of depression for Black adolescents are inconsistent because of variations in sample size, age range assessed, time frame used, study site, and measurement approach (see Table 18.1 for examples). Angold et al. (2002), for example, surveyed four counties in rural North Carolina to assess psychiatric disorders in 920 Black or White 9- to 17-year-olds. They found that 1.4% of Black adolescents were depressed in the previous 3 months using the Child and Adolescent Psychiatric Assessment (based on DSM-IV criteria with impairment) compared to 4.6% of Whites. This result is similar to Roberts and colleagues' (2006) findings for Blacks from a large, ethnically diverse, urban, community-based sample of 11- to 17-year-olds using the DISC-IV with impairment. They found that 1.1% of Black ($n = 1,476$) and 2.3% of White ($n = 1,479$) youth had a mood disorder in the previous 12 months. With the CGAS (Children's Global Assessment Scale) impairment scale, however, the rate for Blacks was 0.5% and it was 1.3% for Whites. When using the DISC (based on DSM-III criteria) without impairment, Doi et al. (2001) found that 13.4% of the 636 Black 12- to 15-year-olds in their urban U.S. sample were depressed. Only 6.1% were depressed when impairment was used in the assessment. Adjusting for functional impairment reduced prevalence by more than half. This decreasing prevalence with impairment was similar for the White (9.6% vs. 4.3%) and Mexican American (16.9% vs. 9.0%) adolescents in their sample as well; however, their estimates of depression remained high when compared with other studies of U.S. youth of color. Perhaps the limited age range in the Doi et al. (2001) study partially accounts for these inconsistencies. Other studies have included prepubertal children, who are of an age when depression is expected to be lower than Doi et al.'s sample of 12- to 15-year-olds. Equivalent age ranges and comparable impairment assessments are necessary to determine consistent prevalence estimates, age of onset, and emergent gender differences in depression. With impairment, prevalence estimates for White youth appear to be more consistent than estimates for youth of color. This finding suggests that the relevance of impairment measures should be examined in multiethnic samples of adolescents.

Ethnic variations among Black adolescents are rarely considered in research, yet differences in depression may exist because of their different life experiences. The National Survey of American Life (Jackson et al., 2004), the most comprehensive, nationally representative study of the mental health of African Americans and Caribbean Blacks ever conducted, provided prevalence estimates for major depressive disorder (MDD) for 18- to 29-year-olds across three racial/ethnic groups (Williams, Gonzalez, et al., 2007). Lifetime prevalence estimates for MDD were 12.8% for young African Americans and 14.7% for young Whites; however, the rate for young Caribbean Blacks was 19.9% using the Composite International Diagnostic Interview (WHO-CIDI, 2004). According to the authors, the pattern for

12-month MDD was similar to the lifetime prevalence rates for all groups. Gender differences in MDD were found among African American and White adults for the total sample, with African American women having higher rates of MDD than African American men and Whites of both genders. No gender differences in MDD were found among Caribbean Black adults. MDD prevalence estimates for the young adults in this study were higher than those in studies of adolescents, perhaps because of the older age range or because the CIDI was the structured interview schedule used. Validity assessments comparing the CIDI with the SCID indicated that Caribbean Blacks had a higher prevalence of MDD with the CIDI than with the SCID, whereas MDD prevalence estimates for African Americans and Whites were comparable across measures. These findings again focus attention on the need to determine cross-cultural equivalence in measurement when conducting multiethnic studies. They also suggest the significance of examining within-group variations in depression for the Black population.

Results of this brief review show that there are Black adolescents who are at risk for depressive symptoms and depression. What is not clear is how mental health research with Black adolescents can incorporate environmental and cultural issues to better understand the meaning of race and ethnicity in psychopathology. The sections that follow present theoretical perspectives and empirical findings on racial discrimination and neighborhood factors as two social contextual issues especially relevant for understanding psychopathology in Black adolescents. These areas were selected because racial discrimination is prevalent in the lives of Black adolescents and neighborhood influences can complement or compete with family socialization efforts to shape the adolescent. Additionally, research in these areas can be conceptualized beyond individual characteristics to offer structural explanations for risk and protective factors associated with depression in Black adolescents when addressing this question: What is it about race or ethnicity that increases or decreases the risk for psychiatric disorders?

Racial Discrimination and Depression

Linking race-related issues to psychopathology allows us to more fully consider the implications of racism as part of the broader sociocultural environment in the lives of adolescents of color. Research involving race often aims to identify how structural conditions may influence racial attitudes and behaviors that have implications for mental health. Thus, the social construction of race is frequently used to explain racial differences observed in mental health outcomes. Most studies of race as a social construction rely on group membership as the defining characteristic (Helms, Jernigan, & Mascher, 2005). The use of the concept of race solely as a demographic variable lacks a depth of understanding of the roles that ethnicity and culture can play in shaping the lives and adaptation of racial subgroups in America. Gabard and Cooper (1998) suggested that "racial identifications serve as frameworks of personal identifications with the groups' accomplishments, histories, political power bases, struggles, and victories" (p. 343). Racial categorizations can be used for purposes of inclusion or exclusion. Research that merely controls for race differences can limit our understanding of underlying factors that may facilitate or prevent psychopathology among different racial groups (LaVeist, 1996).

Scholars have argued that race or ethnicity are markers for more meaningful constructs based on people's lived experiences and malleable social contexts that reflect their social position (Helms et al., 2005; Sampson, Morenoff, & Raudenbush, 2005). Research on racial discrimination and adult mental health has moved beyond examining the effects of race/ethnicity as a demographic variable to recognize the socially embedded meaning of race that blocked opportunity structures such as residential segregation, poverty, or discrimination in access to services may foster. Therefore, we focus on racial discrimination as an example for considering the meaning of race/ethnicity in adolescent depression.

Racial discrimination is often conceptualized within a stress paradigm, suggesting that it is a unique psychosocial stressor that has deleterious consequences for mental and physical health (Sellers, Morgan, & Brown, 2001; Williams, Neighbors, & Jackson, 2003). Cumulative exposures to stress associated with discrimination, economic strain, unsafe neighborhoods, and other social disadvantages contribute to poor mental health. Data on adults consistently show that experiences with racial stress are associated with mental distress (for reviews, see Blaney, 2000; Williams et al., 2003). In one of the few studies to examine the relation between discrimination and psychiatric disorders, Kessler, Mickelson, and Williams (1999) found that lifetime and day-to-day discrimination were associated with major depression in a national sample of racially diverse adults. Blacks (89.7%) attributed discriminatory experiences to race/ethnicity rather than to gender, as Whites did in the study.

The link between racial stress and depressive symptoms exists for Black adolescents as well (Seaton, Caldwell, Sellers, & Jackson, 2008; Simons et al., 2002). One framework for explaining the association between racial discrimination and psychopathology for Black adolescents is Garcia Coll et al.'s (1996) integrative model. This model posits that American society stratifies individuals based on social position, including race, ethnicity, social class, and gender. Social positions are influenced by racial discrimination; therefore, positive developmental pathways for Black youth are expected to be diminished because of the pervasiveness of racial discrimination within society (Garcia Coll et al., 1996; Seaton et al., 2008). Based on national data with ethnically diverse Black youth, Seaton et al. (2008) found that 87% of African American and 90% of Caribbean Black youth reported experiencing a discriminatory episode in the previous year. Other studies found that 52% to 91% of Black adolescents reported at least one encounter with racial discrimination within the prior year (Gibbons, Gerrard, Cleveland,

Wills, & Brody, 2004; Guthrie, Young, Williams, Boyd, & Kintner, 2002; Prelow, Danoff-Burg, Swenson, & Pulgiano, 2004).

The effects of racial stress combined with the normative stresses of adolescence can be especially harmful. Sellers, Caldwell, Schmeelk-Cone, and Zimmerman (2003) found that perceived racial discrimination was associated with higher levels of perceived stress and psychological distress in a sample of late adolescents. Perceived stress mediated the influence of perceived racial discrimination on psychological distress. They concluded that racial hassles may make life more stressful for Black youth, which in turn affects their mental health. Further, Simons et al. (2002) found that both child and caretaker reports of racial discrimination were directly associated with depressive symptoms among rural Black 10- to 12-year-olds, suggesting early exposure to discrimination. These findings support the integrative model's proposition of the pervasiveness and deleterious consequences of racial discrimination on Black adolescents.

Overwhelmingly, research on racial discrimination and Black adolescents has examined its association with depressive symptomatology. Consistent findings have shown that perceived racial discrimination is detrimental to the mental health of Black adolescents, regardless of gender, age, socioeconomic status, or ethnicity when African American and Caribbean Black youth are examined (Caldwell, Guthrie, & Jackson, 2006; Seaton et al., 2008; Sellers et al., 2003; Simons et al., 2002; Stevenson, et al., 1997). The question remains about the extent to which there is an association between perceived racial discrimination and depressive disorders in Black adolescents. Studies of depression and objective experiences with racial discrimination as well as discriminatory practices involving adolescents are also needed to directly demonstrate the effects of racial discrimination on mental health among youth. Research on neighborhoods provides an example of the negative influence of structural racism on the mental health of Black youth.

Neighborhoods and Depression

Neighborhood characteristics (e.g., poverty, violence, social organization, residential mobility) are indicators of family socioeconomic position with implications for adolescent psychopathology. Attempting to separate neighborhood influences from socioeconomic and family influences on adolescent psychopathology can be daunting. Nevertheless, a focus on neighborhoods is critical to understanding environmental conditions that contribute to mental health functioning during adolescence. Cutrona, Wallace, and Wesner (2006) identified three reasons to understand neighborhood context for depression:

> 1) People . . . mistakenly blame themselves for the invisible stressors that affect their well-being . . . ; b) outsiders also fail to realize that residents of adverse neighborhoods are influenced by their surroundings . . . ; and c) when threats to

public health are caused by characteristics of entire communities, it is more efficient to address these threats at the community level rather than to treat each afflicted individual separately. (p. 188)

A focus at the neighborhood level for risk and protective factors also avoids what Silver (2000) has characterized as the "individualistic fallacy." The individualistic fallacy assumes that psychiatric disorders for individuals can be explained by individual characteristics alone (Valkonen, 1967, as cited in Silver, 2000). Research on neighborhood influences on adolescent mental health has increased substantially over the past 20 years, emerging as a critical social context for understanding adolescent development and psychopathology.

Growing evidence has suggested that neighborhood characteristics are associated with mental health functioning beyond individual and family perceptions (Xue, Leventhal, Brooks-Gunn, & Earls, 2005). The residential environment can be a source of both stressors and support. Two divergent sets of theories guide much of the research in this area: (1) social disorganization theories of neighborhood and (2) models of collective efficacy, institutional resources, and social ties. Social disorganization theories suggest that structural characteristics of neighborhoods (e.g., percentage of residential poverty) are important because they facilitate or hinder the formation of community norms, values, and structures that surround residents' behavior (Sampson, Raudenbush, & Earls, 1997). Levels of social organization are expected to determine the degree of public order and monitoring in neighborhoods. Disadvantaged neighborhoods are expected to have low levels of social organization, which is associated with depression because they foster a sense of powerlessness, fear, and despair. A study of the relation between criminal victimization and depressive symptoms among Black 10- to 12-year-olds showed that neighborhood poverty exacerbates the association between criminal victimization and depressive symptoms. On the other hand, racial identification at the community level has been found to moderate this link and protect against escalated depressive symptoms (Simons et al., 2002).

For numerous reasons related to history and discriminatory practices (e.g., segregation, red-lining in mortgage lending, the mismatch between educational attainment and income), Black adolescents disproportionately live in disadvantaged neighborhoods compared to other youth, which puts them at risk for depression. Three complementary models suggest how neighborhood structure and social processes may protect against adolescent depression: (1) norms and collective efficacy, (2) institutional resources, and (3) relationships and social ties (Leventhal & Brooks-Gunn, 2000). The norms and collective efficacy model suggests that the extent of formal and informal social controls for monitoring adolescents accounts for neighborhood influences. The institutional resources model posits that community resources mediate neighborhood effects on youth outcomes. The relationships and social ties model hypothesizes that parental attributes and behaviors, the home environment, and social networks transmit neighborhood influences. The next section discusses the application of these models regarding their influence on the link between depression and risky sexual behaviors.

Problem Behaviors and Black Adolescents

Problem behaviors occur or do not occur as a result of a complex set of risk and protective factors that are dynamic and involve biological, social, and psychological processes. Jessor and Jessor (1977) proposed that adolescent problem behaviors are a function of characteristics of the individual and the social environment. The social environment involves families, friendship networks, schools, and neighborhoods. Arnett (1992) extended influential social environments to include the media and the legal and cultural belief systems. A common element in the conceptualization of problem behavior is that the behaviors cluster together. Further, problem behavior theory suggests that the same risk and protective factors can influence multiple problem behaviors such as sexual, violent, and substance use behaviors.

Studies of adolescents in treatment have shown that behavior problems are the most frequent reason why Black adolescents are referred for mental health services. For example, in a study of the psychiatric profiles of Black and White adolescents at a public university-based mental health facility, Fabrega et al. (1993) found that Black students were assessed with more social aggression symptoms and conduct disorder diagnoses, whereas eating disorders were the most frequent diagnosis for White students. Social impairment was equivalent in both racial groups at intake; however Whites had higher overall symptom levels and comorbidity on Axis I of DSM-III for affective and somatic disorders, and for substance use. They suggested that White intake interviewers may be better able to understand the symptom expression of White patients, which may have resulted in a more elaborate picture of psychopathology in White than Black adolescents. Jainchill et al. (1997) also found that Black youth appeared to be referred to substance abuse treatment while having less severe clinical symptoms than White youth.

Several studies have suggested that a bias in referral and intake procedures against Black youth may account for the disparities in diagnosis between Black and White youth with different symptom levels (Cuffe et al., 1995; Fabrega et al., 1993; Jainchill et al., 1997). Black youth appear to be referred for services with fewer symptoms than White youth. They also appear to receive a diagnosis of conduct and behavioral disorders rather than affective disorders. Embedded within a cultural bias argument, Fabrega et al. (1993) and Jainchill et al. (1997) suggested that limited understanding of the cultural background of Black youth may lead to overreactions by adults to their expressive behaviors.

As a rule, adolescents do not elect to go into treatment. Rather, they are referred by teachers, physicians, parents, or representatives of other systems (e.g., schools, child welfare, and juvenile justice). Consequently, how others respond to Black adolescents can determine their pathway into treatment and their course of treatment. Better preparation and training for mental health professionals working with Black youth are necessary to help them recognize and respond to their actual clinical needs. Myers (1989) asserted, "Valid clinical judgments of the meaning of behaviors should not be based on assumptions about singular norms, but should be tempered by an awareness of the contextual demands that shape and reinforce those behaviors" (p. 130).

For the remainder of the chapter, we focus on one problem behavior that has been linked to depression in Black adolescents: risky sexual behavior. We selected risky sexual behaviors because Black adolescents have been identified as becoming sexually active at an earlier age than other youth. The association between depression and risky sexual behaviors, however, has not been examined as much as other problem behaviors such as substance use and abuse or youth violent behavior. Yet, for several reasons, risky sexual behaviors may be important to understand when considering depression. Risky sexual behaviors among adolescents are often defined as precocious because they are initiated early or "off-time" from a developmental perspective. Determining associations between depression and risky sexual behaviors may be a useful strategy for identifying adolescents whose disorders may be missed through the normal process of problem identification, referral, and treatment as a result of clinicians' focus on precocious behavior (A. Martin et al., 2005). In addition, feelings of despair, loss, helplessness, and hopelessness may be underlying psychological processes associated with both depression and risky sexual behaviors that are precipitated by environmental influences amenable to change. We review what is known about the association between depression and risky sexual behaviors among Black youth as a way to better understand who may be at risk for depression and potential pathways into earlier treatment for depression based on its association with risky sexual behaviors. In the next section, we provide background information on different types of risky sexual behaviors before addressing links between depression and risky sexual behaviors among Black adolescents.

Prevalence of Risky Sexual Behaviors

Although the number of teenagers who engage in sexual intercourse has declined in recent years, approximately 46% of female and 50% of male teenagers 15 to 19 years old had sex at least once in 2007 (Centers for Disease Control and Prevention [CDC], 2007). These figures were higher for Black youth, with 61% of female and 73% of male teenagers being sexually active. Black male youths are at greatest risk for having sex at an early age, with 53% initiating sex by age 15 (Alan Guttmacher Institute, 2002). Early sexual debut is often accompanied by irresponsible sexual behaviors, which puts adolescents at risk for sexually transmitted diseases (STDs), HIV/AIDS, and unintended pregnancies.

Consequently, almost half of the 19 million new STD infections each year are among 15- to 24-year-olds, and about 14% of the new HIV/AIDS diagnoses in 2006 were to youth aged 13 to 24 years (CDC, 2007). Further, between 2005 and 2006, the birth rate for 15- to 17-year-olds rose 3%, and it rose 4% for 18- to 19-year-olds. Among sexually active adolescents, risky sexual behavior is a major public health concern strongly associated with other problem behaviors such as youth violence, substance use, and school dropout. Numerous sexual and nonsexual antecedents have been associated with early sexual debut (see Kirby & Miller, 2002, for a review). The link between depression and risky sexual behaviors for Black adolescents is the focus of a small but growing body of research.

Depression and Risky Sexual Behaviors

The concept of risky sexual behavior is multidimensional and includes early sexual debut, frequency of sexual behavior, multiple sexual partners, inconsistent condom use, and use of alcohol or drugs at the time of sex. Cross-sectional correlational studies, small sample sizes, use of treatment populations, or single-gender studies are pervasive in research on depression and risky sexual behaviors that include adolescents. Further, inconsistent definitions of specific sexual risk behaviors, a lack of precision in conceptualizing concepts (e.g., condom use, regular use of condoms), individualistic versus ecological framing of studies, and limited attention to potential mediators or moderators plague existing research (see Kotchick, Shaffer, Forehand, & Miller, 2001, for a review). Thus clear interpretations and generalizable findings are hampered. Despite these conceptual and methodological flaws, findings from accumulating studies are suggestive as to why it may be important to consider how risky sexual behaviors are associated with depression and pathways into treatment for Black adolescents. One benefit of such an approach may be earlier detection, diagnosis, and treatment of youth at risk for depression who otherwise may not be identified.

In general, depressive symptoms and depression are associated with risky sexual behaviors among Black adolescents regardless of whether studies are based on same- or mixed-gender samples. The evidence for this relationship is modest, and the effects differ depending on the sample and type of sexual behaviors examined or depression measure used. Community samples have tended to find stronger associations than specialized or institutional samples, and the use of self-report measures has resulted in stronger associations than have structured diagnostic or clinical interviews for depression. L. K. Brown et al. (2006), for example, found that inconsistent condom use was four times greater among Black adolescents with depressive symptoms compared to those with fewer symptoms. Depressed juvenile offenders in Tolou-Shams, Brown, Houck, and Lescano's (2008) study were twice as likely to have a history of sexually transmitted infections as those who were not depressed. Further, Bachanas et al. (2002) used an aggregate measure of sexual behavior combining sexual onset, number of partners, and condom use. They found no association between depressive symptoms and risky sexual behavior in their sample of Black female adolescents. Conversely, DiClemente et al.'s (2001) study with a similar sample of female adolescents used separate risky sexual behavior measures and found an association between different behaviors and depressive symptoms.

Several explanations have been offered to explain associations between depressive symptomatology and risky sexual behaviors. First, an adolescent who is depressed may be more willing to engage in risky sexual behaviors with little regard for future consequences because of a sense of hopelessness and a more pessimistic future outlook (Hawkins et al., 1998; A. Martin et al., 2005). Bolland's (2003) research, for example, showed that increased hopelessness among Black youth was associated with increased risky sexual behaviors. Using a different approach, Mandarin, Murray, and Bangi (2003) provided additional support for the hopelessness proposition and for the pessimistic future outlook perspective by showing that the anticipated life expectancy among Black adolescents who were virgins was 10 years longer than the anticipated life expectancy among nonvirgins. In other words, Black adolescents who did not expect to live long were less likely to delay their sexual debut than those with a more positive outlook about their mortality. Based on these findings, future research could examine hopelessness or mortality expectations as potential mediators of the risky sexual behavior–depression link in an effort to identify early warning signs of depression among sexually active Black adolescents.

Much of the research that explores the relationship between symptoms of depression and risky sexual behavior in Black adolescents is female specific. This focus may be attributed to a gender prioritization when the areas of depression and risky sexual behaviors are combined. That is, female adolescents are thought of as more likely than male adolescents to have high levels of depressive symptoms and to be the targets of interventions to reduce risky sexual behaviors. Not surprisingly, gender appears to moderate the depression–risky sexual behavior relationship, with female more likely than male adolescents to be depressed and to engage in multiple types of risky sexual behaviors (Paxton & Robinson, 2008). Research in this area consistently has shown that Black boys who are depressed engage in inconsistent condom use more often than depressed girls (Shrier et al., 2001), whereas depressed girls engage in unprotected sex (DiClementi et al., 2001), have multiple sexual partners (Ethier et al., 2006; Mazzoferro et al., 2006), and are likely to contract sexually transmitted infections more often than depressed boys (Shrier et al., 2001). Thus, observing risky sexual behaviors alone misses the opportunity to address depression as a coexisting problem for some sexually active Black youth, especially girls.

Why does the association between depression and risky sexual behaviors differ among Black male and female adolescents? Some have argued that within Black families and society at large, boys and girls are taught different sexual norms. Girls are taught restrictive sexuality and gender norms, whereas boys are taught more permissive norms (Fasula, Miller, & Wiener, 2007). Restricted sexual norms may leave girls vulnerable to their partners' preferences because they do not have the tools necessary to negotiate safe sex practices. The presence of psychological distress exacerbates this situation, with lasting consequences. In a longitudinal study of sexual risk behavior among sexually active Black female adolescents, DiClemente et al. (2001) found that psychological distress at baseline elevated their fears of the negative consequences of negotiating condom use, increased their perceptions of barriers to condom use, and lowered their sense of self-efficacy to negotiate condom use with a new partner 6 months later.

As with the onset of depression, family factors can be risk or protective factors in the association between depression and risky sexual behaviors. Several studies with Black adolescents have shown that family structure and process factors can protect adolescents from engaging in risky sexual behaviors. Parent–child communication about moral values and expectations demonstrates this point. Dittus, Jaccard, and Gordon (1997) found that perceived paternal disapproval of engaging in sexual intercourse was associated with delayed sexual debut among Black adolescents, regardless of the fathers' residential status. The role of parents in setting norms against risky sexual behaviors may mitigate the influences of depressive symptoms on sexual risk-taking behavior if depressed adolescents are part of supportive family systems. As suggested by research in the economic hardship area (McLoyd, 1990), associated risks may increase for adolescents who have depressed parents because they may be emotionally withdrawn or unavailable to parent. Gutman, McLoyd, and Tokoyawa (2005) modeled parenting practices, neighborhood structural factors (e.g., neighborhood stress), and psychological distress for Black adolescents. They found that stressful neighborhood influences were mediated by parental psychological stress and negative social relations, which in turn were associated with more adolescent depressive symptoms. Further, a lack of parental monitoring, connectedness, and social support has been consistently associated with adolescent risky sexual behaviors. Thus, family factors remain high priority for future research on the depression–risky sexual behavior relationship for Black adolescents, especially within a neighborhood context.

Families embedded within neighborhoods that place youth at risk for both depression and risky sexual behaviors face additional challenges in trying to protect their adolescent children from harm. Neighborhood structural and person factors, such as the racial composition of neighborhoods, social control, and social cohesion, directly contribute to adolescent depression. Decreases in neighborhood cohesion and control are associated with risky sexual behaviors, especially early sexual debut (Baumer & South, 2001; Browning, Leventhal, & Brooks-Gunn, 2004; Kotchick et al., 2001) and its consequences for teenage pregnancy (Sucoff &

Upchurch, 1998). Using data from the Panel Study for Income Dynamics (PSID), Sucoff and Upchurch (1998) found that residence in a lower socioeconomic, racially homogeneous neighborhood increased Black adolescents' rate of premarital first birth by 50%, whereas Browning, Leventhal, and Brooks-Gunn (2004) found that concentrated neighborhood poverty explained a substantial amount of variance in racial/ethnic differences in early sexual initiation.

Although the evidence is modest in its link to depression, some have suggested that living in impoverished and violent neighborhoods contributes to the belief endorsed by some Black adolescents that they will not survive past young adulthood (Bolland, 2003; Kennedy, Nolen, Applewhite, & Waiter, 2007), which creates additional stress beyond that associated with the normal developmental tasks of adolescence. The manifestation of such beliefs differs by gender. For females, sexual activity may be a means of gaining power and protection within an oppressive environment that leaves them vulnerable to victimization from crime and other social problems (Miller-Johnson et al., 1999). For males, violent environments and limited access to traditional means of social status through economic power and educational attainment leave sexual activity as one of few ways to gain social status (Seaton, 2007). In qualitative studies of Black adolescents, Vera, Reese, Paikoff, and Jarrett (1996) found that many girls said that they engaged in sexual activity as a means of gaining protection from gang members or drug dealers, whereas Kennedy et al. (2007) found that some boys planned to impregnate their partners to create an offspring before their perceived premature death. Understanding the meaning of sexual behavior for different groups of adolescents may begin to shed light on why some youth may or may not become vulnerable to depression.

Living in a racially stratified society as part of a marginalized group has led to several unique adaptation strategies for Black people. Determining the role of risky sexual behaviors in the adaptation of Black adolescents may be insightful with regard to symptom expression for depression (Brown, 2003; Seaton, 2007). Brown (2003), for example, used critical race theory as a framework to identify mental disorders that might manifest as a result of racial stratification for Black adults. These included nihilistic tendencies or self-destructive behaviors and anti-self issues. The realities of life in Black, racially homogeneous communities require men, in particular, to learn to repress their anger in specific settings (i.e., settings in which Black rage can be threatening to those in power; Myers, 1989; Spencer, Fegley, Harpalani, & Seaton, 2004). Black men are more vulnerable to victimization by law enforcement and the criminal justice system than men from other racial/ethnic groups (Spencer et al., 2004). Coping responses to such fears can lead to expressions of hypermasculinity as a protective mechanism. Overtly sexual behavior may be an outgrowth of this adaptive coping style that may be linked to depression (Seaton, 2007). Changing neighborhood norms is a strategy that recognizes that patterns of relationships within neighborhoods, rather than individual psychopathology, can be associated with observable risky sexual behaviors among youth living in impoverished neighborhoods. As Myers (1989) noted, recognizing the role of severely disadvantaged and oppressed neighborhoods may be a starting point for scientific explanations of the mental health of Black youth, but understanding how and why such neighborhood conditions persist within the current social order is necessary to make progress toward reducing risks.

Determining causation is not possible because most studies of risky sexual behaviors are based on cross-sectional designs and the approaches to analyses cannot support directional conclusions. Consequently, we do not know if adolescents who were depressed engaged in riskier sexual behaviors or if engaging in riskier sexual behaviors resulted in more depressive symptoms among Black adolescents. Rather than a predictive model in which depression leads to risky sexual behavior, some research has suggested that depressive symptomatology and risky sexual behavior may share an interactive relationship in which depression and risky sexual behaviors emerge simultaneously and are influenced by each other (Ethier et al., 2006; Kotchick et al., 2001). Other studies concluded that risky sexual behavior heightens existing predispositions to depression (Hallsfors, Waller, Bauer, Ford, & Halpern, 2005; Salazar et al., 2006). The few available longitudinal studies suggested that risky sexual behavior exacerbates depressive symptomatology once prior depressive symptoms are controlled (DiClemente et al., 2001; Hallfors et al., 2005). These inconsistencies in findings indicate the need for more long-term longitudinal research that can assess causal order of the observed associations to determine what comes first and in what combination depression and risky sexual behaviors may matter for the mental health of Black adolescents.

Conclusion

Concerns about the mental health of Black adolescents have been evident in the writings of scholars since the 1970s. The limited inclusion of Black youth in large-scale epidemiological studies, however, has resulted in a reliance on institutional data and trend reports to provide information about depression for this group. The growing number of community studies of depression that do include sizable numbers of Black adolescents are well warranted and hold promise for providing better data on the prevalence, onset, course, and correlates of depression for different groups of Black youth. Challenges for future research include the use of measurement scales that may vary in meaning across racial/ethnic groups, the need to be more precise in defining key concepts, and the identification of sociocultural mediators and moderators of the observed relationship between depression and risky sexual behaviors.

Despite the conceptual and methodological limitations identified in research on both depression and risky sexual behaviors, what emerged from this review is modest support for an association between depressive symptoms and different types of risky sexual behaviors based on gender. Few consistent mediators or moderators were identified beyond family and neighborhood factors known to be associated with both outcomes. This gap in the literature limits our ability to fully understand the complexity of the relationship between depression and risky sexual behaviors. Although the association between depression and risky sexual behaviors is complicated, we do know that they seem to influence each other and that observed relationships may be mediated by ecological factors, such as family influences, neighborhood characteristics, and racial discrimination. Many questions remain as to whether risky sexual behaviors are precursors to depression, coexisting symptoms, or even the result of depression. We offer four suggestions for future research when addressing questions in these areas.

1. Current research, although beginning to explore larger macro-level influences in explaining depression in Black adolescents, continues to place emphasis on individual-level factors, perhaps because treatment approaches are focused on the individual. Horwitz (2007) has argued that current treatments of depression that deemphasize social context as critical to vulnerability and protection miss an opportunity to have a larger impact on the social forces that shape an individual's mental health. Broadening research agendas to address explanatory factors beyond the individual will further our understanding of adolescent depression.

2. To answer the question about why race or ethnicity matters in adolescent psychopathology, we must test models that incorporate cultural aspects of adolescents' lived experiences. Research that more closely reflects the meaning of being Black and how that may influence adolescent mental health would be instructive. Examining the role of racial discrimination, neighborhood-level risk, and protective factors, as well as the meaning of risky sexual behaviors, could indicate how macro-level influences may mediate the association between risky sexual behaviors and depression among Black adolescents.

3. Within-group ethnic differences should be incorporated into studies of depression and risky sexual behaviors in recognition of the heterogeneity of ethnicities that exist for Black populations living in the United States. Black adolescents are not a monolithic group. Rather, different ethnic groups are vibrant, including various groups of Caribbean Blacks and Africans. Research focused only on African American adolescents will continue to limit our understanding of the influences of ethnicity on depression because it will not examine customs, practices, beliefs, and historical experiences as contextual factors for explaining observed differences within and across diverse racial and ethnic groups of adolescents.

4. Methodological concerns, specifically those regarding the validity of measurement scales, must be addressed. Frequently used measures of depressive symptomatology and depression should be effectively validated for multiethnic groups of adolescents so that we are confident in what is being measured both with and across racial/ethnic groups in future studies.

With regard to mental health services and intervention, treatment approaches that are holistic in nature, addressing varied environmental and cultural influences as well as individual differences factors, should be applied to diagnosis and treatment with Black adolescents (C. Bell, Williamson, & Chien, 2008). Interventions designed to prevent depression or risky sexual behaviors should address behavioral as well as mental health issues. Black adolescents engaging in risky sexual behaviors can be labeled as pathological with little consideration for the meaning of these behaviors. Although Black adolescents often report higher levels of precocious sexual behaviors and lower levels of depressive symptoms than those in other racial/ethnic groups, we suggest that this may be an early warning sign for depression. Well-designed, culturally specific longitudinal studies with sound instrumentation will be necessary to support this claim. By incorporating cultural, social, and psychological protective factors in research along with biological factors, and not focusing solely on risk factors, the public health agenda of reducing or eliminating inequalities in health and mental health can be more efficiently achieved.

19

Well-Being across the Life Course

John Mirowsky and Catherine E. Ross

Adulthood begins as a time of hopes and tensions as people acquire full adult status. Young adults must complete an education, establish an occupation and household, acquire recognition and prosperity, and develop supportive marriage and family relations. Adulthood begins with high levels of depression, anxiety, anger, economic hardship, marital unhappiness, and distrust. Those negatives decrease rapidly. On the positive side, the overwhelming majority of young Americans feel in control of their lives, responsible for their outcomes, and able to meet the challenges of life. Those perceptions increase as they meet the challenges of adulthood. For most young American adults, the trials and efforts lead to improvements that increase well-being. Late middle age marks the time of life when everything comes together. Earnings and household income reach a peak. The children are grown and probably out of the house. The marriages are more congenial and less discordant. The jobs are more secure and enjoyable. The tensions and conflicts of young adulthood have abated, and the losses of old age have not yet arisen. Later in life, in old age, things are more mixed. Seniors who have health, function, wealth, and marriage intact find old age an enjoyable time of relaxation and companionship. Even those who lose a spouse or suffer a medical crisis often rebuild a gratifying life within a year or two. Eventually, though, physical impairments and the loss of a spouse often leave individuals feeling demoralized, lonely, and hopeless. Emotional well-being in old age rests on economic, interpersonal, and physical well-being built throughout adult life. What are the different aspects of well-being, how do they change across adulthood, and why do they change?

Introduction

The best years of adult life? Some claim the heady springtime must be the best. Looking back on early adulthood, it sparkles with romance, aspiration, adventure, and the elemental energies of life. But what of the golden years – that time of life when the work is done and the harvest is in? Looking forward, late adulthood glows with a relaxed and genial aura. It beckons as a time of mellow reflection retired from obligation. So what time of life is best?

The answer may surprise you: middle age. Forget the midlife crisis. Forget the empty nest. People in their forties and fifties have it best. If you are young, do not pity the middle-aged man with a soft waist and thinning hair or the middle-aged

This research was supported by grants from the National Institute on Aging: Aging, Status, and the Sense of Control (RO1-AG12393), John Mirowsky, P.I., and Education, Resource Substitution, and Health (RO1-AG023380), Catherine E. Ross, P.I. Administrative and facilities support for the Population Research Center are funded in part by an NIH center grant (HD42849–04).

woman with bifocal lenses and crow's feet wrinkles. Some day, with care and perseverance, your life may become as good as theirs.

How do we know that middle age is the best time of life? The term "best" implies a common standard of value by which we can measure and compare. Emotional distress serves as that standard. Research on well-being across the life course usually maps the average levels of depression and anxiety. Depression is a feeling of sadness and dejection marked by trouble sleeping, concentrating, and functioning. Anxiety is a state of unease and apprehension characterized by worry, tension, and restlessness. Both are unpleasant feelings that most persons would rather avoid. They arouse the attention of psychiatrists when they are extreme, prolonged, or inexplicable. More commonly, depression and anxiety come and go with the challenges and adaptations of life. Life course researchers have begun studying other emotions too, particularly anger (Mirowsky & Schieman, 2008; Ross & Van Willigen, 1996; Schieman, 1999, 2003) and positive feelings such as happiness, serenity, and elation (Ross & Mirowsky, 2008; Simon & Nath, 2004). This research adds important details that are summarized here. However, the age-group differences in depression and anxiety tell the main story, as detailed in this chapter. Both forms of distress decline from a peak in early adulthood. The predominant type of distress shifts from active (anxiety and anger) to passive (depression) as persons age.

This chapter has three main sections. The first describes the emotional trajectories of adulthood. The second describes the five views of age that help researchers understand why emotions change as people age. The third describes the conditions and beliefs that change across adulthood, shaping the trajectories of emotions.

Adulthood Trajectories of Emotions

In terms of depression, middle age is the best time of life. Figure 19.1 illustrates results from the survey of Aging, Status and the Sense of Control (ASOC), a 6-year follow-up survey (1995–2001) of about 2,500 U.S. adults selected at random. (Appendix A gives details about the ASOC survey.) It measured depression by asking, "On how many days in the past week have you felt sad? Felt lonely? Felt you couldn't shake the blues? Had trouble getting to sleep or staying asleep? Felt you just couldn't get going? Had trouble keeping your mind on what you were doing? Felt that everything was an effort?" Responses were coded in days, from 0 to 7, and averaged across the seven items. The figure illustrates the results of a latent growth model mapping the level of depression in the first interview and the changes in it over the following 6-year period, as functions of age (Mirowsky & Kim, 2007). Each arrow, called a vector, represents the model's estimate for persons born in a particular year and reaching the same age in each year of the study. The first vector represents the origin level of depression and the following changes, among persons born in 1977, who were aged 18 at the beginning of the study and 24 at

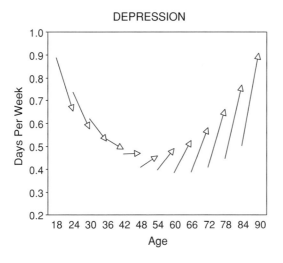

Figure 19.1. Depression vectors showing the initial levels and subsequent changes as birth cohorts aged 6 years (1995–2001 ASOC survey).

the end. The second one represents the origin and changes for persons born in 1971, who were aged 24 at the beginning and 30 at the end, and so on.

Taken together, the vectors illustrate several things about age and depression. In any given survey year, the youngest and oldest adults have the highest levels of depression. Over the follow-up period, levels of depression go down for the young adults and they go up for the old adults. The differences in depression across age groups and the changes in it as persons age reflect two interacting forces. One is the part of adulthood that the individuals are in and aging through. The other is when they were born, as well as the cumulative effects of their history up to the time of observation. Depression follows a U-shaped trajectory, dropping in early adulthood, leveling out in middle age, and then rising in old age. The actual changes in depression as adults age larger than the differences in depression across age groups in a given year. In other words, levels of depression change more as persons go through adulthood than it would seem from just comparing persons of different ages in a particular year.

The depression vectors also show trends among cohorts reaching the same age in different years. In Figure 19.1 the first arrow ends below where the second one begins. This means that the level of depression among 24-year-olds was lower at the end of the study in 2001 than at the beginning of the study in 1995. In other words, there was a trend toward lower age-specific levels of depression in early adulthood. At the other end of adulthood the pattern is reversed, showing a trend toward higher age-specific levels of depression in old age.

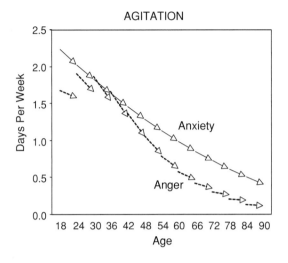

Figure 19.2. Anxiety and anger vectors showing the initial levels and subsequent changes as birth cohorts aged 6 years (1995–2001 ASOC survey).

The aging vectors of anxiety and anger, two forms of emotional agitation, show a different pattern from those of depression (Mirowsky & Schieman, 2008). Anxiety is a state of uneasiness and apprehension focused on threatening events or situations. Anger is a feeling of displeasure and hostility focused on infuriating things or persons. The ASOC survey asked, "On how many days of the past week did you worry a lot about little things? Feel tense or anxious? Feel restless? Feel annoyed with things or people? Feel angry? Yell at someone?" The first three questions index anxiety, and the second three anger. All are scored in days per week, from 0 to 7. Each index takes the mean days per week of its three items.

Emotional agitation declines throughout adulthood, as illustrated in Figure 19.2. The aging vectors of anxiety show the simplest pattern. Anxiety declines at a steady rate, with no sign of trends across birth cohorts. The vectors of anger differ somewhat from those of anxiety. Anger declines fastest between the ages of 40 and 60, and there is a trend toward lower anger in early adulthood. On the whole, though, anxiety and anger show a similar pattern in comparison with depression. Emotional agitation is quite frequent in early adulthood, even more so than depression. Among adults aged 36 and younger, the anxiety and anger symptoms are two or more times as frequent as the depression symptoms. All three negative emotions decline greatly into middle age, but anxiety and anger keep going down, whereas depression goes back up in old age. As a consequence, feelings of distress shift from active to passive across adulthood, from an energetic focus on hazards and conflicts to a devitalized focus on loss and impasse.

Cross-sectional analyses of data from the U.S. General Social Survey indicate that positive emotions also shift from active to passive across adulthood (Ross & Mirowsky, 2008; Simon & Nath, 2004). Positive emotions generally become more common and negative ones become less common with older age. The most common positive emotions shift from forms of elation in early adulthood, such as feeling excited, overjoyed, or proud, to forms of serenity in late adulthood, such as feeling calm, contented, and at ease. So, whether the emotions are positive ones that individuals want and seek or negative ones that they dislike and avoid, the emotions shift to less vigorous forms with older age.

What produces the age-based differences and changes in depression, agitation, and other emotions? Explaining the patterns requires that we understand the five aspects of age, as well as the conditions and beliefs that change over time, giving rise to the emotions that characterize each part of life.

The Five Views of Age

The time elapsed since birth defines a person's age. This simple physical measure marks five distinct aspects of age: (1) maturity, (2) decline, (3) life-cycle stage, (4) generation, and (5) survival (Mirowsky & Ross, 1992). Each aspect contributes its part to the differences in depression among age groups. This section describes each view of age.

Age as Maturity

People become more experienced, accomplished, and seasoned as they age. In a word, they mature. Each human sums a lifetime of experience, composing a self of elements arranged to function efficiently and successfully. Personal growth and development require time. Aging increases a person's practice with living and the extent of self-composition. With growing insight and skill, social and psychological traits merge into an increasingly harmonious and effective whole. Several developments – lower crime rates, safer habits, a more orderly lifestyle, greater satisfaction, and a more positive self-image – suggest that maturity comes with age. Rates of crime decline steeply in early adulthood and continue to decline throughout subsequent ages (Hirschi & Gottfredson, 1983; Ross & Mirowsky, 1987). People in older age groups lead a more routine and orderly life, take fewer risks, avoid fights and arguments, drink more moderately and carefully, and refrain from the recreational use of illegal drugs (Umberson, 1987). Workers in successively older age groups report greater satisfaction with their jobs beyond that due to their higher rank and pay (Kalleberg & Loscocco, 1983). People in successively older age groups rate themselves more helpful, supportive, disciplined, able, and satisfied with life and less emotional, nervous, and frustrated; they report greater self-esteem and, until age 75, less of a sense that life is empty and meaningless (Campbell, Converse, & Rodgers, 1976; Gove, Ortega, & Briggs Style, 1989).

Age as Decline

Just as humans sum and integrate experience, they also sum and integrate failures, faults, injuries, and errors. Often the slow and steady deterioration produces little apparent effect at first. Many defects accrue too slowly for people to notice the changes from year to year. Eventually, though, the accumulation becomes apparent, like the wrinkling of skin or the graying of hair. Many physical problems that accumulate also compound. For example, weight gained in body fat reduces physical activity, and then lower physical activity increases the rate of weight gain. Accumulating and compounding decline may affect behavior and emotions too, as a consequence of physiological decline or as an independent process (Aneshensel, Frerichs, & Huba, 1984).

Several facts point to accelerating decline with advancing age. Many physical and mental abilities hold roughly stable throughout most of the adult years, but erode at a slowly accelerating rate to produce substantial declines after age 70 (Schaie, 1983). The incidence and prevalence of chronic disease increase at an accelerating rate with age (J. G. Collins, 1988; Hartunian, Smart, & Thompson, 1981). So does the average level of dysfunctions such as trouble seeing, hearing, walking, lifting, climbing stairs, grasping, and manipulating (Waldron, 1983; Waldron & Jacobs, 1988). Those dysfunctions interfere with the performance of daily activities such as shopping, cooking, cleaning, gardening, bathing, grooming, dressing, and eating (Berkman & Breslow, 1983; Guralnik & Kaplan, 1989). The peak performance of athletes and the typical levels of physical activity among nonathletes both decline (Shephard, 1987). So does carbohydrate metabolism (i.e., the process that fuels the muscles), lung capacity, and bone density (Rowe & Kahn, 1987). Mental functions also decline, including orientation to time and space, recall, attention, simple calculation, language comprehension, and the speed of perceptual, motor, and cognitive processes (Holzer et al., 1986; House & Robbins, 1983; Rowe & Kahn, 1987; Schaie, 1983).

Age as a Life-Cycle Stage

Age marks a person's stage in the life cycle. Human life progresses through common sequences of roles: from school to job to retirement, from single to married to widowed (Hogan, 1978). Over one's lifetime adult status and prospects rise and fall. The phased roles interlock with a flow and ebb of freedoms, prerogatives, privileges, options, opportunities, scope, and resources. Achievements and acquisitions of early adulthood build the rank and prosperity of middle age that eventually erode in the retrenchment and loss of old age.

Changes in marital, job, and economic status index the social life cycle. Most Americans begin their 18th year single, in school or recently graduated, and with little wealth or personal earnings. The progression to middle age increases the prevalence of marriage, parenthood, and employment. It generally increases the earnings of the employed and the total household income (Mirowsky & Ross, 2003). Beginning around age 60 the progression into old age sharply increases the prevalence of retirement and widowhood, thus decreasing personal earnings and total household income.

Age as Generation

Age marks a person's place in the major trends of recent history. At any given stage in their lives the members of younger generations benefit from material, economic, and cultural progress. In the United States, 20th-century trends increased the average level of education, income, female employment, and life expectancy and decreased family size and rural residence (Bianchi & Spain, 1986; Sagan, 1987). In the past 50 years alone, median family income (adjusted for inflation) more than doubled, life expectancy at birth increased 20%, age-adjusted annual mortality rates dropped 60%, the proportion living in rural areas dropped from 45% to 25%, total fertility rates dropped 20%, and the proportion of women in the labor force more than doubled, from 25% to well over 50% (Bianchi & Spain, 1986; Sagan, 1987). Fifty years ago 6% of Americans aged 25 through 29 had less than 5 years of formal education, and only 6% had completed 4 years of college. Today, under 1% has less than 5 years of education, and 25% have completed 4 years of college. In 1900, 1 American in 10 could not read. In 1940, it was 1 in 25. Today, it is less than 1 in 100. Aggregate increases in education may have generated the favorable trends in income, life expectancy, family size, and female employment (Sagan, 1987).

Age as Survival

Age indirectly indexes traits associated with differences in survival. Other things being equal, traits that confer a selective advantage become more common with age, and those that confer a selective disadvantage become scarce. Being older increases the likelihood of having the traits associated with survival, particularly after age 70. Those traits may create a false impression of aging's effect, perhaps making it appear beneficial or benign when it is actually destructive. Lower survival among the most depressed groups can make aging seem less depressing than it is.

Depression and the things that cause it tend to reduce survival. Severely depressed people die at two to four times the rate of others who are similar in terms of age; gender; socioeconomic status; preexisting chronic health problems such as hypertension, heart disease, stroke, and cancer; and signs of fitness as indicated by blood pressure, blood cholesterol, lung capacity, weight for height, and smoking habits (Bruce & Leaf, 1989; Somervell et al., 1989). Many of the same statuses and conditions that produce depression also reduce survival. Life expectancy at birth is 4.4 years lower for minorities than for others (and 6.4 years lower for Blacks than for others; Kessler & Neighbors, 1986; National Center for Health Statistics, 1990). Unemployment, low education, and poverty all increase the age-specific rates of mortality (Rogers, Hummer, & Nam, 1999). So does being divorced, separated, or widowed.

Although most traits that increase depression also reduce survival, there is one major exception: being female. Women are more depressed than men, but they live an average of 6.8 years longer. This tends to make depression more common among the old, who are disproportionately female. This fact somewhat counterbalances the other survival effects.

Concentric Spheres of Experience

Conditions, beliefs, and emotions form concentric spheres of experience (Mirowsky & Ross, 2003). Conditions make up the most external sphere. They define the hard realities of status and circumstance that enable or restrain action (Aneshensel, 1992). Beliefs form the mental bridge between external conditions and emotional response. Beliefs crystallize around the hard realities, forming interpretations and mental maps that blend observation, judgment, and prediction. Emotions arise from those beliefs. For example, poverty is a condition, hopelessness a belief, and despair an emotion. Maturity, decline, life cycle, generation, and survival define the conditions that shape beliefs and emotions.

This section describes conditions and beliefs that differ across age groups and affect well-being. The facts and figures come from the 1995–2001 ASOC survey, described in Appendix A. References mention reports from other surveys with similar or related findings.

Conditions

People of different ages live under very different conditions. Age is itself one of the most powerful ascribed social statuses. Society assigns many rights, obligations, and opportunities based on age. These include the right to drive, drink alcohol, get married, or vote; the obligation to serve in the military, hold a job, and raise a family; and the opportunity to go to college, run for Congress, or head a corporation. Law prescribes the ages for some rights, obligations, and opportunities, but tradition prescribes the ages for most. In sociological terms, society is stratified by age. The different age groups form the graduated layers in a system of responsibility and privilege.

Economic Prosperity. Our list of conditions that affect emotional well-being begins with economic prosperity. A proverb says that money cannot buy happiness. Technically this may be so. No material or symbolic reward can guarantee happiness: even the rich suffer disappointment and loss. But money goes a long way toward reducing the frequency, intensity, and duration of misery. People in need of money carry more than an equal share of society's total burden of emotional distress (Mirowsky & Ross, 2001, 2003; Ross & Huber, 1985).

The competitive logic of our society guarantees that young adults need money more than others. American society is designed for achievement. For the most part people must earn what they get. Even when society gives an advantage of birth to some over others, that advantage comes chiefly in the form of longer, better education. Rather than give money itself, Americans try to give their children a superior ability to achieve. However, whatever one's advantages or disadvantages, making money takes time. Our system of competition and achievement produces a marked relationship between age and economic prosperity.

Average personal earnings and household income go up in early adulthood, peak in the 50- to 59-year-old bracket, and then go down in old age. Many studies conducted since the 1950s have found that higher earnings and income reduce an individual's probable level of depression and anxiety (Kessler, 1979, 1982; Kessler & Cleary, 1980; Mirowsky & Ross, 2003; Wheaton, 1978, 1980). Why? One factor is that earnings and income mark one's worth and status in the eyes of others. People judge themselves partly by seeing how others judge them. Low earnings or income can make individuals feel inferior, inadequate, or ashamed. Higher earnings and income can make individuals feel proud, respectable, or meritorious. Americans have these feelings, but the main connection between economic and emotional well-being lies elsewhere. Higher earnings and income reduce depression and agitation mostly by reducing economic hardship (Ross & Huber, 1985; Mirowsky & Ross, 2001). People find it distressing to have difficulty paying the bills or buying household necessities such as food, clothing, or medicine. Economic hardship threatens personal security. Worse than that, it threatens the security of children, partners, and others whom one loves and sustains.

Economic hardship is most common in early middle age, when individuals are raising children but earnings, income, and wealth are well below lifetime peaks (Mirowsky & Ross, 1999). Figure 19.3 shows the aging vectors of economic hardship in the 1995–2001 study. Respondents were asked, "During the past 12 months, how often did it happen that you did not have enough money to buy food, clothes, or other things your household needed? . . . did not have enough money to pay for medical care? . . . had trouble paying the bills?" Responses were coded never (0), not very often (1), fairly often (2), or very often (3). The three items were averaged to produce an index of economic hardship. Adults in their mid-20s to mid-40s have the most economic hardship. Those in old age have the least hardship, even though they often have low income and chronic health problems that create economic needs. Life-cycle factors explain part of why economic hardship is low among older persons. They usually do not have economically dependent children, they often already own a home and the usual durable goods, and programs

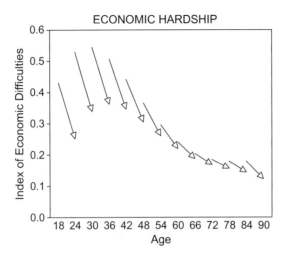

Figure 19.3. Economic hardship vectors showing the initial levels and subsequent changes as birth cohorts aged 6 years (1995–2001 ASOC survey).

such as Social Security and Medicare bolster their income and protect it from the demands of medical expenses. Children are especially important to the life-cycle component. Their absence reduces the risk of economic hardship and reduces the impact of low income on economic hardship. Maturity also plays a big part. Older persons have more temperate lifestyles, which also reduces economic hardship and the effects of low income. Older persons seem to use their income more efficiently, perhaps because of having the time or because of having learned earlier how to do it.

The vectors also show trends toward lower age-specific economic hardship over the period of the study. The trend appears favorable at all adulthood ages. It is particularly large for persons in the first half of adulthood, when the levels of economic hardship are highest. Although the trend has not been analyzed in detail, it seems likely to reflect two factors. One is economic growth during the period, with declining unemployment rates and rising household incomes. The other is the increasing levels of college education among women and the related delay of parenthood. It remains to be seen whether the large decreases in economic hardship of 1995–2001 are being sustained by those cohorts in 2008 and 2009 during the economic recession. One reasonable hypothesis is that trends in economic hardship swing up and down with the economic cycles the most in the first half of adulthood, during the years of child rearing, and prior to the peak of income and wealth. Individuals in late middle age or old age may be more insulated from economic cycles, not benefiting as much during periods of growth, but not suffering as much during the declines.

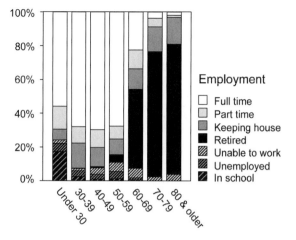

Figure 19.4. Employment status by age group (1995 ASOC data).

Employment. The life cycle of employment generates the rise and fall of earnings and household income. Figure 19.4 illustrates this cycle. Employment also improves emotional well-being apart from its impact on household economics. Adults employed full-time enjoy the lowest average frequency of depression (Gove & Geerken, 1977; Kessler & McRae, 1982; Kessler, Turner, & House, 1989; Pearlin, Lieberman, Menaghan, & Mullan, 1981; Ross, Mirowsky, & Huber, 1983). Full-time employment improves physical health too (Ross & Mirowsky, 1995a). With the exception of full-time students, adults who are not employed full time suffer from depression more frequently than those with full-time jobs. Adults who are unemployed, laid off, or unable to work because of disability carry the highest burden of depression. They experience symptoms two to four times more often than people with full-time jobs. Luckily they comprise less than 10% of the typical random sample. Retirees and part-time employees make up much larger fractions: about 16% and 9%, respectively. Both of these groups have slightly more depression than the full-time employees, but not a lot more (around 10% to 20% more). Women keeping house make up the second largest group not employed full time (after the retirees): about 12% of adults. Women keeping house feel depressed about 37% more often than the women and 75% more often than the men who hold full-time paying jobs. The fact that women often keep house rather than hold a full-time paying job accounts for part of the difference between men and women in the frequency of depression.

The quality of a job affects well-being too. Many aspects of paid jobs improve with age for those who remain employed (Mirowsky & Ross, 2007b). In addition to earnings, these qualities include the ability to decide what to do or how to do

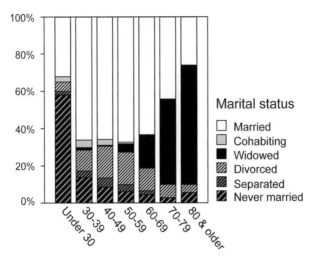

Figure 19.5. Marital status by age group (1995 ASOC data).

it, influence over work group goals, a higher management level, greater prestige and recognition, the freedom to disagree with one's supervisor, and getting to do work that is less routine and more challenging, enjoyable, and creative.

Marriage. Marriage and family form another major aspect of the adult life cycle that affects well-being (M. Hughes & Gove, 1981). Middle-aged adults are the ones most likely to be married, as shown in Figure 19.5. Married people feel depressed about one-third less often than others. People who are recently separated or widowed feel depressed the most often, with two or three times the frequency of symptoms as married persons. The level of depression drops with time for the divorced or widowed, but it remains about 40% to 50% higher than among married persons. Adults who have never been married also experience about 40% to 50% more symptoms than those who are married. People living together with someone as if married are between the married persons and others in their frequency of symptoms.

Marriage reduces depression for two main reasons: social support and household income. Marriage improves well-being by improving emotional and economic security. Adults benefit from a partnership that provides mutual intimacy and reliance (Mirowsky, 1985; Ross, Mirowsky, & Goldsteen, 1990). Of course some marriages meet these needs better than others. The quality of one's marriage affects well-being. A bad marriage can be worse than none (see Chapter 16 in this volume). The quality of marriages improves with age for the ones that stay intact. Older married persons feel happier with their partners, divide housework more

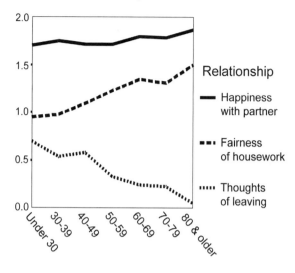

Figure 19.6. Subjective quality of marriage by age group (1995 ASOC data for those with partners).

fairly, and think of separating less often, as shown in Figure 19.6. The quality of marriage improves with age for two reasons. First, people become more adept at managing their relationships as they mature. Second, the worst marriages break up. Learning by trial and error leads to improvement over time.

Children. Child care introduces the major strain associated with marriage (Ross & Huber, 1985; Ross & Mirowsky, 1988). Children improve the well-being of parents in conducive circumstances (e.g., adequate household income and a stable, supportive partnership with a fair sharing of chores and sacrifices). Ready availability of affordable child care helps a lot too. Unfortunately many parents find themselves in circumstances far from this ideal. Some lack the money. Some lack a partner or a helpful partner. Some mothers find themselves in extremely distressing circumstances: a failed or unsupportive marriage, a poorly paid job that does not accommodate family responsibilities, and no ready source of affordable child care. Adults in their 20s, 30s, and 40s bear most of the child care responsibilities, as indicated by Figure 19.7. Few adults over the age of 50 have children in the household. Younger parents bear the greatest child care strains because they have lower income and younger children who need closer attendance.

Most of the conditions discussed so far define the economic and family life cycle and account for much of the relationship between age and depression. The changes between generations account for some of the pattern too. Increasing education leads as the most important of those changes for well-being.

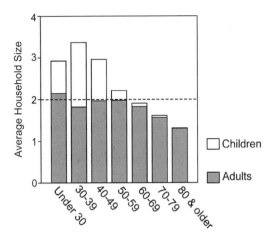

Figure 19.7. Number of adults and children in the household by age group (1995 ASOC data).

Education. Younger generations benefit from higher levels of education. The frequency of distress drops with each additional year of education (Mirowsky & Ross, 1990, 1992; Ross & Huber, 1985). Distress takes an especially big step down at the level of the high school degree. For the most part, though, the years of education rather than the degrees make the difference. The effect of education on depression does not fade with time as people grow old. Likewise, the effect does not fade in successive generations with rising educational standards. Each additional year of education reduces the average level of depression by the same amount as does an additional $40,000 in household income. Remarkably, the education of one's parents has a similar although smaller lifelong effect. Each additional year of one's parents' education reduces the average depression by the same amount as an additional $10,000 in household income. Figure 19.8 shows the average education of the respondents and their parents in 10-year age categories. The middle-aged and older respondents finished about three or four years of education more than their parents did. If Americans under the age of 30 eventually do the same they will complete an average of 16 years of education. That will have two effects. It will help bring their depression down from current levels, and it will help keep their depression below the levels of previous generations at each stage in life.

Childhood Family. The main trends of recent history generally improve the well-being of Americans with each new generation. Unfortunately one harmful trend works against the helpful ones: the increasing breakup of childhood families. Figure 19.9 illustrates that trend. Less than 10% of the adults in their 70s, 80s, and 90s experienced the breakup of their childhood family. In contrast, almost 33%

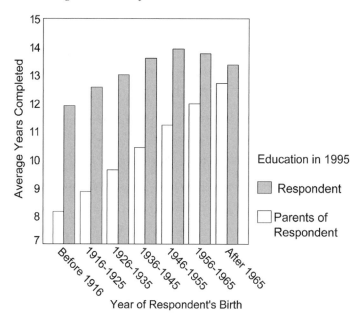

Figure 19.8. Education of the respondent and parents by year of birth (1995 ASOC data).

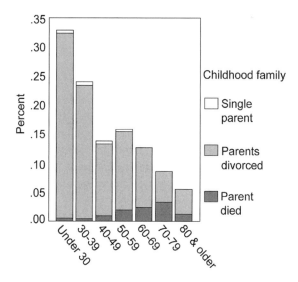

Figure 19.9. Disruption of respondent's childhood family by age group (1995 ASOC data).

of the adults in their 20s did. The death of a parent became less common in succeeding generations, but the divorce of parents increased dramatically. As with the education of one's parents, the breakup of their marriage has a lifelong effect on the frequency of depression. Adults from divorced childhood families feel depressed about 22% more often than adults from families that remained intact. The effect does not vanish as people get older and does not abate as parental divorce becomes more common. The effect remains the same among the young adults with a high prevalence of parental divorce as among the old adults with a low prevalence. Having had only a single parent, or the death of a parent, has even worse effects, raising the frequency of depression by 98% and 57%, respectively (see also Brown & Harris, 1978, on the lifelong effects of parental death). Fortunately those conditions remain relatively uncommon.

Broken childhood family status increases later depression in two ways. First, it reduces the average level of education attained compared to others of the same generation from similar backgrounds (McLanahan & Bumpass, 1988; Ross & Mirowsky, 1999b). Second, it reduces the quality and stability of the respondent's own marital relationships (Ross & Mirowsky, 1999b; Webster, Orbuch, & House, 1995). Adults from divorced or never-married childhood families have more marriages of their own that they find less pleasing, fair, and promising. In fact they feel greater mistrust and suspicion of others in general. The death of a parent does not have these negative interpersonal effects. Thus the breakup of childhood families creates an intergenerational cycle that increases the prevalence of breakups despite the harm done and in part *because* of the harm done.

Health and Physical Function. Like it or not, life comes to an end. Most people think of old age as a time of rising disease and disability leading ultimately to death. As people get old they feel less healthy, have more impairments and medical conditions, and expect to live fewer additional years (Mirowsky, 1997, 1999; Mirowsky & Hu, 1996; Mirowsky & Ross, 2005; Ross & Bird, 1994). Most physical problems increase in prevalence and severity with age. There are a few welcome exceptions: older people report fewer headaches and allergies. Yet their health problems take many forms: discomforting aches and pains, threatening diagnoses, disabling impairments, and a shortening future. A large majority of Americans over the age of 60 have a serious chronic disease such as hypertension, heart disease, diabetes, cancer, osteoporosis, or arthritis. About 70% report some difficulty with everyday activities such as carrying a bag of groceries, and almost one-fourth report a severe impairment of some type. People find all of these types of health problems depressing, but impairments are the worst by far. Employment-aged adults find impairment the most depressing, but the majority of them are unimpaired and few have serious difficulties. The total burden of impairment lies heaviest on the oldest adults.

The ASOC survey measured impairment by asking individuals, "How much trouble do you have climbing stairs? . . . kneeling or stooping? . . . lifting or

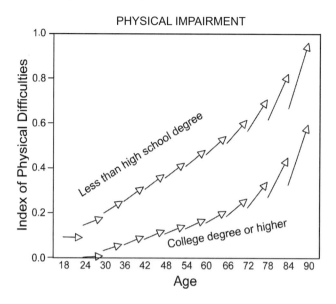

Figure 19.10. Physical impairment vectors at two levels of education, showing the initial levels and subsequent changes as birth cohorts aged 6 years (1995–2001 ASOC survey).

carrying objects under 10 pounds like a bag of groceries?... preparing meals or cleaning and doing other household work?... shopping or getting around town?... seeing, even with glasses?... hearing?" For each item they were asked, "Would you say no difficulty, some difficulty, or a great deal of difficulty?" To make an index, the responses were coded 0, 1, or 2, respectively, and averaged across the items. The adulthood trajectory of physical impairment has two segments, as illustrated by the vectors in Figure 19.10. Before about age 65 the level of impairment rises at a more or less steady rate. This is the phase of health erosion. The changes are not dramatic from year to year, but they add up over the decades. The rate of erosion depends on the level of education (or things indicated by it). The higher the level of education, the lower the average rate of health erosion (Mirowsky & Ross, 2005, 2008). After about age 65 the rate at which impairment increases accelerates, going up faster and faster toward the end of life. This is the phase of health disintegration. In old age the levels of physical impairment rise increasingly quickly at all levels of education. The rate of old-age disintegration is the same across levels of education. However, the more educated still have lower average levels of impairment because of their lower rates of health erosion earlier in life.

Serious impairment can double or triple the frequency of depression. Figure 19.11 compares the average frequency of depression across three categories: persons reporting a great deal of difficulty with one or more of the ASOC physical

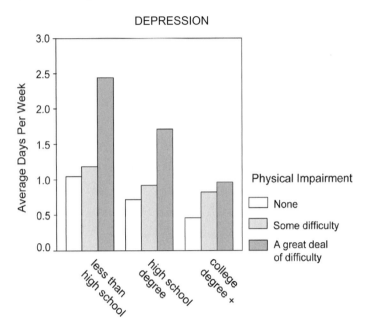

Figure 19.11. Depression by level of education and physical impairment (1995 ASOC data).

functions, those having some difficulty but not a great deal of difficulty with one or more, and those reporting no difficulty with any of them. It also compares across three levels of education: less than a high school degree, high school degree, and college degree (i.e., 4 years or higher). The average frequency of depression goes up with the amount of physical difficulty. The shift from some difficulty to a great deal is especially depressing for persons with a high school degree or less.

Rising levels of education may eventually reduce the amount of depression in old age in two ways, as suggested by Figures 19.10 and 19.11 (Mirowsky & Ross, 2005; Ross & Wu, 1995). Higher levels of education in younger generations may slow the overall rate at which impairment goes up before they reach old age, so that more individuals get there with little or no impairment. In addition, the depression associated with a great deal of difficulty in one or more functions is lower at higher levels of education. Rising levels of education may help today's younger generations delay impairment longer and manage with it better.

Beliefs and Emotions

The members of different age groups live under different conditions. Together those external conditions help shape beliefs that contribute to the age-group differences in depression, anxiety, and anger. A sense of control over one's own life and a mistrust of others are especially relevant for two reasons. Both have substantial effects on depression and agitation, and both follow clear adulthood trajectories, as detailed in this section.

Sense of Control. The perception of being able to direct and regulate one's own life varies by degree, ranging from fatalism and a deep sense of powerlessness and helplessness to instrumentalism and a firm sense of mastery and self-efficacy (Mirowsky & Ross, 1990, 1991, 2003, 2007a; Rodin, 1990). Some people feel that any good things that happen are mostly luck – fortunate outcomes they desire but do not design. They feel that personal problems mostly result from bad breaks and feel little ability to regulate or avoid the bad things that happen. Others feel they can do just about anything they set their minds to. They see themselves as responsible for their own successes and failures and view misfortunes as the results of personal mistakes they can avoid in the future.

Sense of control links socioeconomic, interpersonal, behavioral, and physiological systems. It is the human awareness at their hub. A firm sense of control averts the tendency to become helpless in frustrating and aversive situations (Hiroto, 1974). It also decreases autonomic reactivity. A low sense of control correlates with higher circulating catecholamines and corticosteroids in humans, as does learned helplessness in both humans and animals (Gold, Goodwin, & Chrousos, 1988a, 1988b; Rodin, 1986a, 1986b). The catecholamine norepinephrine (or noradrenaline) is implicated in depression and anxiety. The anti-inflammatory corticosteroid cortisol (hydrocortisone) may produce the sleep disorders related to depression, particularly those involving agitation and early morning rising (Greden et al., 1983). Cortisol regulates the metabolism of cholesterol (its parent compound), mobilizing energy to resist stress. Improving the sense of control of nursing home patients lowers their odds of dying by a factor of 2.5 (at an 18-month follow-up; Rodin, 1986a, 1986b).

Certain objective conditions create a sense of detachment from one's own actions and outcomes that people find demoralizing and distressing (Erikson, 1986; Mirowsky & Ross, 2003; Seeman, 1959, 1983). Many of those conditions represent classic interests of sociology such as alienated labor, powerlessness, structural inconsistency, and dependency. Structural social psychology looks for alienating situations that undermine the individual's sense of control (Kohn, Naoi, Schoenbach, Schooler, & Slomczynski, 1990; Kohn & Slomczynski, 1990; Mirowsky & Ross, 1983, 1984, 1990; Pearlin et al., 1981; Rosenfield, 1989; Ross & Mirowsky, 1992; Wheaton, 1980). Old age is one.

The ASOC survey measured the sense of control by asking respondents how much they agreed with eight statements: "I am responsible for my own successes," "I can do just about anything I really set my mind to," "My misfortunes are the result of mistakes I have made," "I am responsible for my failures," "The really good things that happen to me are mostly luck," "There's no sense planning a lot – if something good is going to happen it will," "Most of my problems are

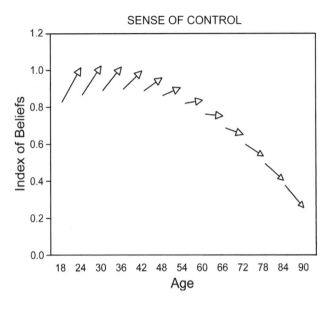

Figure 19.12. Sense of control vectors showing the initial levels and subsequent changes as birth cohorts aged 6 years (1995–2001 ASOC survey).

due to bad breaks," and "I have little control over the bad things that happen to me." Responses to questions claiming control were coded strongly disagree (−2), disagree (−1), neutral (0), agree (1), and strongly agree (2), and responses to questions denying control were coded the opposite way. The index averaged across the eight items.

The sense of control rises from early adulthood until the beginning of old age and then declines. Figure 19.12 shows the overall vectors. The sense of control goes up most steeply at the beginning of adulthood, particularly among those in college or with college degrees (Lewis, Ross, & Mirowsky, 1999; Mirowsky & Ross, 2007a). The increases level off in late middle age and become increasingly steep declines in old age. Young and middle-aged adults typically report a firm sense of directing and regulating their own lives (Mirowsky, 1995; Mirowsky & Ross, 1990, 1991, 2007a). In old age the balance of perceived control shifts from a sense of mastery toward one of helplessness.

A number of factors come together to produce the low and declining sense of control observed among old Americans. They represent many aspects of age, including physical decline; the life cycle of employment, earnings, and marriage; and the generational trends in education and women's employment. Health problems account for much of this decline. The shorter the time people expect to live, the less they feel in control of their own lives and outcomes. People find it hard to plan for a future that looks short, to manage a life that might end soon. Physical impairments have the next biggest effect. Difficulty performing common daily tasks puts real limits on personal control. A general feeling of health and fitness bolsters one's sense of control, but sickness and disease undermine that feeling. Specific diagnoses such as heart disease, cancer, or arthritis reduce the sense of control by making people feel sick, impaired, or near the end of life. Social and economic losses undermine the sense of control too. Widows feel less in control of their own lives than do married people of the same age. A full-time job, substantial personal earnings, and employee medical insurance all increase the sense of control, but they become scarce as people get old.

A large fraction of the fatalism and powerlessness that characterize the elderly comes from having lived in harder times (Mirowsky, 1995). Members of older generations had lower education than is common today, and they were raised by parents who had even less. Both forms of human and social capital affect the sense of control. Together they account for about one-third of the association between old age and a low sense of control. For women the history of employment contributes too. Retirees who held full-time paying jobs most of their lives feel more in control than those who did not. Women who are over the age of 65 lived in a period when few women held full-time jobs over most of the years before retirement.

Mistrust is another belief shaped by conditions. It is not very common, but it has large effects on anxiety, anger, and depression (Ross & Mirowsky, 2009; Ross, Mirowsky, & Pribesh, 2002). The ASOC survey asked, "How many days in the past week have you felt it was not safe to trust anyone? . . . felt suspicious? . . . felt sure everyone was against you?" Responses were coded in number of days, from 0 to 7, and averaged across the three items. Figure 19.13 shows the mistrust vectors. Mistrust is at its peak in the beginning of adulthood, but declines through late middle age, rising slightly in advanced old age.

Although more research needs to be done on the topic, the declining frequency of mistrust in early adulthood probably reflects moves to safer neighborhoods and less adventuresome lifestyles. Younger adults are more likely than middle-aged or older ones to live in dangerous urban neighborhoods. Noise, litter, crime, vandalism, graffiti, people hanging out on the streets, public drinking, run-down and abandoned buildings, drug use, trouble with neighbors, and other incivilities indicate the potential for harm (Geis & Ross, 1998; Ross, 2000; Ross & Mirowsky, 1999a; Ross, Mirowsky, & Pribesh, 2001, 2002; Ross, Reynolds, & Geis, 2000). They suggest that others living nearby are not concerned with public order, do not respect property or each other, and may be dangerous. Mistrust seems reasonable amidst the ambient threat. Economic constraints sometimes force young adults to live in neighborhoods rife with signs of neighborhood disorder. Some young adults, particularly single males, may prefer such neighborhoods, perhaps contributing their share to the signs of disorder. As young adults develop stable careers and

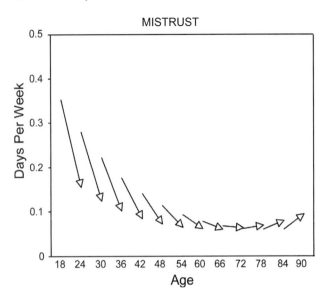

Figure 19.13. Mistrust vectors showing the initial levels and subsequent changes
as birth cohorts aged 6 years (1995–2001 ASOC survey).

relationships and begin raising children, they become more staid and prosperous,
often moving into less exciting but also less threatening neighborhoods.

Well-Being across the Life Course

Adulthood begins as a time of hopes and tensions as people acquire full adult
status. Young adults must complete an education, establish an occupation and
household, acquire recognition and prosperity, and develop marriage and family
relations that profit all involved. The overwhelming majority of young Americans
feel in control of their lives, responsible for their outcomes, and able to meet the
challenges of life. For most, the trials and errors lead to improvements that create
a steady decline in tensions.

Late middle age marks the time of life when everything comes together. Earnings
and household income reach a peak. The children are grown and probably out of
the house. The marriages are more congenial and less discordant. The jobs are
more secure and enjoyable. The tensions and conflicts of young adulthood have
abated, and the losses of old age have not yet arisen.

Later in life, in old age, people walk a narrowing path of improving well-being
along a steepening drop into despair. Those who proceed with health, function,
wealth, and marriage intact find old age an enjoyable time of relaxation and companionship. Even those who lose a spouse or suffer a medical crisis often rebuild

a gratifying life within a year or two. But physical impairment can impose demoralizing limitations. And the shorter and less certain life appears, the less it may seem possible to recover and rebuild. Emotional well-being in old age rests on economic, interpersonal, and physical well-being built throughout adult life. For those not yet old, now is the time to build.

Appendix A

The findings reported in the Concentric Spheres of Experience section and all figures are based on data from the survey of Aging, Status, and the Sense of Control (ASOC). The ASOC survey was supported by a grant from the National Institute on Aging (AG 12393; Principal Investigators John Mirowsky and Catherine E. Ross). It was a national telephone probability sample of 2,592 U.S. households. Sampling, pretesting, and interviewing for the surveys were conducted by the Survey Research Laboratory of the University of Illinois. The ASOC survey has an 80% oversample of people aged 60 or older. At baseline (1995), 58% were ages 18 through 59 ($n = 1,496$) and 42% were ages 60 through 95 ($n = 1,097$).

The ASOC survey had three waves of interviews taken at 3-year intervals, in 1995, 1998, and 2001, with 907 respondents who participated in all three interviews, 470 respondents who participated in the first and second interviews, 237 respondents who participated in the first and third interviews, and 978 respondents who participated only in the first. The latent-growth models represented in the vector graphs adjust for attrition using partitioned full information maximum likelihood estimation, which uses all cases regardless of their follow-up status (Mirowsky & Kim, 2007). The procedure adjusts for data "missing at random" (MAR), meaning random given the observed values in the model.

(quelling political, revolutionary, insurgency, religious, or ethnic movements), or civilian populations (oppressing and brutalizing a population, ethnic cleansing, invasion, or cross-border attacks). Individual civilians and groups of civilians can also commit terrorist-like attacks on states (e.g., assassination of leaders), nonstates, or groups of innocent civilians (e.g., gangs and criminals that terrorize a neighborhood). State-sponsored terrorism occurs when a terrorist group or act is supported with state funding, training, or equipment so it can make its attacks.

The list of types of terrorist attacks is long and includes hijacking, sabotage, kidnapping, detaining, bombings (suicide and others), torture and disfigurement, threats, and assassination. Although bombs are the typical image of a terrorist device, biological, chemical, or nuclear weapons; military or small arms; poison; or any weapon imaginable can be used. The one thing these terrorist devices have in common is the intent to inflict terror as a basic element in the attack.

The Question of Mental Illness as a Cause of Terrorism

Mental illness as a precursor of terrorist acts is not an issue we pursue in this chapter. It should be noted, however, that in fact many people do attribute terrorism to the pathological mind of the terrorist or terrorist leaders, an attribution that is derived probably in no small part from the stereotype that links mental illness and violence (J. K. Martin, Pescosolido, & Tuch, 2000). Social science research on the topic of suicide during war goes back at least as far as Durkheim's work (1897/1951), especially that work associated with the form of altruistic suicide that seems characteristic of today's suicide bombers. Although mental illness as a precursor to suicide attacks and other forms of terrorism may continue to benefit from rigorous analyses derived from theories of chronic stressors, social conditions, labeling, and even the trauma from earlier exposure to terrorism itself (perhaps as a special case of social conditions theories), there are likely mixed motives for these acts and not all or even none may be linked to the mental state of the agent or the leaders of the sponsoring organization (Brym & Araj, 2006; Weatherston & Moran, 2003). Terrorism may just as likely be strategic as it is deranged.

Just as this chapter is not concerned with the mental state of terrorists or terrorist leaders, neither is it concerned too much with the perceived legitimacy of the use or threat of force against the vital interests of another group of people. That is, we do not want to quibble over what is and what is not terrorism. We are instead solely interested in the consequences of the use of that force. We recognize that terrorism and terrorist labels are social constructions designed to define the use of force as illegitimate. It is certainly to the advantage of the targeted group to define the perpetrators as terrorists, in part because it legitimizes the use of force in defense. However, it is not clear whether there is an additional premium for the terrorists to be labeled as such in terms of the impact they have on their targets. Is a population targeted by "terrorists" more vulnerable to the consequences of their attacks than a population targeted by so-called freedom fighters who are putatively resisting oppression? To our knowledge this research question has yet to be addressed, though it probably should be in the near future. In any event, whether acts of terror are committed by freedom fighters attacking the citizenry of their oppressors or states and governments are willing to define collateral damage as acceptable, the consequences for the victims are the same and these are our foci here.

We now turn to the existing scholarship on terrorism. The topic ranges, of course, far into the literatures on science, medicine, the arts, and humanities. We, however, focus our attention on that research that appears in the social science literatures.

Literature Review on Terrorism and Mental Health

An electronic search in March 2008 of Thompson Scientific, Inc.'s "Web of Knowledge" for English-language social science publications on the topic of terrorism[2] revealed 2,442 articles (excluding abstracts, reviews, etc.). The plurality of articles were in the subject area of political science, followed by international relations, law, interdisciplinary social science, and economics. The topics dealt with treaties, trade, stock market fluctuations, emergency management, counter- and antiterrorism, judicial review, national and homeland security, population migration, and diplomacy, to name but a few topics. Of these, only 103 (or slightly more than 4%) focused on the dimensions of health, stress, or the psychological impact of terrorism.

For the majority of the past two and a half decades, terrorism research remained fairly steady and low key. Throughout the two decades leading to the World Trade Center (WTC) terrorist attack, the number of publications per year remained below 50 overall, with the exception of 1987 when there was a brief uptick in numbers. In 15 of the 20 years, there were no publications dealing with terrorism and stress or health. Then, following the September 11, 2001, terrorist attack on the WTC and Pentagon, there was a dramatic upsurge in the number of terrorism articles overall and those specifically related to health and stress (see Figure 20.1). The left axis shows the number of publications overall dealing with terrorism, and the right axis shows the number of publications dealing with health and stress as a consequence of terrorism. By 2002 and 2003 the number on health and stress articles had risen to more than 5, and there were 15 articles by 2004. By 2007 the number had almost doubled to nearly 30 articles. Yet, this is still fewer than 1 in 10 articles published on the topic overall.

---

[2] The euphemistic term *political violence* is sometimes used in an effort to avoid the appearance of bias stemming from the use of the word *terrorism*. We included only those articles that used the term *terrorism* itself.

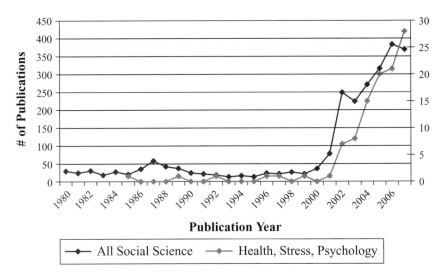

Figure 20.1. Number of social science publications on terrorism per year since 1980.

Over this period of two and a half decades, the vast majority of the articles dealing with terrorism and stress or health addressed Israeli civilian exposure to terrorism or the post-9/11 effects of the terrorist attacks on the WTC, even as most recently the majority of victims of terrorism have been Muslim. The vast majority also focused on mental health consequences of terrorism (78%), followed by increased risk behaviors (12%), use of health services (11%), physical health symptoms (7%), child development (2%), and intervention/prevention (1%). Eleven percent of the studies had two or more of these categories as outcomes (see Figure 20.2).

The following is not intended as a comprehensive review of terrorism and terrorist acts over the last two and a half decades, but is instead a review focusing on English-language social science journals dealing with the topics of terrorism and mental health. It is thus probably reflective of a Western Euro-American bias that must be acknowledged at the outset. In a rough chronology, the earliest study in this group of articles was one of two studies on Guatemalan Mayan children exposed to government-sponsored terrorism during the period from 1981 to 1983 as a result of the Central American civil wars (Melville & Lykes, 1992). The later article (K. E. Miller, 1996) addressed the psychological well-being of children living in the refugee camps but not directly exposed to the civil war because they were born in the camps. Results showed that depressive symptomatology was directly related to the health of the mothers, who did experience the war.

Terrorist attacks in France from 1982 to 1987 yielded one study (Abenhaim, Dab, & Salmi, 1992) of the 254 survivors of 20 bombings and one machine-gun

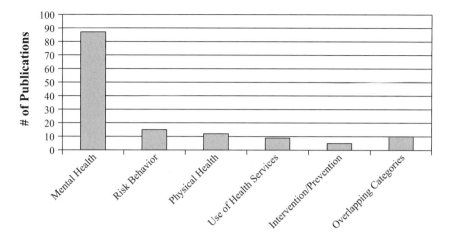

Figure 20.2. Number of publications for various health outcomes of exposure to terrorism, 1992–2008.

attack over that period. They found more than three times the rate of PTSD among the severely injured survivors compared to those who were moderately injured (8.3%) or uninjured (10.5%). This study thus established the first link between the severity of the trauma from terrorism and the severity of the mental health outcome among those who were exposed to it.

The First Gulf War provided a context of both war and terrorism as potential threats to the health of a civilian population caught in the cross-fire. One study (Kiefer, 1992) urged health care providers to consider militarism as a factor in the cause of health problems in developing nations and the world's poor populations. This was a social, political, and economic argument about the effects of diverting resources to war (including the devastating environmental consequences) rather than using them in peaceful endeavors; poor populations were made even more vulnerable to increased poverty and ill health, in part from the effects of increased crime and terrorism in their nations. Hobfoll, Lomranz, et al. (1994) directly investigated the effects of war and state terrorism (i.e., SCUD missile attacks on Israel by Iraq) on mental health. They measured the prevalence of depressive mood in four samples of Israeli citizens, each at one of four time periods: before the crisis leading to the First Gulf War, the approach of hostilities, during the SCUD missile attacks of Iraq on Israel, and shortly after the war. They found, as one might expect, that depressive mood was higher during the period of the SCUD attacks than before the crisis or the start of hostilities. But there was also a rapid return to prewar levels of depressive mood once the hostilities ceased.

On March 1, 1994, a van was targeted by a gunman while crossing the Brooklyn Bridge in New York City. The van was carrying 15 Hasidic students; 1 was killed and 3 were injured. Although initially cast as a case of road rage following a traffic dispute, this attack was later seen as an example of a terrorist attack by a civilian criminal on a local civilian group. It was thus framed as urban terrorism. Trappler and Friedman (1996) described the mental health consequences for 11 of the 14 survivors. More than half of these students (7) suffered from the effects of exposure to this terrorist attack: 4 were diagnosed with both PTSD and major depressive disorder (MDD), 1 with MDD alone, and 2 with adjustment disorder.

In an early study of the effects of terrorist attacks on daily functioning, one team of researchers turned their attention to 50 bus commuters in Israel to determine how frequency of commuting and coping were related to anxiety (Gidron, Gal, & Zahavi, 1999). This small study began to posit that the realistic threat of a terrorist attack might have effects on coping and anxiety, especially in a country like Israel that had experienced fatal terrorist bombings on buses and in marketplaces leading up to this study. The researchers found that anxiety levels were high among approximately 18% of the subjects, and anxiety from terrorism was higher among the commuters who commuted less often. They also found that as problem-focused coping increased (e.g., looking for suspicious objects or unfamiliar faces) so did anxiety. It appears that, as commuters framed their experience in terms of looking out for the possibility of an attack, their anxiety increased. And although the authors did not account for why more frequent commuters experienced less anxiety, it could be a selection effect whereby only the more resilient citizens continued to use the bus regularly.

The Oklahoma City bombing on April 19, 1995, was a criminal terrorist attack against a U.S. federal office building and its civilian occupants. The nation was shocked as it watched rescue workers lead the injured from the building to emergency vehicles and then dig through the rubble to remove the dead and buried bodies. In all, 168 men, women, and children were left dead in what to that point had been the worst terrorist attack on U.S. soil. Four studies assessed the reactions of children and adults in Oklahoma City; see Pfefferbaum et al. (2002); Sprang (2001); Tucker, Dickson, Pfefferbaum, McDonald, & Allen (1997); and Trautman et al. (2002), a study that was conducted among Asian and Middle Eastern immigrants who had high exposure to earlier trauma before emigrating to the United States. Tucker and colleagues (1997) studied 86 adults who sought help after the bombing. They found that the individuals' distress was related to their initial remembered reactions of being upset by what they witnessed in other people's behavior directly after the bombings.

Some of this research also began to build on the idea that especially vulnerable populations such as schoolchildren, immigrants, or those living near the traumatic event might suffer ill health effects even if they were not directly exposed to the terrorist act. Studying more than 2,000 middle school students, Pfefferbaum and her colleagues (2002) found that direct exposure (either personal physical exposure or knowing victims) was no longer relevant in predicting symptoms of PTSD once the students' subjective appraisals of danger and threat at the time of the bombings were taken into account. In a study of 45 Asian and Middle Eastern immigrants living in Oklahoma City and seeking treatment, Trautman et al. (2002) found a high correlation between PTSD symptoms associated with significant prior trauma and those symptoms associated with the Oklahoma City bombings. These prior trauma-related symptoms were more highly related to symptoms associated with the bombing than the level of exposure to the bombing or distress at the time of the bombing, leading the authors to emphasize the unique vulnerability of those who are retraumatized even to varying degrees. Finally, Sprang (2001) used the term *vicarious stress*, finding that the level of victimization symptoms of PTSD did not decline without treatment over the first year among adults not directly exposed to the bombing, although PTSD symptoms of avoidance, reexperiencing the trauma event, and arousal did so even without treatment.

Another series of bombings in France in 1995–1996 that ended in a Paris subway bombing in December 1996 drew the attention of two research teams to their psychological impacts (Jehel et al., 2003; Verger et al., 2004). Among the 32 victims of the Paris subway bombing, more than one-third met PSTD criteria 6 months after the attack, and PTSD persisted among one-fourth up to 32 months after the attack. Severity of the persistent PTSD symptoms was related to physical injury as a result of the attack and drug use prior to it (Jehel et al., 2003). In the second study (Verger et al., 2004), the researchers also found that among the 196 victims the severity of symptoms of PTSD was related not only to the severity of injury in the attack but also to whether the injury caused cosmetic disfiguration.

By the time the last articles on the 1995 Oklahoma City bombing and the 1995–1996 bombings in France appeared in the literature, the first studies of the consequences of the terrorist attacks on September 11, 2001 began to appear, in late 2002 and early 2003 (Herman, Felton, & Susser, 2002; Lee, Isaac, & Janca, 2002; Pantin et al., 2003; L. A. Weiss et al., 2002). Terrorists hijacked four jet planes, crashing two into the World Trade Center Towers, one into the Pentagon near Washington, D.C., and one into the ground in rural Pennsylvania after a group of passengers tried to regain control of the aircraft from the terrorist hijackers. The first study of these attacks focused on PTSD in New York City (NYC) in the first 6 months after the September 11, 2001, terrorist attack on the WTC, and it appeared in late 2003 (Galea et al., 2003). The authors found that one month after the attacks, the prevalence of probable PTSD was 7.5%. However, 6 months after the attack the prevalence of probable PTSD had declined to 0.6% (Galea et al., 2003). The authors concluded that this decrease provided evidence of a "rapid resolution" of symptoms among the general population in NYC. Subsequent studies focused on other NYC residents, continuing the trend to examine those not directly exposed such as college students; particular or vulnerable populations, such as high-exposure survivors of the 9/11 attacks, parents, and children; drug users; first responders; airline employees; displaced Chinese workers; and gay men (Blanchard et al., 2004; Bonanno, Rennicke, & Dekel, 2005; Chiasson et al., 2005; De Bocanegra, Moskalenko, & Chan, 2005; Lating et al., 2004a, 2004b; Liverant, Hofmann, & Litz, 2004; MacGeorge et al., 2004; McCaslin et al., 2005; Perrine et al., 2004). In an early national longitudinal study using a nationally representative sample of 395 adults, B. D. Stein et al. (2004) drove home the point about the potential impact of vicarious or indirect exposure to a terrorist attack on mental well-being. The vast majority of these adults' only exposure to the attacks was through television, radio, the Internet, and newspapers, yet nearly one in six were found to have had persistent distress, first in September and then 2 months later in November. Just over 1 in 10 received counseling or information about distress, and nearly two-thirds with persistent distress reported they were accomplishing less at work.

The two issues of how long these effects of terrorist attacks last and how directly someone must be exposed to experience these effects continued to be examined and debated in many articles to follow in this body of literature. For example, Boscarino, Adams, and Figley (2004) found one year after the WTC attacks that about 13% of New Yorkers reported seeking mental health treatment one or more times for distress related to the attacks. Compared to the year preceding the attack, nearly 9% had increased their use of treatment services, and just over 5% had sought treatment for the first time.

After the spike in research that began with the WTC attacks, research began to appear regarding mental health and terrorist attacks committed in other European settings: the Beslan school hostage crisis on September 1, 2004 (Moscardino, Axia, Scrimin, & Capello, 2007; Scrimin et al., 2006); the London bombings on July 7, 2005 (Rubin et al., 2007); and the March 11, 2004 terrorist attack in Madrid (Conejo-Galindo et al., 2007; Vazquez, Perez-Sales, & Matt, 2006). However, in the last 2 years and 2 months of the period under study, a little more than half of the articles (52%) returned to focus specifically on the events of September 11, 2001 ($n = 19$) or the exposure to terrorism among various Israeli populations ($n = 19$). Thus, just over 88% of all of the articles dealt with issues in the United States or Israel. It appears that, in this age of global terrorism, many victimized and vulnerable populations are being neglected. The importance of the contributions that these studies in the United States and Israel made and should continue to make, however, should not be underestimated. We turn next to the theoretical paradigms and basic constructs that have helped us understand the relationship between mental health and terrorism.

Theoretical Perspectives in the Stress Paradigm

Stress Hierarchy

One of the defining features of human groups is that they form social hierarchies, and today one of the hierarchies that stands out most and has the most persistent influence on a wide range of human experience is organized along the many dimensions of socioeconomic status (SES). Whether power, wealth, and prestige or education, income, and occupation, the many dimensions of SES are perceived by individuals in everyday life and shown by researchers to have beneficial or harmful effects depending on where they stand in the SES hierarchy. Obviously, high SES is commonly found to benefit the welfare of those who have it, and low SES is detrimental to individuals' welfare in many ways. Specifically, SES is directly and positively related to health, and according to what has become called the *stress hierarchy perspective* (Wilkinson, 1997), this relationship is due in part to the absolute level of material living standards and in part to the psychological benefits of a privileged life versus a life of deprivation.

Fundamental or Social Causation

The "persistent association" between some social conditions (e.g., SES, gender, and race) and health is cited as evidence that they play a fundamental role in the cause of disease (Link & Phelan, 1995). Regardless of the intervening risk factors that may be more proximate to disease or illness, these social conditions persist throughout history as a distal cause, sometimes creating the risk for intervening risk factors (and therefore more proximate causes) and sometimes remaining directly linked to disease or illness itself. In addition to maintaining that the fundamental causes of illness are social, this perspective states that illness is influenced by the resources that higher SES provides people with to manage and respond to the risks of their social environment. For example, individuals at the top of the SES ladder have more of these resources than those in the middle or at the bottom. These resources "help individuals avoid diseases and their negative consequences through a variety of mechanisms" (Link & Phelan, 1995, p. 81). Others have more specifically labeled these sources of illness as "social causes" (Ross & Mirowsky, 1989), and they and many more have focused on the actual mechanism by which these social conditions cause illness (Hobfoll, Canetti-Nisim, Johnson, 2006; Hobfoll, Johnson, Ennis, & Jackson, 2003; Link, Lennon, & Dohrenwend, 1993; Pearlin et al., 1981).

Conservation of Resources

Developed independently from both the stress hierarchy and fundamental cause perspectives, yet with a common link to the stress paradigm, conservation of resource (COR) theory (Hobfoll, 1989) incorporates elements of hierarchical position, intervening mechanisms among social causes including risks and resources (i.e., material, social, and psychological), and the use of resources to offset the health consequences of risk. It adds both the notions of conservation and loss of resources to these explanations. People are motivated to conserve the resources they inherit or accumulate, if not even to gain them over the life course. Both the social causation and stress hierarchy perspectives recognize the fundamental health advantage to having these resources, both in an absolute and a relative sense. The motivation to conserve resources is in part a mechanism to maintain this fundamental health advantage, if not other social and psychological advantages as well.

COR theory has been focused primarily on examining the intervening process of the use of resources to offset the effects of specific risks on mental health outcomes (Hobfoll, 1989, 1998, 2001). According to COR theory, resource loss far outweighs the influence of resource gain. Second, COR theory posits that resource gain becomes more salient in the context of high resource loss. Because people require resources to offset resource loss and to foster ongoing resource gain, those who lack resources are at a marked disadvantage. Moreover, a great deal of research has shown that, once resource loss cycles begin, they tend to strengthen and accelerate. The issue of resource loss momentum is unique to COR theory, and it adds to other theories that only speak to the strength of association. Resource loss momentum is critical in the context of terrorism and mass casualty as the major resource loss cycles begin abruptly and acquire great speed. Therefore, intervention must also be implemented quickly and have enough critical mass to offset the power and speed of the resource loss cycles. As resource loss has been repeatedly shown to be the best predictor of mental health outcomes after mass casualty events, this theory should be a critical guide to work in this domain (Freedy et al., 1994; Galea et al., 2003; Hobfoll 2006; Ironson et al., 1997).

All three perspectives make a distinct contribution in the elaboration of the stress process (Pearlin, 1989). Link and Phelan (2000) have argued that the explanations provided by stress hierarchy and fundamental causes are compatible, and Horwitz (2007) placed the concept of loss of resources firmly within the stress paradigm as well. Hobfoll (1989, 2001) amplified the notion of loss of resources, however, by positing a COR theory that makes the distinction between loss and gain, links loss to both location in the hierarchy and the health advantages of having resources, and focuses on the types and uses of resources as mechanisms that explain mental health outcomes.

Hobfoll has often explained the distinction between loss and gain by using the example of trust (Hobfoll, 1998). Trust is a powerful belief, both for those who have it in something and those who have it given to them. It facilitates all sorts of human interactions, many of which would not be possible without it. A person gains trust over a long course of interaction, and a person gives trust over the same long course. As long as the character of the interactions that initially created trust is maintained, it will grow and get stronger. But if the character of the interactions changes to threaten trust, most or all of it can be lost in a very short time. The loss can be precipitous, although regaining that trust is a slow process and may take an even longer course to rebuild than it took initially to form. Thus, loss of trust is more distressful than gain of trust is beneficial, and the gain of trust is a slow process, whereas loss caused by stress can occur rapidly and with great consequences. We can readily recognize how the nature of the loss and gain of a person's trust has direct implications for the effects of loss and gain of resources – psychosocial, personal, and economic.

With an understanding of these theoretical perspectives we can begin to examine the effects of the exposure to terrorism and work toward building a model to illustrate those effects that have been found in the literature.

Exposure to Terrorism

Direct exposure to a terrorist attack is usually considered to mean that the person has in some way become its victim, either through personal injury or loss or the injury or loss of a close family member or friend. We have already seen the results of research that have shown that the severity of injury and disfiguration is related to the severity of PTSD symptoms (Jehel et al., 2003; Verger et al., 2004), and some research has shown how exposure to terrorism is related directly to increased economic and psychosocial loss (Hobfoll et al., 2006). But the question of exposure can be framed in many ways: in terms of distance from the terrorist attack (Blanchard et al., 2004; Ford, Adams, & Dailey, 2006; Perrine et al., 2004), length of time since the attack (Galea et al., 2003; Laugharne, Janca, & Widiger, 2007), or number or recurrence of terrorist attacks (Hobfoll et al., 2006; Laor et al., 2006; Pat-Horenczyk et al., 2007; Shalev et al., 2006; Somer, Ruvio, Sever, & Soref, 2007). The continuous exposure to terrorism in Israel, for example, means that some people can have multiple direct exposures to terrorism (Shalev & Freedman, 2005).

Another issue that is sometimes related to framing the exposure to terrorism is the impact that media coverage of the terrorism attacks has on the well-being of individuals who were not directly affected by the attacks (i.e., were not injured, did not lose a family members, did not have loss of property). Relatedly, others have been interested in whether close physical proximity to the attack is enough to cause damaging effects. Thus, indirect or vicarious exposure, as it has been called, has become the focus of much research into the effects of terrorism on mental health. A recent review of the earlier research concluded as follows:

> At least 28–35% of people exposed to a terrorist attack may develop post-traumatic stress disorder. Whereas persons directly exposed to terrorist attacks have a greater risk of developing post-traumatic stress disorder, the secondary effects of vicarious exposure on people not directly exposed are significant, such that more than 40% of people across the United States experienced substantial symptoms of stress after the attacks of September 11, 2001. (Lee, Isaac, & Janca, 2002, p. 633)

More recent research has continued to show the effects of the media on anxiety (Slone & Shoshani, 2006). In this regard, several studies have shown a generalized effect of terrorism in representative samples of populations that include those who have and have not been directly exposed (Bleich, Gelkopf, Melamed, & Solomon, 2005; Ford, Adams, & Dailey, 2007; Hobfoll et al., 2006; 2008; Pfefferbaum et al., 2008; Solomon, Gelkopf, & Bleich, 2005; B. D. Stein et al., 2004; Stuber, Galea, Boscarino, & Schlesinger, 2006), and the effects of terrorism on those selected populations not directly exposed who were purposely included or specifically studied in their analyses (Hobfoll et al., 2008; Liverant et al., 2004; Shalev et al., 2006; Sprang, 2001; Somer et al., 2005).

Consequences of Exposure to Terrorism

As discussed earlier, the major theoretical approaches to the study of stress and mental health can be used to inform research on terrorism. The basic premise is that individuals are at varying degrees of risk of exposure to or injury from terrorist attacks or both based on social characteristics such as age, sex, being a member of a particular ethnic or race minority, or SES. These characteristics are also directly related to the resources they will have to draw on after experiencing a terrorist attack. These resources are vulnerable to loss as a direct result of the attack (e.g., damaged or destroyed property or workplace, loss of a close loved one who provided support, or a shaken sense of self-mastery); recent research has examined the possibility of some gain or growth from the experience (e.g., support from network members, trust, or other help). The resources or loss thereof mediates the effect of the terrorism and either helps alleviate or exacerbate the experience of distress. In the model depicted in Figure 20.3, social characteristics and terrorism may also directly affect distress (paths C and E) when the full range of mediating resources are not included in the specification and analyses of the model. It is also consistent with some of the theoretical perspectives that hold that the lack of status or low standing itself is distressful. In this section we discuss the major components of the model that are affected by terrorism: resources and distress.

Mental Health Consequences of Exposure to Terrorism (Anxiety and Mood Disorders)

Studies of PTSD or its symptoms dominate the literature on the mental health consequences of terrorism, but also studied are other types of mental disorders including acute stress disorder, depression, risk behaviors, use of health services, intervention or prevention, and in a few examples multiple outcomes (see Figure 20.2). We next describe the unique features of each of the major types of disorder associated with terrorism in the literature, starting with PTSD.

Posttraumatic Stress Disorder (PTSD). Much research already exists on trauma among victims of crime or motor vehicle and other accidents. Terrorism

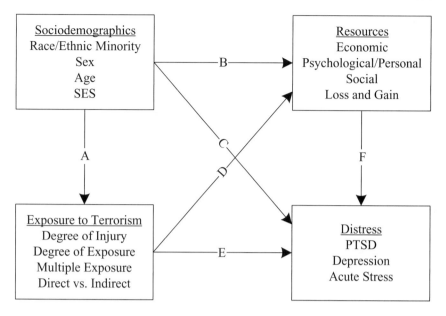

Figure 20.3. General theoretical model of the risks (A), fundamental or social causes (B and C) and effects of terrorism on distress (E), mediated by the loss and gain of resources (D–F).

and mental health research appropriated PTSD from the trauma literature as a primary outcome of exposure to terrorism in much the same way that terrorism exposure was appropriated from the general stress paradigm as a major life event. However, for more than a century, notions of distress similar to PTSD were associated with the violence experienced in warfare, but usually restricted to the experiences of combat soldiers. The shell shock experienced by veterans of World War I and later the combat fatigue suffered by World War II veterans were well studied. The label "PTSD" came into widespread use when large numbers of Vietnam War veterans continued to experience panic disorders long after their service and even the war were over. PTSD was first included in the DSM-III in 1980.

There are six diagnostic criteria for PTSD in DSM IV-R. Criterion A is exposure to a traumatic event in which the "person experienced, witnessed, or was confronted with an event" involving "actual or threatened death or serious injury, or a threat to the physical integrity of self or others." In addition, "the person's response involved intense fear, helplessness, or horror" (American Psychiatric Association, 2000, p. 467). Obviously being the victim of or witnessing a terrorist act fully meets this criterion. Increasingly and cross-culturally, the number of different types of events and event exposure meeting this criterion has been growing, and the research interests in PTSD have broadened enough that it is now almost considered its own specialty.

However, the broadening of the PTSD paradigm, extending it beyond the stress paradigm, has not been without its critics. A recent editorial in the *British Journal of Psychiatry* argued that "Criterion A events are neither necessary nor sufficient to produce PTSD" and that PTSD studies should return to the general stress paradigm (Rosen, Spitzer, & McHugh, 2008). Lending support to this argument was the observation that Criterion A is now defined so broadly that individuals no longer have to directly experience the event, but may experience it through media exposure or interpersonal communication, a phenomenon known as "criterion creep" (Rosen et al., 2008). In our own research we have found that, indeed, exposure is often less important in determining PTSD outcomes than the context in which the exposure occurs or the economic, social, and psychological resources that individuals can bring to bear on the consequences of that exposure (Hall et al., 2008; Hobfoll et al., 2006, 2007, 2008; Palmieri et al., 2008). Others have also found that direct exposure is not a necessary criterion (Lee et al., 2002; B. D. Stein et al., 2004) and that, as discussed earlier, various degrees of exposure can explain various mental health responses. Nevertheless, when dealing with terrorism at the population level one thing is clear: populations exposed to terrorism suffer significantly higher levels of PTSD than those who are not, regardless of the specific parameters of Criterion A that are applied.

Criteria B, C, and D involve 17 distinct experiences that occur as a result of the trauma exposure. There are five items in Criterion B that represent a sense of reexperiencing the traumatic event, seven items in Criterion C that represent avoidance of things associated with the event, and five items in Criterion D that represent a sense of increased arousal. Criterion E stipulates that Criteria B–D must be present for a period longer than one month. Finally, the sixth criterion, F, involves the additional feature of functional impairment. Often this diagnostic criterion for PTSD is expressed as "PTSD with or without functional impairment," depending on whether it is included in the final disposition or not. Finally, the items in Criteria B–D are often measured as ordinal scale items and summed to form a measure of symptom severity. This measure and its relationship to diagnosis are discussed later when we compare measures of diagnosis and symptom severity scales.

Depression. Depression is another common consequence of exposure to terrorism, and sometimes in more comprehensive analyses, it is analyzed along with PTSD. It is one of the mood disorders defined by the DSM, and it can be determined either as a diagnostic category or measured as a symptom scale. In DSM-IV-TR, depression is characterized by extremes of any of the following: depressed mood, loss of interest or pleasure, weight loss without dieting, near daily insomnia or hypersomnia, agitation or sluggishness, fatigue, feeling worthless, difficulty thinking or concentrating, and recurrent thoughts of death or suicide (American Psychiatric Association, 2000). The presence of the first two conditions – depressed mood and loss of interest or pleasure – and three or more of the remaining six are necessary for it to be considered a major depressive disorder (MDD).

Depression and PTSD – Distinctive Comorbidities or Not? It has also been suggested that because PTSD requires a specific etiology (e.g., in this case, exposure to a terrorist event) and such exposure is neither a necessary nor sufficient cause for subjects to report experiencing these symptoms, PTSD may be an "amalgam of other disorders" (Rosen et al., 2008), presumably including depression. To determine whether PTSD and depression are unique sets of symptoms or unique disorders requires research that includes both measures, which is often rare. Recently, some studies have begun to examine these disorders simultaneously with respect to abuse (Vranceanu, Hobfoll, & Johnson, 2007) and terrorism (Hobfoll et al., 2006; Johnson et al., 2007. Although every study has found PTSD and depression to be related, it is probable that each disorder has unique characteristics in terms of the wide range of etiological precursors, the chronic nature of the disorder over time, and the subsequent consequences. Indeed there is preliminary evidence for some of these unique characteristics (Hall et al., 2008; Hobfoll et al., 2006).

Anxiety or Acute Stress Disorder. Although there is less of a focus on anxiety or acute stress disorder (ASD) in studies of terrorism, there is a narrow window of time after exposure to a traumatic terrorist attack during which these disorders are relevant. Because PTSD diagnosis requires that symptoms persist longer than one month, similar symptoms of distress occurring during the first month would be more properly considered ASD. Thus, some have cautioned that PTSD should not be diagnosed automatically in the aftermath of trauma (Rosen et al., 2008). Overdiagnosis or misuse of PTSD, as with psychiatric disorders, runs the risk of reifying mental illness when a person is experiencing normative distress, although the boundary between the two is admittedly "fuzzy, vague, and ambiguous" (Horwitz, 2007).

Measurement of Distress: Diagnosis versus Symptom Severity. The many consumers and producers of research on mental health in general and on mental health and terrorism in particular may be divided along many dimensions when it comes to the measurement of stress. On the one hand, there are the clinicians, health service researchers, and other professional practitioners who adhere more or less strictly to the definition of disorders found in the DSM in diagnosing their patients. Those individuals who do meet the criteria become cases, which are often studied in terms of incidence, prevalence, symptoms, treatment, and recovery. Although "caseness" according to these criteria is not a necessary condition to study these issues, it is fairly standard to adhere to it when researchers want to present their results in outlets that reach other researchers and clinicians. On the other hand, there are researchers (generally nonpractitioners) who adhere to the psychometric principles of measurement and prefer to develop more or less continuous scales of symptoms and their severity.

Other Consequences of Exposure to Terrorism

As this review of the literature revealed and as is shown in Figure 20.2, the consequences of exposure to terrorism other than mental health outcomes are much less frequently studied. Studies of risk behaviors, physical health, use of health services, and intervention/prevention comprise a small percentage of all the studies. As a result the findings are not as clear and consistent as they are beginning to be in studies of PTSD and depression, for example. Some of these results are presented in this section.

Risk behaviors. Increases in risk behaviors including smoking, drinking alcohol, using drugs, suicide, and even sexual behavior have been studied as unhealthy responses to the stress induced by exposure to terrorism (Bleich et al., 2005; Chiasson et al., 2005; Hasin et al., 2007; Knudsen et al., 2005; Perrine et al., 2004; Pfefferbaum et al., 2008; Richman, Cloninger, & Rospenda, 2008; Schiff, 2006; Schiff, Zweig, Benbenishty, & Hasin, 2007; Starkman, 2006; B. D. Stein et al., 2004; Weiss et al., 2002). The findings are decidedly mixed: some found no increase in risk behaviors (e.g., Knudsen et al., 2005; Perrine et al., 2004) whereas others did find an increase (e.g., Chiasson et al., 2005; Hasin et al., 2007; Richman et al., 2008; Shiff, 2006; Schiff et al., 2007; B. D. Stein et al., 2004). It appears that, when results show no or little effect of exposure to terrorism on risk behaviors, the studies were generally done on large representative samples (although some representative studies have found these effects). Generally speaking, when studies are performed among vulnerable populations, exposure is related to an increased risk of unhealthy responses to stress.

Use of health services. Only a handful of studies have examined the impact of terrorist attacks on the use of health services (Green et al., 2006; Levav et al., 2006; Sprang, 2001; Stuber et al., 2006). They all reflected the concern that after the trauma of a terrorist attack some victims may not be served. Sprang (2001) explored why those victimized would not seek treatment. Ford et al. (2006) focused on the receipt of formal services and the public health policies and professional attention needed to provide those services, particularly to the underserved. Stuber et al. (2006) concluded that there was potential unmet need in NYC after the WTC attacks and that particular attention should be paid to those who were vulnerable because of preexisting mental health needs and were not being helped by a professional. Other vulnerable populations were found to include older adults as well as previously hospitalized persons (Levav et al., 2006).

Intervention/prevention. Several studies addressed the prevention of psychological damage from exposure to the violence of terrorism by intervening in communities (De Zulueta, 2007) or schools (Berger, Pat-Horenczyk, & Gelkopf, 2007) to provide the residents with the psychosocial resources to reduce the symptoms of distress. The loss of psychosocial resources has been shown to be among the strongest predictors of such symptoms (Hobfoll et al., 2006), and therefore their provision may have the strongest potential to reduce them. Much more research is called for in this area.

Resilience. In contrast to the focus on the symptoms of PTSD as an outcome of exposure to terrorism, some researchers have been turning their attention to the absence of symptoms as an outcome. Resilience (Bonanno et al., 2005, 2006) has been defined as having no symptoms or only one symptom of PTSD after exposure to a terrorist attack. Bonanno and colleagues' studies, one in the New York area and one among NYC residents, showed large percentages of individuals who were resilient. Rather than a disease-specific outcome of terrorism or a trajectory of recovery over time from that exposure, resilience is a concept that maps the response of individuals without the symptoms of disease. Resilience is not the complete lack of a disturbing response to these terrible events, but rather as Bonanno and his colleagues (2005, p. 985) pointed out, "resilient individuals typically experience only transient and mild disruptions in functioning (e.g., several weeks of variability in negative affect, difficulty concentrating, or sleeplessness) and exhibit relatively stable levels of healthy adjustment across time."

Mediators of the Impact of Traumatic Events

Consistent with most theoretical perspectives, psychological, economic, and social resources are the most common mediators of the impact of traumatic events on psychological distress. These vital resources can be directly threatened by the traumatic event or diminished by the necessity to use them in response to the traumatic event. For example, a terrorist attack can and usually does damage property, causing economic losses. The randomness of the attack and the inability to guard against it can harm psychological resources by lowering one's sense of self-mastery. Or it can disrupt social resources by separating families or communities from the support they provide each other.

Economic Loss

In a terrorist attack, people can lose their jobs, homes, cars, and myriad other personal and other belongings. They may be forced to leave their homes and villages with literally only the shirts on their backs. It is understandable that the greater the magnitude of the attack, the greater the potential for economic loss. And economic loss in turn elevates symptoms of distress (Hobfoll et al., 2008). It is very difficult to determine the true amount of economic loss due to terrorist attacks because individual victims of terrrorism often are not fully aware or able to report how much it cost them, nor can the cost of defending against these attacks be quantified easily, as Kiefer (1992) has argued; in addition, individuals may not fully realize how much they have lost in productivity at work, as B. D. Stein et al. (2004) have pointed out. Often researchers do not have the tools, time, money, or experience to gather such data along with assessments of mental well-being. The economic loss variables tend to be narrowly drawn, and unsophisticated measures that often neglect the full range of the many dimensions of economic resources people have and lose to terrorist attacks.

Psychosocial Resource Loss

Terrorism drains individuals' psychosocial resources similar to the way a destroyed home or workplace drains individuals' financial ones. In particular, terrorism may simultaneously result in the loss of hope, sense of control, belief in the government's ability to protect its citizens, and social bonds (Hobfoll et al., 2007). Indeed, these loss markers have been shown to be the best predictors of both depression and PTSD symptoms after a terrorist attack, illustrating their fundamental nature (Hobfoll et al., 2007; Johnson et al., 2007 Palmieri et al., 2008).

Social Support

One of the variables that demonstrates the different etiology of PTSD and depression is social support, which consistently is found to help reduce symptoms of depression but only sometimes (and often more weakly) to alleviate symptoms of PTSD. For example, Hobfoll et al. (2006) in a study of Israelis found that social support satisfaction was significantly inversely related to both PTSD and depressive symptoms, but the effect was much stronger on the latter. In contrast, in a study of Israelis in Gaza, no beneficial effect of social support was found on symptoms of PTSD, but beneficial effects were found on symptoms of depression (Hall et al., 2008). Sometimes the differences in the findings may be due to the different ways in which social support was conceptualized and measured in any given study. The size of the social support network, type of social support provided, and satisfaction with the social support received measure different dimensions of social support and can produce different findings. Issues of timing may also be important. Specifically, social support may be unavailable immediately after an attack because of safety issues or may even be what is lost in an attack due to death or injury. After a reasonable time period, support structures are reconstituted, and supportive individuals become available to offer help. Work by Kaniasty and Norris (1995, 2008), following COR theory, also has illustrated that traumatic circumstances may drain social support after an initial period of altruistic helping.

Posttraumatic Growth

One of the newer entries into the field of mediators of traumatic events is posttraumatic growth (PTG). It is defined as "positive psychological change experienced as a result of the struggle with highly challenging life circumstances" (Tedeschi & Calhoun, 2004, p. 1). It can be characterized as the silver lining in the dark cloud of trauma's psychological pain and suffering, the potential psychosocial benefit one receives from facing down adversity, even a traumatic one. Theoretically it is one variable among individuals' psychosocial resources that mediates the impact of trauma on distress. PTG has been characterized as self-perceived positive changes in (1) self and life attitudes, (2) philosophy of life, and (3) relations with others (including God). The precise nature of that mediating effect, however, is not uniformly palliative for distress. A recent review by Zoellner and Maercker (2006) showed that there was no consistent relationship between PTG and the symptoms of distress.

In an effort to explain the worsening of symptoms in relation to PTG, it has been suggested that in some contexts the reported increase in this resource occurs in individuals who are deluding themselves, trying to believe things must be better than they are. In the face of severe trauma such as terrorism, cognitive responses alone may be inadequate for coping with the stress and the accompanying loss of resources. In a recent study, for example, those who were relying less on PTG as a mediating resource had better outcomes in terms of symptoms of both depression and PTSD (Hobfoll et al., 2006). However, in another study in Gaza where adaptation to repeated terrorist attacks was accompanied by dedicated, daily, and collective action to resist a government-mandated evacuation, PTG served as a protective factor against PTSD (Hall et al., 2008; Hobfoll et al., 2007).

The close relationship of PTG to resilience has also been a current topic (Hobfoll et al., 2007; Pat-Horenczyk & Brom, 2007). As Zoellner and Maercker (2006) have argued, PTG has two faces. It can represent actual psychological growth and resiliency or a hollow effort to believe something good must come out of the events as a way of justifying tragedy. Research has only begun to explore this distinction, but reviews of PTG in the health literature (Helgeson, Reynolds, & Tomich, 2006) have clearly shown that PTG may be related to both better and worse mental health outcomes in differing circumstances and may both enhance and impede coping. Tedeschi and Calhoun (2004) have argued that PTG takes time to have a positive impact, but their theorizing still fails to consider the potentially more superficial kind of PTG that is often reported on even their own paper-and-pencil scales. Their theorizing speaks to the deeper, more genuine kind of PTG, but it is still unknown if this cognitive coping may nevertheless at times impede behavioral efforts to get beyond the tragedy. Others have also argued that expecting not only reasonable adjustment but also growth after a tragedy such as terrorism may place an excessive burden on people (Hobfoll et al., 2007).

Another attempt to account for the inconsistent findings regarding PTG and distress has focused on the nature of the traumatic events themselves (Stasko & Ickovics, 2007). PTG may be positive in response to some traumas (recovery from accidental events), but not others (terrorism appears to be an event that evokes negative effects from PTG). Exploring this suggestion would be a new, potentially productive direction for research.

Selective effects and differential associations that come from self-selection into groups could also account for some of the inconsistencies in the findings on the relationship between PTG and distress. For example, Wagner, Forstmeier, and Maercker (2007) noted that the protective effects found by Hall et al. (2008) in their Gaza study could be the result of the high levels of religious belief and political commitment among these settlers. Other self-selection factors were also noted as a rationale for this effect (Hall et al., 2008; Hobfoll et al., 2007; Johnson et al., 2007). It is possible that PTG is positive in the context of growth among those who share a highly valued positive outlook (e.g., staying in Gaza and saving their homes), but may be negative in the context of growth among those whose outlook is negative (e.g., revenge or retribution, envy, distrust).

Summary

This chapter provided a glimpse into the increasing interest in the relationship between terrorism and mental health. Some conclusions it provided are necessarily tentative because of the recency of the findings and the difficulty of conducting the studies. Other conclusions are more certain, especially in areas where research is concentrated and converging (e.g., PTSD), although controversies still remain. But because this is a relatively new area of research, we began by defining terrorism and providing examples of the broad range of terrorist tactics used in attacks. In doing so, we acknowledged that some acts of violence are labeled terrorism in order to condemn them and their political motivations while simultaneously pointing out their senselessness and the tragedy for their victims.

We also addressed the issue of whether mental illness played a role in the lives of those who engaged in terrorist acts. The mere senselessness and tragedy associated with terror and violence make it difficult to comprehend how it can be carried out by sane individuals. We concluded, however, that although this issue should be an area for future research there were probably other, more complex reasons why terrorist attacks are plotted and carried out on such a global basis.

Turning to the literature that explicitly dealt with terrorism and mental health outcomes, we noted an increased interest following the WTC attacks on September 11, 2001. We also noted that the types of mental health outcomes examined were predominantly stress responses with a notable focus on PTSD, but also including depression and anxiety. Many fewer studies had examined other outcomes such as risk behaviors, use of professional health services, or intervention/prevention. Thus, further research is needed in these areas in addition to that being conducted on PTSD and depression. The further finding that much of the most recent research is being conducted on post-9/11 responses in the United States or on the ongoing exposure to terrorism in Israel led us to conclude that there is a need to examine terrorism in other places around the world.

Based on the accumulated evidence in the literature, we provided a brief background to current stress theories that we found useful for studying the effects of terrorist attacks on mental health. This allowed us to explore the nature of mental health measures useful in studying responses to terrorist attacks, including measures of the extent and type of exposure to them and the controversies surrounding the measurement of terrorism and mental health. We also explored the explanatory variables known as mediators and modeled their effects within the context of the theoretical framework.

This approach is useful in understanding how mental health outcomes are embedded in the social fabric that includes exposure to violent acts of terrorism and how individuals and their resources are vulnerable to suffering loss, and yet many others seem to be resilient or experience growth. These latter experiences are the object of the most recent inquiries and currently the least well understood. Thus more time and effort are needed before we will have a full understanding of these complex and sometimes perplexing relationships.

Part III
Mental Health Systems and Policy

Teresa L. Scheid and Tony N. Brown

Care of and treatment provided to individuals with mental health problems reflect wider social values and priorities. Hence, the mental health system (i.e., the network of organizations, services, and health care professionals) will change as society changes. Specifically, widely held beliefs about mental health and attitudes toward the mentally ill as well as professional ideologies and treatment preferences will shape the political climate, economic priorities, and type of services available. For this reason, it is difficult both to achieve consensus on what type of system of care will work and to implement change (Mechanic, 2006).

Historically there have been two systems of mental health care: the private and the public. Private mental health care is funded either out of pocket or by insurance and generally serves the "worried well." Public mental health care is funded by federal, state, and local monies and provides services to those with chronic mental health problems. In terms of public policy, the most critical group is those with severe and persistent mental illness. They are often poor and depend on Medicaid to finance their care. The unique needs of those with severe and persistent mental illness have not been adequately recognized; these individuals require long-term care, and there is a notable lack of efficacious treatment technology (Rochefort, 1989). That is, we do not know how to "cure" such illness, and there is wide disagreement over what services can provide the best quality of life to those with severe and persistent mental illness. As noted by Mechanic (2006), although most care for those with severe and persistent illness is provided in the community (rather than the hospital), there is tremendous diversity in treatment programs for this population. Too often, no care is available and many end up in jail or prison, which in some states has become the de facto system of public care.

Care for those with serious (i.e., severe and persistent) mental illness has gone through four general cycles or phases that reflect changing societal values, professional ideologies, and economic priorities:

1. Institutionalization (late 1800s to mid-1900s): In this period of time, the mental hospital was the primary locus of care.

2. Deinstitutionalization (1950s to 1970s): State mental hospitals were deemphasized and community-based care grew.
3. Consolidation of community-based care (1980s to early 1990s): Emphasis was placed on coordinating and integrating community mental health services, developing centralized authorities, and extending services to those most in need.
4. Managed care (early 1990s to present): This period has been characterized by cost cutting, rationing of mental health services, and contracting out of services to private providers (i.e., privatization).

In this overview, we briefly describe each of these trends, thereby providing a framework for understanding our current system of care. The reasons why individuals seek care and the models developed by sociologists to understand help-seeking patterns are described in Chapter 21 by Bernice Pescosolido and Carol Boyer. Pescosolido and Boyer pay particular attention to the influence of patients' social networks on the sorts of services they seek and receive.

Institutionalization

One of the most well-known books in the sociology of mental health is Erving Goffman's *Asylums*, published in 1961. Goffman (1961, p. 4) described the state mental hospital as a total institution designed to care for those who are "felt to be incapable of looking after themselves and a threat to the community." These two criteria – lacking the ability to look after oneself and posing a potential danger to the community – provide the basis for continued debate over appropriate services for those with mental illness. A total institution represents a closed world, where all of the individuals' needs are met and life is highly regimented and controlled.

The state mental hospital became widespread in the 1800s and was the primary locus of care for those with mental illness until the mid-1900s. During that period one either stayed with family or friends or was sent to the state hospital. The varieties of mental health services that exist today simply were not present in that era. Furthermore, although reliance on state hospitals has declined since the 1960s, these institutions continue to dominate mental health policy debates, and many individuals with severe and persistent mental illness will probably spend some time in a state mental hospital.

Dowdall (1996) provided a thorough sociological analysis of the state mental hospital, drawing on organizational theory to explain its growth, decline, and future prospects. He (p. 23) argued that state mental hospitals are "maximalist" organizations; that is, they live very long lives and are unusually resistant to change. This is certainly the case today; most of the several hundred state mental hospitals created since 1773 are still in existence, and a large proportion of state mental health dollars is spent on state hospitals (Dowdall, 1996). However, patient populations have fallen sharply since 1950. If fewer patients are served, why do states still fund state hospitals at such a high level? Vested interests are part of the explanation; communities fight to maintain their state mental hospitals because they provide local jobs. Also, the state hospital provides custodial care to the minority of patients who cannot survive in the community, who cannot afford private residential treatment, or who are unable to utilize community services. State hospitals have also diversified; many now provide a range of outpatient and rehabilitation services to assorted groups of clients. For example, the Buffalo State Mental Hospital that Dowdall studied (1996) now provides day treatment, case management, family care, sheltered workshops, and rehabilitation services. The Boston Psychopathic Hospital has evolved into the Massachusetts Mental Health Center and provides comprehensive treatment to those with serious mental illness, including inpatient, outpatient, and day treatment (Gudeman, 1988). However, the future of the state mental hospital is uncertain because of shrinking state budgets, managed care, and the preference for community treatment.

Deinstitutionalization

Deinstitutionalization, the process of closing state hospitals and transferring inpatients to community-based mental health services, began in the 1950s (see Morrissey, 1982). It received much of its impetus from the conception that public asylums were little more than warehouses for the "custodial care of the poor and immigrant insane" (Williams et al., 1980, p. 57). Goffman's analysis of these total institutions led to the recognition that inpatient care could stigmatize the individual and prevent a return to society. Furthermore, state hospitals provided little therapy or treatment; instead, they served custodial functions and ensured that the most basic needs (i.e., food and shelter) of patients were met.

Harsher critics charged that asylums served primarily to control those with mental illnesses and thereby violated the individual's constitutional rights. Thomas Szasz (1963) argued that civil commitment procedures violated the rights of the individual to be secure in person and possession against unreasonable searches (Fourth Amendment); against self-incrimination (Fifth Amendment); to a speedy trial (Sixth Amendment); to a trail by jury (Seventh Amendment); against cruel and unusual punishment (Eighth Amendment); and, most importantly, due process and protection against deprivation of life, liberty, and property (Fourteenth Amendment). Goffman's (1961, p. 361) observation that in the state hospital the "patient's life is regulated and ordered according to a disciplinary system developed for the management by a small staff of a large number of involuntary inmates" where "quiet, obedient behavior" was rewarded was shockingly portrayed to audiences in the popular movie *One Flew over the Cuckoo's Nest*.

In addition to a change in society's values manifesting in a greater concern for the rights of the mentally ill, the 1950s and 1960s saw the advent of psychotropic drugs (Gronfein, 1985b). Whereas the more liberal attitudes of the 1960s resulted in a series of court cases that mandated care in the least restrictive environment, psychotropic drugs provided community mental health workers with the technology of actually maintaining patients in the community. With the shift from hospital-based care to community-based care, individuals with mental illness became clients rather than patients. In this section, we first discuss the legal impetus behind deinstitutionalization (i.e., the doctrine of the "least restrictive alternative") and then turn to a brief discussion of psychiatric medication.

The legal rationale for asserting state control over those with mental illnesses (i.e., the ability to commit an individual involuntarily to the hospital) originates in the state's police power and *parens patriae* functions. Under its police power the state has the obligation to protect the community from potential harm; under *parens patriae* the state has the obligation to serve the best interests of individuals, which means it must protect those with mental illness from potential harm (Wexler, 1981). Courts have interpreted these obligations to mean that the state can only exercise this power to commit when the individual is found to be dangerous to him- or herself or to others.

The least restrictive alternative ruling represents a second major limitation on the state's power to commit an individual to a mental institution. The ruling in the case heard in the District of Columbia Circuit Court (Reisner, 1985) articulated this concept: "Deprivation of liberty solely because of dangers of the ill persons themselves should not go beyond what is necessary for their protection" (*Lake v. Cameron*, United States Court of Appeals, District of Columbia District Court; 1966, 364 F.2d 657). The state's power to commit is limited by the constitutional imperative that government should use methods that curtail individual freedom to no greater extent than what is essential to secure valid community interests. As delineated by subsequent court rulings, the doctrine of the least restrictive alternative mandates that health officials and courts find or create settings that allow the patient to move from large custodial state institutions to facilities that are smaller, less structured, and integrated into the community and that allow for independent living (Levine, 1981).

Although legal rulings provided formal sanctions for deinstitutionalization, new advances in drug therapy allowed community-based care to become a reality. Because psychiatric drugs do control the overt symptoms of mental illness, medicated individuals are able to live in their communities, outside of hospitals; and, for many, drug therapy has been of tremendous help in the control of their symptoms of mental illness. For example, Prozac (an antidepressant) has helped millions of people deal with their depression; Clozaril and other new psychotropics such as risperidone have helped even those with the most debilitating forms of schizophrenia to live relatively stable lives in their own communities.

In addition to changes in the social environment (i.e., greater liberalization and preference for community-based care), liberalized legal statutes, and the growth in new drug therapies, there were important economic reforms during the first two decades of deinstitutionalization. Changes in the financing of mental health care led to wide-scale institutional reform. New sources of public funding at the federal level for community mental health centers and the extension of welfare benefits to those with mental illnesses in the community allowed community-based care to become a reality. Andrew Scull (1977, p. 131) has argued that the segregative social control of the state hospital simply became too costly to maintain, so those with severe mental illnesses were returned to the community, where costs are lower. Scull's argument, however, ignores the fact that governmental expenses, especially through the federal programs of Medicaid, Medicare, Social Security Income, and Social Security Disability Income, increased dramatically during the period of deinstitutionalization.

The political mechanism for deinstitutionalization was President Kennedy's stated commitment to community mental health, which resulted in the Community Mental Health Centers (CMHC) Act of 1963. The CMHC Act directed each state to develop a statewide plan designating catchment areas that would serve 75,000 to 200,000 people, with a community mental health center serving each catchment area. The legislation was designed in such a way that the federal agency, the NIMH, would deal directly with localities and the CMHCs, bypassing the state governments (Levine, 1981). This bypassing of state authorities was to result in future conflict between state and local roles because states continued to fund state hospitals while local communities assumed fiscal responsibility for CMHCs.

In theory, the CMHC had three main functions (Adler, 1982): (1) to provide focused, individual competency-building programs; (2) to coordinate agencies that serve the mentally ill (i.e., transportation, housing, income maintenance, vocational rehabilitation, crisis intervention, and emergency hospitalization); and (3) to promote social support networks for those with mental illnesses at all levels. These functions of the CMHC reflected a social rather than a medical model of mental illness; the CMHC was to develop the adaptive capacities of the client in the community as well as foster community attitudes of tolerance, respect, and helpfulness toward the patient (Bockoven, 1972).

Yet CMHCs were quickly criticized for having little direct impact (Gronfein, 1985a; Kaplan & Bohr, 1976; Kirk & Therrien, 1975; Stern & Minkoff, 1979). CMHCs neither directly reduced the size of hospital populations nor served the needs of those with severe mental illness; instead they served new patient populations – those with less or acute disorders and segments of the middle class, sometimes referred to as the "worried well." Policies promoting deinstitutionalization assumed that CHMCs would accept responsibility for patients who were released from the state mental hospital and would work to prevent their reinstitutionalization into the hospital or jails. It was also assumed that citizens in the community would accept the mentally ill. Both assumptions were proven false (Morrissey, Goldman, & Klerman, 1980). For former hospital patients, the CMHCs became part of the "shuffle to despair" (H. S. Wilson 1982, p. xviii) as they revolved in and out of state hospitals. These failures were compounded by the programmatic chaos that resulted because deinstitutionalization occurred before a coherent policy was developed and before public consensus was built to support it.

Consequently, deinstitutionalization encountered administrative and system difficulties stemming from the unclear delineation of agency and staff roles, breakdowns in the referral of patients from one agency to another, opposition from the medical profession and from the community, oversaturation of neighborhoods with people with mental health problems, and a lack of residential alternatives (Halpern, Sackett, Binner, & Mohr, 1980). These problems resulted in both the revolving door of frequent hospital admissions (but with shorter stays) when patients could not be maintained in the community, and transinstitutionalization, in which former patients wound up in nursing homes, board and care homes, and other such facilities. Because of the greater difficulties in entering state mental institutions, many seriously mental ill people were jailed or imprisoned for violations that could be attributed to their mental illnesses. Other critics pointed to the rise in homelessness brought about by the wholesale dumping of the mentally ill into the community. Many of the problems associated with deinstitutionalization were attributed to the failure of the local CMHCs to provide or coordinate the necessary support services (Ahmed & Plog, 1976; Mechanic & Rochefort, 1990; Morrissey & Goldman, 1984; Rochefort, 1989; Shadish, Lurigio, & Lewis, 1989).

Gronfein (1985a) charged that CMHCs had neither the incentive nor the means to deal with the seriously or chronically mentally ill. They were inadequately funded, and work with chronic patients involves greater expenditures of time with very little professional return. There is also a notable dearth of solutions or proven technologies beyond psychiatric medication to aid mental health professionals in their work (Mechanic, 1986; Stern & Minkoff, 1979). Consequently, those with severe or persistent mental illness have been characterized as being the least desirable clients (Atwood, 1982; Lang, 1981; Stern & Minkoff, 1979). Much of the necessary care is not therapy, but the provision of supportive services and case management (Mechanic, 1986). Case management involves the coordination of the necessary services and supports (i.e., income, housing, medical care, skills training, medication, therapy) to maintain the client in the community. It has become the primary form of therapy for individuals with severe and persistent mental illness (Harris & Bergman, 1987), but this sort of work is generally not viewed as professionally challenging or rewarding, nor is it well paid. Most mental health professionals are trained in psychotherapy and have neither the skills, training, nor desire to engage in case management.

In a review of studies and evaluations of CMHCs in the 1980s, Dowell and Ciarlo (1989, p. 223) concluded that CMHCs needed to rethink their role and develop a "community based thrust for chronic patient care." The central problem remained of coordinating the various services needed (Aviram, 1990; Dill & Rochefort, 1989); behind these coordination problems were economic and funding constraints.

Consolidation of Community-Based Care

Because those with serious mental illnesses need long-term, continuous care, mental health services must be coordinated. Yet systems of long-term care have been shaped by economic considerations rather than by treatment ideas and philosophies (Frishman & McGuire, 1989). Funding of long-term care is not market driven, but results from governmental policies that affect the funding of CMHCs. The federal government provides direct support to states and local communities via the Alcohol, Drug Abuse, and Mental Health Block Grant, as well as the Social Service Block Grant that helps fund the many supportive services needed by those with severe mental illnesses. Federal policies affecting housing and welfare are also critical. Federal policy is currently in a state of flux, which has serious ramifications for mental health service delivery.

With the decline in government funding that began with President Reagan's Omnibus Reconciliation Act of 1980, mental health researchers, administrators, and advocates turned to a variety of strategies to improve existing service delivery. NIMH provided funding for training programs and services research and also contributed to the development of the Community Support Program (CSP). The CSP is an organizational form that seeks to meet the needs of those with chronic mental illnesses in the community, and many CMHCs subsequently met the standards of CSP certification. As described by Tessler and Goldman (1982) CSPs provided coordinated case management, assessment, emergency intervention, psychiatric treatment, support for activities of daily living, and a wide range of residential, vocational, and recreational services.

Another attempt to improve service delivery to those with severe and persistent illnesses was the Robert Wood Johnson Foundation (RWJF) Program on Chronic Mental Illness (Shern et al., 1994; Shore & Cohen, 1990). The Program on Chronic Mental Illness sought to improve service delivery by establishing centralized authorities that would provide coordinated care. Hence both the CSP and other innovations of the 1980s emphasized integration and coordination of existing services.

Coordination of care operates at three distinct levels: the client, the organization, and the system (Dill & Rochefort, 1989). Case management and multidisciplinary treatment teams operate at the individual level as mental health professionals direct attention to individual clients. Community support systems and other organizational structures such as Assertive Community Treatment that seek to coordinate and integrate the services offered by different community agencies operate at the organization level. Finally, mental health authorities such as those promoted by the RWJF initiative operate at the system level to oversee services to a defined population group. Gary Cuddeback and Joseph Morrissey in Chapter 26 provide a more detailed discussion of various approaches to coordinated care for those with serious mental illnesses.

One consequence of the community mental health care movement has been a growth in rehabilitation as a treatment modality, as opposed to the primary reliance on the reduction of psychiatric symptoms that characterizes the biomedical view of illness. With rehabilitation, the treatment goal is the improvement of social functioning and not just the relief of symptoms. Psychiatric rehabilitation emphasizes "normalization," whereby the client is able to live a normal life in the community, and is based on conformity to the Western ideals of independence and self-reliance. Treatment provides a socialization function – clients learn appropriate social norms and needed skills to "fit in." However, Bayley (1991, p. 88) suggested that such conformity to American ideals of individualist achievement and independence may be "profoundly unhelpful" to those with mental illnesses and disabilities. Lefley (1984) charged that the emphasis on Western ideals represents a type of professional ethnocentrism that may be inappropriate to clients in different cultural contexts as well as members of many minorities. That which is defined as "normal" is culturally specific and valued. Issues regarding cultural diversity and mental health treatment are taken up by Emily Walton, Kateri Berasi, David Takeuchi, and Edwina Uehara in Chapter 22.

In contrast to the focus on normalization are various models for consciousness raising, mutual self-help, and empowerment. Rose and Black (1985) first presented the empowerment paradigm as an alternative to traditional, psychiatric-based mental health care. This paradigm holds that those with mental illnesses should be treated as active agents, rather than subjects, with control and autonomy over their own lives and decisions. An extension of the consumer rights movement, which was part of the original ideology of the community care movement, the empowerment movement calls on "consumers" (those with mental illness who receive services) to take an active role in the creation and delivery of mental health services and argues that mental health professionals should act as "advocates" for their clients. Rather than seeking to rehabilitate or resocialize those with mental illness, this movement believes that mental health providers should work with consumers to help them articulate their concerns and to develop action strategies. Athena McLean provides an analysis of the mental health consumer's movement in Chapter 23. The issues of normalization and empowerment are also central to questions of culturally appropriate treatment and service delivery, as well as alternative forms of mental health care.

Managed Care

Mental health care has been subject to the same attempts to rationalize services as has care of physical health (Brown & Cooksey, 1989). Managed care is any set of techniques used by, or on the behalf of, purchasers of health care to control or influence the quality, accessibility, utilization, and costs of care. That is, managed care is any system that seeks to control access to care or to regulate the type and amount of care received. Cost containment is a driving force behind managed care (Pollack, McFarland, George, & Angell, 1994). The goal is to limit unnecessary services, yet there is also pressure to ensure access to care and to provide quality care. With specific reference to mental health the following types of managed care have been widely used:

- Precertification: Services must be preapproved before a patient may receive them. Most likely one's doctor must make a recommendation and have it approved before the insurance plan or HMO will pay for mental health services.
- Concurrent review: This is also referred to as case management and occurs when there is ongoing review of treatment at regular intervals. The purpose of case management is to allocate services, select less costly treatments, and ensure that those most in need receive appropriate care.
- Gatekeepers: Primary care providers are responsible for allocating mental health care.
- Capitation: A set amount of money is allowed for mental health treatment.

Managed mental health care already exists in many different forms, which is the major reason why there are no conclusive data about the effect of managed care systems on access to care or the quality of care. There are simply too many different kinds of managed care programs to allow for effective evaluation. For example, Medicare's prospective payment system (PPS) is a form of managed care that relies on a preset reimbursement for a given diagnosis-related group (DRG). Many insurance companies also use prospective payment systems. Other types of arrangements (both public or private) may use "carve-out" arrangements in which a managed care firm may contract out its mental health services to a specialty mental health provider (perhaps a group practice or a mental health HMO).

Beyond the wide variety of private insurance arrangements, state mental health authorities (SMHAs) have also "embraced" managed care (Essok & Goldman, 1995). SMHAs have used managed mental health care vendors; that is, managed care firms offer their services to help state and local mental health authorities manage care. These companies, which are private in nature, assist states and public mental health agencies with containing costs, coordinating care, and contracting for services. In general, a managed care manager is hired, or else a consulting firm is brought in for a period of time to assist a public agency with reform. Another device widely used by public mental health agencies to manage care is to contract out services to private organizations. The result of these various mechanisms to manage care is that the historic divide between public and private sector mental health care is crumbling.

An important obstacle to evaluating managed mental health care, in addition to its diversity, is that it is extremely difficult to assess treatment effectiveness. Not only is it difficult to define the nature of the problem, but different types of treatments with different clients and client confidentiality limit the collection of and access to data. Mental health treatment does not result in the same kind of measurable outcomes as does treatment for physical diseases. Even determining whether managed care has resulted in fiscal savings is nearly impossible with the complexity of funding mechanisms for care and the diversity of mental health systems providing treatments (see Wells, Astrachan, Tischler, & Unutzer, 1995). Mental health and substance abuse services are often managed separately, although sometimes services and recipient populations are integrated in an effort to better coordinate care. Michael Polgar in Chapter 25 provides an organizational perspective on how mental health care is currently provided.

Although the cost savings associated with both managed care and mental health carve-outs have been studied, there has been less research on the quality or the continuity of care received by chronic populations. A number of researchers and advocacy groups have found that managed care arrangements are not meeting the needs of chronic care clients. This finding makes sense as the driving force behind managed care, carve-outs, and privatization has been to reduce costs. The only way to accomplish this objective is by limiting access to treatment and the use of more costly services while encouraging the use of less costly services (i.e., focusing on the patient's short-term gains in functional status as opposed to community stability). Even before the advent of managed care, the needs of chronic care populations were never adequately met, so we cannot expect them to be met in a system motivated largely by cost savings rather than by quality care.

There has been widespread concern that "an already vulnerable population" – those with severe and persistent mental illnesses – will be placed at "even great risk for being managed toward the bottom line rather than toward improved client outcomes" (Durham, 1995, p. 117). Of critical importance is the motive behind a given managed care system: Is it to manage care (seeking to improve outcomes as well as care) or to manage reimbursements so as to reduce costs? A concern with cost containment is thought to result in the reduction of services deemed costly, intensive, and long term. Yet those with serious mental illnesses require long-term care and integrated services (Mechanic, 1994). Furthermore, many of those with severe mental illnesses lack insurance and are served largely by the public sector. The private sector has little experience dealing with severe and persistent mental illnesses such as schizophrenia. Mechanic, Schlesinger, and McAlpine (1995, p. 20) have articulated the alternative outcomes of managed mental health care:

"Managed care is a strategy that may increase availability of treatment, contain costs, and increase quality, but it could result as well in denial of needed treatment, reduction in quality of service, and cost shifting to patients, families, professionals, and the community."

Managed care also changes the relationship between a mental health care provider and consumers. Providers must act as gatekeepers and work to keep the costs of care down. Furthermore, their treatment decisions are subject to third-party review. In Chapter 27 Teresa Scheid describes how mental health care providers view managed care and how it has made the work they do to provide for the needs of those with serious mental illness more difficult.

The Current Era: Prospects for Reform?

When Allan Horwitz and Teresa Scheid prepared the first edition of this volume (1999) there was much apprehension over the future of mental health care services. There still is. As David Rochefort has argued (1999), mental health policy has been plagued by recurrent tensions and ambiguities. Mental health care in the public sector is shaped by federal, state, and local policies and varies widely from community to community. Although there has been recent attention to the state of mental health care in the United States (witness the 1999 Surgeon General's Report on Mental Health as well as the 2003 Presidential Commission on Mental Health), there is no clear-cut federal policy such as that which emerged in 1963 with the Community Mental Health Reform Act.[1] As noted by Wolff (2002), in the United States, mental health policy is framed at the state level, and there is tremendous state-by-state variation. Public policy is driven in part by the identification of problems that need to be solved, and part of the reason for the lack of a coherent mental health policy is disagreement over the nature of the problem.

The current era seems to be guided by the principle of recovery. The 1999 Surgeon General's Report on Mental Health devoted an entire chapter to recovery, and the 2003 President's New Freedom Commission of Mental Health (U.S. Department of Health and Human Service, [USDHHS], 1999) also placed attention on recovery. Jacobson and Greenley (2001) have characterized recovery as including internal conditions (i.e., hope, healing, empowerment, and connection) and external conditions (i.e., human rights, positive culture of health, and services to link consumers to the community). Recovery moves beyond the management of symptoms to the idea of building a productive life (Jacobson, 2004; Neugeboren, 1999). Recovery requires collaborative consumer/provider relationships, which involve empowering both providers and consumers.

---

[1] See Grob and Goldman (2006) for an excellent historical overview of mental health policy in the United States. Recent changes at the federal level have been incremental and have not addressed the needs of individuals with serious mental illness.

As described by Jacobson (2004), recovery has multiple meanings and has been used as a slogan by diverse groups to promote different ideological positions. Recovery can mean an expanded service model, as once individuals are stabilized medically they have increased need for social support and skill-building services to obtain independence from the service system (Neugeboren, 1999). Recovery can also mean reduced reliance on service systems and resulting cost savings when it is defined as meeting certain limited functional goals. As described more fully by Jacobson (2004), there have been a number of efforts to develop recovery-based "best practices" and standards for care.

Whether mental health systems can truly promote recovery depends on whether resources are invested into the kinds of supportive services so necessary to community stability. At present, a number of federal programs reimburse individual care for chronic patients, including Supplemental Security Income (SSI), Social Security Disability Income (SSDI), and Medicare. However, funding for public sector mental health care (via Medicaid) has not kept up with demand nor has it allowed for recovery. Community care in many localities is marginal at best, resulting in the criminal justice system becoming the de facto system of care in some states. A recurrent issue is the relationship of the criminal justice system to the mental health system, taken up in Chapter 24 by Virginia Aldigé Hiday and Padraic Burns. Current funding mechanisms simply do not allow for either long-term care or the continuity of care needed by those with severe and persistent mental illness. In addition, this population is aging, and many also face problems with HIV infection (the mental health needs of those with HIV/AIDS are addressed by James Walkup and Stephen Crystal in Chapter 28). Hence, the need for coordinated mental health as well as medical services for populations needing long-term chronic care will continue to put pressures on the service system.

In addition, the stigma attached to mental illness leads to even greater inertia in policy making (McSween, 2002). A *stigma* is an attribute that is discrediting and involves stereotypes that can result in active discrimination; surveys conducted by the National Alliance for the Mental Ill have demonstrated that many people believe those with mental illnesses are dangerous and unpredictable, can never be normal, cannot engage in conversation, and do not make good employees. In other words, those with mental illnesses are feared and shunned. S. Williams (1987) stated that mental illness is the most stigmatizing of conditions; consequently there is a long research tradition examining the course and consequences of stigma. Advocates have engaged in various "stigma-busting" campaigns to change public perceptions to reduce the negative impact of stigma. One recent development that may work to reduce the stigma of mental illness is the passage in October 2008 of parity legislation. Mental health advocates and professionals have been working hard for more than a decade to pass parity legislation, which mandates that basic health care coverage includes reimbursement for mental health services.

Not only does the stigma of mental illness carry negative moral connotations but it can also result in social isolation and withdrawal of the stigmatized individual; ultimately, it may negatively affect ego identity as the individual experiences a devalued sense of self and lowered self-esteem. Link (1982, 1987; Link et al., 1989) has shown how labeling and stigma have negative effects on self-esteem and employment status, as well as on interaction with others, which further isolates the individual who is labeled as mentally ill. In Chapter 29 Bruce Link and Jo Phelan conclude this volume with an extended discussion of labeling theory and stigma, setting forth important considerations for future policies.

21

Understanding the Context and Dynamic Social Processes of Mental Health Treatment

Bernice A. Pescosolido and Carol A. Boyer

This chapter focuses on mental health utilization, commonly referred to as help-seeking. There are four systems of care: (1) the formal system, which consists of specialty mental health care and general medical care; (2) the lay system, which includes friends and family as well as self-help groups; (3) the folk system of religious advisors and alternative healers; and (4) the human/social service system, which includes social service workers, police, and teachers. The chapter provides a review of the research on mental health care utilization and describes and contrasts the dominant theories of help-seeking behavior: the sociobehavioral model, the health belief model, and the theory of reasoned action. These models have provided a profile of the users of services; more recent dynamic approaches also focus on when care is received and attempt to develop models of illness careers. One such model is the help-seeking decision-making model. This is a stage model that has the weakness of assuming that individuals pass through each stage laid out in the model. An alternative, proposed by the authors, is the network-episode model, which views help-seeking as a social process that is managed by the social networks people have in the community, the treatment system, and social service agencies. The network-episode model incorporates four components: the illness career, the social support system, the treatment system, and the social context. What types of services are available in your own community to those seeking help for their mental health problems?

Introduction

I had felt this way before, but this started just before Thanksgiving. I went into a depression.... The feeling that I have is that I've been feeling this way for years and years but to tell somebody about it was, it was silly or it was being childish and ... and a couple of times I called help lines or stress centers and talked to somebody on the phone and they would always either pray with me or just give me enough strength to keep going on.... Well the first person I talked to was Rita. I work with her. And it was just the same day that I came in here. I hadn't done anything prior to that.... I remember going to work so angry inside.... And in my job I have to talk to people all day long on the phone, you know, and I couldn't do it that day ... so Rita asked what was the matter. She goes, "I know something's wrong with you. You don't even have make-up on." So we talked and

We would like to acknowledge financial support from the National Institute of Mental Health (NIMH Research Grants, Independent Research Scientist Award K02MH to the first author).

I just told her, you know. And that's when she told me she'd try to find me some help. "You need help. You don't need to go through this alone." (Pam, diagnosed with major depression; Indianapolis Network Mental Health Study)

When people experience mental health problems – whether stresses associated with the normal "ups and downs" of life, the proverbial "nervous breakdown" still common in public conversation, or problems that come with a diagnosis of a serious mental illness – three basic questions arise: How are these problems seen and interpreted by people? What kinds of help exist? How and when do people use the different sources of care that may be available to them? In this chapter, our focus extends beyond how clinicians define mental illness to examine how people give meaning to psychiatric symptoms and act on them. We pay particular attention to the social processes involved in responding to mental health problems and if, when, and how individuals receive care from a wide range of people in the community – their friends and family, physicians, mental health specialists, alternative healers, the clergy, Web sites, and life coaches. We consider how the fiscal and organizational arrangements seen with changes in the American health care system, particularly the expansion and more recent contraction of stringent managed care strategies, affect how mental health care services are allocated and what this means for people and professionals responding to illness.

Generally, research in mental health utilization, decision making, or help-seeking involves the study of how individuals make contact with the formal system of care. Much of what is known about the use of services focuses on the two major but overlapping sectors that characterize this formal health care system:

1. Specialized mental health care: professionals, including psychiatrists, psychologists, psychiatric nurses, and social workers, as well as specialized hospitals, inpatient psychiatric units of general hospitals, and outpatient mental health programs
2. General medical care: primary care practitioners, community hospitals without specialized psychiatric services, and nursing homes

Even within these sectors, there is considerable variety in the scope, nature, and quality of the clinical resources available to ill individuals and the providers who care for them. What Pam's story indicates is that whether individuals receive formal care eventually often depends on three other sectors: the lay system of care, including friends, family, co-workers, and an increasingly visible set of support or self-help groups (Regier et al., 1993); the alternative or folk system of religious advisors and other healers (Kleinman, 1980); and the human/social service system that includes police, religious advisors, teachers, and social welfare providers (Larson et al., 1988). Together, these sectors of care form a complex web of community resources to treat and manage mental health problems.

Challenges in Understanding the Utilization
of Mental Health Care

To understand the behavior of individuals with mental health problems and their entry into treatment, three basic ideas are important. First, only a limited percentage of people with mental health problems ever receive treatment. Even fewer people are treated by specialized mental health professionals. With research documenting that mental disorders have a high prevalence, can be very disabling, and cause distress not only for individuals but for their families (Mechanic & Schlesinger, 1996), it may seem surprising that the majority of people with psychiatric disorders still do not want care, do not receive treatment or evidenced-based care if they do want it, or, if they make contact, stay in care (e.g., Shapiro, Skinner, Kramer, Steinwachs, & Regier, 1985; J. E. Ware, Manning, Duan, Wells, & Newhouse, 1984).

In the United States, the most recent large-scale national probability samples based on face-to-face interviews for DSM-IV psychiatric disorders (the National Comorbidity Survey Replication; NCS-R) found no notable change in the 12-month prevalence of anxiety disorders, mood disorders, and substance abuse disorders over the decade between 1990–1992 and 2001–2003. Approximately 30% of the population was diagnosed with these disorders in both periods, but several severe mental illnesses (e.g., schizophrenia, schizoaffective disorders) were not targeted in this study. Although the rate of treatment for enumerated psychiatric disorders increased from 20% to 33%, a majority of the population with mental disorders still received no mental health specialty services, general medical care, human social services, or complementary-alternative medical services (Kessler, Berglund, et al., 2005). Even among those individuals who eventually received some sort of care, delays averaged from 6 to 8 years for mood disorders and even longer, from 9 to 23 years, for anxiety disorders (Wang, Berglund, et al., 2005).

Second, the treatment location for mental health problems, as well as the public's view of mental illness, has changed dramatically. While the early 20th century witnessed the growth of the asylum, places intended to provide respite for those with mental illnesses, severe criticism about their operation and effectiveness from mental health providers, former patients, advocates, and families prompted a transfer of care beginning in the 1950s. Persons with severe and persistent mental disorders who had been in state mental institutions and those who later developed problems found treatment services anchored in the community (Bachrach, 1982; Bell, 1989; P. Brown, 1985; Morrissey & Goldman, 1986). Many large state mental hospitals closed, and all decreased their number of beds. Financial arrangements to reimburse care, whether from private or public insurance, also favored the development of outpatient mental health programs (Gronfein, 1985a). However, as the discussion among our focus group participants in Boston has revealed, these newer community-based programs struggled, and continue to struggle, to meet treatment and social needs, even for those with the most serious illnesses.

In an era of state budget deficits, funding for outpatient care competes with other demands for state funding. Similarly, insurance companies have been reluctant to pay for inpatient stays or extended therapeutic visits (e.g., cognitive behavioral therapy), instead favoring reimbursement for the use of psychiatric medications.

Third, major changes in the financing and organization of mental health care in the United States have reshaped available services and patient and provider behaviors. Managed behavioral health care now dominates how mental health services are organized and financed (Mechanic, 2008). Although different forms, financing arrangements, and regulations may be labeled as managed care, every version is designed to control costs, the types of services provided, who provides them, and how they are provided (Wells, Astrachan, Tischler, & Unutzer, 1995). Services are commonly organized as "carve-outs"; that is, mental health benefits are managed separately from the general medical care insurance coverage. Although a public backlash against managed care resulted in diluting rigorous strategies to control access and costs and decrease the utilization of specialists in the general medical sector (Mechanic, 2008), states have continued to introduce managed behavioral health care.

As Mechanic and his colleagues (1995) have explained, managed care organizations make treatment decisions that were previously made by medical care providers together with their patients. Managed care introduces an additional party into models of utilization: an organization that allocates care and may provide care. Managed care plans also place greater responsibility for providing care on those outside the formal treatment system, shifting more of the burden of care to families and neighborhoods (Pescosolido & Kronenfeld, 1995). Researchers are only beginning to understand the extent of the impact of managed behavioral health care plans on individuals' access to care, use of services, quality of care, and outcomes (Mechanic, Schlesinger, & McAlpine, 1995).

Contributions of Sociology to the Study of Utilization

A substantial body of good theory and relevant findings illustrate how social science theory and its methods provide insight into who uses medical or psychiatric care. This research offers an important part of the story of what happens to ill individuals that cannot be known from clinical research alone. In a perfect world, the mere presence of symptoms would be sufficient for people to desire and obtain high-quality and effective treatment. Because this is not the case, knowing who does or does not receive care and who has a propensity to seek care apprises us about what happens to people with mental health problems.

Sociologists have contributed to understanding the use of mental health services through the concept of social selection, the impact of the social context and social structures and the development of theoretical models of utilization. First, sociologists have documented that users and nonusers of mental health services have different sociodemographic characteristics and hold different views of medical and mental health treatment. This systematic difference between people who get treatment and those who do not illustrates a major sociological concept, social selection (Greenley & Mechanic, 1976; Mechanic, 1975). The extent to which individuals and social groups with similar psychiatric symptoms or needs encounter different circumstances in the use of health care poses questions about their personal and social lives quite apart from their symptoms. Many of the earliest (and now classic) studies surprised clinical researchers and medical providers by showing that socioeconomic status (SES) predicted not only who came to treatment but also how they were treated by the health care system. Dunham (1959) found that individuals from poorer neighborhoods in Chicago had higher rates of first psychiatric admissions to hospitals than those from wealthier areas. Hollingshead and Redlich (1958) found that individuals from lower classes were more likely to be brought to Yale-New Haven Hospital by the police than were others. Once hospitalized, these patients were more likely to be given more serious diagnoses than others. It may be tempting to conclude that these actions reflected real differences in mental health problems, but a long tradition of research shows that mental health professionals see the types of problems of persons in lower social classes differently, at times more seriously, and respond to them with more invasive treatments than to those of higher classes (see Loring & Powell, 1988). The effects of sociodemographic factors have, however, been far from consistent. While the search for sociodemographic correlates is now a common research strategy across the medical, public health, and social sciences, concerns about their impact across contexts have been raised, leading to theoretical innovations in thinking about how social factors matter.

Second, sociologists, as well as anthropologists, focus on understanding individuals in the social context in which they live. Whereas early clinical researchers looked at the social and clinical profiles of individuals in care, sociologists were the first to follow individuals from the community into the treatment system. This distinct social science approach provided new and important information. The classic study by Clausen and Yarrow (1955) examined how and when men, later diagnosed with schizophrenia, came to St. Elizabeth's Hospital in Washington, D.C. To the surprise of clinical researchers at the time, this research documented that these men entered care only after years, sometimes decades, of displaying severe and disabling symptoms of schizophrenia. The authors offered a stunning picture of how the men and their wives struggled to understand and normalize strange behaviors before talking to family or friends. Despite extensive and painful delays in getting into treatment, other people in the community – from family and friends to the police and the clergy – played crucial roles in getting these men into care.

Third, sociologists, together with psychologists, have organized psychological, cultural, social, and medical characteristics into comprehensive theoretical frameworks of who enters care and why they seek care. These theories laid the groundwork for empirical studies and interventions that have been conducted since the late 1960s. Revisions of these theories improved their sensitivity to measuring new challenges in health care access, quality, and equity. The detail and history of models, including the sociobehavioral model (R. Andersen, 1995), the health belief model (Rosenstock, 1966), the theory of reasoned action (Fishbein, 1979) and even newer frameworks including the theory of planned behavior (Ajzcn, 1991), the decision-making model (Goldsmith, Jackson, & Hough, 1988) and the network-episode model (Pescosolido, 1991, 1992, 2006; Pescosolido & Boyer, 1999), have been reviewed elsewhere (Gochman, 1997; Pescosolido, Boyer, & Lubell, 1999; Pescosolido & Kronenfeld, 1995). Here, we focus on what we have learned from these models and describe four recent trends in medical sociology, the sociology of mental health, and the larger discipline that call for continued revision of theoretical approaches to mental health service use.

What Do We Know about Who Uses Formal Services?
An Overview of Prior Research on Mental Health Care Use

The single best predictor of the use of mental health services is the need for care. Whether need is defined by the level of psychological distress, one or more psychiatric symptoms, limitations in mental health functioning, self-reports of mental health, risk factors associated with mental illness, or a psychiatric diagnosis, individuals with greater need are more likely to enter treatment (Greenley & Mechanic, 1976; Gurin, Verhoff, & Feld, 1960; Leaf et al., 1985; Portes, Kyle, & Eaton, 1992; Scheff, 1966/1984; Ware et al., 1984). However, the relationship between need for treatment and the use of services by those in need is far from perfect. Although individuals who have the most serious mental health problems are most likely to receive care, the fact that almost two-thirds of other persons with need do not enter treatment is especially troubling. Recent medical research suggests that if persons with schizophrenia are treated in the prodromal stage, the first 6 months after the appearance of symptoms, full-blown onset may be lessened or avoided altogether (McFarlane & Cook, 2007; Miller et al., 2003).

If the magnitude, quality, and seriousness of psychiatric symptoms alone do not lead to treatment, what other factors are important? Drawing on social science research, we discuss four main factors – gender, race and ethnicity, age, and social class – that have been shown to be the most consistent predictors of outpatient mental health care utilization.

Gender

Women are more likely than men to receive treatment for distress or mental illness (Gove, 1984; Greenley & Mechanic, 1976; Kessler, Brown, & Broman 1981; Veroff, 1981). Although this gender difference may reflect the higher prevalence of psychiatric symptoms and disorders in women (Kessler, McGonagle, et al., 1994: Koopmans & Lamers, 2007), gender differences may also be due to the greater propensity of women to recognize, acknowledge, and report psychiatric symptoms or to gender biases in the measures used or in the judgments of clinicians (Horwitz, 1977a, 1977b; Kessler et al., 1981).

Race and Ethnicity

Leading to recent heightened concerns with inequalities or disparities, research has suggested that the gap between need and actual use of outpatient mental health services is greatest among minority populations (Alegría, Pescosolido, & Canino, n.d.; Hough et al., 1978; Padgett et al., 1994; Sussman, Robins, & Earls, 1987; Wells et al., 1988). When symptoms or distress are controlled, significantly fewer Blacks, Mexican Americans, and Asian Americans receive outpatient mental health treatment compared to Whites (Cole & Pilisuk, 1976; Leaf et al., 1985; Mechanic, Angel, & Davies, 1991; Neighbors et al., 1992; Scheffler & Miller, 1989; Sue, 1977; Wells et al., 1988). Even among insured federal employees, Blacks and Hispanics reported both significantly lower probabilities of one mental health visit and lower total visits overall than Whites (Padgett et al., 1994). However, some studies have shown that, once treatment begins, no significant differences exist across ethnic and racial groups in the number of times services were received (Hu et al., 1991; Wells et al., 1988). Complicating this picture are findings that racial and ethnic minority groups are less likely to be treated under evidenced-based guidelines (Cabassa, Zayas & Hansen, 2006; Wang, Demler, & Kessler, 2002).

Age

For the most part, age shows a curvilinear relationship with entering outpatient mental health treatment. Younger and older age groups have the lowest rates of use, whereas the middle aged (25 to 64 years old) use the most outpatient mental health services (Horgan, 1984; Shapiro et al., 1984). Precisely the opposite occurs for physical ailments, where the very young and the elderly are the highest consumers of services (O. W. Anderson & Andersen, 1972). When these groups visit physicians for physical ailments, emotional and psychological problems may be treated as distress related to physical issues. The low rate of mental health treatment may also signal poor detection of mental health problems among the young and the old by physicians, parents or schools, and caretakers (Morlock, 1989; Wells et al., 1986).

Social Class

Perhaps the most intriguing of social selection factors and the most problematic to study is social class. Early researchers constructed summary measures of social class by using occupation, income, and residence and documented important differences in the utilization of mental health services by social class. Hollingshead and Redlich (1958) found that those in the upper social classes were more likely to use outpatient mental health services than persons in a lower social class. More recently, research has focused on the separate components of social class – primarily education and income. The effects of education on the use of services are rather consistent. People with more education have a higher probability of using outpatient mental health services (Greenley, Mechanic, & Cleary, 1987; Veroff, Kulka, & Douvan, 1981). Income effects are far from clear. Several studies have reported that income is not significantly related to the use of mental health services (Kessler, Berglund, et al., 2005; Leaf et al., 1985; Veroff et al., 1981). One suspected cause of this lack of association is the patchwork of insurance coverage in the United States. High use rates among the more affluent may reflect their ability to pay for more services, their better insurance coverage, or their self-selection of better insurance coverage (Wells et al., 1986). For those over 65 and the poor, Medicare and Medicaid have expanded insurance coverage for mental health services, making psychiatric services financially accessible. Although almost all private insurance plans include some coverage for outpatient mental health services, higher co-payments, special deductibles, and lower limits of reimbursable services than for general medical care are likely. Not surprisingly, income may exert its greatest effect on services for the near poor, those less likely to have private health insurance and ineligible for Medicaid (Olfson & Pincus, 1996). In the RAND Health Insurance Experiment, in which the effects of insurance and income could be separated, higher income groups used different providers – specialty mental health providers rather than general medical practitioners – for their mental health problems (Wells et al., 1986).

Combining Social Correlates: Dominant Theories of Help-Seeking

Although enumerating the influence of social correlates is informative, a more comprehensive picture of service use emerges through theories of utilization that bring together these different factors. For the most part, the study findings reported in the previous section drew from one of three major, early theories of utilization: the sociobehavioral model, the health belief model, and the theory of reasoned action.

In the late 1960s, Ronald Andersen (Andersen & Newman, 1968, 1973) developed the sociobehavioral model (SBM). The original model (and still its core) detailed three basic categories of predictors: need, predisposing factors, and enabling factors (see Figure 21.1). Some need for care must be defined or individuals are not likely to consider whether or not to use services, what services to use, and when to go for treatment. Gender, race, age, education, and beliefs are typically defined as predisposing characteristics – those social and cultural factors that are

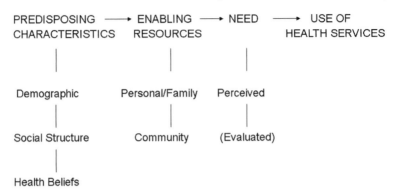

Figure 21.1. The initial sociobehavioral model.

associated with an individual's tendency to seek care. Even in the presence of need and a profile of predisposing social characteristics, individuals must be able to act on a desire to receive care. Enabling characteristics, the centerpiece of a concern with access, are the means and knowledge to get into treatment (Aday, Andersen, & Fleming, 1980). Geographical availability, having a regular source of care, travel time, and financial ability (through income, insurance, or the existence of public clinics and programs) facilitate or limit the use of services. Over time, Andersen revised the SBM by incorporating more variables measuring the organizational structure, goals, and policies of health care systems, the insurance industry, and state regulations (Andersen, 1995). Other revisions in the SBM mirror growing policy concerns about effective (i.e., producing desired or good outcomes in access and quality) and efficient (i.e., achieving cost savings) care (Scheid, 2003).

A second influential theory, the health belief model (HBM; Rosenstock, 1966; Figure 21.2) came originally from social psychology. Where the SBM focuses on the influence of the system and issues of access to understand the use of curative services, the HBM examines the meaning of predisposing characteristics. It analyzes how individuals' general and specific health beliefs (e.g., beliefs about the severity of symptoms), their preferences (e.g., perceived benefits of treatment), their experiences (with health problems and providers), and their knowledge affect decisions to seek care, their health behaviors, and outcomes (Eraker, Kirscht, & Becker, 1984). As major utilization models have taken each other into account, the HBM's multidisciplinary team (including sociologist Marshall Becker) added more structural factors.

In 1980, Ajzen and Fishbein introduced the theory of reasoned action (TRA). Expectancy becomes key as individuals rate how current and alternative actions can reduce their health problems. Like the HBM, this model focuses primarily on

Eraker and associates' 1984 revised health belief model

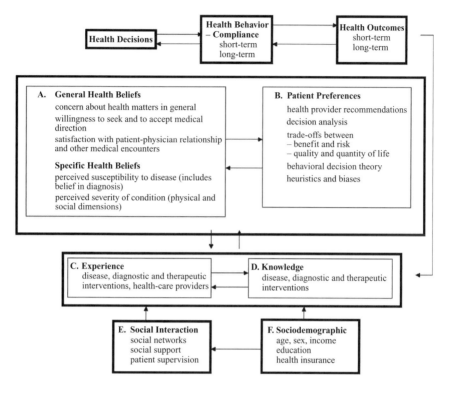

Figure 21.2. The revised health belief model. *Source: Annals of Internal Medicine*, 100, 258–268.

motivations, assessment of risk, and the avoidance of negative outcomes. Individuals evaluate whether or not to engage in healthy (e.g., exercise) or risky (e.g., smoking) behaviors and whether to seek preventive (e.g., mammography) as well as curative medical services. Like the SBM, this model takes into account access to the system.

These utilization models and others provide a comprehensive set of contingencies that affect an individual's decision to use services. The contingencies range from the psychological (e.g., patient preferences in the HBM) to the system level (e.g., external environment in the SBM). Over time, each model broadened its focus to include factors considered central in other approaches. Revised versions of all models have been more inclusive and, in keeping with policy concerns, focus on outcomes (Weinstein, 1993).

Addressing Assumptions and Recent Findings in the Dominant Models and New Directions

The previously described models are still in wide use. Yet starting in the 1990s, trends in social scientific knowledge led to different ways of thinking about service utilization. The motivation for these new theoretical avenues can be found in concerns about a shared image of how service use happens – individuals who notice a physical or mental health problem decide whether or not to use medical services by weighing the costs and benefits of treatment, given the assessment of their health profile and options open to them.

Underlying this approach to utilization stand a series of debatable assumptions. The first suggests that individuals stop and decide to go or not go to a doctor. A second assumption relies on a rational, individual, self-conscious choice. Individuals are thought to weigh whether their need can be met by the resources available (in the SBM) or whether their risk of illness is offset by the health care system treating them (HBM and TRA). A third more implied than explicit assumption equates service use with help-seeking, an active and voluntary action. Fourth, if need for care is seen as one of the consistent findings in using services, the role of culture – beliefs, attitudes, and predispositions about health and health care – is consequently downplayed. Finally, despite an important focus on individuals' income and insurance, the impact of larger fluctuations in health care systems, social structural systemic issues and health system reforms are not examined.

Although existing approaches continued to provide important findings about who uses services and to offer interesting explanations of why individuals seek care, some conclusions about how, when, and why these correlates operated were based more on deduction than empirical findings. What has emerged are four recent trends in utilization research.

Trend 1: From Stagnant Choice to Embedded Careers

More process-oriented approaches to studying the use of services developed in the 1990s, taking their lead from both the emerging prominence of a life course approach in sociology (e.g., Pavalko, 1997) and many early illness career conceptualizations and studies (e.g., Davis, 1963; Roth, 1963; Zola, 1973). Although a focus on dynamics complements traditional models, new versions emphasize that entering treatment often involves a long series of events, some of which happen beneath individuals' levels of awareness. These new approaches focus not only on who receives care but also on when care is received and how the illness episode evolves. Service use is conceptualized as a socially embedded process tied not only to the actions of individuals with psychiatric problems but also to the networks and communities in which they live, the people who surround them, and those encountered in the treatment system.

This research examining the use of services as a social process dates back to early studies by Clausen and colleagues at NIMH's Socio-Environmental Laboratory. These researchers developed the concept of pathways into care, framed the use of health services as part of an illness career, and described the sequence of lay people, professionals, and agencies seen during the course of an illness (Horwitz, 1977a). Anthropologists (Romanucci-Ross, 1977) conceptualized hierarchies of resort – how individuals set priorities to move from one type of health care system to another (Janzen, 1978; Young, 1981).

Some health researchers defined stages – points or phases that individuals pass through as they cope with illness (Parsons, 1951; Roth, 1963). Updates of stage models (e.g., the help-seeking decision-making model, HDM; Goldsmith et al., 1988; Twaddle & Hessler, 1977) blended stage models and the contingency approach of traditional models. Symptoms appear, the problem is recognized, services are used, and particular types of providers are accessed. Alegría and colleagues (1991) added an additional stage, extending the process to events happening after people make initial contact with treatment. Individuals may continue in treatment, change practitioners or services, or discontinue care.

The problem with stage models is twofold: (1) they either tend to be inflexible, with individuals logically passing through each stage specified in the model, or (2) they become labored with many potential feedback loops and lose parsimony. The St. Elizabeth's study described earlier showed that, for some men, the first indication of a serious mental illness was *not* recognizing it but wondering why and how they ended up in a psychiatric hospital. The pathways described revealed that individuals might skip over or repeat stages with advisors, including friends, family, and alternative providers, as well as general and specialty practitioners.

Examining the use of services as embedded in a larger and more complex social process of responding to an illness offers a promising approach to advance our understanding of utilization. However, both data collection and analytic techniques lag behind this theoretical move (see Pescosolido, 1992, 2006). Recent evidence suggested that gender differences in utilization may reflect where men and women go for care rather than if they seek advice and treatment. According to Kessler and his colleagues (2005), women make more mental-health-related visits to general physicians and significantly fewer to complementary-alternative medical services, but do not do not differ significantly from men in their use of outpatient specialty mental health care (Horgan, 1984; Leaf & Bruce, 1987).

Trend 2: From Individual, Rational Choice to Social Influence Models

Dynamic models challenge the underlying, rational person image of traditional utilization models (Pescosolido 1992; Pescosolido & Boyer, 1999). The nature of mental illness and the stress accompanying illness call into question individuals' ability to engage in complicated cognitive processes on which some theories rely. Psychiatric symptoms of confused thinking, cognitive disorganization, delusions, and surges or deficits in affect make a rational choice approach a poor candidate for understanding the mechanisms underlying the use of health services.

With a renewed focus on social networks (see McKinlay, 1972, for an earlier version), how people respond to illness is as much a process of social influence as it is a result of individual action. Using Freidson's (1970a) theoretical conceptualization of the lay referral system, responses to illness vary considerably as social networks suggest, cajole, support, and push individuals toward treatment whereas others may deny, avoid, downplay, and criticize treatment options. Rarely is treatment sought in isolation. Self-conscious decision making may occur at the end of a long process of contemplating treatment, but along the way, social networks have been activated.

Reconsidering the rational choice assumption opens the way to considering other pathways into care. The terms *help-seeking* and *individual choice* assumed in some utilization models do not fit with all patients' experiences. Individuals who use services may have chosen to do so, may have been forced into treatment, or may have struggled haphazardly in coping with psychiatric problems. In the Indianapolis Network Mental Health Study (INMHS), fewer than half of the stories people told interviewers about how they entered the mental health system came close to a cost-benefit assessment, even when it was suggested by supportive friends and relatives (Pescosolido, Gardner, & Lubell, 1995).

Social influence through networks also raises the possibility of coercion as a pathway to care. Family, friends, police, and other institutional agents (e.g., judges, teachers) may suggest that individuals get treatment. Others bring them to treatment at their request or use emergency detentions and involuntary commitments to initiate treatment. Still other individuals are treated over their objections, including the use of an outpatient treatment plan of regular, court-ordered injections of depot antipsychotic medications, such as Prolixin, Haldol, or Risperdal, as occurred to about 24% of the INMHS participants (see also Bennett et al., 1993; Grisso & Applebaum, 1995; Hiday, 1992b; Matthews, 1970; R. D., Miller 1988; Perelberg, 1983; Suchman, 1964). Important and continuing debate exists about the merits of involuntary treatment for individuals and for the public good (Gardner et al., 1993; Mulvey, Gelber, & Roth, 1987). Following individuals and mapping the nature of their contacts, experiences, and outcomes provide the data for evaluating involuntary treatment and its benefits and limitations.

Trend 3: The Cultural Turn in Sociology and the Resurgence of the Study of Health

Beliefs, Attitudes, and Predispositions. Social networks are important because they provide the human links to information on responses to illness and evaluations of these data. What has often been forgotten, even in the studies that have taken a structural approach to health care utilization, is that network structure only provides a measure of how much social influence (e.g., size), likely consistency (e.g., density), or social support (i.e., affect) that individuals access. Not surprisingly, an earlier phase of the social network research on service use yielded contradictory findings: Networks may deter the use of services or have no effect (Geersten et al., 1975; McKinlay, 1972; Salloway & Dillon, 1973; Suchman, 1964). Most studies assumed that networks were good; that is, they would facilitate entry into formal treatment. But, from the earliest conceptualizations, Suchman (1964) differentiated cosmopolitan from parochial networks, and Freidson conceptualized pro-medicine and anti-medicine cultures in the lay referral system. Only the former can be expected to recommend formal health care (Pescosolido, 1991).

The inclusion of beliefs in utilization studies fluctuated over time. Although reliance on existing record-based and large national studies (e.g., Health Interview Survey) accounts for some of this trend, other issues may have played a role. Early research that tended to equate treatment predispositions and actual utilization led to a likely decreased interest in studying health beliefs as social survey researchers documented the lack of correspondence between attitudes and behavior (e.g., Schuman & Johnson, 1976).

More recently, cultural systems have been the subject of an intense and renewed interest in the larger discipline of sociology (Olafsdottir & Pescosolido, 2009). Culture is seen as offering a toolbox for individual action from which individuals can sequentially or simultaneously draw, providing a framework for meaning and suggesting avenues for solving problems (DiMaggio 1997; Swidler, 2001). Perhaps not surprisingly, then, there has been a renewed line of research on health beliefs and attitudes in medical sociology, much of which targets issues of attributions and treatment predispositions. Making hypotheses about the nature of the culture of the study settings helps unravel the inconsistencies in network utilization studies even in the absence of data on network content (e.g., beliefs about and experiences with the health care system) or functions (e.g., support or coercion). Among studies of the middle and upper classes in New York City (e.g., Kadushin, 1966), networks facilitated use of services. Among the poor in Puerto Rico, large and supportive networks promoted informal care and encouraged negative beliefs about the effectiveness of the mental health system, lowering the probability of using formal providers (Pescosolido, Wright, Alegría, & Vera, 1996).

This resurgence in studies of health beliefs has included a renewed look at stigma (e.g., Link et al., 1999; Pescosolido et al., 2000; Rosenfield, 1997). Continued high levels of prejudice and discrimination exist against those with mental illnesses, especially about issues of perceived dangerousness, social rejection, and the long-lasting impact of using services (J. K. Martin, Pescosolido, Olafsdottir, & McLeod, 2007; Martin, Pescosolido, & Tuch, 2000; Pescosolido, McLeod, & Avison, 2007; Pescosolido, Monahan, Link, Stueve, & Kikuzawa, 1999, 2007). At the same time, there has been a decrease in treatment-based stigma with greater support among the public for seeking formal mental health services (Mojtabai, 2007), along with the increase in service use over time (Swindle et al., 2000; Wang et al., 2005).

Perhaps most importantly, some studies have shown that the kinds of attitudes and expectations that were commonly ascribed to the impact of sociodemographic variables do not match reality. African Americans reported a *greater* predisposition to use care in certain circumstances and expressed greater optimism about the effectiveness of care (Schnittker, Freese, & Powell, 2000). Findings about African Americans' use of services are not consistent as with other groups. When asked about the primary reason for not seeking treatment for a major depressive episode, African Americans were significantly more likely than Whites to fear being hospitalized (Sussman et al., 1987).

Research focuses rarely on the simultaneous consideration of actual utilization and beliefs, although some work has been indirectly informative. A few studies have found that when the social network ties of ill persons, especially friends and relatives, hold positive attitudes toward psychiatry or have been in treatment themselves, people are more likely to use medical services (Fisher, 1988; Greenley & Mechanic, 1976; Greenley, Mechanic, & Cleary, 1987; Martin et al., 2000; Pescosolido et al., 2000; Weinstein, 1993). The public believes that psychiatric medications are useful and effective, yet they also report an unwillingness to take them (Croghan et al., 2003).

If we are to bring culture back into the study of utilization, alone or under the network approach, attitudes and utilization must be considered in the same study, and they must be considered directly and broadly. The nature of network encounters that people have helps provide meaning to the symptoms of illness. If individuals see mental health problems as crises of faith or as the result of a bad marriage, they may visit faith healers, spiritualists, or the clergy (Lubchansky, Egri, & Stokes, 1970; Rogler & Hollingshead, 1961). If they, or others around them, see the problem as bad behavior rather than illness, they might seek help from the police and lawyers (Cumming & Harrington, 1963; Hiday, 1992a).

Nowhere is it more critical to examine attitudes than in relation to the finding about the singular importance of need discussed earlier. Need is a relative concept shaped by people who use the term and by their social and cultural circumstances (Cleary, 1989), whereas researchers often define need as a minimum score on symptom scales or through measures of distress, life events, risk factors, self-reports, or diagnostic instruments. Some researchers argue that using the diagnostic approach alone misses a great deal of social phenomena surrounding symptoms, especially how individuals and professionals socially construct mental health problems (Leaf et al., 1985; Mirowsky & Ross, 1989). The nature of the illness, its quality, and severity reflect not merely a biological imperative but also how people perceive need and how they experience symptoms. Carpentier and colleagues (2008) found that social representations were critical in how, if, and when caregivers dealt with their relative's onset of cognitive difficulties, including any delayed entry into the formal treatment system.

Future research needs to embrace, model, and collect data that reflect the complexity of culture in the understanding of illness and treatment options connected to the use of mental health services.

Trend 4: Changing Systems of Care and Their Influence on the Resort to Treatment

Much of the research on managed care focuses on the relationship between systems of care and use. Individuals in prepaid and managed care plans and fee-for-service arrangements have a similar likelihood of making a single outpatient mental health visit, but those in prepaid plans are less likely to have long-term, continuous care (Diehr, Williams, & Martin, 1984; Norquist & Wells, 1991; Wells et al., 1986; see also Sturm et al., 1995). Some studies have addressed the dynamics of the various health care plans. In the Utah Prepaid Mental Health Plan, individuals with serious mental illnesses who participated in the prepaid versus fee-for-service plans had no significant decreases in inpatient or outpatient use of services (Manning et al., 1993; Moscovice et al., 1993). However, in a capitated program in Monroe County, New York, inpatient psychiatric admissions and days hospitalized decreased, whereas the use of outpatient services increased (Babigian, Mitchell, Marshall, & Reed, 1992). In Massachusetts, inpatient admissions from emergency rooms and length of stay declined in both managed care and comparison groups (Stroup & Dorwart, 1995).

Although these studies have documented the importance of system changes in utilization, we have little understanding of how system change works to affect if and how individuals consider their options for care, the opinions held by those around them, and how options and network beliefs translate into service use. By far, this is the area to which sociologists have contributed least.

A Sociological Response: The Network-Episode Model

In response to both concerns about the assumptions underlying the major existing models of utilization and recent theoretical developments in sociology, we continue to develop an alternative – the network-episode model (NEM; Pescosolido, 1991, 2006; Pescosolido & Boyer, 1999). The NEM begins with the foundation that dealing with health problems is a social process managed through the social networks that individuals have in the community, the treatment system, and social service agencies (including support groups, churches, and jails). In the NEM, individuals are seen as pragmatic users with commonsense knowledge and cultural routines

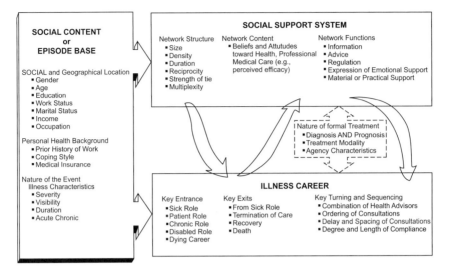

Figure 21.3. The network-episode model.

who seek out and respond to others when psychiatric symptoms or unusual behavior occurs. The NEM does not suggest that people are not rational, but questions whether every action they take in coping with illness is a result of a cost-benefit calculus. Although there are instances when people have to weigh costs and benefits (e.g., when faced with the decision to discontinue aggressive treatment in the face of a relatively immediate, terminal prognosis), individuals face illness in the course of their day-to-day lives by interacting with others who may recognize (or deny) a problem, send them to (or provide) treatment, and support, cajole, or nag them about appointments, medications, or lifestyle (see Figure 21.3).

Incorporating elements of career and stage models, the NEM conceptualizes service use beyond a single, yes–no, one-time decision and rather as patterns and pathways of practices and people consulted during an episode of illness. The illness career marks all of an individual's attempts to cope with the onset of an episode of mental health problems, charting what is done and when it is done. Patterns of care encompass the combination of advisors and practices used during the course of an illness. Some individuals may go only to a psychiatrist; others may visit their family physician and a psychiatrist. Pathways add the element of order – the sequences of advisors and practices used over the course of an illness. Prayer may be used initially before going to a pastor, priest, or rabbi and then to a counselor. Following Freidson (1970a, 1970b), the NEM evaluates the power of social networks and how their structure (e.g., their size and amount of support) and the kinds of advice they offer (e.g., supportive or resistant to mental health treatment) work together. The NEM suggests that the power, structure, and content of social networks must be taken into account to understand how much influence is being exerted on the ill person and the trajectory of the push into or away from mental health treatment.

The NEM also conceptualizes the health care system as a changing set of providers and organizations with which individuals may have contact when they are ill. Changes in the health care system occur over time – on a very different scale from the other two streams in the NEM – but nonetheless in response to the prevalence of new and emerging diseases, advancing technology and expanding medical knowledge, available social resources, and community preferences and demands. In the same way that social networks can help us identify the set of contacts people have, the network perspective allows us to unpack what happens to people when they go for treatment and to think about how their experiences affect whether they stay in treatment, adhere to a treatment regimen, and what outcomes they experience. The treatment system shapes a set of network contacts for ill persons, their families, and other people who become involved in the illness career (e.g., police or social service workers). The treatment system can provide a rich set of helpful, supportive people or can allow contacts that are only brief, impersonal, and antagonistic. The social networks that exist in the treatment setting create a climate of care, affect the work of medical providers, and shape reactions of individuals who come for treatment (Pescosolido, 1996; Pescosolido, Wright, & Sullivan, 1996).

Although only limited information exists about patterns and pathways to care, recent research shows the promise of the NEM. In Rogers and colleagues' (Rogers, Hassell, & Nicolaas, 1999, p. 114) Pathways to Care Study, advice was "proffered or requested, acted upon or ignored." Because advice for psychological or personal problems seemed to be less readily available, the reported level of utilization for problems was lower than typically seen in the national studies. However, their qualitative data suggest that what individuals actually did was not well described by the standard survey questions. Social networks also seem to be critical in determining whether families use in-home services, such as respite and home care, and vocational services (Carpentier et al., 2008; Chou et al., 2008). For migrants, ties to others provided new ideas and practices for health (Lindstrom & Munoz-Franco, 2006), buffering the effects of their low health literacy (Lee, Arozullah, & Cho, 2004).

As a relatively recent addition to the stockpile of theoretical approaches to understanding utilization, the NEM continues to evolve (Pescosolido, 1996). The NEM and other process models provide a more complex picture of what happens when people experience mental health problems. These models raise questions about how we think about, study, and collect data on the complicated realities of experiencing illness and getting help, delaying entry into care, or not receiving treatment.

Conclusion

In this chapter we have provided an overview of the issues and theoretical challenges that surround efforts to understand how, when, and why individuals delay, enter, or fail to enter treatment for mental health problems. A great deal is known about the use of mental health services by different social groups, but we are far from understanding the nature of the process and the timing by which people reach treatment and remain in the mental health system. One way to proceed is to link the community, the illness career, and the treatment system. These links between the day-to-day lives of individuals and their interactions in the community and with the treatment system shape how individuals who may need care – as well as those who provide care – view mental health problems, how they embrace or challenge what the treatment system offers, and whether they are encouraged or dissuaded to receive or provide care.

Two major gaps exist in sociological contributions to mental health utilization research. First, we did not explore in detail the impact of illness and initial treatment choices on later issues in the illness career. The focus on pathways *to* care should be followed by a parallel concern with pathways *across* care. The likelihood of following through with aftercare in the community is quite low (Boyer & Mechanic, 1994). More detail is needed about how different sectors (e.g., psychiatric and medical care, housing, employment, substance abuse) work smoothly or erratically, and in coordination or in opposition, to address individuals' mental health and related social problems (see Alegría et al., 1991; Bachrach, 1980; Morrissey, Calloway, et al., 1994; Pescosolido, 1996; Rosenfield, 1991). Considerably more research needs to examine how to facilitate initial and ongoing treatment and adherence to regimens.

Second, after decades of research on who used what types of mental health services, social scientists have now turned to addressing other challenging sociological questions about patterns and pathways into care. Four theories of utilization were described and how incentives, financial or otherwise, affect the use and quality of services and their allocation in a managed care environment (Mechanic, 2008). With managed care as a mainstay of mental health care delivery in the United States, a process approach may better capture how service use changes over time, how managed care encourages or limits the use of specialty mental health services, how consumerism affects treatment, and how families and social service agencies assume the added responsibilities of care resulting from decreased hospital stays and limits on outpatient visits and treatments.

22

Cultural Diversity and Mental Health Treatment

Emily Walton, Kateri Berasi, David T. Takeuchi, and Edwina S. Uehara

This chapter examines some attempts by service providers and researchers to examine cultural issues in the treatment of ethnic minorities who have mental health problems. It presents data on the use of mental health services by ethnic minorities, including considerations of access to services as well as the use of services. There has been pressure to develop more culturally responsive services, and the authors examine these efforts, distinguishing among provider, agency, and community-level interventions. Empirical studies have found that ethnic and language match are related to a decrease in dropout rate and increase in utilization of services by ethnic minorities. The authors also describe several culturally competent programs (such as cuento therapy for Puerto Rican children). In the second part of the chapter, the authors widen their perspective and examine how recent trends in mental health services at times come into conflict with the goal of developing multicultural mental health service systems. They attribute this conflict to three factors: (1) a tendency to endorse etiologies of mental illness that favor biological causes over social and cultural factors; (2) a tendency to see culture as fixed, historical, and autonomous; and (3) a tendency to overlook the substantial heterogeneity in socioeconomic status and stress-related life experiences within specific ethnic groups. The authors also discuss the societal functions of mental health services, contrasting the social control perspective with views of mental health services as either complementary institutions to the marketplace or compensatory mechanisms for the distribution of resources. Although mental health services are seen as a means to accomplish all of these functions, the question of how to prioritize them is critical to social policy. Finally, the authors describe three service models that emphasize different goals: the clinical services model, the social welfare model, and the empowerment model. The juxtaposition of these models raises a fundamental question: As a society, how broadly are we willing to define the arena of public responsibility for mental health?

Introduction

By the year 2050, it is projected that more than half of the total U.S. population will be members of racial and ethnic minority groups: African American, 15%; Asian, 8%; Latino, 24%; and other racial and ethnic minority groups, 5% (U.S. Census Bureau, 2004h). This projection, if it holds true, will represent a radical departure from the population at the beginning of the 1900s. At the turn of the

---

This study was supported in part by Grants MH 62209, MH 073511, and RWJ DA18715.

439

20th century and continuing until the 1950s, racial and ethnic minority groups, primarily consisting of African Americans, represented about 10% of the adult population. It should be noted that the White population was fairly diverse itself, as 10% of the population was foreign born (U.S. Census Bureau, 1975). Between 1950 and today, the U.S. population has become increasingly more racially and culturally diverse. In the year 2006, for example, minority groups comprised 24% of the total population (U.S. Census Bureau, 2006). Although some of this increase can be attributed to changes in the manner in which the U.S. Census defined racial categories (e.g., by creating "Hispanic" and "Asian/Pacific Islander" categories and allowing respondents to choose more than one race), it nevertheless embodies a real and dramatic change in U.S. demography. In 1990, African Americans were still the largest ethnic minority category, but in the year 2000 they were surpassed by Latino Americans, who currently comprise 15% of the population (U.S. Census Bureau, 2006).

Immigration accounts for a large part of the demographic shift in the United States. Because of various changes in laws and policies over the past four decades, more than 37 million people have come to the United States during that time (U.S. Census Bureau, 2006), an increase that matches the rise in the immigrant population in the early part of this century. Of course, this figure does not consider the large number of undocumented migrants, which could increase the immigrant population by about 9 million (Passel, Capps, & Fix, 2004). Most immigrants settle in a few, large gateway cities – Los Angeles, New York, San Francisco, Chicago, Dallas, Houston, Washington, D.C., and Miami – although recently immigrants have begun to settle directly in smaller metropolitan and nonmetropolitan areas (De Jong & Tran, 2001). A major difference between the rise in the immigrant population in the early 1900s and the current increase is the countries from where immigrants have come. In the early part of the 1900s, most of the immigrants came from Europe and Canada; the recent immigration has come primarily from Asia and Latin America. Muller (1993) noted that the recent waves of immigration have led to a change in the racial composition unseen since the late 17th century, when Black slaves became part of the labor force in the South. This radical racial transformation has strong implications not only for the labor force but also for how social services and health care are delivered to people who may be unaccustomed to Western methods of intervention.

This chapter examines some attempts by service providers and researchers to examine cultural issues in the treatment of ethnic minorities who have mental health problems. It is unavoidable that the constructs of "race" and "class" come into play in discussions of "cultural diversity" (Omi & Winant, 1994). However, we have attempted to keep most of our discussions about culture and treatment issues pointed and focused within the boundaries of this chapter. We begin the chapter with a review of interventions for ethnic minorities, what the empirical research suggests about these interventions, and some direction for future research. We conclude with a discussion about the perspectives that shape views about culture and mental health treatment.

Use of Mental Health Services

Access to Services

Statistics from mental hospitals and outpatient clinics have often been used to draw some conclusions pertinent to ethnic minorities' access to mental health services. That is, the percentage of each group in the hospital or clinic was compared to that group's population size in the United States or in a given community. A higher percentage in treatment was referred to as overrepresentation (sometimes overutilization); a lower percentage as underrepresentation (or underutilization). The use of treatment data has built-in biases such as the questionable assumption that all people who are mentally ill eventually end up in hospitals. However, these types of data analyses were commonly used to assess problems that needed some attention, especially when community epidemiological survey data were not available.

In the early 1900s, African Americans were seen as overrepresented in mental hospitals. The reason for this overrepresentation was often debated. The interpretation of these data was often shaped by the type of perspective one had about mental health services; we discuss this issue in more detail in the concluding section. Data on people admitted into mental hospitals were also used to conclude that immigrants, primarily from Europe, suffered from poorer mental health than native-born residents (Locke, Kramer, & Pasamanick, 1960). Mental health hospital records confirmed early speculations that immigrants undergo social and psychological problems as they adapt to American society (Fabrega, 1969). The reason for the higher rates ranged from the racist (i.e., ethnic minorities and immigrants were inferior) to the social (e.g., ethnic minorities and immigrants endured social problems that accrue because of discrimination in American society; Wade, 1993). A second prevailing theme was that mental health services were another form of a coercive social control agency that was quick to define ethnic minority behavior as deviant (Takeuchi, Bui, & Kim, 1993).

Beginning in the 1940s, survey research methods became a more prominent means to collect community samples of treated and untreated respondents for the estimation of the prevalence of mental disorders (Dohrenwend & Dohrenwend, 1974), a trend that continues into the present. Results from community studies on ethnic minorities and mental health were not as consistently clear as findings from early studies using hospital records. In fact, some studies called into question whether ethnic minorities actually had higher rates of psychopathology than Whites (Vega & Rumbaut, 1991).

Today, research on racial and ethnic disparities in mental health status and care has received increased attention, evidenced by the publication of the Surgeon

General's report *Mental Health: Culture, Race, and Ethnicity* (U.S. Department of Health and Human Services [USDHHS], 2001). The report is the most comprehensive and influential public statement addressing ethnic minority mental health to date. Concomitant with the Surgeon General's report, recent large-scale epidemiological studies, notably the Collaborative Psychiatric and Epidemiology Survey (CPES), which comprises the National Latino and Asian American Study (NLAAS; Alegria et al., 2004), the National Survey of American Life (NSAL; (Jackson et al., 2004), and the National Comorbidity Survey Replication (NCS-R; (Kessler & Merikangas, 2004), have provided much-needed data for research on mental health disparities among previously understudied racial and ethnic groups. The increased public recognition of the need for research on mental health and service use among historically understudied groups and the availability of the rich data from recent community surveys are crucial steps toward ameliorating racial and ethnic service use disparities. These studies have been useful in demonstrating that ethnic minorities, even when their rates of psychopathology are comparable to Whites, often face significant barriers to seeking professional treatment for their mental health problems.

People who suffer from some form of mental health problem, regardless of race or ethnicity, are unlikely to seek professional help (Link & Dohrenwend, 1980). When comparisons are made, however, ethnic minority group members are less likely to use mental health services than Whites (Abe-Kim et al., 2007; Alegria, Mulvaney-Day, Woo, et al., 2007; Jackson et al., 2007). For example, the available evidence has suggested that the use of mental health services is quite distinct for African, Asian, and Latino Americans compared to Whites. After accounting for differences in sociodemographic profiles and need for care, African Americans receive mental health treatment at about half the rate of Whites (Swartz et al., 1998). Asian Americans use mental-health-related services less frequently (8.6%) than the general population (17.9%), and there are important nativity and generational differences within this population, with U.S-born individuals seeking care more often than foreign born and those from the third generation or later reporting higher helpfulness ratings for providers (Abe-Kim et al., 2007). A recent study showed that approximately 11% of Latino Americans used mental health services in the past year, but this use varied by ethnicity (Puerto Ricans reported much higher use at 20%), nativity status, predominant language (English or Spanish), immigration-related factors, and type of insurance coverage (Alegria et al., 2007).

Minority groups may disproportionately belong to groups that have limited access to mental health services. Ethnic minorities are found to comprise a high proportion of these "high-risk" groups. Two examples are the homeless and people who are HIV positive. Tessler and Dennis (1992) synthesized the results of studies from eight large U.S. cities and found that ethnic minorities were over-represented in the homeless population. Regional studies tend to support this general finding. In a study of health services utilization of 832 homeless persons randomly selected from 16 homeless shelters in New York City, 71% were African American and 24.3% were Latino, Asian, or Native American (Padgett, Struening, & Andrews, 1990). Crystal, Ladner, and Towber (1986) conducted a study at 14 New York City public shelters. Of the men and women who reported having psychological problems, 84% (6,363) were from ethnic minority groups. Of 248 homeless persons who were randomly selected from 13 emergency shelters in St. Louis, Missouri, 64.9% were members of ethnic minorities, and all but two of them were African American (Morse & Calsyn, 1986). Yet homelessness does not equalize racial and ethnic differences in access to mental health services. In a study of first mental health service utilization among homeless and runaway adolescents, Berdahl and colleagues (2005) found that racial and ethnic minorities reported more barriers to service utilization than Whites. Fear of racism by mental health care workers is the largest disincentive to seeking treatment among homeless minority youth (Geber, 1997).

HIV disproportionately affects several minority groups, with African and Latino American diagnostic rates 10 and 3 times higher, respectively, than that of Whites (Hall, Lee, Song, & McKenna, 2005). These two groups comprise 64% of all people with HIV, an alarming figure when considering that together they represent less than 30% of the entire U.S. population (Centers for Disease Control and Prevention [CDC], 2008a, 2008b, 2008c). In the early years of the epidemic in the 1980s, the majority of the cases occurred among White men living in large, urban cities like New York, Los Angeles, and San Francisco. In more recent times, there has been an emergence of HIV/AIDS in southern cities, such as Palm Beach and Baton Rouge, primarily among African and Latino Americans. Prevention and research funding efforts have been slow to keep up with the change in demographics of this epidemic, resulting in the drastic increases in rates present today (Mackenzie, 2000).

Some ethnic minority individuals may be severely constrained from seeking professional help. One such constraining factor in gaining needed care is the absence of or limited health insurance coverage. The United States has the most costly health care system among developed nations (Scheiber & Poullier, 1991). A large segment of the American population has found that quality health care is unaffordable. Although health insurance is intended to assist Americans in paying for health care, in 2006, an estimated 47 million Americans (15.8%) were not covered by public or private health insurance (DeNavas-Walt, Proctor, & Smith, 2007). Ethnic minorities comprise a large segment of the uninsured. In a national survey sponsored by the Commonwealth Fund, 20% of White adults reported being without health insurance coverage during the past year; this proportion was lower than the uninsured rates for African Americans (33%), and Latino Americans (62%; Doty & Holmgren, 2006).

Other barriers to care for racial and ethnic minorities, including perceptions of discrimination, stigma, and limited English-language proficiency, are increasingly the subject of investigation. African Americans may exhibit mistrust of health professionals because of experiences with segregation, prejudice, racism, and discrimination (Priest, 1991). Interestingly, one study found that African Americans who reported higher levels of perceived discrimination used more mental health services; however, this relationship was moderated by racial identity, such that those who experienced discrimination and identified more strongly with being African American were less likely to utilize services compared to those with low racial identity who experienced discrimination (Richman, Kohn-Wood, & Williams, 2007). The Surgeon General's report on mental health recognized that shame and stigma associated with mental illness are important obstacles to the receipt of care, but empirical studies addressing these associations are still emerging (USDHHS, 2001). Stigma attached to mental illness may diminish the use of care particularly among foreign-born racial and ethnic minorities because of different cultural beliefs about health and illness. For example, among some groups of Asian Americans mental illness may be viewed as an attack by evil spirits, weak will, or a physical problem (Takeuchi & Kim, 2000). Given that 40% of Latino Americans and 69% of Asian Americans were foreign born in the year 2000, another important consideration in determining access to services for individuals from these minority groups is English-language proficiency. English proficiency may determine individuals' ability to navigate through complex service systems and affect the quality of care they receive (Fiscella, Franks, Doescher, & Saver, 2002; Ngo-Metzger et al., 2003).

In summary, rates of mental disorders have been generally used to indicate the need for professional care. Treatment studies tend to show that some ethnic minorities like African Americans are overrepresented in mental health facilities and other groups like Asian Americans are underrepresented. In contrast, community studies generally provide a mixed assessment as to whether ethnic minorities are more in need of mental health services. Although their assessment of rates has been inconclusive, community studies have typically found that ethnic minorities demonstrate a reluctance to use professional care. Finally, ethnic minorities may belong to populations that are unable to access the mental health system or may be financially constrained by inadequate health insurance coverage, in addition to facing other barriers to receipt of adequate mental health care.

Use of Services

Once ethnic minority consumers navigate around the access barriers and enter hospitals or clinics, there is evidence that they receive differential clinical diagnoses. African Americans, for example, have been diagnosed as having schizophrenic-spectrum disorders more frequently than others, whereas Latinos have been disproportionately diagnosed as having major depression despite exhibiting higher levels of psychotic symptoms (Minsky et al., 2003). Misdiagnosis could result from mislabeling a behavior as deviant when it is normal in certain cultures. Lopez (1989) used the terms "overpathologizing" and "underpathologizing" to classify errors in diagnosis. Although it is difficult to determine when over- and underpathologizing occur, misdiagnosis is relevant to the extent that it determines the type of care received at a mental health facility (Neighbors, Jackson, Campbell, & Williams, 1989; Pavkov, Lewis, & Lyons, 1989).

In addition to receiving differential clinical diagnoses, there is evidence that ethnic minority clients receive different types of care. Asian Americans have been found to stay in inpatient treatment longer than whites (Snowden & Cheung, 1990) and to be overrepresented in outpatient mental health services relative to their representation in the community (Ying & Hu, 1994). African Americans were found to use emergency psychiatric services more than Whites and were much less likely to see private practitioners or therapists, but these differences disappeared after controlling for socioeconomic indicators, suggesting that observed disparities may be attributable to differences in access to care (Snowden, 1999). This study also found that when institutionalized individuals are included in analyses, the disparity in overall rates of service use among racial groups is small; this finding indicates that the overrepresentation of African Americans in jails, prisons, and mental hospitals contributes to their high utilization of mental health services. Latino Americans were less likely to use psychiatrists and more likely to access mental health services through a religious advisor, social worker, or counselor than were Whites (Wang et al., 2006). Among both Latino and Asian Americans with severe mental illness, those with limited English proficiency were less likely to access mental health services through emergency services and more likely to do so through outpatient services (Gilmer et al., 2007).

That the mental health system may be incompatible with the mental health care needs of ethnic minorities is evidenced by their high dropout rate from service (Sue & McKinney, 1975). The dropout rate is still a good barometer of the responsiveness of mental health services (Sue, Zane, & Young, 1994). Some studies have shown this rate to have diminished in recent years (e.g., see O'Sullivan, Peterson, Cox, & Kirkeby, 1989; Snowden, Storey, & Clancey, 1989), whereas others have shown that a significant level of premature termination by ethnic minorities may still occur (e.g., see Sue, Fujino, Hu, Takeuchi, & Zane, 1991). An investigation relying on community epidemiological studies in the United States and Canada showed no significant differences between racial and ethnic groups in their likelihood of dropping out of treatment; however, young age and lack of insurance coverage were important predictors of dropping out (Edlund et al., 2002). Conversely, another recent study concluded that in Canada non-Whites were more likely than Whites to prematurely terminate treatment with psychologists, psychiatrists, and family doctors (Wang, 2007).

Disparate findings in utilization of services could be a function of regional differences. In an evaluation of two California counties, Hu, Snowden, Jerrell, and Nguyen (1991) analyzed the records of 4,000 of the most severely disturbed and disabled clients. They used multivariate models to examine the use of vocational and socialization programs, residential care, partial hospitalization, medication, assessment, and group and individual therapy. The authors also examined psychiatric emergency care and hospitalization, two types of services that indicate a failure of support for the client in the community. Variations in utilization were found across ethnic groups and across counties. In the first county, African Americans were more likely than Whites to receive assessment and medication and were less likely to be hospitalized. In the other county, African Americans were more likely than Whites to use emergency services and to be hospitalized. In one county, Asian Americans clients participated in a wider range of programs than Whites, Latino Americans received medication and individual psychotherapy more than Whites, and Whites used emergency room and inpatient care services more than Asian American and Latino American clients. In the other county, Asian American and Latino American clients were more likely than Whites to be hospitalized, and Asian American clients were less likely than Whites to be assigned to assessment, partial hospitalization, and residential care.

Researchers and service planners have made recommendations for developing mental health care that more closely meets the needs of racial and ethnic minority group members, and many programs have been established in the name of cultural competence. However, the elements of these programs that contribute to cultural competence have not been identified. For example, in a follow-up analysis of a study by Sue and McKinney (1975) that concluded that ethnic minorities were underutilizing community mental health services, O'Sullivan et al. (1989) found a significant decrease in their dropout rate from mental health clinics. The researchers attributed this improvement to mental health clinics being more culturally responsive to the needs of their ethnic minority clients. However, there was no direct evidence to support this finding. The next section examines the issue of cultural responsiveness more closely.

Culturally Responsive Services

Spurred by the civil right movement of the 1960s and with a supportive federal government in the 1970s, many recommendations were advanced to meet the mental health needs of ethnic minority communities. Sue (1977) recommended a three-pronged approach: (1) within existing services, train mental health providers and hire ethnic specialists; (2) establish parallel services devoted specifically to ethnic minority clientele; and (3) establish nonparallel services specifically designed around the culture of ethnic minority clientele. Similarly, Uba (1994) discussed the pros and cons of training personnel within mainstream organizations, establishing a separate team within mainstream organizations for ethnic minority clients, or establishing physically separate facilities staffed by personnel trained in providing culturally sensitive services. Rogler, Malgady, Constantino, and Blumenthal

(1987) used a pyramidal structure as a metaphor for necessary changes. At the base of the pyramid are changes involving linguistic accessibility, coordinating with the ethnic community, and creating an atmosphere open to the cultural values of the community. The second layer of the pyramid involves selecting mainstream treatments that fit the ethnic culture. Crowning the pyramid would be the creation of treatments specifically for the ethnic culture. Recently, another direction of action has emerged that encourages public-health-oriented prevention programs that target and empower diverse communities. These intervention programs recognize that differences in the mental health of individuals are related to structures and social processes operating at the community level, so program effectiveness relies both on individual and community measures of social and psychological health status.

Three themes emerge from these recommendations: (1) the cultural competence of mental health providers can be increased by training existing personnel or hiring ethnic minorities, (2) there is a need for culturally sensitive programs and agencies, and (3) the social and psychological needs of ethnic minorities may be well served by a community-based prevention agenda. Thus, when we examine the responsiveness of mental health services to clients' cultural needs, we distinguish among three levels of analysis: provider, agency, and community (Sue, 2006). First, at the provider level, we are interested in the provider's ability to exhibit cultural awareness and interpersonal sensitivity, build rapport, and establish credibility. Second, we look at how agencies themselves are culturally competent through outreach efforts and marketing of services, collaboration with community organizations, and flexible approaches to therapy that meet the needs of a diverse population. Third, we examine the promise of community-based interventions as a flexible, empowering approach to providing culturally competent services.

Provider-Level Cultural Competence

In line with the first theme, since the mid-1970s more ethnic minority service providers have been employed by psychiatric clinics. Wu and Windle (1980) found that this increase is related to an increase in the numbers of ethnic minority clients. The recommendation to hire more ethnic minority staff is based on the premise that their presence would facilitate the utilization of services by clients of similar backgrounds. Empirical studies have tested this notion by evaluating whether clients are more likely to use mental health services and experience improved outcomes when matched with service providers of similar ethnicity, language ability, and attitudes about therapy.

The largest study on ethnic and language match to date was conducted by Sue et al. (1991). It was an extensive analysis of data from the Los Angeles County outpatient mental health system, involving more than 13,000 African American, Asian American, Mexican American, and White clients over a 5-year period. After sociodemographic and clinical variables were controlled for, ethnic match and language match still predicted a decrease in dropout and an increase in the number of sessions. For clients whose primary language was not English, ethnic match was an important predictor of dropout, number of sessions, and outcome. O'Sullivan and Lasso (1992) analyzed records of 161 Latino clients in the Washington State mental health system. Latino clients who received services through a Latino community mental health center had a lower dropout rate and received more individual therapy sessions than those who did not receive services from Latino staff. Similarly, Blank, Tetrick, Brinkley, Smith, and Doheny (1994) analyzed the records of 677 White and African American clients of a rural community mental health center in Virginia and found that ethnic matching was related to a greater number of made appointments.

However, in outcome studies of African Americans, no relationship was found between ethnic match and treatment outcome. Jones (1978, 1982) paired African American and White clients with therapists of similar and different ethnicity. After analyzing the therapists' assessment of treatment outcome for all cases, it was determined that outcome did not differ as a function of client–therapist racial matching. A number of studies on Asian Americans have had similar results. Ethnic match and language match were related to decreased dropout after one session and an increase in the number of sessions, but for the most part were not related to outcome (Flaskerud & Hu, 1994; Flaskerud & Liu, 1990, 1991; Fujino, Okazaki, & Young, 1994; Ying & Hu, 1994).

In a review of several studies investigating the effectiveness of ethnic match between clients and therapists, Maramba and Nagayama Hall (2002) found small or negligible effect sizes of ethnic match for reducing early termination of services and increasing the number of sessions attended. One reason for the mixed findings may be that other phenomena underlying the ethnic match are responsible for treatment outcomes. Sue (1998) proposed that cognitive match, or similarity between clients and therapists in attitudes, beliefs, and expectations for therapy, may be an important part of the effect of ethnic match on treatment outcomes. In other words, even when clients and therapists are ethnically matched, they may differ in their approaches to therapy, thus rendering the ethnic match ineffective. Zane et al. (2005) conducted a rigorous test of this hypothesis among White and Asian American clients and found that, although different aspects of cognitive match were predictive of specific types of outcomes, whenever cognitive match was significant it always predicted positive treatment outcomes and influenced treatment sessions favorably.

In summary, empirical studies have found that ethnic, language, and cognitive match are related to a decrease in the dropout rate and an increase in utilization of services by ethnic minorities. These results are encouraging in that they indicate a way to provide services from which ethnic minorities can benefit. However, these studies still beg the question, What goes on between a client and a therapist of similar ethnicity, and who speaks the same language that results in culturally responsive mental health services? Rogler et al. (1987, p. 566) called linguistic accessibility the "lowest common denominator of cultural sensitivity," and Bernal, Bonilla, and Bellido (1995, p. 73) described language as the "carrier of the culture." Similarly, ethnic match facilitates mutual understanding, which is more likely to occur between people who are culturally similar (Rosenberg, 1984). Thus, it seems that the traits of ethnicity and language ability may be proxies for cultural characteristics. Therefore, matching a client with a service provider in language and ethnicity traits is related more to the complex issue of cultural similarity.

Lack of funding and the impracticality of conducting randomized efficacy trials for all mental health interventions among multiple ethnic groups have inhibited the adoption of comprehensive policy recommendations for providers of culturally competent care (Sue, 2003). The American Psychological Association has adopted a set of multicultural guidelines for providing efficacious care for ethnic minorities; however, to date these are aspirations and not enforceable policies (American Psychological Association, 2003). Guarnaccia and Rogler (1999) argued that mental health professionals should not use the glossary of 25 culture-bound syndromes from the fourth edition of the *Diagnostic and Statistical Manual of Mental Disorders* (DSM-IV) as their sole resource on pathology in different cultures, as it does not account for differences within and between cultures and individuals. However, the next edition of the DSM, expected to be published in 2012, will elaborate on the previous manual by emphasizing the importance of culture and ethnicity in mental illness diagnosis and effective therapeutic outcome (USDHHS, 2001). In sum, despite limited evidence that provider-centered interventions produce better outcomes, their promise for reducing racial and ethnic mental health disparities is increasingly being recognized.

Agency-Level Cultural Responsiveness

The mental health literature, especially in clinical psychology and psychiatry, has presented a number of techniques and programs that can be used by service agencies working with ethnic minority consumers. These techniques are related to the second common theme found in recommendations for culturally responsive services: the need for culturally competent programs and agencies. Below we describe some specific techniques that have been used. Some are adaptations of Western modalities, others are indigenous techniques taken from ethnic minority cultures, and most fall somewhere in between.

Cuento therapy for Puerto Rican children is a therapeutic modality that involves the telling to children of folktales in which the characters are presented as peer models. Modeling exercises are then used to reinforce the beliefs, values, and behaviors of the characters in the stories (Rogler, Malgady, & Rodriguez, 1989). In working with African American families, Stevenson and Renard (1993) recommended promoting the process of racial socialization in therapy. Racial socialization can be a tool to incorporate into treatment the strengths of the African American family, such as metaphorical parenting (i.e., the use of proverbs, stories, or sayings to teach children about life lessons), spirituality, and ways to cope with racism. In overcoming issues of self-disclosure and trust with African Americans, Mehlman (1994) recommended appropriate self-disclosure by the therapist and attention to nonverbal communication. The South Cove Community Mental Health Center modified Western techniques in recognition of the needs of their clientele in Boston's Chinatown/South Cove area. It was established in response to the lack of bilingual and culturally knowledgeable health and mental health providers in that community. Based on their experience with mostly Chinese American clients, the practitioners at that mental health center modified Western standard therapeutic practices in these ways: (1) developing rapport during intake and directly assigning clients to a therapist, who would then take more detailed information from the client; (2) incorporating educational information early in the treatment process; (3) selectively involving family members in therapy; (4) using short-term therapy; and, (5) making conservative use of pharmacotherapy (Lorenzo & Adler, 1984). Based on his work with Asian American clients, Hong (1988) described a general family practitioner approach. Using this approach, the psychologist provides services to a family in a way similar to that of a family doctor. The therapist is available to all members of the family, either individually or in a group, as needed. Clients are not necessarily seen on a regular basis, and the concept of termination does not apply.

These programs are a sample of the numerous techniques that have been documented. Although there has been some evaluation of the effectiveness of these techniques (e.g., see Malgady, Rogler, & Constantino, 1990), for the most part, they have yet to be empirically tested. Despite the apparent inaction in rigorously testing the efficacy of culturally competent care, the collective evidence is compelling and provides confirmation that ethnic-specific mental health programs that develop and use culturally responsive techniques have been effective in increasing utilization among certain ethnic minority groups (Bestman, 1986; Bobo et al., 1988; Owan, 1981). After controlling for the effects of ethnic match, sociodemographic, and clinical variables, Takeuchi, Sue, and Yeh (1995) found that ethnic-specific programs reduced dropout rates and increased utilization of outpatient services among African American, Asian Americans, and Mexican Americans. Snowden and Hu (1996) also controlled for ethnic match, sociodemographic, and clinical variables in a study of African American, Asian Americans, and Latino Americans and found that ethnic minority programs were effective in reducing the reliance on emergency services. They also noted that programs that served a majority of ethnic minority clients provided more outpatient services but less case management services than programs serving a majority of White clients. Another study demonstrated that, among Asian Americans, ethnic-specific services increased utilization rates, decreased the need to use emergency services, and produced better treatment outcomes (Lau & Zane, 2000). Among county-level ethnic-specific mental health programs in California, the effectiveness of strategies undertaken to increase ethnic access depended on the ethnic community under consideration (Snowden, Masland, Ma, & Ciemens, 2006). For example, Latino and Native Americans responded well to outreach activities, whereas programs targeting Asian Americans increased access by hiring more bilingual and bicultural staff. The only successful intervention across all ethnic groups, including Whites, was increasing the available supply of mental health practitioners.

Community-Level Cultural Responsiveness

Some scholars have proposed that the problems that ethnic minority consumers encounter in receiving appropriate care should be placed in a larger social context (Vega & Murphy, 1990). Chin (1993) has suggested that the "standard practice" mental health service delivery does not take account of other cultures' world views. As an alternative to current service models, Barrera (1982) has argued that priority be given to the social, economic and political problems of the ethnic minority community rather than simply addressing the needs of the seriously mentally ill. These views coincide with those of community psychologists who have advocated that traditional treatment models, emphasizing individual interventions and outcomes, should be complemented by public-health-oriented prevention strategies. These methods focus on creating partnerships between researchers and community members in the design, implementation, and evaluation of services and involving all stakeholders in the process (Case & Robinson, 2003).

Community public-health-oriented interventions are rooted in the notion that individual behavior is influenced by the social environment in which people live. In other words, the values, norms, and behaviors of one's community, such as the level of stigma attached to mental illness or knowledge about the location of language-compatible services, shape individual help-seeking behaviors. Community health interventions seek to capitalize on community strengths to promote prevention and educational campaigns that not only focus on individual outcomes but also target larger societal values that can subsequently affect individual behavior (Bruce, Smith, Miranda, Hoagwood, & Wells, 2002). This orientation to improving well-being has been used more and more over the past three decades, exemplified by the fact that behaviors once considered private matters increasingly are becoming the focus of public policy (e.g., policies that control where smoking is allowed, seatbelt laws, and the provision of fluoride in public drinking water; Thompson, Coronado, Snipes, & Puschel, 2003). Mental health services researchers see this type of "population thinking" as an opportunity to efficiently increase knowledge and decrease stigma among groups that have historically had limited access to and utilization of mental health services (Snowden, 2005; Wells, Miranda, Bruce, Alegria, & Wallerstein, 2004).

The population-based focus in mental health services research involves shifting parameters from individual to population indicators of needs and outcomes (MacCoun, 2004). Approaches to community interventions vary and include social marketing to promote health behavior change, family communication skills training, and school-based social skills training for youth (Anderson et al., 2003; Wandersman & Florin, 2003). The shift to a population perspective also requires evaluating and monitoring progress with measures of community-level social well-being. Siegel and others (2000) described a conceptual model for measuring effectiveness based on the premise that the socioeconomic environment affects the social and mental well-being of community residents. In this model, indicators of social well-being include poverty, employment, criminal justice system involvement, mortality, and the availability of a broad range of public services, such as those addressing homelessness, education, and primary health care.

Community intervention strategies offer unique methods to enhance responsiveness to public health priorities. Wells and colleagues (2004) proposed the evidence-based community/partnership model, which supports health improvement goals by using evidence-based strategies while empowering the community to implement those strategies consistent with their cultural values and strengths. In this model, designing, implementing, and evaluating the interventions are done in several steps. First, community members, researchers, public officials, and community-based agencies work together to negotiate a set of goals. Next, these goals are matched with evidence-based practice strategies and tailored to the community's unmet needs and the particular context. Finally, the research team works with the community to determine the evidence basis for the outcomes in relationship to the designed program. An integral facet of the evidence-based community/partnership model is the participatory process by which goals are defined, interventions are enacted, and evidence is evaluated to respond to the needs, priorities, and culture of the community.

The Los Angeles-based program Talking Wellness provides an illustration of a community intervention with the goal of decreasing the stigma surrounding depression among African Americans (Chung et al., 2006). Part of the mission of Talking Wellness is "to help people in the community begin to dialogue about depression so that friends and family members can recognize depression and help their loved ones reach a greater state of well-being" (Chung et al., 2006). A workgroup of academic researchers and community members met once a month for more than a year to determine the best venues and approaches to engaging the community on the topic of depression. The culminating interventions included a series of outreach events at the Pan African Film Festival: a documentary screening followed by discussion, a poetry/comedy event, a photo exhibit, and the screening of an existing public service announcement. Each of these represented a different format for communication and allowed opportunities to compare their content and effectiveness. Surveys were collected before and after each event to assess changes in audience members' knowledge, attitudes, and beliefs about depression. Challenges arose, namely balancing the competing demands of academic institutional review board deadlines with the need for time to get enough community input in event and evaluation planning. However, the benefits of using the participatory framework outweighed the challenges by helping ensure the creation of better evaluation techniques (e.g., appropriate to the literacy level of the participants and using nonoffensive question formats) and providing invaluable opportunities for mutual exchange of knowledge between academic researchers and their community partners.

Although community interventions have been used extensively to address public health concerns, few mental health studies have employed these strategies and large-scale efficacy studies are not yet available (Wells et al., 2004). To meet the demands of legislative and funding bodies, mental health services researchers must be able to measure the effectiveness of mental health treatments (Glisson & Schoenwald, 2005). At the same time, researchers are challenged to ensure the public health impact of the effective treatments by finding appropriate means to disseminate the information and encourage their widespread adoption (Schoenwald & Hoagwood, 2001). Considering the potential for community-based interventions to efficiently reduce treatment barriers and engage racial and ethnic minority populations in mental health services, this line of research deserves our attention.

Conceptual Issues in Defining Culture and Mental Health Services

In the first part of this chapter, we discussed some of the research conducted in the field of ethnic minority mental health services. We also examined attempts by mental health systems to analyze and respond to the needs of ethnic minorities. Although there are some outstanding examples of carefully conceptualized service models for specific ethnic groups (e.g., see Bestman, 1986), much of the work in this area makes oversimplified assumptions about "culture" and "mental health services." If the programs provide definitions for such terms, they tend to be perfunctory in nature, and assumptions about the fundamental purposes of services – for the individual, the community, and society – are rarely made explicit.

This lack of clarity and precision about the goals and purposes of multicultural mental health services has made it difficult to establish realistic service parameters and evaluation criteria (Vega & Murphy, 1990). Moreover, we suggest that it has failed to provide adequate guidance to advocates in analyzing the potential conflict between multicultural services and certain trends in the "mainstream" mental health service system. Thus, we begin this part of the chapter by summarizing some trends in mental health services that at some level conflict with a commitment to developing "multicultural" mental health service systems. These trends include

(1) a tendency to favor etiological models of mental illness that stress common human biological causes over diverse cultural and social factors; (2) a tendency to reify the construct of culture; that is, to see culture as fixed, historical, and autonomous from social structure; and (3) a tendency to overlook the substantial heterogeneity in socioeconomic status and stress-related life experiences among specific ethnic groups in favor of amalgamating them under four large ethnic categories (i.e., African Americans, Asian Americans, American Indians and Alaska Natives, and Latino Americans).

Conflicting Trends in Mental Health

Biological and Social Origins of Mental Illness. Historically, psychiatrists have played a dominant role in setting the parameters of mental health as a subspecialty of medicine and defining the content of psychiatric disorders (Millon & Klerman, 1986). As a result, mental health has been studied primarily from a non-normative perspective. Marsella, Sartorius, Jablensky, and Fenton (1985) noted that there is a tendency in the mental health field to overlook variation in the expression of mental disorder when developing nosological categories. As indicated earlier, the first studies on minority mental health were derived primarily from clinically based studies and rooted in a disease model (Fabrega, 1990). More recently, a return to biological explanations of mental illness has further discouraged the search for social origins (Kleinman, 1988).

In essence, the idea of a cross-cultural perspective on mental health services conflicts with the tendency in the field to adopt biological models of mental illness. The assumption underlying biological models is that concepts and measurement of mental health and illness are uniform from one cultural group to another. Psychiatric symptoms or syndromes are often assumed to be universally distributed and uniformly manifested. However, this assumption is unwarranted because groups vary in how they define such constructs as "distress," "normality," and "abnormality." These variations affect definitions of mental health and mental illness, expressions of psychopathology, and coping mechanisms (Marsella, 1982). Without adequate attention to cultural variations in health and psychopathology, multicultural programs may be constrained in meeting the needs of minority communities. As Vega and Rumbaut (1991) suggested, the challenge for the mental health field is to understand how best to parcel out cultural influences to achieve more accurate measurement, understanding, and treatment of psychiatric problems.

Reification of "Culture." Westen (1985) focused on the problematic nature of culture theory by differentiating between cognitive anthropologists, for whom shared meaning systems are the essential elements of culture, and ecological anthropologists, for whom culture is firmly anchored in the material world of social structures including power and authority structures. The mental health services field has tended to adopt the cognitive or "ideal" perspective, viewing culture as essentially historically bound, autonomous from social structure, and "located in the realm of expectations, values, ideas and belief systems" (Jayasuriya, 1992, p. 41).

In many respects, a highly cognitive view of culture is both naive and static and fails to capture the lived reality of culture as a form of cultural practice (Westen, 1985). As a system of symbolic meanings, culture is circumscribed by social factors and institutional constraints and cannot be divorced from considerations of power (Jayasuriya, 1992). From this perspective, the changing cultural patterns of ethnic minority groups are inextricably linked to the structural limitations they encounter as the result of discrimination. Ethnic minorities are more likely to face limited access to valued social roles and statuses and constraints to the successful fulfillment of ordinary role requirements such as that of parent or spouse (Vega & Rumbaut, 1991, p. 374). Within groups, cultural expressions of values and behavior will vary along status dimensions such as gender, sexual orientation, and socioeconomic status. Recent research also has shown that the expression of emotion is influenced by culture. For example, compared to European American groups, East Asians have a more dialectical style of thinking, in which contradiction is tolerated and change is expected (Leu et al., 2008). Clearly, mental health service programs that assume uniformity of cultural values and beliefs among the members of ethnic minority communities run the risk of stereotyping consumers. Perhaps even worse, programs that seek to address the "cultural" concerns of ethnic minority communities without attending to issues of power, oppression, and discrimination run the risk of trivializing key aspects of ethnic minority culture as it is lived and experienced by its participants.

Socioeconomic Status and Stress-Related Life Experiences of Ethnic Groups. Ethnic minority status has often been considered a general proxy for life stress. Indeed, analysts have often conceived of minority status itself as a stressor, independent of socioeconomic and demographic predictors of mental health problems (Vega & Rumbaut, 1991). Theoretically at least, stressors are important to mental health because they increase the risk of experiencing certain psychiatric symptoms and disorders. As suggested earlier, however, differences across specific ethnic groups in stress-related life conditions and experiences, such as poverty, war-related physical and emotional trauma, and social role discontinuities, are substantial and warrant more careful attention by service planners. Among foreign-born members of ethnic groups, for example, a general distinction can be made between "immigrants" who must cope with substantial life changes on settling in a new country, and "refugees," who in addition tend to experience more threat, more trauma, and less control over the circumstances surrounding their exit from countries of origin. Such variations in life history imply substantially different mental health service needs (Vega & Rumbaut, 1991).

Differences in the need for mental health services can be as striking within as across the four "catch-all" ethnic minority categories. For example, the category of "Asian Americans" actually encompasses a number of ethnic groups, such as native-born Chinese and Japanese, Chinese and Korean immigrants, and Cambodian and Hmong refugees. These groups differ substantially in levels of education and income, as well as in experiences of dislocation, trauma, and social role disruption. In tailoring services to the specific needs of ethnic minority clients, the utility of such general population categories as "Asians/Pacific Islanders," "Latino Americans," "African Americans," and "Native Americans" must be carefully scrutinized. These categories may conceal more than they reveal.

Assumptions about the Goals and Purposes of Mental Health Programs

Potential conflicts between multicultural service goals and mainstream mental health trends continue at the level of service system assumptions. In this section, we review two basic dimensions along which such conflicts are possible: (1) assumptions about the essential societal functions of mental health services and (2) assumptions about the basic purposes and scope of services for the individual.

In improving services for ethnic minority consumers, it is clearly important to understand how and what service elements contribute to specific outcomes for individuals. Although "services" and "programs" may be presumed to be the most important intervening variables that make a desired difference for clients, surprisingly little thought has gone into conceptualizing these elements. Few service models and evaluation studies of ethnic-specific services adopt a clear theoretical perspective for predicting "effective services" and explaining their effects on specific clients (Rosenfield, 1992a). In mental health services research, for example, service use is often treated as a kind of theoretical black box. Investigators accept terms and definitions as they already exist in the service system's information system (e.g., total hours of individual treatment, group treatment, case management, crisis intervention), despite the fact that existing definitions are driven more by reimbursement and billing needs than by theoretical or clinical concerns. For advocates of culturally appropriate services, accepting "services" and "service units" as they are already and typically defined is problematic for several reasons. For example, doing so precludes the consideration of alternative (culturally appropriate) services and focuses attention on individual- rather than environment-targeted change strategies.

Societal Functions of Mental Health Services. The importance of clarifying the basic purposes of mental health services in contemporary society is exemplified by the service use statistics presented earlier in this chapter. Is the relatively high use of mental health services by some ethnic minority groups an indicator of improved service access or excessive social control – or both? How such phenomena are appraised – indeed, just what constitutes "appropriate service use" and "positive" service use outcomes – is fundamentally shaped by our assumptions about the purposes or functions of mental health services in society. Clarity about these assumptions is necessary for appropriate service improvement and advocacy. The extent to which extensive service use is positive or negative is a particularly controversial subject with respect to ethnic minorities, where issues of discrimination and relative lack of political and economic power come into play.

One helpful way to examine this issue is through a political economy perspective. As the term implies, *political economy* "refers to the interplay between politics and economics – that is, how the institutions and transactions of each sphere impact on the other" (Rochefort, 1987, p. 101). To take a political economy perspective means we view mental health services as an element in the social welfare system, and social welfare in turn is viewed as one of several major institutions within a "market-centered" society (Galper, 1975; Martin & Zald, 1981; Romanyshyn, 1971). In addition, Rochefort (1987, p. 191) suggested that political economy analysts search for a "macro, holistic understanding of the welfare state that encompasses its organization, funding, and effects on the social order." Using a political economy framework is not new; a number of social scientists have conceptualized mental health services in political economy terms (e.g., see Aviram, 1990; Gummer, 1988; Rochefort, 1987). For present purposes, however, the important point is to recognize that different political and theoretical stances can be taken on the relationship between the market economy and mental health services. These perspectives in turn shape such critical factors as how "good" client and system outcomes are defined. Here, we address three of these perspectives.

We can view mental health services as essentially a means to control "deviant" groups (the poor, the chronically mentally ill, ethnic/racial minorities). In a social control perspective, the mental health care system is one of several social institutions (including law enforcement) that operate to facilitate the smoother running of the market, both by fostering and maintaining order and conformity (Aviram, 1990, p. 83) and by creating and maintaining the secondary labor market. From this perspective, the most important outcomes of mental health services are those concerned with the containment of persons with mental illness, particularly those whose behavior has been deemed by "social control agents" to be dangerous, confrontative, or otherwise "inappropriate." The social control perspective can be seen from two vantage points: as "protecting society" (conservative, status quo oriented) or as "protecting the socially controlled" (more reform or change oriented). From the first vantage point, major outcome questions include the following: Do services succeed in restraining/containing clients perceived as "dangerous," "disruptive," or otherwise "offensive" to the general public? Do services succeed in changing those "offensive" client behaviors and in socializing clients to conform to "norms" of "public behavior?" From the second vantage point, major outcome questions revolve around issues of unjust treatment of clients (especially those who enter the mental health system through involuntary treatment or those who are "served" in relatively restricted settings).

A second view sees mental health services as an essentially complementary institution to the marketplace, whose primary function is to improve people's ability to compete and perform adequately within the labor market. From this perspective, the most important outcomes of service are associated with improvements in clients' ability to compete and perform in the labor market and to become and remain as economically self-sufficient as possible. Have mental health services been effective in achieving such service objectives as improving clients' social and vocational skills? Increasing client wage levels? Moving clients from welfare dependency to independent work situations?

A third view proposes that mental health services can serve as a compensatory mechanism for the distribution of resources. In contrast to the first two perspectives, we can view mental health services primarily as providing alternatives to market mechanisms for the distribution of resources (Gummer, 1988, p. 263). From this perspective, the general criterion for service effectiveness is distributional equity and is "simple and straightforward" (though interpretations of equity are anything but): Do mental health services "contribute to a more equal distribution of society's resources" (Gummer, 1988, p. 263)? We would add that in ethnic minority communities, the equity question has often been viewed at the level of the individual consumer. In fact, much of the current debate about whether public mental health expenditures should be distributed on a parity or an equity basis uses the ethnic population/community as a unit of comparison.

In reality, mental health services are seen as means to accomplish some or all of these functions, and few would argue that one or another view totally predominates (Aviram, 1990). As Aviram (1990) has suggested, it is probably unrealistic to assume that Americans would accept a service system that does not have some element of social control. Some tension between these functions is evident, however, and it is also unrealistic to presume that the mental health service system can simultaneously optimize all three. The question of how to prioritize these functions is thus paramount. It is particularly critical in the current climate of reduced public resources for community mental health services and a return to more narrowly circumscribed, medicalized models of practice (Aviram, 1990).

Basic Purposes of Services vis-à-vis the Individual

The term *services* implies work performed and the application of some technology that is useful or beneficial to the client. However, just what constitutes a benefit – that is, what are the desired goals and outcomes for the mental health client – is subject to some debate. At the risk of oversimplifying the distinctions among them, we summarize three service models that emphasize somewhat different goals: the clinical services model, the social welfare model, and the empowerment model. These are not necessarily mutually exclusive (e.g., the social welfare and empowerment models can encompass clinical services), but once again, differences among these models have important consequences for how mental health services are defined, planned, and evaluated.

Under the clinical services model, the primary purpose of mental health services is to alleviate the symptoms and causes of psychological or psychiatric distress experienced by the individual client or patient; it reflects what many analysts refer to as a "medical model" approach (e.g., see Aviram, 1990). This model emphasizes the individual as the focus of service delivery and change and psychiatric interventions as the major means of intervention. Services emphasized include psychiatric assessments; symptom control through drug therapy; and individual, family, and group therapy.

Within the social welfare model, the problems to be addressed by mental health services, although encompassing clinical services, also include a broader range of community living issues, such as poverty, homelessness and the lack of affordable housing, and inaccessibility to primary medical care. The social welfare model sees the majority of problems experienced by consumers less in terms of individual-level causes and more as social structural in nature (e.g., see Aviram, 1990; Neighbors, 1990).

From an empowerment model perspective, mental health services can best help consumers by addressing the psychological, economic, political. and social barriers that create conditions of relative powerlessness and that prevent individual and group empowerment (Rosenfield, 1992). Although empowerment models include service elements of the clinical and social welfare models, they attempt to increase control over services and provide the consumer with access to economic and other resources through consciousness-raising, legislative advocacy, group and community organizing, program development, and administrative skills. This model also most closely fits with consumer-run mental health programs and alternative mental health systems (e.g., see Chamberlin, 1978).

The clinical, social welfare, and empowerment models differ in the scope of desired goals and services, and their juxtaposition raises a fundamental question: As a society, how broadly are we willing to define the arena of public responsibility for mental health? The question is especially critical for members of ethnic minority communities, many of whom have few viable treatment alternatives to publicly funded services (Vega & Murphy, 1990).

As Aviram (1990, p. 74) noted, the restricted focus of the clinical model fits well in many ways with contemporary U.S. welfare ideology, and there is a tendency in the United States to interpret the problems experienced by persons with mental illness in these terms. However, some analysts question the benefit of medicalized service approaches to ethnic minorities. For example, Neighbors (1990) pointed out that the narrower clinical approach is less appropriate for African Americans than wider approaches that address problems disproportionately shared by African Americans that stem from social structural – and not individual pathological – causes. Vega and Murphy (1990, p. 2) concurred, noting that the community mental health services field has "returned to a very narrow disease model of mental illness at the very moment that social models of health are most needed."

Conclusion

As the United States enters a new decade, tensions are likely to increase and become more magnified between the demands placed to meet the social and health care needs of a changing population and the need to standardize care to make services more efficient and cost effective. Although cultural factors are critical to understanding access to mental health services, the proper screening and diagnoses that lead to treatment, and the actual effectiveness of treatment, much of the policy decisions will be based on what assumptions are made about services and which service delivery models are adopted. Sociologists can play an important role by documenting how these tensions are resolved over time, determining whether cultural factors are ignored or incorporated into service delivery models, and continuing the call to examine other social, cultural, and structural factors that can enhance mental health care.

23

The Mental Health Consumers/ Survivors Movement in the United States

Athena McLean

For the last 150 years in the United States, persons who had been committed to psychiatric hospitals and treated against their will have championed the cause for social justice and the right of all persons to exercise self-determination and choice over their bodies and minds. These persons have mobilized political support for change through what is now called the mental health consumers/survivors movement. This chapter briefly reviews the early roots of that movement and then focuses on changes in its development and both its accomplishments and challenges faced in the modern period from about 1970 to 2008. Why have some psychiatric consumers or survivors felt that, although they may have benefited from forced treatment (assertive outpatient treatment), the disadvantages of this form of treatment far outweighed the benefits to them?

Background

The mental health consumer/survivor movement is the modern expression of a 150-year-old social justice, human rights movement devoted to securing the rights and just treatment of persons identified as mentally ill. The movement was initially fueled by reformers in the mid-1800s wanting to improve services and treatments for the indigent insane; these reformers were advocating for a person's right to treatment. A second impetus came from those seeking protection from incarceration and treatment against their will. It also had its early expression in the mid-1800s in the writings of women committed by their husbands, without due process, to asylums. These women and their legal backers were promoting the right to refuse treatment.

During the early 1800s persons involuntarily committed to asylums objected to "moral treatment" as an oppressive form of social control (Hubert, 2002). By the mid-century, as conditions changed, inmates objected instead to abusive treatment by asylum attendants and institutionalized "management" in oversized, impersonal, and inhumane settings. The restriction of human rights had its stark expression in differences in power between the committed and those who committed them – power defined by differences in gender, race, nationality, wealth, ideology, mental health status, and status in the family. Thus the mental health movement has been embedded from the start within deeper social and political struggles.

It would be erroneous, however, to regard the movement as unified and continuous, given the many changes that have occurred in the mental and the legal systems and their impacts on those subjected to their power. These impacts have shaped the contours of the movement throughout its 150-year course. What has persisted is the demand for a more responsive and socially just system to serve its citizens – whatever their gender, nationality, race, beliefs, practices, or mental condition – while protecting their rights to self-determination against the coercive power of the state and treatment system.

Whenever a person's behaviors or ideas are seen as threatening to the state, to the status of those in power, or to that person's or another person's safety, his or her civil rights may be called into question. Mental health advocates have mobilized over the past 150 years in an effort to preserve those civil rights. Their efforts have supported rights ranging from the freedom to express controversial ideas to the right to self-determination over one's body and mind.

This chapter reviews trends in the struggles of activists to achieve these rights. After briefly describing early conditions and moments in the movement, the chapter examines the modern mental health consumer/survivor movement, focusing on (1) the expatients and other advocates who fueled the modern movement, 1970–1980; (2) the reformist turn from antipsychiatry to consumerism, 1980–1986; (3) forces that bolstered or challenged the movement, 1978–1992; (4) subsequent challenges, 1990s–2003; and (5) more recent developments, 2003–2008.

The Early History

In the late 1700s and early 1800s, madness in the United States was viewed as a medical disorder that could only be cured by a doctor's taking complete control over the person, by force if needed (Hubert, 2002). The earliest psychiatric hospitals practiced a form of moral treatment in which social control and conformity to social norms were ensured through isolation, discipline, and forced labor (Hubert, 2002). The influx of immigrants in the second half of the 19th century, many of whom were deemed dangerous or insane (Levine, 1981), added to the ranks of "insane poor" inappropriately placed in overfilled almshouses or prisons. Reformers like Dorothy Dix rallied support for the establishment of huge therapeutic asylums to treat this population. Although she succeeded in ensuring widespread construction of huge institutions throughout the United States, the sheer number of patients (up to 1,000 or more) in each facility impeded the possibility of treatment. As insanity came to be regarded as untreatable (Levine, 1981), psychiatric institutions were transformed into efficient public custodial warehouses that held people, often against their will, for years. Untrained, often abusive attendants controlled inmates and denied them basic rights, like communicating with outsiders, under the guise of treatment. This situation continued well into the 1900s (Hubert, 2002).

When the first psychiatric institutions opened in the late 1700s, only a physician's authorization was needed for involuntary commitment. A family member, backed by a doctor, could also commit a relative who was seen as unwisely using family property (Levine, 1981). Toward the mid-1800s commitment laws enabled family members to secure rapid incarceration, without any judicial hearings (Hubert, 2002), and family members often used these laws to commit their most troublesome members (Levine, 1981). Some states, like Illinois, required minimal evidence of insanity, except for married women, who could be committed at their husband's request without any evidence (Levine, 1981). Thus the lack of rights of female patients was connected to their lack of rights as women.

In 1861 Elizabeth Packard was committed by her pastor husband because of her heretical church teachings. On her release 3 years later, she obtained a writ of habeas corpus[1] to secure a hearing to circumvent his efforts to recommit her. After being found sane, she escaped her husband's control. She later wrote of her ordeal (Packard, 1875/1973) and initiated a national campaign to prevent similar incarceration of others without a jury trial to determine their sanity. She succeeded in having laws passed preventing commitment without a trial (Levine, 1981).

Then in 1900, Clifford Beers, a recent Yale graduate, suffered a psychotic break that led to two major hospitalizations, one lasting 3 years. His experiences of abuse by doctors and attendants moved him to write a book (Beers, 1908) to bring attention to and improve the conditions of other patients. With the support of famous clinicians of his era, he founded the National Committee for Mental Hygiene in 1909, which developed into the national Mental Health Association (MHA) by 1950 (Levine, 1981). To gain public endorsement and financial support he had modulated his intense criticism of the mental health system and was dissuaded from bringing expatients and families into the movement (Dain, 1989). However, by the early 1960s, the national MHA was instrumental in opposing unpaid labor of institutionalized patients and in promoting community mental health legislation (Robbins, 1980) and deinstitutionalization. This legislation was stimulated by a public outcry evoked by the writings of conscientious objectors, who were assigned to work in psychiatric institutions during World War II (e.g., Deutsch, 1948).

Expatients and Allies in the Modern Movement, 1970–1980

Most of the individuals who later drove the mental health consumer/survivor movement had been involuntarily committed to psychiatric hospitals during the early days of deinstitutionalization, where they were often subjected to forced and

---

[1] A writ of habeas corpus is a petition filed by a person with a court in objection to his or her incarceration or to another person's incarceration, on the basis of illegality or factual error.

abusive treatment and to restrictions on their rights and freedom. These people registered their protest to such injustices by calling themselves "antipsychiatric," "expatients," or a term that was even more descriptive of their forced incarceration, "exinmates." Over time, as their cause was heard and later appropriated by traditional sectors within the mental health system, the movement became reconfigured into a consumer/survivor movement by those who called themselves "survivors" or "consumers." As these changes occurred, many who had been vehemently opposed to the psychiatric system dropped out of the movement, fearing it was being gradually co-opted by professionals. Yet, before any expatient groups actually coalesced in the 1970s, individual advocates had brought litigation in support of psychiatric patients' rights during the civil-rights-conscious 1960s. It was in the midst of the emancipatory consciousness of this era, which nurtured gender and racial awareness and self-help movements, that the modern expatient movement was also born (P. Brown, 1981). By the early 1970s the loosely organized Psychiatric Inmates Liberation Movement brought together expatients outraged by their own forced, prolonged, and often abusive treatment in psychiatric hospitals. Because of the oppression they suffered, they were overwhelmingly hostile to psychiatry, the medical model, forced treatment, and involuntary commitment (McLean, 2000). *Madness Network News*, published from 1973 to 1986, was their medium for communication and the National (and later, International) Conference on Human Rights and Against Psychiatric Oppression their meeting forum.

During the early years of this period, radical therapists, a diverse group of mental health professionals dissatisfied with traditional therapies that ignored the contribution of social and economic factors to mental illness (Talbot, 1974; see also Radical Therapist/Rough Times Collective, 1974), joined forces with the expatients. Their journal, *The Radical Therapist*, in print from 1970 to 1972, published articles from both professionals and expatients, who during the early 1970s also engaged together in civil disobedience. However, by the mid-1970s, as the two groups vied for control and the expatients came to doubt their commonality of interests and mission, the two groups parted ways (Chamberlin, 1990; Dain, 1989; Unzicker, personal communication, October 8, 1999).

During this same era, however, a new alliance with legal advocates was formed. Members of the national Mental Health Law Project (founded in 1972 and later called the Brazelon Center), who advocated for civil and treatment rights of institutionalized patients, formed the National Association for Rights Protection and Advocacy (NARPA). Members included legal and other sympathetic professionals and advocates; expatients made up at least one-third of its board of directors. NARPA was unique for supporting the right not only to choose but also to refuse treatment (Scallet, 1980; Unzicker, personal communication, October 8, 1999). Befitting its strong human rights advocacy record, NARPA, which remains a vibrant proactive organization, has sustained ongoing collaboration between expatients and its professional members.

The Reformist Turn: From Antipsychiatry to Consumerism, 1980–1986

During much of the 1970s, expatients who were antipsychiatry refused to work with the mental health system and government agents, whom they feared would co-opt their mission. This resolve began to crumble as ideological differences among expatients surfaced, with some showing a growing willingness to communicate with mental health professionals and many others exhibiting an interest in creating a national organization. A national organization was seen as an urgent means of drawing public attention to the serious problems of deinstitutionalized patients discharged into an unprepared community (e.g., homelessness, inadequate and fragmented services to meet clinical and basic material needs).[2] Although not yet officially organized into an organization, they advocated for change through lobbying, litigation, and the development of their own alternatives to professional mental health services.

In 1977, the National Institute of Mental Health established the Community Support Program (CSP) to respond to continuing problems resulting from the lack of preparation for deinstitutionalization mandated by Congress in 1963 (J. Turner & TenHoor, 1978). CSP shared expatients' views of the medical model's inade-quacy, the need for integrated services, and a rehabilitative approach sensitive to person-defined needs (J. Turner & TenHoor, 1978). Backed by federal legislation, CSP also encouraged consumer involvement in policy making and in running their own alternative services (McLean, 1995), albeit often with inadequate fund-ing (McLean, 2000).

The CSP's offer to fund a consumer conference (the first National Alternatives Conference) in 1985 sparked fierce debate among anarchist, radical reformist, and more conservative expatients, revealing the class differences among them (Dain, 1989). At that first National Alternatives Conference was formed a national orga-nization, the National Mental Health Consumers' Association. Its refusal to take a stand against forced treatment, a central human rights issue for expatients at the conference, led to the formation of a separate organization later that year: the National Alliance of Mental Patients, later called the National Association of Psychiatric Survivors. Whereas the more conservative National Mental Health Consumer's Association supported the medical model and greater access to treat-ment, the expatient survivors' organization vehemently opposed forced treatment legislation. Both agreed on the debilitating effects of institutionalization, the importance of self-determination for recovery (Sproul, 1986), and the value of

---

[2] Although deinstitutionalization was certainly a position that ex-patients favored, given their own horrendous experiences with institutionalization, they objected to the lack of community prepared-ness for the thousands of patients who were discharged without adequate and acceptable housing and support services, both clinical and material.

self-help alternatives. The National Mental Health Consumer Association enjoyed a broader base of supporters, but lacked a clearly unified and trackable membership, whereas the 300 expatients who made up the National Association of Psychiatric Survivors became the intellectual lifeblood of the movement and maintained a newsletter for a time.

The founding of these two organizations destroyed the anarchistic strain of the movement – those who had objected to national organizing and cooperating with mental health professionals and government funders. The ideological strife that had been stirred up was too much for the struggling movement, and the last International Conference on Human Rights and Against Oppression, which had been meeting since the early 1970s, was held in 1985. The next year, *Madness Network News* also ceased publication, blaming the CSP for having co-opted the antipsychiatry movement (McLean, 2000).

By the mid-1980s the antipsychiatry movement had thus become reconfigured into a combined consumer/survivor movement that, though ideologically and politically divergent, was now more organized and better positioned to work with the mental health system and government agencies to advocate for its members. Through most of the 1980s, expatients had resisted the term *consumer*, preferring to see themselves as "survivors" of an oppressive mental health system. They also felt that the label "consumer" deceptively implied a freedom of choice that was simply lacking, especially with involuntary treatment (Chamberlin, 1990). Although many expatients have continued to insist on calling themselves "survivors," there has been some blurring of the two terms. Such a blurring, however, works to erase the political message underlying the choice of the term *survivor*, as it blurs an understanding of *what* one has survived (i.e., mental illness or the service system).

Boosts and Challenges to the Consumer Movement, 1978–1992

Community Support Program (CSP)

Even before the CSP had offered to sponsor the Alternatives Conference in 1985, it had gradually introduced consumers to its national Learning Conferences held from 1978 to 1987. These national conferences were initially designed for psychiatric patients' families, who were themselves seen as consumers by CSP staff, and whose political support CSP had hoped to capture to help promote its own agenda. Many of these families eventually formed the well organized and powerful lobbying group, The National Alliance for the Mentally Ill. (See "Growing Influence of NAMI: the Family Movement" below.) The CSP staff, however, were more tentative about inviting the consumers themselves, because they were not yet regarded as a serious constituency. There were also concerns about handling the legal and financial details of bringing persons still seen as fragile to a conference

(Shifren-Levine, interview with the author, March 5, 1992). The ice broke after CSP took the step to invite Judi Chamberlin, an expatient leader who had just published a book on her experiences (Chamberlin, 1978). The unique consumer perspective and insights she brought to the discussion paved the way for extending invitations to other consumers at future meetings.

Even though there were significantly fewer consumers/ survivors than National Alliance on Mental Illness (NAMI) members and they were less privileged,[3] those who were invited to the CSP conferences made valuable contacts that helped propel their own movement. Through their alliances with researchers, civil rights lawyers, state mental health directors, and government policy makers, they were able to promote favorable legislation that mandated their inclusion in the development of state mental health plans (National Association of State Mental Health Program Directors [NASMHPD], 1989). Consumers/survivors who were also researchers later formed the Consumer/Survivor Research and Policy Workgroup, in which they would regularly discuss their concerns, vision, and goals with CSP leaders, mental health policy administrators, researchers, and program directors at national forums. These forums enabled them to shape both the national mental health policy agenda and processes of knowledge production. By gaining the staunch support of these national leaders (Parrish, 1988), this workgroup helped frame how to conceptualize consumer needs, services, and outcomes (Trochim, Dumont, & Campbell, 1993).

Two significant outcomes of the negotiations of consumers/survivors with national-level mental health professionals were the broad-based expansion of the movement through consumer-run alternatives and increased opportunities for more consumers to engage in advocacy activities. Without the support of CSP and other influential professionals, it is unlikely that these gains would have been possible. For example, the 1990 Alternatives Conference that CSP funded brought 1,300 consumers to Pittsburgh, 43 of them on passes from state psychiatric hospitals (McLean, 2000). Outreach to many of these consumers occurred through the assistance of the mental health system, which now saw the consumer program as working *with* it, rather than against it. The energy generated at this and subsequent Alternatives conferences stimulated hope and a sense of empowerment in participants and encouraged their continued involvement in self-help activities and advocacy. Many became involved in local mental health boards and committees, some in closing down psychiatric hospitals and others in working at local or state consumer offices. Still others worked with state-level policy makers to develop proposals for grants to fund consumer-run services. Most important, a renewed sense of opportunity for consumers to learn about the system, medications, and their

---

[3] In contrast to their families, who were typically successful professionally and economically, most of the consumers, because of their psychiatric history, were unable to secure and sustain the kinds of opportunities their parents enjoyed.

rights helped counter previous dissatisfaction and a pervasive sense of resignation that had come to plague many of them.

Mental Health Associations

The Mental Health Associations (MHAs) that grew out of Clifford Beers' advocacy efforts have continued to support consumers, as well as professionals. Although initially shunning collaboration with either consumers or professionals, their bias toward service-oriented advocacy has led to collaborations with consumers and families on many projects since the 1980s. They have also promoted consumerism by working with consumers on CSP projects. These associations also have a history of promoting the rights of psychiatric patients (Robbins, 1980), most often testifying on behalf of patients in lawsuits (P. Brown, 1982). But their promotion of consumerism for psychiatric patients far predates the term *consumer* (Robbins, 1980).

Mental Health Legislation

The passage of the federal State Comprehensive Mental Health Plan Act of 1986 (P.L. 99–660, Title 5) was advantageous for consumers because it mandated states to provide mental health plans that supported consumer initiatives and involvement in policy planning. Families, however, continued to hold the dominant voice on planning boards, and their perspectives were too often represented as "the consumer voice," even when they contradicted the views of primary consumers. Further, the act itself was passed before funding was made available to implement it and without establishing adequate penalties to encourage compliance (Maury Lieberman, personal communication, April 1992). Even after funding became available for consumer programs, it was often too low to adequately staff them and to pay the consumer staff comparable salaries to those enjoyed by employees of the traditional mental health sector.

Growing Influence of NAMI, the Family Movement

In catering to families of persons diagnosed with mental illness, CSP tried to boost its own power and effectiveness. Its staff realized that families had been marginalized by clinicians who still blamed parents for causing illness in their children. CSP empowered parents by bringing them face to face as equals with mental health professionals (Steven Sharfstein, personal communication, February 27, 1992). This effort helped bolster the incipient family movement, formalized in 1979 as the National Alliance for the Mentally Ill (NAMI). Within one decade its membership rose from 184 to 80,000, and it became one of the most powerful lobbies in Washington.

As NAMI gained force, its top officials and many of its members successfully rallied against a mental health system that had held them responsible for their children's illness. They did this by campaigning to remedicalize psychiatry and constructing mental illness as a disease of the brain (McLean, 1990). Ironically, NAMI's success positioned it to eventually challenge CSP's more comprehensive approach to mental illness (J. Turner & TenHoor, 1986).

NAMI promoted consumerism by encouraging primary consumers to "shop around" for their treatment and to develop a partnership with their doctors – something they had learned as family members working on citizen boards and on policy committees, early in the deinstitutionalization movement (Kenig, 1992). Insofar as this consumerism supported self-determination to make one's own decisions about one's own life and treatment, it was compatible with the views of many consumer/survivors. However, NAMI restricted this approach to the doctor–patient relationship, limiting consumer choice within the existing biomedical marketplace, which was available only to middle-class private-pay consumers. It ignored the larger public system and its treatment mills in which consumers had little choice and in which precious physician time was reserved for renewing prescriptions, not discussing treatment concerns. Thus NAMI supported consumerism only for those who valued the provider–consumer relationship and who had access to it. This kind of consumerism led to uneven empowerment based on class. In advocating biomedical treatment over community support, NAMI opposed services vital to help consumers of the public mental health treatment system with recovery beyond chemotherapeutic management. Even for the more privileged consumer, control over treatment was restricted to the locus of the brain. In light of these limitations, it was not surprising that consumers and expatients felt the need to develop alternative services.

As CSP tightened allegiances with expatients who objected to forced treatment and biomedical approaches alone, NAMI withdrew its support. Gaining influence in its campaign to biomedicalize mental illness, NAMI succeeded by 1992 in its efforts to move the National Institute of Mental Health (NIMH) into the other institutes of medicine. CSP then moved from NIMH to the new Center for Mental Health Services (CMHS) within the Substance Abuse and Mental Health Services Administration (SAMHSA). In its new environment, and under the new ethos favoring brain research over innovative community services, CSP had a significantly reduced capacity to influence change and promote the consumer cause.

NAMI worked against CSP in other ways. When funding became available for consumer grants to develop alternative services (e.g., peer counseling, drop-in centers, or job-training projects), political maneuvering by opponents of consumer projects prevented many of these projects from actualizing their potential (McLean, 1994, 2003a). Dogmatic elements within NAMI, intolerant of non-biomedical interventions, sabotaged 13 demonstration projects funded by CSP in 1988 by placing congressional pressure on NIMH to demonstrate that the CSP projects deserved its funding. These projects had been neither designed nor funded to meet newfound demands for rigorous standardized outcome evaluations. The projects' stage of development was suited more for process evaluations, which would have yielded useful knowledge. Because project directors were forced to adopt the outcome evaluations, this interference by NAMI prevented projects from gaining valuable formative data to address organizational and managerial problems, determine how to best work with state mental health officers, and find subsequent programs (McLean, 2003a). If the criteria for rigorous evaluations had been demanded up front, adequate research designs and funding would have afforded knowledge of both process and outcome. Many state mental health officers and outside evaluators suspected the projects were intended to fail (NASMHPD, 1989). The outcome evaluations produced results suggesting the projects were weak, and CSP lost its authorization to fund similar projects (McLean, 2000).

Costs of Government Dependence and Consumerism

In a political climate in which NAMI had acquired considerable influence, CSP was losing power and had become less favorably positioned to promote the consumer/survivor cause. As CSP became marginalized as a change agent, consumers/survivors lost their key proponent to fund their projects at the federal level. Without government support, they were unable to run their programs, yet in accepting government funding, whenever it was available, consumers risked co-optation of their ideals. It was this dependence that was deplored by anarchists who had dropped out of the movement.

As more people became introduced to the consumer/survivor movement, it became diverted from its empowering principles and participatory democratic values. Many of the new recruits had benefited from improvements wrought by earlier activists, and so did not share their criticism of the system; they fully embraced the medical model and valued the mental health system. Some of the new consumers had been providers themselves and had used their training to secure leadership opportunities in the consumer movement or to become directors of consumer-run projects, even though they were unfamiliar with or did not accept its emancipatory mission (McLean, 1995). They often promoted power hierarchies and abused their power (Zinman, Harp, & Budd, 1987) in ways that rivaled the mental health system.

Some consumer programs and self-help alternatives, even when highly critical of psychiatry or the mental health system (Gartner & Riessman, 1977), became reframed as "consumer options." They thus became part of a collective of options, together with more traditional mental health services, among which consumers could choose. Under such conditions, however, these programs risked losing their original oppositional vision (Grace, 1991).

Subsequent Challenges, 1990s–2003

Despite the manipulation and compromised status of CSP demonstration projects and their subsequent discontinuation, state authorities were convinced of their overall value. After all the projects had ended, at least 35 states continued to independently fund at least one consumer project (Mobray, Grazier, & Holter, 2002).

Managed Care

There were however, new funding developments during the 1990s that further challenged the consumer movement. Since 1965, Medicaid, a joint program of the federal and state governments, had provided fee-for-service health and mental health services to unemployed and underemployed persons. During the 1990s, under the pressures of shrinking state budgets and growing mental health (renamed "behavioral health") costs, many states turned to the private for-profit sector to provide capitated payments (B. McFarland, 2000) and to implement managed care models to keep costs down. Through contracts with states, managed behavioral care organizations began to arrange for service provision, eliminating the need for states to reimburse providers directly.[4] For many consumers, the introduction of managed care was a "breath of fresh air" to a system viewed as entrenched and intransigent. They saw it as providing a welcome opportunity to discard the ideological baggage of the traditional mental health system. They expected that their own input would be welcomed by for-profit competitors intent on competing for consumer satisfaction. Some consumers hoped that managed care organizations would support the cheaper and less invasive services they preferred and might enable them to dismantle and radically transform a system of care that had been recalcitrant to change. Others were more cautious, cognizant that the bottom line would dictate services (McLean, 2003b).

As it turned out, the economic focus of managed care organizations favored time-limited interventions with clear measurable outcomes, targeted to individual symptoms and behaviors, while disregarding the more intractable material conditions that contributed to them. Managed care was better adapted to a reductive biomedical model than to less well-defined continuing support services, such as housing and rehabilitation, which were integral to consumers' preferences for a comprehensive recovery approach. Even though consumers could be involved

---

[4] In order to do this legally, states would need to obtain a Medicaid waiver so as not to violate the federal government's requirement for fee-for-service payment arrangements. Although most states arranged agreements with managed behavioral care companies during the 1990s, some elected to provide their own management through nonprofit managed care arrangements at the state or local level. See Stroup and Dorwart (1997).

in individually oriented "self-change" approaches, their need to comply with therapist-directed assignments impeded the self-determination that was their central principle. Under managed care, many services were eliminated, and forced treatments often provided the only access to any treatment. Noncompliance was cause for disenrolling consumers from programs (Gabriele & Guida, 1998). Others with multiple heavy services needs felt pressured to disenroll after being denied crucial services (Mobray et al., 2002). The influence that consumers had hoped for was simply not realized.

The excesses of a profit-driven model that denied fundamental services and endangered the lives of a vulnerable, indigent population threatened the public trust. A backlash developed (Appelbaum, 2002; Hall, Edgar, & Flynn, 1997; Hopper, 1996), and states were forced to revisit their contractual arrangements under tightening budgetary constraints. Ironically, therefore, the abuses of managed care proved beneficial to consumers. As a corrective, the state overseers of behavioral health have encouraged heightened involvement of consumers in planning and oversight of state behavioral services, greater demand for their perspectives in training providers, and the promotion of their recovery vision (Fisher, 1997; Sabin & Daniels, 1999, 2002).

National Support for Recovery Principles

Beginning in 1999, consumers/survivors enjoyed three significant coups. The U.S. Supreme Court, in its decision in *Olmstead v. L.C.*, 527 U. S. 581, ruled that unnecessary institutionalization severely diminished a person's quality of life and that services that promote integration within the community should be encouraged. That same year the Surgeon General's Report on Mental Health (USDHHS, 1999) articulated the view that behavioral disturbances are immensely varied in etiology, thereby challenging reductionistic biomedical explanations and lending credence to the importance of external factors. Then in 2003, the President's New Freedom Commission on Mental Health recommended "fundamentally transforming" the delivery of care in the United States, shifting from a system that "simply manages symptoms" to one that is "consumer-centered, recovery-oriented" (President's New Freedom Commission Report [NFCR], 2003, p. 86).

Consumers have interpreted the concept of recovery in several ways (cf. Campbell & Schraiber, 1989; Deegan, 1988; Fisher 1992; Leete, 1989). Whereas some, like psychiatrist Dan Fisher, associate recovery with a final cure (Barry, 2002), for others it suggests a satisfying, socially productive life, with or without symptoms (Anthony, 1993; Frese, 1998). And although professional help may facilitate recovery, it is not a prerequisite. Because recovery is seen as constructive, nonthreatening, and focused on transforming the individual, rather than the system, it is one around which consumers, families, and providers alike can rally

(McLean, 2003b). Nonetheless, the processes involved in recovery may entail confrontation of sources of social oppression in one's life.

Oppositional Forces

In spite of apparent gains, opponents continued to challenge the ideologies and goals of consumers. The most vocal opponents included extremist but dominant voices within NAMI and psychiatrists E. Fuller Torrey and Sally Satel. NAMI, for example, backed by funds it received from the pharmaceutical industry (Phillips, 2002), has fiercely advocated for aggressive treatment within the community. Through its Campaign to End Discrimination, NAMI has promoted the Program of Assertive Community Treatment (PACT), which is enforceable by existing outpatient commitment laws. Outpatient commitment, also known as assisted outpatient treatment (AOT), is coercive, court-mandated treatment of persons with a history of medication noncompliance. It is intended to help those whose illness supposedly prevents them from accepting the treatment that AOT proponents insist they need. Through AOT, a person may be forcibly medicated in his or her own home by mental health professionals, and noncompliance can lead to involuntary inpatient commitment (Treatment Advocacy Center [TAC] Briefing Paper, 2005). Although some consumers feel that forced treatment saved their lives (Satel, 2000), others admit its benefits, but argue nonetheless that its damage to their self-esteem outweighed its benefits (Campbell & Schraiber, 1989; Chamberlin, 1978). Still others have found it so aversive that they felt compelled to cross state lines in order to avoid facing it (Fritz, 2006). In addition, while some families support AOT, many blame forced treatment for having eroded their relative's trust in them (Zinman, 2000).

Psychiatrist E. Fuller Torrey has promoted assisted outpatient commitment through the TAC that he founded in 1997, originally as part of NAMI. Under his leadership, TAC has fought successfully for tougher commitment laws, partly by sensationalizing examples of homicides carried out by psychotic individuals (Vine, 2001). By 2003, 39 states had adopted outpatient commitment laws. In 2006 the American Psychiatric Association awarded Torrey the Presidential Award for his exceptional advocacy activities though TAC. A group of public interest lawyers, however, found that New York's Kendra's law,[5] adopted in 1999, was inordinately biased against African Americans and Hispanics. Also, contrary to its claims, it was used to commit people lacking any history of violence (New York Lawyers for the Public Interest, Inc. [NYLPI], 2005). Others found that AOT was used only

---

[5] Like similar laws adopted by other states, the name is taken from that of a young person who was murdered by someone who was presumed to be psychotic and unmedicated. This association thus carries a symbolic message that TAC would approve, even though it is not always borne out by the facts.

because services the person previously sought, when he or she needed them, were not available. Furthermore, there is evidence that AOT may serve to inhibit people from actually seeking help (Carothers & Driscoll, 2004).

Psychiatrist Sally Satel was appointed in 2003 to the influential CMHS National Advisory Council (NAC) that advises the CMHS director and makes judgments on CMHS grant proposals. As a chief mental health advisor to President George W. Bush and a fellow of the conservative Enterprise Institute at the time, she not only advocated outpatient commitment but also blatantly objected to "politically correct" language that elevated consumers above patients (Satel, 2000, pp. 46–47). "Patient is the term I prefer," she announced on her first day at the NAC. She also challenged what she considered to be the "overemphasis" on rights, which leads people to think that coercion is dangerous: "People need to be protected from themselves and the public needs to be protected." She decried laws that frustrated her ability to do her job (Chamberlin, 2002).

These same opponents also targeted the National Consumer Technical Assistance Centers, also funded by the CMHS, and, like the National Empowerment Center (NEC), provide information on self-help, advocacy, services, and policies and foster relations with professionals. The NEC had already received funding approval from the CMHS in 2002, but opponents tried to stop its allocation. Andrew Sperling, NAMI's public policy director, Satel, and Torrey were all instrumental in this effort (McLean, 2003b). Ultimately, funding was allocated, but as a result, consumers felt even more vulnerable, and many were relieved when Satel's term at the CMHS National Advisory Council ended in 2007 (National Coalition of Mental Health Consumer/Survivor Organizations [NMHCSO], 2007).

In spite of this opposition, CMHS has continued to fund consumer programs, adding yet a fourth national technical assistance center in recent years. By 2002, the CMHS budget had grown to $782 million, a more than 200-fold increase over NIMH's original CSP budget of $3.5 million in 1977 (Torrey, 2002). Consumers have been major benefactors of this growth, through initiatives like Community Action Grants (CAGs) from 1999 to 2004, which encouraged consensus building with family and other advocacy groups to improve services; statewide Consumer Network Grant Programs in 2004 and 2007 that fostered unanticipated cooperation among groups who had been seen as adversaries; and the Mental Health Transformation State Incentive Grants (MHT SIG), for system change using recovery principles (Center for Mental Health Services, 2008). Individual states have independently implemented their support for consumer programs. In 2004, California taxpayers passed Resolution 63, which poured almost one billion dollars into its Mental Health Services Act. Consumers/survivors were directly engaged in writing and passing the bill. This act, explicitly guided by the consumer-driven recovery principles articulated in the President's New Freedom Commission Report (California Department of Mental Health, 2005), has promoted the holistic, voluntary community-based services that consumers have long advocated. Sally Zinman, head of one of the nation's largest consumer organization, the California Network for Mental Health Clients, called this act "a monument of what we've gotten done in thirty years" (2006).

Setbacks, however, have been experienced throughout the country. Forty-two states now have outpatient commitment laws despite evidence that challenges their benefits (NYLPI, 2005). Some states have even broadened their commitment criteria and aggressively applied them, causing some consumers to move to other states (Davis, 2006). There has been a resurgence of unpopular treatments, like psychosurgery, electric shock, and aversive therapy, and neglect and needless fatalities still occur in psychiatric facilities (Interlandi, 2008). Psychotropic medications and accompanying profits have also exploded in recent years, and young consumers have been targeted (Oaks, 2006a) through nationwide school programs, like the controversial Teen Screen (cf. "Rutherford Files," 2005).

Still, consumers and survivors have made unquestionable strides through intensified networking, global collaborations, mutual respect, and renewed efforts at unification and compromise. MindFreedom International[6] (MFI), for example, has been a key vehicle of communication and networking for the consumer/survivor movement globally. MFI is a nonprofit alliance of more than 100 grassroots groups and professional organizations in 13 countries. It advocates for human rights and alternatives in the mental health system. Its Web site (http://ww.mindfreedom.org) is an information portal for international news; upcoming local, national, and international events; teleconferences; and countless other material relevant to consumers/survivors around the world. MFI also sends e-mail updates to consumers, families, sympathetic providers, and human rights advocates to mobilize support and advocacy, such as encouraging lawmakers to vote against what it perceives to be destructive bills.[7]

Since 2001, MFI has been accredited as a nongovernmental organization (NGO) by the United Nations, which enables it to participate in international negotiations on the human rights of persons with disabilities. It helped create the legally binding United Nations Convention on the Rights of Persons with Disabilities, ratified by 20 countries on May 12, 2008. Later that month, Interrelate (http://www.Interrelate.info) – another coalition of mental health consumers/survivor organizations from seven countries – was also officially launched.

The unification of disparate consumer and survivor groups in 2006 into the National Coalition of Mental Health Consumer/Survivors Organization also reflected a collaborative spirit (NMHCSO, 2008). Leaders of groups that had

---

[6] MindFreedom International was co-founded by David Oaks and Janet Foner in 1990 as Support Coalition International. The name was changed to MindFreedom International in 2005 (Oaks, 2006a: 1212).

[7] It successfully used its networking capability, for example, to oppose New York Assembly Bill 9986, which would have allowed the use of aversive treatment, including corporeal punishment and solitary confinement, in children and adolescents confined to psychiatric institutions.

parted ways because of ideological differences in 1985 now came to realize the need to unite under a common national front to prevent family and provider groups from speaking for them. Under the new coalition, they proclaimed, "Nothing about us without us." To Sally Zinman, a veteran survivor, this slogan conveys the fundamental message that consumers and survivors must always be at the table to help make decisions to implement, run, monitor, and evaluate any program that will affect them directly (Zinman, 2008). This willingness to collaborate, unthinkable 20 years earlier, has enabled consumers and survivors to advance common causes. For example, survivors who oppose forced treatment and consumers who will support it only in an emergency now are seeking common themes around which both can rally, such as not expanding forced treatment programs (Zinman, 2006). In fact, in California, it was mainly consumers of psychiatric medications whose efforts guaranteed that funding from the new Mental Health Services Act could be used only for voluntary services.

Discussion

Today's compromise and collaboration of consumers and survivors is a far cry from the separatism and militancy that expatients displayed during the early days of the modern movement. Nonetheless, Zinman insists (2008) that the movement's driving values have not changed. The consumer/survivor movement perpetuates the civil rights advanced by Elizabeth Packard to halt forced incarceration and to promote the right to self-determination and choice over one's body and mind. Thirty years ago, the horrors of institutionalization led expatients to oppose the medical model and psychiatry. Today, they advocate for holistic services that may include psychiatric treatment if a person wants it. Thirty years ago, they were adamantly separatist to avoid submitting to an intransigent system that held full control. Because of their advocacy, conditions have improved immensely, but as Zinman argues, "we are not there yet" (2006). In coaching younger advocates, she urges persistence, passion, fairness, inclusiveness, and compromise. She now believes that change must come from inside as well as outside the mental health system and that it "cannot be pushed beyond its box." Yet only by looking back did she realize the extent of changes their activism wrought, changes that occurred incrementally, but were never secure.

Even if the approach to change and the discontinuous pattern of consumer gains were hardly revolutionary, the accomplishments of the consumer/survivor movement have been considerable. Thirty years ago consumer-run programs were virtually nonexistent. Today hundreds of statewide local self-help groups provide alternative services, and in 2006 peer counselors became professionalized and certified under the National Alliance of Peer Specialists ("National Professional Organization," 2006). National and state organizations advance their consumer/ survivor agendas, and every state has a mandated consumer office through which consumers and survivors directly engage with policy makers. National and international consumer/survivor organizations, funded through government or private sources, maintain extensive communication networks through which to mobilize supporters globally. Veteran activists now operate large, broad-based mental health organizations that build community coalitions with families and providers to advance the consumer cause.[8] The principle, "Nothing about us without us," is being realized through collaborations that were unthinkable to ex-patients in the 1970s.

Perhaps the most significant change is found in consumers themselves. Because of strides made by older activists, younger consumers are exposed to a friendlier mental health system and less sedating medications; many can simply not relate to the oppressive experiences that drove the movement's fiercest advocates. Their silence, however, about the adverse consequences, such as diabetes or heart conditions, from taking newer medications is particularly disconcerting to veterans of the movement. Medical control, they argue, is more insidious today than ever before because it is so subtle. We are in the days of empowerment and recovery while being "drugged to the heels" (Oaks, 2006b). Such are the contradictions and textured legacy of decades of consumer/survivor activism and reform. The self-determination so central to their cause has afforded exceptional opportunities, but it has also yielded some unsettling choices that now give many of them pause.

---

[8] For example, in 1986, Joe Rogers founded the Mental Health Consumers Self-Help Clearinghouse through the Southeastern Pennsylvania Mental Health Association. In 1997, he became its executive director, and later, president and CEO of that association, transforming it into one of the largest in the nation.

24

Mental Illness and the Criminal Justice System

Virginia Aldigé Hiday and Padraic J. Burns

Hiday and Burns examine two prevailing beliefs about mental illness and the criminal justice system: that deinstitutionalization has led to the criminalization of mental illness and that mentally ill persons are dangerous and likely to commit crimes. The chapter reviews the available empirical evidence for these beliefs. Although arrest rates and incarceration rates are indeed higher for mentally ill persons than for the general population, criminalization may be too extreme a characterization. Furthermore, most people with mental illnesses are not violent, and only a small proportion becomes violent. The chapter goes on to examine how mentally ill persons are handled by the criminal justice system. The authors follow Hiday and Wales (2009) in suggesting that there are five subgroups of persons with severe mental illness who come into contact with the criminal justice system: (1) those committing only misdemeanor nuisance offenses; (2) those committing offenses involving survival behaviors; (3) those who abuse alcohol and drugs, which leads to high rates of criminal offenses from the use of illegal substances, from attempts to support their habits, and from violence arising out of their use; (4) those with a character disorder who have high rates of felonious criminal offending, especially for violence against others; and (5) a much smaller subgroup whose members fit the stereotypical image of a severely disordered person driven to criminally violent actions by delusions. All five groups tend to live in impoverished, disorganized communities where it is difficult to survive with a major mental illness. The authors conclude that the criminal justice system is left to pick up the pieces after the failure of other social institutions. What types of social stressors contribute to the criminalization of the mentally ill? What failures of social institutions have led to incarceration of those with mental illnesses?

Introduction

Two prevailing beliefs held by the public (and many professionals) connect mental illness to the criminal justice system: first, a belief that deinstitutionalization has led to criminalization of mental illness, and second, a belief that mentally ill persons are dangerous and likely to commit crimes, especially violent crimes. If these beliefs were accurate, then the criminal justice system would be processing and holding significant numbers of sick persons. The first two sections of this chapter examine the evidence to ascertain whether and to what extent empirical evidence supports these beliefs. The third section describes how mentally ill persons are handled and fare in the criminal justice system and, after their release, whether or not these beliefs hold true. The concluding section hypothesizes that there are five distinct types of persons with major mental illness who are arrested, convicted, and incarcerated.

Criminalization of Persons with Mental Illness

Following procedural and substantive legal changes that restricted civil commitment (Appelbaum, 1994, Bloom et al., 1986; Hiday, 1988; LaFond & Durham, 1992), there appeared reports of criminalization of persons with mental illness – reports of large numbers of sick persons arrested and incarcerated in jails and prisons who were previously treated in state mental hospitals (Abramson, 1972; Bonovitz & Guy, 1979; Dickey, 1980; Geller & Lister, 1978; Lamb & Grant, 1982; Rachlin, Pam, & Milton, 1975). Initial reports faulted the legal changes for limiting society's ability to care for mentally ill persons in public hospitals, thus placing substantial numbers of them in the community and at risk for arrest. Soon, however, most observers came to attribute responsibility for criminalization of mentally disordered persons to the larger process of deinstitutionalization, including restrictive civil commitment laws (Goldsmith, 1983; Hiday, 1991, 1992a; Lamb et al., 1995; R. D. Miller, 1987; Roesch & Golding, 1985; Teplin, 1983). Many argued that intolerance and fear of the bizarre, unpredictable, and dangerous nature of some symptoms of mental disorder (Gerbner et al., 1981; Link et al., 1987; Monahan, 1992; Nunnally, 1961; Phelan & Link, 1998; Phelan et al., 2000; Rabkin, 1972; Steadman & Cocozza, 1978; Weiss, 1986) led society to resort to the criminal justice system to arrest and charge mentally ill persons for both nuisance offenses and more serious allegations, with resulting criminal sentences to jail or prison or commitments to mental hospitals. This criminalization thesis suggests that the criminal justice system processes mentally ill persons differently, being quicker to arrest and incarcerate them than persons who are not mentally disordered.

The possibility that society would turn to the criminal justice system after deinstitutionalization should have been anticipated because the police are entrusted with ensuring social order. Undoubtedly, citizens would call law enforcement when they could not control observable disordered behaviors of persons with mental illness, particularly when they felt these behaviors were dangerous. Additionally, many released mentally ill persons would be likely to commit minor infractions such as vagrancy, disorderly conduct, trespassing, and shoplifting because they would return to poor, disorganized neighborhoods with few material and social resources. And because of their vulnerabilities, severely mentally ill persons who did violate the law would be less likely to escape detection and more likely to be caught. But would police involvement lead to criminalization; that is, would it lead to the disproportionate arrest and incarceration of persons with mental illness who previously were held for long periods in state mental hospitals? To answer this question, researchers have investigated police encounters with mentally ill persons, arrest rates, prevalence of mental illness among jail and prison inmates, and mentally ill offenders sent to forensic units.

Police Practices

Even before deinstitutionalization, law enforcement officers frequently dealt with mentally disordered persons (Bittner, 1967; Cumming, Edell, & Cumming, 1965). Since deinstitutionalization, police have increasingly been called on to control persons with mental illness who are disruptive (Bonovitz & Bonovitz, 1981; Lamb, Weinberger, & DeCuir, 2002; Teplin, Filstead, Hefter, & Sheridan, 1980). Sometimes they intervene directly in observed trouble, but family, friends, or others such as landlords, merchants, and physicians call police to quell disorder, check bothersome behavior, or provide transportation to psychiatric emergency facilities (Teplin et al., 1980; Watson, Corrigan, & Uate, 2004). Poor, undereducated urban families often rely on police for these functions (Teplin et al., 1980).

When police are called, they settle encounters (not only those with mentally ill persons) most frequently by informal means – mediating disputes, offering solutions, placating complainants, and in general "cooling out" situations (Bittner, 1967; Bonovitz & Bonovitz, 1981; Brekke, Prindle, Bae, & Long, 2001; Engel & Silver, 2001; Green, 1997; Teplin, 1984b; Watson, Angell, Morabito, & Robinson, 2008; Wolff et al., 1997). Police resort to formal dispositions (including both arrest and hospitalization) infrequently and usually only in those situations that are likely to escalate and require them to return (Bonovitz & Bonovitz, 1981; Teplin, 1984b). Police are likely to opt for hospitalization over arrest when they perceive that the individual lacks criminal intent or needs treatment or when they know the individual to be a former mental patient (Engel & Silver, 2001; Lamb et al., 2002; McNiel et al., 1991; Monahan, Caldeira, & Friedlander, 1979; Teplin et al., 1980). Officers opt for hospitalization and treatment more frequently when their police department has a cooperative program with a mental health facility, especially one that is open 24/7 with a "no-refusal" policy (Borum, Deane, Steadman, & Morrissey, 1998; Deane, Steadman, & Borum, 1999; Kneebone, Rogers, & Hafner, 1995; Lamb et al., 1995, 2002; McNiel et al., 1991; Skeem & Bibeau, 2008; Steadman, Morris, & Dennis, 1995; Teplin et al., 1980).

Police may resort to arrest, even when treatment is preferable, in the following situations: when deviant behavior is serious or so public and visible as to exceed the limits of tolerance, when deviant behavior is likely to proliferate and require later police intervention, when suspects are noncompliant or hostile or fight with officers, or when officers do not recognize symptoms of mental illness (Engel & Silver, 2001; Laberge & Morin, 1995; Lamb et al., 2002; Novak & Engel, 2005; Steadman, Deane, Borum, & Morrissey, 2000; Teplin, 1984b, 1985; Watson et al., 2004). Police also resort to arrest when treatment options are inadequate or facilities refuse to accept a mentally disordered individual (Deane et al., 1999; Fisher,

Roy-Bujnowski, et al., 2006). Mental health practitioners, in attempting to control their work environment, commonly refuse to treat persons with criminal charges or criminal records and persons with substance abuse comorbidity (Borum et al., 1998; Hartwell, 2004; Laberge & Morin, 1995; Lamb & Weinberger, 2005). Substance abuse facility employees likewise refuse substance abusers with comorbid mental illness, leaving police with little choice but to arrest them (Teplin, 1984b, 1985). And police sometimes resort to arrest as a way to get care for mentally disordered persons when psychiatric emergency staff must turn down those who are neither sick enough nor dangerous enough to meet civil commitment criteria for involuntary hospitalization (Lamb & Weinberger, 2005; Steadman, Morrissey, Braff, & Monahan, 1986).

Arrests of Mentally Ill Persons

Before the era of deinstitutionalization, mental patients released from public hospitals had lower arrest rates than the general population; after deinstitutionalization, arrest rates of former mental patients rose both absolutely and in relation to the general population (Melick, Steadman, & Cocozza, 1979; Monahan & Steadman, 1982; Rabkin, 1979). This trend would seem to support a criminalization hypothesis; however, some studies showed that the increased arrest rates could be accounted for by the medicalization of deviance, which sent a new type of patient to mental hospitals – persons whose former criminal behavior came to be viewed as sick rather than bad (Cirincione, Steadman, Robbins, & Monahan, 1994; Horwitz, 2002; Kittrie, 1971; Melick et al., 1979; Steadman, Cocozza, & Melick, 1978; Stone, 1975). As time passed, deinstitutionalization became an established state rather than a process, and community programs were not developed to replace the treatment, clothing, food, shelter, and activities that large public hospitals once provided. Large numbers of poor, highly impaired persons with severe mental illness have been left without needed supports. Although many continue to revolve in and out of state hospitals and psychiatric units of community hospitals for short stays (Kiesler & Sibulkin, 1987; Lamb & Bachrach, 2001; Mechanic, 1999), their treatment is only intermittent, and they face both homelessness and a spreading drug culture. As one might anticipate, recent studies of outpatients have indicated that arrest rates of persons with mental illness are now higher than those of the general population (Borum, Swanson, Swartz, & Hiday, 1997; Cuellar, Snowden, & Ewing, 2007; Fisher, Roy-Bujnowski, et al., 2006; Sheldon et al., 2006; Swanson et al., 2001; Theriot & Segal, 2005).

Most studies of arrest of persons with mental illness have not controlled for comorbidities, despite existing research that shows that mentally ill persons with character disorders and substance abuse are much more likely to offend and have higher arrest rates than other mentally ill persons (Bloom, Shore, & Arvidson, 1981; Bonta, Law, & Hanson, 1998; Crocker et al., 2005; Harry & Steadman,

1988; Holcomb & Ahr, 1988; Monahan et al., 2001; Pandiani, Rosenheck, & Banks, 2003; Poythress, Skeem, & Lelienfeld, 2006; Rice & Harris, 1992; Robins, 1993; Schuerman & Kobrin, 1984; Sheldon et al., 2006; Steadman et al., 1998; Swartz & Lurigio, 2007). Those studies that have been able to place such controls report that substance abuse/dependence and antisocial personality disorder (ASPD) or psychopathy explain much of the elevated arrest rates of persons with mental illness. Another problem is that most samples have consisted of patients in the public mental health system, excluding mentally ill persons who do not get treatment and those who receive treatment in the private sector. Such samples tend to be disproportionately young, male, unmarried, of low socioeconomic status, and living in disadvantaged neighborhoods, all traits associated with criminal offending. Furthermore, a disproportionate number are homeless and live under conditions likely to lead to arrest (Sheldon et al., 2006). Belcher (1988) described homeless mentally ill offenders as persons who self-medicate with alcohol and street drugs (rather than taking their prescribed medication), become increasingly impaired in cognitive and social functioning, wander aimlessly, appear psychotic much of the time, and manifest bizarre and often threatening behaviors in public places. Comparing arrest rates of such samples with arrest rates of the general population without adequate controls for these factors yields too distorted a picture to address the criminalization thesis (Hiday & Wales, 2003; Monahan & Steadman, 1982; Sheldon et al., 2006).

Caution needs to be taken in assessing arrest rates at all because they can be misleading in that they do not indicate the percentage of patients who have been arrested. Arrest rates may be high because of arrests that are concentrated in a minority of patients who revolve in and out of both the mental health and criminal justice systems; such rates would thus not reflect criminalization (Fisher, Roy-Bujnowski, et al., 2006; Hiday, 1991, 1992a).

Incarceration of Mentally Ill Persons

Some researchers have turned to studies of incarcerated populations to investigate whether mentally ill persons have been criminalized since deinstitutionalization. They have analyzed two types of data: archival records on psychiatric hospitalization of prison populations and survey data on the mental status of incarcerated persons. Initially, criminalization adherents pointed to growth in the numbers of persons incarcerated in state prisons after deinstitutionalization as evidence of criminalization of the mentally ill. Clearly, there were substantial increases in prison populations and rates of prison incarceration across the nation after deinstitutionalization (Liska, 1997; Palermo, Smith, & Liska, 1991; Steadman, Fabisiak, Dvoskin, & Holohean, 1987; Steadman & Morrissey, 1987), and jails saw their populations burgeon after the 1970s (Steadman, McCarty, & Morrissey, 1989; Steadman et al., 1995). But although increased prison populations were accompanied in some states by increases in the proportion of inmates with prior mental hospitalization, that proportion decreased in just as many states (Steadman et al., 1984, Steadman & Morrissey, 1987).

Prison and jail surveys consistently have found higher rates of mental illness than found in the general population (Blaauw, Roesch, & Kerkhof, 2000; Brink, Doherty, & Boer, 2001; Collins & Schlenger, 1983; Corrado, Doherty, & Glackman, 1989; Ditton, 1999; Fazel & Danesh, 2002; Fisher, Roy-Bujnowski, et al., 2006; James et al., 1980; James & Glaze, 2006; Jordan et al., 1996; McNiel, Binder, & Robinson, 2005; Teplin, 1990a; Teplin et al., 1996). Part of what accounts for higher rates is inordinately high levels of ASPD and substance abuse or dependence. For instance, male felons in North Carolina had a lifetime ASPD rate 14 times higher, an alcohol abuse/dependence rate 3 times higher, and a drug abuse/dependence rate 23 times higher than the North Carolina Epidemiological Catchment Area (ECA) sample (Collins & Schlenger, 1983). Incorporating ASPD, which often represents no more than a psychiatric label for criminal behavior, and substance abuse/dependence that is either illegal in itself or leads to criminal offending into the definition of mental illness inflates the overall rates of mental illness in prisons and jails and distorts our understanding of causation. Some studies broadened the definition of mental illness with a resulting inflation of rates in other ways: including offenders with only one symptom, which could be caused by other conditions, and including offenders with anxiety and depression, which could arise from incarceration itself (see James & Glaze, 2006).

Research that restricted the definition of mental illness to severe mental illness (bipolar, severe depression, and schizophrenia spectrum disorders) has found lower rates than research using broad definitions, but these rates are still significantly higher than those found in the general population (Blaauw et al., 2000; Corrado et al., 2000; Fazel & Danesh, 2002; Teplin, 1990a; Teplin et al., 1996). For instance, Teplin and colleagues (1990a, 1996) found that approximately 6% of male and 18.5% of female jail detainees met criteria for lifetime severe disorders. The higher lifetime prevalence rate among women was due in large part to their high rate of major depressive episode (16.9%). Comparable levels of major mental disorder have been reported in a review of 62 prison studies in Western nations (Fazel & Danesh, 2002).

Even though higher than the general population, current rates of major mental illness in jails and prisons may be no higher than they were before deinstitutionalization. Because comparable studies of the earlier era are not available, we cannot know from this type of data whether there has been a criminalization of persons with mental illness since deinstitutionalization. One would expect to find greater numbers of mentally ill persons incarcerated in jails and prisons, even if the proportion of mentally ill persons incarcerated remained the same, simply because of the huge overall increases in the number of persons imprisoned owing to other societal trends: spreading illegal drug use, the subsequent war on drugs, and introduction of mandatory minimum and indeterminate sentences (Caplow & Simon, 1999; Ditton, 1999; Wallace, Mullen, & Burgess, 2004).

Mentally Ill Persons in Forensic Units

The fourth type of evidence used to support the criminalization thesis is the number of offenders who are evaluated and treated for mental illness while incarcerated. One study reported an increase in referrals to a prison's psychiatric unit following enactment of restrictive civil commitment criteria and a corresponding increase in the proportion of unit inmates who were less serious offenders (Bonovitz & Guy, 1979). Other studies have supported the criminalization argument with data showing increases in commitment to psychiatric treatment after judgments of both incompetent to stand trial (IST) and not guilty by reason of insanity (NGRI), verdicts that send mentally ill persons to forensic psychiatric units in jails or hospitals or to general units in state hospitals for treatment, instead of punishment (Abramson, 1972; Arvanites, 1988; Dickey, 1980; Morrissey & Goldman, 1986). However, there are alternative interpretations for these data. Commitments of offenders could have increased in response to concurrent reform limitations in length of confinement for IST and NGRI judgments (La Fond & Durham, 1992; Wexler, 1981), or shorter stays could lead to committed offenders revolving in and out of the criminal justice system and forensic treatment units, just as nonoffending mentally ill persons revolve through mental hospitals (Broner, Lattimore, Cowell, & Schlenger, 2004; McMain, Webster, & Menzies, 1989; Menzies, Webster, McMain, & Staley, 1994; Steadman, Cocozza, & Veysey, 1999). Medicalization that redefined as disordered those prisoners previously thought "normal" could also explain increases in these commitments, especially in combination with newly instituted mental health training programs for criminal justice officers (Bonovitz & Bonovitz, 1981; Borum et al., 1998; Finn & Sullivan, 1988) and a more general increased sensitivity throughout society to problems of mental illness (Link et al., 1999; Phelan et al., 2000; Veroff et al., 1981). And, as stated before, increases in jail populations would lead to increased numbers of mentally ill persons in forensic units even if the proportion of mentally ill inmates remained stable from before to after deinstitutionalization.

Although arrest rates and incarceration rates are higher for mentally ill persons than for the general population, and although police may handle, arrest, and incarcerate more mentally ill persons after deinstitutionalization than before, criminalization of mental illness may be too extreme a characterization of these trends, because arrest is not the most frequent response to mentally ill persons whom police encounter (Engel & Silver, 2001; Hartford, Carey, & Mendonca, 2006; Novak & Engel, 2005; Teplin, 1984a, 1985; Watson et al., 2008; Wolff et al., 1997). As well as overstating conditions, the term *criminalization* connotes little appreciation for the role that police play as "street-corner psychiatrists" who not only quell disorder but also assist in maintaining and helping many mentally ill persons in the community (Skeem & Bibeau, 2008; Teplin & Pruett, 1992). Regardless of how one chooses to view the term, there can be no doubt that the criminal justice system is responsible for the care and control of large numbers of severely mentally disordered persons.

Criminality of Mentally Ill Persons

The second belief linking mental illness and the criminal justice system is that mentally ill persons are dangerous and likely to commit crimes, especially violent crimes. Going back at least to the Greco-Roman period, the public has believed that a disproportionate number of mentally ill persons are unpredictable and dangerous (Link et al., 1999; Monahan, 1992; Phelan & Link, 2004; Phelan et al., 2000; Rosen, 1968). This belief is reinforced today in fiction and human interest news stories (Angermeyer & Schulze, 2001; Gerbner, Gross, Morgan, & Signorielli, 1981; McKenna et al., 2007; Steadman & Cocozza, 1978). The frenzied madman, the "psycho" who is driven to harm others, and the delusional paranoid who unexpectedly and randomly kills are regular grist for television and motion picture studios as well as features for the news media (Wahl, 1995). One American organization regularly disseminates stories of criminal and violent behavior by persons with severe mental illness on the Web, in letters to newspapers, and in books in order to obtain funds and legislation for research and coercive treatment of mental illness (Torrey, 2008; Treatment Advocacy Center, 2006).

Unlike criminalization – which holds society responsible for processing mentally ill persons through the criminal justice system instead of treating them more humanely with mental health and social services – the criminality thesis blames mental illness for behavior that the criminal justice system must control. Indeed, the legal verdict of NGRI is premised on the understanding that mental illness can make an individual insane; that is, it can cause a sufficient lack of rational capacity such that the decision to engage in behavior is impaired. Researchers have evaluated the criminality of persons with mental illness by examining arrest rates, incarceration surveys, and data on violent behavior that is not processed by the criminal justice system.

Arrest Data

Some observers have cited the previously discussed higher arrest, conviction, and incarceration rates of mentally disordered persons as evidence supporting the criminality (instead of criminalization) of mentally ill persons (Brennan et al., 2000; Hodgins et al., 1996; Rabkin, 1979; Sosowsky, 1980). But if the criminality thesis is correct – that is, if mentally ill persons are more dangerous as the stereotype holds – then they should be arrested predominantly for violent behavior that threatens or brings physical harm to others. However, most studies have found the distribution of offenses for mental patients to be similar to that of the general population: Most arrests are for misdemeanors rather than felonies, most are for less serious offenses rather than for the more serious FBI "index" crimes, only a minority of the offenses are violent, and few (either absolutely or proportionately) arrests are for the violent crimes that the public most fears: murder, rape, aggravated assault, and arson (Bloom, Williams, & Bigelow, 1992; Borum et al., 1997; Brekke et al., 2001; Desai, Lam, & Rosenheck, 2000; Engel & Silver, 2001; Feder, 1991; Green, 1997; Harry & Steadman, 1988; Hiday, 1991, 1992a; Holcomb & Ahr, 1988; Junginger, Claypoole, Laygo, & Crisanti, 2006; Schuerman & Kobrin, 1984; Swanimath, Mendonca, Vidal, & Chapman, 2002; Swanson et al., 2001; Teplin, 1994; Wolff et al., 1997). A Milwaukee study of persons arrested for deadly and dangerous crimes against others found no support for the stereotypical madman violently out of control (Steury & Choinski, 1995). A 1-year follow-up of severely mentally ill patients after their hospital discharge found that 20% had been arrested. Their most serious charges were for nuisance offenses (41%), substance-related offenses (32%), theft (14%), and assault (13%; Swanson et al., 2001). Two studies that examined arrests of public mental health center clients over much longer time periods (10 years and lifetime) reported comparable arrest rates to those in Swanson and colleagues (2001) and most other such studies (~20%), but higher proportions of those arrested in their samples had more serious charges – for felonies and violent offenses (Cuellar et al., 2007; Fisher, Roy-Bujnowski, et al., 2006).

Studies focusing on violent crime or homicide and major mental disorders have reported that severely mentally ill persons have higher arrest and incarceration rates for these crimes than persons in the general population (Eronen, Hakola, & Tiihonen, 1996; Hodgins et al., 1996; Link, Andrews, & Cullen, 1992; Mullen, Burgess, & Wallace, 2000; Schanda et al., 2004; Simpson, Skipworth, et al., 2006; Wallace et al., 2004). However, as Wessely and Castle (1998) pointed out, one should be cautious in interpreting these studies because of selection bias in cases of severely mentally ill persons. Even more important to remember is that the proportion of persons with mental illness, even severe mental illness, who offend violently is low, approximately 10% of men and 2% of women (Brennan, Grekin, & Vanman, 2000; Hiday, 2006; Link et al., 1992). Severely mentally ill persons are more likely to be victims of violent crime than to be perpetrators of such crime (Brekke et al., 2001; Choe, Teplin, & Abram, 2008; Teplin, McClelland, Abram, & Weiner, 2005).

To address the question of the criminality of mentally ill persons, we need to ascertain whether mental illness causes their violent crime or whether coincidental factors are causal. Robins (1993) reported that the association between crime and major mental illness in the ECA data completely disappeared when controls were placed for age, gender, ASPD symptoms, childhood conduct disorder symptoms (generally considered integral to the ASPD diagnosis), and substance abuse. She concluded that the association of major mental illness with crime is not direct, but occurs when severe mental illness is secondary to ASPD and substance abuse. In a large national sample, Swartz and Lurigio (2007) found the association of severe mental illness with arrest for most types of offenses to be explained by the mediating effect of substance abuse and the association of severe mental illness with violent offenses to be significantly reduced with a control for substance abuse. For Teplin's jail detainees (Teplin, Abram, & McClelland, 1994; Teplin, McClelland, & Abram, 1993), severe mental illness did not predict the probability of arrest or the number of arrests for violent crime over a 3-year or a 6-year postrelease period. Among a sample of defendants admitted to a maximum security forensic institution for competency assessment, four-fifths of whom had at least one violent offense, Rice and Harris (1995) reported that schizophrenia was negatively associated with violent recidivism over an 8-year mean risk period. Psychopathy and alcohol abuse were the factors that placed this sample of defendants at high risk for violent recidivism. In another study examining only defendants with schizophrenia, Rice and Harris (1992) found the predictors of both general and violent recidivism to be the same as those that predict recidivism for nondisordered offenders: prior offenses and aggressive behavior, age, alcohol abuse, and psychopathy. A later meta-analysis of recidivism studies that compared disordered to nondisordered offenders also failed to find severe mental illness or any clinical variables to be causal factors in crime and violence; rather, the significant predictors were age, gender, poverty, disorganized neighborhoods, substance abuse, and prior offense – the same factors that predicted recidivism among persons without mental illness (Bonta et al., 1998).

Incarceration Data

As we have seen, recent studies of random samples of jail and prison inmates reported higher prevalence rates of mental disorder and of major mental disorders than in the general population. Further analyses of samples from two of these studies have revealed that severely mentally disordered inmates tend to be substance abusers or have ASPD disorder or both (Abram, 1989, 1990; Abram & Teplin, 1991; Abram, Teplin, & McClelland, 2003; Coté & Hodgins, 1990). For instance, only 6% of jail detainees with severe mental illness in Teplin's (1990a) sample had neither substance abuse/dependence nor ASPD: 84.8% suffered from alcohol abuse/dependence and 57.9% from drug abuse/dependence, whereas 68.7% met criteria for a diagnosis of ASPD (Abram & Teplin, 1991). Furthermore, these detainees were likely to have been using drugs or alcohol at the time of their arrests (Abram & Teplin, 1991) – as was also reported for Danish male homicide offenders with a major psychosis, 89% of whom were intoxicated at the time of the homicide (Gottlieb, Gabrielsen, & Kramp, 1987). Abram (1990) found that, among those with major depression, ASPD was the primary syndrome in that it appeared in their lives before both substance abuse/dependence and depression. Studies of violent mentally ill offenders have reported that a history of antisocial traits preceded onset of their psychosis and that what distinguished offending from nonoffending mentally disordered persons was an antisocial history or psychopathy (Hafner & Boker, 1982; Rice & Harris, 1995; Tengstrom et al., 2004).

Unofficial Dangerous Behavior

The behaviors of both mentally disordered and nondisordered persons that violate criminal statutes do not always result in arrest. More violence occurs than is revealed in offense charges of arrest records. Many physical assaults and threats by both mentally ill persons and others, especially domestic violence, are not reported to or seen by police and thus cannot result in arrest (Cascardi, Mueser, DeGiralomo, & Murrin, 1996; Felson, Messner, & Hoskin, 1999; Hiday et al., 1998; Lagos, Perlmutter, & Suefinger, 1977). Moreover, as we have seen, much of that behavior that is reported does not result in arrest (Monahan & Steadman, 1982; Teplin, 1984b, 1985). Frequently, lawbreaking behavior by mentally ill persons, including violent behavior toward others, leads instead to mental hospitalization. Studies of legal and medical records have indicated that both voluntary and involuntary mental patients often are hospitalized because of dangerous behavior (Hiday & Markell, 1981; Hiday & Smith, 1987; McNiel & Binder, 1987; Taylor & Schanda, 2000).

Depending on the definition used, rates of violence toward others vary. Definitions restricted to physical assaults and threats of physical harm yield lower rates than definitions including loss of impulse control, hostile verbalizations, and thoughts of harming others (Hiday, 1988; Taylor & Schanda, 2000; Watts et al., 2003). By the more restrictive definition of physical assault and threat with a weapon, studies have reported between 10% and 40% of persons admitted to mental hospitals are violent in the community in the weeks immediately before hospitalization (Monahan, 1992). However, one must use caution in measuring violence mentioned in admission records because physicians and families may use allegations of dangerousness to obtain admission for a person they think is in need of hospital treatment, given that mental hospitalization tends to be limited to those who are dangerous to the self or others (Hiday, 1996; Hiday & Smith, 1987; La Fond & Durham, 1992). As a result, court hearings often find that allegations of violence in commitment petitions and medical records cannot be substantiated (Hiday & Markell, 1981; Warren, 1982).

Inside the hospital, most violence occurs during the first week after admission, especially on the first day (McNiel & Binder, 1987; Yesavage, Werner, Becker, & Mills, 1982). Patients who do behave violently in the hospital tend to do so only once (Werner et al., 1983). Minor violence is common; serious violence is rare

(Quinsey, 2000). Reports of hospital violence have ranged from 10% to 40% of patient samples (Bowers et al., 2005; McNiel & Binder, 1994; Monahan, 1992; Watts et al., 2003), but these rates are likely to be higher than community violence rates because of selection processes, close observation, and rules requiring violence to be recorded in patient charts and institutional reports (Hiday, 1988; Menzies et al., 1994). Still, much violence goes unrecorded in these settings (Lion, Snyder, & Merrill, 1981; Quinsey, 2000). On the other hand, medication, therapy, ward structure, removal from hostile environments in the community, and staff intervention before tense situations erupt are all likely to reduce the amount of violent behavior that would otherwise be expected.

Official legal and medical records indicate that approximately 20% of patients in the community threaten or assault others (Crocker et al., 2005; Hiday, 1990; Steadman & Morrissey, 1987). Although these records have many weaknesses, interviews with patients and their case managers in the public mental health sector have found comparable rates (Crocker et al., 2005; Dean et al., 2006; Swanson et al., 2006). One study of patients who visited an urban psychiatric emergency service found a much higher violence level: 44.3% engaged in a violent incident as defined by laying hands on another or threatening another with a weapon (Lidz, Mulvey, & Gardner, 1993; Newhill, Mulvey, & Lidz, 1995). Most incidents involved hitting and fighting; about one-fifth were minor incidents (involving shoving, slapping, etc.), and just over one-fourth were serious, including murder, attempted murder, assault with injury needing medical treatment, sexual assault, robbery, and use of (or threatening to use) a weapon (Newhill et al., 1995). As with other samples of psychiatric emergency patients, a substantial proportion had no severe mental disorder, and alcohol consumption increased the risk of violence (Lidz, Mulvey, Gardner, & Shaw, 1996; Newhill et al., 1995). The MacArthur study, using similar violence measures with recently hospitalized patients, reported 27.5% had at least one violent act within 1 year after release into the community (Monahan, Steadman, et al., 2001). Psychopathy along with substance abuse/dependence greatly increased the likelihood of violence. Because these last two studies were confined to patients who were recently seen in a psychiatric emergency service or hospitalized because of mental deterioration accompanied by crisis situations, their violence rates cannot be generalized to all mentally ill persons; in addition, because their samples included patients with substance use, personality, and other disorders who did not have severe mental illness, one cannot generalize to patients with major mental disorders. In fact, the MacArthur study found that persons with severe mental illness who had no substance abuse were no more likely to be violent than a matched community sample (Steadman et al., 1998).

Epidemiological studies, which avoid the aforementioned problems, have shown that most mentally ill persons are not violent, that only a small minority with severe mental illness commit any violent act in a year's time, but that their low rate is higher than what is found among those with no mental illness (Eronen et al., 1996;

Link et al., 1992; Link & Stueve, 1994, 1995; Link, Stueve, & Phelan, 1998; Swanson, 1994; Walsh, Buchanan, & Fahy, 2002; Wesseley & Castle, 1998). Although these findings held with controls for age, gender, and socioeconomic status, further analysis of these samples showed that substance abuse or dependence and active psychotic symptoms – especially those that produce feelings of personal threat or involve intrusion of thoughts that can override self-control – accounted for all or most violence differences with the nondisordered (Link & Stueve, 1994; Link et al., 1998; Swanson, 1994). But it must be emphasized that, although these findings are significant, only a small proportion of persons with severe mental illness and active psychotic symptoms become violent. Traits that are far more predictive of violence than severe mental illness include being single, a young adult, male, of low SES, and a substance abuser with psychopathic traits who has been victimized and lives in a disorganized neighborhood (Crocker et al., 2005; Hiday 1995, 2006; Hiday et al., 2001; Link et al., 1992, 1998; Monahan et al., 2001; Silver, Mulvey, & Monahan, 2001).

Mentally Ill Persons in the Criminal Justice System

We have seen that persons with mental illness are more likely to be arrested during encounters with police than are persons without mental disorders and that they are disproportionately convicted and incarcerated. Are they also differentially handled once they enter the criminal justice system?

Based on our society's moral values, legal advocacy system, and presumptions about voluntary behavior, the law provides for different processing when a defendant's mental status impairs his or her capacity to meet the assumptions underlying legal procedures. The law holds that, to be found guilty of a crime and punished for it, a person must be blameworthy – that is, able to choose rationally to commit the offense. In addition, to defend oneself against criminal charges, a person needs to understand the nature and purpose of the criminal proceedings and be able to assist counsel in his or her defense (American Bar Association, 1989). If the accused cannot understand and assist, then that person is incompetent to stand trial (IST; also called "unfit" and "incompetent to proceed"). When the accused is competent at the time of trial but mental illness interfered with his or her ability to make rational choices concerning the offense, then that person is not responsible or blameworthy and thus is legally insane or not guilty by reason of insanity (NGRI). Note that neither legal incompetence nor legal insanity is equivalent to mental illness. A person can be mentally ill, even with a severe psychosis, yet still meet the legal definitions of competence and sanity.

A minority of defendants who are referred for IST evaluations are found to be unfit, approximately 20% to 30%, but there is variation across jurisdictions (Crocker et al., 2005; Hubbard, Zapf, & Ronan, 2003; Melton, Petrila, Poythress, & Slobogin, 1997; Roesch & Golding, 1980; Roesch, Ogloff, & Eaves, 1995; Zapf & Roesch, 1998). The competent are returned for continued criminal processing;

those whom the court finds IST are committed for "fitness treatment"; that is, treatment to bring back competence. After an individual is discharged from IST commitment and restored to competence, the adjudication process resumes on the original charge(s). Many go on to plead NGRI successfully. In fact, 40% to 60% of insanity acquittees are hospitalized and treated as IST prior to NGRI adjudication (Golding, Eaves, & Kowaz, 1989).

Unlike competency proceedings, the insanity defense has generated a degree of controversy that is greatly out of line with the frequency of its use and NGRI judgments. The public tends to dislike the insanity defense because of the perception that NGRI is a common loophole in the law whereby guilty persons who commit murders avoid punishment for their heinous crimes (Callahan, Mayer, & Steadman, 1987; Hans, 1986; Morse, 1985; Pasewark & Pantle, 1979; Pasewark & Seidenzahl, 1979; Steadman, & Cocozza, 1978; Steadman et al., 1993). Even attorneys and judges tend to share these opinions (Burton & Steadman, 1978). However, studies of various states from the 1970s and 1980s reported that the insanity defense was seldom used (pled in less than 1% of all felony cases, on average, across states) and seldom successful – receiving an NGRI verdict in only a fraction of that 1% of cases (Pasewark & Pantle, 1979; Sales & Hafemeister, 1984; Silver, Cirincione, & Steadman, 1994). Many more defendants are held in forensic psychiatric facilities to be evaluated for competency and to be restored to competency after being found IST (Marques, Haynes, & Nelson, 1993; Wack, 1993). Furthermore, the criminal charges that NGRI defendants face cover the full range from nuisance to serious. Although there is variation across jurisdictions, from 20% to 30% of defendants face only lesser charges and 10% to 40% face murder; but the majority of cases judged NGRI involve violent offenses (Crocker et al., 2005; Draine, Salzer, Culhane, & Hadley, 2002; Golding et al., 1989; Hubbard et al., 2003; Silver et al., 1994; Steadman et al., 1993). That there is only a minority of defendants with lesser, nonviolent charges is likely owing to defense attorneys' reluctance to plead NGRI for their clients because of the predictable longer time of incarceration faced by those making this plea (see later discussion).

Some states have enacted a guilty but mentally ill (GBMI) verdict in response to public concern over NGRI leniency, especially after John Hinckley's successful insanity plea for the attempted assassination of President Reagan. Intended to protect society by reducing NGRI verdicts and providing lengthy prison terms instead of brief hospitalization (Callahan et al., 1992; Ogloff, 1991; Steadman et al., 1993), the GBMI verdict holds mentally disordered persons responsible when their mental illness did not make them incapable of rationally choosing to commit the offense. Empirical studies have found GBMI legislation to have little impact on NGRI acquittals because the GBMI verdict has been given primarily to those who previously would have been found guilty (Callahan et al., 1992; Keilitz, 1987). A study in one state, however, did find that the GBMI plea decreased the rate of both guilty and NGRI verdicts out of all insanity pleas (Callahan et al., 1992). The intended effect of more societal protection has been found consistently in that GBMI verdicts lead to more incarceration, longer sentences, and longer imprisonment than guilty or NGRI verdicts for the same offenses (Callahan et al., 1992; Keilitz, 1987; Steadman et al., 1993).

By law, defendants found GBMI are guilty and must be punished despite their mental disorders. Although some state statutes call for evaluation and treatment of their mental illness, in practice no special treatment is given beyond that provided to all inmates under the constitutional right to necessary medical care, which includes psychiatric and psychological services (Callahan et al., 1992; Dvoskin & Steadman, 1989). But because of our moral values and legal philosophy, statutory law provides that those found IST and NGRI are to be treated without punishment. Whereas IST defendants are treated for the purpose of being returned to fitness to stand trial, NGRI acquittees are treated as long as they are mentally ill and dangerous. In both cases, treatment may be for periods that extend beyond what defendants found guilty of the same offenses would serve in prison (Golding et al., 1989).

The public's concern about "coddling" criminals and the subsequent release of NGRI offenders into the community seems to be unwarranted. The overwhelming majority of NGRI acquittees suffer severe mental disorders (Sales & Hafemeister, 1984) and are ordered to treatment in mental hospitals (84.7%) for substantial time periods, with only a small proportion being released outright (1.1%) or ordered to treatment in the community (14.2%; Silver et al., 1994). A multistate study found that courts are more likely to release convicted felons after a verdict than they are to release NGRI acquittees (Silver, 1995). Although results are mixed across jurisdictions and time as to whether NGRI acquittees serve longer confinements than comparable offenders (Sales & Hafemeister, 1984; Silver, 1995), unsuccessful NGRI defendants have been found to have longer detention times than convicted felons who did not raise the insanity defense (Braff, Thomas, & Steadman, 1983). Among NGRI acquittees, those charged with more serious crimes serve longer periods of confinement in the hospital (Golding et al., 1989; Silver, 1995; Silver et al., 1994). In fact, offense seriousness has been found to be the most important predictor of length of confinement – more important than mental disorder or response to treatment (Golding et al., 1989; Pasewark et al., 1982; Silver, 1995).

Although the public and the law give much attention to incompetent defendants and those who raise the insanity defense, only a small proportion of offenders with major mental illness are evaluated for IST and an even smaller proportion raise the insanity defense. Most mentally ill offenders go undetected during pretrial and adjudication stages and proceed through conviction to imprisonment (Freeman & Roesch, 1989; Marques et al., 1993; Teplin, 1990b; Wack, 1993). These legally "fit and sane" mentally ill detainees and prison inmates constitute a minority who serve longer incarceration times than nonmentally ill offenders, require significant management attention by correctional authorities, and need mental health services (Dvoskin & Steadman, 1989; Kropp, Cox, Roesch, & Eaves, 1989; Teplin, 1990b).

They are more likely to be held in custody awaiting trial because of denial of bail, and this "dead time" commonly exceeds the length of sentence ordered for the substantive offense (Freeman & Roesch, 1989). Once imprisoned, they are more likely to be denied parole and to serve a greater proportion of their maximum sentences, in large part because parole boards find few community programs willing to service and supervise offenders with mental illness (Feder, 1994; Hartwell, 2004; Laberge & Morin, 1995; Porporino & Motiuk, 1995). Community agencies frequently refuse to take mental patients with criminal records into their programs, causing mentally ill offenders to be detained longer (once imprisoned) than nondisordered offenders (Borum et al., 1998; Feder, 1994; Lamb & Weinberger, 2005; Porporino & Motiuk, 1995; Skeem, Louden, Polascek, & Camp, 2007; Watson et al., 2008).

Diversion

Some mentally ill suspects are never arrested or incarcerated, or they are held only a short time before being diverted out of the legal system. Commonly, diversion is ad hoc and passive rather than programmatic; that is, court officers merely drop charges and dismiss a case when they learn that the mental health system is treating the defendant's mental illness (Broner et al., 2004; Grudzinskas et al., 2005; Hiday, 1991; McFarland et al., 1989; Steadman et al., 1989). This was true in the past as well: During the 1960s when minor cases increasingly clogged courts and popular rehabilitative and therapeutic philosophies encouraged diversion, courts began to establish pretrial diversion programs to turn minor offenders into law-abiding citizens by linking them with treatment and social services, reducing psychiatric symptoms and substance abuse, and improving their functioning and quality of life (Broner et al., 2004; Grudzinskas et al., 2005; Kittrie, 1971; LaFond & Durham, 1992; Roesch et al., 1995; Steadman & Naples, 2005). Diversion programs have also been used to prevent disruption in the antitherapeutic, crowded, noisy cell blocks of jails (Kropp et al., 1989; Steadman et al., 1989, 1995).

Prebooking diversion programs rely on forensically trained mental health staff to accompany police on emergency calls or on police officers themselves being trained to recognize mental illness, understand its symptoms, manage symptomatic persons, and judge whether diversion is appropriate or arrest is needed. Prebooking programs involve transportation to a treatment facility with a cooperative agreement for both evaluation and treatment of cases that the police deliver (Broner et al., 2004). Most valued by police are those facilities with a 24/7, no-refusal policy (Deane et al., 1999; Hartford et al., 2006). The best-known model of prebooking programs, the Crisis Intervention Team (CIT), which uses a team of police officers who volunteer and are trained to work with mentally ill offenders, has reported success in reducing unnecessary arrests and the use of force and in increasing referrals to psychiatric care (Dupont & Cochran, 2000; Skeem & Bibeau, 2008; Steadman et al., 2000).

Postbooking diversion programs have these components: initial screening of all detainees, evaluation of possible cases by mental health professionals, negotiation with court officers and community mental health providers to agree on treatment and services instead of prosecution or as a condition of a reduction in charges, and referral to the treatment or service itself for residential placement, outpatient treatment, and case management (Steadman et al., 1995). Some programs are based in the jail, and evaluation, negotiation, and placement are done by mental health practitioners working in the jail (Draine & Solomon, 1999). Others are based in either a traditional criminal court or a special mental health court where mental health practitioners are employees of the court and court officers are involved in placement decisions and often in monitoring after placement (Broner et al., 2004). Unfortunately, diversion programs often have no specific follow-up procedure once initial placements are made, and many of those diverted receive no or inadequate treatment and services (Broner et al., 2004; Christy et al., 2005).

Mental health courts, a relatively new type of special jurisdiction court, have specific follow-up procedures with regularly scheduled court hearings on a separate docket to monitor offenders' compliance with court orders for treatment and behavior change. Mentally ill offenders volunteer to participate and follow the court's mandates in return for charges being dismissed in preadjudication cases or, in postadjudication cases, for ending probation or dropping sentences. A mental health court team, consisting of designated prosecution and defense attorneys, probation and parole workers, case managers, mental health and substance abuse providers, and one or more liaisons led by a designated judge, monitors clients in regular team meetings and in open court. Court hearings are notable for being nonadversarial and having the judge speak with each defendant individually to give encouragement and praise, offer a reward, issue a reprimand or warning, or apply sanctions according to the defendant's compliance with court mandates. Recognizing the high risks among these defendants, team members anticipate failure, offer multiple second chances, and stand ready to help them try again. Positive early anecdotal reports of mental health courts' effectiveness have been followed by quantitative research evaluations of single courts, most of which have supported the earlier claims of increased treatment and services, improved compliance with treatment, and reduced arrests and incarceration for new offenses (Boothroyd, Poythress, McGaha, & Petrila, 2003; Christy et al., 2005; Cosden et al., 2003, 2005; Herinckx et al., 2005; Hiday et al., 2005; Hiday & Ray, 2008; McNiel & Binder, 2007; Moore & Hiday, 2006; Ridgely et al., 2007).

Community Tenure and Management

For mentally ill inmates imprisoned or committed to a forensic psychiatric facility, mental health treatment may be a condition of probation or parole on release (Skeem et al., 2007). But mental health services seldom exist for severely disordered persons with antisocial and substance-abusing behaviors, and too often mental health practitioners do not want to engage such persons with criminal records (Borum et al., 1998; Draine & Solomon, 1992; Freeman & Roesch, 1989; Hartwell, 2004, 2005; Lamb & Weinberger, 1998, 2005; Lovell, Gagliardi, & Peterson, 2002; Skeem et al., 2007). Lack of services for mentally ill offenders in the community and their disadvantaged and unstable living situations – along with their comorbidities – lead to a strong likelihood of rearrest and reincarceration, ranging from 24% to 56% (Bieber, Richard, Bosten, & Steadman, 1988; Corrado et al., 1989; Draine et al., 1994; Hartwell, 2004; Solomon, Draine, & Marcus, 2002). However, they are neither more criminal nor more violent than released nondisordered offenders (Bonta et al., 1998; Feder, 1991; Gagliardi, Lovell, Peterson, & Jemelka, 2004; Teplin et al., 1993, 1994). Severely mentally ill persons are also likely to be rehospitalized in psychiatric institutions after criminal justice release, and many have repetitive cycles of institutionalization in both hospitals and prisons (Hartwell, 2003; McMain et al., 1989; McNiel et al., 2005; Menzies et al., 1994).

To break the cycles of institutionalization and to protect society from both feared and actual crime and violence, communities have tried various mandated and nonmandated treatment programs (Grudzinskas et al., 2005; Hartwell, 2005; Simpson, Jones, et al., 2006; Walsh et al., 2001). One such program, forensic assertive community treatment (FACT), is a modified version of assertive community treatment (ACT) that has successfully aided community adjustment of seriously mentally ill patients in multiple areas of functioning but has had little success in reducing arrest rates (Mueser, Bond, Drake, & Resnick, 1998). FACT, like ACT, uses multidisciplinary teams of mental health practitioners to work intensively with individual clients in obtaining services, resources, and social support such as medication, therapy, housing, and financial assistance (Mueser et al., 1998; Stein & Test, 1985). Most treatment and services occur out of the office on the streets and is available after normal work hours, when these clients are likely to get in trouble. FACT modifies ACT for this population by reaching into the prison or forensic unit to assess, plan, and establish a therapeutic relationship with the inmate before discharge, employing careful monitoring and legal leverage, using probation and parole officers as treatment allies or even team members, and continuing case management into the criminal justice system when a client is jailed (Lamberti, Weisman, & Faden, 2004; McCoy et al., 2004; Morrissey, Meyer, & Cuddeback, 2007). Two studies of FACT programs offered preliminary support, showing reduced arrests, jail days, and hospitalization (Lamberti et al., 2004, McCoy et al., 2004); other evaluations have not found these positive outcomes, but they are marked by lack of fidelity to all the components of the FACT model (Morrissey et al., 2007).

Though not developed specifically for mentally ill offenders, supported housing programs designed for homeless severely mentally ill persons have shown the ability to reduce criminal recidivism. These programs tend to follow one of two models: linear residential treatment and the Housing First model. The former model offers case management and intensive treatment along with housing, but requires participation in treatment and sobriety to remain in the program and progress from group to independent housing (Gonzales & Rosenheck, 2002; Skeem, Markos, Tiemann, & Manchak, 2006; Tsemberis & Eisenberg, 2000). The second program, Housing First, offers clients permanent independent apartments with no psychiatric treatment or sobriety requirement. Though an ACT team offers treatment and services, clients are only required to meet with staff twice a month and to participate in a money management plan (Tsemberis & Eisenberg, 2000; Tsemberis, Gulcur, & Nakae, 2004). Empirical research has indicated that both models can increase housing stability, although some studies reported that Housing First got clients housed earlier and longer, with linear residential treatment having high dropout rates (Gulcur et al., 2003; Skeem et al., 2006; Tsemberis & Eisenberg, 2000; Tsemberis et al., 2004). In addition to providing housing, some studies reported that these programs produced mental health and substance abuse improvements and reduced incarceration, hospitalization, victimization, and violence (Culhane, Metraux, & Hadley, 2002; Gonzales & Rosenheck, 2002; Greenwood et al., 2005; Gulcur et al., 2003; Skeem et al., 2006).

Summary

There is no doubt that the criminal justice system deals with large numbers of mentally ill persons on the street and that it processes and holds large numbers of them in its correctional and forensic facilities. But whether there has been a criminalization of mentally ill persons since deinstitutionalization became public policy in the United States cannot be answered definitively because necessary longitudinal data do not exist. Studies in Australia (Mullen et al., 2000; Wallace et al., 2004) and England (P. J. Taylor & Gunn, 1999) with pre- to post-deinstitutionalization data showed no proportional increase in rates of convictions or number of homicides, respectively, of persons with severe mental illness. However, both of those countries provided stronger supportive nets of mental health treatment and services than communities in the United States provided to their deinstitutionalized patients.

The answer to the second question of whether mentally ill persons are dangerous and likely to commit crimes – that is, whether mental illness causes criminality – is both yes and no. There are infrequent cases in which psychosis propels violent acts, which leads to processing in the criminal justice system (McNiel et al., 2000), but in the usual case of mentally ill offenders, other factors in their lives are causal in their violent and nonviolent behaviors that lead to arrest and incarceration (Draine et al., 2002; Fisher, Silver, & Wolff, 2006; Hiday, 2006; Silver, 2006). Hiday and Wales (2009) suggest a categorization of mentally ill offenders according to which such factors are the immediate causes of their offending. We offer it here rather than Hiday's earlier three-group categorization (1999).

Most persons with severe mental illness who come into contact with the criminal justice system for violating laws fall into one of four groups. Members of the first two groups, the largest ones, commit only misdemeanor offenses. Of these, one group consists of mentally ill offenders arrested for nuisance behaviors (e.g., disturbing the peace or loitering) that would not lead to the arrest of nondisordered persons. With nowhere to go and nothing to do, they hang out in malls, fast food stops, parks, and strips of streets with storefronts. The second group consists of mentally ill persons arrested for survival behaviors such as shoplifting and failure to pay for restaurant meals. This group violates the law and becomes criminal not because mental illness forces them to do so but rather because both their social background and mental illness leave them poor, marginal, often homeless, and without the necessary care and services they need to survive in the community without getting into trouble. For these two groups, which overlap, the American Bar Association (1989) recommends mental health diversion, not arrest. Although these two groups would have been hospitalized for much of their adult lives and not at risk for criminal offending and arrest prior to deinstitutionalization, it is failure to provide basic sustaining services and mental health treatment that would reduce their symptoms, improve their functioning, meet their survival needs, and provide somewhere to go and something to do that causes their arrest.

Members of the third group with severe mental illness who come into contact with the criminal justice system abuse or are addicted to alcohol and/or illegal drugs. As with the first two groups, they have few resources and are extremely needy of food, clothing, shelter, direction, and protection. Many of them become homeless. In addition to survival and nuisance crimes, they are arrested for disruptive behavior connected with alcohol and drug intoxication, using illegal substances, prostitution and various forms of stealing to support their habit, and assault involved with procuring drugs and drug money. Some persons in this group fall between the cracks of mental health and substance abuse systems, but others are frequent and demanding users of multiple community agencies such as hospitals, "detox" facilities, emergency shelters, welfare agencies, and community mental health centers along with jails; however, they seldom receive sustained treatment and services sufficient to make a change in their mental, addictive, social, and economic conditions.

The fourth group consists of persons with severe mental illness who are psychopathic or have a diagnosis of ASPD, as do a large proportion of nonmentally ill offenders, and have high rates of substance abuse. They are aggressive, often threatening or intimidating, and likely to have a history of violent acts. Their abusive and uncooperative behavior deprives them of service benefits. They have high rates of criminal offenses, arrests, and incarceration, which are often for violent behavior. Their criminal and violent behavior seems to be driven by their character disorders and not by mental illness.

Finally, there is the much smaller group consisting of severely mentally ill persons who fit the stereotypical image of the madman out of control. Delusions and hallucinations drive them to criminally violent behaviors. This very small group is the one that receives the most news and fictional attention in the media.

Although severely mentally ill offenders in all five groups need mental health medication and psychosocial services, these five groups are different – both from each other and from the large population of mentally ill persons who are not arrested and incarcerated. It is thus incorrect and misleading to generalize from the behavior of any one of these groups to the others. It is also incorrect and misleading to generalize from the behavior of any one of these groups to all persons with major mental illness because they are not representative of that nonoffending population. If we are to reduce their offending, the different causes of offending in each group need to be addressed.

At the same time most members of all five of these groups have harmful social environments in common. They tend to inhabit impoverished communities that have substantially deteriorated in the past quarter-century, making it more difficult for them to survive outside of institutions. Many individuals in these groups come from broken families and disorganized communities that are unable to give desperately needed support and care. In addition, the high prevalence of drugs, alcohol, crime, and violence in their environment entraps these very vulnerable persons in greater pathology. Mental health and social welfare systems with severely inadequate resources try to ameliorate the effects of such deleterious social conditions. The criminal justice system is left to pick up the pieces when these other systems fail.

25

Mental Health Care in Organizations and Systems

Michael Polgar

Social scientists have developed theories and research to describe organizations within systems of mental health care. To learn about the social dynamics that involve mental health care providers, researchers aggregate and study sets of organizations, interorganizational systems, and populations of organizations within changing environments. Macro-social studies apply institutional and population ecology theories to describe groups of organizations evolving over time. Research on systems of mental health care for young adults illustrates the structures and relationships that develop through networks of interorganizational connections. How do the organization and the system influence the care that individuals receive?

Introduction

Mental health problems are understood and explained through biological, psychological, and sociocultural frameworks (Kendler, 2008). They may be conceptualized as personal troubles affecting only individual lives; however, they are also public health concerns that are related to public issues and social systems (Mills, 1959). Research shows that mental disorders have both social antecedents and social consequences (Aneshensel & Phelan, 1999). The need for and use of mental health care across demographic groups are the subject of extensive and ongoing empirical research in psychiatric epidemiology, including clinical and community-based studies in the United States (Kessler, 1994). The mental health care system is used by a variety of individuals experiencing illness trajectories and illness careers, and these individuals are affected by the cultural contexts of both health and health care (Pescosolido, 2006).

Mental health care helps individuals and communities respond to mental health problems. The organization and distribution of mental health care vary across contexts and social structures, within dynamic systems of organizations and institutions (Scheid & Greenberg, 2007). Mental health care is provided by professionals in both public and private sector organizations, led by physicians who are increasingly integrated with hospitals and health care systems (Rundall, Shortell, & Alexander, 2004).

Social scientists have developed extensive theories and research to describe the social context of both mental health and mental health care. Sociology has a long tradition of studying contextual factors that affect the development and care of mental health problems, including social stress and stigma (Pescosolido, McLeod, & Avison, 2007). Social epidemiology describes the distribution of disorders and treatments throughout communities and populations, searching for explanations for correlations between poverty and mental disorder through theories of social causation and social selection (Link & Phelan, 2000). Critical studies examine the social history of mental health care, including some limits to a singularly medical model of mental illness (Horwitz, 2002).

This chapter takes a macro-social view to summarize scholarship that describes organizations and systems of mental health care. At an individual level of measurement and analysis, research aggregates individuals into populations to describe both epidemiology and use of care. At an organizational level, research on mental health care aggregates sets, populations, fields, and systems of organizations within changing environments (Scott & Davis, 2007). Sets and networks of mental health providers and organizations are linked into systems of care, which operate within organizational populations and fields (Evan, 1993; Morrissey, Calloway, Bartko, Ridgely, Goldman, & Paulson, 1994). Organizations work together in systems and also may change in response to institutional environments (Scott, 2003).

Macro-social theories and research analyzing relationships among groups of health providers have shown that health care organizations, including mental health providers, are increasingly structured into social systems and interorganizational networks (Morrissey, 1999). These networks are structured by interorganizational linkages of varying strength. Evaluating the social integration of health care networks is one way to study how systems grow and change.

For example, Morrissey, Calloway, and colleagues (1994) studied cities involved in the Robert Wood Johnson Foundation's program to improve care for people with chronic mental illness. Informed by organizational theories, researchers conducted a survey of organizational representatives to evaluate systemic outcomes of community health programs, including the degree to which interorganizational relationships became more coordinated and centralized under local mental health authorities. This organizational survey examined the extent and strength of social affiliations among mental health care providers. These affiliations were measured as structural linkages through client referrals, information exchanges, and funding relationships among organizations in a system of care. Over time, the research identified complex changes in systems of care, including an inverse relationship between the density of organizations in an urban system and the centralization of local mental health care authority.

With the growth of managed care, the organization and provision of care have been increasingly related to markets (Scott, Ruef, Mendel, & Caronna, 2000), thereby reducing the autonomy of the medical profession (Light, 2004). Studies have shown new forms of medical demand generated by direct marketing to consumers (Conrad & Leiter, 2004), as public and private health care organizations evolve in a changing institutional environment (Scott, 2003).

Earlier chapters in this handbook describe research on mental health and psychiatric disorder as social trends in individual attributes that vary over time. For example, the etiology and social epidemiology of psychiatric disorder help explain social factors in the causation and distribution of individual mental disorders, elaborating social causation and selection theories (Link & Phelan, 2000). Likewise, the stress process model describes how social roles and situations increase strain on individuals and groups of individuals (Aneshensel, 1999; Pearlin, 1998). The remainder of this chapter summarizes research on social groups at a wider level of abstraction, showing how mental health care is provided by organizations working and evolving together within systems of care.

Individuals, Organizations, and Systems

To describe the organization of care for mental health problems, research in social science has created theories, measures, and research methods at three levels of abstraction and analysis:

1. Mental health and disorder among individuals
2. Mental health care provided within organizations
3. Sets and systems of organizations providing care within institutional environments

We can conceive of each of these three levels as nested or layered theoretical perspectives, in the same way as individual behaviors exist in nested organizational contexts (Scott & Davis, 2007) and individual qualities more generally are set in context by social structure and personality frameworks (House, 1981a). Understanding mental health care at all of these three levels requires developing and evaluating theories and methods at higher levels of measurement and analysis, a level of abstraction above and beyond individual health status, individual behavior, and individual use of health care. Therefore, to understand mental health care organizations and systems, we must understand theories of organizations operating within organizational fields and institutional environments (Scott & Davis, 2007).

Different theories and empirical methods are useful when working at each level of abstraction. When developing theories and research on the structure and process of mental health care, scholars create theories and measures using larger units of measurement and analysis, like organizations and systems. Researchers develop key concepts and questions at each analytic level, tied together by theories that integrate these concepts. Even so, it is an ongoing and difficult challenge to integrate both research and data from individual, organizational, and systemic levels. New theories focusing on social processes over the life course attempt to span all three levels (Pescosolido, 2006; Stiffman, Pescosolido, & Cabassa, 2004). Theories of institutional change integrate concepts across even wider levels of abstraction (Scott et al., 2000).

Mental health services research encompasses a variety of studies at the organizational and systemic levels, which analyze the effectiveness of organizations and system of care in communities and measure variations in needs, uses, qualities, and outcomes of mental health care (Bickman, 1999). At a national level, mental health services research examines the availability, quality, use, cost, structure, and effectiveness of mental health services, programs, organizations, and systems (National Institute of Mental Health [NIMH], 1991).

Mental health care problems vary by level. For example, many individual clients need affordable, compassionate, and effective care, which may include case management, but services are complex and often fragmented. Organizations need to offer high-quality care in diverse communities, but have trouble providing continuous and comprehensive care. Health care networks create systems and develop local health authorities, but some organizations and systems may still lack incentives to be cost efficient (Morrissey, 1999).

Mental Health Care Organizations

Mental health services research on organizations has been informed and inspired by institutional theory (Scott, 2003; Scott & Davis, 2007) and by population-ecology theory (Aldrich, 1987). Each of these macro-theoretical perspectives embeds the practice of mental health care within groups and networks of organizations. These perspectives examine the structural forms of mental health care organizations within populations, social networks, and environments, allowing readers to understand the ways that the organization of mental health care is related to larger social contexts.

Institutional theory examines the influence of institutional environments on the structure, function, and adaptation of organizations within organizational fields (Scott, 2001). Within this theory, analyses are grouped into three levels: social-psychological studies of individual relations, organizational studies of structures and processes, and ecological studies of interdependent organizations within institutional environments (Scott & Davis, 2007). Institutional theories have been applied to explain schools as open and loosely coupled systems and later were expanded to understand corporations and health care settings. Institutional theories also became influential in the expansion and evaluation of total quality management in organizations (Scott, 2001).

Institutional theory has helped promote the study of many types of social networks, including both personal networks within organizations and systems of relationships among organizations (Scott & Davis, 2007). In social network studies, organizations and systems are portrayed graphically and are subject to analyses. Organizations are studied as nodes in a network, tied together by relationships into social structures. These structures are known as interorganizational networks. Empirically, links among organizations in networks can be the subject of study and analysis. Researchers can construct a matrix of structural links among

organizations, measuring and evaluating relationships according to different qualities, including distance, centrality, clustering, equivalence, density, and centralization (Scott & Davis, 2007). Network matrix analyses help researchers understand
the roles and relationships among organizations and clusters of organizations in
networks (Wasserman & Faust, 1994), adding a new dimension to our understanding of social structure and improving on traditional social research methods that
use regression analyses of organizational attributes.

Interorganizational and interpersonal networks both involve exchanges and the
sharing of resources, thereby creating interdependence (Scott & Davis, 2007).
Interorganizational networks promote exchanges in market economies, developing social structures in market sectors. Interlocking networks promote information
exchange more than control. There are many classification systems for interorganizational networks and business alliances, which can be used to explain entire
industries and sectors of an economy.

Population-ecology theory is a parallel macro-sociological approach to organizations, developed to understand the structural forces shaping organizations and
populations of organizations over time (Aldrich, 1987). Research using population ecology studies the creation, diffusion, and adaptation of organizational
populations and organizational forms within evolving populations of competing
organizations (Hannan & Freeman, 1998). According to population ecology, organizational forms evolve because of selection processes that operate on multiple
organizations of a similar type. This perspective adapts evolutionary theories,
using biological metaphors and concepts to describe how organizational populations increase and organizational forms evolve, with organizations and forms
being founded, adapting to particular environmental niches, and sometimes dying
off, causing some to become extinct.

This theoretical tradition explains how organizational survival, growth, and evolution take place over many years and in relationship to larger ecologies, sometimes
described as organizational niches. Changes in organizations and populations do
not happen simply as a result of the behavior of individual organizations, any more
than biological evolution takes place based simply on animal or species behavior. This perspective shows how organizations adapt to changing environments,
including local niches for organizations and broader environments like economic
markets.

Population ecology shows how changes in the ecology of organizational populations help diverse sets of organizations and forms to emerge, compete, and die off
(Hannan & Freeman, 1998). Some organizations may specialize within an environmental niche (e.g., providing primarily substance abuse counseling services or
mental health care), whereas others diversify (e.g., expanding a range of mental
health offerings within health care networks). Organizations and organizational
forms compete for legitimacy and resources. Adaptive organizations generally
work with others, create alliances, and span boundaries, becoming interdependent
in systems or networks, like biological organisms in ecological systems. Thus,

organizations and leaders learn the importance of coordination, above and beyond competition, particularly as they are part of larger systems and networks (Alter & Hage, 1993).

From an ecological perspective, mental health care systems are interconnected groups of organizations that work within institutions and environments. They offer help and mental health care to a variety of groups and populations. Initiatives to improve community mental health include both the diffusion of innovative treatments and the expansion of mental health care systems (Morrissey, Calloway, et al., 1994).

At the ecological level, organizational fields and social sectors facilitate the diffusion of institutional effects (DiMaggio & Powell, 1983). Organizations that provide mental health care help diffuse professional practices through a range of occupational groups, including psychiatrists, psychologists, social workers, and a wide variety of family and personal counselors. These professionals help clients, as they compete for business and coordinate care under medical, administrative, and governmental authorities, providing treatments and services for diverse populations experiencing a variety of health problems and conditions.

Mental health care may be one of many services provided by an organization, but it is an organizational attribute of primary interest to mental health services research. To develop research and test hypotheses derived from theories about organizations providing mental health care, researchers identify a list or set of organizations in a specific geographic area and often sample and study these demographic populations of organizations (Carroll & Hannan, 2000). The results both provide evidence to test theories about organizations and also inform us about larger social forms – interorganizational networks of health care providers – often described as systems of care.

Some organizations specialize in mental health care services and thus work within a particular sector of the organizational environment. Specialty mental health organizations often work together with larger social service systems, as is the case with organizations designed to provide care and counseling for children and youth (Stiffman et al., 2001). Other organizations, such as hospitals and schools, provide mental health care along with other types of health care or social services. Many primary or general health care providers also offer medication for mental health disorders, although they are not specialized mental health care providers. Because mental health care services are widely distributed over a range of public and private service providers, creating clear and logical boundaries around organizational sets is complicated but crucial for empirical research (Evan, 1993; Van De Ven & Ferry, 1980).

Mental Health Care Systems and Networks

The mental health care service system comprises both providers and consumers. Although there are both informal and formal providers, the majority are formal providers who work with or within organizations to provide institutional, out-patient, and home-based care. Informal care, provided through nonmedical professions, self-help groups, and families and friends, is a popular and major resource for many people, including people with mental health or substance abuse disorders.

Like medical care systems more generally, mental health provider systems and networks include extensive sets of organizations and medical professionals. These organizations work within institutional environments and organizational fields to provide mental health care, both competing and cooperating, thereby creating expansive systems through exchanges of resources and according to agreements (Alter & Hage, 1993).

In the formal sector, two major distinctions define categories of care. First, institutional or inpatient care is usually distinguished from outpatient care. Over time, there has been a decrease in the use of institutional and inpatient care and corresponding increases in the use of outpatient care (Manderscheid, Henderson, Witkin, & Atay, 1999). This shift is related to historical movements toward community-based mental health care, driven by pressures for deinstitutionalization and aided by improvements in pharmacology. Formal services for mental illness and for substance abuse are usually differentiated, though they are sometimes combined in services for those people with a dual diagnosis.

Second, specialty mental health services are distinguished from mental health services delivered by primary health providers. Over time, there has been an increase in the use of primary providers for mental health care (Miranda, Hohmann, Attkisson, & Larson, 1994; Olfson et al., 1997; Olfson, Weissman, Leon, & Higgins, 1995). By design, diagnosis, severity of illness, and consumer choice affect the use of most types of care (Jacobson, 1998). Services for mental illness and for substance abuse are often provided under the same insurance provisions (e.g., behavioral health care) and sometimes combined into services for those people with a dual diagnosis. As described earlier, informal care is also a major resource for people with mental health or substance abuse disorders, particularly for those with limited resources (Chadiha, Adams, Biegel, Auslander, & Gutierrez, 2004).

Like medical care generally, mental health care is provided by organizations that work within formal and informal social networks. These networks are structurally complex and change over time. Networks are composed of dyads, triads, and larger organizational combinations, which integrate mental health providers into social systems (Calloway et al., 1998; Morrissey, 1999). Networks and systems are connected by many types of social exchange; these exchanges are empirical ties, links, or bonds that create interorganizational social structures. These social structures evolve as systems of care grow and change to help different and broader populations, such as children and youth with mental health problems (Glisson & Hemmelgarn, 1998; Morrissey, Johnsen, & Calloway, 1997).

In research on systems of care, health service systems can be modeled as social networks by creating arrays and matrices of interorganizational relationships

(IORs). The systemic and structural forms created by IORs may be measured using social network analysis (Astley & Van De Ven, 1983; Wasserman & Faust, 1994). These analyses of organizational sets and systems empirically identify structural forms and change, measuring centrality, density, and other network characteristics based on the number and strength of IORs. They can help evaluate the integration and coordination of complex networks, which is one goal of some large-scale health and welfare demonstration projects (Morrissey, 1999).

In many organizational and institutional fields, organizations compete for resources within limited institutional environments. However, in some systems of care, institutional networks are linked because organizations and systems work together toward common goals. For example, systems of mental health care for youth are linked to systems of care for the larger population, requiring social services that work with young people to form interorganizational connections to larger mental health systems (Davis & Vander Stoep, 1997). These connections promote continuity of care and a successful transition from youth to adult mental health systems, as described in the next section.

Transitions from Youth to Adult Mental Health Systems

Both population-ecology and institutional theories explain how organizations evolve and form systematic relationships to provide mental health care within networks and systems. In one example, organizations providing mental health care to young people have grown and changed over time to close the historic gap between health care and social service systems for youths and those for adults (Clark & Davis, 2000). Interorganizational systems and relationships are helpful to teens and young adults who are experiencing difficulties or difficult transitions during stressful turning points early in the life course (Gore & Aseltine, 2003; Gore, Aseltine, & Schilling, 2007). Strong and connected mental health care networks are especially important because young adults experience the onset of mental disorder at rates higher than other age groups (Kessler, 1994).

Growing numbers of organizations and networks serve the mental health care needs of children and youth, thanks in part to developments in medical insurance and assistance through Medicaid (Howell & Teich, 2008). Professionals, organizations, and systems help parents seek mental health care for youth in need (Shanley, Reid, & Evans, 2008). However, these systems of care are sometimes constrained because insurance coverage for dependent children comes to an end for young adults, threatening continuity of care at a crucial time period (Clark & Davis, 2000). In response, organizations and systems may create linkages and span boundaries (Morrissey et al., 2005), creating new structural forms and more extensive systems of care designed to keep vulnerable young people in treatment (Farmer, Burns, Phillips, Angold, & Costello, 2003).

Young adulthood is a dynamic stage in the life course of American life. Patterns in transitions to young adulthood are an important new area of study for family demography (Furstenburg, Kennedy, McLoyd, Rumbaut, & Settersten, 2004; Settersten, Furstenburg, & Rumbaut, 2005). The transition to young adulthood affects many aspects of life, including the allocation of time for work, education, and parenting (Gauthier & Furstenburg, 2002). This transition is particularly stressful and complex for people who experience mental health problems, requiring links and referrals between historically distinct systems of care for children and adults (Clark & Davis, 2000). Policy leaders have championed a mental health care system that provides smooth transitions to adult service systems as youth with mental health problems reach maturity (Stroul et al., 1996). Continuity of care can help improve client outcomes, although research findings on this topic have been mixed (Lehman et al., 1994).

For young people, continuity of care allows predictable and welcome interactions with mental health providers (Vander Stoep, Davis, & Collins, 2000). Accessible pathways to care improve when organizations are informed, diverse, and interconnected (Stiffman et al., 2000, 2004).

Mental health care organizations promote continuity of mental health care by providing specific services, including case management, transition planning, and referrals (Ware, Tugenberg, Dickey, & McHorney, 1999). Organizations can collaborate and facilitate transitions among them when they have wider and stronger relationships within interorganizational networks (Morrissey et al., 1997). Interorganizational relationships can create structural links between mental health care providers that reduce or prevent interruptions in care. In the specialty mental health sector, organizations and systems that have denser and stronger connections may exhibit greater continuity and quality of care (Polgar & Cabassa, 2007).

Studying how mental health systems provide ongoing care to youth and young adults can be done through surveys of organizations within systems of care. These surveys can test predictions of institutional or population-ecology theories, and they can also evaluate specific policies or social interventions. As described earlier, surveys of organizational systems use large units of measurement (agencies or organizations, instead of individuals) to study larger and more complex units of analysis (organizations, networks, and systems). The study of networks and systems requires that researchers collect a lot of data on structural links among organizations, as well as on attributes of organizations.

Testing theories about organizations and systems raises methodological challenges for both researchers and consumers of research. First, we must define and limit our organizational population and environment, listing organizations in a social system, and then we must look within each organization to find organizational representatives (known as key informants) who are willing and able to speak for and about organizations, based on their comprehensive knowledge of organizational behavior (Van De Ven & Ferry, 1980). Second, we must conceptualize and operationalize theories of social systems to identify the nature and range of structural relationships (linkages between organizations) that we should measure. For example, indicators of social cohesion and integration can be based on exchanges of information, resources, and referrals (Morrissey et al., 1994). Third, collecting and analyzing matrices of network data require both extensive and largely complete information from many different organizations, raising the methodological bar even higher. We can then build complex surveys of organizations in a system of mental health care to analyze both attributes of organizations and relational data among systems of care.

Using established research methods to study interorganizational systems of mental health care (Morrissey et al., 1994, 1997), we created a regional survey of organizations for young adults. This survey had three sections, reflecting three complementary approaches to the study of mental health care systems (Polgar & Cabassa, 2007). The first section collected organizational attributes, providing indicators of the range of groups providing services for people with mental health care needs. The second section collected data on interorganizational relationships, the structured ties among organizations. This data provided information about each provider's structural position within a network, enhancing our ability to compare each one's ability to promote continuity of care. A third section of the survey collected data about the availability, accessibility, and quality of care provided by the system as a whole. This data allowed us to evaluate and compare the strengths and weaknesses of the system from the perspective of providers.

Studying data on organizational attributes, such as the size, age, budget, and services offered by an organization, helps one evaluate theories about the role of organizations within a system of care. For example, institutional theory may predict that larger and older organizations are more likely to endure and succeed in competitive environments. This theory can be tested by analysis of organizational attributes in a system of care.

Collecting data on organizational behavior and interorganizational linkages is also helpful in applying theories generated by institutional or population-ecology perspectives. For example, when organizations provide services that promote continuity of care, like case management and transition planning, then there are greater opportunities for young people to continue receiving care from the system when they age out of youth-specific services. When organizations promote and practice principles of cultural competence, they often can help youth make a transition to new settings and work successfully with a wide array of other organizations. Therefore we can analyze data on organizations and their practices to test the predictions of institutional and ecological theories in the context of mental health care.

This example illustrates the salience of both institutional theory and population ecology, which predict changes in organizational relationships and behavior based on changing organizational environments. Organizations and systems must evolve over time to help young adults continue to get necessary mental health care. Organizations and systems must grow and change to span boundaries within the broader environments that provide health care and social services. Although individual organizations and specific providers may specialize in particular areas, the larger ecology, including systems of care, provides an impetus for growth of organizational populations and networks. Growing mental health care systems for youth expand to blend with complex systems of care for adults.

Conclusion

Mental health care organizations work within evolving systems of care. Institutional theory and population ecology provide theoretical frameworks for understanding changes in sets and populations of mental health care organizations. Understanding organizations and their structural networks requires research at multiple and wider levels of abstraction, using larger and more complex units of measurement and analysis. Social scientists can provide ongoing research that describes an evolving structure of mental health care. We can study social dynamics both within and among organizations that operate in changing institutional environments. Understanding the broader context of mental health care helps explain how systems adapt to serve groups of people who experience difficulties, including young adults in need of mental health care.

26

Integrating Service Delivery Systems for Persons with a Severe Mental Illness

Gary S. Cuddeback and Joseph P. Morrissey

Obtaining care for severe mental illness has been a challenge because each service area has its own special purpose and funding mechanisms, whereas those with severe mental illnesses need a broad array of services. Hence there has been much effort to produce service integration. Cuddeback and Morrissey review the experiences of service integration and consider four major innovations: community mental health centers; the Community Support Program and its spin-off, the Child and Adolescent Service System Program; the Program on Chronic Mental Illness; and efforts to introduce managed mental health care. Recent demonstration programs to integrate services have been subjected to comprehensive outcome evaluations. The research from two of these demonstrations produced similar findings; there was strong evidence for service system change and improvement, but little consistent evidence for improved client-level outcomes. The authors include a discussion of the evidence-based practice movement. The chapter concludes by describing opportunities for further research. Without a national policy for health and welfare programs, it is difficult to see how the various needs of those with severe mental illness will be met. List the agencies in your own communities that provide services to those with severe mental illnesses and ask providers about gaps in such services as well as issues of coordination.

Introduction

Over the past 50 years, the U.S. mental health system has shifted from a centralized, institutional model based largely on state mental hospitals to a decentralized, community-based system involving several thousand public and private providers (Grob, 1991). In this process of deinstitutionalization (Mechanic & Rochefort, 1992; Morrissey, 1982) many thousands of long-stay patients who had a severe and persistent mental illness (SPMI) were transferred to nursing homes or released directly to community settings. In addition, the growth of psychiatric services in community mental health centers attracted many more thousands of formerly unserved patients. As a result, the mental health services system expanded enormously and moved from a predominantly inpatient to a predominantly outpatient array of services (Goldman & Taube, 1989). These changes have benefited persons with acute care needs and those with milder conditions, but in a number of respects, they have disadvantaged persons with SPMI. Members of the latter group often present a multiplicity of needs, not only for medical-psychiatric treatment but also for social rehabilitation,income maintenance, housing, health care, employment, social supports, and substance abuse counseling (Rosenblatt & Atkisson, 1993). Obtaining appropriate care to meet these needs in community settings has been a challenge because the human service system in the United States is organized largely on a categorical or single problem basis. Each categorical program area or service sector has its own special purpose, its specific sources of financing, its particular eligibility requirements, its own geographical service area, and its individual mode of operation. Moreover, persons with SPMI often have cognitive and functional impairments that reduce their motivation to seek care or comply with treatment plans once contact is established.

The disjuncture between the needs of persons with SPMI and the contours of the community care system have led to a variety of efforts to decategorize the various service sectors and to integrate or bundle the services in a more accessible and effective way. The quest for improved service arrangements has been advanced under the banner of "services integration" (SI). SI is a broad-based movement that has sought to develop linkages among sectors at the service delivery and administrative levels that enhance the effectiveness, efficiency, and economy of human service programs for persons at risk such as the poor, the disabled, persons with mental illness, dependent children, and delinquents (Kusserow, 1991).

This chapter reviews the experiences with SI in the broader U.S. health and welfare arena as a context for considering its applications in the mental health field over the past few decades. It then considers four major innovations as examples of SI in the mental health field – community mental health centers (CMHCs); the Community Support Program (CSP) and its spin-off, the Child and Adolescent Service System Program (CASSP); the Program on Chronic Mental Illness (PCMI) cosponsored by the Robert Wood Johnson Foundation (RWJF) and the U.S. Department of Housing and Urban Development; and the introduction of managed mental health care. The chapter then considers the effectiveness of SI with a focus on evaluation findings from the RWJF, PCMI (Goldman, Morrissey, & Ridgely, 1994) and the Ft. Bragg children's mental health demonstration (Bickman et al., 1995). In addition, the ACCESS Demonstration for persons who are homeless and severely mentally ill (Randolph, 1995) is discussed as the most comprehensive effort yet undertaken to demonstrate the client-level effects of service system integration in the mental health field. These reviews lead to a brief discussion of the emergence of the evidence-based practice (EBP) movement and the interface between SI and EBP.

Services Integration: Setting the Context

Although the roots of SI as a health and welfare policy can be traced to the charity organization societies in the late 1800s and early 1900s (Kagan, 1993), the real impetus came from the New Frontier and Great Society programs spawned by the Kennedy-Johnson administrations during the 1960s. Initiatives were undertaken on juvenile delinquency, Neighborhood Service Centers, Community Action, community mental health centers, Model Cities, Head Start, Older Americans Act, and the War on Poverty, to name just a few. Between 1962 and 1966 the number of federal categorical grant programs increased from 160 to 349, and by 1971 there were 500 (Banfield, 1971). These projects focused on substance (target group needs) over structure (coordination within and between programs). Their funding was appropriated on a categorical basis that was restricted and restrictive with tight eligibility, accountability, and personnel requirements (Kagan, 1993).

By the early 1970s, services coordination had become a watchword within the Department of Health, Education, and Welfare (DHEW). In speeches, Secretary Richardson often lamented that these programs were suffering from a "hardening of the categories" (Kusserow, 1991). He initiated a number of reforms that would foster the integration of services across categorical program areas, including research and demonstration projects, proposed legislation, technical assistance efforts, and internal departmental reforms. His successors continued these efforts throughout the 1970s and 1980s. Most of these projects promoted linkages, coordination, and comprehensiveness in the context of federal categorical legislation. The 1970s saw a shift in strategy from redesigning the system with the aid of the federal government to "capacity building" at the level of local government (Morris & Hirsch-Lescohier, 1978). At the state level, strategies included the development of comprehensive human resource departments, "umbrella agencies," or interdepartmental planning councils; information and referral systems; community-based care; case management; and other forms of service coordination mechanisms. Service Integration Targets of Opportunity (SITO) projects focused on interagency program linkages, core services, and case coordination. Partnership Projects targeted the management of service systems at the state/local levels, program planning, and design.

Despite the DHEW's demonstration projects and capacity-building efforts, progress in services integration was slow throughout the 1970s and 1980s due, in part, to the lack of documentation of examples of successful SI or of the efficacy of state-level administrative reorganizations. Baumheier (1982), for example, described how in much of the public administration literature of the 1970s no established causal links were made between interorganizational and intraorganizational coordination, even with well-controlled structures of authority. So the question remained largely unanswered whether changes in formal structures would enhance coordination among organizational units. Overall, services integration projects of the 1970s and 1980s showed little impact (Kusserow, 1991). Therefore, attention began to shift dramatically from broad national initiatives to narrower initiatives focused at the level of the provider and the client; this shift was sustained into the 1990s. Service needs emphasized case management strategies and networking among agencies and providers within a community (Kagan, 1993; Kahn & Kammerman, 1992).

Past SI efforts have been criticized for lacking accountability, evaluation, and measurable outcomes. Evaluations that did take place only identified implementation problems and failures to be avoided in future efforts. Baumheier (1982) offered four reasons for the failure of integration efforts: (1) target grant programs were inadequately funded; (2) coordination was aimed at existing service techniques and approaches that had been proven to be inadequate; (3) the root barriers to coordination were not susceptible to managerial solutions – revised national policy was needed rather than administrative coordination; and (4) the true sources of the coordination problem were the fragmentation and pluralism of American policies, opinions, and interests.

SI's failure leads to the question of why interest in services integration has persisted. Warren (1973) answered this question by identifying the latent functions of services coordination that sustain interest in integration given its limited success. He used the example of the Model Cities project to describe the ways in which the project succeeded not in improving the conditions of the inner city, but in reinforcing the reliance on policies of comprehensive planning and coordination. The various projects he studied met with varying levels of success and were burdened by local political shifts, economic conditions, and unemployment. However, the critics of these projects were largely ignored while proponents offered statements about unrealistic expectations and suggestions for subsequent integration projects. Consequently, Warren identified a number of latent functions as the factors that sustain interest in coordination. In his view, the coordination strategy serves to strengthen existing local agencies, reduce competition, provide money for agency expansion, define poverty in terms of needed services, secure roles for agencies in channeling efforts, produce an aura of change without threatening the status quo, and provide a stimulus for additional funds and employment. Finally, he noted that the habit of simply writing about how to improve subsequent SI efforts avoids the question of how outcomes can be measured.

Similarly, Morris and Hirsh-Lescohier (1978, p. 22) stated as follows:

> Integration and coordination are often turned to because the real problems of social organization and social distress are too difficult to deal with frontally or directly. Inequity, inequality, serious deprivation, and disability are impossible to overcome without serious expenditure of resources.... [Integration is a] less painful way to make the existing welfare system function more efficiently by presumably stretching its resources further.

These authors opted for identifying specific defects in the service system that integration or coordination might likely improve, rather than working to reconstruct the entire human services system.

Table 26.1. *Profile of service integration strategies for persons with a severe mental illness*

Level of integration	Mechanisms	Problem to be solved
Client	Case management	Fragmented and uncoordinated office-based services
Organization	Community mental health centers	Lack of comprehensive services and of continuity of care
System	Local mental health authorities	Lack of organization and accountability at system level
	Managed care	Lack of incentives for cost-efficient performance

Mental Health Services Integration Strategies

The experience with services integration in the welfare field underscores that it is a multilevel process that can be focused at system, organization, or client interventions (Agranoff, 1991; Kagan, 1993; Kahn & Kammerman, 1992). Table 26.1 presents a profile of the major SI mechanisms that have been pursued in the public mental health system for persons with SPMI. This configuration is based on discussions by Mechanic (1991) and by Hoge and colleagues (1994). Each strategy emerged as a response to a specific set of problems, and in many respects each in isolation is only a partial solution for SI problems facing SPMI persons.

At the system level two main interventions have been attempted – creating mental health authorities and, more recently, implementing managed care. Both strategies focus on the organization and financing of services. A mental health authority was the central focus in the Robert Wood Johnson Foundation Program on Chronic Mental Illness (see later discussion). The assumption was that the lack of accountability and organization within the mental health system made it difficult to meet the needs of SPMI persons so that a single entity had to be created to assume systemwide responsibility for the clinical, fiscal, and administrative aspects of care.

Managed mental health care is a way of financing services that shifts risk from the payer to the provider of services, limits the choice of provider, and manages utilization through use of a gatekeeper, periodic reviews, and authorizations. The main problem that it addresses is the lack of incentives for cost-efficient performance in the traditional fee-for-service or indemnity insurance reimbursements (Frank & Morlock, 1997).

At the organizational level, the principal mental health innovation of the past 25 years has been the community mental health centers program (Schulberg & Killilea, 1982). Here the goal was to create a new community-based treatment program that would supplant the state mental hospitals. The underlying problems that the centers address are the lack of comprehensive and coordinated services and the discontinuity of care.

At the client level, two interventions have been carried out within an SI framework – case management and assertive community treatment. Both focus on the needs of individual clients and avoid efforts to reorganize the structure or financing of services. Case management is an effort to increase the accessibility of services and entitlements provided by a complex and diverse network of provider agencies. Assertive community treatment attempts to integrate major responsibilities for patient care within a single, multidisciplinary, and largely self-contained team. It represents a response to the fragmented and uncoordinated care and largely office-based practices of most community mental health programs.

Mechanic (1991) has argued that systems that employ mutually reinforcing combinations of these strategies provide a more viable framework for achieving true SI and overcoming some of these barriers that have undermined or constrained individual strategies when used in isolation. Such a framework would provide incentives and foster favorable professional behavior for integrated service delivery. The next section highlights the evolution of these strategies as a basis for considering current research evidence on their effectiveness.

The Evolution of Mental Health Services Integration

The issue of services integration, especially the linkage between state mental hospitals and community programs, was an active concern throughout the 1950s. This concern intensified between the years 1960–1995, a period of rapid and tumultuous change in mental health care. This section focuses on the applications of SI to mental health in four programmatic efforts – community mental health centers, the Community Support Program, mental health authorities, and managed mental health care.

Community Mental Health Centers (CMHCs)

The most ambitious effort to deliberately integrate the delivery of mental health services on a national scale was the CMHC program initiated by the National Institute of Mental Health (NIMH) in the mid-1960s (Schulberg & Killilea, 1982). The goal was to develop closer-to-home or community-based services (vs. the often distant state mental hospitals) that were comprehensive (e.g., providing emergency, inpatient, outpatient, and partial hospitalization services), had catchmented responsibilities (serving population areas of 125,000 to 250,000 persons), and were organized under one administrative umbrella (either as a freestanding center or a consortium of providers with affiliation agreements) to promote early treatment, continuity of care, and a preventive orientation. Citizen boards and consultation-education services to schools and other community agencies were also key features.

Such centers would seem to be ideally suited to meet the multiple needs of persons with SPMI. Ironically, however, at the outset, the CMHC system was never fully intended nor utilized for such persons. For much of their early history, CMHCs concentrated largely on heretofore unserved populations and those persons with acute, episodic, or less severe conditions (Chu & Trotter, 1974; Windle & Scully, 1974). Indeed, despite the clustering of services and their delivery often in "single-stop" locations, most CMHC patients were one-service (predominantly outpatient) users (Morrissey & Lindsey, 1987). Gradually, with the growing concerns about deinstitutionalization beginning in the 1970s, the CMHCs began to serve SPMI persons. This trend was accelerated in 1981 when the Omnibus Budget Reconciliation Act (P.L. 97–35) repealed the major provisions of the Mental Health Systems Act, thereby eliminating authorization for using federal funds specifically earmarked for community-based services for persons with a SPMI. Federal funding for substance abuse and mental health programs was consolidated into a block grant and allocated to the states, which resulted in reduced funding levels (Tessler & Goldman, 1982). Roughly at the same time, Medicaid funds were capped, which also reduced the availability of federal funds for mental health services to the poor (Morrissey & Goldman, 1984; Sharfstein, 1982). With the transfer of operational responsibility for the CMHCs from NIMH to state governments, the centers became much more dependent on state funding (Tessler & Goldman, 1982). As states began to give priority to SPMI persons, CMHCs were induced to increase their services to this population to secure state funding. Today, CMHCs are among the primary (outpatient) service providers for SPMI persons.

With the growing prevalence of the homeless mentally ill across the country and with widespread concern about the adequacy of funding for public mental health services, however, CMHCs in many large cities were often seen as impediments to, rather than vehicles for, alleviating these problems (Shore & Cohen, 1990). It was thought that catchmenting (assigning specific geographic districts to each center) and the decline in federal funding of CMHCs led to a fragmentation of services for those SPMI persons with stable housing (i.e., there was not enough of a critical mass of chronic patients in any one catchment area to warrant the development of multiple, specialized services) while encouraging the denial of responsibility for problems seen as "out of area" or citywide in scope such as those presented by persons who are mentally ill, homeless, and on the streets. For example, homeless mentally ill persons often congregated in center city areas, thereby overburdening the assigned CMHC, whereas other contiguous CMHCs might have fewer homeless persons to serve.

Community Support Program

Beginning in the early 1970s and intensifying throughout the decade, the concept of deinstitutionalization was severely criticized because of the emergence of new patterns of exclusion, neglect, and abuse among persons with SPMI. The General Accounting Office issued a report in November 1977 that called for immediate efforts to address the needs of the thousands of state mental hospital patients who had been deinstitutionalized into local communities without adequate provision for their overall care (Morrissey, Goldman, & Klerman, 1985). In 1978 the President's Commission on Mental Health issued a similar call for action.

In response to this criticism NIMH created the Community Support Program (CSP). It was designed "to improve services for one particularly vulnerable population – adult psychiatric patients whose disabilities are severe and persistent but for whom long-term skilled or semi-skilled nursing care is inappropriate" (J. Turner & TenHoor, 1978, p. 319). Initially, $3.5 million was allocated annually for contracts with 19 states for 3-year pilot demonstration programs designed to provide psychosocial rehabilitation services, medical and mental health care, case management for the chronically mentally ill, supportive living and working arrangements, and crisis care services (Tessler & Goldman, 1982). In addition, state-level planning and policy development activities were supported by NIMH in an effort to induce legislative changes and new sources of funding for local programs.

In a sense, CSP may be viewed as a fourth cycle of reform in that it advocated a whole system of care and treatment approach for the mentally ill (Goldman & Morrissey, 1985; Morrissey & Goldman, 1984). Unlike earlier reform efforts, (asylums, psychopathic hospitals, and CMHCs), CSP offered direct care and rehabilitation for the chronically mentally ill rather than a focus on preventing chronicity by the early treatment of acute cases. An additional difference was the importance of developing a system of support services for persons with SPMI among the currently existing community agencies. Advocates of CSP recognized that, first and foremost, SPMI is a social welfare problem. And as such, they did not recommend mental health solutions to social problems; rather, they proposed social welfare solutions to mental health problems (Goldman & Morrissey, 1985). They proposed a "community support system" that included health and mental health services while also wrapping around the critical entitlement programs that assist with income supports, transportation, and housing.

Despite the repeal of the Mental Health Systems Act in 1980, CSP continued to receive an annual appropriation (approximately $6 million in the early 1980s), and though limited, the block grants also contained provisions for continued financial support of community-based mental health services. In the early 1980s the program was expanded to younger age groups with the Child and Adolescent Service System Program (CASSP), which followed a similar advocacy, planning, and local service development strategy. The central concept was a system or continuum of care providing individualized mental health services in the least restrictive setting in the community, involving families and close collaboration among child-serving agencies, particularly schools, social services, youth services, the courts, and health care providers (Behar, 1988; Knitzer, 1982; Looney, 1988; Stroul & Friedman, 1986). In 1989, CASSP was a key stimulant for the RWJF Mental Health Services Program for Youth, a 5-year, $20.4 million initiative designed to demonstrate that mental health and community support services for young people with serious mental illness could be organized, financed, and delivered more effectively (Beachler, 1990).

Local Mental Health Authorities

The next, and in many respects, the most well-conceived effort to create a truly comprehensive system of care for persons with SPMI was launched by the Robert Wood Johnson Foundation (RWJF) on a pilot demonstration basis (Aiken, Somers & Shore, 1986; Shore & Cohen, 1990). The Program on Chronic Mental Illness (PCMI) was a unique public–private partnership between RWJF and the U.S. Department of Housing and Urban Development (HUD). Nine cities from among the nation's largest were selected on a competitive basis in 1986 to receive support in the form of grants, low-interest loans, and federal rent subsidies (Section 8s) to develop more effective systems of care and housing for the chronically mentally ill. The demonstration was funded for a 5-year period from January 1987 through December 1992.

The mandate to the demonstration sites had several components: create local mental health authorities to take clinical, fiscal, and administrative responsibility for services to persons with SPMI; develop mechanisms to promote continuity of care; create independent and supported housing for the target population; develop flexible and expanded funding arrangements; and promote psychosocial supports for persons with SPMI. The form and function of these authorities varied widely among the nine cities (Goldman, Morrissey, & Ridgely, 1990).

Local mental health authorities (LMHAs), in large part because of the publicity surrounding the PCMI, were touted as the systems development model for the 1990s. As a result, the MHA concept has come under a lot of scrutiny, and not all of the commentary to date has been favorable. Rosenberger (1990) criticized LMHAs as politically flawed because, similar to the CMHCs, they are an organizational solution imposed on communities from above rather than a negotiated agreement between agencies and government units whereby they give up voluntarily some of their authority and power so that systemwide needs can be accomplished. Dill and Rochefort (1989) made a related point in arguing that the most serious obstacle for services integration and consolidation of funding streams under a local mental health authority is "geopolitical" – the operation of federal, state, county, and municipal public and private providers under many separate local jurisdictions. Rarely have the prerequisites been present for such integration to occur. These include not only a special will and energy for system transformation on the part of service workers, recipients, and citizens but also mechanisms to organize and channel these sentiments. As a result, Dill and Rochefort believed that the promise of local or substate mental health authorities still exceeded their performance.

Greenley (1992) questioned the viability of LMHAs because their design failed to address a number of organization and management issues. Reflecting on the experience with local mental health authorities in Wisconsin (Stein & Ganser, 1983), he pointed out that services were highly variable across the state even though county-level LMHAs had control and responsibility for service delivery. In his view, LMHAs would not succeed unless managers and others in these systems went beyond administrative structures to "pay attention to issues of setting goals, monitoring care, giving feedback, and promoting desirable interorganizational cultures" (Greenley, 1992, p. 382).

Managed Care

The concept of health care reform was in no way a new idea introduced by the Clinton administration. Virtually every political platform since the Great Depression in the 1930s has grappled with health care costs. Yet, if Clinton's tenure is remembered for no other reason, he and Hilary Rodham Clinton should be credited with bringing the issue of health care reform to the forefront of public consciousness in America during 1992 to 1994. Armed with the knowledge that escalating health costs had a stranglehold on the national economy, Clinton's health care reform plan took aim at both providing universal coverage and reducing cost through capitation.

"Managed care" equates to cost containment and is a catchall term coined to encompass a broad range of financing arrangements, organizational forms, and regulatory mechanisms that affect patient care (Mechanic, Schlesinger, & McAlpine, 1995). In 1989, the Institute of Medicine defined managed care as "a set of techniques used by or on behalf of purchasers of health care benefits to manage health care costs by influencing patient care decision making through case-by-case assessment of the appropriateness of care prior to its provision" (Institute of Medicine, 1989; see also Frank & Morlock, 1997; Wells, Astrachan, Tischler, & Unutzer, 1995). More generally, the term is now used to define programs that control access to care, the types of care delivered, and the amount or costs of care. Managed care has developed within the private health care sector over the past 20 years through health maintenance organizations (Paley, 1993) and other prepaid arrangements; in the late 1980s and early 1990s there was growth in mental health and substance abuse benefits being specified and managed separately from general health benefits in employer-sponsored insurance (Hoy, Curtis, & Rice, 1991). In these "carve-out" situations a managed care organization is often used to provide mental health care and manage costs.

Medicaid-managed behavioral health care for persons with SPMI has been the focus of ongoing research and evaluation over the past decade or longer. For example, in a five-site study that compared traditional Medicaid fee-for-service to managed care arrangements for persons with severe mental illness, no differences were found in measures of quality of services, consumer satisfaction, and symptoms (Leff et al., 2005). However, consumers under managed care arrangements were less likely to receive inpatient services and received more primary health services compared to their peers under fee-for-service arrangements (Leff et al., 2005). Other studies about the effects of Medicaid managed care have produced mixed results. For example, Ray and colleagues (2003) found that a transition from a fee-for-service model to a fully capitated Medicaid managed care carve-out program resulted in decreased use of antipsychotic medications for persons with severe mental illness and a disruption in the continuity of care (Ray, Daugherty, & Meader, 2003). Conversely, Bianconi and colleagues (2006) found no deterioration in outcomes among persons with severe mental illness who were transitioned from fee-for-service arrangements to managed behavioral health care. The relationship between managed behavioral health care and incarceration for persons with SPMI has also been explored in a handful of studies with mixed results (Domino, Norton, Morrissey, & Thakur, 2004; Fisher, Dickey, Normand, Packer, Grudzinskas, & Azeni, 2002; Norton, Yoon, Domino, & Morrissey, 2006).

Medicaid is now the largest payer of mental health services (Frank, Goldman, & Hogan, 2003), and states will continue to wrestle with how to adequately fund mental health services with Medicaid while putting a cap on increasing Medicaid budgets. Ongoing evaluations of financing arrangements under the broad umbrella of managed care will need to continue to ensure that the needs of consumers with severe mental illness are met in ways that are efficient and cost effective.

Effectiveness of Mental Health Services Integration

Unlike earlier efforts in human services integration, recent demonstration programs seeking to integrate services for persons with SPMI have been subjected to comprehensive outcome evaluations sponsored by both government agencies and private foundations. Media reports throughout the late 1970s and 1980s about the failures of deinstitutionalization contributed to the interest in services for persons with SPMI, as did the increasing visibility of homeless mentally ill persons living on the streets of urban America (Goldman & Morrissey, 1985). The rise of mental health advocacy and consumerism also contributed to the critique of mental health policies and to public demands for reform. In response to criticisms of its role in encouraging deinstitutionalization, NIMH began in the early 1980s to shift its goals and research programs toward persons with SPMI. Increased NIMH grant funding in these areas spawned the growth of a mental health services research community that attracted many young social and behavioral scientists and clinicians to study ways in which services can be improved for persons with SPMI. Findings from three of these demonstrations – the PCMI for adults sponsored by the Robert Wood Johnson Foundation, the Ft. Bragg demonstration for children and youth sponsored by the U.S. Department of the Army, and the ACCESS program sponsored by the Substance Abuse and Mental Health Services Administration – highlight evidence about the effectiveness of SI strategies.

Program on Chronic Mental Illness

The PCMI systems evaluation focused on the extent of change in the performance of the local mental health authorities and on the development of community support systems for nine demonstration cities (Goldman, Lehman, et al., 1990). Parallel measures of local mental health authority and community support system performance were obtained from two data sources (key informant and interorganizational network surveys) conducted at each site at two times during the demonstration (1989 and 1991). Findings indicated that the local mental health authorities were successfully implemented in coordination with the CSPs at most demonstration sites, but changes in the community support systems lagged behind authority performance levels (Morrissey, Ridgely, et al., 1994).

The outcome study was fielded at two points in time in four of the nine demonstration cities (Lehman et al., 1994). Two cohorts of clients were followed for a 12-month period, one cohort beginning in late 1988 and extending through late 1989 and the other beginning in late 1990 and extending through late 1991. Clients entered the study cohorts just prior to discharge from local inpatient or crisis residence units, on the assumption that such clients were most likely to be exposed to the sites' services (e.g., case management, housing, entitlements, rehabilitation). Data were collected on each client's personal and treatment history, current level of psychosocial functioning, housing, continuity of care, and quality of life. The core hypothesis tested was that Cohort 2 would outperform Cohort 1 on all outcome measures because the system of care would be better developed later in the demonstration. The improvement in services at the system/provider level was expected to translate into improvements in services at the client level, leading in turn to better client outcomes.

Contrary to expectations, the results showed that there was no detectable improvement in outcomes between the two cohorts across multiple domains in any of the cities (Lehman et al., 1994). Positive results were found for case management in three of the four cities where a significantly higher proportion of clients in Cohort 2 received this service during the 2-month period after hospitalization. In addition, a greater proportion of Cohort 1 changed case managers (a measure of discontinuity of care) compared with Cohort 2 during the 1 year period in two of the cities (there was a clear trend in this direction for all four sites). Both of these findings supported the hypothesis that improvements at the system level are associated with improvements in the services available to clients. However, for all five client outcome measures, the only significant difference between cohorts was on symptomatology at 12 months, and it was in the opposite direction than that predicted: Cohort 2 had more symptoms than Cohort 1. Similar findings of no out-come effects were also reported for a companion study of the PCMI demonstration in Denver (Shern et al., 1994).

Ft. Bragg Demonstration

Would a continuum of services for children and youth lead to improved treatment outcomes and lower costs per client in comparison to usual care? This was the central question addressed in the Ft. Bragg Child and Adolescent Mental Health Demonstration that was sponsored by the U.S. Department of the Army from 1989 to 1995 (Bickman et al., 1995). A private mental health agency implemented the $80 million demonstration project for an eligible pool of 42,000 military dependents residing in south central North Carolina. Families seeking services for their children were required to use the demonstration's clinical services, which were free, or seek and pay for services on their own. The contract agency either provided services directly (outpatient) or contracted with local providers (for both outpatient care and acute hospitalization) to form a continuum of community-based nonresidential and residential services. The continuum offered intake and assessment, outpatient therapy, day treatment, acute inpatient hospitalization, in-home therapy, afterschool group treatment, therapeutic homes, case management and interdisciplinary treatment teams (for cases requiring more intensive care), and 24-hour crisis services.

The evaluation consisted of a 3-year assessment of program implementation, quality, mental health outcomes, and cost/utilization components (Bickman et al., 1995). The "usual care" comparison group consisted of children receiving tra-ditional CHAMPUS (health insurance for military dependents) services at two other comparable army posts. Families were interviewed at intake and 6 and 12 months later. Findings indicated that the demonstration successfully implemented a coordinated, individualized, community-based, and family-focused system of care. Quality of care results showed that the demonstration had greater continuity of care and fewer dropouts, used less restrictive settings, provided more individu-alized care, and delivered services quicker than the comparison sites. Furthermore, most of the children at each site improved on a battery of clinical outcomes over the 12-month follow-up period, although few were free of mental health problems at year's end (e.g., 80% of the children had at least one diagnosis at the 12-month interview). However, and this is the key finding vis-à-vis the central question addressed, no consistent clinical outcome differences were found to favor the demonstration site (Ft. Bragg) over the comparison sites, and the costs per treated child were greater at the demonstration site ($7,777) than at the comparison sites ($4,904). Finally, and not surprisingly given the free and virtually unlimited needs-based care, parents and adolescents at the demonstration site did show a higher level of satisfaction with services.

The Ft. Bragg demonstration was replicated in Stark County, Ohio (see Bickman, Noser, & Summerfelt, 1999), and the replication study featured a stronger research design than what was implemented in the original Ft. Bragg demonstration. Specifically, study participants were randomly assigned to experimental and control conditions within the same treatment environment and participated in five waves of data collection. The results of this replication study, however, were no different from those of the original Ft. Bragg demonstration in that the effects of SI were limited to system-level outcomes, and SI did not appear to affect individual clinical outcomes.

Access to Community Care and Effective Services and Supports (ACCESS)

In May 1990, the Federal Interagency Council on the Homeless convened the Federal Task Force on Homelessness and Severe Mental Illness to develop a plan of action to end homelessness among people who are severely mentally ill (Center for Mental Health Services [CMHS], 1995). On the task force were representatives from all major federal departments whose policies and programs directly affected the homeless population with severe mental illness, including the Departments of Health and Human Services, Housing and Urban Development, Labor, Education, Veterans Affairs, and Agriculture. The task force also sought advice from experts in mental health research and housing administration, citizen advocates, mental health consumers, and state and local officials. Recognizing that there was no single, simple solution to the problems of homelessness among this population across the nation, the task force recommended the development of new incentives to promote integrated systems of care that offered access to essential services and to affordable and safe housing. To advance this agenda, the Access to Community Care and Effective Services and Supports (ACCESS) initiative was proposed (Randolph et al., 1997).

Applications were solicited from the states, and ultimately, nine were selected for participation in a 5-year demonstration sponsored by the Center for Mental Health Services (CMHS) involving grants totaling about $45 million (Randolph, 1995). Two communities in each state were identified as demonstration sites to participate in a quasi-experimental program design. Both sites received funding to recruit and enroll 100 homeless mentally ill persons each year and to engage them into comprehensive services. One site selected at random (integration site) received additional funding to develop SI strategies, whereas the other (enhancement site) did not receive such funds. In this way, the ACCESS program was designed to assess what gains in quality of life and psychosocial functioning are obtained by systems integration over and above what can be accomplished by an array of comprehensive services alone. Many of the sites implemented assertive community treatment teams as part of the services plan.

The ACCESS evaluation was carried out by a consortium of private and public organizations under contract with CMHS (Randolph et al., 1997). The component parts included an implementation study, a systems integration study (Morrissey, Calloway, Johnsen, & Ullman, 1997), and a client outcome study (Rosenheck & Lam, 1997). Because it was a formative evaluation, feedback was provided to demonstration sites on a regular basis, and the CMHS gave technical assistance to each site to ensure full implementation. The implementation study involved periodic site visits and semi-annual reporting on progress from the sites. The client outcome study involved baseline, 2-month, and 12-month follow-up interviews with enrolled clients covering a wide array of clinical, social, housing, and service utilization topics. The systems study component, in turn, obtained data at three points in time (1994, 1996, 1998) about interagency relationships in the local systems of care (density, fragmentation, and centralization of interorganizational networks) and ratings of the performance of the overall system (services accessibility and coordination).

In brief, findings from the ACCESS study mirrored those of the PCMI and Ft. Bragg demonstrations. Specifically, SI was associated with better access to housing and other supports for persons with SPMI (Rosenheck, Morrissey, Lam, et al., 1998; Rothbard, Min, Kuno, & Wong, 2004); however, SI did not result in better clinical outcomes for persons with SPMI (Rosenheck, Lam, Morrissey, et al., 2002).

Interpretations

All three of these demonstrations produced similar findings in that there was strong evidence for service system change and improvement, but no consistent evidence for client-level improvements. The PCMI investigators interpreted their findings as evidence that service system change was a necessary but not a sufficient condition for positive outcome effects for clients (Goldman et al., 1994; Lehman et al., 1994). They suspected that this set of results might reflect the lack of attention to improving clinical services in the design and conduct of the demonstration. From the outset, the focus of the PCMI was on structural change and continuity of care, not on developing specific clinical services other than case management. As a result, attention was deflected from the treatment needs of persons with SPMI, and no consistency was achieved in delivering services according to models with demonstrated efficacy such as assertive community treatment (Santos, Henggeler, Burns, Arana, & Meisler, 1995) and other quality clinical, rehabilitative, and supportive services (Lehman et al., 1994).

The Ft. Bragg evaluators suggested that, in any situation where there are no outcome effects, several alternative explanations must be considered; that is, the results are due either to theory failure or implementation failure or both (Bickman, 1996). In this case, they ruled out implementation failure because their data clearly indicated that the continuum of care at the demonstration site was implemented successfully and with fidelity. Instead, they suggested that the most parsimonious interpretation of their findings was that the program theory underlying the continuum of care idea is wrong (i.e., exposure to a continuum does not improve child and family outcomes as assumed). The underlying issue in their view was the general ineffectiveness of clinical services in community (noncontrolled) settings. The meta-analyses conducted by Weisz and Weiss (1993) documenting the ineffectiveness of psychotherapy for children in community mental health were consistent with this view. These authors found that children were as likely to improve while on the waiting lists as they were after receiving treatment services.

The ACCESS evaluators suggested three possible reasons why SI does not result in better clinical outcomes (Rosenheck et al., 2002). First, SI is unrelated to client-level clinical outcomes, with the exception of housing. Second, SI is related to clinical outcomes, but a greater dose, so to speak, than what was realized in the ACCESS study is needed to affect those outcomes. Third, SI has a minimal impact on clinical outcomes in the presence of effective treatment, such as the assertive community treatment services provided in the study.

Thus, investigators associated with the PCMI and Ft. Bragg evaluations pointed to failures associated with clinical interventions as the most plausible explanation for the negative results, and the ACCESS evaluators suggested that the effects of SI may have been minimized in the presence of delivery of an effective service. Collectively, these findings suggested that the methods for improving service system performance (e.g., mental health governance or financing strategies) are far more developed than are the clinical interventions (e.g., parent/child counseling) employed in everyday community settings.

Evidence-Based Practices for Persons with Severe Mental Illness

The waning enthusiasm for SI as a solution to the needs of persons with SPMI has given way to the emergence of the evidence-based practice (EBP) movement. In 1998, the Robert Wood Johnson Foundation catalyzed the EBP movement by sponsoring a conference during which a national consensus panel identified six evidence-based practices for persons with SPMI (Mueser, Torrey, Lynde, Singer, & Drake, 2003): (1) supported employment, (2) assertive community treatment, (3) illness management and recovery, (4) family psychoeducation, (5) integrated dual disorders treatment, and (6) medication management (Bond, Salyers, Rollins, Rapp, & Zipple, 2004).

Evidence-based practices are interventions for which there is consistent evidence showing that they improve client outcomes and that are shown to be superior over alternatives, including no intervention (Drake et al., 2001). Assertive community treatment (ACT), for example, is an EBP for persons with severe and persistent mental illness (Dixon, 2000; Phillips et al., 2001; Stein & Test, 1980).

ACT is best viewed as a platform for delivering services such as medication management, vocational and housing services, and psychosocial interventions (Stein & Santos, 1998) and is a multidisciplinary team-based approach with a small (1:10) staff-to-consumer ratio, 24/7 hour staff availability, and aggressive outreach and engagement (Bond et al., 2001).

ACT, in particular, is one of the most widely studied interventions for persons with mental illness. There have been more than 25 randomized controlled studies examining its effectiveness in reducing psychiatric hospital days (Bond et al., 2001; Burns & Santos, 1995; Dixon, 2000; Marshall & Lockwood, 1998), and a number of qualitative studies have examined consumers' perceptions of what they like least about ACT (McGrew, Wilson, & Bond, 2002) and what is helpful about ACT (McGrew, Wilson, & Bond, 1996) and consumers' experiences with ACT (Watts & Priebe, 2002).

Despite dramatic changes in mental health practice and policy over the past three decades or longer, including the deinstitutionalization of our state hospitals, the diffusion of persons with mental illness across multiple public health and safety sectors, and changes in the way mental health services are financed and delivered, the core principles of ACT have changed little. Despite its status as an evidence-based practice, however, the widespread dissemination of ACT has been slow, and few communities have developed enough ACT capacity to meet local demand (Cuddeback, Morrissey, & Meyer, 2006).

The Dissemination of EBPs and Services Integration

There is consensus that the implementation of ACT or any other evidence-based practice for persons with SPMI requires capable leadership, adequate financing, flexible administrative rules and regulations that can support the incorporation of an EBP into routine agency operations, and staff who buy in to the model and have the training to implement it (Phillips et al., 2001). Indeed, the challenges associated with the widespread dissemination of evidence-based practices like ACT have been well documented (Drake et al., 2001). ACT, for example, is expensive but cost effective for consumers who are frequent users of local or state hospitals (i.e., those with length of stays from 16 to 50 days; Cuddeback et al., 2006; Latimer, 1999), and funding ACT is a particular challenge for mental health authorities given the misalignment between who benefits from and who pays for ACT. For instance, in the seminal study on the cost effectiveness of ACT, Weisbrod (1983) illuminated the dissonance between ACT beneficiaries (i.e., state and local hospitals) and those who finance ACT (i.e., community mental health authorities). Put simply, local and state hospitals benefit from ACT to the extent that consumers with severe mental illness frequent local and state emergency rooms and psychiatric units less often; however, the costs of operating ACT teams are shouldered exclusively by community mental health centers, and savings realized by local and state hospitals do not necessarily get reinvested toward the support of the ACT team.

A growing literature on the implementation and dissemination of EBPs has emerged (Corrigan, Steiner, McCracken, Blaser, & Barr, 2001; Isett et al., 2007; Mueser, Torrey, Lynde, et al., 2003; Schoenwald & Hoagwood, 2001). In brief, EBPs have not been widely implemented because of provider barriers (i.e., training needed to implement EBPs), organizational barriers (i.e., inflexible organizational rules that inhibit the delivery of EBPs, lack of leadership and top-down buy in), and system barriers (i.e., access, regulations, and funding issues; Corrigan et al., 2001; Isett et al., 2007; Schoenwald & Hoagwood, 2001).

Do SI principles have the potential to create environments in which EBPs can be widely disseminated? The extent to which SI can address the intraorganizational and interorganizational barriers that inhibit the widespread dissemination of EBPs is unclear. However, the findings of the PCMI, Ft. Bragg, and ACCESS studies discussed earlier do suggest that SI results in greater access to services. Can the combination of SI and EBPs realize better access and clinical outcomes for persons with severe mental illness? Research is needed to explore the benefits of SI and disseminating EBPs such that the gulf between effective mental health services and persons with severe mental illness can be bridged.

Conclusions

The public asylums that were created in the early part of the 19th century were the first mental health service "carve-outs." The mentally ill were placed in separate facilities under the superintendency of psychiatrists for short-term care and restoration to functioning. Policies over the succeeding century led to the segregation of the mentally ill in a separate system of care that was governed by considerations of public welfare, charity, and the care of dependent populations cut off from developments in the broader health care field (Grob, 1973, 1983). The progressive dismantling of the asylum system during the past 50 years under policies of deinstitutionalization has returned responsibility for the care of mentally ill persons to local communities (Mechanic & Rochefort, 1992; Morrissey, 1982; Morrissey, Goldman, & Klerman, 1985). The underdeveloped system of care in most communities and the inadequate health and welfare coverage for persons with SPMI place them in an extremely vulnerable position.

At this time point it is difficult to be prescient. A few things seem certain, however. For one, there is little chance of a wholesale return of persons with SPMI to the public asylum system, yet "asylum" (the function, not the facility) is needed in community settings for a relatively small group of such clients. For another, services may become more fragmented and less integrated with the absence of national policy and the growth of 50 different state mental health systems. And third, the mismatch between the needs of persons with SPMI (e.g., for social rehabilitative care) and public spending (e.g., acute care hospitals) may continue indefinitely. Until these issues are addressed as national policy for all citizens, it is difficult to see how the needs of persons with SPMI can be adequately met at the community level.

In this political and economic climate, many of the key decisions about financing and organization will not be made on the basis of research findings. The knowledge base about the costs and benefits of alternative service delivery arrangements is still exceedingly primitive. In such situations interest group politics often prevails. The mental health services research community – including social scientists, clinicians, economists, and health policy analysts – that crystallized within the past decade is now addressing issues of the organization and financing of mental health care in a rigorous way. Whether and how this research capacity is sustained during this period of transition and innovation in the delivery of mental health services will have a lot to do with how soon persons with SPMI will receive effective services and community supports.

27

Consequences of Managed Care for Mental Health Providers

Teresa L. Scheid

This chapter examines the effect of managed care on the work of mental health care providers. Even before the advent of managed care, mental health care workers experienced high levels of psychological burnout and job-related stress. This is because mental health care providers engage in emotional labor in their roles as caregivers and are subject to psychological burnout if they become overinvolved with clients (emotional exhaustion) or too detached from the emotional needs of their clients (depersonalization). Past research has seen burnout as a consequence of doing either too much emotional labor with needy clients or seeking too much distance from clients because of their excessive demands. However, managed care has changed the way in which mental health care workers are able to provide care. Managed health care emphasizes cost containment, performance assessment, and measurable outcomes and subjects the treatment actions of health care providers to increased organizational control. Rather than requiring workers to display emotions they do not necessarily feel, managed care imposes limits on the emotional labor of caregivers. The degree to which workers are prevented from making a meaningful investment of self in their work is critical to the experience of burnout; burnout is a consequence not only of excessive emotional demands but can also be attributed to the failure of emotional labor. Scheid uses longitudinal data obtained from providers working in a large public sector mental health organization to analyze changes in working experiences with the advent of managed care. Disagreement with organizational priorities (goal incongruence) emerges as a major source of both indicators of burnout (emotional exhaustion and depersonalization). The findings demonstrate that burnout is exacerbated under managed care because the emotional labor of providers is subject to increased organizational control. What effect is this likely to have on the quality of care?

Introduction

As noted by Mechanic (2006), most people receive mental health care in their community, at an outpatient mental health center. Who provides this care? Most people tend to think of a psychiatrist in a white coat as the typical mental health provider, but in fact most people will see a social worker or a nurse. Although both social workers and nurses are professionals, they do not have the same degree of autonomy and authority as psychiatrists or health care providers with a PhD. Consequently their work is subject to higher levels of organizational control. Historically, a major divide between mental health care providers was whether they worked in the private or the public sector. The distinction was based on whether care was reimbursed by private insurance (or self-pay) or by public monies (Medicaid). However, with managed care the distinction between private and public is no longer as meaningful as many public sector agencies have been privatized. Furthermore, insurance-based care is also subject to managed care oversight and restrictions on care.

Therefore, the most valid distinction is whether the client has a short-term acute mental health problem that can be resolved with medication or with short-term therapy or has a serious mental illness and requires long-term care and case management. Case management involves the coordination of the many services and supports (e.g., income, housing, medical care, medication) needed by individuals with a chronic mental illness. Case managers also provide a great deal of both emotional and tangible social support (Dill, 2001). This chapter focuses on the work of case managers who provide care to those with chronic mental illnesses.

Providing mental health care requires an unusually high degree of emotional involvement with clients. Mental health care providers (and many other caretakers) engage in emotional labor; emotional labor occurs when work involves dealing with others' feelings in addition to the regulation of one's own feelings (Hochschild, 1983, 1990; James, 1989). Caring work is different from other jobs involving emotional labor as the emotional labor is a desirable part of the job (Himmelweit, 1999; Treweek, 1996); "care giving is a balancing act of attachment to and detachment from others" (Kahn, 1993, p. 554). Luhrmann (2000, p. 67) described the emotional labor of psychotherapists as learning to be "deeply, emotionally engaged with their patients, and yet not respond to their own needs." Mental health care workers do more than maintain a smile or a friendly demeanor; they must develop an intense personal relationship that directly involves the emotions of their clients.

Mental health care providers must learn to manage their emotional labor; that is, to fulfill the emotional demands of their caring role. If they become overinvolved with clients (a lack of detachment) or too detached (cynical and hardened), they risk psychological burnout and will be less competent caregivers. However, the organization, the insurer, or a supervisor may assume varying degrees of control over how an emotional laborer will enact his or her professional role. Hochschild (1983) has provided insight into the ways in which organizations exercise control over emotional labor and the consequences this control has for workers, but analysis of organizational control has not been extended to caregivers for whom emotional labor is a desirable aspect of the job and an extension of one's self (England & Folbre, 1999). With caring work one is managing one's own feelings as well as those of another. Because of their professional training, those performing caring labor hold themselves accountable to normative standards that dictate a certain kind and degree of emotional labor (i.e., feeling rules). The critical factor that affects care providers' ability to do their work in accordance with their own professional logics of care (treatment ideologies) is the degree of autonomy and control they have over treatment decisions. Autonomy allows providers to perform necessary emotional labor in the manner to which they have been professionally socialized to believe is appropriate.

Managed care emphasizes cost containment, performance assessment, and measurable outcomes, and it subjects the treatment actions of health care providers to increased scrutiny and organizational control. As described by Dill (2001), with managed care the role of the mental health case manager is changing from linking clients to services to keeping down the costs of care (i.e., not providing services). Managed care uses a variety of means to control the work of caregivers to reduce the costs of care and limit their autonomy. What happens when treatment decisions are made by third-party payers whose principal motivation is cost savings? What happens when providers are not allowed to render the type of care they believe is professionally appropriate and necessary to achieve the mental health outcomes their clients seek? What happens when the emotional labor of caregivers is curtailed? It is likely that psychological burnout will be exacerbated. In this chapter I present longitudinal data from mental health care providers in one large public sector agency to describe how their caregiving work has changed with managed care.

Psychological Burnout, Emotional Labor, and the Investment of Self

Psychological burnout is a concept that has received a great deal of empirical attention and has most often been measured with the Maslach Burnout Inventory (Jackson, Schwab, & Schuler, 1986). The Maslach Burnout Inventory conceptualizes burnout in terms of three distinct dimensions that govern the relations workers have with their clients: emotional exhaustion (an inability to feel compassion for clients), depersonalization (callousness toward clients), and a lack of personal accomplishment (a tendency to negatively evaluate oneself). These dimensions of burnout contain an obvious reference to emotional labor as well as the need for an investment of self into the work role. Wharton (1993) argued that burnout is a consequence of emotional labor, and recent research has made the linkage between emotional labor and burnout explicit (Brotheridge & Grandey, 2002; Erickson & Ritter, 2001; Zapf et al., 2001).

There has been an overwhelming amount of research on the conditions that cause burnout. Aiken and Sloane (1997) noted that more than 100 factors have been found to be associated with burnout (see Golembiewski, Boudreau, Munzenrider, & Luo, 1996, for an extensive description of the diverse sources of burnout). Empirical assessments of burnout, both quantitative (Aiken & Sloane, 1997; Schulz, Greenley, & Brown, 1995) and qualitative (Meyerson, 1994), have pointed to the central role played by organizational context (see also Handy, 1988, and Hoff, Whitcomb, & Nelson, 2002). As with earlier research on alienation, and consistent with research on the emotional labor of service workers (Erickson &

Wharton, 1997; Leidner, 1993), researchers studying burnout have focused on the negative effects of bureaucratic working conditions and restrictions of worker's autonomy and control (Arches, 1991; Aiken & Sloane, 1997; Cherniss, 1980; Handy, 1988; Hoff et al., 2002; Meyerson, 1994; Schulz et al., 1995; Wolpin et al., 1991). Foner (1995, p. 58) demonstrated that "the bureaucratization of nursing home care has had the effect of officially devaluing the supportive emotional labor nursing aids provide." I argue that burnout can result when the job demands an emotional investment in one's work role (especially relevant for care workers), yet the organization prevents the worker from meeting the feeling rules associated with this emotional labor.

Emotional labor has most commonly been associated with service work, or work that involves interactions with clients and entails the management of feeling and the expression of appropriate emotions (Hochschild, 1983). Morris and Feldman (1996, p. 987) defined emotional labor as the "act of expressing organizationally desired emotions during service transactions." Emotional labor requires conformity to display rules and involves "surface acting," a form of impression management in which workers display emotions they do not necessarily feel. Emotional labor can also involve "deep acting," in which the worker actually feels the emotions expressed and must conform to feeling rules.

Caregiving work involves deep acting to a greater extent than service work; deep acting also calls for a greater investment of self into the work role. Hochschild (1983, p. 7) has argued that self-concept or identity is central to emotional labor: "this kind of labor calls for coordination of mind and feeling, and it sometimes draws upon a source of self we honor as deep and integral to our individuality." The importance of self has also been recognized by those who have examined the relationship between emotional labor and feelings of authenticity (Bulen, Erickson, & Wharton, 1997; Erickson, 1995; Erickson & Ritter, 2001; Erickson & Wharton, 1997; Leidner, 1993). Researchers have found that when emotional labor is controlled and routinized, feelings of inauthenticity can result because workers are required to express emotions they do not feel (Erickson & Wharton, 1997; Leidner, 1993). When workers must actually feel the emotions they express (deep acting), they are more likely to experience psychological burnout because of overinvolvement with their work role (Ashforth & Humphrey, 1993; Hochschild, 1983).

The emotional labor produced by mental health workers is typical of deep acting, in which they draw on emotional memory and actually experience the emotion they are to display with clients (i.e., concern, regret, empathy). Mental health workers (and many other types of health care workers) are caregivers and must be responsive emotionally to their clients (P. Smith, 1992, 1999). Their relationships with their clients involve accessibility, inquiry, attention, validation, empathy, support, compassion, and consistency (Kahn, 1993). Such deep acting fundamentally involves self and identity in a way that surface acting may not. The feeling rules associated with this deep acting become part of the caregiver's self-identity. However, even when feeling rules are internalized, workers can still exhibit a degree of detachment; however, this faking is in "good faith" because it can enhance workers' well-being (Rafaeli & Sutton, 1989). That is, caregivers learn that some degree of detachment is necessary if they are to effectively fulfill the emotional demands of their caring roles. If they become overinvolved with clients (a lack of detachment) or too detached (hardened and cynical) they risk psychological burnout and will be less competent caregivers as a result. Hence, professional norms specify the appropriate feeling rules (i.e., the emotions necessary to performance of a specific work role) and provide some guidance on how one can avoid the negative consequences of emotional labor.

However, emotional labor is also constrained by organizational factors over which the worker may have little control. As Bulen, Erickson, and Wharton (1997, p. 238) noted, the "identity dilemma may be aggravated further by employee's lack of control over their work conditions." Organizational control over emotional labor that involves deep acting (in which workers actually feel the emotions they are to express) is likely to produce both burnout and feelings of inauthenticity. Managed care has resulted in greater bureaucratic control over the treatment decisions of health care providers and is likely to affect both emotional labor and psychological burnout.

Managed Mental Health Care

The primary ways in which managed care controls costs are by limiting access to services and by limiting the utilization of more costly services while encouraging the use of less costly services. To determine the cost effectiveness of a given treatment, managed care systems must assess empirically verifiable "success," or outcomes. Mental health treatment must be "medically necessary"; increasingly, managed care companies or payers will only reimburse services that have been scientifically validated as efficacious. An important obstacle to evaluating managed mental health care is the difficulty in evaluating treatment effectiveness; there is little consensus on the etiology of mental illness or on appropriate treatments (Mechanic, 1999). Not only is it difficult to define the nature of the problem but also different types of treatment work with different types of clients. Persons with chronic and severe mental illness may not show noticeable signs of improvement, even if treated within excellent programs (Mechanic, 1986); it is also far more difficult to determine standards for medical necessity (Manderscheid et al., 2000). Moreover, client confidentiality limits collection of and access to data. Yet managed care does rely on the assessment of client outcomes and has led to the development of a scientifically (as opposed to professionally based) system of treatment and practice guidelines.

In the United States managed care has resulted in fewer inpatient care episodes and reduced hospital stays and has thus reduced the overall costs of mental health care, as inpatient care is more costly than outpatient care (Durham, 1995; Manderscheid et al., 2000). This has been at the cost of restricted access to care (Weissman, Pettigre, Stosky, & Regier, 2000). Many managed care plans do not cover chronic mental illness in their standard benefit packages, and the amount of money generally allocated for mental health services is not considered sufficient for adequate treatment (Iglehart, 1996; Manderscheid et al., 2000). Furthermore, providers often face pressure from their managed care organization to provide even less treatment than what is covered by a patient's benefit plan, especially when fees are capitated. Mechanic and McAlpine (1999) have argued that managed care has produced a democratization of care – in which everyone gets a similar level of services and those with greater service needs (chronic mental illness) do not get the services they need. With reduced inpatient stays, individuals with chronic care needs have higher rates of readmissions. Furthermore, following criteria of medical necessity and relying on measurable outcomes have resulted in a reliance on short-term therapy, group sessions, and psychiatric medications.

Managed care represents a direct challenge to the autonomy and control providers have over their work; "by design, managed care is intended to alter clinical practices" (Schlesinger & Gray, 1999, p. 441). The decline in professional power has been characterized in terms of deprofessionalization (loss of trust in one's professional prerogative), proletariatization (loss of autonomy), or corporatization (Wolinsky, 1993). Schlesinger, Gray, and Perreira (1997) have argued that utilization review and the development of protocols to standardize treatment threaten autonomy by challenging professional authority and expertise. Soderfelt et al. (1996, p. 1222) suggested that "cost containment and market mechanisms may increasingly set limits" on providers' job control, decision-making authority, and input into organizational goals and premises for action. Reduced autonomy and higher levels of bureaucratic control over treatment decisions are likely to result in higher levels of psychological burnout.

Managed care may also curtail the emotional labor of health care providers by setting limits on the types of care authorized and the number of treatment sessions, subjecting clinical decisions and client records to third-party review, and imposing bureaucratic controls on therapeutic relationships. Managed care forces health care providers to act as gatekeepers or double agents; rather than advocating for their clients, providers must meet the standards of care determined by the managed care entity. The main role of the provider is no longer to advocate for the best possible care for the client but to keep the costs of care low. Providers experience a series of ethical dilemmas as they deal with conflicts of interest (between patients and their own preferences for care versus the standards imposed by the managed care entity) as well as violations of client confidentiality (Furman, 2003; LaRoche & Turner, 2002; Turner & Conway, 2000). Managed care not only controls the emotional labor of health care providers but it also may actually prohibit them from fulfilling their therapeutic role. Burnout may arise not so much because of excessive emotional demands, but from the inability of providers to adequately perform their emotional labor.

In a recent study of the effect of managed care on hospital physicians, Hoff, Whitcomb, and Nelson (2002) found that favorable relationships with colleagues and patients are more important to the experience of burnout than the type of fiscal and clinical restraints imposed by managed care. Of course, doctors do tend to maintain a high degree of control over clinical decisions by virtue of their professional expertise (Griffiths & Hughes, 1999; Hoff & McCaffrey, 1996; M. Weiss & Fitzpatrick, 1997). We know less about those health care providers who do not have claim to professional status by virtue of an advanced degree. Furthermore, where treatment technologies are ambiguous or contradictory, as in mental health, there is an increased likelihood that bureaucratic standards of care will prevail. In an ethnographic study of mental health care workers, Kirschner and Lachicotte (2001) found that providers felt threatened by managed care. Ware et al. (2000) reported that these same providers feared that the quality of care would deteriorate. However, there is little research that addresses what effect managed care has had on the emotional labor of health care providers or whether it has indeed exacerbated burnout. I used longitudinal data collected from providers in a public sector mental health agency that underwent a purposive move to managed care to examine the impact of managed care on work experiences.

Setting

In this study I analyzed data collected from one public sector mental health care organization that provides services in a large urban county in the United States (this data site is referred to as CARE). CARE provides services to more than 1,500 clients with severe, chronic mental illnesses. CARE began planning for a movement to managed care in 1996 and hired a managed care director to develop and implement a strategy to manage care. During the 4-year period of organizational transition, I interviewed directors and administrators responsible for implementing managed care and attended staff meetings and development meetings with groups of providers. In the spring of 1998 I distributed a questionnaire to all direct care providers ($N = 90$) to collect data on the organization before the advent of managed care. The questionnaire was extensive and took close to an hour to complete and had a good number of open-ended questions as well as fixed-choice questions. The questionnaire was replicated in 2000 to evaluate the impact of managed care. The response rate in 1998 was 56.6% ($n = 51$), and it was 49% ($n = 46$) in 2000. The majority of respondents were female (76% in 1998 and 70% in 2000), White (64% in 1998 and 60% in 2000), and had a master's degree, generally the MSW (25% in 1998 and 33% in 2000); about one-fourth of the respondents were nurses (22% in 1998 and 26% in 2000). The majority of respondents were case managers. Respondents were representative of the larger population of providers at CARE. I relied on the open-ended questions to describe providers' experience of managed care and the quantitative data to examine changes over time as well as the relationships among key variables.

In terms of its orientation to community-based care, CARE is remarkably similar to a sample of 19 mental health outpatient programs in Wisconsin (Scheid & Greenley, 1997), with the exception that CARE places greater emphasis on substance abuse services. CARE is unique in its proactive movement toward managed care and in its attempt to preserve the ideology of community-based care as well as professional control of mental health care services (Scheid, 2003). CARE was the first public sector agency to obtain accreditation from the National Committee for Quality Assurance. Consequently, CARE is both a substantively and a theoretically significant case and so warrants in-depth study (Berg, 1990; Ragin, 1999). There has also been recognition that health services research on managed care has suffered from a focus on large-scale studies (where diversity makes any kind of generalization difficult) and from a dearth of empirically grounded case study research (Devers, Sofaer, & Rundall, 1999). The data on CARE are important because they tell us about the impact of managed care in an organization that worked hard to preserve the ideals of community-based care.

Measures of Key Concepts

Burnout was assessed using the items in the Maslasch Burnout Inventory to measure emotional exhaustion, depersonalization, and lack of accomplishment. I created an index of emotional labor for the second wave of data collection based on interviews conducted with mental health care providers and responses to open-ended questions in the first wave of data collection. I also used some items from the emotional labor index developed by Steinberg and Figart (1999) that seemed most relevant to caring work. Providers were asked how often (never to almost always) they (1) had to work with clients to establish a relationship, (2) work with clients on many different aspects of their lives, (3) understand what their clients are feeling, and (4) understand the unique needs of their clients. This summed index could go from 0 (no emotional labor) to 12. Of the 45 providers who answered these questions in 2000, only 33.3% had scores below 10. Forty percent had a score of 12 (the highest level of emotional labor possible). The overall mean was 10.27 with a standard deviation of 1.84. Although an index (and additive in nature), the emotional labor measure also had good scale properties, with a reliability of .7075, indicating that the measures of emotional labor were highly interrelated. A second measure of emotional labor was the percent of time spent in direct client contact (excluding phone calls). Providers reported spending close to half their time in direct client contact (49.55% with a standard deviation of 25.28).

A good working environment is important to the effective management of emotional labor as well as of psychological burnout. The questionnaire included five subscales to assess aspects of the organization's work climate: innovation, job involvement, clarity, cohesion, and supervisory support. Several scales assessed job satisfaction, and one scale measured the degree to which the worker was subject to bureaucratic control. I also included a scale that assessed pride in work, which referred to the degree to which workers found their job meaningful; this variable provided an indication of the degree to which an individual's self was involved in the job. Autonomy is also critical to the degree of control providers have over decisions about client care, and the questionnaire assessed their input into organizational decisions, as well as their autonomy.

Providers directly assessed managed care by responding to a series of questions about the effect of managed care on services. Five questions that examined how financial mechanisms to manage care changed services (reduction in the use of community services, reduction in the duration of treatment, provision of less intensive services, greater reliance on medication, and reduced lengths of stay) were added together to indicate the degree to which providers were critical of managed care. This index ranged from 0 to 10 with a higher score indicating the belief that managed care had resulted in reduced services and care (the mean was 6.68 with a standard deviation of 2.62).

I also collected information on goal incongruence – the degree to which providers felt that current organizational goals and practices varied from what they thought the organization ought to be doing. In this regard, I evaluated both client-level goals (more outreach, high technical quality, improvement in client functioning, client satisfaction, client's families' satisfaction, protection of the community from violent and unwanted behavior, improvement in the quality of the client's life) and organizational goals (contain costs, enhance revenues, satisfy staff, innovate, increase interagency collaboration, expand service offerings, integrate services to diverse client populations). Respondents were asked to indicate a percentage (0 to 100) for how important to the organization they thought achievement of a goal currently was and another percentage for how important they thought achievement of the goal ought to be. I subtracted goals from ideal goals to arrive at a goal incongruence score. Positive numbers indicated that providers thought a goal should be more important than it was; negative numbers indicated that the providers thought the organization placed too much emphasis on a given goal. The measure of goal incongruence is a direct measure of conflict between organizational priorities and individual or professional standards for care.

In the next section, I first describe the providers' experience with managed care and how it has changed their work. I used the methods of grounded theory (Glaser & Strauss, 1967; Strauss & Corbin, 1990) to analyze the qualitative data collected from open-ended questions. Quotes from individual providers cited in the next section exemplified common experiences and general themes; for each one, I provided respondent ID numbers, as well as the year of the interview (interviews from 1998 and 2000 were matched by ID number). Except where noted, responses came from case managers (as three-fourths of the sample were case managers). Several longer quotes came from nurses, which may be due to their greater willingness to make extensive notes given their professional socialization. I then assess changes in the work environment, working conditions, goal incongruence, and burnout between 1998 and 2000. I used ordinary least squares regression with the data from 2000 to examine the effect of managed care, organizational working conditions, goal incongruence, and emotional labor on burnout.

The "Lived Experience" of Managed Care

The providers I interviewed and who completed questionnaires in 1998 expressed concern that managed care would limit access to services and that the "over concern with the cost of care might prohibit clients with severe and persistent mental illnesses from getting the services they needed" (1998, #28: MSW provider). Providers knew their clients well and realized that severe mental illnesses require long-term care and intensive social supports. It was unclear in 1998 how managed care would meet the needs of their clients, as one nurse administer lamented in a personal interview with me:

> When we first started hearing about managed care I wondered – how is this going to work with a person who can't hold a job, who needs ongoing services, but they aren't in the hospital? Who is going to pay for that?

Yet some providers in 1998 felt that managed care had the potential to integrate delivery systems, increase accountability, and widen access to the underserved population. However, 2 years later the only benefits of managed care were felt to be cost containment and increased accountability. Only one respondent (2000, #88) felt that "services seem to be more streamlined and a little better coordinated," and another felt services had increased (both respondents were administrators). The majority of respondents did not feel that managed care provided any benefits, or they shared the more cynical critique of managed care as focused on managing money, not care:

> Managed care is a plan created to pretend to provide quality care and be account-able. Anyone who has ever had to navigate a managed care system for their own care knows it has nothing to do with care. It has to do with making money, laying on multiple layers of staff who monitor success (or prevent them), and destroying any bond you have with your consumers (2000, #58: nurse).

Providers at CARE were quite outspoken in identifying the problems with managed care. Most prevalent were concerns about the quality of the care provided and the limitations placed on long-term services. Providers reported that patients were often discharged without adequate treatment or did not get the services they needed. One nurse (2000, #52) reported that managed care had resulted in a

> shortened length of stay in the hospital for the seriously mentally ill, resulting in clients being ill and sent into the community before they are stabilized. The community resources are not in place for our client population, housing and other supports. . . . Consequently clients get sick, they never stabilize, they have to return to the hospital – it's a revolving door.

The revolving door was associated with the early days of deinstitutionalization, when community supports for those with chronic and severe illnesses were nonexistent. However, now there are community supports, but providers cannot get authorization because treatment decisions are based primarily on principles of cost containment.

Responses to the fixed-choice questions about managed care also revealed dissatisfaction with managed care (data not shown). Although some providers felt managed care affords an opportunity to develop a better system of mental health services (17.8%), a larger proportion disagreed with this statement (35.5%). Close to 80% percent disagreed that managed care had improved the quality of care, 64.4% disagreed that clinical outcomes had improved, and slightly more than 50% felt that managed care inevitably results in underservice to clients. Providers believed that the institutional logic of cost containment (operationalized as the use of financial considerations to manage care) resulted in the reduced use of community-based services (31.8%), reduced duration of treatment (52.3%), less intensive treatment (47.6%), a greater reliance on psychiatric medication than providers would prefer (31.8%), and reduced duration of outpatient care for clients (56.8%).

Organizational Control and Burnout

In describing how their work had changed since the advent of managed care, providers at CARE universally complained about excessive paperwork and difficulties with the management information system (a computer system that contained client data). Consequently they were able to provide less direct client care. Providers reported a twofold increase in time spent documenting care and felt that efficiency was hindered by the requirement to have all services certified by the review panel rather than the treatment team. One comment from a nurse (2000, #75) demonstrated the impact that managed care had had on her ability to provide care to her clients:

> The paperwork has expanded at least fourfold, and is taking additional time from patient care. There is not time to build a relationship with a patient or his family, and trust is lost, the frustration level in providing care because of cumbersome pre-approval procedures and denials of needed services has increase to a level where I will be glad to leave nursing.

Table 27.1. *Work environment and working experiences (means and standard deviations)*

Changes	1998 ($n = 51$)	2000 ($n = 47$)
Work environment (all scales from 4 to 20; higher score indicates better work environment)		
Innovation	11.80 (3.46)	10.85 (3.80)
Involvement in job*	14.35 (3.05)	12.91 (3.51)
Role clarity*	13.24 (4.05)	11.15 (4.24)
Supervisory support	13.57 (3.48)	12.49 (3.79)
Group cohesion*	14.22 (2.99)	12.64 (3.89)
Work experiences (higher score indicates better work experiences)		
Autonomy (2–5)*	3.56 (0.68)	3.30 (0.70
Decision input (0–9)	7.25 (2.67)	6.23 (2.45)
Pride in work (2–5)**	3.99 (0.56)	3.65 (0.75)
Satisfaction with pay (1–4)	2.78 (0.85)	2.67 (0.78)
Satisfaction with professional status (2–5)	3.74 (0.53)	3.60 (0.56)
Satisfaction with bureaucratic control (1–5)	2.87 (0.83)	2.65 (0.77)
Burnout (higher score indicates higher levels of burnout)		
Emotional exhaustion (0–6)*	1.86 (1.21)	2.42 (1.48)
Depersonalization (0–6)	1.01 (0.98)	0.92 (1.02)
Lack of personal accomplishment	1.00 (0.72)	1.08 (0.76)

*$p < .05$; ** $p < .01$; *** $p < .001$.

Providers reported they "treat the computer, not the consumer," and the "human connection feels more automated, its assembly like maintenance" (2000, #88: case manager). Everyone reported spending less time with clients and far more time meeting bureaucratic demands. Once again, these impressions were supported by the quantitative assessment of changes in the work environment and in work experiences with managed care (see Table 27.1). Providers found the work environment to be less supportive of their work in that there was less job involvement in the job, reduced role clarity, and lower levels of group cohesion. Providers also reported significantly less satisfaction with the nature of their work and less autonomy. Although not reaching statistical significance, providers experienced less input into decisions and reduced satisfaction with pay, professional status, and operating procedures. In addition, levels of emotional exhaustion had significantly increased since 1998.

In the open-ended questions several providers also commented that levels of burnout were higher, and they noted that the tremendous amount of turnover in the organization was a consequence of burnout. A majority cited managed care as a significant source of stress and felt that the increases in bureaucratic control over decisions had resulted in a lack of support from supervisors and administrators, which was producing higher levels of burnout. One case manager (2000, #88) wrote that the "contribution to burnout is frustration over the never ending barriers and obstacles to the job created by the managed care system." Another case manager (2000, #75) stated, "I like my patient contact but I dislike foolish administrative decisions."

Close to half of the providers who completed the questionnaire cited concerns with the quality of care under managed care. Providers were frustrated that treatment decisions were now being made on the basis of cost, rather than clinical need, and that volume was a higher priority than quality of care. Almost all of the providers provided feedback on the open-ended questions about the negative effect of cost-containment strategies on the quality of care and the "devastating effect of shortened lengths of stay for chronically ill clients" (2000, #91). The emphasis on cost was felt to directly interfere with client care, and clients were getting sick and sicker. In response to a question about the problems with managed care, one male case manager (2000, #63) reported,

> Fiscal issues are more important than client related ones, there is a lack of information to ground level clinicians regarding changes, there is staff burnout – look at the number of new hires in case management over the past year. Case managers and other professionals seem to have to fight for services; our hard jobs are getting harder.

Providers at CARE overwhelmingly cited changes in the organization and lack of support for their work as the major sources of burnout. Burnout resulted "when client needs far outweigh what I (and the system) could provide"; when "no matter how much you work you will never have met the expected need" (2000, #77). "I am very burned out – it started with this job. I feel very hopeless about this job" (2000, #78). Almost everyone surveyed stated that a lack of support, mainly from upper level administrators, was the major contributing factor to burnout. Closely related to the lack of support was the lack of decision-making authority and input – these two factors were often mentioned in conjunction – "not having input into decisions which impact my job and a lack of support from higher level supervisors" (2000, #80). Providers at CARE felt their immediate team supervisors and clinical supervisors were great – it was the higher level of management at which decisions about managed care and organizational restructuring were being made that was targeted as the source of the problem. Because care work had become a commodity and emotional labor was being curtailed, providers "spend less time with consumers, (and) more time documenting doing less for the consumers" (2000, #58). Providers felt that burnout could be alleviated by more organizational supports and incentives and a greater focus on client care.

These negative feelings about organizational priorities can be empirically validated by examining changes in goal incongruence. Table 27.2 examines changes in the degree of goal incongruence between 1998 and 2000. The overall goal incongruence score was 21.97 for 2001, compared to 20.35 in 1998, and although there is no significant difference between the summary scores there were in fact significant

Table 27.2. *Goal incongruence (mean percentages and standard deviations)*

Organizational goals	1998	2000	p value
Reach out to more clients	15.0 (22.97)	18.78 (26.04)	.460
High technical quality	27.79 (24.64)	21.46 (32.31)	.301
Improved client functioning	20.94 (18.95)	23.95 (23.84)	.501
Client satisfaction	13.87 (22.66)	23.26 (29.51)	.089
Satisfaction of client's family	13.33 (20.03)	20.71 (29.51)	.132
Protect community from violent/ unwanted behavior	16.80 (25.52)	19.52 (25.15)	.600
Improve quality of client's life	22.91 (23.96)	28.17 (18.07)	.343
Contain costs	−4.55 (23.73)	−9.88 (24.77)	.006
Enhance revenues	−9.77 (29.27)	−8.95 (28.29)	.003
Satisfy staff	40.95 (33.32)	45.24 (26.27)	.506
Innovate	32.95 (26.35)	31.30 (34.41)	.793
Improve interorganizational relations	30.42 (28.18)	34.41 (29.48)	.513
Expand service offerings	20.31 (23.76)	29.53 (25.74)	.081
Integrate service offerings to diverse client populations	19.89 (25.89)	27.14 (29.57)	.219

Note: A higher number indicates that providers thought the goal should be more important than it currently was; a negative number indicates they thought the organization placed too much emphasis on a given goal.

changes in the levels of goal incongruence for individual goals. Providers felt that more emphasis needed to be placed on client satisfaction and the satisfaction of client's families. Providers also felt more emphasis needed to be placed on improving the quality of the client's life. They also felt too much emphasis was being placed on containing costs and enhancing revenues and that more emphasis had to be placed on satisfying staff, expanding service offerings, and integrating services (Table 27.2). It is apparent from the changes in goal incongruence that organizational priorities were more about managing costs rather than care – producing a situation in which providers felt frustrated because they were not able to provide the care their clients needed. Consequently, managed care is likely to exacerbate psychological burnout. I turn next to an examination of the factors that influenced the higher levels of burnout reported in 2000.

Causal Analysis of the Effect of Managed Care on Burnout

The survey data allow for a quantitative consideration of the relationship among organizational working conditions, feelings about work, emotional labor, and burnout. Because the sample was small, I limited the number of variables in the analysis. I used extent of bureaucratic control over work and autonomy because these factors have been associated with both emotional labor and burnout in the literature. I included pride in work as one measure of the investment of self

Table 27.3. *Correlations among key organizational variables, emotional labor, and burnout*

Variable	(1)	(2)	(3)	(4)	(5)	(6)	(7)	(8)
1. Emotional exhaustion	1.0							
2. Depersonalization	.695***							
3. Satisfaction with bureaucracy	−.723***	−.377*						
4. Pride in work	−.393*	−.442**	.426**					
5. Autonomy	−.732***	−.431**	.817***	.414**				
6. % direct client care	−.444**	−.148	.402**	.175	.326*			
7. Goal incongruence	.166	−.036	−.449**	−.294*	−.431**	−.039		
8. Emotional labor	.034	−.044	.036	−.072	−.276*	.091	.249	
9. Critical of managed care	.222	.052	−.307	−.017	−.286*	.170	.486**	.350*

Note: Here, $n = 35$.
$^*p < .05; ^{**}p < .01; ^{***}p < .001$.

in work. As noted earlier,levels of autonomy and pride in work had decreased between 1998 and 2000. I also included levels of goal incongruence, the summary index for feeling that managed care had resulted in reduced services, the scale for emotional labor, and the percent of direct client contact as a second measure of emotional labor.

The analysis focuses on two dimensions of burnout: emotional exhaustion and depersonalization. A lack of personal accomplishment (the third dimension of burnout commonly measured) can also be attributed to a lack of professional recognition as well as burnout. Emotional exhaustion and depersonalization are also more clearly tied to work with clients and to the performance of emotional labor.

Examination of the correlation matrix yields some interesting findings. The correlations between the indices of psychological burnout (emotional exhaustion and a sense of depersonalization) show that burnout is significantly associated with bureaucratic control (increased paperwork and rules), a lack of pride in work (or feeling work is meaningless), decreased job autonomy, and critical attitudes toward the cost-containment emphasis of managed care (see Table 27.3). Emotional exhaustion is also significantly related to decreased (not increased) client contact. Emotional labor is not related to burnout, although it is negatively related to autonomy and positively related to goal incongruence (meaning that those doing more emotional labor had less authority and were more likely to disagree with organizational priorities). Goal incongruence is associated with greater dissatisfaction with bureaucratic control, feeling less pride in one's work, and lower levels of autonomy. Critical views of managed care are also associated with dissatisfaction with bureaucratic control, with lower levels of autonomy, with goal incongruence,

544   *Teresa L. Scheid*

Table 27.4. *Causal analysis of burnout under managed care*

Independent variables	Emotional exhaustion			Depersonalization		
	β	SE	p value	β	SE	p value
Satisfaction with bureaucracy	−.214	.442	.391	.095	.389	.782
Pride in work	−.136	.250	.288	−.389	.220	.033
Autonomy	−.524	.463	.029	−.517	.407	.111
% client contact	−.201	.007	.125	.026	.006	.883
Goal incongruence	−.281	.014	.052	−.362	.012	.068
Emotional labor	−.098	.130	.499	−.187	.115	.353
Critical of managed care	.210	.077	.155	.163	.068	.418
R^2		.678	.000	.385	.047	

Note: Here, $n = 35$; standardized coefficients, standard error, and *p* values are shown.

and with higher levels of emotional labor, indicating that managed care is having an impact on providers' ability to do their work in a manner they consider meaningful.

Table 27.4 provides the ordinary least squares regression analysis of burnout. Reduced autonomy and goal incongruence are significant predictors of emotional exhaustion, and the measure of critical attitudes toward managed care approaches statistical significance, which is noteworthy given the small sample size. Goal incongruence and pride in work are significant predictors of depersonalization. The significance of goal incongruence for both indicators of burnout demonstrates that it is not emotional labor per se, or bureaucratic constraints, or client demands; instead, it is the feeling that the organization is NOT meeting professional-based criteria for care that is the source of burnout.

Because burnout results when providers are prevented from fulfilling their therapeutic roles in the manner they consider viable – when they feel they "lacked control" – managed care at CARE is leading to disillusionment. A good number of providers at CARE responded to my question about how they thought their work would change in the next 10 years with plans to leave mental health work: "I'm going to retire and escape this mess." Not "caring" about the mental health needs of clients or of the wider public is certainly a powerful indicator of burnout.

Conclusions

It is important to acknowledge the limitations of this study. The data were collected from one organization, and the sample was accordingly small. Although CARE's orientation to care is similar to that of other outpatient mental health programs, there is tremendous diversity in approaches to managed care. However, CARE is unique in that it was the first public sector mental health agency to receive certification by the National Committee for Quality Assurance as a Managed Behavioral

Health Organization. It has also actively sought to preserve professional-based principles underlying community-based care within a managed care framework and has worked hard to involve its providers in the decisions about managed care. As a case study, CARE is both substantively and theoretically significant (Ragin, 1999) because it allows us to examine the impact of managed care under reasonably good circumstances.

In terms of specific findings, critical attitudes toward managed care, a lack of autonomy, and disagreement with organizational priorities are significant predictors of emotional exhaustion. Disagreement with organizational priorities and a lack of pride in one's work are significant predictors of depersonalization. The significance of goal incongruence for both indicators of burnout demonstrates that the feeling that the organization is NOT meeting professional-based criteria for care is the source of burnout. These data support my theoretical argument that burnout results when the emotional labor of providers is curtailed such that they are not able to perform their clinical role in the manner that they feel is professional and personally appropriate and their professional identity is not confirmed or enhanced. As found by Smith (1992), supportive organizational environments (or organizational leaders) are necessary for the effective performance of emotional labor or care work. Burnout is a likely consequence when the organization limits the emotional labor of providers. Burnout not only arises from excessive emotional demands (i.e., a consequence of emotional labor) but can also be attributed to the failure of emotional labor.

This chapter addresses the larger question of how caregiving work has been constrained by managed care, as well as the effects of managed care on the quality of patient care. Providers at CARE were deeply concerned about the quality of the care received by their clients and denials for needed services. No one I interviewed had a positive view of managed care or felt that managed care would lead to greater service integration or more effective treatment. Although some providers felt that increased accountability was probably good, they did not believe that accountability in and of itself would lead to better care. This perception makes sense, because mechanisms to ensure accountability (third-party review, authorization, and standardization of treatment practices) all decrease autonomy and limit providers' ability to provide quality care or to maintain the type of relationship they feel is best for their clients. Third-party review undermines the therapeutic relationship by introducing distrust of the clinician and places constraints on the emotional labor of providers. Providers expressed a sense of dismay, as the gains that had been made during the years of community mental health were being lost. As one nurse lamented,

> Almost everything I used to do in this job was important. I had a great relationship with consumers assigned to my caseload, I have worked frontline for almost 20 years. I have been recognized by individuals and organizations for my advocacy

on behalf of mentally ill consumers. With the changes in Medicaid and the introduction of this Case Management system, all of this has changed. I got into this profession because I like consumers and their families. I'm good at what I do, and I make a real difference in folks' lives. With the death of a real community support system, I worry what is to become of our consumers. Why can't people learn from what works? Now we are going backwards. We are doomed to repeat our mistakes.

This dismay is echoed in the professional and academic literatures on mental health. As Shore and Beigel (1996, p. 77) have argued, managed care provides a "controversial" challenge to "traditional definitions of mental illness and treatment goals." Providers are experiencing conflict between their professional logics of care and the commodification of care, and consequently they face what has been described in the literature as ethical dilemmas (Boyle & Callahan, 1995; Furman, 2003; Galambos, 1999; LaRoche & Turner, 2002; Turner & Conway, 2000). Many mental health advocacy groups are highly critical of managed mental health care (for example the National Alliance for the Mentally Ill and the Bazelon Center for Mental Health Law) and are working to provide safeguards for quality care.

The quality of care is also influenced by the degree to which providers are burned out. Managed care has a direct impact on burnout in two ways. First, by seeking to specify the type of treatment model or role the provider is to assume with a client, managed care seeks to change the work identity of providers. Mental health providers have been socialized into a model of care that emphasizes long-term continuous care and the provision of supports for clients with severe mental illnesses. Yet managed care emphasizes short-term, brief, focused therapy that is results oriented. As described in this chapter, when providers disagree with organizational priorities for care and when their caregiving labor is controlled, they experience higher levels of burnout. Second, cost containment is likely to further reduce resources, and subsequently providers will experience the acceleration of multiple demands and simply having too many clients. The speedup provides an organizational context that is likely to produce not only increased stress but also burnout, because it prevents providers from meeting professional prescribed norms about appropriate care for their clients. The negative consequences of managed care are not limited to mental health, but have implications for other health care providers, especially those dealing with chronic care populations for whom long-term care and social supports are necessary.

Managed care is one aspect of a more general commodification in which organizations and providers must meet cost-containment goals (whether for increased profits or to save public dollars). As described by Light (1997), health care has moved to a system characterized by a distrust of professional authority, a focus on external accountability and monitoring, and the rise of corporate health systems. The era of managed care values cost containment above quality care, although there have been efforts to implement quality-based performance indicators (and these are in use at CARE). Ensuring that services are delivered in a cost-effective manner requires that the emotional labor of providers be monitored and ultimately curtailed. Managed care seeks to reduce professional prerogatives and to control the emotional labor of health care providers; consequently, burnout will be exacerbated under managed care. The commodification of care and its curtailment of emotional labor and the exacerbation of burnout will further lower the quality of care we all receive. We need to insist that health be measured by a wider social ethic than that of cost containment. As Mechanic noted (1999, p. xii), "Managed care is simply a framework. What takes place in this framework will continue to be affected by our economic and social philosophies and values."

28

Mental Health and the Changing Context of HIV

James Walkup and Stephen Crystal

The mental health challenges associated with HIV/AIDS have evolved and changed as the dynamics of the epidemic have developed. These challenges include knowledge of HIV status and disclosure to members of social networks, the impact of stigma on people living with HIV, alternative styles of coping with HIV illness and their consequences, suicidality among people with HIV, and the special challenges of HIV among persons with severe mental illness and among injection drug users. Key issues include these: How have mental health needs and policies as related to HIV/AIDS been affected by changes over time in public fears of infection? How has the context for mental health treatment in the HIV/AIDS population changed as the social, cultural, and economic profile of this population has evolved? How is this care affected by evolving organizational and financing factors?

The HIV Mental Health Challenge

The Centers for Disease Control (CDC) first noted five cases of the disease we now know as acquired immunodeficiency syndrome (AIDS) in the June 1981 issue of the *Morbidity and Mortality Weekly Report* (*MMWR*): It described young men who had sex with men who were treated in the prior 8 months at three different hospitals in Los Angeles for a type of pneumonia that appears almost exclusively in immunosuppressed patients (*Pneumocystis carinii* pneumonia; CDC 1981). From that time to the present, the challenges posed to mental health professionals and policy makers by AIDS and its cause, human immunodeficiency virus (HIV), have been conditioned by multiple, sometimes rapidly changing, influences. These influences include disease-related characteristics, such as its epidemiology, symptoms, common comorbidities, course, and outcome; developments in our understanding of the disease and how best to respond to it in terms of prevention, therapeutics, and palliation; and the evolving social and cultural contexts that assign meaning to the disease, the battle against it, and the effort to live with it. In this chapter we update and revise material from this *Handbook's* first edition,

This work was supported by the National Institute of Mental Health (MH058984, MH076206) and by the Agency for Healthcare Research and Quality (AHRQ) through a cooperative agreement for the Center for Research and Education on Mental Health Therapeutics at Rutgers (U18HS016097), as part of AHRQ's Centers for Education and Research on Therapeutics program. The content is solely the responsibility of the authors and does not necessarily reflect the official views of NIMH or AHRQ.

emphasizing how the mental health issues associated with the epidemic have been significantly affected by changes in disease context. As in the first edition, our focus is on the epidemic in the United States.

Changing Contexts and Changing Mental Health Needs

It can be helpful to identify some historical landmarks and use them to organize periods in the epidemic (Forstein, 2008). By 1983, case reports had supplied the basic facts, profiling a disease that was somehow transmitted sexually and by blood and was commonly found among men who have sex with men (MSM), but the causative agent was identified only by further research over the next several years. From 1981 until roughly 1984, when reliable serological tests were developed, uncertainty fueled fear, both in the public and among health professionals. Activists in the gay community responded with diverse sentiments, some sounding an alarm at a health crisis in their midst and others fearing that efforts to identify and contain disease risk would serve as devices to impose social controls motivated by homophobia. Prominent mental health issues included fears of infection; psychological responses to illness, including consideration of planned suicide and end-of-life issues; and coping with public attitudes expressed in stigma.

After HIV was identified as the cause of AIDS and reliable serological tests were developed, there followed a period when only prophylaxis for opportunistic infections was available. Zidovudine (AZT), a nucleoside analogue reverse transcriptase inhibitor (NRTI), was the first antiretroviral treatment for HIV and was introduced in March 1987. The availability of treatment increased incentives to be tested and introduced psychological issues related to living with HIV for longer periods of time. AZT was approved as a preventive treatment in 1990, and its use was adapted to stop mother-to-child transmission of pregnant women. Perinatal transmission dropped more than 90% between 1992 and 2003, drastically reducing the need for assessment and remediation of infant and early childhood HIV-related developmental problems, as well as reducing the incidence of new mothers struggling with the self-blame when a child was born infected (Ybarra, 1991). The availability of a potentially efficacious treatment again changed the psychological calculus regarding testing, made medication adherence a central issue, and increased the salience of systemic issues related to disparities, access to care, and the diffusion of innovations.

Early antiretroviral treatments for HIV produced only limited improvements in survival because of emergent drug resistance; however, beginning in the mid-1990s research advances allowed the introduction of treatment based on the use of multiple classes of agents, called highly active antiretroviral therapy (HAART). The availability of HAART only amplified the earlier emphasis on the necessity of adherence, first because the new regimens were complex and demanding and, second, because it was feared that even with combination therapy incomplete adherence would lead to development of drug resistance, limiting therapeutic options for the individual patient and posing potential public health threats from the spread of multiple new resistant strains of the virus. Shifts in disease epidemiology intersected with the heightened concern with adherence, as more patients were drawn from socially marginal groups identified by behavioral or mental health conditions that did not inspire physician confidence in their ability or willingness to meet adherence requirements, such as injection drug users and people with severe mental illness. As we discuss later in the chapter, although many people living with HIV/AIDS (PLWHA) from these groups proved able to achieve unexpectedly good adherence, provider skepticism, perhaps fed in some cases by stigma, meant that access to new treatments was a focus of clinical and research attention (Walkup, Sambamoorthi, & Crystal, 2001; Walkup, Wei, Sambamoorthi, & Crystal, 2008).

As HIV/AIDS has increasingly become a chronic, manageable disease, concern with mental health problems is no longer so dominated by crisis issues involving fear/guilt related to contracting the disease, the stresses of symptom management and social network depopulation, and end-of-life preparation. The spread of the disease into populations with high rates of addiction or psychiatric illness has complicated treatment because of the concentration of comorbidities and the demands of coordination of care for services from multiple treatment settings.

By the close of 2006, more than 1 million cases of HIV/AIDS had been reported to the CDC (CDC, 2008a). Rates went sharply upward in the 1980s, peaked in 1992, and stabilized in 1998. Surprisingly few data exist describing the extent of mental health needs and treatment in this population today. Using data collected in the 1990s, Burnam and colleagues (2001) found that 61% of a national sample of PLWHA receiving medical care had received mental health or substance abuse services in the preceding half-year. Few data are available on treatment patterns in more recent periods, in a much-changed, and changing, environment continually influenced by numerous social, epidemiological, medical, and cultural factors.

Knowledge of HIV Status

Psychological aspects of HIV testing illustrate how important it is to consider changing contexts in the discussion of mental health and HIV. One constant is that choosing to be tested can be conceptualized as involving a tradeoff between the reduction of uncertainty and the fear of having to deal with bad news. Before effective antiretroviral care became available, a person might avoid testing out of skepticism that providers had anything useful to offer and the fear of an inevitable progression to severe morbidity and death. Social implications of a positive test could intensify fears as well – both because a person acquired a new status (having a stigmatized disease) and because a positive test could suggest a status that was the object of stigma (e.g., homosexual, injection drug user). Today, much has changed. The testing process itself has changed, as more rapid and more convenient technologies have been developed. The nature of the "bad news" that must figure in any calculation has also changed, having been affected by reductions in mortality and morbidity. It also seems likely – although more difficult to demonstrate empirically – that changes in legal, institutional, and social contexts have influenced the cultural meanings ascribed to testing.

Anxiety seems to play a less pervasive role in determining testing patterns. Data from the Kaiser Family Foundation Survey of Americans on HIV/AIDS, conducted in spring 2006, indicated that the percentage of people in the general population who say that they are personally "very concerned" about contracting HIV trended downward between November 1995 and March 2006 for African Americans (55% to 34%), Latinos (38% to 31%), and Whites (16% to 9%). Just under half (48%) of those surveyed said they had been tested for HIV, including 19% who were tested in the past year. Fear of stigma associated with being tested was a concern for only a minority (21%), who said they believe people would think less of them if they found out they had been tested. Most (61%) respondents thought it would make no difference in how people they know think about them. People who had not been tested for HIV rarely named fear of testing positive as a reason (3%). Worries regarding confidentiality were not commonly cited either (13%).

For some in the general population, a decision to forgo testing may reflect an accurate assessment that their risk is negligible, but in samples of people at high risk, the decision to forgo testing seems to suggest that psychological factors are at work other than a clear-eyed assessment of risk alone. In a cross-sectional community sample of HIV-negative men and women judged to be at risk (due to drug use or sexual behavior), perceived risk was not significantly related to prior testing. However, a strong association was found between testing and a "decisional balance" scale, based around a weighing of perceived advantages and disadvantages of being tested (Lauby, Bond, Eroglu, & Batson, 2006). In the HIV Testing Survey (HITS), a high-risk sample was recruited at gay bars (men having sex with men; MSM), street intercept (injecting drug users; IDUs), and a sexually transmitted disease (STD) clinic (high-risk heterosexuals; HRH) in 1995–1996 and then again in 1998–1999 (Kellerman et al., 2002). Given that HAART was introduced and diffused during this period, the authors were surprised that the proportion tested increased only slightly (from 77% to 80%). However, although the proportion not tested was not much smaller in the more recent study, the psychological perspectives of those not tested may have been affected by HAART. They were significantly less likely to cite fear of finding out they were HIV-positive as the main reason for not being tested: they were less likely to cite as a reason that they "didn't want to think about being HIV-positive" or "there's little you can do if you test positive for HIV" (Kellerman et al., 2002).

In theory, rates of failure to return (FTR) for testing could provide a behavioral index of mixed feelings about testing, because they indicate that individuals have taken a key step to learning their serostatus, but fail to get the results. In the first round of the HIV Testing Survey with high-risk populations (described earlier), at least one case of FTR was reported by 10% of MSM, 20% of HRHs, and 27% of IDUs. Approximately one-quarter of respondents said that fear of getting test results was an important reason for their FTR, and those with higher perceived risk were more likely to have FTR (Sullivan, Lansky, Drake, & HITS-2000 Investigators, 2004). Although FTR rates certainly have public health implications, interpretation of their psychological significance is made more complicated because the motivation implied by the act of getting tested can be so variable. (For example, an FTR may not reflect much ambivalence for a person whose original testing was informally coerced by social or institutional forces.)

A 2006 Kaiser survey found that most respondents (72%) said increasing the number of people tested for HIV was a "very important" prevention priority. The most recent national figures available (2006) indicate that about two-fifths (40.4%) of U.S. adults aged 18 to 64 report having been tested for HIV at some time – a rate that had remained essentially unchanged over the previous 5 years. Testing in the past year was reported by 10.4% of all adults and by 23% of those who acknowledge their risk factors (CDC, 2008b). Money spent on prevention seems to make a difference, because data suggest the odds of having been tested are higher in areas where CDC funding was more generous (Linas, Zheng, Losina, Walensky, & Freedberg, 2006). Doubts have accumulated regarding testing policies that emphasize the selective use of testing with persons with identified risks (Koo, Begier, Henn, Sepkowitz, & Kellerman, 2006). It has become clear that many people who should get tested do not (Bond, Lauby, & Batson, 2005; Liddicoat et al., 2004; Rust, Minor, Jordan, Mayberry, & Satcher, 2003) or do so only after the disease is relatively advanced (Bozzette et al., 1998; Samet et al., 1998). In a multisite study of 2,621 young MSM, just over one-fifth had never been tested (22%), and 71% had not been tested recently (Sumartojo et al., 2008). CDC statistics from 2002 indicated that 39% of those with a positive HIV test received an AIDS diagnosis within a year (CDC, 2002). A recent change in CDC policy now calls for routine testing in medical settings, but little empirical evidence is available on its implementation.

Disclosure of HIV-Positive Serostatus

Disclosure of HIV-positive status can be a psychologically consequential decision. One approach is to look at individual predictors of disclosure. A 2008 review of the literature examined disclosure among heterosexual PLWHA adults (omitting parental disclosure; Mayfield, Rice, Flannery, & Rotheram-Borus, 2008). Disclosure was more likely among women compared to men, Latino and White families compared to African American families, and younger compared to older adult PLWHA. A recent article not included in that review used in-depth interviews to examine themes related to disclosure among 25 older adults

(50 to 72 years of age), concluding that many of the concerns expressed echo those found in younger PLWHA (Emlet, 2007).

Studies commonly consider disclosure in the contexts of specific relationships between the PLWHA and the person told, but a few studies have examined the decision to disclose as a more general expression of personal identity (Mayfield et al., 2008). One recent qualitative study examined how, as HIV/AIDS is increasingly viewed as a chronic disease, individuals incorporate the disease into their identity (Baumgartner, 2007). Cultural identity, at least as indexed by language choice, may play some role in influencing disclosure, because disclosure was less likely among Spanish-speaking Latino men (Mason, Marks, Simoni, Ruiz, & Richardson, 1995) and women (Simoni et al., 1995) than their English-speaking counterparts.

Another approach is to see whether people who have disclosed their status regretted it afterward. Generally, when the anticipated consequences of those who have not disclosed are compared with the reported consequences of those who have disclosed, the actual consequences are more positive both with employers (Simoni, Mason, & Marks, 1997) and personal relations (Mansergh, Marks, & Simoni, 1995). Of course studies such as these cannot show definitively that the nondisclosers have it wrong and are too pessimistic in their anticipated consequences. It could simply be that people are good at judging whether to disclose and that those who chose to disclose had what turned out to be good reasons to anticipate more positive consequences. Another possibility is that once individuals have gone ahead and committed themselves by disclosing their HIV-positive status, they may be particularly alert to consequences that justify that prior action.

Patterns of regret over disclosure may have changed over time. Whereas studies of this topic were common in the early and mid-1990s, one more recent study reported on regret in a group of HIV-positive gay men, most of whom were recruited from an AIDS Clinical Trial Unit at a Midwestern university between 1998 and 2000 (Serovich, Mason, Bautista, & Toviessi, 2006). There was very little reported regret. Most (63%) reported 0% regret. Not surprisingly, findings differed by relationship: 77.2% of men said some in their nuclear family knew (of whom 8.2% expressed regret); 88.9% had a friend who knew (of whom 24% expressed regret); and 49.4% said someone at work knew (of whom 7.6% expressed regret).

While regret is probably the most common consequence studied, other correlates of disclosure have received some attention. A 2008 meta-analysis found that, across studies, disclosure was positively correlated with social support and negatively correlated with stigma (Smith, Rossetto, & Peterson, 2008). Concerns over serostatus disclosure sometimes have a negative impact on antiviral adherence, and, in a study of serodiscordant couples, greater disclosure was correlated with better adherence even after controlling for other explanatory variables (Stirratt et al., 2006). A common assumption is that encouraging PLWHA to disclose their serostatus to partners leads to safer sex, but the evidence supporting this assumption has been criticized as inadequate (Simoni & Pantalone, 2004). Inconsistent disclosure – telling some partners and not others – was relatively common in a large group of MSM recruited in San Francisco and New York City (Parsons et al., 2005).

Stigma and Societal Attitudes

In a national sample of PLWHA receiving medical care during the 1990s, approximately one-quarter (26%) reported they had suffered some type of discrimination (Schuster et al., 2005). More generally, there is wide agreement that stigma against PLWHA exists and has implications for mental health. Efforts to study it empirically have made clear that the topic may be complex in at least three ways. First, stigma assessment is complicated by real-world "layering," or co-occurrence of multiple stigmatized identity elements in PLWHA (e.g., IDU and commercial sex worker). Second, stigma effects are embedded in changing historical contexts, influenced by changes in public awareness and knowledge, disease epidemiology, and treatment responsiveness. Finally, as a construct, stigma has been conceptualized as existing at multiple levels of analysis (interpersonal, institutional, etc.) and is capable of having both a direct effect on mental health and indirect effects, by promoting opposition to AIDS-directed service and support programs. In some formulations, for example, exclusionary practices are treated as a component of stigma or as a subtype (e.g., enacted stigma), whereas in others stigma is said to produce discrimination, which can be conceptualized as a consequence of stigma, rather than a component or subtype (Nyblade, 2006).

Conceptualization and measurement of HIV/AIDS-related stigma have both benefited from and been complicated by the prior existence of extensive social science research on health-related stigma developed long before HIV. The extensive attention devoted to HIV/AIDS stigma has required considering longstanding issues in the literature, such as whether stigma should be approached as a generic concept applicable across diseases and groups or as a more disorder-specific or culturally local concept. A typical generic component of stigma is social distance, such as unwillingness to work with PLWHA or have them as a neighbor; this construction of the stigma concept is familiar from sociological work that pre-dates HIV by more than 50 years (Bogardus, 1925). More HIV-specific components concern such elements as fear of infection or support for coercive behavior by the government (e.g., quarantine). Application of existing social distance items to HIV can introduce ambiguities (Nyblade, 2006). For example, an item that measures the reluctance to eat with PLWHA could reflect fear of infection or, alternatively, an aversion to the social reciprocity and intimacy implied by eating together, just as it might for reluctance to eat with, say, someone who had been to prison.

Performance characteristics of HIV-specific stigma measures may sometimes differ by race. Item response analysis suggests that, among Blacks, indications of stigmatization come largely from items describing situational discrimination. Among Whites, these indications come from items describing concerns about secrecy and interpersonal rejection (Rao, Pryor, Gaddist, & Mayer, 2008). A recent literature review stressed that, despite evidence that many of the consequences of stigma are similar across multiple different conditions and groups, research on generic measurement is underdeveloped (Van Brakel, 2006). Across conditions, stigma assessments have been categorized into five groups: those based on experienced discrimination, attitudes toward sufferers, felt stigma, internalized stigma, or stigmatizing institutional practices (Van Brakel, 2006).

One influential AIDS-specific approach, exemplified by the extensive work by Herek and colleagues, is to distinguish between instrumental stigma – which is directly linked to disease features such as transmissibility, visibility, and severity – and symbolic stigma, involving the expression of negative attitudes toward groups and practices (e.g., homosexual sex, drug use; Herek, Capitanio, & Widaman, 2002, 2003; Herek et al., 1998). Herek has stressed the contrasting function of instrumental attitudes, which serve both an evaluative function and a function to satisfy a need to understand the social world in terms of utility or harm, versus the expressive function served by the value-laden, self-defining function of symbolic stigma.

Rather than conceptualizing HIV-related stigma as multicomponent, incorporating negative attitudes toward transmission-related characteristics such as homosexual sex or injection drug use, others have described a person's membership in multiple stigmatized groups as a "layering" of stigma (McBride, 1998). Nyblade has recently named this topic ("layering") as a key knowledge gap in HIV stigma assessment (Nyblade, 2006). One approach to layering measurement issues is the general framework proposed by Reidpath and Chan (2005). They start with two stigma sources (e.g., being a MSM or being an injection drug user). They then construct a 2×2 table: MSM vs. not-MSM and IDU vs. not-IDU. In the not-MSM/not-IDU cell, neither factor contributes to stigma. In the MSM/not-IDU cell and the not-MSM/IDU cell, there is a single unique source (i.e., MSM or IDU, respectively). In the MSM/IDU cell, the two are combined. In this cell, the stigma can be conceptualized either as a shared stigma or as a "synergistic" stigma, which they have defined as measured stigma that exceeds the additive sum of the two sources independently. Thus, for example, if the stigma score for an IDU is largely equivalent to that for an IDU who was also an MSM, there would be little evidence for a synergistic stigma.

Although Reidpath and Chan (2005) are concerned with how layering may increase stigma, it is not obvious a priori that all stigma combinations necessarily act synergistically to *increase* stigma (or have no effect). Synergism could decrease stigma. If perceived responsibility for infection is associated with greater stigma, as was found by investigators interested in so-called innocent PLWHA who had acquired the virus perinatally or through transfusions, then the combination of

HIV/AIDS with a stigmatized condition that decreased perceived responsibility for infection might produce stigma levels lower than that for HIV/AIDS alone. Far from being an abstract speculation, this exact issue was raised when evidence indicated that HIV was spreading among people with severe mental illness (who might be perceived as less responsible than other PLWHA). If perceived as less responsible, then the predicted synergistic stigma ought to be less than the additive sum of the two unique sources (probably because in the absence of mitigating considerations, people assume a PLWHA who does not have a mental illness is more "responsible" for his or her own infection). Using a narrative vignette approach, Walkup, Cramer, and Yeras (2004) tested this notion and found that the additional presence of mental illness did not significantly reduce stigma ratings. More recent vignette-based work by Chan and colleagues has found that layering can produce both stigma increases and stigma reductions: for example, the stigma of commercial sex alone was greater than combined AIDS and commercial sex, and the stigma of IDU alone was greater than for combined AIDS and IDU (Chan & Reidpath, 2007).

The historical dimension of HIV-related stigma introduces additional causal complexity. Discussions by journalists and historians offer narratives of the changes in social attitudes toward HIV/AIDS, but empirical approaches to time-dependent changes are less common. Using cross-sectional data from surveys conducted in 1991, 1997, and 1999, Herek and colleagues compared various items to characterize trends through the decade of the 1990s (Herek, 2002). Support for coercive policies, such as quarantine, declined, as did the percentage of respondents expressing negative feelings toward PLWHA, such as anger, fear, or disgust.

Determining just how developments in the HIV epidemic may influence stigma poses analytic challenges, because population-level attitude changes are inherently difficult to study. In the general population, older cohorts have been replaced by younger, typically more educated counterparts, who have a quite different historical experience. In contrast to the adult population who first learned about AIDS in the early 1980s, most U.S. adults who are today younger than 40 experienced their sexual debut in a world where HIV was a concern, and many college students and young adults have lived their whole lives during the period of the epidemic. One effort to address these analytic challenges focused on the link between time-specific state-level AIDS incidence patterns from the CDC and homophobia, as indexed by items from a geographically stratified probability sample of U.S. adults, the General Social Survey (GSS), from 1973 through 1998 (Ruel & Campbell, 2006). Because prior work had found increases in support for the rights of people who are homosexual despite evidence of negative moral or social evaluations, the authors distinguished between attitudes toward rights and attitudes toward the morality of homosexual behavior. Contrary to their expectation that the impact of AIDS incidence rates would taper off over time as society adjusted to it, they found that, after controlling for the complexities posed by various compositional, cohort, and period effects, higher state-level AIDS incidence rates were associated with more negative views of rights for people who are homosexual throughout the period studied. Although negative attitudes toward the morality of homosexual behavior increased, particularly during the early period of the epidemic, this rise was not tied to AIDS incidence.

Stress, Coping, and Social Support

A large literature now exists regarding the impact of HIV/AIDS-related stresses on various psychological and biological outcomes. The multiple models used to study stress are discussed in Chapter 6 by Thoits, Chapter 9 by Wheaton and Montazer, Chapter 10 by Turner and Lewis Brown, and Chapter 11 by Lennon and Limonic in this volume, but most share a common starting point: the dual observation, first, that challenging or noxious features of a situation (e.g., a positive HIV test, pain, or the development of disfiguring symptoms) often seem to have an impact on outcomes related to psychological/physical health or well-being, and, second, that the correlation between stresses and these outcomes is far from perfect. To explain how and why outcomes may vary, theories look to differences in the resources people can call on to help them cope (e.g., support from a spouse) or differences in the strategies they use to cope (e.g., taking an analgesic to reduce pain).

Broadly speaking, resources can either moderate or mediate the effects of stressors. For example, when individuals learn they have HIV, the impact may be lessened if they have supportive friends. If people who have supportive friends are not hit as hard as others by the news of a diagnosis and so have better well-being outcomes, then the presence of friends may moderate the stress effect of the diagnosis (by, for example, buffering its impact). Alternatively, if, for another person, the news of a positive HIV test prompts the departure of a spouse or partner and this loss itself produces worsened well-being outcomes, the impact of the stressor is said to be mediated by its impact on resources. (Often a mediational effect such as this does not occur by itself, in which case the only negative impact of the positive HIV test is transmitted via its impact on a person's spouse or partner; instead the stressor has various other negative effects, some of which may be direct effects, as well as those mediated by the departure.)

A number of studies have identified coping style as a significant predictor of psychosocial functioning. These typically draw on a well-developed literature in this area associated with the stress-coping work of Lazarus and Folkman (1984), which was recently reviewed by Walkup and Cramer-Berness (2007). This framework has promoted research and made possible linkages to the broader coping literature related to other diseases. One problem for readers unfamiliar with this literature is that it uses many different terms as models have been elaborated. Often a two-stage process is envisioned, with a first stage consisting of a primary appraisal of threat, followed by a secondary appraisal of whether and how a person can respond to affect his or her situation. The resulting coping responses focus either on trying to change facts about the situation ("problem focused" or "active" coping) or changing one's emotional response to the situation ("emotion-focused" or "passive" coping; Fleishman et al., 2000; Schmitz & Crystal, 2000). For example, a person who has disclosed a recent diagnosis to a primary sexual partner may feel frightened and depressed in the face of that partner's anger or alienation (the stressor or threat). Problem-focused coping might include efforts to reestablish emotional connections by working to improve communication or going for couples therapy. Emotion-focused coping might include efforts to step back from the dysphoric mood and to quit fighting it, find distractions, or somehow promote positive feelings.

Some research has examined the impact of specific stressors. Anyone older than 50 who lived in an AIDS epicenter in the 1980s can recall the terrible toll associated with the high mortality rates. It is the period that was portrayed retrospectively in Jonathan Demme's movie *Philadelphia*, with clinics filled with emaciated figures approaching death. Conceptualized as a "community stressor" in a lecture in the 1980s, AIDS was described in terms of two stress-inducing sources: both the uncertainty around one's own death and the death of loved ones due to AIDS (J. L. Martin, Dean, Garcia, & Hall, 1989). For loved ones, family members, and those in social networks with PLWHA, as well as for many who delivered services to them, funerals and bereavement were a constant occurrence. The impact of these losses was magnified for many PLWHA, because the net effect was to deplete social networks of valued sources of support (J. L. Martin & Dean, 1993; J. L. Martin et al., 1989; Neugebauer et al., 1992).

In a diverse group of PLWHA reported on by Sikkema and colleagues, four of five participants had lost someone close to AIDS, and most of these had lost several people (Sikkema et al., 2000). Grief symptoms within the prior month were reported by two-thirds of those with losses. In later publications, the severity of the grief reaction was associated with loss type and coping strategies (i.e., escape-avoidance and self-controlling), as well as with depressive symptoms and a history of IDU (Sikkema, Kochman, DiFranceisco, Kelly, & Hoffmann, 2003). Participants randomized to a cognitive behavioral group intervention to promote improved coping with grief (vs. individual psychotherapy on request) showed improved health-related quality of life (Sikkema, Hansen, Meade, Kochman, & Lee, 2005). Both groups showed decreases in grief severity, but among those with higher levels of psychiatric distress, grief severity scores were significantly lower for patients in the group intervention (Sikkema et al., 2006).

Improvements in medical treatments have unquestionably made life better in many different ways for many PLWA, but the impact of HAART on stress and coping can be complicated. By directly comparing women with HIV before HAART's introduction to a matched sample after HAART, an interesting study by Siegel and Schrimshaw (2005) found that the second group faced more stress associated with

HIV-related disclosure and stigma and more often had recourse to escape-avoidant coping or other negative strategies (Schrimshaw, Siegel, & Lekas, 2005). Thus, HAART may be better described as reconfiguring, rather than simply eliminating, stressors. As part of the Healthy Living Project, a large, multicity, randomized control trial of a cognitive behavioral intervention with HIV-positive women in the HAART era, Remien and colleagues conducted a cross-sectional analysis of recruited subjects; they found that, although high levels of depressive symptomatology were present, these were not predicted by HAART utilization or clinical markers of disease state (Remien et al., 2006). Using a stress and coping model, they found higher depressive symptom levels were predicted by illness-related factors, such as the number of physical symptoms and illness intrusiveness, as well as perceived stress. Stress mediated the impact of health status on depression. Lower depression levels were predicted by coping self-efficacy and social support. Coping self-efficacy mediated the impact of psychosocial resources on depression.

Leserman (2008) reviewed published longitudinal studies conducted between 1990 and 2007, concluding that evidence indicated that variation in HIV disease progression can be influenced by chronic depression, stressful events, and trauma. In one group of PLWHA, fatigue intensity and fatigue-related impairment were associated with lower income, childhood trauma, more recent stressful events, and more depressive symptoms (Leserman, Barroso, Pence, Salahuddin, & Harmon, 2008). In a longitudinal study of 490 PLWHA, those with more lifetime trauma were more likely to die (Leserman et al., 2007). In an unusual study, researchers compared a group of PLWHA ($n = 37$) who had shown an atypically favorable disease course with an HIV-positive comparison group ($n = 100$), asking each to write about their reactions to past traumas. Coding of essays showed emotional disclosure/processing was more common in the "healthy survivor" group (O'Cleirigh, Ironson, Fletcher, & Schneiderman, 2008).

High-quality reviews are available describing the impact of stress management for PLWHA (Brown & Vanable, 2008), including two recent meta-analytic reviews (Crepaz et al., 2008; Scott-Sheldon, Kalichman, Carey, & Fielder, 2008). In the first, Crepaz and colleagues identified 15 randomized controlled trials of cognitive behavioral interventions on depression, anxiety, anger, stress, and CD4 cell counts. Evidence for effects on CD4 cell counts was limited, but aggregated effect size estimates were significant for depression and anxiety in trials with 11 or more sessions that included stress management (Crepaz et al., 2008). In the second review, Scott-Sheldon and colleagues (2008) identified 35 randomized controlled trials conducted between 1989 and 2006. They found little evidence of benefit from stress management for various biological measures (e.g., CD4 counts, viral load, hormonal outcomes), but effect sizes were significant for such outcomes as anxiety, depression, distress, fatigue, and quality of life (Scott-Sheldon et al., 2008). However, possible benefits of stress management for physical health recently received support in a randomized control trial comparing a wait-list control to three treatment conditions (a cognitive behavioral relaxation training, focused tai chi training, and groups to promote spiritual growth), all of which produced improvements in lymphocyte function (McCain et al., 2008).

Suicidality and Suicide

In considering research on suicidality, it is helpful to keep in mind how thoughts of ending one's life have been subject to varying interpretations during the course of the epidemic. From a psychiatric perspective these thoughts are often viewed as symptoms, potential indicators of depressive disorder. Alternatively, in the early days of the epidemic, ending one's life rather than endure the psychological and physical miseries of end-stage AIDS was sometimes viewed as a positive expression of autonomy. For example, physician-assisted suicide was considered as an option by 55% of a group of ambulatory PLWHA (Breitbart, Rosenfeld, & Passik, 1996).

A key development was the changing association between HIV and slow, certain death, as treatments became more effective in reducing morbidity and mortality of PLWHA. Early research investigated suicidality in relation to disease stage. In the pre-HAART era, some research indicated that early stages of HIV infection were more closely associated with suicide than was full-blown AIDS (O'Dowd & McKegney, 1990). More recently, time since diagnosis was found important in a study of 207 women with HIV/AIDS in New York City. Approximately one-quarter (26%) reported a suicide attempt in the period since HIV diagnosis, 42% of which occurred within the first month after diagnosis and 27% within the first week (Cooperman & Simoni, 2005).

Suicidal ideation was examined in a diverse sample of 2,909 HIV-positive individuals from San Francisco, Los Angeles, Milwaukee, and New York City, who were screened for a prevention trial between July 2000 and January 2002 (Carrico et al., 2007). Past-week suicidal ideation was found in 19% of those screened and was associated with not being heterosexual, having more severe HIV-related symptoms and medication side effects, regular marijuana use, and symptoms of depression. Past-week suicidal ideation was higher (38%) in an eight-state sample of PLWHA outside urban areas (Heckman et al., 2002). Inadequately controlled pain likely played a role as well. In one group of 75 PLWHA, pain intensity independently predicted suicidal ideation even after controlling for reported psychiatric and substance abuses diagnoses (Dafoe & Stewart, 2004).

HIV and Psychiatric Illness

Research on HIV and mental health has historically been concerned with multiple psychosocial stressors and nonpathological emotional and functional outcomes, but over the past 10 to 15 years, research on the intersection of HIV and diagnosable psychiatric illness has become an increasingly differentiated and active area of investigation. Psychiatric publications in the 1980s that included reports on treated cases largely originated in a handful of research-oriented consultation services at Johns Hopkins, New York Hospital, University of California, San Francisco, and elsewhere. Reflecting the early epidemiology, this research often focused on gay, male groups of patients in treatment and was concerned with adjustment to illness, complicating comorbidities, and occasional neuropsychiatric complications of infection. A review of the literature to 1987 suggested that rates of psychopathology were high among PLWHA (Catalan, 1988). Further examination of the nature of this association required large community cohort studies that incorporated seronegative comparison groups and used standardized diagnostic instruments (e.g., G. R. Brown et al., 1992; Perkins et al., 1994; Rosenberger et al., 1993; J. B. Williams, Rabkin, Remien, Gorman, & Ehrhardt, 1991).

Depression has been the foremost focus of attention, and a review published in 1997 identified 11 studies using clinician diagnostic assessments according to specified diagnostic criteria for prevalence estimates of major depression in HIV-positive populations (Stober, Schwartz, McDaniel, & Abrams, 1997). Rates ranged from 0% to 35%, with the authors speculating that some of the variability resulted from differences over how to count physical symptoms, such as fatigue or loss of appetite, which could reflect depression, HIV disease, or medication side effects. Examination of the HIV–depression linkage pointed to the importance of considering base rates of disorder among those who contract HIV. Longitudinal studies, including uninfected controls (Dew et al., 1997) and a meta-analysis comparing HIV-positive and HIV-negative at risk patients (Ciesla & Roberts, 2001), eventually clarified that, although recurrences of depression contribute to the point prevalence among PLWA, there is likely some distinctive association between HIV and depression.

The need to consider disorders that may precede HIV infection arose in another area – the study of more enduring and severe disorders, such as bipolar illness or schizophrenia. Recognition of the significance of the serious mental illness (SMI)–HIV linkage was initially so limited that some investigators using structured assessments opted to drop the psychosis screen to save interview time (Holmes et al., 1997; J. B. Williams et al., 1991). Only after the Cournos group in New York City published reports regarding HIV in psychiatric inpatient settings did concern begin to focus on this linkage.

AIDS was first identified in a state psychiatric hospital in New York City in 1983 when a 25-year-old young woman developed a low white blood cell count. AIDS was considered a gay men's disease at the time, and her condition was at first attributed to her antipsychotic medicine. When stopping her medicine did not help, she was transferred to a general hospital. Lacking an HIV antibody test at the time, her AIDS diagnosis was made only when the cause of her pneumonia was found to be *Pneumocystis carinii* (Cournos, 1996).

Case reports mounted, and in 1987 more than 40 medically ill HIV-infected patients had been treated in New York City state hospitals. Many of the most important initial studies of HIV and SMI were motivated by a need to learn more about these institutional inpatient settings. Multiple settings reported elevated seroprevalence rates, often calculated from examination of waste blood drawn at intake (Cournos et al., 1991; Cournos, Empfield, Horwath, & Schrage, 1990; Cournos, Horwath, Guido, McKinnon, & Hopkins, 1994; Cournos & McKinnon, 1997; Empfield et al., 1993; McKinnon, Carey, & Cournos, 1997; Meyer, Empfield, Engel, & Cournos, 1995; Meyer et al., 1993). Reviews cited rates ranging from 4% to 23% in studies published between 1991 and 2001 (Cournos & McKinnon, 2008).

By the end of the 1990s, other data sources yielded results broadly consistent with the seroprevalence studies. Archival and administrative data documented lower but still elevated rates in population-based studies and community-dwelling populations (Blank, Mandell, Aiken, & Hadley, 2002; Stoskopf, Kim, & Glover, 2001), as well as treated prevalence rates of SMI significantly higher among PLWHA than in the general population (Walkup, Crystal, & Sambamoorthi, 1999). Prompted by early prevalence data, several studies also profiled risk behaviors among people with serious mental illness (Carey, Carey, & Kalichman, 1997; Carey, Carey, Maisto, Gordon, & Vanable, 2001; Carey et al., 2004; Carey, Carey, Weinhardt, & Gordon, 1997; Weinhardt, Carey, & Carey, 1998).

The nature of the epidemiological linkages between serious mental illness and HIV is not clear. Psychiatric symptoms, risky sex, and substance abuse have all been examined as influences; the relations among them seem complex (Walkup et al., 2008). The most pronounced elevations among the institutionally based studies came from treatment settings focused on patients with psychiatric illness and substance abuse (Krakow, Galanter, Dermatis, & Westreich, 1998; Silberstein et al., 1994). In a study conducted in the Veterans Administration system, a comparison was made between a national sample who received a diagnosis of schizophrenia, bipolar illness, or other, nonorganic psychosis and a national random sample who had received none of these diagnoses (Himelhoch et al., 2007). HIV diagnosis was recorded for 1.0% of the first group, which was lower than most institutional and claims-based studies, but still elevated in comparison to the veteran group without serious mental illness (0.5%). However, further analysis indicated that, although patients with schizophrenia and a substance abuse diagnosis were more likely than those with neither to have HIV, patients with schizophrenia and no substance abuse diagnosis were less likely, not more likely, to have HIV. Other work has indicated that substance abuse problems may differ in how they affect sexual risk among people with serious mental illness, because lifetime substance use diagnosis seems to predict partner-related risks (e.g., sex trade), but only active substance use disorder predicts condom-related risks (Meade, 2006).

Not all studies reporting on rates of HIV among people with serious mental illness have found the very high elevations that have been the focus of attention (Himelhoch et al., 2007; Rosenberg et al., 2001), but it is not yet clear what factors best account for rate variation. The literature cited in the preceding paragraph certainly suggests that one factor may be local infection rates among drug users, especially IDUs, along with the local overlap between drug-using populations and those with serious mental illness and the level of social network ties uniting the groups. Future work needs to examine contextual factors responsible for local epidemics in this vulnerable group, including housing, employment rates, methadone and syringe exchange programs, and local institutional policies that make it difficult for people with substance abuse problems to get psychiatric treatment for major mental illness, and vice versa.

Documentation of the association between SMI and HIV in disease epicenters and the suggestive evidence of risky behaviors in this population have raised a range of clinical and policy issues involving HIV testing (Walkup, McAlpine, Olfson, Boyer, & Hansell, 2000; Walkup, Satriano, Barry, Sadler, & Cournos, 2002), the possible impact of stigma (Walkup, Cramer, et al., 2004), and physician concerns about adherence on initiation of antiretroviral care, as well as the ability of patients to achieve acceptable levels of adherence (Tegger et al., 2008; Walkup, Sambamoorthi, & Crystal, 2004) and the role of clinical and other services in promoting adherence.

An active area of investigation is the extent to which receipt of psychiatric care affects initiation of and adherence to HAART (Tegger et al., 2008). Early survey-based findings suggested that physicians might be reluctant to commence antiretroviral treatment for patients with psychiatric conditions (Bogart, Kelly, Catz, & Sosman, 2000). Claims-based studies of Medicaid patients with HIV and SMI tended not to find evidence of access barriers (Walkup et al., 2001), and there is evidence that in some circumstances patients with HIV and SMI are more likely than others to initiate antiretroviral care (Walkup, Sambamoorthi & Crystal, 2004). These studies did not consider the role that psychiatric medication use may play in making antiretroviral care more likely. In a large observational study, it was found that, although compared to patients without mental illness, those with depression or anxiety were equally likely to initiate HAART if they received antidepressant/antianxiety medication; however, they were significantly less likely to receive that therapy if they did not get that medicine (Tegger et al., 2008). A similar result was found in a study of Medicaid claims in which patients diagnosed with depression who were receiving antidepressants were more likely to receive antiretroviral care than those not receiving antidepressants (Sambamoorthi, Walkup, Olfson, & Crystal, 2000).

Once antiretroviral care has been initiated, receipt of ongoing psychiatric care may play some role in promoting antiretroviral adherence, but definitive evidence is lacking. Observational studies relying on administrative claims have found that patients diagnosed with depression who received an antidepressant were more likely to adhere to antiretrovirals in the following month (Walkup, Wei, et al., 2008; Yun, Maravi, Kobayashi, Barton, & Davidson, 2005), and possibly antiretroviral adherence may show more improvement over time among those receiving antidepressants. It is challenging to demonstrate these effects with data of this kind (see comment of I. B. Wilson & Jacobson, 2006 on Yun et al., 2005), yet ethical considerations argue against random assignment of depressed patients to nontreatment conditions. Further study of this topic is a high priority.

HIV and Injection Drug Use

CDC estimates suggest that more than one-quarter of the cumulative HIV/AIDS cases in the United States are attributable to injection drug use (CDC, 2005). Historically recognition of the IDU connection to AIDS lagged behind the MSM linkage somewhat because the initial AIDS cases identified among IDUs (in 1981) often came to clinical attention in patients who were also MSM. This created some uncertainty around the source of infection in the days before HIV was identified as that source. Experts examining historically collected sera have concluded that HIV was probably introduced into the IDU population in New York City around 1977 and then spread rapidly, with south Manhattan samples from 1980 showing 40% seropositivity (Des Jarlais, 1990). Incidence among IDUs has varied across geographic areas, with rates historically higher in East Coast cities than in West Coast cities, and it has shown pronounced changes over time (Quan et al., 2002; Santibanez et al., 2006).

Multiple sources have suggested that HIV incidence in this group peaked in the 1980s and declined steadily through the 1990s. National trends were documented in a 25-state group with available surveillance data (CDC, 2003), and other studies examined trends in Baltimore, San Francisco, Chicago, and New York City (Santibanez et al., 2006). Cross-sectional findings from the period between 2001 to 2004 indicated that there might be a convergence in New York City between infection rates of injecting and noninjecting drug users (Des Jarlais et al., 2007), which may suggest a growing predominance of sexual transmission among drug users. The factors responsible for these changes are not known with certainty. Data collected in the late 1980s indicated that injecting drug users' understanding of HIV transmission did not differ appreciably from that of the general public (Celentano, Vlahov, Menon, & Polk, 1991). Experts have stressed the likely role played by IDUs themselves, as they have adopted and promoted protective and harm-reduction behaviors (S. R. Friedman et al., 2007).

Mixed-method and qualitative research studies have contributed to a better understanding of the social psychology of risk and infection among IDUs and have also explored race differences. Patterns of risk behavior and infection in San Francisco, for example, have been explored ethnographically. Social hierarchies exist: Those with higher rank inject before lower ranked members, who are left to obtain drugs from used cottons (Bourgeois, 1998). Risk differences between African American and White heroin injectors have been interpreted as reflecting differences in their experiences with law enforcement, family ties, and self-presentation (Bourgeois et al., 2006). For example, Whites were described as seeing themselves as abject outcasts, injecting heroin not to seek pleasure but to stave off withdrawals; by contrast, African American IDUs were described as self-consciously cultivating an "outlaw" identity and as characterizing heroin injection primarily as a source of pleasure. The authors argued that these differences in self-presentation and style are reflected in characteristic risks. Expressing an identity-related commitment to achieving an ecstatic rush, African American IDUs probe themselves extensively with needles to find a useful vein for injection, in circumstances in which White IDUs would tend to opt for subcutaneous injection, which produces patterns of abscesses. Residential segregation may play a role in race differences in adolescent initiation of injection drug use (Fuller et al., 2005). Drawing from three datasets with information on people seeking substance abuse treatment, Broz and Ouellet (2008) found indications of race-specific changes in drug use practices. Between 1992 and 2004, the proportion of admissions who inject declined much more sharply for African Americans than for Whites (44% vs. 14%; Broz & Ouellet, 2008). Age may play a role as well, because younger White substance abusers were much more likely to inject than younger African Americans.

Mental health problems are frequent, consequential accompaniments of injection drug use, both for those with HIV/AIDS and those without (Chander, Himelhoch, & Moore, 2006; Cook et al., 2007; Klinkenberg & Sacks, 2004), and levels of unmet need are high (M. D. Stein & Friedmann, 2002). Depression is common among PLWHA who inject drugs, particularly among women and those with limited social support (Valverde et al., 2007). In a meta-analysis that included studies of IDU samples from both clinical venues and the community, significant associations were found between depression and a range of drug use behaviors, including concurrent substance use and needle sharing (Conner, Pinquart, & Duberstein, 2008). In a six-city sample of women with HIV/AIDS, drug use and depression were found to interact to suppress HAART use after controlling for a range of clinical and demographic variables (Cook et al., 2007). A systematic review of studies of IDUs, most of whom were PLWHA, found active substance abuse to be associated with low adherence to antiretroviral therapy (Malta, Strathdee, Magnanini, & Bastos, 2008).

There are reasons for concern about the care received by PLWHA who are IDUs. In one national study IDUs were more than twice as likely as non-IDUs to visit an emergency room in a 1-year period and were almost twice as likely to be hospitalized. Elements of standard care processes, such as CD4 and viral load testing, were about half as likely to be performed in a 6-month period (Barash, Hanson, Buskin, & Teshale, 2007). Indications of poor health care for IDUs, such as fewer than two outpatient visits in the past 6 months or reporting the emergency room as a usual source of care, are predicted by the absence of health insurance (Mizuno et al., 2006). Some specific types of treatment contact may improve treatment access. After controlling for a range of variables, case management and substance abuse treatment were associated with the use of outpatient services, and, among those with an AIDS diagnosis, with optimal outpatient use (Knowlton et al., 2001). Receipt of drug abuse services can positively affect both antiretroviral use and adherence (Kapadia et al., 2008; Sambamoorthi, Warner, Crystal, & Walkup, 2000). Treatment contact per se does not invariably reduce risk, however. In a sample of IDUs, those with more drug treatment contact were more likely, not less likely, to share needles. However, although needle sharing was significantly associated with anxiety, it was negatively associated with the use of psychotropic medication (Lundgren, Amodeo, & Chassler, 2005).

Syringe exchange programs (SEPs) have proved a distinctly powerful intervention for reducing HIV transmission among IDUs, but historically their impact has been drastically slowed by determined political opposition. Efforts to secure federal funding for SEPs, based on extensive evidence for their effectiveness, became entangled in the war on drugs (Des Jarlais & Friedman, 1998; Vlahov et al., 2001). Nevertheless, surveys of known SEPs have shown steady growth through the 1990s. A 2002 survey of 148 known SEPs yielded data from 126 SEP directors, reporting on programs in 102 cities in 31 states, in which almost 25 million syringes were exchanged (CDC, 2005). During this period of SEP growth, between 1994 and 2000, new HIV diagnoses among adolescent/adult IDUs declined 42% overall in the 25 states from which HIV surveillance data were collected (CDC, 2003).

Despite the utility of SEPs, research has also clarified some of their limitations. One is that they seem to have a less pronounced impact when introduced into cities where there are already alternative sources of syringes; this reduced impact is referred to as a "dilution" effect (Gibson et al., 2001). Another is the occasional finding of associations between SEP participation and either higher rates of HIV (Strathdee et al., 1997) or seroconversion (Bruneau et al., 1997). Although opponents have suggested possible unintended negative consequences of SEPs, such as the creation of new needle sharing networks, the more likely explanation seems to be that SEPs may attract more high-risk IDUs, as has been found in other programs (Hahn, Vranizan, & Moss, 1997; Schoenbaum, Hartel, & Gourevitch, 1996). Finally, perhaps not surprisingly, SEP benefits tend to be circumscribed, with additional services needed to have an impact on a broader range of downstream outcomes (Strathdee et al., 1997).

Development of Mental Health Services

Many early institutional efforts to respond to the psychological needs of PLWHA took place outside the formal mental health service system, in what came to be called AIDS service organizations, which were organized to provide practical and psychosocial support (Altman, 1994; Perrow & Guillen, 1990). Sometimes existing organizations were refocused on AIDS, such as the San-Francisco-based Shanti Project, which was originally founded (in 1974) to deal with the problems of death and dying and then was subsequently funded by the City of San Francisco to provide psychosocial services to persons with HIV and their families, friends, and loved ones. Shanti provided a practical support program and an emotional support program in addition to a residence and a counseling program at San Francisco General Hospital. By fiscal year 1984–1985, the project had provided more than 50,000 hours of "emotional support" services to 950 clients in its AIDS service program (Arno & Hughes, 1987). In other cases, organizations developed directly in response to AIDS, as advocacy groups mobilized around a mixture of political, self-help, and community service agendas. Comparable in some respects to the mental health consumer empowerment movement discussed in Chapter 23 by McLean, these groups often drew on social networks and a spirit of solidarity – in this case cultivated during the preceding period of gay rights activism. The mental health help provided to PLWHA often stressed overcoming stigma (and homophobia), creating and sustaining solidarity, and building self-esteem through empowerment.

It is difficult to reconstruct retrospectively what percentage of the mental health problems presented in these settings were diagnosable psychological or psychiatric disorders. Volunteers, rather than professionals, often staffed the services. The subsequent incorporation of formal mental health services and biomedical models of mental disorder was probably slowed both by a reluctance commonly seen in social-movement-based programs to surrender the direct, mission-focused vitality of volunteerism and by a distrust of psychiatry. Less than a decade before AIDS was identified, psychiatric nomenclature still designated homosexuality as a disorder (Bayer, 1987), an example of what Gamson (1989) described as a kind of sociological "control through the creation of abnormality" (p. 352).

In the formal health care system, AIDS patients were greeted with trepidation. Veteran AIDS psychiatrist Mary Ann Cohen has described her first psychiatric consultation for a PLWHA patient in 1981 (Cohen, 2008, p. 4). She found a young man, "almost skeletal" in appearance, who had covered his head with a sheet. Entering his room, she found the floor sticky, covered with food spilled by the patient and body fluids from his failed attempts to make it from the bed to the bathroom. Looking back on the episode, she described how it reflected both the extreme weakness and physical deterioration caused by the unchecked disease and the staff's fearful reluctance to clean the floor. Ironically, alongside anxiety so extreme that staff failed to perform their duties, other reports suggest that something like denial sometimes operated, making staff slow to adopt universal precautions. Another veteran psychiatrist, Francine Cournos, has described how when an agitated patient broke a window and cut his hand, staff failed to use gloves or take other precautions, only to be distraught when they later learned that his blood tested positive for HIV (Cournos, 1996). In psychiatry, as elsewhere, providing high-quality care required workers to overcome fears and sometimes stigmatizing attitudes. Leadership promoting affirmative responses to HIV was provided by psychiatrists and other mental health professionals in major urban settings, drawing on many of their backgrounds in consultation-liaison services, community psychiatry, and community-based and activist groups.

From an institutional perspective, meeting the mental health needs of PLWHA has been complicated by a historical legacy of fragmentation in the formal delivery system. Services for psychiatric conditions, substance abuse, and HIV care are typically located in quite different institutional environments, are accountable to different licensing and regulatory bodies, draw funds from different budgets, and commonly develop differing professional cultures and sources of legitimacy. Historically, providers in these sectors have been suspicious of efforts to expand responsibility to treat "someone else's patients," particularly because such efforts are often unaccompanied by access to new funding streams (Ridgely, Goldman, & Willenbring, 1990). For example, state mental health authorities have traditionally had ultimate public responsibility for people with mental illness. Reformers in the 1980s were veterans of efforts to limit the scope of state responsibility in order to concentrate on the needs of people with highly disabling psychiatric conditions and so were sometimes initially reluctant to configure state service systems to serve PLWHA, particularly because it was seen as nearly impossible to estimate the fiscal bottom line of these expanded responsibilities.

Much of what is known about the response of statewide psychiatric systems to HIV comes from a limited number of studies. Studies conducted in general hospital inpatient psychiatric units (Walkup, Satriano, Hansell, & Olfson, 1998) and outpatient clinics (McKinnon et al., 1999; Satriano, McKinnon, & Adoff, 2007) in New York State suggested that sites became more active in identifying patient risk behaviors during the decade. Reporting on New York State, Markson et al. (1997) found only limited evidence for services integration: Substance abuse counselors were unavailable in 26% of sites and psychologists/mental health counselors in 21%.

Hospital stays are a high-cost service, and the role of psychiatric conditions in inpatient HIV care has been studied (Uldall, Koutsky, Bradshaw, & Hopkins, 1994; Uldall, Koutsky, Bradshaw, & Krone, 1998). As HAART access decreases the need for inpatient care related to opportunistic infections, a higher proportion of hospital use by PLWHA likely will be devoted to stays by PLWHA who also have an SMI. Using data from the mid-1990s, including the period after the introduction of HAART, Hoover and colleagues found a longer adjusted length of stay associated with patients with severe mental illness, but not other psychiatric diagnoses (Hoover et al., 2008).

The high levels of need found in many populations with HIV have meant that efforts to develop comprehensive care systems have sometimes produced ironic results. In particular, efforts to target tailored services to special populations have sometimes been overwhelmed and diverted from their original missions. Other high-need patients have tended to gravitate to new programs in a resource-limited environment. Programs to serve PLWHA who have a serious mental illness have instead been filled with patients with anxiety or depression who nevertheless are difficult to treat (Sullivan et al., 1999). Among PLWHA, those with serious mental illness may be most in need of services such as housing. As a consequence, a long-term care facility for PLWHA in New York City found that these patients were least likely to die or be discharged, resulting in a "silting up" of these patients who came to occupy a growing proportion of total beds (Goulet, Molde, Constantino, Gaughan, & Selwyn, 2000).

Conclusion

Understanding mental health in the context of HIV illustrates in a particularly vivid fashion some of the challenges facing behavioral and social scientific research on mental health and illness. A survey of today's mental health aspects of the HIV epidemic makes clear that there has been a dramatic – if difficult to quantify – shift in the social representation of AIDS in the United States. Discussions were once dominated by metaphors of invasion and crisis. Fear coexisted with the determination to do battle with AIDS and eventually eradicate it. But neither cures nor effective vaccines have been forthcoming, and today HIV is an unwelcome presence that seems unlikely to depart any time soon.

Many of the mental health challenges to be faced need to be considered in this changed context. Despite the enormous benefits made possible by new, life-prolonging medications, they are not easily achieved. PLWHA must make a place in their lives for a demanding medication regimen they are unlikely to be able ever to stop. Social networks are called on to sustain the needed support without the inspirational "movement" atmosphere common two decades ago. Life-span developmental issues now intersect with HIV in ways that were not imagined in the early days. Along with the burden of illness, many PLWHA now face many of the same psychological demands everyone else faces in negotiating life challenges and transitions: work, establishing lasting partnerships, parenthood, and aging. Yet the increasing normalization of HIV and the increasing number of PLWHA for whom it is a chronic illness have not undone the infectious risks it poses. With the waning of the crisis mentality and the improved prospects for those who become ill, there is concern that younger people in some quarters, who never experienced firsthand the most visibly destructive period in the United States, may feel less commitment to risk reduction. But as risk reduction messages have made headway at the population level and incidence has stabilized, there is the risk that new cases will become increasingly concentrated in very high-risk individuals living in high-prevalence areas. When infected, these PLWHA pose challenges to mental and physical health delivery systems that must often help them manage HIV/AIDS while they deal with substance abuse and psychiatric problems.

Despite the challenges there are impressive examples of success. Syringe exchange programs are one, and there is also evidence of behavior changes among IDUs that constrain spread. Early fears that adequate adherence could not be achieved by highly disadvantaged patients with severe mental illness have proved exaggerated. Stigma continues to exert a negative impact, particularly in some subgroups, but support for coercive and exclusionary practices has diminished significantly in the course of the epidemic.

Change has been a constant of the epidemic in the United States. Despite progress, uncertainty surrounds many key questions regarding the epidemiology of HIV in populations heavily burdened with psychiatric illness, the impact on antiretroviral adherence of psychological and psychiatric care, psychological and institutional impediments to HIV testing, and how to overcome barriers to the integration of medical, mental health, substance abuse, and social welfare services.

29

Labeling and Stigma

Bruce G. Link and Jo C. Phelan

This chapter provides a frame for examining extant issues and evidence concerning labeling and stigma as they pertain to mental illnesses. The issues addressed are (1) the conceptualization of labeling and stigma, (2) evidence about trends in stigma-relevant public attitudes and beliefs, and (3) how labeling and stigma affect individuals who develop mental illnesses. Both modified labeling theory and the conceptualization of stigma developed by Link and Phelan point to the importance of attitudes and beliefs, leading to questions about how such attitudes and beliefs are faring over time. The research reviewed in this chapter shows that the public recognizes mental illnesses as illnesses with genetic and biological bases; however, the core stereotypes of dangerousness and incompetence have either changed little or actually become stronger. No change in social distancing responses has accompanied the increasingly medical conception of mental illnesses. Discrimination against people with mental illnesses occurs through multiple mechanisms, including direct person-to-person discrimination, discrimination operating through the stigmatized person, discrimination that emerges silently but perniciously through social interaction, and structural stigma. What are the policy implications of this chapter?

Introduction

When we ask who is labeled mentally ill and what the consequences of such labeling are, we ask questions that are central to the sociological understanding of mental disorder. Such questions are relevant to those who are concerned that so many people with serious mental illnesses go unlabeled and untreated (Regier et al., 1993; Wang et al., 2005). Such questions are also relevant to people attempting to recover from mental illnesses, who often feel that they suffer as much from being labeled mentally ill as they do from mental illnesses itself (Deegan, 1993).

As a society, we have created specific professions (including psychiatry, clinical psychology, psychiatric social work, and psychiatric nursing) on whose members we confer the authority to define, label, and treat mental illnesses. Social processes determine who encounters these professionals and many of the important consequences that might follow from such an encounter. The treatment patients receive may ameliorate their symptoms, improve their well-being, and enhance their social and occupational functioning. At the same time, along with treatment comes the possibility of pejorative labeling and stigma. Social science research on labeling and stigma can help us understand the processes involved and, by bringing those processes to light, open the possibility of addressing some of their negative consequences.

This chapter begins with some background on how a consideration of these issues developed in mental health sociology. This selective review provides a frame for examining extant issues and evidence concerning labeling and stigma as they pertain to mental illnesses. The issues addressed are (1) the conceptualization of labeling and stigma, (2) evidence about trends in stigma-relevant public attitudes and beliefs, and (3) how labeling and stigma affect individuals who develop mental illnesses.

The Labeling Debate

The issue of whether and to what extent labeling and stigma are important in the area of mental illness was brought into sharp relief by the labeling debate that emerged within sociology in the 1960s and 1970s. Scheff (1966/1984) constructed a formal labeling theory of mental illnesses that strongly endorsed labeling processes in the production of stable mental illnesses. In Scheff's theory, the act of labeling was strongly influenced by the social characteristics of the labelers, the person being labeled, and the social situation in which their interactions occurred. Labeling was driven as much by these social factors as it was by anything that might be called the symptoms of mental illness. Moreover, according to Scheff, once a person is labeled, powerful social forces come into play to produce a stable pattern of "mental illness." Key aspects of Scheff's theory are captured in the following quotation:

> In a crisis, when the deviance of an individual becomes a public issue, the traditional stereotype of insanity becomes the guiding imagery for action, both for those reacting to the deviant and, at times, for the deviant himself. When societal agents and persons around the deviant react to him uniformly in terms of the stereotypes of insanity, his amorphous and unstructured rule-breaking tends to crystallize in conformity to these expectations, thus becoming similar to behavior of other deviants classified as mentally ill and stable over time. The process of becoming uniform and stable is completed when the traditional imagery becomes a part of the deviant's orientation for guiding his own behavior (Scheff 1966/1984, p. 82).

Critics of the theory, especially Walter Gove, took sharp issue with Scheff's characterization of the labeling process. Gove argued that labels are applied far less capriciously and with many fewer pernicious consequences than the labeling theory indicates. In Gove's view, research supports the idea that, if people with mental illnesses are rejected, it is because of responses to their symptomatic behavior rather than because of any label they received. Moreover, he argued, labeling is not an important cause of further deviant behavior. "The available evidence," Gove concluded, "indicates that deviant labels are primarily a consequence of deviant behavior and that deviant labels are not a prime cause of deviant careers" (Gove, 1975, p. 296).

Although some observers despaired at the protracted and seemingly irresolvable labeling debate, the sharply opposed stances that Scheff and Gove provided served to clarify what was at issue and thereby set the stage for subsequent theory and research.

Modified Labeling Theory

In the 1980s Link and his colleagues developed a "modified" labeling theory that derived insights from the original labeling theory, but stepped away from the claim that labeling is a direct cause of mental illness (Link, 1982, 1987; Link et al., 1989). Instead the theory postulated a process through which labeling and stigma jeopardize the life circumstances of people with mental illnesses, harming their employment chances, social networks, and self-esteem. By creating disadvantage in these domains and others like them, people who have experienced mental illness labels are put at greater risk of the prolongation or reoccurrence of mental illness. The "modified" labeling theory also provided an explanation as to how labeling and stigma might produce these effects and how key concepts and measures could be used in testing the explanation with empirical evidence.

The theory begins with the observation that people develop conceptions of mental illness early in life as part of socialization (Angermeyer & Matschinger, 1996; Scheff, 1966/1984; Wahl, 1995). Once in place, people's conceptions become a lay theory about what it means to have a mental illness (Angermeyer & Matschinger, 1994; Furnham & Bower, 1992). People form expectations as to whether most people will reject an individual with mental illness as a friend, employee, neighbor, or intimate partner and whether most people will devalue a person with mental illness as less trustworthy, intelligent, and competent. These beliefs have an especially poignant relevance for a person who develops a serious mental illness, because the possibility of devaluation and discrimination becomes personally relevant. If one believes that others will devalue and reject people with mental illness, one must now fear that this rejection will apply personally. The person may wonder, "Will others look down on me, reject me, simply because I have been identified as having a mental illness?" Then, to the extent that it becomes a part of a person's world view, that perception can have serious negative consequences. Expecting and fearing rejection, people who have been hospitalized for mental illness may act less confidently and more defensively, or they may simply avoid a potentially threatening contact altogether. The result may be strained and uncomfortable social interactions with potential stigmatizers (Farina et al., 1968), more constricted social networks (Link et al., 1989), a compromised quality of life (Rosenfield, 1997), low self-esteem (Wright, Gronfein, & Owens, 2000), depressive symptoms (Link et al., 1997), unemployment, and income loss (Link, 1982, 1987).

To test this explanation, Link (1987) constructed a 12-item scale measuring the extent to which a person believes that people who have been labeled by treatment contact will be devalued and discriminated against. Respondents are asked the extent to which they agree or disagree with statements indicating that most people devalue current or former psychiatric patients by seeing them as failures, as less intelligent than other persons, or as individuals whose opinions need not be taken seriously. The scale also includes items that assess perceived discrimination by most people in jobs, friendships, and romantic relationships. The scale was administered to people with mental illnesses and to community residents from the same general area of New York City in a case-control study of major depression and schizophrenia. Link (1987) showed that the degree to which a person expects to be rejected is associated with demoralization, income loss, and unemployment. This association occurs in individuals labeled mentally ill but not in unlabeled individuals, thereby supporting the idea that labeling activates beliefs that lead to negative consequences.

Link and colleagues (1989) extended the forgoing reasoning in two ways. First they brought into the analysis empirical measures of coping orientations of secrecy (concealing a history of treatment), withdrawal (avoiding potentially threatening situations), and education (attempting to teach others in order to forestall the negative effects of stereotypes). Consistent with the idea that the stigma associated with mental illness creates expectations of rejection, they showed that people with mental illnesses tend to endorse these strategies as a means of protecting themselves. Second, the researchers extended the analysis to a consideration of the effects of these processes on social network ties. They found that people who fear rejection most and who endorse the strategy of withdrawal have insular support networks consisting mainly of household members.

Aspects of the theory have since been tested with a broader range of outcomes, in different samples, by different investigators, and often using longitudinal data. These studies generally showed that the perceived devaluation-discrimination measure is associated with outcome variables including quality of life (Rosenfield, 1997), low self-esteem (Link et al., 2001, 2008; Wright et al., 2000), social networks (Link et al., 1989; Perlick et al., 2001) depressive symptoms (Link et al., 1997; Perlick et al., 2007), treatment adherence (Sirey, Bruce, Alexopoulos, Perlick, Friedman, et al., 2001), and treatment discontinuation (Sirey, Bruce, Alexopoulos, Perlick, Raue, et al., 2001). But one particular aspect of the theory, the idea that cultural conceptions (perceived devaluation and discrimination) have effects on outcome variables in labeled persons but not in unlabeled ones, has not been as thoroughly tested in subsequent research. One study that did do so was undertaken by Kroska and Harkness (2006) using samples of psychiatric hospital patients and community residents in Indianapolis. This study operationalized cultural conceptions in a completely different way than Link and his colleagues did. Patients and community residents were asked to evaluate the concept of "mentally ill person," using a seven-point semantic differential scale with opposing adjectives such as "good/bad," "useful/useless," and "powerless/powerful." Respondents also rated the concepts of "myself as I really am" and "myself as others see me" with the same adjective pairings. The researchers' modified labeling theory hypothesis was that associations between ratings of the concepts of "mentally ill person" and "myself as I really am" and "myself as others see me" would be stronger in the labeled group (where a mental illness label is potentially personally relevant) than in the unlabeled group (where it is not personally relevant). Their results were generally consistent with this prediction, providing additional support for this key prediction of modified labeling theory.

Understanding the "Package Deal"

Evidence from modified labeling theory and other approaches to labeling, stereo-typing, and rejection strongly suggest that negative consequences associated with labeling are experienced by many people. At the same time, evidence from a voluminous body of research indicates that a variety of psychotherapies and drug therapies can be helpful in treating many mental illnesses. Given this, existing data simply do not justify a continued debate concerning whether the effects of labeling are positive or negative – clearly they are both. Rosenfield (1997) was the first to bring this point to light in a single study. She examined the effects of both treatment services and stigma in the context of a model program for people with severe mental illnesses. She showed that both the receipt of services (spe-cific interventions that some people in the program receive and others do not) and stigma (Link's 1987 measure of perceived devaluation and discrimination) are related – in opposite directions – to multiple dimensions of a quality of life measure. Receipt of services had positive effects on dimensions of quality of life, such as living arrangements, family relations, financial situation, safety, and health, whereas stigma had equally strong negative effects on such dimensions.

A second study that explores the idea of joint effects in opposite directions is one by Link and colleagues (1997). In a longitudinal study, men who were dually diagnosed with mental disorder and substance abuse were followed from entry into treatment (when they were highly symptomatic and addicted to substances) to a follow-up point 1 year later (when they were far less symptomatic and largely drug and alcohol free). Despite these dramatic benefits, the results also showed that perceptions of devaluation and discrimination and reported experiences of discrimination continued to affect the men's level of depressive symptoms. Sim-ilar results, showing evidence of improvement in symptoms with treatment but enduring effects of stigma on self-esteem, were reported in a recent study by Link and colleagues (2008). The effects of stigma and discrimination endure and are apparently unaffected by any benefits of treatment.

Thus the evidence indicates a bundling of labeling effects that are currently joined in a kind of "package deal." People seeking mental health treatment nav-igate this deal in one way or another. Sometimes they do so in ways that mental health professionals think they should not, such as avoiding treatment, denying their illness, or ending treatment earlier than their treatment team thinks they should. A kind of collective finger wagging ensues that at times shifts from admonitions and warnings to using the "leverage" of housing or financial benefits to ensure treatment compliance (Monahan et al., 2001). If leverage fails, more direct forms of coercion are also possible such as involuntary inpatient commitment or the ascendant "outpatient commitment" (Hiday, 2003). Of course, there is an intense debate about the utility and effectiveness of leverage and coercion, with some believing that these practices are necessary (Torrey & Zdanowicz, 2001) and others seeing them as counterproductive (Pollack, 2004). What a sociological perspective adds to this debate is evidence that there is indeed a package deal and that people face real choices and real dilemmas as they navigate its parameters. It also suggests that the ingenuity invested in constructing strategies to leverage compliance or to coerce it needs to be complemented or replaced by efforts that really change the balance of the package deal to one that delivers more benefit and less stigma. When that happens, more people will choose treatment, and less leveraging and coercion will be required. Mental health sociologists can help by continuing to unpack the package deal so that its existence is more widely acknowledged and our understanding of the mechanisms that undergird it more complete. Recent research by mental health sociologists is engaged in precisely these issues. Rosenfield (2008), for example, queried people with mental illnesses as to sources of stigmatizing reactions and found that the reactions of treatment providers are the ones that have the most harmful impact. Markowitz and Angell (2008) elaborated on the modified labeling theory to probe more deeply into the mechanisms involved by including the reflected appraisals of family members in their empirical analysis. Phelan, Lucas, and Link (2008) conducted experimental work integrating paradigms from the expectation-states tradition in sociology (Berger, Cohen, & Zelditch, 1972) with work in psychology on the sources of stigma in interaction processes to investigate whether and to what extent a mental illness label reduces influence in interactions and engenders behavioral social distance. Morrison (2008) described an effort to break the cycles of stigma by developing a kind of rapid-response mechanism that includes the evaluations of consumers of mental health treatment in planning services that suit their needs. Identifying sources, probing mechanisms, and evaluating novel attempts to respond to stigma will deepen our understanding and enable us to address the stigma processes that affect people with mental illnesses.

The Rise of Interest in Stigma

Although the reasons are far from fully understood, it is very clear that there has been a dramatic increase in interest in stigma since the labeling debate emerged and Goffman's (1963) seminal book was first published. One indicator of this rise in interest is the number of published articles with the word *stigma* in the title or abstract. According to Link and Phelan (2001) the number of such articles in 1980 stood at 19 for Medline and 14 for Psych Info, but rose dramatically by the end of the century in 1999 to 114 for Medline and 161 for Psych Info. Incredibly, just 6 years later in 2006 the numbers had more than doubled to 416 for Medline and 462 for Psych Info. This crude quantitative accounting coheres with evidence from other sources, including the prominence given to stigma in Surgeon General Satcher's report on mental health (1999, p. 6). This report described the importance of stigma as follows:

> Stigma erodes confidence that mental disorders are valid, treatable conditions. It leads people to avoid socializing, employing or working with, or renting to or living near persons who have a mental disorder, especially a severe disorder like schizophrenia. Stigma deters the public from wanting to pay for care and, thus, reduces consumers' access to resources and opportunities for treatment and social services. A consequent inability or failure to obtain treatment reinforces destructive patterns of low self-esteem, isolation and hopelessness. Stigma tragically deprives people of their dignity and interferes with their full participation in society. It must be overcome.

From what could be a long list of additional indicators of a growing interest in stigma, we mention only two more. First, the National Institute of Mental Health (NIMH) convened a "stigma working group" and released a Request for Applications designed to stimulate research aimed at reducing the impact of stigma on people's lives. Second, enormous effort has been undertaken to address aspects of the stigma of mental illness in the United States and around the world. In the midst of all of this interest, questions have arisen as to precisely what the term *stigma* means and whether it is the most appropriate concept to use to convey the circumstances that people with mental illness confront.

Conceptualizing Stigma in Relation to Labeling, Stereotyping, and Discrimination

In the literature on stigma, the term has been used to describe what seem to be quite different concepts. It has been used to refer to the "mark" or "label" that is used as a social designation, the linking of the label to negative stereotypes, or the propensity to exclude or otherwise discriminate against the designated person. Even Goffman's (1963) famous essay included somewhat different, albeit very instructive, definitions. As a consequence of this variability in its usage, there has been confusion as to what the term means. Additionally, an intense dissatisfaction with the concept emerged in some circles for at least two reasons. First, it was argued that the stigma concept identifies an "attribute" or a "mark" residing in the person as something the person possesses. The process of selecting and affixing labels was not taken to be as problematic as it should have been. In particular, far too little attention was focused on the identification of only a single characteristic for social salience from a vast range of possible characteristics that might have been selected instead. Second, too much emphasis was placed on cognitive processes of category formation and stereotyping and too little on the broad and very prominent fact of discrimination and the influence that such discrimination has on the distribution of life chances.

In light of this confusion and controversy, Link and Phelan (2001) put forward a conceptualization of stigma that recognized the overlap in meaning among concepts like stigma, labeling, stereotyping, and discrimination. The conceptualization they offered defined stigma in the relationship among those interrelated components. It also responded to criticisms of the concept by making the social selection of designations a prominent feature, by incorporating discrimination into the concept, and by focusing on the importance of social, economic, and political power in the production of stigma. Link and Phelan described their conceptualization as follows:

> In our conceptualization, stigma exists when the following interrelated components converge. In the first component, people distinguish and label human differences. In the second, dominant cultural beliefs link labeled persons to undesirable characteristics – to negative stereotypes. In the third, labeled persons are placed in distinct categories so as to accomplish some degree of separation of "us" from "them." In the fourth, labeled persons experience status loss and discrimination that lead to unequal outcomes. Stigmatization is entirely contingent on access to social, economic and political power that allows the identification of differentness, the construction of stereotypes, the separation of labeled persons into distinct categories and the full execution of disapproval, rejection, exclusion and discrimination. Thus we apply the term stigma when elements of labeling, stereotyping, separation, status loss and discrimination co-occur in a power situation that allows them to unfold (Link & Phelan, 2001, p. 367).

Although a detailed exposition of each of these components is available elsewhere (Link & Phelan, 2001), we provide a brief description of each component as follows.

Distinguishing and labeling differences. The vast majority of human differences, such as hairy ears or preferred vegetables, are not considered to be socially relevant. However, some differences, such as skin color and sexual preferences, are currently awarded a high degree of social salience. Both the selection of salient characteristics and the creation of labels for them are social achievements that need to be understood as essential components of stigma.

Associating differences with negative attributes. In this component, the labeled difference is linked to negative stereotypes in such a manner, for example, that a person who has been hospitalized for mental illness is thought to represent a violence risk.

Separating "us" from "them." A third aspect of the stigma process occurs when social labels connote a separation of "us" from "them." For example, certain ethnic or national groups (Morone, 1997), people with mental illnesses, or people with a different sexual orientation may be considered fundamentally different kinds of people from "us."

Emotional responses. The Link and Phelan conceptualization of stigma was expanded to include emotional responses in Link and colleagues' (2004) paper on measuring mental illness stigma. They noted that the stigmatizer is likely to experience emotions of anger, irritation, anxiety, pity, and fear. These emotions are important because they can be detected by the person who is stigmatized, thereby providing an important statement about a stigmatizer's response to them. Second, emotional responses may shape subsequent behavior toward the stigmatized person or group through processes identified by attribution theory (Weiner, Perry, & Magnusson, 1988). From the vantage point of the person who is stigmatized, emotions of embarrassment, shame, fear, alienation, or anger are possible. Thomas Scheff (1998) has, for example, argued that the emotion of shame is central to stigma and that shaming processes can have powerful and hurtful consequences for stigmatized persons.

Status loss and discrimination. When people are labeled, set apart, and linked to undesirable characteristics, a rationale is constructed for devaluing, rejecting, and excluding them. This process can occur in several ways that we describe more fully later in the chapter.

The dependence of stigma on power. A unique feature of Link and Phelan's (2001) conceptualization is the idea that stigma is entirely dependent on social, economic, and political power. Groups with lower amounts of power (e.g., psychiatric patients) may label, stereotype, and separate themselves from higher power groups (e.g., psychiatrists). But in these cases, stigma as Link and Phelan define it does not exist, because the potentially stigmatizing groups do not have the social, cultural, economic, and political power to imbue their cognitions with serious discriminatory consequences.

The Link and Phelan (2001) conceptualization is meant to be useful, not definitive or comprehensive. Readers interested in the stigma concept should attend to other conceptualizations, especially for particular purposes. If the project seeks to understand how stigma differs from circumstance to circumstance, the Jones et al. (1984) conceptualization of dimensions of stigma is particularly useful. It identifies six dimensions: concealability (how obvious or detectable the characteristic is), course (how reversible the condition is), disruptiveness (the extent to which a designation leads to strained interactions), aesthetics (the extent to which a condition elicits an instinctive and affective reaction of disgust), origin (how the condition came into being), and peril (the extent to which the condition induces fear or threat in others). Readers especially interested in the issue of what causes people to stigmatize should refer to the evolutionary psychology theory of Kurzban and Leary (2001) and to the social science perspective of Phelan, Link, and Dovidio (2008). Kurzban and Leary identified three potential evolutionary origins of stigma. They argued that humans have developed cognitive adaptations designed to avoid poor social exchange partners (e.g., cheaters and individuals with little social capital), to compete with and exploit outgroups, and to avoid individuals likely to carry communicable pathogens. Each of these strategies, they argue, is likely to have survival value from an evolutionary perspective. Phelan, Link and Dovidio (2008) also identified three functions of stigmatization: exploitation and domination, norms enforcement, and disease avoidance. Readers with an anthropological bent should refer to the conceptualization of Yang and colleagues (2007) that identifies stigma in "moral experience" and argues that what matters about stigma is rooted in a local context of meanings. Readers interested in a mapping of concepts and theories relevant to stigma are referred to Phelan, Link and Dovidio (2008) and Pescosolido, Martin, Lang, et al. (2008).

Trends in Public Attitudes Relevant to Stigma

An interest in public attitudes and beliefs assumes that such attitudes and beliefs are important. But do public attitudes and beliefs matter in the lives of people who develop mental illnesses? Some argue that it matters little whether members of the public harbor negative attitudes or false beliefs. What matters is whether they actually discriminate against people with mental illnesses. But both the modified labeling theory and the Link and Phelan conceptualization of stigma assign critical importance to the ambient attitudes, emotions, and beliefs of dominant groups in their relations between a more powerful "us" and a less powerful "them." For modified labeling theory, these attitudes, emotions, and beliefs are what people learn early in life that then confound their capacity to obtain desired goals at some later point in their lives when they develop a mental illness. In Link and Phelan's article, "Conceptualizing Stigma," attitudes, emotions, and beliefs are, along with power differences, the prime drivers of stigma processes.

From these vantage points, an inclination to focus only on blocking discrimination misses the capacity of more powerful groups to find new, perhaps less obvious ways to discriminate. Indeed if the attitudes, emotions, and beliefs remain unchanged and power differences also remain unchanged, blocking one form of discrimination is likely to simply increase the need for new and perhaps more subtle forms. Consistent with this idea is Monahan et al.'s (2001) observation that in the period of deinstitutionalization with its quest for "least restrictive environments," a powerful new form of control has emerged and spread in the form of "leveraging." Instead of old forms of control conferred by the mental hospital system, a new form that restricts access to housing and withholds benefits until "compliance" is secure has emerged and proliferated. For all of these reasons, the extant attitudes and beliefs of the general public are important to the stigma of mental illness. Whether and to what extent these attitudes are changing over time and whether new knowledge about the determinants of mental illnesses is influencing attitudes in expected directions are matters of considerable importance.

The Dangerousness Stereotype from 1950 to 1996

In 1996, teams of investigators at Columbia and Indiana Universities constructed the MacArthur module of the General Social Survey (GSS; Pecosolido, Martin, Long, et al., 2008a). Interested in trends over time, the team directed attention to the first nationwide study of public attitudes conducted in 1950 by Shirley Star. Unfortunately, the questions in the original study generally used language that had become "dated" by 1996. However, the following open-ended question was available and could be repeated: "Of course, everyone hears a good deal about physical illness and disease, but now, what about the ones we call mental or nervous illness. . . . When you hear someone say that a person is "mentally-ill," what does that mean to you?" In both the Star study and the MacArthur module of the 1996 survey, answers were recorded verbatim. Fortunately, every tenth interview of the original Star survey had been saved by the librarian at the National Opinion Research Center in Chicago where both studies were conducted. This allowed trained coders to reliably rate the 1950 and 1996 responses to this question with respect to whether the respondent spontaneously referred to violent behavior in describing a person with mental illness. Thereby the study allowed a rare glimpse at trends in one key stereotype associated with the stigma of mental illnesses involving psychosis. Remarkably, the analysis revealed that, despite massive efforts to educate the public about mental illness and enormous advances in treatment, respondents whose descriptions indicated a person with psychosis were nearly two and a half times as likely to mention violent behavior in 1996 (31.0%) as in 1950 (12.7%; Phelan, Link, Stueve, & Pescosolido, 2000). Whatever the reasons for this change, at the very least, it represents a discomforting fact for people with a psychotic illness who are seeking broader social acceptance.

Trends in Causal Attributions, Stereotypes, and Social Distancing Responses, 1996–2006

In keeping with an interest in monitoring trends in public attitudes and beliefs, the same team of investigators involved in the 1996 MacArthur module secured funding from NIMH to replicate the identical module in 2006. Both studies used identical vignettes describing individuals with major depression, schizophrenia, alcohol dependence, and, to provide a no-disorder contrast, a so-called troubled person who has mild worries but no diagnosable disorder. Each respondent was randomly assigned one of these vignettes and then asked questions about what might have caused the problem, whether the described person should seek medical or psychiatric help, whether the person was a violence risk, and whether the person would be able to manage his or her own money, as well as social distance questions that asked the respondent whether he or she would be willing to interact with the described person in a variety of circumstances. In keeping with a strong push to educate the public that mental illnesses were illnesses like other illnesses, respondents in 2006 as compared to those in 1996 were more likely to see the conditions as caused by biological and genetic factors. Additionally, respondents to the 2006 survey were more likely to recommend medical and psychiatric treatment for the described cases. At the same time, there was no evidence whatsoever that stereotypes of violence and incompetence, or the willingness to interact with people with mental illnesses, changed for the better over the period between the studies. This evidence challenges the idea that stigma will dissipate when the public is moved toward a more medical view of mental illnesses (Pescosolido, Martin, Long, et al., 2008a).

Reflecting on these trends can induce either pessimistic or optimistic thoughts about the future of mental illness stigma. From a pessimistic stance, at least one highly touted approach to addressing mental illness stigma seems to have yielded few if any benefits for stereotyping or social distance. From a more optimistic vantage point, however, one notes that the public was receptive to the main message delivered – mental illnesses are biologically based and can be effectively treated by medical professionals. From this optimistic vantage point, the reason the public has not changed beliefs about dangerousness or incompetence or its attitudes toward interacting with people with mental illnesses is that these beliefs and attitudes were not directly targeted. The GSS studies have shown that attitudes can change; we just need to complete the process by addressing a fuller range of attitudes and beliefs with effective messages.

A pessimistic response takes two forms. The first argues that stereotypes of dangerousness and incompetence are inherently more intransigent than the beliefs that have changed. They are intransigent because they are strongly supported by countervailing forces such as the portrayal of people with mental illness in the media as violent and incompetent and the "kernel of truth" idea that says that sometimes people with mental illnesses are violent because of their illness. The second pessimistic response contends that the selection of attitudes and beliefs targeted for change was driven by powerful forces with different aims than the eradication of stigma. For psychiatry, promulgating the idea that the disorders its treats are valid, biologically based illnesses counters stereotypes about psychiatry and brings this specialty more fully and equally into the medical fold. Additionally, the interests of pharmaceutical companies are strongly served when the public sees mental illnesses as biologically based conditions that can be medically treated with the compounds the industry has developed for sale. If it takes clout to target and change attitudes, what will the interests be that push for change in stereotypes and social distancing responses?

Geneticization and Stigma

One emerging social phenomenon that is likely to alter causal attributions for mental illness is the genetics revolution. Research focusing on genetic sources of mental illness and a general focus on genetics and genomics are pervasive in the current culture. What will the consequences be for stigma? To address this question, Phelan (2005) conducted a vignette experiment in which a person with schizophrenia or major depressive disorder was described and causal attribution (genetic or not genetic) was randomly varied. She found that genetic attributions affected respondents' perceptions and beliefs about the illness; for example, they increased the perceived seriousness and persistence of the mental illness and the belief that the mentally ill person's siblings or children might develop the same problem. Looking at more direct indicators of stigma, a genetic attribution did not significantly affect blame, anger, sympathy, or social distance from the ill person, but it did increase social distance from the person's sibling, particularly regarding intimate forms of contact such as dating, marriage, and having children. These findings suggest that "associative stigma" affecting biological family members of people with mental illness may be the aspect of stigma that is most strongly affected by geneticization.

How Labeling and Stigma Affect the Lives of People with Mental Illnesses

People who have been hospitalized for serious mental illnesses are disadvantaged when it comes to a general profile of life chances like income, education, psychological well-being, housing status, medical treatment, and health (e.g., Druss et al., 2000; Link, 1987). How does this happen? Although some part of the difference may be due to the directly debilitating consequences (given existing social circumstances) of the illness, we attend to ways in which stigma-related processes may be involved.

Status Loss

An almost immediate consequence of successful negative labeling and stereotyping is a general downward placement of a person in a status hierarchy. The person is connected to undesirable characteristics that reduce his or her status in the eyes of most others. The fact that human beings create hierarchies is, of course, evident in organizational charts, who sits where in meetings, who defers to whom in conversational turn-taking, and so on. One strand of sociological research on social hierarchies, the so-called expectation-states tradition, is particularly relevant to the study of stigma and status loss (Berger, Fisek, Norman, & Zelditch, 1977;

Ridgeway & Walker, 1995). Based on finding a reliable tendency of even unac-quainted individuals to form fairly stable status hierarchies when placed in group situations, researchers set out to understand these processes. This research showed that external statuses, like race and gender, shape status hierarchies within small groups of unacquainted persons, even though the external status has no bearing on proficiency at a task the group is asked to perform. Men and Whites were more likely than women and Blacks to attain positions of power and prestige – they talked more frequently, had their ideas more readily accepted by others, and were more likely to be voted group leader (Mullen, Salas, & Driskell, 1989). This finding implies that status loss has immediate consequences for a person's power and influence and thus his or her ability to achieve desired goals.

Discrimination

We conceptualize four broad mechanisms of discrimination as part of the stigma process: individual discrimination, discrimination that operates through the stig-matized individual, interactional discrimination, and structural discrimination.

Individual discrimination. What usually comes to mind when thinking about discrimination is the classic model of individual prejudice and discrimination, in which Person A discriminates against Person B based on Person A's prejudicial attitudes or stereotypes connected to a label applied to Person B (Allport, 1954). For example, if, as in Page's experimental study (Page, 1977), a landlord learns about a renter's history of psychiatric hospitalization and consequently denies that an advertised apartment is available, we would say that individual discrimination has occurred. This rather straightforward process doubtless occurs with consid-erable regularity, although it may often be hidden from the discriminated-against person; one rarely learns why one is turned down for a job, an apartment, or a date. We believe, however, that this relatively straightforward process represents the tip of the discrimination iceberg. Most discrimination, we argue, is extremely subtle in its manifestation, if not in its consequences, and occurs without full awareness. For example, Druss et al. (2000) have shown that people with schizophrenia are less likely to receive optimal treatment for heart disease even after controlling for the nature of the condition and the availability of services. This is an instance of individual discrimination, as it results from the behavior of individual physicians who make treatment decisions. Yet it is unlikely that the physicians are aware of their discriminatory behavior or the reasons for it. Comparing demographically similar samples of medical and psychiatric inpatients, Bromley and Cunningham (2004) found that, whereas the medical patients received gifts like flowers, bal-loons, and chocolate, psychiatric patients generally received more practical gifts of toiletries, nonluxury foodstuffs, and tobacco. Again, this differential gift-giving behavior on the part of friends and family members is surely not deliberate or conscious; rather it reflects and reinforces societal attitudes about what it means to have a medical versus a psychiatric problem. Individual discrimination can come from many sources, including community members, employers, mental health caregivers, family members, and friends (Dickerson et al., 2002; Wahl, 1999).

Discrimination that operates through the stigmatized individual. Another form of discrimination that is subtle in its manifestation and insidious in its consequences operates within stigmatized individuals themselves. As explicated earlier, Link and colleagues (Link, 1982, 1987; Link et al., 1989, 1997) proposed in their modified labeling theory that all people are exposed to common, ambient stereotypes about mental illness as part of socialization. If a person then develops a mental illness, these beliefs about how others will treat a person with mental illness become personally relevant (Link, 1982; Link et al., 1989). This process has been referred to as "internalized stigma" and is central to understanding the inner psychological harm caused by stigma (Corrigan, 1998; Corrigan & Watson, 2002). Internalized stigma consists of the devaluation, shame, secrecy, and withdrawal triggered by negative stereotypes that one believes that others harbor (Corrigan, 1998).

Interactional discrimination. A third type of discrimination emerges in the back-and-forth between individuals in interaction. A classic study that brings this form of discrimination to light was an experimental study conducted by Sibicky and Dovidio (1986). In the study, 68 male and 68 female introductory psychology students were randomly assigned in mixed-sex pairs to one of two conditions. In one condition, a "perceiver" (random assignment here as well) was led to believe that a "target" was recruited from the psychotherapy clinic at the college. In the other condition, the perceiver was led to believe that the individual was a fellow student in introductory psychology. In fact, the target was always recruited from the class, and targets and perceivers both were led to believe that the study was focusing on "the acquaintance process in social interaction." Each member of a pair completed a brief inventory of his or her courses, hobbies, and activities. Then the experimenter exchanged the inventories and provided the perceiver with the labeling information (student or therapy client). Subsequently the two engaged in a tape-recorded interaction that was later reliably evaluated by two raters blind to the experimental conditions. Even before meeting them, perceivers rated the therapy targets less favorably than the student targets. Moreover the judges' ratings revealed that, in their interactions with therapy targets, perceivers were less open, secure, sensitive, and sincere. Finally, the results showed that the behavior of the labeled targets was adversely affected as well, even though they had no knowledge of the experimental manipulation. Thus, expectations associated with psychological therapy color subsequent interactions, actually calling out behaviors that confirm those expectations.

An important lesson for stigma researchers is embedded in these studies of interactional discrimination – substantial differences in influence and social distance can occur even when it is difficult for participants to specify a discriminatory event that produced the unequal outcome.

Structural discrimination. Finally, structural discrimination occurs when social policy, laws, or other institutional practices disadvantage stigmatized groups cumulatively over time. Prominent examples are the policies of many health insurance companies that provide less coverage for psychiatric illnesses than they do for physical ones (Schulze & Angermeyer, 2003) or laws restricting the civil rights of people with mental illnesses (Corrigan, Markowitz, & Watson, 2004). Structural discrimination need not involve direct or intentional discrimination by individuals in the immediate context (Corrigan et al., 2004); it can result from a practice or policy that is the residue of past intentional discrimination. For example, if a history of not-in-my-backyard (NIMBY) reactions has influenced the location of board-and-care homes over time so that they are situated in disorganized sections of the city where rates of crime, violence, pollution, and infectious disease are high, people with serious mental illnesses are more likely to be exposed to these noxious circumstances as a consequence. Again, although the unequal outcomes resulting from structural discrimination – unequal coverage for mental and physical health problems or undesirable location of board-and-care homes – may be readily apparent, the fact that these outcomes represent discrimination is only obvious on reflection and analysis.

Summary and Conclusion

The original labeling theory of mental illness strongly emphasized the negative consequences of labeling and stigma, whereas the critics emphasized the benefits of treatment and denied those negative consequences. The strongly stated positions in this debate brought into focus key issues that mental health sociologists have effectively pursued in subsequent research. Modified labeling theory stepped back from direct etiological claims to indicate how individuals' employment opportunities, social networks, self-esteem, and quality of life are influenced by labeling and stigma. As evidence supporting modified labeling theory grew, a potential resolution of the more strongly stated positions of the original theorists began to emerge. Both positions were partially correct: Labeling induced both positive and negative consequences in a sort of "package deal." On average, treatments and services brought benefits, whereas stigma and the discrimination it entails produced harm. As evidence from modified labeling theory and other approaches within mental health sociology evolved, a parallel explosion of interest in stigma emerged in the social science literature more generally. But with this growth came confusion about the stigma concept and whether it was a useful concept at all. Link and Phelan (2001) responded by defining stigma as a phenomenon dependent on the exercise of power that inheres in the confluence of labeling, stereotyping, setting apart, status loss, and discrimination. Both modified labeling theory and the Link and Phelan conceptualization of stigma point to the importance of attitudes and beliefs, leading to questions about how such attitudes and beliefs are faring in trends over time. In this regard, research shows that progress toward a recognition of mental illnesses as illnesses with genetic and biological bases has emerged and grown over time, but that core stereotypes of dangerousness and incompetence have either changed little or actually become stronger. No change in social distancing responses has accompanied the increasingly medical conception of mental illness. Discrimination against people with mental illnesses occurs through multiple mechanisms, including direct person-to-person discrimination, discrimination operating through the stigmatized person, discrimination that emerges silently but perniciously through social interaction, and structural stigma.

References

Abe-Kim, J., Takeuchi, D. T., Hong, S., Zane, N., Sue, S., Spencer, M. S., et al. (2007). Use of mental health-related services among immigrant and US-born Asian Americans: Results from the National Latino and Asian American Study. *American Journal of Public Health, 97*, 91–98.

Abenhaim, L., Dab, W., & Salmi, L. R. (1992). Study of civilian victims of terrorist attacks (France 1982–1987). *Journal of Clinical Epidemiology, 45*, 103–109.

Abou-Saleh, M. T. (2006). Neuroimaging in psychiatry: An update. *Journal of Psychosomatic Research, 61*, 289–293.

Abram, K. M. (1989). The effect of co-occurring disorders on criminal careers: Interaction of antisocial personality, alcohol and drug disorders. *International Journal of Law and Psychiatry, 12*, 133–148.

Abram, K. M. (1990). The problem of co-occurring disorders among jail detainees: Antisocial disorder, alcoholism, drug abuse, and depression. *Law and Human Behavior, 14*, 333–345.

Abram, K. M., & Teplin, L. A. (1991). Co-occurring disorders among mentally ill jail detainees. *American Psychologist, 46*, 1036–1045.

Abram, K. M., Teplin, L. A., & McClelland, G. M. (2003). Comorbidity of severe psychiatric disorders and substance use disorders among women in jail. *American Journal of Psychiatry, 160*, 1007–1010.

Abramson, M. L. (1972). The criminalization of mentally disordered behavior: Possible side effects of a new mental health law. *Hospital and Community Psychiatry, 23*, 101–105.

Achenbach, T. M. (1984). The status of research related to psychopathology. In A. W. Collins (Ed.), *Development during middle childhood: The years from six to twelve* (pp. 370–397). Washington, DC: National Academy Press.

Acs, G., Loprest, P., & Roberts T. (2001). *Final synthesis report of findings from ASPE 'Leavers' Grants*. Washington, DC: Urban Institute. Retrieved June 20, 2008, from http://www.urban.org/uploadedPDF/410809_welfare_leavers_synthesis.pdf.

Aday, L. A., Andersen, R., & Fleming, G. V. (1980). *Health care in the U.S. – Equitable for whom?* Beverly Hills, CA: Sage.

Adebimpe, V. R. (2004). A second opinion on the use of White norms in psychiatric diagnosis of Black patients. *Psychiatric Annals, 34*, 543–551.

Adler, A. (1927). *The practice and theory of individual psychology*. New York: Harcourt, Brace, and World.

Adler, P. T. (1982.) An analysis of the concept of competence in individuals and social systems. *Community Mental Health Journal, 18*, 34–45.

Afifi, T. O., Cox, B. J., & Enns, M. W. (2006). Mental health profiles among married, never-married, and separated/divorced mothers in a nationally representative sample. *Social Psychiatry and Psychiatric Epidemiology, 41*, 122–129.

Agerbo, E., Byrne, M., Eaton, W. W., & Mortensen, P. B. (2004). Schizophrenia, marital and labor market status in the long run. *Archives of General Psychiatry, 61*, 28–33.

589

Agranoff, R. (1991). Human services integration: Past and present challenges in public administration. *Public Administration Review, 51*, 533–542.

Ahmed, F., Brown, D. R., Gary, L. E., & Sadatmaad, F. (1994). Religiosity as a predictor of cigarette smoking among women of childbearing age. *Journal of Behavioral Medicine, 20*, 34–43.

Ahmed, A., Mohammed, S., & Williams, D. R. (2007). Racial discrimination & health: Pathways & evidence. *Indian Journal of Medical Research, 126*, 21–30.

Ahmed, P. I., & Plog, S. C. (Eds.). (1976). *State mental hospitals: What happens when they close?* New York: Plenum Press.

Ahnert, L., Pinquart, M., & Lamb, M. E. (2006). Security of children's relationships with nonparental care providers: A meta-analysis. *Child Development, 77*, 664–679.

Aiken, L. H., & Sloane, D. M. (1997). Effects of specialization and client differentiation on the status of nurses: The case of AIDs. *Journal of Health and Social Behavior, 38*, 203–222.

Aiken, L., Somers, S., & Shore, M. (1986). Private foundations in health affairs: A case study of a national initiative for the chronically mentally ill. *American Psychologist, 41*, 1290–1295.

Ajzen, I. (1991). The theory of planned behavior. *Organizational Behavior and Human Decision Processes, 50*, 179–211.

Ajzen, I., & Fishbein, M. (1980). *Understanding attitudes and predicting behavior.* Englewood Cliffs, NJ: Prentice-Hall.

Akbar, N. (1991). The evolution of human psychology for African Americans. In R. L. Jones (Ed.), *Black psychology* (pp. 99–123). Berkeley: Cobb & Henry.

Alan Guttmacher Institute. (2002). *In their own right: Addressing the sexual and reproductive health needs of American men.* New York: Author.

Alberman, E. (1984). Low birthweight. In M. Bracken (Ed.), *Perinatal epidemiology* (pp. 86–98). New York: Oxford University Press.

Alcantara, C., & Gone, J. P. (2007). Reviewing suicide in Native American communities: Situating risk and protective factors within a transactional-ecological framework. *Death Studies, 31*, 457–477.

Aldrich, H. (1987). New paradigms for old: The population perspective's contribution to health services research. *Medical Care Review, 44*, 257–277.

Alegría, M., Canino, G., Ríos, R., Vera, M., Calderón, J, Rusch, D., et al. (2002). Inequalities in use of specialty mental health services among Latinos, African Americans, and non-Latino Whites. *Psychiatric Services, 53*, 1547–1555.

Alegría, M., Canino, G., Shrout, P. E., Woo, M., Duan, N., Vila, D., et al. (2008). Prevalence of mental illness in immigrant and non-immigrant Latino groups. *American Journal of Psychiatry, 165*, 359–369.

Alegría, M., Mulvaney-Day, N., Torres, M., Polo, A., Cao, Z., & Canino, G. (2007). Prevalence of psychiatric disorders across Latino subgroups in the United States. *American Journal of Public Health, 97*, 68–75.

Alegría, M., Mulvaney-Day, N., Woo, M., Torres, M., Gao, S., & Oddo, V. (2007). Correlates of past-year mental health service use among Latinos: Results from the National Latino and Asian American Study. *American Journal of Public Health, 97*, 76–83.

Alegría, M., Pescosolido, B. A., & Canino, G. (n.d.). *A socio-cultural framework for health service disparities: Illustrating the case of mental health and substance abuse.* Presented at the 2008 American Sociological Association Meeting, Boston, MA, August.

Alegría, M., Robles, R., Freeman, D. H., Vera, M., Jimenez, A. L., Rios, C., et al. (1991). Patterns of mental health utilization among island Puerto Rican poor. *American Journal of Public Health, 81*, 875–879.

Alegría, M., Takeuchi, D., Canino, G., Duan, N., Shrout, P., Meng, X.-L., et al. (2004). Considering context, place and culture: The National Latino and Asian American Study. *International Journal of Methods in Psychiatric Research, 13*, 208–220.

Alexander, J. F., Holtzworth-Munroe, A., & Jameson, P. B. (1994). The process and outcome of marital and family therapy: Research review and evaluation. In A. E. Bergin & S. L. Garfield (Eds.), *Handbook of psychotherapy and behavior change* (4th ed, pp. 595–630). New York: Wiley.

Al-Issa, I. (1982). Gender and adult psychopathology. In I. Al-Issa (Ed.), *Gender and psychopathology* (pp. 83–110). New York: Academic Press.

Allen, L., & Britt, D. W. (1983). Black women in American society: A resource development perspective. *Issues in Mental Health Nursing, 5*, 1–4, 61–79.

Allen, L., & Mitchell, C. (1998). Racial and ethnic differences in patterns of problematic and adaptive development: An epidemiological review. In V. McLoyd (Ed.), *Racial and ethnic differences in studying minority adolescents: Conceptual, methodological, and theoretical issues* (pp. 29–54). Mahwah, NJ: Erlbaum.

Allport, G. W. (1954). *The nature of prejudice.* Garden City, NY: Doubleday.

Almeida-Filho, N., Lessa, I., Magalhães, L., Araújo, M. J., Aquino, E., James, S. H., et al. (2004). Social inequality and depressive disorders in Bahia, Brazil: Interactions of gender, ethnicity, and social class. *Social Science & Medicine, 59*, 1339–1353.

Alon, S., & Haberfeld, Y. (2007). Labor force attachment and the evolving wage gap between White, Black and Hispanic young women. *Work and Occupations, 34*, 369–398.

Alonso, J., Angermeyer, M. C., Bernert, R., Bruffaerts, T. S., Brugha, H., Bryson, G., et al. (2004). Use of mental health services in Europe: Results from the European Study of the Epidemiology of Mental Disorders (ESEMeD) Project. *Acta Psychiatrica Scandinavica, 109* (Suppl. 420), 47–54.

Alter, C., & Hage, J. (1993). *Organizations working together.* Newbury Park, CA: Sage.

Altman, D. (1994). *Power and community: Organizational and cultural responses to AIDS.* London: Taylor & Francis.

Amaddeo, F., & Jones, J. (2007). What is the impact of socio-economic inequalities on the use of mental health services? *Epidemiological Psychiatric Sociology, 16*, 16–19.

Amato, P. R., & Keith, B. (1991). Parental divorce and the well-being of children: A meta-analysis. *Psychological Bulletin, 110*, 26–46.

American Bar Association Criminal Justice Standards Committee. (1989). *American Bar Association Criminal Justice and Mental Health Standards.* Washington, DC: Author.

American Psychiatric Association. (1980). *Diagnostic and statistical manual of mental disorders* (3rd ed.). Washington, DC: Author.

American Psychiatric Association. (1987). *Diagnostic and statistical manual of mental disorders* (3rd ed. rev.). Washington, DC: Author.

American Psychiatric Association. (1994). *Diagnostic and statistical manual of mental disorders* (4th ed.). Washington, DC: Author.

American Psychiatric Association. (2000). *Diagnostic and statistical manual of mental disorders* (4th ed. rev.). Washington, DC: Author.

American Psychological Association. (2003). Guidelines on multicultural education, training, research, practice, and organizational change for psychologists. *American Psychologist, 58*, 377–402.

Anastasi, A. (1988). *Psychological testing* (6th ed.) New York: Macmillan.

Andersen, R. (1995). Revisiting the behavioral model and access to care: Does it matter? *Journal of Health and Social Behavior, 36*, 1–10.

Andersen, R., & Newman, J. (1968). *A behavioral model of families' use of health services* (Research Series No. 25). Chicago: University of Chicago, Center for Health Administration Studies.

Andersen, R., & Newman, J. (1973). Societal and individual determinants of medical care utilization in the United States. *Milbank Quarterly, 51*, 95–124.

Anderson, C. M., Robins, C. S., Greeno, C. G., Cahalane, H., Copeland, V. C., & Andrews, R. M. (2006). Why lower income mothers do not engage with the formal mental health care system: Perceived barriers to care. *Qualitative Health Research, 16*, 926–943.

Anderson, L. M., Scrimshaw, S. C., Fullilove, M. T., Fielding, J. E., & the Task Force on Community Preventive Services. (2003). The community guide's model for linking the social environment to health. *American Journal of Preventive Medicine, 24*, 12–20.

Anderson, M., & Fienberg, S. E. (1995). Black, white, and shades of gray (and brown and yellow). *Chance, 8*, 15–18.

Anderson, O. W., & Andersen, R. (1972). Patterns of use of health services. In H. E. Freeman, S. Levine, & L. G. Reeder (Eds.), *Handbook of medical sociology* (2nd ed., pp. 386–406). Englewood Cliffs, NJ: Prentice-Hall.

Anderson, S. G., Halter, A. P., & Gryzlak, B. M. (2004). Difficulties after leaving TANF: Inner-city women talk about reasons for returning to welfare. *Social Work, 49*, 185–194.

Andreasen, N. (1984). *The broken brain: The biological revolution in psychiatry.* New York: Harper & Row.

Andreasen, N. (1999). Understanding the causes of schizophrenia. *New England Journal of Medicine, 340,* 645–647.

Andreasen, N., & Black, D. (1995). *Introductory textbook of psychiatry.* Washington, DC: American Psychiatric Association.

Andreasen, N., & Swayze, V. (1989). Neuroimaging. In J. A. Silva & C. C. Nadelson (Eds.), *International review of psychiatry* (pp. 355–393). Washington, DC: American Psychiatric Association.

Aneshensel, C. S. (1992). Social stress: Theory and research. *Annual Review of Sociology, 18,* 15–38.

Aneshensel, C. S. (1996). The neighborhood context of adolescent mental health. *Journal of Health and Social Behavior, 37,* 293–310.

Aneshensel, C. S. (1999). Outcomes of the stress process. In A. V. Horwitz & T. L. Scheid (Eds.), *A handbook for the sociology of mental health* (pp. 211–227). New York: Cambridge University Press.

Aneshensel, C. S., Botticello, A. L., & Yamamoto-Mitani, N. (2004). When caregiving ends: The course of depressive symptoms after bereavement. *Journal of Health and Social Behavior, 45,* 422–440.

Aneshensel, C. S., Frerichs, R. R., & Huba, G. J. (1984). Depression and physical illness: A multiwave, nonrecursive causal model. *Journal of Health and Social Behavior, 25,* 350–371.

Aneshensel, C. S., & Phelan, J. C. (Eds.). (1999). *Handbook of the sociology of mental health.* New York: Plenum Press.

Aneshensel, C. S., Rutter, C. M., & Lachenbruch, P. A. (1991). Competing conceptual and analytic models: Social structure, stress, and mental health. *American Sociological Review, 56,* 166–178.

Aneshensel, C. S., & Sucoff, C. A. (1996). The neighborhood context of adolescent mental health. *Journal of Health and Social Behavior, 37,* 293–310.

Angermeyer, M. C., & Matschinger, H. (1994). Lay beliefs about schizophrenic disorder: The results of a population survey in Germany. *Acta Psychiatrica Scandinavica, 89,* 39–45.

Angermeyer, M. C., & Matschinger, H. (1996). Public attitudes towards psychiatric treatment. *Acta Psychiatrica Scandinavica, 94,* 326–336.

Angemeyer, M., & Schulze, B. (2001). Reinforcing stereotypes: How the focus on forensic cases in news reporting may influence public attitudes towards the mentally ill. *International Journal of Law and Psychiatry, 24,* 469–486.

Angold, A., Erkanli, A., Farmer, E. M. Z., Fairbank, J. A., Burns, B. J., Keeler, G., et al. (2002). Psychiatric disorder, impairment, and service use in rural African American and White youth. *Archives of General Psychiatry,* 893–901.

Angst, J., Gamma, A., Benazzi, F., Ajdacic V., Eich, D., & Rössler, W. (2003). Toward a definition of subthreshold bipolarity: Epidemiology and proposed criteria for Bipolar-II, Minor Bipolar Disorders and Hypomania. *Journal of Affective Disorders, 73,* 133–146.

Anthony, J. C., Folstein, M., Romanoski, A. J., Von Korff, M. R., Nestadt, G. R., Chahal, R., et al. (1985). Comparison of the lay Diagnostic Interview Schedule and a standardized psychiatric diagnosis: Experience in eastern Baltimore. *Archives of General Psychiatry, 42,* 667–675.

Anthony, J. C., & Petronis, K. R. (1991). Suspected risk factors for depression among adults 18–44 years old. *Epidemiology, 2,* 123–132.

Anthony, W. (1993). Recovery from mental illness: The guiding vision of the mental health service system in the 1990s. *Psychosocial Rehabilitation Journal, 16,* 11–23.

Antonovsky, A. (1979). *Health, stress, and coping.* San Francisco: Jossey-Bass.

Appelbaum, P. (1994). *Almost a revolution: Mental health law and the limits of change.* New York: Oxford University Press.

Appelbaum, P. (2002). Starving in the midst of plenty: The mental health care crisis in America. *Psychiatric Services, 53,* 1247–1249.

Appleby, L., Luchins, D. J., Freels, S., Smith, M. E., & Wasner, D. (2008). The impact of immigration on psychiatric hospitalization in Illinois from 1993 to 2003. *Psychiatric Services, 59,* 648–654.

Arches, J. (1991). Social structure, burnout, and job satisfaction. *Social Work, 36,* 202–206.

Arnett, J. (1992). Socialization and adolescent reckless behavior: A reply to Jessor. *Developmental Review, 12,* 391–409.

Arno, P. S., & Hughes, R. G. (1987). Local policy responses to the AIDS epidemic: New York and San Francisco. *New York State Journal of Medicine, 87*, 264–272.

Artis, M. E. (2007). Maternal cohabitation and child well-being among kindergarten children. *Journal of Marriage and Family, 69*, 222–236.

Arvanites, T. M. (1988). The impact of state mental hospital deinstitutionalization on commitments for incompetency to stand trial. *Criminology, 26*, 307–320.

Aseltine, R. H., & Kessler, R. C. (1993). Marital disruption and depression in a community sample. *Journal of Health and Social Behavior, 34*(3), 237–251.

Ashforth, B. E., & Humphrey, R. H. (1993). Emotional labor in service roles: The influence of identity. *Academy of Management Review, 18*, 88–115.

Astley, W. G., & Van de Ven, A. H. (1983). Central perspectives and debates in organization theory. *Administrative Science Quarterly, 28*, 245–273.

Asuni, T. (1990). Nigeria: Report on the care, treatment, and rehabilitation of people with mental illness. *Psychosocial Rehabilitation Journal, 14*, 35–44.

Atwood, N. (1982). Professional prejudice and the psychotic patient. *Social Work, 27*, 172–177.

Auffarth, I., Busse, R., Dietrich, D., & Emrich, H. (2008). Length of psychiatric inpatient stay: Comparison of mental health care outlining a case mix from a hospital in Germany and the United States of America, *German Journal of Psychiatry, 11*, 40–44.

Aviram, U. (1990). Community care of the seriously mental ill: Continuing problems and current issues. *Community Mental Health Journal, 26*, 69–88.

Avison, W. R. (1999). Family structure and processes. In A. V. Horwitz & T. L. Scheid (Eds.), *A handbook for the study of mental health* (pp. 228–240). New York: Cambridge University Press.

Avison, W. R., Ali, J., & Walters, D. (2007). Family structure, stress, and psychological distress: A demonstration of the impact of differential exposure. *Journal of Health and Social Behavior, 48*(30), 301–317.

Avison, W. R., & McAlpine, D. (1992). Gender differences in symptoms and depression among adolescents. *Journal of Health and Social Behavior, 33*, 77–96.

Babcock, J. (1895). The colored insane. *Alienist and Neurologist, 16*, 423–447.

Babigian, H., Mitchell, O., Marshall, P., & Reed, S. (1992). A mental health capitation experiment: Evaluating the Monroe-Livingston experience. In R. Frank & W. G. Manning (Eds.), *Economics and mental health* (pp. 307–331). Baltimore: Johns Hopkins University Press.

Bachanas, P., Morris, M. K., Lewis-Gess, J. K., Sarett-Cuasay, E. J., Sirl, K., Ries, J. K., et al. (2002). Predictors of risky sexual behavior in African American adolescent girls: Implications for prevention interventions. *Journal of Pediatric Psychology, 27*, 519–530.

Bachrach, L. L. (1980). Overview: Model programs for chronic mental patients. *American Journal of Psychiatry, 137*, 1023–1030.

Bachrach, L. L. (1982). *Deinstitutionalization: An analytical review and sociological perspective* (DHEW Publication No. ADM 76–351). Washington, DC: U.S. Government Printing Office.

Badawi, M. A., Eaton, W. W., Myllyluoma, J., Weimer, L. G., & Gallo, J. (1999). Psychopathology and attrition in the Baltimore ECA 15-year follow-up, 1981–1996. *Social Psychiatry and Psychiatric Epidemiology, 34*, 91–98.

Bakketeig, L. S., Hoffman, H. J., & Titmuss-Oakley, A. R. (1984). Perinatal mortality. In M. B. Bracken (Ed.), *Perinatal epidemiology* (pp. 99–151). New York: Oxford University Press.

Baltes, P. B., Reese, H. W., & Lipsitt, L. P. (1980). Life-span developmental psychology. *Annual Review of Psychology, 31*, 65–110.

Baltrus, P. T., Lynch, J. W., Everson-Rose, S., Raghunathan, T. E., & Kaplan, G. A. (2005). Race/ethnicity, life-course socioeconomic position, and body weight trajectories over 34 years: The Alameda County Study. *American Journal of Public Health, 95*(9), 1595–1601.

Bandura, A. (1969). *Principles of behavior modification*. New York: Holt, Rinehart & Winston.

Bandura, A. (1986). *Social foundations of thought and action*. Englewood Cliffs, NJ: Prentice-Hall.

Banfield, E. (1971). Revenue sharing in theory and practice. *Public Interest, 23*, 33–44.

Banks, K. H.. & Kohn-Wood, L. P. (2007). The influence of racial identity profiles on the relationship between racial discrimination and depressive symptoms. *Journal of Black Psychology, 33*, 331–354.

Barash, E. T., Hanson, D. L., Buskin, S. E., & Teshale, E. (2007). HIV-infected injection drug users: Health care utilization and morbidity. *Journal of Health Care for the Poor and Underserved, 18,* 675–686.

Barbee, E. (2003). Violence and mental health. In D. R. Brown & V. M. Keith (Eds.), *In and out of our right minds: The mental health of African American women* (pp. 99–115). New York: Columbia University Press.

Barber, C. (2008). *Comfortably numb: How psychiatry is medicating a nation.* New York: Pantheon.

Barnett, P., & Gotlib, I. (1988). Dysfunctional attitudes and social stress: The differential prediction of future psychological symptomatology. *Motivation and Emotion, 12,* 251–270.

Barrera, M., Jr. (1982). Raza populations. In L. R. Snowden (Ed.), *Reaching the underserved: Mental health needs of neglected populations* (pp. 119–142). Beverly Hills, CA: Sage.

Barrett, A. E. (2000). Marital trajectories and mental health. *Journal of Health and Social Behavior, 41,* 451–464.

Barrett, A., & White, H. R. (2002). Trajectories of gender role orientations in adolescence and early adulthood: A prospective study of the mental health effects of masculinity and femininity. *Journal of Health and Social Behavior, 43,* 451–468.

Barry, E. (2002, March 3). Group stirs debate over schizophrenia. *Boston Globe,* p. B2. Retrieved September 21, 2008, from http://www.resourcepartnership.org/webdocs/Documents/Resource%20Library/Mental%20Health/Group_stirs_debate_over_schizophrenia.pdf.

Bartley, S. J., Blanton, P. W., & Gilliard, J. L. (2005). Husbands and wives in dual-earner marriages: Decision-making, gender role attitudes, division of household labor, and equity. *Marriage & Family Review, 37,* 69–94.

Bassett, A. S., Jones, B. D., McGillivray B. C., et al. (1988). Partial trisomy chromosome 5 cosegregating with schizophrenia. *Lancet, 1,* 799–801.

Bassoff, E. S., & Glass, G. (1982). The relationship between sex roles and mental health: A meta-analysis of twenty-six studies. *Counseling Psychologist, 10,* 105–112.

Bateson, G., Jackson, D. D., Haley, J., & Weakland, J. (1956). Toward a theory of schizophrenia. *Behavioral Science, 1,* 251–264.

Baumer, E., & South, S. (2001). Community effects on youth sexual activity. *Journal of Marriage and the Family, 63,* 540–554.

Baumgartner, L. M. (2007). The incorporation of the HIV/AIDS identity into the self over time. *Qualitative Health Research, 17,* 919–931.

Baumheier, E. C. (1982). Services integration in the field of health and human services. In *Health services integration: Lessons for the 1980s: Vol. 4. Commissioned papers.* Washington DC: Institute of Medicine, National Academy of Sciences.

Bayer, R. (1987). *Homosexuality and American psychiatry: The politics of diagnosis.* Princeton, NJ: Princeton University Press.

Bayley, M. (1991). Normalization or "social role" valorization: An adequate philosophy? In S. Baldwin & J. Hattersley (Eds.), *Mental handicap: Social sciences perspectives* (pp. 87–99). New York: Routledge.

Beachler, M. (1990). The mental health services program for youth. *Journal of Mental Health Administration, 17,* 115–121.

Beals, J., Manson, S. M., Whitesell, N. R., Spicer, P., Novins, D. K., & Mitchell, C. M. (2005). Prevalence of DSM-IV disorders and attendant help-seeking in 2 American Indian reservation populations. *Archives of General Psychiatry, 62,* 99–108.

Beals, J., Novins, D. K., Spicer, P., Orton, H. D., Mitchell, C. M., Baron, A. E., et al. (2004). Challenges in pperationalizing the DSM-IV clinical significance criterion. *Archives of General Psychiatry, 61,* 1197–207.

Beals, J., Piasecki, J., Nelson, S., Jones, M., Keane, E., Dauphinais, P., et al. (1997). Psychiatric disorder among American Indian adolescents: Prevalence in Northern Plains youth. *Journal of the American Academy of Child & Adolescent Psychiatry, 36,* 152–159.

Beardslee, W. R., Bemporad, J., Keller, M., & Klerman, G. (1983). Children of parents with major affective disorder: A review. *American Journal of Psychiatry, 140,* 825–832.

Beauboeuf-Lafontant, T. (2007). "You have to show strength": An exploration of gender, race, and depression. *Gender & Society, 21,* 128–151.

Beck, A., Rush, J., Shaw, B., & Emery, G. (1979). *Cognitive theory of depression*. New York: Guilford.

Becker, G. S. (1976). *The economic approach to human behavior*. Chicago: University of Chicago Press.

Becker, H. S. (1973). *Outsiders: Studies in the sociology of deviance*. New York: The Free Press.

Beers, C. (1908). *A mind that found itself*. New York: Longmans, Green.

Behar, L. (1988). An integrated state system of services for seriously disturbed children. In J. Looney (Ed.), *Chronic mental illness in children and adolescents* (pp. 131–138). Washington, DC: American Psychiatric Press.

Belcher, J. R. (1988). Are jails replacing the mental health system for the homeless mentally ill? *Community Mental Health Journal, 24*, 185–194.

Belkic, K. L., Landsbergis, P. A., Schnall, P. L., & Baker, D. (2004). Is job strain a major source of cardiovascular disease risk? *Scandinavian Journal of Work, Environment and Health, 30*, 85–128.

Bell, C., Williamson, J. L., & Chien, P. (2008). Cultural, racial, and ethnic competence and psychiatric diagnosis. *Ethnicity and Inequalities in Health and Social Care, 8*, 32–39.

Bell, D. (1973). *The coming of post-industrial society*. New York: Basic Books.

Bell, L. V. (1989). From the asylum to the community in U.S. mental health care: A historical overview. In D. Rochefort (Ed.), *Mental health policy in the United States* (pp. 89–120). New York: Greenwood.

Belle, D. (1982). *Lives in stress: Women and depression*. Beverly Hills, CA: Sage.

Belle, D. (1987). Gender differences in the social moderators of stress. In R. C. Barnett, L. Biener, & G. K. Baruch (Eds.), *Gender & stress* (pp. 257–277). New York: The Free Press.

Belmaker, R. H., & Agam G. (2008). Major depressive disorder. *New England Journal of Medicine, 358*, 55–68.

Belsky, J., & Eggebean, D. (1991). Early and extensive maternal employment and young children's socioemotional development: Children of the National Longitudinal Survey of Youth. *Journal of Marriage and Family, 53*, 1083–1110.

Belsky, J., Vandell, D. L., Burchinal, M., Clarke-Stewart, K. A., McCartney, K., Owen, M. T., et al. (2007). Are there long-term effects of child care? *Child Development, 78*, 681–701.

Bengtson, V. L., & Allen, K. R. (1993). The life course perspective applied to families over time. In P. G. Boss, W. J. Doherty, R. LaRossa, W. R. Schumm, & S. K. Steinmetz. (Eds.), *Sourcebook of family theories and methods: A contextual approach* (pp. 469–499). New York: Plenum Press.

Benin, M., & Keith, V. M. (1995). The social support of employed African American and Anglo mothers. *Journal of Family Issues, 16*, 275–297.

Bennett, N. S., Lidz, C. W., Monahan, J., Mulvey, E. P., Hoge, S. K., Roth, L. H., et al. (1993). Inclusion, motivation and good faith: The morality of coercion in mental hospital admission. *Behavioral Science and the Law, 11*, 295–306.

Berdahl, T. A., Hoyt, D. R., & Whitbeck, L. B. (2005). Predictors of first mental health service utilization among homeless and runaway adolescents. *Journal of Adolescent Health, 37*, 145–154.

Berg, D. (1990). A case in print. *Journal of Applied Behavioral Science, 26*, 67–70.

Berger, J., Cohen, B. P., & Zelditch, M., Jr. (1972). Status characteristics and social interaction. *American Sociological Review, 37*, 241–255.

Berger, J., Fisek, M. H., Norman, R. Z., & Zelditch, M,. Jr. (1977). *Status characteristics and social interaction*. New York: Elsevier.

Berger, R., Pat-Horenczyk, R., & Gelkopf, M. (2007). School-based intervention for prevention and treatment of elementary-students' terror-related distress in Israel: A quasi-randomized controlled trial. *Journal of Traumatic Stress, 20*, 541–551.

Berk, S. F. (1985). *The gender factory: The apportionment of work in American households*. New York: Plenum Press.

Berk, R. A., & Berk, S. F. (1979). *Labor and leisure at home: Content and organization of the household day*. Beverly Hills, CA: Sage.

Berkman, L. F., & Breslow, L. (1983). *Health and ways of living: The Alameda County Study*. New York: Oxford University Press.

Berkman, L. F., & Glass, T. (2000). Social integration, social networks, social support and health. In L. F. Berkman & I. Kawachi. (Eds.), *Social epidemiology* (pp. 137–173). New York: Oxford University Press.

Bernal, G., Bonilla, J., & Bellido, C. (1995). Ecological validity and cultural sensitivity for the cultural adaptation and development of psychosocial treatment with Hispanics. *Journal of Abnormal Child Psychology, 23*, 67–82.

Bernard, J. S. (1972). *The future of marriage.* New Haven, CT: Yale University Press.

Bestman, E. W. (1986). Cross-cultural approaches to service delivery to ethnic minorities: The Miami model. In M. Miranda & H. Kitano. (Eds.), *Mental health research and practice in minority communities: Development of culturally sensitive training programs* (pp. 199–226). Washington, DC: National Institute of Mental Health.

Beutler, L. E., Crago, M., & Arizmendi, T. G. (1986). Research on therapist variables in psychotherapy. In S. L. Garfield & A. E. Bergin (Eds.), *Handbook of psychotherapy and behavior change* (3rd ed.). New York: Wiley.

Bhatia, S. K., & Bhatia, S. C. (2007). Childhood and adolescent depression. *American Family Physician, 75*, 73–80.

Bianchi, S. M. (1995). Changing economic roles of women and men. In R. Farley (Ed.), *State of the union* (pp. 107–154). New York: Russell Sage Foundation.

Bianchi, S. M., Robinson, J. P., & Milkie, M. A. (2006). *Changing rhythms of family life.* New York: Russell Sage Foundation.

Bianchi, S. M., & Spain, D. (1986). *American women in transition.* New York: Russell Sage Foundation.

Bianconi, J., Mahler, J., & McFarland, B. (2006). Outcomes for rural Medicaid clients with severe mental illness of fee for service versus managed care. *Administration and Policy in Mental Health and Mental Health Services Research, 33*, 411–422.

Bickman, L. (1996). A managed continuum of care: More is not always better. *American Psychologist, 51*, 689–701.

Bickman, L. (1999). Introductory statement. *Health Services Research, 1*, 1–3.

Bickman, L., Guthrie, P., Foster, E., Summerfelt, W., Lambert, E., Breda, C., et al. (1995). *Evaluating managed mental health services: The Fort Bragg experiment.* New York: Plenum Press.

Bickman, L., Noser, K., & Summerfelt, W. (1999). Long-term effects of a system of care on children and adolescents. *Journal of Behavioral Health Services and Research, 26*, 185–202.

Bieber, S. L., Richard A. P., Bosten, K., & Steadman, H. J. (1988). Predicting criminal recidivism of insanity acquittees. *International Journal of Law and Psychiatry, 11*, 105–112.

Bilder, R. M. (2008). Phenomics: Building scaffolds for biological hypotheses in the post-genomic era. *Biological Psychiatry, 63*, 439–440.

Bilder, R. M., Lipschutz-Bruch, L., Reiter, G., Geisler, S. H., Mayerhoff, D. I., & Lieberman, J. A. (1992). Intellectual deficits in first-episode schizophrenia: Evidence for progressive deterioration. *Schizophrenia Bulletin, 18*, 437–448.

Billingsley, A. (1992). *Climbing Jacob's ladder: The enduring legacy of Black families.* New York: Simon & Schuster.

Bilu, Y., & Witztum, E. (1993). Working with Jewish ultra-Orthodox patients: Guidelines for a culturally sensitive therapy. *Culture, Medicine and Psychiatry, 17*, 197–233.

Bird, C. E. (1999). Gender, household labor, and psychological distress: The impact of the amount and division of housework. *Journal of Health and Social Behavior, 40*, 32–45.

Bird, C. E., & Ross, C. E. (1993). Houseworkers and paid workers: Qualities of the work and effects on personal control. *Journal of Marriage and the Family, 55*, 913–925.

Bird, H. R., Canino, G. J., Davis, M., Zhang, H., Ramirez, R., & Lahey, B. B. (2001). Prevalence and correlates of antisocial behaviors among three ethnic groups. *Journal of Abnormal Child Psychology, 29*(6), 465–478.

Bittner, E. (1967). Police discretion in apprehension of mentally ill persons. *Social Problems, 14*, 278–292.

Blaauw, E., Roesch, R., & Kerkhof, A. (2000). Mental disorders in European prison systems. *International Journal of Law and Psychiatry, 23*, 649–663.

Black, D. R., Gleser, L. J., & Kooyers, K. J. (1990). A meta-analytic evaluation of couples weight-loss programs. *Health Psychology, 9*, 330–347.

Blanchard, E. B., Kuhn, E., Rowell, D. L., Hickling, E. J., Wittrock, D., Rogers, R. L., et al. (2004). Studies of the vicarious traumatization of college students by the September 11th attacks: Effects of proximity, exposure and connectedness. *Behaviour Research and Therapy, 42*, 191–205.

Blaney, P. H. (2000). Stress and depression: A personality-situation interaction approach. In S. L. Johnson. (Ed.), *Stress, coping, and depression* (pp. 89–116). Mahwah, NJ: Erlbaum.

Blank, M. B., Mandell, D. S., Aiken, L., & Hadley, T. R. (2002). Co-occurrence of HIV and serious mental illness among Medicaid recipients. *Psychiatric Services, 53*, 868–873.

Blank, M. B., Tetrick, F. L., III, Brinkley, D. F., Smith, H. O., & Doheny, V. (1994). Racial matching and service utilization among seriously mentally ill consumers in the rural South. *Community Mental Health Journal, 30*, 271–281.

Blank, R. M., & Dabady, M. (2004). *Measuring racial discrimination.* Washington, DC: National Academies Press.

Blau, P. M., & Duncan, O. D. (1967). *The American occupational structure.* New York: Wiley.

Blauner, R. (1964). *Alienation and freedom.* Berkeley: University of California Press.

Blazer, D. G., Hughes, D., George, L. K., Swartz, M., & Boyer, R. (1991). Generalized anxiety disorder. In L. N. Robins & D. A. Regier (Eds.), *Psychiatric disorders in America: The Epidemiological Catchment Area Study* (pp. 180–203). New York: The Free Press.

Bleich, A., Gelkopf, M., Melamed, Y., & Solomon, Z. (2005). Emotional impact of exposure to terrorism among young-old and old-old Israeli citizens. *American Journal of Geriatric Psychiatry, 13*, 705–712.

Bloom, J. D., Rogers, J. L., Manson, S. M., & Williams, M. H. (1986). Lifetime police contacts of discharged psychiatric security review board clients. *International Journal of Law and Psychiatry, 8*, 189–202.

Bloom, J. D., Shore J. H., & Arvidson, B. (1981). Local variations in arrests of psychiatric patients. *Bulletin of the American Academy of Psychiatry and Law, 9*, 203–210.

Bloom, J. D., Williams, M. H., & Bigelow, D.A. (1992). The involvement of schizophrenic insanity acquittees in the mental health and criminal justice systems. *Clinical Forensic Psychiatry, 15*, 591–604.

Boardman, J. D., Finch, B. K., Ellison, C. G., Williams, D. R., & Jackson, J. S. (2001). Neighborhood disadvantage, stress, and drug use among adults. *Journal of Health and Social Behavior, 42*, 151–165.

Bobo, J. L., Gilchrist, L. D., Cvetkovich, G. T., Trimble, J. E., & Schinke, S. P. (1988). Cross cultural service delivery to minority communities. *Journal of Community Psychology, 16*, 263–272.

Bockoven, J. S. (1972). *Moral treatment in community mental health.* New York: Springer.

Bogardus, E. S. (1925). Measuring social distances. *Journal of Applied Sociology, 9*, 299–308.

Bogart, L. M., Kelly, J. A., Catz, S. L., & Sosman J. M. (2000). Impact of medical and nonmedical factors on physician decision making for HIV/AIDS antiretroviral treatment. *Journal of Acquired Immune Deficiency Syndromes and Human Retrovirology, 23*, 396–404.

Bogerts, B., & Lieberman, J. (1989). Neuropathology in the study of psychiatric disease. In J. A. Silva & C. C. Nadelson (Eds.), *International review of psychiatry* (pp. 515–555). Washington, DC: American Psychiatric Press.

Bolland, J. (2003). Hopelessness and risk behavior among adolescents living in high-poverty inner-city neighborhoods. *Journal of Adolescence, 26*, 145–158.

Bollini, P., & Mollica, R. (1989). Surviving without the asylum: An overview of the studies of the Italian Reform Movement. *Journal of Nervous and Mental Disease, 177*, 607–615.

Bonanno, G. A., Rennicke, C., & Dekel, S. (2005). Self-enhancement among high-exposure survivors of the September 11th terrorist attack: Resilience or social maladjustment? *Journal of Personality and Social Psychology, 88*, 984–998.

Bonanno, G. A., Galea, S., Bucciarelli, A., & Vlahov, D. (2006). Psychological resilience after disaster: New York City in the aftermath of the September 11th terrorist attack. *Psychological Science, 17*, 181–186.

Bond, G., Drake, R., Mueser, K., & Latimer, E. (2001). Assertive community treatment: Critical ingredients and impact on patients. *Disease Management and Health Outcomes, 9*(3), 141–159.

Bond, G., Salyers, M., Rollins, A., Rapp, C., & Zipple, A. (2004). How evidence-based practices contribute to community integration. *Community Mental Health Journal, 40*(6), 569–588.

Bond, L., Lauby, J., & Batson, H. (2005). HIV testing: The role of individual- and structural-level barriers and facilitators. *AIDS Care, 17*, 125–140.

Bonovitz, J. C., & Bonovitz, J. S. (1981). Diversion of the mentally ill into the criminal justice system: The police intervention perspective. *American Journal of Psychiatry, 138*, 973–976.

Bonovitz, J. C., & Guy, E. B. (1979). Impact of restrictive civil commitment procedures on a prison psychiatric service. *American Journal of Psychiatry, 13*, 1045–1048.

Bonta, J., Law, M., & Hanson, K. (1998). The prediction of criminal and violent recidivism among mentally disordered offenders: A meta-analysis. *Psychological Bulletin, 123*, 123–142.

Booth, A., & Amato, P. (1991). Divorce and psychological stress. *Journal of Health and Social Behavior, 32*, 396–407.

Boothroyd, R. A., Poythress, N. G., McGaha, A., & Petrila, J. (2003). The Broward mental health court: Process, outcomes and service utilization. *International Journal of Law and Psychiatry, 26*, 55–71.

Borum, R., Deane, M. W., Steadman, H. J., & Morrissey, J. (1998). Police perspectives on responding to mentally ill people in crisis: Perceptions of program effectiveness. *Behavior Sciences and the Law, 16*, 393–405.

Borum, R., Swanson, J., Swartz, M., & Hiday, V. 1997. Substance abuse, violent behavior, and police encounters among persons with severe mental disorders. *Journal of Contemporary Criminal Justice, 13*, 236–249.

Boscarino, J. A., Adams, R. E., & Figley, C. R. (2004). Mental health service use 1 year after the World Trade Center disaster: Implications for mental health care. *General Hospital Psychiatry, 26*(5), 346–358.

Bourbonnais, R., Brisson, C., Moisan, J., & Vézina, M. (1996). Job strain and psychological distress in white-collar workers. *Scandinavian Journal of Work, Environment and Health, 22*(2), 139–145.

Bourdon, K. H., Rae, D. S., Locke, B. Z., Narrow, W. E., & Regier, D. A. (1992). Estimating the prevalence of mental disorders in U.S. adults from the Epidemiologic Catchment Area Study. *Public Health Report, 107*, 663–668.

Bourgois, P. (1998). The moral economies of homeless heroin addicts: Confronting ethnography, HIV risk, and everyday violence in San Francisco shooting encampments. *Substance Use & Misuse, 33*, 2323–2351.

Bourgois, P., Martinez, A., Kral, A., Edlin, B. R., Schonberg, J., & Ciccarone, D. (2006). Reinterpreting ethnic patterns among White and African American men who inject heroin: A social science of medicine approach. *PLoS Medicine, 3*(10), e452.

Bowers, L., Douzenis, A., Galeazzi, M. G., Forghieri, M., Tsopelas, C., Simpson, A., et al. (2005). Disruptive and dangerous behavior by patients on acute psychiatric wards in 3 European centres. *Social Psychiatry and Psychiatric Epidemiology, 40*, 822–828.

Bowlby, J. (1969). *Attachment and loss: Vol. 1. Attachment*. London: Hogarth.

Bowlby, J. (1973). *Attachment and loss: Vol. 2. Separation, anxiety and anger*. London: Hogarth.

Boyer, C. A., & Mechanic, D. (1994). Psychiatric reimbursement reform in New York State: Lessons in implementing change. *Milbank Quarterly, 72*, 621–651.

Boyle, P. J., & Callahan, D. (1995). Managed care in mental health: The ethical issues. *Health Affairs, 14*, 7–23.

Bozzette, S. A., Berry, S. H., Duan, N., Frankel, M. R., Leibowitz, A. A., Lefkowitz, D., et al. (1998). The care of HIV-infected adults in the United States: HIV Cost and Services Utilization Study Consortium. *New England Journal of Medicine, 339*, 1897–1904.

Bracken, M. B. (1984). *Perinatal epidemiology*. New York: Oxford University Press.

Bradbury, T., & Miller, G. (1985). Season of birth in schizophrenia: A review of evidence, methodology and etiology. *Psychological Bulletin, 98*, 569–594.

Bradley, R. H. (1985). The HOME Inventory: Rationale and research. In J. Lachenmeyer & M. Gibbs (Eds.), *Recent research in developmental psychopathology* (pp. 191–201). New York: Gardner.

Bradley, R. H., & Corwyn, R. F. (2002). Socioeconomic status and child development. *Annual Review of Psychology, 53*, 371–399.

Braff, J., Thomas A., & Steadman, H. J. (1983). Detention patterns of successful and unsuccessful insanity defendants. *Criminology, 21*, 439–448.

Braginsky, B. M., Braginsky, D. D., & Ring, K. (1969). *Methods of madness: The mental hospital as a last resort*. New York: Holt, Rinehart & Winston.

Brambilla, P., & Tansella, M. (2008). Can neuorimaging studies help us in understanding the biological causes of schizophrenia? *International Review of Psychiatry, 19*, 313–314.

Bramesfeld, A., Wedegartner, F., Elgeti, H., & Bisson, S. (2007). How does mental health care perform in respect to service users' expectations? Reevaluating inpatient and outpatient care in Germany with the WHO responsiveness concept. *BMC Health Services Research, 7*, 99.

Bratter, J., & Eschbach, K. (2005). Race/ethnic differences in nonspecific psychological distress: Evidence from the National Health Interview Survey. *Social Science Quarterly, 86*(3), 20–42.

Breitbart, W., Rosenfeld, B. D., & Passik, S. D. (1996). Interest in physician-assisted suicide among ambulatory HIV-infected patients. *American Journal of Psychiatry, 153*(2), 238–242.

Brekke, J. S., Prindle, C., Bae, S. W., & Long, J. D. (2001). Risks for individuals with schizophrenia that are living in the community. *Psychiatric Services, 52*(10), 1358–1366.

Brennan, P. A., Grekin, E. R., & Vanman E. J. (2000). Major mental disorders and crime in the community: A focus on patient populations and cohort investigations. In S. Hodgins (Ed.), *Violence among the mentally ill: Effective treatments and management strategies* (pp. 3–18). London: Kluwer.

Brenner, M. H. (1974). *Mental illness and the economy*. Cambridge, MA: Harvard University Press.

Breslau, N., & Davis, G. C. (1985). DSM-III generalized anxiety disorder: An empirical investigation of more stringent criteria. *Psychiatry Research, 15*, 231.

Bresnahan, M., Begg, M. D., Brown, A., Schaefer, C., Sohler, N., Insel, B., et al. (2007). Race and risk of schizophrenia in a U.S. birth cohort: Another example of health disparity? *International Journal of Epidemiology, 36*, 751–758.

Brewster, K. L., & Padavic, I. (2002). No more kin care?: Change in Black mothers' reliance on relatives for child care, 1977–94. *Gender & Society, 16*, 546–563.

Briggs, J. L. (1970). *Never in anger: Portrait of an Eskimo family*. Cambridge, MA: Harvard University Press.

Brines, J., & Joyner, K. (1999). The ties that bind: Principles of cohesion in cohabitation and marriage. *American Sociological Review, 64*(3), 333–355.

Brink, J. H., Doherty, D., & Boer, A. (2001). Mental disorder in federal offenders: A Canadian prevalence study. *International Journal of Law and Psychiatry, 24*, 339–357.

Brody, E. B. (2000, February 4). The other consumer movement: Psychiatric users/survivors. *Psychiatric News, 35*, 2–3.

Broman, C. (1988). Household work and family life satisfaction among Blacks. *Journal of Marriage and the Family, 50*, 743–748.

Broman, C. L. (1991). Gender, work-family roles, and psychological well-being of Blacks. *Journal of Marriage and Family, 53*, 509–520.

Broman, C. L. (1993). Race differences in marital well-being. *Journal of Marriage and the Family, 55*, 732.

Bromet, E. J., Dew, M. A., Parkinson, D. K., et al. (1988). Predictive effects of occupational and marital stress on mental health of a male workforce. *Journal of Organizational Behavior, 9*, 1–13.

Bromley, J. S., & Cunningham, S. J. (2004). You don't bring me flowers any more: An investigation into the experience of stigma by psychiatric in-patients. *Psychiatric Bulletin, 28*, 371–374.

Broner, N., Lattimore, P. K., Cowell A. J., & Schlenger, W. E. (2004). Effects of diversion on adults with co-occurring mental illness and substance use: Outcomes from a national multi-site study. *Behavioral Sciences and the Law, 22*, 519–541.

Brooks, T. L., Harris, S. K., Thrall, J. S., & Woods, E. R. (2002). Association of adolescent risk behaviors with mental health symptoms in high school students. *Journal of Adolescent Health, 31*, 240–246.

Brotheridge, C., & Grandey, A. (2002). Emotional labor and burnout: Comparing two perspectives of "people work." *Journal of Vocational Behavior, 60*, 17–39.

Brown, D. R. (1988). Employment and health among older Black women: Implications for their economic status (Working Paper Series). Wellesley, MA: Wellesley College Center for Research on Women.

Brown, D. R. (1996). Marriage and mental health. In J. S. Jackson & H. W. Neighbors (Eds.), *Mental health in Black America* (pp. 434–441). Thousand Oaks, CA: Sage.

Brown, D. R., Eaton, W. W., & Sussman, L. (1990). Racial differences in prevalence of phobic disorders. *Journal of Nervous and Mental Disease, 178*, 434–441.

Brown, D. R., & Keith, V. M. (2003). The epidemiology of mental disorders and mental health among African American women. In D. R. Brown & V. M. Keith (Eds.), *In and out of our right minds: The mental health of African American women* (pp. 23–59). New York: Columbia University Press.

Brown, D. R., & Monye, D. B. (1995). *Midlife and older caregivers of urban school-aged children* (Final Report). Washington, DC: AARP Andrus Foundation.

Brown, G. R., Rundell, J. R., McManis, S. E., Kendall, S. N., Zachary, R., & Temoshok, L. (1992). Prevalence of psychiatric disorders in early stages of HIV infection. *Psychosomatic Medicine, 54*, 588–601.

Brown, G. W. (2002). Social roles, context and evolution in the origins of depression. *Journal of Health and Social Behavior, 4*, 255–276.

Brown, G. W., Bhrolchain, M. N., & Harris, T. (1975). Social class and psychiatric disturbance among women in an urban population. *Sociology, 2*, 225–254.

Brown, G. W., & Harris, T. O. (1978). *Social origins of depression: A study of psychiatric disorder in women*. New York: The Free Press.

Brown, G. W., Harris, T. O., & Bifulco, A. (1986). Long-term effects of early loss of a parent. In M. Rutter, G. E. Izard, & P. B. Read (Eds.), *Depression in young people* (pp. 251–296). New York: Guilford.

Brown, J. L., & Vanable, P. A. (2008). Cognitive-behavioral stress management interventions for persons living with HIV: A review and critique of the literature. *Annals of Behavioral Medicine, 35*(1), 26–40.

Brown, L. K., Tolou-Shams, M., Lescano, C., Houck, C., Zeidman, J., Pugatch, D., et al. (2006). Depressive symptoms as a predictor of sexual risk among African American adolescents and young adults. *Journal of Adolescent Health, 39*, 444e1–444e8.

Brown, P. (1981). The mental patients' rights movement and mental health institutional change. *International Journal of Health Services, 11*(4), 523–540.

Brown, P. (1982). Attitudes towards the rights of mental patients. *Social Science and Medicine, 16*, 2025–2039.

Brown, P. (1985). *The transfer of care*. London: Routledge & Kegan Paul.

Brown, P., & Cooksey, E. (1989). Mental health monopoly: Corporate trends in mental health services. *Social Science and Medicine, 28*, 1129–1138.

Brown, S. L. (2000). The effect of union type on psychological well-being: Depression among cohabitors versus marrieds. *Journal of Health and Social Behavior, 41*(3), 241–255.

Brown, S. L. (2004). Family structure and child well-being: The significance of parental cohabitation. *Journal of Marriage and Family, 66*, 351–367.

Brown, S. L., & Booth, A. (1996). Cohabitation versus marriage: A comparison of relationship quality. *Journal of Marriage and the Family, 58*(3), 668–678.

Brown, T. (2003). Critical race theory speaks to the sociology of mental health: Mental health problems produced by racial stratification. *Journal of Health and Social Behavior, 44*(3), 292–301.

Brown, T. N., Sellers, S. L., & Gomez, J. P. (2002). The relationship between internalization and Black Americans' self-esteem. *Sociological Focus, 35*, 55–71.

Brown, T. N., Williams, D. R., Jackson, J. S., Neighbors, H. W., Torres, M., Sellers, S. L., et al. (2000). Being Black and "feeling blue": The mental health consequences of racial discrimination. *Race and Society, 2*, 117–131.

Browning, C., Leventhal, T., & Brooks-Gunn, J. (2004). Neighborhood context and racial differences in early adolescent sexual activity. *Demography, 41*(4), 697–720.

Broz, D., & Ouellet, L. J. (2008). Racial and ethnic changes in heroin injection in the United States: Implications for the HIV/AIDS epidemic. *Drug and Alcohol Dependence, 94*(1–3), 221–233.

Bruce, M. L., & Leaf, P. J. (1989). Psychiatric disorders and 15-month mortality in a community sample of older adults. *American Journal of Public Health, 79*, 727–730.

Bruce, M. L., Smith, W., Miranda, J., Hoagwood, K., & Wells, K. B. (2002). Community-based interventions. *Mental Health Services Research, 4*(4), 205–214.

Bruce, M. L., Takeuchi, D. T., & Leaf, P. J. (1991). Poverty and psychiatric status. *Archives of General Psychiatry, 48*, 470–474.

Bruder, C. E., Piotrowski, A., Gijsbers, A., Andersson, R., Erickson, S., et al. (2008). Phenotypically concordant and discordant monozygotic twins display different DNA copy-number-variation profiles. *American Journal of Human Genetics, 82*, 763–771.

Brugha, T. S., Bebbington P. E., & Jenkins, R. (1999). A difference that matters: Comparisons of structured and semi-structured psychiatric diagnostic interviews in the general population. *Psychological Medicine, 29*, 1013–1020.

Bruneau, J., Lamothe, F., Franco, E., Lachance, N., Desy, M., Soto, J., et al. (1997). High rates of HIV infection among injection drug users participating in needle exchange programs in Montreal: Results of a cohort study. *American Journal of Epidemiology, 146*, 994–1002.

Bryer, J. B., Nelson, B. A., Milller, J. B., & Krol, P. A. (1987). Childhood sexual and physical abuse as factors in adult psychiatric illness. *American Journal of Psychiatry, 144*, 1426–1430.

Brym, R. J., & Araj, B. (2006). Suicide bombing as strategy and interaction: The case of the second Intifada. *Social Forces, 84*(4), 1969–1986.

Buchwald, D., Manson, S. M., Dinges, N. G., Keane, E. M., & Kinzie, J. D. (1993). Prevalence of depressive symptoms among established Vietnamese refugees in the United States: Detection in a primary care setting. *Journal of General Internal Medicine, 8*, 76–81.

Buehler, C., Lange, G., & Lange, K. L. (2007). Adolescents' cognitive and emotional responses to marital hostility. *Child Development, 78*, 775–789.

Bulen, H. F., Erickson, R. J., & Wharton, A. S. (1997). Doing for others on the job: The affective requirements of service work, gender, and emotional well being. *Social Problems, 44*, 235–256.

Bullard, R. (1993). *Confronting environmental racism: Voices from the grassroots.* Boston: South End Press.

Bullmore, E. T., & Suckling, J. (2001). Functional magnetic resonance imaging. *International Review of Psychiatry, 13*, 24–33.

Bumpass, L., & Lu, H. (2000). Trends in cohabitation and implications for children's family contexts. *Population Studies, 54*, 29–41.

Burgess, K. B., Wojslawowicz, J. C., Rubin, K. H., Rose-Krasnor, L., & Booth-LaForce, C. (2006). Social information processing and coping strategies of shy/withdrawn and aggressive children: Does friendship matter? *Child Development, 77*, 371–383.

Burnam, A., Karno, M., Hough, R. L., Escobar, J. I., & Telles, C. (1987). Acculturation and lifetime prevalence of psychiatric disorders among Mexican Americans in Los Angeles. *Journal of Health and Social Behavior, 28*, 89–92.

Burnam, M. A., Bing, E. G., Morton, S. C., Sherbourne, C., Fleishman, J. A., London, A. S., et al. (2001). Use of mental health and substance abuse treatment services among adults with HIV in the United States. *Archives of General Psychiatry, 58*, 729–736.

Burnam, M. A., Stein, J. A., Golding, J. M., Siegel, J. M., Sorenson, S. B., Forsythe, A. B., et al. (1988). Sexual assault and mental disorders in a community population. *Journal of Consulting and Clinical Psychology, 56*, 843–850.

Burns, B., & Santos, A. (1995). Assertive community treatment: An update of randomized trials. *Psychiatric Services, 46*(7), 669–675.

Burt, K. B., Obradovic, J., Long, J. D., & Masten, A. S. (2008). The interplay of social competence and psychopathology over 20 years: Testing transactional and cascade models. *Child Development, 79*, 359–374.

Burton, N. M., &.Steadman, H. J. (1978). Legal professionals' perceptions of the insanity defense. *Journal of Psychiatry and Law, 6*, 173–187.

Byrne, M., Agerbo, E., Eaton, W. W., & Mortensen, P. B. (2004). Parental socio-economic status and risk of first admission with schizophrenia – A Danish National Register Based Study. *Social Psychiatry and Psychiatric Epidemiology, 39*(2), 87–96.

Cabassa, L. J., Zayas, L. H., & Hansen, M. C. (2006). Latino adults' access to mental health care: A review of epidemiological studies. *Administration and Policy in Mental Health, 33*(3), 316–330.

Cadoret, R. (1978). Evidence for genetic inheritance of primary affective disorder in adoptees. *American Journal of Psychiatry, 133*, 463–466.

Cadoret, R. J. (1991). Adoption studies in psychosocial epidemiology. In M. T. Tsuang, K. S. Kendler, & M. J. Lyons (Eds.), *Genetic issues in psychosocial epidemiology* (pp. 33–46). New Brunswick: Rutgers University Press.

Cadoret, R., O'Gorman, T. W., & Heywood, E. (1985). Genetic and environmental factors in major depression. *Journal of Affective Disorders, 9*, 155–164.

Cairney, J., & Krause, N. (2005). The social distribution of psychological distress and depression in older adults. *Journal of Aging and Health, 17*(6), 807–835.

Caldwell, C. H., Guthrie, B. J., & Jackson, J. S. (2006). Identity development, discrimination and psychological well-being in African American and Caribbean Black adolescents. In A. J. Schulz & L. Mullings (Eds.), *Race, class, gender and health: Intersectional approaches* (pp. 163–191). San Francisco: Jossey-Bass.

California Department of Mental Health. (2005, February 16). *Vision statement and guiding principles for DMH implementation of the Mental Health Services Act.* Retrieved October 1, 2008, from www.dmh.ca.gov/prop_63/MHSA/docs/Vision_and_Guiding_Principles_2-16-05.pdf.

Callahan, L. A., Mayer, C., & Steadman, H. J. (1987). Insanity defense reform in the United States – post Hinckley. *Mental and Physical Disability Law Reporter, 11*, 54–59.

Callahan, L. A., McGreevy M. A., Cirincione, C., & Steadman V. (1992). Measuring the effects of the Guilty but Mentally Ill (GBMI) verdict: Georgia's 1982 BMI reform. *Law and Human Behavior, 6*, 447–462.

Callinicos, A., & Harman, C. (1989). *The changing working class.* Chicago: Bookmarks.

Calloway, M. O., Morrissey, J. P., & Paulson, R. I. (1998). A method for analyzing and comparing social structure in networks of mental health organizations. *Research in Community and Mental Health, 9*, 139–162.

Campbell, A., Converse, P. E., & Rodgers, W. L. (1976). *The quality of American life.* New York: Russell Sage Foundation.

Campbell, J., & Schraiber, R. (1989). *The Well-Being Project: Mental health clients speak for themselves.* Sacramento, CA: California Department of Mental Health.

Cancian, M., & Meyer, D. R. (2000). Work after welfare: Women's work effort, occupation and economic well-being. *Social Work Research, 24*, 69–86.

Canino, G. J., Bird, H. R., Rubio-Stipic, M., & Woodbury, M. A. (1987). Reliability of child diagnosis in a Hispanic sample. *Journal of the American Academy of Child and Adolescent Psychiatry, 25*, 254–259.

Cannon, C. P., Braunwald, E., McCabe, C. H., Rader, D. J., Rouleau, J. L., Belder, R., et al. (2004). Comparison of intensive and moderate lipid lowering with statins after acute coronary syndromes. *New England Journal of Medicine, 350*, 1495–1504.

Caplan, P. J. (1995). *They say you're crazy: How the world's most powerful psychiatrists decide who's normal.* Reading, MA: Addison-Wesley.

Caplan, R. D., Vinokur, A. D., & Price, R. H. (1997). From job loss to re-employment: Field experiments in prevention-focused coping. In G. W. Albee & T. P. Gullotta (Eds.), *Primary prevention works* (pp. 341–379). Thousand. Oaks, CA: Sage.

Caplow, T., & Simon, J. (1999). Understanding prison policy and population trends. In M. H. Tonry & J. Petersilla (Eds.), *Prisons* (pp. 63–120). Chicago: University of Chicago Press.

Carey, M. P., Carey, K. B., & Kalichman, S. C. (1997). Risk for human immunodeficiency virus (HIV) infection among persons with severe mental illnesses. *Clinical Psychology Review, 17*(3): 271–291.

Carey, M. P., Carey, K. B., Maisto, S. A., Gordon, C. M., & Vanable, P. A. (2001). Prevalence and correlates of sexual activity and HIV-related risk behavior among psychiatric outpatients. *Journal of Consulting and Clinical Psychology, 69*(5), 846–850.

Carey, M. P., Carey, K. B., Maisto, S. A., Schroder, K. E., Vanable, P. A., & Gordon, C. M. (2004). HIV risk behavior among psychiatric outpatients: Association with psychiatric disorder, substance use disorder, and gender. *Journal of Nervous and Mental Disease, 192*(4), 289–296.

Carey, M. P., Carey, K. B., Weinhardt, L. S., & Gordon, C. M. (1997). Behavioral risk for HIV infection among adults with a severe and persistent mental illness: Patterns and psychological antecedents. *Community Mental Health Journal, 33*(2), 133–142.

Carlson, E. D., & Chamberlain, R. M. 2005. Allostatic load and health disparities: A theoretical orientation. *Research in Nursing and Health, 28*, 306–315.

Carlson, G., & Grant, K. (2008). The roles of stress and coping in explaining gender differences in risk for psychopathology among African American urban adolescents. *Journal of Early Adolescence, 28*, 375–404.

Carothers, C., & Driscoll, P. (2004). An advocacy perspective. In-Patient safety: An Advocacy Perspective. *Psychiatric Services, 55*, 698–702.

Carpenter, K. M., Hasin, D. S., Allison, D. B., & Faith, M. S. (2000). Relationships between obesity and DSM-IV major depressive disorder, suicide ideation, and suicide attempts: Results from a general population study. *American Journal of Public Health, 90*(2), 251–257.

Carpiano, R. M. (2006). Towards a neighborhood resource-based theory of social capital for health: Can Bourdieu and sociology help? *Social Science & Medicine, 62*, 165–175.

Carpentier, N., Ducharme, F., Kergoat, M.-J., & Bergman, H. (2008). Barriers to care and social representations early in the career of caregivers of persons with Alzheimer's disease. *Research on Aging, 30*(3), 334–357.

Carr, D., House, J. S., Kessler, R. C., Nesse, R. M., Sonnega, J., & Wortman, C. (2000). Marital quality and psychological adjustment to widowhood among older adults: A longitudinal analysis. *Journal of Gerontology, 55B*(4), S197–S207.

Carrico, A. W., Johnson, M. O., Morin, S. F., Remien, R. H., Charlebois, E. D., Steward, W. T., et al. (2007). Correlates of suicidal ideation among HIV-positive persons. *AIDS, 21*(9), 1199–1203.

Carroll, G. R., & Hannan, M. T. 2000. *The demography of corporations and industries*. Princeton, NJ: Princeton University Press.

Cascardi, M., Mueser, K. T., DeGiralomo, J., & Murrin, M. (1996). Physical aggression against psychiatric inpatients by family members and partners. *Psychiatric Services, 47*(5), 531–532.

Case, M. H., & Robinson, W. L. (2003). Interventions with ethnic minority populations: The legacy and promise of community psychology. In G. Bernal, J. E. Trimble, A. K. Burlew, & F. T. L. Leong (Eds.), *Handbook of racial and ethnic minority psychology* (pp. 573–590). Thousand Oaks: Sage.

Caspi, A., Roberts, B. W., & Shriner, R. (2005). Personality development: Stability and change. *Annual Review of Psychology, 56*, 453–484.

Caspi, A., Sugden, K., Moffitt, T. E., Taylor, A., Craig, I. W., Harrington, H., et al. (2003). Influence of life stress on depression: Moderation by a polymorphism in the 5-HTT gene. *Science, 301*, 386–389.

Cassel, J. (1974). Psychosocial processes and "stress": Theoretical formulation. *International Journal of Health Services, 4*, 471–482.

Cassel, J. (1976). The contribution of the social environment to host resistance. *American Journal of Epidemiology, 14*, 107–123.

Castle, D. J., & Morgan, V. (2008). Epidemiology. In K. T. Mueser & D. V. Jeste (Eds.), *Clinical handbook of schizophrenia*. New York: Guilford.

Castle, D., Wessely, S., Der, G., & Murray, R. M. (1991). The incidence of operationally defined schizophenia in Camberwell, 1965–84. *British Journal of Psychiatry, 159*, 790–794.

Castonguay, L. G., & Goldfried, M. R. (1994). Psychotherapy integration: An idea whose time has come. *Applied and Preventive Psychology, 3*, 159–172.

Catalan, J. (1988). Psychosocial and neuropsychiatric aspects of HIV infection: Review of their extent and implications for psychiatry. *Journal of Psychosomatic Research, 32*, 237–248.

Catalano, R. (1981). Contending with rival hypotheses in correlation of aggregate time series (CATS): An overview for community psychologists. *American Journal of Community Psychology, 9*, 667–679.

Catalano, R., & Dooley, D. (1977). Economic predictors of depressed mood and stressful life events in a metropolitan community. *Journal of Health and Social Behavior, 18*, 292–307.

Catalano, R., & Dooley, D. (1983). The health effects of economic instability: A test of the economic stress hypothesis. *Journal of Health and Social Behavior, 24*, 46–60.

Catalano, R., Dooley, D., & Jackson, R. (1981). Economic predictors of admissions to mental health facilities in a nonmetropolitan community. *Journal of Health and Social Behavior, 22*, 284–297.

Catalano, R., & Hartig, T. (2001). Communal bereavement and the incidence of very low birthweight in Sweden. *Journal of Health and Social Behavior, 42*, 333–341.

Cavalli-Sforza, L. L., & Menozi, P., & Piazza, A. (1994). *The history and geography of human genes.* Princeton, NJ: Princeton University Press.

Celentano, D. D., Vlahov, D., Menon, A. S., & Polk, B. F. (1991). HIV knowledge and attitudes among intravenous drug users: Comparisons to the U.S. population and by drug use behaviors. *Journal of Drug Issues, 21*(3), 635–649.

Center for Mental Health Services. (1995). *First year interim status report on the evaluation of the ACCESS demonstration program.* Rockville, MD: Author.

Center for Mental Health Services. (2008). *Consumer/peer-run activities and services grant programs, 2004 and 2007.* Retrieved September 29, 2008, from http://mentalhealth.samhsa.gov/cmhs/CommunitySupport/consumers/2004network.asp.

Centers for Disease Control and Prevention. (1981). Pneumocystis pneumonia – Los Angeles. *Morbidity Mortality Weekly Report, 30*(21), 1–3. Retrieved October 7, 2008, from http://www.cdc.gov/mmwr/preview/mmwrhtml/june_5.htm.

Centers for Disease Control and Prevention. (2002). *HIV/AIDS Surveillance Report, 2002.* Retrieved October 7, 2008, from http://www.cdc.gov/hiv/topics/surveillance/resources/reports/2002report/pdf/2002SurveillanceReport.pdf.

Centers for Disease Control and Prevention. (2003). HIV diagnoses among injection-drug users in states with HIV surveillance – 25 states, 1994–2000. *Morbidity Mortality Weekly Report, 52*, 634–636. Retrieved October 7, 2008, from http://www.cdc.gov/mmwr/preview/mmwrhtml/mm5227a2.htm.

Centers for Disease Control and Prevention. (2005). Update: Syringe exchange programs – United States, 2002. *Morbidity Mortality Weekly Report, 54*, 673–676.

Centers for Disease Control and Prevention. (2007). *Sexual risk behaviors.* Youth Risk Behavior Survey (National Center for Health Statistics). Retrieved from http://www.cdc.gov/HealthyYouth/sexualbehaviors/#1.

Centers for Disease Control and Prevention. (2008a). HIV prevalence estimates – United States, 2006. *Morbidity Mortality Weekly Report, 57*, 1073–1076. Retrieved October 7, 2008, from http://www.cdc.gov/mmwr/PDF/wk/mm5739.pdf.

Centers for Disease Control and Prevention. (2008b). *HIV/AIDS surveillance report, 2006.* Atlanta: Author.

Centers for Disease Control and Prevention. (2008c). Persons tested for HIV – United States, 2006. *Morbidity Mortality Weekly Report, 57*, 845–849. Retrieved October 7, 2008, from http://www.cdc.gov/mmwr/preview/mmwrhtml/mm5731a1.htm.

Cervantes, R. C., & Arroyo, W. (1994). DSM-IV: Implications for Hispanic children and adolescents. *Hispanic Journal of Behavioral Sciences, 16*, 8–27.

Chadiha, L. A., Adams, P., Biegel, D. E., Auslander, W., & Gutierrez, L. (2004). Empowering African American women informal caregivers: A literature synthesis and practice strategies. *Social Work, 49*, 97.

Chamberlin, J. (1978). *On our own: Patient controlled alternatives to the mental health system.* New York: Hawthorne.

Chamberlin, J. (1990). The ex-patients' movement: What we've been and where we're going. *Journal of Mind and Behavior, 11*(3 & 4), 323–336.

Chamberlin, J. (2002, September 11). *President Bush's newest mental health advisor reports for duty: Sally Satel's first National Advisory Council meeting, September 5 to 6, 2002.* Retrieved September 26, 2008, from http://www.independenceinc.org/alerts/091702.htm.

Chan, K. Y., & Reidpath, D. D. (2007). Stigmatization of patients with AIDS: Understanding the interrelationships between Thai nurses' attitudes toward HIV/AIDS, drug use, and commercial sex. *AIDS Patient Care and STDs, 21*(10), 763–775.

Chander, G., Himelhoch, S., & Moore, R. D. (2006). Substance abuse and psychiatric disorders in HIV-positive patients: Epidemiology and impact on antiretroviral therapy. *Drugs, 66*(6), 769–789.

Chen, X., & French, D. C. (2008). Children's social competence in cultural context. *Annual Review of Psychology, 59*, 591–616.

Cherlin, A. (1998). Marriage and marital dissolution among Black Americans. *Journal of Comparative Family Studies, 29*, 147–158.

Cherlin, A. (1992). *Marriage, divorce, remarriage.* (Rev. ed.) Cambridge, MA: Harvard University Press.

Cherniss, C. (1980). *Staff burnout: Job stress in the human services.* Beverly Hills, CA: Sage.

Chiasson, M. A., Hirshfield, S., Humberstone, M., DiFilippi, J., Koblin, B. A., & Remien, R. H. (2005). Increased high risk sexual behavior after September 11 in men who have sex with men: An Internet survey. *Archives of Sexual Behavior, 34*(5), 527C–535C.

Chien, W. T., & Wong, K.-F. (2007). A family psychoeducation group program for Chinese people with schizophrenia in Hong Kong. *Psychiatric Services, 58*, 1003–1006.

Chin, J. L. (1993). Toward a psychology of difference: Psychotherapy for a culturally diverse population. In J. L. Chin. (Ed.), *Diversity psychotherapy* (pp. 69–92). Westport, CT: Praeger.

Chisholm, J. F. (1996). Mental health issues in African American women. *Annals of the New York Academy of Sciences, 789*, 161–179.

Chodorow, N. (1974). Family structure and feminine personality. In M. Rosaldo & L. Lamphere (Eds.), *Women, culture and society* (pp. 42–66). Stanford, CA: Stanford University Press.

Chodorow, N. (1978). *The reproduction of mothering: Psychoanalysis and the sociology of gender.* Berkeley: University of California Press.

Choe, J. Y., Teplin, L. A., & Abram, K. (2008). Perpetration of violence, violent victimization, and severe mental illness: Balancing public health concerns. *Psychiatric Services, 59*(2), 153–164.

Chomsky, N. (1989). *Necessary illusions: Thought control in democratic societies.* Boston: South End Press.

Chou, Y.-C., Lee, Y.-C., Lin, L.-C., Chang, A.-N., & Huang, W.-Y. (2008). Social services utilization by adults with intellectual disabilities and their families. *Social Science and Medicine, 66*(12), 2474–2485.

Christoffersen, M. N. (1994). A follow-up study of long-term effects of unemployment on children: Loss of self-esteem and self-destructive behavior among adolescents. *Childhood, 2*(4), 212–220.

Christie, K. A., Burke, J. D. J., Regier, D. A., Rae, D. S., Boyd, J. H., & Locke, B. Z. (1988). Epidemiologic evidence for early onset of mental disorders and higher risk of drug-abuse in young-adults. *American Journal of Psychiatry, 145*, 971–975.

Christy, A., Poythress, N. G., Boothroyd, R. A., Petrila, J., & Mehra, S. (2005). Evaluating the efficiency and community safety goals of the Broward County mental health court. *Behavioral Sciences & the Law, 23*, 227–243.

Chu, F., & Trotter, S. (1974). *The madness establishment.* New York: Grossman.

Chua, S. E., & McKenna. P. J. (1995). Schizophrenia – a brain disease?: A critical review of structural and functional cerebral abnormality in the disorder. *British Journal of Psychiatry, 166*, 563–582.

Chung, B., Corbet, C. E., Boulet, B., Cummings, J. R., Paxton, K., McDaniel, S., et al. (2006). Talking wellness: A description of a community-academic partnered project to engage an African-American community around depression through the use of poetry, film, and photography. *Ethnicity and Disease, 16*(Suppl. 1), S1-67–S61–78.

Cicchetti, D., & Rogosch, R. A. (2002). A developmental psychopathology perspective on adolescence. *Journal of Consulting and Clinical Psychology, 70*, 6–20.

Ciesla, J. A., & Roberts, J. E. (2001). Meta-analysis of the relationship between HIV infection and risk for depressive disorders. *American Journal of Psychiatry, 158*, 725–730.

Cirincione, C., Steadman, H. J., Robbins, P. C., & Monahan, J. (1994). Mental illness as a factor in criminality: A study of prisoners and mental patients. *Criminal Behavior and Mental Health, 4*, 33–47.

Clark, H. B., & Davis, M. (2000). Transition to adulthood. In B. A. Stroul & R. M. Friedman (Eds.), *Systems of care for children's mental health.* Baltimore: Paul Brookes.

Clark, L. A. (2005). Temperament as a unifying basis for personality and psychopathology. *Journal of Abnormal Psychology, 114*, 505–521.

Clausen, J., & Yarrow, M. (1955). Pathways to the mental hospital. *Journal of Social Issues, 11*, 25–32.

Cleary, P. D. (1989). The need and demand for mental health services. In C. A. Taube, D. Mechanic, & A. A. Hohmann (Eds.), *The future of mental health services research* (DHHS Publication No. ADM 89–1600; pp.161–184). Washington, DC: U.S. Government Printing Office.

Cobb, S. (1976). Social support as a moderator of life stress. *Psychosomatic Medicine, 38*, 300–314.

Cobb, S. (1979) Social support and health through the life course. In M. W. Riley (Ed.), *Aging from birth to death: Interdisciplinary perspectives* (pp. 93–206). Boulder, CO:Westview.

Cochrane, R., & Bal, S.S. (1989). Mental hospital admission rates of immigrants to England: A comparison of 1971 and 1981. *Social Psychiatry & Psychiatric Epidemiology, 24*, 2–11.

Cohen, A., Kleinman, A., & Saraceno, B. (Eds.). (2002). *World mental health casebook: Social and mental health programs in low-income countries*. New York: Kluwer.

Cohen, A., & Saraceno, B. (2002). The risk of freedom: Mental health services in Trieste. In A. Cohen, A. Kleinman, & B. Saraceno (Eds.), *World mental health casebook: Social and mental programs in low-income countries* (pp. 191–220). New York: Kluwer.

Cohen, C. I., Magai, C., Yafee, R., & Walcott-Brown, L. (2006). The prevalence of anxiety and associated factors in a multiracial sample of older adults. *Psychiatric Services, 57*(12), 1719–1725.

Cohen, M. A. (2008). History of AIDS psychiatry: A biopsychosocial approach – paradigm and paradox. In M. A. Cohen & J. M. Gorman (Eds.), *Comprehensive textbook of AIDS psychiatry* (pp. 3–14). New York: Oxford University Press.

Cohen, P., & Huffman, L. (2003). Individuals, jobs, and labor markets: The devaluation of women's work. *American Sociological Review, 68*, 443–463.

Cohen, S. (1992). Models of the support process. In H. O. F. Veil & U. Baumann (Eds.), *The meaning and measurement of social support* (pp. 109–124). New York: Hemisphere.

Cohen, S. (1996). Psychological stress, immunity, and upper respiratory infections. *Current Directions in Psychological Science, 5*, 86–90.

Cohen, S., Janicki-Deverts, D., & Miller, G. E. (2007). Psychological stress and disease. *Journal of the American Medical Association, 298*, 1685–1687.

Cohen, S., & Syme, S. L. (Eds.). (1985). *Social support and health*. New York: Academic Press.

Cohen, S., Underwood, L. G., & Gottlieb, B. H. (2000). *Social support measurement and intervention: A guide for health and social scientists*. New York: Oxford University Press.

Cohen, S., & Wills, T. A. (1985). Stress, social support, and the buffering hypothesis. *Psychological Bulletin, 98*, 310–357.

Cole, E. R., & Stewart, A. J. (2001). Invidious comparisons: Imagining a psychology of race and gender beyond differences. *Political Psychology, 22*, 293–308.

Cole, J., & Pilisuk, M. (1976). Differences in the provision of mental health services by race. *American Journal of Orthopsychiatry, 46*, 510–525.

Collins, C. F. (2003). *Sources of stress and relief for African American women*. Westport, CT: Praeger.

Collins, J. G. (1988). Prevalence of selected chronic conditions, United States, 1983–85. *NCHS Advancedata, 155*, 1–16.

Collins, J. J., & Schlenger, W. E. (1983, November). *The prevalence of psychiatric disorder among admissions to prisons*. Paper presented at the annual meeting of the American Society of Criminology, Denver.

Collins, P. H. (2000). *Black feminist thought*. New York: Routledge.

Collins, R. (1994). *Four sociological traditions*. New York: Oxford University Press.

Collins, S. (1997). *Black corporate executives: The making and breaking of a Black middle class*. Philadelphia: Temple University Press.

Commander, M. J., Odell, S. M., Surtees, P. G., & Sashidharan S. O. (2003). Characteristics of patients and patterns of psychiatric service use in ethnic minorities. *International Journal of Social Psychiatry, 49*, 216–224.

Commission on Lunacy, 1. (1971). *Report on insanity and idiocy in Massachusetts*. Cambridge, MA: Harvard University Press. (Original work published 1855)

Commission on the Social Determinants of Health. (2008). Closing the gap in a generation: Health equity through action on the social determinants of health. In *Final Report of the Commission on Social Determinants of Health*. Geneva: World Health Organization.

Compas, B., Orosan, P., & Grant, E. K. (1993). Adolescent stress and coping: Implications for psychopathology during adolescence. *Journal of Adolescence, 16*, 331–349.

Conejo-Galindo, J., Medina, O., Fraguas, D., Teran, S., Sainz-Corton, E., & Arango, C. (2007). Psychopathological sequelae of the 11 March terrorist attacks in Madrid. *European Archives of Psychiatry and Clinical Neuroscience, 258*(1), 28–34.

Conger, J. J., Sawrey, W., & Turrell, E. S. (1958). The role of social experience in the production of gastric ulcers in hooded rats placed in a conflict situation. *Journal of Abnormal Psychology, 57*, 214–220.

Conger, R. D., Conger, K. J., Elder, G. H., Lorenz, F. O., Simons, R. L. & Whitbeck, L. B. (1992). A family process model of economic hardship and adjustment of early adolescent boys. *Child Development, 63*, 526–541.

Conger, R. D., Conger, K. J., Matthews, L. S., & Elder, G. H. (1999). Pathways of economic influence on adolescent adjustment. *American Journal of Community Psychology, 27*, 519–541.

Conger, R. D., & Elder, G. H., Jr. (1994). *Families in troubled times: Adapting to change in rural America*. New York: Aldine de Gruyter.

Conger, R. D., Elder, G. H., Jr., Larenz, F. O., & Simons, R. I. (1994). Economic stress, coercive family process, and developmental problems of adolescents. *Child Development, 65*, 541–561.

Conger, R. D., Wallace, L. E., Sun, Y., Simons, R. L., McLoyd, V. C., & Brody, G. H. (2002). Economic pressure in African American families: A replication and extension of the family stress model. *Developmental Psychology, 38*, 179–193.

Connell, R. W. (1995). *Masculinities*. Berkeley: University of California Press.

Conner, K. R., Pinquart, M., & Duberstein, P. R. (2008). Meta-analysis of depression and substance use and impairment among intravenous drug users (IDUs). *Addiction, 103*(4), 524–534.

Conrad, P. (2005). The shifting engines of medicalization. *Journal of Health and Social Behavior, 46*, 3–14.

Conrad, P. (2007). *The medicalization of society: The transformation of human conditions into medical disorders*. Baltimore: Johns Hopkins University Press.

Conrad, P., & Leiter, V. (2004). Medicalization, markets and consumers. *Journal of Health and Social Behavior, 45*, 158–176.

Cook, J. A., Grey, D. D., Burke Miller, J. K., Cohen, M. H., Vlahov, D., Kapadia, F., et al. (2007). Illicit drug use, depression and their association with highly active antiretroviral therapy in HIV-positive women. *Drug and Alcohol Dependence, 89*(1), 74–81.

Cooper, C. L. (2005). *Handbook of stress medicine and health*. London: CRC Press.

Cooper, R. S., & David, R. (1986). The biological concept of race and its application to public health and epidemiology. *Journal of Health and Politics, Policy and Law, 11*, 97–116.

Cooper, R., & Simmons, B. (1985). Cigarette smoking and ill health among Black Americans. *New York State Journal of Medicine, 7*, 344–349.

Cooperman, N. A., & Simoni, J. M. (2005). Suicidal ideation and attempted suicide among women living with HIV/AIDS. *Journal of Behavioral Medicine, 28*(2), 149–156.

Coopers, B. (1991). Sociology in the context of social psychiatry. *British Journal of Psychiatry, 61*, 594–598.

Corcoran, M., Danziger, S., Kalil, A., & Seefeldt, K. S. (2000). How welfare reform is affecting women's work. *Annual Review of Sociology, 26*, 241–269.

Corrado, R. R., Cohen, I., Hart, S., & Roesch, R. (2000). Comparative examination of the prevalence of mental disorders among jailed inmates in Canada and the United States. *International Journal of Law and Psychiatry, 23*(5–6), 633–647.

Corrado, R. R., Doherty, D., & Glackman, W. (1989). A demonstration program for chronic recidivists of criminal justice, health and social service agencies. *International Journal of Law and Psychiatry, 12*, 211–230.

Corrigan, P. (1998). The impact of stigma on severe mental illness. *Cognitive & Behavioral Practice, 5*, 201–222.

Corrigan, P., Steiner, L., McCracken, S., Blaser, B., & Barr, M. (2001). Strategies for disseminating evidence-based practices to staff who treat people with serious mental illness. *Psychiatric Services, 52*(12), 1598–1606.

Corrigan, P. W., Markowitz, F. E., & Watson, A. C. (2004). Structural levels of mental illness stigma and discrimination. *Schizophrenia Bulletin, 30,* 481–491.

Corrigan, P. W., & Watson, A. C. (2002). The paradox of self-stigma and mental illness. *Clinical Psychology: Science & Practice, 9,* 35–53.

Cosden, M., Ellens, J., Schnell, J., & Yamini-Diouf, Y. (2005). Efficacy of a mental health treatment court with assertive community treatment. *Behavioral Sciences and the Law, 23,* 199–214.

Cosden, M., Ellens, J., Schnell, J., Yamini-Diouf, Y., & Wolfe, M. (2003). Evaluation of a mental health court with assertive community treatment. *Behavioral Sciences and the Law, 21,* 415–427.

Costello E. J. (1982). Locus of control and depression in students and psychiatric outpatients. *Journal of Clinical Psychology, 36,* 661–667.

Costello, E. J., Egger, H., & Angold, A. (2005). 10-year research update review: The epidemiology of child and adolescent psychiatric disorders: I. Methods and public health burden. *Journal of the American Academy of Child & Adolescent Psychiatry, 44,* 972–986.

Costello, E. J., Mustillo S., Erkanli, A., Keeler, G., & Angold, A. (2003). Prevalence and development of psychiatric disorders in childhood and adolescence. *Archives of General Psychiatry, 60,* 837–843.

Coté, G., & Hodgins, S. (1990). Co-occurring mental disorders among criminal offenders. *Bulletin of the American Academy of Psychiatry and Law, 18,* 271–281.

Cotter, D. A., Hermsen, J. M., & Vanneman, R. (2004). *Gender inequality at work.* Retrieved June 10, 2008, from http://www.bsos.umd.edu/socy/vanneman/papers/Cotter_etal.pdf.

Cournos, F. (1996). Epidemiology of HIV. In F. Cournos & N. Bakalar (Eds.), *AIDS and people with severe mental illness: A handbook for mental health professionals.* New Haven, CT: Yale University Press.

Cournos, F., Empfield, M., Horwath, E., McKinnon, K., Meyer, I., Schrage, H., et al. (1991). HIV seroprevalence among patients admitted to two psychiatric hospitals. *American Journal of Psychiatry, 148*(9), 1225–1230.

Cournos, F., Empfield, M., Horwath, E., & Schrage, H. (1990). HIV infection in state hospitals: Case reports and long-term management strategies. *Hospital & Community Psychiatry, 41*(2), 163–166.

Cournos, F., Horwath, E., Guido, J. R., McKinnon, K., & Hopkins, N. (1994.) HIV-1 infection at two public psychiatric hospitals in New York City. *AIDS Care, 6*(4), 443–452.

Cournos, F., & McKinnon, K. (1997). HIV seroprevalence among people with severe mental illness in the United States: A critical review. *Clinical Psychology Review, 17*(3), 259–269.

Cournos, F., & McKinnon, K. (2008). Epidemiology of psychiatric disorders associated with HIV and AIDS. In M. A. Cohen & J. M. Gorman (Eds.), *Comprehensive textbook of AIDS psychiatry* (pp. 39–48). New York: Oxford University Press.

Cowan, W. M., Harter, D. H., & Kandel, E. R. (2000). The emergence of modern neuroscience: Some implications for neurology and psychiatry. *Annual Review of Neuroscience, 23,* 343–391.

Cox, G. L., & Merkel, W. T. (1989). A qualitative review of psychosocial treatments for bulimia. *Journal of Nervous and Mental Disease, 177,* 77–84.

Coyne, J. C., & Marcus, S. C. (2006). Health disparities in care for depression possibly obscured by the clinical significance criterion. *American Journal of Psychiatry, 163*(9), 1577–1579.

Craighead, L., & Green, B. (1989). Relationships between depressed mood and sex-typed personality characteristics in adolescents. *Journal of Youth and Adolescence, 18,* 467–474.

Creed, P. A., & Macintyre, S. R. (2001). The relative effects of deprivation of the latent and manifest benefits of employment on the well-being of unemployed people. *Journal of Occupational Health Psychology, 6*(4), 324–331.

Crepaz, N., Passin, W. F., Herbst, J. H., Rama, S. M., Malow, R. M., Purcell, D. W., et al. (2008). Meta-analysis of cognitive-behavioral interventions on HIV-positive persons' mental health and immune functioning. *Health Psychology, 27*(1), 4–14.

Crespo, M. (1977). *Deviance and aspirations in adolescence: The influence of school absenteeism, drug use, and mental disorder on educational and occupational aspirations.* Montreal: McGill University.

Crocker, A. G., Mueser, K. T., Drake R. E., Clark, R. E., & McHugo, G. J. (2005). Antisocial personality, psychopathy and violence in persons with dual disorders: A longitudinal analysis. *Criminal Justice and Behavior, 32,* 452–476.

Croghan, T. W., Tomlin, M., Pescosolido, B. A., Martin, J. K., Lubell, K. M., & Swindle, R. (2003). Americans' knowledge and attitudes towards and their willingness to use psychiatric medications. *Journal of Nervous and Mental Disease, 191,* 166–174.

Cropley, M., Steptoe, A., & Joekes, K. (1999). Job strain and psychiatric morbidity. *Psychological Medicine, 29*(6), 1411–1416.

Crosnoe, R., Frank, K., & Mueller, A. S. (2008). Gender, body size, and social relations in American high schools. *Social Forces, 86,* 1189–1216.

Crouter, A. C., MacDermid, S. M., McHale, S. M., & Perry-Jenkins, M. (1990). Parental monitoring and perceptions of children's school performance and conduct in dual and single-earner families. *Developmental Psychology, 26,* 649–657.

Crow, T. (1994). Prenatal exposure to influenza as a cause of schizophrenia. *British Journal of Psychiatry, 164,* 588–592.

Crum, R. M., Green, K. M., Storr, C. L., Chan, Y. F., Ialongo, N., Stuart, E. A., et al. (2008). Depressed mood in childhood and subsequent alcohol use through adolescence and young adulthood. *Archives of General Psychiatry, 65,* 702–712.

Crystal, S., Ladner, S., & Towber, R. (1986). Multiple impairment patterns in the mentally ill homeless. *International Journal of Mental Health, 14,* 61–73.

Cuddeback, G., Morrissey, J., & Meyer, P. (2006). How many ACT teams do we need? Results from a large, urban community. *Psychiatric Services, 57*(12), 1803–1806.

Cuellar, A. E., Snowden, L. M., & Ewing, T. (2007). Criminal records of persons served in the public mental health system. *Psychiatric Services, 58,* 114–120.

Cuffe, P., Waller, J. L., Cuccaro, M. L., Pumariega, A. J., & Garrison, C. Z. (1995). Race and gender differences in the treatment of psychiatric disorders in young adolescents. *Journal of the American Academy of Child & Adolescent Psychiatry, 34,* 1536–1543.

Culhane, D. P., Metraux, S., & Hadley, T. (2002). Public service reductions associated with placement of homeless persons with serious mental illness in supportive housing. *Housing Policy Debate, 13,* 107–163.

Cumming, E., Edell, L., & Cumming, I. (1965). Policeman as philosopher, guide and friend. *Social Problems, 12,* 278–286.

Cumming, E., & Harrington, C. (1963). Clergyman as counselor. *American Journal of Sociology, 69,* 234–243.

Cutrona, C. E. (1986). Objective determinants of perceived social support. *Jounal of Personality & Social Problems, 12,* 178–186.

Cutrona, C., Russell, D., Hessling, R. M., Brown, P. A., & Murry. V. (2000). Direct and moderating effects of community context on the psychological well-being of African American women. *Journal of Personality and Social Psychology, 79,* 1088–1101.

Cutrona, C. E., Wallace, G., & Wesner, A. (2006). Neighborhood characteristics and depression: An examination of stress processes. *Current Directions in Psychological Science, 15,* 188–192.

Dafoe, M. E., & Stewart, K. E. (2004). Pain and psychiatric disorders contribute independently to suicidal ideation in HIV-positive persons. *Archives of Suicide Research, 8*(3), 215–226.

Dain, N. (1989). Critics and dissenters: Reflections on "anti-psychiatry" in the United States. *Journal of the History of Behavioral Sciences, 23,* 2–25.

Danziger, S., Heflin, C., Corcoran, M., Oltmans, E., & Wang, H. C. (2002). Does it pay to move from welfare to work? *Journal of Policy Analysis and Management, 21,* 674–693.

D'Aunno, J., Sutton, R., & Price, R. (1991). Isomorphism and external support in conflicting institutional environments. *Academy of Management Review, 34,* 636–661.

Davila, J. (2008). Depressive symptoms and adolescent romance: Theory, research, and implications. *Child Development Perspectives, 2,* 26–31.

Davis, F. (1963). *Passage through crisis: Polio victims and their families.* Indianapolis: Bobbs-Merrill.

Davis, G. Y., & Stevenson, H. C. (2006). Racial socialization experiences and symptoms of depression among Black youth. *Journal of Child and Family Studies, 15,* 303–317.

Davis, K., & Moore, W. (1974). Some principles of stratification. In J. Lopreato & L. S. Lewis (Eds.), *Social stratification: A reader* (pp. 64–71). New York: Harper & Row.

Davis, M., & Vander Stoep, A. (1997). The transition to adulthood for youth who have serious emotional disturbance: Developmental transition and young adult outcomes. *Journal of Mental Health Administration, 24*, 400–427.

Davis, S. (2006, March 1). Forced drugging. *Saginaw News*. Retrieved September 30, 2008, from http://www.intenex.net/pipermail/mindfreedom-news/2006-March/000030.html.

Day, R., Nielsen, A., Korten, A., Ernberg, G., Dube, K., Gebhart, J., et al. (1987). Stressful life events preceding the acute onset of schizophrenia: A cross-national study from the World Health Organization. *Culture, Medicine, and Psychiatry, 11*, 123–205.

Deakin, J. F. W. (1996). Neurobiology of schizophrenia. *Current Opinion in Psychiatry, 9*, 50–56.

Dean, A., & Lin, N. (1977). The stress buffering role of social support. *Journal of Nervous & Mental Disease, 165*, 403–417.

Dean, K., Walsh, E., Moran, P., Tyrer, P., Creed, F., Byford, S., et al. (2006). Violence in women with psychosis in the community: Prospective study. *British Journal of Psychiatry, 188*, 264–270.

Deane, M. W., Steadman, H. J., & Borum, R. (1999). Emerging partnerships between mental health and law enforcement. *Psychiatric Services, 50*, 99–101.

De Bocanegra, H. T., Moskalenko, S., & Chan, P. (2005). PTSD and depression among displaced Chinese workers after the World Trade Center attack: A follow-up study. *Journal of Urban Health–Bulletin of the New York Academy of Medicine, 82*(3), 364–369.

DeBruyn, L. M., Hymbaugh, K., & Valdez, N. (1988). Helping communities address suicide and violence: The special initiatives team of the Indian Health Service. *American Indian and Alaska Native Mental Health Research, 1*, 56–65.

Deegan, P. (1988). Recovery: The experience of rehabilitation. *Psychosocial Rehabilitation Journal, 11*(4), 11.

Deegan, P. E. (1993). Recovering our sense of value after being labeled. *Journal of Psychosocial Nursing, 31*, 7–11.

De Jong, G. F., & Tran, Q.-G. (2001). Warm welcome, cool welcome: Mapping receptivity toward immigrants in the U.S. *Population Today, 29*(8), 1–4.

De Marneffe, D. (1997). Bodies and words: A study of young children's genital and gender knowledge. *Gender and Psychoanalysis, 2*, 3–33.

Demerouti, E., Bakker, A. B., de Jonge, J., Janssen, P. P., & Schaufeli, W. B. (2001). Burnout and engagement at work as a function of demands and control. *Scandinavian Journal of Work, Environment and Health, 27*(4), 279–286.

Demyttenaere, K., Bruffaerts, R., Posada-Villa, J., Gasquet, I., Kovess, V., Lepine, J. P., et al. (2004). Prevalence, severity and unmet need for treatment of mental disorders in the World Health Organization World Mental Health surveys. *Journal of the American Medical Association, 291*, 2581–2590.

DeNavas-Walt, C., Proctor, B. D., & Smith, J. (2007). *Income, poverty, and health insurance coverage in the United States: 2006* (Current Population Reports P60–223). Washington, DC: U.S. Census Bureau.

DePaulo, B. (2006). *Singled out: How singles are stereotyped, stigmatized, and ignored, and still live happily ever after*. New York: St. Martin's Press.

Desai, R. A., Lam, J., & Rosenheck, R. A. (2000). Childhood risk factors for criminal justice involvement in a sample of homeless people with serious mental illness. *Journal of Nervous and Mental Disease, 188*, 324–332.

DeSchipper, E. J., Riksen-Walraven, J. M., & Geurts, S A. (2006). Effects of child-caregiver ratios on the interactions between caregivers and children in child-care centers: An experimental study. *Child Development, 77*, 861–874.

Des Jarlais, D. C. (1990). Stages in the response of the drug abuse treatment system into the AIDS epidemic in New York City. *Journal of Drug Issues, 20*, 335–347.

Des Jarlais, D. C., Arasteh, K., Perlis, T., Hagan, H., Abdul-Quader, A., Heckathorn, D. D., et al. (2007). Convergence of HIV seroprevalence among injecting and non-injecting drug users in New York City. *AIDS, 21*(2), 231–235.

Des Jarlais, D. C., & Friedman, S. R. (1998). Fifteen years of research on preventing HIV infection among injecting drug users: What we have learned, what we have done, what we have not done. *Public Health Reports, 113*(Suppl. 1), 182–188.

Detera-Wadleigh, S. D., & McMahon, F. J. (2004). Genetic association studies in mood disorders: Issues and promise. *International Review of Psychiatry, 16,* 301–310.

Deutsch, A. (1948). *A shame of the states.* New York: Harcourt Brace.

Devers, K. J., Sofaer, S., & Rundall, T. G. (1999). Introduction to the Special Issue on Qualitative Methods in Health Services Research. *Health Services Research, 34*(Part II), 1096–1101.

Dew, M. A., Penkower, L., & Bromet, E. J. (1991). Effects of unemployment on mental health in the contemporary family. *Behavior Modification, 15,* 501–544.

DeWitt, K. N. (1978). The effectiveness of family therapy: A review of outcome research. *Archives of General Psychiatry, 35,* 549–561.

De Zulueta, C. F. (2007). Mass violence and mental health: Attachment and trauma. *International Review of Psychiatry, 19*(3), 221–233.

Dickerson, F. B., Sommerville, J., Origoni, A. E., Ringel, N. B., & Parente, F. (2002). Experiences of stigma among outpatients with schizophrenia. *Schizophrenia Bulletin, 28,* 143–155.

Dickey, W. (1980). Incompetency and the nondangerous mentally ill client. *Criminal Law Bulletin, 16,* 22–40.

DiClemente, R.,Wingood, G. M., Crosby, R. A., Sionean, C., Brown, L. K., Rothbaum, B., et al. (2001). A prospective study of psychological distress and sexual risk behavior among Black adolescent females. *Pediatrics, 108,* 85–91.

Diehr, P., Williams, S. J., & Martin, D. P. (1984). Ambulatory mental health services utilization in three provider plans. *Medical Care, 2,* 1–13.

Diener, E., Lucas, R. E., & Oishi, S. (2002). Subjective well being: The science of happiness and life satisfaction. In C. R. Synder & S. J. Lopez (Eds.), *Handbook of positive psychology* (pp. 63–73). Oxford: Oxford University Press.

Dill, A. P. (2001). *Managing to care: Case management and service system reform.* New York: Aldine de Gruyter.

Dill, A., & Rochefort, D. (1989). Coordination, continuity, and centralized control: A policy perspective on service strategies for the chronically mentally ill. *Journal of Social Issues, 45*(3), 145–159.

Dilworth-Anderson, P., Williams, I. C., & Gibson, B. E. (2002). Issues of race, ethnicity, and culture in caregiving research: A 20-year review (1980–2000). *Gerontologist, 42,* 237–272.

DiMaggio, P. J. (1997). Culture and cognition. *Annual Review of Sociology, 23,* 263–287.

DiMaggio, P. J., & Powell, W. W. (1983). The iron cage, revisited: Institutional isomorphism and collective rationality in organizational fields. *American Sociological Review, 48,* 147–160.

Ditton, P. M. (1999). *Bureau of Justice Statistics special report: Mental health treatment of inmates and probationers (NCJ 174463).* Washington, DC: U.S. Department of Justice.

Dittus, P. J., Jaccard, J., & Gordon, V. (1997). The impact of African American fathers on adolescent sexual behavior. *Journal of Youth and Adolescence, 26,* 445–465.

Dixon, L. (2000). Assertive community treatment: Twenty-five years of gold. *Psychiatric Services, 51*(6), 759–765.

Dixon, L., & Lehman, A. (1996). Family interventions for schizophrenia. *Schizophrenia Bulletin, 21,* 631–643.

Dodge, K. A. (1993). Social-cognitive mechanisms in the development of conduct disorder and depression. *Annual Review of Psychology, 44,* 559–584.

Dodge, K. A. (2006). Translational science in action: Hostile attributional style and the development of aggressive behavior problems. *Development and Psychopathology, 18,* 791–814.

Dodge, K. A., Lansford, J. E., Burks, V. S., Bates, J. E., Pettit, G. S., Fontaine, R., et al. (2003). Peer rejection and social information-processing factors in the development of aggressive behavior problems in children. *Child Development, 74,* 374–393.

Dohrenwend, B. P. (1990). Socioeconomic status (SES) and psychiatric disorders: Are the issues still compelling? *Social Psychiatry and Psychiatric Epidemiology, 25,* 4–47.

Dohrenwend, B. P. (1995). The problem of validity in field studies of psychological disorders – revisited. In M. T. Tsuang, M. Tohen, & G. E. P. Zahner (Eds.), *Textbook in psychiatric epidemiology* (pp. 3–22). New York: Wiley.

Dohrenwend, B. P. (2000). The role of adversity and stress in psychopathology: Some evidence and its implications for theory and research. *Journal of Health and Social Behavior, 41,* 1–19.

Dohrenwend, B. P., & Dohrenwend, B. S. (1969). *Social status and psychological disorder: A casual inquiry.* New York: Wiley.

Dohrenwend, B. P., & Dohrenwend, B. S. (1974). Social and cultural influences on psychopathology. *Annual Review of Psychology, 25*, 417–452.

Dohrenwend, B. P., & Dohrenwend, B. S. (1982). Perspectives on the past and future of psychiatric epidemiology. *American Journal of Public Health, 72*, 1271–1279.

Dohrenwend, B. P., Dohrenwend, B. S., Dodson, M., & Shrout, P. E. (1984). Symptoms, hassles, social supports, and life events: The problem of confounded measures. *Journal of Abnormal Psychology, 93*, 222–230.

Dohrenwend, B. P., Levav, I., Shrout, P. E., Schwartz, S., Naveh, G., Link, B. G., et al. (1992). Socioeconomic status and psychiatric disorders: The causation-selection issue. *Science, 255*, 946–952.

Dohrenwend, B. P., Shrout, P. E., Egri, G., & Mendelsohn, F. S. (1980). Nonspecific psychological distress and other dimensions of psychopathology: Measures for use in the general population. *Archives of General Psychiatry, 37*, 1229.

Dohrenwend, B. S., Krasnoff, L., Askenasy, A. R., & Dohrenwend, B. P. (1978). Exemplification of a method for scaling life events: The PERI Life Events Scale. *Journal of Health and Social Behavior, 19*, 205–229.

Doi, Y., Roberts R. E., Takeuchi, K., & Suzuki, S. (2001). Multiethnic comparison of adolescent major depression based on DSM-IV criteria in a U.S.-Japan study. *Journal of the American Academy of Child & Adolescent Psychiatry, 11*, 1308–1315.

Domino, M., Norton, E., Morrissey, J., & Thakur, N. (2004). Cost shifting to jails after a change to managed mental health care. *Health Services Research, 39*(5), 1379–1401.

Dooley, D., & Catalano, R. (1979). Economic, life, and disorder changes: Time-series analyses. *American Journal of Community Psychology, 7*, 381–396.

Dooley, D., & Catalano, R. (1984). Why the economy predicts help-seeking: A test of competing explanations. *Journal of Health and Social Behavior, 25*, 160–175.

Dooley, D., Catalano, R., & Rook, K. (1988). Personal and aggregate unemployment and psychological symptoms. *Journal of Social Issues, 44*, 107–123.

Doty, M. M., & Holmgren, A. L. (2006). *Health care disconnect: Gaps in coverage and care for minority adults: Findings from the Commonwealth Fund Biennial Health Insurance Survey (2005).* New York: Commonwealth Fund.

Dowdall, G. W. (1996). *The eclipse of the state mental hospital: Policy, stigma and organization.* Albany: State University of New York Press.

Dowdall, G, W., & Golden, J. (1989). Photographs as data: An analysis of images from a mental hospital. *Qualitative Sociology, 12*, 183–212.

Dowell, D., & Ciarlo, J. A. (1989). An evaluative overview of the community mental health centers program. In D. Rochefort (Ed.), *Handbook on mental health policy in the U.S.* (pp. 195–236). Westport, CT: Greenwood.

Downey, G., & Coyne, J. C. (1990). Children of depressed parents: An integrative review. *Psychological Bulletin, 108*, 50–76.

Downey, G., & Coyne, J. C. (1991). Social factors and psychopathology: Stress, social support and coping processes. *Annual Review of Psychology, 42*, 401–425.

Draine, J., Salzer, M. S., Culhane, D. P., & Hadley, T. R. (2002). Role of social disadvantage in crime, joblessness, and homelessness among persons with serious mental illness. *Psychiatric Services, 53*(5), 565–573.

Draine, J., & Solomon, P. (1992). Comparison of seriously mentally ill case management clients with and without arrest histories. *Journal of Psychiatry and Law, 3*, 335–349.

Draine, J., & Solomon, P. (1999). Describing and evaluating jail diversion services for persons with serious mental illness. *Psychiatric Services, 50*(1), 56–61.

Draine, J., Solomon, P., & Meyerson, A. T. (1994). Predictors of reincarceration among patients who received psychiatric services in jail. *Hospital and Community Psychiatry, 45*, 163–167.

Drake, R., Goldman, H., Leff, H., Lehman, A. F., Dixon, L., Mueser, K., et al. (2001). Implementing evidence-based practices in routine mental health settings. *Psychiatric Services, 52*(2), 179–182.

Drapalski, A. L., Marshall, T., Seybolt, D., Medoff, D., Peer, J., Leith, J., et al. (2008). Unmet needs of families of adults with mental illness and preferences regarding family services. *Psychiatric Services, 59,* 655–662.

Drentea, P. (2000). Age, debt and anxiety. *Journal of Health and Social Behavior, 41,* 437–450.

Drevets, W. C. (1998). Functional neuroimaging studies of depression: The anatomy of melancholia. *Annual Review of Medicine, 49,* 341–361.

Drillien, C. M. (1964). *The growth and development of the prematurely born infant.* Baltimore: Williams & Wilkins.

Druss, B. G., Marcus, S. C., Rosenheck, R. A., Olfson, M., Tanielian, T., & Pincus, H. A. (2000). Understanding disability in mental and general medical conditions. *American Journal of Psychiatry, 157,* 485–491.

Dunham, H. W. (1959). *Sociological theory and mental disorder.* Detroit: Wayne State University Press.

Dunham, H. W. (1965). *Community and schizophrenia: An epidemiological analysis.* Detroit: Wayne State University Press.

Dunn, R. L., & Schwebel, A. I. (1995). Meta-analytic review of marital therapy outcome research. *Journal of Family Psychology, 9,* 58–68.

Dupont, R., & Cochran, S. 2000. Police response to mental health emergencies – barriers to change. *Journal of the American Academy of Psychiatry and the Law, 28*(3), 338–344.

Durham, M. L. (1995). Can HMOs manage the mental health benefit? *Health Affairs, 14,* 116–122.

Durkheim, E. (1951). *Suicide: A study in sociology.* New York: The Free Press. (Original work published 1897)

Dvoskin, J. A., & Steadman, H. J. (1989). Chronically mentally ill inmates: The wrong concept for the right services. *International Journal of Law and Psychiatry, 12,* 203–211.

Dwork, A. (1996). Recent progress and future directions for neuropathologic studies of schizophrenia. In C. A. Kauffmann & J. M. Gorman (Eds.), *Schizophrenia: New directions for clinical research and treatment* (pp. 63–78). New York: Mary Ann Liebert.

Dye, J. L. (2005). *Fertility of American women: June 2004* (Current Population Reports). Washington DC: U.S. Census Bureau.

Eaton, W. W. (1974). Residence, social class, and schizophrenia. *Journal of Health and Social Behavior, 15,* 289–299.

Eaton, W. W. (1980). A formal theory of selection for schizophrenia. *American Journal of Sociology, 86,* 149–158.

Eaton, W. (1985). The epidemiology of schizophrenia. *Epidemiologic Reviews, 7,* 105–126.

Eaton W. (2000). Epidemiology, social deprivation, and community psychiatry. *Current Opinion in Psychiatry, 13*(2), 185–187.

Eaton, W. W., Anthony, J. C., Gallo, J., Cai, G., Tien, A., Romanoski, A., et al. (1997). Natural history of DISDSM major depression: The Baltimore ECA followup. *Archives of General Psychiatry,* 993–999.

Eaton, W. W., Dryman, A., & Weissman, M. M. (1991). Panic and phobia. In L. N. Robins & D. A. Regier (Eds.), *Psychiatric disorders in America: The Epidemiologic Catchment Area Study* (pp. 155–179). New York: The Free Press.

Eaton, W., & Harrison, G. (2000). Ethnic disadvantage and schizophrenia. *Acta Psychiatrica Scandinavica, 102*(Suppl.), 38–43.

Eaton, W. W., & Kessler, L. G. (1981). Rates of symptoms of depression in a national sample. *American Journal of Epidemiology, 114,* 528–538.

Eaton, W. W., & Kessler, L. G. (1985). *Epidemiologic field methods in psychiatry: The NIMH Epidemiologic Catchment Area Program.* Orlando, FL: Academic Press.

Eaton, W. W., & Keyl, P. M. (1990). Risk factors for the onset of DIS/DSM-III agoraphobia in a prospective, population-based study. *Archives of General Psychiatry, 47,* 819–824.

Eaton, W. W., & Lasry, J.-C. (1978). Mental health and occupational mobility in a group of immigrants. *Social Science & Medicine, 12,* 53–58.

Eaton, W. W., & Merikangas, K. R. (2000). Psychiatric epidemiology: Progress and prospects in the year 2000. *Epidemiologic Reviews, 22,* 29–34.

Eaton, W. W., Regier, D. A., Locke, B. Z., & Taube, C. A. (1981). The Epidemiologic Catchment Area Program of the National Institute of Mental Health. *Public Health Reports, 96,* 319–325.

Eaton, W. W., Muntaner, C., Smith, C. B., & Tien, A. Y. (2004). Revision of the Center for Epidemiologic Studies – Depression (CESD) scale. In M. Maruish (Ed.), *The use of psychological testing for treatment planning and outcomes assessment* (Mahwah, NJ: Erlbaum.

Edin, K., & Kefalas, M. (2005). *Promises I can keep.* Berkeley: University of California Press.

Edlund, M. J., Wang, P. S., Berglund, P. A., Katz, S. J., Lin, E., & Kessler, R. C. (2002). Dropping out of mental health treatment: Patterns and predictors among epidemiological survey respondents in the United States and Ontario. *American Journal of Psychiatry, 159*(5), 845–851.

Edwards R. (1979). *Contested terrain: The transformation of the workplace in the twentieth century.* New York: Basic Books.

Egan, M., Tannahill, C., Petticrew, M., & Thomas, S. (2008). Psychosocial risk factors in home and community settings and their associations with population health and health inequalities: A systematic meta-review. *BMC Public Health, 8,* 239.

Egeland, J., & Hostetter. A. (1983). Amish Study I: Affective disorders among the Amish. *American Journal of Psychiatry, 140,* 56–61.

Egeland, J., Hostetter, A., & Eshleman. S. K. (1983). Amish Study III: The impact of cultural factors in the diagnosis of bipolar illness. *American Journal of Psychiatry, 140,* 67–71.

Eisenberg, L. (1995). The social construction of the human brain. *American Journal of Psychiatry, 152,* 1563–1575.

Eisenberg P., & Lazarsfeld, P. F. (1938). The psychological effects of unemployment. *Psychological Bulletin, 35,* 358–390.

Elder, A. G. H., & Caspi, A. (1988). Human development and social change: An emerging perspective on the life course. In N. Bolger, A. Caspi, G. Downey, & M. Morehouse (Eds.), *Persons in context: Developmental perspectives* (pp. 77–113). Cambridge: Cambridge University Press.

Elder, G. H., Jr. (1974). *Children of the Great Depression.* Chicago: University of Chicago Press.

Elder G. H., Jr. (1977). *Children of the Great Depression: Social change in life experience.* Chicago: University of Chicago Press.

Elder, G. H., Jr. (1985). *Life course dynamics: Transitions and trajectories.* Ithaca, NY: Cornell University Press.

Elder, G. H., George, L. K., & Shanahan, M. (1996). Psychosocial stress over the life course. In H. Kaplan (Ed.), *Psychosocial stress* (pp. 247–284). New York: Academic Press.

Ellenberger, H. F. (1970). *The discovery of the unconscious.* New York: Basic Books.

Elliott, C. (2003). *Better than well: American medicine meets the American dream.* New York: Norton.

Ellis, A. (1962). *Reason and emotion in psychotherapy.* New York: Stuart.

Elster, A., Jarosik, J., VanGeest, J., & Fleming, M. (2003). Racial and ethnic disparities in health care for adolescents: A systematic review of the literature. *Archives of Pediatric & Adolescent Medicine, 157,* 867–874.

Emlet, C. A. (2007). Experiences of stigma in older adults living with HIV/AIDS: A mixed-methods analysis. *AIDS Patient Care and STDs, 21*(10), 740–752.

Emmelkamp, P. M. G. (1994). Behavior therapy with adults. In A. E. Bergin & S. L. Garfield (Eds.), *Handbook of psychotherapy and behavior change* (4th ed., pp. 379–427). New York: Wiley.

Empfield, M., Cournos, F., Meyer, I., McKinnon, K., Horwath, E., Silver, M., et al. (1993). HIV seroprevalence among homeless patients admitted to a psychiatric inpatient unit. *American Journal of Psychiatry, 150*(1), 47–52.

Engel, G. L. (1980). The clinical application of the biopsychosocial model. *American Journal of Psychiatry, 137,* 535–544.

Engel, R. S., & Silver, E. (2001). Policing mentally disordered suspects: A reexamination of the criminalization hypothesis. *Criminology, 39,* 225–252.

Engels, F. (1958). *The condition of the working class in England.* Stanford, CA: Stanford University Press.

Engels, G. I., Garnefski, N., & Diekstra, R. F. W. (1993). Efficacy of rational-emotive therapy: A quantitative analysis. *Journal of Consulting and Clinical Psychology, 61,* 1083–1090.

England, P., & Folbre, N. (1999). The costs of caring [Special Issue]. Annals of the *American Academy of Political and Social Sciences*, *561*, 39–51.

Eraker, S. A., Kirscht, J. P., & Becker, M. H. (1984). Understanding and improving patient compliance. *Annals of Internal Medicine*, *100*, 258–268.

Erickson, R. J. (1995). The importance of authenticity for self and society. *Symbolic Interaction*, *18*, 117–136.

Erickson, R. J., & Ritter, C. (2001). Emotional labor, burnout and inauthenticity: Does gender matter? *Social Psychological Quarterly*, *64*, 146–163.

Erickson, R. J., & Wharton, A. S. (1997). Inauthenticity and depression: Assessing the consequences of interactive service work. *Work and Occupations*, *24*, 188–213.

Erikson, E. (1963). *Childhood and society* (2nd ed.). New York: Norton. (Original work published 1950)

Erikson, K. T. (1976a). *Everything in its path: Destruction of community in the Buffalo Creek Flood.* New York: Simon & Schuster.

Erikson, K. T. (1976b). Loss of community at Buffalo Creek. *American Journal of Psychiatry*, *133*, 302–305.

Erikson, K. T. (1986). On work and alienation. *American Sociological Review*, *51*, 1–8.

Erikson, R. E. & Goldthorpe, J. H. (1993). *The constant flux: A study of class mobility in industrial societies.* Oxford: Clarendon.

Eronen, M., Hakola, P., & Tiihonen, J. (1996). Mental disorders and homicidal behavior in Finland. *Archives of General Psychiatry*, *53*(6), 497–501.

Essed, P. (1991). *Understanding everyday racism.* Newbury Park, CA: Sage.

Essok, S. M., & Goldman, H. H. (1995). States' embrace of managed mental health care. *Health Affairs*, *14*, 34–44.

Estroff, S. E. (1981). *Making it crazy: An ethnography of psychiatric patients in an American community.* Berkeley: University of California Press.

Estroff, S. E. (1989). Self, identity, and subjective experiences of schizophrenia: In search of the subject. *Schizophrenia Bulletin*, *15*, 189–196.

Ethier, K., Kershaw, T., Lewis, J., Milan, S., Niccoli, L., & Ickovics, J. (2006). Self-esteem, emotional distress and sexual behavior among adolescent females: Inter-relationships and temporal effects. *Journal of Adolescent Health*, *38*, 268–274.

Evan, W. M. (1993). *Organization theory: Research and design.* New York: MacMillan.

Evans, M. D. R., & Kelley, J. (2004). Effect of family structure on life satisfaction: Australian evidence. *Social Indicators Research*, *69*, 303–349.

Even-Chen, M. S., & Itzhaky, H. (2007). Exposure to terrorism and violent behavior among adolescents in Israel. *Journal of Community Psychology*, *35*(1), 43–55.

Fabrega, H. (1969). Social psychiatric aspects of acculturation and migration: A general statement. *Comprehensive Psychiatry*, *10*(4), 314–326.

Fabrega, H. (1990). Hispanic mental health research: A case for cultural psychiatry. *Hispanic Journal of Behavioral Sciences*, *23*, 339–365.

Fabrega, H., Ulrich, R., & Mezzich, J. E. (1993). Do Caucasian and Black adolescents differ at psychiatric intake? *Journal of the American Academy of Child & Adolescent Psychiatry*, *32*, 407–413.

Falloon, I. R. H., Montero, I., Sungur, M., Mastroeni, A., Malm, U., Economou, A., et al. (2004). Implementation of evidence-based treatment for schizophrenic disorders: Two-year outcome of an international field trial of optimal treatment. *World Psychiatry*, *3*(2), 104–109.

Faraone, S., & Tsuang, M. T. (1995). Methods in psychiatric genetics. In M. T. Tsuang, M. Tohen, & G. Zahner (Eds.), *Textbook in psychiatric epidemiology* (pp. 81–133). New York: Wiley-Liss.

Fariante, C, Salis, M. P., Dazzan, P., Carta, M. G., & Carpiniello. B. (1996). Outcome of patients after reform in Italy (Letter). *Psychiatric Services*, *47*, 1266–1267.

Farina A., Allen, J. G., & Saul, B. (1968). The role of the stigmatized in affecting social relationships. *Journal of Personality*, *36*, 169–182.

Faris, R. E. L., & Dunham, H. W. (1939). *Mental disorders in urban areas: An ecological study of schizophrenia and other psychoses.* Chicago: University of Chicago Press.

Farkas, M., & Anthony, W. (1989). *Psychiatric rehabilitation*. Baltimore: Johns Hopkins University Press.

Farley, J. E. (1994). *Sociology* (3rd ed.). Englewood Cliffs, NJ: Prentice-Hall.

Farmer, E. M. Z., Burns, B. J., Phillips, S. D., Angold, A., & Costello, E. J. (2003). Pathways into and through mental health services for children and adolescents. *Psychiatric Services, 54*, 60–66.

Farmer, T. W., Price, L. N., O'Neal, K. K., Leung, M.-C., Goforth, J. C., Cairns, D. C., et al. (2004). Exploring risk in early adolescent African American youth. *American Journal of Community Psychology, 33*, 51–59.

Fasula, A., Miller, K., & Wiener, J. (2007). The sexual double standard in African American adolescent women's sexual risk reduction socialization. *Women & Health, 46*, 3–21.

Fava, M., & Kendler, K. (2000). Major depressive disorder. *Neuron, 28*(2), 335–341.

Fazel, S., & Danesh, J. (2002). Serious mental disorder in 23,000 prisoners: A systematic review of 62 surveys. *Lancet, 359*, 545–550.

Feagin, J. R. (1991). The continuing significance of race: Anti-Black discrimination in public places. *American Sociological Review, 56*, 101–116.

Feather, N. T. (1989). Reported changes in behavior after job loss in a sample of older unemployed men. *Australian Journal of Psychology, 41*(2), 175–185.

Feder, L. (1991). A comparison of the community adjustment of mentally ill offenders with those from the general prison population: An 18 month followup. *Law and Human Behavior, 15*, 477–494.

Feder, L. (1994). Psychiatric hospitalization history and parole decisions. *Law and Human Behavior, 18*, 395–410.

Feel blue? Say "I do." (2006). *Reuters UK*. Retrieved August 12, 2006, from http://today.reuters.co.uk/news/.

Feinberg, M. E., Kan, M. L., & Hetherington, E. M. (2007). The longitudinal influence of coparenting conflict on parental negativity and adolescent maladjustment. *Journal of Marriage and Family, 69*, 687–702.

Felson, R. B., Messner, S. F., & Hoskin, A. (1999). The victim-offender relationship and calling the police in assaults. *Criminology, 37*(4), 931–947.

Fenwick, R., & Tausig, M. (1994). The macroeconomic context of job stress. *Journal of Health and Social Behavior, 35*(3), 266–282.

Ferguson, T. (1995). *Golden rule: The investment theory of party competition and the logic of money-driven political systems*. Chicago: University of Chicago Press.

Fernando, S., & Keating, F. (2008). *Mental health in a multi-ethnic society*. London: Routledge.

Ferrie, J. E., Head, J., Shipley, M. J., Vahtera, J., Marmot, M. G., & Kivimäki, M. (2006). Injustice at work and incidence of psychiatric morbidity: The Whitehall II study. *Occupational and Environmental Medicine, 63*, 443–450.

Festinger, L. (1957). *A theory of cognitive dissonance*. Evanston: Row, Peterson.

Fields, J., & Casper, L. M. (2001). *America's families and living arrangements: March 2000* (Current Population Reports, Series P-20, No. 537). Washington, DC: U.S. Census Bureau.

Finch, B. K., Kolody, B., & Vega, W. A. (2000). Perceived discrimination and depression among Mexican-origin adults in California. *Journal of Health and Social Behavior, 41*, 295–313.

Finkelhor, D., Ormrod, R. K., Turner, H. A., & Hamby, S. L. (2005). The victimization of children and youth: A comprehensive, national survey. *Child Maltreatment, 10*, 5–25.

Finn, P. E., & Sullivan, M. (1988). Police respond to special populations. *National Institute of Justice Reports, 209*, 2–8.

First, M. B. (2005). Clinical utility: A prerequisite for the adoption of a dimensional approach in DSM. *Journal of Abnormal Psychology, 114*, 560–654.

First, M. B., & Westen, D. (2007). Classification for clinical practice: How to make ICD and DSM better able to serve clinicians. *International Review of Psychiatry, 19*, 473–481.

First, M. B., & Zimmerman, M. (2006). Including laboratory tests in DSM-V diagnostic criteria. *American Journal of Psychiatry, 163*, 12–13.

Fiscella, K., Franks, P., Doescher, M. P., & Saver, B. G. (2002). Disparities in health care by race, ethnicity, and language among the insured: Findings from a national sample. *Medical Care, 40*(1), 52–59.

Fischer, J. (1969). Negroes and Whites and rates of mental illness: Reconsideration of a myth. *Psychiatry, 32*, 428–446.

Fishbein, M. (1979). A theory of reasoned action: Some applications and implications. *Nebraska Symposium on Motivation, 27*, 65–116.

Fisher, D. (1992). Thoughts on recovery. *Resources: Workforce Issues in Mental Health Systems, 4*, 7–8.

Fisher, D. (1997). Self-managed care: Meaningful participation of consumer/survivors in managed care. In K. Minkoff & D. Pollack (Eds.), *Managed mental health care in the public sector* (pp. 283–293). Amsterdam: Harwood.

Fisher, J. D. (1988). Possible effects of reference group-based social influence on AIDS-risk behavior and AIDS prevention. *American Psychologist, 43*, 914–920.

Fisher, W., Dickey, B., Normand, S., Packer, I., Grudzinskas, A., & Azeni, H. (2002). Use of a state inpatient forensic system under managed mental health care. *Psychiatric Services, 53*(4), 447–451.

Fisher, W. H., Roy-Bujnowski, K., Grudzinskas, A. J., Clayfield, J. C., Banks, S. M., & Wolff, N. (2006). Patterns and prevalence of arrest in a statewide cohort of mental health care consumers. *Psychiatric Services, 57*, 1623–1628.

Fisher, W. H., Silver, E., & Wolff, N. (2006). Beyond criminalization: Toward a criminologically informed framework for mental health policy and services research. *Administration, Policy, Mental Health and Mental Health Services Research, 33*, 544–557.

Fitchett, G., Murphy, P. E., Kravitz, H., Everson-Rose, S., Krause, N., & Powell, L. (2007). Racial/ethnic differences in religious involvement in a multi-ethnic cohort of midlife women. *Journal for the Scientific Study of Religion, 46*(1), 119–132.

Fix, M., & Struyk, R. J. (1993). *Clear and convincing evidence: Measurement of discrimination in America*. Washington, DC: Urban Institute Press.

Flaherty, J. A., & Richman, J. A. (1986). Effects of childhood relationships on the adult's capacity to form social supports. *American Journal of Psychiatry, 59*, 143–153.

Flanagan, J. G. (1989). Hierarchy in simple egalitarian societies. *Annual Review of Anthropology, 18*, 245–266.

Flaskerud, J. H., & Hu, L.-T. (1992). Relationship of ethnicity to psychiatric diagnosis. *Journal of Nervous and Mental Disease, 180*, 296–303.

Flaskerud, J. H., & Hu, L.-T. (1994). Participation in and outcome of treatment for major depression among low income Asian-Americans. *Psychiatry Research, 53*(3), 289–300.

Flaskerud, J. H., & Liu, P. Y. (1990). Influence of therapist ethnicity and language on therapy outcome of Southeast Asian clients. *International Journal of Social Psychiatry, 36*(1), 18–29.

Flaskerud, J. H., & Liu, P. Y. (1991). Effects of Asian client-therapist ethnicity and gender match on utilization and outcome of therapy. *Community Mental Health Journal, 27*(1), 31–42.

Flax, J. (1993). *Disputed subjects: Essays on psychoanalysis, politics, and philosophy*. New York: Routledge.

Fleishman, J., Sherbourne, C., Crystal, S., Collins, R., Marshall, G., Kelly, M., et al. (2000). Coping, conflictual social interactions, social support, and mood among HIV-infected persons. *American Journal of Community Psychology, 28*, 421–453.

Fleming, J. E., & Offord, D. R. (1990). Epidemiology of childhood depressive disorder: A critical review. *Journal of the American Academy of Child & Adolescent Psychiatry, 29*, 571–580.

Folkman, S. (1984). Personal control and stress and coping processes: A theoretical analysis. *Journal of Personality and Social Psychology, 46*, 839–852.

Folkman, S., & Lazarus, R. S. (1980). An analysis of coping in a middle-aged community sample. *Journal of Health & Social Behavior, 21*, 219–239.

Folkman, S., & Moskowitz, J. T. (2004). Coping: Pitfalls and promise. *Annual Review of Psychology, 55*, 745–774.

Foner, N. (1995). *The caregiving dilemma: Work in an American nursing home*. Berkeley: University of California Press.

Ford, J. D., Adams, M. L., & Dailey, W. F. (2006). Factors associated with receiving help and risk factors for disaster-related distress among Connecticut adults 5–15 months after the September 11th terrorist incidents. *Social Psychiatry and Psychiatric Epidemiology, 41*(4), 261–270.

Formby, P., & Cherlin, A. J. (2007). Family instability and child well-being. *American Sociological Review, 72*, 181–204.

Forstein, M. (2008). Young adulthood and serodiscordant couples. In M. A. Cohen & J. M. Gorman (Eds.), *Comprehensive textbook of AIDS psychiatry* (pp. 341–356). New York: Oxford University Press.

Forsyth, B. H., & Lessler, J. T. (1991). Cognitive laboratory methods: A taxonomy. In P. P. Biemer et al. (Eds.), *Measurement errors in surveys* (pp. 393–418). New York: Wiley.

Foster, E. M., & Kalil, A. (2007). Living arrangements and children's development in low-income White, Black, and Latino families. *Child Development, 78*, 1657–1674.

Foucault, M. (1988). *Madness and civilization: A history of insanity in the age of reason*. New York: Vintage. (Original work published 1965)

Fox, K. R. (1999). The influence of physical activity on mental well-being. *Public Health Nutrition, 2*(3A), 411–418.

Frances, A. (1998). Problems in defining clinical significance in epidemiological studies. *Archives of General Psychiatry, 55*, 119.

Frances, A. J., Widiger, T. A., & Fyer, M. R. (1990). The influence of classification methods on comorbidity. In J. D. Maser & C. R. Cloninger (Eds.), *Comorbidity of mood and anxiety disorders* (pp. 41–59). Washington, DC: American Psychiatric Press.

Frank, R., Goldman, H., & Hogan, M. (2003). Medicaid and mental health: Be careful what you ask for. *Health Affairs, 22*, 101–113.

Frank, R., & Morlock, L. (1997). *Managing fragmented public mental health services*. New York: Milbank Memorial Fund.

Frankenhaeuser, M., Lundberg, U., & Chesney, M. (Eds.). (1991). *Women, work and health: Stress and opportunities*. New York: Plenum Press.

Frankl, V. E. (1975). Paradoxical intention and dereflection. *Psychotherapy: Theory, Research, and Practice, 12*, 226–237.

Franko, D. L., Striegel-Moore, R. H., Bean, J., Barton, B. A., Biro, F., Kraemer, H. C., et al. (2005). Self-reported symptoms of depression in late adolescence to early adulthood: A comparison of African-American and Caucasian females. *Journal of Adolescent Health, 37*, 526–529.

Frech, A., & Williams, K. (2007). Depression and the psychological benefits of entering marriage. *Journal of Health and Social Behavior, 48*(2), 149–163.

Freedy, J. R., Saladin, M. E., Kilpartick, D. G., Resnick, H. S., & Saunders, B. E. (1994). Understanding acute psychological distress following natural disaster. *Journal of Traumatic Stress, 7*, 257–273.

Freeman, R. J., & Roesch, R. (1989). Mental disorder and the criminal justice system: A review. *International Journal of Law and Psychiatry, 12*, 105–116.

Freidson, E. (1970a). *Profession of medicine*. New York: Dodd Mead.

Freidson, E. (1970b). *Professional dominance*. Chicago: Aldine.

Fremont, A. M., & Bird, C. E. (1999). Integrating sociological and biological models. *Journal of Health and Social Behavior, 40*, 126–129.

Frerichs, R., Aneshensel, C., & Clark, V. (1981). Prevalence of depression in Los Angeles County. *American Journal of Epidemiology, 113*, 691–699.

Frese, F. J. (1998). Advocacy, recovery, and the challenges of consumerism for schizophrenia. *Psychiatric Clinics of North America, 21*, 233–249.

Frese M., & Zapf, D. (1989). Methodological issues in the study of work stress: Objective vs. subjective measurement of work stress and the question of longitudinal studies. In C. L. Cooper & R. Payne (Eds.), *Causes, coping and consequences of stress at work* (pp. 375–411). New York: Wiley.

Freud, A. (1937). *The ego and the mechanisms of defense*. London: Hogarth Press.

Freud, S. (1949). An example of psycho-analytic work. In H. Ragg-Kirkby (Trans.), *An outline of psychoanalysis*. New York: Norton.

Freud, S. (1950). Project for a scientific psychology. In J. Strachey (Ed. and Trans.), *The standard edition of the complete psychological works of Sigmund Freud* (Vol. I). London: Hogarth Press. (Original work published 1895)

Freud, S. (1953). The interpretation of dreams. In J. Strachey (Ed. and Trans.), *The standard edition of the complete psychological works of Sigmund Freud* (Vol. IV). London: Hogarth Press. (Original work published 1900)

Freud, S. (1959a). Some psychological consequences of the anatomical distinction between the sexes. In *Collected papers* (Vol. 5). New York: Basic Books.

Freud, S. (1959b). Female sexuality. In *Collected papers* (Vol. 5). New York: Basic Books.

Freud, S. (1959c). The passing of the Oedipus complex. In *Collected papers* (Vol. 2). New York: Basic Books.

Freud, S. (1961). Civilization and its discontents. In J. Strachey (Ed. and Trans.), *The standard edition of the complete psychological works of Sigmund Freud* (Vol. XXI). London: Hogarth Press. (Original work published 1930)

Freud, S. (1966a). Femininity. In *The complete introductory lectures on psychoanalysis*. New York: Norton.

Freud, S. (1966b). Anxiety and instinctual life. In *New introductory lectures*. New York: Norton.

Friedman, E. S., Thase, M. E., & Wright, J. H. (2008). Cognitive and behavioral therapies. In A. Tasman, J. Kay, J. A. Lieberman, M. B. First, & M. Maj (Eds.), *Psychiatry* (Vol. 2, 3rd ed., pp. 1920–1947). New York: Wiley.

Friedman, R., & Downey J. (2008). Sexual differentiation of behavior: The foundation of a developmental model of psychosexuality. *Journal of the American Psychoanalytic Association, 53*(1), 147–175.

Friedman, S. R., de Jong, W., Rossi, D., Touze, G., Rockwell, R., Des Jarlais, D. C., et al. (2007). Harm reduction theory: Users' culture, micro-social indigenous harm reduction, and the self-organization and outside-organizing of users' groups. *International Journal of Drug Policy, 18*(2), 107–117.

Frishman, L. K., & McGuire, T. G. (1989). The economics of long-term care for the mentally ill. *Social Issues, 45*, 119–130.

Fritz, M. (2006, February 1). Mr. Hadd goes underground. *Wall Street Journal*, p. A1. Retrieved September 30, 2008, from http://trouble.philadelphiaweekly.com/archives/2006/02/wall_street_jou.html.

Froehlich, T. E., Bogardus, S. T., Jr., & Inouye, S. K. (2001). Dementia and race: Are there differences between African Americans and Caucasians? *Journal of the American Geriatric Society, 49*(4), 477–484.

Froggatt, D., Fadden G., Johnson D. L., Leggatt, M., & Shankar, R. (2007). *Families as partners in care: A guidebook for implementing family work.* Toronto: World Fellowship for Schizophrenia and Allied Disorders.

Fromm, E. (1947). *Man for himself.* New York: Rinehart.

Fryer, D. M. (1986). Employment deprivation and personal agency during unemployment: A critical discussion of Jahoda's explanation of the psychological effects of unemployment. *Social Behaviour, 1*, 3–23.

Fujino, D. C., Okazaki, S., & Youth, K. (1994). Asian-American women in the mental health system: An examination of ethnic and gender match between therapist and client. *Journal of Community Psychology, 22*(2), 164–176.

Fuller, C. M., Borrell, L. N., Latkin, C. A., Galea, S., Ompad, D. C., Strathdee, S. A., et al. (2005). Effects of race, neighborhood, and social network on age at initiation of injection drug use. *American Journal of Public Health, 95*(4), 689–695.

Funch, D. P., & Mettlin, C. (1982). The role of support in relation to recovery from breast surgery. *Social Science & Medicine, 16*, 91–98.

Furman, R. (2003). Frameworks for understanding value discrepancies and ethical dilemmas in managed mental health for social work in the U.S. *International Social Work, 46*, 37–52.

Furner, S., Wallace, K., Arguelles, L., Miles, T., & Goldberg, J. (2006). Twin study of depressive symptoms among older African-American women. *Journal of Gerontology: Psychological Sciences, 61B*, P355–P361.

Furnham, A., & Bower, P. (1992). A comparison of academic and lay theories of schizophrenia. *British Journal of Psychiatry, 161*, 201–210.

Furnham, A., & Shiekh, S. (1993). Gender, generational and social support correlates of mental health in Asian immigrants. *International Journal of Social Psychiatry, 39*, 22–33.

Furstenburg, F., Kennedy, S., McLoyd, V., Rumbaut, R., & Settersten, R. (2004). Growing up is harder to do. *Contexts, 3*, 33–41.

Gabard, D. L., & Cooper, T. L. (1998). Race: Constructs and dilemmas. *Administration & Society, 30,* 339–346.

Gabriele, R., & Guida, A. (1998). Privatization of the public trust: Devolution of disaster? *Behavioral Healthcare Tomorrow, 7*(1), 34–35, 47.

Gadalla, T. M. (2008). Comparison of users and non-users of mental health services among depressed women: A national study. *Women Health, 47*(1), 1–19.

Gagliardi, G. J., Lovell, D., Peterson, P. D., & Jemelka, R. (2004). Forecasting recidivism in mentally ill offenders released from prison. *Law and Human Behavior, 28,* 133–156.

Gaines, A. D. (Ed.). (1992). *Ethnopsychiatry: The cultural construction of professional and folk psychiatrists.* Albany: State University of New York.

Galambos, C. (1999). Resolving ethical conflicts in a managed health care environment. *Health and Social Work, 24,* 91–98.

Galea, S., D. Vlahov, H., Resnick, J., Ahern, E., Susser, J., Gold, M., et al. (2003). Trends of probable post-traumatic stress disorder in New York City after the September 11 terrorist attacks. *American Journal of Epidemiology, 158*(6), 514–524.

Galper, J. H. (1975). *The politics of social services.* Englewood Cliffs, NJ: Prentice-Hall.

Gamson, J. (1989). Silence, death, and the invisible enemy: AIDS activism and social movement 'newness.' *Social Problems, 36,* 351–367.

Ganster, D. C. (1989). Worker control and well-being: A review of research in the workplace. In S. L. Lauter, J. J. Hurrell, & C. L. Cooper (Eds.), *Job control and worker health* (pp. 2–23). New York: Wiley.

Garcia Coll, C., Lamberty, G., Jenkins, R., McAdoo, H. P., Crnic, K., Wasik, B. H., et al. (1996). An integrative model for the study of developmental competencies in minority children. *Child Development, 67,* 1891–1914.

Gardner, H. (1985). *The mind's new science: A history of the cognitive revolution.* New York: Basic Books.

Gardner, W., Hoge, S. K., Bennett, N. S., Roth, L. H., Lidz, C. W., Monahan, J., et al. (1993). Two scales for measuring patients' perceptions of coercion during mental hospital admission. *Behavioral Sciences and the Law, 11,* 307–322.

Gartner, A., & Riessman, F. (1977). *Self-help in the human services.* San Francisco: Jossey-Bass.

Gauthier, A., & Furstenburg, F. (2002). The transition to adulthood: A time use perspective. *Annals of the American Academy of Political and Social Sciences, 580,* 153–171.

Geber, G. M. (1997). Barriers to health care for street youth. *Journal of Adolescent Health, 21*(5), 287–290.

Geertsen, R., Klauber, M. R., Rindflesh, M., Kane, R. L., & Gray, R. (1975). A re-examination of Suchman's views on social factors in health care utilization. *Journal of Health and Social Behavior, 16,* 226–237.

Geis, K. J., & Ross, C. E. (1998). A new look at urban alienation: The effect of neighborhood disorder on perceived powerlessness. *Social Psychology Quarterly, 61,* 232–246.

Geistel, N., Riessman, C., & Rosenfield, S. (1985). Explaining the symptomatology of separated and divorced men and women: The role of material conditions and social networks. *Social Forces, 64,* 84–101.

Geller, J. L., & Lister, E. D. (1978). The process of criminal commitment for pretrial psychiatric examination: An evaluation. *American Journal of Psychiatry, 135,* 53–60.

Gelles, R. J., & Conte, J. R. (1990). Domestic violence and sexual abuse of children: A review of research in the eighties. *Journal of Marriage and the Family, 52,* 1045–1058.

George, L. K. (1999). Life course perspectives on mental health. In C. Aneshensel & J. C. Phelan, (Eds.), *Handbook of the sociology of mental health* (pp. 565–583). New York: Kulwer.

Gerbner, G., Gross, L., Morgan, M., & Signorielli, N. (1981). Health and medicine on television. *New England Journal of Medicine, 305,* 901–904.

Geronimus, A., Hicken, M., Keene, D., & Bound, J. (2006). "Weathering" and age patterns of allostatic load scores among Blacks and Whites in the United States. *American Journal of Public Health, 96*(5), 826–833.

Gershon, E., & Nurnberger, J. I. (1995). Bipolar illness. In J. Oldham & M. B. Riba (Eds.), *Review of psychiatry* (Vol. 14, pp. 339–423) Washington, DC: American Psychiatric Press.

Gershon, E. S., Hamovit, J., Guroff, J. J., Dibble, E., Leckman, J. F., Sceery, W., et al. (1982). A family study of schizoaffective bipolar I, bipolar II, unipolar and normal control probands. *Archives of General Psychiatry, 39,* 1157–1167.

Gershon, E., Targum, S., Matthysee, S. et al. (1979). Color blindness not closely linked to bipolar illness. Report of a new pedigree series. *Arch. General Psychiatry, 36,* 1423–30.

Gerstel, N., & Sarkisian, N. (2006). Marriage: The good, the bad, and the greedy. *Contexts, 5*(4), 16–21.

Gersten, J. C., Langner, T. S., Eisenberg, J. G., & Orzeck, L. (1974). Child behavior and life events: Undesirable change or change per se? In B. S. Dohrenwend & B. P. Dohrenwend (Eds.), *Stressful life events: Their nature and effects* (pp. 159–170). New York: Wiley.

Giaconia, R. M., Reinherz, H. Z., Silverman, A. B., Pakiz, B., Frost, A. K., & Cohen, E. (1994). Ages of onset of psychiatric disorders in a community population of older adolescents. *Journal of the American Academy of Child Adolescent Psychiatry, 33,* 706–717.

Gibbons, F. X., Gerrard, M., Cleveland, M. J., Wills, T. A., & Brody, G. (2004). Perceived discrimination and substance use in African American parents and their children: A panel study. *Journal of Personality and Social Psychology, 86,* 517–529.

Gibson, D., Flynn, N., & Perales D. (2001). Effectiveness of syringe exchange programs in reducing HIV risk behavior and HIV seroconversion among injecting drug users. *AIDS, 15*(11), 1329–1341.

Gidron, Y., Gal, R., & Zahavi, S. (1999). Bus commuters' coping strategies and anxiety from terrorism: An example of the Israeli experience. *Journal of Traumatic Stress, 12*(1), 185–192.

Gilkes, C. T. (2000). *If it wasn't for the women.* New York: Orbis.

Gilmer, T. P., Ojeda, V. D., Folsom, D. P., Fuentes, D., Garcia, P., & Jeste, D. V. (2007). Initiation and use of public mental health services by persons with severe mental illness and limited English proficiency. *Psychiatric Services, 58*(12), 1555–1562.

Gilmore, K. (1998). Cloacal anxiety in female development. *Journal of the American Psychoanalytic Association, 46,* 443–470.

Giordano, P. C., Cernkovich, S. A., & Pugh, M. D. (1986). Friendships and delinquency. *American Journal of Sociology, 91,* 1170–1202.

Giordano, P. C., Longmore, M. A., & Manning, W. A. (2006). Gender and the meanings of adolescent romantic relationships: A focus on boys. *American Sociological Review, 71,* 260–287.

Gittleman, M. B., & Howell, D. R. (1995). Changes in the structure and quality of jobs in the United States: Effects by race and gender, 1973–1990. *Industrial and Labor Relations Review, 48*(3), 420–440.

Glaser, B. G., & Strauss, A. L. (1967). *The discovery of grounded theory: Strategies for qualitative research.* Chicago: Aldine.

Glisson, C., & Hemmelgarn, A. (1998). The effects of organizational climate and interorganizational coordination on the quality and outcomes of children's service systems. *Child Abuse & Neglect, 22,* 401–421.

Glisson, C., & Schoenwald, S. K. (2005). The ARC organization and community intervention strategy for implementing evidence-based children's mental health treatments. *Mental Health Services Research, 7*(4), 243–259.

Gochman, D. S. (1997). *Handbook of health behavior research.* New York: Plenum Press.

Goffman, E. (1961). *Asylums.* Garden City, NY: Doubleday.

Goffman, E. (1963). *Stigma: Notes on the management of spoiled identity.* New York: Simon & Schuster.

Gold, P., Goodwin, F. K., & Chrousos, G. P. (1988a). Clinical and biochemical manifestations of depression: Relation to the neurobiology of stress (first of two parts). *New England Journal of Medicine, 319,* 348–353.

Gold, P., Goodwin, F. K., & Chrousos, G. P. (1988b). Clinical and biochemical manifestations of depression: Relation to the neurobiology of stress (second of two parts). *New England Journal of Medicine, 319,* 413–420.

Goldberg, E., & Comstock, G. (1980). Epidemiology of life events: Frequency in general populations. *American Journal of Epidemiology, 111,* 736–752.

Goldberg, E. M., & Morrison, S. L. (1963). Schizophrenia and social class. *British Journal of Psychiatry, 109,* 785–802.

Golding, S. L., Eaves, D., & Kowaz, A. M. (1989). The assessment, treatment and community outcome of insanity acquittees: Forensic history and response to treatment. *International Journal of Law and Psychiatry, 12*, 149–179.

Goldman, H., Lehman, A., Morrissey, J., Newman, S., Frank, R., & Steinwachs, D. (1990). Design for the national evaluation of the Robert Wood Johnson Foundation program on chronic mental illness. *Hospital and Community Psychiatry, 41*(11), 1217–1230.

Goldman, H., & Morrissey, J. (1985). The alchemy of mental health policy: Homelessness and the fourth cycle of reform. *American Journal of Public Health, 75*(7), 727–731.

Goldman, H., Morrissey, J., & Ridgely, M. (1990). Form and function of mental health authorities at RWJ Foundation Program sites: Preliminary observations. *Hospital and Community Psychiatry, 41*(11), 1222–1230.

Goldman, H., Morrissey, J., & Ridgely, M. (1994). Evaluating the Robert Wood Johnson Foundation Program on chronic mental illness. *Milbank Quarterly, 72*(1), 37–47.

Goldman, H., & Taube, C. (1989). State strategies to restructure psychiatric hospitals: A selective review. *Inquiry, 26*(2), 146–157.

Goldsmith, H. F., Jackson, D. J., & Hough, R. (1988). Process model of seeking mental health services: Proposed framework for organizing the literature on help-seeking. In H. F. Goldsmith, E. Lin, & R. A. Bell (Eds.), *Needs assessment: Its future* (DHHS Publication No. ADM 88–1550; pp. 49–64). Washington, DC: U.S. Government Printing Office.

Goldsmith, M. F. (1983). From mental hospitals to jails: The pendulum swings. *Journal of the American Medical Association, 250*, 3017–3018.

Goldstein, R. B., Prescott, C. A., & Kendler, K. S. (2001). Genetic and environmental factors in conduct problems and adult antisocial behavior among adult female twins. *Journal of Nervous and Mental Disease, 189*(4), 201–209.

Goldstrom, I. D., Campbell, J., Rogers, J. A., Lambert, D. B., Blacklow, B., Henderson, M. J., et al. (2006). National estimates for mental health mutual support groups, self-help organizations, and consumer-operated services. *Administration and Policy in Mental Health and Mental Health Services Research, 33*, 92–103.

Golembiewski, R. T., Boudreau, R. A., Munzenrider, R. F., & Luo, H. (1996). *Global burnout: A worldwide pandemic explored by the phase model.* Greenwich, CT: JAI Press.

Gonzales, G., & Rosenheck, R. (2002). Outcomes and service use among homeless persons with serious mental illness and substance abuse. *Psychiatric Services, 53*, 437–446.

Goodman, A. B. (1996). Medical conditions in Ashkenazi schizophrenic pedigrees. *Schizophrenia Bulletin, 20*, 507–517.

Goodman, W. B., Crouter, A. C., Lanza, S. T., & Cox, M. J. (2008). Paternal work characteristics and father-infant interactions in low-income rural families. *Journal of Marriage and Family, 70*, 640–653.

Goodwin, P. Y. (2003). African American and European American women's marital well-being. *Journal of Marriage and Family, 65*(3), 550–560.

Gore, S., & Aseltine, R. (2003). Race and ethnic differences in depressed mood following the transition from high school. *Journal of Health & Social Behavior, 44*, 370–389.

Gore, S., Aseltine, R. H., & Colten, M. E. (1993). Gender, social-relational involvement, and depression. *Journal of Research on Adolescence, 3*(2), 101–125.

Gore, S., Aseltine, R., & Schilling, E. (2007). Transition to adulthood, mental health, and inequality. In W. R. Avison, J. D. McLeod, & B. A. Pescosolido (Eds.), *Mental health, social mirror* (pp. 191–218). New York: Springer Science.

Gorenstein, E. E. (1984). Debating mental illness: Implications for science, medicine, and social policy. *American Psychologist, 39*, 50–56.

Gottlieb, B. H. (1981a). Social networks and social support in community mental health. In B. H. Gottlieb (Ed.), *Social networks and social support* (pp. 11–42). Beverly Hills, CA: Sage.

Gottlieb, B. H. (1981b). *Social networks and social support.* Beverly Hills, CA: Sage.

Gottlieb, B. H. (1983). *Social support strategies: Guidelines for mental health practice.* Beverly Hills, CA: Sage.

Gottlieb, P., Gabrielsen, G., & Kramp, P. (1987). Psychotic homicides in Copenhagen from 1959 to 1983. *Acta Psychiatrica Scandinavica, 76*(3), 285–292.

Gottschalck, A. O. (2008). *Net worth and the assets of households: 2002* (Current Population Reports). Retrieved from http://www.census.gov/hhes/www/wealth/1998_2000/wlth00-.

Goulet, J. L., Molde, S., Constantino, J., Gaughan, D., & Selwyn, P. A. (2000). Psychiatric comorbidity and the long-term care of people with AIDS. *Journal of Urban Health, 77*, 213–221.

Gove, W. R. (1975). *The labeling of deviance: Evaluating a perspective.* New York: Sage.

Gove, W. R. (1982). The current status of the labelling theory of mental illness. In W. R. Gove (Ed.), *Deviance and mental illness* (pp. 273–300). Beverly Hills, CA: Sage.

Gove, W. R. (1984). Gender differences in mental and physical illness: The effects of fixed roles and nurturant roles. *Social Science and Medicine, 19*, 77–91.

Gove, W. R., & Geerken, M. R. (1977). The effect of children and employment on the mental health of married men and women. *Social Forces, 56*, 66–76.

Gove, W. R., Hughes, M., & Style, C. B. (1983). Does marriage have positive effects on the psychological well-being of the individual? *Journal of Health and Social Behavior, 24*(2), 122–131.

Gove, W. R., Ortega, S. T., & Briggs Style, C. (1989). The maturational and role perspectives on aging and self through the adult years: An empirical evaluation. *American Journal of Sociology, 94*, 1117–1145.

Gove, W. R., & Tudor, J. F. (1973). Adult sex roles and mental illness. *American Journal of Sociology, 78*(4), 813–835.

Grace, V. (1991). The marketing of empowerment and the construction of the health consumer: A critique of health promotion. *International Journal of Health Services, 21*(2), 329–343.

Gracia, E., & Herrero, J. (2004). Personal and situational determinants of relationship-specific perceptions of social support. *Social Behavior and Personality, 32*(5), 459–476.

Grandberg, E. M., Simons, R. L., Gibbons, F. X., & Melby, J. N. (2008). The relationship between body size and depressed mood: Findings from a sample of African American middle school girls. *Youth & Society, 39*(3), 294–315.

Granovetter, M. (1995). *Getting a job: A study of contacts and careers.* Chicago: University of Chicago Press.

Grant, K., Lyons, A. L., Finkelstein, J. S., Conway, K. M., Reynolds, L. K., O'Koon, J. H., et al. (2004). Low-income, urban, African American youth: A test of two mediational hypotheses. *Journal of Youth and Adolescence, 33*, 523–533.

Greden, J. F., Gardner, R., King, D., Grunhaus, L., Carroll, B., & Kronfol, Z. (1983). Dexamethasone suppression tests in antidepressant treatment of melancholia: The process of normalization and test-retest reproducibility. *Archives of General Psychiatry, 40*, 493–500.

Green, B. L., Grace, M. C., Vary, M. G., & Kramer, T. L. (1994). Children of disaster in the second decade: A 17-year follow-up of Buffalo Creek survivors. *Journal of the American Academy of Child and Adolescent Psychiatry, 33*, 71–79.

Green, B. L., Lindy, J. D., Grace, M. C., & Gleser, G. C. (1990). Buffalo Creek survivors in the second decade: Stability of stress symptoms. *American Journal of Orthopsychiatry, 60*, 43–54.

Green, D. C., Buehler, J. W., Silk, B. J., Thompson, N. J., Schild, L. A., Klein, M., et al. (2006). Trends in healthcare use in the New York City region following the terrorist attacks of 2001. *Biosecurity and Bioterrorism-Biodefense Strategy Practice and Science, 4*(3), 263–275.

Green, T. M. (1997). Police as frontline mental health workers: The decision to arrest or refer to mental health agencies. *International Journal of Law and Psychiatry, 20*, 469–486.

Green, V. (1978). The Black extended family in the United States: Some research suggestions. In D. B. Shimkin, E. M. Shimkin, & D. A Frate (Eds.), *The extended family in Black societies.* The Hague: de Gruyter.

Greenberg, J. R., & Mitchell, S. A. (1983). *Object relations in psychoanalytic theory.* Cambridge, MA: Harvard University Press.

Greenberg, L. S., Elliott, R. K., & Lietar, G. (1994). Research on experiential psychotherapies. In A. E. Bergin & S. L. Garfield (Eds.), *Handbook of psychotherapy and behavior change* (4th. ed.) (pp. 509–539). New York: Wiley.

Greene, B. 1996. African-American women: Considering diverse identities and societal barriers in psychotherapy. *Annals of the New York Academy of Sciences, 789*, 191–209.

Greene, B., White, J. C., & Whitten, L. (2000). Hair texture, length and style as a metaphor in the African American mother-daughter relationship. In L. C. Jackson & B. Greene (Eds.), *Psychotherapy with African American women* (pp. 166–193). New York: Guilford.

Greenley, J. (Ed.). (1995). *Research in community and mental health: Vol. 8. The family and mental illness.* Greenwich, CT: JAI Press.

Greenley, J. R. (1992). Neglected organization and management issues in mental health systems development. *Community Mental Health Journal, 28*(5), 371–384.

Greenley, J. R., & Mechanic, D. (1976). Social selection in seeking help for psychological problems. *Journal of Health and Social Behavior, 17,* 249–262.

Greenley, J. R., Mechanic, D., & Cleary, P. D. (1987). Seeking help for psychologic problems. *Medical Care, 25,* 1113–1128.

Greenspoon, P. J., & Saklofske, D. H. (2001). Toward integration of subjective well-being and psychopathology. *Social Indicators Research, 54,* 81–108.

Greenstein, T. N. (2000). Economic dependence, gender, and the division of labor in the home: A replication and extension. *Journal of Marriage and the Family, 62,* 322–335.

Greenwood, R. M., Schaefer-McDaniel, N. J., Winkel, G., & Tsemberis, S. J. (2005). Decreasing psychiatric symptoms by increasing choice in services for adults with histories of homelessness. *American Journal of Community Psychology, 36,* 223–238.

Griffiths, L., & Hughes, D. (1999). Talking contracts and taking care: Managers and professional in the British National Health Service internal market. *Social Science and Medicine, 44,* 1–13.

Grisso, T., & Appelbaum, P. S. (1995). The MacArthur Treatment Competence Study: III. Abilities of patients to consent to psychiatric and medical treatment. *Law and Human Behavior, 19,* 149–174.

Grob, G. (1973). *Mental institutions in America: Social policy to 1875.* New York: The Free Press.

Grob, G. (1983). *Mental illness and American society, 1875–1940.* Princeton, NJ: Princeton University Press.

Grob, G. (1991). *From asylum to community.* Princeton, NJ: Princeton University Press.

Grob, G. (1995). *The mad among us: A history of the care of America's mentally ill.* Cambridge, MA: Harvard University Press.

Grob, G. N. (1971). Introduction. In *Report of the Commission on Lunacy, 1855.* Cambridge, MA: Harvard University Press.

Grob, G. N., & Goldman, H. H. (2006). *The dilemma of federal mental health policy: Radical reform or incremental change?* New Brunswick, NJ: Rutgers University Press.

Gronfein, W. (1985a). Incentives and intentions in mental health policy: A comparison of the Medicaid and Community Mental Health programs. *Journal of Health and Social Behavior, 26,* 192–206.

Gronfein, W. (1985b). Psychotropic drugs and the origins of deinstitutionalization. *Social Problems, 32,* 437–452.

Grudzinskas, A. J., Jr., Clayfield, J. C., Roy-Bujnowski, K., Fisher, W. H., & Richardson, M. H. (2005). Integrating the criminal justice system into mental health service delivery: The Worcester diversion experience. *Behavioral Sciences and the Law, 23*(2), 277–293.

Guarnaccia, P. J. (1992). Ataques de nervios in Puerto Rico: Culture-bound syndrome or popular illness. *Medical Anthropology, 15,* 1–14.

Guarnaccia, P. J., & Rogler, L. H. (1999). Research on Culture-Bound Syndromes: New Directions. *American Journal of Psychiatry, 156,* 1322–1327.

Gudeman, J. E. (1988). The evolution of a public psychiatric hospital and its system of care. In M. F. Shore & J. E. Gudeman (Eds.), *Serving the chronically mentally ill in an urban setting* (pp. 25–32). San Francisco: Jossey-Bass.

Guillin, O., Abi-Dargham, A., & Laruelle, M. (2007). Neurobiology of dopamine in schizophrenia. *International Review of Neurobiology, 78,* 1–39.

Guisinger, S., & Blatt, S. J. (1994). Individuality and relatedness: Evolution of a fundamental dialectic. *American Psychologist, 49,* 104–111.

Gulcur, L., Stefancic, A., Shinn, M., Tsemberis, S., & Fischer, S. N. (2003). Housing, hospitalization, and cost outcomes for homeless individuals with psychiatric disabilities participating in continuum of care and Housing First programmes. *Journal of Community and Applied Social Psychiatry, 13,* 171–186.

Gummer, B. (1988). Competing perspectives on the concept of 'effectiveness' in the analysis of social services. *Administration in Social Work, 11*, 257–270.

Guralnik, J. M., & Kaplan, G. A. (1989). Predictors of healthy aging: Prospective evidence from the Alameda County Study. *American Journal of Public Health, 79*, 703–708.

Gurin, G., Veroff, J., & Feld, S. (1960). *Americans view their mental health*. New York: Basic Books.

Guthrie, B. J., Young, A. M., Williams, D. R., Boyd, C. J., & Kintner, E. K. (2002). African American girls' smoking habits and day-to-day experiences with racial discrimination. *Nursing Research, 51*, 183–190.

Gutman, L., McLoyd, V., & Tokoyawa, T. (2005). Financial strain, neighborhood stress, parenting behaviors and adolescent adjustment in urban African American families. *Journal of Research on Adolescence, 15*, 425–449.

Ha, J.-H., Hong, J., Seltzer, M. M., & Greenberg, J. S. (2008). Age and gender differences in the well-being of midlife and aging parents with children with mental health or developmental problems: Report of a national study. *Journal of Health and Social Behavior, 49*, 301–316.

Haavio-Mannila, E. (1986). Inequalities in health and gender. *Social Science and Medicine, 22*(2), 141–149.

Hafner, H., & Boker, W. (1982). *Crimes of violence by mentally abnormal offenders – A psychiatric and epidemiological study in the Federal German Republic*. Cambridge: Cambridge University Press.

Hagan, J. (1991). Destiny and drift: Subcultural preferences, status attainments, and the risks and rewards of youth. *American Sociological Review, 56*, 567–582.

Hagan, J., Gillis, A. R., & Simpson, J. (1985). The class structure of gender and delinquency: Toward a power-control theory of common delinquent behavior. *American Journal of Sociology, 90*, 1151–1178.

Hagedoorn, M., Van Yperen, N. W., Coyne, J. C., & van Jaarsveld, C. H. M. (2006). Does marriage protect older people from distress? The role of equity and recency of bereavement. *Psychology and Aging, 21*(3), 611–620.

Hahn, J. A., Vranizan, K. M., & Moss, A. R. (1997). Who uses needle exchange? A study of injection drug users in treatment in San Francisco, 1989–1990. *Journal of Acquired Immune Deficiency Syndromes and Human Retrovirology, 15*, 157–164.

Halaby, C. N., & Weakliem, D. L. (1989). Worker control and attachment to the firm. *American Journal of Sociology, 95*, 549–591.

Halaby, C. N., & Weakliem, D. L. (1993). Ownership and authority in the earnings function: Nonnested tests of alternative specifications. *American Sociological Review, 58*, 16–30.

Haley, J. (1973). *Uncommon therapy: The psychiatric techniques of Milton H. Erickson, M.D.* New York: Norton.

Haley, J. (1976). *Problem-solving therapy*. San Francisco: Jossey-Bass.

Haley, J. (1987). *Problem-solving therapy* (2nd ed.). San Francisco: Jossey-Bass.

Hall, B. J., Hobfoll, S. E., Palmieri, P., Canetti-Nisim, D., Shapira, O., Johnson, R. J., et al. (2008). The psychological impact of impending forced settler disengagement in Gaza: Trauma and posttraumatic growth. *Journal of Traumatic Stress, 21*(1), 22–29.

Hall, H. I., Lee, L. M., Li, J., Song, R., & McKenna, M. T. (2005). Describing the HIV/AIDS epidemic: Using HIV case data in addition to AIDS case reporting. *Annals of Epidemiology, 15*(1), 5–12.

Hall, L., Edgar, E. & Flynn, L. (1997, September). *Stand and deliver: Action call to a failing industry.* Arlington, VA: NAMI.

Hallfors, D., Waller, M., Bauer, D., Ford, C., & Halpern, C. (2005). Which comes first in adolescence – sex and drugs or depression? *American Journal of Preventive Medicine, 29*(3), 163–170.

Halli, S. S., & Rao, K. V. (1992). *Advanced techniques of population analysis*. New York: Plenum Press.

Hallmayer, J., Maier, W., Ackenheil, M., Ertl, M. A., Schmidt, S., Minges, J., et al. (1992). Evidence against linkage of schizophrenia to chromosome Sq11-q13 markers in systematically ascertained families. *Biological Psychiatry, 31*, 83–94.

Halpern, J., Sackett, K. L., Binner, P. R., & Mohr, B. C. B. (1980). *The myths of deinstitutionalization: Policies for the mentally disabled*. Boulder, CO: Westview Press.

Hamad, R., Fernald, L. C., Karlan, D. S., & Zinman, J. (2008). Social and economic correlates of depressive symptoms and perceived stress in South African adults. *Journal of Epidemiology and Community Health, 62*(6), 538–544.

Hammer, M., Makiesky-Barrow, S., & Gutwirth, L. (1978). Social networks and schizophrenia. *Schizophrenia Bulletin, 4*, 522–545.

Handy, J. (1988). Theoretical and methodological problems within occupational stress and burnout research. *Human Relations, 41*, 351–369.

Hannan, M. T., & Freeman, J. (1998). *Organizational ecology.* Cambridge: Cambridge University Press.

Hans, V. P. (1986). An analysis of public attitudes toward the insanity defense. *Criminology, 4*, 393–415.

Harknett, K., & McLanahan, S. S. (2004). Racial and ethnic differences in marriage after the birth of a child. *American Sociological Review, 69*, 790–881.

Harlow, H. E. (1959). Love in infant monkeys. *Scientific American, 200*, 68–74.

Harlow, S. D., Goldberg, E. L., & Comstock, G. W. (1991). A longitudinal study of risk factors for depressive symptomatology in elderly widowed and married women. *American Journal of Epidemiology, 134*(5), 526–538.

Harper, S., Lynch, J., Hsu, W. L., Everson, S. A., Hillemeier, M. M., Raghunathan, T. E., et al. (2002). Life course socioeconomic conditions and adult psychosocial functioning. *International Journal of Epidemiology, 31*(2), 395–403.

Harris, M., & Bergman, H.C. (1987). Case management with the chronically mentally ill: A clinical perspective. *American Journal of Orthopsychiatry, 57*, 296–302.

Harrison, G., Glazebrook, C., Brewin, J., Cantwell, R., Dalkin, T., Fox, R., et al. (1997). Increased incidence of psychotic disorders in migrants from the Caribbean to the United Kingdom. *Psychological Medicine, 27*, 799–806.

Harrison, G., Hopper, K., Craig, E., Laska, C., Siegel, J., Wanderling, K. C., et al. (2001). Recovery from psychotic illness: A 15- and 25-year international follow-up study. *British Journal of Psychiatry, 178*, 506–517.

Harry, B., & Steadman, H. J. (1988). Arrest rates of patients treated at a community mental-health center. *Hospital and Community Psychiatry, 39*(8), 862–866.

Hart, D., Atkins, R., & Matsuba, M. K. (2008). The association of neighborhood poverty with personality change in childhood. *Journal of Personality and Social Psychology, 94*, 1048–1061.

Hartford, K., Carey, R., & Mendonca, J. (2006). Pre-arrest diversion of people with mental illness: Literature review and international survey. *Behavioral Sciences and the Law, 24*, 845–856.

Hartmann, H. (1939). *Ego psychology and the problem of adaptation.* New York: International Universities Press.

Hartunian, N. S., Smart, C. N., & Thompson, M. S. (1981). *The incidence and economic costs of major health impairments: A comparative analysis of cancer, motor vehicle injuries, coronary heart disease, and stroke.* Lexington, MA: Lexington.

Hartwell, S. W. (2003). Short-term outcomes for offenders with mental illness released from incarceration. *International Journal of Offender Therapy and Comparative Criminology, 47*, 145–158.

Hartwell, S. W. (2004). Comparison of offenders with mental illness only and offenders with dual diagnoses. *Psychiatric Services, 55*(2), 145–150.

Hartwell, S. W. (2005). The organizational response to community re-entry. *Research in Social Problems and Public Policy, 12*, 197–217.

Hasenfled, Y. (Ed). (1992). *Human services as complex organizations.* Newbury Park, CA: Sage.

Hasin, D. S., Keyes, K. M., Hatzenbuehler, M. L., Aharonovich, E. A., & Alderson, D. (2007). Alcohol consumption and posttraumatic stress after exposure to terrorism: Effects of proximity, loss, and psychiatric history. *American Journal of Public Health, 97*(12), 2268–2275.

Hawkins, D. N., & Booth, A. (2005). Unhappily ever after: Effects of long-term, low-quality marriage on well-being. *Social Forces, 84*(1), 451–471.

Hawkins, W. E., Hawkins, M. J., Sabatino, C., & Ley, S. (1998). Relationship of perceived future opportunity to depressive symptomatology of inner-city African-American adolescents. *Children and Youth Services Review, 20*, 757–764.

Haworth, J. T. (1997). *Work, leisure and well-being.* London: Routledge.

Haynes, F. E. (2000). Gender and family ideals: An exploratory study of Black middle-class Americans. *Journal of Family Issues, 21*(7), 811–837.

Hayward, C., Killen J. D., & Taylor, C. B. (1989). Panic attacks in young adolescents. *American Journal of Psychiatry, 146*, 1061–1062.

Hayward, M. D., Crimmins, E. M., Miles, T. P., & Yang, Y. (2000). 'The significance of socioeconomic status in explaining the racial gap in chronic health conditions. *American Sociological Review, 65*, 910–930.

Headey, B. W., Kelley, J., & Wearing, A. J. (1993). Dimensions of mental health: Life satisfaction, positive affect, anxiety, and depression. *Social Indicators Research, 29*, 63–82.

Health United States. (2004). Washington, DC: National Center for Health Statistics.

Healy, D. (2004). *Let them eat Prozac*. New York: New York University Press.

Heckman, T., Miller, J., Kochman, A., Kalichman, S. C., Carlson, B., & Silverthorn, M. (2002). Thoughts of suicide among HIV-infected rural persons enrolled in a telephone-delivered mental health intervention. *Annals of Behavioral Medicine, 24*(2), 141–148.

Heeringa, S., Wagner, G. J., Torres, M., Duan, N., Adams, T., & Berglund, P. (2004). Sample designs and sampling methods for the Collaborative Psychiatric Epidemiology Studies (CPES). *International Journal of Methods in Psychiatric Research, 13*(4), 221–240.

Heider, F. (1958). *The psychology of interpersonal relations*. New York: Wiley.

Heimer, K. (1995). Gender, race and the pathways to delinquency: An interactionist explanation. In J. Hagan & R. D. Peterson (Eds.), *Crime and inequality* (pp. 140–173). Stanford, CA: Stanford University Press.

Heimer, K., & De Coster, S. (1999). The gendering of violent delinquency. *Criminology, 37*, 277–317.

Heinrichs, R. (1993). Schizophrenia and the brain: Conditions for a neuropsychology of madness. *American Psychologist, 48*, 221–233.

Helgeson, V. S., Reynolds, K. A, & Tomich, T. L. (2006). A meta-analytic review of benefit finding and growth. *Journal of Consulting and Clinical Psychology, 74*(5), 797–816.

Heller, K. (1979). The effects of social support: Prevention and treatment implications. In A. P. Goldstein & F. H. Kanfer (Eds.), *Maximizing treatment gains: Transfer enhancement in psychotherapy*. New York: Academic Press.

Helms, J. E., Jernigan, M., & Mascher, J. (2005). The meaning of race in psychology and how to change it: A methodological perspective. *American Psychologist, 60*, 27–36.

Helzer, J. E., & Canino, G. (1992). Comparative analysis of alcoholism in 10 cultural regions. In J. E. Helzer & G. Canino (Eds.), *Alcoholism in North America, Europe and Asia* (pp. 289–308). New York: Oxford University Press.

Helzer, J. E., Stoltzman, R. K., Farmer, A., Brockington, I. F., Plesons, D., Singerman, B., et al. (1985). Comparing the DIS with a DIS/DSM-III-based physician reevaluation. In W. W. Eaton & L. G. Kessler (Eds.), *Epidemiologic field methods in psychiatry* (pp. 285–308). Orlando, FL: Academic Press.

Henderson, A. S. (1992). Social support and depression. In H. O. F. Veil & U. Baumann (Eds.), *The meaning and measurement of social support* (pp. 85–92). New York: Hemisphere.

Henderson, S. (1977). The social network, support and neurosis: The functions of attachment in adult life. *British Journal of Psychiatry, 131*, 185–191.

Heninger, G. R. (1999). Psychiatric research in the 21st century: Opportunities and limitations. *Molecular Psychiatry, 4*, 429–436.

Henry, J. P., & Cassel, J. C. (1969). Psychosocial factors in essential hypertension: Recent epidemiologic and animal experimental evidence. *American Journal of Epidemiology, 90*, 3, 171–200.

Henry, W. P., Strupp, H. H., Schacht, T. E., & Gaston, L. (1994). Psychodynamic approaches. In A. E. Bergin & S. L. Garfield (Eds.), *Handbook of psychotherapy and behavior change* (4th ed.). New York: Wiley.

Herek, G. M. (2002). Heterosexuals' attitudes toward bisexual men and women in the United States. *Journal of Sex Research, 39*(4), 264–274.

Herek, G. M., Capitanio, J. P., & Widaman, K. F. (2002). HIV-related stigma and knowledge in the United States: Prevalence and trends, 1991–1999. *American Journal of Public Health, 92*(3), 371–377.

Herek, G. M., Capitanio, J. P., & Widaman, K. F. (2003). Stigma, social risk, and health policy: Public attitudes toward HIV surveillance policies and the social construction of illness. *Health Psychology, 22*(5), 533–540.

Herek, G. M., Mitnick, L., Burris, S., Chesney, M., Devine, P., Fullilove, M. T., et al. (1998). Workshop report: AIDS and stigma: A conceptual framework and research agenda. *AIDS & Public Policy Journal, 13*(1), 36–47.

Herinckx, H. A., Swart, S. C., Ama, S. M., Dolezal, C. D., & King, S. (2005). Rearrest and linkage to mental health services among clients of the Clark County mental health court program. *Psychiatric Services, 56*, 853–857.

Herman, D., Felton, C., & Susser, E. (2002). Mental health needs in New York State following the September 11th attacks. *Journal of Urban Health–Bulletin of the New York Academy of Medicine, 79*(3), 322–331.

Herz, D. E., Meisenheimer, J. R., & Weinstein, H. G. (2000). Health and retirement benefits: Data from two BLS surveys. *Monthly Labor Review, 123*(3), 3–20.

Heston, L. L. (1982). Mending minds: A guide to the new psychiatry of depression, anxiety, and other serious mental disorders. New York: Freeman.

Hetherington, E. M., Henderson, S. H., & Reiss, D. (1999). Adolescent siblings in step-families: Family functioning and adolescent adjustment. *Monographs of the Society for Research in Child Development, 64*(4), 1–218.

Hetherington, E. M., & Kelly, J. (2003). *For better or for worse: Divorce reconsidered.* New York: Norton.

Hiday, V. A. (1988). Civil commitment: A review of empirical research. *Behavioral Sciences and the Law, 6*, 15–43.

Hiday, V. A. (1990). Dangerousness of civil commitment candidates: A six months follow-up. *Law and Human Behavior, 14*, 551–567.

Hiday, V. A. (1991). Hospitals to jails: Arrests and incarceration of civil commitment candidates. *Hospital and Community Psychiatry, 42*, 729–734.

Hiday, V. A. (1992a). Civil commitment and arrests: An investigation of the criminalization thesis. *Journal of Nervous and Mental Disease, 180*, 184–191.

Hiday, V.A. (1992b). Coercion in civil commitment: Process, preferences and outcome. *International Journal of Law and Psychiatry, 15*, 359–377.

Hiday, V. A. (1995). The social context of mental illness and violence. *Journal of Health and Social Behavior, 36*, 122–137.

Hiday, V. A. (1996). Involuntary commitment as a psychiatric technology. *International Journal of Technology Assessment in Health Care, 12*, 585–603.

Hiday, V. A. (1999). Mental illness and the criminal justice system. In A. V. Horwitz & T. S. Scheid (Eds.), *A handbook for the study of mental health: social contexts, theories, and systems* (pp. 508–525). New York: Cambridge University Press.

Hiday, V. A. (2003). Outpatient commitment: The state of empirical research on its outcomes. *Psychology, Public Policy, & Law, 9*, 8–32.

Hiday, V. A. (2006). Putting community risk in perspective: A look at correlations, causes, and controls. *International Journal of Law and Psychiatry, 29*, 451–468.

Hiday, V. A., Gurrera, M., Lamoureaux, M., & DeMagistris, J. (2005). North Carolina's mental health court. *Popular Government, 70*, 24–30.

Hiday, V. A., & Markell, S. J. (1981). Components of dangerousness: Legal standards in civil commitment. *International Journal of Law and Psychiatry, 34*, 5–19.

Hiday, V. A., & Ray, B. (2008). A court for offenders with mental illness. *Trial Briefs.*

Hiday, V. A., & Smith, L. N. (1987). Effects of the dangerousness standard in civil commitment. *Journal of Psychiatry and Law, 15*, 433–454.

Hiday, V. A., Swanson, J. W., Swartz, M. S., Borum, R., & Wagner, H. R. (2001). A link between mental illness and violence? *International Journal of Law and Psychiatry, 24*, 559–572.

Hiday, V. A., Swartz, M. S., Swanson, J. W., Borum, R., & Wagner, H. R. (1998). Male and female differences in the setting and construction of violence among people with severe mental illness. *Social Psychiatry and Psychiatric Epidemiology, 33*, 68–74.

Hiday, V. A., & Wales, H. W. (2003). Civil commitment and arrests. *Current Opinion in Psychiatry, 16*, 575–580.

Hiday, V. A., & Wales, H. W. (2009). Criminalization of mental illness. In E. Vingilis & S. State (Eds.), *Applied research and evaluation in community mental health services: An overview*. Montreal: McGill-Queens.

Hill, R. (1972). *The strengths of Black families*. New York: Emerson-Hall.

Hill, T. D., Ross, C. E., & Angel, R. J. (2005). Neighborhood disorder, psychophysiological distress, and health. *Journal of Health and Social Behavior, 46*(2), 170–186.

Himelhoch, S., McCarthy, J. F., Ganoczy, D., Medoff, D., Dixon, L. B., & Blow, F. C. (2007). Understanding associations between serious mental illness and HIV among patients in the VA health system. *Psychiatric Services, 58*(9), 1165–1172.

Himmelweit, S. (1999). Caring labor [Special issue]. *Annals of the American Academy of Political and Social Science, 561*, 27–38.

Hine, D. C. (1995). For pleasure, profit, and power: The sexual exploitation of Black women. In G. Smitherman (Ed.), *African American women speak out on Anita Hill–Clarence Thomas* (pp. 168–177). Detroit, MI: Wayne State University Press.

Hinkle, L. (1987). Stress and disease: The concept after 50 years. *Social Science and Medicine, 25*, 561–567.

Hiroto, D. S. (1974). Locus of control and learned helplessness. *Journal of Experimental Psychology, 102*, 187–193.

Hirsch, B. (1980). Natural support systems and coping with major life changes. *American Journal of Community Psychology, 8*, 159–172.

Hirsch, S., Bowen, J., Emami, J., Cramer, P., Jolley, A., Haw, C., et al. (1996). A one year prospective study of the effect of life events and medication in the etiology of schizophrenic relapse. *British Journal of Psychiatry, 168*, 49–56.

Hirsch, S. R., & Weinberger, D. (Eds.). (1996). *Schizophrenia*. Oxford: Blackwell.

Hirschfeld, R., Klerman, G. L., Chodoff, P., Korchin, S., & Barrett, J. (1976). Dependency: Self-esteem–clinical depression. *Journal of the American Academy of Psychoanalysis, 4*, 373–388.

Hirschi, T., & Gottfredson, M. (1983). Age and the explanation of crime. *American Journal of Sociology, 89*, 552–584.

Hobfoll, S. E. (1989). Conservation of resources: A new attempt at conceptualizing stress. *American Psychologist, 44*, 513–524.

Hobfoll, S. E. (1998). *Stress, culture, and community: The psychology and philosophy of stress*. New York: Plenum Press.

Hobfoll, S. E. (2001). The influence of culture, community, and the nested-self in the stress process: Advancing conservation of resources theory. *Applied Psychology: An International Review, 50*(3), 337–421.

Hobfoll, S. E., Canetti-Nisim, D., & Johnson, R. J. (2006). Exposure to terrorism, stress-related mental health symptoms, and defensive coping among Jews and Arabs in Israel. *Journal of Consulting and Clinical Psychology, 74*(2), 207–218.

Hobfoll, S. E., Canetti-Nisim, D., Johnson, R. J., Varley, J., Palmieri, P. A., & Galea, S. (2008). The association of exposure, risk and resiliency factors with PTSD among Jews and Arabs exposed to repeated acts of terrorism in Israel. *Journal of Traumatic Stress, 21*(1), 9–21.

Hobfoll, S. E., Hall, B. J., Canetti-Nisim, D., Galea, S., Johnson, R. J., & Palmieri, P. A. (2007). Refining our understanding of traumatic growth in the face of terrorism: Moving from meaning cognitions to doing what is meaningful. *Applied Psychology: An International Review, 56*(3), 345–366.

Hobfoll, S. E., Johnson, R. J., Ennis, N. E., & Jackson, A. P. (2003). Resource loss, resource gain, and emotional outcomes among inner-city women. *Journal of Personality and Social Psychology, 84*(3), 632–643.

Hobfoll, S. E., Lomranz, J., Johnson, R. J., Eyal, N., & Zemach, M. (1994). A nation's response to attack: Israelis' depressive reactions to the Gulf War. *Journal of Traumatic Stress, 7*(1), 59–73.

Hochschild, A., & Machung, A. (1989). *The second shift: Working parents and the revolution at home*. New York: Academic Press.

Hochschild, A. R. (1983). *The managed heart: Commercialization of human feeling*. Berkeley: University of California Press.

Hochschild, A. R. (1990). Ideology and emotion management: A perspective and path for future research. In T. D. Kemper (Ed.), *Research agendas in the sociology of emotions* (pp. 117–142). Albany: SUNY Press.

Hochschild, J. L. (1995). *Facing up to the American dream*. Princeton, NJ: Princeton University Press.

Hodges, K. (1994). Evaluation of depression in children and adolescents using diagnostic clinical interviews. In W. M. Reynolds & H. F. Johnson (Eds.), *Handbook of depression in children and adolescents* (pp. 183–208). New York: Plenum Press.

Hodgins, S., Mednick, S., Brennan, P. A., Schulsinger, F., & Engberg, M. (1996). Mental disorder and crime. Evidence from a Danish birth cohort. *Archives of General Psychiatry, 53*(6), 489–496.

Hoff, T., & McCaffrey, D. P. (1996). Adapting, resisting, and negotiating how physicians cope with organizational and economic change. *Work and Occupations, 23,* 165–189.

Hoff, T., Whitcomb, W. F., & Nelson, J. R. (2002). Thriving and surviving in a new medical career: The case of hospital practice. *Journal of Health and Social Behavior, 43,* 15–42.

Hofferth, S. L. (2006). Residential father family type and child well-being: Investment versus selection. *Demography, 43,* 53–77.

Hogan, D. P. (1978). The variable order of events in the life course. *American Sociological Review, 43,* 573–586.

Hogan, R., & Perrucci, C. C. (2007). Truly disadvantaged in the transition from employment to retirement income. *Social Science Research, 36,* 1184–1199.

Hoge, M., Davidson, L., Griffith, E., Sledge, W., & Howenstine, R. (1994). Defining managed care in public-sector psychiatry. *Hospital & Community Psychiatry, 45,* 1085–1089.

Holcomb, W. R., & Ahr, P. R. (1988). Arrest rates among young adult psychiatric patients treated in inpatient and outpatient settings. *Hospital and Community Psychiatry, 39,* 52–57.

Hollingshead, A. B., & Redlich, F. C. (1958). *Social class and mental illness*. New York: Wiley.

Hollon, S. D., & Beck, A. T. (1994). Cognitive and cognitive-behavioral therapies. In A. E. Bergin & S. L. Garfield (Eds.), *Handbook of psychotherapy and behavior change* (4th ed., pp. 428–468). New York: Wiley.

Holmes, T. H., & Rahe, R. H. (1967). The social readjustment rating scale. *Journal of Psychosomatic Research, 11,* 213–218.

Holmes, W. C., Bix, B., Meritz, M., Turner, J., & Hutelmyer, C. (1997.) Human immunodeficiency virus (HIV) infection and quality of life: The potential impact of Axis I psychiatric disorders in a sample of 95 HIV seropositive men. *Psychosomatic Medicine, 59,* 187–192.

Holzer, C. E., Shea, B. M., Swanson, J. W. Leaf, P. J., Myers, J. K., George, L., et al. (1986). The increased risk for specific psychiatric disorders among persons of low socioeconomic status: Evidence from the Epidemiologic Catchment Area surveys. *American Journal of Social Psychiatry, 6*(4), 259–271.

Hong, G. K. (1988). A general family practitioner approach for Asian-American mental health services. *Professional Psychology: Research and Practice, 19*(6), 600–605.

Hoover, D. R., Akincigil, A., Prince, J. D., Kalay, E., Lucas, J. A., Walkup, J. T., et al. (2008). Medicare inpatient treatment for elderly non-dementia psychiatric illnesses 1992–2002: Length of stay and expenditures by facility type. *Administration and Policy in Mental Health, 35*(4), 231–240.

Hope, S., Power, C., & Rodgers, B. (1999). Does financial hardship account for elevated psychological distress in lone mothers? *Social Science & Medicine, 49*(12), 1637–1649.

Hopper, K. (1996) Regulation from without: The shadow side of coercion. In D. Dennis & J. Monahan (Eds.), *Coercion and aggressive community treatment: A new frontier in mental health law*. New York: Plenum Press.

Horgan, C. M. (1984). *Demand for ambulatory mental health services from specialty providers*. Rockville, MD: National Center for Health Services Research.

Horney, K. (1937). *Neurotic personality of our times*. New York: Norton.

Horney, K. (1967). *Feminine psychology*. New York: Norton. (Original work published 1926)

Horwitz, A. (1977a). The pathways into psychiatric treatment: Some differences between men and women. *Journal of Health and Social Behavior, 18,* 169–178.

Horwitz, A. (1977b). Social networks and pathways to psychiatric treatment. *Social Forces, 56*, 86–105.

Horwitz, A. (1982). *The social control of mental illness*. New York: Academic Press.

Horwitz, A. (1984). The economy and social pathology. *Annual Review of Sociology, 10*, 95–119.

Horwitz, A. (1987). Help-seeking processes and mental health services. In D. Mechanic (Ed.), *Improving mental health services: What the social sciences can tell us* (pp. 33–45). San Francisco: Jossey-Bass.

Horwitz, A. (2002). Outcomes in the sociology of mental health and illness: Where have we been and where are we going? *Journal of Health and Social Behavior, 43*, 143–151.

Horwitz, A. (2007). Transforming normality into pathology: The DSM and the outcomes of stressful social arrangements. *Journal of Health and Social Behavior, 48*, 211–222.

Horwitz, A. V., & Davies, L. (1994). Are emotional distress and alcohol problems differential outcomes to stress? *Social Science Quarterly, 75*, 607–621.

Horwitz, A. V., & Wakefield, J. C. (2007). *The loss of sadness: How psychiatry transformed normal sorrow into depressive disorder*. New York: Oxford University Press.

Horwitz, A. V., & White, H. (1987). Gender role orientations and styles of pathology among adolescents. *Journal of Health and Social Behavior, 28*, 158–170.

Horwitz, A. V., & White, H. (1991). Becoming married, depression, and alcohol problems among young adults. *Journal of Health and Social Behavior, 32*, 221–237.

Horwitz, A. V., & White, H. R. (1998). The relationship of cohabitation and mental health: A study of a young adult cohort. *Journal of Marriage and the Family, 60*(2), 50.

Horwitz, A. V., White, H. R., & Howell-White, S. (1996a). Becoming married and mental health: A longitudinal study of a cohort of young adults. *Journal of Marriage and Family, 58*(4), 895–907.

Horwitz, A. V., White, H. R., & Howell-White, S. (1996b). The use of multiple outcomes in stress research: A case study of gender differences in responses to marital dissolution. *Journal of Health and Social Behavior, 37*, 278–291.

Horwitz, A. V., Widom, C. S., McLaughlin, J., & White, H. R. (2001). The impact of childhood abuse and neglect on adult mental health: A prospective study. *Journal of Health and Social Behavior, 42*, 184–201.

Hough, R. L., Landsverk, J. A., Karno, M., Burnam, A., Timbers, D. M., & Escobar, J. I. (1978). Utilization of health and mental health services by Los Angeles Mexican Americans and non-Hispanic Whites. *Archives of General Psychiatry, 44*, 702–709.

House, J. S. (1981a). Social structure and personality. In M. Rosenberg & R. H. Turner (Eds.), *Social psychology: Sociological perspectives* (pp. 525–561). New York: Basic Books.

House, J. S. (1981b). *Work stress and social support*. Reading, MA: Addison-Wesley.

House, J. S. (1987). Social support and social structure. *Sociological Forum, 2*, 135–146.

House, J. S., Landis, K. R., & Umberson, D. (1988). Social relationships and health. *Science, 241*, 540–545.

House, J. S., & Robbins, C. (1983). Age, psychosocial stress, and health. In M. W. Riley, B. H. Hess, & K. Bond (Eds.), *Aging and society: Selected reviews and recent research* (pp. 175–197). Hillsdale, NJ: Erlbaum.

House, J. S., Umberson, D., & Landis, K. R. (1988). Structures and processes of social support. *Annual Review of Sociology, 14*, 293–318.

Howell, E., & Teich, J. (2008). Variations in Medicaid mental health service use and cost for children. *Administration and Policy in Mental Health and Mental Health Services Research, 35*, 220–228.

Hoy, E., Curtis, R., & Rice, T. (1991). Change and growth in managed care. *Health Affairs, 10*, 18–36.

Hsu, F. L. K. (1972). American core values and national character. In F. L. K. Hsu (Ed.), *Psychological anthropology*. Cambridge MA: Schenkman.

Hu, T.-W, Snowden, L. R., Jerrell, J. M., & Nguyen, T. D. (1991). Ethnic populations in public mental health: Services choice and level of use. *American Journal of Public Health, 81*, 1429–1434.

Hubbard, K. L., Zapf, P. A, & Ronan, K. A. (2003). Competency restoration: An examination of the differences between defendants predicted restorable and not restorable to competency. *Law and Human Behavior, 27*, 127–140.

Hubert, S. J. (2002). *Questions of power: The politics of women's madness narratives*. Newark: University of Delaware Press.

Hughes, C. C. (1996). The culture-bound syndromes and psychiatric diagnosis. In J. E. Mezzich, A. Kleinman, H. Fabrega, & D. L. Parron (Eds.), *Culture and psychiatric diagnosis: A DSM-IV perspective* (pp. 289–312). Washington, DC: American Psychiatric Press.

Hughes, D. (2003). Correlates of African American and Latino parents' messages to children about ethnicity and race: A comparative study of racial socialization. *American Journal of Community Psychology, 31*, 15–33.

Hughes, J. R., Oliveto, A. H., Helzer, J. E., Higgens, S. T., & Bickel, W. K. (1992). Should caffeine abuse, dependence, or withdrawal be added to DSM-IV and ICD-10? *American Journal of Psychiatry, 149*, 33–40.

Hughes, M., & Gove, W. R. (1981). Living alone, social integration and mental health. *American Journal of Sociology, 87*, 48–74.

Hughes, M., & Thomas, M. E. (1998). The continuing significance of race revisited: A study of race, class, and quality of life in America, 1972 to 1996. *American Sociological Review, 63*, 785–795.

Hummer, R. A. (1996). Black-White differences in health and mortality: A review and conceptual model. *Sociological Quarterly, 37*, 105–125.

Hunter, M. (2005). *Race, gender, and the politics of skin tone*. New York: Routledge–Taylor Francis.

Huselid, R., & Cooper, M. L. (1992). Gender roles as mediators of sex differences in adolescent alcohol use and abuse. *Journal of Health & Social Behavior, 33*, 348–362.

Idler, E. L. (1995). Religion, health, and nonphysical senses of self. *Social Forces, 74*, 683–704.

Iglehart, J. K. (1996). Managed care and mental health. *New England Journal of Medicine, 334*, 131–135.

Institute of Medicine. (1989). *Controlling costs and changing patient care? The role of utilization management*. Washington, DC: National Academies Press.

Interlandi, J. (2008, July 12). The woman who died in the waiting room. *Newsweek*. Retrieved September 30, 2008, from http://www.newsweek.com/id/145870.

Iritani, S. (2007). Neuropathology of schizophrenia: A mini review. *Neuropathology, 27*, 604–608.

Ironson, G., Wynings, C., Schneiderman, N., Baum, A., Rodriguez, M., Greenwood, D., et al. (1997). Post-traumatic stress symptoms, intrusive thoughts, loss, and immune function after Hurricane Andrew. *Psychosomatic Medicine, 59*(2), 128–141.

Isett, K., Burnam, A., Coleman-Beattie, B., Hyde, P., Morrissey, J., Magnabosco, J., et al. (2007). The state policy context of implementation issues for evidence-based practices in mental health. *Psychiatric Services, 58*(7), 914–921.

Jablensky A., Sartorius, N., Ernberg, G., Anker, M., Korten, A., Cooper, J. E., et al. (1991). Schizophrenia: Manifestations, incidence, and course in different cultures. World Health Organization Ten Country Study. *Psychological Medicine* (Suppl. 20).

Jackson, J. S., Neighbors, H. W., Torres, M., Martin, L. A., Williams, D. R., & Baser, R. (2007). Use of mental health services and subjective satisfaction with treatment among Black Caribbean immigrants: Results from the National Survey of American Life. *American Journal of Public Health, 97*, 60–67.

Jackson, J. S., Torres, M., Caldwell, C. H., Neighbors, H. W., Nesse, R. M., Taylor, R. J., et al. (2004). The National Survey of American Life: A study of racial, ethnic and cultural influences on mental disorders and mental health. *International Journal of Methods in Psychiatric Research, 13*(4), 196–207.

Jackson, P. B., & Stewart, Q. T. (2003). A research agenda for the Black middle class: Work stress, survival strategies, and mental health. *Journal of Health and Social Behavior, 44*, 442–455.

Jackson, P. R., Stafford, E. M., Banks, M. H., & Warr, P. B. (1983). Unemployment and psychological distress in young people: The moderating role of employment commitment. *Journal of Applied Psychology, 68*(3), 525–535.

Jackson, S. E., Schwab, R. A., & Schuler, R. (1986). Toward an understanding of the burnout phenomenon. *Journal of Applied Psychology, 71*, 630–640.

Jaco, E. G. (1960). *The social epidemiology of mental disorders*. New York: Russell Sage Foundation.

Jacobson, J. W. (1998). Psychological services utilization: Relationship to severity of behaviour problems in intellectual disability services [Special issue]. *Journal of Intellectual Disability Research II, 42*, 307–315.

Jacobson, N. (2004). *In recovery: The making of mental health policy.* Nashville, TN: Vanderbilt University Press.

Jacobson, N., & Greenley, D. (2001). What is recovery? A conceptual model and explication. *Psychiatric Services, 52,* 482–485.

Jacobson, N. S., & Addis, M. E. (1993). Research on couples and couple therapy: What do we know? Where are we going? *Journal of Consulting and Clinical Psychology, 61,* 85–93.

Jacobson, N. S., Holtzworth-Munroe, A., & Schmaling, K. B. (1989). Marital therapy and spouse involvement in the treatment of depression, agoraphobia, and alcoholism. *Journal of Consulting and Clinical Psychology, 57,* 5–10.

Jahoda, M. (1958). *Current concepts of positive mental health.* New York: Basic Books.

Jahoda, M. (1981). Work, employment, and unemployment: Values, theories, and approaches in social research. *American Psychologist, 36*(2), 184–191.

Jahoda, M. (1982). *Employment and unemployment: A social psychological analysis.* New York: Cambridge University Press.

Jahoda, M. (1997). Manifest and latent functions. In N. Nicholson (Ed.), *The encyclopedic dictionary of organizational psychology* (pp. 317–318). Oxford: Blackwell.

Jainchill, N., De Leon, G., & Yagelka, J. (1997). Ethnic differences in psychiatric disorders among adolescent substance abusers in treatment. *Journal of Psychopathology and Behavioral Assessment, 19,* 133–148.

James, D. J., & Glaze, L. E. (2006). Mental health problems of prison and jail inmates. *Bureau of Justice Statistics Bulletin, 674–677.*

James, F., Gregory, D., & Jones, R. K. (1980). Psychiatric morbidity in prisons. *Hospital and Community Psychiatry, 140,* 674–677.

James, N. (1989). Emotional labour: Skill and work in the regulation of feelings. *Sociological Review, 37,* 15–42.

Janzen, J. M. (1978). *The quest for therapy in Lower Zaire.* Berkeley: University of California Press.

Jayasuriya, L. (1992). The problematic of culture and identity in social functioning. *Journal of Multicultural Social Work, 2,* 37–58.

Jehel, L., Paterniti, S., Brunet, A., Duchet, C., & Guelfi, J. D. (2003). Prediction of the occurrence and intensity of post-traumatic stress disorder in victims 32 months after bomb attack. *European Psychiatry, 18*(4), 172–176.

Jekelek, S. M. (1998). Parental conflict, marital disruption, and children's emotional well-being. *Social Forces, 76,* 905–935.

Jencks, C. (1980). Heredity, environment, and public policy reconsidered. *American Sociological Review, 45,* 723–736.

Jenkins, J., Simpson, A., Dunn, J., Rasbash, J., & O'Connor, T. G. (2005). Mutual influence of marital conflict and children's behavior problems: Shared and nonshared family risks. *Child Development, 76,* 24–39.

Jensen, A. R. (1969). How much can we boost IQ and scholastic achievement? *Harvard Educational Review, 39,* 1–123.

Jessor, R., & Jessor, S. L. (1977). *Problem behavior and psychosocial development: A longitudinal study of youth.* New York: Academic Press.

Jilek, W. (1993). Traditional medicine relevant to psychiatry. In N. Sartorius, G. de Girolamo, G. Andrews, G. A. German, & L. Eisenberg (Eds.), *Treatment of mental disorders: A review of effectiveness* (pp. 341–383). Washington, DC: American Psychiatric Press.

Joffe, R. T. (2001). Progress in the biology of psychiatry. *Journal of Psychiatry and Neuroscience, 26,* 101–102.

Johnson, D. (1994). Stress, depression, substance abuse, and racism. *Journal of the National Center for American Indian and Alaska Native Health Research, 6,* 29–33.

Johnson, D. L. (2007). Models of family intervention. In D. Froggatt, G. Fadden, D. L. Johnson, M. Leggatt, & R. Shankar (Eds.), *Families as partners in care: A guidebook for implementing family work* (pp. 10–19). Toronto: World Fellowship for Schizophrenia and Allied Disorders.

Johnson, D. R., Amoloza, T., & Booth, A. (1992). Stability and developmental change in marital quality: A three-wave panel analysis. *Journal of Marriage and the Family, 54,* 582–594.

Johnson, D. R., & Wu, J. (2002). An empirical test of crisis, social selection, and role explanations of the relationship between marital disruptions and psychological distress: A pooled time-series analysis of four-wave panel data. *Journal of Marriage and the Family, 64*, 211–224.

Johnson, J. V., & Hall, E. M. (1988). Job strain, work place social support, and cardiovascular disease: A cross-sectional study of a random sample of the Swedish working population. *American Journal of Public Health, 78*(10), 1336–1342.

Johnson, J. V., Hall, E. M., & Theorell, T. (1989). Combined effects of job strain and social isolation on cardiovascular disease morbidity and mortality in a random sample of the Swedish male working population. *Scandinavian Journal of Work, Environment and Health, 15*(4), 271–279.

Johnson, R. J., Hobfoll, S. E., Hall, B. J., Canetti-Nisim, D., Palmieri, P. A., & Galea, S. (2007). Response, "Posttraumatic Growth: Action and Reaction." *Applied Psychology International, 56*(3), 428–436.

Jones, C. P. (2000). Levels of racism: A theoretical framework and a gardener's tale. *American Journal of Public Health, 90*(8), 1212–1215.

Jones, E. E. (1978). Effects of race on psychotherapy process and outcome: An exploratory investigation. *Psychotherapy: Theory, Research and Practice, 15*, 226–236.

Jones, E. E. (1982). Psychotherapists' impressions of treatment outcome as a function of race. *Journal of Clinical Psychology, 38*(4), 722–731.

Jones, E. E., Farina, A., Hastorf, A. H., Markus, H., Miller, D. T., & Scott, R. (1984). *Social stigma: The psychology of marked relationships.* New York: Freeman.

Jones, K., & Poletti. A. (1985). The Italian transformation of the asylum. *International Journal of Mental Health, 13*, 210–215.

Jordan, B. K., Schlenger, W. E., Fairbank, J. A., & Caddell, J. M. (1996). Prevalence of psychiatric disorders among incarcerated women: Convicted women felons entering prison. *Archives of General Psychiatry, 53*, 513–519.

Jordan, C., Lewellen, A., & Vandiver, V. (1995). Psychoeducation for minority families: A social work perspective. *International Journal of Mental Health, 23*, 27–43.

Jordan, J. V., Kaplan, A. G., Miller, J. B., Stiver, I. B., & Surrey, J. L. (1991). *Women's growth in connection.* New York: Guilford.

Joshi, P., & Bogen, K. (2007). Nonstandard schedules and young children's behavioral outcomes among working low-income families. *Journal of Marriage and Family, 69*, 139–156.

Joyner, K., & Udry, J. R. (2000). You don't bring me anything but down: Adolescent romance and depression. *Journal of Health and Social Behavior, 41*, 369–391.

Judd, L. L., Akiskal, H. S., & Paulus, M. P. (1997). The role and clinical significance of subsyndromal depressive symptoms (SSD) in unipolar major depressive disorder. *Journal of Affective Disorders, 45*, 5–18.

Jung, C. G. (1924). *Psychological types.* New York: Random House.

Junginger, J., Claypoole, K., Laygo, R., & Crisanti, A. (2006). Effects of serious mental illness and substance abuse on criminal offenses. *Psychiatric Services, 57*(6), 879–882.

Kadushin, C. (1966). The friends and supporters of psychotherapy: On social circles in urban life. *American Sociological Review, 31*, 786–802.

Kagan, S. (1993). *Integrating services for children and families.* New Haven, CT: Yale University Press.

Kahn, A. J., & Kammerman, S. B. (1992). *Integrating services integration: An overview of initiatives, issues and possibilities.* New York: National Center for Children in Poverty, Columbia University School of Public Health.

Kahn, J. R., & Pearlin, L. I. (2006). Financial strain over the life course and health among older adults. *Journal of Health and Social Behavior, 47*, 17–31.

Kahn, R. L. (1981). *Work and health.* New York: Wiley.

Kahn, W. (1993). Caring for the caregivers: Patterns of organizational caregiving. *Administrative Science Quarterly, 38*, 539–563.

Kaiser Family Foundation. (2006). *Survey of Americans on HIV/AIDS.* Retrieved October 2008, from http://www.kff.org/kaiserpolls/pomr050806pkg.cfm.

Kalil, A., & Ziol-Guest, K. M. (2005). Single mothers' employment dynamics and adolescent well-being. *Child Development, 76*, 196–211.

Kalleberg, A. L., & Loscocco, K. A. (1983). Aging, values, and rewards: Explaining age differences in job satisfaction. *American Sociological Review, 48*, 78–90.

Kalmijn, M., & Monden, C. W. S. (2006). Are the negative effects of divorce on well-being dependent on marital quality? *Journal of Marriage and Family, 68*, 1197–1213.

Kaniasty, K., & Norris, F. (1995). In search of altruistic community: Patterns of social support mobilization following Hurricane Hugo. *American Journal of Community Psychology, 23*, 447–477.

Kaniasty, K., & Norris, F. (2008). Longitudinal linkages between perceived social support and post-traumatic stress symptoms: Sequential roles of social causation and social selection. *Journal of Traumatic Stress, 21*(3), 274–281.

Kanner, A. D., Coyne, J. C., Schaefer, C., & Lazarus, R. S. (1981). Comparison of two modes of stress measurement: Daily hassles and uplifts versus major life events. *Journal of Behavioral Medicine, 4*, 1–39.

Kapadia, F., Vlahov, D., Wu, Y., Cohen, M. H., Greenblatt, R. M., Howard, A. A., et al. (2008). Impact of drug abuse treatment modalities on adherence to ART/HAART among a cohort of HIV seropositive women. *American Journal of Drug and Alcohol Abuse, 34*(2), 161–170.

Kaplan, G. A., & McNeil, J. E. (1993). Socioeconomic factors and cardiovascular disease: A review of the literature. *Circulation*, 1973–1998.

Kaplan, H. (1996). Themes, lacunae, and directions in research in psychosocial stress. In H. B. Kaplan (Ed.), *Psychosocial stress: Perspectives on structure, theory, life-course, and methods* (pp. 369–403). New York: Academic Press,

Kaplan, H., & Bohr, R. H. (1976). Change in the mental health field? *Community Mental Health Journal, 12*, 244–251.

Kaplan, H., Sadock, B. J., & Grebb, J. A. (1994). *Kaplan and Sadock's synopsis of psychiatry: Behavioral sciences, clinical psychiatry*. Baltimore: Williams & Wilkins.

Karasek, R. (1979). Job demands, job decision latitude, and mental strain: Implications for job redesign. *Administrative Science Quarterly, 24*(2), 285–308.

Karasek, R., Gardell, B., & Windell, J. (1987). Work and nonwork correlates of illness and behavior in male and female Swedish white-collar workers. *Journal of Occupational Behavior, 8*, 87–207.

Karasek, R., & Theorell, T. (1990). *Healthy work: Stress, productivity and the reconstruction of working life*. New York: Basic Books.

Karasek, R., Theorell, T., Schwartz, J., Schnall, P., Pieper, C., & Michela, J. (1988). Job characteristics in relation to the prevalence of myocardial infarction in the U.S. HES and HANES. *American Journal of Public Health, 78*, 910–918.

Karayiorgou, M., & Gogos, J. A. (2006). Schizophrenia genetics: Uncovering positional candidate genes. *European Journal of Human Genetics, 14*, 512–519.

Kasarda, J. D. (1995). Industrial restructuring and the changing location of jobs. In R. Farley (Ed.), *State of the union: American in the 1990s* (pp. 215–267). New York: Russell Sage Foundation.

Kasl, S. V. (1989). An epidemiological perspective on the role of control in health. In S. L. Sauter, J. J. Hurrell, & C. L. Cooper (Eds.), *Job control and worker health* (pp. 161–189). New York: Wiley.

Kasl, S. V., & Cobb, S. (1979). Some mental health consequences of plant closing and job loss. In L. Ferman & J. Gordus (Eds.), *Mental health and the economy* (pp. 255–300). Kalamazoo, MI: Upjohn Institute for Employment Research.

Kaslow, N. J., Croft, S. S., & Hatcher, C. A. (1999). Depression and bipolar disorder in children and adolescents. In S. D. Netherton, D. Holmes, & C. E. Walker (Eds.), *Child and adolescent psychological disorders: A comprehensive textbook* (pp. 264–281). New York: Oxford University Press.

Katz, S. J., Kessler, R. C., Frank, R. G., Leaf, P., Lin, E., & Edlund, M. (1997). The use of outpatient mental health services in the United States and Ontario: The impact of mental morbidity and perceived need for care. *American Journal of Public Health, 87*, 1136–1143.

Kawachi, I. (2006). Injustice at work and health: Causation or correlation? Commentary on the paper by Ferrie et al. (Occupational and Environmental Medicine, July 2006). *Occupational and Environmental Medicine, 63*, 578–579.

Kawachi, I., & Berkman, L. F. (2001). Social ties and mental health. *Journal of Urban Health–Bulletin of the New York Academy of Medicine, 78*(3), 458–467.

Keilitz, I. (1987). Researching and reforming the insanity defense. *Rutgers Law Review, 39*, 289–322.

Kellam, S. G., Simon, M. B., & Ensminger, M. (1983). Antecedents in first grade of teenage substance use and psychological well-being: A ten-year community wide prospective study. In D. B. Ricks (Ed.), *Origins of psychopathology* (pp. 17–42). New York: Cambridge University Press.

Kellerman, S. E., Lehman, J. S., Lansky, A., Stevens, M. R., Hecht, F. M., Bindman, A. B., et al. (2002). HIV testing within at-risk populations in the United States and the reasons for seeking or avoiding HIV testing. *Journal of Acquired Immune Deficiency Syndromes, 31*(2), 202–210.

Kelly, G. A. (1955). *The psychology of personal constructs*. New York: Norton.

Kelsoe, J. R. (2004). Genomics and the human genome project: Implications for psychiatry. *International Review of Psychiatry, 16*, 294–300.

Kendell, R. E. (2002). Five criteria for an improved taxonomy of mental disorders. In J. E. Helzer & J. J. Hudziak (Eds.), *Defining psychopathology in the 21st century: DSM-V and beyond* (pp. 3–17). Washington, DC: American Psychiatric Press.

Kendall-Tackett, K. A., Williams, L. M., & Finkelhor, D. (1993). Impact of sexual abuse on children: A review and synthesis of recent and empirical studies. *Psychological Bulletin, 113*, 164–180.

Kendler, K. (1983). Overview: A current perspective on twin studies of schizophrenia. *American Journal of Psychiatry, 140*, 1413–25.

Kendler, K., & Gardner, C. O. (1998). Boundaries of major depression: An evaluation of DSM-IV criteria. *American Journal of Psychiatry, 155*, 172–177.

Kendler, K., Kessler, R., Heath, A., Neale, M., & Eaves, L. (1991). Coping: A genetic epidemiological investigation. *Psychological Medicine, 21*, 337–346.

Kendler, K., Lyons, M., & Tsuang, M. T. (1991). Introduction. In M. T. Tsuang, K. S. Kendler, & M. J. Lyons (Eds.), *Genetic issues in psychosocial epidemiology* (pp. 1–11). New Brunswick, NJ: Rutgers University Press.

Kendler, K., Neale, M., Kessler, R., Heath, A., & Eaves, L. (1992). A population-based twin study of major depression in women: The impact of varying definitions of illness. *Archives of General Psychiatry, 49*, 257–266.

Kendler, K., Neale, M., Kessler, R., Heath, A., & Eaves, L. (1993). A twin study of recent life events and difficulties. *Archives of General Psychiatry, 50*, 789–796.

Kendler, K., Neale, M., Prescott, C. A., & Kessler, R. (1996). Childhood parental loss and alcoholism in women: A causal analysis using a twin-family design. *Psychological Medicine, 26*, 79–95.

Kendler, K., Neale, M., Thornton, L. M., Aggen, S. H., Gilman, S. E., & Kessler, R. C. (2002). Cannabis use in the last year in a US national sample of twin and sibling pairs. *Psychological Medicine, 32*, 1–4.

Kendler, K. S. (2005). Psychiatric genetics: A methodologic critique. *American Journal of Psychiatry, 162*, 3–11.

Kendler, K. S. (2008). Explanatory models for psychiatric illness. *American Journal of Psychiatry, 165*, 695–702.

Kenig, S. (1992). *Who pays? Who cares? A case study in applied sociology, political economy and the community mental health centers movement*. Amityville, NY: Baywood.

Kennedy, C. (1989). Community integration and well-being: Toward the goals of community care. *Journal of Social Issues, 45*, 65–77.

Kennedy, J. L., Giuffra, L. A., Moises, H. W., Cavalli-Sforza, L. L., Pakstis, A. J., Kidd, J. R., et al. (1988). Evidence against linkage of schizophrenia to markers on chromosome 5 in a northern Swedish pedigree. *Nature, 336*, 167–170.

Kennedy, S., Nolen, S., Applewhite, J., & Waiter, E. (2007). Urban African American males' perceptions of condom use, gender and power, and HIV/STD prevention program. *Journal of the National Medical Association, 99*(12), 1395–1401.

Kennelly, I. (1999). That single-mother element: How White employers typify Black women. *Gender and Society, 13*, 168–192.

Kessler, R. C. (1979). Stress, social status, and psychological distress. *Journal of Health and Social Behavior, 20*, 259–272.

Kessler, R. C. (1982). A disaggregation of the relationship between socioeconomic status and psychological distress. *American Sociological Review, 47*, 752–764.

Kessler, R. C. (1993). *The National Comorbidity Study*. Paper presented at a meeting of the American Sociological Association, Miami Beach.

Kessler, R. C. (1994). The National Comorbidity Survey of the United States. *International Review of Psychiatry, 4*, 81–94.

Kessler, R. C. (2000). Gender differences in the prevalence and correlates of mood disorders in the general population. In M. Steiner, K. A. Yonkers, & E. Erikson (Eds.), *Mood disorders in women* (pp. 15–33). London: Martin Dunitz.

Kessler, R. C. (2002). The categorical versus dimensional assessment controversy in the sociology of mental illness. *Journal of Health and Social Behavior, 43*, 171–188.

Kessler, R. C. (2003). Epidemiology of women and depression. *Journal of Affective Disorders, 74*, 5–13.

Kessler, R. C., Adler, L., Barkley, R., Biederman, J., Conners, C. K., Demler, O., et al. (2006). The prevalence and correlates of adult ADHD in the United States: Results from the National Comorbidity Survey Replication. *American Journal of Psychiatry, 163*, 716–723.

Kessler, R. C., Andrews, G., Mroczek, D., Ustun, B., & Wittchen, H–U. (1998). The World Health Organization Composite International Diagnostic Interview Short Form (CIDI–SF). *International Journal of Methods in Psychiatric Research, 7*, 171–185.

Kessler, R. C., Angermeyer, M., Anthony, J. C., De Graaf, R., Demyttenaerem K., Gasquet, I., et al. (2007). Lifetime prevalence and age-of-onset distributions of mental disorders in the World Health Organization's World Mental Health Survey initiative. *World Psychiatry, 6*(3), 168–176.

Kessler, R. C., Berglund, P., Demler, O., Jin, R., Koretz, D., Merikangas, K. R., et al. (2003). The epidemiology of major depressive disorder: Results from the National Comorbidity Survey Replication. *Journal of the American Medical Association, 289*, 3095–3105.

Kessler, R. C., Berglund, P., Demler, O., Jin., R., & Walters, E. E. (2005). Lifetime prevalence and age-of-onset distributions of DSM-IV disorders in the National Comorbidity Survey Replication. *Archives of General Psychiatry, 62*, 593–602.

Kessler, R. C., Berglund, P. A., Walters, E. E., Leaf, P. J., Kouzis, A. C., Bruce, M. L, et al. (1995). *Estimation of the 12-month prevalence of serious mental illness* (SMI) (NCS Working Paper #8). Ann Arbor: University of Michigan, Institute for Social Research.

Kessler, R. C., Brandenburg, N., Lane, M., Roy-Byrne, P., Stang, P. D., Stein, D. J., et al. (2005). Rethinking the duration requirement for Generalized Anxiety Disorder: Evidence from the National Comorbidity Survey Replication. *Psychological Medicine, 35*, 1073–1082.

Kessler, R. C., Brown, R. L., & Broman, C. L. (1981). Sex differences in psychiatric help-seeking: Evidence from four large scale surveys. *Journal of Health and Social Behavior, 22*, 49–64.

Kessler, R. C., Chiu, W. T., Demler, O., Merikangas, K. R., & Walters, E. E. (2005). Prevalence, severity, and comorbidity of 12-month DSM-IV disorders in the National Comorbidity Survey Replication. *Archives of General Psychiatry, 62*, 617–627.

Kessler, R. C., & Cleary, P. D. (1980). Social class and psychological distress. *American Sociological Review, 45*, 463–478.

Kessler, R. C., Coccaro, E. F., Fava, M., Jaeger, S., Jin, R., & Walters, E. (2006). The prevalence and correlates of DSM-IV intermittent explosive disorder in the National Comorbidity Survey Replication. *Archives of General Psychiatry, 63*, 669–678.

Kessler, R. C., Demler, O., Frank, R. G., Olfson, M., Pincus, H. A., Walters, E. E., et al. (2005). Prevalence and treatment of mental disorders, 1990 to 2003. *New England Journal of Medicine, 352*, 2515–2523.

Kessler, R. C., Foster, C. L., Saunders, W. B., & Stang, P. E. (1995). Social consequences of psychiatric disorders, I: Educational attainment. *American Journal of Psychiatry, 152*, 1026–1032.

Kessler, R. C., Galea, S., Gruber, M. J., Sampson, N. A., Ursana, R. J., & Wessely, S. (2008). Trends in mental illness and suicidality after Hurricane Katrina. *Molecular Psychiatry, 13*, 374–384.

Kessler, R. C., House, J. S., Anspach, R., & Williams, D. R. (1995). Social psychology and health. In K. S. Cook, G. A. Fine, & J. S. House (Eds.), *Sociological perspectives on social psychology* (pp. 548–570). Boston: Allyn & Bacon.

Kessler, R. C., & Magee, W. (1994). Childhood family violence and adult recurrent depression. *Journal of Health and Social Behavior, 35, 13–27.*

Kessler, R. C., McGonagle, K.A., Schwartz, M., Glazer, D. G., & Nelson, C. B. (1993). Sex and depression in the National Comorbidity Survey I: Lifetime prevalence, chronicity, and recurrence. *Journal of Affective Disorders, 25*, 85–96.

Kessler, R. C., McGonagle, K., Zhao, S., Nelson, C., Hughes, M., Eshleman, S., et al. (1994). Lifetime and 12-month prevalence of DSM III–R psychiatric disorders among persons aged 15–54 in the United States: Results from the National Comorbidity Survey. *Archives of General Psychiatry, 51*, 8–19.

Kessler, R. C., & McLeod, J. D. (1984). Sex differences in vulnerability to undesirable life events. *American Sociological Review, 49*, 620–631.

Kessler, R. C., & McLeod, J. D. (1985). Social support and mental health in community samples. In S. Cohen & S. L. Syme (Eds.), *Social support and health* (pp. 219–240). Orlando, FL: Academic Press.

Kessler, R. C., McLeod, J. D., & Wethington, E. (1985). The costs of caring: A perspective on the relationship between sex and psychological distress. In I. G. Sarason & B. R. Sarason (Eds.), *Social support: Theory, research and application* (pp. 491–506). Dordrecht: Martinus Nijhoff.

Kessler, R. C., & McRae, J. A. (1982). The effect of wives' employment on the mental health of married men and women. *American Sociological Review, 47*, 216–227.

Kessler, R. C., & Merikangas, K. R. (2004). The National Comorbidity Survey Replication (NCS-R): Background and aims. *International Journal of Methods in Psychiatric Research, 13*(2), 60–68.

Kessler, R. C., Merikangas, K. R., Berglund, P., Eaton, W. E., Koretz, D. S., & Walters, E. E. (2003). Mild disorders should not be eliminated from the DSM-V. *Archives of General Psychiatry, 60*, 1117–1122.

Kessler, R. C., Mickelson, K. D., & Williams, D. R. (1999). The prevalence, distribution, and mental health correlates of perceived discrimination in the United States. *Journal of Health and Social Behavior, 40*, 208–230.

Kessler, R. C., & Neighbors, H. W. (1986). A new perspective on the relationships among race, social class, and psychological distress. *Journal of Health and Social Behavior, 27*, 107–115.

Kessler, R. C., & Price, R. H. (1993). Primary prevention of secondary disorders: A proposal and agenda. *American Journal of Community Psychology, 21*, 607–633.

Kessler, R. C., Turner, J. B., & House, J. S. (1989). Unemployment, reemployment and emotional functioning in a community sample. *American Sociological Review, 54*, 648–657.

Kessler, R. C., & Üstun, T. B. (2004). The World Mental Health (WMH) Survey Initiative version of the World Health Organization (WHO) Composite International Diagnostic Interview (CIDI). *International Journal of Methods in Psychiatric Research, 13*, 93–121.

Kessler, R. C., Walters, E. E., & Wittchen, H.-U. (2004). Epidemiology. In R. G. Heimberg, C. L. Turk, & D. S. Mennin (Eds.), *Generalized anxiety disorder: Advances in research and practice* (pp. 29–50). New York: Guilford.

Kessler, R. C., Wittchen, H.-U., Abelson, J. M., McGonagle, K. A., Schwarz, N., Kendler, K. S., et al. (1998). Methodological studies of the Composite International Diagnostic Interview (CIDI) in the US National Comorbidity Survey. *International Journal of Methods in Psychiatric Research, 7*, 33–55.

Kessler, R. C., Zhao, S., Blazer, D. G., & Swartz, M. (1997). Prevalence, correlates, and course of minor depression and major depression in the National Comorbidity Survey. *Journal of Affective Disorders, 45*, 19–30.

Keyes, C. (1998). Social well being. *Social Psychology Quarterly, 61*(2), 121–140.

Keyes, C. L. M. (2002). The mental health continuum: From languishing to flourishing in life. *Journal of Health and Social Behavior, 43*, 207–222.

Keyes, C. L. M. (2004). The nexus of cardiovascular disease and depression revisited: The complete mental health perspective and the moderating role of age and gender. *Aging and Mental Health, 8*, 266–274.

Keyes, C. L. M. (2005a). Mental illness and/or mental health? Investigating axioms of the complete state model of health. *Journal of Consulting and Clinical Psychology, 73*, 539–548.

Keyes, C. L. M. (2005b). Chronic physical disease and aging: Is mental health a potential protective factor? *Ageing International, 30*, 88–104.

Keyes, C. L. M. (2005c). The subjective well-being of America's youth: Toward a comprehensive assessment. *Adolescent and Family Health, 4*, 3–11.

Keyes, C. L. M. (2006). Subjective well-being in mental health and human development research worldwide: An introduction. *Social Indicators Research, 77*, 1–10.

Keyes, C. (2007). Promoting and protecting mental health as flourishing: A complementary strategy for improving national mental health. *American Psychologist, 62*(2), 95–108.

Keyes, C. L. M., & Grzywacz, J. G. (2005). Health as a complete state: The added value in work performance and healthcare costs. *Journal of Occupational and Environmental Medicine, 47*, 523–532.

Keyes, C. L. M., Shmotkin, D., & Ryff, C. D. (2002). Optimizing well-being: The empirical encounter of two traditions. *Journal of Personality and Social Psychology, 82*, 1007–1022.

Keyl, P., & Eaton, W. W. (1990). Risk factors for the onset of panic attacks and panic disorder. *American Journal of Epidemiology, 131*, 301–311.

Kibria, N., Barnett, C., Baruch, G. K., Marshall, N. L., & Pleck, J. H. (1990). Homemaking-role quality and the psychological well-being and distress of married women. *Sex Roles, 22*, 327–347.

Kiefer, C. W. (1992). Militarism and world health. *Social Science & Medicine, 34*(7), 719–724.

Kiesler, C. A., & Sibulkin, A. E. (1987). *Mental hospitalization: Myths and facts about a national crisis.* Newbury Park, CA: Sage.

Kiesler, D. J. (2001). *Beyond the disease model of mental disorders.* Greenwood, CT: Praeger.

Kilbourne, B. S., England, P., Farkas, G., Beron, K., & Weir, D. (1994). Returns to skill, compensating differentials, and gender bias: Effects of occupational characteristics on the wages of White women and men. *American Journal of Sociology, 100*, 689–719.

Kim, H. K., & McKenry, P. C. (2002). The relationship between marriage and psychological well-being: A longitudinal analysis. *Journal of Family Issues, 23*(8), 885–911.

Kinzie, J. D., Boehnlein, J. K., Leung, P. K., Moore, L. J., Riley, C., & Smith, D. (1990). The prevalence of posttraumatic stress disorder and its clinical significance among Southeast Asian refugees. *American Journal of Psychiatry, 147*, 913–917.

Kirby, D., & Miller, B. (2002). Interventions designed to promote parent-teen communication about sexuality. *New Directions for Child and Adolescent Development, 97*, 93–110.

Kirk, S. A., & Kutchins, H. (1992). *The selling of the DSM: The rhetoric of science in psychiatry.* New York: Aldine de Gruyter.

Kirk, S. A., & Kutchins, H. (1994, June 20). Is bad writing a mental disorder? *New York Times*, p. A17.

Kirk, S. A., & Therrien, M. E. (1975). Community mental health myths and the fate of former hospitalized patients. *Psychiatry, 38*, 209–217.

Kirsch, I., Deacon, B. J., Huedo-Medina, T. B., Scoboria, A., Moore, T. J., et al. (2008). Initial severity and antidepressant benefits: A meta-analysis of data submitted to the Food and Drug Administration. *PLoS Med, 5*(2), e45.

Kirschner, S. R., & Lachicotte, W. S. (2001). Managing managed care: Habitus, hysteresis and the end(s) of psychotherapy. *Culture and Medicine in Psychiatry, 25*, 441–456.

Kishiyama, M. M., Boyce, W. T., Jimenez, A. M., Perry, L. M., & Knight, R. T. (2009). Socioeconomic disparities affect prefrontal function in children. *Journal of Cognitive Neuroscience, 21*(6), 1106–1115.

Kittrie, N. N. (1971). *The right to be different.* Baltimore: Johns Hopkins University Press.

Kivimäki, M., Gunnell, D., Lawlor, D. A., Davey Smith, G., Pentti, J., Virtanen, M., et al. (2007). Social inequalities in antidepressant treatment and mortality: A longitudinal register study. *Psychological Medicine, 37*(3), 373–382.

Klein, D., & Wender, P. (1993). *Understanding depression: A complete guide to its diagnosis and treatment.* New York: Oxford University Press.

Klein, D. F. (1978). A proposed definition of mental illness. In R. L. Spitzer & D. F. Klein (Eds.), *Critical issues in psychiatric diagnosis* (pp. 41–71). New York: Raven Press.

Kleinman, A. (1980). *Patients and healers in the context of culture.* Berkeley: University of California Press.

Kleinman, A. (1988). *Rethinking psychiatry: From cultural category to personal experience.* New York: The Free Press.

Kleinman, A., & Good, B. (Eds.) 1985. *Culture and depression.* Berkeley: University of California Press.

Klinkenberg, W. D., & Sacks, S. (2004). Mental disorders and drug abuse in persons living with HIV/AIDS. *AIDS Care, 16*(Suppl. 1), 22–42.

Kneebone, P., Rogers, J., & Hafner, R. J. (1995). Characteristics of police referrals to a psychiatric emergency unit in Australia. *Psychiatric Services, 46,* 620–622.

Knitzer, J. (1982). *Unclaimed children.* Washington, DC: Children's Defense Fund.

Knowlton, A. R., Hoover, D. R., Chung, S., Celentano, D. D., Vlahov, D., & Latkin, C. A. (2001). Access to medical care and service utilization among injection drug users with HIV/AIDS. *Drug and Alcohol Dependence, 64*(1), 55–62.

Knudsen, H. K., Roman, P. M., Johnson, J. A., & Ducharme, L. J. (2005). A changed America? The effects of September 11th on depressive symptoms and alcohol consumption source. *Journal of Health and Social Behavior, 46*(3), 260–273.

Kohen, D. E., Leventhal, T., Dahinten, V. S., & McIntosh, C. N. (2008). Neighborhood disadvantage: Pathways of effects for young children. *Child Development, 79,* 156–169.

Kohlberg, L. (1969). Stage and sequence: The cognitive-development approach to socialization. In D. A. Goslin (Ed.), *Handbook of socialization theory and research* (pp. 347–480). Chicago: Rand McNally.

Kohn, M. (1977). *Class and conformity* (2nd ed.) Chicago: University of Chicago Press.

Kohn, M. L. (1968). Social class and schizophrenia: A critical review. *Journal of Psychiatric Research, 6* (Suppl.), 155–173.

Kohn, M. L., Naoi, A., Schoenbach, C., Schooler, C., & Slomczynski, K. M. (1990). Position in the class structure and psychological functioning in the United States, Japan, and Poland. *American Journal of Sociology, 95,* 964–1008.

Kohn, M. L., & Schooler, C. (1982). Job conditions and personality: A longitudinal assessment of their reciprocal effects. *American Journal of Sociology, 87,* 1257–1286.

Kohn, M. L., & Schooler, C. (Eds.). (1983). *Work and personality: An inquiry into the impact of social stratification.* Norwood, NJ: Ablex.

Kohn, M. L., & Slomczynski, K. M. (1990). *Social structure and self-direction: A comparative analysis of the United States and Poland.* Cambridge: Blackwell.

Koo, D. J., Begier, E. M., Henn, M. H., Sepkowitz, K. A., & Kellerman, S. E. (2006). HIV counseling and testing: Less targeting, more testing. *American Journal of Public Health, 96,* 962–964.

Koopmans, G. T., & Lamers, L. M. (2007). Gender and health care utilization: The role of mental distress and help-seeking propensity. *Social Science and Medicine, 64*(6), 1216–1230.

Koss, J. (1987). Expectations and outcomes for patients given mental health care or Spiritist healing in Puerto Rico. *American Journal of Psychiatry, 144,* 56–61.

Kotchick, B., Shaffer, A., Forehand, R., & Miller, K. S. (2001). Adolescent sexual risk behavior: A multi-system perspective. *Clinical Psychology Review, 21,* 493–519.

Kovacs, M. (1992). *Children's Depression Inventory (CDI) manual.* North Tonawanda, NY: Multi-Health Systems.

Kowaleski-Jones, L. (2000). Staying out of trouble: Community resources and problem behavior among high-risk adolescents. *Journal of Marriage and Family, 62,* 449–464.

Krakow, D. S., Galanter, M., Dermatis, H., & Westreich, L. M. (1998). HIV risk factors in dually diagnosed patients. *American Journal of Addiction, 7,* 74–80.

Kramer, P. D. (2005). *Against depression.* New York: Viking.

Krause, N., & Markides, K. A. (1985). Employment and well-being in Mexican American women. *Journal of Health and Social Behavior, 26,* 15–26.

Krieger, N. (1987). Shades of difference: Theoretical underpinnings of the medical controversy on Black/White differences in the United States, 1830–1870. *International Journal of Health Services, 17,* 259–278.

Krieger, N. (1990). Racial and gender discrimination: Risk factors for high blood pressure? *Social Science and Medicine, 30,* 1273–1281.

Krieger, N. (1999). Embodying inequality: A review of concepts, measures, and methods for studying health consequences of discrimination. *International Journal of Health Services, 29*(2), 295–352.

Krieger, N., Barbeau, E. M., & Soobader, M. J. (2005). Class matters: U.S. versus U.K. measures of occupational disparities in access to health services and health status in the 2000 U.S. National Health Interview Survey. *International Journal of Health Services, 35*(2), 213–236.

Krieger, N., Rowland, D. L., Herman, A. A., Avery, B., & Phillips, M. T. (1993). Racism, sexism, and social class: Implications for studies of health, disease, and well-being. *American Journal of Preventive Medicine, 9*, 82–122.

Krieger, N., Williams, D. R., & Moss, N. E. (1997). Measuring social class in U.S. public health research: Concepts, methodologies, and guidelines. *Annual Review of Public Health, 18*, 341–378.

Kroeger, R. A., & Williams, K. (2007). *Interracial relationships and psychological well-being among young adults.* Paper presented at the annual meeting of the American Sociological Association, New York.

Kropp, P. R., Cox, D. N., Roesch, R., & Eaves, D. (1989). The perceptions of correctional officers toward mentally disordered offenders. *International Journal of Law and Psychiatry, 12*, 181–188.

Kroska, A., & Harkness, S. K. (2006). Stigma sentiments and self-meanings: Exploring the modified labeling theory of mental illness. *Social Psychology Quarterly, 69*, 325–348.

Krueger, R. F., Markon, K. E., & Patrick, C. J. (2005). Externalizing psychopathology in adulthood: A dimensional-spectrum conceptualization and its implications for DSM-V. *Journal of Abnormal Psychology, 114*, 537–550.

Krueger, R. F., Watson, D., & Barlow, D. H. (2005). Introduction to the special section: Toward a dimensionally based taxonomy of psychopathology. *Journal of Abnormal Psychology, 114*, 491–493.

Kuh, D., & Ben-Shlomo, Y. (1997). *A life course approach to chronic disease epidemiology.* Oxford: Oxford University Press.

Kuo, E. S., Vander Stoep, A., & Stewart, D. G. (2005). Using the short mood and feelings questionnaire to detect depression in detained adolescents. *Assessment, 12*, 374–383.

Kuo, W. H. (1984). Prevalence of depression among Asian-Americans. *Journal of Nervous and Mental Disorders, 172*, 449–457.

Kurdek, L. A. (1991). The relations between reported well-being and divorce history, availability of a proximate adult, and gender. *Journal of Marriage and the Family, 53*, 71–78.

Kuruvilla, A., & Jacob, K. S. (2007). Poverty, social stress & mental health. *Indian Journal of Medical Research, 126*(4), 273–278.

Kurzban, R., & Leary, M. R. (2001). Evolutionary origins of stigmatization: The functions of social exclusion. *Psychological Bulletin, 127*, 187–208.

Kusserow, R. (1991). *Services integration: A twenty-year retrospective.* Washington, DC: Department of Health and Human Services, Office of the Inspector General.

Kuyken, W., & Orley. J. (1994). Quality of Life Assessment: Cross-cultural issues – 1. *International Journal of Mental Health, 23*(2).

Laberge, D., & Morin, D. (1995). The overuse of criminal justice dispositions: Failure of diversionary policies in the management of mental health problems. *International Journal of Law and Psychiatry, 18*, 389–414.

Ladd, G. W. (2006). Peer rejection, aggressive or withdrawn behavior, and psychological maladjustment from ages 5 to 12: An examination of four predictive models. *Child Development, 77*, 822–846.

Ladd, G. W., & Troop-Gordon, W. (2003). The role of chronic peer adversity in the development of children's psychological adjustment problems. *Child Development, 74*, 1344–1367.

Ladner, J. (1972). *Tomorrow's tomorrow.* Garden City, NY: Anchor Books.

La Fond, J. Q., & Durham, M. L. (1992). *Back to the asylum: The future of mental health law and policy in the United States.* New York: Oxford University Press.

Lagos, J. M., Perlmutter, K., & Suefinger, H. (1977). Fear of the mentally ill: Empirical support for the common man's response. *American Journal of Psychiatry, 134*, 1134–1137.

Laing, R. D. (1959). *The divided self.* London: Tavistock.

Lakey, B., & Cassady, P. B. (1990). Cognitive processes in perceived social support. *Journal of Personality & Social Psychology, 59,* 337–348.

Lakey, B., & Dickinson, L. G. (1994). Antecedents of perceived support: Is perceived family environment generalized to new social relationships? *Cognitive Therapy & Research, 18,* 39–53.

Lakey, B., & Scoboria, A. (2005). The relative contribution of trait and social influences to the links among perceived social support, affect, and self-esteem. *Journal of Personality, 73*(2), 361–388.

Lamb, H. R. (1982). *Treating the long-term mentally ill.* San Francisco: Jossey-Bass.

Lamb, H. R., & Bachrach, L. L. (2001). Some perspectives on deinstitutionalization. *Psychiatric Services, 52,* 1039–1045.

Lamb, H. R., & Grant, R. W. (1982). The mentally ill in an urban county jail. *Archives of General Psychiatry, 39,* 17–22.

Lamb, H. R., Shaner, R., Elliot, D. M., De Cuir, W. J., & Foltz, J. T. (1995). Outcome for psychiatric emergency patients seen by an outreach police–mental health team. *Psychiatric Services, 46,* 1267–1271.

Lamb, H. R., & Weinberger, L. E. (1998). Persons with severe mental illness in jails and prisons: A review. *Psychiatric Services, 49,* 483–492.

Lamb, H. R., & Weinberger, L. E. (2005). The shift of psychiatric inpatient care from hospitals to jails and prisons. *Journal of the American Academy of Psychiatry and Law, 33,* 529–534.

Lamb, H. R., Weinberger, L. E., & DeCuir, W. J., Jr. (2002). The police and mental health. *Psychiatric Services, 53,* 1266–1271.

Lamb, K. A., Lee, G. R., & DeMaris, A. (2003). Union formation and depression: Selection and relationship effects. *Journal of Marriage and Family, 65,* 953–962.

Lamberti, S. J., Weisman, R., & Faden, D. I. (2004). Forensic assertive community treatment: Preventing incarceration of adults with severe mental illness. *Psychiatric Services, 55*(11), 1285–1293.

Lambourn, S., Mounts, N., & Steinberg, L. (1991). Patterns of competence and adjustment among adolescents from authoritative, authoritarian, indulgent, and neglectful homes. *Child Development, 62,* 1049–1065.

Lane, C. (2007). *Shyness: How normal behavior became a sickness.* New Haven, CT: Yale University Press.

Lang, C. L. (1981). Good cases–bad cases: Client selection and professional prerogative in a community mental health center. *Urban Life, 10,* 289–309.

Langner, T. S. (1962). A twenty-two item screening score of psychiatric symptoms indicating impairment. *Journal of Health and Human Behavior, 3,* 269–276.

Langner, T. S., & Michael, S. T. (1963). *Life stress and mental health.* New York: The Free Press.

Lantz, P. M., House, J. S., Mero, R. P., & Williams, D. R. (2005). Stress, live events, and socioeconomic disparities in health: Results from the Americans' Changing Lives Study. *Journal of Health and Social Behavior, 46,* 274–288.

Laor, N., Wolmer, L., Alon, M., Siev, J., Samuel, E., & Toren, P. (2006). Risk and protective factors mediating psychological symptoms and ideological commitment of adolescents facing continuous terrorism. *Journal of Nervous and Mental Disease, 194*(4), 279–286.

LaRoche, M. J., & Turner, C. (2002). At the crossroads: Managed mental health care, the Ethics Code, and ethnic minorities. *Cultural Diversity and Ethnic Minority Psychology,* 187–198.

Larson, D. B., Hohmann, A. A., Kessler, L. G., Meador, K. G., Boyd, J. H., & McSherry, E. (1988). The couch and the cloth: The need for linkage. *Hospital and Community Psychiatry, 39,* 1064–1069.

Latimer, E. (1999). Economic impacts of assertive community treatment: A review of the literature. *Canadian Journal of Psychiatry, 44*(5), 443–455.

Lating, J. M., Sherman, M. F., Everly, G. S., Lowry, J. L., & Peragine, T. F. (2004a). PTSD reactions and functioning of American Airlines Flight attendants in the wake of September 11. *Journal of Nervous and Mental Disease, 192*(6), 435–441.

Lating, J. M., Sherman, M. F., Everly, G. S., Lowry, J. L., & Peragine, T. F. (2004b). PTSD reactions and coping responses of East Coast and West Coast American Airlines flight attendants after September 11: A possible psychological contagion effect? *Journal of Nervous and Mental Disease, 192*(12), 876–879.

Latkin, C., & Curry, A. D. (2003). Stressful neighborhoods and depression: A prospective study of the impact of neighborhood disorder. *Journal of Health and Social Behavior, 44*, 34–44.

Lau, A., & Zane, N. (2000). Examining the effects of ethnic-specific services: An analysis of cost-utilization and treatment outcome for Asian American clients. *Journal of Community Psychology, 28*(1), 63–77.

Lauby, J. L., Bond, L., Eroglu, D., & Batson, H. (2006). Decisional balance, perceived risk and HIV testing practices. *AIDS and Behavior, 10*(1), 83–92.

Laufer, R. S., Gallops, M. S., & Frey-Wouters, E. (1984). War stress and trauma: The Vietnam veteran experience. *Journal of Health and Social Behavior, 25*, 65–85.

Laugharne, J., Janca, A., & Widiger, T. (2002). Posttraumatic stress disorder and terrorism: 5 years after 9/11. *Current Opinion in Psychiatry, 20*(1), 36–41.

Laurin-Frenette, N. (1976). *Functionalist theories of social class: Sociology and bourgeois ideology.* Paris: Editions Anthropos.

LaVeist, T. (1996). Why we should continue to study race . . . but do a better job: An essay on race, racism, and health. *Ethnicity and Disease, 6*, 21–29.

Lawton, M. P., Rajagopal, D., Brody, E., & Kleban, M. H. (1992). The dynamics of caregiving for a demented elder among Black and White families. *Journal of Gerontology: Social Sciences, 47*(4), S156–S164.

Lazarus, R. S., & Folkman, S. (1984). *Stress, appraisal, and coping.* New York: Springer.

Leaf, P. J., & Bruce, M. L. (1987). Gender differences in the use of mental health-related services: A re-examination. *Journal of Health and Social Behavior, 28*, 171–183.

Leaf, P. J., Livingston, M. M., Tischler, G. L., Weissmann, M. M., Holzer, C. E., & Myers, J. K. (1985). Contact with health professionals for the treatment of psychiatric and emotional problems. *Medical Care, 23*, 1322–1337.

Leavy, R. L. (1983). Social support and psychological disorder: A review. *Journal of Consulting & Clinical Psychology, 54*, 438–446.

Lebow, J, L., & Gurman, A. S. (1995). Research assessing couple and family therapy. *Annual Review of Psychology, 46*, 27–57.

LectLaw n.d. Lectric Law Library. (n. d.). *Habeas corpus.* Retrieved October 3, 2008, from http://www.lectlaw.com/def/h001.htm.

Lee, A., Isaac, M., & Janca, A. (2002). Post-traumatic stress disorder and terrorism. *Current Opinion in Psychiatry, 15*(6), 633–637.

Lee, G. R., & DeMaris, A. (2007). Widowhood, gender, and depression: A longitudinal analysis. *Research on Aging, 29*(1), 56–72.

Lee, S.-Y. D., Arozullah, A. M., & Cho,Y. I. (2004). Health literacy, social support, and health: A research agenda. *Social Science and Medicine, 58*(7), 1309–1321.

Leete, E. (1989). How I perceive and manage my illness. *Schizophrenia Bulletin, 8*, 605–609.

Leff, H., Wieman, D., McFarland, B., Morrissey, J., Rothbard, A., Shern, D., et al. (2005). Assessment of Medicaid managed behavioral health care for persons with serious mental illness. *Psychiatric Services, 56*, 1245–1253.

Leff, J. (1988). *Psychiatry around the globe: A transcultural view* (2nd ed.). London: Gaskell.

Leff, J. (2005). *Advanced family work for schizophrenia: An evidence-based approach.* London: Gaskell.

Leff, J., &Vaughn, C. (1985). *Expressed emotion in families: Its significance for mental illness.* New York: Guilford.

Lefley, H. P. (1984). Delivering mental health services across cultures. In Pederson, P. B., N. Sartorius, & A. J. Marsell (Eds.) (1984). *Mental Health Services: The Cross-Cultural Context.* Beverly Hills, CA: Sage, 135–71.

Lefley, H. P. (1990). Culture and chronic mental illness. *Hospital and Community Psychiatry, 41*, 277–286.

Lefley, H. P. (1994). Mental health treatment and service delivery in cross-cultural perspective. In L. L Adler & U. Gielen (Eds.), *Cross-cultural topics in psychology* (pp. 179–200). New York: Praeger.

Lefley, H. P. (1996). *Family caregiving in mental illness.* Thousand Oaks, CA: Sage.

Lefley, H. P. (2004). Intercultural similarities and differences in family caregiving and family interventions in schizophrenia. *Psychiatric Times, 21*(13), 70.

Lefley, H. P., & Bestman, E. W. (1991). Public-academic linkages for culturally-sensitive community mental health. *Community Mental Health Journal, 27*, 473–488.

Lefley, H. P., & Johnson, D. L. (Eds.). (2002). *Family interventions in mental illness: International perspectives*. Westport, CT: Praeger.

Lefley, H. P., Sandoval, M., & Charles, C. (1997). Traditional healing systems in a multi-cultural setting. In S. Okpaku (Ed.), *Clinical methods in transcultural psychiatry* (pp. 88–109). Washington, DC: American Psychiatric Press.

Lehman, A., Postrado, L., Roth, D., McNary, S., & Goldman, H. (1994). An evaluation of continuity of care, case management, and client outcomes in the Robert Wood Johnson Program on chronic mental illness. *Milbank Quarterly, 72*(1), 105–122.

Leidner, R. (1993). *Fast food, fast talk: Service work and the routinization of everyday life*. Berkeley: University of California Press.

Leigh, W., & Lindquist, M. (1999). *Women of color health data book*. Washington, DC: Office on Women's Health, National Institutes of Health, U.S. Department of Health and Human Services.

Lemert, E. M. (1951). *Social pathology*. New York: McGraw-Hill.

Lemstra, M., Neudorf, C., D'Arcy, C., Kunst, A., Warren, L. M., & Bennett, N. R. (2008). A systematic review of depressed mood and anxiety by SES in youth aged 10–15 years. *Canadian Journal of Public Health, 99*(2), 125–129.

Lennon, M. C. (1987). Sex difference in distress: The impact of gender and work roles. *Journal of Health and Social Behavior, 28*, 290–305.

Lennon, M. C. (1994). Women, work, and well-being: The importance of work conditions. *Journal of Health and Social Behavior, 35*, 235–247.

Lennon, M. C. (1995). Work conditions as explanations for the relation between status, gender, and psychological disorders. *Epidemiologic Reviews, 17*, 120–127.

Lennon, M. C. (1998). Domestic arrangements and depression: An examination of household labor. In B. P. Dohrenwend (Ed.), *Adversity, stress, and psychopathology* (pp. 409–421). New York: Oxford University Press.

Lennon, M. C., & Rosenfield, S. (1992). Women and mental health: The interaction of work and family conditions. *J. Health and Social Behavior, 33*, 316–327.

Lennon, M. C., & Rosenfield, S. (1994). Relative fairness and the division of family work: The importance of options. *American Journal of Sociology, 100*, 506–531.

Lenzenweger, M. F., Lane, M. C., Loranger, A. W., & Kessler, R. C. (2007). DSM-IV personality disorders in the National Comorbidity Survey Replication. *Biological Psychiatry, 62*, 553–564.

Lerman, R. (2002). *How do marriage, cohabitation, and single parenthood affect the material hardships of families with children?* Washington, DC: Urban Institute. Retrieved June 30, 2006, from http://www.urban.org/UploadedPDF/410539_SippPaper.pdf.

Leserman, J. (2008). Role of depression, stress, and trauma in HIV disease progression. *Psychosomatic Medicine, 70*(5), 539–545.

Leserman, J., Barroso, J., Pence, B. W., Salahuddin, N., & Harmon, J. L. (2008). Trauma, stressful life events and depression predict HIV-related fatigue. *AIDS Care, 20*(10), 1–8.

Leserman, J., Pence, B. W., Whetten, K., Mugavero, M. J., Thielman, N. M., Swartz, M. S., et al. (2007). Relation of lifetime trauma and depressive symptoms to mortality in HIV. *American Journal of Psychiatry, 164*(11), 1707–1713.

Leu, J., Mesquita, B., Ellsworth, P. C., Zhi Yong, Z., Huijian, Y., Buchtel, E., et al. (2008). *Dialectical emotions among East Asians and European Americans: Co-occurring pleasantness and unpleasantness and readiness emotions*. Unpublished manuscript.

Levav, I., Novikov, I., Grinshpoon, A., Rosenblum, J., & Ponizovsky, A. (2006). Health services utilization in Jerusalem under terrorism. *American Journal of Psychiatry, 163*(8), 1355–1361.

Leventhal, T., & Brooks-Gunn, J. (2000). The neighborhoods they live in: The effects of neighborhood residence on child and adolescent outcomes. *Psychological Bulletin, 126*, 309–337.

Levine, M. (1981). *The history and politics of community mental health*. New York: Oxford University Press.

Levinson, D. F. (2006). The genetics of depression: A review. *Biological Psychiatry, 60*, 84–92.

Lewinsohn, P. M., & Essau, C. A. (2002). Depression in adolescents. In I. Gotlib & C. L. Hammen (Eds.), *Handbook of depression* (pp. 541–559). New York: Guilford.

Lewinsohn, P. M., Hops, H., Roberts, R. E., Seeley, J. R., & Andrews, J. A. (1993). Adolescent psychopathology: I. Prevalence and incidence of depression and other DSM-III-R disorders in high school students. *Journal of Abnormal Psychology, 102*, 133–144.

Lewis, D. A., & Levitt, P. (2002). Schizophrenia as a disorder of neurodevelopment. *Annual Review of Neuroscience, 25*, 409–432.

Lewis, D. A., & Lieberman, J. A. (2000). Catching up on schizophrenia: Natural history and neurobiology. *Neuron, 28*, 325–334.

Lewis, S. K., Ross, C. E., & Mirowsky, J. (1999). Establishing a sense of personal control in the transition to adulthood. *Social Forces, 77*, 1573–1599.

Lewis, S. (1990). Computerized tomography in schizophrenia 15 years on. *British Journal of Psychiatry, 157*, 16–24.

Lewontin, R. C. (1972). The apportionment of human diversity. In T. Dobzhansky, M. K. Hecht, & W. C. Steere (Eds.), *Evolutionary biology* (Vol. 6, pp. 381–386). New York: Appleton-Century-Crofts.

Lewontin, R. C., Rose, S., & Kamin, L. (1984). *Not in our genes: Biology, ideology and human nature.* New York: Pantheon.

Liberatos, P., Link, B. G., & Kelsey, J. L. (1988). The measurement of social class in epidemiology. *Epidemiologic Reviews, 10*, 87–122.

Lichter, D., & Jayakody R. (2002). Welfare reform: How do we measure success? *Annual Review of Sociology, 28*, 117–141.

Lichter, D. T., Qian, Z., & Mellott, L. M. (2006). Marriage or dissolution? Union transitions among poor cohabiting women. *Demography, 43*(2), 233–250.

Lickey, M. E., & Gordon, B. (1991). *Medicine and mental illness: The use of drugs in psychiatry.* New York: Freeman.

Liddell, H. S. (1950). Some specific factors that modify tolerance for environmental stress. In H. G. Wolff, S. Wolf, & C. Hare (Eds.), *Life stress and bodily disease* (pp. 155–171). Baltimore: Williams & Wilkins.

Liddicoat, R. V., Horton, N. J., Urban, R., Maier, E., Christiansen, D., & Samet, J. H. (2004). Assessing missed opportunities for HIV testing in medical settings. *Journal of General Internal Medicine, 19*(4), 349–356.

Lidz, C. W., Mulvey E. P., & Gardner, W. P. (1993). The accuracy of predictions of violence to others. *Journal of the American Medical Association, 269*, 1007–1111.

Lidz, C. W., Mulvey, E. P., Gardner, W. P., & Shaw, E. C. (1996). Conditional clinical predictions of violence: The condition of alcohol use. *Law and Human Behavior, 20*, 35–48.

Lidz, T. (1975). *The origin and treatment of schizophrenic disorders.* London: Hutchinson.

Lieberman, J. (2006). Neurobiology and the natural history of schizophrenia. *Journal of Clinical Psychiatry, 67*, 14.

Lieberman, J., Brown, A., & Gorman, J. (1994). *Schizophrenia.* Washington, DC: American Psychiatric Press.

Lieberman, J., Chakos, M., Wu, H., Alvir, J., Hoffman, E., Robinson, D., et al. (2001). Longitudinal study of brain morphology in first episode schizophrenia. *Biological Psychiatry, 49*, 487–499.

Lieberman, J. A., &. Rush. A. J. (1996). Redefining the role of psychiatry in medicine. *American Journal of Psychiatry, 153*, 1388–1397.

Lieberson, S. (1985). *Making it count: The improvement of social research and theory.* Berkeley: University of California Press.

Light, D. (1997). The rhetorics and reality of community health care: The limits of countervailing powers to meet the needs of the twenty-first century. *Journal of Health Politics, Policy and Law, 22*, 106–145.

Light, D. W. (2004). Ironies of success: A new history of the American health care "system." *Journal of Health and Social Behavior, 45*, 1–24.

Lin, K.-M. (1996). Cultural influences on the diagnosis of psychotic and organic disorders. In J. E. Mezzich, A. Kleinman, H. Fabrega, & D. L. Parron (Eds.), *Culture and psychiatric diagnosis: A DSM-IV perspective* (pp. 49–62). Washington, DC: American Psychiatric Press.

Lin, K.-M., & Kleinman. A. (1988). Psychopathology and clinical course of schizophrenia: A cross-cultural perspective. *Schizophrenia Bulletin, 14*, 555–567.

Lin, N., Ye, X., & Ensel, W. M. (1999). Social support and depressed mood: A structural analysis. *Journal of Health and Social Behavior, 40*, 344–359.

Linas, B. P., Zheng, H., Losina, E., Walensky, R. P., & Freedberg, K. A. (2006). Assessing the impact of federal HIV prevention spending on HIV testing and awareness. *American Journal of Public Health, 96*, 1038–1043.

Lincoln, K. D., Chatters, L. M., & Taylor, R. J. (2003). Psychological distress among Black and White Americans: Differential effects of social support, negative interactions and personal control. *Journal of Health and Social Behavior, 44*, 390–407.

Lind, J. (1914). The color complex in the Negro. *Psychoanalytic Review, 1*, 404–414.

Lindstrom, D. P., & Munoz-Franco, E. (2006). Migration and maternal health services utilization in rural Guatemala. *Social Science and Medicine, 63*(3), 706–721.

Link, B. G. (1982). Mental patient status, work and income: An examination of the effects of a psychiatric label. *American Sociological Review, 47*, 202–215.

Link, B. G. (1987). Understanding labeling effects in the area of mental disorders: An assessment of the effects of expectations of rejection. *American Sociological Review, 52*, 96–112.

Link, B. G., Andrews, H., & Cullen, F. T. (1992). The violent and illegal behavior of mental patients reconsidered. *American Sociological Review, 57*, 275–292.

Link, B., Castille, D., & Stuber, J. (2008). Stigma and coercion in the context of outpatient treatment for people with mental illnesses. *Social Science & Medicine, 67*, 409–419.

Link, B. G., Cullen, F. T., Frank, J., & Wozniak, J. F. (1987). The social rejection of ex-mental patients: Understanding why labels matter. *American Journal of Sociology, 92*, 1461–1500.

Link, B. G., Cullen, F. T., Struening, E., Shrout, P., & Dohrenwend, B. P. (1989). A modified labeling theory approach in the area of the mental disorders: An empirical assessment. *American Sociological Review, 54*, 400–423.

Link, B. G., & Dohrenwend B. P. (1980). Formulation of hypotheses about the true relevance of demoralization in the United States. In B. P. Dohrenwend et al. (Eds.), *Mental illness in the United States* (pp. 114–132). New York: Praeger.

Link, B. G., Dohrenwend, B. P., & Skodol, A. E. (1986). Socio-economic status and schizophrenia: Noisome occupational characteristics as a risk factor. *American Sociological Review, 51*, 242–258.

Link, B. G., Lennon, M., & Dohrenwend, B. P. (1993). Socioeconomic status and depression: The role of occupations involving direction, control, and planning. *American Journal of Sociology, 98*, 1351–1387.

Link, B. G., & Phelan, J. C. (1995). Social conditions as fundamental causes of disease [Extra Issue]. *Journal of Health and Social Behavior, 35*, 80–94.

Link, B. G., & Phelan, J. C. (2000). Evaluating the fundamental cause explanation for social disparities in health. In C. E. Bird, P. Conrad, & A. M. Fremont (Eds.), *Handbook of medical sociology* (pp. 33–46). Upper Saddle River, NJ: Prentice-Hall.

Link, B. G., & Phelan, J. C. (2001). Conceptualizing stigma. *Annual Review of Sociology, 27*, 363–385.

Link, B. G., Phelan, J., Bresnahan, M., Stueve, A., & Pescosolido, B. A. (1999). Public conceptions of mental illness: Labels, causes, dangerousness, and social distance. *American Journal of Public Health, 89*, 1328–1333.

Link, B. G., Struening, E. L., Neese-Todd, S., Asmussen, S. & Phelan, J. C. (2001). Stigma as a barrier to recovery: The consequences of stigma for the self-esteem of people with mental illnesses. *Psychiatric Services, 52*, 1621–1626.

Link, B. G., Struening, E. L., Rahav, M., Phelan, J. C., & Nuttbrock, L. (1997). On stigma and its consequences: Evidence from a longitudinal study of men with dual diagnoses of mental illness and substance abuse. *Journal of Health & Social Behavior, 38*, 177–190.

Link, B. G., & Stueve, A. (1994). Psychotic symptoms and the violent/illegal behavior of mental patients compared to community controls. In J. Monahan & H. J. Steadman (Eds.), *Violence and mental disorder* (pp. 137–160). Chicago: University of Chicago Press.

Link, B. G., & Stueve, A. (1995). Evidence bearing on mental illness as a possible cause of violent behavior. *Epidemiological Review, 17*, 172–180.

Link, B. G., Stueve, A., & Phelan, J. (1998). Psychotic symptoms and violent behaviors: Probing the components of "threat/control-overrride" symptoms. *Social Psychiatry and Psychiatric Epidemiology, 33*, S55–S60.

Link, B. G., Yang, L., Phelan, J. C., & Collins, P. C. (2004). Measuring mental illness stigma. *Schizophrenia Bulletin, 30*, 11–42.

Lion, J. R., Snyder, W., & Merrill, G. L. (1981). Under reporting of assaults on staff in a state hospital. *Hospital and Community Psychiatry, 32*, 497–498.

Lipscomb, H. J., Loomis, D., McDonald, M. A., Argue, R. A., & Wing, S. (2006). A conceptual model of work and health disparities in the United States. *International Journal of Health Services, 36*(1), 25–50.

Liska, A. E. (1997). Modeling the relationships between macro forms of social control. *Annual Review of Sociology, 23*, 39–61.

Liu, H., & Umberson, D. J. (2008). 'The times they are a changin': Marital status and health differentials from 1972 to 2003. *Journal of Health and Social Behavior, 49*, 239–253.

Liverant, G. I., Hofmann, S. G., & Litz, B. T. (2004). Coping and anxiety in college students after the September 11(th) terrorist attacks. *Anxiety, Stress and Coping, 17*(2), 127–139.

Locke, B., Kramer, M., & Pasamanick, B. (1960). Immigration and insanity. *Public Health Reports, 75*(4), 301–306.

Loeb, S., Fuller, B., Kagan, S. L., & Carrol, B. (2004). Child care in poor communities: Early learning effects of type, quality, and stability. *Child Development, 75*, 47–65.

Loeber, R., Burke, J. D., Lahey, B. B., Winters, A., & Zera, M. (2000). Oppositional defiant and conduct disorder: A review of the past 10 years, Part I. *Journal of American Academy of Child & Adolescent Psychiatry, 39*, 1468–1484.

London, A., Scott, K. E., Edin, K., & Hunter, V. (2004). Welfare reform: Work-family tradeoffs, and child well-being. *Family Relations, 53*(2), 148–158.

Lonely? Feeling low? Try a walk . . . down the aisle. (2006). *Scientific American*. Retrieved August 14, 2006, from http://www.scientificamerican.com.

Loo, C., Tong, B., & True, R. (1989). A bitter bean: Mental health status and attitudes in Chinatown. *Journal of Community Psychology, 17*, 283–296.

Looney, J. (1988). *Chronic mental illness in children and adolescents*. Washington, DC: American Psychiatric Press.

Lopez, S. R. (1989). Patient variable biases in clinical judgment: Conceptual overview and methodological considerations. *Psychological Bulletin, 106*(2), 184–203.

Lopez, S. R., & Guarnaccia, P. J. J. (2000). Cultural psychopathology: Uncovering the social world of mental illness. *Annual Review of Psychology, 51*, 571–598.

Lopez-Leon, S., Anssens, A. C., Gonzalez-Zuloeta, A. M., Del-Faveo, J., Claes, S. J., Oostra, B. A., et al. (2008). Meta-analyses of genetic studies on major depressive disorder. *Molecular Psychiatry, 13*, 772–785.

Lorant, V., Deliege, D., Eaton, W., Robert, A., Philippot, P., & Ansseau, M. (2003). Socio-economic inequalities in mental health: A meta-analysis. *American Journal of Epidemiology, 157*, 98–112.

Lorenzo, M. K., & Adler, D. A. (1984). Mental health services for Chinese in a community health center. *Journal of Contemporary Social Work, 65*(10), 600–609.

Loring, M., & Powell, B. (1988). Gender, race and the study of DSM-III: A study of the objectivity of psychiatric diagnostic behavior. *Journal of Health and Social Behavior, 29*, 1–22.

Louden, D. M. (1995). The epidemiology of schizophrenia among Caribbean-born and first- and second-generation migrants in Britain. *Journal of Social Distress and the Homeless, 4*(3), 237–253.

Lovejoy, M. (2001). Disturbances in the social body: Differences in body image and eating problems among African American and White women. *Gender and Society, 15*(2), 239–261.

Lovell, D., Gagliardi, G. J., & Peterson, P. J. (2002). Recidivism and use of services among persons with mental illness after release from prison. *Psychiatric Services, 53*(10), 1290–1296.

Lubchansky, I., Egri, G., & Stokes, J. (1970). Puerto Rican spiritualists view mental illness: The faith healer as paraprofessional. *American Journal of Psychiatry, 127*, 88–97.

Luborsky, L. (1984). *Principles of psychoanalytic psychotherapy*. New York: Basic Books.

Lucas, R. E. (2005). Time does not heal all wounds: A longitudinal study of reaction and adaptation to divorce. *Psychological Science, 16*(12), 945–950.

Lucas, R. E., Clark, A. E., Georgellis, Y., & Diener, E. (2003). Reexamining adaptation and the set point model of happiness: Reactions to changes in marital status. *Journal of Personality and Social Psychology, 84*(3), 527–539.

Luhrmann, T. M. (2000). *Of two minds: The growing disorder in American psychiatry.* New York: Alfred Knopf.

Lui, W. T., & Yu, E. (1985). Asian/Pacific American elderly: Mortality differentials, health status and use of health services. *Journal of Applied Gerontology, 4,* 35–63.

Lum, O. M. (1995). Health status of Asians and Pacific Islanders. *Ethnogeriatrics, 11,* 53–67.

Lund, D. A., Caserta, M. S., & Dimond, M. F. (1993). The course of spousal bereavement in later life. In M. S. Stroebe, W. Stroebe, & R. O. Hansson (Eds.), *Handbook of bereavement: Theory, research, and intervention* (pp. 240–254). New York: Cambridge University Press.

Lundgren, L. M., Amodeo, M., & Chassler, D. (2005). Mental health status, drug treatment use, and needle sharing among injection drug users. *AIDS Education and Prevention, 17*(6), 525–539.

Luster, T., Rhoades, K., & Haas, B. (1989). The relation between parental values and parental behavior: A test of the Kohn hypothesis. *Journal of Marriage and Family, 51,* 139–147.

Lynch, J. (1977). *The broken heart.* New York: Basic Books.

Lyons, M., Kendler, K., Gersony Provet, A., & Tsuang, M. T. (1991). The genetics of schizophrenia. In M. T. Tsuang, K. S. Kendler, & M. J. Lyons (Eds.), *Genetic issues in psychosocial epidemiology* (pp. 119–152), New Brunswick, NJ: Rutgers University Press.

MacCoun, R. (2004). Population thinking as an adjunct to the clinical trial perspective. *Psychiatric Services, 55*(5), 509–515.

MacGeorge, E. L., Samter, W., Feng, B., Gillihan, S. J., & Graves, S. J. (2004). Stress, social support, and health among college students after September 11, 2001. *Journal of College Student Development, 45*(6), 655–670.

Mackenzie, S. (2000). Scientific silence: AIDS and African Americans in the medical literature. *American Journal of Public Health, 90,* 1145–1146.

Macmillan, R., McMorris, B. J., & Kruttschnitt, C. (2004). Linked lives: Stability and change in maternal circumstances and trajectories of antisocial behavior in children. *Child Development, 75,* 205–220.

Magee, W. J. (1993). *Psychosocial predictors of agoraphobia, simple phobia, and social phobia onset in a U.S. national sample.* Unpublished doctoral dissertation, University of Michigan, Ann Arbor.

Magee, W. J., Eaton, W. W., Witchen, H. J., McGonagle, K. A., & Kessler, R. C. (1996). Agoraphobia, simple phobia, and social phobia in the National Comorbidity Survey. *Archives of General Psychiatry, 53,* 159–168.

Magliano, L., & Fiorillo, A. (2007). Psychoeducational family interventions for schizophrenia in the last decade: From explanatory to pragmatic trials. *Epidemiologia e Psichiatria Sociale, 16*(1), 22–34.

Magliano, L., Fiorillo, A., Malangone, C., De Rosa, C., Favata, G., Sasso, A., et al. (2006). Family psychoeducational interventions for schizophrenia in routine settings: Impact on patients' clinical status and social functioning and on relatives' burden and resources. *Epidemiologia e Psichiatria Sociale, 15*(3), 219–227.

Maher, B. (2005). Why marriage should be privileged in public policy. *Family Research Council's Insights,* Retrieved August 15, 2005, from http://www.frc.org/get.cfm?i=IS03D1.

Mahoney, M. J. (1974). *Cognition and behavior modification.* Cambridge, MA: Ballinger.

Mail, P. D. (1989). American Indians, stress, and alcohol. *American Indian and Alaska Native Mental Health Research, 3,* 7–26.

Mail, P. D., & Johnson, S. (1993). Boozing, sniffing, and toking: An overview of the past, present, and future of substance use by American Indians. *American Indian and Alaska Native Mental Health Research, 5,* 1–33.

Malaspina, D., Kegeles, L., & Van Heertum, L. (1996). Brain imaging in schizophrenia. In C. A. Kauffmann & J. M. Gorman (Eds.), *Schizophrenia: New directions for clinical research and treatment* (pp. 35–61). New York: Mary Ann Leibert.

Malgady, R. G., Rogler, L. H., & Constantino, G. (1990). Culturally sensitive psychotherapy for Puerto Rican children and adolescents: A program of treatment outcome research. *Journal of Consulting and Clinical Psychology, 58*(6), 704–712.

Malhi, G. S., Moore, J., & McGuffin, P. (2000). The genetics of major depressive disorder. *Current Psychiatry Reports, 2,* 165–169.

Malta, M., Strathdee, S. A., Magnanini, M. M. F., & Bastos, F. I. (2008). Adherence to antiretroviral therapy for human immunodeficiency virus/acquired immune deficiency syndrome among drug users: A systematic review. *Addiction, 103*(8), 1242–1257.

Malzberg, B. (1944). Mental disease among American Negroes: A statistical analysis. In O. Klineberg (Ed.), *Characteristics of the American Negro* (pp. 373–402). New York: Harper.

Mandarin, J., Murray, C. B., & Bangi, A. K. (2003). Predictors of African American adolescent sexual activity: An ecological framework. *Journal of Black Psychology, 29*, 337–356.

Manderscheid, R. W., Henderson, M. J., Witkin, M. J., & Atay, J. E. (1999). Contemporary mental health systems and managed care. In A. Horwitz & T. Scheid (Eds.), *A handbook for the study of mental health: Social contexts, theories, and systems* (pp. 412–426). New York: Cambridge University Press.

Manderscheid, R. W., Henderson, M. J., Witkin, M. J., & Atay, J. E. (2000). The U.S. mental health system of the 1990s: The challenges of managed care. *International Journal of Law and Psychiatry, 23*, 245–259.

Manning, W. D., & Smock, P. J. (2005). Measuring and modeling cohabitation: New perspectives from qualitative data. *Journal of Marriage and Family, 67*, 989–1002.

Manning, W., Stoner, T., Lurie, N., Christianson, J. B., Gray, D. Z., & Popkin, M. (1993). *Outcomes for Medicaid beneficiaries with schizophrenia in the first year of the Utah Prepaid Mental Health Plan.* Paper presented at the annual meeting of the American Public Health Association, San Francisco.

Manoleas, P. (Ed.). (1996). *The cross-cultural practice of clinical case management in mental health.* New York: Haworth.

Manor, O., Matthews, S., & Power, C. (2003). Health selection: The role of inter- and intra-generational mobility on social inequalities in health. *Social Science & Medicine, 57*(11), 2217–2227.

Manor, O., Matthews, S., & Power, C. (2003). Childhood and adult risk factors for socioeconomic differentials in psychological distress: Evidence from the 1958 British birth cohort. *Social Science & Medicine, 57*(1), 2217–2227.

Manschreck, T. C., Duckworth, K. S., Halpern, L., & Blockel, L. M. (2008). Schizophrenia recovery: Time for optimism? *Current Psychiatry, 7*(5), 41–58.

Mansergh, G., Marks, G., & Simoni, J. M. (1995). Self-disclosure of HIV infection among men who vary in time since seropositive diagnosis and symptomatic status. *AIDS, 9*(6), 639–644.

Manson, S. (1995). Culture and major depression. *Psychiatric Clinics of North America, 18*, 487–501.

Manson, S., Walker, R. D., & Kivlahan, D. R. (1987). Psychiatric assessment and treatment of American Indians and Alaska Natives. *Hospital and Community Psychiatry, 38*, 165–173.

Maramba, G. G., & Nagayama Hall, G. C. (2002). Meta-analysis of ethnic match as a predictor of dropout, utilization, and level of functioning. *Cultural Diversity and Ethnic Minority Psychology, 8*(3), 290–297.

Marcussen, K. (2005). Explaining differences in mental health between married and cohabiting individuals. *Social Psychology Quarterly, 68*(3), 239–257.

Markowitz, F., & Angell, B. (2008). *Extending modified labeling theory: Self, family, and recovery processes.* Presented at the annual meeting of the Society for the Study of Social Problems, Boston.

Marks, N. F., & Lambert, J. D. (1998). Marital status continuity and change among young and mid-life adults: Longitudinal effects on psychological well-being. *Journal of Family Issues, 19*(6), 652–686.

Marks, N. F., & McLanahan, S. S. (1993). Gender, family structure, and social support among parents. *Journal of Marriage and the Family, 55*, 481–494.

Markson, L. E., Turner, B. J., Cocroft, J., Houchens, R., & Fanning, T. R. (1997). Clinic services for persons with AIDS. *Journal of General Internal Medicine, 12*, 141–149.

Marmot, M., & Wilkinson, R. G. (Eds.). (1999). *Social determinants of health.* New York: Oxford University Press.

Marmot, M. G., & Koveginas, E. M. A. (1987). Social/economic status and disease. *Annual Review of Public Health, 8*, 111–135.

Marques, J. K., Haynes, R. L., & Nelson, C. (1993). Forensic treatment at Atascadero State Hospital. *International Journal of Law and Psychiatry, 16*, 57–70.

Marsella, A. J. (1982). Culture and mental health: An overview. In A. J. Marsella & G. M. White (Eds.), *Cultural conceptions of mental health and therapy* (pp. 359–388). Boston: Reidel.

Marsella, A. J., Sartorius, N., Jablensky, A., & Fenton, F. R. (1985). Cross-cultural studies of depressive disorders: An overview. In A. Kleinman & B. Good (Eds.), *Culture and depression* (pp. 299–324). Berkeley: University of California Press.

Marsh, C. E. (1993). Sexual assault and domestic violence in the African American community. *Western Journal of Black Studies, 17*(3), 149–155.

Marshall, M., & Lockwood, A. (1998). Assertive community treatment for people with severe mental disorders. *Cochrane Database of Systematic Reviews, 2,* CD001089.

Martin, A., Ruchkin, V., Caminis, A., Vermeiren, R., Henrich, C., & Schwab-Stone, M. (2005). Early to bed: A study of adaptation among sexually active urban adolescent girls younger than sixteen. *Journal of the American Academy of Child & Adolescent Psychiatry, 44,* 358–367.

Martin, G. T., Jr., & Zald, M. N. (1981). *Social welfare in society.* New York: Columbia University Press.

Martin, J. A., Hamilton, B. E., Sutton, P. D., Ventura, S., Menacker, F., & Munson, M. (2005). Births: Final data for 2003. *National Vital Statistics Report, 54,* 2. Retrieved from http://www.cdc.gov/nchs/data/nvsr/nvsr54/nvsr54_02.pdf.

Martin, J. K., Pescosolido, B. A., Olafsdottir, S., & McLeod, J. D. (2007). The construction of fear: Modeling Americans' preferences for social distance from children and adolescents with mental health problems. *Journal of Health and Social Behavior, 48,* 50–67.

Martin, J. K., Pescosolido, B. A., & Tuch, S. A. (2000). Of fear and loathing: The role of disturbing behavior, labels and causal attributions in shaping public attitudes toward persons with mental illness. *Journal of Health and Social Behavior, 41,* 208–233.

Martin, J. K., Tuch, S. A., & Roman, P. M. (2003). Problem drinking patterns among African Americans: The impact of reports of discrimination, perceptions of prejudice, and "risky" coping strategies. *Journal of Health and Social Behavior, 44,* 408–425.

Martin, J. L., & Dean, L. (1993). Effects of AIDS-related bereavement and HIV-related illness on psychological distress among gay men: A 7-year longitudinal study, 1985–1991. *Journal of Consulting and Clinical Psychology, 61*(1), 94–103.

Martin, J. L., Dean, L., Garcia, M., & Hall, W. (1989). Barbara Snell Dohrenwend Memorial Lecture: The impact of AIDS on a gay community: Changes in sexual behavior, substance use, and mental health. *American Journal of Community Psychology, 17*(3), 269–293.

Marwaha, S., Johnson, S., Bebbington, P., Angermeyer, M. C., Brugha, T., Azorin, J.-M., et al. (2008). Correlates of subjective quality of life in people with schizophrenia: Findings from the EuroSC study. *Journal of Nervous and Mental Disease, 196,* 87–94.

Marx, K. (1967). *Capital: A critique of political economy.* New York: International Publishers.

Mashburn, A. J., Pianta, R. C., Hamre, B. K., Downer, J. T., Barbarin, O. A., Bryant, D., et al. (2008). Measures of classroom quality in prekindergarten and children's development of academic, language, and social skills. *Child Development, 79,* 732–749.

Maslach, C., & Jackson, S. E. (1981). The measurement of experienced burnout. *Journal of Occupational Behavior, 2,* 99–113.

Maslow, A. H. (1966). *The psychology of science: A reconnaissance.* New York: Harper & Row.

Maslow, A. H. (1970). *Motivation and personality* (2nd ed.). New York: Harper & Row.

Mason, H. R., Marks, G., Simoni, J. M., Ruiz, M. S., & Richardson, J. L. (1995). Culturally sanctioned secrets? Latino men's nondisclosure of HIV infection to family, friends, and lovers. *Health Psychology, 14*(1), 6–12.

Mastekaasa, A. (1994). Marital status, distress, and well-being: An international comparison. *Journal of Comparative Family Studies, 25*(2), 183–205.

Mastekaasa, A. (1995). Marital dissolution and subjective distress: Panel evidence. *European Sociological Review, 11,* 173–185.

Matthews, A. R. (1970). Observations on policy, policing and procedures for emergency detention of the mentally ill. *Journal of Criminal Law, Criminology and Police Science, 61,* 283–295.

Matthews, S., Hertzman, C., Ostry, A., & Power, C. (1998). Gender, work roles and psychosocial work characteristics as determinants of health. *Social Science & Medicine, 46*(11), 1417–1424.

Mattlin, J. A., Wethington, E., & Kessler, R. C. (1990). Situational determinants of coping and coping effectiveness. *Journal of Health and Social Behavior, 31*, 103–122.

Matras, J. (1984). *Social inequality, stratification, and mobility* (2nd ed.) Englewood Cliffs, NJ: Prentice-Hall.

Matza, D. (1967). The disreputable poor. In R. Bendix & S. M. Lipset (Eds.), *Class, status, and power.* London: Routledge & Kegan Paul.

Mausner-Dorsch, H., & Eaton W. W. (2000). Psychosocial work environment and depression: Epidemiologic assessment of demand-control model. *American Journal of Public Health, 90*, 1765–1770.

Mayfield, A. E., Rice, E., Flannery, D., & Rotheram-Borus, M. J. (2008). HIV disclosure among adults living with HIV. *AIDS Care, 20*(1), 80–92.

Mazzoferro, K., Murray, P., Ness, R., Bass, D., Tyus, N., & Cook, R. (2006). Depression, stress and social support as predictors of high-risk sexual behavior and STIs in young women. *Journal of Adolescent Health, 39*, 601–603.

McBride, C. A. (1998). The discounting principle and attitudes toward victims of HIV infection. *Journal of Applied Social Psychology, 28*, 595–608.

McCain, N. L., Gray, D. P., Elswick, R. K., Robins, J. W., Tuck, I., Walter, J. M., et al. (2008). A randomized clinical trial of alternative stress management interventions in persons with HIV infection. *Journal of Consulting and Clinical Psychology, 76*(3), 431–441.

McCarthy, J. D., & Yancey, W. L. (1971). Uncle Tom and Mr. Charlie: Metaphysical pathos in the study of racism and personal disorganization. *American Journal of Sociology, 76*, 648–672.

McCaslin, S. E., Jacobs, G. A., Metzler, T. J., & Marmar, C. R. (2005). How does negative life change following disaster response impact distress among Red Cross responders? *Professional Psychology: Research and Practice, 36*(3), 246–253.

McCoy, M. L., Roberts, D. L., Hanrahan, P., Clay, R., & Luchins, D. J. (2004). Jail linkage assertive community treatment services for individuals with mental illnesses. *Psychiatric Rehabilitation Journal, 27*, 243–250.

McCrae, R. R., & Costa, P. T., Jr. (1993). Psychological resilience among widowed men and women: A 10-year follow-up of a national sample. In M. S. Stroebe, W. Stroebe, & R. O. Hansson (Eds.), *Handbook of bereavement: Theory, research, and intervention* (pp. 196–207). New York: Cambridge University Press.

McDowell, I., & Newell, C. (2006). *Measuring health: A guide to rating scales and questionnaires* (3rd ed.). New York: Oxford University Press.

McEwen, B. S., & Stellar, E. (1993). Stress and the individual: Mechanism leading to disease. *Archives of Internal Medicine, 153*, 2093–2101.

McFarland, B. (2000). Overview of Medicaid managed behavioral health care. *New Directions for Mental Health Services, 85*, 17–22.

McFarland, B. H., Faulkner, L. R., Bloom, J. D., Hallaux, R., & Bray, J. D. (1989). Chronic mental illness and the criminal justice system. *Hospital and Community Psychiatry, 40*, 718–723.

McFarland, D. (1969). Measuring the permeability of occupational structures: An information-theoretic approach. *American Journal of Sociology, 75*, 41–61.

McFarlane, W. R. (2002). *Multifamily groups in the treatment of severe psychiatric disorders.* New York: Guilford.

McFarlane, W. R., & Cook, W. L. (2007). Family expressed emotion prior to onset of psychosis. *Family Process, 46*(2), 185–197.

McGoldrick, M., Pearce, J., & Giordano, J. (1995). *Ethnicity and family therapy* (Rev. ed.). New York: Guilford.

McGraw, S. A., McKinley, J. B., Crawford, S. L., & Costa, L. A. (1992). Health survey methods with minority populations: Some lessons from recent experience. *Ethnicity and Disease, 2*, 273–287.

McGregor, I., & Little, B. R. (1998). Personal projects, happiness, and meaning: On doing well and being yourself. *Journal of Personality and Social Psychology, 74*, 494–512.

McGrew, J., Wilson, R., & Bond, G. (1996). Client perspectives on helpful ingredients of assertive community treatment. *Psychiatric Rehabilitation Journal, 19*(3), 13–21.

McGrew, J., Wilson, R., & Bond, G. (2002). An exploratory study of what clients like least about assertive community treatment. *Psychiatric Services, 53*(6), 761–763.

McGuffin, P., Asherson, P., Own, M., & Farmer, A. (1994). The strength of the genetic effect: Is there room for an environmental influence in the aetiology of schizophrenia? *British Journal of Psychiatry, 164*, 593–599.

McKelvey, M. W., & McKenry, P. C. (2000). The psychosocial well-being of Black and White mothers following marital dissolution. *Psychology of Women Quarterly, 24*, 4–14.

McKenna, B., Thom, K., & Simpson, A. (2007). Media coverage of homicide involving mentally disordered offenders: A matched comparison study. *International Journal of Forensic Mental Health, 6*(1), 57–63.

McKeown, R. E., Garrison, C. Z., Jackson, K. L., Cuffe, S. P., Addy, C. L., & Waller, J. L. (1997). Family structure and cohesion, and depressive symptoms in adolescents. *Journal of Research on Adolescence, 7*, 267–281.

McKinlay, J. (1972). Some approaches and problems in the study of the use of services: An overview. *Journal of Health and Social Behavior, 13*, 115–152.

McKinnon, K., Carey, M. P., & Cournos, F. (1997). Research on HIV, AIDS, and severe mental illness: Recommendations from the NIMH national conference. *Clinical Psychology Review, 17*(3), 327–331.

McKinnon, K., Cournos, F., Herman, R., Satriano, J., Silver, B. J., & Puello, I. (1999). AIDS-related services and training in outpatient mental health care agencies in New York. *Psychiatric Services, 50*(9), 1225–1228.

McKusick, V. A. (1967). The ethnic distribution of disease in the United States. *Journal of Chronic Disease, 20*, 115–118.

McLanahan, S. (2004). Diverging destinies: How children are faring under the second demographic transition. *Demography, 44*, 607–627.

McLanahan, S., & Percheski, C. (2008). Family structure and the reproduction of inequalities. *Annual Review of Sociology, 34*, 267–276.

McLanahan, S. S., & Bumpass, L. L. (1988). Intergenerational consequences of family disruption. *American Journal of Sociology, 94*, 130–152.

McLaughlin, A. E., Campbell, F. A., Pungello, E. P., & Skinner, M. (2007). Depressive symptoms in young adults: The influences of the early home environment and early educational child care. *Child Development, 78*, 746–756.

McLaughlin, K. A., Hilt, L. M., & Nolen-Hoeksema, S. (2007). Racial/ethnic differences in internalizing and externalizing symptoms in adolescents. *Journal of Abnormal Child Psychology, 35*, 801–816.

McLean, A. (1990). Contradictions in the social production of clinical knowledge: The case of schizophrenia. *Social Science and Medicine, 30*, 969–985.

McLean, A. (1994). *The role of consumers in mental health services research and evaluation* (Report and Concept Paper No. 92MF03814201D). Rockville, MD: Substance Abuse and Mental Health Services Administration.

McLean, A. (1995). Empowerment and the psychiatric consumer/ex-patient movement in the United States: Contradictions, crisis and change. *Social Science and Medicine, 40*(8), 1053–1071.

McLean, A. (2000). From ex-patient alternatives to consumer options: Consequences of consumerism for psychiatric consumers and the ex-patient movement. *International Journal of Health Services, 30*(4), 821–847.

McLean, A. (2003a). Legitimization of the consumer movement and obstacles to it. Part I: "Recovering" consumers and a broken mental health system in the United States: Ongoing challenges for consumers/survivors and the New Freedom Commission on Mental Health. *International Journal of Psychosocial Rehabilitation, 8*, 47–57.

McLean, A. (2003b). Impact of managed care and continuing challenges. Part II: "Recovering" consumers and a broken mental health system in the United States: Ongoing challenges for consumers/survivors and the New Freedom Commission on Mental Health. *International Journal of Psychosocial Rehabilitation, 8*, 58–70.

McLean, D., & Link, B. G. (1994). Unraveling complexity: Strategies to refine concepts, measures and research designs in the study of life events and mental health. In W. R. Avison & I. H. Gotlib (Eds.), *Stress and mental health: Contemporary issues and prospects for the future* (pp. 15–42). New York: Plenum.

McLean, D., & Link, B. G. (2002). Measurement for a human science. *Journal of Health and Social Behavior, 43,* 152–170.

McLeod, J., & Owens, T. (2004). Psychological well-being in the early life course: Variations by socioeconomic status, gender, and race/ethnicity. *Social Psychology Quarterly, 67,* 257–278.

McLeod, J. D. (1991). Childhood parental loss and adult depression. *Journal of Health and Social Behavior, 32,* 205–220.

McLeod, J. D., & Nonnemaker, J. M. (1999). Social stratification and inequality. In C. S. Aneshensel & J. C. Phelan (Eds.), *Handbook of the sociology of mental health* (pp. 321–344). New York: Kluwer/Plenum.

McLeod, J. D., & Shanahan, M. J. (1993). Poverty, parenting, and children's mental health. *American Sociological Review, 58,* 351–366.

McLoyd, V. C. (1990). The impact of economic hardship on Black families and children: Psychological distress, parenting, and socioeconomic development. *Child Development, 61,* 311–346.

McLoyd, V. C. (1998). Socioeconomic disadvantage and child development. *American Psychologist, 53,* 185–204.

McLoyd, V. C., Jayaratne, T. E,. Ceballo, R., & Borquez, J. (1994). Unemployment and work interruption among African American single mothers: Effects on parenting and adolescent socioemotional functioning. *Child Development, 65*(2), 562–589.

McMain, S., Webster, C. D., & Menzies, R. J. (1989). The postassessment careers of mentally disordered offenders. *International Journal of Law and Psychiatry, 12,* 189–201.

McNiel, D. E., & Binder, R. L. (1987). Predictive validity of judgments of dangerousness in emergency civil commitment. *American Journal of Psychiatry, 144,* 197–200.

McNiel, D. E., & Binder, R. L. (1994). The relationship between acute psychiatric symptoms, diagnosis and short-term risk of violence. *Hospital and Community Psychiatry, 45,* 133–137.

McNiel, D. E., & Binder, R. L. (2007). Effectiveness of a mental health court in reducing criminal recidivism and violence. *American Journal of Psychiatry, 164,* 1395–1403.

McNiel, D. E., Binder, R. L., & Robinson, J. C. (2005). Incarceration associated with homelessness, mental disorder, and co-occurring substance abuse. *Psychiatric Services, 56*(7), 840–846.

McNiel, D. E., Eisner, J. E., & Binder, R. L. (2000). The relationship between command hallucinations and violence. *Psychiatric Services, 51,* 1288–1292.

McNiel, D. E., Hatcher, C., Zeiner, H., Wolfe, H. L., & Myers, R. S. (1991). Characteristics of persons referred by police to the psychiatric emergency room. *Hospital and Community Psychiatry, 42,* 425–427.

McSween, J. L. (2002). The role of group interest, identity, and stigma in determining mental health policy preferences. *Journal of Health Politics, Policy, and Law, 27,* 773–800.

Mead, G. H. (1934). *Mind, self, and society.* Chicago: University of Chicago Press.

Meade, C. S. (2006). Sexual risk behavior among persons dually diagnosed with severe mental illness and substance use disorder. *Journal of Substance Abuse Treatment, 77,* 227–233.

Mechanic, D. (1975). Sociocultural and socio-psychological factors affecting personal responses to psychological disorder. *Journal of Health and Social Behavior, 16,* 393–404.

Mechanic, D. (1978). *Medical sociology* (2nd ed.) New York: The Free Press.

Mechanic, D. (1986). The challenge of chronic mental illness: A retrospective and prospective view. *Hospital and Community Psychiatry, 37,* 891–896.

Mechanic, D. (1991). Strategies for integrating public mental health services. *Hospital & Community Psychiatry, 42*(8), 797–801.

Mechanic, D. (1994). Establishing mental health priorities. *Milibank Q, 72,* 501–14.

Mechanic, D. (1999). *Mental health and social policy: The emergence of managed care* (4th ed.) Boston: Allyn & Bacon.

Mechanic, D. (2006). *The truth about health care: Why reform is not working in America.* New Brunswick, NJ: Rutgers University Press.

Mechanic, D. (2008). *The truth about health care: Why reform is not working in America* (paperback ed.). New Brunswick, NJ: Rutgers University Press.

Mechanic, D., Angel, R., & Davies, L. (1991). Risk and selection processes between the general and the specialty mental health sectors. *Journal of Health and Social Behavior, 32,* 49–64.

Mechanic, D., & McAlpine, D. (1999). Mission unfulfilled: Potholes on the road to mental health parity. *Health Affairs, 18,* 7–21.

Mechanic, D., & Rochefort, D. (1990). Deinstitutionalization: An appraisal of reform. *Annual Review of Sociology, 16*, 301–327.

Mechanic, D., & Rochefort, D. (1992). A policy of inclusion for the mentally ill. *Health Affairs, 11*(1), 128–150.

Mechanic, D., & Schlesinger, M. (1996). The impact of managed care on patients' trust in medical care and their physicians. *Journal of the American Medical Association, 275*, 1693–1697.

Mechanic, D., Schlesinger, M., & McAlpine, D. D. (1995). Management of mental health and substance abuse services: State of the art and early results. *Milbank Quarterly, 73*(1), 19–55.

Mehlman, E. (1994). Enhancing self-disclosure of the African-American college student in therapy with the Caucasian therapist. *Journal of College Student Psychotherapy, 9*(1), 3–20.

Meichenbaum, D. (1977). *Cognitive behavior-modification: An integrative approach.* New York: Plenum Press.

Melick, M. E., Steadman, H. J., & Cocozza, J. J. (1979). The medicalization of criminal behavior among mental patients. *Journal of Health and Social Behavior, 20*, 228–237.

Melton, G. B., Petrila, J., Poythress, N. G., & Slobogin, C. (1997). *Psychological evaluations for the courts: A handbook for mental health professionals and lawyers* (2nd ed.). New York: Guilford.

Melville, M. B., & Lykes, M. B. (1992). Guatemalan Indian children and the sociocultural effects of government-sponsored terrorism. *Social Science & Medicine, 34*(5), 533–548.

Menaghan, E. G. (1991). Work experiences and family interaction processes: The long reach of the job? *Annual Review of Sociology, 17*, 419–444.

Menaghan, E. G., & Parcel, T. L. (1991). Determining children's home environments: The impact of maternal characteristics and current occupational and family conditions. *Journal of Marriage and Family, 53*, 417–431.

Menaghan, E. G., & Parcel, T. L. (1995). Social sources of change in children's home environments: Effects of parental occupational experiences and family conditions over time. *Journal of Marriage and Family, 57*, 69–84.

Mendlewicz, J., & Rainer, J. D. (1977). Adoption study supporting genetic transmission in manicde-pressive illness. *Nature*, 268–329.

Mendes de Leon, C. F., Rapp, S. S., & Kast, S. V. (1994). Financial strain and symptoms of depression in a community sample of elderly men and women. *Journal of Aging and Health, 6*(4), 448–468.

Menzies, R., Webster, C. D., McMain, S., & Staley, S. (1994). The dimensions of dangerousness revisited: Assessing forensic predictions about violence. *Law and Human Behavior, 18*(1), 1–28.

Merikangas, K. R., Ames, M., Cui, L., Stang, P. E., Ustun, T. B., Von Korff, M., et al. (2007). The impact of comorbidity of mental and physical conditions on role disability in the US adult household population. *Archives of General Psychiatry, 64*, 1180–1188.

Merikangas, K., Angst, J., Eaton, W., Canino, G., Rubio-Stipec, M., Wacker, H., et al. (1996). Comorbidity and boundaries of affective disorders with anxiety disorders and substance misuse: Results of an International Task Force. *British Journal of Psychiatry, 168*, 58–67.

Merikangas, K. R., Avenevoli, S., Costello, E. J., Koretz, D., & Kessler, R. C. (2009). Background and measures in the National Comorbidity Survey Adolescent Supplement (NCS-A). *Journal of American Academy of Child & Adolescent Psychiatry, 48*(4), 367–379.

Merton, R. K. (1956). *Social theory and social structure* (Rev. ed.) New York: The Free Press.

Merton, R. K. (1968). Social structure and anomie. In R. K. Merton (Ed.), *Social theory and social structure* (pp. 185–214). New York: The Free Press. (Original work published 1938)

Meyer, I., Empfield, M., Engel, D., & Cournos, F. (1995). Characteristics of HIV-positive chronically mentally ill inpatients. *Psychiatric Quarterly, 66*(3), 201–207.

Meyer, I., McKinnon, K., Cournos, F., Empfield, M., Bavli, S., Engel, D., et al. (1993). HIV seroprevalence among long-stay patients in a state psychiatric hospital. *Hospital & Community Psychiatry, 44*(3), 282–284.

Meyerson, D. E. (1994). Interpretations of stress in institutions: The cultural production of ambiguity and burnout. *Administrative Science Quarterly, 39*, 628–653.

Mezzich, J. E., Lewis-Fernandez, R., & Ruiperez, M. A. (2008). Cultural and psychiatric diagnosis. In A. Tasman, J. Kay, J. A. Libeman, M. B. First, & M. Maj (Eds.), *Psychiatry* (Vol. 1, 3rd ed). Chichester, UK: Wiley.

Michels, R., & Marzuk, R. M. (1993). Progress in psychiatry. Part I. *New England Journal of Medicine, 329*, 552–560.

Mickelson, K. D., & Kubzansky, L. D. (2003). Social distribution of social support: The mediating role of life events. *American Journal of Community Psychology, 32*(3/4), 265–281.

Miech, R., Eaton, W., & Brennan, K. (2005). Mental health disparities across education and sex: A prospective analysis examing how they persist over the life course. *Journal of Gerontology: Social Sciences, 60B*, S93–S98.

Miedzian, M. (1991). *Boys will be boys: Breaking the link between masculinity and violence.* New York: Doubleday.

Milkie, M., & Peltola, P. (1999). Playing all the roles: Gender and the work-family balancing act. *Journal of Marriage and the Family, 61*, 476–490.

Miller, J., Schooler, C., Kohn, M. L., & Miller, K. A. (1979). Women and work: The psychological effects of occupational conditions. *American Journal of Sociology, 85*, 66–94.

Miller, K. E. (1996). The effects of state terrorism and exile on indigenous Guatemalan refugee children: A mental health assessment and an analysis of children's narratives. *Child Development, 67*(1), 89–106.

Miller, R. D. (1987). *Involuntary civil commitment of the mentally ill in the post-reform era.* Springfield, IL: Thomas.

Miller, R. D. (1988). Outpatient civil commitment of the mentally ill: An overview and update. *Behavioral Science and the Law, 6*, 99–118.

Miller, R. R., & Browning, S. L. (2000). Sharing a man: Insights from research. *Journal of Comparative Family Studies, 31*, 339–346.

Miller, T. J., McGlashan, T. H., Rosen, J. L., Cadenhead, K., Cannon, T., Ventura, J., et al. (2003). Prodromal assessment with the structured interview for prodromal syndromes and the Scale of Prodromal Symptoms; Predictive validity, interrater reliability, and training to reliability. *Schizophrenia Bulletin, 29*(4), 703–715.

Miller-Johnson, S., Winn, D. M., Coie, J., Maumary-Gremaud, A., Hyman, C., Terry, R., et al. (1999). Motherhood during the teen years: A developmental perspective on risk factors for childbearing. *Development and Psychopathology, 11*, 85–100.

Millon, T., & Klerman, J. G. (1986). *Contemporary directions in psychopathology: Toward the DSM-IV.* New York: Guilford.

Mills, C. W. (1956). *The power elite.* New York: Oxford University Press.

Mills, C. W. (1959). *The sociological imagination.* New York: Oxford University Press.

Minkoff, K. (1994). Community mental health in the nineties: Public sector managed care. *Community Mental Health Journal, 30*(4), 317–321.

Minsky, S., Vega, W., Miskimen, T., Gara, M., & Escobar, J. (2003). Diagnostic patterns in Latino, African American, and European American psychiatric patients. *Archives of General Psychiatry, 60*, 637–644.

Minuchin, S. (1974). *Families and family therapy.* Cambridge, MA: Harvard University Press.

Miranda, J., Hohmann, A. A., Attkisson, C., & Larson, D. (1994). *Mental disorders in primary care.* San Francisco: Jossey-Bass.

Mirowsky, J. (1985). Depression and marital power: An equity model. *American Journal of Sociology, 91*, 557–592.

Mirowsky, J. (1995). Age and the sense of control. *Social Psychology Quarterly, 58*, 31–43.

Mirowsky, J. (1997). Age, subjective life expectancy, and the sense of control: The horizon hypothesis. *Journal of Gerontology: Social Sciences, 52B*, S125–S134.

Mirowsky, J. (1999). Subjective life expectancy in the U.S.: Correspondence to actuarial estimates by age, sex, and race. *Social Science and Medicine, 49*, 967–979.

Mirowsky, J., & Hu, P. N. (1996). Physical impairment and the diminishing effects of income. *Social Forces, 74*, 1073–1096.

Mirowsky, J., & Kim, J. (2007). Graphing age trajectories: Vector graphs, synthetic and virtual cohort projections, and cross-sectional profiles of depression. *Sociological Methods and Research, 35*, 497–541.

Mirowsky, J., & Ross, C. E. (1983). Paranoia and the structure of powerlessness. *American Sociological Review, 48*, 228–239.

Mirowsky, J., & Ross, C. E. (1984). Mexican culture and its emotional contradictions. *Journal of Health and Social Behavior, 25*, 2–13.

Mirowsky, J., & Ross, C. E. (1988). Childcare and emotional adjustment to wives' employment. *Journal of Health and Social Behavior, 29*, 127–138.

Mirowsky, J., & Ross, C. E. (1989a). Psychiatric diagnosis as reified measurement. *Journal of Health and Social Behavior, 30*, 11–25.

Mirowsky, J., & Ross, C. E. (1989b). *Social causes of psychological distress.* New York: Aldine de Gruyter.

Mirowsky, J., & Ross, C. E. (1990). The consolation prize theory of alienation. *American Journal of Sociology, 95*, 1505–1535.

Mirowsky, J., & Ross, C. E. (1991). Eliminating defense and agreement bias from measures of the sense of control: A 2 × 2 index. *Social Psychology Quarterly, 54*, 127–145.

Mirowsky, J., & Ross, C. E. (1992). Age and depression. *Journal of Health and Social Behavior, 33*, 187–205.

Mirowsky, J., & Ross, C. E. (1995). Sex differences in distress: Real or artifact? *American Sociological Review, 60*, 449–468.

Mirowsky, J., & Ross, C. E. (1999). Economic hardship across the life course. *American Sociological Review, 64*, 548–569.

Mirowsky, J., & Ross, C. E. (2001). Age and the effect of economic hardship on depression. *Journal of Health and Social Behavior, 42*, 132–150.

Mirowsky, J., & Ross, C. E. (2002). Measurement for a human science. *Journal of Health and Social Behavior, 43*, 152–170.

Mirowsky, J., & Ross, C. E. (2003). Social causes of psychological distress (2nd ed.). New Brunswick, NJ: Aldine Transaction.

Mirowsky, J., & Ross, C. E. (2005). Education, cumulative advantage and health. *Aging International, 30*, 27–62.

Mirowsky, J., & Ross, C. E. (2007a). Creative work and health. *Journal of Health and Social Behavior, 48*, 385–403.

Mirowsky, J., & Ross, C. E. (2007b). Life course trajectories of perceived control and their relationship to education. *American Journal of Sociology, 112*, 1339–1382.

Mirowsky, J., & Ross, C. E. (2008). Education and self-rated health: Cumulative advantage and its rising importance. *Research on Aging, 30*, 93–122.

Mirowsky, J., & Schieman, S. (2008). Gender, age, and the trajectories and trends of anxiety and anger. In H. Turner & S. Schieman (Eds.), *Advances in life course research: Stress processes across the life course* (pp. 45–73). New York: Elsevier.

Mischel, W., Ebbesen, E. B., & Zeiss, A. R. (1973). Selective attention to the self: Situational and dispositional determinants. *Journal of Personality and Social Psychology, 27*, 129–142.

Miyamoto, S., LaMantia, A. S., Cuncan, G. E., Sullivan, P., Gilmore, J. H., & Lieberman, J. A. (2003). Recent advances in the neurobiology of schizophrenia. *Molecular Interventions, 3*, 28–39.

Mizuno, Y., Wilkinson, J. D., Santibanez, S., Dawson Rose, C., Knowlton, A., Handley, K., et al. (2006). Correlates of health care utilization among HIV-seropositive injection drug users. *AIDS Care, 18*(5), 417–425.

Mobray, C. T., Grazier, K. L., & Holter, M. (2002). Managed behavioral health care in the public sector. *Psychiatric Services, 53*, 157–170.

Mojtabai, R. (2007). Americans' attitudes toward mental health treatment seeking: 1990–2003. *Psychiatric Services, 58*(5), 642–651.

Mollica, R. F., Donelan, K., Tor, S., Lavelle, J., Elias, C., Frankel, M., et al. (1993). The effect of trauma and confinement on functional health and mental health status of Cambodians living in Thailand-Cambodia border camps. *Journal of the American Medical Association, 270*, 581–586.

Monahan, J. (1992). Mental disorder and violent behavior: Perceptions and evidence. *American Psychologist, 47*, 511–521.

Monahan, J., Bonnie, R. J., Appelbaum, P. S. Hyde, P. S., Steadman, H. J., & Swartz, M. S. (2001). Mandated community treatment: Beyond outpatient commitment. *Psychiatric Services, 52*, 1198–1205.

Monahan, J., Caldeira, C., & Friedlander, H. D. (1979). Police and the mentally ill: A comparison of committed and arrested persons. *International Journal of Law and Psychiatry, 2*, 509–518.

Monahan, J., & Steadman, H. J. (1982). Crime and mental disorder: An epidemiological approach. In M. Tonry & N. Morris (Eds.), *Crime and justice: An annual review of research* (Vol. 4, pp. 145–189). Chicago: University of Chicago Press.

Monahan, J., Steadman, H. J., Silver, E., Appelbaum, P., Robbins, P., Mulvey, E., et al. 2001. *Rethinking risk assessment: The MacArthur Study of Mental Disorder and Violence*. Oxford: Oxford University Press.

Monroe, S. M., & Hadjiyannakis, K. (2002). The social environment and depression: Focusing on severe life stress. In I. Gotlib & C. L. Hammen (Eds.), *Handbook of depression* (pp. 314–340). New York: Guilford.

Monroe, S. M., Roberts, J. E., Kupfer, D. J., Frank, E. (1996). Life stress and treatment course of recurrent depression: II. Postrecovery associations with attrition, symptom course, and recurrence over 3 years. *Journal of Abnormal Psychology, 105*, 313–328.

Montagu, A. (1965). *The concept of race*. New York: The Free Press.

Moodley, R. (2000). Representation of subjective stress in Black and ethnic minority patients: Constructing a research agenda. *Counseling Psychology Quarterly, 13*, 159–174.

Moore, M. E., & Hiday, V. A. (2006). Mental health court outcomes: A comparison of re-arrest and re-arrest severity between mental health court and traditional court participants. *Law and Human Behavior, 30*, 659–674.

Moreno, C., Laje, G., Blanco, C., Jiang, H., Schmidt, A. B., & Olfson, M. (2007). National trends in the outpatient diagnosis and treatment of bipolar disorder in youth. *Archives of General Psychiatry, 64*, 1032–1039.

Morgan, C., McKenzie, K., & Fearon, P. (Eds.). (2008). *Society and psychosis*. Cambridge: Cambridge University Press.

Morlock, L. L. (1989). Recognition and treatment of mental health problems in the general health sector. In C. A. Taube, D. Mechanic, & A. A. Hohmann (Eds.), *The future of mental health services research* (DHHS Publication No. ADM 89–1600; pp. 39–61). Washington, DC: U.S. Government Printing Office.

Morone, J. A. (1997). Enemies of the people: The moral dimension to public health. *Journal of Health, Politics, Policy & Law, 22*, 993–1020.

Morris, J. A., & Feldman, D. C. (1996). The dimensions, antecedents, and consequences of emotional labor. *Academy of Management Review, 21*, 986–1010.

Morris, R., & Hirsch-Lescohier, I. (1978). Service integration: Real vs. illusory solutions to welfare dilemmas. In R. Sarri & Y. Hassenfeld (Eds.), *The management of human services*. New York: Columbia University Press.

Morrissey, J. (1982). Deinstitutionalizing the mentally ill: Process, outcomes, and new directions. In W. Gove (Ed.), *Deviance and mental illness* (pp. 147–176). Beverly Hills, CA: Sage.

Morrissey, J. P. (1999). Integrating service delivery systems for persons with a severe mental illness. In A. V. Horwitz & T. L. Scheid (Eds.), *A handbook for the study of mental health: Social contexts, theories, and systems* (pp. 449–466). New York: Cambridge University Press.

Morrissey, J. P., Calloway, M., Bartko, W., Ridgely, M. S., Goldman, H., & Paulson, R. I. (1994). Local mental health authorities and service system change: Evidence from the Robert Wood Johnson Foundation program on Chronic Mental Illness. *Milbank Quarterly, 72*(1), 49–80.

Morrissey, J., Calloway, M., Johnsen, M., & Ullman, M. (1997). Service system performance and integration: A baseline profile of the ACCESS demonstration sites. *Psychiatric Services, 48*, 374–380.

Morrissey, J., & Goldman, H. (1984). Cycles of reform in the care of the chronically mentally ill. *Hospital and Community Psychiatry, 35*, 785–793.

Morrissey, J. P. & Goldman, H. H. (1986). Care and treatment of the mentally ill in the United States: Historical developments and reforms. *Annals of the American Academy of Political and Social Science, 484*, 12–27.

Morrissey, J., Goldman, H., & Klerman, L. (1980). *The enduring asylum: Cycles of institutional reform at Worcester State Hospital*. New York: Grune & Stratton.

Morrissey J. P., Goldman H., Klerman L. (1985) Cycles of reform in mental helth care. In: Brown P. ed. *Mental Health Care and Social Policy*. Boston: Routledge and Kegan Paul, 70–98.

Morrissey, J. P., Johnsen, M. C., & Calloway, M. O. (1997). Evaluating performance and change in the mental health systems serving children and youth: An interorganizational network approach. *Journal of Mental Health Administration, 24*, 4–21.

Morrissey, J. P., Johnsen, M. C., & Calloway, M. O. (2005). Methods for system-level evaluations of child mental health service networks. In M. Epstein, K. Kutash, & A. Duchnowski (Eds.), *Outcomes for children and youth with emotional and behavioral disorders and their families: Programs and evaluations, best practices* (pp. 297–307). Austin TX: Pro-Ed.

Morrissey, J., & Lindsey, M. (1987). *Organizational structure and continuity of care: A study of community mental health centers*. Albany: New York State Office of Mental Health.

Morrissey, J., Meyer, P., & Cuddeback, G. (2007). Extending assertive community treatment to criminal justice settings: Origins, current evidence and future directions. *Community Mental Health Journal, 43*, 527–544.

Morrissey, J. P., Ridgely S. M., Goldman, H. H., & Barko, T. W. (1994). Assessment of community mental health support systems: A key informant approach. *Community Mental Health Journal, 30*, 565–579.

Morrison, L. (2008). *Making it work: Consumer voices and service transformation in mental health*. Paper presented at the annual meeting of the American Sociological Association, Boston.

Morse, G., & Calsyn, R. J. (1986). Mentally disturbed homeless people in St. Louis: Needy, willing, but underserved. *International Journal of Mental Health, 14*(4), 74–94.

Morse, N., & Weiss, R. S. (1955). The function and meaning of work. *American Sociological Review, 20*, 191–198.

Morse, S. J. (1985). Excusing the crazy: The insanity defense reconsidered. *Southern California Law Review, 58*, 777–836.

Moscardino, U., Axia, G., Scrimin, S., & Capello, F. (2007). Narratives from caregivers of children surviving the terrorist attack in Beslan: Issues of health, culture, and resilience. *Social Science & Medicine, 64*(8), 1776–1787.

Moscicki, E. E., Locke, B., Rar, D., & Boyd, J. H. (1989). Depressive symptoms among Mexican Americans: The Hispanic Health and Nutrition Examination Survey. *American Journal of Epidemiology, 130*, 348–360.

Moscovice, I., Lurie, N., Christianson, J. B., Finch, M., Atchtar, M. R., & Popkin, M. (1993). Access and use of health services by chronically mentally ill Medicaid beneficiaries. *Health Care Financing Review, 14*, 75–87.

Mossakowski, K. (2003). Coping with perceived discrimination: Does ethnic identity protect mental health? *Journal of Health and Social Behavior, 44*, 318–331.

Mowbray, C., Grazier, K., & Holter, M. (2002). Managed behavioral health care in the public sector: Will it become the third shame of the states? *Hospital and Community Psychiatry, 53*(2), 157–170.

Mrazek, P. J., & Haggerty, R. J. (1994). *Reducing risks for mental disorders*. Washington, DC: National Academies Press.

Muchtler, J. E. & Burr, J. A. (1991). Racial differences in health and health service utilization in later life: The effect of SES. *Journal of Health and Social Behavior, 32*, 342–356.

Mueser, K. T., Bond, G. R., Drake, R. E., & Resnick, S. G. (1998). Models of community care for severe mental illness: A review of research on case management. *Schizophrenia Bulletin, 24*(1), 37–74.

Mueser, K. T., & Jeste, D. V. (2008). *Clinical handbook of schizophrenia*. New York. Guilford.

Mueser, K. T., Torrey, W., Lynde, D., Singer, P., & Drake, R. (2003). Implementing evidence-based practices for people with severe mental illness. *Behavior Modification, 27*(3), 387–411.

Muijen, M. (2008). Mental health services in Europe: An overview. *Psychiatric Services, 59*, 479–482.

Mukherjee, S., Shukls, S., Woodle, J., Rosen, A. M., & Olarte, S. (1983). Misdiagnosis of schizophrenia in bipolar patients: A multiethnic comparison. *American Journal of Psychiatry, 14*, 1571–1574.

Mullen B., Salas, E., & Driskell, J. E. (1989). Salience, motivation, and artifact as contributions to the relation between participation rate and leadership. *Journal of Experimental Social Psychology, 25*, 545–559.

Mullen, P. E., Burgess, P., & Wallace, C. (2000). Community care and criminal offending in schizophrenia. *Lancet, 35*, 614–617.

Muller, T. (1993). *Immigrants and the American city*. New York: New York University Press.

Mulvey, E. P., Gelber, J. L., & Roth, L. H. (1987). The promise and peril of involuntary outpatient commitment. *American Psychologist, 42*, 571–584.

Muntaner, C., & Eaton, W. W. (1996). Psychosocial and organizational factors: Chronic outcomes: Mental illness. In J. Stellman (Ed.), *ILO encyclopedia of occupational health and safety* (pp. 137–140). Geneva: International Labor Office.

Muntaner, C., Eaton, W. W., & Chamberlain, C. D. (2000). Social inequalities in mental health: A review of concepts and underlying assumptions. *Health, 4*(1), 89–113.

Muntaner, C., Tien, A. Y., Eaton, W. W., & Garrison, R. (1991). Occupational characteristics and the occurrence of psychotic disorders. *Social Psychiatry and Psychiatric Epidemiology, 26*, 273–280.

Murphy, G. C., & Athanasou, J. A. (1999). The effect of unemployment on mental health. *Journal of Occupational and Organizational Psychology, 72*(1), 83–99.

Murphy, H. B., & Vega, G. (1982). Schizophrenia and religious affiliation in Northern Ireland. *Psychological Medicine, 12*(3), 595–605.

Murray, C. J. L., & Lopez, A. D. (1996). *Global health statistics*. Cambridge, MA: Harvard University Press.

Murry, V. M., Harrell, A. W., Brody, G. H., Chen, Y., Simons, R. L., Black, A. R., et al. (2008). Long-term effects of stressors on relationship well-being and parenting among rural African American women. *Family Relations, 57*, 117–127.

Musick, K., & Bumpass, L. (2006). Cohabitation, marriage, and trajectories in well-being and relationships. *California Center for Population Research Working Paper Series* (CCPR-003–06). Retrieved November 15, 2006, from http://www.ccpr.ucla.edu/asp/papers.asp.

Myers, H. F. (1989). Urban stress and mental health in Black youth: An epidemiologic and conceptual update. In R. L. Jones (Ed.), *Black adolescents* (pp. 123–152). Berkeley: Cobb & Henry.

Nagaswami, V. (1990). Integration of psychosocial rehabilitation in national health care programmes. *Psychosocial Rehabilitation Journal, 14*, 53–65.

Napholz, L. (1994). Mental health and American Indian women's multiple roles. *American Indian and Alaska Native Mental Health, 6*, 57–75.

Narrow, W. E., Rae, D. S., Robins, L. N., & Regier, D. A. (2002). Revised prevalence estimates of mental disorders in the United States: Using a clinical significance criterion to reconcile 2 surveys' estimates. *Archives of General Psychiatry, 59*, 115–123.

Narrow, W. E., Rae, D. S., Moscicki, E. K., Locke, B. Z., & Regier, D. A. (1991). Depression among Cuban Americans: The Hispanic Health and Nutrition Examination Survey. *Social Psychology and Psychiatric Epidemiology, 25*, 260–268.

Nathan, K. I., & Schatzberg A. F. (1994). Mood disorders. In J. Oldham & M. B. Riba (Eds.). *Review of Psychiatry*, vol. 13. Washington, DC: American Psychiatric Press.

Nathan, P. E., & Gorman, J. M. (2002). *A guide to treatments that work* (2nd ed.). New York: Oxford University Press.

National Advisory Mental Health Council. (1993). Health care reform for Americans with severe mental illnesses: Report of the National Advisory Mental Health Council. *American Journal of Psychiatry, 150*, 1447–1465.

National Advisory Mental Health Council. (1996). Basic behavioral science research for mental health: Sociocultural and environmental processes. *American Psychologist, 51*, 722–731.

National Association of State Mental Health Program Directors (NASMHPD). (1989). *Position paper on consumer contributions to mental health service delivery systems*. Alexandria, VA: Author.

National Center for Health Statistics. (1990). Advance report of final mortality statistics, 1988. *Monthly Vital Statistics Report, 39*, 1–47.

National Center for Health Statistics. (2007). *Health, United States, 2007 with chartbook on trends in the health of Americans*. Retrieved from http://www.cdc.gov/nchs/data/hus/hus07.pdf.

National Coalition of Mental Health Consumer/Survivor Organizations (NCMHCSO). (2007, June 7). *Teleconference transcription*. Retrieved September 27, 2008, from http://www.ncmhcso.org/downloads/6.7.2007.pdf.

National Coalition of Mental Health Consumer/Survivor Organizations (NCMHCSO). (2008). *History of the National Coalition of Mental Health Consumer/Survivor Organizations.* Retrieved September 15, 2008, from http://www.ncmhcso.org/how-formed.htm.

National Counterterrorism Center. (2007). *National Counterterrorism Center: Annex of statistical information.* Retrieved June 16, 2008, from http://www.state.gov/s/ct/rls/crt/2006/82739.htm.

National Institute of Mental Health. (1987). *Mental health, United States, 1987* (DHHS Publication No. ADM 87-1518). Washington DC: U.S. Government Printing Office.

National Institute of Mental Health. (1991). *Caring for people with severe mental disorders: A national plan of research to improve services.* Washington, DC: U.S. Government Printing Office.

National Institute of Mental Health. (2001). *Blueprint for change: Research on child and adolescent mental health.* Washington, DC: U.S. Government Printing Office.

National professional organization of people in recovery from psychiatric disabilities is created. (2006, July 29). *Medical News Today.* Retrieved September 29, 2008, from www.medicalnewstoday.com/articles/48210.php.

National Research Council, Commission on Behavioral and Social Sciences and Education. (1993). *Losing generations: Adolescents in high risk settings.* Washington, DC: National Academies Press.

Natsuaki, M. N., Ge, X., Brody, G. H., Simons, R. L., Gibbons, F. X., & Cutrona, C. E. (2007). African American children's depressive symptoms: The prospective effects of neighborhood disorder, stressful life events, and parenting. *American Journal of Community Psychology, 39,* 163–176.

Navarro, V. (1994). *The politics of health policy: The US reforms, 1980–1994.* Boston: Blackwell.

Nebbitt, V. E., & Lombe, M. (2007). Environmental correlates of depressive symptoms among African American adolescents living in public housing. *Journal of Human Behavior in the Social Environment, 15,* 435–454.

Needleman, H. L. (1995). Behavioral toxiocology. *Environmental Health Perspectives, 103,* 77–79.

Needleman, H. L., & Bellinger, D. (1991). The health effects of low level exposure to lead. *Annual Review of Public Health, 12,* 111–140.

Neighbors, H. W. (1984). The distribution of psychiatric morbidity in Black Americans. *Community Mental Health Journal, 20,* 169–181.

Neighbors, H. W. (1990). The prevention of psychopathology in African Americans: An epidemiological persepective. *Community Mental Health Journal, 26,* 167–179.

Neighbors, H. W., Bashshur, R., Price, R., Selig, S., Donabedian, A., & Shannon, G. (1992). Ethnic minority mental health service delivery: A review of the literature. *Research in Community Mental Health, 7,* 53–69.

Neighbors, H. W., Caldwell, C., Williams, D. R., Nesse, R., Taylor, R. J., McKeever Bullard, K., et al. (2007). Race, ethnicity, and the use of services for mental disorders. *Archives of General Psychiatry, 64,* 485–494.

Neighbors, H. W., Jackson, J. S., Campbell, L., & Williams, D. (1989). The influence of racial factors on psychiatric diagnosis: A review and suggestions for research. *Community Mental Health Journal, 25*(4), 301–311.

Neighbors, H. W., Trierweller, S. J., Ford, B. C., & Muroff, J. R. (2003). Racial differences in DSM diagnosis using a semi-structured instrument: The importance of clinical judgment in the diagnosis of African Americans. *Journal of Health and Social Behavior, 44,* 237–256.

Neugebauer, R., Rabkin, J. G., Williams, J. B., Remien, R. H., Goetz, R., & Gorman, J. M. (1992). Bereavement reactions among homosexual men experiencing multiple losses in the AIDS epidemic. *American Journal of Psychiatry, 149*(10), 1374–1379.

Neugeboren, J. (1999). *Transforming madness: New lives for people living with mental illness.* Berkeley: University of California Press.

New treatment for depression – Marriage. (2007). *MSNBC.* Retrieved June 4, 2007, from http://www.msnbc.msn.com/id/19032614/.

New York Lawyers for the Public Interest, Inc. (NYLPI). (2005, April 7). *Implementation of "Kendra's Law" is severely biased.* New York: Author.

Newhill, C. E., Mulvey, E. P., & Lidz, C. W. (1995). Characteristics of violence in the community by female patients seen in a psychiatric emergency service. *Psychiatric Services, 46,* 785–789.

Ngo-Metzger, Q., Massagli, M. P., Clarridge, B. R., Manocchia, M., Davis, R. B., Iezzoni, L. I., et al. (2003). Linguistic and cultural barriers to care: Perspectives of Chinese and Vietnamese immigrants. *Journal of General Internal Medicine, 18*(1), 44–52.

NICHD Early Child Care Research Network. (1997). Familiar factors associated with the characteristics of nonmaternal care for infants. *Journal of Marriage and Family, 59,* 389–408.

NICHD Early Child Care Research Network. (2002). The interaction of child care and family risk in relation child development at 24 and 36 months. *Applied Developmental Science, 6,* 144–156.

NICHD Early Child Care Research Network. (2003). Does the amount of time spend in child care predict socioemotional adjustment during the transition to kindergarten? *Child Development, 74,* 976–1005.

NICHD Early Child Care Research Network. (2004). Trajectories of physical aggression from toddlerhood to middle childhood. *Monographs of the Society for Research in Child Development, 69*(1, Serial No. 278).

NICHD Early Child Care Research Network. (2005). Duration and developmental timing of poverty and children's cognitive and social development from birth through third grade. *Child Development, 76,* 795–810.

Niedhammer, I., Bugel, I., Goldberg, M., Leclerc, A., & Gueguen, A. (1998). Psychosocial factors at work and sickness absence in the GAZEL cohort: A prospective study. *Occupational & Environmental Medicine, 55*(11), 735–741.

Nissen, S. E., Tuzcu, E. M., Schoenhagen, P., Brown, B. G., Ganz, P., Vogel, R. A., et al. (2004). Effect of intensive compared with moderate lipid-lowering therapy on progression of coronary atherosclerosis: A randomized controlled trial. *Journal of the American Medical Association, 291,* 1071–1080.

Nobles, M. (2000). History counts: A comparative analysis, of racial/color categorization in US and Brazilian censuses. *American Journal of Public Health, 50,* 1738–1745.

Nock, S. L. (2005). Marriage as a public issue. *The Future of Children, 15,* 13–32.

Nolan, W. J. (1917). Occupational and dementia praecox. *State Hospitals Quarterly, 3,* 127–154.

Nolen-Hoeksema, S. (1987). Sex differences in unipolar depression: Evidence and theory. *Psychological Bulletin, 101,* 259–282.

Nolen-Hoeksema, S. (1994). *Sex differences in depression.* Stanford, CA: Stanford University Press.

Nolen-Hoeksema, S. (2002). Gender differences in depression. In I. Gotlib & C. L. Hammen (Eds.), *Handbook of depression* (pp. 492–509). New York: Guilford.

Nolen-Hoeksema, S., & Girgus, J. S. (1994). The emergence of gender differences in depression during adolescence. *Psychological Bulletin, 115,* 424–443.

Norquist, G. S., & Wells, K. B. (1991). How do HMOs reduce outpatient mental health care costs? *American Journal of Psychiatry, 148,* 96–101.

Norris, F. H. (1992). Epidemiology of trauma: Frequency and impact of different potentially traumatic events on different demographic groups. *Journal of Consulting and Clinical Psychology, 60,* 409–418.

North, C. S., Nixon, S. J., Shariat, S., Mallonee, S., Curtis, J., McMillen, E. L., et al. (1999). Psychiatric disorders among survivors of the Oklahoma City bombing. *Journal of the American Medical Association, 282,* 755–762.

Norton, E., Yoon, J., Domino, M., & Morrissey, J. (2006). Transitions between the public mental health system and jail for persons with severe mental illness: A Markov analysis. *Health Economics, 15*(7), 719–733.

Novak, K. J., & Engel, R. S. (2005). Disentangling the influence of suspects' demeanor and mental disorder on arrest. *Policing, 28,* 493–512.

Nunnally, J. C. (1961). *Popular conceptions of mental health.* New York: Holt, Rinehart & Winston.

Nuru-Jeter, A., Williams, C. T., & LaVeist, T. S. (2008). A methodological note on modeling the effects of race: The case of psychological distress. *Stress and Health,* DOI: 10.1002/smi.

Nyblade, L. C. (2006). Measuring HIV stigma: Existing knowledge and gaps. *Psychology, Health & Medicine, 11*(3), 335–345.

Oakes, J. M., & Rossi, P. H. (2003). The measurement of SES in health research: Current practice and steps toward a new approach. *Social Science & Medicine, 56*(4), 769–784.

Oakley A. (1974). *The sociology of housework.* New York: Pantheon.

Oaks, D. (2006a). The evolution of the consumer movement [Letter to the editor]. *Psychiatric Services, 57*(8), 1212.

Oaks, D. (2006b, August 22). *Comments made during David Oaks' interview with Sally Zinman.* Retrieved September 23, 2008, from http://www.mindfreedom.org/campaign/media/mfradio/archived-shows/sally-zinman.mp3/view.

O'Cleirigh, C., Ironson, G., Fletcher, M. A., & Schneiderman, N. (2008). Written emotional disclosure and processing of trauma are associated with protected health status and immunity in people living with HIV/AIDS. *British Journal of Health Psychology, 13*(1), 81–84.

O'Dowd, M.A., & McKegney, F. P. (1990). AIDS patients compared with others in psychiatric consultation. *General Hospital Psychiatry, 12*, 50–55.

O'Farrell, T. J. (1989). Marital and family therapy in alcoholism treatment. *Journal of Substance Abuse Treatment, 6*, 23–29.

Office of Management and Budget. (1997, October 30). Revisions to the standards for the classification of federal data on race and ethnicity. *Federal Register,* 62FR58781–58790.

Ogloff, J. R. P. (1991). A comparison of insanity defense standards on juror decision making. *Law and Human Behavior, 15*, 509–532.

Ohbuchi, K., Ohno, T., & Mukai, H. (1992). Empathy and aggression: Effects of self-disclosure and fearful appeal. *Journal of Social Psychology, 133*, 243–253.

Okun, M. A., & Keith, V. M. (1998). Effects of positive and negative social exchanges with various sources on depressive symptoms. *Journal of Gerontology: Psychological Sciences, 53B*, P14–P20.

Olafsdottir, S., & Pescosolido, B. A. (2009). Drawing the line: The cultural cartography of utilization recommendations for mental health problems. *Journal of Health and Social Behavior, 50.*

Olfson, M., Blaco, C., Liu, L., Moreno, C., & Laje, G. (2006). National trends in the outpatient treatment of children and adolescents with antipsychotic drugs. *Archives of General Psychiatry, 63*, 679–685.

Olfson, M., Fireman, B., Weissman, M., Leon, A. C., Sheehan, D. V., Kathol, R. G., et al. (1997). Mental disorders and disability among patients in a primary care group practice. *American Journal of Psychiatry, 154*, 1734–1740.

Olfson, M., Gameroff, M. J., Marcus, S. C., & Jensen, P. S. (2003). National trends in the treatment of attention deficit hyperactivity disorder. *American Journal of Psychiatry, 160*, 1071–1077.

Olfson, M., Marcus, S. C., Druss, B., & Pincus, H. A. (2002). National trends in the use of outpatient psychotherapy. *American Journal of Psychiatry, 159*, 1914–1920.

Olfson, M., & Pincus, H. A. (1996). Outpatient mental health care in nonhospital settings: Distribution of patients across provider groups. *American Journal of Psychiatry, 153*, 1353–1356.

Olfson, M., Weissman, M. W., Leon, A. C., & Higgins, E. S. (1995). Psychological management by family physicians. *Journal of Family Practice, 41*, 543–550.

Oliver, M. N., & Muntaner, C. (2005). Researching health inequities among African Americans: The imperative to understand social class. *International Journal of Health Services, 35*(3), 485–498.

Olvera, R. L. (2002). Intermittent explosive disorder: Epidemiology, diagnosis and management. *CNS Drugs, 16*, 517–526.

Omer, H. (1993). The integrative focus: Coordinating symptom- and person-oriented perspectives in therapy. *American Journal of Psychotherapy, 47*, 283–295.

Omi, M., & Winant, H. (1994). *Racial formation in the United States: From the 1960s to the 1990s.* New York: Routledge.

Oppenheimer, V. (2000). The continuing importance of men's economic position in marriage formation. In L. Waite. (Ed.), *The ties that bind* (pp. 283–301). New York: Aldine de Gruyter.

Ortega, S. T., & Corzine, J. (1990). Socioeconomic status and mental disorders. In J. R. Greenley (Ed.), *Research in community and mental health: A research annual: Mental disorder in social context* (pp. 149–182). Greenwich, CT: JAI Press.

Osborne, C., Manning, W. D., & Smock, P. J. (2007). Married and cohabiting parents' relationship stability: A focus on race and ethnicity. *Journal of Marriage and Family, 69*, 1345–1366.

Osborne, C., & McLanahan, S. (2007). Relationship instability and child well-being. *Journal of Marriage and Family, 69*, 1065–1083.

O'Sullivan, M. J., & Lasso, B. (1992). Community mental health services for Hispanics: A test of the culture compatibility hypothesis. *Hispanic Journal of Behavioral Sciences, 14*(4), 455–468.

O'Sullivan, M. J., Peterson, P. D., Cox, G. B., & Kirkeby, J. (1989). Ethnic populations: Community mental health services ten years later. *American Journal of Community Psychology, 17*(1), 17–30.

Overbeek, G., Vollbergh, W., de Graaf, R., Scholte, R., de Kemp, R., & Engels, R. (2006). Longitudinal associations of marital quality and marital dissolution with the incidence of DSM-III-R disorders. *Journal of Family Psychology, 20*(2), 284–291.

Owan, T. (1981). Neighborhood-based mental health: An aproach to overcome inequities in mental health services delivery to racial and ethnic minorities. In D. D. Biegal & A. J. Naparstek (Eds.), *Community support systems and mental health: Practice, policy, and research* (pp. 282–300). New York: Springer.

Oxford illustrated dictionary. (2nd ed.). (1975). Oxford: Clarendon.

Packard, E. (1973). *Modern persecution or insane asylums unveiled.* Mental illness and social policy: The American experience (2 vols). New York: Arno Press. (Original work published 1875)

Padgett, D. K., Patrick, C., Burns, B. J., & Schlesinger, H. J. (1994). Ethnicity and the use of outpatient mental health services in a national insured population. *American Journal of Public Health, 84*, 222–226.

Padgett, D., Struening, E. L., & Andrews, H. (1990). Factors affecting the use of medical, mental health, alcohol, and drug treatment services by homeless adults. *Medical Care, 28*(9), 805–821.

Page, M. E., & Stevens, A. H. (2005). Understanding racial differences in the economic costs of growing up in a single parent family. *Demography, 42*, 75–90.

Page, S. (1977). Effects of the mental illness label in attempts to obtain accommodations. *Canadian Journal of Behavioral Science, 9*, 85–90.

Paikoff, R. L., Brooks-Gunn, J., & Warren, M. P. (1991). Effects of girls' hormonal status on depressive and aggressive symptoms over the course of one year. *Journal of Youth and Adolescence, 20*, 191–215.

Pakenham, K. I., & Rinaldis, M. (2001). The role of illness, resources, appraisal, and coping strategies in adjustment to HIV/AIDS: The direct and buffering effects. *Journal of Behavioral Medicine, 24*, 259–279.

Palermo, G. B., Smith, M. B., & Liska, F. J. (1991). Jails versus mental hospitals: A social dilemma. *International Journal of Offender Therapy and Comparative Criminology, 35*, 97–106.

Paley, W. D. (1993). Overview of the HMO movement. *Psychiatric Quarterly, 64*(1), 5–12.

Palmieri, P. A., Canetti-Nisim, D., Galea, S., Johnson, R. J., & Hobfoll, S. E. (2008). The psychological impact of the Israel-Hezbollah War on Jews and Arabs in Israel: The impact of risk and resilience factors. *Social Science and Medicine, 67*(8), 1208–1216.

Pandiani, J. A., Rosenheck, R., & Banks, S. M. (2003). Elevated risk of arrest for Veteran's Administration behavioral health service recipients in four Florida counties. *Law and Human Behavior, 27*, 289–298.

Pantin, H. M., Schwartz, S. J., Prado, G., Feaster, D. J., & Szapocznik, J. (2003). Posttraumatic stress disorder symptoms in Hispanic immigrants after the September 11th attacks: Severity and relationship to previous traumatic exposure. *Hispanic Journal of Behavioral Sciences, 25*(1), 56–72.

Paradies, Y. (2006). A systematic review of empirical research on self-reported racism and health. *International Journal of Epidemiology, 35*(4), 888–901.

Parcel, T. L., & Menaghan, E. G. (1994). *Parents' jobs and children's lives.* New York: de Gruyter.

Pardoen, D., Bauwens, F., Dramaix, M., Tracy, A., Genevrois, C., Staner, L., et al. (1996). Life events and primary affective disorders: A one year prospective study. *British Journal of Psychiatry, 169*, 160–166.

Parke, R. D., Coltrane, S., Duffy, S. Buriel, R., Dennis, J., Powers, J., et al. (2004). Economic stress, parenting, and child adjustment in Mexican American and European American families. *Child Development, 75*, 1632–1656.

Parker, G. (1987). Are the lifetime prevalence estimates in the ECA study accurate? *Psychological Medicine, 17*, 275–282.

Parker, S., & Kleiner, R. J. (1966). *Mental illness in the urban Negro community*. New York: The Free Press.

Parrish, J. (1988). The consumer movement: A personal perspective. *Community Support Network News, 5*, 1, 3.

Parsey, R. V., Hastings, R. S., Oquendo, M. A., Huang, Y. Y., Simpson, N., Arcement, J., et al. (2006). Lower serotonin transporter binding potential in the human brain during major depressive episodes. *American Journal of Psychiatry, 163*, 52–58.

Parsons, J. T., Schrimshaw, E. W., Bimbi, D. S., Wolitski, R. J., Gomez, C. A., & Halkitis, P. N. (2005). Consistent, inconsistent, and non-disclosure to casual sexual partners among HIV-seropositive gay and bisexual men. *AIDS, 19* (Suppl. 1), S87–S97.

Parsons, T. (1951). *The social system*. Glencoe, IL: The Free Press.

Pasamanick, B. (1963). Some misconceptions concerning differences in the racial prevalence of mental disease. *American Journal of Orthopsychiatry, 33*, 72–86.

Pasamanick, B., & Knobloch, H. (1961). Epidemiologic studies on the complications of pregnancy and birth process. In G. Caplan (Ed.), *Prevention of mental disorders in children* (pp. 74–94). New York: Basic Books.

Pasewark, R. A., & Pantle, M. L. (1979). Insanity plea: Legislator's view. *American Journal of Psychiatry, 136*, 222–223.

Pasewark, R. A, Pantle, M. L., & Steadman, H. J. (1982). Detention and rearrest rates of persons found not guilty by reason of insanity and convicted felons. *American Journal of Psychiatry, 139*, 892–897.

Pasewark, R. A., & Seidenzahl, D. (1979). Opinions concerning the insanity plea and criminality among mental patients. *Bulletin of the American Academy of Psychiatry and Law, 7*, 199–202.

Passel, J. S., Capps, R., & Fix, M. E. (2004). *Undocumented immigrants: Facts and figures*. Washington, DC: Urban Institute.

Patel, V., & Winston, M. (1994). "Universality of mental illness" revisited: Assumptions, artifacts and new directions. *British Journal of Psychiatry, 165*, 437–439.

Paterniti, S., Niedhammer, I., Lang, T., & Consoli, S. (2002). Psychosocial factors at work, personality traits and depressive symptoms: Longitudinal results from the GAZEL Study. *British Journal of Psychiatry, 181*, 111–117.

Pat-Horenczyk, R., Abramovitz, R., Peled, O., Brom, D., Daie, A., & Chemtob, C. M. (2007). Adolescent exposure to recurrent terrorism in Israel: Posttraumatic distress and functional impairment. *American Journal of Orthopsychiatry, 77*(1), 76–85.

Pat-Horenczyk, R., & Brom, D. (2007). The number of faces of post-traumatic growth. *Applied Psychology International, 56*, 379–385.

Pat-Horenczyk, R., Peled, O., Miron, T., Brom, D., Villa, Y., & Chemtob, C. M. (2007). Risk-taking behaviors among Israeli adolescents exposed to recurrent terrorism: Provoking danger under continuous threat? *American Journal of Psychiatry, 164*(1), 66–72.

Patterson, G. R. (2002). The early development of coercive family process. In J. B. Reid, G. R. Patterson, & J. Snyder (Eds.), *Antisocial behavior in children and adolescents: A developmental analysis and model for intervention* (pp. 25–44). Washington, DC: American Psychological Association.

Pattillo-McCoy, M. (1999). *Black picket fences: Privilege and peril among the Black middle class*. Chicago: University of Chicago Press.

Pavalko, E. K. (1997). Beyond trajectories: Multiple concepts for analyzing long-term process. In M. A. Hardy (Ed.), *Studying aging and social change: Conceptual and methodological issues* (pp. 129–147). Thousand Oaks, CA: Sage.

Pavkov, T. W., Lewis, D. A., & Lyons, J. S. (1989). Psychiatric diagnoses and racial bias: An empirical investigation. *Professional Psychology: Research and Practice, 20*(6), 364–368.

Paxton, K., & Robinson, W. L. (2008). Depressive symptoms, gender and sexual risk behavior among African American adolescents: Implications for prevention and intervention. *Journal of Prevention and Intervention in the Community, 35*(2), 49–62.

Pearlin, L. I. (1983). Role strains and personal stress. In H. B Kaplan (Ed.), *Psychosocial stress: Trends in theory and research* (pp. 3–32). New York: Academic Press.

Pearlin, L. I. (1998). The stress process revisited. In C. Aneshensel & J. Phelan (Eds.), *Handbook of the sociology of mental health* (pp. 395–415). New York: Plenum.

Pearlin, L. I. (1989). The sociological study of stress. *Journal of Health and Social Behavior, 30,* 241–256.

Pearlin, L. I., & Lieberman, M. A. (1979). Social sources of emotional distress. In R. G. Simmond (Ed.), *Research in community and mental health* (pp. 217–48). Greenwich CT: JAI Press.

Pearlin, L. I., Lieberman, M. A., Menaghan, E. G., & Mullan, J. T. (1981). The stress process. *Journal of Health and Social Behavior, 22,* 337–356.

Pearlin, L. I., Nguyen, K., Schieman, S., & Milkie, M. A. (2007). The life-course origins of mastery among older people. *Journal of Health and Social Behavior, 48,* 164–179.

Pearlin, L. I., Schieman, S., Fazio, E. M., & Meersman, S. C. (2005). Stress, health, and the life course: Some conceptual perspectives. *Journal of Health and Social Behavior, 46,* 205–219.

Pearlin, L. I., & Schooler. C. (1978). The structure of coping. *Journal of Health and Social Behavior, 19,* 2–21.

Pearlin, L. I., & Skaff, M. (1996). Stress and the life course: A paradigmatic alliance. *Gerontologist, 36,* 239–247.

Peck, M. C., & Scheffler, R. M. (2002). An analysis of the definitions of mental illness used in state parity laws. *Psychiatric Services, 53,* 1089–1095.

Pedersen, S., Vitaro, F., Barker, E. D., & Borge, A. I. (2007). The timing of middle-childhood peer rejection and friendship: Linking early behavior to early-adolescent adjustment. *Child Development, 78,* 1037–1405.

Perelberg, R. J. (1983). Mental illness, family and networks in a London borough. *Social Science and Medicine, 17,* 481–491.

Perkins, D., Stern, R., Golden, R., Murphy, C., Naftolowitz, D., & Evans, D. L. (1994). Mood disorders in HIV infection: Prevalence and risk factors in a non-epicenter of the AIDS epidemic. *American Journal of Psychiatry, 151,* 233–236.

Perlick, D. A., Miklowitz, D. J., Link, B. G., Struening, E., Kaczynski, R., Gonzalez, J., et al. (2007). Perceived stigma and depression among caregivers of patients with bipolar disorder. *British Journal of Psychiatry, 190,* 535–536.

Perlick, D. A., Rosenheck, R. A., Clarkin, J. F., Sirey, J. A., Salahi, J., Struening, E. L., et al. (2001). Stigma as a barrier to recovery: Adverse effects of perceived stigma on social adaptation of persons diagnosed with bipolar affective disorder. *Psychiatric Services, 52,* 1627–1632.

Perreira, K. A., Deeb-Sossa, N., Harris, K. M., & Bollen, K. (2005). What are we measuring? An evaluation of the CES-D across race/ethnicity and immigrant generation. *Social Forces, 83,* 1567–1602.

Perrine, M. W. B., Schroder, K. E. E., Forester, R., McGonagle-Moulton, P., & Huessy, F. (2004). The impact of the September 11, 2001, terrorist attacks on alcohol consumption and distress: Reactions to a national trauma 300 miles from Ground Zero. *Journal of Studies on Alcohol, 65*(1), 5–15.

Perrow, C., & Guillen, M. (1990). *The AIDS disaster: The failure of organizations in New York and the nation.* New Haven, CT: Yale University Press.

Perrucci, C., & Perrucci, R. (1990). Unemployment and mental health: Research and policy implications. In J. Greenley (Ed.), *Research in community and mental health: Vol. 6* (pp. 237–264). Greenwich, CT: JAI Press.

Perrucci, C., Perrucci, R., & Targ, D. (1997). Gender differences in the economic, psychological and social effects of plant closings in an expanding economy. *Social Science Journal, 34*(2), 217–233.

Perrucci, R. (1974). *Circle of madness: On being insane and institutionalized in America.* Englewood Cliffs, NJ: Prentice-Hall.

Persons, J. B. (1986). The advantages of studying psychological phenomena rather than psychiatric diagnoses. *American Psychologist, 41,* 1252–1260.

Pescosolido, B. A. (1991). Illness careers and network ties: A conceptual model of utilization and compliance. In G. L. Albrecht & J. A. Levy (Eds.), *Advances in medical sociology* (pp. 161–184). Greenwich, CT: JAI Press.

Pescosolido, B. A. (1992). Beyond rational choice: The social dynamics of how people seek help. *American Journal of Sociology, 97,* 1096–1138.

Pescosolido, B. A. (1996). Bringing the 'community' into utilization models: How social networks link individuals to changing systems of care. In J. J. Kronenfeld (Ed.), *Research in the sociology of health care* (pp. 171–198). Greenwich, CT: JAI Press.

Pescosolido, B. A. (2006). Of pride and prejudice: The role of sociology and social networks in integrating the health sciences. *Journal of Health and Social Behavior, 47*, 189–208.

Pescosolido, B. A., & Boyer, C. A. (1999). How do people come to use mental health services? Current knowledge and changing perspectives. In A. V. Horwitz & T. L. Scheid (Eds.), *A handbook for the study of mental health: Social contexts, theories, and systems* (pp. 392–411). New York: Cambridge University Press.

Pescosolido, B. A., Boyer, C. A., & Lubell, K. M. (1999). The social dynamics of responding to mental health problems: Past, present, and future challenges to understanding individuals' use of services. In C. Aneshensel & J. Phelan (Eds.), *Handbook of the sociology of mental health* (pp. 441–460). New York: Plenum Press.

Pescosolido, B. A., Gardner, C. B, & Lubell, K. (1998). How people get into mental health services: Stories of choice, coercion, and 'muddling through' from 'first-timers.' *Social Science & Medicine, 46*, 275–286.

Pescosolido, B. A., & Kronenfeld, J. J. (1995). Health, illness and healing in an uncertain era: Challenges from and for medical sociology. *Journal of Health and Social Behavior, 36* [Extra Issue], 5–33.

Pescosolido, B. A., Martin, J. K., Lang, A., & Olafsdottir, S. (2008). Rethinking theoretical approaches to stigma: A framework integrating normative influences on stigma. *Social Science & Medicine, 67*, 431–440.

Pescosolido, B. A., Martin, J. K., Link, B. G., Kikuzawa, S., Burgos, G., & Swindle, R. (2000). *Americans' views of mental illness and health at century's end: Continuity and change. Public report on the MacArthur Mental Health Module, 1996 General Social Survey.* Bloomington: Indiana Consortium for Mental Health Services Research.

Pescosolido, B. A., Martin, J. K., Long, J. S., Medina, T. R., Link, B. G., & Phelan, J. C. (2008a). *A decade of continuity and change in the stigma of mental illness: Evidence from two national surveys.* Paper presented at the annual meeting of the Society for the Study of Social Problems, Boston.

Pescosolido, B. A., Martin, J. K., Long, J. S., Medina, T. R., Phelan, J., & Link, B. G. (2008b). *Can medical science erase the stigma of mental illness?* Paper presented at the annual meeting of the American Sociological Association, August.

Pescosolido, B. A., McLeod, J. D., & Avison, W. R. (2007). Reflections through the sociological looking glass. In W. R. Avison, J. D. McLeod, & B. A. Pescosolido (Eds.), *Mental health, social mirror* (pp. 3–32). New York: Springer Science.

Pescosolido, B. A., Monahan, J., Link, B. G., Stueve, A., & Kikuzawa, S. (1999). The public's view of the competence, dangerousness, and need for legal coercion of persons with mental health problems. *American Journal of Public Health, 89*, 1339–1345.

Pescosolido, B. A., Perry, B. L., Martin, J. K., McLeod, J. D., & Jensen, P. S. (2007). Stigmatizing attitudes and beliefs about treatment and psychiatric medications for children with mental illness. *Psychiatric Services, 58*, 613–618.

Pescosolido, B. A., Wright, E., Alegría, M., & Vera, M. (1996). *Social networks and patterns of use among the poor with mental health problems in Puerto Rico.* Paper presented at the annual meeting of the American Public Health Association.

Pescosolido, B. A., Wright, E. R., & Sullivan, W. P. (1996). Communities of care: A theoretical perspective on case management models in mental health. In G. Albrecht (Ed.), *Advances in medical sociology: Vol 6* (pp. 37–79). Greenwich, CT: JAI Press.

Petersen, A. C., Compas, B. E., Brooks-Gunn, J., Stemmler, M., Ey, S., & Grant, K. E. (1993). Depression in adolescence. *American Psychologist, 48*, 155–168.

Petersen, A. C., Sarigani, P. A., & Kennedy, R. E. (1991). Adolescent depression: Why more girls? *Journal of Youth & Adolescence, 20*, 247–271.

Peterson, C. (1992). *Personality* (2nd ed.). Fort Worth, TX: Harcourt Brace.

Peterson, C. (1996). *The psychology of abnormality.* Fort Worth, TX: Harcourt Brace.

Peyrot, M. (1991). Institutional and organizational dynamics in community based drug abuse treatment. *Social Problems, 38*, 20–33.

Pfefferbaum, A., Lim, K., Rosenbloom, M., & Zipursky, R. B. (1990). Brain magnetic resonance imaging: Approaches for investigating schizophrenia. *Schizophrenia Bulletin, 16*, 452–476.

Pfefferbaum, B., Doughty, D. E., Reddy, C., Patel, N., Gurwitch, R. H., Nixon, S. J., et al. (2002). Exposure and peritraumatic response as predictors of posttraumatic stress in children following the 1995 Oklahoma City bombing. *Journal of Urban Health–Bulletin of the New York Academy of Medicine, 79*(3), 354–363.

Pfefferbaum, B., North, C. S., Pfefferbaum, R. L., Christiansen, E. H., Schorr, J. K., Vincent, R. D., et al. (2008). Change in smoking and drinking after September 11, 2001, in a national sample of ever smokers and ever drinkers. *Journal of Nervous and Mental Disease, 196*(2), 113–121.

Phelan, J. (1992). The paradox of the contented female worker: An assessment of alternative explanations. *Social Psychology Quarterly, 57*, 95–107.

Phelan, J. C. (2005). Geneticization of deviant behavior and consequences for stigma: The case of mental illness. *Journal of Health & Social Behavior, 46*, 307–322.

Phelan, J. C., & Link, B. G. (1998). The growing belief that people with mental illnesses are violent: The role of the dangerousness criterion for civil commitment. *Social Psychiatry and Pschiatric Epidemiology, 33*, S7–S12.

Phelan, J. C., & Link, B. G. (2004). Fear of people with mental illnesses: The role of personal and impersonal contact and exposure to threat or harm. *Journal of Health and Social Behavior, 45*, 68–80.

Phelan, J. C., Link, B. G., & Dovidio, J. F. (2008). Stigma and discrimination: One animal or two? *Social Science & Medicine, 67*, 358–367.

Phelan, J. C., Link, B. G., Stueve, A., & Pescosolido, B. A. (2000). Public conceptions of mental illness in 1950 and 1996: What is mental illness and is it to be feared? *Journal of Health and Social Behavior, 41*(2), 188–207.

Phelan, J. C., Lucas, J. W., & Link, B. G. (2008). *Comparison of status and stigma processes in interpersonal interactions.* Paper presented at the annual meeting of the Society for the Study of Social Problems, Boston.

Phillips, P. (2002). *Censored 2003: The top 25 censored stories.* New York: Seven Stories Press.

Phillips, S., Burns, B., Edgar, E., Mueser, K., Linkins, K., Rosenheck, R., et al. (2001). Moving assertive community treatment into standard practice. *Psychiatric Services, 52*, 771–779.

Pierce, G. R., Sarason, B. R., Sarason, I. G., Joseph, H. J., & Henderson, C. A. (1996). Conceptualizing and assessing social support in the context of the family. In G. R. Pierce, B. R. Sarason, & I. G. Sarason (Eds.), *Handbook of social support and the family* (pp. 3–24). New York: Plenum Press.

Pilowksy, L. S. (2001). Research methods and biological psychiatry. *International Review of Psychiatry, 13*, 5–6.

Pleck, J. (1985). *Working wives, working husbands.* Beverly Hills, CA: Sage.

Plomin, R. (1990). *Nature and nurture: An introduction to human behavioral genetics.* Pacific Grove: Brooks/Cole.

Plomin, R., DeFries, J., McClearn, G., & McGuffin, P. (2000). *Behavioral genetics.* New York: Worth.

Plotnik, R. (1993). *Introduction to psychology.* Pacific Grove: Brooks/Cole.

Polgar, M., & Cabassa, L. (2007). Helping young adults with mental health problems: Providers evaluate a regional system of care. *Sociological Viewpoints, 83*, 85–100.

Pollack, D. A. (2004). *Moving from coercion to collaboration in mental health services* (DHHS Publication No. SMA 04-3869). Rockville, MD: Substance Abuse and Mental Health Services Administration.

Pollack, D., McFarland, B. H., George, R. A., & Angell, R. H. (1994). Prioritization of mental health services in Oregon. *Milbank Quarterly, 72*, 515–550.

Porporino, F. J., & Motiuk, L. L. (1995). The prison careers of mentally disordered offenders. *International Journal of Law and Psychiatry, 18*, 29–44.

Portes, A., Kyle, D., & Eaton, W. W. (1992). Mental illness and help-seeking behavior among Mariel Cuban and Haitian refugees in South Florida. *Journal of Health and Social Behavior, 33*, 283–298.

Poythress, N., Skeem, J., & Lelienfeld, S. (2006). Associations among early abuse, disassociation and psychopathy among offenders. *Journal of Abnormal Psychology, 115*, 288–297.

Poznanski, E. O., & Mokros, H. B. (1994). Phenomenology and epidemiology of mood disorders in children and adolescents. In W. M. Reynolds & H. F. Johnson (Eds.), *Handbook of depression in children and adolescents* (pp. 19–39). New York: Plenum Press.

Pratt, L. A., & Brody, D. J. (2008). *Depression in the United States household population, 2005–2006* (National Center for Health Statistics, Data Brief). Hyattsville, MD: U.S. Department of Health and Human Services.

Prelow, H. M., Danoff-Burg, S., Swenson, R. R., & Pulgiano, D. (2004). The impact of ecological risk and perceived discrimination on the psychological adjustment of African American and European American youth. *Journal of Community Psychology, 32*, 375–389.

Presidential Commission. (1988). *Report of the Presidential Commission on the human immunodeficiency virus epidemic*. Washington, DC: U.S. Government Printing Office.

President's Commission on Mental Health and Illness. (1978). *Report to the president from the President's Commission on Mental Health: Vol, 1*. Washington, DC: U.S. Government Printing Office.

President's New Freedom Commission on Mental Health. (2003). *Achieving the promise: Transforming mental health care in America. Final report* (DHHS Publication No. SMA-03-3832). Rockville, MD: Author.

Presser, H. B. (2005). *Working in a 24/7 economy: Challenges for American families*. New York: Russell Sage Foundation.

Priebe, S., Frottier, P., Gaddini, A., Kilian, R., Lauber, C., Martinez-Leal, R., et al. (2008). Mental health care institutions in nine European countries, 2002–2006. *Psychiatric Services, 59*, 570–575.

Priest, R. (1991). Racism and prejudice as negative impacts on African American clients in therapy. *Journal of Counseling and Development, 70*(1), 213–215.

Pryor Brown, L. J., Powell, J., & Earls, F. (1989). Stressful life events and psychiatric symptoms in Black adolescent females. *Journal of Adolescent Research, 4*, 140–151.

Pudrovska, T., Schieman, S., & Carr, D. (2006). Strains of singlehood in later life: Do race and gender matter? *Journal of Gerontology: Social Sciences, 61B*, S315–S322.

Pugliesi, K. (1995). Work and well-being: Gender differences in the psychological consequences of employment. *Journal of Health and Social Behavior, 36*, 57–71.

Putnam, F. W., Guroff, J. J., Silberman, E. K., Barban, L., & Post, R. M. (1986). The clinical phenomenology of multiple personality disorder: Review of 100 recent cases. *Journal of Clinical Psychiatry, 47*, 285–293.

Quan, V. M., Steketee, R. W., Valleroy, L., Weinstock, H., Karon, J., & Janssen R. (2002). HIV incidence in the United States, 1978–1999. *Journal of Acquired Immune Deficiency Syndromes, 31*, 188–201.

Quinsey, V. L. (2000). Institutional violence among the mentally ill. In S. Hodgins (Ed.), *Violence among the mentally ill: Effective treatments and management strategies* (pp. 213–236). London: Kluwer.

Rabkin, J. G. (1972). Opinions about mental illness: A review of the literature. *Psychological Bulletin, 72*, 153–171.

Rabkin, J. (1979). Criminal behavior of discharged mental patients: A critical appraisal of the research. *Psychological Bulletin, 86*, 1–27.

Rachlin, S., Pam, A., & Milton, J. (1975). Civil liberties versus involuntary hospitalization. *American Journal of Psychiatry, 132*, 89–191.

Radloff, L. S. (1977). The CES-D Scale: A self-report depression scale for research in the general population. *Applied Psychological Measurement, 1*, 385–401.

Radloff, L. S. (1991). The use of the Center for Epidemiologic Studies Depression Scale in adolescents and young adults. *Journal of Youth and Adolescence, 20*, 149–166.

Radical Therapist/Rough Times Collective (Eds.). (1974). *The radical therapist*. Harmondsworth, England: Penguin.

Rafaeli, A., & Sutton, R. (1989). The expression of emotion in organizational life. In L. L. Cummings & B. M. Staw (Eds.), *Research in organizational behavior* (Vol. 11, pp. 1–42). Greenwich, CT: JAI Press.

Rafferty, Y., Friend, R., & Landsbergis, P. A. (2001). The association between job skill discretion, decision authority and burnout. *Work & Stress, 15*(1), 73–85.

Ragin, C. C. (1999). The distinctiveness of case-oriented research. *Health Services Research, 34*, 1137–1151.

Raley, R. K., & Bumpass, L. (2003). The topography of the divorce plateau: Levels and trends in union stability in the United States after 1980. *Demographic Research, 8*(8), 245–260.

Randolph, F. (1995). Improving service systems through systems integration: The ACCESS program. *American Rehabilitation, 21*(1), 36–38.

Randolph, F., Blasinsky, M., Leginski, W., Parker, L., & Goldman, H. (1997). Creating the integrated service systems for homeless persons with mental illness: The ACCESS Program. *Psychiatric Services, 48*, 369–373.

Rao, D., Pryor, J. B., Gaddist, B. W., & Mayer, R. (2008). Stigma, secrecy, and discrimination: Ethnic/racial differences in the concerns of people living with HIV/AIDS. *AIDS and Behavior, 12*(2), 265–271.

Rapaport, D. (1959). The structure of psychoanalytic theory: A systematizing attempt. In S. Koch (Ed.), *Psychology: A study of a science* (Vol. 1). New York: McGraw-Hill.

Raudenbush, S. W., & Bryk, A. S. (2002). *Hierarchical linear models: Applications and data analysis methods* (2nd ed.). Thousand Oaks: Sage.

Ray, W., Daugherty, J., & Meader, K. (2003). Effect of a mental health "carve-out" program on the continuity of antipsychotic therapy. *New England Journal of Medicine, 348*, 1185–1894.

Raz, S., & Raz, N. (1990). Structural brain abnormalities in the major psychoses: A quantitative review of the evidence from computerized imaging. *Psychological Bulletin, 16*, 391–402.

Rector, R. E., Pardue, M. G., & Noyes, L. R. (2003, August 22). "Marriage Plus": Sabotaging the president's efforts to promote healthy marriage. *Heritage Foundation Backgrounder No. 1677.* Retrieved from www.heritage.org/Research/Welfare/GB1677.cfm.

Regier, D. A., Kaelber, C. T., Rae, D. S., Farmer, M. E., Knauper, B., Kessler, R. C., et al. (1998). Limitations of diagnostic criteria and assessment instruments for mental disorders: Implications for research and policy. *Archives of General Psychiatry, 55*, 109–115.

Regier, D. A., Myers, J. K., Kramer, M., Robins, L. N., Blazer, D. G., Hough, R. L., et al. (1984). The NIMH Epidemiologic Catchment Area (ECA) Program: Historical context, major objectives, and study population characteristics. *Archives of General Psychiatry, 41*, 934–941.

Regier, D. A., Narrow, W. E., Rae, D. S., Manderscheid, R. W., Locke, B. Z., & Goodwin, F. K. (1993). The de facto US mental and addictive disorders service system: Epidemiologic catchment area prospective 1-year prevalence rates of disorders and services. *Archives of General Psychiatry, 50*, 85–94.

Regoeczi, W. C. (2008). Crowding in context: An examination of the differential responses of men and women to high-density living environments. *Journal of Health and Social Behavior, 49*, 254–268.

Reid, L. (2002). Occupational segregation, human capital, and motherhood: Black women's higher exit rates from full-time employment. *Gender and Society, 16*, 728–747.

Reidpath, D. D., & Chan, K. Y. (2005). A method for the quantitative analysis of the layering of HIV-related stigma. *AIDS Care, 17*(4), 425–432.

Reisner, R. (1985). *Law and the mental health system* (American Casebook Series). St. Paul, MN: West.

Reiss, D., Plomin, R., & Hetherington, E. (1991). Genetics and psychiatry: An unheralded window on the environment. *American Journal of Psychiatry, 148*, 283–291.

Remien, R. H., Exner, T., Kertzner, R. M., Ehrhardt, A. A., Rotheram-Borus, M. J., Johnson, M. O., et al. (2006). Depressive symptomatology among HIV-positive women in the era of HAART: A stress and coping model. *American Journal of Community Psychology, 38*(3–4), 275–285.

Renou, S., Hergueta, T., Flament, M., Mouren-Simeoni, M. C., & Lecrubier, Y. (2004). Diagnostic structured interviews in child and adolescent's psychiatry. *Encephale, 30*, 122–134.

Reynolds, W. M. (1994). Assessment of depression in children and adolescents by self-report questionnaires. In W. M. Reynolds & H. F. Johnson (Eds.). *Handbook of depression in children and adolescents* (pp. 209–234). New York: Plenum Press.

Reynolds, S. & Gilbert, P. (1991). Psychological impact of unemployment: Interactive effects of vulnerability and protective factors on depression. *Journal of Counseling Psychology, 38*, 76–84.

Rex, T. R. (2005). Job quality nationally and in all states. *William Seidman Research Institute at Arizona State University*. Retrieved June 10, 2008, from http://www.wpcarey.asu.edu/seid/Reports. cfm.

Ribar, D. C. (2003). What do social scientists know about the benefits of marriage? A review of quantitative methodologies. *IZA Discussion Paper No. 998*. Retrieved July 7, 2008, from http://ssrn. com/abstract=500887.

Rice, M., & Harris, G. T. (1992). A comparison of criminal recidivism among schizophrenic and nonschizophrenic offenders. *International Journal of Law and Psychiatry, 15*, 397–408.

Rice, M., & Harris, G. T. (1995). Psychopathy, schizophrenia, alcohol abuse and violent recidivism. *International Journal of Law and Psychiatry, 18*, 249–263.

Richman, J. A., Cloninger, L., & Rospenda, K. M. (2008). Macrolevel stressors, terrorism, and mental health outcomes: Broadening the stress paradigm. *American Journal of Public Health, 98*, 323–329.

Richman, J., & Rospenda, K. (1991). *Gender roles and alcohol abuse: Costs of non-caring*. Paper presented at the Society for the Study of Social Problems. Washington, DC.

Richman, L. S., Kohn-Wood, L. P., & Williams, D. R. (2007). The role of discrimination and racial identity for mental service utilization. *Journal of Social and Clinical Psychology, 26*(8), 960–981.

Ridgely, M. S., Engbereg, J., Greenberg, M. D., Turner S., DeMartini, C., & Dembosky, J. W. (2007). *Justice, treatment and cost: An evaluation of the fiscal impact of Allegheny County Mental Health Court*. Santa Monica, CA: RAND.

Ridgely, M. S., Goldman, H. H., & Willenbring, M. (1990). Barriers to the care of persons with dual diagnoses: Organizational and financing issues. *Schizophrenia Bulletin, 16*(1), 123–132.

Ridgeway, C. L., & Walker, H. (1995). Status structures. In K. Cook, G. Fine, & J. House (Eds.), *Sociological perspectives on social psychology*. New York: Allyn & Bacon.

Rieger, G., Linsenmeier, J. A., Gygax, L., & Bailey, J. M. (2008). Sexual orientation and childhood gender non-conformity: Evidence from home videos. *Developmental Psychology, 44*, 46–58.

Riley, A. L., & Keith, V. M. (2003). Life aint' been no crystal stair: Employment, job conditions, and life satisfaction among African American women. In D. R. Brown & V. M. Keith (Eds.), *In and out of our right minds: The mental health of African American women* (pp. 191–206). New York: Columbia University Press.

Risch, N. (1991). Genetic linkage studies in psychiatry: Theoretical aspects. In M. T. Tsuang, K. S. Kendler, & M. J. Lyons (Eds.), *Genetic issues in psychosocial epidemiology* (pp. 71–93). New Brunswick, NJ: Rutgers University Press.

Rizzolatti, G., & Craighero, L. (2004). The mirror-neuron system. *Annual Review of Neuroscience, 27*, 169–192.

Robbins, H. (1980). Influencing mental health policy: The MHA approach. *Hospital and Community Psychiatry, 31*(9), 610–613.

Roberts, R. E. (1980). Prevalence of psychological distress among Mexican Americans. *Journal of Health and Social Behavior, 21*, 134–145.

Roberts, R. E. (1992). Manifestation of depressive symptoms among adolescents: A comparison of Mexican Americans with the majority and other minority populations. *Journal of Nervous and Mental Disease, 180*, 627–633.

Roberts R. E., Attkisson C., & Rosenblatt, A. (1998). Prevalence of psychopathology among children and adolescents. *American Journal of Psychiatry, 155*, 715–725.

Roberts, R. E., Deleger, S., Strawbridge, W. J., & Kaplan, G. A. (2003). Prospective association between obesity and depression: Evidence from the Alameda County Study. *International Journal of Obesity, 27*, 514–521.

Roberts, R. E., & Roberts, C. R. (2007). Ethnicity and risk of psychiatric disorder among adolescents. *Research in Human Development, 4*, 89–117.

Roberts, R. E., Roberts, C. R., & Chen, R. (1997). Ethnocultural differences in prevalence of adolescent depression. *American Journal of Community Psychology, 25*, 95–110.

Roberts, R. E., Roberts, C. R., & Xing, Y. (2006). Prevalence of youth-reported DSM-IV psychiatric disorders among African, European, and Mexican American adolescents. *Journal of the Academy of Child and Adolescent Psychiatry, 45*, 1329–1337.

Roberts, R. E., & Sohban, M. (1992). Symptoms of depression in adolescence: A comparison of Anglo, African, and Hispanic Americans. *Journal of Youth and Adolescence, 21*, 639–651.

Roberts, R. E., Solovitz, B. L., Chen, Y., & Casat, C. (1996). Retest stability of DSM-III-R diagnoses among adolescents using the Diagnostic Interview Schedule for Children (DISC-2.1C). *Journal of Abnormal Child Psychology, 24*, 349–362.

Robins, E., & Guze, S. (1970). Establishment of diagnostic validity in psychiatric illness: Its application to schizophrenia. *American Journal of Psychiatry, 126*(7), 983–987.

Robins, L. (1985). Epidemiology: Reflections on testing the validity of psychiatric interviews. *Archives of General Psychiatry, 42*, 918–924.

Robins, L. (1993). Childhood conduct problems, adult psychopathology and crime. In S. Hodgins (Ed.), *Mental disorder and crime* (pp. 173–193). London: Sage.

Robins, L. N., Clayton, P. J., & Wing, J. K. (1980). *The social consequences of psychiatric illness.* New York: Brunner/Mazel.

Robins, L. N., Helzer, J. E., Croughan, J., & Ratcliff, K. S. (1981). The NIMH Diagnostic Interview Schedule: Its history, characteristics and validity. *Archives of General Psychiatry, 28*, 381–389.

Robins, L. N., Helzer, J. E., Orvaschel, H., Anthony, J. C., Blazer, D. G., Burnam, A., et al. (1985). The Diagnostic Interview Schedule. In W. W. Eaton & L. G. Kessler (Eds.), *Epidemiologic field methods in psychiatry: The NIMH Epidemiologic Catchment Area Program* (pp. 143–170). New York: Academic Press.

Robins, L. N., Locke, B. Z., & Regier, D. A. (1991). An overview of psychiatric disorders in America. In L. N. Robins & D. A. Regier (Eds.), *Psychiatric disorders in America: The Epidemiologic Catchment Study* (pp. 328–366). New York: The Free Press.

Robins, L. N., & Regier, D. A. (Eds.). (1991). *Psychiatric disorders in America: The Epidemiologic Catchment Area Study.* New York: The Free Press.

Robins, L. N., Wing, J., Wittchen, H. U., Helzer, J. E., Babor, T. F., Burke, J., et al. (1988). The Composite International Diagnostic Interview: An epidemiologic instrument suitable for use in conjunction with different diagnostic systems and in different cultures. *Archives of General Psychiatry, 45*, 1069–1077.

Robins, P. K., Spiegelman, R. G., Weiner, S., & Bell, J. G. (Eds.). (1980). *A guaranteed annual income.* New York: Academic Press.

Robinson, R. V., & Kelley, J. (1990). Class as conceived by Marx and Dahrendorf: Effects on income inequality, class consciousness, and class conflict in the US and Great Britain. *American Sociological Review, 55*, 827–841.

Rochefort, D. A. (1987). The political context of mental health care. In D. Mechanic. (Ed.), *Improving mental health services: What the social sciences can tell us* (pp. 93–106). San Francisco: Jossey-Bass.

Rochefort, D. A. (Ed.). (1989). *Handbook on mental health policy in the U.S.* New York: Greenwood Press.

Rochefort, D. A. (1999). Mental health policy making in the intergovernmental system. In A. V. Horwitz & T. L. Scheid (Eds.), *A handbook for the study of mental health* (pp. 467–483). New York: Cambridge University Press.

Rodin, J. (1986a). Aging and health: Effects of the sense of control. *Science, 233*, 1271–1276.

Rodin, J. (1986b). Health, control, and aging. In M. M. Baltes & P. B. Baltes (Eds.), *The psychology of control and aging* (pp. 139–165) Hillsdale, NJ: Erlbaum.

Rodin, J. (1990). Control by any other name: Definitions, concepts and processes. In J. Rodin, C. Schooler, & K. W. Schaie (Eds.), *Self-directedness: Causes and effects throughout the life course* (pp. 1–18). Hillsdale, NJ: Erlbaum.

Roesch, R., & Golding S. L. (1980). *Competency to Stand Trial.* Urbana: University of Illinois Press. (1995). The impact of deinstitutionalization. In D. P. Farrington & J. Gunn (Eds.), *Aggression and Dangerousness*, pp. 209–39. New York: Wiley.

Roesch, R., & Golding, S. L. (1985). The impact of deinstitutionalization. In D. P. Farrington & J. Gunn (Eds.), *Aggression and dangerousness* (pp. 209–239). New York: Wiley.

Roesch, R., Ogloff, J. R. P., & Eaves, D. (1995). Mental health research in the criminal justice system: The need for common approaches and international perspectives. *International Journal of Law and Psychiatry, 18*, 1–14.

Rogers, A., Hassell, K., & Nicolaas, G. (1999). *Demanding patients? Analysing the use of primary care.* Philadelphia: Open University Press.

Rogers, C. R. (1942). *Counseling and psychotherapy: Newer concepts in practice.* Boston: Houghton Mifflin.

Rogers, C. R. (1951). *Client-centered therapy: Its current practice, implications, and theory.* Boston: Houghton Mifflin.

Rogers, C. R. (1961). *On becoming a person.* Boston: Houghton Mifflin.

Rogers, R. G., Hummer, R. A., & Nam, C. B. (1999). *Living and dying in the USA: Behavioral, health, and social forces of adult mortality.* New York: Academic Press.

Rogers, S. J., & DeBoer, D. D. (2001). Changes in wives' income: Effects on marital happiness, psychological well-being, and the risk of divorce. *Journal of Marriage and the Family, 63,* 458–472.

Rogers, S. J., Parcel, T. L., & Menaghan, E. G. (1991). The effects of maternal working conditions and mastery on children's behavior problems: Studying the intergenerational transmission of social control. *Journal of Health and Social Behavior, 32,* 145–164.

Rogler, L. H. (1989). The meaning of culturally sensitive research in mental health: Issues of memory in the Diagnostic Interview Schedule. *Journal of Nervous and Mental Disease, 146,* 296–303.

Rogler, L. H. (1999). Methodological sources of cultural insensitivity in mental health research. *American Psychologist 54*(6), 424–433.

Rogler, L. H., Cortes, D. E., & Malgady, R. G. (1991). Acculturation and mental health status among Hispanics. *American Psychologist, 46,* 585–597.

Rogler, L., Gendlin, E. T., Kiesler, D. V., & Truax, C. B. (1967). *The therapeutic relationship and its impact: A study of psychotherapy with schizophrenics.* Madison: University of Wisconsin Press.

Rogler, L., & Hollingshead. A. (1961). The Puerto-Rican spiritualist as psychiatrist. *American Journal of Sociology, 67,* 17–21.

Rogler, L. H., Malgady, R. G., Constantino, G., & Blumenthal, R. (1987). What do culturally sensitive mental health services mean? The case of Hispanics. *American Psychologist, 42*(6), 565–570.

Rogler, L. H., Malgady, R. G., & Rodriguez, O. (1989). *Hispanics and mental health: A framework for research.* Malabar, FL: Krieger.

Rogler, L. H., Malgady, R. G., & Tryon, W. W. (1992). Evaluation of mental health: Issues of memory in the Diagnostic Interview Schedule. *Journal of Nervous and Mental Disease, 180,* 215–222.

Rollins, B. C., & Thomas, D. L. (1979). Parental support, power, and control techniques in the socialization of children. In W. R. Burr, R. Hill, F. I. Nye, & I. L. Reiss (Eds.), *Contemporary theories about the family: Vol. 1.* New York: The Free Press.

Romanucci-Ross, L. (1977). The hierarchy of resort in curative practices: The Admiralty Islands, Melanesia. In D. Landy (Ed.), *Culture, disease and healing* (pp. 481–486). New York: Macmillan.

Romanyshyn, J. M. (1971). *Social welfare: Charity to justice.* New York: Random House.

Rose, R. (1991). Twin studies and psychosocial epidemiology. In M. T. Tsuang, K. S. Kendler, & M. J. Lyons (Eds.), *Genetic issues in psychosocial epidemiology* (pp. 12–32). New Brunswick, NJ: Rutgers University Press.

Rose, S. P., & Black, B. L. (1985). *Advocacy and empowerment: Mental health care in the community.* Boston: Routledge.

Rosen, G. (1968). *Madness in society.* Chicago: University of Chicago Press.

Rosen, G. M., Spitzer, R. L., & McHugh, P. R. (2008). Problems with the post-traumatic stress disorder diagnosis and its future in DSM-V. *British Journal of Psychiatry, 192,* 3–4.

Rosenbaum, J. L. (1987). Social control, gender, and delinquency: An analysis of drug, property, and violent offenders. *Justice Quarterly, 4,* 117–142.

Rosenberg, M. (1965). *Society and adolescent self-image.* Princeton, NJ: Princeton University Press.

Rosenberg, M. (1979). The self concept: Source, product and force. In M. Rosenberg & R. H. Turner (Eds.), *Social psychology: Sociological perspectives.* New York: Basic Books.

Rosenberg, M. (1984). A symbolic interactionist view of psychosis. *Journal of Health and Social Behavior, 25,* 289–302.

Rosenberg, M. (1985). Self-concept and psychological well-being in adolescence. In R. L. Leahy (Ed.), *Development of the self* (pp. 205–256). Orlando, FL: Academic Press.

Rosenberg, M. (1989). Self-concept research: A historical overview. *Social Forces, 68,* 34–44.

Rosenberg, S. D., Goodman, L. A., Osher, F., Swartz, M. S., Essock, S. M., Butterfield, M. I., et al. (2001). Prevalence of HIV, Hepatitis B, and Hepatitis C in people with severe mental illness. *American Journal of Public Health, 91,* 31–37.

Rosenberger, J. (1990). Central mental health authorities: Politically flawed? *Hospital and Community Psychiatry, 41*, 1171.

Rosenberger, P. H., Bornstein, R. A., Nasrallah, H. A., Para, M. F., Whitaker, C. C., Fass, R. J., et al. (1993). Psychopathology in human immunodeficiency virus infection: Lifetime and current assessment. *Comprehensive Psychiatry, 34*, 150–158.

Rosenblatt, A., & Atkisson, C. (1993). Assessing outcomes for sufferers of severe mental disorder: A conceptual framework and review. *Evaluation and Program Planning, 16*, 347–363.

Rosenfield, S. (1980). Sex differences in depression: Do women always have higher rates? *Journal of Health and Social Behavior, 21*, 33–42.

Rosenfield, S. (1984). Race differences in involuntary hospitalization: Psychiatric vs. labeling perspectives. *Journal of Health and Social Behavior, 25*, 14–23.

Rosenfield, S. (1989). The effects of women's employment: Personal control and sex differences in mental health. *Journal of Health and Social Behavior, 30*, 77–91.

Rosenfield, S. (1991). Homelessness and rehospitalization: The importance of housing for the chronically mentally ill. *Journal of Community Psychology, 19*, 60–69.

Rosenfield, S. (1992a). Factors contributing to the subjective quality of life of the chronically mentally ill. *Journal of Health and Social Behavior, 33*, 299–315.

Rosenfield, S. (1992b). The costs of sharing: Wives' employment and husbands' mental health. *Journal of Health and Social Behavior, 33*, 213–225.

Rosenfield, S. (1995, August). *Gender stratification, stress, and mental illness.* Paper presented at the workshop sponsored by NIMH on Social Structure, Stress, and Mental Illness, Washington, DC.

Rosenfield, S. (1997). Labeling mental illness: The effects of received services and perceived stigma on life satisfaction. *American Sociological Review, 62*, 660–672.

Rosenfield, S. (1999). Splitting the difference: Gender, psychopathology, and the self. In C. Aneshensel & J. Phelan (Eds.), *Handbook of psychiatric sociology* (pp. 209–224). New York: Plenum Press.

Rosenfield, S. (2008). *Taking the bad with the good: Stigma and quality of life among persons with serious mental illness.* Paper presented at the annual meeting of the Society for the Study of Social Problems, Boston.

Rosenfield, S., Lennon, M. C., & White, H. R. (2005). The self and mental health: Self salience and the emergence of internalizing and externalizing problems. *Journal of Health and Social Behavior, 46*, 323–340.

Rosenfield, S., Phillips, J. & White, H. R. (2006). Gender, race, and the self in mental health and crime. *Social Problems, 53*, 161–185.

Rosenfield S., Vertefuille, J., & McAlpine, D. (2000). Gender stratification and mental health: An exploration of dimensions of the self. *Social Psychology Quarterly, 63*, 208–223.

Rosenfield, S., & Wenzel, S. (1996). *Social support and chronic mental illness: A test of four hypotheses.* Paper presented at the Society for the Study of Social Problems, Cincinnati.

Rosenhan, D. (1973). On being sane in insane places. *Science, 179*, 250–258.

Rosenheck, R., & Lam, J. (1997). Homeless mentally ill clients' and providers' perceptions of service needs and clients' use of services. *Psychiatric Services, 48*, 381–386.

Rosenheck, R., Lam, J., Morrissey, J., Calloway, M., Stolar, M., Randolph, F., et al. (2002). Service systems integration and outcomes for mentally ill homeless persons in the ACCESS program. *Psychiatric Services, 53*(8), 958–966.

Rosenheck, R., Morrissey, J., Lam, J., Calloway, M., Johnsen, M., Goldman, H., et al. (1998). Service system integration, access to services, and housing outcomes in a program for homeless persons with severe mental illness. *Psychiatric Services, 88*(11), 1610–1615.

Rosenthal, D. (1970). *Genetic theory and abnormal behavior.* New York: McGraw-Hill.

Rosenstock, I. M. (1966). Why people use health services. *Milbank Quarterly, 44*, 94–106.

Ross, C. E. (1995). Reconceptualizing marital status as a continuum of social attachment. *Journal of Marriage and the Family, 57*, 129–140.

Ross, C. E. (2000). Neighborhood disadvantage and adult depression. *Journal of Health and Social Behavior, 41*, 177–187.

Ross, C. E., & Bird, C. E. (1994). Sex stratification and health lifestyle: Consequences for men's and women's perceived health. *Journal of Health and Social Behavior, 35*, 161–178.

Ross, C. E., & Huber, J. (1985). Hardship and depression. *Journal of Health and Social Behavior, 26*, 312–327.

Ross, C. E., & Mirowsky, J. (1979). A comparison of life event weighting schemes: Change, undesirability, and effect-proportional indices. *Journal of Health and Social Behavior, 20*, 166–177.

Ross, C. E., & Mirowsky, J. (1987). Normlessness, powerlessness, and trouble with the law. *Criminology, 25*, 257–278.

Ross, C. E., & Mirowsky, J. (1988). Child care and emotional adjustment to wives' employment. *Journal of Health and Social Behavior, 29*, 127–138.

Ross, C. E., & J. Mirowsky. (1989). Explaining the social patterns of depression: Control and problem solving or support and talking? *Journal of Health and Social Behavior, 30*, 206–219.

Ross, C. E., & Mirowsky, J. (1992). Households, employment, and the sense of control. *Social Psychology Quarterly, 55*, 217–235.

Ross, C. E., & Mirowsky, J. (1995a). Does employment affect health? *Journal of Health and Social Behavior, 36*, 230–243.

Ross, C. E., & Mirowsky, J. (1995b). Sex differences in distress: Real or artifact? *American Sociological Review, 60*, 449–468.

Ross, C. E., & Mirowsky, J. (1999a). Disorder and decay: The concept and measurement of perceived neighborhood disorder. *Urban Affairs Review, 34*, 412–432.

Ross, C. E., & Mirowsky, J. (1999b). Parental divorce, life course disruption and adult depression. *Journal of Marriage & the Family, 61*, 1034–1045.

Ross, C. E., & Mirowsky, J. (2001). Neighborhood disadvantage, disorder, and health. *Journal of Health and Social Behavior, 44*, 258–276.

Ross, C. E., & Mirowsky, J. (2002). Age and the gender gap in the sense of personal control. *Social Psychology Quarterly, 65*, 25–45.

Ross, C. E., & Mirowsky, J. (2008). Age and the balance of emotions. *Social Science and Medicine, 66*, 2391–2400.

Ross, C. E., & Mirowsky, J. (2009). Neighborhood disorder, subjective alienation, and distress. *Journal of Health and Social Behavior, 50*(1), 49–64.

Ross, C. E., Mirowsky, J., & Goldsteen, K. (1990). The impact of the family on health: The decade in review. *Journal of Marriage and the Family, 52*, 1059–1078.

Ross, C. E., Mirowsky, J., & Huber, J. (1983). Dividing work, sharing work, and in-between: Marriage patterns and depression. *American Sociological Review, 48*, 809–823.

Ross, C. E., Mirowsky, J., & Pribesh, S. (2001). Powerlessness and the amplification of threat: Neighborhood disadvantage, disorder, and mistrust. *American Sociological Review, 66*, 568–591.

Ross, C. E., Mirowsky, J., & Pribesh, S. (2002). Disadvantage, disorder and urban mistrust. *City and Community, 1*, 59–82.

Ross, C. E., Reynolds, J. R., & Geis, K. J. (2000). The contingent meaning of neighborhood stability for residents' psychological well-being. *American Sociological Review, 65*, 581–597.

Ross, C. E., & Van Willigen, M. (1996). Gender, parenthood and anger. *Journal of Marriage and the Family, 58*, 572–584.

Ross, C. E., & Wu, C. (1995). The links between education and health. *American Sociological Review, 60*, 719–745.

Roth, J. A. (1963). *Timetables*. Indianapolis: Bobbs-Merrill.

Rothbard, A., Min, S., Kuno, E., & Wong, I. (2004). Long-term effectiveness of the ACCESS program in linking community mental health services to homeless persons with serious mental illness. *Journal of Behavioral Health Services & Research, 31*(4), 441–449.

Rotter, J. B. (1966). Generalized expectancies for internal vs. external control of reinforcement. *Psychological Monographs, 80*, 1–28.

Rowe, J. W., &. Kahn, R. J. (1987). Human aging: Usual and successful. *Science, 143*, 143–149.

Rowley, K. M., & Feather, N. T. (1987). The impact of unemployment in relation to age and length of unemployment. *Journal of Occupational Psychology, 72*, 83–89.

Roxburgh, S. (2004). 'There just aren't enough hours in the day': The mental health consequences of time pressure. *Journal of Health and Social Behavior, 45*, 115–131.

Rubin, G. J., Brewin, C. R., Greenberg, N., Hughes, J. H., Simpson, J., & Wessely, S. (2007). Enduring consequences of terrorism: 7-month follow-up survey of reactions to the bombings in London on 7 July 2005. *British Journal of Psychiatry, 190,* 350–356.

Ruel, E., & Campbell, R. T. (2006). Homophobia and HIV/AIDS: Attitude change in the face of an epidemic. *Social Forces, 84*(4), 2167–2178.

Ruesch, J. (1949). Social techniques, social status and social change. In C. Kluckhohn & H. A. Murray (Eds.), *Personality in nature, society and culture* (pp. 117–130). New York: Knopf.

Rundall, T. G., Shortell, S. M., & Alexander, J. A. (2004). A theory of physician-hospital integration: Contending instititutional and market logics in the health care field. *Journal of Health and Social Behavior, 45,* 102–117.

Ruscio, A. M., Lane, M., Roy-Byrne, P., Stang, P. E., Stein, D. J., Wittchen, H. U., et al. (2005). Should excessive worry be required for a diagnosis of generalized anxiety disorder? Results from the US National Comorbidity Survey Replication. *Psychological Medicine, 35,* 1761–1772.

Rush, A. J., Beck, A. T., Kovacs, M., & Hollon, S. D. (1977). Comparative efficacy of cognitive therapy and imipramine in the treatment of depressed outpatients. *Cognitive Therapy and Research, 1,* 17–37.

Rushing, W. A., & Ortega, S. T. (1979). Socioeconomic status and mental disorder: New evidence and a socio-medical formulation. *American Journal of Sociology, 84,* 1175–1200.

Russell, G. (1996). Internalized classism: The role of class in the development of self. *Women & Therapy, 18,* (3–4), 59–71.

Rust, G., Minor, P., Jordan, N., Mayberry, R., & Satcher, D. (2003). Do clinicians screen Medicaid patients for syphilis or HIV when they diagnose other sexually transmitted diseases? *Sexually Transmitted Diseases, 30,* 723–727.

Rutherford Files. (2005, September 19). *Rutherford files mental health screening lawsuit.* Retrieved September 30, 2005, from http://www.ahrp.org/infomail/05/09/19a.php.

Rutter, M. (1970). Sex differences in children's responses to family stress. In E. J. Anthony & C. Koupernik (Eds.), *The child in his family* (pp. 165–196). New York: Wiley.

Rutter, M. (2004). Pathways of genetic influences on psychopathology. *European Review, 12,* 19–33.

Rutter, M. (2006a). Gene-environment interplay and psychopathology: Multiple varieties but real effects. *Journal of Child Psychology and Psychiatry, 47,* 226–261.

Rutter, M. (2006b). *Genes and behavior: Nature-nurture interplay explained.* Malden: Blackwell.

Rutter, M., Kim-Cohen, J., & Maughan, B. (2006). Continuities and discontinuities in psychopathology between childhood and adult life. *Journal of Child Psychology and Psychiatry, 47,* 276–295.

Rutter, M., Moffitt, T. E., & Caspi, A. (2006). Gene-environment interplay and psychopathology: Multiple varieties but real effects. *Journal of Child Psychology and Psychiatry, 47,* 226–261.

Ryan, R. M., & Deci, E. L. (2001). On happiness and human potentials: A review of research on hedonic and eudaimonic well-being. *Annual Review of Psychology, 52,* 141–166.

Ryff, C. D. (1989). Happiness is everything, or is it? Explorations on the meaning of psychological well being. *Journal of Personality and Social Psychology, 57,* 1069–1081.

Ryff, C. D., Keyes, C., & Hughes, D. (2003). Status inequalities, perceived discrimination, and eudemonic well-being: Do the challenges of minority life hone purpose and growth? *Journal of Health and Social Behavior, 44,* 275–291.

Sabin, J., & Daniels, N. (1999). Managed care: Public-sector managed behavioral health care: III. Meaningful consumer and family participation. *Psychiatric Services, 50,* 883–885.

Sabin, J., & Daniels, N. (2002). Managed care: Strengthening the consumer voice in managed care: V. Helping professionals listen. *Psychiatric Services, 53,* 805–811.

Sacks, F. M. (2004). High-intensity statin treatment for coronary heart disease. *Journal of the American Medical Association, 291,* 1132–1134.

Sadock, B. J., & Sadock, V. A. (2003). *Kaplan and Sadock's synopsis of psychiatry: Behavioral sciences, clinical psychiatry.* Baltimore: Williams & Wilkins.

Sagan, L. A. (1987). *The health of nations: True causes of sickness and well-being* New York: Basic Books.

Salazar, L. F., DiClemente, R. J., Wingood, G. M., Crosby, R. A., Lang, D. L., & Harrington, K. (2006). Biologically confirmed sexually transmitted infection and depressive symptomatology among African American female adolescents. *Sexually Transmitted Infections, 82,* 55–60.

Salem, D., Seedman, E., & Rappaport, J. (1988). Community treatment of the mentally ill: The promise of mutual help organizations. *Social Work, 33*, 403–408.

Saler, L. (1992). Childhood parental death and depression in adulthood: Roles of surviving parent and family environment. *American Journal of Orthopsychiatry, 62*, 504–516.

Sales, B., & Hafemeister, T. (1984). Empiricism and legal policy on the insanity defense. In L. Teplin (Ed.), *Mental health and criminal justice* (pp. 253–278). Beverly Hills, CA: Sage.

Salloway, J. C. & Dillon, P. B. (1973). A comparison of family networks in health care utilization. *Journal of Comparative Family Studies, 68*, 57.

Saluja, G., Iachan, R., Scheidt, P. C., Overpeck, M. D., Sun, W., & Giedd, J. N. (2004). Prevalence of and risk factors for depressive symptoms among young adolescents. *Archives of Pediatric and Adolescent Medicine, 158*, 760–765.

Sambamoorthi, U., Walkup, J., Olfson, M., & Crystal, S. (2000). Antidepressant treatment and health services utilization among HIV-infected Medicaid patients diagnosed with depression. *Journal of General Internal Medicine, 15*(5), 311–320.

Sambamoorthi, U., Warner, L. A., Crystal, S., & Walkup, J. (2000). Drug abuse, methadone treatment, and health services use among injection drug users with AIDS. *Drug and Alcohol Dependence, 60*(1), 77–89.

Samet, J. H., Freedberg, K. A., Stein, M. D., Lewis, R., Savetsky, J., Sullivan, L., et al. (1998). Trillion virion delay: Time from testing positive for HIV to presentation for primary care. *Archives of Internal Medicine, 158*, 734–740.

Sampson, R. J., Morenoff, J. D., & Raudenbush, S. (2005). Social anatomy of racial and ethnic disparities in violence. *American Journal of Public Health, 95*, 224–232.

Sampson, R. J., Raudenbush, S. W., & Earls, R. (1997). Neighborhoods and violent crime: A multilevel study of collective efficacy. *Science, 277*, 918–924.

Santibanez, S., Garfein, R., Swartzendruber, A., Purcell, D., Paxton, L., & Greenberg, A. (2006). Update and overview of practical epidemiologic aspects of HIV/AIDS among injection drug users in the United States. *Journal of Urban Health, 83*, 86–100.

Santos, A., Henggeler, S., Burns, B., Arana, G., & Meisler, N. (1995). Research on field-based services: Models for reform in the delivery of mental health care to populations with complex clinical problems. *American Journal of Psychiatry, 152*, 1111–1123.

Sapolsky, R. M. (1994). *Why zebras don't get ulcers: Guide to stress, stress-related diseases and coping.* New York: Freeman.

Sarason, B. R., Pierce, G. R., & Sarason, I. G. (1990). Social support: The sense of acceptance and the role of relationships. In B. R. Sarason, I. G. Sarason, & G. R. Pierce (Eds.), *Social support: An interactional view* (pp. 97–129). New York: Wiley.

Sarason, B. R., Sarason, I. G., & Pierce, G. R. (1990). Traditional views of social support and their impact on assessment. In B. R. Sarason, I. G. Sarason, & G. R. Pierce (Eds.), *Social support: An interactional view* (pp. 9–25). New York: Wiley.

Sarason, I. G., & Sarason, B. R. (Eds.). (1985). *Social support: Theory, research, and applications.* Boston: Martinus Nijhoff.

Sarason, I. G., Sarason, B. R., & Shearin, E. N. (1986). Social support as an individual difference variable: Its instability, origins and relational aspects. *Journal of Personality & Social Psychology, 50*, 845–855.

Sarkisian, N., & Gerstel, N. (2004). Kin support among blacks and whites: Race and family organizations. *American Sociological Review, 69*, 812–837.

Sarkisian, N., & Gerstel, N. (2008). Till marriage do us part: Adult children's relationships with their parents. *Journal of Marriage and Family, 70*, 360–376.

Satel, S. (2000). *PC, M.D.: How political correctness is corrupting medicine.* New York: Basic Books.

Sartorius, N., de Girolamo, G., Andrews, G., Allen. G., German, G. A., & Eisenberg. L. (1993). *Treatment of mental disorders: A review of effectiveness.* Washington, DC: American Psychiatric Press.

Sartorius, N., Jablensky, A.,. Korten, A., Emberg, G., Anker, M., Cooper, J. E., et al. (1986). Early manifestations and first contact incidence of schizophrenia in different cultures. *Psychological Medicine, 16*, 909–928.

Sassler, S. (2004). The process of entering into cohabiting unions. *Journal of Marriage and Family, 66,* 491–505.

Satriano, J., McKinnon, K., & Adoff, S. (2007). HIV service provision for people with severe mental illness in outpatient mental health care settings in New York. *Journal of Prevention & Intervention in the Community, 33*(1–2), 95–108.

Sawa, A., & Snyder, S. H. (2002). Schizophrenia: Diverse approaches to a complex disease. *Science, 296,* 692–695.

Saxena, S., Sharan, P., Garrido, M., & Saraceno, B. (2006). World Health Organization's Mental Health Atlas 2005: Implications for policy development. *World Psychiatry, 5*(3), 179–184.

Saxena, S., Sharan, P., & Saraceno, B. (2003). Budget and financing of mental health services: Baseline information on 89 countries from WHO's project atlas. *Journal of Mental Health Policy and Economics, 6*(3), 135–143.

Saxena, S., Thornicroft, G., Knapp, M., & Whiteford, H. (2007). Resources for mental health: Scarcity, inequity, and inefficiency. *Lancet, 8370*(9590), 878–889.

Scahill, L., & Schwab-Stone, M. (2000). Epidemiology of ADHD in school-age children. *Child & Adolescent Psychiatric Clinics of North America, 9,* 541–555.

Scallet, L. (1980). Mental health law and public policy. *Hosptial and Community Psychiatry, 31,* 614–616.

Scarr, S. K., & McCartney, K. (1983). How people make their own environments: A theory of genotype environmental effects. *Child Development, 54,* 424–435.

Schaie, K. W. (1983). The Seattle Longitudinal Study: A 21-year exploration of psychometric intelligence in adulthood. In K. W. Schaie (Ed.), *Longitudinal studies of adult psychological development* (pp. 64–135). New York: Guilford.

Schanda, H., Knecht, G., Schreinzer, D., Stompe, T., Ortwein-Swoboda, G., & Waldhoer, T. (2004). Homicide and major mental disorders: A 25-year study. *Acta Psychiatrica Scandinavia, 110,* 98–107.

Scheff, T. J. (1966). Users and nonusers of a student psychiatric clinic. *Journal of Health and Social Behavior, 7,* 1114.

Scheff, T. J. (1984). *Being mentally ill: A sociological theory.* Chicago: Aldine. (Original work published 1966)

Scheff, T. J. (1998). Shame in the labeling of mental illness. In P. Gilbert & B. Andrews (Eds.), *Shame: Interpersonal behavior, psychopathology, and culture.* New York: Oxford University Press.

Scheffler, R. M., & Miller, A. G. (1989). Demand analysis of mental health service use among ethnic subpopulations. *Inquiry, 26,* 202–215.

Scheiber, G. J., & Poullier, J.-P. (1991). International health spending: Issues and trends. *Health Affairs, 10,* 106–116.

Scheid, T. L. (2003). Managed care and the rationalization of mental health services. *Journal of Health and Social Behavior, 44,* 142–161.

Scheid, T. L., & Greenberg, G. (2007). An organizational analysis of mental health care. In W. R. Avison, J. D. McLeod, & B. A. Pescosolido (Eds.), *Mental health, social mirror* (pp. 379–406). New York: Springer Science.

Scheid, T. L., & Greenley, J. R. (1997). Evaluations of organizational effectiveness in mental health care programs. *Journal of Health and Social Behavior, 38,* 403–426.

Schieman, S. (1999). Education and the activiation, course, and management of anger. *Journal of Health and Social Behavior, 41,* 20–39.

Schieman, S. (2003). Socioeconomic status and the frequency of anger across the life course. *Sociological Perspectives, 46,* 207–222.

Schieman, S., Pearlin, L. I., & Meersman, S. C. (2006). Neighborhood disadvantage and anger among older adults: Social comparisons as effect modifiers. *Journal of Health and Social Behavior, 47,* 156–172.

Schieman, S., Whitestone, Y. K., & Van Gundy, K. (2006). The nature of work and the stress of higher status. *Journal of Health and Social Behavior, 47,* 242–257.

Schiff, M. (2006) Living in the shadow of terrorism: Psychological distress and alcohol use among religious and non-religious adolescents in Jerusalem. *Social Science & Medicine, 62*(9), 2301–2312.

Schiff, M., Zweig, H. H., Benbenishty, R., & Hasin, D. R. (2007). Exposure to terrorism and Israeli youths' cigarette, alcohol, and cannabis use. *American Journal of Public Health, 97*, 1852–1858.

Schlesinger, M. J., & Gray, B. H. (1999). Institutional change and its consequences for the delivery of mental health services. In A. V. Horwitz & T. L. Scheid (Eds.), *A handbook for the study of mental health* (pp. 427–448). New York: Cambridge University Press.

Schlesinger, M. J., Gray, B. H., & Perreira, K. M. (1997). Medical professionalism under managed care: The pros and cons of utilization review. *Health Affairs, 16*(1), 106–124.

Schmitz, M., & Crystal, S. (2000). Social relations, coping, and psychological distress among persons with HIV/AIDS. *Journal of Applied Social Psychology, 30*(4), 665–685.

Schnittker, J., Freese, J., & Powell, B. (2000). Nature, nurture, neither, nor: Black-White differences in beliefs about the causes and appropriate treatment of mental illness. *Social Forces, 78*, 1101–1130.

Schoen, R., Landale, N., & Daniels, K. (2007). Family transitions in young adulthood. *Demography, 44*(4), 807–820.

Schoenbach, V. J., Kaplan, B. H., Wagner, E. H., Grimson, R. C., & Miller, F. T. (1983). Prevalence of self-reported depressive symptoms in young adolescents. *American Journal of Public Health, 73*, 1281–1287.

Schoenbaum, E. E., Hartel, D. M., & Gourevitch, M. N. (1996). Needle exchange use among a cohort of injecting drug users. *AIDS, 10*, 1729–1734.

Schoenwald, S., & Hoagwood, K. (2001). Effectiveness, transportability, and dissemination of interventions: What matters when? *Psychiatric Services, 52*(9), 1190–1197.

Schooler, C., Kohn, M. L., Miller, K. A., & Miller, J. (1983). Housework as work. In M. L. Kohn & C. Schooler (Eds.), *Work and personality: An inquiry into the impact of social stratification* (pp. 242–60). Norwood, NJ: Ablex.

Schooler, C., Mulatu, M. S., & Oates, G. (2004). Occupational self-direction, intellectual functioning, and self-directed orientation in older workers: Findings and implications for individuals and societies. *American Journal of Sociology, 110*, 161–197.

Schrimshaw, E. W., Siegel, K., & Lekas, H. (2005). Changes in attitudes toward antiviral medication: A comparison of women living with HIV/AIDS in the pre-HAART and HAART eras. *AIDS and Behavior, 9*(3), 267–279.

Schuerman, L. A., & Kobrin, S. (1984). Exposure of community mental health clients to the criminal justice system: Client/criminal or patient/prisoner. In L. A. Teplin (Ed.), *Mental health and criminal justice* (pp. 87–118). Beverly Hills, CA: Sage.

Schulberg, H., & Bromet, E. (1981). Strategies for evaluating the outcome of mental health services for the chronically mentally ill. *American Journal of Psychiatry, 138*, 930–935.

Schulberg, H., & Killilea, M. (Eds.). (1982). *The modern practice of community mental health.* San Francisco, Jossey-Bass.

Schulz, A., Gravlee, C., Williams, D. R., Israel, B., Mentz, G., & Rowe, Z. (2006). Discrimination, symptoms of depression, and self-rated health among African American women in Detroit: Results from a longitudinal analysis. *American Journal of Public Health, 96*, 1265–1270.

Schulz, A., Israel, B., Zenk, S., Parker, E., Lichtenstein, R., Sellman-Weir, S., et al. (2006). Psychosocial stress and social support as mediators of relationships between income, length of residence and depressive symptoms among African American women on Detroit's east side. *Social Science and Medicine, 62*, 510–522.

Schulz, A., Williams, D. R., Israel, B., Becker, A., Parker, E., James, S. A., et al. (2000). Unfair treatment, neighborhood effects, and mental health in the Detroit metropolitan area. *Journal of Health and Social Behavior, 41*, 314–332.

Schulz, R., Greenley, J. R., & Brown, R. (1995). Organization, management, and client effects on staff burnout in care for persons with severe mental illness. *Journal of Health and Social Behavior, 36*, 333–345.

Schulze, B., & Angermeyer, M. C. (2003). Subjective experiences of stigma: A focus group study of schizophrenic patients, their relatives and mental health professionals. *Social Science & Medicine, 56*, 299–312.

Schuman, H. S., & Johnson, M. (1976). Attitudes and behavior. *Annual Review of Sociology, 2*, 161–207.

Schuster, M. A., Collins, R., Cunningham, W. E., Morton, S. C., Zierler, S., Wong, M., et al. (2005). Perceived discrimination in clinical care in a nationally representative sample of HIV-infected adults receiving health care. *Journal of General Internal Medicine, 20*, 807–813.

Schwalbe, M. L. (1985). Autonomy in work and self-esteem. *Sociological Quarterly, 26*, 519–535.

Schwartz, B. (1984). *Psychology of learning and behavior* (2nd ed.). New York: Norton.

Schwartz, J., Pickering, T., & Landsbergis, P. (2001). Work-related stress and blood pressure: Current theoretical models and considerations from a behavioral medicine perspective. *Journal of Occupational Psychology, 1*(3), 287–310.

Schwartz, S. (1991). Women and depression: A Durkheimian prspective. *Social Science and Medicine, 32*, 127–140.

Schwartz, S., & Susser, E. (2006). Twin studies of heritability. In E. Susser, S. Schwartz, A. Morabia, & E. J. Bromet (Eds.), *Psychiatric epidemiology: Searching for the causes of mental disorders* (pp. 375–388). New York: Oxford University Press.

Scott, R. W. (2003). The old order changeth: The evolving world of health care organizations. In S. S. Mick (Ed.), *Advances in health care organization theory* (pp. 29–48). New York: Jossey-Bass.

Scott, W. R. (2001). *Institutions and organizations*. Thousand Oaks, CA: Sage.

Scott, W. R., & Davis, G. F. (2007). *Organizations and organizing*. Upper Saddle River, NJ: Prentice-Hall.

Scott, W. R., Ruef, M., Mendel, P. J., & Caronna, C. A. (2000). *Institutional change and health care organizations: From professional dominance to managed care*. Chicago: University of Chicago Press.

Scott-Sheldon, L. A., Kalichman, S. C., Carey, M. P., & Fielder, R. L. (2008). Stress management interventions for HIV+ adults: A meta-analysis of randomized controlled trials, 1989 to 2006. *Health Psychology, 27*(2), 129–139.

Scrimin, S., Axia, G., Capello, F., Moscardino, U., Steinberg, A. M., & Pynoos, R. S. (2006). Post-traumatic reactions among injured children and their caregivers 3 months after the terrorist attack in Beslan. *Psychiatry Research, 141*(3), 333–336.

Scull, A. (1977). *Decarceration: Communitiy treatment and the deviant*. Englewood Cliffs, NJ: Prentice-Hall.

Seaton, E. K., Caldwell, C. H., Sellers, R. M., & Jackson, J. S. (2008). The prevalence of perceived discrimination among African American and Caribbean Black youth. *Developmental Psychology, 44*, 1288–1297.

Seaton, G. (2007). Towards a theoretical understanding of hypermasculine coping among urban Black adolescent males. *Journal of Human Behavior in the Social Environment, 15*(2/3), 367–390.

Seeman, M. (1959). On the meaning of alienation. *American Sociological Review, 24*, 783–791.

Seeman, M. (1983). Alienation motifs in contemporary theorizing. *Social Psychology Quarterly, 46*, 171–184.

Segel, S. P., & Aviram, U. (1978). *The mentally ill in community based care*. New York: Wiley.

Seligman, M. E. P. (1975). *Helplessness: On Depression, Development, and Death*. San Francisco: Freeman.

Sellers, R. M., Caldwell, C. H., Schmeelk-Cone, K. H., & Zimmerman, M. A. (2003). Racial identity, racial discrimination, perceived stress, and psychological distress among African American young adults. *Journal of Health and Social Behavior, 44*, 302–317.

Sellers, R. M., Morgan, L., & Brown, T. N. (2001). A multidimensional approach to racial identity: Implications for African American children. In A. Neal-Barnett, J. M. Contreras, & K. A. Kerns (Eds.), *Forging links: Clinical-developmental perspectives on African American children*. Greenwood, CT: Praeger.

Sellers, S. L., & Neighbors, H. W. (2008). Effects of goal-striving stress on the mental health of Black Americans. *Journal of Health and Social Behavior, 49*, 92–103.

Selten, J. P., & Sijben, N. (1994). First admission rates for schizophrenia immigrants to the Netherlands: The Dutch National Register. *Social Psychiatry & Psychiatric Epidemiology, 29*, 71–77.

Selye, H. (1956). *The stress of life*. New York: McGraw-Hill.

Semmer N. (1982). Stress at work, stress in private life and psychological well-being. In W. Bachmann & I. Udris (Eds.), *Mental load and stress in activity: European approaches*. New York: Elsevier-North Holland.

Serovich, J. M., Mason, T. L., Bautista, D., & Toviessi, P. (2006). Gay men's report of regret of HIV disclosure to family, friends, and sex partners. *AIDS Education and Prevention, 18(2)*, 132–138.

Settersten, R., Furstenburg, F., & Rumbaut R. (2005). *On the frontiers of adulthood: Theory, research, and public policy*. Chicago: University of Chicago Press.

Sewell, W. H., Haller, A. O., & Ohlendorf, G. W. (1970). The educational and early occupational status attainment process: Replication and revision. *American Sociological Review, 35*, 1014–1027.

Shadish, W. R., Lurigio, A. J., & Lewis, D. A. (1989). After deinstitutionalization: The present and future of mental health long-term policy. *Journal of Social Issues, 45*, 1–15.

Shaffer, D., Fisher, P., Dulcan, M. K., Davies, M., Piacentini, J., Schwab-Stone, M. E., et al. (1996). The NIMH Diagnostic Interview Schedule for Children Version 2.3 (DISC 2.3): Description, acceptability, prevalence rates and performance in the MECA study. *Journal of the American Academy of Child & Adolescent Psychiatry, 35*, 865–877.

Shalev, A. Y., & Freedman, S. (2005). PTSD following terrorist attacks: A prospective evaluation. *American Journal of Psychiatry, 162(6)*, 1188–1191.

Shalev, A. Y., Tuval, R., Frenkiel-Fishman, S., Hadar, H., & Eth, S. (2006). Psychological responses to continuous terror: A study of two communities in Israel. *American Journal of Psychiatry, 163(4)*, 667–673.

Shanley, D., Reid, G., & Evans, B. (2008). How parents seek help for children with mental health problems. *Administration and Policy in Mental Health and Mental Health Services Research, 35*, 135–146.

Shanok, A. F., & Miller, L. (2007). Depression and treatment in inner city pregnant and parenting teens. *Archives of Women's Mental Health, 10*, 199–210.

Shapiro, S., Skinner, E. A., Kessler, L. G., Von Korff, M., German, P. S., Tischler, G. L., et al. (1984). Utilization of health and mental health services: Three epidemiologic catchment area sites. *Archives of General Psychiatry, 41*, 971–978.

Shapiro, S., Skinner, E. A., Kramer, M., Steinwachs, D. M., & Regier, D. A. (1985). Measuring need for mental health services in a general population. *Medical Care, 23*, 1033–1043.

Sharfstein, S. (1982). Medicaid cutbacks and block grants: Crisis or opportunity for community mental health. *American Journal of Psychiatry, 139*, 466–470.

Sharif, Z. (1996). Neurochemistry of schizophrenia. In C.A. Kauffmann & J. M. Gorman (Eds.), *Schizophrenia: New directions for clinical research and treatment* (pp. 79–103). New York: Mary Ann Liebert.

Sheldon, C. T., Aubry, T. D., Arboleda-Florez, J., Wasylenki, D., Goering, P. N., & CMHEI Working Group. (2006). Social disadvantage, mental illness and predictors of legal involvement. *International Journal of Law and Psychiatry, 29*,249–256.

Shenton, M. E., Dickey, C. C., Frumin, M., & McCarley, R. W. (2001). A review of MRI findings in schizophrenia. *Schizophrenia Research, 49*, 1–52.

Shephard, R. L. (1987). *Physical activity and aging* (2nd ed.). Rockville, MD: Aspen.

Shern, D., Wilson, N., Saranga Coen, A., Patrick, D., Foster, M., & Bartsch, D. (1994). Client outcomes II: Longitudinal client data from the Colorado Treatment Outcome Study. *Milbank Quarterly, 72(1)*, 123–148.

Sherrington, R., Bynjolfsson, J., Petursson, H., et al. (1988). Localization of a susceptibility locus for schizophrenia on chromosome 5. *Nature, 336*, 164–169.

Shifren-Levine, I. (1992). Interview with author, March 5, 1992.

Shih, R. A., Belmonte, P. L., & Zandi, P. (2004). A review of the evidence from family, twin and adoption studies for a genetic contribution to adult psychiatric disorders. *International Review of Psychiatry, 16*, 260–283.

Shore, J. M. (1987). A pilot study of depression among American Indian patients with research diagnostic criteria. *American Indian and Alaska Native Mental Health Research, 1*, 4–15.

Shore, M. F., & Biegel, A. (1996). The challenges posed by managed behavioral health care. *The Milibank Quarterly, 73*, 77–93.

Shore, M., & Cohen, M. (1990). The Robert Wood Johnson Foundation Program on Chronic Mental Illness: An overview. *Hospital and Community Psychiatry, 41(11)*, 1212–1216.

Shrier, L., Harris, S. K., Sternberg, M., & Beardslee, W. (2001). Associations of depression, self-esteem and substance use with sexual risk among adolescents. *Preventive Medicine, 33*, 179–189.

Sibicky, M., & Dovidio, J. F. (1986). Stigma of psychological therapy: Stereotypes, interpersonal reactions, and the self-fulfilling prophecy. *Journal of Consulting & Clinical Psychology, 33*, 148–154.

Siegel, C., Laska, E., Haugland, G., O'Neill, D., Cohen, N., & Lesser, M. (2000). The construction of community indexes of mental health and social and mental well-being and their application to New York City. *Evaluation and Program Planning, 12*, 315–327.

Siegel, K., & Schrimshaw, E. W. (2005). Stress, appraisal, and coping: A comparison of HIV-infected women in the pre-HAART and HAART eras. *Journal of Psychosomatic Research, 58*, 225–233.

Siegrist, J. (1996). Adverse health effects of high-effort/low-reward conditions. *Journal of Occupational Health Psychology, 1*(1), 27–41.

Sigle-Rushton, W., & McLanahan, S. S. (2002). The living arrangements of new unmarried mothers. *Demography, 39*(3), 415–433.

Sikkema, K. J., Hansen, N. B., Ghebremichael, M., Kochman, A., Tarakeshwar, N., Meade, C. S., et al. (2006). A randomized controlled trial of a coping group intervention for adults with HIV who are AIDS bereaved: Longitudinal effects on grief. *Health Psychology, 25*(5), 563–570.

Sikkema, K. J., Hansen, N. B., Meade, C. S., Kochman, A., & Lee, R. S. (2005). Improvements in health-related quality of life following a group intervention for coping with AIDS-bereavement among HIV-infected men and women. *Quality of Life Research, 14*(4), 991–1005.

Sikkema, K. J., Kalichman, S. C., Hoffmann, R., Koob, J. J., Kelly, J. A., & Heckman, T. G. (2000). Coping strategies and emotional well-being among HIV-infected men and women experiencing AIDS-related bereavement. *AIDS Care, 12*(5), 613–624.

Sikkema, K. J., Kochman, A., DiFranceisco, W., Kelly, J. A., & Hoffmann, R. G. (2003). AIDS-related grief and coping with loss among HIV-positive men and women. *Journal of Behavioral Medicine, 26*(2), 165–181.

Silberstein, C., Galanter, M., Marmor, M., Lifshutz, H., & Krasinski, K. (1994). HIV-1 among inner city dually diagnosed inpatients. *American Journal of Drug and Alcohol Abuse, 20*, 101–131.

Silver, E. (1995). Punishment or treatment? Comparing the lengths of confinement of successful and unsuccessful insanity defendants. *Law and Human Behavior, 19*, 375–388.

Silver, E. (2000). Race, neighborhood disadvantage, and violence among persons with mental disorders: The importance of contextual measurement. *Law and Human Behavior, 24*, 449–456.

Silver, E. (2006). Understanding the relationship between mental disorder and violence: The need for a criminological perspective. *Law and Human Behavior, 30*, 685–706.

Silver, E., Cirincione, C., & Steadman, H. J. (1994). Demythologizing inaccurate perceptions of the insanity defense. *Law and Human Behavior, 18*, 63–70.

Silver, E., Mulvey, E. P., & Monahan, J. (2001). Assessing violence risk among discharged psychiatric patients: Toward an ecological approach. *Law and Human Behavior, 23*, 235–253.

Silver, E., Mulvey, E. P., & Swanson, J. W. (2002). Neighborhood structural characteristics and mental disorder: Faris and Dunham revisited. *Social Science & Medicine, 55*, 1457–1470.

Silver, R,, Cohen, E., Holman, A., McIntosh, D. N., Poulin, M., & Gil-Rivas, V. (2002). Nationwide longitudinal study of psychological responses to September 11. *Journal of the American Medical Association, 288*, 1235–1241.

Simon, G. E., Goldberg, D. P., Von Korff, M., & Ustun, T. B. (2002). Understanding cross-national differences in depression prevalence. *Psychological Medicine, 32*, 585–594.

Simon, R. (1995). Gender, multiple roles, role meaning, and mental health. *Journal of Health and Social Behavior, 36*, 182–194.

Simon, R. (1997). The meanings individuals attach to role identities and their implications for mental health. *Journal of Health and Social Behavior, 38*, 256–274.

Simon, R. (2002). Revisiting the relationships among gender, marital status, and mental health. *American Journal of Sociology, 107*(4), 1065–1096.

Simon, R. W. (2007). Contributions of the sociology of mental health for understanding the social antecedents, social regulation, and social distribution of emotion. In W. R. Avison, J. D. Mcleod, & B. A. Pescosolido (Eds.) *Mental Health, Social Mirror*. New York: Springer, pp. 239–274.

Simon, R. W., & Marcussen, K. (1999). Marital transitions, marital beliefs, and mental health. *Journal of Health and Social Behavior, 40*(2), 111–125.

Simon, R. W., & Nath, L. E. (2004). Gender and emotion in the United States: Do men and women differ in self-reports of feelings and expressive behavior? *American Journal of Sociology, 109,* 1137–1176.

Simoni, J. M., Mason, H. R., & Marks, G. (1997). Disclosing HIV status and sexual orientation to employers. *AIDS Care, 9*(5), 589–599.

Simoni, J. M., Mason, H. R., Marks, G., Ruiz, M. S., Reed, D., & Richardson, J. L. (1995). Women's self-disclosure of HIV infection: Rates, reasons, and reactions. *Journal of Consulting and Clinical Psychology, 63*(3), 474–478.

Simoni, J. M., & Pantalone, D. W. (2004). Secrets and safety in the age of AIDS: Does HIV disclosure lead to safer sex? *Topics in HIV Medicine, 12*(4), 109–118.

Simons, R. L., Murry, V., McLoyd, V., Lin, K., Cutrona, C., & Conger, R. D. (2002). Discrimination, crime, ethnic identity, and parenting as correlates of depressive symptoms among African American children: A multilevel analysis. *Development and Psychopathology, 14,* 371–393.

Simpson, A. I. F., Jones, R. M., Evans, C., & McKenna, B. (2006). Outcome of patients rehabilitated through a New Zealand forensic psychiatry service: A 6 year retrospective study. *Behavioral Sciences and the Law, 24,* 833–844.

Simpson, A. I. F., Skipworth, J., McKenna, B., Moskowitz, A., & Barry-Walsh, J. (2006). Mentally abnormal homicide in New Zealand as defined by legal and clinical criteria: A national study. *Australian and New Zealand Journal of Psychiatry, 40,* 804–809.

Singh-Manoux, A., Clarke, P., & Marmot, M. (2002). Multiple measures of socio-economic position and psychosocial health: proximal and distal measures. *International Journal of Epidemiology, 31,* 1192–1199.

Singh-Manoux, A., Ferrie, J. E., Chandola, T., & Marmot, M. (2004). Socioeconomic trajectories across the life course and health outcomes in midlife: Evidence for the accumulation hypothesis? *International Journal of Epidemiology, 33*(5), 1072–1079.

Sirey, J. A., Bruce, M. L., Alexopoulos, G. S., Perlick, D. A., Friedman, S. J., & Meyers, B. S. (2001). Stigma as a barrier to recovery: Perceived stigma and patient-rated severity of illness as predictors of antidepressant drug adherence. *Psychiatric Services, 52,* 1615–1620.

Sirey, J. A., Bruce, M. L., Alexopoulos, G. S., Perlick, D. A., Raue, P., Friedman, S. J., et al. (2001). Perceived stigma as a predictor of treatment discontinuation in young and older outpatients with depression. *American Journal of Psychiatry, 158,* 479–481.

Skapinakis, P., Weich, S., Lewis, G., Singleton, N., & Araya, R. (2006). Socio-economic position and common mental disorders: Longitudinal study in the general population in the UK. *British Journal of Psychiatry, 189,* 109–117.

Skeem, J. L., & Bibeau, L. (2008). How does violence potential relate to crisis intervention team responses to emergencies? *Psychiatric Services, 59,* 201–204.

Skeem, J. L., Louden, J. E., Polascek, D., & Camp, J. (2007). Assessing relationship quality in mandated community treatment: Blending care with control. *Psychological Assessment, 19,* 397–410.

Skeem, J. L., Markos, P., Tiemann, J., & Manchak, S. (2006). "Project HOPE" for homeless individuals with co-occurring mental and substance abuse disorders: Reducing symptoms, victimization, and violence. *International Journal of Forensic Mental Health, 5,* 1–14.

Slade, T. B., & Andrews, G. (2002). Empirical impact of the DSM-IV diagnostic criterion for clinical significance. *Journal of Nervous and Mental Disease, 190,* 334–337.

Slone, M., & Shoshani, A. (2006). Evaluation of preparatory measures for coping with anxiety raised by media coverage of terrorism. *Journal of Counseling Psychology, 53*(4), 535–542.

Smith, B. (1968). Competence and socialization. In J. A. Clausen (Ed.), *Socialization and society* (pp. 270–320). Boston: Little, Brown.

Smith, D. (1978). K is mentally ill. *Sociology, 12,* 23–53.

Smith, M. R. (1990). What is new in "new structuralist" analyses of earnings? *American Sociological Review, 55,* 827–841.

Smith, P. (1992). *The emotional labor of nursing: How nurses care.* Basingstoke: Macmillan.

Smith, P. (1999). Emotional labor. *Soundings, 11,* 14–19.

Smith, R., Rossetto, K., & Peterson, B. L. (2008). A meta-analysis of disclosure of one's HIV positive status, stigma and social support. *AIDS Care, 20*(10), 1–10.

Smith, W. K. (1987). The stress analogy. *Schizophrenia Bulletin, 13,* 215–220.

Smock, P. J. (1994). Gender and the short-run economic consequences of marital disruption. *Social Forces, 73,* 243–262.

Snowden, L. R. (1999). African American service use for mental health problems. *Journal of Community Psychology, 27*(3), 303–313.

Snowden, L. R. (2005). Racial, cultural and ethnic disparities in health and mental health: Toward theory and research at community levels. *American Journal of Community Psychology, 35*(1/2), 1–8.

Snowden, L. R., & Cheung, F. (1990). Use of inpatient mental health services by members of ethnic minority groups. *American Psychologist, 45*(3), 347–355.

Snowden, L. R., & Hu, T.-W. (1996). Outpatient service use in minority-serving mental health programs. *Administration and Policy in Mental Health and Mental Health Services Research, 24*(2), 149–159.

Snowden, L. R., Masland, M., Ma, Y., & Ciemens, E. (2006). Strategies to improve minority access to public mental health services in California: Description and preliminary evaluation. *Journal of Community Psychology, 34*(2), 225–235.

Snowden, L. R., Storey, C., & Clancey, T. (1989). Ethnicity and continuation in treatment at a Black community mental health center. *Journal of Community Psychology, 17*(2), 111–118.

Soderfeldt, B., Soderfeldt, M., Muntaner, C., O'Campo, P., Warj, L., & Ohlsom, C. (1996). Psychosocial work environment in human service organizations: A conceptual analysis and development of the demand-control model. *Social Science and Medicine, 42,* 1217–1226.

Solomon, P. (1992). The efficacy of case-management services for severely mentally disabled clients. *Community Mental Health Journal, 28,* 163–180.

Solomon, P., Draine, J., & Marcus, S. C. (2002). Predicting incarceration of clients of a psychiatric probation and parole service. *Psychiatric Services, 53,* 50–56.

Solomon, Z., Gelkopf, M., & Bleich, A. (2005). Is terror gender-blind? Gender differences in reaction to terror events. *Social Psychiatry and Psychiatric Epidemiology, 40*(12), 947–954.

Somer, E., Ruvio, A., Soref, E., & Sever, I. (2005). Terrorism, distress and coping: High versus low impact regions and direct versus indirect civilian exposure. *Anxiety, Stress and Coping, 18*(3), 165–182.

Somer, E., Ruvio, A., Sever, I., & Soref, E. (2007). Reactions to repeated unpredictable terror attacks: Relationships among exposure, posttraumatic distress, mood, and intensity of coping. *Journal of Applied Social Psychology, 37*(4), 862–886.

Somervell, P. D, Kaplan, B. H., Heiss, G., Tyroler, T. A., Kleinbaum, D. G., & Oberist, P. A. (1989). Psychological distress as a predictor of mortality. *American Journal of Epidemiology, 130,* 1013–1023.

Sorlie, P., Backlund, E., & Keller, J. B. (1995). US mortality by economic, demographic and social characteristics: The National Longitudinal Mortality Study. *American Journal of Public Health, 85,* 903–905.

Sosowsky, L. (1980). Explaining the increased arrest rate among mental patients: Cautionary note. *American Journal of Psychiatry, 137,* 1602–1605.

Spector, P. E. (1986). Perceived control by employees: A meta-analysis of studies concerning autonomy and participation at work. *Human Relations, 39*(11), 1005–1016.

Spencer, M., Fegley, S., Harpalani, V., & Seaton, G. (2004). Understanding hypermasculinity in context: A theory driven analysis of urban adolescent males' coping responses. *Research in Human Development, 1*(4), 229–257.

Spitz, R. A. (1946). Anaclitic depression: An inquiry into the genesis of psychiatric conditions in early childhood II. *Psychoanalytic Study of the Child, 2,* 313–342.

Spitzer, R. L. (1998). Diagnosis and need for treatment are not the same. *Archives of General Psychiatry, 55,* 120.

Spitzer, R. L., & Endicott, J. (1978). Medical and mental disorder: Proposed definition and criteria. In R. L. Spitzer & D. F. Klein (Eds.), *Critical issues in psychiatric diagnosis* (pp. 15–39). New York: Raven Press.

Spitzer, R. L., & Wakefield, J. C. (1999). DSM-IV diagnostic criterion for clinical significance: Does it help solve the false positives problem? *American Journal of Psychiatry, 156,* 1856–1864.

Spitzer, R. L., & Williams, J. B. W. (1982). The definition and diagnosis of mental disorder. In W. R. Gove (Ed.), *Deviance and mental illness* (pp. 15–31). Beverly Hills, CA: Sage.

Sprang, G. (2001). Vicarious stress: Patterns of disturbance and use of mental health services by those indirectly affected by the Oklahoma City bombing. *Psychological Reports, 89*(2), 331–338.

Sproul, B. (1986). *Models of community support service approaches to helping persons with long-term mental illness.* Boston: NIMH Consumer Support Program. Boston University.

Srole, L., Langner, T. S., Michael, S. T., Kirkpatrick, P., Opler, M. K., & Rennie, T. A. C. (1978). *Mental health in the metropolis: The Midtown Manhattan Study* (Rev. ed.). New York: New York University Press.

Srole, L., Langner, T. S., Michael, S. T., Opler, M. K., & Rennie, T. A. C. (1961). *Mental health in the metropolis* (Vol. 1). New York: McGraw-Hill.

St. Jean, Y., & Feagin, J. R. (1998). *Double burden: Black women and everyday racism.* New York: Sharpe.

Stack, S., & Eshleman, J. R. (1998). Marital status and happiness: A 17-nation study. *Journal of Marriage and the Family, 60,* 527–536.

Stansfeld, S. A., Bosma, H., Hemingway, H., & Marmot, M. G. (1998). Psychosocial work characteristics and social support as predictors of SF-36 health functioning: The Whitehall II study. *Psychosomatic Medicine, 60*(3), 247–255.

Stansfeld, S. A., Fuhrer, R., Shipley, M., & Marmot, M. G. (1999). Work characteristics predict psychiatric disorders: Prospective results from the Whitehall II study. *Occupational and Environmental Medicine, 56,* 302–307.

Stansfeld, S., Head, J., Bratley, M., & Fonagy, P. (2008). Social position, early deprivation and the development of attachment. *Social Psychiatry and Psychiatric Epidemiology, 43*(7), 516–526.

Stanton, M. (1981). An integrated structural/strategic approach to family therapy. *Journal of Marital and Family Therapy, 74,* 427–440.

Stanton, M. D. (1981). Strategic approaches to family therapy. In A. S. Gurman & D. P. Kniskern (Eds.), *Handbook of family therapy.* New York: Brunner/Mazel.

Starkman, M. N. (2006). The terrorist attacks of September 11, 2001, as psychological toxin – increase in suicide attempts. *Journal of Nervous and Mental Disease, 194*(7), 547–550.

Stasko, E., & Ickovics, J. (2007). Traumatic growth in the face of terrorism: Threshold effects and action-based growth. *Applied Psychology: An International Review, 56*(3), 386–395.

Steadman, H. J., & Cocozza, J. J. (1978). Selective reporting and the public's misconceptions of the criminally insane. *Public Opinion Quarterly, 42,* 523–533.

Steadman, H. J., & Cocozza, J. J. (1987). The impact of deinstitutionalization on the criminal justice system: Implications for understanding changing modes of social control. In J. Lawman, R. J. Menzies, & T. S. Palys (Eds.), *Transcarceration: Essays in the sociology of social control* (pp. 227–248). Aldershot, England: Gower.

Steadman, H. J., Cocozza, J. J., & Melick, M. E. (1978). Explaining the increased crime rate of mental patients: The changes in clientele of state hospitals. *American Journal of Psychiatry, 135,* 816–820.

Steadman, H. J., Cocozza, J. J., & Veysey, B. M. (1999). Comparing outcomes for diverted and nondiverted jail detainees with mental illness. *Law and Human Behavior, 23,* 615–627.

Steadman, H. J., Deane, M. W., Borum, R., & Morrissey, J. P. (2000). Comparing outcomes of major models for police responses to mental health emergencies. *American Journal of Public Health, 51,* 645–649.

Steadman, H. J., Fabisiak, S., Dvoskin, J., & Holohean, E. J.(1987). A survey of mental disability among state prison inmates. *Hospital and Community Psychiatry, 38,* 1086–1090.

Steadman, H. J., McCarty, D. W., & Morrissey, J. P. (1989). *The mentally ill in jail: Planning for essential services.* New York: Guilford.

Steadman, H. J., McGreevy, M. A., Morrissey, J., Callahan, L. A., Robbins, P. C., & Cirincione, C. (1993). *Before and after Hinkley: Evaluating insanity defense reform.* New York: Guilford.

Steadman, H. J., Monahan, J., Duffee, B., Hartstone, E., & Pamela, C. (1984). The impact of state mental hospital deinstitutionalization on U.S. prison populations, 1968–1978. *Journal of Criminal Law and Criminology, 75,* 474–490.

Steadman, H. J., Morris, S. M., & Dennis, D. L. (1995). The diversion of mentally ill persons from jails to community based services: A profile of programs. *American Journal of Public Health, 85,* 1630–1635.

Steadman, H. J., & Morrissey, J. P. (1987). The impact of deinstitutionalization in the criminal justice system: Implications for understanding changing modes of social control. In J. Lowman, R. J. Menzies, & T. S. Palys (Eds.), *Transcarceration: Essays in the sociology of social control* (pp. 227–248). Aldershot, England: Gower.

Steadman, H. J., Morrissey, J. P., Braff, J., & Monahan, J. (1986). Psychiatric evaluations of police referrals in a general hospital emergency room. *International Journal of Law and Psychiatry, 8,* 39–47.

Steadman, H. J., Mulvey, E. P., Monahan, J., Robbins, P. C., Appelbaum, P. S., Grisso, T., et al. (1998). Violence by people discharged from acute psychiatric inpatient facilities and by others in the same neighborhoods. *Archives of General Psychiatry, 55,* 393–401.

Steadman, H. J., & Naples, M. (2005). Assessing the effectiveness of jail diversion programs for persons with serious mental illness and co-occurring substance use disorders. *Behavioral Sciences and the Law, 23,* 163–170.

Steen, R. G., Mull, C., McClure, R., Hamer, R. M., & Jeffrey, A. (2006). Brain volume in first-episode schizophrenia: Systematic review and meta-analysis of magnetic resonance imaging studies. *British Journal of Psychiatry, 188,* 510–518.

Steffensmeier, D., & Allan, E. (1991). Gender, age, and crime. In J. F. Sheley (Ed.), *Criminology: A contemporary handbook* (pp. 67–93). Belmont, CA: Wadsworth.

Stein, B. D., Elliott, M. N., Jaycox, L. H., Collins, R. H., Berry, S. H., Klein, D. J., et al. (2004). A national longitudinal study of the psychological consequences of the September 11, 2001 terrorist attacks: Reactions, impairment, and help-seeking. *Psychiatry – Interpersonal and Biological Processes, 67*(2), 105–117.

Stein, L., & Ganser, L. (1983). Wisconsin's system for funding mental health services. In J. Talbott (Ed.), *Unified mental health systems: Utopia unrealized.* San Francisco: Jossey-Bass.

Stein, L., & Santos, A. (1998). *Assertive community treatment of persons with severe mental illness.* New York, Norton.

Stein, L., & Test, M. (1980). Alternative to mental hospital treatment. *Archives of General Psychiatry, 37,* 392–397.

Stein, L., & Test, M. (1985). The evolution of the training in community living model. *New Directions for Mental Health Services, 26,* 7–16.

Stein, M. D., & Friedmann, P. (2002). Need for medical and psychosocial services among injection drug users: A comparative study of needle exchange and methadone maintenance. *American Journal on Addictions, 11*(4), 262–270.

Steinberg, R, J., & Figart, D. M. (1999). Emotional demands at work: A job content analysis. *Annals of the American Academy of Political and Social Science, 561,* 177–191.

Stern, D. (1985). *The interpersonal world of the infant: A view from psychoanalysis and developmental psychology.* New York: Basic Books.

Stern, R., & Minkoff, K. (1979). Paradoxes in programming for chronic patients in a community clinic. *Hospital and Communitiy Psychiatry, 30,* 613–617.

Sternberg, R. J. (1995). For whom the bell curve tolls: A review of *The Bell Curve. Psychological Science, 6,* 257–261.

Steury, E. H., & Choinski, M. (1995). "Normal" crimes and mental disorder: A two group comparison of deadly and dangerous felonies. *International Journal of Law and Psychiatry, 18,* 183–207.

Stevens, J. A., Hasbrouck, L. M., Durant, T. M., Dellinger, A. M., & Batabyal, P. K. (1999). Surveillance for injuries and violence among older adults. *Morbidity and Mortality Weekly, 48*(8), 27–50.

Stevenson, H. C., & Renard, G. (1993). Trusting ole' wise owls: Therapeutic use of cultural strengths in African-American families. *Professional Psychology: Research and Practice, 24*(4), 433–442.

Stevenson, H. C., Reed, J., Bodison, P., & Bishop, A. (1997). Racism stress management: Racial socialization beliefs and the experience of depression and anger in African American youth. *Youth and Society, 29*(2): 197–222.

Stiffman, A. R., Striley, C., Horvath, V. E., Hadley-Ives, E., Polgar, M., Elze, D., et al. (2001). Organizational context and provider perception as determinants of mental health service use. *Journal of Behavioral Health Services & Research, 28,* 188–204.

Stiffman, A. R., Horwitz, S. M., Hoagwood, K., Compton, W., III, Cottler, L., Bean, D. L., et al. (2000). The Service Assessment for Children and Adolescents (SACA): Adult and child reports. *Journal of the American Academy of Child & Adolescent Psychiatry, 39,* 1032–1039.

Stiffman, A. R., Pescosolido, B., & Cabassa, L. (2004). Building a model to understand youth service access: The gateway provider model. *Mental Health Services Research, 6,* 189–198.

Stirratt, M. J., Remien, R. H., Smith, A., Copeland, O. Q., Dolezal, C., Krieger, D., et al. (2006). The role of HIV serostatus disclosure in antiretroviral medication adherence. *AIDS and Behavior, 10*(5): 483–493.

Stober, D. R., Schwartz, J. A. J., McDaniel, J. S., & Abrams, R. F. (1997). Depression and HIV disease: Prevalence, correlates and treatment. *Psychiatric Annals, 27*(5), 372–377.

Stockdale, S. E., Wells, K. B., Tang, L., Belin, T. R., Zhang, L., & Sherbourne. C. D. (2007). The importance of social context: Neighborhood stressors, stress-buffering mechanisms, and alcohol, drug, and mental health disorders. *Social Science & Medicine, 65,* 1867–1881.

Stone, A. A. (1975). *Mental health and law: A system in transition.* Washington, DC: Department of Health, Education, and Welfare.

Stoskopf, C. H., Kim, Y. K., & Glover, S. H. (2001). Dual diagnosis: HIV and mental illness, a population-based study. *Community Mental Health Journal, 37,* 469–479.

Strathdee, S. A., Patrick, D. M., Currie, S. L., Cornelisse, P. G., Rekart, M. L., Montaner, J. S., et al. (1997). Needle exchange is not enough: Lessons from the Vancouver injecting drug use study. *AIDS, 11,* F59–F65.

Strauss, A. L., & Corbin, J. (1990). *Basics of qualitative research: Grounded theory proceedures and techniques.* Newbury Park, CA: Sage.

Strazdins, L., Clements, M. S., Korda, R. J., Broom, D. H., & D'Souza, R. M. (2006). Unsociable work? Nonstandard work schedules, family relationships, and children's well-being. *Journal of Marriage and Family, 68,* 394–410.

Stressed out? Say "I do." (2005). *Knight-Ridder.* Retrieved March 1, 2005, from.

Strobino, D. M., Ensminger, M. E., Kim, Y. J., & Nanda, J. (1995). Mechanisms for maternal age differences in birth weight. *American Journal of Epidemiology, 142,* 504–514.

Stroebe, W., & Stroebe, M. S. (1993). Determinants of adjustment to bereavement in younger widows and widowers. In M. S. Stroebe, W. Stroebe, & R. O. Hansson (Eds.), *Handbook of bereavement: Theory, research, and intervention* (pp. 208–226). New York: Cambridge University Press.

Strohschein, L. (2002). Parental divorce and child mental health trajectories. *Journal of Marriage and Family, 67,* 1286–1300.

Strohschein, L. (2005). Household income histories and child mental health trajectories. *Journal of Heath and Social Behavior, 46,* 359–375.

Strohschein, L., McDonough, P., Monette G., & Shao, Q. (2005). Marital transitions and mental health: Are there gender differences in the short-term effects of marital status change? *Social Science & Medicine, 61*(11), 2293–2303.

Ström S. (2003). Unemployment and families: A review of research. *Social Service Review, 77*(3), 399–431.

Stroul, B., & Friedman, R. (1986). *A system of care for severely emotionally disturbed children and youth.* Washington, DC: Georgetown University Child Development Center, CASSP Technical Assistance Center.

Stroul, B., Friedman, R., Hernandez, M., Roebuck, L., Lourie, I., & Koyanagi, C. (1996). Conclusion: Systems of care in the future. In B. Stroul (Ed.), *Children's mental health: Creating systems of care in a changing society* (pp. 591–612). Baltimore: Paul H. Brookes.

Stroup, S., & Dorwart, R. (1995). Impact of a managed mental health program on Medicaid recipients with severe mental illness. *Psychiatric Services, 46,* 885–889.

Stroup, S., & Dorwart, R. (1997). Overview of public sector managed health care. In K. Minkoff & D. Pollack (Eds.), *Managed mental health care in the public sector* (pp. 1–13). Amsterdam: Harwood.

Strümpfer, D. J. W. (1995). The origins of health and strength: From 'salutogenesis' to 'fortigenesis.' *South African Journal of Psychology, 25,* 81–89.

Stuber, J., Galea, S., Boscarino, J. A., & Schlesinger, M. (2006). Was there unmet mental health need after the September 11, 2001 terrorist attacks? *Social Psychiatry and Psychiatric Epidemiology, 41*(3), 230–240.

Sturge-Apple, M. L., Davies, P. T., & Cummings, E. M. (2006). Impact of hostility and withdrawal in interparental conflict on parents' emotional unavailability and children's adjustment difficulties. *Child Development, 77,* 1623–1641.

Sturm, R., Jackson, C. A., Meredith, L. S., Yip, W., Manning, W. G., Rogers, W. H., et al. (1995). Mental health care utilization in prepaid and fee-for-service plans among depressed patients in the Medical Outcomes Study. *Health Services Research, 30,* 319–340.

Stutzer, A., & Frey, B. S. (2006). Does marriage make people happy, or do happy people get married? *Journal of Socio-Economics, 35*(2), 326–347.

Substance Abuse and Mental Health Services Administration. (1993). Final notice establishing definitions for (1) children with a serious emotional disturbance, and (2) adults with a serious mental illness. *Federal Register, 58,* 29,422–29,455.

Suchman, E. (1964). Sociomedical variation among ethnic groups. *American Journal of Sociology, 70,* 319–331.

Sucoff, C. A., & Upchurch, D. M. (1998). Neighborhood context and the risk of childbearing among metropolitan-area Black adolescents. *American Sociological Review, 63*(4), 571–585.

Sue, S. (1977). Community mental health services to minority groups: Some optimism, some pessimism. *American Psychologist, 32*(8), 616–624.

Sue, S. (1998). In search of cultural competence in psychotherapy and counseling. *American Psychologist, 53,* 440–448.

Sue, S. (2003). In defense of cultural competency in psychotherapy and treatment. *American Psychologist, 58*(11), 964–970.

Sue, S. (2006). Cultural competency: From philosophy to research and practice. *Journal of Community Psychology, 34*(2), 237–245.

Sue, S., & Chu, J. Y. (2003). The mental health of ethnic minority groups: Challenges posed by the supplement to the Surgeon General's Report on Mental Health. *Culture, Medicine and Psychiatry, 27,* 447–465.

Sue, S., Fujino, D. C., Hu, L.-T., Takeuchi, D. T., & Zane, N. W. S. (1991). Community mental health services for ethnic minority groups: A test of the cultural responsiveness hypothesis. *Journal of Consulting and Clinical Psychology, 59*(4), 522–540.

Sue, S., & McKinney, H. L. (1975). Asian Americans in the community mental health care system. *American Journal of Orthopsychiatry, 45,* 111–118.

Sue, S., Sue, D. W., Sue, L., & Takeuchi, D. T. (1995). Psychopathology among Asian Americans: A model minority? *Cultural Diversity and Mental Health, 1,* 39–51.

Sue, S., Zane, N. W. S., & Young, K. (1994). Research on psychotherapy with culturally diverse populations. In A. Bergin & S. L. Garfield (Eds.), *Handbook of psychotherapy and behavior change* (pp. 783–817). New York: Wiley.

Suldo, S. M., & Shaffer, E. J. (2008). Looking beyond psychopathology: The dual-factor model of mental health in youth. *School Psychology Review, 37,* 52–68.

Sullivan, G., Koegel, P., Kanouse, D. E., Cournos, F., McKinnon, K., Young, A. S., et al. (1999). HIV and people with serious mental illness: The public sector's role in reducing HIV risk and improving care. *Psychiatric Services, 50*(5), 648–652.

Sullivan, H. S. (1947). *Conceptions of modern psychiatry.* Washington, DC: William Alanson White Psychiatric Foundation.

Sullivan, P. F., Kessler, R. C., & Kendler, K. S. (1998). Latent class analysis of lifetime depressive symptoms in the National Comorbidity Survey. *American Journal of Psychiatry, 155,* 1398–1406.

Sullivan P. F., Neale, M. C., & Kendler, K. S. (2000). Genetic epidemiology of major depression: Review and meta-analysis. *American Journal of Psychiatry, 157,* 1552–1562.

Sullivan, P. S., Lansky, A., Drake, A., & HITS-2000 Investigators. (2004). Failure to return for HIV test results among persons at high risk for HIV infection: Results from a multistate interview project. *Journal of Acquired Immune Deficiency Syndromes, 35,* 511–518.

Sumartojo, E., Lyles, C., Choi, K., Clark, L., Collins, C., Grey, C. G., et al. (2008). Prevalence and correlates of HIV testing in a multi-site sample of young men who have sex with men. *AIDS Care, 20*, 1–14.

Summerville, M. B., Abbate, M. F., Siegel, A. M., Serravezza, J., & Kaslow, N. (1992). Psychopathology in urban female minority adolescents with suicide attempts. *Journal of the Academy of Child and Adolescent Psychiatry, 31*, 663–668.

Surgeon General of the United States. (1999). Mental health: A report of the Surgeon General. *U.S. Public Health Service.* Retrieved September 21, 2008, from http://www.surgeongeneral.gov/library/mentalhealth/home.html.

Susser, E., & Lin, S. P. (1992). Schizophrenia after prenatal exposure to the Dutch hunger winter of 1944–1945. *Archives of General Psychiatry, 49*, 983–988.

Susser, M. W., Watson, W., & Hopper, K. (1985). *Sociology in medicine* (3rd ed.) Oxford: Oxford Univeristy Press.

Sussman, L. K., Robins, L. N., & Earls, F. (1987). Treatment-seeking for depression by Black and White Americans. *Social Science & Medicine, 24*, 187–196.

Sutton, J. R. (1991). The political economy of madness: The expansion of the asylum in progressive America. *American Sociological Review, 56*, 665–678.

Swaminath, R. S., Mendonca, J. D., Vidal, C., & Chapman, P. (2002). Experiments in change: Pretrial diversion of offenders with mental illness. *Canadian Journal of Psychiatry, 47*, 450–458.

Swanson, J. W. (1994). Mental disorder, substance abuse and community violence: An epidemiological approach. In J. Monahan & H. J. Steadman (Eds.), *Violence and mental disorder* (pp. 101–136). Chicago: University of Chicago Press.

Swanson, J. W., Borum, R., Swartz, M. S., Wagner, H. R., Burns, B. J., & Hiday, V. A. (2001). Can involuntary outpatient commitment reduce arrests among persons with severe mental illness? *Criminal Justice and Behavior, 28*, 156–189.

Swanson, J. W., Swartz, M. S., Van Dorn, R. A., Elbogen, E. B., Wagner, H. R., Rosenheck, R. A., et al. (2006). A national study of violent behavior in persons with schizophrenia. *Archives of General Psychiatry, 63*, 490–499.

Swartz, J. A., & Lurigio, A. J. (2007). Serious mental illness and arrest: The generalized mediating effects of substance use. *Crime and Delinquency, 53*, 581–604.

Swartz, M. S., Wagner, H. R., Swanson, J. W., Burns, B. J., George, L. K., & Padgett, D. K. (1998). Comparing use of public and private mental health services: The enduring barriers of race and age. *Community Mental Health Journal, 34*, 133–144.

Sweet, A. A., & Loizeaux, A, L. (1991). Behavioral and cognitive treatment methods: A critical comparative review. *Journal of Behavior Therapy and Experimental Psychiatry, 22*, 159–185.

Swidler, A. (2001). *Talk of love: How culture matters.* Chicago: University of Chicago Press.

Swindle, R., Heller, K., Pescosolido, B. A., & Kikuzawa, S. (2000). Responses to 'nervous breakdowns' in America over a 40-year period: Mental health policy implications. *American Psychologist, 55*, 740–749.

Swinnerton, K. A., & Wial, H. (1995). Is job stability declining in the U.S. economy? *Industrial & Labor Relations Review, 48*, 293–304.

Symonds, P. (1939). *The psychology of parent-child relationships.* New York: Appleton-Century-Crofts.

Szasz, T. (1961). *The myth of mental illness.* New York: Harper & Row.

Szasz, T. (1963). *Law, liberty, and psychiatry: An inquiry into the social use of mental health practices.* New York: Macmillian.

Szyf, M., McGowan, P., & Meaney, M. J. (2008). The social environment and the epigenome. *Environmental and Molecular Mutagenesis, 49*, 46–60.

Takeuchi, D. T., Bui, K.-V. T., & Kim, L. (1993). The referral of minority adolescents to community mental health centers. *Journal of Health and Social Behavior, 34*, 53–64.

Takeuchi, D. T., Chun, C., Gong, F. & Shen, H. (2002). Cultural Expression of Distress. *Health: An Interdisciplinary Journal for the Social Study of Health, Illness and Medicine, 6*, 221–235.

Takeuchi, D. T., Sue, S., & Yeh, M. (1995). Return rates and outcomes from ethnicity-specific mental health programs in Los Angeles. *American Journal of Public Health, 85*, 638–643.

Takeuchi, D. T., & Kim, K. F. 2000. Enhancing mental health services delivery for diverse populations. *Contemporary Sociology, 29*(1), 74–83.

Takeuchi, D. T, Uehara, E., & Maramba, G. (1999). Cultural diversity and mental health treatment. in A. V. Horwitz & T. L. Scheid (Eds.), *A handbook for the study of mental health* (pp. 550–565). New York: Cambridge University Press.

Takeuchi, D. T., Zane, N., Hong, S., Chae, D. H., Gong, F., Gee, G. C., et al. (2007). Immigration-related factors and mental disosrders among Asian Americans. *American Journal of Public Health, 97*, 84–90.

Talbot, J. (1974). Radical psychiatry: An examination of the issues. *American Journal of Psychiatry, 13*(2), 121–128.

Tasman, A., Kay, J., Lieberman, J. A., First, M., & Maj, M. (Eds.). (2008). *Psychiatry* (2 vols). Chichester, UK: Wiley.

Tausig, M., & Fenwick R. (1999). Recession and well-being. *Journal of Health and Social Behavior, 40*, 1–16.

Tavris, C. (1992). *Mismeasure of woman: Why women are not the better sex, the inferior sex, or the opposite sex.* New York: Simon & Schuster.

Taylor, J., Henderson, D., & Jackson, B. B. (1991). A holistic model for understanding and predicting depressive symptoms in African-American women. *Journal of Community Psychology, 19*, 306–320.

Taylor, J., & Turner, J. (2004). A longitudinal study of the role and significance of mattering to others for depressive symptoms. *Journal of Health and Social Behavior, 42*, 310–325.

Taylor, J., & Jackson, B. (1990). Factors affecting alcohol consumption in Black women, Part II. *International Journal of Addictions, 25*, 1415–1427.

Taylor, J., & Jackson, B. (1991). Evaluation of a holistic model of mental health symptoms in African American women. *Journal of Black Psychology, 18*, 19–45.

Taylor, P. J., & Gunn, J. (1999). Homicides by people with mental illness: Myth and reality. *British Journal of Psychiatry, 174*, 9–14.

Taylor, P. J., & Schanda, H. (2000). Violence against others by psychiatric hospital inpatients with psychosis: Prevention strategies and challenges to their evaluation. In S. Hodgins (Ed.), *Violence among the mentally ill: Effective treatments and management strategies* (pp. 251–276). London: Kluwer.

Taylor, R. D., Casten, R., & Flickinger, S. M. (1993). Influence of kinship social support on the parenting experiences and psychosocial adjustment of African-American adolescents. *Developmental Psychology, 29*, 382–388.

Taylor, R. J., Chatters, L. M., & Levin, J. (2004). *Religion in the lives of African Americans: Social, psychological, and health perspectives.* Thousand Oaks, CA: Sage.

Taylor, S. E. (1981). The interface of cognitive and social psychology. In J. Harvey (Ed.), *Cognition, social behavior, and the environment.* Hillsdale, NJ: Erlbaum.

Taylor, S. E. (1989). *Positive illusions: Creative self-deception and the healthy mind.* New York: Basic Books.

Taylor, S. E. (2007). Coping resources, coping processes, and mental health. *Annual Review of Clinical Psychology, 3*, 377–401.

Taylor, S. E., & Aspinwall, L. G. (1996). Mediating and moderating processes in psychosocial stress: Appraisal, coping, resistance, and vulnerability. In H. B. Kaplan (Ed.), *Psychosocial stress: Perspectives on structure, theory, life-course, and methods* (pp. 71–110). San Diego: Academic Press.

Teachman, J., Tedrow, L., & Crowder, K. (2000). The changing demography of America's families. *Journal of Marriage and Family, 62*, 1234–1246.

Tedeschi, R. G., & Calhoun, L. G. (2004). Post-traumatic growth: Conceptual foundations and empirical evidence. *Psychological Inquiry, 15*(1), 1–18.

Tegger, M. K., Crane, H. M., Tapia, K. A., Uldall, K. K., Holte, S. E., & Kitahata, M. M. (2008). The effect of mental illness, substance use, and treatment for depression on the initiation of highly active antiretroviral therapy among HIV-infected individuals. *AIDS Patient Care STDS, 22*, 233–243.

Tengstrom, A., Hodgins, S., Grann, M., Langstrom, N., & Kullgren, G. (2004). Schizophrenia and criminal offending: The role of psychopathy and substance use disorders. *Criminal Justice and Behavior, 31*, 367–391.

Tennant, C. (1999). Life stress, social support and coronary heart disease. *Australian and New Zealand Journal of Psychiatry, 33*, 636–641.

Teplin, L. A. (1983). The criminalization of the mentally ill: Speculation in search of data. *Psychological Bulletin, 94*, 54–67.

Teplin, L. A. (1984a). Criminalizing mental disorder: The comparative arrest rate of the mentally ill. *American Psychologist, 39*, 794–803.

Teplin, L. A. (1984b). *Mental health and criminal justice.* Beverly Hills, CA: Sage.

Teplin, L. A. (1985). The criminality of the mentally ill: A dangerous misconception. *American Journal of Psychiatry, 142*, 593–599.

Teplin, L. A. (1990a). The prevalence of severe mental disorder among male urban jail detainees: Comparison with the Epidemiologic Catchment Area program. *American Journal of Public Health, 80*, 663–669.

Teplin, L. A. (1990b). Detecting disorder: The treatment of mental illness among jail detainees. *Journal of Consulting and Clinical Psychology, 58*, 233–236.

Teplin, L. A. (1994). Psychiatric and substance abuse disorders among male urban jail detainees. *American Journal of Public Health, 84*, 290–293.

Teplin, L. A. (1996). The prevalence of psychiatric disorder among incarcerated women. *Archives of General Psychiatry, 53*, 505–512.

Teplin, L. A., Abram, K. M., & McClelland, G. (1994). Does psychiatric disorder predict violent crime among released jail detainees? A six-year longitudinal study. *American Psychologist, 49*, 335–342.

Teplin, L. A., Abram, K. M., & McClelland, G. (1996). The prevalence of psychiatric disorder among incarcerated women. *Archives of General Psychiatry, 53*, 505–512.

Teplin, L. A., Filstead, W. J., Hefter, G. M., & Sheridan, E. P. (1980). Police involvement with the psychiatric emergency patient. *Psychiatric Annals, 10*, 46–54.

Teplin, L. A., McClelland, G. M., & Abram, K. M. (1993). The role of mental disorder and substance abuse in predicting violent crime among released offenders. In S. Hodgins (Ed.), *Mental disorder and crime* (pp. 86–103). Newbury Park, CA: Sage.

Teplin, L. A., McClelland, G. M., Abram, K. M., & Weiner, D. A. (2005). Crime victimization in adults with severe mental illness: Comparison with the National Crime Victimization Survey. *Archives of General Psychiatry, 62*(8), 911–921.

Teplin, L. A., & Pruett, N. S. (1992). Police as street corner psychiatrists: Managing the mentally ill. *International Journal of Law and Psychiatry, 15*, 157–170.

Terr, L. C. (1991). Childhood traumas: An outline and overview. *American Journal of Psychiatry, 148*, 10–20.

Tessler, R. C., & Dennis, D. L. (1992). Mental illness among homeless adults: A synthesis of recent NIMH-funded research. *Research in Community and Mental Health, 7*, 3–53.

Tessler, R., & Goldman, H. (1982). *The chronically mentally ill: Assessing community support programs.* Cambridge: Ballinger.

Theodossiou I. (1998). The effects of low-pay and unemployment on psychological well-being: A logistic regression approach. *Journal of Health Economics, 17*(1), 85–104.

Theorell, T., Alfredsson, L., Knox, S., Perski, A., Svensson, J., Waller, D. (1984). On the interplay between socioeconomic factors, personality and work environment in the pathogenesis of cardiovascular disease. *Scandinavian Journal of Work, Environment and Health, 10*, 373–380.

Theorell, T., & Karasek, R. (1996). Current issues relating to psychosocial job strain and cardiovascular disease research. *Journal of Occupational Health Psychology, 1*, 9–26.

Theriot, M. T., & Segal, S. P. (2005). Involvement with the criminal justice system among new clients at outpatient mental health agencies. *Psychiatric Services, 56*, 179–185.

Thoits, P. A. (1983). Dimensions of life events that influence psychological distress: An evaluation and synthesis of the literature. In H. B. Kaplan (Ed.), *Psychosocial stress: Trends in theory and research* (pp. 33–103). New York: Academic Press.

Thoits, P. A. (1984). Coping, social support, and psychological outcomes: The central role of emotion. In T. Millon, M. J. Lerner, & I. B. Weiner (Eds.), *Review of personality and social psychology* (Vol. 5, pp. 219–238). Beverly Hills, CA: Sage.

Thoits, P. A. (1985). Self-labeling processes in mental illness: The role of emotional deviance. *American Journal of Sociology, 92*, 221–249.

Thoits, P. A. (1992). Identity structures and psychological well-being: Gender and marital status comparisons. *Social Psychology Quarterly, 55*, 236–256.

Thoits, P. A. (1995). Stress, coping and social support processes: Where are we? What next? *Journal of Health & Social Behavior* [Extra issue], 53–79.

Thoits, P. A. (2003). Personal agency in the accumulation of multiple role-identities. In P. J. Burke, T. J. Owens, R. Serpe, & P. A. Thoits (Eds.), *Advances in identity theory and research* (pp. 179–194). New York: Kluwer.

Thoits, P. A., & Hewitt, L. N. (2001). Volunteer work and well-being. *Journal of Health and Social Behavior, 42*, 115–131.

Thomas, C., Conrad, P., Casler, R., & Goodman, E. (2006). Trends in the use of psychotropic medications among adolescents, 1994–2001. *Psychiatric Services, 57*, 63–69.

Thomas, W. I., & Thomas, D. S. (1928). *The child in America: Behavior problems and programs.* New York: Knopf.

Thompson, B. W. (1996). A way outa no way: Eating problems among African American, Latina, and White women. In E. N. Chow, D. Y. Wilkinson, & M. Baca-Zinn (Eds.) *Race, class & gender: Common bonds, different voices* (pp. 62–69). Thousand Oaks, CA: Sage.

Thompson, B., Coronado, G., Snipes, S. A., & Puschel, K. (2003). Methodologic advances and ongoing challenges in designing community-based health promotion programs. *Annual Review of Public Health, 24*, 315–340.

Thompson, C. (1942). Cultural pressures on the psychology of women. In C. Zandari. (Ed.), *Essential papers on the psychology of women.* New York: New York University Press.

Thompson, M. S., & Keith, V. M. (2001). The blacker the berry: Gender, skin tone, self-esteem, and self-efficacy. *Gender and Society, 15*, 336–357.

Thomson, E., & Colella, U. (1992). Cohabitation and marital stability: Quality or commitment? *Journal of Marriage and the Family, 54*, 259–267.

Tolou-Shams, M., Brown, L. K., Houck, C., & Lescano. C. M. (2008). The association between depressive symptoms, substance use, and HIV risk among youth with an arrest history. *Journal of Studies on Alcohol and Drugs, 69*(1), 58–64.

Topol, E. J. (2004). Intensive statin therapy – a sea change in cardiovascular prevention. *New England Journal of Medicine, 350*, 1562–1564.

Torrey, E. F. (1992). Are we overestimating the genetic contribution to schizophrenia? *Schizophrenia Bulletin, 18*, 159–170.

Torrey, E. F. (2002, April). Hippie healthcare policy. *Washington Monthly*. Retrieved September 22, 2008, from http://findarticles.com/p/articles/mi_m1316/is_4_34/ai_85107346/pg_1?tag=artBody; col 1.

Torrey, E. F. (2008). *The insanity offense: How America's failure to treat the seriously mentally ill endangers its citizens.* New York: Norton.

Torrey, E. F., Bowler, A. E., Taylor, E. H., & Gottesman, I. I. (1994). *Schizophrenia and manic-depressive disorder.* New York: Basic Books.

Torrey, E. F., & Zdanowicz, M. (2001). Outpatient commitment: What, why, and for whom. *Psychiatric Services, 52*, 337–341.

Torrey, W. C., Drake, R. E., Dixon, L., Burns, B. J., Flynn, L., Rush, A. J., et al. (2001). Implementing evidence-based practices for persons with severe mental illness. *Psychiatric Services, 52*, 45–50.

Trappler, B., & Friedman, S. (1996). Posttraumatic stress disorder in survivors of the Brooklyn Bridge Shooting. *American Journal of Psychiatry, 153*(5), 705–707.

Trautman, R., Tucker, P., Pfefferbaum, B., Lensgraf, S. J., Doughty, D. E., Buksh, A., et al. (2002). Effects of prior trauma and age on posttraumatic stress symptoms in Asian and Middle Eastern immigrants after terrorism in the community. *Community Mental Health Journal, 38*(6), 459–474.

Treatment Advocacy Center (TAC). (2005). *Assisted outpatient treatment.* Retrieved September 25, 2008, from http://www.treatmentadvocacycenter.org/BriefingPapers/BP4.htm.

Treatment Advocacy Center (TAC). (2006). *Treatment Advocacy Center wins 2006 APA Presidential Commendation.* Retrieved September 29, 2008, from http://www.psychlaws.org/pressroom/rls-2006PresidentialCommendation.htm.

Treweek, G. L. (1996). Emotion work: Order, and emotional power in care assistant work. In V. James & J. Gabe (Eds.), *Health and the sociology of emotions* (pp. 159–172). Oxford: Blackwell.

Triandis, H, C. (1995). *Individualism and collectivism.* Boulder, CO: Westview Press.

Trochim, W., Dumont, J., & Campbell, J. (1993). *Mapping mental health outcomes from the perspective of consumers/survivors: A report for the state mental health agency profiling system* (Technical report). Alexandria, VA: National Association of State Mental Health Program Directors.

Tsemberis, S., & Eisenberg, R. F. (2000). Pathways to housing: Supported housing for street-dwelling homeless individuals with psychiatric disabilities. *Psychiatric Services, 51*(4), 487–493.

Tsemberis, S., Gulcur, L., & Nakae, M. (2004). Housing First consumer choice, and harm reduction for homeless individuals with a dual diagnosis. *American Journal of Public Health, 94*, 651–656.

Tsuang, M. T., & Faraone, S. (1990). *The genetics of mood disorders.* Baltimore: Johns Hopkins University Press.

Tsuang, M. T., Faraone, S., & Lyons, M. (1989). Advances in psychiatric genetics. In J. A. C. Silva & C. C. Nadelson (Eds.), *International review of psychiatry* (Vol. 1, pp. 395–439). Washington, DC: American Psychiatric Press.

Tsuang, M. T., Winokur, G., & Crowe, R. R. (1980). Morbidity risks of schizophrenia and affective disorders among first-degree relatives of patients with schizophrenia, mania, depression, and surgical conditions. *British Journal of Psychiatry, 137*, 497–504.

Tsutsumi, A., Kayaba, K., Theorell, T., & Siegrist, J. (2001). Association between job stress and depression among Japanese employees threatened by job loss in a comparison between two complementary job-stress models. *Scandinavian Journal of Work, Environment and Health, 27*(2), 146–153.

Tucker, C., McKay, R., Kojetin, B., Harrison, R., dela Puente, M., Stinson, L., et al. (1996). Testing methods of collecting racial and ethnic information: Results of the Current Population Survey supplement on race and ethnicity. *Bureau of Labor Statistical Notes, 40*, 1–149.

Tucker, M. B. (2003). Intimate relationships and psychological well-being. In D. R. Brown & V. M. Keith (Eds.), *In and out of our right minds: The mental health of African American women* (pp. 139–159). New York: Columbia University Press.

Tucker, M. B., & Mitchell-Kernan, C. (1995). Marital behavior and expectations: Ethnic comparisons of attitudinal and structural correlates. In M. B. Tucker & C. Mitchell-Kernan (Eds.), *The decline in marriage among African Americans: Causes, consequences, and policy implications* (pp. 145–171). New York: Russell Sage Foundation.

Tucker, P., Dickson, W., Pfefferbaum, B., McDonald, N. B., & Allen, G. (1997). Traumatic reactions as predictors of posttraumatic stress six months after the Oklahoma City Bombing. *Psychiatric Services, 48*(9), 1191–1194.

Tucker, W. H. (1994). *The science and politics of racial research.* Urbana: University of Illinois Press.

Turner, B. S. (1987). *Medical power and social knowledge.* London: Sage.

Turner, H. A. (1994). Gender and social support: Taking the bad with the good? *Sex Roles, 30*, 521–541.

Turner, H. A., Finkelhor, D., & Ormrod, R. (2006). The effect of lifetime victimization on the mental health of children and adolescents. *Social Science & Medicine, 62*, 13–27.

Turner, H. A., & Turner, R. J. (1999). Gender, social status, and emotional reliance. *Journal of Health and Social Behavior, 40*, 360–373.

Turner, H. M. & P. Conway. (2000). Managed mental health care: Implications for social work practice and social work education. *Journal of Family Social Work, 5*, 5–19.

Turner, J. B. (1995). Economic context and the health effects of unemployment. *Journal of Health and Social Behavior, 36*(3), 213–229.

Turner, J., & TenHoor, W. (1978). The NIMH community support program: Pilot approach to a needed social reform. *Schizophrenia Bulletin, 4*(3), 319–408.

Turner, R. J. (1981). Social support as a contingency in psychological well-being. *Journal of Health & Social Behavior, 22*, 357–367.

Turner, R. J. (1983). Direct, indirect and moderating effects of social support upon psychological distress and associated conditions. In H. H. Kaplan (Ed.) *Psychosocial stress: Trends in theory and research.* New York: Academic Press.

Turner, R. J. (1995). The epidemiology of social stress. *American Sociological Review, 60*, 104–125.

Turner, R. J. (1999). Social support and coping. In A. Horwitz & T. Scheid (Eds.), *A handbook for the study of mental health: Social contexts, theories, and systems* (pp. 198–210). New York: Cambridge University Press.

Turner, R. J., Frankel, B. G., & Levin, D. M. (1983). Social support: Conceptualization, measurement and implications for mental health. In J. R. Greeley (Ed.), *Research in community mental health* (Vol. 3). Greenwich, CT: JAI Press.

Turner, R. J., & Lloyd, D. A. (1995). Lifetime traumas and mental health: The significance of cumulative adversity. *Journal of Health and Social Behavior, 36,* 360–376.

Turner, R. J., & Lloyd, D. (1999). The stress process and the social distribution of depression. *Journal of Health and Social Behavior, 40,* 374–404.

Turner, R. J., & Marino, F. (1994). Social support and social structure: A descriptive epidemiology. *Journal of Health & Social Behavior, 35,* 193–212.

Turner, R. J., & Noh, S. (1983). Class and psychological vulnerability among women: The significance of social support and personal control. *Journal of Health & Social Behavior, 24,* 2–15.

Turner, R. J., & Roszell, P. (1994). Psychosocial resources and the stress process. In W. R. Avison & I. H. Gotlib (Eds.), *Stress and mental health: Contemporary issues and prospects for the future* (pp. 179–210). New York: Plenum Press.

Turner, R. J., Russell, D., Glover, R., & Hutto, P. (2007). The social antecedents of anger proneness in young adulthood. *Journal of Health and Social Behavior, 48,* 68–83.

Turner, R. J., & Wagenfeld, M. O. (1967). Occupational mobility and schizophrenia. *American Sociological Review, 32,* 104–113.

Turner, R. J., Wheaton, B., & Lloyd, D. A. (1995). The epidemiology of stress. *American Sociological Review, 60,* 104–125.

Twaddle, A. C., & Hessler, R. M. (1977). *A sociology of health.* St. Louis: Mosby.

Twenge, J., & Nolen-Hoeksema, S. (2002). Age, gender, race, SES, and birth cohort differences on the Children's Depression Inventory: A meta-analysis. *Journal of Abnormal Psychology, 111,* 578–588.

Uba, L. (1994). *Asian Americans: Personality patterns, identity, and mental health.* New York: Guilford.

Ulbrich, P. M., Warheit, G. J., & Zimmerman, R. S. (1989). Race, socioeconomic status, and psychological distress: An examination of differential vulnerability. *Journal of Health and Social Behavior, 30,* 131–146.

Uldall, K. K., Koutsky, L. A., Bradshaw, D. H., & Hopkins, S. G. (1994). Psychiatric comorbidity and length of stay in hospitalized AIDS patients. *American Journal of Psychiatry, 151*(10), 1475–1478.

Uldall, K. K., Koutsky, L. A., Bradshaw, D. H., & Krone, M. (1998). Use of hospital services by AIDS patients with psychiatric illness. *General Hospital Psychiatry, 20*(5), 292–301.

Umberson, D. (1987). Family status and health behaviors: Social control as a dimension of social integration. *Journal of Health and Social Behavior, 28,* 306–319.

Umberson, D., Chen, M. D., House, J. S., Hopkins, K., & Slaten, E. (1996). The effect of social relationships on psychological well-being: Are men and women really so different? *American Sociological Review, 61*(5), 837–857.

Umberson, D., & Williams, C. (1993). Divorced fathers, parental role strain, and psychological distress. *Journal of Family Issues, 14*(3), 378–400.

Umberson, D., & Williams, K. (1999). Family status and mental health. In C. Aneshensel & J. Phelan (Eds.), *Handbook of the sociology of mental health* (pp. 225–254). New York: Kluwer.

Umberson, D., Williams, K., & Anderson, K. (2002). Violent behavior: Measure of emotional upset? *Journal of Health and Social Behavior, 43*(2), 189–206.

Umberson, D., Williams, K., Powers, D., Chen, M. & Campbell, A. (2005). As good as it gets? A life course perspective on marital quality. *Social Forces, 84,* 493–511.

Umberson, D., Wortman, C. B., & Kessler, R. C. (1992). Widowhood and depression: Explaining long-term gender differences in vulnerability. *Journal of Health and Social Behavior, 33,* 10–24.

Unzicker, R. (1999). Personal communication, October 8.

Urban, H. B. (1983). Phenomenological-humanistic approaches. In M. Hersen, A. E. Kazdin, & A. S. Bellack (Eds.), *The clinical psychology handbook.* New York: Pergamon.

U.S. Census Bureau. (1975). *Historical statistics of the United States: Colonial times to 1970*. Washington, DC: U.S. Government Printing Office.

U.S. Census Bureau. (1998). *Statistical abstract of the United States* (118th ed.). Washington, DC: U.S. Government Printing Office.

U.S. Census Bureau. (2000). *Educational attainment of people 15 years of age and over by age, sex, race and Hispanic origin* (Current Population Report, P20–536). Washington, DC: U.S. Government Printing Office.

U.S. Census Bureau. (2004a, March). *Family and nonfamily household type, for Black alone and White alone, not Hispanic, March 2004*. http://www.census.gov/population/www/socdemo/race/ppl-186_aoic.html.

U.S. Census Bureau. (2004b, March). *Table 2. Marital status of the population 15 years and over by sex, for Black alone and White alone, not Hispanic, March 2004*. http://www.census.gov/population/www/socdemo/race/ppl-186_aoic.html.

U.S. Census Bureau. (2004c, March). *Table 6. Families by size and type, for Black alone and White alone, not Hispanic families, March 2004*. http://www.census.gov/population/www/socdemo/race/ppl-186_aoic.html.

U.S. Census Bureau. (2004d, March). *Table 7. Educational attainment of the population 25 years of age and over by sex, for Black alone and White alone, not Hispanic, March 2004*. http://www.census.gov/population/www/socdemo/race/ppl-186_aoic.html.

U.S. Census Bureau. (2004e, March). *Table 11. Major occupation group of the employed civilian population 16 years and over by sex, for Black alone and White alone, not Hispanic, March 2004*. http://www.census.gov/population/www/socdemo/race/ppl-186_aoic.html.

U.S. Census Bureau. (2004f, March). *Table 16. Poverty status of the population by sex and age, for Black alone and White alone, not Hispanic, March 2004*. http://www.census.gov/population/www/socdemo/race/ppl-186_aoic.html.

U.S. Census Bureau. (2004g, March). *Table 17. Poverty status of families in 2003 by type, for Black alone and White alone, not Hispanic, March 2004*. http://www.census.gov/population/www/socdemo/race/ppl-186_aoic.html.

U.S. Census Bureau. (2004h). *U.S. interim projections by age, sex, race, and Hispanic origin*. Washington, DC: U.S. Government Printing Office.

U.S. Census Bureau. (2006). *American Community Survey*. Washington, DC: U.S. Government Printing Office.

U.S. Census Bureau. (2007). *Current Population Survey, 2007: Annual social and economic supplement*. Retrieved July 12, 2008, from http://pubdb3.census.gov/macro/032007/pov/new02_100_01.htm.

U.S. Congress, Office of Technology Assessment. (1992). *The biology of mental disorders* (OTA-BA-538). Washington, DC: U.S. Government Printing Office.

U.S. Department of Health and Human Services. (1999). *Mental health: A report of the Surgeon General*. Washington, DC: U.S. Governmental Printing Office, Rockville, MD.

U.S. Department of Health and Human Services. (2001). *Mental health: Culture, race, ethnicity supplement to mental health: Report of the Surgeon General*. Rockville, MD: Author.

U.S. Department of Labor. (2007). *America's dynamic workforce: 2007*. Retrieved June 18, 2008, from http://www.dol.gov/asp/media/reports/workforce2007/ADW2007_Full_Text.pdf.

U.S. Bureau of Labor Statistics. (2005), Table 3: Employment status by race, age, sex, and Hispanic or Latino ethnicity. 2005 Annual Averages. http://www.dls/gov/cps/wif-table3-2006.pdef, retrieved July 31, 2008.

U.S. Department of Labor, Bureau of Labor Statistics. (2008a). *Current employment statistics*. Retrieved June 24, 2008, from ftp://ftp.bls.gov/pub/suppl/empsit.cpseea23.txt.

U.S. Department of Labor, Bureau of Labor Statistics. (2008b). *EconStats*. Retrieved June 30, 2008, from http://www.econstats.com/BLS/blsnea14.htm.

Vaillant, G. E. (1977). *Adaptation to life*. Boston: Little, Brown.

Valverde, E. E., Purcell, D. W., Waldrop-Valverde, D., Malow, R., Knowlton, A. R., Gomez, C. A., et al. (2007). Correlates of depression among HIV-positive women and men who inject drugs. *Journal of Acquired Immune Deficiency Syndromes, 46* (Suppl. 2), S96–100.

Van Brakel, W. H. (2006). Measuring health-related stigma – a literature review. *Psychology, Health & Medicine, 11*(3), 307–334.

Vandell, D. L. (2004). *Early child care: The known and the unknown.* Merrill-Palmer Quarterly, *50*, 387–415.

Vander Stoep, A., Davis, M., & Collins, D. (2000). Transition: A time of developmental and institutional clashes. In H. B. Clark & M. Davis (Eds.), *Transition to adulthood* (pp. 2–28). Baltimore: Paul H. Brookes.

Van De Ven, A., & Ferry, D. (1980). *Measuring and assessing organizations.* New York: Wiley.

Vanitallie, T. B. (2002). Stress: A risk for serious illness. *Metabolism, 51.* 40–45.

Van Laningham, J., Johnson, D., & Amato, P. R. (2001). Marital happiness, marital duration, and the U-shaped curve: Evidence from a 5-wave panel study. *Social Forces, 78*, 1313–1341.

Van Vegchel, N., de Jonge, J., Bosma, H., & Schaufeli, W. (2005). Reviewing the effort–reward imbalance model: Drawing up the balance of 45 empirical studies. *Social Science & Medicine, 60*(5), 1117–1131.

Van Voorhees, B. W., Paunesku, D., Kuwabara, S. A., Basu, A., Gollan, J., Hankin, B., et al. (2008). Protective and vulnerability factors predicting new-onset depressive episode in a representative sample of U.S. adolescents. *Journal of Adolescent Health, 42*, 605–616.

Vaux, A. (1988). *Social support: Theory, research and intervention.* New York: Praeger.

Vazquez, C., Perez-Sales, P., & Matt, G. (2006). Post-traumatic stress reactions following the March 11, 2004 terrorist attacks in a Madrid community sample: A cautionary note about the measurement of psychological trauma. *Spanish Journal of Psychology, 9*(1), 61–74.

Vega, W. A., Chen, K. W., & Williams, J. (2007). Smoking, drugs, and other behavioral health problems among multiethnic adolescents in the NHSDA. *Addictive Behaviors, 32*, 1949–1956.

Vega, W. A., & Murphy, J. W. (1990). *Culture and the restructuring of community mental health.* Westport, CT: Greenwood.

Vega, W. A., & Rumbaut, R. G. (1991). Ethnic minorities and mental health. *Annual Review of Sociology, 17*, 351–383.

Veil, H. O. F., & Baumann, U. (1992). The many meanings of social support. In H. O. F. Veil & U. Baumann (Eds.), *The meaning and measurement of social support* (pp. 1–7). New York: Hemisphere.

Vera, E. M., Reese, L. E., Paikoff, R. L., & Jarrett, R. C. (1996). Contextual factors of sexual risk-taking in urban African American preadolescent children. In B. Leadbeater & N. Way (Eds.), *Urban girls: Resisting stereotypes, creating identities* (pp. 291–304). New York: NYU Press.

Verger, P., Dab, W., Lamping, D. L., Loze, J. Y., Deschaseaux-Voinet, C., Abenhaim, L., et al. (2004). The psychological impact of terrorism: An epidemiologic study of posttraumatic stress disorder and associated factors in victims of the 1995–1996 bombings in France. *American Journal of Psychiatry, 161*(8), 1384–1389.

Vernon, S. W., & Roberts, R. E. (1982). Prevalence of treated and untreated psychiatric disorders in three ethnic groups. *Social Science & Medicine, 16*, 1575–1582.

Veroff, J. B. (1981). The dynamics of help-seeking in men and women: A national survey study. *Psychiatry, 44*, 189–200.

Veroff, J., Kulka, R. A., & Douvan, E. (1981). *Mental health in America: Patterns of help-seeking from 1957 to 1976.* New York: Basic Books.

Vine, P. (2001, May/June). Mindless and deadly: Media hype on mental illness and violence. *FAIR (Fairness and Accuracy in Reporting).* Retrieved September 28, 2008, from http://www.fair.org/index.php?page=1064.

Vinokur, A., Schul, Y., & Caplan, R. D. (1987). Determinants of perceived social support: Interpersonal transactions, personal outlook, and transient affect states. *Journal of Personality & Social Psychiatry, 53*, 1137–1145.

Visser, S. N., Lesesne, C., & Perou, R. (2007). National estimates and factors associated with medication treatment for childhood attention-deficit/hyperactivity disorder. *Pediatrics, 119* (Suppl. 1), S99–S106.

Vlahov, D., Safaien, M., Lai, S., Strathdee, S. A., Johnson, L., Sterling, T., et al. (2001). Sexual and drug risk-related behaviours after initiating highly active antiretroviral therapy among injection drug users. *AIDS, 15*, 2311–2316.

Von Knorring, A., Cloninger, R., Bohman, M., & Sigvadsson, S. (1983). An adoption study of depressive disorders and substance abuse. *Archives of General Psychiatry, 40*, 943–950.

Votruba-Drzal, E., Coley, R. L., & Chase-Landale, P. L. (2004). Child care and low-income children's development. Direct and moderated effects. *Child Development, 75*, 296–312.

Vranceanu, M., Hobfoll, S. E., & Johnson, R. J. (2007). Child multi-type maltreatment and associated depression and PTSD symptoms: The role of social support and stress. *Child Abuse & Neglect, 31*(1), 71–84.

Wack, R. C. (1993). Treatment services at Kirby Forensic Psychiatric Center. *International Journal of Law and Psychiatry, 16*, 83–104.

Wade, J. C. (1993). Institutional racism: An analysis of the mental health system. *American Journal of Orthopsychiatry, 63(4)*, 536–544.

Wade, T. J., & Pevalin, D. J. (2004). Marital transitions and mental health. *Journal of Health and Social Behavior, 45*(2), 155–170.

Wagner, B., Forstmeier, S., & Maercker, A. (2007). Posttraumatic growth as a cognitive process with behavioral components: A commentary on Hobfoll et al. (2007). *Applied Psychology: An International Review, 56*(3), 407–416.

Wahl, O. (1995). *Media madness: Public images of mental illness*. New Brunswick, NJ: Rutgers University Press.

Wahl, O. F. (1999). Mental health consumers' experience of stigma. *Schizophrenia Bulletin, 25*, 467–478.

Waite, L. J. (2009). Marital history and well-being in later life. In P. Uhlenberg (Ed.), *International handbook of population aging* (pp. 691–704). New York: Springer.

Waite, L. J., & Gallagher, M. (2000). *The case for marriage: Why married people are happier, healthier, and better off financially*. New York: Doubleday.

Wakefield, J. C. (1992a). The concept of mental disorder: On the boundary between biological facts and social values. *American Psychologist, 47*, 373–388.

Wakefield, J. C. (1992b). Disorder as harmful dysfunction: A conceptual critique of DSM-III-R's definition of mental disorder. *Psychological Review, 99*, 232–247.

Wakefield, J. C. (1993). Limits of operationalization: A critique of Spitzer and Endicott's (1978) proposed operational criteria for mental disorder. *Journal of Abnormal Psychology, 102*, 160–172.

Wakefield, J. C. (1996). DSM-IV: Are we making diagnostic progress? *Contemporary Psychology, 41*, 646–652.

Wakefield, J. C. (1997). Diagnosing DSM-IV, Part 1: DSM-IV and the concept of mental disorder. *Behavior Research and Therapy, 35*, 633–650.

Wakefield, J. C. (1998). Meaning and melancholia: Why DSM cannot (entirely) ignore the patient's intentional system. In J. W. Barron (Ed.), *Making diagnosis meaningful: Enhancing evaluation and treatment of psychological disorders* (pp. 29–72). Washington, DC: American Psychological Association.

Wakefield, J. C. (1999a). Evolutionary versus prototype analyses of the concept of disorder. *Journal of Abnormal Psychology, 108*, 374–399.

Wakefield, J. C. (1999b). Disorder as a black box essentialist concept. *Journal of Abnormal Psychology, 108*, 465–472.

Wakefield, J. C. (2008). The perils of dimensionalization: Distinguishing personality traits from personality disorders. *Psychiatric Clinics of North America, 31*, 379–393.

Wakefield, J. C., & First, M. B. (2003). Clarifying the distinction between disorder and non-disorder: Confronting the overdiagnosis ("false positives") problem in DSM-V. In K. A. Phillips, M. B. First, & H. A. Pincus (Eds.), *Advancing DSM: Dilemmas in psychiatric diagnosis* (pp. 23–56). Washington, DC: American Psychiatric Press.

Wakefield, J. C., Schmitz, M. F., First, M. B., & Horwitz, A. V. (2007). Extending the bereavement exclusion for major depression to other losses: Evidence from the National Comorbidity Survey. *Archives of General Psychiatry, 64*, 433–440.

Wakefield, J. C., & Spitzer, R. L. (2002a). Lowered estimates – But of what? *Archives of General Psychiatry, 59*, 129–130.

Wakefield, J. C., & Spitzer, R. L. (2002b). Why requiring clinical significance does not solve epidemiology's and DSM's validity problem. In J. E. Helzer & J. J. Hudziak (Eds.), *Defining psychopathology in the 21st century: DSM-V and beyond* (pp. 31–40). Washington, DC: American Psychiatric Press.

Waldron, I. (1983). Sex differences in illness incidence, prognosis and mortality: Issues and evidence. *Social Science & Medicine, 17*, 1107–1123.

Waldron, I., & Jacobs, J. A. (1988). Effects of labor force participation on women's health: New evidence from a longitudinal study. *Journal of Occupational Medicine, 30*, 977–983.

Walker, P. S.. & Kivlahan, D. (1993). Treatment implications of comorbid psychopathology in American Indians and Alaska natives. *Culture, Medicine and Psychiatry, 16*, 555–572.

Walkup, J., Blank, M. B., Gonzalez, J. S., Safren, S., Schwartz, R., Brown, L., et al. (2008). The impact of mental health and substance abuse factors on HIV prevention and treatment. *Journal of Acquired Immune Deficiency Syndromes, 47* (Suppl. 1), S15–9.

Walkup, J., Cramer, L. J., & Yeras, J. (2004). How is stigmatization affected by the "layering" of stigmatized conditions, such as serious mental illness and HIV? *Psychological Reports, 95* (3 Pt 1), 771–779.

Walkup, J. T.. & Cramer-Berness, L. (2007). Coping with AIDS: The challenges of an evolving disease. In E. Martz & H. Livneh (Eds.), *Coping with chronic illness and disability: Theoretical, empirical, and clinical aspects* (pp. 129–153). New York: Springer.

Walkup, J., Crystal, S., & Sambamoorthi, U. (1999). Schizophrenia and major affective disorder among Medicaid recipients with HIV/AIDS in New Jersey. *American Journal of Public Health, 89*, 1101–1103.

Walkup, J., McAlpine, D. D., Olfson, M., Boyer, C., & Hansell, S. (2000). Recent HIV testing among general hospital inpatients with schizophrenia: Findings from four New York City sites. *Psychiatric Quarterly, 71*(2), 177–193.

Walkup, J., Sambamoorthi, U., & Crystal, S. (2001). Incidence and consistency of antiretroviral use among HIV-infected Medicaid beneficiaries with schizophrenia. *Journal of Clinical Psychiatry, 62*(3), 174–178.

Walkup, J., Sambamoorthi, U., & Crystal, S. (2004). Use of newer antiretroviral treatments among HIV-infected Medicaid beneficiaries with serious mental illness. *Journal of Clinical Psychiatry, 65*, 1180–1189.

Walkup, J., Satriano, J., Barry, D., Sadler, P., & Cournos, F. (2002). HIV testing policy and serious mental illness. *American Journal of Public Health, 92*(12), 1931–1940.

Walkup, J., Satriano, J., Hansell, S., & Olfson, M. (1998). Practices related to HIV risk assessment in general hospital psychiatric units in New York State. *Psychiatric Services, 49*(4), 529–530.

Walkup, J., Wei, W., Sambamoorthi, U., & Crystal, S. (2008). Antidepressant treatment and adherence to combination antiretroviral therapy among patients with AIDS and diagnosed depression. *Psychiatric Quarterly, 79*(1), 43–53.

Wallace, C., Mullen, P. E., & Burgess, P. (2004). Criminal offending in schizophrenia over a 25-year period marked by deinstitutionalization and increasing prevalence of comorbid substance use disorders. *American Journal of Psychiatry, 161*(4), 716–727.

Wallgrena, L. G., & Hanse, J. J. (2007). Job characteristics, motivators and stress among information technology consultants: A structural equation modeling approach. *International Journal of Industrial Ergonomics, 37*(1), 51–59.

Walsh, E., Buchanan, A., & Fahy, T. (2002). Violence and schizophrenia: Examining the evidence. *British Journal of Psychiatry, 180*, 490–495.

Walsh, E. G., Samele, C., Harvey, K., Manley, C., Tyrer, C., Creed, F., et al. (2001). Reducing violence in severe mental illness: Randomised controlled trial of intensive case management compared with standard care. *British Medical Journal, 323*(7321), 1092–1095.

Wandersman, A., & Florin, P. (2003). Community interventions and effective prevention. *American Psychologist, 58*(6–7), 441–448.

Wang, J. (2007). Mental health treatment dropout and its correlates in a general population sample. *Medical Care, 45*(3), 224–229.

Wang, P. S., Angermeyer, M., Borges, G., Bruffaerts, R., Chiu, W. T., De Girolamo, G. et al. (2007). Delay and failure in treatment seeking after first onset of mental disorders in the World Health Organization's Mental Heath Survey Initiative. *World Psychiatry, 6*(3), 177–185.

Wang, P. S., Berglund, P., Olfson, M., Pincus, H. A., Wells, K. B., & Kessler, R. C. (2005). Failure and delay in initial treatment contact after first onset of mental disorders in the National Comorbidity Survey Replication. *Archives of General Psychiatry, 62*, 603–613.

Wang, P. S., Demler, O., & Kessler, R. C. (2002). Adequacy of treatment for serious mental illness in the United States. *American Journal of Public Health, 92*, 92–98.

Wang, P. S., Demler, O., Olfson, M., Pincus, H. A., Wells, K. B., & Kessler, R. C. (2006). Changing profiles of service sectors used for mental health care in the United States. *American Journal of Psychiatry, 163*, 1187–1198.

Wang, P. S., Lane, M. Olfson, M., Pincus, H. A., Wells, K. B., & Kessler, R. C. (2005). Twelve-month use of mental health services in the United States: Results from the National Comorbidity Survey Replication. *Archive of General Psychiatry, 62*, 629–640.

Ward, K. B., & Mueller, C. W. (1985). Sex differences in earnings: The influence of industrial sector, authority hierarchy, and human capital variables. *Work and Occupations, 12*, 437–463.

Ware, J. E., Manning, W. G., Duan, N., Wells, K. B., & Newhouse, J. P. (1984). Health status and the use of outpatient mental health services. *American Psychologist, 39*, 1090–1100.

Ware, N. C., Lachiocotte, W. S., Kirschner, S. R., Cortes, D. E., & Good, B. J. (2000). Clinician experiences of managed mental health. *Medical Anthropology Quarterly, 14*, 3–27.

Ware, N. C., Tugenberg, T., Dickey, B., & McHorney, C. (1999). An ethnographic study of the meaning of continuity of care in mental health services. *Psychiatric Services, 50*, 395–400.

Warner, L. A., Kessler, R. C., Hughes, M., Anthony, J. C., & Nelson, C. B. (1995). Prevalence and correlates of drug use and dependence in the United States: Results from the National Comorbidity Survey. *Archives of General Psychiatry, 52*, 219–229.

Warner, R. (1985). *Recovery from schizophrenia: Psychiatry and political economy*, London: Routledge & Kegan Paul.

Warner, R. (1992). Commentary on Cohen: Prognosis for schizophrenia in the Third World. *Culture, Medicine and Psychiatry, 16*, 85–88.

Warner, R. (1994). *Recovery from schizophrenia: Psychiatry and political economy* (2nd. ed.). London: Routledge.

Warner, R. (2000). *The environment of schizophrenia: Innovations in practice, policy, and communication*. London: Routledge.

Warr, P., Jackson, P., & Banks, M. (1988). Unemployment and mental health: Some British studies. *Journal of Social Issues, 44*, 47–68.

Warren, C. A. B. (1977). Involuntary commitment for mental disorder: The application of California's Lanterman-Petris-Short Act. *Law and Society Review, 11*, 629–650.

Warren, C. A. B. (1982). *Court of last resort*. Chicago: University of Chicago Press.

Warren, R. (1973). Comprehensive planning and coordination: Some functional aspects. *Social Problems, 20*, 355–364.

Wasserman, S., & Faust, K. (1994). *Social network analysis: Methods and applications*. New York: Cambridge University Press.

Waters, L. E., & Moore, K. A. (2002). Reducing latent deprivation during unemployment: The role of meaningful leisure activity. *Journal of Occupational and Organizational Psychology, 75*(1), 15–32.

Watson, A. C., & Angell, B. 2007. Applying procedural justice theory to law enforcement's response to persons with mental illness. *Psychiatric Services, 58*, 787–793.

Watson, A. C., Angell, B., Morabito, M. S., & Robinson, N. (2008). Defying negative expectations: Dimensions of fair and respectful treatment by police officers as perceived by people with mental illness. *Administration and Policy in Mental Health and Mental Health Services Research, 35*(6), 449–457.

Watson, A. C., Corrigan, P. W., & Uate, V. O. (2004). Police responses to persons with mental illness: Does the label matter? *Journal of the American Association of Psychiatry and Law, 32*, 378–385.

Watson, D. (2005). Rethinking the mood and anxiety disorders: A quantitative hierarchical model for DSM-V. *Journal of Abnormal Psychology, 114*, 522–536.

Watts, D., Leese, M., Thomas, S., Atakan, Z., & Wykes, T. (2003). The prediction of violence in acute psychiatric units. *International Journal of Forensic Mental Health, 2*, 173–180.

Watts, J., & Priebe, S. (2002). A phenomenological account of users' experiences of assertive community treatment. *Bioethics, 16*, 5, 439–354.

Weatherston, D., & Moran, J. (2003). Terrorism and mental illness: Is there a relationship? *International Journal of Offender Therapy and Comparative Criminology, 47*(6), 698–713.

Webster, B. H., & Bishaw, A. (2006). *Income, earnings, and poverty: Data from the 2005 American Community Survey (ACS-02)*. Washington DC: U.S. Government Printing Office.

Webster, P., Orbuch, T., & House, J. S. (1995). Effects of childhood family background on adult marital quality and perceived stability. *American Journal of Sociology, 101*, 404–432.

Weinberger, D. R., Egan, M. F., Bertonlino, A., Callicott, J. H., Mattay, V. S., Lipsaka, B. K., et al. (2001). Prefrontal neurons and the genetics of schizophrenia. *Biological Psychiatry, 50*, 825–844.

Weiner, B., Perry, R. P., & Magnusson, J. (1988). An attributional analysis of reactions to stigmas. *Journal of Personality & Social Psychology, 55*, 738–748.

Weinhardt, L. S., Carey, M. P., & Carey, K. B. (1998). HIV-risk behavior and the public health context of HIV/AIDS among women living with a severe and persistent mental illness. *Journal of Nervous and Mental Disease, 186*(5), 276–282.

Weinstein, N. D. (1993). Testing four competing theories of health protective behavior. *Health Psychology, 12*, 325–333.

Weisbrod, B. (1983). A guide to benefit-cost analysis, as seen through a controlled experiment in treating the mentally ill. *Journal of Health Politics, Policy and Law, 7*(4), 808–845.

Weiss, C. I. (1992). Controlling domestic life and mental illness: Spiritual and aftercare resources used by Dominican New Yorkers. *Culture, Medicine, and Psychiatry, 16*, 237–271.

Weiss, L., Fabri, A., McCoy, K., Coffin, P., Netherland, J. & Finkelstein, R. (2002). A vulnerable population in a time of crisis: Drug users and the attacks on the World Trade Center. *Journal of Urban Health–Bulletin of the New York Academy of Medicine, 79*(3), 392–403.

Weiss, M. F. (1986). Children's attitudes toward the mentally ill: A developmental analysis. *Psychological Reports, 58*, 11–20.

Weiss, M., & Fitzpatrick, R. (1997). Challenges to medicine: The case of prescribing. *Sociology of Health and Illness, 19*, 297–327.

Weiss, R. (1974). The provisions of social relationship. In Z. Rubin (Ed.), *Doing unto others*. Englewood Cliffs, NJ: Prentice-Hall.

Weissman, E., Pettigre, K., Stosky, S., & Regier, D. A. (2000). The cost of access to mental health services in managed care. *Psychiatric Services, 51*, 664–666.

Weissman, M. M., Bland, R. C., Canino, G. J., Faravelli, C., Greenwald S., Hwu, H. G., Joyce, P. R., et al. (1996). Cross-national epidemiology of major depression and bipolar disorder. *Journal of the American Medical Association, 276*, 293–299.

Weissman, M., Gershon, E., & Kidd, K. (1984). Psychiatric disorders in the relatives of probands with affective disorders: The Yale-NIMH collaborative family study. *Archives of General Psychiatry, 41*, 13–21.

Weissman, M. M., & Myers, J. K. (1978). Affective disorders in a US urban community: The use of research diagnostic criteria in an epidemiological survey. *Archive of General Psychiatry, 35*, 1304–1311.

Weissman, M. M., Myers, J. K., & Ross., C. E. (1986). *Community surveys of mental disorders*. New Brunswick, NJ: Rutgers University Press.

Weissman, M. M., Wickramaratne, P., Nomura, Y., Warner, V., Pilowsky, D., & Verdeli, H. (2006). Offspring of depressed parents: 20 years later. *American Journal of Psychiatry, 163*, 1001–1008.

Weissman, M. M., Wickramaratne, P., Nomura, Y., Warner, V., Verdeli, H., Pilowsky, D., et al. (2008). Families at high and low risk for depression: A 3-generation study. *Archives of General Psychiatry, 62*, 29–36.

Weisz, J., & Weiss, B. (1993). *Effects of psychotherapy with children and adolescents*. Newbury Park, CA: Sage.

Wellman, B. (1981). Applying network analysis to the study of support. In B. Gottlieb (Ed.), *Social networks and social support* (pp. 171–200). Beverly Hills, CA: Sage.

Wellman, B. (1990). The place of kinfolk in personal community networks. *Marriage & Family Review, 15*, 195–227.

Wellman, B., & Wortley, S. (1989). Brother's keepers: Situating kin relations in broader networks of social support. *Sociological Perspectives, 32*, 273–306.

Wells, J. C., Tien, A. Y., Garrison, R., & Eaton, W. W. (1994). Risk factors for the incidence of social phobia as determined by the Diagnostic Interview Schedule according to DSM-III in a population-based study. *Acta Psychiatrica Scandinavica, 90*, 84–90.

Wells, K. B., Astrachan, B. M., Tischler, G. T., & Unutzer, J. (1995). Issues and approaches in evaluating managed mental health care. *Milbank Quarterly, 73*, 57–74.

Wells, K. B., Golding, J. M., Hough, R. L., Burnam, A., & Karno, M. (1988). Factors affecting the probability of use of general and medical health and social/community services for Mexican Americans and non-Hispanic Whites. *Medical Care, 26*, 441–452.

Wells, K. B., Manning, W. G., Duan, N., Newhouse, J. P., & Ware, J. E. (1986). Sociodemographic factors and the use of outpatient mental health services. *Medical Care, 24*, 75–85.

Wells, K., Miranda, J., Bruce, M. L., Alegria, M., & Wallerstein, N. (2004). Bridging community intervention and mental health services research. *American Journal of Psychiatry, 161*(6), 955–963.

Wender, P., Kety, S., Rosenthal, D., Schulsinger, F., Ortmann, J., & Lunde, I. (1986). Psychiatric disorders in the biological and adoptive families of adopted individuals with affective disorders. *Archives of General Psychiatry, 43*, 923–929.

Werner, P. D., Yesavage, J. A., Becker, J., Brunsting, D. W., & Issacs, J. (1983). Hostile words and assaultive behavior on an acute inpatient unit. *Journal of Nervous and Mental Disease, 171*, 385–387.

Wessely, S., & Castle, D. (1998). Mental disorder and crime. *Archives of General Psychiatry, 55*, 86–88.

Westen, D. B. (1985). *Self and society*. London: Cambridge University Press.

Western, M., & Wright, E. O. (1994). The permeability of class boundaries to intergenerational mobility among men in the United States, Canada, Norway and Sweden. *American Sociological Review, 59*, 606–629.

Wethington, E., Brown, R. W., & Kessler, R. C. (1995). Interview measurement of stressful life events. In S. Cohen, R. C. Kessler, & L. U. Gordon (Eds.), *Measuring stress: A guide for health and social scientists* (pp. 59–79). New York: Oxford University Press.

Wethington, E., & Kessler, R. C. (1986). Perceived support, received support, and adjustment to stressful life events. *Journal of Health & Social Behavior, 27*, 78–89.

Wetzel, J. R. (1995). Labor force, unemployment, and earnings. In R. Farley (Ed.), *State of the union: American in the 1990s* (pp. 59–105). New York: Russell Sage Foundation.

Wexler, D. B. (1981). *Mental health law: Major issues*. New York: Plenum Press.

Wharton, A. (1993). The affective consequences of service work: Managing emotions on the job. *Work and Occupations, 20*, 205–232.

Wheaton, B. (1978). The sociogenesis of psychological disorder: Reexamining the causal issues with longitudinal data. *American Sociological Review, 43*, 383–403.

Wheaton, B. (1980). The sociogenesis of psychological disorder: An attributional theory. *Journal of Health and Social Behavior, 21*, 100–124.

Wheaton, B. (1983). Stress, personal coping resources, and psychiatric symptoms: An investigation of interactive models. *Journal of Health and Social Behavior, 24*, 100–124.

Wheaton, B. (1990). Life transitions, role theories, and mental health. *American Sociological Review, 55*, 209–223.

Wheaton, B. (1991, August). *Chronic stress: models and measurement*. Paper presented at the Society for Social Problems, Cincinnati.

Wheaton, B. (1994). Sampling the stress universe. In W. R. Avison & I. H. Gotlib (Eds.), *Stress and mental health: Contemporary issues and prospects for the future* (pp. 77–114). New York: Plenum Press.

Wheaton, B. (1997). The nature of chronic stress. In B. H. Gottlieb (Ed.), *Coping with chronic stress* (pp. 43–73). New York: Plenum Press.

Wheaton, B. (1999). Social stress. In C. S. Aneshenshel & J. C. Phelan (Eds.), *Handbook of the sociology of mental health* (pp. 277–300). Dordrecht: Kluwer.

Wheaton, B., & Clarke, P. (2003). Space meets time: Integrating temporal and contextual influences on mental health in early adulthood. *American Sociological Review, 68*, 680–706.

Wheaton, B., Roszell, P., & Hall, K. (1997). The impact of twenty childhood and adult traumatic stressors on the risk of psychiatric disorder. In I. Gotlib & B. Wheaton (Eds.), *Stress and adversity over the life course: Trajectories and turning points* (pp. 50–72). New York: Cambridge University Press.

Whitbeck, L. B., Hoyt, D., Johnson, K., & Chen, X. (2006). Mental disorders among parents/caretakers of American Indian early adolescents in the Northern Midwest. *Social Psychiatry and Psychiatric Epidemiology, 41*(8), 632–640.

White, B. J., & Madara E. J. (Eds.). (2002). *The self-help group source book: Your guide to community and online support groups* (7th ed). Denville, NJ: American Self-Help Clearinghouse.

White, R. W. (1959). Motivation reconsidered: The concept of competence. *Psychological Review, 66*, 297–333.

Whitehead, M. (1990). *The concepts and principles of equity in health* (EUR/ICP/RPD 414 7734r). Copenhagen: World Health Organization.

Whitley, B. E., & Gridley, B. E. (1993). Sex role orientation, self-esteem, and depression: A latent variables analysis. *Personality and Social Psychology Bulletin, 19*, 363–369.

Whitsett, D., & Land, H. (1992). Role strain, coping, and marital satisfaction of stepparents. *Families in Society, 73*(2), 79–92.

Widiger, T. A., & Clark, L. A. (2000). Toward DSM-V and the classification of psychopathology. *Psychological Bulletin, 126*, 946–963.

Widiger, T. A., & Samuel, D. B. (2005). Diagnostic categories or dimensions? A question for the *Diagnostic and Statistical Manual of Mental Disorders* – fifth edition. *Journal of Abnormal Psychology, 114*, 494–504.

Wiemann, C. M., Berenson, A. B., & San Miguel, V. V. (1994). Tobacco, alcohol and illicit drug use among pregnant women: Age and racial/ethnic differences. *Journal of Reproductive Medicine, 39*(10), 769–776.

Wiersma, D., Giel, R., DeJong, A., & Slooff, C. J. (1983). Social class and schizophrenia in a Dutch cohort. *Psychological Medicine, 13*(1), 141–150.

Wight, R. G., Cummings, J. R., Miller-Martinez, D., Karlamangla, A. S., Seeman, T. E., & Aneshensel, C. S. (2008). A multilevel analysis of urban neighborhood socioeconomic disadvantage and health in late life. *Social Science & Medicine, 66*, 862–872.

Wilcox, S., Evenson, K. R., Aragaki, A., Wassertheil-Smoller, S., Mouton, C. P., & Loevinger, B. L. (2003). The effects of widowhood on physical and mental health, health behaviors, and health outcomes: The Women's Health Initiative. *Health Psychology, 22*(5), 513–522.

Wilens, T. E., Faraone, S. V., & Biederman, J. (2004). Attention-deficit/hyperactivity disorder in adults. *Journal of the American Medical Association, 292*, 619–623.

Wilkinson, R. G. (1997). Health inequalities: Relative or absolute standards. *British Medical Journal, 314*, 591–595.

Williams, D. H., Bells, E. C., & Wellington, S. W. (1980). Deinstitutionalization and social policy: Historical perspective and present dilemmas. *American Journal of Orthopsychiatry, 50*, 54–64.

Williams, D. R. (1990). Socioeconomic differentials in health: A review and redirection. *Social Psychology Quarterly, 53*, 81–99.

Williams, D. R. (1996a). Race/ethnicity and socioeconomic status: Measurement and methodological issues. *International Journal of Health Services, 26*, 483–505.

Williams, D. R. (1996b). Racism and health: A research agenda. *Ethnicity and Disease, 6*(1/2), 1–6.

Williams, D. R. (1997a). Race and health: Basic questions, emerging directions. *Annals of Epidemiology, 7*(5), 322–333.

Williams, D. R. (1997b). *Race, stress and mental health: Findings from the Commonwealth Minority Health Survey*. Ann Arbor: University of Michigan, Survey Research Center.

Williams, D. R. (2002). Racial/ethnic variations in women's health: The social embeddedness of health. *American Journal of Public Health, 92*, 588–597.

Williams, D. R. (2004). Racism and health. In K. E. Whitfield (Ed.), *Closing the gap: Improving the health of minority elders in the new millennium* (pp. 69–80). Washington, DC: Gerontological Society of America.

Williams, D. R. (2005). The health of U.S. racial and ethnic populations [Special issue II]. *Journal of Gerontology: Social Sciences, 60B*, S53–S62.

Williams, D. R., & Chung, A.-M. (in press). Racism and health. In R. Gibson & J. S. Jackson (Eds.), *Health in Black America.* Thousand Oaks, CA: Sage.

Williams, D. R., & Collins, C. (1995). U.S. socioeconomic and racial differences in health. *Annual Review of Sociology, 21*, 349–386.

Williams, D. R., & Fenton, B. (1994). The mental health of African Americans: Findings, questions, and directions. In I. L., Livingston (Ed.), *Handbook of Black American health: The mosaic of conditions, issues, policies, and prospects* (pp. 253–268). Westport, CT: Greenwood.

Williams, D. R., Gonzalez, H. M., Neighbors, H., Nesse, R., Abelson, J. M., Sweetman, J., et al. (2007). Prevalence and distribution of major depressive disorder in African Americans, Caribbean Blacks, and Non-Hispanic Whites: Results from the National Survey of American Life. *Archives of General Psychiatry, 64*, 305–315.

Williams, D. R., Haile, R., Gonzalez, H. M., Neighbors, J., Baser, R., & Jackson, J. S. (2007). The mental health of Black Caribbean immigrants: Results from the National Survey of American Life. *American Journal of Public Health, 97*, 52–59.

Williams, D. R., & Harris-Reid, M. (1999). Race and mental health: Emerging patterns and promising approaches. In A. V. Horowitz & T. L. Scheid (Eds.), *A handbook for the study of mental health: Social contexts, theories, and systems* (pp. 295–314). New York: Cambridge University Press.

Williams, D. R., Lavizzo-Mourey, R., & Warren, R. C. (1994). The concept of race and health status in America. *Public Health Reports, 109*, 26–41.

Williams, D. R., & Mohammed, S. A. (2009). Discrimination and racial disparities in health: Evidence and needed research. *Journal of Behavioral Medicine, 32*(1), 20–47.

Williams, D. R., Neighbors, H. W., & Jackson, J. S. (2003). Racial/ethnic discrimination and health: Findings from community studies. *American Journal of Public Health, 93*, 200–208.

Williams, D. R., Takeuchi, D. T., & Adair, R. K. (1992a). Marital status and psychiatric disorders among Blacks and Whites. *Journal of Health and Social Behavior, 33*, 140–157.

Williams, D. R., Takeuchi, D. T., & Adair, R. K. (1992b). Socioeconomic status and psychiatric disorder among Blacks and Whites. *Social Forces, 71*, 179–194.

Williams, D. R,. & Whitfield, K. E. (2004). *Racism and health.* Washington, DC: Gerontological Society of America.

Williams, D. R. & Williams-Morris, R. (2000). Racism and mental health: The African American experience. *Ethnicity and Health, 5*, 243–268.

Williams, D. R., Yu, Y., Jackson, J. S., & Anderson, N. B. (1997). Racial differences in physical and mental health: Socioeconomic status, stress, and discrimination. *Journal of Health Psychology, 2(3)*, 335–351.

Williams, J. B., Rabkin, J. G., Remien, R. H., Gorman, J. M., & Ehrhardt, A. A. (1991). Multidisciplinary baseline assessment of homosexual men with and without human immunodeficiency virus infection. II. Standardized clinical assessment of current and lifetime psychopathology. *Archives of General Psychiatry, 48*, 124–130.

Williams, K. (2003). Has the future of marriage arrived? A contemporary examination of gender, marriage, and psychological well-being. *Journal of Health and Social Behavior, 44*, 470–487.

Williams, K., & Dunne-Bryant, A. (2006). Marital dissolution and adult psychological well-being: Clarifying the role of gender and child age. *Journal of Marriage and Family, 68*, 1178–1196.

Williams, K., Sassler, S., & Nicholson, L. (2008). For better or for worse? The consequences of marriage and cohabitation for the health and well-being of single mothers. *Social Forces, 86*(4), 1481–1511.

Williams, S. (1987). Goffman, interactionism, and the management of stigma in everyday life. In G. Scrambler (Ed.), *Sociological theory and medical sociology* (pp. 135–164). London: Tavistock.

Williams-Morris, R. (1996). Racism and children's health: Issues in development. *Ethnicity and Disease, 6*, 69–82.

Willie, C. W., Rieker, P., Kramer, B., & Brown, B. (Eds). (1995). *Mental health, racism, and sexism.* Pittsburgh: University of Pittsburgh Press.

Wilson, C., Civic, D., & Glass, D. (1994). Prevalence and correlates of depressive syndromes among adults visiting an Indian health service primary care clinic. *American Indian and Alaska Native Mental Health Research, 6*, 1–12.

Wilson, C., & Williams, D. R. (2004). Mental health of African Americans. In I. L. Livingston (Ed.), *Praeger handbook of Black American health: Policies and issues behind disparities in health* (Vol. 1, pp. 369–382). Westport, CT: Praeger.

Wilson, H. S. (1982). *Deinstitutionalized residential care for the mentally disordered.* New York: Greene & Smith.

Wilson, I. B., & Jacobson, D. (2006). Regarding antidepressant treatment improves adherence to antiretroviral therapy among depressed HIV-infected patients. *Journal of Acquired Immune Deficiency Syndromes, 41*, 254–255.

Wilson, M. (1993). DSM-III and the transformation of American psychiatry: A history. *American Journal of Psychiatry, 150*, 399–410.

Wilson, W. J. (1985). Urban poverty. *Annual Review of Sociology, 11*, 231–258.

Wilson, W. (1993). *The Ghetto Underclass: Social Science Perspectives.* Newbury Park, CA: Sage Publications.

Wilson, W. J. (2003). Race, class and urban poverty: A rejoinder. *Ethnic and Racial Studies, 26*(6), 1096–1114.

Windle, C., & Scully, D. (1974). Community mental health centers and the decreasing use of state mental hospitals. *Community Mental Health Journal, 12*, 239–243.

Wittchen, H. U. (1994). Reliability and validity studies of the WHO–Composite International Diagnostic Interview (CIDI): A critical review. *Journal of Psychiatric Research, 28*, 57–84.

Wolff, E. N. (1995). *Top heavy: A study of wealth inequality in America.* New York: Twentieth Century Fund.

Wolff, N. (2002). Risk, response, and mental health policy: Learning from the experience of the United Kingdom. *Journal of Health Politics, Policy, and Law, 27*, 801–832.

Wolff, N., Diamond, R. J., & Helminiak, T. W. (1997). A new look at an old issue: People with mental illness and the law enforcement system. *Journal of Mental Health Administration, 24*, 152–165.

Wolinsky, F. (1993). The professional dominance, deprofessionalization, proletariatization, and corporatization perspectives: An overview. In F. W. Hafferty & J. B. McKinley (Eds.), *The changing medical profession: An international perspective* (pp. 1–11). New York: Oxford University Press.

Wolpe, J. (1958). *Psychotherapy by reciprocal inhibition.* Stanford: Stanford University Press.

Wolpin, J., Burke, R. J., & Greenglass, E. R. (1991). Is job stress an antecedent or a consequence of psychological burnout? *Human Relations, 44*, 193–209.

World Health Organization. (1948). World Health Organization constitution. In *Basic documents.* Geneva: Author.

World Health Organization. (1990). *Composite International Diagnostic Interview (CIDI)* (Version 1.0). Geneva: Author.

World Health Organization. (1991). *International classification of diseases.* Geneva: Author.

World Health Organization. (1992). *The ICD-10 classification of mental and behavioral disorders.* Geneva: Author.

World Health Organization. (2000). *World Health Report 2000. Health systems: Improving performance.* Geneva: Author.

World Health Organization. (2004). *Promoting mental health: Concepts, emerging evidence, practice* (Summary report). Geneva: Author.

World Health Organization. (2005). *Mental health atlas 2005.* Geneva: Author.

World Health Organization International Consortium in Psychiatric Epidemiology. (2000). Cross-national comparisons of the prevalences and correlates of mental disorders. *Bulletin of the World Health Orgaization, 78*, 413–426.

World Health Organization World Mental Health Survey Consortium. (2004). The prevalence, severity, and unmet need for treatment of mental disorders in the World Health Organization World Mental Health Surveys. *Journal of the American Medical Association, 291*, 2581–2590.

Worthington, C. (1992). An examination of factors influencing the diagnosis and treatment of Black patients in the mental health system. *Archives of Psychiatric Nursing, 6*, 195–204.

Wright, E. O. (1979). *Class structure and income determination*. New York: Academic Press.

Wright, E. O. (1985). *Classes*. London: Verso.

Wright, E. O. (1993). Typologies, scales, and class analysis: A comment on Halaby and Weakliem. *American Sociological Review, 58*, 31–34.

Wright, E. O. (2000). *Class counts: Comparative studies in class analysis*. Cambridge: Cambridge University Press.

Wright E. R., Gronfein, W. F. I., & Owens, T. J. (2000). Deinstitutionalization, social rejection, and the self-esteem of former mental patients. *Journal of Health & Social Behavior, 41*, 68–90.

Wu, I.-H., & Windle, C. W. (1980). Ethnic specificity in the relative minority use and staffing of community mental health centers. *Community Mental Health Journal, 16*(2), 156–168.

Wu, Z., & Hart, R. (2002). The effects of marital and nonmarital union transition on health. *Journal of Marriage and Family, 64*, 420–432.

Wu, Z., Penning, M. J., Pollard, M. S., & Hart, R. (2003). In sickness and in heath: Does cohabitation count? *Journal of Family Issues, 24*(6), 811–838.

Wyatt, G. E., & Riederle, M. H. (1995). The prevalence and context of sexual harassment among African American and White American women. *Journal of Interpersonal Violence, 10*, 309–321.

Xiong, W., Phillips, M. R., Hu, X., Wang, R., Dai, Q., Kleinman, J., et al. (1994). Family-based intervention for schizophrenic patients in China. *British Journal of Psychiatry, 165*, 239–247.

Xue, Y., Leventhal, T., Brooks-Gunn, J., & Earls, F. J. (2005). Neighborhood residence and mental health problems of 5- to 11-year olds. *Archives of General Psychiatry, 62*, 554–563.

Yang, L. H., Kleinman, A., Link, B. G., Phelan, J. C., Lee, S., & Good, B. (2007). Culture and stigma: Adding moral experience to stigma theory. *Social Science & Medicine, 64*, 1524–1535.

Yang, Y. (2008). Social inequalities in happiness in the United States, 1972 to 2004: An age-period-cohort analysis. *American Sociological Review, 73*, 204–226.

Ybarra, S. (1991). Women and AIDS: Implications for counseling. *Journal of Counseling & Development, 69*(3), 285–287.

Yesavage, J. A., Werner, P. D., Becker, J., & Mills, M. J. (1982). Short term civil commitment and the violent patient: A study of legal status and inpatient behavior. *American Journal of Psychiatry, 139*, 1145–1149.

Yeung, W. J., & Conley, D. (2008). Black-White achievement gap and family wealth. *Child Development, 79*, 303–324.

Ying, Y.-W., & Hu, L.-T. (1994). Public outpatient mental health services: Use and outcome among Asian Americans. *American Journal of Orthopsychiatry, 64*(3), 448–455.

Yoon, J. H., Minzenberg, M. J., Ursu, S., Walters, R., Wendelken, C., Ragland, J. D., et al. (2008). Association of dorsolateral prefrontal cortex dysfunction with disrupted coordinated brain activity in schizophrenia: Relationship with impaired cognition, behavioral disorganization, and global function. *American Journal of Psychiatry, 165*, 1006–1014.

Young, J. C. (1981). *Medical choices in a Mexican village*. New Brunswick, NJ: Rutgers University Press.

Young, M. (1994). *The rise of the meritocracy*. New Brunswick, NJ: Transaction.

Yucun, S., Chen, C., Zhang, W., Tingming, X., & Yunhua. T. (1990). An example of community-based health/home care programme. *Psychosocial Rehabilitation Journal, 14*, 29–34.

Yun, L., Maravi, M., Kobayashi, J., Barton, P., & Davidson, A. (2005). Antidepressant treatment improves adherence to antiretroviral therapy among depressed HIV-infected patients. *Journal of Acquired Immune Deficiency Syndromes, 38*(4), 432–438.

Zane, N., Sue, S., Chang, J., Huang, L., Huang, J., Lowe, S., et al. (2005). Beyond ethnic match: Effects of client-therapist cognitive match in problem perception, coping orientation, and therapy goals on treatment outcomes. *Journal of Community Psychology, 33*(5), 569–585.

Zapf, D., Seifert, C., Schmutte, B., Mertini, H., & Holz, M. (2001). Emotion work and job stressors and their effect on burnout. *Psychology and Health, 16*, 527–545.

Zapf, P. A., & Roesch, R. (1998). Fitness to stand trial: Characteristics of remands since the 1992 criminal code amendments. *Canadian Journal of Psychiatry, 43*, 287–293.

Zhang, M. Y., & Yan, H. Y. (1993). Effectiveness of psychoeducation of relatives of schizophrenic patients: A prospective cohort study in five cities in China. *International Journal of Mental Health, 22,* 47–57.

Zimmerman, A. C., & Easterlin, R. A. (2006). Happily ever after? Cohabitation, marriage, divorce, and happiness in Germany. *Population and Development Review, 32*(3), 511–528.

Zimmerman, M., McGlinchey, J. B., Chelminski, I., & Young, D. (2006). Diagnosing Major Depressive Disorder V: Applying the DSM-IV exclusion criteria in clinical practice. *Journal of Nervous and Mental Disease, 194,* 530–533.

Zinman, S. (2000, June). *Keynote speech.* Presented at the National Mental Health Consumers Summit Conference.

Zinman, S. (2006, August 22). *Interview with David Oaks.* Retrieved September 23, 2008, from http://www.mindfreedom.org/campaign/media/mfradio/archived-shows/sally-zinman.mp3/view.

Zinman, S. (2008, June 18). *Comments made during interview with Jay Mahler and Sally Zinman.* Retrieved September 6, 2008, from http://www.mpuuc.org/mentalhealth/mentalTVconsumer.html.

Zinman, S., Harp, H. T., & Budd, S. (Eds.). (1987). *Reaching across: Mental health clients helping each other.* Riverside, CA: California Network of Mental Health Clients.

Zoellner, T., & Maercker, A. (2006). Posttraumatic growth in clinical psychology: A critical review and introduction of a two component model. *Clinical Psychology Review, 26,* 626–653.

Zola, I. K. (1973). Pathways to the doctor – from person to patient. *Social Science & Medicine, 7,* 677–689.

Zsembik, B. A. (1995). Issues for women of racial and ethnic groups. *Research in Human Social Conflict, 1,* 257–273.

Zuvekas, S. H., Vitiello, B., & Norquist, G. S. (2006). Recent trends in stimulant medication use among U.S. children. *American Journal of Psychiatry, 163,* 579–585.

Index

707